THE TIMETABLES OF AMERICAN HISTORY

Millennial Edition

Laurence Urdang, Editor

**WITH AN INTRODUCTION BY
HENRY STEELE COMMAGER
AND A NEW FOREWORD BY
ARTHUR SCHLESINGER, JR.**

A TOUCHSTONE BOOK
Published by Simon & Schuster
New York   London   Toronto   Sydney   Singapore

TOUCHSTONE
Rockefeller Center
1230 Avenue of the Americas
New York, NY 10020

We gratefully acknowledge the help given by The Bettman Archive, Inc., especially the personal attention
accorded us by Victoria Dungan.

A LAURENCE URDANG REFERENCE BOOK

"The Timetables of" is a trademark of Simon & Schuster, Inc.
The Timetables of American History is part of a best-selling series of books including
The Timetables of Science, The Timetables of History, The Timetables of Technology,
The Timetables of Jewish History, The Timetables of Women's History, and
The Timetables of African-American History.

For information about special discounts for bulk purchases
please contact Simon & Schuster Special Sales:
1-800-456-6798 or business@simonandschuster.com

Manufactured in the United States of America

1 3 5 7 9 10 8 6 4 2

Library of Congress Cataloging-in-Publication Data is available.

ISBN 0-7432-0261-9

Introduction

We speak of Time as a stream—thus the philosopher Marcus Aurelius, "Time is a river of passing events, aye a rushing torrent." It is a very apt metaphor: Time is a stream sometimes placid and peaceful, sometimes turbulent and dangerous. And like a stream, it can never be neatly divided at any one point: it flows on and on, like life itself. Longfellow put this most poetically:

> What is Time? The shadow on the dial, the striking of the clock, the running of the sand, centuries—these are but arbitrary and outward signs, the measure of Time, not Time itself. Time is the life of the soul.

"Time," like "space," is a profound intellectual concept. But our use of that concept is intensely practical. Doubtless, our chronological divisions are artificial: our division of the calendar into minutes, hours, weeks, months, years; our divisions of human life itself into infancy, childhood, adolescence, maturity, and old age are commonplaces we could not do without. Doubtless, too, the artificiality of those chronological divisions we have imposed upon history: Ancient, Medieval, Renaissance, Reformation, and Modern—all are arbitrary, and not only arbitrary but parochial, for certainly the Chinese, the Indians, and the Arabs would not try to impose these same chronological divisions on their concepts of history. But how convenient they are, nay, how essential! Imagine doing without chronology, without fixed periods, artificial or even arbitrary as some of them may be. Time, even exact time, is one of the fixtures of our system: eighteen years for voting and for signing legal documents; twenty-five years for membership in the House of Representatives, thirty for the Senate, thirty-five for the Presidency; Congressional terms of two years and of six; Presidential terms of four; Social Security effective at a series of precise ages; exact, though arbitrary, distinctions between crimes before six and after six o'clock, and so forth, *ad infinitum.*

Granted that dates are tiresome—but what would we do without them? What would Americans do without 1492, 1776, 1787, and 1861; what would the English do without 1066, 1215, 1588, and 1689?

Facts by themselves are all but meaningless. No wonder the great historians of the era of the Enlightenment poured scorn upon them. "Let us begin," wrote Rousseau in his *Essay on the Inequalities of Mankind,* "by laying facts aside." That is the way most historians of the Enlightenment did, in fact, begin. "Confound details," said its greatest spokesman, François Voltaire, "they are the vermin which destroy books. Posterity forgets them all." And his own histories—perhaps the most widely read of their day—inspired a tribute from that other great philosopher of the Enlightenment, Diderot (who edited a great encyclopedia crammed with facts): "Other historians teach us facts—you excite our souls to a hatred of lying, ignorance and hypocrisy." And Edward Gibbon, who devoted six massive volumes to tracing the *Decline and Fall of the Roman Empire,* acknowledged that "events are the least interesting part of history."

Yet they did not really scorn facts, these scholars and philosophers who created modern history; they rejected, instead, the notion that facts could stand by themselves, that facts had any meaning except in connection with hundreds of other facts.

In all this, Rousseau, Voltaire, and other historians of the Enlightenment were, of course, right. The passion for neatness is one of the hazards of Politics, Philosophy, and History: indeed, after 2500 years (note even that figure is hopelessly imprecise!) we still do not agree on the definition of any of these terms—Politics, Philosophy, History, or Education. Nevertheless, this passion for neatness and for precision is not only legitimate, it is essential: without it there could be neither politics, nor law, nor history, nor education. Certainly if we had to delay all education until there was general agreement on its character and its content, we should have to close all schools and colleges. Historians, lawyers, teachers, and scholars are committed to bringing some kind of order out of what would otherwise be chaos: they are committed to the task of organizing in usable form such facts as they can discover and explain.

Henry Adams, the American historian who combined the best qualities of both Voltaire and Gibbon, put the problem of the dependence of History upon facts most cogently. It was, he wrote, "the function of history to arrange such facts as seemed sure, in such order as seemed rigorously consequent, in order to fix for a familiar moment a necessary sequence of human movement."

What Adams here acknowledged is the inescapable duty of every historian to select out of the myriad facts which confront him those that are of interest to more than a single individual and those that have contributed in some fashion to society, economy, law, culture, and morals: those, in short, that appear to be *significant.*

But appear so to whom? The view, after all, depends upon the point of view, and the points of view of an American and a Russian are quite different; so, too, the points of view of a frontiersman "planning civilization" on the Ohio River and an Indian determined to protect his hereditary hunting grounds. For that matter, the points of view of members of the same society are often very different: an economist and an anthropologist do not think the same things significant; neither do a Protestant and a Catholic, a Democrat and a Republican. Yet there is, on the whole, a substantial consensus.

Both the diversity and the consensus come out dramatically in the *Timetables of American History.* The diversity is dramatized by all the historic or economic or cultural "facts" that occur together; the consensus is dramatized precisely by the extent to which so many of these "facts" are interrelated and interdependent.

Consider, for example, the year 1492, to which most Americans ascribe almost global significance. It is for Americans and for a great many Europeans the year of the Discovery. But Asians had discovered America several thousand years before that date, and over these centuries innumerable Asians, whom Columbus mistakenly called "Indians," swarmed over the American continents. The Norsemen, too, had "discovered" America some five centuries before Columbus set sail on his hazardous voyage. Nor was America "discovered" all at once: the discovery went on and on, all through the seventeenth, the eighteenth, and the nineteenth centuries; parts of it—in Alaska, in back-country Brazil—are still being discovered. What, then, is important about 1492? It is important because historians everywhere have come to see it as a dramatic point in the emergence of that culture we associate with the Renaissance, in the birth of modern science, modern navigation, and modern thought, and in the first stirrings of nationalism. Thus the date takes on larger significance: it helps to "fix for a moment a necessary sequence of human movement." It is only when we put this elementary fact of Columbus' great venture into the larger context that it takes on global significance.

Or consider that most famous of all American dates, 1776, a date now generally acknowledged throughout the Western world as one of the most dramatic in history. And surely the drama is clear enough. Yet the history of every nation is filled with drama. The "significance" of 1776 is, however, in no sense a discovery of later generations, as was the case with 1492. Jefferson, Washington, Franklin, and their associates all read a fateful fame into their act. Here is John Adams, who was, as Jefferson said, "The Atlas of Independence," writing to his wife Abigail after signing the Declaration of Independence.

> It ought to be commemorated as the day of deliverance, by solemn acts of devotion to God. It ought to be solemnized with pomp and parade, with shows, games, sports, guns, bells, bonfires, and illuminations from one end of the continent to the other, from this time forward forevermore.
>
> You will think me transported with enthusiasm, but I am not. I am well aware of the toil and blood and treasure it will cost us to maintain this declaration and support and defend these States. Yet through all the gloom I can see the rays of ravishing light and glory. . . .

I cite this moving letter, not just for its own sake, but as a reminder that just as the Declaration of Independence is itself a fact, so are the role of John Adams and the spirit and the vision which he and his associates in the great enterprise revealed. It is all part of what we call "The Spirit of '76," a spirit which in turn is immortalized in the painting which is both a fact and an artifact. . . .

The Declaration of Independence, then, is a Fact which, like a magnet, attracts and clusters about itself a thousand other facts.

No one would think of ignoring great Facts, like the Declaration of Independence; but the small, the fortuitous fact has its own significance, and we ignore, at our peril, the day-by-day events that somehow find their way into the historical record, often because of their association with those facts which we have decided are significant. In the same way that the Significant Facts can be understood only in the light of other developments and against a broad background, so the fortuitous facts derive their meaning from circumstances. Consider the fact that on the night of December 25–26, Washington crossed the Delaware. In itself that fact is meaningless; after all, thousands of people cross the Delaware every day. It is only when we surround that historic episode with all that we know about the American struggle for independence, the desperation of the retreat of the Continental Army through New Jersey, the indomitable figure of Washington, the heroism of his ragged army, the Hessians sleeping off their Christmas debauch, the electrical impact of the astonishing victory at Trenton on the American cause at home and abroad—it is only when we reflect on what might have happened had the crossing ended in disaster that we can appreciate the meaning and importance of the famous, though grossly misleading painting of *Washington Crossing the Delaware* by the German, Emanuel Leutze. Historically, of course, it was all wrong: it was painted in Germany; the river was the Rhine; Washington was an American artist visiting Düsseldorf; the Flag had not yet been made. But no matter; the painting itself made history and became part of that American mythology which is itself a chapter of American cultural history.

Facts, then, take on meaning only in connection with a hundred or a thousand other facts. By themselves they are like bricks, lying about in hopeless disarray; it is only when the historian fits them together in some formal design that they build a harmonious structure.

It is perhaps here that comparative chronology has its special function to perform. Chronology provides the latitude and longitude of History. It is to History what the multiplication tables are to mathematics, what grammar is to literature, and what scales are to music. It imposes order on that which is otherwise anarchical.

Thus, this *Timetables of American History* is a reflection of what may be called a general consensus on the part of the historical profession about what is significant and therefore memorable, in a comparative arrangement that enables each reader to draw meaning from and impart meaning to significant and fortuitous events. Although History is not by itself harmonious, this book can help us to give to each fact some larger significance and thus to impose upon the infinite profusion of historical facts some degree of harmony. *Timetables of American History* is designed to make the connections, to provide the meanings, and, by implication, to illuminate the significance of facts which are otherwise lifeless.

Henry Steele Commager

Amherst, Massachusetts
1981

EDITOR'S FOREWORD

I HAVE LONG BEEN CONCERNED about the insular nature of the educational system in the United States. Students are traditionally exposed to American history, usually in secondary school, where little is learned about historical and cultural events taking place in other parts of the world—unless those events have had some direct influence on the history of the U.S. In college, where they are exposed, in a survey course, to European history, American history and culture are ignored unless a direct correlation chanced to occur. The result is that few graduates of high schools and colleges in the U.S. have gained the insight into history that can come from only a thoughtful overview of world events —a *Weltanschauung* recognition that all human accomplishments are interrelated.

Although an occasional, gifted teacher may impart this sense of "world view," the education of most students is so remiss that only a handful graduate from college with the realization that da Vinci, Michelangelo, and Bosch were active while Columbus was discovering the New World, or that Shakespeare's *Coriolanus* and *Timon of Athens* were being written (and *Antony and Cleopatra* completed) in the same year that Jamestown was settled; it was the same year (1607) that Caravaggio, Cervantes, Bacon, Jonson, Dekker, Lope de Vega, Drayton, and others were active and only one year after Guy Fawkes had been put to death for the Gunpowder Plot. Only scholars seem to be aware that the eighteenth century was characterized by the development (and implementation) of a totally new philosophy—freedom of the individual—that manifested itself in the American and French revolutions, although it took America almost another century to abolish slavery, while the British parliament had abolished the slave trade in 1788.

People grow up in America looking inward but without the wisdom that a knowledgeable *Weltanschauung* can bring to introspection. Because of their insularity, Americans find it difficult to understand the politics and cultures of the Soviet Union, of the Far East, of the Middle East, of Africa, and of South America.

It would be presumptuous to suggest that *The Timetables of American History* could change a tradition of two centuries. But I hope that it will be recognized as an attempt to help rectify the narrowly detached attitudes reflected in American educational policy.

In 1975, under the direction of Peter Schwed, Chairman of the Editorial Board, Simon and Schuster published *The Timetables of History,* based on *Kulturfahrplan,* a very successful work created by Werner Stein and originally published in Germany in 1946. *The Timetables of History,* a more international and updated version of that classic, was translated, expanded, and edited by Bernard Grun and has proved to be a comparable success. I am grateful to Simon and Schuster for the opportunity to present this new and specifically American *Timetables* to the public, for although it is inspired by the previous work, it is quite different and serves a unique and separate function.

LAURENCE URDANG, *Editor*

Essex, Connecticut
May 1980

FOREWORD TO THE UPDATED EDITION

THE TIMETABLES OF AMERICAN HISTORY offers a useful and beguiling approach to the understanding of the past— nor should any of us, consumed as we all are by the urgencies of the present, dismiss the past as something irrelevant and expendable.. History, when you think about it, is an indispensable key to life. As memory is to the individual, so history is to a nation. Individuals deprived of memory become rudderless and disoriented; they know neither where they have been nor where they are going. In the same way, nations that forget their past are disabled in dealing with their future.

But if we cannot live without history, history itself is not, alas, a fixed quantity. It has its share of mysteries and ambiguities. For the past is, after all, past. It is beyond recovery in its totality. How we conceive the past derives in part from what concerns us, pleasures us, scares us in the present. Historians, like everyone else, are prisoners of their own experience, and the history they write reflects that experience.

In my lifetime the writing of American history has been reshaped by two great revolutions—the civil rights revolution and the women's rights revolution. These revolutions have forced historians to look back afresh and suddenly discover things in the nation's past that had always been there but had not thus far been spotlighted by what Federalist 70 calls "the dim light of historical research." In this sense, the present recreates the past. History itself is enlarged as the questions we ask the past widen and deepen.

"The one duty we owe to history," said Oscar Wilde, "is to rewrite it." Another aspect of the past that demands fresh attention comes from the fact that we live in an incessantly shrinking and increasingly interdependent world. Nations are no longer so self-sufficient as they once were, and purely national history is no longer quite so satisfactory. We have also become aware of the perils of nationalist history—history converted into a weapon sanctifying one's own nation and trashing other people's nations, such as dictators rely on as one of their instruments of rule. "Who controls the past controls the future," the Party slogan runs in *1984*, George Orwell's great evocation of a totalitarian state; "who controls the present controls the past."

It is to prevent such corruption of history that our Declaration of Independence recommends "a decent respect to the opinions of mankind" and Federalist 63 declares, "An attention to the judgment of other nations is important to every government." Knowledge of other nations, their interests and their vicissitudes, may help inoculate us against national vainglory and mindless jingoism.

To embrace the widening reach of history and to escape the parochialism and abuse of nationalist history, we must begin to see history in comparative terms. We must view the experience of our own nation in a broad social context, and we must view that experience in light of the experiences of other nations. In *The Timetables of American History* we see a thousand years in the life of North America spread out from one millennium to the next, from Leif Ericson arriving along the Atlantic coast in his Viking long ship to the spacecrafts Viking 1 and 2 sending back photographs from distant Mars. We see these thousand years in terms not only of politics and war but of the arts, science, technology, commerce, industry, demography, medicine, education, religion, and sports. And we see the life of the American nation against the backdrop of contemporaneous developments in the rest of the world.

This is a fascinating volume for browsing, and it is a rich volume for learning. It will broaden understanding and lift spirits and, I hope, leave the reader with a realistic sense of our achievements, frustrations, failures—and dreams.

Arthur Schlesinger, Jr.

New York
1995

HOW TO USE THIS BOOK

The Timetables of American History is arranged in chronological order. Except for HISTORY: ELSEWHERE, the early period is not described in year-by-year listings because the records of events are not sufficiently detailed or because they were of minor significance. But once events begin to crowd upon one another, the years are listed individually.

Major events in HISTORY & POLITICS, THE ARTS, and SCIENCE & TECHNOLOGY are briefly identified and, in many cases, their significance is noted. Philosophy that is linked to the publication of a particular work is covered under THE ARTS, as are literature, theater, visual arts, and music. The subjects included under HISTORY & POLITICS and SCIENCE & TECHNOLOGY are described by those headings. Under MISCELLANEOUS are listed sports, day-to-day events of human interest, religious happenings, population and other statistics, natural and man-made disasters, and other topics not conveniently listed under one of the other classifications.

Each of the classifications is divided in two, describing in one column events that took place in America and, in the other, events Elsewhere in the world. For convenience, before the year 1764, America is interpreted as including all of the New World—South, Central, and North America; after 1764, the column headed AMERICA confines itself to areas that were later to be parts of the United States; and Central America, the Caribbean, and Canada are listed under ELSEWHERE.

For ease of reference, every item listed in *The Timetables of American History* can be identified by year, column, and individual, sequential reference number. For example:

1801	History and Politics		The Arts	
	America	Elsewhere	America	Elsewhere
	1 Lorem ipsum dolor sit amet tempor incidunt ut labore et do veniam, quis nostrund exercita commodo consequat. Duis aut esse molestiae consequat, vel ill et iusto odio dignissim qui blan excepteur sint occaecat cupidit deserunt mollit anim id est lab distinct. Nam liber tempor cun maxim 2 Temporibud autem quinsud err epudiand sint et molestia nc delectus au aut prefer endis d quid est cur verear ne ad eam n memorite tum etia ergat. Nos cum conscient	3 Concupis plusque in ipsinu Itaque ne iustitial dem rect qui Nam dilig et carum esse iucun non ob ea solu incommod qu mult etiam mag quod cuis. G expetend quam nostras expetc tuent tamet eum locum seque f: dictum est, sic amicitiand neg amicis insidar et metus plena si confirmatur animuset a spe par despication 4 Lorem ipsum dolor sit amet tempor incidunt ut labore et dc veniam, quis nostrund	1 Lorem ipsum dol tempor incidunt ut la veniam, quis nostrun commodo consequat esse molestiae consec et iusto odio dignissi excepteur sint occaec deserunt mollit anim distinct. Nam liber te quod	2 Temporibud aute err epudiand sint et n delectus au aut prefe quid est cur verear ne memorite tum etia e cum conscient 3 Nam dilig et caru non ob ea solu inco mult etiam mag quo expetend quam nost tuent tamet eum locu dictum est, sic amici amicis insidar et met confirmatur animuse despication

Thus, any item listed can more quickly be found by using the date, the category of information, and the item's individual number.

Here and there at the end of a text entry, a cross-reference to another, related entry is given, in this form: [1920:ARTS/6] The abbreviations used are:

HIST—HISTORY & POLITICS   SCI—SCIENCE & TECHNOLOGY

ARTS—THE ARTS   MISC—MISCELLANEOUS

Not all possible related entries can be listed, and again the Index should be used for a detailed search for information.

The Index contains more than 2,500 listings, including names of events, names of people and places, and names of works of art. In addition, certain categories of information (population, for example) have ben grouped together under a single listing. To save space in the main part of *The Timetables of American History,* birth and (where appropriate) death dates of people are in the Index.

References appear in the Index in this form: 1920:A/6. The abbreviations used are:

H—HISTORY & POLITICS   S—SCIENCE & TECHNOLOGY

A—THE ARTS   M—MISCELLANEOUS

	History and Politics		The Arts	
	America	**Elsewhere**	**America**	**Elsewhere**
1000	**1** Norsemen under Leif Ericson land on the coast of North America. Because they find grapes there, they call the region *Vinland.* Sites from Newfoundland to Virginia have been identified as *Vinland,* but its location is generally thought to be the coast of Nova Scotia or New England.	**2** Olaf I, King of Norway, is killed during his defeat at the naval Battle of Svoldor. Kings of Sweden and Denmark divide Norway. There follows a period of feudal disorder. **3** Norsemen raid the coasts of England. **4** Boleslaus I, King of Poland, continues to add territory to his domain and frees the Polish church from German control.		**1** First English epic, *Beowulf,* appears in writing. Its story of a hero fighting monsters had been passed on orally for 200 years. **2** Gregorian chant or plainsong declines as the dominant church music. **3** Murasaki Shikibu completes *Tale of Genji,* the oldest known novel and the greatest classic in Japanese literature.
1010	**1** Norsemen under Thorfinn Karlsefni set out to settle in *Vinland.* They spend three winters on the North American continent. Sites from Labrador to New England have been identified as localities visited by them.	**2** Robert II, King of France, seeks to strengthen the royal power of his country, conquering several towns and acquiring the duchy of Burgundy. **3** Caliph Hakim renounces the Holy City of Jerusalem one year after the Arabs sack the Holy Sepulcher.		
1492	**1** Christopher Columbus, Ital. navigator in the service of Spain, searches for a western route to Asia. He lands on Guanahaní, one of the Bahama Islands (Oct. 12), and names the land San Salvador, claiming it for Spain. He discovers Cuba and Haiti.	**2** Spanish forces conquer the Moorish kingdom of Granada, strengthening the monarchy of Ferdinand II of Aragon and Isabella I of Castile. **3** Henry VII, King of England, invades France, which had previously raided Brittany and supported Perkin Warbeck as claimant to the English throne.		**1** Leonardo da Vinci, Ital. painter, sculptor, and engineer, sketches flying machine and helicopter. **2** Albrecht Dürer, Ger. engraver, works on illustrations for *Ship of Fools.* **[1494:ARTS/2]**
1493	**1** On a second voyage, Columbus lands on Puerto Rico, Jamaica, and other islands in the West Indies.	**2** Maximilian I becomes Holy Roman Emperor, succeeding his father Frederick III. **3** Pope Alexander VI divides the New World (America) between Spain and Portugal.		
1494	**1** Treaty of Tordesillas is signed, by which Spain and Portugal officially divide the non-Christian world between them. **[1493:HIST/3]** **2** Charles VIII, King of France, invades Italy, marching victoriously through Florence and Rome.			**1** Da Vinci draws figures of symmetrical bodies for *On Divine Proportion* by Lucas Pacioli, Ital. mathematician. **2** Sebastian Brant, Ger. satirist, publishes *Ship of Fools,* most famous German work of the century. **[1492:ARTS/2]**

2

Science & Technology		Miscellaneous		
America	**Elsewhere**	**America**	**Elsewhere**	
Painting of Christopher Columbus by Luigi Gregori		**1** According to the Icelandic *Saga of Eric the Red,* Leif Ericson, Norse mariner, introduces Christianity along the North American coast.		**1000**
				1010
1 Hopi Indians in the Southwest have been using coal for cooking and heating since the 12th century and since the 14th century for firing pottery. **2** Columbus discovers American Indians using tobacco in religious ceremonies and as a medicine.	**3** Martin Behaim, Ger. navigator and geographer, builds the first globe.		**1** Thousands die from bubonic plague in Cairo, Egypt. **2** About 800,000 Jews refuse to convert to Christianity and are expelled from Spain.	**1492**
1 On his second voyage to the New World, Columbus brings cattle, sugar cane, wheat, and other European animals and plants to the West Indies.			**1** *The Nuremberg Chronicle,* an illustrated world history, is published in Bavaria.	**1493**
				1494

	History and Politics		The Arts	
	America	Elsewhere	America	Elsewhere
				3 Sandro Botticelli, Ital. artist, paints "Calumny." **4** Aldine Press, Venice, is founded as one of the first publisher-printers.
1495		**1** Charles VIII of France captures Naples, but he is forced to retreat. Pope Alexander VI forms Holy League to drive Charles out of Italy. The League's forces are defeated at the Battle of Fornovo. Charles returns to France. **2** Diet (assembly) of Worms establishes an imperial court of justice to settle disputes among princes and to apply Roman law throughout the Holy Roman Empire.		**1** Hieronymus Bosch, Dutch artist known for grotesque portrayals of evil, paints his most famous work, "The Garden of Earthly Delights." **2** Da Vinci begins his fresco "The Last Supper" on the wall of a monastery dining hall in Milan. **3** Dürer opens his studio in Nuremberg. Here he executes his most famous engravings, woodcuts, and watercolors. **4** Aldus Manutius, Ital. printer and scholar, starts publishing *Aldine* editions of Greek classics.
1496		**1** James IV, King of Scotland, invades northern England in support of Perkin Warbeck, pretender to the English throne. **[1492:HIST/3]**		**1** Michelangelo Buonarrotti, Ital. sculptor, painter, and architect, arrives in Rome for the first time.
1497	**1** John Cabot, Ital. navigator in the service of England, reaches the North American coast.	**2** Warbeck's rebel army is crushed by the troops of Henry VII at Exeter, England. Warbeck is captured, imprisoned, and hanged (1499) for plotting against the king. **[1496:HIST/1]**		**1** Under the reign of Savonarola in Florence, musical instruments and books are burned, leaving gaps in our knowledge of secular music.
1498	**1** On a second voyage, Cabot sails along the New England coast and then south, possibly as far as Maryland. **2** Columbus, on a third voy-	**3** Vasco da Gama, Port. navigator, discovers a sea route to India. By rounding the Cape of Good Hope (1497) he reaches Calicut, India.		**1** Michelangelo begins his famous sculpture, the "Pietà." **2** Dürer publishes his woodcut series illustrat-

4

Science & Technology		Miscellaneous		
America	Elsewhere	America	Elsewhere	
	1 The writings of Da Vinci include a wide scope of scientific topics, ranging from mechanics to aerodynamics to human anatomy.		**1** England allows very poor people to bring law suits in the courts.	**1495**

Nicolaus Copernicus, Polish astronomer

Science & Technology		Miscellaneous		
	1 Roller bearings and rolling mill are designed by Da Vinci.	**1** Spaniards bring sugar cane, cotton, and cattle to Santo Domingo. Gold is exported.	**2** Jews and Muslims in Portugal are forced to convert to Christianity or be expelled from the country. **3** Scottish Parliament requires schooling for eldest sons.	**1496**
	1 Alsatian physician Hieronymus Brunschwig publishes the first known work on the surgical treatment of gunshot wounds. **2** Pol. astronomer Nicolaus Copernicus notes an eclipse of a star by the Moon in his first recorded observation of the heavens.		**1** Girolamo Savonarola, Ital. monk and reformer, is excommunicated (expelled from membership) by the Catholic Church because of his attempt to overthrow the Pope. **2** Severe famine occurs in Florence, Italy.	**1497**
			1 First pawnshop is opened in Nuremberg, Bavaria. **2** Savonarola is strangled, then burnt, at Flor-	**1498**

History and Politics		The Arts	
America	**Elsewhere**	**America**	**Elsewhere**
age, discovers Trinidad. He lands in South America at the mouth of the Orinoco River.	**4** Louis XII becomes King of France, succeeding his cousin, Charles VIII.		ing the *Book of Revelation.*
1499 **1** Amerigo Vespucci, Ital. navigator after whom America is named, explores the northern and eastern coasts of South America.	**2** Emperor Maximilian I grants Switzerland independence (eight cantons). **3** Louis XII of France conquers Milan and Genoa but fails to secure Naples. **4** Turks wage war against Venice until peace treaty is signed (1503).		**1** Giorgione, Ital. painter, completes "Portrait of a Young Man." **2** Luca Signorelli, Ital. painter, begins frescoes at Orvieto Cathedral. (Completed 1504.)
1500 **1** Gaspar Corte Real, Port. navigator, sails along the east coast of North America.	**2** Under pressure from Germany, Emperor Maximilian I creates an imperial council and court of justice for administering the Holy Roman Empire. **3** Pedro Álvares Cabral, Port. navigator, discovers Brazil and claims it for Portugal. **4** Lodovico Sforza with the aid of Swiss mercenaries tries unsuccessfully to retake Milan. He is captured and dies a prisoner in France.	**1** Indians in Florida area produce beautiful wood carvings. **2** Indians of Mississippi region attain artistic peak. An existing diorite bowl shaped as a crested duck shows their achievement.	**3** Famous English morality play *Everyman* appears about this time. Morality plays taught Christian principles of ethics to the common man. **4** Anecdotes about the popular 14th-cent. German prankster and folk hero Till Eulenspiegel are published.
1501 **1** On a second voyage, Corte Real, with his brother, explores further south; he is lost during the expedition.	**2** Moors in the kingdom of Granada resist the Spanish army. **3** French conquests in upper Italy are recognized by Emperor Maximilian I. **4** The Pope seeks, but does not secure, aid from Henry VII of England against the Turks. **5** Rodrigo de Bastidas, Span. conquistador, explores the coasts of Colombia and Panama.		**1** Michelangelo begins work on the "David," a 14-foot marble statue symbolizing the artistic supremacy of his native city, Florence. [1504:ARTS/3] **2** Manuscripts of plays by Roswitha of Gandersheim, a nun who lived about 1000 A.D., are discovered at Nuremberg, Ger.
1502 **1** Columbus sails on his fourth and last voyage, hoping to find Asia and Japan. He lands on Honduras and Panama.	**2** Imperial council of the Holy Roman Empire is dissolved by Emperor Maximilian I. [1500:HIST/2] **3** Cesare Borgia, Ital. soldier and son of Pope Alexander VI, completes his conquests of small neighboring states and adds them to the Papal domain. **4** Vasco da Gama leads a fleet of 20 ships on his second voyage to India. [1498:HIST/3]	Michelangelo's *David*	**1** Ludovico Ariosto, Ital. poet and playwright, begins work on *Orlando Furioso,* epic which greatly influenced European literature. [1516:ARTS/2] **2** Da Vinci begins the "Mona Lisa." **3** Dürer does watercolor of a hare. **4** *Cornucopiae,* a multilingual dictionary, is completed by Ambrogio Calepino.

6

Science & Technology		Miscellaneous		
America	**Elsewhere**	**America**	**Elsewhere**	
			ence, Italy, for sedition and "religious errors." [1497:MISC/1]	
			1 Spanish Muslims rebel unsuccessfully against forced conversions to Christianity. Many are expelled. **2** First known political cartoon (on the subject of King Louis XII of France and the Italian war).	**1499**
	1 The first recorded Caesarean section in which both mother and child survive is performed in Switzerland. **2** The first clock run by springs is built by Ger. locksmith Peter Henlein.			**1500**
		1 Portuguese fishing boats reach the east coast of North America.		**1501**
	1 Henlein invents the watch. **2** Da Vinci suggests the building of a canal to link Florence, Italy, with the sea.			**1502**

Mona Lisa, painting by Leonardo daVinci

7

	History and Politics		The Arts		
	America	Elsewhere	America	Elsewhere	
1503		1 Spanish win victories over the French, taking control of Naples and southern Italy. 2 Poland gives up the left bank of Dnieper River to Russia.		1 Cathedral at Canterbury, Eng., begun 1070, is completed.	
1504		1 Isabella of Castile dies; Ferdinand secures from the Spanish legislature control over Castile as regent for his daughter.		1 Raphael (Raffaello Sanzio), Ital. Renaissance artist known for his madonnas, visits Florence where he is influenced by the art of da Vinci and Michelangelo. 2 Michelangelo completes "David." **[1501:ARTS/1]** 3 Lucas Cranach the Elder, Ger. painter, completes one of his finest works, "Rest on the Flight into Egypt."	
1505		1 Louis XII consents to the Treaties of Blois, keeping Genoa and Milan but ceding Naples to Spain. **[1499:HIST/3; 1503:HIST/1]**		1 Donato Bramante undertakes design of new St. Peter's, in Rome. **[1615:ARTS/2]**	
1506		1 Sigismund I becomes King of Poland and begins strengthening his domain through alliances and laws.		1 The Laocoön, a famous sculpture of the 2nd century B.C., is unearthed in Rome.	
1507	1 Martin Waldseemüller, Ger. geographer, is the first mapmaker to call the New World "America."	2 Diet (assembly) of Constance establishes imperial chamber, stressing unity of the Holy Roman Empire. 3 Francisco de Almeida as viceroy of Portuguese India builds forts on the African and Indian coasts, taking control of the spice trade from the Arabs.		1 A Dance of Death pageant is performed at the Tuscan court in Italy.	
1508		1 League of Cambrai is formed by Holy Roman Emperor Maximilian I, King Louis XII of France, King Ferdinand of Aragon, Pope Julius II, and several Italian states to break the power of Venice.		1 The writings of Baldassare Castiglione, Ital. diplomat and courtier, include comment on dances of the period. 2 Michelangelo begins work on the ceiling of the Sistine Chapel. This masterpiece depicts the Biblical story	

Science & Technology		Miscellaneous		
America	Elsewhere	America	Elsewhere	
	1 The refinement of raw sugar is developed.			1503
		1 Fishing boats from France sail to North America's east coast.		1504
			1 India and Persia are struck by a disastrous earthquake.	1505
			1 Europe imports spices from the East Indies. 2 Ital. political philosopher Niccolò Machiavelli forms the Florentine militia, the first national army in Italy.	1506
			1 Martin Luther, Ger. theologian, is ordained a priest.	1507
1 First New World sugar mill is established in the West Indies.			1 Luther teaches and studies theology at Wittenberg University. 2 An earthquake destroys the city of Constantinople (Istanbul), Turkey.	1508

St. Peter's in Rome, Italy

9

History and Politics		The Arts	
America	**Elsewhere**	**America**	**Elsewhere**
			of creation. [1512:ARTS/1]
1509	**1** French defeat the Venetians at Agnadello; Venice loses many possessions but is not crushed. [1508:HIST/1] **2** Henry VIII becomes King of England, succeeding his father Henry VII.		**1** Desiderius Erasmus (Erasmus of Rotterdam), Renaissance scholar and friend of Sir Thomas More, writes *In Praise of Folly,* one of most famous satires of all time. [1516:ARTS/1] **2** Andrea del Sarto, Ital. painter, completes "Miracles of St. Philip."
1510	**1** Pope Julius II, fearful of the power of France, withdraws from the League of Cambrai and joins Venice. [1508:HIST/1]		
1511	**1** Pope Julius II forms the Holy League to drive the French from Italy. League consists of Venice, Aragon, England, and the Papal States.		
1512	**1** After French victory at Ravenna, the Swiss cantons and the Holy Roman Emperor join the Holy League. French are driven out of Milan. [1511:HIST/1] **2** Diet of Cologne undertakes further reorganization of the Holy Roman Empire. [1495:HIST/2] **3** Ten-year war between Poland and Russia begins over White Russian region.		**1** Michelangelo completes the ceiling of the Sistine Chapel. **2** Raphael paints his greatest altarpiece, the "Sistine Madonna."
1513	**1** Juan Ponce de León, Span. explorer in search of the Fountain of Youth, lands on the Florida peninsula and claims it for Spain. **2** Vasco Núñez de Balboa, Span. conquistador, leads an expedition across the Isthmus of Panama. He becomes the first European to see the Pacific from the New World.	**3** Henry VIII of England defeats the French at the Battle of the Spurs in northern France. **4** English forces defeat invading Scots at Flodden Field in northern England.		**1** Niccolò Machiavelli, Ital. statesman, writes *The Prince,* in which he describes the model ruler.
1514	**1** Selim I, Ottoman sultan, defeats the Persians and annexes territory, thus begin-		**1** Raphael takes over plans for St. Peter's Basilica after the death

Science & Technology		Miscellaneous		
America	**Elsewhere**	**America**	**Elsewhere**	
	1 Attempts are made to require the licensing of physicians.		**1** Jews are persecuted in Germany. Their books are confiscated and burned.	**1509**
			1 John Colet, Eng. educator, founds St. Paul's School in London.	**1510**
		1 Catholic bishops are appointed in America; two in Hispaniola and one in Puerto Rico.		**1511**
			1 English navy builds double-deck ships weighing 1000 tons, with 70 guns.	**1512**
	1 Martin Waldseemüller, Ger. mapmaker, prepares a book of more than 200 maps.			**1513**
	1 Copernicus privately discloses the theory that the Earth and other plan-		**1** European ships from Portugal sail into Chinese waters to trade with the	**1514**

Raphael, self portrait in Florence's Uffizi Gallery

11

History and Politics		The Arts		
America	Elsewhere	America	Elsewhere	
	ning a lasting rivalry between the Persians and the Ottomans (Turks). **2** In Hungary, revolt of the peasants against ruthless aristocrats is suppressed.		of Bramante. **2** Da Vinci sketches concept of parachute.	
1515	**1** Francis I becomes King of France. He reconquers Milan for France, winning a great victory at Marignano over the Swiss.			
1516	**1** Treaty of Fribourg is signed by France and the Swiss; peace lasts until the French Revolution. **[1789:HIST/6]** **2** Concordat (agreement) between Francis I of France and Pope Leo X secures French independence in church appointments. **3** Juan Díaz de Solís, Span. explorer, enters the Río de la Plata. He lands on the coast of Uruguay, where he is slain by hostile Indians.		**1** Sir Thomas More, Eng. statesman, publishes *Utopia,* a political work presenting his ideas about an ideal society. **2** Ariosto's *Orlando Furioso* is published. **[1502:ARTS/1]** **3** Da Vinci goes to France at invitation of Francis I.	
1517	**1** Francisco Fernández de Córdoba discovers the Yucatan peninsula in Mexico.	**2** Selim I defeats the Mamelukes in Syria and Egypt, which he adds to the Ottoman Empire. Ottoman Turks capture holy cities of Mecca and Medina and control much of Arabia. **[1514:HIST/1]**		**1** Raphael is appointed commissioner of antiquities for Rome. **2** Luther uses psalms sung to melodies rather than chanted in worship service. This leads to development of hymns and chorales.	
1518	**1** Juan de Grijalva lands on the coast of Mexico and hears of Montezuma's empire.	**2** Thomas Wolsey, Cardinal and Lord Chancellor of England, devises a treaty of peace embracing England, France, Spain, the Holy Roman Empire, and the Pope. **3** Barbarossa, Turkish pirate, captures Algiers from the Spanish, placing Algeria under Turkish rule.			
1519	**1** Hernando Cortés, Span. conquistador, captures Tenochtitlán (now Mexico City), capital of the Aztec empire. Cortés imprisons Montezuma, the Aztec emperor, who later dies in battle. **2** Alonso Alvarez de Piñeda	**3** Charles I of Spain becomes Holy Roman Emperor as Charles V, succeeding his grandfather Maximilian I. **4** Ferdinand Magellan, Port. navigator in the service of Spain, attempts to sail around the world. He is killed		**1** Construction of the chateau at Chambord, France, is begun. It is considered the finest example of early Renaissance style.	

| Science & Technology | | Miscellaneous | | |
America	Elsewhere	America	Elsewhere	
	ets orbit the Sun (the heliocentric theory).		Orient. **2** Pineapples are brought to Europe.	
				1515
				1516

Renaissance style chateau at Chambord, France

| Science & Technology | | Miscellaneous | | |
America	Elsewhere	America	Elsewhere	
	1 Girolamo Fracastoro, Ital. physician and scientist, suggests that fossils are the remains of ancient life.		**1** Coffee is introduced in Europe. **2** Luther publicly protests the sale of indulgences (reductions in punishment for sins) in the Catholic Church. The Protestant Reformation begins. [1507:MISC/1]	**1517**
	1 The Royal College of Physicians is established in London.		**1** Luther refuses to withdraw his condemnation of the sale of indulgences. **2** Charles I, King of Spain, grants the first license to import African slaves to the colonies in America.	**1518**
1 Hernando Cortés, Span. conqueror of Mexico, brings wheat to Mexico from Spain.			**1** Ulrich Zwingli, Swiss priest and reformer, stops the sale of indulgences in Zurich. The Protestant Reformation begins in Switzerland. **2** Luther questions the authority of the Pope.	**1519**

13

History and Politics		The Arts	
America	**Elsewhere**	**America**	**Elsewhere**
explores the coast of Gulf of Mexico from Florida to Veracruz.	in the Philippines. One of his ships, under Juan Sebastian del Cano, reaches Spain in 1522, completing the first circumnavigation of the globe.		

1520

	Elsewhere		Elsewhere
	1 Christian II, King of Denmark and Norway, massacres Swedish nobles at Stockholm and asserts claim to Sweden. **2** England and France sign commercial treaty.		**1** First plays of John Heywood appear. He introduced comic elements into English drama. **2** King Francis I founds Royal Library of France at Fontainebleau.

1521

America	Elsewhere		Elsewhere
1 Francisco de Gordillo sails up the Atlantic coast from Florida to South Carolina.	**2** Gustavus Eriksson leads the Swedes to victory over the Danes. **[1520:HIST/1; 1523:HIST/1]** **3** Sulayman I, Ottoman sultan, conquers Belgrade, continuing his father's (Selim I) conquests in the Balkans.		

Ferdinand Magellan

1522

	Elsewhere		Elsewhere
	1 Sulayman I expels the Knights Hospitalers from Rhodes. **2** Spanish quarrel and fight among themselves for control of Panama, Costa Rica, and Nicaragua.		**1** Luther's translation of the New Testament influences style of later German writers.

1523

	Elsewhere		Elsewhere
	1 Gustavus Eriksson becomes King of Sweden as Gustavus I. He founds the House of Vasa, under whom Sweden becomes the strongest Baltic power. **[1521:HIST/2]**		**1** Hans Holbein the Younger, Ger. painter best known for his portraits, begins woodcut series, *The Dance of Death*. **2** Luther's liturgical reforms change church music, giving rise to more communal song.

1524

America	Elsewhere	America	Elsewhere
1 Giovanni da Verrazano, Ital. navigator in the service of France, explores the east coast from Maine to North Carolina. He sails into New York Bay and finds Hudson River.	**2** Spanish invade Provence and advance to Marseilles.	**1** Spaniards found a school of music in Texcoco, near modern Mexico City.	**2** *Mémoires* by Philippe de Comnynes, Fr. statesman, are published after his death. He is considered the first modern French historian.

1525

America	Elsewhere		
1 Esteban Gómez, sailing from Spain, explores the coast from Nova Scotia to Florida.	**2** French are defeated by the Germans and Spanish at Pavia; Francis I of France is captured. He is released after agreeing to give up his Italian		

14

Science & Technology		Miscellaneous		
America	**Elsewhere**	**America**	**Elsewhere**	
			1 Luther is excommunicated (expelled from membership) by the Catholic Church. He refuses to accept the Pope's action. **2** Chocolate in slab form is sold in Spain.	**1520**
Luther and Melachthon translating the Bible			**1** Luther is banned from the Holy Roman Empire (the German states in Central and Western Europe). In prison, he begins a German translation of the Bible. **2** Silk manufacture begun in France.	**1521**
	1 Cuthbert Tunstall, Eng. clergyman, publishes the first arithmetic book in England.		**1** A Polyglot Bible (printed in four languages) is published in Spain. **2** Luther returns to Wittenberg, Germany. He finishes his translation of the Bible. [1521:MISC/1]	**1522**
		1 Franciscan missionaries start a school for Indians in Mexico.	**2** Insurance policies on trading vessels are first issued in Florence, Italy.	**1523**
	1 Petrus Apianus, Ger. geographer, publishes an illustrated textbook of science and history.		**1** Soap is first made in London. **2** Turkeys from South America are eaten in England for the first time.	**1524**
			1 William Tyndale, Eng. religious reformer, translates the New Testament into English. **2** Thomas Wolsey, Eng.	**1525**

15

History and Politics		The Arts	
America	Elsewhere	America	Elsewhere
	claims and ceding Burgundy to Emperor Charles V. **3** Peasants' War in southern Germany is crushed.		
1526 **1** Verrazano, sailing from France, explores the West Indies and is killed by the Indians.	**2** Emperor Babar founds Mogul empire in India. **3** Turks under Sulayman I defeat the Hungarians at Mohács, beginning more than 150 years of Ottoman rule in Hungary. **4** Francis I of France creates the League of Cognac with the Pope, Henry VIII of England, Venice, and Florence against Holy Roman Emperor Charles V and the Spanish. [1525:HIST/2]		**1** The Palace of Charles V, the first building in Spain in the Italian Renaissance style, is constructed within the Alhambra at Granada. **2** Lucas Cranach paints portrait of Martin Luther. **3** William Tyndale's English translation of the New Testament replaces that of John Wycliffe as the dominant one.
1527	**1** Troops of the Holy Roman Empire sack Rome and hold the Pope prisoner for some months. **2** Sebastian Cabot, Eng. navigator and son of John Cabot, builds forts in Paraguay. Hostile Indians force him to leave.		**1** Holbein paints the portrait, "Thomas More and His Family."
1528 **1** Pánfilo de Narváez, Span. conquistador, lands in Florida with colonists from Spain and marches inland in search of gold. His expedition later sails for Mexico. All except Cabeza de Vaca and three others are lost off the Texas coast. [1536:HIST/1]	**2** Henry VIII and Cardinal Wolsey make unpopular alliance with France to curb the power of the Holy Roman Empire. **3** Turks seize Ofen (now Budapest), Hungary, and support John Zápolya (John I of Hungary) against Ferdinand of Austria and Bohemia (later Holy Roman Emperor Ferdinand I).		**1** Titian (Tiziano Vecellio), Ital. painter noted for his use of color, completes painting of "Madonna with Saints and Members of the Pesaro Family" in church in Venice. **2** Johannes Agricola, compiles and publishes German proverbs.
1529	**1** Francis I and Charles V sign the Treaty of Cambrai; Francis renounces claims on Italy, Flanders, and Artois; Charles leaves Burgundy to France and releases the French princes. **2** Garrison at Vienna resists the Turkish siege. **3** Henry VIII of England deprives Cardinal of the chancellorship and gives it to Sir Thomas More.		

16

Science & Technology		Miscellaneous		
America	**Elsewhere**	**America**	**Elsewhere**	
			cardinal and statesman, endows Cardinal College at Oxford, England.	
1 Gonzalo de Oviedo y Valdés, Span. historian, publishes *Natural History of the West Indies,* which includes a list and description of New World plants and animals.			**1** The Capuchins, a religious order of monks, is founded.	**1526**
			1 Philipps-Universität, Europe's first Protestant university, is founded in Germany. **2** Denmark and Sweden make Lutheranism their state religion.	**1527**
		1 Juan de Zumárraga becomes the first Catholic bishop in Mexico.	**2** Typhus epidemic kills about 21,000 people in Italy. **3** Philipp Melanchthon, Ger. Protestant reformer, proposes educational changes in Germany.	**1528**
				1529

Sir Thomas More, engraving based on Holbein painting

	History and Politics		The Arts	
	America	Elsewhere	America	Elsewhere
1530		**1** Charles V is crowned Holy Roman Emperor by the Pope at Bologna; he is the last German emperor to be crowned by the Pope. **2** Charles V establishes the Knights Hospitalers on the island of Malta. **[1522:HIST/1]**		**1** Antonio Allegri Correggio, Ital. artist, completes altar painting "The Holy Night."
1531		**1** Catholic cantons in Switzerland suppress Protestant Zürich. Ulrich Zwingli, leader of the Swiss Reformation, is killed.		
1532		**1** Sulayman I attacks Carinthia in southern Austria. **2** Francisco Pizarro, Span. conquistador, conquers Inca city of Cuzco in Peru. He seizes Atahualpa, Inca leader, exacts a huge ransom, and then kills him.	**1** The highly-wrought metal objects of the great Inca civilization are plundered by Spanish treasure seekers.	**2** François Rabelais, Fr. satirist, publishes first book of his masterpiece *Pantagruel*. **[1535:ARTS/1]** **3** Albrecht Altdorfer, Ger. painter and engraver, paints first landscape, a scene without a theme or human figure.
1533		**1** Thomas Cranmer as Archbishop of Canterbury declares marriage between Henry VIII and Catherine of Aragon invalid. He crowns Anne Boleyn, who is already secretly married to Henry, queen. The Pope, who refused to allow a divorce, excommunicates Henry.		**1** Luther's popular hymn "A mighty fortress is our God" appears in print for the first time.
1534	**1** Jacques Cartier, Fr. navigator, makes the first of three voyages (1534-42) to the New World. He lands on the Gaspé Peninsula and claims the region for France.	**2** Act of Supremacy makes King Henry VIII head of the Church of England, breaking the union of the English church with Rome.		**1** Michelangelo takes up permanent residence in Rome.

Science & Technology		Miscellaneous		
America	**Elsewhere**	**America**	**Elsewhere**	
	1 Fracastoro publishes work on syphilis written in rhyme. **2** Georgius Agricola, Ger. scientist, publishes his first book on mineralogy. **3** Otto Brunfels, Ger. botanist, publishes *Living Pictures of Herbs,* thus establishing botany as a modern science.		**1** English merchants trading in Spain form a company. **2** A criminal code and police regulations are drawn up for the Holy Roman Empire.	**1530**
1 Cultivation of tobacco begins in the West Indies.	**2** Comet appears which is later described by Johannes Kepler and Edmund Halley.		**1** Sir Thomas Elyot writes *The Boke Named the Governour,* first treatise in English to treat specifically of education. **2** "Poor law" in England forbids able-bodied beggars. **3** English Parliament sentences convicted poisoners to be boiled to death (repealed in 1547). **4** An earthquake in Lisbon, Portugal, kills 30,000 people.	**1531**
			1 John Calvin, Fr. theologian and reformer, begins the Reformation in Paris. It becomes known as the Huguenot Movement. **2** Robert Estienne, Fr. scholar and printer, publishes a Latin-English dictionary.	**1532**
				1533
			1 St. Ignatius Loyola, Span. priest, founds the Society of Jesus (Jesuits) in Paris.	**1534**

ANNO · ETATIS ·   · SVÆ · XLIX ·

Henry VIII, King of England

	History and Politics		The Arts	
	America	Elsewhere	America	Elsewhere
1535		**1** Sir Thomas More refuses to take the oath of the king's supremacy. He is tried for treason and beheaded. [1529:HIST/3] **2** Emperor Charles V conquers Tunis, which the Spanish control until 1569.		**1** Rabelais publishes *Gargantua*, Book II of his four book masterpiece. It later usually appears first, with the title given as *Gargantua and Pantagruel*.
1536	**1** Alvar Núñez Cabeza de Vaca and three companions arrive in Culcán, Mexico, after wandering through Texas, New Mexico, and Arizona. [1528:HIST/1] **2** Seeking a waterway to China (Northwest Passage), Cartier sails up the St. Lawrence River as far as Quebec, then to Montreal.	**3** Queen Anne Boleyn, who gave Henry VIII no son, is executed on a charge of adultery. [1533:HIST/1] **4** Henry VIII marries Jane Seymour third of his six wives. She gives birth to a son, who later becomes Edward VI. **5** Pedro de Mendoza, Span. conquistador, founds Buenos Aires.		**1** Holbein paints his celebrated portrait of Henry VIII. **2** Michelangelo begins painting the "Last Judgment" in the Sistine Chapel.
1537		**1** War between Venice and Ottoman Empire begins after Turks threaten to block the Straits of Otranto.		**1** Holbein becomes court painter to Henry VIII. His portraits of the royal household give a vivid picture of the people of the period.
1538		**1** Venice allies itself with the Pope and Emperor Charles V, who fails to buy off the Turks. **2** Two years of war between Charles V and Francis I ends with the Truce of Nice. Francis I seeks alliance with Sulayman I, who sends his Turkish fleets to raid the coasts of Italy.		
1539	**1** Hernando de Soto, Span. explorer, lands in Florida and leads an expedition inland in search of gold. He travels through parts of Georgia, Alabama, and Arkansas before dying on the banks of the Mississippi.	**2** Barbarossa as admiral of the Turkish fleet under Sulayman I besieges Corfu and ravages the coasts of Greece, Italy, and Spain. [1518:HIST/3]		
1540	**1** Francisco Vázquez de Coronado, Span. explorer, leads an expedition from Mexico into the American Southwest in search of gold. His lieutenant, Garcia Lopez de Cardenas, discovers the Grand Canyon; Coronado discovers the Pueblos of New Mexico.	**2** After a defeat at sea (Battle of Prevesa), Venice signs peace treaty with Ottoman Empire. **3** Thomas Cromwell, Eng. statesman, is beheaded on a charge of treason. He had displeased Henry VIII, having persuaded the king to ally		**1** Holbein paints famous miniature, "Anne of Cleves." **2** Titian begins his well known untitled portrait called "A Young Englishman."

20

Science & Technology		Miscellaneous		
America	**Elsewhere**	**America**	**Elsewhere**	
Hernando de Soto			**1** Most English bishops refuse to accept the Pope's authority. **2** The Ursuline Order of nuns is founded in Italy. **3** Parliament limits the power of English land-owners.	**1535**
	1 Paracelsus, Swiss al-chemist and physician, publishes the first surgical manual.		**1** Catholic monasteries in England are closed. **2** Parliament declares that the Pope has no au-thority in England.	**1536**
	1 Niccolò Fontana Tar-taglia, Ital. mathemati-cian, establishes the science of ballistics.		**1** First complete edition of the Bible is printed in England.	**1537**
	1 Fracastoro suggests that planets follow spheri-cal orbits.		**1** A public school is started in Strassburg, Germany.	**1538**
1 First New World printing press is estab-lished in Mexico City by Antonio de Mendoza, first Viceroy of Mexico.	**2** Olaus Magnus, Swed. author, completes the first detailed map of Scandina-via.	**1** First book is printed in Mexico. [1539:SCI/1]	**2** A public lottery is held in France. **3** *The Great Bible,* a new edition of earlier ver-sions, is published in Eng-land.	**1539**
		1 Priests traveling with Hernando de Soto, Span. explorer, baptize their In-dian guide. It is the first recorded baptism in the New World.		**1540**

	History and Politics		The Arts	
	America	**Elsewhere**	**America**	**Elsewhere**
		himself with the German Protestant princes by marrying Anne of Cleves. Henry disliked Anne and divorced her.		
1541		**1** Charles V launches unsuccessful expedition against Algiers, base of the Turkish fleet that preys upon Christian trade in the Mediterranean. **[1518:HIST/3]**		
1542	**1** Juan Rodríguez Cabrillo, Span. conquistador, explores the California coast, particularly San Diego Bay, and claims the region for Spain.	**2** War between England and Scotland ends with the defeat of James V of Scotland at Solway Moss. **3** James V of Scotland dies and his infant daughter Mary Queen of Scots ascends the throne six days later.	**1** Span. explorer Alvar Núñez Cabeza de Vaca publishes *Relación,* an account of his walk across the area of the present Texas, New Mexico, and Arizona.	
1543		**1** Portuguese arrive on a Chinese ship in Japan. They bring muskets and are the first Europeans to visit Japan. Portugal begins maritime trade with lords in western Japan.		**1** The first academy primarily for the study of music is established in Verona, Italy.
1544		**1** Parliament recognizes Elizabeth (daughter of Henry VIII and Anne Boleyn) and Mary (daughter of Henry VIII and Catherine of Aragon) as heirs to the crown in the event of the death of Edward without children. **[1536:HIST/4]**	The Council of Trent	
1545		**1** Council of Trent assembles intermittently until 1563 to make reforms in the Roman Catholic Church and to reaffirm the Pope's supremacy. Emperor Charles V supports the Catholic Reformation. **[1544:MISC/1]**		**1** Michelangelo completes a much modified version of the tomb of Julius II. Its most famous section is the sculpture of Moses. The work is in the church of St. Peter in Chains, Rome.

Science & Technology		Miscellaneous		
America	**Elsewhere**	**America**	**Elsewhere**	
	1 Rhäticus, Aust. mathematician and astronomer, publishes work in which he supports the Copernican heliocentric theory. **[1514:SCI/1]**	1 Earthquake destroys Guatemala City.	2 John Knox, Scot. reformer, leads the Calvinist Reformation in Scotland. **[1532:MISC/1]** 3 English Parliament passes a law to maintain archery, which is necessary for warfare.	**1541**
	1 Leonhard Fuchs, Ger. physician and botanist, publishes *Historia Stirpium,* a highly organized, illustrated description of plants.		1 St. Francis Xavier, Span. priest and missionary, arrives in India and establishes the first mission.	**1542**
	1 The heliocentric theory by Copernicus is published, amid much religious and political opposition. **[1514:SCI/1]** 2 Andreas Vesalius, Belg. anatomist, publishes *De fabrica,* the most accurate anatomy textbook of his day.		1 Protestants are burned at the stake by the Spanish Inquisition.	**1543**
	1 Sebastian Münster, Ger. cartographer, publishes the first major Ger. geographical work.		1 Pope Paul III calls for a general council of the Catholic Church at Trent, Italy. **[1545:HIST/1]**	**1544**
	1 Conrad Gesner, Swiss naturalist and physician, publishes work on the nutritive merits of milk. 2 Public botanical gardens are opened in Padua, Italy. 3 Ambroise Paré, Fr. surgeon, publishes work which results in better treatment of gunshot wounds. **[1497:SCI/1]** 4 Ital. mathematician Gerolama Cardona pub-		1 Typhus epidemic in Cuba kills about 250,000 people.	**1545**

	History and Politics		The Arts	
	America	**Elsewhere**	**America**	**Elsewhere**
1546		**1** Charles V attacks Schmalkaldic League, which was formed (1531) to counter the Emperor's threat to stamp out Lutheranism in Germany.		**1** Rebuilding of the Louvre Palace in Paris is begun. Only half of the original design of Fr. architect Pierre Lescot was ever completed. Today the structure is one of the most famous museums in the world.
1547		**1** Edward VI becomes King of England, succeeding Henry VIII. [1536:HIST/4] **2** Ivan IV ("the Terrible") is crowned Czar of Russia. **3** Henry II becomes King of France, succeeding his father Francis I. **4** Charles V defeats the Schmalkaldic League at the Battle of Mühlberg. [1546:HIST/1]		
1548	**1** Pedro de la Gasca defeats Gonzalo Pizarro at the Battle of Xaquixaguana and restores order to Peru. Pizarro, who led a revolt and became governor (1544), is executed.	**2** Ottoman Turks occupy Tabriz, Persia.	**1** The Spanish bring traditions of religious and secular drama to Peru.	**2** Tintoretto (Jacopo Robusti), Ital. artist, paints first important work, "St. Mark Rescuing the Slave." Many of his paintings are of his native Venice.
1549		**1** Ivan IV convenes the first national assembly in Russia. He seeks to broaden the support of the crown and to weaken the powers of the provincial governors.		**1** The first edition of *The Book of Common Prayer* is published in England. Its style influenced English prose writers.
1550		**1** Spain is at the peak of her political and economic power and remains so until the end of the century.	**1** Reports of Spanish explorers tell of great temple mounds of wood in southeast North America.	**2** Tintoretto executes famous painting of "St. George and the Dragon." **3** Andrea Palladio, Ital. architect, designs the Villa Rotonda, an example of 16th century Italian mannerist style. **4** Benvenuto Cellini, Florentine sculptor and goldsmith, completes

Science & Technology		Miscellaneous		
America	**Elsewhere**	**America**	**Elsewhere**	
	lishes *Ars Magna,* on which much of modern algebra is based.			
	1 Fracastoro publishes *De Contagione,* in which he suggests that many diseases are spread by germs.		**1** Henry VIII founds Trinity College in Cambridge, England.	**1546**
	1 Nostradamus, Fr. physician and astrologer, uses novel methods in fighting the plague in several French cities.		**1** In England, the Hospital of St. Mary of Bethlehem (Bedlam) is incorporated as an asylum for lunatics. **2** Moscow is destroyed by fire. **3** After the reign of Henry VIII dancing is no longer permitted as part of the Christian service.	**1547**
			1 St. Francis Xavier establishes a mission in Japan.	**1548**
			1 *Book of Common Prayer* becomes the official service of the Church of England. **2** Jesuits convert about 300,000 Japanese to Christianity. Missionaries also travel to South America. [1534:MISC/1]	**1549**
	1 Agricola's *De re metallica* becomes the foundation of the science of metallurgy.		**1** Billiards is played for the first time in Italy.	**1550**

Louvre Palace in Paris, France

	History and Politics		The Arts	
	America	**Elsewhere**	**America**	**Elsewhere**
				statue of Perseus, in Florence.
1551		**1** Ottoman Turks capture Tripoli but fail to take Malta.		
1552		**1** War between Emperor Charles V and Henry II of France ends in a truce, leaving France with the cities of Metz, Toul, and Verdun. **2** Persians capture Erzerum from the Turks.	Pieter Brueghel the Elder, Flemish painter.	
1553		**1** Ivan IV conquers Kazan and Astrakhan from the Tatars. Russia now controls the entire course of the Volga River. **2** Mary I becomes Queen of England. [1544:HIST/1] **3** Chinese repel attacks by Japanese pirates.		**1** Pieter Brueghel the Elder, Flemish painter known for scenes of peasant life, is in Rome where he produces his earliest signed and dated painting. **2** *Ralph Roister Doister* by Nicholas Udall is presented. This early English comedy was based on Latin models. **3** The first truly native English comedy, *Gammer Gurton's Needle*. Its author is anonymous.
1554		**1** Princess Elizabeth is imprisoned for suspected participation in plot against Mary I, Queen of England. **2** Turks seize Mehedia on the Tunisian coast from the Spaniards.		
1555	**1** French establish a colony at Rio de Janeiro.	**2** Sulayman I makes peace with the Turks and keeps his conquests in Mesopotamia. **3** Peace of Augsburg allows German princes to choose Catholicism or Lutheranism, but not Calvinism, as the religion of their states. Lutheranism prevails in north Germany; Catholicism in south.		**1** Michelangelo completes "Pietá" sculpture.

Science & Technology		Miscellaneous		
America	Elsewhere	America	Elsewhere	
	1 Gesner publishes *Historiae animalium,* which deals with mammals and their habits. **2** Pierre Belon, Fr. naturalist, publishes work on dolphins and other marine animals. **3** Gerardus Mercator, Belgian map-maker, makes a celestial globe.		**1** Population in Lisbon, Portugal, is about 100,000, including 10,000 African slaves. **2** Alehouses and taverns in England are licensed for the first time.	**1551**
	1 Astronomy and geometry are considered magic; all books on these subjects are burned in England.		**1** About 35 grammar schools are founded in the name of Edward VI, King of England.	**1552**
	1 Michael Servetus, Span. physician and theologian, puts forth theory of blood circulation through the lungs. **2** Belon publishes description of eastern Mediterranean plants and animals.		**1** Europeans first learn about the potato.	**1553**
	1 Mercator publishes map of Europe. **2** The first guns are cast in England.		**1** Catholicism is restored in England. **[1536:MISC/1]** **2** Tobacco is brought to Spain from America.	**1554**
	1 Nostradamus publishes *Centuries,* in which he makes many astrological predictions. **2** Belon publishes an illustrated book on birds, in which he classifies some 200 species.		**1** Wallpaper is used in Spain and in Holland.	**1555**

	History and Politics		The Arts	
	America	**Elsewhere**	**America**	**Elsewhere**
1556		**1** Emperor Charles V abdicates, giving Spain and the colonies to his son Philip II and giving the imperial crown and the Hapsburg lands to his brother Ferdinand I. Charles retires to the monastery of Yuste. **2** Akbar becomes Mogul emperor of India.	**1** First book with music is printed in the New World by Giovanni Paoli at Mexico City. It is the *Ordinary of the Mass*.	
1557		**1** Portuguese establish permanent trading post at Macao in south China. **2** Spanish defeat the French at the Battle of St. Quentin.		**1** Michelangelo designs the dome of St. Peter's, Rome.
1558		**1** French capture Calais from the English. **2** Elizabeth I becomes Queen of England at the death of Queen Mary I.		**1** Gioseffe Zarlino, Ital. musical theorist, publishes work on harmony in which he establishes the major and minor chords.
1559		**1** Francis II becomes King of France; his wife, Mary Queen of Scots, assumes title of Queen of England.		**1** Thomas Sackville, Eng. statesman and poet, publishes *Induction*, often described as first work marking Elizabethan literary style.
1560		**1** Charles IX becomes King of France; his mother Catherine de' Medici rules as regent.		**1** The Cathedral of St. Basil the Blessed, an outstanding example of medieval Russian architecture, is completed. **2** The Uffizi Palace in Florence is begun. Originally government offices, it now houses the world's greatest collection of Italian Renaissance art. **3** Tintoretto completes the painting, "Susannah and the Elders."
1561		**1** Mary Queen of Scots, returns to Scotland and accepts establishment of the Presbyterian Church. **2** Eric XIV, King of Sweden, strengthens the power of the crown by limiting the rights of the royal dukes.		

| Science & Technology | | Miscellaneous | | |
America	Elsewhere	America	Elsewhere	
	1 The first of a three-volume work by Tartaglia on elementary mathematics is published. **2** Gesner completes several more works, in which he describes fishes, birds, and aquatic mammals.		**1** Earthquake strikes Shensi, China, killing 830,000. **2** Pope Paul IV issues the Catholic Church's first list of forbidden books.	**1556**
			1 Influenza epidemic spreads throughout Europe.	**1557**
	1 Giambattista della Porta, Ital. scientist, invents the camera obscura.		**1** Jean Nicot, Fr. ambassador in Spain, sends tobacco ("Nicotine") to Paris. The Portuguese introduce snuff, a preparation of powdered tobacco, to Europe.	**1558**
	1 Matteo Realdo Colombo, Ital. anatomist, describes the circulation of blood.			**1559**
	1 Tycho Brahe, Dan. astronomer, observes a total eclipse.		**1** The Church of Scotland is founded. **2** The Geneva Bible is published in England. **3** Scottish Parliament abolishes the Pope's authority in Scotland. The Catholic Mass is made a penal offense, with death for the third conviction.	**1560**
	1 Gabriel Fallopius, Ital. anatomist, publishes *Observationes anatomicae,* in which he greatly increased the knowledge of the ear and genital organs.		**1** Modern technique of playing chess is developed in Spain. **2** St. Paul's Cathedral in London is badly damaged by fire.	**1561**

	History and Politics		The Arts	
	America	**Elsewhere**	**America**	**Elsewhere**
1562	**1** Jean Ribaut, Fr. colonizer, lands in Florida and claims the region for France. He sails north and establishes a colony on Parris Island, S.C., which is later abandoned when supplies do not come.	**2** Huguenots (French Protestants) take up arms to fight for freedom of worship and political rights. **3** Akbar the Great subdues the Rajputs, the most warlike of the Hindu peoples. He establishes a uniform system of rule and a policy of religious toleration throughout his empire. **[1556:HIST/2]**		**1** English exiles in Geneva produce the psalm book brought to the Colonies by the Puritans. **2** Cellini completes his *Autobiography*. It gives us a vivid picture of the 16th century. **3** Veronese (Paulo Cagliari), Venetian painter, completes "The Marriage at Cana."
1563		**1** Peace of Ambroise ends first War of Religion in France; Huguenots are given limited religious freedom. **[1562:HIST/2]** **2** Ivan IV conquers part of Livonia (now Estonia and part of Latvia), securing an outlet to the Baltic Sea.	**1** Construction of the cathedral in Mexico City is begun. This church, in Spanish Renaissance style, is the largest cathedral on the North American continent.	**2** Brueghel moves to Brussels, where he produces his greatest paintings. One of the first is "The Flight into Egypt."
1564	**1** French Huguenots under René Goulaine de Laudonnière establish a colony called Fort Caroline near the mouth of the St. Johns River, Fla.	**2** Peace of Troyes ends war between France and England; English give up claims to Calais for 222,000 crowns. **[1558:HIST/1]** **3** Maximilian II becomes Holy Roman Emperor, succeeding his father Ferdinand I. **4** Powerful Russian boyars (nobles) force Ivan IV to withdraw from Moscow. Ivan takes horrible revenge on them and begins reign of terror.	**1** Jacques LeMoyne, Fr. Huguenot explorer, paints scenes of Indian life in Florida.	**2** Construction of the original Tuileries Palace, Paris, begins. Architect is the Frenchman Philibert Delorme. **3** Religious musical works of Lassus are published in Paris. He dominates this field for the remainder of the century. **4** Andrea Amati, Ital. violin maker, produces his first instruments.
1565	**1** Pedro Menéndez de Avilés, Span. colonizer, establishes colony of St. Augustine, Fla. (oldest permanent city in the U.S.). Menéndez destroys the French colony at Fort Caroline. **[1564:HIST/1; 1565:MISC/1]**	**2** Knights of Malta (formerly Knights Hospitalers) defend Malta against the Turks. **[1530:HIST/2]**	**1** The architecture of St. Augustine (Florida) is Spanish Colonial, based on the Renaissance and Baroque styles of Spain and Mexico.	**2** Tintoretto paints his immense "Crucifixion" in a room of St. Roch's School in Venice.
1566		**1** The Netherlands, led by William of Orange, rebels against Spanish rule and the Inquisition (Catholic council engaged in punishing heresy).	**1** Nicholas LeChalleux writes an account of the French in Florida.	**2** George Gascoigne writes the first English comedy in prose, *Supposes*. **3** Giuseppe Arcimboldo's grotesque painting of reformer John Calvin is one of the earliest examples of

Science & Technology		Miscellaneous		
America	**Elsewhere**	**America**	**Elsewhere**	
				1562
1 John Hawkins, Eng. slave trader, brings tobacco and sweet potatoes from America to England.	**2** Mills for making wire are developed at Nuremberg. **3** Brahe makes his first recorded observation—the conjunction of Jupiter and Saturn.		**1** A general outbreak of the bubonic plague in Europe spreads to England, killing more than 20,000 people.	**1563**
			1 The horse-drawn coach is introduced to England from Holland.	**1564**

The great Cathedral in Mexico City

Science & Technology		Miscellaneous		
America	**Elsewhere**	**America**	**Elsewhere**	
	1 Dissections of human bodies are allowed at the Royal College of Physicians in England. **2** Bernadino Telesio, Ital. philosopher and scientist, establishes the scientific method of observation and experimentation.	**1** Spanish priests found the first Catholic parish in St. Augustine, Fla. **2** Game of billiards is brought to the New World by Spanish settlers.	**3** Thomas Gresham, Eng. economist, starts the Royal Exchange, a center for business, in London. **4** Graphite pencil is invented by Konrad Gesner who first describes the writing instrument, a wooden holder into which graphite is inserted.	**1565**
		1 Jesuits establish a mission in Florida.	**2** One of the first newspapers is published in Venice.	**1566**

31

History and Politics		The Arts	
America	**Elsewhere**	**America**	**Elsewhere**
			caricature. **4** Brueghel paints "The Wedding Dance," now in the Detroit Institute of Arts.
1567	**1** Mary Queen of Scots abdicates in favor of her son James and makes her stepbrother regent. Mary had lost the support of the people because of her personal intrigues.		**1** Brueghel paints "The Conversion of St. Paul."
1568 **1** Dominique de Gourgues, Fr. soldier, destroys, with the help of Indians, the Spanish colony of San Mateo (formerly Fort Caroline under the French). **[1565:HIST/1]**	**2** Peace of Longjumeau ends second War of Religion in France; Protestant Huguenots are persecuted less. **3** Maximilian II signs truce with Ottoman Turks.		
1569	**1** Sigismund II, King of Poland, unites the duchy of Lithuania with the Polish kingdom.	**1** Jesuit missionaries encourage and build on theatrical activities in Peru.	**2** Miguel de Cervantes, greatest Span. literary figure of all time, publishes first work, an elegy for wife of Philip II.
1570	**1** Treaty of Saint-Germain ends third War of Religion in France; Huguenots are given new liberties. **[1568:HIST/2]** **2** Turks attack Cyprus and declare war on Venice. **3** Japan opens Nagasaki to foreign trade. **4** The Pope excommunicates Elizabeth I of England for imposing harsh penalties upon Catholics who continue to recognize papal authority and not the Church of England.		**1** Nicholas Hilliard, Eng. painter, is appointed Court Miniaturist and Goldsmith to Elizabeth I. He influenced the development of miniature portraiture as a serious art form.
1571	**1** Turks capture Famagusta, Cyprus. Turkish fleet is defeated at Battle of Lepanto by Spanish and Italian fleet. **2** Crimean Tatars sack and burn Moscow. **3** Spanish found colony at Manila in the Philippines.		
1572	**1** Hundreds of Protestant Huguenots are murdered at the massacre of St. Bartholomew's Day, which Catherine de' Medici helped plan. Fourth War of Religion begins in France.		**1** Luis Vaz de Camões, Port. poet, publishes *The Lusiads,* an epic celebrating the history of Portugal and the voyages of Vasco da Gama.

Science & Technology		Miscellaneous		
America	Elsewhere	America	Elsewhere	

Gerardus Mercator, famous 16th century map-maker, with Iudocus Hondius

Science & Technology		Miscellaneous		
America	Elsewhere	America	Elsewhere	
			1 Typhoid fever kills 2 million Indians in South America.	**1567**
			1 A college is founded in Douai, France, to train Jesuits for missionary work in England.	**1568**
1 Nicolás Monardes, Span. physician, describes medicinal uses of American plants.	**2** Mercator establishes the use of latitude and longitude in world maps.		**1** Almost 40,000 inhabitants of Lisbon, Portugal, die in an epidemic of carbuncular fever.	**1569**
	1 Abraham Ortelius, Dutch map-maker, prepares the first world atlas.		**1** Roger Ascham, stresses importance of the English language in *The Scholemaster*. He is tutor to Queen Elizabeth. **2** Postal service is organized in Nuremberg, Bavaria (Germany).	**1570**
			1 Cambridge University is founded in England.	**1571**
	1 Brahe observes a nova in the constellation Cassiopeia.		**1** An epidemic in Algiers in North Africa kills one third of the population.	**1572**

Miguel de Cervantes, Spanish novelist

History and Politics		The Arts	
America	**Elsewhere**	**America**	**Elsewhere**
			2 Pierre de Ronsard, Fr. poet, publishes *La Franciade,* epic poem about kings of France.
1573	**1** Edict of Boulogne ends war favorably for the Huguenots. **[1572:HIST/1]** **2** Venetians desert the Spanish and make peace with the Turks, who continue to ravage the coasts of the western Mediterranean. **[1571:HIST/1]** **3** Akbar conquers the rich territory of Gujarat in western India. **[1562:HIST/3]**		
1574	**1** Turks drive the Spanish out of Tunis. **2** Portuguese found colony in Angola. **3** Fifth War of Religion begins in France. **4** Henry III becomes King of France, succeeding his brother Charles IX.		
1575	**1** Mogul Emperor Akbar conquers Bengal from the Afghans.		**1** Giacomo Della Porta, Ital. architect, designs facade of a Roman church in Baroque style. Della Porta completed many of Michelangelo's projects.
1576 **1** English begin expeditions to North America in search of the Northwest Passage, a water route around America to Asia. Martin Frobisher makes his first voyage to Arctic regions in search of the passage.	**2** Fifth War of Religion in France ends with the Peace of Monsieur, ratified by the Edict of Beaulieu, giving freedom of worship throughout France, except in Paris. **[1574:HIST/3]** **3** Ghent joins William of Orange in the revolt of the Netherlands against Spain. **[1566:HIST/1]**		**1** The first London theater is built by James Burbage outside the city limits to escape censorship by the Lord Mayor. When it is later dismantled by his son, its timber is used to build the Globe. **[1599:ARTS/1]**
1577 **1** Frobisher explores eastern passages to Hudson and Baffin Bays on his second voyage to the Arctic.	**2** French Catholics persuade Henry III to repeal the Edict of Beaulieu; Huguenots revolt once more. This sixth war ends with the Peace of Bergerac, which renews the terms of the Peace of Monsieur. **[1576:HIST/2]**		**1** El Greco "The Greek" (Doménikos Theotokópoulous) paints high altarpiece in Toledo, Spain. **2** The *Chronicles* of Raphael Holinshed are published. Shakespeare used this history of Britain when writing many of his plays.

Science & Technology		Miscellaneous		
America	**Elsewhere**	**America**	**Elsewhere**	
	1 Brahe publishes his observations in *De nova stella,* a work which establishes him as the leading European astronomer.			**1573**
	1 Ulisse Aldrovandi, Ital. scientist, writes a pharmacopoeia in which the uses and properties of drugs are described.			**1574**

The Plague in Milan, painting by Casper de Crayer

Science & Technology		Miscellaneous		
			1 Paris' population is approximately 300,000; that of London, about 100,000. **2** Bubonic plague breaks out in Italy. It spreads north from Sicily to Florence and Milan.	**1575**
	1 Carolus Clusius, Dutch botanist, publishes a work on flowers.		**1** There are 40,000 African slaves in South America.	**1576**
	1 Brahe proves that the orbits of comets lie beyond the Moon.	**1** With 150 vessels, France is the most active country in the fishing industry. Spain is next with 100 ships, followed by Portugal and England.	**2** State monopoly (control) of trade is abolished in Portugal.	**1577**

	History and Politics		The Arts	
	America	Elsewhere	America	Elsewhere
1578	**1** Sir Francis Drake, Eng. navigator and admiral, lands on the California coast and claims the region for England.	**2** Swedes defeat the Russians at Cesis, Latvia, in the struggle for Baltic territory. **3** Sebastian, King of Portugal, invades Morocco. His army is defeated and he is killed at Alcazarquivir.		
1579		**1** Union of Utrecht, consisting of seven provinces of the Netherlands, proclaims independence from Spain.		**1** John Lyly, Eng. dramatist and novelist, publishes *Euphues,* a novel of polite society written in an elaborate style that gives us the word *euphuistic.* **2** The Corral de la Cruz, the most important theater in Madrid, opens. **3** Edmund Spenser, Eng. poet, publishes *The Shepheard's Calendar,* 12 pastoral poems.
1580		**1** Seventh War of Religion in France breaks out but soon ends with the Treaty of Felix, which grants the Huguenots amnesty. **2** Spanish invade Portugal and occupy Ceuta. **3** Sir Francis Drake arrives in England after voyage around the world. [1578:HIST/1]		**1** Fr. writer Michel de Montaigne, publishes two volumes of *Essays.* He originated this form for expressing personal views. **2** A group of Florentines form the Camerata. Their revivals of Greek theater emphasize its musical aspects and give rise to European opera. **3** The first mention is recorded of the English folk melody "*Greensleeves.*"
1581		**1** Spanish defeat Portuguese near Lisbon. Philip II of Spain becomes King of Portugal. **2** Stephen Báthory, King of Poland, invades Russia and fights war against Ivan IV for control of Livonia. [1563:HIST/2]		**1** *Ballet Comique de la Reine,* considered the first ballet, is presented by Catherine de' Medici as a court festival in France. **2** Tintoretto paints mythological scenes for the Doge's Palace in Venice. The most famous is "Ariadne, Bacchus, and Venus."
1582	**1** Antonio de Espejo travels down the Conchos River and up the Rio Grande, exploring	**2** Russia makes peace with Poland and Sweden; Russia loses access to Baltic and	**1** Richard Hakluyt's *Divers Voyages* brings American discoveries to	**2** El Greco completes "The Martyrdom of St. Maurice," known for

36

Science & Technology		Miscellaneous		
America	**Elsewhere**	**America**	**Elsewhere**	
			1 The catacombs, underground burial places of early Christians, are discovered in Rome. **2** Levant Trading Company is founded in London for trade with Turkey.	**1578**
	1 François Viète, Fr. mathematician, publishes *Mathematical Laws Applied to Triangles,* in which algebraic notation is introduced.	**1** First Protestant religious service is held in California by the crew of Sir Francis Drake. [1578:HIST/1]	**2** Portuguese merchants set up a trading station in India. **3** The English Eastland Company is established for trade with Scandinavia.	**1579**
1 Cultivation of tobacco begins in Cuba.			**1** About 500 head of cattle and 1000 horses are brought to South America. **2** Earthquake in London. **3** Copper money comes into use in France.	**1580**
			1 Demand for beaver wool for hats in Paris stimulates trade with North America. **2** More than 100 priests from the college at Douai, France, are working in England. [1568:MISC/1]	**1581**

Queen Elizabeth knighting Sir Francis Drake

			1 The Douai-Rheims Bible, an English translation of the New Testa-	**1582**

	History and Politics		The Arts	
	America	**Elsewhere**	**America**	**Elsewhere**
	much of the American Southwest before returning to Mexico in 1583.	abandons Livonia. [1581:HIST/2]	the attention of the English-speaking world.	its startling color contrasts. Philip II ordered the work for El Escorial, but later rejected it. [1584:ARTS/1]
1583		**1** Persecution of the Catholics leads to plots to murder Queen Elizabeth I and to seat the Catholic Mary Queen of Scots. **2** William of Orange rules over the northern Netherlands.	**1** Bernardino de Sahagún, Span. friar and linguist, publishes *Psalmodia Christiana* in Mexico City. It contains psalms in the Aztec language set to native melodies.	**2** Claudio Monteverdi, Ital. composer, publishes his first work at the age of 16, a book of sacred madrigals.
1584	**1** Sir Walter Raleigh, Eng. explorer and writer, sends expedition to explore the New World. Expedition lands in Virginia. (Raleigh names it in honor of Queen Elizabeth I, the "virgin queen.")	**2** Russian government falls into the hands of the boyars and Boris Godunov, regent for Ivan's young son. [1547:HIST/2; 1564:HIST/4]		**1** The palace-monastery of Philip II, El Escorial near Madrid, Spain, is completed. Its starkness contrasts with the ornate palace of his father, Charles V. Its architect was the Spaniard Juan de Herrera. [1526:ARTS/1]
1585	**1** English colonists sent by Raleigh land on Roanoke Island, N.C., and build a settlement.	**2** English expedition is sent to aid the Dutch in their fight against the Spanish governor of the Netherlands. **3** Ottoman Empire begins to decline due to the corruption of the sultans and the military organization. [1514:HIST/1] **4** Toyotomi Hideyoshi is appointed civil dictator in central Japan.	**1** John White, Eng. artist and surveyor, paints scenes of Indian life in Virginia.	**2** Teatro Olimpico, the first permanent indoor theater, is completed in Vicenze, Italy.
1586	**1** Sir Francis Drake ravages the Spanish settlements in the West Indies and Florida, including St. Augustine. Drake rescues the English colonists on Roanoke Island, who had fared badly and asked to return to England. [1585:HIST/1]	**2** England's secretary of state discovers conspiracy to murder Queen Elizabeth I and to free Mary Queen of Scots. Conspirators are executed, and Mary is put on trial.		**1** Christopher Marlowe, Elizabethan playwright who influenced development of poetic tragedy, writes the drama *Tamburlaine* in blank verse. **2** El Greco begins his masterpiece, "The Burial of Count Orgaz." El Greco's work is characterized by long, narrow human figures. **3** Kabuki theater begins in Japan, developing out of the Nō drama.

Science & Technology		Miscellaneous		
America	**Elsewhere**	**America**	**Elsewhere**	
			ment, is published. **2** Pope Gregory XIII introduces a new ("Gregorian") calendar in which the year begins on January 1.	
			1 First known life insurance policy is issued in England.	**1583**
			1 First book is printed in Peru.	**1584**

El Escorial, the palace-monastery of King Philip II, near Madrid, Spain

Science & Technology		Miscellaneous		
1 Iron is discovered in North Carolina.	**2** Simon Stevin, Dutch mathematician, publishes *The Tenth,* in which the current use of decimal fractions is introduced.			**1585**
	1 The potato is introduced into Europe. **2** Galileo Galilei, Ital. physicist and astronomer, describes hydrostatic balance.			**1586**

	History and Politics		The Arts	
	America	**Elsewhere**	**America**	**Elsewhere**
1587	**1** John Davis, Eng. navigator, attempts to find Northwest Passage to Asia. [1576:HIST/1] **2** Raleigh sends out another group to colonize Roanoke Island. Virginia Dare is born there, the first white child of English parents born in America.	**3** Mary Queen of Scots is convicted of treason and beheaded by order of Elizabeth I. [1586:HIST/2] **4** Hideyoshi completes conquest of western Japan and banishes Portuguese missionaries from Japan. [1585:HIST/4]		**1** Thomas Kyd's *The Spanish Tragedy* is performed. **2** Osaka Castle, with its huge stone walls and wide moats, is completed in Japan.
1588	**1** Second English colony on Roanoke Island disappears, known as the Lost Colony.	**1** English fleet defeats Spanish Armada, sent by Philip II of Spain to overthrow Queen Elizabeth I and put Philip on the English throne. Spain's power begins to fade; Elizabethan England flourishes.	**2** The first book in English about the English colonies is published. [1588:MISC/1]	**2** Thoinot Arbeau, Fr. priest, writes *Orchesography,* one of the first works on dance. **3** Marlowe writes *Dr. Faustus.*
1589		**1** Henry, King of Navarre and Protestant leader, becomes King of France as Henry IV.		**1** Monteverdi publishes *First Book of Madrigals.*
1590		**1** Turks and Persians make peace after a long, erratic war that began in 1577. Turks acquire lands, extending their frontier to the Caspian Sea. **2** Henry IV of France defeats Holy League and besieges Paris. **3** Hideyoshi becomes ruler of a united Japan after conquering the eastern and northern parts.		**1** Spenser publishes the first books of *The Fairie Queene.* The medieval characters and plot represent people and events of his own day. **2** Shakespeare completes *Henry VI, Parts 2* and *3. Part 1* is written in 1591.
1591		**1** The Pope excommunicates Henry IV of France. **2** Godunov strengthens the power of the Russian state and its people at the expense of the boyars. [1584:HIST/2]		**1** Sir Philip Sidney's sonnets are published. They influenced love lyrics of the period.
1592		**1** Hideyoshi of Japan attempts to conquer China. He invades Korea on route to China. Chinese army forces Japanese to withdraw to south coast.		**1** Shakespeare's *Richard III* is presented by the Lord Chamberlain's Men, an acting company for which Shakespeare performed and wrote. The play enjoys immediate popularity.
1593		**1** Henry IV converts to Catholicism, remarking "Paris is well worth a Mass." [1590:HIST/2] **2** Portuguese and Dutch es-	**1** Anonymous artist draws Fort of St. Augustine in Florida.	**2** The plague causes the closing of London theaters for a year. **3** Shakespeare completes *Titus Andron-*

Science & Technology		Miscellaneous		
America	**Elsewhere**	**America**	**Elsewhere**	
		1 Manteo, the first American Indian to be converted to Protestant Christianity, is baptized in the Church of England.	**2** *History of the Reformation in Scotland* by Knox is published after his death. **[1541:MISC/2]** **3** English Guinea Company is founded for trade with the Guinea coast areas of West Africa.	**1587**
	1 Bombs are invented.	**1** In *A Briefe and True Report of the New Found Land of Virginia,* Thomas Harriot, Eng. scientist, attempts to describe the natural resources to be found in America.		**1588**
			1 Forks are used for the first time at the French court.	**1589**
1 José d'Acosta, Span. missionary, publishes a natural history of the West Indies and suggests that the differences between American and European animals may be due to mutations.	**2** Zacharias Janssen, Dutch optician, with the aid of his father, builds the first compound microscope.		**1** Jesuits establish a second mission in India.	**1590**
	1 Viète publishes an elementary textbook of algebra.		**1** Skittle, an early form of bowling, becomes popular in Germany.	**1591**
	1 Cornelius Drebbel, Dutch scientist, builds an air-water thermometer.		**1** Site of Pompeii in Italy is rediscovered. The city had been destroyed when Mt. Vesuvius erupted in A.D. 79. **2** Bubonic plague kills 15,000 people in London.	**1592**
				1593

	History and Politics		The Arts	
	America	**Elsewhere**	**America**	**Elsewhere**
		tablish settlements on the east and west coast of Africa respectively.		*icus* and *The Taming of the Shrew.*
1594		**1** Henry IV enters Paris, having been crowned King of France at Chartres. He wins popular support. **2** Turks and Austrians battle on the Austria-Hungary border.		**1** Shakespeare's *Comedy of Errors*, written earlier, is performed at Gray's Inn. Its story comes from a play by the Roman dramatist Plautus. *Romeo and Juliet, The Two Gentlemen of Verona,* and *Love's Labour's Lost* are completed. **2** The first opera, *Dafne* by Jacopo Peri with story by Ottavio Rinuccini, is performed at the Corsi Palace.
1595	**1** Sir Walter Raleigh leads an expedition 300 miles up the Orinoco River in Venezuela in search of the fabled city of El Dorado.	**2** To rid France of Spanish influence, Henry IV declares war on Spain.		**1** El Greco paints "View of Toledo," a stormy, ominous scene and one of his few landscapes. **2** Shakespeare completes *Richard II* and *A Midsummer Night's Dream.*
1596	**1** Sebastián Vizcaíno, Span. explorer, makes unsuccessful attempt to colonize southern California.	**2** English attack and partly destroy Cádiz, Spain; Spanish seize Calais, France. **3** Turks defeat army of the Holy Roman Empire in northern Hungary. **4** Willem Barents, Dutch navigator, discovers Spitsbergen while searching for a northeast passage to Asia.		**1** Shakespeare writes *King John* and *The Merchant of Venice.* **2** Spenser's *The Faerie Queene*, Books 4–6, completed.
1597		**1** Chinese repel Japanese invasions in Korea. **2** Portuguese, English, and Dutch begin to fight over control of the spice trade in the East Indies.		**1** Caravaggio (Michelangelo Merisi), Ital. painter whose realistic religious paintings are considered revolutionary, decorates the chapel of a Roman church with scenes from life of St. Matthew. **2** Shakespeare writes *Henry IV, Parts 1* and *2.* **3** Aldine Press, founded by Aldus Manutius in Venice, closes after publishing 908 works. [1494:ARTS/4]

Science & Technology		Miscellaneous		
America	**Elsewhere**	**America**	**Elsewhere**	
			1 Richard Hooker, Eng. author and clergyman, writes a defense of the Church of England. **2** James Lancaster, Eng. navigator, breaks the Portuguese trade monopoly in India. **[1579:MISC/2]**	**1594**
			1 Shoes with heels first appear in Europe. **2** English army no longer uses the bow as a weapon. **[1541:MISC/3]**	**1595**
	1 The first trigonometric tables, devised by Rhäticus, are published 20 years after his death.		**1** Gresham College is founded in London for education in 7 liberal sciences.	**1596**
	1 John Gerard, Fr. botanist, publishes *The Herball, or Generall Historie of Plants*.		**1** English Parliament orders workhouses built to house and feed paupers. Convicted criminals are transported to the colonies.	**1597**

William Shakespeare, English dramatist and poet

	History and Politics		The Arts	
	America	**Elsewhere**	**America**	**Elsewhere**
1598	**1** Juan de Oñate, Span. explorer, leads an expedition into New Mexico and claims the region for Spain; he establishes a settlement.	**2** Henry IV issues the Edict of Nantes, which grants political rights and religious toleration to the Huguenots in France. [1685:MISC/3] **3** Boris Godunov is chosen Czar of Russia by the national assembly. [1584:HIST/2] **4** France and Spain sign Treaty of Vervins; Philip II gives up claims to the French throne.	**1** The performance of a Spanish play in the area of present-day El Paso is one of the earliest theatrical presentations on the North American continent.	**2** Lope de Vega, Span. poet and playwright, publishes *La Dragontea*, an epic about the last voyage and death of Sir Francis Drake. **3** Ben Jonson's *Every Man in His Humour* is performed. **4** Shakespeare writes *Much Ado about Nothing* and *Henry V*.
1599		**1** Swedish Diet (assembly) deposes Sigismund III as King of Sweden.		**1** The Globe Theater is built. Most of Shakespeare's plays are performed here. **2** Shakespeare writes *Julius Caesar, As You Like It,* and *Twelfth Night*.
1600		**1** Ieyasu defeats rival Japanese lords at the Battle of Sekigahara. He establishes Japan's military capital at Edo (now Tokyo).		**1** Thomas Dekker's *The Shoemaker's Holiday* is printed. It is one of the first realistic comedies with ordinary people from everyday life. **2** Shakespeare writes *Hamlet* and *The Merry Wives of Windsor*. **3** Hans Leo Hassler, Ger. composer, is appointed musical director at Nuremberg.
1601		**1** English suppress rebellion in Ireland. Queen Elizabeth I checks uprising against her in London. **2** Ieyasu welcomes Spanish traders to Japan. [1600:HIST/1]		**1** Thomas Campion, Eng. poet, composer, and musical theorist, publishes *A Book of Ayres*. **2** Ben Jonson's *The Poetaster* is performed by one of the many children's companies popular in the Elizabethan theater.
1602	**1** Bartholomew Gosnold, Eng. explorer, sails along the American coast, from Maine to Rhode Island. He names Cape Cod and builds a fort on Cuttyhunk, one of the Elizabeth Islands.	**2** War breaks out between the Persians and Turks. **3** Spanish army, sent to aid Catholic Irish chiefs in their fight against Protestant England, surrenders to English at Kinsale, Ireland.		**1** *Hamlet,* the most often performed and most popular of Shakespeare's tragedies, is first presented. **2** Shakespeare writes *All's Well That Ends Well*.

44

Science & Technology		Miscellaneous		
America	**Elsewhere**	**America**	**Elsewhere**	
			1 After being destroyed by fire, The Oxford University Library in England is rebuilt. Supported by Thomas Bodley, diplomat and scholar, it is renamed the Bodleian Library.	**1598**
			1 Bubonic plague breaks out in Spain. **2** Copper money comes into use in Spain. [1580:MISC/3]	**1599**
	1 Hieronymus Fabricius, Ital. scientist, publishes an exhaustive study of embryology, in which the larynx is established as the human vocal organ. **2** William Gilbert, Eng. physician, publishes *Concerning Magnetism,* which explains how a compass works.		**1** English East India Company is founded to carry on spice trade with Asia. **2** India's population is estimated at 100 million.	**1600**
	1 Julius Casserius, Ital. scientist, publishes an illustrated work on hearing and speech.			**1601**
1 Bartholomew Gosnold, Eng. navigator, plants wheat at Buzzards Bay, Mass.	**2** Santorio Santorio, Ital. physician, develops a clock to measure the pulse.		**1** Dutch East India Company is founded to expand the spice trade in Asia.	**1602**

Ship of the Dutch East India Company

	History and Politics		The Arts	
	America	Elsewhere	America	Elsewhere
1603	**1** Samuel de Champlain, Fr. explorer, sails up the St. Lawrence River on the first of many expeditions to the New World.	**2** James VI of Scotland, son of Mary Queen of Scots, becomes King James I of England. [1567:HIST/1] **3** Sir Walter Raleigh is found guilty of intrigues with Spain against England and of plotting to dethrone King James I. **4** Abbas I, Shah of Persia, conquers much territory from the Ottoman Turks.		**1** Peter Paul Rubens, Flemish artist, scholar, and diplomat, paints "Democritus and Heraclitus."
1604		**1** England makes peace with Spain. **2** Spanish take Ostend from the Dutch after a three-year siege. **3** "False Dmitri" appears, claiming title to the Russian throne.	**1** Span. missionary Cristóbal de Quinoñes is the first music teacher in what is now the U.S., the area of present-day New Mexico. **2** The Habitation of Fr. explorer Samuel de Champlain is built at Port Royal in Nova Scotia. It is an example of French Colonial architecture in Canada's maritime provinces.	**3** Annibale Carracci, Ital. painter, completes a ceiling of Rome's Farnese Palace with scenes from Ovid. **4** Shakespeare writes *Measure for Measure*.
1605	**1** Sieur de Monts, Fr. colonizer, founds the first permanent French settlement in North America at Port Royal (now Annapolis Royal), Nova Scotia.	**2** Godunov's son becomes Czar of Russia. He is assassinated. Dmitri is crowned Czar. [1604:HIST/3] **3** Guy Fawkes and others are arrested (and later executed) for planning to blow up the English Parliament. Plan is called the "Gunpowder Plot."	**1** Construction is begun on the Jesuit church La Compañía in Quito, Ecuador. It is an outstanding example of Spanish-Moorish architecture in the Americas.	**2** Eng. architect Inigo Jones designs a masque (performance) for the Queen. He executes the scenes, costumes, and effects. **3** Cervantes publishes *Don Quixote,* a parody of chivalrous romances. Next to the Bible, it becomes the world's most translated book. **4** Shakespeare completes *King Lear* and *Macbeth*.
1606	**1** Virginia Company of London is granted a charter by King James I to found colonies in America.	**2** Russian boyars murder Czar Dmitri. New pretenders to the Russian throne appear; Cossacks and peasants rise in revolt. [1605:HIST/2] **3** Austrians and Turks sign peace Treaty of Zsitva-Török.	**1** A performance of a French theatrical masque in Port Royal, Acadia, is among the first plays presented in the New World.	**2** Ben Jonson's *Volpone* is first performed. It is a bitterly comical treatment of the serious theme of greed. **3** The earliest known examples of multi-color woodblock printing are in "Mr. Ch'eng's Ink Miscellany."
1607	**1** First permanent English colony in North America is established at Jamestown,	**2** House of Commons blocks King James's proposed union of Scotland with England.		**1** Shakespeare writes *Timon of Athens* and *Coriolanus*.

Science & Technology		Miscellaneous		
America	Elsewhere	America	Elsewhere	
	1 Fabricius publishes the first description of the valves of the blood veins.		1 Bubonic plague breaks out in England; more than 30,000 people die in London. 2 James I, King of England, announces tolerance for Catholics in England. [1603:HIST/2]	1603
	1 Galileo proves his law of gravity, supposedly after dropping weights from the Leaning Tower of Pisa.		1 Dutch establish trading posts on the west coast of Borneo, in the South China Sea. 2 French East India Company is founded.	1604
			1 Jesuits first arrive in South America. 2 Sir Francis Bacon, Eng. essayist and philosopher, publishes *The Advance of Learning*.	1605

Galileo, Italian physicist and astronomer

Science & Technology		Miscellaneous		
America	Elsewhere	America	Elsewhere	
	1 Porta describes the steam engine. 2 Andreas Libavius, Ger. chemist, publishes *Alchemy,* the first chemistry textbook.		1 A commercial treaty is agreed to between France and Germany.	1606
	1 Galileo constructs an elementary air thermometer.	1 First wedding takes place in Virginia.		1607

History and Politics		The Arts	
America	Elsewhere	America	Elsewhere
Virginia. Capt. John Smith holds colonists together through periods of hardship.			**2** *Orfeo,* an opera by Monteverdi, is presented under the auspices of Duke Francesco Gonzaga.

1608

1 Champlain establishes French colony at Quebec.	**2** German cities and states form Protestant Union to defend their lands, persons, and rights against any reestablishment of Roman Catholicism by the Holy Roman Emperor. **3** Matthias forces his brother, Holy Roman Emperor Rudolf II, to cede Hungary, Austria, and Moravia to him.	**1** Captain John Smith's written account of the Virginia colony is considered the first American book. The work was printed in London.	**2** Shakespeare writes *Pericles.* **3** Monteverdi's opera *Arianna* is an immense success.

1609

1 Henry Hudson, Eng. navigator then in the service of the Dutch East India Company, explores Chesapeake Bay, Delaware Bay, and the Hudson River as far as Albany.	**2** Duke of Bavaria forms Catholic League to oppose Protestant Union. **[1608:HIST/2]** **3** Complicated dynastic quarrel begins between Brandenberg and Neuburg for the succession of the duchy of Jülich-Cleves. **4** Moriscos (Moors converted to Christianity) are expelled from Spain.	**1** The Governor's Palace at Sante Fe is built. The oldest surviving non-Indian building in the U.S., it combines Spanish and Pueblo architectural styles. **2** An anonymous engraving pictures the explorer Champlain at Ticonderoga.	**3** Shakespeare writes *Cymbeline.* **4** Thomas Ravenscroft, Eng. composer, publishes the first collection of rounds and catches in English. It includes "Three Blind Mice."

1610

1 Spanish found Santa Fe, N. Mex., on the site of ancient Indian ruins. **2** English colonists at Jamestown endure "starving time," when many die of hunger and disease.	**3** Boyars in Russia struggle for control and seek aid from Poles and Swedes, who both take advantage of the confused state to try to secure the throne for themselves. **[1606:HIST/2]** **4** After the assassination of Henry IV of France, Marie de' Medici (Henry's second wife) becomes regent for her son Louis XIII.	**1** Flemish historian Emanuel van Meteren publishes the first account of voyages of Henry Hudson. **2** William Strachey writes of a New World settlement in the area of the Bermudas. Some scholars think Shakespeare used this source when writing *The Tempest.*	**3** The church of S. Giorgio Maggiore in Venice, designed by Palladio, is completed. **4** Ben Jonson's *The Alchemist,* known for perfection of plot, is performed.

1611

	1 James I of England dissolves Parliament. Except for the Addled Parliament of 1614, he rules without one until 1621. **2** Gustavus II (Gustavus Adolphus) becomes King of Sweden. War of Kalmar begins between Denmark and Sweden. **3** Rudolf II cedes Bohemia to Matthias. **[1608:HIST/3]**		**1** George Chapman, Eng. poet and dramatist, completes his famous translation of Homer's *Iliad.* **2** Shakespeare writes *The Tempest.* **3** *The Maid's Tragedy* by John Fletcher and Francis Beaumont is their most successful playwriting venture.

48

Science & Technology		Miscellaneous		
America	Elsewhere	America	Elsewhere	
	1 Hans Lippershey, Dutch optician, invents the telescope.	1 Cargo, consisting of tar, pitch, soap, and glass, is shipped from Jamestown, Va., to England. 2 Of the 105 men in Jamestown, 35 are considered gentlemen.	3 Checks, or cash letters, are first used in Holland. 4 First recorded use of forks in Italy. [1589:MISC/1]	1608
	1 Galileo builds a telescope. 2 Casserius publishes *Pentaessteseion,* which presents new information on the sense organs. 3 Johann Kepler, Ger. astronomer, discovers the elliptical orbit of Mars.	1 Church of England is established by law in Virginia. 2 Eng. colonial leader Capt. John Smith requires that the Virginia colonists grow maize (corn).	3 Old Testament of the Rheims-Douai Bible is published. [1582:MISC/1] 4 Tea is shipped from China to Europe by the Dutch East India Company.	1609
1 Dr. Lawrence Bohun is appointed by the London Company as the first official physician to the colonies. 2 Samuel de Champlain, Fr. explorer, establishes a botanical garden in Canada near Mount Royal (Montreal).	3 Galileo discovers the rings of Saturn, the stellar composition of the Milky Way, and the Moon's rough surface. 4 Simon Marius, Bavarian astronomer, names the moons of Jupiter.	1 Number of settlers in the colonies is estimated at 210.	2 St. Francis de Sales, Fr. bishop, helps found the Order of the Visitation nuns.	1610
	1 Marius makes the first recorded observation of the Andromeda nebula. 2 Johannes Fabricius, Dutch astronomer, makes the first known observation of sunspots. 3 Caspar Bartholin, Dan. physician, writes *The Textbook of Modern Anatomy,* perhaps the most complete anatomy work of its time.	1 First recorded recreation of European settlers is a game of bowls, played in Jamestown. 2 First Presbyterian congregation is established in Virginia.	3 Authorized Version of the Bible, called the King James Bible, is published in England. 4 Dutch merchants trade in Japan.	1611

	History and Politics		The Arts	
	America	Elsewhere	America	Elsewhere
1612		**1** Matthias becomes Holy Roman Emperor on the death of Rudolf II. **2** Russian national militia drives the Poles out of Moscow. **[1610:HIST/3]**		**1** Henry Ainsworth's *Psalm Book*, containing English, French, and Dutch tunes, is published in Amsterdam. **[1620:ART/1]**
1613	**1** English colonists from Virginia destroy rival French colony on Mount Desert Island, Me.	**2** Representative assembly elects Michael Romanov Czar of Russia, thus ending the Time of Troubles. Romanov dynasty rules until 1917. **3** Gustavus II of Sweden ends War of Kalmar with Denmark by buying off the Danes. He begins war with Russia. **[1611:HIST/2]**	**1** French explorer Samuel de Champlain publishes the first account of his explorations in the New World. **2** Rev. Alexander Whitaker writes to London of *Good News from Virginia* describing an ideal land.	**3** The original Globe Theater burns down. Its thatched roof caught fire when a cannon was discharged during a performance.
1614	**1** Capt. John Smith explores the coast of New England, hoping to start a settlement there. **2** Adriaen Block, Dut. navigator, explores Long Island Sound, Connecticut River, and Narragansett Bay; he makes a map of the region. **3** Dutch build a fur-trading post called Fort Nassau at Albany. **4** English colonists destroy the French colony at Port Royal, Nova Scotia. **[1613:HIST/1]**	**5** Gustavus II of Sweden captures city of Novgorod from the Russians. **6** Marie de' Medici summons the Estates-General (legislative body) to oppose the power of the nobles, the last before the Revolution of 1789.		**1** One of the most powerful of post-Shakespearean tragedies, *The Duchess of Malfi* by John Webster, is presented. **2** The Globe Theater, rebuilt with tiled roof, reopens.
1615	**1** Franciscan friars (monks) arrive in Quebec and begin French missionary activity.	**2** Dutch seize the Moluccas (Spice Islands) from the Portuguese. Dutch East India Company secures a monopoly in the clove trade. **[1602:MISC/1]**		**1** John Donne, Eng. poet whose love lyrics and religious sonnets have had a profound influence on modern verse, is ordained a priest in the Church of England. Many of his best-known poems were written before this time. **2** The new St. Peter's in Rome is completed. **[1505:ARTS/1]** **3** Chapman completes his translation of Homer's *Odyssey*.

Science & Technology		Miscellaneous		
America	**Elsewhere**	**America**	**Elsewhere**	
1 First American bricks are made in Virginia. **2** Captain John Smith publishes *A Map of Virginia* giving geological features and a description of the area. **3** John Rolfe, Eng. colonist, discovers method of curing tobacco so that large amounts can be exported.	**4** Santorio develops the clinical thermometer for human use.	**1** Dutch use Manhattan Island as a fur-trading center.	**2** Two Unitarians are burnt at the stake, the last heretics to be burnt in England.	**1612**
1 Large-scale cultivation of tobacco begins in Jamestown, Va. **2** John Rolfe crosses tobacco from the West Indies with native plants, producing a hybrid that quickly becomes popular in England.	**3** Galileo gives public support to Copernicus in three letters on sunspots.	**1** Pocahontas is the first Indian convert to Protestant Christianity in Virginia.	**2** Copper coins come into use in England. **[1599:MISC/2]**	**1613**
 Captain John Smith, Admiral of New England	**1** Scot. mathematician John Napier invents logarithms.	**1** First important lottery in the English colonies is held by the Virginia Company. The prize is 4500 English crowns.	**2** New Netherlands Company of Amsterdam is given a 3-year monopoly of the fur trade in North America. **3** All foreign missionaries are ordered to leave Japan. Their churches are destroyed.	**1614**
	1 Gaspard Bauhin, Swiss anatomist, botanist, and physician, publishes *Mircocosmographia,* an anatomy textbook.		**1** Jesuits have 13,112 members in their Order. **[1534:MISC/1]** **2** Merchant Adventurers are given a monopoly for exporting English cloth.	**1615**

	History and Politics		The Arts	
	America	**Elsewhere**	**America**	**Elsewhere**
1616	**1** William Baffin, Eng. explorer, searches for the Northwest Passage, sailing far into Baffin Bay.	**2** Raleigh is released from prison to lead another expedition to the Orinoco in search of gold. **[1595:HIST/1; 1603:HIST/3]** **3** Through the favor of Marie de' Medici, Armand Jean du Plessis, Duke of Richelieu becomes Minister of State for Foreign Affairs and War in France. **4** Tartars from Manchuria invade China.	**1** Oil painting of Pocahontas is done by anonymous artist.	**2** Francisco de Zurbarán, Span. Baroque painter of religious subjects, completes his first known work, "Immaculate Conception."
1617		**1** Treaty of Stolbovo ends war between Russia and Sweden. Sweden acquires Karelia and Ingria and returns Novgorod to Russia. **[1610:HIST/3]** **2** Persecution of Christians builds up in Japan. **[1614:MISC/3]**		**1** The Marquise de Rambouillet's salon devoted to literary and cultured conversation influences French literature of the 17th century. **2** Gian Lorenzo Bernini, Ital. sculptor and architect credited with creation of the Baroque, executes his sculpture "St. Sebastian" for Cardinal Maffeo Barberini, later Pope Urban VIII.
1618		**1** Thirty Years' War begins with a revolt in Prague, where two Imperial officers are thrown from a window by Protestants in the Bohemian diet. German Protestant princes and foreign powers begin struggle against oppression of the Holy Roman Empire (the Hapsburgs) and the Catholic princes. **2** Raleigh returns to England after failing to find gold on the Orinoco. He is executed under the old sentence of treason as redress to Spain. **[1603:HIST/3; 1616:HIST/2]**		**1** Diego Velázquez paints "Old Woman Frying Eggs." Such domestic scenes became popular in Spanish painting.
1619	**1** House of Burgesses, first colonial legislature, meets for the first time in Jamestown, Va. **2** Dutch ship carries first Negroes to Jamestown and sells them as slaves to colonists.	**3** Marie de' Medici opposes power of her son Louis XIII of France. **4** Ferdinand II becomes Holy Roman Emperor. His Catholicism angers the Bohemian nobles, who choose Frederick V (the Winter King) as King of Bohemia.		**1** Jan Sweelinck, Dutch organist and teacher who established the fugue form used by J. S. Bach, publishes *Cantiones sacrae*.

Science & Technology		Miscellaneous		
America	Elsewhere	America	Elsewhere	
1 Captain John Smith writes *Description of New England* telling of the excellent farming and fishing conditions and including the first accurate map of the area.		**1** Smallpox epidemic kills almost all of the Indians in New England.	**2** Trade treaty is settled between the Dutch and the Japanese.	**1616**
1 Tobacco becomes the major industry in the New World. 50,000 lbs. are exported to England.	**2** Willebrond Snell, Dutch astronomer and mathematician, develops a way to measure the Earth. **3** Henry Briggs, Eng. mathematician, establishes common logarithms. **4** Napier devises a means of multiplying and dividing, using a system of small rods called Napier's bones—the forerunner of the slide rule.	**1** Criminals in England are transported to Virginia as punishment.	**2** Guide to 11 languages, including Welsh, Dutch, Greek, and Hebrew, is published in London. **3** Sweden forbids the practice of Catholicism.	**1617**
1 Colonists begin growing wheat in Jamestown, Va. Arrival of wives for the settlers of Jamestown, Virginia		**1** Women arrive in Virginia. This brings stability to the settlement. **2** Dancing, fiddling, card playing, hunting, and fishing are forbidden on Sunday in Virginia.	**3** Diphtheria epidemic kills about 8000 people in Naples, Italy. **4** Dutch West African Company is founded. **5** Puritans in England object to the playing of popular sports.	**1618**
	1 John Bainbridge, Eng. astronomer, publishes *Astronomical Description of the Comet of 1618,* in which he suggests that the comet was an omen of disaster. **2** Kepler devises a reliable method for determining the distance of planets from the Earth.	**1** Population of Virginia is approximately 2000. **2** Everyone is required to attend religious services on the Sabbath in Virginia.	**3** Pestilence kills 330,000 people in Egypt. **4** Banks are founded in Hamburg and Venice.	**1619**

	History and Politics		The Arts	
	America	Elsewhere	America	Elsewhere
1620	**1** Pilgrims, chartered by the Virginia Company of London to settle in Virginia, reach the coast of Cape Cod after a hard, three-month voyage on *Mayflower* from England. They establish a colony at Plymouth, Mass. **2** Pilgrims sign Mayflower Compact, the first basis of government established in the American colonies.	**3** Armies of the Catholic League and Imperial forces of the Holy Roman Empire defeat army of King Frederick V of Bohemia at the Battle of the White Mountain, near Prague. Bohemian rebels are executed; nobles' lands are seized; Protestant clergy are expelled. Bohemia loses its independence for 300 years. **[1609:HIST/2]** **4** Gustavus II of Sweden begins war with Poland and seizes Livonia.	**1** Pilgrims bring with them Henry Ainsworth's *Psalm Book* for use at religious services. It is the first music book in the country. **2** A library is established in Virginia in conjunction with plans for a college.	**3** Michael Praetorius, Ger. composer and music historian, completes *Syntagma musicum*, a 3-volume work containing information on the musical instruments and practices of the time.
1621	**1** William Bradford is elected governor of Plymouth Colony on the death of the first governor, John Carver. **2** Plymouth Colony makes a treaty with Massasoit, chief of the Wampanoag Indians. Peace is kept for nearly 20 years.	**3** Protestant Union in Germany is dissolved; Thirty Years' War moves from Bohemia to Palatinate in Germany. **[1618:HIST/1]** **4** Spain resumes war with Holland, breaking Twelve Years' Truce.		**1** Ravenscroft compiles and publishes *The Whole Book of Psalms*, usually called *Ravenscroft's Psalter*. **2** Van Dyck completes his painting, "Rest on the Flight into Egypt."
1622		**1** Richelieu is made cardinal and puts down Protestant uprising in France. **[1616:HIST/3]** **2** Spanish control of Valtelline Pass leads to war between France and Spain. **3** Parliament rebukes James I of England for meddling in affairs of the state; James dissolves Parliament. **4** Catholic League with Imperial forces defeats revolutionary forces in the Palatinate. **[1620:HIST/3]**	**1** *Mourt's Relation*, compiled by George Morton from notes and memoranda of William Bradford and Edward Winslow, contains the first published firsthand account of the voyage of the Mayflower and the landing at Plymouth.	**2** The Banqueting House at Whitehall is completed. It is considered the greatest achievement of Inigo Jones. **3** Marie de' Medici commissions Rubens to do a series of paintings for the galleries of the Luxembourg Palace in Paris.
1623	**1** English build settlements at Dover and Portsmouth, N.H. **2** Dutch West India Company is established for the purpose of trading and colonizing in the New World.	**3** Imperial forces win at Stadtlohn; Holy Roman Emperor Ferdinand II grants Maximilian I, Duke of Bavaria, the Upper Palatinate.		**1** The first single volume containing all of Shakespeare's undisputed plays is published by Heminges & Condell. This is referred to as the *First Folio*. **2** Velázquez paints a portrait of Philip IV and shortly thereafter is appointed court painter.

Science & Technology		Miscellaneous		
America	**Elsewhere**	**America**	**Elsewhere**	
	1 Sir Francis Bacon, Eng. philosopher and statesman, publishes *Novum Organum,* in which the nature of heat is studied. **2** Edmund Gunter, Eng. mathematician, coins the terms *cosine* and *cotangent.* **3** Bainbridge translates several ancient Greek works on astronomy. **4** Drebbel invents a "diving boat," the forerunner of the modern submarine.	**1** Pilgrims in Massachusetts, called Separatists, reject the Church of England. They practice "congregationalism," based on the teachings of Calvin, and establish a Congregational Church at Plymouth. [1532:MISC/1]	**2** Fabrics with colored designs, called tapestries, are manufactured in England.	**1620**
1 First American blast furnace for processing iron is established at Falling Creek, Va.	**2** Snell devises a law concerning the refraction of light. France's Cardinal Richelieu	**1** Gov. William Bradford of Plymouth Colony is shocked to find newcomers to the settlement playing games in the street on Christmas day. He stops the games by taking their equipment. **2** Pilgrims celebrate their first year in the New World.	**3** Nathaniel Butter, the "father of English journalism," first publishes *Corante, or newes from Italy, Germany, Hungarie, Spaine and France.* It is the first authorized newspaper to carry foreign news in England.	**1621**
1 Indians destroy blast furnace.			**1** First turnpike act is passed in England for the road between Biggleswade and Baldock in Bedfordshire. **2** Pope Gregory XV founds the Sacred Congregation for the Propagation of the Faith to promote missions. This is the beginning of the modern missionary activity of the Catholic Church.	**1622**
	1 Galileo writes his exposition on the new scientific method. **2** Bauhin publishes *Illustrated Exposition of Plants,* in which he classifies 6000 species.	**1** Women and children arrive in New England to join their husbands and fathers. They are feasted with "a lobster or a piece of fish without bread or anything else but a cup of spring water." Lobsters and fish are essential to the diet of early settlers.	**2** Patent laws are passed in England to protect inventors.	**1623**

History and Politics		The Arts	
America	**Elsewhere**	**America**	**Elsewhere**
1624 **1** Dutch establish colony of New Netherlands, with the town of New Amsterdam (now New York City) at the lower tip of Manhattan. Dutch families also settle at Fort Orange (now Albany) and on the Delaware River.	**2** Cardinal Richelieu becomes first minister in France. **3** Spanish are driven from Japan.	**1** Capt. John Smith publishes a *General History* of the New England and Virginia colonies. This contains the famous story of Pocahontas.	**2** Ger. organist Samuel Scheidt's *Tabulatura nova* sets new standards for organ playing. **3** Bernini begins the gilt-bronze baldachin (an ornamental canopy) in St. Peter's Basilica. Its columns are as tall as a 4-story building. **4** Frans Hals, Dutch portraitist, paints "The Laughing Cavalier." **5** First theater is opened in Yedo, Japan.
1625	**1** Charles I becomes King of England, succeeding his father James I. **2** Spanish capture city of Breda from the Dutch. **[1621:HIST/4]** **3** Cádiz, Spain, repels attack by English fleet.	**1** Dutch publishers put out *New World,* an account of all Dutch colonies including New Amsterdam.	**2** Sir Francis Bacon publishes the final and enlarged edition of his *Essays.* **[1605:MISC/2]**
1626 **1** Peter Minuit with new Dutch colonists arrives at New Amsterdam and builds 30 houses. He buys Manhattan Island from the Indians for trinkets worth $24.	**2** Imperial army of Emperor Ferdinand II defeats Protestant forces at Dessau and helps Catholic League defeat Danish king at Lutter. **3** Cardinal Richelieu concentrates all royal and political power in France in his hands.	**1** George Sandys, official for the colony of Virginia, translates Ovid's *Metamorphoses,* the first translation of this work by an American.	
1627 **1** English establish settlement in Barbados. French, Dutch, and English begin settling the West Indies region and fighting for control of the islands. **2** Swedish company is granted charter for first colony in America. **[1638:HIST/1]**	**3** Huguenots revolt in France; England sends fleets to aid them at La Rochelle. **4** Imperial armies conquer Holstein and subdue Schleswig, Jutland, and Mecklenburg. **[1626:HIST/2]** **5** Manchus invade Korea.		**1** Rembrandt van Rijn, Dutch painter, paints "The Moneychanger" and "The Flight into Egypt," the first known outdoor night scene. It shows early mastery of light effects. **2** Heinrich Schütz composes the first German opera, *Daphne,* to a German translation of Rinuccini's text. **[1594:ARTS/2]**
1628 **1** Puritans led by John Endecott arrive at Massachusetts Bay and settle at Salem.	**2** English Parliament forces Charles I to sign Petition of Rights; it prohibits arbitrary taxation, imprisonment, martial law, and billeting of soldiers. Charles is given badly needed money. **3** Cardinal Richelieu cap-	**1** William Bradford describes May Day dancing and merry-making in the Colonies. The festivities are later banned.	**2** Hals paints "The Merry Toper." The work illustrates his infusion of gaiety and exuberance into the formerly serious, somber art of portraiture. **3** Work is begun on

56

Science & Technology		Miscellaneous		
America	**Elsewhere**	**America**	**Elsewhere**	
1 Cattle are introduced into New England by Edward Winslow, founder (later, governor) of Plymouth Colony.	**2** Briggs publishes *Arithmetica Logarithmica,* containing the logarithms for 30,000 numbers.		**1** Fire destroys Oslo, Norway.	**1624**
			1 Bubonic plague in London kills 35,000 people.	**1625**

Peter Minuit, Dutch colonist, purchasing Manhattan Island from the Indians

1 Plymouth colony passes first conservation laws limiting the cutting and sale of colonial lumber.		**1** Plymouth requires the approval of the governor and the council to sell or transport lumber out of the colony.	**2** An edict is published in France condemning to death anyone who kills an opponent in a duel. **3** Order of the Sisters of Mercy is founded in France.	**1626**
		1 About 1500 children kidnapped in Europe are brought to the colonies. Many become great successes. One 6-year-old, kidnapped by a sailor and sold in America, later marries his master's daughter and inherits his fortune.	**2** Swedish South Sea Company is founded. **3** Typhus epidemic kills about 60,000 people in Lyons, France. **4** Jesuits in Africa establish 11 missions in Ethiopia.	**1627**
	1 William Harvey, Eng. physician, describes the circulation of blood.	**1** Dutch Reformed Church is founded at New Amsterdam.		**1628**

	History and Politics		The Arts	
	America	**Elsewhere**	**America**	**Elsewhere**
		tures La Rochelle after 14-month siege; Huguenots are subdued. **4** In the Thirty Years' War, Stralsund on the Baltic withstands a siege by Imperial army.		Taj Mahal, a white marble mausoleum built by Shah Jahan, Mogul emperor, to commemorate one of his wives.
1629	**1** Endecott becomes governor of the Salem colony, which receives more settlers from the Massachusetts Bay Company, an English-chartered colonization company. **2** Dutch West India Company grants special rights to rich persons willing to transport colonists to New Netherlands (now New York and New Jersey). Much land is granted along the Hudson, Connecticut, and Delaware rivers. [1623:HIST/2]	**3** Parliament is dissolved; Charles I of England rules without it for 11 years. **4** Emperor Ferdinand II issues the Edict of Restitution, ordering restoration of church lands secularized since 1552. **5** Peace of Lübeck between Holy Roman Empire and Denmark assures Ferdinand II that the Danes will not interfere in Germany. **6** Peace of Alais ends political power of Huguenots but assures them religious toleration.		**1** John Milton, giant of Eng. literature, writes his first great poem, "On the Morning of Christ's Nativity." **2** Span. dramatist Pedro Calderón de la Barca writes *The Phantom Lady,* a comedy of intrigue.
1630	**1** John Winthrop, with members of the Massachusetts Bay Company, founds a settlement at Boston. Puritans from England begin the "Great Migration" to Massachusetts and Connecticut.	**2** Swedish forces under Gustavus II invade Germany to support the Protestant cause and to gain control of the Baltic coast. **3** Cardinal Richelieu crushes plot by Marie de' Medici to regain control in France.	**1** John Winthrop, first governor of the Mass. Bay Colony, begins a detailed journal which he keeps until his death. It is a prime source of information about life in early New England. **2** William Bradford begins *History of Plymouth Plantation,* the first account of a Puritan settlement in New England.	**3** Inigo Jones designs Covent Garden, London's first residential square. This is an early example of urban design.
1631		**1** Imperial forces sack Magdeburg and other cities; Swedish and Saxon troops defeat Imperial forces at Battle of Breitenfeld, securing north Germany. **2** Pope secures Urbino, completing the dominions of the Papal States.		**1** Ital. architect Francesco Borromini collaborates with Bernini in designing the baldachin in St. Peter's and the Barberini Palace in Rome. **2** Velázquez' "Christ on the Cross," painted after his return from Italy, shows a new depth of devotion and advance in technique.
1632		**1** Swedish forces defeat imperial forces at Lech and Lützen, where Gustavus II of Sweden is killed in battle.	**1** The Franciscan missionary, Brother Gabriel Sagard, writes an account of the Huron Indians which contains	**3** Rembrandt receives commission from the Amsterdam Surgeon's Guild to paint "The Anatomy Lesson of Dr.

Science & Technology		Miscellaneous		
America	**Elsewhere**	**America**	**Elsewhere**	

Taj Mahal, white marble mausoleum in India

Science & Technology		Miscellaneous		
America	Elsewhere	America	Elsewhere	
		1 First ordained minister arrives at Plymouth, Mass. **2** First non-Separatist Congregational Church is established at Salem, Mass.	**3** Cardinal Richelieu, Fr. statesman, forms the Company of New France for trade in Canada. **[1624:HIST/2]**	**1629**
	1 Peter Chamberlen, Eng. surgeon, invents forceps for use in childbirth.	**1** First church is founded in Boston. **2** Population in the colonies is estimated at 5700. **[1610:MISC/1]** **3** First criminal executed in the colonies is hanged for murder.	**4** Beginning of public advertising, in Paris. **5** Cribbage, a card game invented by Eng. poet Sir John Suckling, is first played in England.	**1630**
1 Cultivation of tobacco begins in Maryland. **2** *Blessing of the Bay*, the first ship built in America, is launched.	**3** The greater than ($>$) and less than ($<$) symbols are established in a posthumous work of Thomas Harriot, Eng. mathematician. **4** William Oughtred, Eng. mathematician, establishes the symbol *"x"* for multiplication.	**1** Boston has its first serious fire. Because of it, Cambridge, Mass., prohibits wooden chimneys and thatched roofs on houses.	**2** Earthquake in Naples, Italy. Mt. Vesuvius erupts, killing more than 3000 people.	**1631**
	1 Francesco Cavalieri, Ital. mathematician, introduces the use of logarithms into Italy.	**1** Gov. John Winthrop of Massachusetts receives information that Dixy Bull and 15 other Englishmen have become	**2** Russia establishes a fur-trading center in Siberia.	**1632**

History and Politics		The Arts	
America	**Elsewhere**	**America**	**Elsewhere**
		a dictionary of their language. **2** Champlain's final and best known book, *Les Voyages de la Nouvelle France,* is published.	Nicolaes Tulp." His treatment of group portraiture was original and revolutionary. **4** Charles I appoints Van Dyck principal painter. His portraits give us our image of England before the 1648 revolution.
1633 **1** Dutch build trading post on Connecticut River near what is now Hartford.	**2** Protestant forces capture Regensburg in the Thirty Years' War; Imperial troops retake the city in 1634.		**1** The poems of Eng. clergyman George Herbert are published. These religious verses establish him as an outstanding poet of the era.
1634 **1** Roman Catholic colony is founded in Maryland under patent granted to Cecilius Calvert, 2nd Lord Baltimore.	**2** Charles I of England issues ship-money tax on ports and later on inland towns. Charles's tyranny of taxation leads to public indignation and defiance. **3** Imperial forces defeat the Swedes at Nördlingen; Germany is in economic ruin, her fields ravaged. **4** King of Poland renounces claim to Russian throne.	A soldier of the Thirty Years' War	**1** The first Oberammergau (Germany) Passion Play is presented. Every ten years since, the villagers of this Bavarian town reenact the drama of Christ's Passion in thanksgiving for having been spared from the plague. **2** Rubens paints the ceiling of the royal Banqueting House at Whitehall with scenes from the reign of James I, whose son, Charles I, commissioned the work.
1635 **1** English build Fort Saybrook at the mouth of the Connecticut River. English compete with Dutch for control of the region.	**2** Peace of Prague between Ferdinand II and the elector of Saxony is accepted by German princes; it helps to reconcile Catholics and Protestants in Holy Roman Empire. **3** France forms alliance with Sweden against the House of Hapsburg and enters the Thirty Years' War.	**1** Eng. clergyman Richard Mather keeps a journal of his voyage to America.	**2** The Académie Française (French Academy) is founded to study and regulate the French language and to compile a dictionary.

Science & Technology		Miscellaneous		
America	**Elsewhere**	**America**	**Elsewhere**	
		pirates and have raided Bristol, Me. Bull is probably the first pirate to appear on the New England coast.		
	1 Thomas Johnson, Eng. botanist, revises and expands *Herball*. The new book is known as *Gerardus Immaculatus*. **[1597:SCI/1]** **2** Oughtred makes the first slide rule. **3** Briggs publishes *Trigonometria Brittannica,* containing detailed trigonometric tables that are used for the next 200 years.	**1** In New England, strong liquor, games, and dancing are not allowed at inns and taverns.	**2** An English trading post is established in Bengal, India.	**1633**
		1 Boston purchases 45 acres of land to use as a military training field and a common pasture. **2** A schoolmaster arrives in New Amsterdam and establishes the first school. **3** Puritans in Massachusetts forbid the wearing of clothes with silver, gold, silk, or lace.	**4** Bubonic plague strikes Canada. **5** Forgery is made a capital offense in England. **6** Use of tobacco is forbidden by Russian clergy; the penalty is death. This is changed later to a tax.	**1634**
1 John Winthrop, Jr., governor of Conn., opens the first American chemical plant in Boston to produce saltpeter for gunpowder. **2** Jacques Philippe Cornuti, Fr. physician, publishes *Canadensium Plantarum* with descriptions and illustrations of Canadian plants and medicines.		**1** A hurricane strikes the Plymouth Colony. **2** Boston Public Latin School is founded.	**3** In Britain, public mail service is set up by royal proclamation; postal service is introduced between London and Edinburgh, Scotland. **4** Museum of Natural History is founded in Paris.	**1635**

	History and Politics		The Arts	
	America	Elsewhere	America	Elsewhere
1636	**1** Roger Williams, Eng. minister banished (1635) from the Puritan colony at Salem, founds Providence, R.I., on land bought from the Indians. **2** Thomas Hooker, Puritan minister unhappy with the strict religious rule in Massachusetts, founds Hartford, Conn.	**3** Swedish forces defeat Imperial and Saxon forces at Wittstock. **4** Manchus proclaim the Ch'ing dynasty and invade China.	**1** The house of Adam Thoroughgood near Norfolk, Va., is built. Today, it is the oldest house in the English-speaking colonies.	
1637	**1** Pequot Indians of Connecticut are nearly wiped out by colonial forces, thus stopping four years of Indian raids against English traders and settlers. Pequot War is first Indian War in New England.	**2** Ferdinand III becomes Holy Roman Emperor, succeeding his father Ferdinand II. **3** Dutch recapture city of Breda from the Spanish. [1625:HIST/2]	**1** *New English Canaan* by Thomas Morton provides an account of the more festive side of New England life.	**2** Fr. landscape architect André LeNôtre redesigns the Tuileries gardens and lays out the Champs-Élysées, Paris' main boulevard. **3** *Le Cid* by Fr. dramatist Pierre Corneille is first performed, marking the beginning of French classical tragedy. **4** Milton writes *Lycidas,* an elegy on the death of a classmate.
1638	**1** Swedish settlers in Dutch ships found Fort Christina (now Wilmington), Del. **2** Puritans settle New Haven, Conn. **3** Anne Hutchinson, banished (1637) as a heretic from Massachusetts Bay Colony, founds town of Pocasset (now Portsmouth), R.I.	**4** Swedish and Protestant armies defeat Imperial forces at Breisach on the Rhine River. **5** Ottoman Turks recapture Baghdad from the Persians. **6** Japan's rulers crush peasant revolt over economic and religious oppression; Dutch and Portuguese traders are expelled and Christianity is suppressed. [1543:HIST/1]	**1** The Swedish settlement along the lower Delaware contributes the log cabin style of architecture. **2** The first almanac in the English colonies is published. **3** Construction of Old College at Harvard is begun. It is the most ambitious building project in the Colonies. **4** Stephen Day establishes a printing press in Cambridge, Mass.	**5** William Davenant, Eng. playwright and theater manager, is named poet laureate.
1639	**1** Connecticut Colony adopts the Fundamental Orders, one of the first written legal documents in the New World.	**2** First Bishops' War in Scotland ended without fighting by the Pacification of Berwick. Charles I of England accepts Scottish right to a free church assembly and a free parliament. **3** English build trading outpost at Madras, India.	**1** The Governor's Castle is built in St. Mary, Maryland. It was the largest building in the English colonies. **2** The Whipple House in Ipswich, Mass., is a typical New England domestic building of the salt-box style.	

Science & Technology		Miscellaneous		
America	Elsewhere	America	Elsewhere	
		1 Pension Act is passed in Plymouth Colony. A soldier who is maimed will be supported by the Colony for the rest of his life. **2** Rhode Island is the first colony to grant complete religious freedom. **[1636:HIST/1]** **3** Harvard College is founded in Cambridge, Mass.	**4** Dutch East India Company establishes itself on Ceylon (Sri Lanka). **[1602:MISC/1]**	1636
	1 René Descartes, Fr. mathematician, publishes *Discourse on Method,* containing the basic concepts of analytical geometry. He also put forth his law of refraction and an explanation of rainbows.	**1** Taunton, Mass., is founded by an "ancient maid" of 48. Unmarried women have a difficult time making a living, and marriages usually take place early. After they reach 25, unmarried women are often ridiculed and restricted by law.	**2** Emigration from England to America is restricted. **3** Christianity is prohibited in Japan, and missionaries are forced to leave. **[1614:MISC/3]** **4** Prayer Book of the Church of Scotland is approved.	1637
	1 Descartes proposes the existence of luminiferous ether, an invisible substance that exists everywhere and carries light through the air.	**1** First Lutheran congregation is established by Swedish settlers in Delaware. **2** Colonial justice is harsh: a New Amsterdam man, having drawn a knife on another person, is sentenced to throw himself into the water from the yardarm of a ship 3 times and to receive 3 lashes from each sailor.	**3** Torture as a punishment is abolished in England.	1638
1 First colonial printing press is established at Harvard College in Cambridge, Mass. **[1539:SCI/1]**	**2** Jeremiah Horrocks, Eng. astronomer, becomes the first person to observe a transit of Venus. **3** Girard Desargues, Fr. mathematician, publishes *An Attempt to Deal With the Events of the Meeting of a Cone With a Plane,* in which he introduces the Desargues theorem for conic sections.	**1** New England laws governing men's clothing show the gay attire of the day: men are censured for wearing "immoderate great breeches," broad shoulder-bands, capes, and double ruffles; silk roses are worn on shoes. **2** A woman of Plymouth, Mass., convicted of adultery is sentenced to be whipped and to wear a		1639

	History and Politics		The Arts	
	America	Elsewhere	America	Elsewhere
1640		**1** Scots invade England in Second Bishops' War and defeat English at Newburn-on-Tyne. Charles I makes peace at Ripon; his promise to pay the Scottish army £850 a day forces him to call Parliament. **2** Portugal revolts and becomes independent from Spanish rule.	**1** The first book issued in the Colonies is the *Bay Psalm Book* for use at church services. It contains no music, but suggests 48 melodies to which psalms might be sung. Published in Cambridge, it has a preface by Richard Mather.	**2** Velázquez begins doing the portraits of dwarfs of the Spanish court. **3** Rembrandt paints one of his most famous works, "Self-Portrait."
1641	**1** General Court of Massachusetts Bay Colony adopts legal code, which asserts the authority of church magistrates and contains hints of growing colonial independence.	**2** English Parliament passes bill to prevent its dissolution without its own consent; it cites grievances against Charles I, suspecting him of involvement in the Irish massacre of 30,000 Protestants in Ulster.	**1** Thomas Shepard's *The Sincere Convert* is a popular collection of sermons.	
1642	**1** French establish settlement at Montreal.	**2** Swedish army again defeats imperial forces at Breitenfeld. [1631:HIST/1] **3** Charles I rejects English Parliament's demands for control of militia and church affairs and for selection of king's ministers. English Civil War begins with Cavaliers (king's supporters) against Roundheads (Puritans and Parliament's supporters). **4** Abel Tasman, Dut. navigator, discovers Tasmania and New Zealand.	**1** Gov. William Berkeley builds the first Virginia mansion, "Greenspring," near Jamestown.	**2** "Virgin of the Rosary" by Span. religious painter Bartolomé Murillo shows Italian and Flemish influences. **3** Eng. poet Richard Lovelace, imprisoned for Royalist sympathies, writes "To Althea, from Prison."
1643	**1** Massachusetts Bay, Plymouth, Connecticut, and New Haven colonies form New England Confederation for common defense against the Indians and to resist possible Dutch and French intrusion.	**2** English Parliament accepts the Solemn League and Covenant, which establishes the Presbyterian Church in England, Ireland, and Scotland. Scots send army to aid Roundheads. [1642:HIST/3] **3** War begins between Denmark and Sweden.	**1** Roger Williams, missionary to the Indians, compiles a dictionary of the language of New England natives.	**2** Molière (Jean-Baptiste Poquelin), one of the greatest comic writers in world literature, forms an acting company in Paris, Illustre Théâtre, which for many years tours the provinces. **3** *Polyeucte,* considered by some Corneille's finest play, is first presented.

Science & Technology		Miscellaneous		
America	Elsewhere	America	Elsewhere	
		badge with the letters "AD" on her left sleeve. If found in public without the badge, she is to be branded on the face with a hot iron.		
Blaise Pascal, French scientist and philosopher	**1** Blaise Pascal, Fr. mathematician, publishes a work on conic sections. **2** Desargues publishes work on stonecutting.	**1** Public land in New-port, R.I., is given to support a school. Income from the land is to be used to educate poor children. **2** Log cabins, introduced from Sweden, are built in Swedish settlements on the Delaware River; after about 1700 they become common frontier dwellings.	**3** Eight postal lines are running in England.	**1640**
	1 Arsenic is prescribed for the first time.	**1** A patent is issued in Massachusetts for making salt.	**2** *Diurnal Occurrences,* a weekly periodical, is published in London. **3** René Descartes, Fr. philosopher, publishes *Meditations.* [1637:SCI/1]	**1641**
	1 Bainbridge publishes *Antiprognosticon,* in which he retracts his former superstitions about comets. [1619:SCI/1]	**1** Education is made compulsory in Massachusetts, with fines imposed if it is neglected. **2** First Dutch Reformed Church is founded in New Amsterdam.	**3** A seawall at Kaifeng, China, is destroyed and 300,000 people drown. **4** Income and property taxes are introduced in England.	**1642**
1 First American wool mill is established in Rowley, Mass. **2** Winthrop is the first to bring a telescope to America.	**3** Evangelista Torricelli, Ital. scientist, invents the mercury barometer.	**1** First restaurant or "cook's shop" opens in Boston.	**2** Parcel post is established in France. **3** *Cristiania Almanack* is the first book printed in Norway.	**1643**

65

	History and Politics		The Arts	
	America	Elsewhere	America	Elsewhere
1644		**1** Roundheads under Oliver Cromwell defeat Cavaliers at Marston Moor. **2** French capture the Rhineland. **3** Ming dynasty, having ruled China since 1368, falls to the Manchus.	**1** Williams, a staunch advocate of religious freedom, publishes *The Bloody Tenent*, defending liberty of conscience.	**2** Choral music in Eng. church services is forbidden by Act of Parliament. **3** Bernini's sculpture, "The Vision of St. Theresa," is erected for the side altar of a church in Rome.
1645		**1** Cromwell defeats Charles I at Naseby; Cavalier cause appears lost in England. **2** Sweden is victorious in war with Denmark, which loses some territory. [1643:HIST/3] **3** Swedish army defeats Imperial forces at Jankau.		**1** Sakaida Kakiemon makes the first enamel-decorated porcelain in Japan. He paints red flower-and-bird designs on white porcelain using a technique patterned on the Chinese. **2** Nicolas Poussin exhibits the oil painting, "St. John on Patmos."
1646		**1** Charles I of England gives himself up to the Scottish army. **2** Swedish and French forces overrun Bavaria and threaten Vienna.		**1** David Teniers the Younger, Flemish Baroque painter of peasant life, completes "The Village Fête." **2** Eng. poet Richard Crashaw publishes a volume of religious and secular verse in Latin and English. **3** Englishman Henry Vaughan publishes *Poems*. His later verse is on religious subjects.
1647	**1** Peter Stuyvesant arrives in New Amsterdam and begins harsh rule as governor of the Dutch colony of New Netherlands. **2** Rhode Island General Assembly drafts code of civil law that separates church and state.	**3** Scots surrender Charles I to Parliament; English army leaders, suspicious of Parliament, seize Charles, who later escapes and concludes an agreement with the Scots. Charles accepts Presbyterianism in return for military support.	**1** In *The Simple Cobler of Agawam in America*, Nathaniel Ward expresses his reflections on current fashions and customs. **2** Rev. John Cotton of Boston publishes a tract stressing the importance of church singing. **3** An early painting of New York by an anonymous artist shows a 4-striped flag. **4** A new edition of the *Bay Psalm Book* contains "spiritual songs" as well as psalms.	**5** Dutch Baroque landscapist Jacob van Ruisdael paints "Dunes," a work illustrating his interest in trees. **6** Academy of Arts is founded in Dresden, Germany.

Science & Technology		Miscellaneous		
America	**Elsewhere**	**America**	**Elsewhere**	
1 First successful ironworks in America is established on the Saugus River near Boston.	**2** Marin Mersenne, Fr. mathematician, devises a formula to represent prime numbers. **[1963:SCI/3]** **3** Pascal completes a calculating device—the forerunner of the modern digital calculator.		**1** Descartes' *Principles of Philosophy* is published. **[1641:MISC/3]** **2** English Parliament forbids merriment or religious festivals at Christmas. **3** Schools at Port Royal, France, are organized, with special series of textbooks on logic, grammar, and mathematics.	**1644**
				1645
	1 Sir Thomas Browne, Eng. physician, coins the term *electricity*. **2** Pascal invents the hypodermic syringe.	**1** Massachusetts' heresy law makes death the punishment for any person who denies that the Holy Scriptures are the Word of God. **2** Because of the danger of fire, Massachusetts makes smoking unlawful within 5 miles of a town. **3** First Protestant service for Indians is held in Massachusetts.		**1646**
	1 Johannes Hevelius, Dan. astronomer, publishes the first atlas of the Moon. **2** Cavalieri's *Six Geometrical Exercises,* an early work on calculus, is published.	**1** Massachusetts requires all towns of 50 families to provide a teacher to teach reading and writing. Towns of 100 families must establish a Latin grammar school. **2** Massachusetts forbids Catholic priests to enter any Puritan territory.	**3** First newspaper advertisement appears in London. **4** Yellow fever epidemic breaks out in Barbados, the West Indies.	**1647**

History and Politics		The Arts	
America	**Elsewhere**	**America**	**Elsewhere**
1648			
	1 Second English Civil War begins; Cromwell defeats the Scots at Preston and seizes Charles I. **2** Peace of Westphalia ends Thirty Years' War; France and Sweden obtain territory; republics of the Netherlands and Switzerland are independent; Catholic and Protestant states are accepted.		**1** Carel Fabritius' "Abraham de Potter" shows his originality in a style of portraiture that will influence de Hooch and Vermeer. **2** Calderón de la Barca writes a 2-act play with spoken and sung dialogue. **3** Eng. poet Robert Herrick publishes *Hesperides,* a collection of 1000 lyrics.
1649			
	1 Charles I of England is found guilty of treason and beheaded. England forms a Commonwealth with Cromwell as leader of the army. Cromwell suppresses rebellion in Ireland. **2** Treaty of Ruel ends unsuccessful rebellion of the Parliament of Paris against the French court led by Jules (Cardinal) Mazarin.	**1** Edward Winslow writes *Glorious Progress of the Gospel Amongst the Indians in New England.*	**2** Francisco Pacheco, Span. painter and writer, publishes *The Art of Painting.* It provides important information on the careers of Spanish painters.
1650			
1 English and Dutch try to decide respective boundaries of their American colonies.	**2** Cardinal Mazarin fights rebellion of the French nobility. **3** Charles II is proclaimed king in parts of England and Ireland.	**1** Anne Bradstreet, the first poet in New England, publishes a volume of verse in London, *The Tenth Muse.*	**2** Taj Mahal, in Agra, India, is completed. **[1628:ARTS/3]**
1651			
	1 Charles II is proclaimed king in Scotland. He escapes to France after Cromwell defeats him at Worcester. **2** French nobles force Cardinal Mazarin to leave France. **[1649:HIST/2; 1650:HIST/2]** **3** Shogun (ruler) of Japan puts down two rebellions at Edo (now Tokyo). **4** Treaty is signed by Poles and Ukrainian Cossacks, who have fought for 50 years against Polish domination.	**1** Eng. portrait painter Robert Walker completes an oil portrait of Edward Winslow. It is the only existing authentic likeness of any of the Mayflower Pilgrims.	**2** John Playford's *The English Dancing-Master* which contains known songs and ballads, shows that dancing remained popular during the Puritan regime of Cromwell.
1652			
1 Massachusetts General Court rules that Maine is part of the Bay colony.	**2** English and Dutch go to war over English Navigation Act, which restricts Dutch trade with English possessions. **3** Louis XIV, King of France, declares lawful government and recalls Mazarin.		**1** Rembrandt's etching, "Christ Preaching," accurately reproduces the dress and appearance of the inhabitants of Amsterdam's Jewish quarter.

68

Science & Technology		Miscellaneous		
America	**Elsewhere**	**America**	**Elsewhere**	
Oliver Cromwell, General of the British Army	1 Jan Baptist van Helmont, Belg. chemist, demonstrates the existence of carbon dioxide. 2 Pascal publishes work on vacuums.	1 Margaret Jones of Charlestown, Mass., is the first person in the colonies to be executed as a witch. 2 Shoemakers and coopers (barrelmakers) in Boston are allowed to meet as a group of workers. 3 Margaret Brent, a landowner and an attorney, asks for a vote in the Maryland Assembly, an unheard action by a woman at this time. Her request is rejected.	4 George Fox, Eng. religious leader, founds Society of Friends (Quakers).	**1648**
		1 Maryland Assembly passes the Act of Toleration for Christians.	2 English replaces Latin (for a time) as the language used for all legal documents in England.	**1649**
1 Fishing increases as a New England industry.	2 Otto von Guericke, Ger. engineer, invents the air pump.	1 Population in the colonies is estimated at 52,000. **[1630:MISC/2]** 2 Iron is exported from Lynn, Mass., to England. **[1644:SCI/1]**	3 World population is estimated at 500 million. 4 Thomas Hobbes, Eng. political philosopher, publishes *The Elements of Law, Moral and Political.*	**1650**
1 Parliament prohibits trade with the colonies, a move which stimulates New England shipbuilding.	2 Gilbert's *A New Philosophy of Our Sublunar World,* published posthumously, suggests that the planets are held in their orbits by magnetism. 3 Harvey publishes work concerning the embryology of chickens and deer.	1 Two Baptist ministers, John Clarke and Obediah Holmes, are arrested in Massachusetts during a service in a private home. Clarke is released against his wishes because a friend pays his fine, but Holmes is whipped in the streets of Boston.	2 Hobbes publishes his major work, *Leviathan,* a defense of absolute monarchy.	**1651**
	1 Thomas Bartholin, Dan. anatomist, describes the lymphatic system of humans.	1 A form of miniature golf is popular in the New Netherlands Colony. 2 Coins ("pine-tree" shillings) are minted at Boston. 3 New Amsterdam regulates the speed of traffic.		**1652**

History and Politics		The Arts	
America	Elsewhere	America	Elsewhere
	[1651:HIST/2] 4 Dutch found Capetown, South Africa.		
1653 1 Resistance against Stuyvesant's harsh rule forces him to give local self-government to New Amsterdam. [1647:HIST/1]	2 English army officers draw up document by which Cromwell becomes Lord Protector of England. 3 Peasants' revolt in Bern is suppressed by other Swiss cantons (states). For the next century, the Swiss cantons fight over religious issues.	1 Puritan missionary John Eliot prints *Catechism in the Indian Language,* probably the first book in Indian in the Colonies.	2 Rembrandt paints "Aristotle Contemplating the Bust of Homer." 3 Izaak Walton, Eng. writer, publishes *The Compleat Angler,* a treatise on fishing. 4 Louis XIV appears as the Sun in the *Ballet de la Nuit* and is thereafter known as the Sun King.
1654	1 English defeat Dutch off Portland, England, regaining control of the English Channel. Peace treaty ends Anglo-Dutch war. 2 War begins between Russia and Poland for possession of the Ukraine. 3 Portuguese drive the Dutch out of Brazil.		
1655 1 Stuyvesant, with Dutch forces, seizes Swedish forts on the Delaware River.	2 Cromwell dissolves Parliament and divides England into 11 districts, each governed by a major-general. [1655:MISC/3] 3 Swedish army invades Poland and seizes Warsaw and Cracow. 4 English capture Jamaica from the Spanish.	1 David Pieterson de Vries recounts his travels to Dutch settlements along the Delaware.	
1656	1 Russia, Denmark, and the Holy Roman Empire declare war on the Swedes. 2 English capture Spanish treasure ships off Cádiz, Spain. 3 Dutch take Colombo (capital of Sri Lanka) from the Portuguese.		1 A science fantasy of imaginary journeys to the sun and the moon, by Fr. satirist and dramatist Savinien Cyrano de Bergerac, is published. 2 Velázquez paints "Las Meninas." It depicts a scene in the artist's studio as he paints the King and Queen. 3 Murillo paints his celebrated "Vision of St. Anthony." His religious art appeals to popular taste and often illustrates the teachings of the Counter-Reformation.

70

Science & Technology		Miscellaneous		
America	**Elsewhere**	**America**	**Elsewhere**	
		1 Boston has its first "great fire," after which it adopts a fire code.	**2** London Polyglot Bible is published (in 10 languages). **3** First mailboxes are used in Paris.	**1653**
	1 Guericke demonstrates the force of air pressure to the Holy Roman emperor.	**1** Twenty-four Jewish immigrants arrive in New Amsterdam.	**2** First picture-book for children (the world in pictures) is published in Nuremberg, Bavaria (now part of Germany).	**1654**
			1 Bubonic plague in Angola, Africa: half the population dies. **2** First regular newspaper is published in Berlin. **3** Oliver Cromwell, Puritan statesman, readmits Jews into England.	**1655**
		1 Members of the Society of Friends (Quakers) arrive in Boston. They are imprisoned for 15 weeks and then deported. Quakers are prohibited from coming to Massachusetts. **[1648:MISC/4]**	**2** Blaise Pascal, Fr. philosopher, publishes *Les Provinciales,* an attack against the Jesuits. **[1534:MISC/1]**	**1656**

Peter Stuyvesant's surrender of New Amsterdam

	History and Politics		The Arts	
	America	**Elsewhere**	**America**	**Elsewhere**
1657		**1** Cromwell refuses English crown; he sets up second legislative chamber and increases his power. England makes alliance with France.	**1** Construction begins on the monastery of San Francesco at Lima, Peru. Its architecture, with colorful geometric designs on the plasterwork, shows the influence of the Spanish Moors.	
1658		**1** French and English defeat the Spanish at the Battle of the Dunes near Dunkirk. **2** Cromwell dies; his son is the new Lord Protector. Army and Parliament struggle for power. **3** Danes successfully defend Copenhagen against the Swedes.	Molière, French dramatist	**1** Dutchman Pieter de Hooch paints "The Pantry," a typical simple domestic scene. **2** George Stiernhielm, Swed. poet, completes *Hercules,* first epic in that language. **3** Molière returns to Paris where one of his "entertainments" is warmly received by the King, marking the beginning of his successful stage career.
1659		**1** France and Spain sign Peace of the Pyrenees; Spanish border is set at the Pyrenees Mountains. France receives Roussillon and much land in Flanders. **2** Army forces new Lord Protector to dissolve Parliament; Rump Parliament assembles itself, forces the Lord Protector to resign, and reestablishes the Commonwealth. [1658:HIST/2]		**1** Molière's first Paris play, *Les Précieuses ridicules,* makes fun of two provincial young women. Many believe Molière was satirizing salons such as that of the Marquise de Rambouillet. [1617:ARTS/1]
1660	**1** Virginia Colony proclaims Charles II King of England. It restores Sir William Berkeley as governor. Puritans had ousted him in 1652.	**2** Parliament calls for the restoration of the English monarchy; Charles II accepts Parliament's conditions of amnesty, returns to England, and is proclaimed king. **3** Sweden and Poland sign Peace of Oliva. Poland gives up claim to Swedish throne and cedes Livonia to Sweden. Sweden also makes peace with Denmark.		**1** Samuel Pepys begins his famous *Diary.* It gives a valuable picture of the London of Charles II. **2** The restoration of the English monarchy brings about the reopening of the theaters and the re-introduction of choral music into the church service, forbidden since 1642 by Cromwell.

Science & Technology		Miscellaneous		
America	Elsewhere	America	Elsewhere	
	1 Oughtred publishes *Trigonometria,* which deals with complex trigonometric concepts. **2** Academia del Cimento, the first school of science, is established in Italy.	**1** Measles epidemic strikes Boston. **2** Virginia organizes a postal system. **3** Quakers arrive in New Amsterdam. They are imprisoned, then freed to go to Rhode Island. **[1656:MISC/1]**	**4** Drinking chocolate is sold in London. **5** Pendulum clock is invented.	**1657**
	1 Cristiaan Huygens, Dutch mathematician and astronomer, discovers the time-keeping ability of pendulums. **2** John Swammerdam, Dutch naturalist and microscopist, observes and describes red blood cells.	**1** Typhoid fever epidemic strikes New Amsterdam. **2** Police force of 10 men is formed in New Amsterdam. The men are paid about 50 cents a night.	**3** First bank note is used by the Swedish state bank.	**1658**
1 Joseph Jencks, ironworker, builds the first "fire engine," a portable water pump with a self-contained water supply.	**2** Huygens discovers the true shape of Saturn's rings.	**1** Two Quakers who return to Massachusetts after having been banished are hanged on Boston Common. **2** First classical elementary school is established in New Amsterdam.		**1659**
	1 Robert Hooke, Eng. physicist, states his law of elasticity (Hooke's Law). **2** Robert Boyle, Anglo-Irish scientist, invents an air pump. **3** Isaac Barrow, Eng. mathematician and theologian, translates ancient Greek mathematical works. **4** The Royal Society of London, an organization designed to promote scientific research, is established.	**1** Massachusetts fines violators 5 shillings for celebrating Christmas. **[1644:MISC/2]** **2** John Eliot, colonial missionary, establishes the first American Indian church in Massachusetts. **3** Wigs come into fashion. The authorities in Massachusetts try to prevent their use. **4** Connecticut requires all men to live with their wives. A man separated from his wife for more than 3 years is ordered out of the colony.		**1660**

	History and Politics		The Arts	
	America	**Elsewhere**	**America**	**Elsewhere**
1661		**1** Ottoman Empire and Venice are at war. **2** Sweden and Russia sign Peace of Kardis, reestablishing status quo. **3** Cavalier Parliament passes statute to strengthen the Church of England.	**1** John Eliot's translation of the New Testament into Algonkian is printed by Samuel Green of Cambridge, Mass. It is the first Bible printed in North America. **[1663:ARTS/1]**	**2** Fr. finance minister Jean-Baptiste Colbert founds the Royal Academy of Dance.
1662		**1** France buys Dunkirk from England. **2** Portugal gives Tangier to England. **3** English build fort at the mouth of the Gambia River in Africa.	**1** Michael Wigglesworth's terrifying poetic description of the Last Judgment, *The Day of Doom,* is a bestseller of the time.	**2** Charles Le Brun decorates the Gallery of Mirrors at Versailles, near Paris. Le Nôtre designs the gardens. **3** Molière's first big hit, *The School for Wives,* causes a scandal.
1663		**1** Charles II of England signs charter of Royal African Company, establishing its rights to slave trade with Spanish America. **2** Ottoman Turks declare war on Holy Roman Empire and invade Transylvania, Hungary and Slovakia.	**1** John Eliot completes his translation of the Old Testament into Algonkian. **[1661:ARTS/1]**	**2** K'un-ts'an, abbot of a Buddhist monastery near Nanking, paints the landscape, "Pao-en Temple." **3** London's Drury Lane Theater, officially the Theater Royal, opens.
1664	**1** English forces capture New Amsterdam (rename it New York) and Fort Orange (rename it Albany). Dutch power in the region is broken. **2** England's attempt to regulate its New England colonies is opposed by General Court of Massachusetts.	**3** Austrians defeat the Turks at St. Gotthard, Hungary; a 20-year truce is concluded at Vasvar. **[1663:HIST/2]** **4** Sweden sells its colonies on Africa's Gold Coast to the Dutch.	**1** *A Call to the Unconverted* by Eng. preacher Richard Baxter is a bestselling book of sermons in America. **2** Wills and diaries attest to the presence of viols, guitars, and virginals in the Mass. Bay Colony. Drums and trumpets were used for military and civil purposes throughout New England.	**3** Molière collaborates with Jean-Baptiste Lully, court musician and choreographer, on *Le Mariage Forcé,* a play which includes much dancing. **4** *Tartuffe,* Molière's attack on religious hypocrisy, is banned at Versailles after its first performance.
1665	**1** New Haven colony unites with Connecticut. **2** English laws are introduced into New York, providing for organization of courts and militia. **3** Colony of New Jersey is founded. **4** English colony, called Clarendon Colony, is established near Wilmington, N.C.	**5** English defeat the Dutch during sea battle off Lowestoft, England. **6** Portuguese army wins series of victories over Spain. **[1668:HIST/3]**	**1** *Ye Bare and Ye Cubb* by Philip Alexander Bruce is performed in Virginia. It is the first theatrical performance in the North American colonies.	**2** François, duc de La Rochefoucauld, publishes *Maximes,* a book of reflections and epigrams. **3** Jan Vermeer, Dutch artist known for subtle light effects, executes "Allegory of Painting," one of his finest works.

Science & Technology		Miscellaneous		
America	**Elsewhere**	**America**	**Elsewhere**	
1 Winthrop is elected as the first American Fellow of the Royal Society of London.	**2** In his work *The Sceptical Chymist,* Boyle disputes the views of Aristotle and Paracelsus on the composition of matter. **3** Marcello Malpighi, Ital. physician and microscopist, discovers the network of blood vessels that link the small veins and arteries.	**1** Persecution of Quakers ends in Massachusetts. [1656:MISC/1]		**1661**
1 Winthrop gives complete description of maize (Indian corn) to the Royal Society.		**1** Virginia requires that children be baptized. If they are not, parents are fined. **2** Printed material is censored in Puritan New England.	**3** Population of China is estimated at 100 million. **4** More than 1500 Quakers are imprisoned in England because they refuse to accept the Anglican Church. Many other nonconformists are persecuted and put into prison. [1661:MISC/1]	**1662**
	1 Guericke invents the electric generator.	**1** A New Amsterdam court sentences a man to be flogged and to have his right ear cut off for selling his wife.	**2** Turnpike tolls are introduced into England. **3** Gold guinea pieces are coined in England.	**1663**
1 Winthrop claims to have discovered a fifth moon of Jupiter.	**2** Hooke suggests that Jupiter rotates on an axis. **3** Thomas Willis, Eng. physician, describes the human brain and nervous system.	**1** Marriage by a justice of the peace instead of by a clergyman is made legal in New York. **2** Maryland law provides for life-long servitude of Negro slaves. Similar laws are passed in other colonies. **3** Horse races are run regularly on Long Island, N.Y. [1668:MISC/1]	**4** Trappist Order is founded in Normandy, France.	**1664**
	1 Hooke publishes *Small Drawings,* in which he analyzes snowflakes, devises methods of making synthetic fibers, and applies the term *cell* scientifically for the first time. **2** *Philosophical Transactions,* the journal of the Royal Society of London, is published.	**1** First American Indian graduates from Harvard College.	**2** Great Plague of London begins. **3** First modern census is taken in Quebec, Canada. **4** First issue of the official government newspaper, *London Gazette,* is printed.	**1665**

History and Politics		The Arts	
America	**Elsewhere**	**America**	**Elsewhere**
1666			
1 Puritans from Connecticut settle Newark, N.J.	**2** France and Denmark support the Dutch in their war against England. **3** Treaty of Cleves gives the duchy of Cleves to Brandenburg and Jülich to Neuburg. **[1609:HIST/3]** **4** French, English, and the Dutch battle over islands in the West Indies.	**1** George Alsop's account of life in early Maryland, *A Character of the Province of Maryland,* is known for its liveliness and humor. Alsop was an indentured servant in that colony and published the account on his return to London.	**2** Italian Antonio Stradivari (Stradivarius), greatest violin maker of all time, produces the first violin bearing his name. **3** Molière's masterpiece *Le Misanthrope* satirizes self-righteousness.
1667		 Louis XIV of France	
	1 By the Peace of Breda, trade laws are changed in favor of the Dutch, who give up claims to New Netherlands but keep Surinam (Dutch Guiana) in South America. **2** Louis XIV of France begins War of Devolution and captures Spanish Netherlands. **3** By the Treaty of Andrussovo, Poland cedes Smolensk and the eastern Ukraine to Russia. **[1654:HIST/2]**		**1** John Milton's epic *Paradise Lost* is known for its powerful portrayal of Satan. **2** *Andromaque,* the first important play of Fr. classical tragedian Jean Racine, is produced.
1668			
1 French establish Jesuit mission and fur-trading post at Sault Ste. Marie, Mich.	**2** Triple Alliance of England, Sweden, and the Netherlands is formed against France. War of Devolution ends with the Treaty of Aix-la-Chapelle; France restores Franche-Comté to Spain but keeps most of its conquests in Flanders. **[1667:HIST/2]** **3** By the Treaty of Lisbon, Spain recognizes Portugal's independence. **[1665:HIST/6]** **4** English East India Company takes control of Bombay, India. **[1600:MISC/1]**		**1** Ger. composer Dietrich Buxtehude is appointed organist of the church in Lübeck, which becomes the most important music center in northern Europe. **2** Fr. poet Jean de La Fontaine publishes *Fables*. His versions of these stories from Aesop are noted for their wit and characterization.
1669			
1 Plan of government for Carolina is drawn up; religious freedom is granted, but revision in 1670 officially recognizes only the Church of England.	**2** Ottoman Turks capture Crete from the Venetians after a 24-year siege. **3** Aurangzeb, Mogul Emperor of India, prohibits the Hindu religion.	**1** Nathaniel Morton, secretary of Plymouth colony, publishes *New England's Memorial* documenting life there at that time.	**2** Permission for performance of Molière's *Tartuffe* is finally obtained. The play enjoys a long run. **[1664:ARTS/4]** **3** The Académie Royale de Musique is established by Louis XIV. **4** Christopher Wren, Eng. astronomer, geometrician, and archi-

Science & Technology		Miscellaneous		
America	**Elsewhere**	**America**	**Elsewhere**	
	1 Sir Isaac Newton, Eng. mathematician and physicist, invents the reflecting telescope. 2 Giovanni Borelli, Ital. physiologist, publishes work concerning the moons of Jupiter. 3 Giovanni Domenico Cassini, Ital. astronomer, determines the rotational period of Mars. 4 Thomas Sydenham, Eng. physician, publishes work on fevers.	1 First Presbyterian Church is established in New Jersey.	2 Great Plague of London at its height; kills 68,000 people. 3 Great Fire of London destroys St. Paul's Cathedral, many other churches and buildings. It leaves 200,000 people homeless.	**1666**
Sir Isaac Newton, English mathematician and physicist		1 Smallpox spreads throughout Virginia.	2 An earthquake in Shemaka (in Russian Caucasia) kills 80,000.	**1667**
	1 Cassini publishes a table describing the positions of Jupiter's moons.	1 First sports trophy, a silver porringer, is presented to the winner of a horse race on Long Island, N.Y.		**1668**
	1 Nicolaus Steno, Dan. geologist, publishes a work containing topics ranging from crystals to mountain building to fossils.		1 Mt. Etna erupts in Catania, Italy, killing about 20,000 people. 2 Outbreak of cholera in China.	**1669**

History and Politics		The Arts	
America	**Elsewhere**	**America**	**Elsewhere**
			tect, is appointed Surveyor of Works to Charles II.
1670 **1** First permanent colony in South Carolina is established by the English at Albemarle Point, near present-day Charleston. **2** Act of Virginia says that servants who are not Christians before coming to America are slaves for life. Act is repealed in 1682.	**3** Russian troops of the czar crush great peasant revolt led by the Don Cossacks. **4** Louis XIV of France signs private Treaty of Dover with Charles II of England, securing the disruption of the Triple Alliance. **[1668:HIST/2]**	**1** Daniel Denton writes *A Brief Description of New York,* the first printed account of that city. **2** The first section of Salem's House of the Seven Gables, made famous by Hawthorne's novel, is built. **[1851:ARTS/2]** **3** Unidentified artist completes an oil painting of a young girl, Alice Mason.	**4** *The Forc'd Marriage,* a tragi-comedy by Mrs. Aphra Behn, the first professional woman dramatist, is performed at Dorset. **5** Christopher Wren undertakes the rebuilding of 51 London churches that were destroyed by the Great Fire of 1666. **[1666:MISC/3]** **6** Dryden is named poet laureate. **7** Molière's *Le Bourgeois Gentilhomme,* a ballet-comedy, is staged.
1671	**1** Don Cossacks appeal to the Turks for aid against the Polish and Russian governments. **[1670:HIST/3]**	**1** A hand-colored engraving is made of Capt. John Smith's 1616 map of Virginia.	**2** Marie de Rabutin-Chantal, the Marquise de Sévigné, begins writing letters to her daughter that are noted examples of epistolary style. **3** Milton's *Paradise Regained* and *Samson Agonistes* are published.
1672	**1** England and France declare war on the Dutch. French overrun southern Netherlands, but Dutch stop French advance on Amsterdam by opening the dikes. French reject Dutch peace proposals. William of Orange (later William III of England) becomes Dutch Captain-General.		**1** Eng. violinist John Banister begins London's first public concerts. **2** Drury Lane Theater is destroyed by fire. **3** The Clarendon Press, official printers of Oxford University, is founded.
1673 **1** Dutch forces occupy New York until the English regain control in early 1674. **2** Jacques Marquette, Fr. missionary, and Louis Joliet, Fr. explorer, travel down the Mississippi River as far as the Arkansas River.	**3** Parliament forces Charles II to approve the Test Act, which excludes from public office nonconformists and Roman Catholics. **4** Polish army defeats the Turks in the Ukraine.		**1** Petrovich Avvakum, Russ. religious leader imprisoned for his beliefs, writes his *Life,* the first Russian autobiography.

Science & Technology		Miscellaneous		
America	**Elsewhere**	**America**	**Elsewhere**	
	1 John Ray, Eng. naturalist, publishes *The Catalogue of English Plants.* **2** The bayonet is invented.	**1** An American Indian church is founded on Martha's Vineyard, an island off the coast of Massachusetts. **2** Population in the colonies is estimated at 114,500. Virginia has 40,000 residents. [1650:MISC/1]	**3** Hudson's Bay Company is established in England for trade in America. **4** Pascal's *Pensées,* his ideas on Christianity, are published after his death. [1656:MISC/2]	**1670**
	1 Willis describes two childhood diseases, myasthenia gravis and puerperal fever, and introduces techniques for detecting diabetes.	**1** First Seventh-Day Baptist Church is founded in Newport, R.I.	**2** First edition of the Bible in Arabic is printed in Rome. **3** French Senegal Company is founded.	**1671**
1 John Josselyn, Eng. naturalist, publishes *New England's Rarities Discovered* describing the area's animals, plants, medicines, and minerals.	**2** Nehemiah Grew, Eng. botanist, coins many botanical terms in his work on plant anatomy. **3** Hooke discovers the diffraction of light. **4** Newton publishes a work on light and color. **5** Guericke becomes the first person to describe electroluminescence.		**1** Bubonic plague kills 60,000 people in Lyon, France, and 400,000 in Naples, Italy.	**1672**
	1 Gottfried Leibniz, Ger scientist and philosopher, designs a crude adding machine. **2** Malpighi discovers the aortic arches and other embryonic structures. **3** Swammerdam publishes extensive descriptions of observations made through the microscope.	**1** Regular mounted mail service begins between New York and Boston.		**1673**

	History and Politics		The Arts	
	America	**Elsewhere**	**America**	**Elsewhere**
1674	**1** By the Treaty of Westminster between England and the Netherlands, the inhabitants of New York and New Sweden are recognized as English subjects.	**2** England makes peace with the Dutch. [1672:HIST/1] **3** Holy Roman Empire declares war on France; French forces defeat Dutch at Seneff and Imperial forces at Sinzheim. Spain joins fight against France, which is allied with Sweden. **4** Sivaji is crowned king of the Mahratta state in India; he resists successfully the Moguls.	**1** Samuel Sewall begins the diary which he kept for more than 50 years. Much of our knowledge of colonial life comes from its pages.	**2** Christopher Wren's plans for the new St. Paul's Cathedral are accepted.
1675		**1** Brandenburg, an ally of the Holy Roman Empire, defeats Swedish forces at the Battle of Fehrbellin. **2** French retreat across the Rhine and suffer defeat at Trier. France makes an alliance with Poland.		**1** *The Country Wife,* a comedy by William Wycherley, Eng. poet and dramatist, is staged.
1676	**1** Indian tribes under Philip, son of Massasoit, are subdued after a year of vicious Indian attacks on settlements (King Philip's War). Philip is shot and killed, thus ending the bloodiest Indian war in New England. **2** Nathaniel Bacon leads rebellion against severe rule of governor of Virginia in attempt to gain protection against the Indians; Bacon dies, but Indian attacks end.	**3** Poland and the Ottoman Empire conclude the Treaty of Zuravno, by which the Turks acquire the Polish Ukraine and Podolia, thus coming in contact with Russia. [1673:HIST/4]	**1** Peter Folger writes *A Looking-Glass for the Times,* a ballad satire which criticizes the religious intolerance of New England Christians.	**2** Wycherley, whose plays are often coarse and indecent, writes *The Plain Dealer,* the most effective of his works.
1677	**1** Quakers from England settle in Burlington, N.J.	**2** Swedes defeat the Danes, allies of the Dutch, at Landskrona. French defeat the Dutch at Cassel and seize Freiburg. Combined Dutch-Danish fleet defeats Swedes off Öland.		**1** John Dryden writes *All For Love.* It deals with the Antony and Cleopatra theme. **2** After the production of *Phèdre,* his last and most powerful play, Racine retires from the stage.

Science & Technology		Miscellaneous		
America	**Elsewhere**	**America**	**Elsewhere**	
1 Josselyn publishes *An Account of Two Voyages to New England* with expanded descriptions of New England's plants. He also claims to have seen a merman in the North Atlantic.	**2** Antonie van Leeuwenhoek, Dutch microscopist, observes bacteria and protozoa.	**1** First commercial corporation, the New York Fishing Company, is chartered.	**2** First description of billiards in English appears in the *Compleat Gamester.*	**1674**
	1 Cassini discovers the space between two of Saturn's rings—now known as Cassini's Division. **2** Leibniz lays the groundwork for the development of modern calculus. **3** Newton examines optical phenomena in *An Hypothesis Explaining the Properties of Light.*	**1** More than 600 ships and 4000 men are now involved in New England fishing. **2** Fire in Boston destroys 46 houses and other buildings. **3** Massachusetts passes laws to control fashions, particularly that of men wearing long hair—whether it be their own hair or wigs. **4** Massachusetts law requires that church doors be locked during services because too many people leave before the long sermon is completed.	**5** Paris is the cultural center in Europe; has approximately 500,000 inhabitants. **6** Baruch Spinoza, Dutch philosopher, finishes his major work, *Ethica.*	**1675**
 Antonie van Leeuwenhoek, Dutch microscopist	**1** Ole Rømer, Dan. astronomer, is the first to estimate the speed of light. **2** Ray publishes *The Ornithology of F. Willughby,* a bird catalogue written in part by his colleague Francis Willughby. **3** Sydenham publishes *Observationes Medicae,* which becomes a standard medical textbook for 200 years.	**1** Connecticut forbids anyone to wear clothes that do not match their place in society. This applies to the wearing of silk, gold or silver lace, or any other luxurious fabric or metal. **2** Massachusetts regulates the price of shoes: five pence half penny for all plain and wooden heeled shoes, and more than seven pence half penny for well-made "French falls."	**3** Influenza epidemic sweeps through England. **4** Observance of the Sabbath is made legal in England.	**1676**
	1 Leeuwenhoek is the first to describe the spermatozoa of humans and other mammals.		**1** Ice cream becomes popular as a dessert in Paris.	**1677**

	History and Politics		The Arts	
	America	**Elsewhere**	**America**	**Elsewhere**
				3 Eng. musician Henry Purcell is appointed composer to the King's violins.
1678		**1** False "Popish Plot" to murder King Charles II and establish Roman Catholicism in England results in wave of anti-Catholic hatred with executions of innocent people. **2** France signs peace Treaties of Nijmegen with the Netherlands and Spain. Dutch get all lands back; French get Franche-Comté and border towns in return for evacuating Spanish Netherlands.	**1** Anne Bradstreet publishes *Several Poems* in Boston.	**2** John Bunyan, Eng. preacher, publishes *Pilgrim's Progress,* an allegory about a Christian's life and struggles.
1679	**1** England proclaims New Hampshire a royal colony, separate from Massachusetts.	**2** France signs Treaties of Nijmegen with Holy Roman Emperor, Sweden, and Denmark. Sweden makes peace with the Netherlands, Brandenburg, and Denmark. [1678:HIST/2] **3** Habeas Corpus Act in England establishes protection against unlawful imprisonment of persons.	**1** Samuel Hardy's *A Guide to Heaven* is published in Boston. This book of Puritan rules and practices is a colonial bestseller.	**2** Ital. composer Alessandro Scarlatti produces the first opera. He is a key figure in the development of the opera form. **3** Jap. poet Matsuo Bashō writes verses in a new haiku style, greatly enriching that form.
1680	**1** French plan colonial empire stretching from Quebec to the mouth of the Mississippi River.	**2** Louis XIV of France, now at the height of his power, sets up Chambers of Reunion to find legal French claims on various towns, which he promptly annexes. **3** Swedish Parliament passes law repossessing crown lands from the nobles.		**1** Eng. organist and composer John Blow begins *Venus and Adonis,* the first English opera. **2** France's national theater, the Comédie Française, is founded by the merger of two acting companies.
1681	**1** Sieur de La Salle (Robert Cavelier), Fr. explorer, travels to the mouth of the Mississippi River, claims entire region from Quebec to Gulf for France, and names it Louisiana after King Louis XIV. **2** William Penn, Eng. Quaker, receives charter from King Charles II of England for lands that become the state of Pennsylvania. He founds the city of Philadelphia.	**3** Turks give up much of Turkish Ukraine to Russia. **4** Brandenburg makes defensive alliances with both France and Sweden.	**1** William Penn writes an account designed to attract settlers to Pennsylvania. **2** The Old Ship Meeting House is built at Hingham, Mass. Representative of colonial "four-square" church construction, it lacks a spire and cross, but has a bell tower with a weathervane. **3** The first American edition of Bunyan's *Pilgrim's Progress* is a popular seller.	**4** *Le Triomphe de l'Amour,* a court entertainment, is presented, marking the first public appearance of a female dancer. **5** Dryden's verse satire *Absalom and Achitophel* supports the King against the Whigs and the Earl of Shaftesbury.

Science & Technology		Miscellaneous		
America	**Elsewhere**	**America**	**Elsewhere**	
William Penn, English Quaker (engraving from a painting by Benjamin West)	**1** *Isagoge Phytoscopia,* by Ger. philosopher Joachim Jungius, sets new standards for describing and classifying plants. **2** Hooke describes planetary motion using the inverse square law. **3** Giovanni Ceva, Ital. mathematician, publishes *Concerning Straight Lines.*	**1** Year-long smallpox epidemic ends in New England.		**1678**
	1 Hevelius shows that the position of a star can be determined without a telescope. **2** Denis Papin, Fr. physicist, invents the pressure cooker. **3** Leibniz establishes the advanced mathematical field of topology.	**1** First plan for naming streets in Newport, R.I. **2** Fire in Boston destroys the dockyard, warehouses, and 150 houses; thereafter, all houses are required to be of stone or brick, covered with slate or tile roofs.	**3** Elias Ashmole founds the Ashmolean Museum at Oxford, England.	**1679**
1 Thomas Brattle, merchant, contributes his observations on comets to Newton's *Principia.*	**2** Leeuwenhoek studies the composition of yeast.	**1** Population in the colonies is estimated at 155,000. **[1670:MISC/2]**	**2** In London, William Dockwra sets up the "Penny Post." For the first time, letters are prepaid and stamped, showing where they are posted and the time they are sent out.	**1680**
1 William Penn, founder of Pennsylvania, decrees that at least 20% of the land in Pennsylvania must remain forested.	**2** Borelli publishes *De Motu Animalium,* in which he describes the mechanics of muscular movement.	**1** William Penn, Quaker leader, writes *Frame of Government,* giving his ideas on religious liberty. **[1681:HIST/2]** **2** First dancing master appears in Boston and is quickly driven out by the authorities. Dancing is a constant source of complaint among ministers.	**3** Bank checks are first used in England.	**1681**

	History and Politics		The Arts	
	America	**Elsewhere**	**America**	**Elsewhere**
1682	**1** French establish first white settlement in Arkansas.	**2** Ottoman Empire begins war with Austria, which is allied to Poland.	**1** Edward Taylor, Mass. minister and physician considered the finest poet of colonial times, begins writing religious verses *Preparatory Meditations*. Though he bound his poems himself, he never had them published. **2** Gov. Berkeley suppresses an attempt to establish a printing press in Virginia.	**3** French Jesuit Claude-François Menestrier writes the first history of the ballet. **4** With Ts'ang Ying-hsuan's appointment as director of the Imperial kilns, Chinese porcelain attains a new level of excellence. **5** Eng. dramatist Thomas Otway's tragedy, *Venice Preserv'd*, is produced.
1683	**1** Mennonites from Germany settle Germantown, near Philadelphia.	**2** Combined Imperial and Polish forces raise the Turkish siege of Vienna and defeat the larger Turkish army. **3** Manchus of China conquer the island of Formosa.	**1** Franciscan Father Louis Hennepin writes a description of the Louisiana territory and the upper Mississippi Valley.	**2** Purcell's first composition appears: *Sonatas of III Parts*.
1684	**1** England issues new royal charter making Maine and Plymouth part of Massachusetts, revoking original charter of Massachusetts Bay Colony.	**2** Holy Roman Empire, Poland, and Venice join with the Pope to form Holy League against the Turks. **3** English abandon Tangier to the Moroccans. **4** French fleet bombards Algerian coastal towns and forces deys (Turkish governors) to surrender Christian slaves.	**1** Increase Mather writes *An Essay for the Recording of Illustrious Providences*, a collection of stories about the hand of God rescuing people from disasters.	**2** Richard Steele meets Joseph Addison when both attend Charterhouse school in London. [1709:ARTS/3] **3** Bunyan publishes *Pilgrim's Progress, Second Part*.
1685	**1** La Salle leads French expedition that explores east Texas.	**2** James II becomes King of England, Scotland, and Ireland, succeeding his brother Charles II. Uprising against James is crushed. **3** Manchus open all Chinese ports to foreign trade.	**1** William Bradford sets up a printing press in Philadelphia, the first outside Boston. **2** Increase Mather is named president of Harvard College, a post he holds until 1701.	**3** Christopher Wren's stark design for the Royal Hospital at Chelsea complements its military nature.
1686	**1** England establishes a Dominion of New England, including New York, New Jer-	**2** Austrians capture Budapest from the Turks. Russia declares war on Ottoman		

Science & Technology		Miscellaneous		
America	**Elsewhere**	**America**	**Elsewhere**	
	1 Grew publishes *The Anatomy of Plants,* in which he correctly describes their sex organs. **2** Ray publishes work in which plants are classified according to their type of seed germination.	**1** First recorded tornado hits New Haven, Conn.		**1682**
1 Increase Mather, clergyman, publishes *Kometographia* describing the 1682 return of Halley's comet and giving a history of all comets "since creation." **2** Mather and others form the Philosophical Society in Boston to promote scientific research and experimentation in the colonies.	**3** Leeuwenhoek publishes the first drawing of bacteria. **4** Sydenham publishes a work on gout. **5** Newton suggests that the attraction of the Sun and Moon governs the tides.		**1** About 50,000 French Huguenots are forced to convert to Catholicism.	**1683**
	1 Newton submits his work *De Motu (On Motion)* to Eng. astronomer Edmund Halley.	**1** First excise tax on liquor goes into effect in Pennsylvania.	-	**1684**
	1 Ray publishes *A History of Fish.*	**1** Pennsylvania orders evacuation of caves being used for homes in order to fill them in. Because early settlers lacked sawmills, saws, and facilities for cutting and using stone, many of them lived in caves dug into sides of hills. **2** Huguenots flee France and settle in Massachusetts, Rhode Island, Virginia, and South Carolina.	**3** Edict of Nantes, which gives religious freedom to French Huguenots, is revoked. Thousands of Huguenots are exiled from France. **[1598:HIST/2]**	**1685**
1 John Banister, botanist, publishes his description of Virginia plants in	**2** Edmund Halley publishes the first weather chart.	**1** Diphtheria epidemic spreads throughout Virginia.	**2** Leibniz, Ger. philosopher, publishes *Discourse on Metaphysics.*	**1686**

History and Politics		The Arts	
America	**Elsewhere**	**America**	**Elsewhere**
sey, and Pennsylvania. It is governed by Sir Edmund Andros. Harsh rulings by Andros cause much colonial dissent.	Empire. **3** Louis XIV of France proclaims the annexation of Madagascar. **4** Holy Roman Emperor with various German states and with Sweden forms the League of Augsburg, opposing French expansion.		
1687 **1** Yamasee Indians revolt under Spanish rule in Florida and Georgia and flee northward.	**2** James II issues Declaration of Liberty of Conscience, suspending laws against Catholics and dissenters in England and Scotland. **3** Imperial troops defeat the Turks at the Battle of Mohács. **4** Hungarian diet fixes the succession to the throne in the male line of the Hapsburgs.		**1** The premiere of Carlo Pallavincini's opera, *La Gerusalemme liberata,* is held in Dresden. His 20 other operas are produced in Venice.
1688	**1** Protestants, fearing the restoration of Catholicism in England, demand "Glorious Revolution." Dutch Prince William of Orange and Mary, his English wife, are invited to England; James II flees to France. **[1672:HIST/1]** **2** French invade Palatinate and seize Heidelberg; war of the League of Augsburg begins against France.	**1** Francis Bacon's *Essays* is first published in America. The volume becomes one of the most widely read books in colonial times.	**2** Fr. satirist and moralist Jean de La Bruyère publishes his masterwork on the manners and morals of his age.
1689 **1** England and France seek to gain control of eastern North America. King William's War begins; French, aided by Indians from Maine and Canada, attack English settlements. Iroquois Indians aid English. **2** Colonists rebel in Boston against Governor Andros, who is ousted and sent to England to stand trial for misconduct. **[1686:HIST/1]**	**3** Parliament declares William and Mary joint sovereigns, King William III and Queen Mary II of England. They sign English Bill of Rights, limiting royal power and barring any Catholic from the throne. **[1688:HIST/1]** **4** England and the Netherlands join the League of Augsburg, forming Grand Alliance against France. **[1686:HIST/4]** **5** Peter I (the Great) becomes Czar of Russia.		**1** Dutch landscapist Meindert Hobbema paints his greatest work, "The Avenue, Middelharnis."
1690 **1** French and Indians attack and burn English settlements at Schenectady, N.Y., and Casco Bay, Me. **2** English forces seize Port Royal, Nova Scotia, from the French, who recapture it.	**3** William III crushes Jacobites' hope of restoring James II to the English throne by his victory at the Battle of Boyne, Scotland. **4** French defeat the English fleet at the Battle of Beachy	**1** Benjamin Harris puts out the *New England Primer,* an elementary textbook whose rhymed sayings are designed to teach colonial youth Chris-	**3** Purcell composes the music for Dryden's comedy *Amphitryon* and completes the opera *Dido and Aeneas.*

86

Science & Technology		Miscellaneous		
America	**Elsewhere**	**America**	**Elsewhere**	
John Ray's *Historia Plantarum.*				
1 John Clayton writes about medical practices among the Indians. This is his first in a series of scientific papers about the New World.	**2** Newton publishes *Philosophiae Naturalis Principia Mathematica,* in which he establishes his laws of motion and gravity, the foundation of modern science. **3** Guillaume Amontons, Fr. inventor and scientist, invents the hygrometer, an instrument used to measure humidity.	**1** First Anglican service (Church of England) is held in Boston. **2** Malaria epidemic strikes Virginia.		**1687**
1 The Philosophical Society of Boston disbands. [1683:SCI/2]		**1** Year-long measles epidemic ends in New England. An influenza epidemic strikes Virginia.	**2** Smyrna (Izmir), Turkey, is destroyed by an earthquake.	**1688**
Peter the Great, Czar of Russia		**1** First public school is founded in Philadelphia. Tuition is charged only to those who can afford it.		**1689**
1 William Rittenhouse and William Bradford establish the first American paper mill in Roxborough, a town near Philadelphia, Pa.	**2** Jakob Bernoulli, Swiss mathematician, coins the calculus term *integral.* **3** *Prodromus Astronomiae,* a catalogue and atlas of the heavens compiled by Hevelius, is	**1** Population in the colonies is estimated at 213,000. **2** Paper money is issued in Massachusetts.	**3** First English periodical to answer reader's letters, *The Athenian Gazette,* is published. **4** John Locke, Eng. philosopher, writes *An Essay Concerning Human*	**1690**

87

History and Politics		The Arts	
America	**Elsewhere**	**America**	**Elsewhere**
	Head and defeat the Dutch and their allies at Fleurus, Belgium. **5** Spain joins the War of the Grand Alliance against France. **[1689:HIST/4]**	tian virtues along with reading. **2** The first newspaper in the colonies, *Publick Occurrences,* is soon suppressed by Boston authorities.	
1691 **1** English forces regain control of New York. Jacob Leisler, Ger. trader who led a revolt in the name of William and Mary of England and seized control (1689), is caught, tried for treason, and hanged.	**2** Austrians defeat the Turks at Slankamen; Turks continue to ravage the country.		
1692	**1** English and Dutch defeat the French fleet at La Hogue. **2** Macdonald clan is massacred at Glencoe, Scotland, for allegedly failing to take oath to King William III.	 Francois Couperin, French composer	**1** Eng. playwright Nahum Tate is named poet laureate. He is best known for hymns such as "While shepherds watched their flocks by night."
1693	**1** French defeat the English fleet off Lagos, Portugal. **2** National debt begins in England.		**1** Fr. composer François Couperin becomes organist of the Royal Chapel.
1694	**1** Bank of England is founded by company of merchants, who, in return for banking privileges, lend the government £1,200,000. **2** French towns of Dieppe, Le Havre, and Dunkirk are heavily bombarded by English and Dutch navies.	**1** Samuel Willard's election sermon, *The Character of a Good Ruler,* is published in Boston. It demonstrates that politics, religion, and literature are closely related in colonial times.	**2** Jap. poet Bashō publishes *The Narrow Road to the Deep North,* a sensitively written account of his travels in northern Japan. **3** Reinhard Keiser becomes principal composer to the Hamburg opera. He produced 116 operas in the next 40 years.
1695	**1** Namur, Belgium, seized by the French in 1695, is retaken by the Dutch and English. **2** Licensing Act lapses in England, a great step toward freedom of the press.	**1** The first building at William and Mary College is begun. This example of Georgian architecture was reputedly designed by Sir Christopher Wren. **[1669:ARTS/4]**	**2** Fr. playwright Jean François Regnard writes the comedy *Le Joueur (The Gamester).*

Science & Technology		Miscellaneous		
America	**Elsewhere**	**America**	**Elsewhere**	
	published three years after the author's death.		*Understanding* **5** England's population is about 5 million. **6** An early form of the bicycle, the *celérifère,* is invented.	
The arrest of a Salem witch		**1** Ducking stool, a form of punishment for scolds, is built in New York. Although not used frequently in New York, it is common in the South.	**2** First directory of addresses is published in Paris.	**1691**
		1 Trials for witchcraft begin in Salem, Mass. Of the 20 people condemned as witches, 18 are executed and two die in prison. **2** Maryland officially recognizes the Church of England.	**3** An earthquake strikes Jamaica, in the West Indies.	**1692**
1 Bradford establishes a printing press in New York.	**2** Ray's *Synopsis of Quadrupeds,* an important work on the taxonomy (classification) of animals, is published. **3** Cassini publishes three rules, known as Cassini's Laws, concerning the Moon's rotation.	**1** William and Mary College is founded in Virginia. **2** Postal service is established between New York and Philadelphia.	**3** In Catania, Italy, an earthquake kills 60,000 people. **4** Locke publishes *Some Thoughts Concerning Education,* in which he stresses teaching through practice rather than by memorization of rules.	**1693**
	1 Rudolph Camerarius, Ger. botanist, proves that plants have sexes.			**1694**
	1 Jakob Bernoulli applies calculus to bridge construction. **2** Amontons perfects the mercury barometer.		**1** A model school for children who are paupers is opened in Halle (Germany).	**1695**

89

	History and Politics		The Arts	
	America	**Elsewhere**	**America**	**Elsewhere**
1696	**1** French successfully hold Quebec against attacks by the English and Iroquois.	**2** Czar Peter I of Russia captures Azov from the Turks. **3** Plot to murder William III of England is discovered, and the conspirators are executed.	**1** The first book printed in New York is *Advice to a Young Gentleman Leaving the University* by Richard Lyon.	**2** *Love's Last Shift,* the first of the "sentimental comedies" popular in the 18th century, is produced. It was written by Colley Cibber, Eng. actor, playwright, and theater manager.
1697	**1** King William's War ends; Treaty of Ryswick restores all possessions to status quo before the war. **[1689:HIST/1]**	**2** France signs Treaty of Ryswick with England, Spain, and the Netherlands, ending the War of the Grand Alliance. France loses most of her conquests made since 1679. **3** Imperial forces defeat the Turkish army at the Battle of Zenta. **4** China gains control of Outer Mongolia.		**1** Charles Perrault, Fr. storyteller and poet, publishes *Contes de ma mère l'oye (Tales of Mother Goose),* a collection of fairy tales and folk tales for children.
1698		**1** Czar Peter I suppresses a revolt of the streltsy (soldiers of the Moscow garrison); he prepares for war with Sweden, hoping to gain possession of the Baltic coast.	**1** The new edition of the *Bay Psalm Book* contains music for the first time—13 tunes, in 2-part harmony. It is the oldest existing music of American imprint. The tunes come from Playford's book. **[1651:ARTS/2]**	**2** Eng. clergyman Jeremy Collier publishes *Short View of the Immorality and Profaneness of the English Stage,* attacking the obscenity of Restoration drama.
1699	**1** Sieur d'Iberville (Pierre le Moyne) founds Old Biloxi (now Ocean Springs, Miss.)—first permanent white settlement in the French territory of Louisiana.	**2** Ottoman Empire signs the Treaty of Karlowitz with Austria, Poland, and Venice. Hungary, Croatia, and Slavonia are ceded to Austria; Podolia passes to Poland; Morea and most of Dalmatia pass to Venice.	**1** Jonathan Dickinson writes an adventurous bestseller, *God's Protecting Providence.* **2** Distinctive regional architecture develops in the Louisiana colony.	**3** Fr. writer François Fénelon publishes *Les Adventures de Télémarque,* a book considered by many to be a satire of the king and his policies.
1700		**1** Great Northern War begins; Russia, Poland, and Denmark fight Sweden to break Swedish supremacy in the Baltic area. **2** Charles XII of Sweden forces the Danes to make peace and defeats Peter I of Russia at Narva. **3** Poles invade Livonia.	**1** Samuel Sewall writes *The Selling of Joseph,* an anti-slavery tract. **2** Henrietta Johnson of Charleston, S.C., is the first known woman painter in America.	**3** The best known comedy of Restoration dramatist William Congreve, *The Way of the World,* is presented at Lincoln's Inn. **4** Fr. dancer and choreographer Raoul Feuillet publishes a system of dance notation, *Choreography, or*

Science & Technology		Miscellaneous		
America	**Elsewhere**	**America**	**Elsewhere**	
	1 Ray describes peppermint. **2** Sir Hans Sloane, Eng. naturalist, publishes a catalogue of more than 800 new plant species.		**1** First company is formed to issue property insurance in England. **2** Journeymen hatters, who have formed a trade union, call a strike in London. **3** Schools are established in every parish in Scotland.	**1696**
  Whaling in New England		**1** Smallpox strikes Charleston, S.C. **2** Massachusetts law provides that anyone denying the divine nature of the Bible can be imprisoned for 6 months, confined to a pillory, whipped, or have his tongue bored through with a hot iron.	**3** Daniel Defoe, Eng. writer, in *An Essay Upon Projects*, recommends an income tax and urges higher education for women. **4** Whitehall Palace in London is destroyed by fire.	**1697**
1 Colonies offer prizes of tobacco to the colonists who produce the best linen.			**1** New East India Company is founded. **2** African trade is opened to all English subjects.	**1698**
1 Connecticut exempts the New Haven Ironworks from taxes for seven years. Such financial inducements are becoming common and do much to stimulate increased industrialization in the colonies.	**2** Amontons publishes work on the nature of friction.	**1** Yellow fever epidemic in Charleston, S.C., and Philadelphia kills nearly one sixth of the population. **2** Captain Kidd, the notorious pirate, visits a friend in Narragansett, R.I., and leaves some treasure. Legend says that Kidd murdered a helper and buried him with the treasure to keep others away.	**3** Persecution of Huguenots in France lessens.	**1699**
1 Whaling increases along the New England coast.	**2** Fr. mapmaker Guillaume Delisle publishes map in which locations were determined by astronomical observations. **3** Fr. botanist Joseph de Tournefort publishes illustrated work on Mediterranean plant life.	**1** Approximately 275,000 people live in the Colonies. Boston, the largest city, has about 7000 inhabitants; New York, 5000; Newport, R.I. fewer than 2000. 250 families live in Charleston, S.C., and Philadelphia has about 700 houses. [1680:MISC/1]	**3** Population in France is 19 million, in England and Scotland 7.5 million, in the Hapsburg dominions (Central Europe) 7.5 million, and in Spain 6 million. **4** English Royal Company loses its trade monopoly between the African Gold Coast and	**1700**

History and Politics		The Arts	
America	**Elsewhere**	**America**	**Elsewhere**
			the Art of Describing the Dance.
1701			
1 Antoine de la Mothe Cadillac, with a band of French colonists, establishes Fort Pontchartrain (now Detroit, Mich.). French soon build other forts and fur-trading posts in Michigan and Illinois region.	**2** War of the Spanish Succession begins. England, Holland, and most of the German states oppose France, Spain, Portugal, Bavaria, and Savoy. Louis XIV of France makes last effort to dominate the continent. **3** Elector of Brandenburg crowns himself King of Prussia.	**1** An anonymous writer calling himself "An American" publishes, in London, *An Essay Upon the Government of the English Plantations on the Continent of America,* which includes a proposed plan for a union of the colonies.	**2** Ger. composer J.S. Bach starts giving organ lessons. **3** Ogata Kōrin, Jap. decorative painter known for colorful screen designs, decorates his famous iris screen. **4** Jeremy Collier, Eng. clergyman, publishes a dictionary of the English language.
1702			
1 Queen Anne's War begins; England fights France and Spain for control of territory. English sack and burn St. Augustine, Fla.	**2** Charles XII of Sweden invades Poland and captures Warsaw and Cracow. **3** French seize the lower Rhine. Duke of Marlborough, Eng. general, captures Venlo and Liège. **4** Anne becomes Queen of England.	**1** Cotton Mather, son of Increase Mather, publishes *Magnalia Christi Americana,* an ecclesiastical history of America from the founding of New England until his own time.	**2** John Weaver, Eng. ballet master, adopts the comic characters of Italian plays for the first English pantomime ballet, *The Tavern Bilkers*. **3** The 16-year-old J.S. Bach walks 30 miles to hear organist Jan Reinken. **4** A. Scarlatti composes operas in Florence for the private theater of Prince Ferdinand III.
1703			
1 Quaker colony of Pennsylvania gives three Delaware counties the right to a separate assembly.	**2** French threaten Vienna; Marlborough captures Bonn, Huy, Limburg, and Guelders. **3** Archduke Charles of Austria (later Holy Roman Emperor Charles VI) invades Spain with English troops and proclaims himself King of Spain (Charles III). **4** Hungarians revolt against Austrian government.	**1** Instrumental and organ music flourishes in some colonies of Pennsylvania. **2** The first professional actors to perform in the colonies present a play in Charleston, S.C.	**3** Fr. painter Jean-Antoine Watteau begins studying with Claude Gillot, a decorator of theater scenery. Watteau's paintings are often of theatrical subjects. **4** Ger. composer George Frederick Handel begins his musical career in Hamburg. **5** Eng. dramatist Nicholas Rowe writes *The Fair Penitent,* a play that introduces the character Lothario.
1704			
1 French and Indians massacre 50 men, women, and children at Deerfield, Mass., and carry off more than 100	**3** English-Austrian army under Marlborough and Prince of Savoy defeat decisively French-Bavarian army at the	**1** Schoolmistress Sarah Kemble Knight keeps a diary of her journey from Boston to	**2** The religious satire, *A Tale of a Tub,* is published anonymously by Jonathan Swift,

92

Science & Technology		Miscellaneous		
America	**Elsewhere**	**America**	**Elsewhere**	
		2 Catholic priests are banned from Massachusetts. The penalty for their being found in the colony is either life in prison or execution.	Britain. 5 Fire sweeps through Edinburgh, Scotland.	
	1 Halley publishes magnetic charts of the Atlantic and Pacific Oceans.	1 Yale College is founded in New Haven, Conn.	2 Society for Propagation of the Gospel in Foreign Parts (SPG) is founded in London. Its goal is to help the Church of England in America by establishing missions and founding churches. [1710:MISC/2]	1701
	1 Amontons invents the air pressure thermometer.	1 To combat delinquency in Massachusetts, Mather forms the "Society for the Suppression of Disorders," a sort of vigilante committee to keep an eye and ear open for swearing, blaspheming, and patronage of bawdy houses. 2 Act of Establishment in Maryland officially recognizes the Church of England.	3 First daily newspaper, *The Daily Courant,* is published in London. 4 French set up a factory in Sierra Leone, Africa. 5 Peter the Great orders the publication of the *Moscow Gazette.* [1689:HIST/5] 6 Queen Anne approves horse racing in England. She encourages a sweepstakes.	1702
			1 Earthquake kills almost 200,000 people in Tokyo. 2 Port wine becomes popular in England when the duties are lowered by a treaty between England and Portugal. 3 First A-Z treatment of knowledge in an English publication is the *Universal, Historical, Geographical, Chronological and Classical Dictionary.*	1703

Yale College, New Haven, Connecticut

| | 1 John Harris, Eng. editor, publishes one of the first encyclopedias.
2 Giovanni Battista | 1 First continuous newspaper, the *News-Letter,* is printed in Boston.
2 Ministers in Maryland | 3 Earthquake destroys many buildings in Gondar, Ethiopia.
4 Protestant dissenters | 1704 |

History and Politics		The Arts	
America	Elsewhere	America	Elsewhere
others. **2** English colonial forces attack the French fort of Port Royal, Nova Scotia.	Battle of Blenheim in Bavaria. **4** English take Gibraltar from the Spanish.	New York. It is a realistic account of early colonial life.	Eng. clergyman and satirist. **3** Eng. organist Jeremiah Clark, composer of the famous *Trumpet Voluntary*, becomes organist of the Chapel Royal.

1705

1 Virginia's slavery act states all imported Negroes are to be life-long slaves unless they are Christians. [1670:HIST/2]	**2** English forces seize Barcelona, Spain. **3** Tunis throws off Turkish rule; Husseinite dynasty is founded.	**1** Robert Beverley publishes, in London, *The History and Present State of Virginia . . . by a Native of the Place,* in which he severely criticizes the royal governors.	**2** Eng. architect John Vanbrugh designs Blenheim Palace for the Duke of Marlborough, later the birthplace of England's wartime leader Winston Churchill. **3** Domenico Scarlatti, son of Alessandro, studies in Florence. A harpsichord virtuoso, he is considered the father of modern piano-playing. **4** J.S. Bach walks 200 miles to Lübeck to hear Buxtehude.

1706

1 Invading Spanish-French flotilla (small naval ships) is driven out of the harbor at Charleston, S.C. **2** Customhouse (government office for collecting revenue) is built at Yorktown, Va.—port of entry for New York, Philadelphia, and other northern towns.	**3** English, Dutch, and Danish troops under Marlborough defeat the French at the Battle of Ramillies and seize the Spanish Netherlands. **4** Prince of Savoy, aided by the Prussians, defeats the French at Turin, which results in the French evacuation of northern Italy. **5** Swedes invade and overrun Saxony. Charles XII of Sweden forces Augustus II to recognize Stanislaus I as King of Poland and to end his alliance with Russia.	**1** Construction begins on the Governor's Palace in Williamsburg, Va.	**2** Handel begins three years in Italy which contribute greatly to his musical development.

1707

1 English expedition tries to capture the French colony of Acadia (now Nova Scotia, New Brunswick, and Prince Edward Island).	**2** Great Britain is formed by Act of Union between England and Scotland. English and Scots sit in one British Parliament. **3** Mogul empire in India begins falling apart when Emperor Aurangzeb dies. [1669:HIST/3] **4** French-Spanish forces defeat the British at the Battle of Almanza.	**1** *The Redeemed Captive* by John Williams is popular reading among colonists. Like many favorite works of the era, it tells of its author's reputed capture by Indians.	**2** The publication of Eng. minister Isaac Watts' *Hymns and Spiritual Songs* marks an advance in the quality of church music. This collection sees much use in the colonies. **3** *The Beaux' Stratagem,* a comedy by George Farquhar, Eng. playwright, is produced in London.

Science & Technology		Miscellaneous		
America	Elsewhere	America	Elsewhere	
	Morgagni, Ital. anatomist, publishes *Anatomy and Diseases of the Ear.*	have the right to separate a man and a woman if the minister disapproves of her. If the man does not obey, he can be brought into court, and, if convicted, can be fined, or whipped until blood begins to flow.	in Ireland are excluded from holding public office by the Test Act. **5** Earliest subscription library opens in Berlin.	
	1 Halley publishes *A Synopsis of the Astronomy of Comets,* in which he correctly predicts the reappearance of Halley's Comet.	**1** Thomas Odell of Boston, arrested for counterfeiting the new pound note, is sentenced to pay a fine and to spend a year in jail. Counterfeiting is a new crime, since paper money is just coming into use. **2** Anglican Church is established by law in North Carolina.		**1705**
		1 Hunting season on deer is limited on Long Island, N.Y., because continued hunting has almost eliminated them. **2** First Latin grammar is published. **3** First Anglican parish is established in Connecticut. **4** First Presbytery, an organization of the Presbyterian Church, is established in Philadelphia.	**5** First evening newspaper, *The Evening Post,* is published in London. **6** First life insurance office opens in London.	**1706**
	1 Papin builds the first steam engine.	**1** First meeting of the Baptist Association is held in Philadelphia.		**1707**

The Governor's Palace in Williamsburg, Virginia

History and Politics		The Arts	
America	**Elsewhere**	**America**	**Elsewhere**

1708

History and Politics — America

1 French and Indians destroy colony at Haverhill, Mass.

Johann Sebastian Bach, German composer

History and Politics — Elsewhere

2 Marlborough and the Prince of Savoy defeat the French at Oudenaarde, Belgium.
3 British occupy Minorca and bombard Sardinia.
4 Charles XII of Sweden secures secret pact with Ukrainian Cossack hetman (leader) and invades Russia.

The Arts — America

1 *The Sot-Weed Factor,* a verse satire ridiculing contemporary life in Maryland, is published in London. Its author is reputedly Ebenezer Cook. **[1960:ARTS/10]**

The Arts — Elsewhere

2 J.S. Bach accepts a post as organist at Weimar in the chapel of Duke Wilhelm Ernst. Here he writes some of his greatest preludes and fugues for organ.
3 As concert master at Eisenach, Ger. composer Georg Philipp Telemann meets and begins a close friendship with J.S. Bach.

1709

History and Politics — Elsewhere

1 Peter I of Russia decisively defeats Charles XII of Sweden at the Battle of Poltava in the Ukraine.
2 Marlborough and the Prince of Savoy defeat the French at the Battle of Malplaquet.
3 Austrians defeat Philip V, King of Spain, at Almenara and Zaragoza. **[1703:HIST/3]**

The Arts — America

1 Scot. adventurer John Lawson publishes, in London, *A New Voyage to Carolina,* promotional literature aiming to increase immigration.
2 An unknown artist chisels a detailed portrait on the gravestone of Rev. Jonathan Pierpoint in Wakefield, Mass.

The Arts — Elsewhere

3 Richard Steele starts publishing *The Tatler,* a thrice-weekly periodical of essays. Addison is a frequent contributor.
4 Ital. harpsichord maker Bartolomeo Cristofori replaces that instrument's plucking mechanism with a hammer action, thus inventing the piano.
5 "For He's a Jolly Good Fellow" becomes a popular song.

1710

History and Politics — America

1 New Englanders, aided by British ships and marines, capture Port Royal from the French. It is renamed Annapolis Royal, and part of Acadia becomes the British province of Nova Scotia. **[1704:HIST/2]**

History and Politics — Elsewhere

2 Charles XII (a refugee in Turkey) persuades the Ottoman Turks to fight Russia. **[1709:HIST/1]**
3 Philip V and the French win victories at Brihuega and Villaviciosa, Spain. **[1709:HIST/3]**
4 French seize Mauritius from the Dutch.

The Arts — America

1 The Pennsylvania Dutch architectural style develops in the southeastern counties of the colony.
2 Cotton Mather writes *Bonifacius, or Essays to Do Good,* a favorite work of Benjamin Franklin's.

The Arts — Elsewhere

3 The production of Handel's opera *Agrippina* in Venice marks the high point of his years in Italy.

1711

History and Politics — America

1 Tuscarora Indians massacre more than 150 settlers in North Carolina.
2 Campaign by British colonials against Montreal and Quebec fails.

History and Politics — Elsewhere

3 Turkish army surrounds the Russians on the Pruth River. By the Peace of Pruth, Peter I restores Azov to the Turks.
4 Marlborough, falsely accused of misusing public funds, is dismissed as English Commander-in-Chief.
5 Charles VI becomes Holy Roman Emperor and, by the Peace of Szatmar, restores religious and constitutional freedom to the Hungarians.

The Arts — America

1 Newspaper ads for the sale of organs document the presence of that instrument in New England.

The Arts — Elsewhere

2 Alexander Pope, Eng. man of letters, publishes *An Essay on Criticism.*
3 Following the success of his first London opera *Rinaldo,* Handel settles permanently in England.
4 St. Paul's, London, is completed.
5 Steele inaugurates *The Spectator,* a joint venture with Addison.

Science & Technology		Miscellaneous		
America	**Elsewhere**	**America**	**Elsewhere**	
	1 Papin builds a self-propelled paddle-wheel boat.	1 Saybrook Platform, or Constitution, is accepted by Connecticut Congregational churches. It brings them closer to the Presbyterian way of church organization and away from the democratic ideas of Massachusetts Congregationalism.	2 United Company of Merchants of England is organized for trade with the West Indies. 3 Alexander Mack, Ger. clergyman, founds the German Baptist United Brethren (Moravians). **[1735:MISC/1]**	**1708**
	1 Gabriel Fahrenheit, Ger. physicist, invents the alcohol thermometer.	1 German and Swiss Protestants flee from Europe and settle in the Carolinas. 2 Quakers of Philadelphia establish the first private home for mental illness. In 1751 it becomes part of Pennsylvania Hospital.	3 First Copyright Act is passed in England. 4 Postage rates in England are regulated by mileage. 5 Abraham Darby, an ironmaster in Shropshire, England, devises a furnace for smelting pig-iron with coke. As a result coal becomes an important fuel.	**1709**
	George Frederick Handel, German composer	1 Colonial population is estimated at 357,000. **[1700:MISC/1]** 2 Trinity School is established in New York City under the Society for the Propagation of the Gospel. **[1701:MISC/3]** 3 Colonial fashion includes high heels and stiff stays (corsets). Large curled wigs are worn by both men and women.	4 English South Sea Company is founded. 5 George Berkeley, Ir. philosopher, publishes *A Treatise Concerning the Principles of Human Knowledge*.	**1710**
1 Sperm whale is captured by a whaling boat from Nantucket. 2 Parliament prohibits Americans from cutting trees in the colonies. All lumber is reserved for use by the Royal Navy.		1 Bookselling flourishes. There are almost 30 shops in Boston doing a profitable business.	2 Bubonic plague kills more than 500,000 people in Austria and Germany. 3 Horse racing is established at Ascot, England. **[1702:MISC/6]**	**1711**

	History and Politics		The Arts	
	America	**Elsewhere**	**America**	**Elsewhere**
1712	**1** Carolina militia, aided by friendly Indians, attacks and kills more than 300 Tuscarora Indians near the Neuse River. **2** Negro slave uprising in New York City results in the execution of more than 100 Negroes.	**3** Swiss Protestants defeat the Catholics at Villmergen, after which the Protestant cantons dominate in Switzerland. **4** Moguls suppress the Sikhs, a militant religious order, in India.	**1** Rev. John Tufts of Newbury (Mass.) publishes a collection of psalm tunes with music. Issued in Boston, it is the first book of sacred music published in America.	**2** Eng. painter William Hogarth, later known for his comic engravings, becomes apprenticed to a silversmith and learns to engrave gold and silver. **3** Pope publishes *The Rape of the Lock,* a mock-heroic poem which treats insignificant events as if they were momentous.
1713	**1** Territory of Carolina is divided into North and South Carolina. **2** Tuscarora War ends with the capture of the Indians' stronghold in South Carolina. Tuscarora Indians flee north and join the Iroquois Confederation. **3** Treaty of Utrecht ends Queen Anne's War. Britain receives Hudson Bay region, Newfoundland, and Nova Scotia. France retains Cape Breton Island. [1702:HIST/1]	**4** Peace of Utrecht ends War of the Spanish Succession. Treaties among Britain, France, Holland, Spain, Portugal, Savoy, and Prussia establish Protestant succession in England, separation of the crowns of France and Spain, and the kingship of Prussia. Savoy receives Sicily. Britain receives Gibraltar and Minorca. Spain signs the *Asiento,* giving Britain sole right to the African slave trade with Spanish America. [1713:HIST/3]		**1** Joseph Addison's popular tragedy, *Cato,* is first performed at Drury Lane. **2** Members of the literary Scriblerus Club begin collaborating on satirical pieces eventually published as *The Memoires of Martinus Scriblerus.* Members include Alexander Pope, Jonathan Swift, and John Gay.
1714	**1** Natchitoches, La., is founded as a French military and trading post.	**2** Treaty of Rastatt between Louis XIV of France and Holy Roman Emperor Charles VI confirms Austrian possession of the Spanish Netherlands. Treaty of Baden restores Rhine's right bank to the Empire; France keeps Alsace and Strasbourg. **3** Charles XII returns to his Swedish kingdom from Turkey. [1710:HIST/2] **4** George I, Elector of Hanover, becomes King of England, succeeding Queen Anne.	**1** The first pipe organ used in a church in the colonies is played during an Anglican service in King's Chapel, Boston. Its use was denounced by Puritans who forbade instrumental music during service. **2** The first play composed and printed in the colonies is *Androboros,* a political satire by Robert Hunter, the governor of New York.	**3** Antonio Vivaldi, Ital. violinist and composer, becomes director of choir and orchestra concerts at a school for orphans in Venice. **4** Gottfried Silbermann, the first German piano maker, builds the great organ at the Cathedral in Freiburg.
1715	**1** Yamasee Indians go on the warpath and massacre more than 200 settlers in South Carolina. The Indians are driven southward into Georgia and Florida, where they become allies of the Spanish against the British. [1687:HIST/1]	**2** Jacobite uprising in Scotland, opposing King George I, ends in disastrous Battles of Preston and Sheriffmuir. **3** Polish nobles rebel against strict policies of Augustus II, who drove out Stanislaus I in 1709. [1706:HIST/5]		**1** Alain-René Lesage, Fr. writer, publishes the first installment of *Gil Blas,* a novel about the travels of a rogue. **2** Karlskirche, Vienna, is begun. It represents one of the most famous designs of Fischer von Erlach.

Science & Technology		Miscellaneous		
America	Elsewhere	America	Elsewhere	
 George I, King of England	**1** Mathematics is applied to economics for the first time in Ceva's *Concerning Money Matters*.		**1** In the last English trial for witchcraft, Jane Wenham is convicted but not executed.	**1712**
	1 Bernardino Ramazzini, Ital. physician, introduces the concept of job-related diseases. **2** The term *species* is introduced in the naming of natural classifications. **3** Jakob Bernoulli publishes *The Conjectural Arts,* in which he introduces several important mathematical concepts.	**1** New York City prohibits children from sleighing and coasting in the winter.	**2** Smallpox epidemic strikes the Cape Colony in South Africa.	**1713**
	1 Fahrenheit invents the mercury thermometer and devises the Fahrenheit temperature scale.	**1** Tea is introduced into the colonies. The favorite nonalcoholic beverage is chocolate, but rum is popular in New England and beer in the Middle Colonies.	**2** Peter the Great institutes public education in Russia. **3** French Senegal Company sets up factories in Guinea, Africa.	**1714**
1 Alexander Spotswood, governor of Virginia, opens an iron plant near Fredericksburg and establishes the town of Germanna for the workers, most of whom are German.	**2** Brook Taylor, Eng. mathematician, publishes work on perspective.		**1** Annual rowing race on the Thames River is started in England.	**1715**

	History and Politics		The Arts	
	America	**Elsewhere**	**America**	**Elsewhere**
1716		**1** Jacobite pretender to the throne of England flees to France. **2** Emperor Charles VI declares war on the Turks, who have been at war with Venice for two years. Prince of Savoy defeats the Turks at Petrovaradin, Yugoslavia. **3** Dutch receive several strongholds along the French frontier of the Austrian Netherlands, as protection against an attack by France. **[1714:HIST/2]**	**1** Edward Enstone runs a dancing and music school in Boston. He also sells and repairs a variety of musical instruments.	**2** Giovanni Battista Tiepolo paints his first public work, "The Sacrifice of Isaac," for a church in Venice. **3** Couperin publishes an important work on playing keyboard instruments. **4** Watteau paints "The Italian Comedy."
1717	**1** John Law, Scot. financier in France, acquires monopoly of trade rights in Louisiana and forms the Mississippi Company. **[1720:HIST/6]**	**2** Spain seizes Sardinia. **3** Prince of Savoy defeats the Turks at Belgrade. **4** Mongols occupy Lhasa, Tibet. **5** Charles XII of Sweden leads military invasion of Norway (then ruled by Denmark), where he is killed in 1718.		**1** J.S. Bach becomes choirmaster to Prince Leopold at Cöthen. Here he writes his chief orchestral works. **2** Fr. man of letters Voltaire (François-Marie Arouet) is imprisoned in the Bastille for mocking the regent, Duc d'Orléans.
1718	**1** New Orleans, La., is founded by French settlers from Canada and France. **[1681:HIST/1]** **2** San Antonio, Tex., is founded as a Spanish mission and presidio (military post).	**3** Quadruple Alliance is formed by Great Britain, France, The Netherlands, and the Holy Roman Empire to counteract the attempts of Philip V of Spain to overturn the Peace of Utrecht. **[1713:HIST/4]** **4** Treaty of Passarowitz ends war between Holy Roman Empire and Ottoman Empire (Turkey). Turks lose the Banat of Temesvar, northern Serbia and Bosnia, and Lesser Wallachia, but they keep Morea (Peloponnesus). **5** Britain declares war on Spain.	**1** Cotton Mather publishes a new book of psalms, *Psalterium Americanum*.	**2** Watteau's "Fête in a Park" shows the characteristically dreamy quality of his works.
1719	**1** French Mississippi Company encourages settlement in the southern Mississippi Valley.	**2** Sweden and Hanover (lower Saxony) sign Peace of Stockholm. **3** France declares war on Spain. **4** British Parliament issues Declaratory Act, affirming its right to legislate for Ireland. **5** Liechtenstein becomes an independent principality.	**1** *American Weekly Mercury* begins publication in Philadelphia. William Brooker founds the *Boston Gazette*. **2** *The Psalms of David Imitated* becomes the dominant hymn book in most Protestant churches in the colonies.	**3** Eng. journalist and pamphleteer Daniel Defoe publishes *Robinson Crusoe*. **4** Baron Ludvig Holberg, writer credited with founding the literature of Denmark, publishes the epic *Peder Paars,* the first Danish classic.

| Science & Technology | | Miscellaneous | |
America	Elsewhere	America	Elsewhere
			1 Earthquake kills about 20,000 people in Algiers, North Africa. **2** Japan allows works in Western languages to be brought into the country. Dutch writings make an appearance, and the Japanese translate medical and military works. **3** General Bank is established in Paris. **4** First Italian newspaper, *Diario di Roma,* is issued. **1716**
			1 Grand Lodge of Freemasons is established in London. **1717**
1 William Douglass opens medical practice as one of the first colonial physicians with a medical degree and license.	**2** Étienne-François Geoffroy, Fr. chemist, publishes tables listing the attractions of different substances to each other.	**1** Alexander Spotswood, governor of Virginia, offers rewards for pirates—dead or alive. Aimed chiefly at Blackbeard who has a hideout in North Carolina, it brings results. The Governor's men capture Blackbeard's ship and bring his head back on a pole.	**2** First bank notes are issued in London. **1718**
1 Aurora borealis (northern lights) is described for the first time in America.	**2** Morgagni's *Adversaria Anatomica* establishes pathological anatomy as a science.	**1** New Jersey law states that a person under 21 years of age cannot be married without the consent of a parent or guardian.	**2** Protestant dissenters are tolerated in Ireland. **[1704:MISC/4]** **3** Oriental Company is founded in Vienna to trade with the East. **4** Cricket match is played in London. **5** James Figg, becomes the first boxing champion in England; he remains undefeated for 15 years. **1719**

Voltáire, French philosopher, historian, dramatist and essayist

101

	History and Politics		The Arts	
	America	**Elsewhere**	**America**	**Elsewhere**
1720	**1** William Burnet, Eng. governor in New York and New Jersey, extends trade with the Indians. He seeks to bind the Iroquois to the British, away from the French. **2** French Canadians begin settling the Illinois region. [1680:HIST/1] **3** Spanish set up missions in Texas to counter the French threat from Louisiana.	**4** Treaty of The Hague revises Peace of Utrecht. Savoy is given Sardinia in place of Sicily, which is handed over to Austria. Naples goes to Austria, which promises Parma, Piacenza, and Tuscany to Philip's son Charles (later Charles III of Spain). Spain joins the Quadruple Alliance. [1713:HIST/4; 1718:HIST/3] **5** By the Treaties of Stockholm and Frederiksborg, Sweden makes peace with both Prussia and Denmark. Prussia receives Stettin (now Szczecin) and part of west Pomerania, but pays Sweden two million thalers (dollars). Denmark restores all conquests for a payment and freedom from customs duties in the Sound. **6** John Law's Mississippi Company, merged with the French royal bank, collapses because of wild speculation in its assets in Louisiana. [1717:HIST/1]	**1** The Governor's Palace in Williamsburg is completed. It is considered the finest colonial residence of the time.	**2** Canaletto (Giovanni Antonio Canal), Ital. painter known for views of Venice, is in Rome painting scenes for the operas of A. Scarlatti. **3** Giovanni Battista Tiepolo, Ital. painter, completes "Martyrdom of St. Bartholomew."
1721		**1** Sir Robert Walpole becomes Chancellor of the Exchequer. He restores public credit after the failure (1720) of the South Sea Company, formed (1711) to trade (mainly in slaves) with Spanish America. The "Bubble" burst from overspeculation in the company, which had also assumed England's national debt. **2** Treaty of Nystad between Russia and Sweden concludes the Great Northern War. Russia acquires Livonia, Ingermanland, part of Karelia, and some Baltic islands. Sweden retains Finland. [1700:HIST/1]	**1** Swed. artist Gustavus Hesselius receives the first art commission in the colonies: to paint "The Last Supper" as an altarpiece for a Maryland church. **2** Rev. Thomas Walter of Roxbury edits a singing book, the first with bars of music.	**3** Montesquieu (Charles-Louis de Secondat), Fr. satirist and political philosopher, publishes *Lettres persanes,* satirizing Parisian society. **4** J.S. Bach composes the six Brandenburg concertos for the Margrave of Brandenburg. **5** Handel's first oratorio, *Esther,* is composed.
1722	**1** Iroquois Confederation of Six Nations (Mohawk, Oneida, Onondaga, Cayuga, Seneca, and Tuscarora Indians) makes treaty with Virginia settlers, agreeing not to cross the Potomac River or the Blue Ridge Mountains.	**2** Afghan army invades Persia and captures the capital, Isfahan. **3** Manchu dynasty flourishes in China, despite periodic war against the Mongols and western tribesmen.	**1** Benjamin Franklin contributes a series of 14 satirical essays to the *New-England Courant* under the pseudonym "Silence Dogood." **2** Newspaper accounts attest to the existence of trained choral	**4** Jean Philippe Rameau, Fr. composer, publishes the first important work on harmony, *Traité de l'Harmonie.* **5** J.S. Bach completes volume I of *The Well-Tempered Clavier.*

Science & Technology		Miscellaneous		
America	**Elsewhere**	**America**	**Elsewhere**	
1 Paul Dudley, Mass. judge, writes the first in a series of 12 letters to the Royal Society of London about American animals and earthquakes.	**2** René-Antoine Ferchault de Réaumur, Fr. scientist, invents the cupola furnace for melting iron. Protection clothes of a plague physician	**1** Colonial population is estimated at 474,388: Boston, 12,000; Philadelphia, 10,000; New York, 7000; Charleston, S.C., 3500; Newport, R.I., 3800. **[1710:MISC/1]**	**2** Bubonic plague kills about 60,000 people in Marseilles, France.	**1720**
1 Cotton Mather, clergyman, publishes the first report on American hybrid plants. **2** Smallpox epidemic strikes Boston. **3** Douglass leads opposition of smallpox inoculations. **[1718:SCI/1]** **4** Zabdiel Boylston, Boston physician, is the first American to inoculate patients against smallpox. When 6 of 250 patients die, riots break out.	**5** John Hadley, Eng. mathematician, builds an improved reflecting telescope.	**1** Connecticut law provides that no person may leave home on Sunday except to attend worship or to do some essential task. **2** William Smith of Charlestown, Mass., and Hannah Travis, also known as Dancing Hannah, are convicted of theft by a Philadelphia court and sentenced to death, the usual penalty for theft.		**1721**
1 Boylston uses statistics to prove the success of his smallpox inoculations.	**2** Lady Mary Wortley Montagu wins public's approval of inoculation against smallpox in England.	**1** *New-England Courant* reports that a public house in Charlestown, Mass., has set up a table for customers who want to "Recreate themselves with a Game of Billiards."		**1722**

| History and Politics | | The Arts | |
America	Elsewhere	America	Elsewhere
		groups. **3** The role of music in the church is a controversial topic. Many tracts and sermons are devoted to it.	**6** Defoe publishes *Moll Flanders* and *A Journal of the Plague Year*.
1723	**1** British African Company takes control of the Gambia region. **2** Peter I of Russia conquers Derbent, Baku, and the southern coast of the Caspian Sea in a war with Persia. **3** Prussia builds a strong army, which helps to unify the state; it establishes a government-controlled economy.	**1** The cornerstone is laid for Boston's "Old North Church." Its design by William Price shows the influence of Christopher Wren. **[1669:ARTS/4]**	**2** J.S. Bach is appointed to the Cantorship in Leipzig. Here he conducts the first performance of his *St. John Passion* on Good Friday.
1724 **1** To protect settlers from Indians, English build Fort Dummer (near Brattleboro), first permanent white settlement in Vermont.	**2** Two-year reign of terror begins in Isfahan when Afghan ruler orders massacre of Persian nobility, many soldiers, and inhabitants.	**1** Rev. Hugh Jones publishes *The Present State of Virginia*, a straightforward factual account of that colony.	**2** Antonio Palomino, Span. court painter and art scholar, publishes an important work on Spanish painting. **3** Eng. organist and composer William Croft publishes *Musica Sacra*. Its setting of the burial service is still used in the Church of England.
1725 **1** Brit. settlers in northern Maine kill French Jesuit missionary for inciting trouble among the Abenaki Indians. British build border forts to contain French expansion. Abenakis ally themselves with French against British.	**2** Louis XV, King of France, marries the daughter of Stanislaus I, deposed king of Poland. **[1715:HIST/3]** **3** Philip V of Spain allies himself with Austria. Britain, France, Holland, and Prussia form an alliance in opposition. Both alliances are short-lived. **4** Russia gives the western part of Transcaucasia to the Turks, who are driven out (1730) in a war with Persia.		**1** Fr. architect Gabriel-Germain Boffrand undertakes the restoration of the rose window in the transept of Notre-Dame de Paris. **2** Alexander Pope completes his translation of Homer's *Odyssey*.
1726 **1** Brit. governor puts down riot by the poor in Philadelphia.	**2** Cardinal André Fleury is made minister of state by Louis XV of France. By skillful diplomacy, Fleury lessens France's involvement in European conflicts. His rule brings economic prosperity and stability to France. **3** Afghans defeat the Turks, who are marching on Isfahan. **[1722:HIST/2]**	**1** William Parks establishes a printing press at Annapolis, Md.	**2** Voltaire is banished from France and settles in England. **3** Scottish poet James Thomson publishes "Winter," the first part of *The Seasons* (1730). Its emphasis on nature foreshadows much romantic poetry. **4** The first edition of *Gulliver's Travels,* by

Science & Technology		Miscellaneous		
America	Elsewhere	America	Elsewhere	
		1 Boston police force consists of 12 men. Their beats are designated by the Selectmen, who instruct them to walk silently and slowly, to stand still now and then and listen to what is going on. They are not allowed to smoke on their rounds.	**2** Christianity is banned in China.	**1723**
1 Dudley describes the cross-fertilization of several varieties of corn. **2** Irrigation of rice fields begins in South Carolina.	**3** Hermann Boerhaave, Dutch physician, publishes work on chemical elements.		**1** First woolen factory is established in Sweden. **2** Gin becomes popular in England.	**1724**
1 Dudley discovers that ambergris, a fragrant liquid later used in perfume, is produced by male sperm whales.	**2** An accurate star catalogue by Eng. astronomer John Flamsteed is published 6 years after his death.	**1** First newspaper in New York is the *Gazette,* operated by William Bradford. **2** First separate church of Colored Baptists is established at Williamsburg, Va.	**3** First circulating library opens in Edinburgh, Scotland. **4** English Quakers publicly denounce slavery. **[1648:MISC/4]**	**1725**
				1726

Jonathan Swift, British satirist and clergyman

105

History and Politics		The Arts	
America	Elsewhere	America	Elsewhere

	History and Politics		The Arts	
	America	Elsewhere	America	Elsewhere
				Swift, is published. It is considered by many to be the greatest satire in the English language.
1727		**1** Gibraltar is besieged unsuccessfully by the Spanish; war begins between Britain and Spain. **2** George II becomes King of Great Britain and Ireland. **3** Kiakhta Treaty establishes the Amur border between China and Russia.	**1** Rev. Jonathan Edwards goes to the church at Northampton, Mass., the most influential parish in the Connecticut valley. He remains there more than 20 years. **2** James Franklin establishes the first printing press in Rhode Island.	**3** John Arbuthnot, Scot. mathematician and physician, publishes his collection of 5 pamphlets, *The History of John Bull*. This political allegory made John Bull a symbol of Britain.
1728	 Old South Meeting House, Boston, Massachusetts	**1** Persians led by Nadir Shah defeat the Afghans and retake Isfahan. [1726:HIST/3]	**1** One of the first church organs in America is installed in Philadelphia's Christ Church.	**2** John Gay's lighthearted political satire, *The Beggar's Opera*, begins a 62-performance run, the longest then known. **3** Hogarth's first dated painting depicts a scene from *The Beggar's Opera*. **4** Jean-Baptiste-Siméon Chardin, Fr. still-life painter, completes "La Raie" ("The Skate"). **5** Pope completes the first 3 books of *The Dunciad*. **6** Ephraim Chambers, Scot. scholar, publishes *Cyclopaedia, or An Universal Dictionary of Arts and Sciences*.
1729	**1** North and South Carolina become royal colonies after giving up their charters. **2** Indian raids force French settlements in Mississippi Valley to be confined to the lower part (now the state of Louisiana). **3** Baltimore, Md., is founded.	**4** Britain, France, and Spain sign the Treaty of Seville: all conquests are restored; Britain keeps Gibraltar; Spanish succession in the Italian duchies is accepted. **5** Portuguese briefly occupy the city of Mombasa, Kenya. **6** Corsica rebels against harsh Genoese rule.	**1** Benjamin Franklin acquires the *Pennsylvania Gazette*. **2** Boston's Old South Meeting House is built. **3** John Smibert, Scot. painter who settled in New England, paints "Dean George Berkeley and His Entourage."	**4** Ital. composer Giovanni Battista Pergolesi writes his best known work, the *Stabat Mater*. He also composed operas, comic operas, and oratorios. **5** J.S. Bach's *St. Matthew Passion* is first performed. **6** Perrault's fairy tales for children are published in English. They include "Little Red Riding Hood" and "Puss in Boots." **7** Swift's satirical essay, "A Modest Pro-

Science & Technology		Miscellaneous		
America	**Elsewhere**	**America**	**Elsewhere**	
	1 Stephen Hales, Eng. botanist, introduces various concepts of plant physiology in *Vegetable Staticks.*	**1** Benjamin Franklin establishes *Junto,* a society for scientific and philosophical discussion. *Junto* later inspires the formation of the American Philosophical Society. [1743:SCI/1]		**1727**
1 John Bartram, botanist, plants America's first botanical gardens near Philadelphia and begins experiments with hybrids. **2** Samuel Higby (or Higley), Conn. blacksmith, produces America's first steel in Hartford. **3** William Byrd surveys border between North Carolina and Virginia.	**4** James Bradley, Eng. astronomer, proves the validity of the Copernican heliocentric theory. [1514:SCI/1] **5** Francesco Bianchini, Ital. astronomer, estimates the rotational period of Venus.	**1** Boston begins to enclose the Common to preserve the grass from carts and horses. Soon it becomes the custom after tea for people to stroll about the green. **2** Jews in New York build the first synagogue.	**3** Copenhagen is almost totally destroyed by fire.	**1728**
1 Isaac Greenwood publishes *Arithmetick Vulgar and Decimal,* America's first textbook in mathematics.		**1** First arithmetic textbook is published in Boston. **2** Third Anglican parish is established in Trinity Church in Boston.	**3** English Act of Parliament requires attorneys to serve a 5-year apprenticeship.	**1729**

History and Politics		The Arts	
America	**Elsewhere**	**America**	**Elsewhere**
			posal," suggests that to prevent poor children from being a burden on their parents and society, they should be fattened and served as food to the rich.

	America	**Elsewhere**	**America**	**Elsewhere**
1730	**1** French construct a stone fort at Crown Point on Lake Champlain, N.Y.	**2** Persians under Nadir Shah decisively defeat the Afghans near the city of Shiraz. Afghans retreat to Kandahar.	**1** Benjamin Franklin ridicules the superstition of witchcraft in *A Witch Trial at Mount Holly*. He later prints a book of German hymns. **2** A printing press is established in Virginia by William Parks of Maryland. **[1726:ARTS/1]**	**3** Eng. novelist Henry Fielding satirizes heroic tragedy in *Tragedy of Tragedies, or The History of Tom Thumb the Great*. **4** Ital. composer Francesco Geminiani publishes *The Art of Playing on the Violin*, an important source for performance of late Baroque music. **5** The style of rococo is most popular.
1731	 James Oglethorpe, British General, founder of the colony of Georgia	**1** Britain, Holland, Spain, and the Holy Roman Empire sign the Treaty of Vienna. Emperor Charles VI dissolves the Ostend East India Company, rival of the Dutch and British East India Companies, in return for acceptance of the Pragmatic Sanction (imperial law by which Charles's daughter inherits the Hapsburg lands). **2** Russia, Prussia, and the Holy Roman Empire agree to oppose Stanislaus I of Poland. **[1715:HIST/3]**	**1** Naturalist Mark Catesby illustrates his *Natural History of Carolina and Florida* with 100 engravings of American birds. **2** The first known concert given in the colonies is presented in Mr. Pelham's great room (Boston). Admission is 5 shillings.	**3** Johann Hasse, the most popular operatic composer of his day, becomes director of the Dresden Opera. **4** George Lillo's *The London Merchant* is the first serious play with a lower-class hero. **5** Fr. novelist Abbé Prévost publishes *Manon Lescaut*.
1732	**1** Royal charter is granted to James Oglethorpe for an English colony in Georgia.	**2** Genoa receives help from the Holy Roman Emperor in making peace in Corsica. **[1729:HIST/6]** **3** Spanish recapture Oran, Algeria, from the Turks, who seized the city in 1708. **4** By the Treaty of Rasht, Russia gives land it has claimed to Persia.	**1** New Theater, one of the earliest theater buildings in the colonies, opens in New York City. It presents *The Recruiting Officer* by Eng. dramatist George Farquhar. **2** Benjamin Franklin begins publishing *Poor Richard's Almanac*.	**3** One of the first musical dictionaries is published by Ger. organist Johann Gottfried Walther. **4** Hogarth completes "A Harlot's Progress," a series of narrative prints. **5** The Covent Garden Opera House opens in London.
1733	**1** Oglethorpe founds Savannah in Georgia, the last of the original 13 colonies to be settled. Oglethorpe's colony is a defense against the Spanish in Florida and the French in	**3** War of the Polish Succession begins after the death of Augustus II. Russia and Austria support Augustus III; France, Spain, and the Polish nobles claim Stanislaus I is	**1** John Peter Zenger publishes the *New York Weekly Journal*, which opposes policies of the colonial governor.	**3** Pope's *Essay on Man* is published. **4** Jean Philippe Rameau, Fr. composer, becomes leading operatic figure in France on

Science & Technology		Miscellaneous		
America	**Elsewhere**	**America**	**Elsewhere**	
1 Thomas Godfrey invents the reflecting quadrant, an instrument for determining position at sea. At about the same time, Eng. inventor John Hadley makes a similar device.	**2** Anders Celsius, Swed. astronomer, estimates the distance between the Sun and the Earth. **3** The Réaumur scale, in which 80° is water's boiling point, is introduced.	**1** Population in the colonies is estimated at 655,000. **[1720:MISC/1]** **2** A craze for white stockings for both men and women sets in. Made mostly of silk or cotton thread, they are supported by means of fancy garters. Often the name of a gentleman or a lady is woven into the garter.	**3** Earthquake kills 137,000 people in Hokkaido, Japan. **4** *The Daily Advertiser* is published in London. It is considered the first modern newspaper because it depends mainly on advertisements for its revenues.	**1730**
1 Mark Catesby Eng. naturalist, publishes *The Natural History of Carolina, Florida, and the Bahama Islands*.		**1** First circulating library is founded in Philadelphia by Franklin.	**2** English factory workers are forbidden to emigrate to America. **3** French Parliament places the clergy under the jurisdiction of the Crown.	**1731**
1 Isaac Greenwood establishes a department of mathematics and natural philosophy (science) at Harvard.		**1** For the first time, the game of ninepins is played in New York City. Land at the south end of Broadway is used as a bowling green. **2** First stagecoach line is established between Burlington and Amboy, N.J.		**1732**
	1 Celsius compiles his observations of the aurora borealis. **2** John Kay, Eng. engineer, invents the flying shuttle, a great improve-	**1** Social clubs are formed in New York City. One of the earliest is the Political Club, followed by the Hum Drum Club, the Hungarian Club, and the	**5** Latin is abolished as the language of the courts in England. **6** Charter schools for Protestants only are founded in Ireland.	**1733**

	History and Politics		The Arts	
	America	Elsewhere	America	Elsewhere
	Louisiana and is a refuge for the poor and the persecuted. **2** Molasses Act puts prohibitive duties on sugar, rum, and molasses brought to the colonies from the French, Spanish, and Dutch West Indies.	entitled to the Polish throne. **4** Turks defeat Persians at the Battle of Kirkuk. Nadir Shah restores Persian control and blockades Baghdad.	**2** Benjamin Franklin is public printer for the colonies of Pennsylvania, New Jersey, Delaware, and Maryland.	presentation of *Hippolyte et Aricie.* **5** *Rosamond,* the first opera staged by Eng. composer Thomas Augustine Arne, begins 40 years of performances.
1734	**1** French families settle at Vincennes on the Wabash River—first permanent colony in Indiana.	**2** Spanish forces seize Naples and Sicily. Russians take Danzig, Poland, after 8-month siege. Stanislaus I flees to Prussia during the War of the Polish Succession. **3** Ottoman Empire and Persia battle in the Transcaucasian region.	**1** In his Northampton parish, Jonathan Edwards delivers a series of sermons on salvation by faith alone.	**2** Jean-Baptiste Oudry, Fr. designer, illustrator, and painter known for depictions of animals, becomes head of the Beauvais tapestry works. **3** Voltaire's *Lettres philosophiques* attack established religion and argue for religious tolerance. Soon after their publication, a warrant is issued for his arrest.
1735		**1** Russia establishes control of Polish affairs. Stanislaus I renounces rights in favor of Augustus III but keeps royal title. [1733:HIST/3] **2** Russia joins in alliance with Persia against the Ottoman Empire. Nadir Shah defeats the Turks at Baghavand and captures city of Tiflis (now Tbilisi).	**1** Dutch farm life of the Hudson Valley is documented in "Van Bergen Overmantle," a landscape by an anonymous itinerant painter.	**2** Hogarth publishes "A Rake's Progress," a series of engravings satirizing social abuses and portraying the punishment of vice. **3** England passes copyright legislation to protect the works of artists. Hogarth is instrumental in obtaining its passage.
1736	**1** Britain can not enforce the Molasses Act. New England merchants continue to import low-priced sugar, rum, and molasses from other than British islands in the West Indies. [1733:HIST/2]	**2** Turks protest against Russian control in Poland and begin war. Russians recapture Azov and raid the Crimea. **3** Stanislaus I abdicates; Augustus III becomes King of Poland. **4** Nadir Shah becomes ruler	**1** The German Charles Theodore Pachelbel gives organ concerts in New York City. He brings the Bach tradition to the New World. **2** William Parks be-	**3** Fr. engraver and type founder Pierre-Simon Fournier sets up a foundry in Paris whose fame extends throughout western Europe. He later publishes several technical works on

Science & Technology		Miscellaneous		
America	**Elsewhere**	**America**	**Elsewhere**	
	ment for the weaving industry. *A Rake's Progress*, satiricial engraving by William Hogarth	New Club. **2** First serious outbreak of influenza sweeps through New York City and Philadelphia. About three fourths of the population are affected. **3** Jonathan Edwards, clergyman, preaches "The Great Awakening," in New England. It is a religious revival that stresses man's sinful nature. **4** John Peter Zenger, publisher of the *New York Weekly Journal*, is arrested for seditious libel. His later acquittal is a landmark for freedom of the press (1735).	**7** Conscription, or compulsory enrollment of men for military service, is put into effect in Prussia (now a part of Germany).	
1 James Logan, colonial politician, describes the function of pollen and various plant organs in the sexual reproduction of corn.	**2** Réaumur publishes the first of several comprehensive volumes about insects.			**1734**
	1 George Hadley, Eng. meteorologist, develops the Hadley cell, a model of the Earth's wind circulation. **2** Carolus Linnaeus, Swed. botanist, devises a classification method for plants and animals.	**1** First Moravian (United Brethren) community is established at Savannah, Ga. **[1708:MISC/3]** **2** Increasing wealth in the colonies causes a change in the status of women. More women leave their husbands when they find living together incompatible; newspapers tell of runaway wives and elopements.	**3** John Wesley, Eng. clergyman and founder of Methodism, writes his *Journals*.	**1735**
1 Douglass gives first accurate and detailed description of scarlet fever.	**2** Celsius proves that the Earth's poles are somewhat flattened.	**1** Regular stagecoach service begins between Boston and Newport, R.I.	**2** First Protestant missions are established at the Cape Colony in South Africa. **3** There have been no trials for witchcraft in England for more than 20 years; laws against witch-	**1736**

111

	History and Politics		The Arts	
	America	**Elsewhere**	**America**	**Elsewhere**
		of Persia. **[1733:HIST/4]** **5** German Baron is made King of Corsica until he is driven out by the Genoese and French (1738). **6** Ch'ien Lung becomes Emperor of China, which attains its greatest territorial expansion under him.	gins a literary newspaper in Williamsburg, the *Virginia Gazette*.	the arts of engraving and typeface. **4** Oudry designs a tapestry series, "The Fables of LaFontaine."
1737	**1** William Byrd, colonial official and writer, founds the city of Richmond, Va.	**2** Russia, allied with Austria, suffers some reverses in its war against the Turks. **[1736:HIST/2]**		**1** Fr. portraitist Maurice-Quentin de La Tour exhibits his paintings of such well-known subjects as Voltaire, Rousseau, and Louis XV. **2** Lexicographer Samuel Johnson arrives in London.
1738		**1** By the Treaty of Vienna, which ends the War of the Polish Succession, Spain receives Naples and Sicily and cedes to Austria its claims to Parma. (Austria also retains Lombardy.) Russian-Austrian policy is assured in Poland. **[1733:HIST/3]** **2** Turks drive Austrian forces back to Belgrade.		**1** Carl Philipp Emanuel Bach, son of J.S. Bach, goes to Berlin in the service of Frederick of Prussia. **2** The Imperial St. Petersburg School is founded by Jean Baptiste Landé to train children of court serfs to dance in palace ballets. **3** J.S. Bach's *Mass in B minor* is completed in its full version.
1739	**1** English colonists of South Carolina and Georgia declare war on the Spanish in Florida. Border difficulties and mistreatment of captured British seamen are the chief grievances against the Spanish. British begin raiding Spanish towns in the Caribbean.	**2** Persians under Nadir Shah defeat huge army of the Mogul Emperor of India. Delhi and Lahore are sacked, much treasure is seized, and Persian territory is extended to the Indus River. **3** Russians defeat the Turks and advance into Moldavia. **4** Austria, alarmed by Russian success in the Balkans, concludes the Treaty of Belgrade. Russia demilitarizes Azov and agrees not to build a fleet on the Black Sea.	**1** The appearance of the American edition of Watts' *Hymns and Spiritual Songs* profoundly influences the course of American music. **[1707:ARTS/2]**	**2** Josiah Wedgwood, renowned designer and manufacturer of pottery, begins working in the family business.
1740	**1** Oglethorpe leads an unsuccessful expedition against St. Augustine, Fla. **[1739:HIST/1]**	**3** War of the Austrian Succession begins. After Maria Theresa, daughter of Charles VI, becomes Hapsburg ruler,	**1** Jonathan Edwards begins writing the religious thoughts and reflections later published	**3** Swed. writer Olof von Dalin publishes *Sagan om hästen (The Tale About the Horse)*,

Science & Technology		Miscellaneous		
America	Elsewhere	America	Elsewhere	
			craft are repealed. **[1712:MISC/1]**	
	1 Linnaeus publishes work on the plant life of Lapland.	**1** Copper money is first coined in Connecticut. The coins are stamped "I am good copper" and "Value me as you will."	**2** Tornado and earthquake kill approximately 300,000 people in Calcutta, India.	**1737**
1 John Lining begins recording daily weather observations and theorizes that weather affects—and may cause—certain diseases. **2** Caspar Wistar starts America's first successful glass factory in Salem County, N.J. **3** Thomas Clap, president of Yale College, begins teaching astronomy and natural philosophy (science). **4** Joseph Breintnall describes the aurora borealis.	**5** Joseph-Nicolas Delisle, Fr. astronomer, devises a way to determine the location of sunspots.	**1** One of the first umbrellas is owned by Edward Shippen. There is much religious opposition to the use of umbrellas, particularly among Quakers. **2** Population in the colonies is estimated at 880,000. **[1730:MISC/1]** **3** Strict codes of behavior in New England are relaxed somewhat. Permission is given to Charles Bradstreet to teach French dancing, "so long as he keeps good order." **[1681:MISC/2]**	**4** Excavation of Herculaneum begins. The city in southwest Italy was buried along with Pompeii by the eruption of Mt. Vesuvius in A.D. 79. **[1592:MISC/1]** **5** Wesley and George Whitefield travel to America. They plan to start a Methodist mission. **[1735:MISC/3]**	**1738**
	Carolus Linnaeus Swedish botanist, in Lapland dress		**1** David Hume, Scot. philosopher, writes *A Treatise on Human Nature.*	**1739**
1 John Winthrop observes and describes a transit of Mercury and a lunar eclipse.	**2** Celsius builds the Uppsala observatory in Sweden.	**1** Great fire destroys half of Charleston, S.C.	**2** Smallpox epidemic in Berlin. **3** Frederick II, King of Prussia, abolishes torture;	**1740**

	History and Politics — America	History and Politics — Elsewhere	The Arts — America	The Arts — Elsewhere
	2 British bombard Spanish town of Cartagena, Colombia, and raid foreign colonies in the West Indies.	a general European war breaks out among claimants to the Austrian inheritance. Frederick II (the Great), King of Prussia, invades and occupies Silesia, offering his aid to Maria Theresa if she gives Silesia to him. (She refuses.)	as *Personal Narrative.* **2** Laws prohibit slaves from using drums.	a popular allegory satirizing the Swedish people and their leaders. **4** Samuel Richardson publishes *Pamela.* Written in the form of letters, this extremely popular work is considered the first English novel. **5** Colley Cibber's autobiography contains much information on the theater of his time. **6** Handel's *Water Music,* composed in 1717, is published.
1741	**1** Capt. Vitus Bering, Dan. explorer in the service of Russia, discovers Alaska. He dies after his ship is wrecked on the shore of Bering Island. **2** British make unsuccessful attack on Santiago, Cuba, and seize Spanish treasure ships.	**3** Victorious at Mollwitz, Frederick II joins the alliance of France, Spain, Bavaria, and Saxony against Austria. Bavarians, French, and Saxons seize Prague. Maria Theresa gets support from Hungary and Great Britain. **4** Sweden begins war with Russia.	**1** *A True and Historical Narrative of the Colony of Georgia* is published by enemies of the colony's founder, Gen. James Oglethorpe. It is a bitter attack on his governance. **2** Jonathan Edwards delivers the most famous sermon of colonial times, "Sinners in the Hands of an Angry God."	**3** Eng. playwright and actor David Garrick makes his first appearance on the stage as Richard III. His acting style has a profound influence on other performers. **4** The first opera of Ger. composer Christoph Gluck, *Artaserse,* is presented in Milan. He influenced opera by integrating the music and story line. **5** Handel composes *The Messiah* in 18 days.
1742	**1** Spanish attack Georgia. They withdraw after being defeated by Oglethorpe's forces at the Battle of Bloody Marsh on St. Simons Island.	**2** Austrian army conquers Bavaria. After Prussian victories, Maria Theresa makes peace with Frederick II by ceding most of Silesia. **[1740:HIST/3]**	**1** Handel's *The Messiah* is performed in Bethlehem, Penn., where music flourishes in a Moravian religious settlement. **[1741:ARTS/5]** **2** John Smibert draws plans for Boston's Faneuil Hall.	**3** Fielding expands *Shamela* (1741), a spoof of *Pamela,* into *Joseph Andrews,* a comic novel of social criticism. **4** Religious reformer John Wesley publishes his first collection of hymns. He encouraged congregational singing. **5** Edward Young, Eng. poet, publishes *Night Thoughts* (–1745), "graveyard poems." **6** Handel's most popular work, *The Messiah,* is first performed in Dublin.
1743	**1** Oglethorpe again invades Florida but fails to capture	**2** Austrians drive the French out of Bohemia. George II of	**1** *American Magazine and Historical Chron-*	**3** Hogarth's series of satirical engravings,

Science & Technology		Miscellaneous		
America	Elsewhere	America	Elsewhere	
			grants freedom of worship and the press.	
1 Lining completes a year-long experiment on human metabolism, using himself as the subject.		**1** Drunkenness is prevalent. Each colony has strict laws to control drinking. Boston goes so far as to post the names of drunkards. **2** First strike takes place in New York City when bakers protest the regulation of the price of bread.	**3** Yellow fever epidemic kills about 10,000 people in Cadiz, Spain. **4** Population of China is 143 million. **5** In England, Highway Act is passed to improve roads. **6** Hume publishes *Essays: Moral and Political.* [1739:MISC/1]	1741
1 Winthrop begins 21 years of recording weather observations three times a day.	**2** Celsius devises the centigrade temperature scale, in which the freezing point of water is at 0° and its boiling point at 100°. **3** Johann Bernoulli, Swiss mathematician, publishes work on integral calculus. **4** Benjamin Robins, Eng. mathematician, publishes *New Principles of Geometry.*	**1** Fishing industry grows in New England; there are almost 1000 fishing ships.	**2** Cotton factories are established in Northampton and Birmingham in England. **3** Jews are expelled from Russia.	1742
1 Franklin establishes the American Philosophi-	**5** Jean Le Rond d'Alembert, Fr. mathematician,		**1** Yarn from the East Indies is imported to Lan-	1743

History and Politics		The Arts	
America	**Elsewhere**	**America**	**Elsewhere**
St. Augustine. [1740:HIST/1]	Britain defeats the French at the Battle of Dettingen. Saxony makes peace and joins Austria as an ally. **3** By the Treaty of Abo, Sweden cedes to Russia territory in Finland. **4** Persians under Nadir Shah resume war with the Turks.	*icle,* edited by Jeremiah Gridley, appears in Boston. Its content is largely political. **2** William Price publishes the map, "View of Boston," on which he also advertises the sale of musical instruments and books.	"Marriage à la Mode," appears.
1744 **1** French make unsuccessful attack on Annapolis Royal, Nova Scotia. King George's War begins between British and French colonies. **2** Iroquois Confederation cedes Ohio Valley territory north of the Ohio River to Britain.	**3** Frederick II of Prussia, alarmed at rising Austrian power, invades Bohemia, seizes Prague, but is driven back by Austrian and Saxon forces. **4** Dutch join Britain in alliance with Maria Theresa against France and Prussia. **5** Persians defeat the Turks near Kars, Turkey. [1743:HIST/4]	**1** Moravians in Bethlehem, Penn., establish a Collegium Musicum for the performance of chamber music and symphonies by European composers. **2** Richardson's *Pamela* is published in America.	**3** Samuel Johnson's *Account of the Life of Mr. Richard Savage,* an outstanding English biography is published anonymously. Savage, poet and satirist, was a personal friend of Johnson's. **4** J.S. Bach completes Part 2 of *The Well-Tempered Clavier.* **5** "God Save the Queen" is published in *Thesaurus Musicus.*
1745 **1** New Englanders, supported by a British fleet, capture the French fortress at Louisburg on Cape Breton Island, Canada. **2** French and Indians raid Maine towns and forts and burn Saratoga, N.Y.	**3** Jacobites, opposing King George II, defeat British forces at Prestonpans, Scotland, and advance into England. **4** French defeat the British at Fontenoy, Belgium, and begin conquest of Austrian Netherlands. **5** Prussians win victories at Hohenfriedburg, Soor, and Kesseldorf. Maria Theresa concludes Treaty of Dresden with Frederick II of Prussia. Prussia secures Silesia, and Maria's husband becomes Holy Roman Emperor. [1740:HIST/3]	**1** The writings of Montesquieu appear in American periodicals. They influence the formation of the Constitution. [1721:ARTS/3; 1748:ARTS/4] **2** The first carillon in America is installed in the belfry of Christ Church, Boston.	**3** Eng. poet Thomas Warton writes *The Pleasures of Melancholy,* a work that influences later writers. **4** Gluck is invited to England by Lord Middlesex, director of Italian opera at Haymarket Theater. **5** Tiepolo completes "Antony and Cleopatra" frescoes for Labia Palace, in Venice. **6** Giambattista Piranesi, Ital. etcher, completes his most famous series of plates, "Carceri d'invenzione" ("Imaginary Prisons").
1746 **1** French fail to retake Cape Breton and Nova Scotia from the British.	**2** Jacobites are defeated at the Battle of Culloden Moor, England. The pretender to the English throne flees to France, ending Catholic hopes for the crown forever. [1715:HIST/2]	**1** The hymnody of the Ephrata Cloister in Pennsylvania is printed in beautifully illuminated songbooks that include chorales for as many as 7 parts.	**2** Eng. painter Joshua Reynolds' large group portrait "The Eliot Family" shows the influence of Van Dyck. **3** Handel and Gluck give a joint concert at

116

Science & Technology		Miscellaneous		
America	**Elsewhere**	**America**	**Elsewhere**	
cal Society in Philadelphia to promote colonial science. **2** Colden describes and classifies American plants in *Acta Upsaliensis* by Linnaeus. **3** John Clayton collects and describes plants in *Flora Virginica* published by the Dutch botanist, John Gronovius. **4** Lining links weather and epidemics. **[1738:SCI/1]**	expands on Newton's laws of motion.		caster, England. **2** Handkerchiefs are first manufactured in Paisley, Scotland. **3** First Methodist Association is formed in Wales.	
1 Franklin invents the Pennsylvania Fireplace (or Franklin Stove) which provides much more heat on much less fuel than regular fireplaces.			**1** Rubber is first used in Europe about this time. **2** First General Conference of Methodists is held in England. **3** Population of Calcutta is estimated to be 100,000; that of Bombay 70,000.	**1744**

Benjamin Franklin, American author and inventor

Science & Technology		Miscellaneous		
1 Thomas Cadwalader, Pa. surgeon, publishes America's first medical pamphlet describing the treatment of lead poisoning caused by drinking rum distilled in lead pipes. **2** Colden incorrectly claims to have discovered the cause of gravity, causing confusion among English and American scientists.	**3** Ewald Georg von Kleist, Ger. scientist, invents the capacitor, or condenser, a device used to store electricity.	**1** Whist, a popular card game, is played by men and women.	**2** The quadrille becomes a fashionable dance in France. **3** Earliest meeting of the Independent Order of Odd Fellows, a secret social and benevolent group, is held in England.	**1745**
1 Franklin explains weather patterns, pressure systems, and water spouts. He begins his experiments with electricity. **2** Winthrop claims that lightning is a sign of	**4** A geological survey of France and England is published by the Fr. geologist Jean-Étienne Guettard.	**1** Princeton University is founded. **2** First boarding school for girls is started in Pennsylvania by the Moravians. **[1735:MISC/1]**	**3** Denis Diderot, Fr. philosopher and author, publishes *Pensées philosophiques*.	**1746**

117

History and Politics		The Arts	
America	**Elsewhere**	**America**	**Elsewhere**
	3 French defeat Austria's allies at Raucoux and conquer the Austrian Netherlands. **4** French seize Madras, India, but the British recover the city in 1748.		Haymarket Theater, London. **4** Johnson contracts for *A Dictionary of the English Language.*
1747 **1** Ohio Company is formed to extend colonial settlements of Virginia westward. Rivalry for the West, especially for the upper Ohio Valley, increases between France and Great Britain.	**2** China begins campaign to pacify the tribes on the Tibetan border. **3** Persia makes peace with Ottoman Empire. Nadir Shah fights rebellious Kurds and is killed by his own officers.	**1** William Stith publishes *The History of the First Discovery and Settlement of Virginia.* Covering the years to 1624, it is one of the most accurate accounts of a colonial settlement. **2** Pope's *Essay on Man* appears in the colonies. [1733:ARTS/3]	**3** Eng. poet Thomas Gray publishes *Ode on a Distant Prospect of Eton College,* the poem containing the lines, "Where ignorance is bliss,/'Tis folly to be wise." **4** Drury Lane begins to flourish under the management of David Garrick. **5** Aleksandr Petrovich Sumarokov, Russ. dramatist, publishes *Khorev,* Russia's first classic tragedy.
1748 **1** King George's War ends; Louisburg is returned to France. British strengthen hold on Nova Scotia by founding the town of Halifax (1749). [1744:HIST/1]	**2** Treaty of Aix-la-Chapelle ends the War of the Austrian Succession, confirming the Pragmatic Sanction and Russian possession of Silesia. [1740:HIST/3] **3** Chieftains compete for control in Persia. **4** India becomes battleground for Great Britain and France, each trying to control Indian trade and to oust the other. [1746:HIST/4]		**1** Eng. portraitist Thomas Gainsborough paints "Cornard Wood," an early landscape. **2** The Kabuki masterpiece *Treasury of Royal Retainers* is presented. **3** Eng. novelist Tobias Smollett publishes *The Adventures of Roderick Random,* about the travels of a rogue. **4** Montesquieu's *Spirit of the Laws* is a philosophical treatise on law and government. **5** Richardson publishes *Clarissa, or The History of a Young Lady.*
1749 **1** Ohio Company obtains royal charter with a large land grant around the forks of the Ohio River. [1747:HIST/1] **2** In an effort to break the British-Iroquois alliance, the French establish a mission and trapping-post at Ogdensburg, N.Y. French build Fort Rouille (near Toronto) to	**3** French East India Company pursues aggressive policy of expansion in India against the British East India Company.	**1** Architect Peter Harrison designs the new King's Chapel, Boston. Built of Quincy granite, it represents the Georgian style of architecture. **2** Addison's *Cato* is performed in Philadelphia by an English acting troupe.	**3** Fielding publishes his most popular work, *Tom Jones,* known for its vivid portrayal of 18th-century England. **4** Carlo Goldoni, Ital. dramatist influential in the development of comedy, presents his first successful work, *The Respectable Girl.*

Science & Technology		Miscellaneous		
America	**Elsewhere**	**America**	**Elsewhere**	
God's anger. He begins experiments in physics. **3** Breintnall publishes a paper about rattlesnake bites.				
1 Catesby publishes *On Migration* claiming that birds migrate to areas where there is better weather and more food. Catesby is later called the "Father of American Ornithology."	**2** Mikhail Lomonosov, Russ. scientist, publishes *Cause of Heat and Cold.* **3** Albrecht von Haller, Swiss biologist, publishes work on respiration and heart function.	**1** First legal society, the New York Bar Association, is established in New York City.		**1747**
1 John Mitchell classifies American plants and animals by the Linnaean system of scientific names and claims to have discovered 25 new plant genera. He is the first to describe accurately the lifestyle and pouch of the opossum.	**2** John Fothergill, Eng. physician, is the first to describe the symptoms of diphtheria. **3** Leonhard Euler, Swiss mathematician, relates the functions of variables (unknown quantities) in equations.		**1** Dutch begin to trade on Africa's east coast. **2** Cricket is ruled a legal sport in England. **3** First silk factory is established in Berlin. **4** Hume publishes *Philosophical Essays Concerning Human Understanding.* **[1739:MISC/1]** **5** Excavation begins at Pompeii. **[1592:MISC/1]**	**1748**
1 Franklin invents the lightning rod and installs one on his Philadelphia home.	**2** d'Alembert explains the regular variations in the Earth's orbit. **3** Leibniz's *Protogeae,* which suggests that the Earth was once composed of molten material, is published, 35 years after his death.	**1** Severe drought occurs in New England. A shortage of hay requires that it be imported from Pennsylvania and England.	**2** A study of chess is published in France.	**1749**

119

	History and Politics		The Arts	
	America	**Elsewhere**	**America**	**Elsewhere**
	counteract British trade and influence in the Niagara region. French also send expedition to take possession of the Ohio Valley.			
1750	**1** Ohio Company sends Christopher Gist to explore its western lands. He descends the Ohio River, explores eastern Kentucky, and maps the region. **[1749:HIST/1]**	**2** By the Treaty of Madrid, Spain recognizes Portugal's claims to areas in South America. **3** Karim Khan becomes ruler of Persia.	**1** Shakespeare's *Richard III* is presented in New York City by Murray and Kean's acting troupe. **2** The first playhouse opens in New York City. **3** Parlange, a classic plantation house of Fr. colonial architecture, is built at New Roads, La.	**4** Samuel Johnson begins publication of the *Rambler,* a periodical containing moralistic essays. **5** Gray publishes *Elegy Written in a Country Church Yard.* **6** Ger. printer Johann Breitkopf invents a system of movable musical type. **7** In *Discours sur les sciences et les arts,* Fr. philosopher, writer, and social reformer Jean-Jacques Rousseau attacks science and art as tools of the rich that undermine morality.
1751	**1** Ohio Company engages in active British colonization of the Ohio Valley. Rivalry between Britain and France for control of the area increases.	**2** British capture town of Arcot from the French in southern India. **[1748:HIST/4]** **3** China invades Tibet and establishes control of the Dalai Lama (chief monk).	**1** James Logan's library of 3000 books is bequeathed to the city of Philadelphia. **2** The *Halifax Gazette,* first English language newspaper in Canada, begins publication.	**3** Smollett's *The Adventures of Peregrine Pickle,* one of his better comic works, is published. **4** The first volumes of Diderot's *Encyclopédie* are published. This work is one of the first to attempt a summation of knowledge in the arts, sciences, philosophy, and history.
1752	**1** French begin building forts across Pennsylvania and into Ohio to stop British invasion of their territory.	**2** British turn aside the French siege of Trichinopoly in southern India. French control the Carnatic and Deccan regions.	**1** The George Muller house, the best surviving example of Pennsylvania Dutch architecture, is built at Milbach, Pa. **2** Rev. John Barnard publishes a new version of the psalms. **3** Jonathan Edwards publishes *Misrepresen-*	**5** Fielding publishes *Amelia,* his last novel.

Science & Technology		Miscellaneous		
America	**Elsewhere**	**America**	**Elsewhere**	
1 Parliament passes the Iron Act of 1750, ordering all colonial finishing plants to close and dropping import taxes on pig iron to encourage the colonists to produce raw iron for finishing in England. **2** First American coal mine opens on the James River in Virginia. **3** Potash is exported to England.	**4** Nicolas-Louis de Lacaille, Fr. astronomer, plots 10,000 Southern Hemisphere stars.	**1** First appearance in Pennsylvania of the flatboat for navigating the inland rivers and of the Conestoga wagon, eventually the common pioneer transportation and original form of prairie schooner. **2** Edwards is forced to resign from his church in Northampton, Mass., by members of his congregation who oppose his emphasis on the sinful nature of man. Edwards' departure marks the end in New England of "The Great Awakening." [1733:MISC/3]	**3** Europe's population reaches 140 million. **4** English Jockey Club is founded. **5** Hambledon Cricket Club is founded in Hampshire, England.	**1750**
1 Franklin publishes *Experiments and Observations on Electricity* describing electricity as a single fluid and using the terms *positive* and *negative* for the first time. **2** Colden publishes *Principles of Action in Matter* to explain his theories of gravity and planetary motion. **3** Bartram publishes *Observations* and other papers describing North American plants and botanical medicines. **4** Calculus is introduced into the Harvard curriculum by John Winthrop, Jr.	**5** Lomonosov publishes *Discourse on the Usefulness of Chemistry.*	**1** First cricket match is held in New York City. **2** Franklin publishes *Observations Concerning the Increase of Mankind,* containing his economic ideas. **3** First sugar cane grown in America is introduced in Louisiana by Catholic missionaries from Santo Domingo. It is used to make taffia, a kind of rum.	**4** British calendar is changed by Parliament. January 1 is to be the beginning of the year. [1582:MISC/2]	**1751**
1 Franklin performs his famous kite experiment, demonstrating that lightning is electricity.	**2** Réaumur identifies gastric juices and their role in digestion.	**1** An early fire insurance company, the Philadelphia Contributorship for the Insurance of Homes, is founded in Pennsylvania. **2** Thomas Bond establishes the first general hospital in the colonies in Philadelphia. Pest-houses (contagious-disease hospi-	**3** Missionaries from the Society for the Propagation of the Gospel in Foreign Parts first arrive at the Cape Colony, South Africa. **4** Fire in Moscow destroys about 18,000 houses.	**1752**

History and Politics		The Arts	
America	Elsewhere	America	Elsewhere
		tations Corrected and Truth Vindicated in which he defends his strong religious principles. **4** *The Merchant of Venice* is presented at Williamsburg, Va., by a group calling itself the "American Company."	
1753 **1** Governor of Virginia sends George Washington to demand French withdrawal from the Ohio territory. French plan further advances.	**2** Wenzel Anton Kaunitz becomes Chancellor of Austria. He persuades Austria and France to sign a defense treaty, recognizing Prussia as Austria's chief enemy. **3** Frederick II of Prussia fights coalition of Austria, Russia, and France.	**1** The first theater in New York City is built by a theatrical repertory company headed by Lewis Hallam, an Eng. immigrant.	**2** Carl Philipp Emanuel Bach publishes Part I of *Essay on Keyboard Instruments,* an influential work essential to an understanding of the style of 18th-century music.
1754 **1** French build Fort Duquesne (Pittsburgh) at the forks of the Ohio River. French defeat Virginia militiamen led by Washington at Great Meadows—the first battle of the French and Indian War.	**2** France recalls its colonial governor in India, making a French empire in India impractical.	**1** Benjamin Franklin publishes, in the *Pennsylvania Gazette,* a cartoon calling for unity against the French. It is believed to be the first such cartoon in America. **2** The Deblois brothers build the first public structure with a special room for musical performances, called the "Concert Hall" or "Music Hall." **3** Quaker John Woolman publishes *Some Considerations on the Keeping of Negroes,* in which he urges Quakers to give up their slaves. **4** J. Edwards publishes his influential work, *Inquiry into Freedom of the Will.*	**5** Thomas Chippendale, Eng. furniture maker and designer, publishes *The Gentleman and Cabinetmaker's Director.* **6** David Hume, Scot. historian, publishes the first volume of *History of England.*
1755 **1** French and Indians ambush and defeat colonial militiamen and British regulars under Gen. Edward Braddock, near Fort Duquesne. Braddock is mortally wounded; Washington takes command.	**2** Emperor Ch'ien Lung of China takes control of Sinkiang (Chinese Turkistan). **3** Pasquale Paoli, Corsican patriot, leads successful revolt against Genoese and becomes president under a republican constitution. [1736:HIST/5]	**1** Joseph Blackburn paints "The Winslow Family."	**2** Johnson completes *Dictionary of the English Language.* **3** Gotthold E. Lessing, Ger. dramatist, publishes *Miss Sara Sampson,* the first German domestic tragedy.

Science & Technology		Miscellaneous		
America	**Elsewhere**	**America**	**Elsewhere**	
		tals) had been started earlier in Boston, Philadelphia, and Charleston, S.C.		
1 Franklin is the first American to be awarded the Copley Medal by the Royal Society of London. He becomes a Fellow of the Royal Society, an Associate of the Académie des Sciences (France), and receives honorary degrees from three American colleges.	**2** Linnaeus publishes *Species Plantarum,* in which the names of species are established.		**1** Marriage Act in Britain stops marriages by unlicensed ministers and requires notice to be given by publishing of banns. **2** Jockey Club establishes a permanent race course at Newmarket, England. **3** Parliament allows the naturalization (the rights and privileges of citizenship) of Jews in England.	**1753**
		1 Columbia University is founded in New York City.	**2** Population in China is 185.4 million. **3** St. Andrews Royal and Ancient Golf Club is founded in Scotland.	**1754**

Benjamin Franklin's cartoon calling for unity against the French

Science & Technology		Miscellaneous		
1 Thomas Prince, clergyman and historian, reprints his 1727 sermon, *Earthquakes, The Work of God and Tokens of His Just Displeasure,* adding that Bostonians caused the Portugal earthquake	**4** Johann Tobias Mayer, Ger. astronomer, publishes lunar tables which prove helpful to navigators.		**1** Smallpox epidemic hits the Cape Colony, South Africa. **2** An earthquake in Lisbon, Portugal, kills about 60,000 people; another in Northern Persia kills about 40,000.	**1755**

123

History and Politics		The Arts	
America	**Elsewhere**	**America**	**Elsewhere**
			4 Franz Joseph Haydn, Austrian composer, writes his first string quartet. **5** Karl Heinrich Graun, Ger. composer in Ital. style, writes the oratorio, *Der tod Jesu.* For more than 100 years, it is performed annually during Holy Week.
1756 **1** French under Gen. Louis Joseph de Montcalm capture Fort Oswego and restore control of Lake Ontario to France.	**2** Seven Years' War begins in Europe, India, and North America. France, Austria, Russia, Saxony, Sweden, and (after 1762) Spain oppose Prussia, Great Britain, and Hanover. War involves colonial rivalry between Britain and France and struggle for power in Germany between Austria and Prussia. **3** Frederick II of Prussia invades Saxony, seizes Dresden, and defeats the Austrians at Lobositz and the Saxons at Pirna.	**1** *New Hampshire Gazette,* one of the longest running newspapers in America, is established.	**2** Son of J.S. Bach, Johann Christian Bach, called "the English Bach," begins study in Bologna. **3** Sumarokov is appointed director of the first permanent theater in St. Petersburg (Russia). **4** Johnson establishes *The Literary Magazine, or Universal Review.*
1757 **1** French under Montcalm capture Fort William Henry on Lake George from the British. Indian allies of the French massacre many British prisoners in the garrison.	**2** British recapture Calcutta from the nawab (viceroy) of Bengal. **3** Victorious at first, Frederick II of Prussia is defeated by the Austrians at Kolin and has to evacuate Bohemia. In Saxony and Silesia, he wins great victories at Rossbach and Leuthen against the French and Austrians respectively. **[1756:HIST/3]** **4** Emperor Ch'ien Lung of China restricts foreign maritime trade to the city of Canton.	**1** George Washington acquires Mount Vernon. **2** *The American Magazine and Monthly Chronicle,* a literary periodical, is founded by editor William Smith, provost of the College of Philadelphia. **3** A colonial newspaper reports the theft of a bassoon.	**4** Étienne-Maurice Falconet, Fr. sculptor, becomes director of the porcelain factory at Sèvres. He completes "The Bather," a marble statue. **5** The Academy of Fine Arts is founded in St. Petersburg, Russia. The school is directed primarily by French artists.
1758 **1** French under Montcalm repulse British attack on Fort Ticonderoga, N.Y. British capture Louisburg on Cape Breton Island, and Fort Frontenac on Lake Ontario. French burn and abandon Fort Duquesne, which the British rebuild and rename Fort Pitt. **[1754:HIST/1]**	**2** British and Hanoverians defeat the French at Krefeld. Prussians defeat invading Russian army at Zorndorf. Austrians defeat Prussians at Hochkirch but are unable to drive them out of Saxony and Silesia. **3** British take control of the Bengal region in India.	**1** The *Bay Psalm Book* is completely revised by Rev. Thomas Prince. Reprinted in England, it comes into wide use there and in Scotland. **2** J. Edwards publishes a religious work defending the doctrine of original sin.	**3** Haydn writes his first symphony.

Science & Technology		Miscellaneous		
America	Elsewhere	America	Elsewhere	
by using lightning rods. **2** John Winthrop, Jr. publishes *Lectures on Earthquakes* to oppose Prince's theory. Winthrop refers to earthquakes as "waves." **3** Maps of Virginia and the Middle British Colonies are printed.				
1 Clap theorizes that there are three "terrestrial comets" (meteors) that constantly orbit the earth. He builds a simple orrery (planetarium) to help demonstrate the orbits of planets. **2** Patrick Browne publishes *Civil and Natural History of Jamaica.* **3** Bartram proposes a geological survey of the colonies in hopes of discovering buried minerals.	**4** Lomonosov publishes *Theory of Electricity* and *Origin of Light and Color.*	**1** "Bosom Bottles" are worn at this time. These small glasses, decorated with ribbons, contain flowers and serve much the same purpose as corsages do today. **2** Through stagecoach line is established between Philadelphia and New York City.	**3** First chocolate factory is started in Germany.	**1756**
Mount Vernon, George Washington's home in Virginia		**1** Lewis Morris' famous horse, "American Childers," wins a race around Beaver Pond at Jamaica, Long Island (N.Y.). **2** First street lights are used in Philadelphia: whale-oil lamps, designed by Franklin, are installed on a few streets.	**3** *London Chronicle* is first published.	**1757**
		1 A school for Negroes is established in Philadelphia by the Anglican missionary group. **2** First North American Indian reservation is established in New Jersey.		**1758**

	History and Politics		The Arts	
	America	**Elsewhere**	**America**	**Elsewhere**
1759	**1** British capture Fort Niagara. French abandon Fort Ticonderoga and Crown Point, N.Y., as British threaten siege. **2** Colonial troops destroy village of the Saint Francis Indians in southern Canada. **3** British under Gen. James Wolfe defeat the French under Gen. Montcalm at the Battle of the Plains of Abraham, near Quebec. Both generals are killed. Quebec surrenders to the British.	**4** French win at Bergen but lose at Minden against the British and Hanoverians. Austrians and Russians decisively defeat the Prussians under Frederick II at Kunersdorf. Austrians capture Dresden and later 13,000 Prussians at Maxen. **5** Chinese conquer the city of Kashgar from the Turkish Khojar dynasty.	**1** Peter Harrison designs the Touro Synagogue in Newport, R.I. It is the first synagogue in the U.S. **2** Thomas Godfrey, Eng. playwright in America, writes *The Prince of Parthia*, a tragedy. **3** In Pennsylvania, religious opposition to the theater results in a penalty of 500 pounds for performing a play.	**4** Voltaire's *Candide*, a philosophical novel and his best-known work, is published. **5** Johnson publishes *Rasselas*, a novel about the futility of seeking happiness. **6** Laurence Sterne, an Anglican clergyman and author of humorous novels, publishes the first two volumes of *Tristram Shandy*.
1760	**1** British capture Montreal; French Governor of Canada surrenders the entire province to the British. **2** French surrender Detroit to the British. **3** Cherokee Indians massacre the garrison at Fort Loudoun on the Tennessee River. **4** Governors of frontier colonies are told not to honor land grants that have permitted trespass on Indian lands.	**5** Austrians defeat Prussians at Landshut but are defeated by Frederick II at Liegnitz and Torgau. Russians burn Berlin. **6** George III becomes King of Great Britain and Ireland. **7** Dutch in South Africa explore beyond the Orange River.	**1** A concert by amateur "gentlemen" musicians in Charleston includes vocal and instrumental music. **2** Benjamin West, American painter who later emigrates to England, goes to Italy to study.	**3** George Stubbs, Eng. painter known as a superb anatomical draftsman, completes "Mares and Foals in a Landscape." **4** Jean-Georges Noverre publishes *Letters on the Dance and on Ballet* in France, marking a turning point in the art. **5** Scot. poet James Macpherson publishes *Fragments of Ancient Poetry, Collected in the Highlands*. Supposedly by Ossian, a legendary 3rd century poet and hero, they are later proved a fraud. **6** Royal Society of Arts is founded in London. First public exhibition of contemporary art is held.
1761	**1** James Otis opposes British writs of assistance (search warrants), claiming they violate the natural rights of the British colonials.	**2** Austrians capture Schweidnitz and Russians occupy Kolberg. Frederick II of Prussia is deprived of subsidies by Great Britain. **3** Afghans defeat the Mahrattas (Hindu warriors) at Panipat in northwestern India.	**1** James Lyons of Philadelphia publishes *Urania,* the largest collection of hymns and psalms in the colonies. **2** Benjamin Franklin invents a musical percussion instrument played by tapping tuned glasses. Called the *glassychord,* later the harmonica, it bears no resemblance to the mouth organ. **3** "Springfield Mountain," the earliest recorded American folk	**5** At the age of 5, Wolfgang Amadeus Mozart, Aust. composer, begins writing minuets. **6** Rousseau publishes *Julie, or La Nouvelle Heloise,* a moralistic novel. **7** "Parnassus" a fresco by Anton Raphael Mengs, Ger. painter living in Rome, marks start of the neo-classical movement in Italy. **8** Gasparo Angiolini,

Science & Technology		Miscellaneous		
America	Elsewhere	America	Elsewhere	
1 Winthrop publishes *Two Lectures on Comets*. **2** Colonial shipbuilders are producing nearly 400 vessels each year.	**3** Franz Aepinus, Ger. physicist, applies mathematics to electricity and magnetism. **4** John Smeaton, Eng. engineer, builds a lighthouse in which underwater blocks and mortar are used.	**1** Thomas and Richard Penn establish the first recorded life insurance company, the Presbyterian Ministers fund, in Philadelphia.	**2** Jesuits are expelled from Spain and Portugal, and the Jesuit University at Evora in Portugal is closed. **3** Earthquake in Baalbek, Lebanon, kills 30,000 people.	1759
1 Tobacco prices in England drop sharply forcing many colonists to begin planting corn and wheat instead. **2** New York requires that all physicians and surgeons pass a test and be licensed to practice medicine. **3** Jared Eliot, Conn. agriculturist, writes *Essays Upon Field Husbandry in New England,* modifying British farming techniques for use in America.	**4** Lomonosov publishes work on the formation of icebergs.	**1** Population in the colonies is estimated at 1.6 million. **[1738:MISC/2]** **2** Students at William and Mary College in Virginia petition for a change in menus. They do not mind leftovers ("scraps") so long as everyone gets the same. They request salt and frest meat for dinner, and desserts, either pies or puddings, 3 times a week.	**3** Laurence Shirley, 4th Earl of Ferrers, is the last nobleman in England to be hanged as a felon for murder. **4** First school in Britain for teaching the deaf and mute opens in Edinburgh, Scotland. **5** Rules of whist are set down by Edmond Hoyle. **6** The silk hat is introduced in Florence, Italy.	1760
1 Winthrop leads a group of scientists to Newfoundland to observe a transit of Venus. **2** George Washington begins experimenting with crop rotation, soil fertilization, and livestock management and breeding.	**3** Josef Kobreuter, Ger. botanist, recognizes the role of the wind and insects in the pollination of plants.	**1** One of the earliest known cookbooks, *The Complete Housewife,* is published in New York City.		1761

History and Politics		The Arts	
America	**Elsewhere**	**America**	**Elsewhere**
		ballad, is sung in New England. **4** The first musical society in America, the St. Cecilia Society, is founded in Charleston, S.C.	Ital. choreographer in Vienna, composes *Don Juan,* the most dramatic ballet of the later 18th century.
1762 **1** By the Treaty of Fontainebleau, France secretly cedes the Louisiana Territory to Spain, thus keeping it from falling under British control.	**2** Peter III becomes Czar and takes Russia out of the Seven Years' War. He concludes alliance with Frederick II of Prussia. Peter is murdered, and his wife becomes Czarina of Russia as Catherine II (the Great). **3** Treaty of Hamburg between Sweden and Prussia restores status quo before the Seven Years' War. **4** Prussians defeat the Austrians at Burkersdorf and Freiberg. **5** British seize Cuba and the Philippines from Spain. Spain recovers them by treaty the next year.	**1** The Moravians publish a collection of hymns in the language of the Delaware Indians.	**2** James Boswell, Scot. author, begins his journal. **3** Giovanni Pannini, Ital. artist, completes the sculpture for the Fountain of Trevi, Rome. **4** Christoph Willibald Gluck, Ger. composer, completes *Orpheus and Eurydice,* the most famous opera of his Vienna period. **5** Mozart goes on his first concert tour at age 6. **6** Tiepolo paints frescoes in the Royal Palace in Madrid.
1763 **1** Treaty of Paris ends the French and Indian War. France cedes to Great Britain all its territories east of the Mississippi River, except the Island of Orleans. Spain gives up Florida to Britain for return of Cuba and the Philippines. France and Britain exchange and receive islands in the West Indies. [1754:HIST/1] **2** Indian tribes attack forts and settlements, now held by the British in the Ohio-Great Lakes region. Indians destroy all forts except Forts Pitt and Detroit before making peace in 1766.	**3** Treaty of Paris among Great Britain, France, and Spain and the Treaty of Hubertusburg among Prussia, Austria, and Saxony end the Seven Years' War. France loses Canada, India, and Senegal to Great Britain; France withdraws its troops from Germany. Prussia retains Silesia and promises to support Archduke Joseph (later Joseph II) as Holy Roman Emperor. Saxony is restored to its prewar limits. [1756:HIST/2]	**1** The technology of printing is firmly established in all 13 colonies. **2** Henry William Stiegel, Ger. manufacturer, establishes the American Flint Glass Manufactory in Manheim, Pa. **3** Benjamin West arrives in London and introduces the Neoclassical style into English painting.	**4** Johnson meets Boswell, who becomes his devoted follower and biographer, in an accidental encounter at a bookshop in London. **5** Mozart publishes four violin sonatas—his first compositions—in Paris. **6** The first edition of the letters of Lady Mary Wortley Montagu is published. The more interesting letters concern her experiences as wife of the British ambassador to Constantinople.
1764 **1** British Parliament enacts the Sugar Act to raise money in the colonies to pay the British war debt. The Currency Act prohibits the plantation colonies from issuing money (colonies of New England had been under such restriction since 1751). Colonials protest against the two acts.	**2** Stanislaus II becomes King of Poland. By agreement, Russia and Prussia arrange to cooperate in Polish affairs. **3** British defeat the nawab of Oudh at Buxar, giving them uncontested control of Bengal and Bihar in India.	**1** *The Connecticut Courant,* perhaps the American newspaper in longest continuous publication, is established in Hartford, Conn.	**2** Thomas Chatterton, a 12-year-old Eng. poet, begins an amazing literary hoax by forging "original" manuscripts of an imaginary 15th-century monk named Thomas Rowley. **3** Mozart (8 years old) writes his first sym-

Science & Technology		Miscellaneous		
America	**Elsewhere**	**America**	**Elsewhere**	
1 Ethan Allen establishes an ironworks and blast furnace in Salisbury, Conn. This plant will produce many of the cannons used by colonists in the Revolutionary War. **2** Eliot describes new process for removing iron ore from black, magnetic sand. **3** Second edition of *Flora Virginica* is published using the Linnaean system of scientific names. **[1743:SCI/3]**	**4** John Harrison, Eng. inventor, builds a marine chronometer. **5** Charles Bonnet, Swiss naturalist, suggests that species which reproduce asexually will never become extinct. **6** Peter Collinson, Eng. naturalist, asks Linnaeus to reconsider his belief that swallows winter beneath the mud of pond bottoms.		**1** Jean Jacques Rousseau publishes *Émile*, advice on rearing children in a natural way, and *Du Contrat Social*, political theories on freedom and equality. Both are condemned by the Fr. Parliament, and Rousseau is forced to flee to Switzerland.	**1762**
1 America's first medical society is formed in New London, Conn.	**2** Nevil Maskelyne, Eng. astronomer, publishes *The British Mariner's Guide*.	**1** Beginnings of the free Negro tradition in New England is seen: there are 5214 Negroes in Massachusetts' population of 235,810. Most Negroes, however, work at menial jobs in shipyards and homes.	**2** Frederick the Great, King of Prussia, establishes village schools in his country.	**1763**
1 Smallpox epidemic sparks the opening of two inoculation hospitals in the Boston area. **2** Harvard Hall burns, destroying its collection of scientific equipment.	**3** Joseph-Louis Lagrange, Fr.-Ital. mathematician, explains librations (the apparent vibrations of the Moon).	**1** Connecticut silversmith Abel Buell is imprisoned for counterfeiting five-pound notes. **[1705:MISC/1]** **2** First minister of the Dutch Reformed Church preaches at New York City. He tries to have dancing banned in the colony.	**3** François Marie Arouet Voltaire, Fr. philosopher, publishes his *Philosophical Dictionary*. **4** Practice of numbering houses is started in London.	**1764**

129

	History and Politics		The Arts	
	America	**Elsewhere**	**America**	**Elsewhere**
				phony. **4** Pierre-Simon Fournier, Fr. engraver and typographer, publishes a work on typefaces and printing. **5** James and Robert Adam are designing many famous buildings in England.
1765	**1** British Parliament enacts the Stamp Act, requiring the purchase of tax stamps to be affixed to newspapers, pamphlets, documents, playing cards, licenses, dice, etc. **2** Quartering Act requires the colonies to provide food and lodging for British soldiers. **3** Virginia Assembly opposes Stamp Act. Sons of Liberty force British stamp agents to resign. Stamp Act Congress in New York City adopts Declaration of Rights and Grievances to be submitted to the King and Parliament. Colonial policy of nonimportation of British goods goes into effect.	**4** Joseph II becomes Holy Roman Emperor and rules Hapsburg lands jointly with his mother, Maria Theresa, until 1780. **5** British East India Company assumes control of the administration of Bengal, Bihar, and part of Orissa in India. **6** Chinese invade Burma but fail to reach Ava, the Burmese capital.	**1** William Paterson, Princeton College student, founds the Well Meaning Society, later known as the Cliosophic Society, the first college society of arts and letters in America. **2** John Dickinson, "Penman of the Revolution," criticizes the Stamp Act in *Late Regulations Respecting the Colonies Considered.* **3** A letter from Benjamin Franklin to his brother Peter includes an early example of original musical criticism. **4** The London Book-Store, Boston, sells music and has a circulating library of more than 1200 volumes.	**5** Jean-Baptiste Greuze, Fr. painter, completes two of his most popular works, "The Father's Curse" and "Prodigal Son." **6** Horace Walpole, Eng. writer known chiefly for his letter-writing, publishes *The Castle of Otranto,* a popular Gothic novel. **7** Jean-Honoré Fragonard, Fr. rococo painter, exhibits "Corèsus and Callirhoé." **8** Suzuki Harunobu, Jap. artist, develops technique of multicolor printing from wood blocks, designed to illustrate haiku poetry.
1766	**1** Stamp Act is repealed after London merchants cite business failures caused by loss of American market for their goods. [1765:HIST/3] **2** British Parliament enacts Declaratory Act, stating its right to make laws for the colonies. **3** Mason-Dixon Line marks boundary between Pennsylvania and Maryland.	**4** France obtains the duchies of Bar and Lorraine. **5** Catherine II of Russia interferes in the affairs of Poland, where one of her favorites, Stanislaus II, had been put on the throne in 1764. **6** Ottoman Turks concede some self-rule to the Mamelukes (warrior caste) in Egypt.	**1** St. Paul's Chapel, the oldest surviving church in Manhattan, is constructed. **2** *Ponteach, or The Savages of America* is written by Major Robert Rogers. It is the first play on an American subject. **3** The Southwark Theater, one of the earliest permanent buildings for theatrical productions, is built in Philadelphia. **4** John Singleton Copley, portrait painter, sends a portrait of Henry Pelham, his half-brother, to a London exhibition.	**5** Oliver Goldsmith, Ir. author, publishes *The Vicar of Wakefield,* a novel that includes the famous ballad, "The Hermit." **6** Haydn becomes music director at the court of Prince Paul Esterházy, one of the most influential families in the Austrian empire. **7** Johann Zumpe constructs England's first pianoforte.

Science & Technology		Miscellaneous		
America	**Elsewhere**	**America**	**Elsewhere**	
1 Benjamin Gale studies the use of mercury in smallpox inoculations. **2** John Morgan establishes America's first medical school at the College of Philadelphia. William Shippen is appointed professor of anatomy. **3** Winthrop calculates the mass and density of several comets.	**4** James Watt, Scot. scientist, invents a more efficient steam engine. **5** Jean Baptiste de Gribeauval, Fr. general, suggests that cannon cartridges be made one standard size so they will be interchangeable. [1798:SCI/1] James Watt, Scottish scientist	**1** Chocolate is first manufactured at Dorchester, Mass. **2** Latin schools are maintained in at least 40 of 140 Massachusetts communities of more than 100 families. **3** Curriculum for wealthy young Southerners includes Latin, Greek, Hebrew, reading, writing, arithmetic-vulgar, plane geometry, surveying, Italian bookkeeping, and navigation. **4** Horse racing in Maryland becomes popular and fashionable. The course at Annapolis is one of the best in the country.	**5** Sir William Blackstone, Eng. jurist, begins publishing the *Commentaries on the Laws of England,* a history of the common law in England. **6** Bank of Prussia is founded by Frederick the Great.	**1765**
1 Morgan establishes the Philadelphia Medical Society. Other short-lived societies are formed in Conn. **2** George Croghan discovers fossils (mastodon bones) at Big Bone Lick along the Ohio River.	**3** Henry Cavendish, Eng. scientist, publishes work on the preparation of gases. **4** Horace-Benedict de Saussure, Swiss geologist and physicist, invents the electrometer. **5** Haller publishes his 8-volume *Physiological Elements of the Human Body,* a milestone of medicine.	**1** Stagecoach between New York City and Philadelphia advertises itself as a "flying-machine, a good stagewagon set on springs." Trips take two days (in good weather). **2** Games popular in New York City are indicated by advertisements for battledores, shuttlecocks, cricket balls, pellets, racquets for tennis and fives, and backgammon tables. **3** Gloucester Fox Hunting Club, the first regular fox-hunting group, is organized in New Jersey.	**4** Famine in Bengal, India.	**1766**

	History and Politics		The Arts	
	America	Elsewhere	America	Elsewhere
1767	**1** New York Assembly is suspended for refusing to comply fully with the Quartering Act. [1765:HIST/2] **2** Townshend Acts are passed, requiring the colonies to pay import duties on tea, glass, lead, oil, paper, and painters' colors. Nonimportation policy is revived by the colonies.	**3** British, allied with the Mahrattas, begin war against Haidar Ali, Hindu ruler of the state of Mysore, India. [1761:HIST/3] **4** Burmese invade Siam (Thailand) and destroy capital city of Ayutthaya.	**1** Charles Willson Peale, painter, is sent to London to study under Benjamin West. **2** The first professional production of a native play, *The Prince of Parthia,* is presented in Philadelphia. [1759:ARTS/2]	**3** Jean-Antoine Houdon, Fr. Rococo sculptor, establishes his reputation in Rome with his statue of St. Bruno. **4** Bernardo Bellotto (Canaletto), Venetian artist, becomes court painter to Stanislaw II in Warsaw. His paintings of European cities are so accurate that they are referred to for the restoration of famous buildings destroyed during World War II. **5** Sterne completes *Tristram Shandy* and *A Sentimental Journey.*
1768	**1** Colonial assemblies urge opposition to Townshend Acts. **2** Cherokee and Iroquois Indians negotiate treaties. Indian land in Virginia extends to the Ohio River. British control western New York and Pennsylvania. **3** Colonists refuse to provide quarters to British troops in Boston. [1765:HIST/2]	**4** Genoa sells Corsica to France. **5** Polish nobles form the Confederation of Bar, an anti-Russian union supporting Poland's independence. Civil war breaks out; Catherine II sends Russian troops to crush rebels. **6** Ottoman Turks, alarmed by the Russian policy in Poland and urged by France, declare war on Russia. **7** Gurkhas conquer Nepal.	**1** Sheet music is published and sold in Boston. **2** B. West paints "Agrippina Landing at Brundisium with the Ashes of Germanicus," a favorite of George III.	**3** J.C. Bach performs, in London, the first piano solo ever heard in a concert in England. **4** The first edition of *Encyclopaedia Britannica* appears in Edinburgh. **5** Mozart, now 12 years old, composes his first operettas. **6** The Royal Academy is founded in London. Joshua Reynolds is its president.
1769	**1** British governor dissolves Virginia Assembly for its resolutions against the British taxes and other policies. **2** Colonial seaports draw up nonimportation agreements against the British.	**3** Russian troops overrun Moldavia and Wallachia and enter Bucharest. **4** French forces oust President Paoli in Corsica; he flees to England. [1755:HIST/3] **5** Haidar Ali forces the British to sign a peace treaty of mutual assistance. **6** Frederick II of Prussia and Holy Roman Emperor Joseph II meet in Silesia to discuss the partition (separation) of Poland. Austria occupies the Lwow and Zips regions in Poland.	**1** John Harris, Boston harpsichord maker, constructs the first spinet made in the colonies. **2** San Diego de Alcala, the first California mission, is founded by the Franciscan friars. It presents religious plays with music.	**3** Reynolds delivers the first *Discourse* (-1790), his annual address to the Royal Academy. **4** Greuze completes the historical painting, "Septimus Severus Reproaching Caracalla." **5** Eng. painter Thomas Gainsborough demonstrates his elegant and formal style in the portrait, "Isabella, Countess of Sefton."
1770	**1** British soldiers kill several colonists in Boston. Colonial resentment over the Town-	**3** Frederick North (Lord North) becomes British Prime Minister.	**1** Parts of Handel's *Messiah* are presented in New York City for	**5** Karl Ditters von Dittersdorf, Aust. violinist and early com-

Science & Technology

America

Elsewhere

Miscellaneous

America

Elsewhere

Science & Technology		Miscellaneous		
America	Elsewhere	America	Elsewhere	
1 David Rittenhouse, astronomer, invents a detailed and accurate orrery (planetarium). **2** King's College in New York opens America's second medical school.	**3** Joseph Priestley, Eng. scientist and clergyman, writes *The History and Present State of Electricity.*	**1** Daniel Boone, starting from North Carolina, makes his first exploration west of the Appalachian Mts.; he travels along the present-day Kentucky-West Virginia border.	**2** Jesuits are expelled from Spain and France. **3** Emperor Joseph II and his mother, Maria Theresa, introduce educational reforms in Austria. [1765:HIST/4]	**1767**

Daniel Boone's first view of Kentucky.

1 Bodo Otto, Ger. physician, produces cottonseed oil in Bethlehem, Pa. **2** Alexander Garden, physician, discovers the Congo eel, a native American amphibian belonging to a previously unknown order. He also contributes to Linnaeus' 12th edition of *Systema Natura.* **3** Medical School at Philadelphia College graduates its first physicians.	**4** Lazzano Spallanzani, Ital. physiologist, determines that lower animals are able to regenerate lost body parts better than higher animals.	**1** New York Chamber of Commerce, probably the first of its kind, elects John Cruger its first president. **2** First Methodist Church is established in New York City.	**3** New criminal code, based on more humane principles, is put into effect in Austria.	**1768**
1 Abel Buell, Conn. silversmith, produces the first American-made type fonts for printing presses. **2** Rittenhouse builds an observatory and telescope to observe a transit of Venus.	**3** Bonnet suggests that the Earth is subject to occasional disasters, followed by an evolutionary advance of the survivors. **4** Nicolas-Joseph Cugnot, Fr. military engineer, builds the first automobile—with a steam-powered engine. **5** Euler introduces new mathematical symbols, such as π (pi).		**1** First day nursery opens at Steintal, Alsace.	**1769**
1 John Warren and several other Harvard students form a society for		**1** Population in the colonies is estimated at 2.2 million. [1760:MISC/1]	**4** First public restaurant opens in Paris. **5** Elementary education	**1770**

History and Politics

America

Elsewhere

The Arts

America

Elsewhere

	History and Politics		The Arts	
	America	Elsewhere	America	Elsewhere
	shend and Quartering Acts cause the incident, now known as the Boston Massacre. **2** British Parliament repeals the Townshend Acts, but retains the tax on tea. Colonists end their embargo on British goods.	**4** Russian fleet defeats and destroys the Turkish fleet at the Battle of Çeşme on the Aegean Sea. **5** Capt. James Cook, Eng. navigator, explores and maps the coast of New Zealand and sights the coast of Australia.	the first time by Eng. born organist William Tuckey. **2** Copley completes a portrait of Paul Revere. [1775:HIST/2] **3** Paul Revere publishes the engraving "The Bloody Massacre." It is actually a copy of an earlier rendition by Peter Pelham, another important engraver of the period. **4** *The New England Psalm Singer, or American Chorister,* by William Billings, marks the beginning of publishing of American compositions.	poser of the Viennese classical school, writes several comic operas and an oratorio. **6** Goldsmith completes "The Deserted Village," a poem calling for a return to an agricultural society. **7** Gainsborough completes "The Blue Boy," one of the world's most popular paintings. **8** Fragonard is commissioned by Mme. du Barry to decorate the Pavillon de Louveciennes.
1771	**1** British troops suppress uprising of back-country farmers in North Carolina, who protest discriminatory laws, excessive taxes, and under-representation in the colonial legislature.	**2** Russia conquers the Crimea. Russian successes alarm the Austrians and Prussians. Frederick II arranges the first partition of Poland in order to prevent war between the powers. [1769:HIST/6] **3** James Bruce, Scot. explorer in Africa, follows the Blue Nile to its confluence with the White Nile.	**1** Music of Handel is performed at concert given by Josiah Flagg in Boston. **2** Shortly after his arrival in Boston, Eng. organist William Selby is appointed organist at King's Chapel. **3** West, in England, breaks many artistic conventions in his historical paintings, "The Death of Wolfe" and "Penn's Treaty with the Indians." **4** *Poems on Various Subjects* by Phillis Wheatley, a black poet from Boston, is published in London.	**5** George Romney, Eng. portrait painter, completes "Mrs. Yates as the Tragic Muse" reflecting an artificial, classical style. **6** Sophie von LaRoche, Ger. writer, completes *History of Lady Sophia Sternheim,* considered by many the first original novel by a woman. **7** Smollett's novel, *The Expedition of Humphry Clinker,* is a masterpiece of character development and portrayal.
1772	**1** Governors and judges in Massachusetts are to be paid by the Crown, making them independent of the Assembly's financial control. **2** Rhode Islanders attack and burn the British revenue cutter *Gaspee* in Narragansett Bay. **3** Samuel Adams leads Committees of Correspondence in revolt against Britain.	**4** Gustavus III, King of Sweden, restores absolute government by a military coup d'etat. He reforms finances and poor laws, proclaims religious toleration, encourages trade, and builds a fleet. **5** First Partition of Poland gives Latgale and part of Belorussia to Russia, Pomerelia and Ermeland to Prussia, and Galicia to Austria. Poland loses about one third of its territory. [1771:HIST/2]	**1** Charles Willson Peale, the most important painter of the Revolutionary period, completes a life-sized portrait of George Washington. **2** West becomes history painter to George III.	**3** Johann Gottfried von Herder, Ger. writer and leading figure in the Sturm und Drang (Storm and Stress) literary movement, publishes *Essay on the Origin of Language.* **4** Lessing publishes *Emilia Galotti,* a social tragedy. **5** Johan Herman Wessel, Dan. playwright, completes *Love Without Stockings,* a

Science & Technology		Miscellaneous		
America	**Elsewhere**	**America**	**Elsewhere**	
the secret dissection of animals. This society later becomes the Massachusetts Medical Society. **2** Benjamin Banneker builds a wooden clock that keeps accurate time for more than 50 years.		**2** College of Charleston, the first municipal college, is established in South Carolina. **3** Popular form of hair style among rich colonial women is the "tower." Hair is piled high over pads until there is a mountain of curls. It is then greased with pomatum, powdered, and finally decked with such things as beads, jewels, ribbons, lace, feathers, and flowers. Hairdressing takes hours and hairdressers are in great demand.	is established in the Austrian Empire (present-day Central Europe).	
1 First issue of *Transactions,* the journal of the American Philosophical Society, is published. **2** Lining gives a detailed description of yellow fever. **3** Hugh Williamson suggests that comets are inhabited.	 *The Blue Boy,* painting by Thomas Gainsborough		**1** Edict in Spain requires the modernization of textbooks.	**1771**
1 Andrew Oliver, lieutenant governor of Mass., publishes his *Essay on Comets.* **2** John Hobday invents the threshing machine and is awarded a gold medal by the Virginia Society for Promoting Useful Knowledge. **3** William DeBrahm publishes *The Atlantic Pilot,* a navigational guide.	**4** Karl Wilhelm Scheele, Swed. chemist, is popularly thought to have discovered oxygen, which he called "fire water." **5** Euler clarifies the basic principles of optics, acoustics, mechanics, and astronomy.		**1** English court rules that a slave is free on landing in England. **2** Inquisition is abolished in France. **3** First carriage traffic crosses the Brenner Pass in the Alps, on the border between Italy and Austria.	**1772**

History and Politics		The Arts	
America	**Elsewhere**	**America**	**Elsewhere**
	6 Warren Hastings, Brit. statesman, becomes Governor of Bengal and initiates financial and judicial reform.		parody of French tragedies and Italian operas.
1773 **1** Parliament passes the Tea Act to save British East India Company from bankruptcy and to reassert its right to tax the colonies. Colonial anger leads to the Boston Tea Party, in which men dressed as Indians dump British tea shipment into the Boston harbor.	**2** Cossacks, peasants, and serfs of southeastern Russia rebel unsuccessfully against the government of Catherine II. **3** Lord North's Regulating Act reforms the British East India Company in India. [1770:HIST/3] **4** Denmark cedes duchy of Oldenburg to Russia, with which it concludes an alliance.	**1** The Philadelphia Museum is established. **2** A theater, larger than those in Philadelphia and New York, is opened in Charleston, S.C.	**3** Johann Wolfgang von Goethe, Ger. writer and philosopher, publishes *Götz von Berlichingen,* a tragedy that marks the start of the Sturm und Drang movement. [1776:ARTS/2] **4** Goldsmith's comedy, *She Stoops to Conquer,* is staged at Covent Garden, London. **5** Greuze's "Broken Pitcher" portrays one of his favorite themes: a young, innocent girl saddened by the loss of a favorite object. **6** A dance class established at the Moscow Orphanage later evolves into the Bolshoi Ballet Company. [1825:ARTS/4]
1774 **1** British Parliament passes measures ("Intolerable Acts") to punish the Massachusetts colonists for the Boston Tea Party. Boston port is closed until payment is made for the tea destroyed. Colonists are forced to quarter British soldiers and are deprived of many chartered rights. [1773:HIST/1] **2** First Continental Congress meets in Philadelphia with delegates from all the colonies except Georgia. Petitions of grievances are sent to the king.	**3** Russia and the Ottoman Empire sign the Treaty of Kuchuck Kainarji. Russia gains territory in the Crimea and free navigation in the Black Sea. Turks retain Moldavia and Wallachia. **4** Louis XVI becomes King of France. **5** Manchus suppress rebellion in the Shantung province of China.	**1** Thomas Paine arrives in America and becomes the editor of *Pennsylvania Magazine.* **2** Copley leaves Boston for England. **3** Thomas Jefferson writes his first important work, *A Summary View of the Rights of British America,* in which he asserts that the British have no right to rule or legislate for the colonies.	**4** Goethe's *The Sorrows of Young Werther,* first novel of the Sturm und Drang movement, brings its author fame throughout Europe. **5** Now in Paris, Gluck composes *Iphigenia in Aulis,* an opera. **6** The letters of Philip Dormer Stanhope (Lord Chesterfield) to his son are published. They give advice on the moral principles and behavior of gentlemen.
1775 **1** Patrick Henry delivers speech against tyrannical British rule, closing with "Give me liberty or give me death." **2** Paul Revere alerts colonists that British soldiers are on the way to Concord to destroy arms. Minutemen fight	**6** Catherine II of Russia reorganizes the provincial administration to increase the government's control over rural regions. **7** Karim Khan of Persia seizes the city of Basra (in Iraq).	**1** Colonial government regulations curb sport and entertainment during the Revolution. Theaters close. **2** Ralph Earl sketches scenes at the battles of Lexington and Concord, which he later de-	**5** Richard Brinsley Sheridan, Eng. comic playwright, stages *The Rivals,* a lively farce that introduces Mrs. Malaprop. **6** Romney paints "Mrs. Carwardine and Son" which shows a

Science & Technology		Miscellaneous		
America	Elsewhere	America	Elsewhere	
1 William Alexander, astronomer, publishes *Variations of the Compass,* an attempt to form a general rule for computing true north from magnetic north. **2** Benjamin Rush, physician, compares the medical values of mineral water taken from various springs. **3** Charleston (Va.) Library Society opens the first American museum of natural history. **4** Oliver Evans proposes steam-powered "horseless carriage."	**5** Spallanzani finds that the digestive juices contain certain substances which act on specific foods.	**1** First annual conference of American Methodists meets at Philadelphia. **2** An early mental hospital, the Public Hospital for Persons of Insane and Disordered Minds, opens in Williamsburg, Va. **3** First large-scale street lighting begins in Boston: 310 street lamps are installed and kept lighted evenings from October to May. **[1757:MISC/2]**	**4** Jesuits are suppressed by the Pope and expelled from the Holy Roman Empire by Emperor Joseph II.	**1773**
1 Rush describes Indian medical practices. **2** Winthrop suggests that writings found at Dighton Rock in eastern Mass. were made by ancient Indians. **3** Abraham Chovet, Pa. physician, opens anatomical wax museum showing internal structures and the effects of disease on internal organs.	**4** Priestley discovers what he calls "dephlogisticated air." **[1777:SCI/2]** **5** Scheele discovers the element chlorine. **6** Johan Gahn, Swed. mineralogist, discovers the element manganese.	**1** *Royal American Magazine,* the first to use illustrations regularly, is published. Paul Revere contributes engravings attacking the British oppression of the colonies. **2** Ann Lee arrives from England with a group of followers called the United Society of Believers in Christ's Second Coming (Shakers). She establishes a community at New Lebanon, N.Y.	**3** Jesuits are expelled from Poland. **4** Swiss educator Johann Pestalozzi founds a school for orphaned and neglected children in Zurich, Switzerland.	**1774**
1 David Bushnell invents a one-man, hand-operated submarine, the "American Turtle." **2** Colonies are supplying nearly 15% of the world's iron. **3** Bernard Romans, Dutch engineer, publishes	**6** Franz Anton Mesmer, Ger. physician, suggests that attractions between certain persons are the result of "animal magnetism." **7** Alessandro Volta, Ital. physicist, invents the electrophorus, a device	**1** Postal system is established by the Second Continental Congress, and Franklin is appointed Postmaster General. **2** Indians in Florida are described as playing lacrosse, using a deerskin ball and deerskin nets on	**4** First Thames Regatta, a rowing race, is held in England.	**1775**

History and Politics | The Arts

	America	Elsewhere	America	Elsewhere
	British at Lexington and Concord, beginning the American Revolution. **3** Green Mountain Boys under Col. Ethan Allen capture Fort Ticonderoga from the British. **4** Second Continental Congress meets in Philadelphia and appoints Washington Commander-in-Chief of the Continental Army. **5** British defeat colonial forces at the Battle of Bunker Hill.		velops into a series of historical paintings. **3** Gilbert Stuart, American painter, goes to London to study under Benjamin West. **4** "Yankee Doodle" becomes popular as a rallying song with which to taunt the British.	neoclassical influence—an effect of 3 years of study in Italy. **7** Pierre Augustin Beaumarchais, Fr. dramatist, writes *The Barber of Seville,* a comedy. **8** Johnson writes *A Journey to the Western Islands of Scotland.*
1776	**1** British forces evacuate Boston. **2** Congress adopts the Declaration of Independence, drafted by Thomas Jefferson. **3** Gen. William Howe leads British troops in the successful Battle of Long Island, captures New York City, and defeats the Continental Army at White Plains, N.Y. Washington retreats; he defeats Hessians (German soldiers hired by the British) at the Battle of Trenton, N.J. **4** British hang (without trial) Nathan Hale as a spy. **5** British defeat small colonial fleet under Benedict Arnold on Lake Champlain.	**6** Russia forms naval fleet in the Black Sea. **7** Six edicts in France make reforms in taxation and dissolve the old trade guilds. King, queen, and privileged groups oppose edicts (later repealed) and any prison reform.	**1** Philip Freneau, "Poet of the American Revolution," writes biting satires against the British.	**2** Friedrich von Klinger, Ger. dramatist, writes *Der Wirrwarr, oder Sturm und Drang,* an emotional play that gives the Sturm und Drang (Storm and Stress) movement its name. **3** Edward Gibbon, Eng. historian, publishes the first volume of *The History of the Decline and Fall of the Roman Empire* (-1788). **4** Two important works on the history of music are published in England: a 5-volume history by John Hawkins and the first of several volumes by Charles Burney. **5** Theater of Drama, Opera and Ballet begins performances in Moscow.
1777	**1** Washington defeats the British at the Battle of Princeton. **2** British forces under Gen. John Burgoyne seize Fort Ticonderoga, but fail to capture Albany. Revolutionary forces surround and defeat Burgoyne at the Battle of Saratoga, ending the British plan to split the colonies along the Hudson River. **3** British forces under Gen. Howe defeat Washington's forces at Brandywine and Germantown, Pa. British con-	**5** Portugal builds up Brazil, unifies administration, and incorporates state of Maranhão with Brazil. (Rio de Janeiro replaced Bahia as Brazil's capital in 1763.) Native Brazilians are given important government posts. **6** Spain and Portugal settle disputes about their colonies in South America. **7** Burmese are driven out of Siam.	**1** The New Testament of the Bible is published in English for the first time in America. **2** California's oldest building still in existence, the chapel of the San Juan Capistrano mission, is built.	**3** Sheridan writes *School for Scandal,* a comedy. **4** Reynolds completes his most ambitious portrait, "The Family of the Duke of Marlborough." **5** Maruyama Ōkyo, founder of the Maruyama school of naturalistic Japanese painting, completes "Bamboo in Wind and Rain."

Science & Technology		Miscellaneous		
America	**Elsewhere**	**America**	**Elsewhere**	
a natural history of Florida with navigational charts and maps. **4** Garden describes electric eels. **5** John Lorimer invents the dipping needle compass.	used to create static electricity.	sticks. **3** First abolition society, the Society for the Relief of Free Negroes Unlawfully Held in Bondage, is organized in Philadelphia by Franklin and Benjamin Rush, physician and political leader.		
1 Bushnell unsuccessfully tries to sink a British warship by attaching time bombs to the hull. **2** Lionel Chalmers publishes *An Account of the Weather and Diseases in South Carolina.*	**3** Haller publishes a bibliography of 52,000 scientific works. **4** Peter Pallas, Ger. naturalist, advances a theory on mountain formation.	**1** Fire destroys most of the old parts of New York City. **2** Thomas Paine's *Common Sense* is published and sells more than 100,000 copies in 3 months. It urges the end of the union with England. **3** The *Pennsylvania Evening Post,* a 4-page paper, devotes its entire front page and part of the 2nd page to the text of Declaration of Independence.	**4** Famine strikes Bengal, India; one third of the population dies. **5** St. Leger horse race is established at Doncaster, England.	**1776**
1 Washington orders his soldiers to be inoculated against smallpox.	**2** Antoine-Laurent Lavoisier, Fr. chemist, coins the term *oxygen* for the "dephlogisticated air" discovered by Priestley. **[1774:SCI/4]** **3** Scheele suggests that the atmosphere is made up of two gases—one which causes fire and the other which prevents it.	**1** Congress specifies the design of the U.S. flag: "thirteen strips alternate red and white . . . thirteen stars of white on a blue field."	**2** First French newspaper, *Journal de Paris,* is published. **3** A cooperative workshop for tailors is formed in Birmingham, England, to employ men on strike.	**1777**

History and Politics		The Arts	
America	**Elsewhere**	**America**	**Elsewhere**

	America	Elsewhere	America	Elsewhere
	trol Philadelphia. Washington sets up winter quarters at Valley Forge, Pa. **4** Congress adopts Articles of Confederation and Perpetual Union.			
1778	**1** Congress ratifies treaty of alliance with France and rejects British peace offer. British evacuate Philadelphia, fearing blockade by French fleet. **2** Baron Friedrich von Steuben and Marquis de Lafayette help Washington train Continental Army. **3** Washington defeats British at the Battle of Monmouth, N.J. British capture Savannah, Ga. **4** British Tories and Indians massacre inhabitants of Wyoming Valley, Pa., and Cherry Valley, N.Y.	**5** France enters war for American independence against Great Britain. **[1778:HIST/2]** **6** Capt. Cook discovers the islands of Hawaii, naming them the Sandwich Islands. **[1770:HIST/5]** **7** War of the Bavarian Succession begins. Holy Roman Emperor Joseph II tries to acquire Bavaria by secret treaty. Frederick II of Prussia protests, declares war on Austria, and invades Bohemia. **8** French regain their possessions in the Senegal, Africa.	**1** Francis Hopkinson writes the satiric ballad, *Battle of the Keys*.	**2** Fanny Burney, Eng. writer, anonymously publishes *Evelina,* the story of a young girl's entrance into society. **3** Mozart's ballet, *Les Petits Riens,* is performed in Paris. He also composes *Symphony No. 31 in D Major* (*Paris Symphony*). **4** Herder publishes *Volkslieder,* a popular collection of folk songs. **5** At the age of 8, Ger. composer Ludwig van Beethoven is presented by his father as a 6-year-old child prodigy.
1779	**1** Virginians under George Rogers Clark complete their conquest of the Old Northwest, capturing Vincennes, Ind. **2** Gen. Anthony Wayne defeats the British at Stony Point, N.Y. **3** *Bonhomme Richard,* commanded by John Paul Jones, wins naval victory against British frigate *Serapis* off the east coast of England. **4** French and colonial land-sea forces fail to recapture Savannah, Ga. **[1778:HIST/3]**	**5** Treaty of Teschen ends the War of the Bavarian Succession, in which no serious battles are fought. Austria renounces its claims to Bavaria but retains the Inn district (Upper Austria). **[1778:HIST/7]** **6** Spain declares war on Great Britain. **7** British fight the Mahrattas in India. **8** French capture the islands of St. Vincent and Grenada from the British, who recover them in 1783. French post of Gorée in the Senegal is seized by the British. **[1778:HIST/8]**	**1** Billings publishes *Music in Miniature.*	**2** Eng. poet William Cowper writes his famous ballad, *John Gilpin.* **3** Hokusai, Jap. artist of the Ukiyo-e school, publishes his first color prints. **4** James Gillray, Eng. political cartoonist known for satires of King George III, publishes his first caricature, "Paddy on Horseback." **5** Antonio Canova, Ital. neoclassical sculptor, exhibits his first major work, "Daedalus and Icarus." **6** Sheridan publishes *The Critic,* a farce. **7** Lessing publishes *Nathan the Wise,* an emotional poem that urges religious tolerance.
1780	**1** British capture Charleston and overrun South Carolina. **2** Benedict Arnold's plot to	**4** Dutch go to war with Britain over the right to search ships at sea.	**1** The American Academy of Arts and Sciences is organized in	**3** Giovanni Paisello, Ital. composer, produces the opera, *The*

Science & Technology		Miscellaneous		
America	**Elsewhere**	**America**	**Elsewhere**	
1 Gotthilf Henry Muhlenberg, botanist, begins systematic study of American plants. **2** William Brown, Va. physician, publishes *Pharmacopoeia,* a guide to medicines and drugs.	**3** Jean-Baptiste de Lamarck, Fr. biologist, publishes a work on French plant life. **4** Volta discovers methane gas. **5** Scheele discovers the element molybdenum.	**1** Jonathan Carver's *Travels Through the Interior of North America* contains information on Indian customs and the natural history of the Great Lakes and the upper Mississippi region. **2** Phillips Andover Academy is founded in Massachusetts. The academy school has a broader and more practical curriculum than that of the Latin Grammar School.	**3** Admissions to and the size of monasteries are regulated in France.	**1778**
1 Benjamin Thompson, later known as Count Rumford, studies ballistics, specifically, recoil and bullet momentum. **2** Physicians from Connecticut, Massachusetts, and New York establish the Sharon Medical Society.	**3** Spallanzani studies the role of semen in fertilization.	**1** Under Thomas Jefferson, statesman and author, William and Mary College creates schools of medicine, law and modern languages. The system allowing students to choose courses is introduced. **2** John Murray establishes the First Universalist Congregation at Gloucester, Mass. **3** Popular sport around Charlottesville, Va., is sprint racing, quarter-mile races between two horses.	**4** The Derby is established in Surrey, England, at the Epsom Racecourse.	**1779**
1 Philadelphia Humane Society is established to teach first aid (reviving	**3** d'Alembert publishes the eighth of the 8-volume *Opuscubs Mathema-*	**1** Horse racing on Long Island, N.Y., includes: Gentleman's Purse, La-	**3** *The British Gazette and Sunday Monitor,* the first Sunday newspaper, is	**1780**

141

History and Politics		The Arts	
America	**Elsewhere**	**America**	**Elsewhere**
surrender West Point to the British is discovered through the capture of a British spy. Arnold flees and joins the British, with whom he campaigns. **3** British win the Battle of Camden, S.C. Colonial frontiersmen win the Battle of King's Mountain, S.C.	**5** Haidar Ali, aided by the French, attacks the British in the Carnatic region, India. [1767:HIST/3] **6** Protestants march on British Parliament to present a petition against Catholic Relief Act of 1778; riots ensue with many deaths. **7** Indians and Creoles rebel against the Spanish government in Peru.	Boston. **2** Winthrop Chandler paints portraits of "Captain Samuel Chandler" and "Mrs. Samuel Chandler," his brother and sister-in-law.	*Barber of Seville,* for Catherine II in St. Petersburg, Russia. **4** The bolero, a lively Spanish dance, is invented by Sebastian Cerezo. **5** Frederick the Great (Frederick II of Prussia) writes *De la Littérature allemande.*
1781 **1** Colonials win the Battle of Cowpens, S.C., but lose at Guilford Court House, N.C. British suffer heavy losses. **2** French fleet defeats British naval force at Hampton Roads and blockades the Chesapeake Bay. Revolutionary troops surround the British at Yorktown, Va. Gen. Charles Cornwallis surrenders to Washington, ending hostilities of the American Revolution. [1775:HIST/2] **3** Articles of Confederation and Perpetual Union are ratified. Congress charters Bank of North America.	**4** Emperor Joseph II and Catherine II of Russia conclude treaty. Catherine's Greek Scheme aims at breaking up the Ottoman Empire and restoring a Greek (Christian) empire. Austria is to get the western half of the Balkans. **5** Emperor Joseph II abolishes serfdom and feudal dues. His Patent of Tolerance provides extensive freedom of worship. **6** British defeat Haidar Ali near Madras, India.	**1** Virginia commissions Fr. artist Jean-Antoine Houdon to sculpt a statue of Lafayette.	**2** Johann Christoph Friedrich von Schiller, Ger. poet, publishes his first tragedy, *Die Räuber (The Robbers),* a protest against tyranny. **3** Johann Heinrich Voss, Ger. poet, publishes his most famous work, a translation of Homer's *Odyssey.* **4** Rousseau's *Confessions* is published posthumously. **5** Immanuel Kant, Ger. philosopher, publishes *Critique of Pure Reason.* **6** Gainsborough is commissioned to paint portraits of the King and Queen.
1782 **1** Benjamin Franklin, John Adams, and John Jay negotiate peace treaty with British in Paris. **2** British troops evacuate Savannah, Ga., and Charleston, S.C. **3** Holland recognizes U.S. independence.	**4** Spanish seize Minorca, Honduras, and Florida, but fail to take Gibraltar from the British. **5** British interference in Mahratta affairs in India having led to war, British and Mahrattas sign peace Treaty of Salbai. [1767:HIST/3] **6** Chakkri dynasty is founded in Siam, whose capital is moved from Thon Buri to Bangkok.	**1** J. Hector St. John Crèvecoeur publishes *Letters from an American Farmer,* a series of 12 essays about his extensive travels in North America. [1925:ARTS/13] **2** John Trumbull publishes *M'Fingal,* his most important work, considered at the time to contain much anti-loyalist propaganda. **3** Robert Aitken, printer, publishes the first complete English-language Bible in America.	**4** Sarah Siddons, considered England's greatest tragic actress, has her first success at Drury Lane. **5** Mozart composes *The Abduction from the Seraglio,* an opera, and *Symphony in D Major (Haffner Symphony).* **6** Burney publishes her second novel, *Cecilia.* **7** Pierre Laclos, Fr. author, publishes his popular psychological novel, *Les Liaisons Dangereuses.* **8** Giovanni Battista Viotti, (Ital.) father of modern violin technique, debuts in Paris.

Science & Technology		Miscellaneous		
America	**Elsewhere**	**America**	**Elsewhere**	
drowning victims). Franklin proposes mouth-to-mouth resuscitation. **2** Samuel Williams observes eclipse, gives first description of droplets of sunlight along the moon's edge during the eclipse.	*tiques,* a cornerstone of modern calculus. **4** Guettard publishes a geological atlas of France.	dies' Subscription, and a race with women riders. **2** U.S. population is estimated at 2.7 million. [1770:MISC/1]	published in England. **4** Catholic population of England is 70,000. **5** Steel pens are first used.	
1 Cotton Tufts establishes the Massachusetts Medical Society. **2** Jeremiah Wilkinson produces cold-cut iron nails from iron plate.	**3** William Herschel, Eng. astronomer, discovers the planet Uranus.	**1** A French traveler to Annapolis, Md., reports on its splendor. Fine women, elegant horses, coaches, sumptuous dinners and balls are described. He notes that "A French hairdresser is a man of importance . . ., and it is said, a certain dame here hires one . . . at a thousand crowns a year salary."	**2** Pestalozzi gives his educational theories in his four-volume novel, *Leonard and Gertrude.* [1774:MISC/4] **3** Emperor Joseph II orders religious tolerance and freedom of the press in the Austrian Empire. [1781:HIST/5]	**1781**

Marble bust of Lafayette by French sculptor Jean-Antoine Houdon

Science & Technology		Miscellaneous		
1 Harvard Medical School opens. **2** Hugh Martin, physician, proposes a secret cure for cancer—a powder containing arsenic, a common cancer treatment at the time.	**3** Watt patents an engine in which the pistons both push and pull.	**1** First Catholic parochial school is founded by St. Mary's Catholic Church in Philadelphia. **2** Great seal of the United States is adopted. **3** Town Meeting in Worcester, Mass., opposes a state liquor tax because it is felt that liquor is necessary for the morale of farm workers. **4** Use of the scarlet letter for adulterers in New England is discontinued. [1639:MISC/2]		**1782**

History and Politics		The Arts	
America	**Elsewhere**	**America**	**Elsewhere**

1783

America (History):
1 Treaty of Paris between Britain and the U.S. ends American Revolution; Britain recognizes U.S. independence.
2 British evacuate New York City.
3 Continental Army is disbanded; Washington resigns as Commander-in-Chief. [1775:HIST/4]
4 U.S. independence recognized by Sweden, Denmark, Spain, and Russia. [1782:HIST/3]

Elsewhere (History):
5 William Pitt is made British Prime Minister by King George III.
6 Frederick II of Prussia tries to form a union of the German princes in order to resist the advances of the Holy Roman Emperor.
7 Russia annexes the Crimea on the excuse of restoring order. Britain and Austria dissuade the Turks from declaring war.

America (Arts):
1 The first daily newspaper in the U.S., *The Pennsylvania Evening Post,* begins publication.

Elsewhere (Arts):
2 William Blake, Eng. poet and artist, publishes his early poems in *Poetical Sketches.*
3 John Philip Kemble, Eng. actor, debuts at Drury Lane as Hamlet. His unusual reading first confuses, then captivates the audience.
4 Beethoven's first compositions are published.
5 Eng. poet George Crabbe writes "The Village" as a protest against Goldsmith's sentimental idealism. [1770:ARTS/6]

1784

America (History):
1 Congress adopts Jefferson's plan for governing western lands.
2 North Carolina cedes its western lands to the U.S. The state of Franklin (present-day east Tennessee) exists until 1888, when settlers accept renewed jurisdiction of North Carolina.
3 Congress, with no power of taxation under the Articles of Confederation, is unable to raise needed revenue. [1781:HIST/3]

Elsewhere (History):
4 Pitt's India Act strengthens the government's control of the British East India Company.
5 China suppresses revolts by Muslims, including the Wahabis, in Kansu province.
6 British make peace with Tippoo Sahib, ruler of Mysore, India.
7 Emperor Joseph II revokes constitution in Hungary; riots break out.

America (Arts):
1 *Gentlemen and Ladies' Town and Country Magazine,* one of the first periodicals designed especially for female readers, begins publication.
2 Joel Barlow, poet, establishes a weekly newspaper, *American Mercury,* in Hartford, Ct.
3 Jefferson publishes *Notes on Virginia.*
4 Joseph-Siffred Duplessis, Fr. portraitist, executes portrait of Benjamin Franklin.

Elsewhere (Arts):
5 Jacques-Louis David, prominent Fr. neoclassical painter, exhibits "Andromache Mourning Hector."
6 Francisco de Goya, Span. painter, completes "Don Manuel de Zuniga."
7 Thomas Rowlandson, Eng. cartoonist, publishes his first caricatures.
8 Beaumarchais' comedy *Le Mariage de Figaro,* attacks privileges of aristocracy.
9 *K'un ch'ii,* a style of Chinese music devised in the 16th century, reaches its height with a performance for the emperor.

1785

America (History):
1 U.S. and Spain argue over navigation rights on the Mississippi River and the boundaries of Florida (returned to

Elsewhere (History):
4 Frederick II creates the Fürstenbund (League of Princes) among Prussia, Electoral Saxony, and Hanover,

America (Arts):
1 Ralph Earl is active as an itinerant portrait painter in rural Connecticut.

Elsewhere (Arts):
5 David's painting, "Oath of the Horatii," firmly establishes the neoclassical movement:

144

Science & Technology		Miscellaneous		
America	**Elsewhere**	**America**	**Elsewhere**	
1 Buell makes first map of the United States. **2** Josiah Flagg, America's first native-born dentist, opens practice in Boston.	**3** Lavoisier correctly suggests that water is a compound of hydrogen and oxygen. **4** The first hot-air balloon is launched by Joseph Montgolfier and his brother Jacques. **[1785:MISC/5]** **5** Saussure invents the hair hygrometer, a device for measuring humidity.	**1** Lexicographer Noah Webster publishes *The American Spelling Book,* popularly called "Blue-Backed Speller." It is the first part of *A Grammatical Institute of the English Language,* the other parts being a grammar (1784) and a reader (1785). The work helps standardize spelling of American English. **2** Population of the U.S. is estimated at 2.4 million. Decrease is due mainly to war deaths and the departure of Loyalists during the Revolutionary War. **[1780:MISC/2]** **3** It takes Thomas Jefferson five days to travel by public transportation from Philadelphia to Baltimore, Md., a distance of about 90 mi. **4** Enrollment at Yale College is 270.	**5** Series of six earthquakes kills about 50,000 people in southern Italy and Sicily. **6** Bank of Ireland is founded. **7** Civil marriage and divorce are established in the Austrian Empire. **8** Mt. Skaptar erupts in Iceland, killing one fifth of the population.	**1783**
1 Franklin invents bifocal eyeglasses. **2** Charles Willson Peale, portrait painter, opens the Philadelphia Museum with displays of animals, minerals, and art. **3** John Foulke, physician, flies a small paper balloon. **4** Peter Carnes pays a 13-year-old boy to make America's first manned balloon flight. **5** Oliver Evans establishes an automatic production line in a flour mill near Philadelphia. **6** Jedidiah Morse publishes *Geography Made Easy* and includes descriptions of American plants and animals. **7** Andrew Ellicot surveys and extends the Mason-Dixon Line.	**8** Joseph Bramah, Eng. engineer, invents a pick-proof lock. **9** Henry Cort, Eng. inventor, patents the puddling process of iron production.	**1** *Empress of China* sails to Canton, China. This trade route enables American commerce to recover from the British blockade of the Revolutionary War. Salem, Mass., becomes the center in New England for the China trade. **2** Deer hunting at night in the Carolinas is made a misdemeanor because of the accidental slaughter of many cows and horses.	**3** First school for the blind is started in Paris. **4** Wesley signs the deed of declaration in England as the charter of Wesleyan Methodism and ordains two Presbyters, or clergy, for a mission in America. **[1735:MISC/3]** **5** In England, stagecoaches are used for the first time to transport mail.	**1784**
1 Philip Freneau suggests that balloons could be used for travel to other planets.	**7** Charles-Augustin de Coulomb, Fr. physicist, establishes the relationship between electric	**1** Protests by reformers and better heating of houses weaken the arguments in favor of bun-	**4** London Society for the Establishment of Sunday Schools is founded. **5** Jean Pierre Blanchard	**1785**

America	Elsewhere	America	Elsewhere
Spain by Britain in 1783). **[1763:HIST/1]** **2** U.S. and Prussia sign treaty of commerce and friendship. **3** Thomas Jefferson becomes Minister to France; John Adams becomes Minister to Great Britain.	thwarting Emperor Joseph's plan to exchange the Austrian Netherlands for Bavaria. **[1783:HIST/6]** **5** Catherine II of Russia issues charter to the nobles, freeing them from taxation and giving them absolute control of their lands and peasants. **6** Isfahan is reestablished as Persia's capital. **[1728:HIST/1]** **7** Russians settle in the Aleutian Islands.	**2** Virginia commissions Houdon for a statue of George Washington. **3** First American edition of *Mother Goose Rhymes* is published by Isaiah Thomas. **4** Mathew Carey founds the *Pennsylvania Herald*.	a return to clean lines, bold simplicity, bright colors, and idealistic subjects. **6** Cowper publishes *The Task,* a poem in blank verse. **7** Kemble's portrayal of Macbeth establishes him as the leading actor on the English stage. **8** Rev. James Wilmot of Warwickshire claims that Shakespeare's plays were actually written by Eng. author Francis Bacon.
1786 **1** Britain tells U.S. it will not evacuate Great Lakes region until U.S. debts to Britain are paid. **2** Barbary pirates raid U.S. ships in the Mediterranean Sea. **3** Debt-ridden farmers in western Massachusetts, led by Daniel Shays, revolt against the state government, protesting high taxes, shortage of money, and insistent creditors. Shays's Rebellion is crushed (1787).	**4** Cornwallis becomes Governor-General of India. He makes administrative and judicial reforms. **5** France, with a huge public debt and a worsening financial situation, tries to initiate a direct land tax and other reforms. **6** Sultan of Kedah cedes Pinang Island, Malaysia, to the British East India Company.	**1** Mathew Carey founds the *Columbian Magazine,* an important periodical of the day. **2** *Lans Deo!,* a collection of sacred music for schools, is published in Worcester, Mass. It is the first American book printed with movable type (all previous books were engraved). **3** C. W. Peale opens exhibition gallery near his Philadelphia studio. It is considered the first art gallery in the U.S.	**4** Scot. poet Robert Burns receives immediate acclaim for *Poems, Chiefly in the Scottish Dialect.* **5** Mozart composes *Symphony in D (Prague Symphony)* and *The Marriage of Figaro,* the first of his great operas. **6** Fr. ballet dancer Jean Dauberval establishes comic ballet as a legitimate art form by choreographing his *La Fille mal gardée* and Vincenzo Galeotti's *Whims of Cupid and the Ballet Master.* **7** Dittersdorf composes the comic opera, *Doctor and Apothecary,* a popular example of a singspiel.
1787 **1** Congress enacts Northwest Ordinance, providing for government for the Northwest Territory east of the Mississippi River and north of the Ohio. Territory is to be divided into three to five states when population is large enough. **[1800:HIST/3]** **2** Congress calls for Constitutional Convention in Philadelphia. Delegates draft and	**3** Louis XVI of France calls the Assembly of Notables and asks its permission to tax the privileged classes. The Notables refuse; the Parliament of Paris demands the summoning of the Estates-General (national legislative body). **4** Austrian Netherlands is declared a Hapsburg possession. **5** Ottoman Empire declares	**1** George Washington attends a concert given by Alexander Reinagle, finest pianist in the U.S. at the time. Later, Washington engaged him to give music lessons to his daughter. **2** *Contrast* by Royall Tyler is performed. It is considered the first American comedy.	**4** Mozart composes the opera, *Don Giovanni.* **5** Fr. author Marquis de Sade, imprisoned for numerous crimes, writes *The Adversity of Virtue,* a book that establishes him as the first modern *écrivain maudit (damned writer).* He is later

Science & Technology		Miscellaneous		
America	**Elsewhere**	**America**	**Elsewhere**	
2 Thomas Jefferson publishes *Notes on the State of Virginia* with detailed sections on natural history. **3** John Greenwood, George Washington's dentist, begins using porcelain for false teeth. **4** Manasseh Cutler publishes *Account,* a highly regarded scientific study of American vegetables. **5** First issue of *Memoirs,* the journal of the American Academy of Arts and Sciences, is published. **6** Humphry Marshall, botanist, publishes *The American Grove,* a systematic catalog of trees.	charges (Coulomb's Law). **8** Cavendish determines that water is a compound, not an element.	dling, a custom which approves of a fully clothed, unmarried couple being in bed together. **2** Regular stagecoach routes linking New York City, Boston, and Philadelphia begin operations. **3** Continental Congress provides that a section of each township in the Western Reserve (northeast Ohio) be set aside for the support of public schools.	and John Jeffries cross the English Channel in a balloon from England to France. **[1783:SCI/4]**	
1 Rush suggests that some illnesses may be psychosomatic. He publishes "Observations on the Cause and Cure of the Tetanus." **2** Rittenhouse describes the molecular theory of magnetism and experiments with diffraction gratings and light dispersion.	**3** Claude-Louis Berthollet, Fr. chemist, discovers the chemical makeup of ammonia and introduces chlorine as a bleaching agent.	**1** First ice cream is made commercially in New York City. **2** Pennsylvania Hospital opens an outpatient dispensary, a forerunner of free clinics. **3** A "golf club" is established at Charleston, S.C. **[1887:MISC/4]**	**4** Mt. Blanc in the Alps is climbed for the first time.	**1786**
1 John Fitch launches first American steamboat on the Delaware River. **2** First American cotton mill opens in Beverly, Mass. **3** Casper Wistar and Samuel Latham Mitchill conduct independent experiments on evaporation. **4** College of Physicians of Philadelphia, a profes-	Wolfgang Amadeus Mozart, Austrian composer		**1** Flood in eastern India kills about 10,000 people. **2** Marylebone Cricket Club is founded in London. **3** Bubonic plague kills about 17,000 people in Algiers. **4** Edict of Versailles grants religious freedom and legal status to French Protestants.	**1787**

History and Politics		The Arts	
America	**Elsewhere**	**America**	**Elsewhere**
sign the Constitution of the United States, which is sent to the states for ratification (approval). Delaware, Pennsylvania, and New Jersey ratify it.	war on Russia. **6** China suppresses revolt in Formosa.	**3** One of the first non-religious song-books, *A Select Collection of the Most Favorite Scots Tunes,* is published in the U.S.	(1803) committed to an insane asylum where he convinces the other inmates to be actors in his plays.
1788			
1 Georgia, Connecticut, Massachusetts, Maryland, South Carolina, and New Hampshire ratify the Constitution, thereby achieving the necessary nine-state acceptance to put it into effect. Virginia and New York ratify it after heated debate. Rhode Island and North Carolina refuse to ratify it. Bill of Rights is recommended by anti-Federalists.	**2** Austria enters Russo-Turkish war as Russia's ally. **3** Gustavus III of Sweden invades Russian Finland. Danes invade Sweden but are repulsed. **4** Assembly of Notables fails to solve the financial crisis in France. King Louis XVI orders elections for the Estates-General. [1787:HIST/3] **5** Temporary insanity of King George III causes regency crisis in England for a year.	**1** The publication of *Miscellaneous Works of Freneau* establishes the author as the new country's greatest poet. **2** Francis Hopkinson, claiming himself to be the first native-born American composer, publishes *Seven Songs for the Harpsichord.* **3** *The Federalist* papers are published.	**4** Goethe publishes *Egmont,* a psychological tragedy, and develops a friendship with Schiller that results in literary collaboration until Schiller's death. **5** Jap. artist Kitagawa Utamaro publishes *Insects,* a book illustrated with his color prints. **6** Mozart composes his three greatest symphonies: *Jupiter Symphony, Symphony in E flat,* and *Symphony in G minor.*
1789			
1 Supporters of ratification of the Constitution form the Federalist Party. George Washington and John Adams (both Federalists) are chosen President and Vice President, respectively. **2** Federal Judiciary Act creates Supreme Court, 13 district courts, and three circuit courts. John Jay becomes first Chief Justice. **3** Congress creates Departments of State, War, and Treasury and adopts the first ten amendments to the Constitution (the Bill of Rights). **4** North Carolina ratifies the Constitution (Rhode Island ratifies it in 1790). [1787:HIST/2; 1788:HIST/1] **5** New York City becomes first capital of the U.S.	**6** Estates-General meets at Versailles, France. Third Estate (Commons) declares itself the National Assembly and swears not to disband until King Louis XVI has granted France a constitution. Third Estate votes with First (nobles) and Second (clergy) Estates despite Louis's opposition. Paris mob storms the Bastille (fortress and prison), symbol of royal power, to capture ammunition, setting off the French Revolution. National Assembly adopts the Declaration of the Rights of Man, abolishes France's feudal structure, and nationalizes church lands. Royal family is confined in the Tuileries Palace, Paris. **7** Austrians capture Belgrade; Russians advance to the Danube against the Turks. **8** Austrian Netherlands pro-	**1** *The Children's Magazine,* first periodical directed at this audience, is published in Hartford, Ct. **2** William Hill Brown writes *The Power of Sympathy,* often considered the first American novel. It deals with such topics as incest, desertion, and suicide. **3** Secular music is being published in Boston and Philadelphia. **4** William Selby, important figure in Boston's musical life, directs a concert of sacred music which includes voice and instruments.	**5** Blake publishes *Songs of Innocence,* a collection of his lyrical poems illustrated with his own etchings. **6** François Pascal Gérard, Fr. painter, completes "Joseph and His Brothers." **7** William Jones, Eng. linguist, completes the translation of *Sakuntala,* a 5th century Sanskrit work by Kàlidàsa, one of India's foremost poets. **8** Goethe publishes *Torquato Tasso,* a tragedy.

Science & Technology		Miscellaneous		
America	**Elsewhere**	**America**	**Elsewhere**	
sional medical organization, is founded. **5** James Rumsey invents a "jet-propelled" steamboat which shoots a stream of water through the stern (rear). **6** Benjamin Barton, Pa. physician, publishes *Observations* describing Indian tools found in Ohio.				
1 Mobs riot in New York and Boston to protest the use of cadavers (human bodies) for dissection in medical schools. **2** John Fraser and Thomas Walter publish *Flora Caroliniana,* a description of plants in the Carolinas. **3** *Cases and Observations,* America's first collection of medical papers, is published by the Medical Society of New Haven. **4** *Northwest America,* the first American ship built on the west coast, is launched.	**5** Andrew Meikle, Scot. millwright, patents a thrasher for removing husks from grain. **6** Lagrange publishes *Mécanique analytique,* a 100-year summary of advances in mechanics.	**1** Fire destroys more than 800 buildings in New Orleans, La. **2** Maryland and Virginia give land on the Potomac River to the Congress as the site for a federal capital.	**3** In London, John Walter, founder of the *Daily Universal Register* (1785), changes its name to *The Times.* **4** Rules for cricket are set down at the Marylebone Cricket Club in London.	**1788**
1 Christopher Colles publishes the first American road map. **2** John Churchman suggests that magnetic variation (true north vs. magnetic north) is due to small satellites moving around at the Poles, either in space or below the ground. **3** Edward Holyoke, physician, publishes life expectancy table showing that Americans live longer than Europeans.	**4** Martin Klaproth, Ger. chemist, discovers the elements uranium and zirconium. **5** W. Herschel builds the largest telescope of his time. **6** *Traité élémentaire de chimie* establishes Lavoisier as the father of modern chemistry.	**1** Methodists establish the Methodist Book Concern to publish religious material and to further Christian education. **2** Some suggestions for the style of address for the first U.S. president include "Excellency" and "Highness." **3** Thanksgiving Day is celebrated as a national holiday for the first time. **4** First organized temperance group is formed by 200 farmers in Connecticut, who pledge not to drink alcoholic beverages during farming season. **5** Political buttons first appear.	**6** Jeremy Bentham, Eng. philosopher and writer, publishes *An Introduction to the Principles of Morals and Legislation.* He states that the object of the law is to achieve the "greatest happiness of the greatest number."	**1789**

	History and Politics		The Arts	
	America	**Elsewhere**	**America**	**Elsewhere**
		claims its independence as Belgium; Austria regains control in 1790.		
1790	**1** Congress adopts financial programs of Secretary of the Treasury Alexander Hamilton. Federal government assumes national debt; Bank of the United States is proposed; revenue is raised by import tariffs and excise taxes. **2** Seat of government moves from New York City to Philadelphia, which becomes the new capital. **[1789:HIST/5]**	**3** National Assembly in France drafts a constitution, creating a limited monarchy with a unicameral legislature elected by qualified voters. **4** Sweden wins naval victory against Russia. Peace treaty is signed between the countries, leaving Finland and Karelia in Russian hands. **[1788:HIST/3]** **5** Tippoo Sahib battles against the British in India. **[1784:HIST/6]**	**1** Winthrop's diary is published in two volumes. **2** Noah Webster is instrumental in gaining passage of the Copyright Act. **3** Rufus Hathaway, Mass. itinerant painter, executes "Lady with Her Pets." **4** Mathew Carey publishes the first Roman Catholic Bible in the U.S.	**5** In Vienna, Mozart composes the comic opera, *Cosi fan tutte (All Women Are Like That)*. **6** Burns publishes *Tam O'Shanter,* an elegant narrative poem. **7** George Morland, Eng. painter, completes one of his best works, "Inside of a Stable."
1791	**1** Indians armed by the British attack settlements in the Northwest Territory. Indians defeat U.S. forces near the Wabash River in Ohio. **2** Vermont becomes 14th state, ending 14 years as an independent republic. **3** States ratify the Bill of Rights, which becomes part of the Constitution. **[1789:HIST/3]**	**4** Louis XVI, trying to flee France, is stopped and returned to Paris. He is forced to accept the constitution, which makes him a figurehead. **5** Austria, urged by Prussia, signs Treaty of Sistova, returning Belgrade to the Turks in exchange for part of northern Bosnia. **[1788:HIST/2]** **6** British pass Canada Constitutional Act, dividing Quebec into Upper Canada (present-day Ontario) and Lower Canada (present-day Quebec). **7** French suppress mulatto and Negro slave rebellion in Haiti.	**1** George Washington attends a concert of the St. Cecilia Society. **2** Franklin's *Autobiography* is published in Paris. **3** *The Death Song of an Indian Chief,* the first orchestral score published in the U.S., appears as an insert in the *Massachusetts Magazine.* **4** Pierre-Charles L'Enfant, engineer, completes the design of Washington, D.C. **5** The Théâtre de St. Pierre, the first opera house in the U.S., opens in New Orleans.	**6** Mozart conducts the first performance of his fairy-tale opera, *The Magic Flute.* Later that year, he dies before completing *Requiem (Mass for the Dead).* His student, Franz Xaver Süssmayr, completes the work by following Mozart's sketches and deathbed instructions. **7** Boswell publishes *The Life of Samuel Johnson,* one of the most popular biographies ever written. **8** Haydn composes *Surprise Symphony,* one of his so-called "London Symphonies" (No. 93–104). **9** Ital. composer Luigi Cherubini completes *Lodoïska,* a Fr. opera that marks the transition from solo to ensemble performances.
1792	**1** Republican Party (later Democratic-Republican) is formed to oppose the Federal-	**3** Russian army invades Poland, which is recovering from the partition of 1772. Prussia	**1** Robert B. Thomas founds *The Farmer's Almanac.*	**6** Claude-Joseph Rouget de Lisle composes *La Marseillaise,* the

Science & Technology		Miscellaneous		
America	**Elsewhere**	**America**	**Elsewhere**	
1 John Greenwood invents foot-powered dental drill. **2** Samuel Slater builds the first American steam-powered cotton-processing machines in Rhode Island, an event that marks the beginning of the Industrial Revolution in America. **3** Congress rejects a proposal by Thomas Jefferson, Secretary of State, that the U.S. adopt a decimal system of measurement (an early metric system). **4** First American patent is awarded to Samuel Hopkins for his process of manufacturing potash.	**5** Watt invents the pressure gauge.	**1** First national census sets U.S. population at 4 million; approximately 25% in New England, 25% in the Middle States, and 50% in the South. The largest city is Philadelphia with 42,000 inhabitants, followed in order by New York, Boston, Charleston, and Baltimore. **[1783:MISC/2]**	**2** Jews in France are granted civil liberties. **3** Eng. statesman Edmund Burke publishes *Reflections on the Revolution in France,* a passionate criticism of its excesses.	**1790**
1 William Bartram, ornithologist, publishes *Travels* describing and illustrating many birds of the Southeast. **2** Rumsey receives patents for his improved steam boiler. **3** Ellicot and Banneker survey Washington, D.C. **4** First successful American sugar refinery is opened in New Orleans by Antonio Méndez. **5** Anthracite coal is discovered in Pennsylvania.	**6** Klaproth discovers and names the element titanium.	**1** Congress passes the first internal revenue law. Fourteen revenue districts are set up, and a tax of 20 to 30 cents a gallon is put on distilled spirits. **2** First important turnpike is opened, a 62-mile road between Philadelphia and Lancaster, Pa. It is the first macadam road.	**3** Political philosopher and author Thomas Paine publishes in England the first part of *The Rights of Man,* supporting the French Revolution and calling for an overthrow of the English monarchy. **4** First general strike occurs in Hamburg, Germany.	**1791**
		Thomas Paine, U.S. patriot and writer		
1 Timothy Palmer builds Essex Merrimac Bridge in Massachusetts.	**5** Joseph Montgolfier invents the hydraulic ram.	**1** Congress passes a national conscription act to require "each and every	**5** Newspaper *The Northern Star* is first published in Belfast, Ireland.	**1792**

History and Politics		The Arts	
America	**Elsewhere**	**America**	**Elsewhere**

	History and Politics — America	History and Politics — Elsewhere	The Arts — America	The Arts — Elsewhere
	ists. Republicans led by Jefferson feel Federalists' policies favor urban financial and commercial groups and are harmful to the farmers. Republicans, who are pro-French, oppose a strong centralized government favored by the Federalists, who are pro-British. [1789:HIST/1; 1790:HIST/1] **2** Kentucky becomes 15th state.	invades the country in turn. **4** Treaty of Jassy ends Russo-Turkish war. Russia receives Oczakov and a boundary along the Dniester River, but gives back Moldavia and Bessarabia. **5** Francis II becomes the last Holy Roman Emperor. **6** France declares war on Austria and Prussia, which hope to restore Louis XVI to the throne. **7** Invading Austrian and Prussian forces are repulsed at the Battle of Valmy. France seizes the Austrian Netherlands.	**2** Barlow writes *Advice to the Privileged Orders,* in which he defends human rights over property rights. **3** Ralph Earl paints the portrait "Chief Justice Oliver Ellsworth and His Wife, Abigail Ellsworth." **4** Architect Charles Bulfinch designs the State House in Hartford, Ct., the oldest such building still standing. **5** The New Exhibition Room opens in Boston. Plays are presented under the guise of "moral lectures."	French national anthem. **7** Domenico Cimarosa, Ital. composer, stages his comic opera, *The Secret Marriage,* in Vienna. It is so successful that the Emperor orders an encore performance. **8** Beethoven begins studying with Haydn in Vienna.
1793	**1** Washington declares U.S. neutrality in British-French war. Washington and Adams are reelected President and Vice President, respectively. **2** Congress passes the Fugitive Slave Act, making it illegal to aid or to prevent the arrest of runaway Negro slaves.	**3** The monarchy is abolished in France. King Louis XVI and Queen Marie Antoinette are executed. **4** Britain, Holland, and Spain join Austria, Prussia, and Sardinia in the First Coalition against France. **5** Committee of Public Safety begins Reign of Terror as political measure in France. Many are guillotined for treason. New French armies are raised. **6** Second Partition of Poland gives most of Lithuania and western Ukraine to Russia; Prussia gets Danzig, Thorn, and Great Poland. Poland loses another third of its territory. [1772:HIST/5]	**1** An early anthology, *American Poems, Selected and Original,* draws mostly from the works of the "Connecticut Wits." **2** Ir.-Amer. architect James Hoban designs the White House. **3** George Washington lays the cornerstone of the U.S. Capitol building. **4** Gilbert Stuart paints "Mrs. Richard Yates." **5** Noah Webster founds the pro-Federalist newspaper *The American Minerva.*	**6** William Wordsworth, Eng. poet, publishes his first poems. **7** Nicolò Paganini, at the age of 11, debuts in Genoa as a violin virtuoso. **8** Goya completes two paintings, "Village Bullfight" and "The Madhouse." **9** David's "The Dead Marat" portrays the recently assassinated revolutionary leader. **10** Eng. artist John Flaxman prepares engravings to illustrate new editions of the *Iliad* and the *Odyssey.* **11** The Louvre (Paris) becomes a national gallery.
1794	**1** Neutrality Act forbids U.S. citizens to serve in the military forces of foreign countries and forbids the giving of supplies to foreign warships in U.S. ports. **2** Militia puts down Whiskey Rebellion in western Pennsylvania. Farmers protest the excise tax placed on liquor in 1791. **3** U.S. Army under Gen. Wayne defeats the Indians at Fallen Timbers. Indian resist-	**5** Thaddeus Kosciusko leads unsuccessful Polish national uprising against Russians and Prussians. **6** Rivalry between groups in France leads to executions of political leaders and their followers. French forces defeat the Austrians and advance south along the Rhine. **7** Britain suspends the Habeas Corpus Act as a measure against revolutionary agitation. [1679:HIST/3]	**1** James Hewitt writes *Tammany or the Indian Chief,* one of the first American operas. **2** Duncan Phyfe is listed as a cabinetmaker in the *New York Directory and Register.* By 1800, Phyfe had transmitted the elegant Sheraton, Regency, and French Directoire furniture styles to the	**4** Ann Ward Radcliffe, Eng. novelist, publishes *Mysteries of Udolpho,* a Gothic novel. **5** David, imprisoned in Luxembourg after the French revolution, paints "Self-Portrait" and "View of the Luxembourg Gardens." **6** Scot. portraitist Henry Raeburn paints "Sir John Sinclair."

Science & Technology		Miscellaneous		
America	**Elsewhere**	**America**	**Elsewhere**	
2 Chemical Society of Philadelphia, the world's first, is established. **3** Benjamin Waterhouse, R.I. physician, publishes *The Rise, Progress, and Present State of Medicine.* **4** James Mease, Pa. physician, reports on rabies.		free able-bodied white male citizen of the republic" to serve in the U.S. militia. **2** A mint is established in Philadelphia. **3** New York Stock Exchange is organized. **4** Twelve-hundred-mile Columbia River (in present-day Canada and Washington) is discovered by Captain Robert Gray of Boston in his ship *Columbia* on a fur-trading expedition.	**6** Eng. writer Mary Wollstonecraft publishes *Vindication of the Rights of Women.* **7** An earthquake in Hizen, Japan, kills about 15,000 people; another in Quito, Ecuador, kills 41,000. **8** Bubonic plague in Egypt; about 80,000 people die. **9** Baptist Missionary Society is founded in London. **10** David Mendoza becomes the English boxing champion.	
1 François Jean Pierre Blanchard, Fr. ballonist, makes first American free-flight from Philadelphia to New Jersey. **2** Work begins on the Middlesex Canal in Mass. (Completed in 1803.) **3** Work begins on the Santee Canal in South Carolina. (Completed in 1800.) **4** Eli Whitney invents the cotton gin. ("Gin" is short for *engine.*)	**5** Lamarck links fossils with similar living organisms. **6** John Dalton, Eng. chemist and physicist, publishes *Meteorological Observations and Essays.* Eli Whitney's cotton gin	**1** Yellow fever in Philadelphia kills 5000, the worst epidemic in any U.S. city up to this time. **2** Eli Whitney's cotton gin greatly increases cotton production and revives the dying slave economy of the South. **[1793:SCI/4]**	**3** English law gives recognition to insurance companies and friendly societies (mutual-aid groups). **4** Compulsory education from the age of six takes effect in France.	**1793**
1 David Wilkinson invents the sliding rest lathe for making delicate pieces of machinery. **2** Thomas Cooper publishes *Some Information Respecting America,* a report on the state of Science.	**3** Claude Chappe, Fr. engineer, invents the semaphore, a device for communicating via visual signals. **4** *Elements of Geometry,* by Fr. mathematician Adrien-Marie Legendre, becomes the standard geometry text throughout Europe and North America. **5** Erasmus Darwin, Eng. physician, suggests a the-	**1** Paine publishes the first part of *The Age of Reason,* which is popular with those who resent religious and political tyranny. **[1776:MISC/2; 1791:MISC/3]** **2** Postal rates are usually paid by the person receiving the mail: 6¢ up to 30 mi., 15¢ up to 200 mi., and 25¢ over 400 mi. **3** Use of powder on men's hair goes out of		**1794**

153

History and Politics		The Arts	
America	**Elsewhere**	**America**	**Elsewhere**
ance in the Northwest Territory is broken. **4** U.S. and Britain conclude Jay's Treaty. British promise to evacuate Great Lakes posts, but British interference with neutral U.S. ships continues.	**8** Belgium is occupied by the French.	U.S. **3** The New Theater in Philadelphia opens with an opera by Eng. composer Samuel Arnold.	**7** Burns composes "Auld Lang Syne." **8** Jean Paul (Johann Friedrich Richter), Ger. author, publishes *Hesperus*. **9** Goya, now deaf after a 2-year illness, paints "Procession of the Flagellants."
1795			
1 Naturalization Act makes five-year residence a requirement for citizenship. Members of the nobility entering the U.S. must give up titles. **2** Gen. Wayne signs Treaty of Greenville with the chiefs of 12 Indian tribes. Indians cede lands in the Northwest Territory to white settlers. **3** Treaty of San Lorenzo between Spain and the U.S. establishes Florida boundary and gives U.S. right of navigation on the Mississippi River.	**4** The Netherlands, occupied by the French, is reconstituted as the Batavian Republic. [1806:HIST/7] **5** French troops under Napoleon Bonaparte put down a royalist uprising. Napoleon becomes commander of the army in Italy. **6** All of Poland is divided among Russia, Prussia, and Austria in the Third Partition. Russia annexes Courland and receives the most territory. [1793:HIST/6] **7** Prussia makes peace, ceding left bank of the Rhine to France. Spain makes peace, too. [1793:HIST/4] **8** Third French Constitution forms Directory government, which continues war against Austria, Britain, and Sardinia. **9** British conquer Ceylon (now Sri Lanka) from the Dutch.	**1** The American Academy of Fine Arts holds its first exhibition in Philadelphia's Philosophical Hall. **2** C.W. Peale paints "The Staircase Group," famous trompe d'oeil, a style of photographically realistic painting. **3** Stuart executes famous portraits of Washington. The engraving of one of them is now on the $1 bill. **4** Bulfinch designs the Massachusetts State House.	**5** Goethe's *Wilhelm Meister's Apprenticeship* describes a young man's education and social development—a classic example of a novel in the *Bildungsroman* genre. [1821:ARTS/3] **6** Eng. author Robert Southey publishes *Poems*. **7** Wordsworth and Samuel Taylor Coleridge form a literary partnership. **8** Goya completes the portrait, "The Duchess of Alba." **9** Paris Conservatoire de Musique is established.
1796			
1 Tennessee becomes 16th state. **2** Washington's "Farewell Address" warns against U.S. involvement in foreign affairs. He refuses the Presidency for a third term. **3** John Adams (Federalist) is elected President; Thomas Jefferson (Democratic-Republican) is elected Vice President.	**4** Spain joins France in the war against Britain. **5** French forces under Napoleon win victories against the Austrians at Lodi and Arcole in northern Italy. Napoleon forces Sardinia to make peace, establishes the Lombard Republic, and obtains armistices from the King of Naples and the Pope. **6** Austrian forces defeat the French at Amberg and Wurzberg in southern Germany, forcing the French to retreat to the Rhine.	**1** The first complete works of Shakespeare are published in the U.S. **2** Joel Barlow writes *The Hasty Pudding*, the humorous epic poem for which he is best known. **3** The Haymarket Theater opens. It is the largest building in Boston at the time. **4** *The Archers; or, the Mountaineers of Switzerland,* an opera by Benjamin Carr, is produced in New York. It is considered the forerunner of the American musical play.	**6** In his production of *Zéphyr et Flore,* Fr. choreographer Charles Didelot introduces the use of "flights" as dancers glide through the air on wires. **7** Burney publishes *Camilla*. **8** Eng. novelist Matthew Gregory Lewis writes the Gothic romance, *Ambrosio, or the Monk*. **9** Thomas Morton, Eng. playwright, publishes *The Way to Get Married,* a sentimental comedy.

154

Science & Technology		Miscellaneous		
America	**Elsewhere**	**America**	**Elsewhere**	
	ory of evolution more than 50 years before his grandson, Charles, formulates his theory. **[1859:SCI/5]**	fashion after more than 100 years. Hair is still worn in a braid, tied with black ribbon.		
1 Thompson explains that clothes keep the body warm by trapping body-heated air near the skin. **2** Robert Fulton patents the first power-shovel for digging canals.	**3** Georges Cuvier, Fr. zoologist, publishes work concerning the classification of mammals.	**1** One of the earliest unions, the Federal Society of Journeymen Cordwainers (shoemakers), is organized in Philadelphia.	**2** Irish Parliament founds a Catholic seminary to prevent priests from traveling to the Continent for study where they might be influenced by revolutionary ideas. **[1789:HIST/6]** **3** Speenhamland Act goes into effect in England. To relieve the poor, wages are supplemented by aid from the government.	**1795**

State House in Boston designed by Charles Bulfinch

Science & Technology		Miscellaneous		
1 Fulton writes *Treatise on the Improvement of Canal Navigation.* **2** America's first suspension bridge is built across Jacob's Creek in Westmoreland, Pa., by James Finley. **3** Ellicot surveys the border between Florida and the United States.	**4** Edward Jenner, Eng. physician, inoculates a boy with matter from a cowpox lesion. The boy becomes immune to smallpox. **5** Saussure coins the term *geology* in his work *Travels in the Alps.*	**1** Billiards is played frequently in the South. **2** Travelers along the Philadelphia-Baltimore roads complain of chasms 6–10 ft. deep along the way, sometimes causing vehicles to overturn. It often takes a stagecoach 5 days to make the trip. **3** Congress authorizes the construction of Zane's Trace, a road from Wheeling (now in West Virginia) to Limestone (now Maysville), Ky. It becomes one of the main routes traveled by westbound settlers.	**4** Glasgow Missionary Society is founded in Scotland.	**1796**

History and Politics		The Arts	
America	Elsewhere	America	Elsewhere
		5 Houdon's marble statue of George Washington is set up in the state capitol at Richmond, Va.	
1797			
1 France, believing Jay's Treaty shows U.S. bias toward Britain, interferes with U.S. shipping. Three agents of Charles Maurice de Talleyrand try to extort money from U.S. commissioners in Paris (the XYZ Affair). [1794:HIST/4]	**2** Austria and France sign preliminary Peace of Leoben, which is confirmed by the Treaty of Campo Formio. Austria cedes Belgium to France and receives Venice, Istria, and Dalmatia. France keeps the Ionian Islands. Secret promises are made. **3** Napoleon creates the Cisalpine Republic and the Ligurian Republic in Italy. **4** Talleyrand becomes French Foreign Minister. France orders seizure of all neutral ships carrying British goods. **5** British defeat Spanish fleet off Cape St. Vincent, Portugal.	**1** The San Xavier del Bac church in Arizona is completed. It represents the height of Spanish-Mexican baroque style in the U.S. **2** *The Pocket Hymn Book,* used at revivalist camp meetings, is published in Philadelphia. It contains words but no music.	**3** Awaking from an opium-induced dream, Coleridge writes "Kubla Khan," a mysterious poem that is left unfinished. (Published in 1816.) **4** Goya completes two of his most famous paintings, "Maja desnuda" and "Maja vestida." **5** August Wilhelm von Schlegel, Ger. scholar, begins his translation of Shakespeare. **6** Haydn composes the *Emperor Quartet.* **7** Joseph Mallord William Turner, Eng. landscape painter, exhibits "Moonlight at Millbank."
1798			
1 Congress repeals all treaties with France and orders navy to capture French armed ships. **2** Federalist majority in Congress amends Naturalization Act to require a residence period of 14 years. Alien and Sedition Acts permit the arrest and deportation of any "dangerous" alien and restrict political opposition. **3** Virginia and Kentucky Resolutions, framed by James Madison and Thomas Jefferson respectively, declare the Alien and Sedition Acts unconstitutional; states may nullify acts (states' rights).	**4** French capture Rome and proclaim revolutionary Roman Republic. Pope moves to southern France. **5** French invade Switzerland, create Helvetic Republic, and annex Geneva. **6** Napoleon plans to attack the British Empire by way of Egypt. He seizes Malta and Alexandria. He defeats the Mamelukes at the Battle of the Pyramids and takes Cairo. **7** Horatio Nelson, Brit. admiral, destroys the French fleet in Abukir Bay, thus cutting Napoleon's forces off from Europe. **8** Britain, Austria, Russia, Portugal, Naples, and the Ottoman Empire form Second Coalition against France. [1793:HIST/4]	**1** Charles Brockden Brown, "Father of the American Novel," publishes *Wieland,* which deals with mystery, terror, and crime. He also publishes *Alcium,* considered the first feminist novel. **2** Joseph Hopkinson writes the patriotic song "Hail Columbia." **3** *The Columbian Songster and Free Mason's Pocket Companion,* one of the first collections of secular music, is published in Boston.	**4** Coleridge's "The Rime of the Ancient Mariner" and Wordsworth's "Lines Composed a Few Miles Above Tintern Abbey" are included in *Lyrical Ballads,* a collection of works by the two poets. **5** Haydn composes one of his greatest oratorios, *The Creation.* **6** Charles Lamb's most famous poem, "The Old Familiar Faces," is included in *Blank Verse,* a collection of poems published jointly by him and Charles Lloyd. **7** Southey writes *The Battle of Blenheim,* one of his most popular ballads.
1799			
1 Settlement of the Mississippi Territory, created by Congress in 1798, is hampered	**3** Napoleon's invasion of Syria is repelled by the Turks at Acre. Napoleon, back in	**1** Gracie Mansion, now the official residence of the New York	**4** Friedrich von Schlegel, Ger. writer, publishes the semiautobio-

Science & Technology		Miscellaneous		
America	**Elsewhere**	**America**	**Elsewhere**	
1 Mitchill publishes *The Medical Repository,* America's first medical magazine. **2** James Woodhouse publishes *The Young Chemist's Pocket Companion.* **3** Charles Newbold patents America's first cast iron plow amid reports that the iron would poison the soil and increase the weeds. **4** Thompson designs a vacuum bottle.	**5** Caroline Herschel, Eng. astronomer, discovers her eighth comet in eleven years. **6** Louis-Nicolas Vauquelin, Fr. chemist, discovers the element chromium. **7** The Royal Society rejects Jenner's smallpox vaccination technique.		**1** First copper pennies are minted in England, and the first one-pound notes (paper money) are issued. **[1613:MISC/2]**	**1797**

Maja Vestida by Goya

Science & Technology		Miscellaneous		
1 Whitney invents a milling machine to produce muskets with standard and interchangeable parts. He is later hailed as the "Father of Mass Production." **2** Rush publishes the five-volume *Medical Inquiries and Observations.* **3** Thompson discovers convection currents (heat) and publishes *Enquiry Concerning the Source of Heat Which is Excited by Friction.* **4** Fulton invents the *Nautilus,* a hand-operated, four-man submarine.	**5** Vauquelin discovers the element beryllium. **6** Aloys Senefelder, Ger. author, invents lithography. **7** Jenner publishes the results of his successful inoculation procedure and soon gains worldwide recognition.	**1** Yellow fever epidemic kills 2086 people in New York City.	**2** Eng. economist Thomas Malthus publishes *Essays on the Principle of Population,* his most influential work.	**1798**
1 Nathaniel Bowditch revises J. H. Moore's error-filled *The New Practi-*	**4** Alexander von Humboldt, Ger. scientist, leaves on a five-year tour	**1** First recorded use of the word "scab" comes in the strike of shoemakers	**3** Russia grants the Russian-American Company a monopoly of trade in	**1799**

	History and Politics		The Arts	
	America	**Elsewhere**	**America**	**Elsewhere**
	by hostile Indians and by Spanish control of the Gulf ports. **2** Pres. Adams avoids war with France by reopening negotiations; pro-war group of Federalists, led by Hamilton, bitterly attacks Adams's friendly policy toward France.	Egypt, defeats invading Turks and British at Abukir. He returns to France, overthrows the Directory, and sets up the Consulate, with himself as First Consul. **4** Austrian forces defeat the French at Stockach, Magnano, and Zürich. Russo-Austrian forces win victories at Cassano, Trebbia, and Novi. Disunity brings Russia's withdrawal from the coalition. **5** British suppress rebellion of the United Irishmen who seek independence for Ireland. **6** Russo-Turkish fleet seizes the Ionian Islands, which are reclaimed by France in 1807.	City mayor, is constructed in upper Manhattan. **2** The quarterly *American Review and Literary Journal* begins publication. **3** C.B. Brown publishes two novels: *Ormond* describes a woman who, through her personal resources, saves her own life; *Edgar Huntly,* the first mystery novel in an American setting, introduces the Indian as a character.	graphical novel, *Lucinde.* **5** Goya completes "The Caprices," a series of 82 satirical etchings that includes a self-portrait. **6** Schiller's historical trilogy, *Wallenstein,* is published. **7** Turner paints "Battle of the Nile." **8** After his release from prison, David reestablishes his reputation with "The Intervention of the Sabine Women," a painting often incorrectly called "Rape of the Sabines."
1800	**1** Seat of government moves from Philadelphia to Washington, D.C., which becomes the new capital. **2** Thomas Jefferson and Aaron Burr (Democratic-Republicans) run for President against John Adams and Charles Pinckney (Federalists). Because candidates for President and Vice President are not separately nominated, Jefferson and Burr end in a tie with 73 votes each in the electoral college. **[1801:HIST/1]** **3** Congress enacts a law dividing the Northwest Territory into two territories, Indiana and Ohio. **[1787:HIST/1]**	**4** By secret treaty, Spain cedes the Louisiana Territory to France. **5** Napoleon defeats the Austrians at the Battle of Marengo and conquers Italy. French forces seize Munich and defeat the Austrians at the Battle of Hohenlinden. French advance on Vienna. **6** British capture Malta. East India concludes political and commercial treaty with the Shah of Persia.	**1** The Library of Congress is founded. **2** Rembrandt Peale paints a portrait of Thomas Jefferson. **3** Benjamin Carr begins the weekly *Musical Journal.* **4** C.B. Brown publishes *Arthur Mervyn,* a realistic depiction of the yellow fever epidemic in Philadelphia.	**5** Beethoven composes *Symphony No. 1 in C Major.* **6** Novalis (Friedrich von Hardenberg), publishes *Hymnen an die Nacht,* six prose poems written in 1797 after the death of his fiancée. **7** Goya completes his most famous group portrait, "Family of Charles IV." **8** Cherubini composes *Les Deux Journées,* his greatest opera. **9** Fr. composer François-Adrien Boieldieu completes *Le Caliphe de Bagdad,* one of his early romantic operas. **10** Fr. writer Anne Louise Germaine de Staël publishes *On Literature.* **11** Morton's comedy, *Speed the Plough,* introduces Mrs. Grundy, a character who has given English the name for a narrow-minded prude.
1801	**1** House of Representatives chooses Jefferson for President and Burr for Vice President.	**4** United Kingdom of Great Britain and Ireland is established with one parliament and one monarch.	**1** Crèvecoeur publishes work describing his travels through Pennsylvania and New	**5** Fr. writer François René de Chateaubriand publishes *Atala,* a novel that marks the start

Science & Technology		Miscellaneous		
America	**Elsewhere**	**America**	**Elsewhere**	

cal Navigator.
[1802:SCI/2]
2 Alexander Hamilton describes the state of American industry in *Report on the Subject of Manufactures.*
3 John Beale Bordley, agriculturist, publishes *Essays and Notes on Husbandry and Rural Affairs,* a book that deals with the management of crops and livestock.

of the Spanish colonies.

in Philadelphia. The term of abuse refers to workers hired to replace strikers.
[1795:MISC/1]
2 A 14-year-old boy graduates from Rhode Island College. Intellectual ability among children is not uncommon during colonial times. Infants of 3 are sometimes taught to read Latin as soon as they are taught English. Timothy Dwight (President of Yale College) was able to read the Bible at age 4.

Alaska.
4 Church Missionary Society is founded in London.
5 Rosetta stone, found near Rosetta (Egypt), makes possible the deciphering of hieroglyphics.
6 Carcass of extinct mammoth, a large elephantlike mammal, is discovered preserved in Siberia.

---

1 Waterhouse gives America's first smallpox vaccination to his son.
2 Semaphore communication system is set up on a series of "telegraph hills" between Boston and Martha's Vineyard, Mass.
3 Fireboats are used in New York Harbor.

4 W. Herschel discovers infrared light.
5 Volta invents the electric battery.
6 Henry Bell, Scot. engineer, designs the first European steamship.
7 Marie-François Bichat, Fr. physiologist, studies the changes that occur in human organs following death.

1 Second national census shows a population of 5.3 million, including more than 800,000 slaves.
[1790:MISC/1]
2 William Young of Philadelphia is the first shoemaker in America to make different shoes for the right and left feet.
3 4-tined forks come into common use in American homes at this time, replacing 2- or 3-tined forks.
4 John Chapman ("Johnny Appleseed") visits pioneer settlements in the Ohio Valley, distributing religious material and apple seeds.

5 India's population is estimated at 130 million, and Japan's at about 29 million.
6 Socialism develops in Europe as a reaction to the wretched conditions of industrial workers.
7 Welsh social reformer Robert Dale Owen begins social reform in the mills of England.
8 Postal service for letters is introduced in Berlin.
9 Yellow fever epidemic kills about 80,000 people in Spain.

1800

Ludwig van Beethoven, German composer

---

1 Robert Hare, Pa. chemist, invents a blowpipe (cutting torch) that uses oxygen and hydrogen

2 Lamarck devises a classification system for invertebrates.
3 Johann Bode, Ger. as-

1 *New York Evening Post* is established.
2 American Company of Booksellers is organized

6 Ger. philosophers Georg Hegel and Friedrich Schelling publish their *Critical Journal of*

1801

History and Politics		The Arts	
America	**Elsewhere**	**America**	**Elsewhere**
2 Pasha of Tripoli declares war on the U.S., demanding that U.S. ships pay more tribute to the pirates of the Barbary States (Morocco, Algiers, Tunis, and Tripoli). Jefferson sends naval ships to Mediterranean area. **3** John Marshall becomes Chief Justice of the Supreme Court. [1803:HIST/3]	**5** British fleet under Nelson defeats the Danes, allies of Napoleon, near Copenhagen. **6** Treaty of Lunéville between France and Austria practically ends the Holy Roman Empire. France also makes peace with Naples and Portugal. **7** Czar Paul I of Russia is assassinated and succeeded by his son, Alexander I. **8** British force the French to surrender in Egypt.	York. **2** J.M. Sewall publishes *Miscellaneous Poems.* **3** John Brewster, Jr. paints "Sarah Prince," which portrays a young girl at a piano. **4** Architect Benjamin H. Latrobe transmits the Greek revival form of architecture to the U.S. with his design of the Bank of Pennsylvania.	of the French romantic movement. **6** Beethoven composes *Piano Sonata in C Sharp Minor* (Moonlight Sonata) and *Die Geschöpfe des Prometheus,* his only ballet. **7** Schiller publishes *Die Jungfrau von Orleans,* the story of Joan of Arc. **8** Paganini begins composing a series of 24 *capricci* for solo violin (–1807). **9** Haydn completes *The Seasons,* one of his greatest oratorios. **10** Canova sculpts "Perseus with Medusa's Head."
1802 **1** Act of Congress recognizes Tripolitan War against the U.S. and empowers President to arm merchant ships. Act does not explicitly declare war but states the intent of the U.S. to protect its ships at sea. **2** Government repeals excise taxes, the Naturalization Act, and the Judiciary Act (which had allowed Pres. Adams to appoint more than 200 "midnight judges" just before he left office). Alien and Sedition Acts are allowed to expire. [1798:HIST/2] **3** Georgia cedes its western territory to the U.S.	**4** France, Spain, and Britain sign the Treaty of Amiens by which all conquests are restored to France. Malta is to be restored to the Knights Hospitalers. France also signs a treaty restoring Egypt to the Ottoman Empire. **5** Napoleon becomes President of the Italian Republic and First Consul for life in France. He annexes Piedmont, Parma, Piacenza, and Elba. **6** French suppress Negro rebellion led by Haitian François Dominique Toussaint L'Ouverture on the island of Hispaniola.	**1** Benjamin West paints "Death on the Pale Horse."	**2** Sir Walter Scott publishes *Minstrelsy of the Scottish Border,* a collection of ancient British poetry. **3** Literary critics Francis Jeffrey (Scot.), Henry Brougham (Scot.), and Sydney Smith (Eng.) establish the *Edinburgh Review,* a powerful and influential periodical known for its frank critiques. **4** Beethoven composes *Symphony No. 2 in D Major.* **5** Classicist Empire style dominates European art and architecture.
1803 **1** Ohio becomes 17th state. **2** U.S. negotiates the Louisiana Purchase from France. Napoleon sells the Louisiana Territory (828,000 sq. mi.) to the U.S. for $15 million. ($3.75 million of this sum covers debt to U.S. citizens owed by France and assumed by the U.S.) **3** Supreme Court under	**4** Robert Emmet leads Irish patriots in unsuccessful uprising against English rule. He is tried for treason and hanged. **5** Britain refuses to restore Malta to the Knights Hospitalers, thereby resuming war with France. [1802:HIST/4] **6** France captures Hanover, part of the Holy Roman Empire, and threatens to invade	**1** New York City Hall, a classic example of Georgian architecture, is constructed.	**2** Thomas Sheraton, Eng. furniture maker, publishes *The Cabinet Dictionary,* a collection of his designs.

160

| Science & Technology | | Miscellaneous | | |
America	Elsewhere	America	Elsewhere	
to produce a high-temperature flame.	tronomer, publishes *Uranographia,* an atlas of stars and nebulae. 4 Cavendish determines the Earth's density by the method later known as the Cavendish experiment. 5 Bichat publishes *Anatomie générale.*	in New York City by Mathew Carey. 3 "Plan of Union" by Congregationalists and Presbyterians permits their ministers to serve in each other's churches, helping to spread religion to scattered frontier settlements. 4 Complete skeleton of a mastodon is unearthed on a New York farm. 5 Josiah Bent popularizes hardwater crackers made in his factory in Milton, Mass.	*Philosophy.* 7 Bank of France is founded. 8 Italy's population is 17.2 million; Spain's 10.5 million; Britain's 10.4 million. London's population is 864,000; Paris' 547,000; Vienna's 231,000; and Berlin's 183,000. 9 Union Jack becomes the official flag of the United Kingdom of Great Britain and Ireland. 10 Catholics are excluded from voting in the United Kingdom and Ireland.	
1 John C. Stevens, N.Y. inventor, builds a screw-driven steamboat. 2 Bowditch publishes *The New American Practical Navigator,* the "bible" of navigation. 3 James Smith, Md. physician, opens a clinic that gives free smallpox vaccinations to the poor. 4 Abel Porter, Conn. metalworker, opens America's first brass rolling mill in Waterbury, Conn.	5 Franz-Joseph Gall, Ger. physiologist, is punished for practicing phrenology (the determination of intelligence by features of the skull). 6 Joseph-Louis Gay-Lussac, Fr. chemist, demonstrates that all gases increase by the same percentage of their volume when subjected to the same increase in temperature. 7 Lamarck coins the term *biology.* 8 Sir Charles Bell, Eng. anatomist, publishes engravings of the brain. 9 H.W.M. Olbers, Ger. astronomer, discovers the asteroid Pallas.	1 Merino sheep are brought from Spain by Col. David Humphreys, establishing the industry of raising sheep for fine wool. 2 Congress establishes a military academy at West Point, N.Y. 3 New York State prohibits public horse races. The only races held are by private jockey clubs. 4 First hotel, the Union Hotel, is built at Saratoga, N.Y. by Gideon Putnam. 5 First chess book, *Chess Made Easy,* is published in Philadelphia.	6 Bentham publishes *Civil and Penal Legislation,* which introduces the theory of utilitarianism. 7 Englishman John Truter and William Somerville explore Bechuanaland (now Botswana), Africa. 8 Yellow fever epidemic kills about 29,000 of Napoleon's soldiers in Santo Domingo (Dominican Republic). 9 First important labor law protecting children, the Health and Morals Act, is enacted in Great Britain. 10 French system of public instruction is reformed. Lycées (secondary schools maintained by the state) are erected.	1802
1 John C. Otto, Pa. physician, publishes a detailed description of hemophilia. 2 John James Audubon, ornithologist, performs first banding studies on wild American birds. 3 Barton publishes *Elements of Botany.*	4 Dalton devises a table of elements. 5 Jöns Jacob Berzelius, Swed. chemist, discovers the element cerium. 6 William H. Wollaston, Eng. scientist, discovers the element palladium.	1 John Sibley sets out to explore the Red River as far as the present site of Shreveport, La. 2 A doctor, setting up practice, advertises that he would be glad to wait on the public but that his first concern is for "his friends in particular." 3 Explorers Meriwether	4 Henry Shrapnel, Eng. soldier, invents the shell case shot, in which a small explosive charge causes the bullets to scatter.	1803

History and Politics		The Arts	
America	**Elsewhere**	**America**	**Elsewhere**
Chief Justice Marshall declares unconstitutional and void an act of Congress for the first time (*Marbury* v. *Madison*). Decision establishes the principle of judicial review.	Britain. **7** Through various annexations, the British extend control over most of southern India and put down hostilities. **8** Napoleon's Act of Mediation establishes a Swiss confederation of 19 cantons.		

1804

America	Elsewhere	America	Elsewhere
1 U.S. expedition under Stephen Decatur enters the harbor of Tripoli and destroys the U.S. frigate *Philadelphia,* which had been captured by the Tripolitans. **2** Extremists plan separate northern confederacy in alliance with Aaron Burr. Plan fails when Hamilton blocks Burr's attempt to be governor of New York. Hamilton also attacks Burr's character. Burr challenges Hamilton to a pistol duel, in which Hamilton is fatally wounded. **3** Jefferson is reelected President in the first election with separate balloting for President and Vice President. George Clinton is elected Vice President. They are Democratic-Republicans.	**4** Plot to murder Napoleon fails. French Senate and Tribunate proclaim Napoleon Emperor; Napoleon crowns himself before the Pope. **5** Francis II assumes the title Emperor of Austria as Francis I. [1792:HIST/5] **6** Spain, allied with France, declares war on Britain. **7** Russians fail to capture the city of Yerevan from the Persians. Fighting continues in northwest Persia. **8** Negroes and mulattoes defeat a large French army in Haiti (western part of Hispaniola). Haiti declares its independence. [1802:HIST/6] **9** Karageorge leads the Serbs in a successful revolt against the cruel Janissaries (elite Turkish army corps). [1826:HIST/4]	**1** Washington Allston, leading figure in American Romantic art, paints "The Deluge."	**2** Schiller writes *Wilhelm Tell,* a play based on the legendary 15th-century Swiss hero. **3** Nearly deaf, Beethoven composes two of his greatest works, *Symphony No. 3 in E Flat Major ("Eroica")* and *Piano Sonata in F Major ("Appassionata").* **4** Turner completes the watercolor "The Great Falls of the Reichenbach" and opens a private gallery in London.

1805

America	Elsewhere	America	Elsewhere
1 Michigan Territory is formed out of the northern part of the Indiana Territory. [1800:HIST/3] **2** U.S. forces capture the seaport of Derna in North Africa, a stronghold of the Barbary pirates. Peace treaty ends the Tripolitan War; U.S. prisoners are ransomed, and Tripoli grants free passage to U.S. ships in the Mediterranean. U.S. and Tunis sign treaty. However, piracy by the Barbary States continues until 1815.	**3** Napoleon proclaims himself King of Italy and annexes Genoa. **4** Britain, Austria, Russia, and Sweden form Third Coalition against France. **5** Napoleon defeats the Austrians at Ulm and the combined Russian and Austrian forces at the Battle of Austerlitz. The Russians retreat, and the Austrians sign the harsh Treaty of Pressburg, ceding much territory to France, Italy, and Bavaria. **6** British under Lord Nelson defeat the combined French and Spanish fleets at the Battle of Trafalgar. **7** Ottoman Sultan appoints Muhammad Ali viceroy of Egypt.	**1** Charles W. Peale is instrumental in founding the Pennsylvania Academy of the Fine Arts.	**2** Scott publishes "The Lay of the Last Minstrel," his best-known poem. **3** Turner's "The Shipwreck" exemplifies a new, more powerful romanticism in landscape paintings. **4** *Fidelio,* Beethoven's only opera, is performed in Vienna.

Science & Technology		Miscellaneous		
America	**Elsewhere**	**America**	**Elsewhere**	
		Lewis and William Clark begin exploring lands west of the Mississippi River. They follow the Ohio, Missouri, and Columbia Rivers to the Pacific Ocean and return by a similar route, a total of 8000 mi.		
1 William C. Bond, astronomer, designs a ship's chronometer. **2** Bananas are imported from Cuba.	**3** Olbers observes the asteroid Juno. **4** Wollaston discovers the element rhodium. **5** Friedrich William Bessel, Ger. astronomer, calculates the orbit of Halley's comet. **6** Thomas Bewick, Eng. printmaker, illustrates *A History of British Birds*. **7** Humboldt returns from South America with a wealth of botanical, geological, and meteorological data. **[1799:SCI/4]**	**1** "Coonskin Libraries" founded in Marietta, Ohio, come into being when settlers along the Ohio River barter coonskins for books from Boston merchants.	**2** British and Foreign Bible Society is founded in London. **3** Laws in France are revised and unified with the establishment of the Code Napoleon. It influences civil codes of most countries of continental Europe and Latin America in the 19th century.	**1804**
1 Richard Gallagher, Conn. scientist, describes "Wildoc syndrome," later called "shell shock" or "battle fatigue."	**2** Gay-Lussac proves that water is composed of two parts hydrogen and one part oxygen. **3** Cuvier's *Lessons on Comparative Anatomy* establishes comparative anatomy as a science. **4** Pierre-André Latreille, Fr. zoologist, publishes *Comprehensive Natural History of Crustaceans and Insects*.	**1** German pietist group, Harmonists, also known as Rappites after their leader George Rapp, establish a communal settlement near Pittsburgh, Pa., which they call Harmony. **2** First American to win distinction as a boxer is Bill Richmond, a Negro, who knocks out Jack Holmes (Tom Tough) in the 26th round in England. Richmond never fought in the U.S. **3** First important shipment of ice from New England is made by Frederick Tudor, who exports it to Martinique (West Indies). Shipping ice to the East, especially India, becomes a profitable business.	**6** Scot. explorer Mungo Park begins his 2nd exploration of the Niger River in Africa.	**1805**

	History and Politics		The Arts	
	America	Elsewhere	America	Elsewhere
1806	**1** Jefferson protests Britain's interference with and France's restrictions on neutral U.S. shipping. Congress passes Nonimportation Act, forbidding the purchase of British goods. The act is suspended. **2** Burr plans to establish an independent republic in the Southwest. Plot fails when Pres. Jefferson orders his arrest. **[1804:HIST/2]**	**3** Napoleon forms the Confederation of the Rhine (league of German states), forcing Francis II to renounce the title of Holy Roman Emperor. Empire formally ends. **[1804:HIST/5]** **4** Prussia declares war on France. French armies defeat the Prussians at Jena and Auerstädt. Napoleon occupies Berlin. **5** British blockade French ports. Napoleon issues Berlin Decree, initiating Continental System (closure of Continental ports to British ships). **6** France and Saxony make peace. **7** Napoleon transforms Batavia into the Kingdom of Holland. **[1795:HIST/4]**	**1** Noah Webster publishes his *Compendious Dictionary of the English Language,* in which he establishes *i* and *j* and *u* and *v* as separate letters. **2** John Trumbull, architect (first cousin of the poet), designs the Congregational Meeting House in Lebanon, Ct., his only architectural work still standing. **3** Latrobe designs his greatest work, the Basilica of the Assumption of the Blessed Virgin Mary (Baltimore), the first Roman Catholic cathedral in the U.S.	**4** Ann and Jane Taylor publish *Rhymes for the Nursery,* a collection that includes Jane's "Twinkle, Twinkle, Little Star." **5** Fr. sculptor Clodion (Claude Michel) begins work on the Arc de Triomphe, Paris. **6** At the age of 14, Ital. composer Gioacchino Antonio Rossini produces his first opera, *Demetrio a Polibio.* **7** Beethoven composes *Symphony No. 4 in B Flat Major* and *Violin Concerto.*
1807	**1** British frigate *Leopard* attacks U.S. frigate *Chesapeake;* four seamen, alleged to be British subjects, are seized. Jefferson, opposed to war, orders British warships to leave U.S. waters. **2** Burr is tried for treason and acquitted. **[1806:HIST/2]** **3** Congress passes Embargo Act, which prohibits U.S. trade with any foreign country. Act tries to force Britain and France to remove restrictions on and stop interference with U.S. trade. New England merchants oppose Act as scheme to deprive them of business.	**4** Combined Russian and Prussian armies fight the French in the indecisive Battle of Eylau. French defeat the Russians at the Battle of Friedland. **5** Napoleon concludes the Treaties of Tilsit with the Czar and the King of Prussia. Russia recognizes the Grand Duchy of Warsaw and other territorial changes; Prussia loses half its territory. **6** French army occupies Portugal. Portugal's royal family flees to Brazil. **7** Russia fights the Ottoman Turks for control of Moldavia and Wallachia.	**1** Joel Barlow publishes *The Columbiad,* an enlarged version of *Vision of Columbus.* **2** Robert Mills designs the wings of Independence Hall, Philadelphia. **3** Washington Irving and James Paulding found *Salmagundi,* a periodical which satirizes local events.	**4** Charles and Mary Lamb publish *Tales From Shakespeare,* a collection of children's stories based on the plays. **5** Eng. poet Lord Byron (George Gordon) publishes *Hours of Idleness,* a collection of poems that draws savage criticism in the *Edinburgh Review.* **[1809:ARTS/5]** **6** Wordsworth writes "Ode on Intimations of Immortality."

Science & Technology		Miscellaneous		
America	**Elsewhere**	**America**	**Elsewhere**	
		4 U.S. general Zebulon Pike explores the Upper Mississippi River. **5** Free School Society (later Public School Society) is founded in New York City as a private charitable group interested in establishing an alternative to the pauper school system.		
1 Bowditch publishes accurate charts of Mass. harbors. Noah Webster and his *Compendious Dictionary*	**2** Morphine becomes the first drug to be isolated from a plant, through the work of Ger. chemist F.W.A. Sertürner.	**1** Pike explores the southwestern territory, traveling through Kansas, southern Nebraska, Colorado, and New Mexico. He first sees Pike's Peak on this trip. **2** First horse to trot a mile in under 3 minutes is "Yankee," covering the distance in 2 min. 59 sec. **3** Trial of the striking Philadelphia cordwainers (shoemakers) is the first prosecution of a trade union in a criminal conspiracy for the purpose of increasing their wages. The union is disbanded. **4** Gas street lighting is introduced by David Melville, who sets up lamps on a street in Newport, R.I.	**5** British cotton industry employs 90,000 factory workers and 184,000 handloom weavers.	**1806**
1 Fulton launches the *Clermont,* a 150-ft.-long steamboat that travels 150 miles up the Hudson River in 32 hours. **2** Huge meteor lands in Weston, Conn. **[1815:SCI/1]** **3** Barton publishes his studies of American natural history and makes suggestions for further scientific research.	**4** Sir Humphry Davy, Eng. chemist, discovers the elements potassium and sodium.	**1** Boston Athenaeum is founded. It combines the activities of a subscription library limited to commercial, academic, and professional citizens of Boston, a social meeting place for the group, a reference library, and a museum of natural history. **2** Eli Terry and Seth Thomas of Connecticut begin the manufacture in quantity of clocks with interchangeable parts.	**3** Napoleon, Emperor of France, introduces a commercial law code into France. **4** First Ascot Gold Cup in horse racing is held in England.	**1807**

	History and Politics		The Arts	
	America	**Elsewhere**	**America**	**Elsewhere**
1808	**1** Congress prohibits the importation of African slaves. **2** Congress tries to enforce the Embargo Act. U.S. farmer and merchant opposition results in smuggling and other illegal trade. France confiscates U.S. ships and cargoes in European ports. **3** James Madison is elected President, and George Clinton is reelected Vice President on the Democratic-Republican ticket.	**4** French invade Spain and capture Barcelona and Madrid. Napoleon's brother Joseph Bonaparte is made King of Spain. Spanish rise in revolt. **5** British land in Portugal and defeat the French at Vimeiro. French, British, and Portuguese negotiate the Convention of Cintra, by which the French surrender Lisbon. **6** Congress of Erfurt between Napoleon and Alexander I renews Franco-Russian alliance concluded at Tilsit in 1807. **7** Napoleon's occupation of Spain encourages the birth of separatist movements in Mexico and South American countries.		**1** Beethoven composes his *Fifth Symphony* (*No. 5 in C Minor*) and *Pastoral Symphony* (*No. 6 in F Major*). **2** Schiller convinces Goethe to complete the first part of *Faust*. **3** Scott publishes *Marmion*, a poem in six cantos. **4** Blake completes *Milton*, an epic poem. **5** The art world is divided on the bold and original use of light in "The Cross on the Mountain," an oil painting by Ger. artist Kaspar David Friedrich.
1809	**1** Congress passes Nonintercourse Act, repealing the Embargo Act and resuming trade with all countries except France and Britain. **2** Illinois Territory is formed from the western part of the Indiana Territory. [1800:HIST/3] James Madison, 4th U.S. President	**3** British and Portuguese forces under Arthur Wellesley (later Duke of Wellington) drive the French out of Portugal, invade Spain, and with the help of a Spanish army defeat the French at Talavera. **4** Napoleon captures Vienna, is defeated at Aspern, and defeats the Austrians at Wagram. By the Peace of Schonbrunn, Austria loses territory to France, Russia, Bavaria, and the Grand Duchy of Warsaw. **5** Russia conquers Finland (ruled by Sweden) and annexes it. **6** Napoleon annexes the Papal States and imprisons Pope Pius VII. **7** Treaty of Amritsar between Britain and the Sikhs establishes the northwest boundary of the East India Company's territories in India.	**1** Irving publishes *History of New York . . . by Diedrich Knickerbocker,* the first American comic literature. **2** Thomas Sully, leading portraitist of the period, studies under West in England. **3** Royall Tyler publishes the satire *The Yankee in London.*	**4** Beethoven composes *Piano Concerto No. 5 in E Flat Major* (The Emperor). **5** Byron answers the *Edinburgh Review* with biting satire in *English Bards and Scotch Reviewers.* **6** Cherubini's *Mass in F Major* marks his decision to compose church music.
1810	**1** Macon's Bill No. 2 repeals restrictions on trade with France and Britain. It states that if either nation removes its restrictions on U.S. trade, the President will break off trade with the other. Madi-	**3** Klemens von Metternich, Foreign Minister of Austria, arranges the marriage of Archduchess Marie Louise, daughter of Francis I of Austria, to Napoleon. **4** Napoleon annexes Hol-	**1** I. Thomas publishes the 2-volume *History of Printing in America.* **2** *Repository of Sacred Music,* an important source of U.S. folk hymnody, is published	**4** Beethoven composes music to Goethe's *Egmont* (1778). **5** Scott publishes the poem, "The Lady of the Lake." **6** Goya begins "The

Science & Technology		Miscellaneous		
America	**Elsewhere**	**America**	**Elsewhere**	
1 Stevens launches the *Phoenix,* a 100-ft.-long steamboat powered by a low-pressure engine.	**2** Gay-Lussac states that when gases combine at constant temperature and pressure, they do so in simple proportions (Gay-Lussac's law). **3** Davy discovers the elements boron and strontium. **4** Joseph-Louis Proust, Fr. chemist, proves that any given compound, regardless of its source, has the same composition of elements.	**1** Earliest legal periodical, the *American Law Journal,* is founded in Baltimore, Md., by John Elkin Hall. **2** John Jacob Astor establishes the American Fur Company, the first of several companies founded by him in the West that make him the dominant figure in the industry. **3** Great popularity of horse racing is seen in the widespread mourning in Virginia for the death of a famous race horse named "Diomed." **4** First Bible Society is established in Philadelphia, its first president the Rev. William White.	**5** Napoleon abolishes the Inquisition in Spain and Italy. **6** Source of the Ganges River in India is discovered. **7** Extensive excavations begin at Pompeii in Southern Italy. **8** Scottish judicial system is reformed. **9** First printing press is established in Brazil.	**1808**
1 The *Phoenix* becomes the first sea-going steamboat as it travels from New York to Philadelphia. **2** William Maclure, "Father of American Geology," publishes the first detailed geological survey of the United States. (Revised in 1817.)	**3** George Cayley, Eng. inventor, builds the first successful glider. **4** In *Philosophie Zoölogique,* Lamarck suggests that the giraffe evolved its long legs and neck by its continual stretching for treetop food.	**1** An exhibit in New York City features a Grand Panorama, a view of New York and the surrounding county. Admission is 50¢, children half price. A $2.00 lifetime ticket is also available. **2** First cricket club is founded at Boston. **3** Americans buy Hamilton's "Essence and Extract of Mustard" as a remedy for rheumatism, gout, palsy, swelling, and numbness.	**4** Pall Mall section of London is lighted by gas. **5** National society is formed to promote Church of England schools.	**1809**
1 Yale Medical School is established. **2** François Michaux, Fr. botanist, publishes a 3-volume description of North American trees.	**3** Dalton publishes *New System of Chemical Philosophy,* a foundation of modern chemistry. **4** Nicolas-François Appert, Fr. chef, preserves food in sealed containers.	**1** Third U.S. census shows a population of 7.2 million, including 60,000 immigrants and about 1.2 million slaves. Population west of the Appalachian Mountains is slightly	**5** First public billiards rooms open at the Piazza, Covent Garden in London. **6** Yellow fever epidemic kills about 25,000 people in Spain.	**1810**

	History and Politics		The Arts	
	America	**Elsewhere**	**America**	**Elsewhere**
	son, believing France has removed her restrictive decrees, reopens trade with France and renews Nonintercourse Act with Britain. France continues to seize U.S. ships. **2** Southerners revolt against Spanish rule in West Florida. U.S. annexes the area.	land, Hanover, Bremen, Hamburg, Lauenburg, and Lübeck. He issues the Decree of Fontainebleau, ordering the seizure of all British goods. **5** Struggle for independence begins in Mexico and South America.	by John Wyeth. **3** Gottlieb Graupner organizes the Philharmonic Society in Boston.	Disasters of War," a series of 65 savage and gruesome etchings. **7** Ger. painter Johann Friedrich Overbeck establishes the Nazarenes (also known as Pre-Raphaelites) to revive religious themes in art. **8** de Staël publishes *De l'Allemagne,* her best known novel.
1811	**1** Gen. William Henry Harrison, Governor of the Indiana Territory, defeats the Indians in the Battle of Tippecanoe. **2** Western "War Hawks" in Congress urge U.S. expansion and protest British interference with U.S. shipping.	**3** British and Portuguese armies win victories against the French in Spain and Portugal. **4** Revolutionary forces overthrow the Spanish royal governor in Paraguay. **5** British seize control of the island of Java. **6** Muhammad Ali kills the leader of the Mamelukes, rulers of Egypt and Syria since 1250. **[1805:HIST/7]** **7** Napoleon annexes Oldenburg (German state).	**1** Allston paints "The Poor Author and the Rich Bookseller." **2** Construction begins on the buildings of Boston's aristocratic Colonnade Row, designed by Bulfinch.	**3** With the anonymous publication of *Sense and Sensibility,* Eng. author Jane Austen establishes the modern novel and its realistic portrayal of everyday life. **4** Ger. novelist Friedrich Heinrich La Motte-Fouqué publishes *Undine.* **5** Eng. architect John Nash designs London's fashionable Regent's Park and Regent Street.
1812	**1** Congress declares war (War of 1812) on Great Britain. Canadians, allies of the British, defeat U.S. forces at Detroit. Northwest Indians under Tecumseh join the British. **2** U.S. frigate *Constitution* defeats British frigate *Guerrière* off Nova Scotia and destroys British frigate *Java* off	**5** British under Wellington defeat the French at Salamanca, Spain, and enter Madrid. **6** Russia makes peace with the Turks at Bucharest. **7** Napoleon's Grand Army (about 500,000 men) invades Russia. French destroy Smolensk and defeat the Russians at the bloody Battle of Boro-	**1** I. Thomas founds the American Antiquarian Society and becomes the organization's first president. **2** William Rush sculpts "Nymph of the Schuylkill."	**3** Ger. writers Jacob Grimm and Wilhelm Grimm publish *Grimm's Fairy Tales.* **4** Byron publishes the narrative poem, *Childe Harold's Pilgrimage* (–1818). **5** Eng. writer William Combe collaborates with caricaturist Row-

Science & Technology		Miscellaneous		
America	**Elsewhere**	**America**	**Elsewhere**	
	5 Charles Bell's *Anatomy of the Brain,* the "bible" of neurology, studies the difference between sensory and motor nerves. **6** Robert Brown, Scot. scientist, publishes work on Australian plant life. **7** Samuel Hahnemann, Ger. physician, advocates homeopathy, a form of therapy in which a disease is treated by tiny doses of a drug that would normally produce the disease's symptoms in a healthy person.	more than 1 million. **2** American Board of Commissioners for Foreign Missions is established. This is the beginning of a wide missionary effort in the U.S. **3** Lottery is held at Union College in which the winning ticket has a chance of drawing $100,000. **4** First unofficial heavyweight boxing champion, Tom Molineaux, a freed Virginia slave, is beaten in the 40th round in a match in England.		
1 Using his simple "transit finder," Bond discovers a comet. **2** Wistar publishes *A System of Anatomy,* America's first anatomy textbook.	**3** Hahnemann publishes a catalogue of homeopathic drugs. [1810:SCI/7] **4** W. Herschel suggests that a nebula is an early stage in the development of a galaxy. **5** Sir David Brewster, Scot. physicist, announces his work on polarized light. **6** Count Amadeo Avogadro, Ital. physicist, states that, under identical conditions, equal volumes of different gases contain the same number of molecules (Avogadro's number).	**1** Earthquake rocks the Ohio–Mississippi Valleys. Tremors are felt over an area of 300,000 sq. mi. **2** First steamboat to sail down the Mississippi River reaches New Orleans, La., (in January 1812), and causes a sensation. Boat then makes a regular New Orleans-Natchez run, charging $18 for the trip downstream and $25 for the trip upstream. **3** Beginning of the Cumberland Road at Cumberland, Md. By 1840 the road reaches Vandalia, Ill., at a cost of $7 million. It becomes an important route during the period of western exploration. **4** Competitive rowing races are popular. A race between *Knickerbocker* of New York City and *Invincible* of Long Island attracts thousands. *Knickerbocker* wins.	**5** In a "Great Schism" (division or separation) about two-thirds of the Welsh Protestants leave the Anglican Church. **6** Swiss mountaineer Johann Meyer climbs the 13,668-foot–high Jungfrau in the Alps. **7** Eng. naval captain Philip Beaver surveys Africa's eastern coast.	**1811**
1 James Thacher, Mass. physician, publishes a book about rabies. **2** Rush publishes *Medical Inquiries and Observation Upon the Diseases of the Mind.* **3** Large-scale drug production begins in Philadelphia as America's first drug mill opens.	**4** Cuvier discovers that fossils follow an increasing age sequence as one probes deeper into layers of rock and soil.	**1** William Monroe of Concord, Mass., begins manufacturing lead pencils. **2** Lucy Brenner, serving under the name of Nicholas Baker, is a member of the crew of the *Constitution.* She serves for 3 years, successfully disguising her sex.	**5** The waltz is danced in English ballrooms. **6** Swiss historian J.L. Burckhardt discovers the Great Temple at Abu Simbel in Egypt. **7** Fire started in Moscow after the French occupation destroys 30,000 houses. **8** Earthquake kills	**1812**

History and Politics		The Arts	
America	**Elsewhere**	**America**	**Elsewhere**
Brazil, thus earning herself the nickname "Old Ironsides." U.S. frigate *United States* under Capt. Decatur captures British frigate *Macedonian.* **3** Madison is reelected President, and Elbridge Gerry is elected Vice President on the Democratic-Republican ticket. **4** Louisiana becomes 18th state. Louisiana Territory becomes the Missouri Territory.	dino. Russians retreat and abandon (later burn) Moscow. Lacking shelter and supplies, Napoleon retreats. Many of Napoleon's men die from hunger, severe cold, and Cossack attacks. **8** Napoleon puts down conspiracy against him, strengthens his dictatorship, and raises money to support a new army.		landson to create the first of three *Tours of Dr. Syntax.* **6** The "Elgin Marbles," a collection of Parthenon sculptures obtained from the Turks by Lord Elgin, give Londoners their first taste of original classical Greek art. **7** Turner paints "Snowstorm: Hannibal and his Army Crossing the Alps." **8** Ger. philosopher Georg Wilhelm Hegel publishes *Die Objektive Logik.*
1813 **1** U.S. forces capture York (now Toronto). British seize Fort Niagara and burn Buffalo, N.Y. British blockade coastal ports. **2** U.S. fleet under Capt. Oliver Hazard Perry defeats the British in the Battle of Lake Erie. **3** British evacuate Detroit. Gen. Harrison defeats the British in the Battle of the Thames, Ont., in which Shawnee Indian Chief Tecumseh is killed. Powerful Indian confederacy in Northwest collapses, depriving the British of their Indian allies.	**4** Napoleon wins victories at Lützen (against Russo-Prussian forces), Bautzen, Wurschen, and Dresden. Allied armies defeat French armies at Grossbeeren, Katzbach, Kulm, and Dennewitz. Allied Austrian, Russian, and Prussian armies decisively defeat Napoleon's army at the Battle of Leipzig. **5** Wellington defeats the French at Vittoria, captures San Sebastian, and invades France. **6** Treaty of Gulistan ends Russo-Persian war. Persia loses territory.	**1** A choirbook is composed for use in the Span. missions of the Southwest.	**2** Austen publishes *Pride and Prejudice,* a novel begun in 1794 as "First Impressions." **3** Southey publishes *Life of Nelson.* [1798:HIST/7] **4** Rossini composes *The Italian Girl in Algiers,* an opera. **5** Eng. poet Percy Bysshe Shelley publishes "Queen Mab," an antireligious poem. **6** Ger. Writer Aldebert von Chamisso publishes *Peter Schlemihl,* a Faustian tale. **7** London Philharmonic Society is founded.
1814 **1** Creek Indian War ends when Gen. Andrew Jackson defeats the Creeks at the Battle of Horseshoe Bend, Ala. **2** U.S. fleet defeats British fleet on Lake Champlain, halting the British drive from Canada into the Hudson Valley. **3** British win at Bladensburg, capture Washington, D.C., and burn the Capitol and the White House. British fleet bombards Fort McHenry in Baltimore harbor but fails to capture it. **4** Federalists at Hartford Convention, opposed to the	**5** Allied armies defeat the French at La Rothière, Barsur-Aube, Laon, Arcis-sur-Aube, and La Fère-Champenoise. Allies capture Paris. Napoleon abdicates and is exiled to Elba. **6** Ferdinand VII is restored to the Spanish throne. [1808:HIST/4] **7** Spanish defeat revolutionary forces in Chile, Venezuela, Mexico, and Guatemala. **8** Louis XVIII is restored to the French throne. Congress of Vienna opens to restore European balance of power.	**1** During the Brit. bombardment of Fort McHenry, Francis Scott Key writes the lyrics to "The Star-Spangled Banner," now the U.S. national anthem. **2** In the Park Street Church, Boston, a flute, bassoon, and cello are used to accompany the singing.	**3** Scott anonymously publishes *Waverly,* based on the Jacobite rebellion. [1745:HIST/3] **4** Aust. composer Franz Peter Schubert publishes his first lieder (songs). **5** Edmund Kean, one of England's greatest tragic actors, debuts as Shylock, in Shakespeare's *The Merchant of Venice,* in London. **6** Fr. painter Jean Auguste Dominique Ingres completes "Grande

170

170

170

Science & Technology		Miscellaneous		
America	**Elsewhere**	**America**	**Elsewhere**	
		3 Pennsylvania Company for Insurance on Lives is incorporated in Philadelphia. It is the first insurance company primarily involved with life insurance. **4** Samuel Wilson, a meat-packer from Troy, N.Y., becomes the original "Uncle Sam." Soldiers call the meat "Uncle Sam's" because of the stamp "U.S." on the provision boxes.	20,000 in the Caracas region of Venezuela.	
		1 Celebrated witch Molly Pitcher dies in Lynn, Mass. Her fame had spread throughout the country and hundreds went to her for prophecies, love potions, and information about lost property. **2** Craps is first introduced into New Orleans, La. It was adapted from a French dice game, "hazards."	**3** East India Company's trade monopoly is abolished, but its monopoly in China continues. **4** Methodist Missionary Society is founded.	**1813**
1 Jacob Bigelow, Mass. physician, publishes *Flora Bostoniensis,* the standard botany manual for years. [1848:SCI/2] **2** Francis C. Lowell, Mass. industrialist, opens the first totally mechanized factory for processing raw cotton into finished cloth. **3** Eli Terry, Conn. clockmaker, invents a 30-hour shelf clock that uses interchangeable parts. **4** Based on his collection of fossils, Barton publishes a report on extinct	**5** Berzelius publishes his *Theory of Chemical Proportions and the Chemical Action of Electricity.*	**1** First large library network west of the Alleghenies is established from several circulating libraries in Pittsburgh, Pa. **2** First school for the higher education of women is started by Emma Hart Willard in Middlebury, Vt. **3** Cost of education at Harvard College in Cambridge, Mass., is about $300 a year.	**4** Pope Pius VII on returning to Rome revives the Inquisition and restores the Jesuits and the Index. **5** First Anglican bishop is appointed in India.	**1814**

Napoleon Bonaparte, French General, at age 34

History and Politics

America

Elsewhere

The Arts

America

Elsewhere

	History and Politics		The Arts	
	America	**Elsewhere**	**America**	**Elsewhere**
	war, propose to revise Constitution. Convention ends in ridicule with news of the Treaty of Ghent between Britain and the U.S. Territory seized during the war is returned; commissions settle disputed boundaries.			Odalisque." **7** Austen publishes *Mansfield Park,* a novel.
1815	**1** Gen. Jackson defeats the British at the Battle of New Orleans, fought two weeks after the Treaty of Ghent is signed. **[1814:HIST/4]** **2** U.S. flotilla under Decatur captures two Algerine warships. Decatur forces the Dey of Algiers to sign a treaty ending U.S. tribute. He exacts similar treaties from Tunis and Tripoli, and the Algerine War is ended. **3** Anglo-American commercial treaty ends discriminatory British duties against U.S. ships, and vice versa.	**4** Napoleon returns to France and rules for the "Hundred Days." Austria, Britain, Russia, and Prussia form new alliance against him. **5** British (under Wellington) and Prussian forces defeat the French under Napoleon at the Battle of Waterloo, Belgium. Napoleon abdicates again and is exiled to St. Helena. **6** Congress of Vienna reestablishes Austrian and Prussian monarchies and creates the German Confederation, the Kingdom of the Netherlands, and a Polish kingdom. Britain retains Malta, Heligoland, and some former French and Dutch colonies. Sweden retains Norway, which had been acquired by the Treaty of Kiel with Denmark in 1814.	**1** Latrobe supervises the rebuilding of the Capitol and White House following the burning of Washington, D.C., by the British. **[1814:HIST/3]** **2** A musical jubilee is held at King's Chapel in Boston to celebrate the Peace of Ghent. On Christmas Eve, the first concert of the Handel and Haydn Society is held in the same building.	**3** Scott publishes *Guy Mannering,* an adventure novel set in 18th-century Scotland. **4** The quadrille, a formal French ballroom dance, becomes fashionable among English aristocracy.
1816	**1** James Monroe and Daniel D. Tompkins are elected President and Vice President, respectively, on the Democratic-Republican ticket. **2** Indiana becomes 19th state. **3** Supreme Court affirms right of federal courts to review decision of state courts. **4** First tariff bill to protect domestic industry rather than to raise revenue is enacted by Congress.	**5** Louis XVIII of France dissolves the extreme reactionary Chamber of Deputies. **6** Metternich seeks Austrian domination of the German Confederation—a loose union of 39 states formed for mutual aid and defense. **7** United Provinces of La Plata (now part of Argentina) declare their independence from Spain. **8** Spanish authority is reestablished in Mexico. **9** British defeat the Gurkhas in northern India and force them back into Nepal. **[1768:HIST/7]**	**1** Bulfinch designs the Congregational Church in Lancaster, Mass. **2** Ananias Davisson publishes *Kentucky Harmony,* a collection of music of the South and Midwest U.S.	**3** The first performance of Rossini's opera, *The Barber of Seville,* is hissed by the audience. Later, however, it is a popular success. **4** Leigh Hunt, Eng. writer, publishes the poem, "Story of Rimini." **5** P.B. Shelley writes "Alastor," his first major poem.

Science & Technology		Miscellaneous		
America	**Elsewhere**	**America**	**Elsewhere**	
plants and animals of North America.				
1 Bowditch examines a Conn. meteor (1807) and determines that it once weighed 6 million tons. **2** Fulton launches America's first steam-powered warship, the *Demologos* (also called *Fulton the First* or *U.S.S. Fulton*). **3** New England textile mills are processing 90,000 bales of cotton a year—up from only 500 bales in 1800.	**4** Davy invents the miner's safety lamp. James Monroe, 5th U.S. President	**1** Chief imports are woolen and cotton items, sugar, and coffee. The main export item is cotton. **2** Most colorful method of transportation during this time is the Conestoga wagon with its lively colors, a 4-to-6 horse team decorated with bells. It carries a load of several tons; is about 60 ft. long. **3** Boston Society for the Moral and Religious Instruction of the Poor is established. It promotes Sunday school education in the city.	**4** Volcano on Sumbawa Island, Indonesia, erupts, killing about 12,000 people. **5** Apothecaries Act in Britain forbids unqualified doctors from practicing medicine.	**1815**
1 Parker Cleaveland, Mass. mineralogist, publishes *Elementary Treatise on Mineralogy and Geology,* America's first book in this field. **2** World's first wire suspension bridge is built over the Schuylkill River near Philadelphia.	**3** René-Théophile Laënnec, Fr. physician, invents the stethoscope. **4** Brewster invents the kaleidoscope.	**1** American Bible Society is founded in New York City. Its purpose is to increase the circulation of texts of the Bible, particularly to the poor. **2** Freak summer in New England brings 10 in. of snow on June 6. July and August are no better, with half an inch of ice spread over Vermont and New Hampshire. This year is recorded as the "year in which there was no summer." **3** First savings banks are established in Boston and Philadelphia. **4** Jacob Hyer beats Tom Beasley in a grudge fight and calls himself America's first boxing champion.	**5** William Cobbett's *Weekly Political Register,* the first cheap periodical, is published in England. **6** Typhus epidemic breaks out in Ireland. It lasts three years and kills about one-fourth of the population.	**1816**

History and Politics		The Arts	
America	**Elsewhere**	**America**	**Elsewhere**

1817

America (History and Politics)
1 Rush-Bagot Agreement between the U.S. and Britain limits naval forces on the Great Lakes.
2 Mississippi Territory is divided; western part becomes Mississippi, the 20th state; eastern part becomes Alabama Territory.
3 Seminole Indians attack white settlers in Florida and Georgia.

Elsewhere (History and Politics)
4 Revolutionary army under José de San Martín crosses the Andes and defeats the Spanish at Chacabuco, Chile.
5 Milosh Obrenovich has his rival, Karageorge, murdered and becomes Prince of Serbia. [1804:HIST/9]
6 British government passes Coercion Acts to stop radical demands for parliamentary reform.

Elsewhere (The Arts)
1 Jeffrey, an opponent of Romanticism and mysticism, uses the term "Lake Poets" to ridicule Coleridge, Southey, and Wordsworth.
2 Rossini composes two operas, *Cinderella* and *The Thieving Magpie*.
3 William Hazlitt establishes himself as a leading English critic with the publication of *Characters of Shakespeare's Plays*.
4 Coleridge publishes *Biographia Literaria*.

1818

America (History and Politics)
1 U.S. and Britain establish U.S.-Canadian boundary at the 49th parallel from Lake of the Woods to the Rocky Mts. Oregon boundary is left undecided.
2 U.S. forces under Jackson invade Florida to punish the hostile Seminoles. Jackson captures Pensacola and kills two British men accused of aiding the Indians. Spain is told either to control the Indians or cede Florida to the U.S. [1819:HIST/1]
3 Illinois becomes 21st state.

Elsewhere (History and Politics)
4 San Martín defeats the Spanish royalist army at Maipú and assures the independence of Chile. [1817:HIST/4]
5 Jean Pierre Boyer, mulatto who fought under Toussaint L'Ouverture, becomes President of Haiti.
6 British suppress Pindari tribes in India.
7 Allies evacuate their troops from France.

America (The Arts)
1 The first complete performance of an oratorio in the U.S. is presented in Boston by the Handel and Haydn Society.
2 Paulding publishes "The Backwoodsman," a poem about the westward movement.
3 Sully paints "Lady With a Harp: Eliza Ridgely."

Elsewhere (The Arts)
4 Eng. author Mary Wollstonecraft Shelley, writes *Frankenstein,* a horror story.
5 Austen's last novels, *Northanger Abbey* and *Persuasion* are published posthumously.
6 With the publication of "Endymion," John Keats abandons his career as a surgeon and becomes a full-time poet.
7 Scot. writer Thomas Bowdler publishes *Family Shakespeare,* a censored, rewritten version of the plays that later gives rise to the word "bowdlerize."
8 Scott publishes *The Heart of Midlothian* and *Rob Roy,* two novels.
9 Prado Museum, Madrid, opens.

1819

America (History and Politics)
1 Spain cedes Florida to the U.S. in the Adams-Onís Treaty. Western border of Louisiana Purchase is agreed on; U.S. assumes $5 million

Elsewhere (History and Politics)
4 Peterloo Massacre occurs when soldiers break up crowd listening to speeches on parliamentary reform and repeal of the corn laws in England.

America (The Arts)
1 William Strickland, architect and engineer, bases his design of the Second Bank of the U.S. in Philadelphia on

Elsewhere (The Arts)
5 Prominent Eng. landscape painter John Constable exhibits "Flatford Mill on the River Stour."

Science & Technology		Miscellaneous		
America	**Elsewhere**	**America**	**Elsewhere**	
1 Construction of the Erie Canal begins. It is designed by DeWitt Clinton, governor of N.Y., to connect the Great Lakes with the Hudson River (and thus, the Atlantic Ocean). **2** Bigelow publishes the 3-volume *American Medical Botany.* **3** Baltimore lights its streets with gas lamps.	**4** Berzelius discovers the element selenium. **5** Cuvier publishes *The Animal Kingdom, Distributed According to Its Organization,* an important taxonomic work.	**1** Wild accounts of a sea serpent off the coast of Gloucester, Mass., describe a strange undulating creature, 3 ft. in diameter and from 70 to 100 ft. long. It has a long tongue that shoots out from its gaping mouth. **2** A significant force in early frontier education is the American Tract Society. It circulates religious literature by means of circuit riders. **3** American Society for the Return of Negroes to Africa is founded in Richmond, Va. Headed by a succession of distinguished Virginians, the Society first sends Negroes to Sierra Leone, then buys and establishes a neighboring area called Liberia.	**4** Hegel publishes the *Encyclopedia of Philosophy.*	**1817**
1 Benjamin Silliman, Conn. chemist, establishes the *American Journal of Sciences and Arts,* known popularly as *Silliman's Journal.* **2** Thomas Blanchard, Mass. inventor, designs a lathe for making irregularly shaped objects such as gun stocks. **3** Thomas Cooper, Eng.-Amer. scientist, publishes *Discourse on the Connexion Between Chemistry and Medicine.* **4** The *Savannah,* using its sails through most of the journey, becomes the first steam-powered ship to cross the Atlantic.	**5** Jean-Baptiste Dumas, Fr. chemist, uses iodine as treatment for goiter.	**1** First recorded trotting contest occurs when "Boston Blue" does the mile in less than three minutes, winning his supporters $1000. **2** Englishman Peter Durand introduces the tin can in America. He hit upon the idea of selling hot perishable foods in suitable containers, and he put tin at the top of the list of recommended materials. **3** School for children as young as 4 years is made part of the public school system in Boston. **4** Transatlantic packet lines (under sail) begin operation between New York City and Liverpool, Eng. The average time for the trip is 30 days.	**5** Scot. explorer John Ross leads an expedition to the Arctic to discover the Northwest Passage. **6** Population of Canada is estimated at 800,000.	**1818**
1 Stephen Long, N.H. explorer, leads an expedition to the Rocky Mountains (-1820). **2** American Geological	**3** Johann Encke, Ger. astronomer, discovers a comet with an orbital period of only 3½ years. **4** Laënnec publishes the	**1** Ebenezer Brown begins the Methodist mission to convert the French-speaking population of New Orleans, La.,	**4** A maximum 12-hour working day for children is established in England. **5** Eng. explorer John Barrow discovers Bar-	**1819**

History and Politics		The Arts	
America	Elsewhere	America	Elsewhere
claims of its citizens against Spain. **2** Supreme Court under Chief Justice Marshall upholds the right of Congress to create the Bank of the United States and expresses strongly the doctrine of implied powers in the Constitution (*McCulloch* v. *Maryland*). **3** Alabama becomes 22nd state.	**5** Congress of Angostura elects Simón Bolívar President of Venezuela. Bolívar with his army crosses the Andes and defeats the Spanish royalist army at Boyacá. Bolívar is made President of Greater Colombia (present-day Colombia, Venezuela, Ecuador, and Panama). **6** British East India Company establishes colony at Singapore.	the Parthenon in Athens, Greece. **2** John W. Jarvis, painter, does the famous oil portrait "Andrew Jackson." **3** Allston paints "Moonlit Landscape" and "The Flight of Florimel." **4** Sully paints "The Passage of the Delaware," his best-known painting.	**6** Byron publishes the first two cantos of *Don Juan*, a satirical account of an adventurous rogue. **7** Keats begins "Hyperion" (published in 1856). **8** The *Complete Works* of André Chénier, one of France's greatest classical poets, are published. **9** Goya paints "The Last Communion of St. Joseph of Calasanz."
1820			
1 Congress passes the Missouri Compromise, whereby slavery is prohibited in the Louisiana Territory north of latitude 36°30′. Maine is admitted to the Union as free state; Missouri as slave state in 1821. **[1854:HIST/2]** **2** Monroe and Tompkins are reelected President and Vice President, respectively, on the Democratic-Republican ticket. **3** Government offers land to settlers at $1.25 an acre, reduces minimum purchase to 80 acres, and abolishes credit provisions.	**4** Cato Street plot to murder British cabinet members is discovered; the leaders are executed. **5** Revolutionary movements occur in Spain; King Ferdinand VII restores the Constitution. **6** San Martín moves his forces to Peru by sea. Spanish viceroy abandons Lima. Spain refuses to acknowledge independence of Greater Colombia. **7** Revolution overthrows the regency in Portugal; liberal constitution is drafted.	**1** Irving's *The Sketch Book* introduces the short story as a literary form with such works as "Rip Van Winkle" and "The Legend of Sleepy Hollow."	**2** Scott publishes *Ivanhoe,* a historical novel. **3** "Venus de Milo," a classical Greek statue carved c. 150 B.C., is discovered in Melos. **4** P.B. Shelley publishes "Prometheus Unbound," a dramatic poem. **5** Keats publishes a volume of poems that includes some of his greatest works: "Ode to a Nightingale," "Ode on a Grecian Urn," "Lamia," etc. **6** After publication of his "Ode to Liberty," Russ. poet Aleksandr Sergeyevich Pushkin is exiled to South Russia. **7** Alphonse de Lamartine, Fr. Romantic poet, publishes *Méditations Poétiques*.
1821			
1 Spanish governor grants charter to Moses Austin for the settlement of 300 families in Texas. His son, Stephen Fuller Austin, establishes the first legal settlement of Anglo-Americans in Texas in 1822. **2** New York abolishes property qualifications for voting, following similar action by Connecticut in 1818 and Massachusetts in 1821. **3** Official U.S. occupation of Florida takes place; Andrew	**4** Bolívar defeats the Spanish royalist army at Carabobo and assures the independence of Venezuela. **5** Peru, Mexico, and Guatemala become independent from Spain. **6** Turks put down revolts in Wallachia and Moldavia. **7** Greeks seize Tripolitsa, the main Turkish fortress in the Peloponnesus, and massacre 10,000 Turks. Greek War of Independence begins. **8** Congress of Laibach	**1** Sequoya develops an Indian alphabet that is used to teach thousands of Cherokees to read and write. **2** James Fenimore Cooper writes *The Spy*, a Revolutionary War novel which establishes Cooper's literary prowess.	**3** Goethe begins *Wilhelm Meister's Travels* (–1829), a sequel in which Wilhelm completes his education. **[1795:ARTS/5]** **4** Carl Maria von Weber, creator of the German romantic opera, composes *Der Freischütz*. **5** E.T.A. Hoffmann, Ger. writer and composer, publishes the 4-volume *Die Serapions-*

Science & Technology		Miscellaneous		
America	**Elsewhere**	**America**	**Elsewhere**	

Society is formed at Yale College in Conn. (Disbands in 1828.)

results of three years of stethoscopic chest medicine research. [1816:SCI/3]
5 Eilhardt Mitcherlich, Ger. chemist, realizes that compounds of similar chemical makeup often have similar crystalline structures (theory of isomorphism).
6 John McAdam, Scot. inventor, introduces "macadam" roadmaking technique using crushed stone.

but the mission fails.
2 Norwich University opens in Vermont, specializing in technical training. This is something that has been neglected in most colleges at the time, except for the West Point Military Academy.
3 William Ellery Channing leads the formation of the Unitarian Church in Boston.

row's Straits in the North Arctic.
6 Ger. philosopher Arthur Schopenhauer publishes the *World as Will and Idea*.

---

1 William Underwood, Eng.-Amer. industrialist, opens a canning factory in Boston.
2 Henry Burden, N.Y. ironmaster, invents an improved plow and cultivator.
3 Daniel Treadwell, Mass. inventor, builds a horse-powered printing press.
4 John Gorham, Mass. physician, publishes the 2-volume *Elements of Chemical Science* which serves as the standard textbook for years.
5 New York Eye Infirmary opens.
6 Granite is mined in Quincy, Mass.

7 John Herschel, Eng. astronomer, and Charles Babbage, Eng. mathematician, help found the Royal Astronomical Society.
8 John Frederic Daniell, Eng. chemist and meteorologist, invents a dew point hygrometer.
9 Augustin-Jean Fresnel, Fr. physicist, invents a special lens for lighthouse use.

1 Fourth national census shows that population is 9.6 million. New York is the largest city, with a population of approximately 124,000, followed by Philadelphia (113,000), Baltimore (63,000), Boston (43,000), and New Orleans (27,000). Population west of the Appalachian Mountains is 2.2 million.
2 First football games are played in American colleges, especially as a form of hazing at Yale and Harvard.
3 Expedition led by Maj. Stephen Long sets out from Pittsburgh, Pa., to explore the region between the Missouri River and the Rocky Mountains.

4 Russian explorer F.G. Bellinghausen first sights land in the Antarctic Circle.

1820

Simón Bolivar, South American statesman

---

1 Zachariah Allen, R.I. inventor, designs a hot-air heating system for homes.
2 Hare invents the copper-zinc battery.
3 America's first tunnel—450 ft. long, 18 ft. high, 20 ft. wide—opens near Auburn, Pa.
4 Congress rejects a proposal by John Quincy Adams, Secretary of State, that the U.S. convert to the metric system.

5 Michael Faraday, Eng. chemist and physicist, discovers electromagnetic rotation.
6 George Dollond, Eng. optician, builds a rock-crystal micrometer for measuring stars.
7 Thomas Seebeck, Est. physicist, discovers the thermoelectric, or Seebeck effect.

1 Public horse racing becomes popular, and tracks are opened in Queens County, N.Y.
2 First women's college-level school, the Troy Female Seminary, is founded by Emma Willard in Troy, N.Y.
3 First public high school, English Classical School, is established in Boston.

4 French archaeologist and linguist Jean-François Champollion deciphers Egyptian hieroglyphics using the Rosetta Stone.
5 *Manchester Guardian* is founded by J.E. Taylor in England.
6 France's population is 30.4 million, Germany's 26 million, Great Britain's 20.8 million, Italy's 18 million, and Austria's 12 million.

1821

History and Politics		The Arts	
America	**Elsewhere**	**America**	**Elsewhere**
Jackson is made military governor. **[1818:HIST/2; 1819:HIST/1]**	among European powers authorizes the use of Austrian troops to suppress revolts in Naples and Piedmont.		*brüder,* tales of the supernatural. **[1881:ARTS/8]** **6** P.B. Shelley publishes "Adonaïs," an elegy on the death of John Keats. **7** Thomas DeQuincey publishes *Confessions of an English Opium Eater.* **8** Hazlitt publishes *Table Talk, or Original Essays on Men and Manners* (–1822). **9** Scott publishes *Kenilworth,* a novel.
1822 **1** Florida is organized as a territory. **2** Pres. Monroe proposes U.S. recognition of newly independent Latin American republics. Congress passes measure to establish diplomatic relations with them. **3** Rebellion of Negro slaves is discovered and suppressed in Charleston, S.C. Negro leader Denmark Vesey is hanged along with 34 others.	**4** Greeks draw up liberal constitution and declare independence. Turks seize the island of Chios and massacre most of the Greek inhabitants. Turkish army invades mainland Greece. **5** Augustín de Iturbide is proclaimed Emperor of Mexico. **6** Brazil becomes independent from Portugal. **7** Congress of Verona discusses European problems, especially the rebellion in Spain against King Ferdinand VII. **8** Haitians take control of all Hispaniola, forming the republic of Haiti. **[1844:HIST/5]**	**1** Clement C. Moore writes the familiar Yuletide ballad "'Twas the night before Christmas" for his children. **2** Paulding satirizes the British in *A Sketch of Old England, by a New England Man.* **3** Timothy Dwight publishes *Travels in New England and New York.* **4** C.W. Peale does the self-portrait "The Artist in His Museum." **5** Irving publishes *Bracebridge Hall,* a sequel to *The Sketch Book.* **[1820:ARTS/1]** **6** A collection of psalm tunes by Lowell Mason is published by the Handel and Haydn Society.	**7** Pushkin writes *Eugene Onegin,* a Romantic novel in verse. (Published in 1832.) **8** Inspired by Dante's *Inferno* (1321), Fr. Romantic artist Ferdinand Delacroix paints "Dante and Virgil Crossing the Styx." **9** At the age of 11, Hung. piano virtuoso and composer Franz Liszt makes his debut in Vienna. **10** Royal Academy of Music, London, is founded. **11** Cherubini is named director of the Paris Conservatoire. **12** Charles Nodier, Fr. author, publishes *Trilby,* a romantic novel.
1823 **1** Pres. Monroe announces the Monroe Doctrine in his annual message to Congress. European nations are warned not to interfere in Western Hemisphere. U.S. intends not to take part in European wars.	**2** Ferdinand VII, backed by French arms, revokes Spain's Constitution. Cruel repression follows. **[1820:HIST/5]** **3** Iturbide, Emperor of Mexico, is forced to abdicate. **4** Guatemala, San Salvador, Nicaragua, Honduras, and Costa Rica form the confederated United Provinces of Central America. **5** Treaty of Erzurum ends war between Persians and Turks.	**1** Samuel F.B. Morse paints "The Old House of Representatives." **2** Cooper publishes *The Pioneer,* a brilliant portrait of frontier life and the first of his "Leatherstocking Tales," and *The Pilot,* the first of several sea novels. **3** Raphaelle Peale paints "After the Bath."	**4** Schubert composes the music for *Rosamunde,* a drama by Ger. writer Wilhelmine de Chézy. **5** C. Lamb publishes *Essays of Elia.* **6** Eng. architect Robert Smirke designs the British Museum. **7** *Clari, or the Maid of Milan,* an opera by Eng. composer Henry Rowley Bishop and Amer. librettist J. H. Payne, introduces the

Science & Technology		Miscellaneous		
America	Elsewhere	America	Elsewhere	
1 William Beaumont, Conn. physician, begins his famous digestion experiments in the exposed stomach of Alexis St. Martin, an injured soldier. **[1833:SCI/1]** **2** Quinine production begins in Philadelphia.	**3** Jean-Baptiste Fourier, Fr. mathematician, publishes work on heat conduction.	**1** Football is prohibited at Yale. Violators are reported and fined. **2** Hobart College is established in Geneva, N.Y. It offers an "English Course" designed for "the practical business of life." First course diploma, in English, is awarded in 1827. **3** First patent for making false teeth is awarded to W.C. Graham. **4** Cotton mills begin production in Massachusetts with water-powered machinery. By 1826, one plant in Lowell turns out 2 million yards of cloth a year. A female labor force is used.	**5** Earthquake in Aleppo, Syria, kills 22,000 people. **6** The *Sunday Times* is founded in London.	**1822**
1 America's first ophthalmology book, *A Treatise on the Diseases of the Eye,* is published by George Frick, Md. eye surgeon.	**2** Faraday liquefies chlorine. **3** Berzelius isolates the element silicon. **4** Charles Macintosh, Scot. chemist, invents method for waterproofing cloth. **5** Daniell's *Meteorological Essays and Observations* studies the atmosphere and trade winds. **6** Sir William Hamilton, Ir. mathematician, discovers conical refraction.	**1** First gymnasium to offer systematic instruction is started by the Round Hill School in Northampton, Mass. Gymnastics is scheduled from 5 to 7 p.m. **2** First great horse race is between the North's "American Eclipse" and "Sir Henry," the challenger from the South, for a purse of $20,000. About 1000 spectators jam Union Course on Long Island, N.Y., to see "Ameri-	**3** Death penalty is abolished for more than 100 crimes in Britain. **4** Eng. explorer Walter Oudney, on an expedition from Tripoli, discovers Lake Chad in Central Africa. **5** Rugby football originates in England at the Rugby School. **6** Politician and philanthropist William Wilberforce forms an anti-slavery society to abolish the slave trade and slavery it-	**1823**

179

History and Politics		The Arts	
America	Elsewhere	America	Elsewhere
			song, "Home, Sweet Home."

	History and Politics — America	History and Politics — Elsewhere	The Arts — America	The Arts — Elsewhere
1824	**1** None of the four Presidential candidates receives an electoral majority: Andrew Jackson, 99 votes; John Quincy Adams, 84 votes; William H. Crawford, 41 votes; and Henry Clay, 37 votes. All are Democratic-Republicans, except Adams, who is a National Republican. [1825:HIST/1] **2** U.S. signs territorial treaty with Russia, which agrees to 54°40′ as the southern limit of her territory. **3** Congress enacts General Survey Bill authorizing federal plans for roads which may be needed for national and commercial purposes.	**4** Civil war breaks out in the Ottoman Empire. Ottoman Sultan appeals to Muhammad Ali of Egypt for help. Egyptians seize Crete. **5** Revolutionary forces defeat Spanish royalist forces at Junin and Ayacucho in Peru. **6** Anglo-Burmese war begins; British capture Rangoon. **7** Dutch cede Malacca to Britain in return for Bengkulen in Sumatra. **8** Mexico is set up as a republic.		**1** Beethoven, now totally deaf, composes *Symphony No. 9 in D Minor.* **2** After years of controversy, Parliament establishes the National Gallery, London. **3** John Wilson Croker, Eng. Tory leader and writer, founds the Athenaeum Club in London.

Grain-boat on the Erie Canal

	History and Politics — America	History and Politics — Elsewhere	The Arts — America	The Arts — Elsewhere
1825	**1** House of Representatives chooses Adams (National Republican) as President. John C. Calhoun (Democratic-Republican) was elected Vice President during 1824 election. **2** Texas (Mexican territory) is opened to settlement by U.S. citizens. **3** Creek Indians reject treaty ceding to the U.S. government all their lands in Georgia. [1814:HIST/1] **4** Congress adopts policy of removal of eastern Indian tribes to territory west of the Mississippi River. Whites settle on Indian lands; Indian frontier is established.	**5** Czar Nicholas I crushes uprising of the Decembrists, members of secret revolutionary society in Russia. **6** Turks subdue the Greeks in the Peloponnesus. **7** Bolivia proclaims its independence. **8** British begin war against the Ashanti on the Gold Coast (Ghana) of Africa. **9** Java revolts against Dutch control. Javanese are subdued in 1830; Dutch extend their control to the interior. **10** France's Law of Indemnity compensates the nobles for losses during the revolution. **11** Portugal recognizes Brazil's independence.	**1** Phyfe begins producing furniture in the Empire style. **2** Thomas Cole establishes the Hudson River School of landscape painting. **3** Sarah Knight's diary is published as *The Journal of Mme. Knight.*	**4** The Bolshoi Ballet is established in Moscow. **5** Esaias Tegnér, Swed. poet, publishes *Frithjofs Saga,* an epic poem considered one of the best in Scandinavian literature. **6** Manzoni publishes *The Betrothed,* one of Italy's greatest historical novels. **7** Pushkin writes *Boris Godunov,* a historical tragedy. **8** The *Diary* of Samuel Pepys is published. [1660:ARTS/1]

Science & Technology		Miscellaneous		
America	**Elsewhere**	**America**	**Elsewhere**	
		can Eclipse" take 2 out of 3 races.	self in British possessions overseas.	
1 Thomas Say, "Father of Descriptive Entomology," publishes the 3-volume *American Entomology; or Descriptions of the Insects of North America.* (-1828) **2** America's first school of science and engineering opens. It is later called Rensselaer Polytechnic Institute.	**3** Berzelius isolates the element zirconium. **4** Niels Henrick Abel, Norw. mathematician, proves that an algebraic solution to a fifth-degree equation is impossible. **5** J. Herschel publishes work on gravity in outer space. **6** Joseph Aspdin, Eng. bricklayer, patents the process for making Portland cement. **7** Charles Bell publishes *Injuries of the Spine and Thigh Bone.* **8** Sadi Carnot, Fr. military engineer, publishes *Reflections on the Motive Power of Fire,* in which the efficiency of steam engines is examined.	**1** Jedediah Smith of the Rocky Mountain Fur Company discovers the gateway to the West through the Rocky Mountains at South Pass, Wyo. **2** Weavers' strike at Pawtucket, R.I., is the first recorded strike by women. **3** Great Salt Lake is discovered by James Bridger. **4** Auburn (N.Y.) Penitentiary houses prisoners in cell blocks, and they perform labor in groups. An alternative to this system is that of Pennsylvania in which prisoners are in solitary confinement and they work alone. **5** American Sunday School Union is established in Philadelphia to promote and coordinate Sunday school activity in America.	**6** Anglican bishops are appointed in Barbados and Jamaica.	**1824**
1 Erie Canal is completed. **2** Stevens builds *Action,* an experimental steam locomotive. **3** Yale College purchases a collection of 10,000 minerals from George Gibbs, R.I. mineralogist. **4** Thomas Kensett, N.Y. canner, patents tin-plated cans.	**5** Faraday isolates benzene. **6** Berzelius isolates the element titanium. **7** Cuvier suggests that great catastrophes have altered the earth, causing the extinction of whole animal species. **8** André Ampère, Fr. physicist, develops the electromagnetic theory, which relates electricity to magnetism.	**1** Scottish-born social reformer, Frances Wright, establishes the Nashoba community near Memphis, Tenn., for training Negroes to make possible their colonization outside the U.S. **2** New York Governor DeWitt Clinton opens the Erie Canal. It becomes an important commercial route connecting the East with the Ohio and Mississippi valleys. **3** Robert Dale Owen establishes a community at New Harmony, Ind. **[1800:MISC/7]** **4** First significant strike for a 10-hour day is called in Boston by 600 carpenters. **5** New York Trotting Club builds a race course on Long Island.	**6** Eng. philosopher John Stuart Mill, age 19, publishes *Analysis of the Phenomena of the Human Mind,* a basic work of modern psychology. **7** British workers are allowed to organize into labor unions.	**1825**

	History and Politics		The Arts	
	America	**Elsewhere**	**America**	**Elsewhere**
1826	**1** Senate reluctantly approves U.S. delegates to Panama Congress, called by Latin American republics to plan union against Spain and Europe. One delegate dies on route; another arrives after the Congress adjourns. **2** Creek Indians sign Treaty of Washington which voids previous treaty and cedes less land to the government. Indians must move in 1827. **[1825:HIST/3]**	**3** Persia attacks Russian possessions in Transcaucasia. Russia declares war on Persia. **4** Ottoman Sultan has the unruly Janissaries (elite Turkish corps) massacred in their barracks at Constantinople. **5** Treaty of Yandabu ends Anglo-Burmese War. British secure Assam, Arakan, and the Tenasserim coast. British also sign treaty with Siam. **6** Dost Muhammad becomes Emir (prince) of Afghanistan.	**1** Cooper publishes *Last of the Mohicans,* the second "Leatherstocking Tale." **2** S.F.B. Morse founds the National Academy of Design.	**3** Felix Mendelssohn establishes himself as a leading Ger. composer with his *Overture* to Shakespeare's *A Midsummer Night's Dream.* **4** Benjamin Disraeli, Brit. politician and writer, anonymously publishes his first novel, *Vivian Grey.* **5** Weber composes *Oberon,* one of his most popular operas. **6** Jap. artist Hokusai begins his famous series of wood-block prints, "Thirty-six Views of Mt. Fuji" (–1833). **7** Fr. author Alfred Victor de Vigny publishes *Cinq Mars,* a historical novel, and *Poèmes antiques et modernes,* a collection of his poetry.
1827	**1** Protectionists (mainly northern manufacturers) demand higher tariffs at Harrisburg convention. Southerners oppose tariffs. Sectional differences in U.S. increase between the North and South. **2** U.S. and Britain agree to joint occupation of the Oregon Territory. **[1818:HIST/1]** **3** Congress gives the President the right to call out the militia.	**4** France, Britain, and Russia demand an armistice from the Turks to end war with Greece. Sultan refuses. French, British, and Russian squadrons destroy the Turkish and Egyptian fleets at the Battle of Navarino. **5** Argentine and Uruguayan forces defeat the Brazilians at the Battle of Ituzaingó. Argentina and Brazil both claim Uruguay. **[1828:HIST/4]** **6** Russia defeats Persia and seizes Tabriz and Erivan (part of Armenia).	**1** Cooper publishes *The Prairie,* the third "Leatherstocking Tale," and *The Red Rover,* a sea novel. **2** Thomas Cole paints "Last of the Mohicans."	**3** The preface to Fr. writer Victor Hugo's drama, *Cromwell,* calls for freedom from rigid literary styles and is later adopted as the rallying call of Romantic writers in France. **4** Fr. landscape painter Jean-Baptiste-Camille Corot exhibits his first important work, "Le Pont de Narni." **5** Ger. poet Heinrich Heine publishes *Buch der Lieder,* a popular songbook.
1828	**1** Democratic Party is formed, advocating Jeffersonian principles. Andrew Jack-	**4** Through British mediation, Uruguay gains its independence as a buffer state	**1** Nathaniel Hawthorne publishes *Fanshawe,* his first novel.	**4** Hunt unleashes bitter criticism in *Lord Byron and Some of his*

Science & Technology		Miscellaneous		
America	**Elsewhere**	**America**	**Elsewhere**	
1 Samuel Morey, Conn. inventor, patents an internal combustion engine. **2** America's first reflecting telescope is built by Amasa Holcomb in Mass. Bald eagle by Audubon	**3** Abel founds the *Journal for Pure and Applied Mathematics.* **4** Davy's last lecture, *On the Relation of Electrical and Chemical Changes,* wins him the Royal Medal. **5** Bessel designs a pendulum that requires exactly one second per swing.	**1** Smith of the Rocky Mountain Fur Company leads an expedition from Great Salt Lake to explore the Southwest, and blazes the first overland route to California. **2** First railroads built are short-line systems, powered by cable systems, horses, or sails. The Mauch Chunk Railroad in Pennsylvania carries coal, and a railroad in Massachusetts carries granite. The first passenger line is the Baltimore and Ohio. **3** Charles Follen, an instructor at Harvard, introduces physical education into college education. **4** Millbury Lyceum Number 1 is established at Millbury, Mass., by Josiah Holbrook. This is the beginning of the adult self-improvement and education movement.	**5** First railroad tunnel in England is built on the Liverpool-Manchester Railway.	**1826**
1 Audubon publishes *Birds of America* (-1838), a collection of 435 lifelike paintings, many showing birds in action. Unable to interest American printers, Audubon's drawings are released in Europe where he is acclaimed a genius. **2** Isaac Adams, N.H. printer, invents and manufactures "Adams Power Printing Presses" which are widely used for more than 50 years. **3** Isaac Coffin, British admiral born in Boston, opens America's first nautical school in Nantucket, Mass.	**4** Georg Ohm, Ger. physicist, publishes important work on the theory and uses of electrical currents. **5** Karl Ernst von Baer, Est. physician, discovers the mammalian ovum (egg), thus proving that mammals actually develop from eggs. **6** Richard Bright, Eng. physician, describes the symptoms of the kidney disorder later known as Bright's disease. **7** Sir William Hamilton, Ir. mathematician, publishes *Theory of Systems of Rays.*	**1** First Negro newspaper, *Freedom's Journal,* is published in New York City, edited by John Brown Russwurm and Samuel Cornish. **2** *American Shooter's Manual,* a handbook for sportsmen, is published in Philadelphia. **3** Massachusetts requires a high school in every town having more than 500 families. **4** First city central trade union, the Mechanics Trade Union Association, is established in Philadelphia. **5** French-American students in New Orleans, La., organize a procession of street maskers on Shrove Tuesday, starting the Mardi Gras celebration.	**6** Eng. politician and reformer Henry Brougham founds the Society for the Diffusion of Useful Knowledge, which works to make good books available at low prices to workingmen. **7** Friction matches, called Lucifers, are introduced in England. **8** Anglican clergyman John Darby secedes from the Church of England and forms the Plymouth Brethren.	**1827**
1 Joseph Henry, N.Y. physicist, invents the electromagnet.	**2** Berzelius discovers the element thorium. **3** Johann Lukas Schön-	**1** First Indian newspaper, *Cherokee Phoenix,* is published in Echota, Ga.	**4** British Test and Corporation Acts are repealed; Catholics and	**1828**

History and Politics		The Arts	
America	**Elsewhere**	**America**	**Elsewhere**

	History and Politics — America	History and Politics — Elsewhere	The Arts — America	The Arts — Elsewhere
	son is elected first Democratic U.S. President. John Calhoun is reelected Vice President on the Democratic ticket. **2** Congress passes the protectionist "Tariff of Abominations." Northern mercantile interests conflict with the Southern agricultural economy dependent on foreign markets. **[1827:HIST/1]** **3** Resolutions by South Carolina legislature declare Tariff of Abominations oppressive and unconstitutional. Legislatures of Georgia, Mississippi, and Virginia issue similar protests.	between Argentina and Brazil. **5** Duke of Wellington becomes Prime Minister of Great Britain. **6** Russia declares war on the Ottoman Empire. Russians cross the Danube and seize Varna from the Turks. **7** By the Treaty of Turkmanchai, Persia cedes to Russia the provinces of Erivan and Nakhchivan and pays a large indemnity.	**2** Noah Webster publishes *American Dictionary of the English Language,* in which many of the American characteristics of the English language are introduced. **3** Thomas ("Jim Crow") Rice introduces the song "Jim Crow" between acts of a play. It is the first international song hit of American popular music.	*Contemporaries.* **5** Daniel François Esprit Auber, Fr. composer, collaborates with librettist Augustin Eugène Scribe on *The Mute Girl of Portici,* one of the first grand operas.
1829	**1** Jackson introduces the spoils system into national politics—the practice of basing appointments on party service. Jackson's unofficial political advisers are called his "Kitchen Cabinet." **2** Workingmen's Party is formed in New York. Party advocates social reform, free public education, new banking laws, and non-imprisonment for debt. Movement spreads to other states in the North.	**3** Cantonal constitutions of Switzerland are revised to include universal suffrage, freedom of the press, and equality before the law. **4** Russians capture Adrianople, Kars, and Erzerum. Ottoman Empire on the verge of collapse concludes the Treaty of Adrianople. Russia secures the mouth of the Danube and the east coast of the Black Sea. Turks raze all fortresses in Wallachia and Moldavia and recognize Greek autonomy. **5** Irish political leader Daniel O'Connell agitates for repeal of the parliamentary union of Great Britain and Ireland. **[1801:HIST/4]**	**1** Edgar Allan Poe anonymously publishes his first work *Tamerlane and Other Poems.*	**2** Mendelssohn performs Bach's *St. Matthew Passion,* sparking renewed interest in Bach's works. **[1729:ARTS/5]** **3** Fr. novelist Honoré de Balzac publishes *The Chouans,* a description of military life. **4** Rossini completes his final major composition, the opera *William Tell.* **5** Delacroix paints "The Death of Sardanapalus," often considered to be his masterpiece.
1830	**1** Senators Robert Y. Hayne (S.C.) and Daniel Webster (Mass.) engage in debate on the nature of the Union. Hayne upholds states' rights; Webster defends the Constitution and the Union. **2** Mexico forbids further U.S. colonization in Texas. **[1825:HIST/2]** **3** Congress passes Removal Bill, authorizing resettlement of eastern Indians in the Oklahoma Territory. Sauk and Fox Indians in Illinois forced to move west of the	**4** Louis Philippe becomes King of the French ("the Citizen King") as revolution forces Charles X to abdicate. France invades Algeria. **5** Poles rebel in Warsaw against Russian rule. **6** Venezuela and Ecuador separate from Greater Colombia to become independent republics. The rest of Greater Colombia (Colombia and Panama) is renamed New Granada. **[1819:HIST/5]** **7** Serbia becomes autonomous state with Milosh	**1** Oliver Wendell Holmes writes the poem "Old Ironsides" about the battleship *USS Constitution.* The poem, which brought the author great popularity, prevented the planned scrapping of the historic vessel. **2** Daniel Emmett composes "Old Dan Tucker," one of the most popular minstrel tunes. **3** Joseph E. Worces-	**4** Balzac announces plans to incorporate nearly 100 novels and short stories into *La Comédie Humaine (The Human Comedy).* (Published in 1842.) **5** Hugo's drama, *Hernani,* marks the start of the Romantic movement in France. **6** Hector Berlioz, France's most important Romantic composer, produces *Symphonie fantastique.*

Science & Technology		Miscellaneous		
America	**Elsewhere**	**America**	**Elsewhere**	
	lein, Ger. physician, describes and names the blood disease hemophilia. **4** Brown proposes the concept of Brownian movement.	Its editor is Elias Budinot, a full-blooded Cherokee. **2** First recorded strike of textile factory workers occurs in Paterson, N.J. The militia is called in to control the violence. The workers strike for a 10-hour day, but the strike fails. **3** First archery club is formed in Philadelphia. Members pay an initiation fee of $5 and 50¢ dues a month.	Nonconformists may hold public office. **5** Earthquake in Echigo, Japan, kills 30,000 people.	
1 William A. Burt, Mass. surveyor, invents the "typographer," an early typewriter. **2** Bigelow coins the word "technology" and publishes *The Elements of Technology.* **3** Allen publishes *The Science of Mechanics.* **4** William E. Horner, Va. physician, publishes *A Treatise on Pathological Anatomy,* America's first pathology text.	**5** Thomas Graham, Scot. chemist, publishes work on the diffusion of gases. **6** Gustav-Gaspard Coriolis, Fr. engineer, publishes *On the Calculation of Mechanical Action,* in which he coins the term *kinetic energy.* **7** Franz Ressel, Aust. inventor, devises a screw propeller for steamships. **8** Nikolai Ivanovich Lobachevsky, Russ. mathematician, publishes work which establishes him as the founder of non-Euclidian geometry.	**1** First modern hotel, the Tremont, opens in Boston. It has 170 rooms. **2** *American Turf Register and Sporting Magazine* is published in Baltimore, Md., by John Skinner. It is devoted to thoroughbred horses, racing, hunting, shooting, and the habits of game. **3** First school for the blind opens in Boston. **4** Earliest recorded "Fat Ladies" in America are Deborah Tripp, who at age 3 weighs 125 pounds, and Susan Tripp, 5 years old, 205 pounds. **5** *Encyclopedia Americana* is published in Philadelphia by Francis Lieber. It is the first American encyclopedia.	**6** Catholic Emancipation Act in Britain allows Catholics to sit in Parliament and to hold public office. **7** Eng. statesman Robert Peel founds the Metropolitan Police force in London. The police become known as "Bobbies." **8** First Cambridge-Oxford boat race takes place at Henley, England; Oxford wins.	**1829**
1 Henry discovers electromagnetic induction and electromotive force when he uses magnetism to produce electricity. **2** Peter Cooper, N.Y. manufacturer, builds *Tom Thumb,* America's first commercially successful steam locomotive. It loses a race against a horse when an engine belt slips. **3** Constantine Rafinesque, Fr.-Amer. naturalist, publishes *Medical Flora of the United*	**6** In Charles Bell's *The Nervous System of the Human Body,* different types of nerves are distinguished. **7** Charles Lyell, Eng. geologist, publishes *Principles of Geology,* a thorough work based on exhaustive observations and collections. **8** Dumas develops a method for finding the nitrogen content of an organic compound.	**1** Fifth national census shows a population of 12.8 million, including about 150,000 immigrants who arrived between 1820 and 1830. Census also shows that 8.8% of the population lives in cities of 2500 or more inhabitants. **2** *Lady's Book* (later *Godey's Lady's Book*), an influential woman's magazine, is published in Philadelphia. **3** Joseph Smith founds	**4** First epidemic of cholera occurs in Europe. **5** Eng. explorers Richard and John Lander travel the lower course of the Niger River. **6** National education system is introduced into Ireland. English is the only language of instruction.	**1830**

	History and Politics		The Arts	
	America	**Elsewhere**	**America**	**Elsewhere**
	Mississippi.	Obrenovich as hereditary prince. **[1817:HIST/5]** **8** Belgians revolt against the Dutch King.	ter, lexicographer, publishes the *Comprehensive Pronouncing and Explanatory Dictionary of the English Language*.	**7** Frédéric François Chopin, Pol. composer, debuts in Warsaw with a performance of his *Piano Concerto No. 2 in F Minor*. **8** Stendhal (Marie Henri Beyle), Fr. novelist, publishes *The Red and the Black*. **9** *Anna Bolena* establishes Gaetano Donizetti as one of Italy's leading opera composers.
1831	**1** Nat Turner leads unsuccessful Negro slave revolt in which about 55 white people are killed in Southampton County, Va. Turner is captured and hanged. **2** Anti-Masonic Party, first political third party in U.S., meets in Baltimore, Md. Party is opposed to Pres. Jackson and is absorbed by the Whigs after 1836. **3** Supreme Court upholds Georgia's order for the removal of the Cherokee Indians beyond the Mississippi.	**4** Belgium separates from the Netherlands. Leopold I becomes King of the Belgians. **5** Russians suppress Polish rebellion. "Russification" of Poland begins. **6** Austria crushes uprisings in Modena, Parma, and the Papal States but fails to suppress Italy's nationalist movement. **7** British take control of the state of Mysore, India. **8** Radical agitation, violence, and workers' uprisings occur in France. French king and legislature are unresponsive to the political and economic desires of the lower classes.	**1** *The Floating Theater,* the first showboat, is built. **2** John Greenleaf Whittier, the "Quaker poet," publishes *Legends of New England.* **3** *Poems by Edgar Allan Poe* is published. **4** Paulding publishes *The Dutchman's Fireside* about life in upstate N.Y. during the French and Indian War. **5** William Lloyd Garrison founds the Abolitionist periodical *The Liberator,* which urges the immediate release of all slaves. **[1865:ARTS/3]** **6** The Trumbull Gallery at Yale, the first U.S. art gallery associated with a university, is founded by Benjamin Silliman, John Trumbull's nephew.	**7** Hugo publishes *The Hunchback of Notre Dame,* one of the most popular historical novels ever written. **8** Giacomo Meyerbeer (Jakob Liebmann Beer), Ger. composer, produces the opera, *Robert Le Diable.* **9** Bellini and Romani collaborate on two operas, *La Sonnambula* and *Norma.*
1832	**1** Black Hawk War occurs when Chief Black Hawk with Sauk Indians returns to Illinois to plant crops. State militia and U.S. troops massacre Black Hawk's tribe at the Bad Axe River in Wisconsin. **[1830:HIST/3]** **2** Jackson (Democrat) is re-elected President; Martin Van Buren is elected Vice President on the Democratic ticket. **3** South Carolina convention	**4** Giuseppe Mazzini founds the secret society Giovine Italia (Young Italy), which seeks Italy's unification under a republican government. **5** Reform bill redistributes seats in the British Parliament in the interest of larger communities. **6** Swiss liberal cantons form the *Siebenerkonkordat* to guarantee their new liberal constitutions. Conservative cantons form the *Sarnen-*	**1** The Boston Academy of Music is founded. It offers free music lessons to children and classes for adults and music teachers. **2** Paulding publishes *Westward Ho!* **3** John Quidor, Hudson River School painter, begins a series of paintings depicting characters created by	**4** Amantine Lucile Aurore Dupin adopts the pen name "George Sand" for the publication of *Indiana,* a novel. **5** Ital. ballet master Filippo Taglioni composes *La Sylphide,* one of the first Romantic ballets. His daughter Marie is featured in the title role. **6** Adam Mickiewicz,

Science & Technology		Miscellaneous		
America	**Elsewhere**	**America**	**Elsewhere**	
States. **4** Silliman publishes *Elements of Chemistry.* **5** Charles Grice, America's first veterinarian, opens an animal hospital in New York City.		the Church of Jesus Christ of Latter-day Saints (Mormon) in Fayette, N.Y. Mormons are forced by opposition to their beliefs to go to Ohio, then Missouri, and then Illinois. They finally settle in Utah under the leadership of Brigham Young.		
1 Henry builds the first electric motor, electrical relay, electromagnetic telegraph, and electric bell. **2** Samuel Guthrie, Mass. inventor, develops a process for producing chloroform. **3** Robert L. Stevens, R.I. engineer, buys the 30-horsepower British locomotive, the *John Bull,* and sets up America's first steam railway. He also invents a flanged railroad track called the "T-rail" or "Stevens rail."	**4** Brewster publishes *Treatise on Optics.* **5** Brown discovers and names the cell nucleus. **6** Faraday produces electric current by a change in magnetic intensity (electromagnetic induction). **7** Charles Darwin, Eng. naturalist, embarks on a 5-year voyage aboard the *HMS Beagle* as the ship's naturalist.	**1** A popular weekly racing sheet, the *Spirit of the Times,* is founded by William Trotter. Its aim is to raise the reputation of racing and other sports. **2** *Lady Sherbrooke,* a ship carrying a large number of immigrants, sinks off Cape May, N.J., killing 263 people. **3** First use of the term "Old Glory" to mean the U.S. flag. The term caught on during the Civil War when Union troops commonly used it.	**4** Eng. navigator James Ross plants the British flag at the north magnetic pole. Samuel F. B. Morse, U.S. artist and inventor	**1831**
1 Samuel F. B. Morse, Mass. inventor, designs an improved electromagnetic telegraph. (He applies for a patent in 1837.) **2** Walter Hunt invents, but does not patent, a lock-stitch sewing machine. **3** Horsedrawn streetcars are used in New York City.	**7** Thomas Hodgkin, Eng. physician, describes the illness later known as Hodgkin's disease. **8** Sir Charles Wheatstone, Eng. physicist, invents the stereoscope. **9** Mitscherlich makes nitrobenzene in the laboratory.	**1** *History of Women,* the first work to treat women in a completely distinctive way, is published. **2** First of the famous American sailing clipper ships, the *Ann McKim,* is launched at Baltimore, Md. Its structure is completely new, and its design is later preferred to all others. **3** New York & Harlem Railroad (New York City)	**6** Great cholera epidemic, which began in India in 1826 and spread from Russia into Central Europe, reaches Scotland. **7** First railroad in Europe is completed.	**1832**

187

	America	Elsewhere	America	Elsewhere
	passes Ordinance of Nullification, declaring the tariffs of 1828 and 1832 null and void.	bund, opposed to a strong central government. **[1829:HIST/3]** **7** Egyptian army under Ibrahim Pasha, son of Muhammad Ali, captures Acre, Damascus, and Aleppo and defeats the main Turkish army at the Battle of Konia. Russia offers help to the Ottoman Sultan.	Washington Irving.	Pol. poet, publishes his epic, *Pan Tadeusz (Master Thaddeus)* (–1834). **7** Goethe publishes *Faust: Part II.* **8** Ando Hiroshige, prominent Jap. artist in the Ukiyo-e movement, publishes "Fifty-three stages of the Tokaido," a series of color prints. **9** Fr. political cartoonist Honoré Daumier is imprisoned for his satirical lithographs of King Louis Philippe. **10** Tennyson's *Poems* includes "Lady of Shalott" and "The Lotus Eaters."
1833	**1** Congress passes Force Bill, giving Pres. Jackson authority to use the armed forces to execute the tariff laws. After enactment of a compromise tariff, South Carolina rescinds its Ordinance of Nullification. **[1832:HIST/3]** **2** Pres. Jackson orders public funds to be withdrawn from the Bank of the United States and deposited in state ("pet") banks. He charges the Bank is a monopoly. **3** American Anti-Slavery Society is founded by abolitionist groups from New York and New England.	**4** Antonio López de Santa Anna is elected President of Mexico. **5** Slavery is abolished in the British Empire. **6** Muhammad Ali of Egypt acquires control of all Syria. **7** Facing defeat by Muhammad Ali, the Ottoman Sultan accepts Russian military aid and concludes the Treaty of Hunkar Iskelesi. **8** Bavarian prince becomes the first King of Greece as Otto I. **9** German states join the Zollverein, a union organized to eliminate trade barriers among the members of the German Confederation. **[1816:HIST/6]**	**1** Thomas Ustick Walter, architect, designs Founder's Hall at Girard College, Pa. It is considered the finest example of Greek revival architecture in the U.S. **2** Architects Ithiel Town and Alexander Jackson Davis design the U.S. Custom House in New York City.	**3** Tennyson, mourning the death of his friend, Eng. essayist Arthur Henry Hallam, begins work on his great elegy, *In Memoriam* (–1850). **4** Mendelssohn composes *Italian Symphony,* his fourth and most popular symphony. **5** Balzac publishes *Eugénie Grandet,* a description of provincial life.
1834	**1** Whig Party is formed, succeeding the National Republicans as the anti-Jackson party. Party ends after 1852 election. **2** Senate adopts Henry Clay's resolution censuring Pres. Jackson for removing public funds from the Bank of the United States.	**6** Quadruple Alliance (Great Britain, France, Portugal, and Spain) is formed to support Spain's constitutional government and the throne of Isabella II against the Carlists, supporters of Don Carlos who claims the throne. Civil war occurs in Spain. **7** War occurs between the	**1** William Dunlap publishes *History of the Rise and Progress of the Arts of Design in the United States.*	**2** Southey's prose collection, *The Doctor* (–1847) introduces and popularizes the fairy tale, "The Three Bears." **3** Lytton publishes his detailed historical novel, *The Last Days of Pompeii.*

Science & Technology		Miscellaneous		
America	**Elsewhere**	**America**	**Elsewhere**	

4 Mass. legalizes the dissection of cadavers in medical schools.
5 Cholera epidemic sweeps major American cities.
6 Thomas Nuttall, Eng.-Amer. ornithologist, publishes a guide to North American birds.

Felix Mendelssohn, German composer

begins operating with the first streetcar in the world. Built by John Stephenson, it is the "John Mason," a horse-drawn car which runs on lower Fourth Ave.
4 A reaper invented by Cyrus H. McCormick is successfully demonstrated.
5 Asian cholera breaks out in New York City where there are 2251 deaths. Within a 12-day period, 6000 people die in New Orleans.

1833

1 Beaumont publishes *Experiments and Observations on the Gastric Juice and the Physiology of Digestion* stating that digestion is caused by chemicals released by the stomach wall. **[1822:SCI/1]**
2 Edward Hitchcock, Mass. geologist, completes a geological survey of Massachusetts.

3 J. Herschel embarks on a trip to the southern hemisphere to make astronomical observations.
4 Faraday coins the terms *electrolysis, electrolyte, anode,* and *cathode.*
5 Wilhelm Weber, Ger. physicist, develops an electromagnetic telegraph.
6 Fr. mathematician Siméon-Dénis Poisson publishes *Treatise on Mechanics,* which becomes the standard text on mechanics.

1 Early form of baseball is played in Philadelphia by the Olympic Ball Club. Many of the rules are like those of English cricket.
2 Expedition led by Joseph R. Walker climbs the Sierra Nevada from the east, reaches Yosemite Valley in Mexican Upper California.
3 Oberlin College is established in Ohio as a center of Abolitionist activity. It is the first college to admit both men and women. In 1835 it becomes the first to admit Negroes.
4 Publication of the *Sketches and Eccentricities of Col. David Crockett, of West Tennessee,* helps launch the legend of Davy Crockett throughout America.

5 First state grant for public education is made in England.
6 East India Company's monopoly of trade in China ends.
7 Scot. explorer Alexander Burns crosses the Hindu Kush mountain range in Central Asia.
8 Factory Act forbids the employment in the textile industry of children under 9 years, restricts labor of those between 9 and 13 to a 9-hour day, and of those from 13 to 18 to a 12-hour day. Children under 13 are to have 2 hours' schooling a day.
9 Grand National Consolidated Trades Union is formed in London.

1834

1 Allen patents an automatic cutoff valve for steam engines.
2 Cyrus H. McCormick, Va. inventor, patents a successful reaper which he invented in 1831.
3 Jacob Perkins, Mass. inventor, patents a compressor. Later models are

5 Babbage discovers the principle of the analytical engine, which eventually leads to the construction of the first computer.
6 Robert Bunsen, Ger. chemist, discovers an antidote for arsenic poisoning.
7 Dumas proves that

1 First printed rules for a game resembling baseball are published in *The Book of Sports.*
2 Methodist minister Jason Lee leads an expedition that explores the Willamette Valley in Oregon and founds the first mission and first farming

4 Slavery is abolished in the British Empire.
5 Fire in London destroys the Houses of Parliament and part of the city.
6 Fr. teacher Louis Braille perfects a system of characters enabling the blind to read.

History and Politics		The Arts	
America	**Elsewhere**	**America**	**Elsewhere**
3 Anti-abolition riots break out in New York City and Philadelphia. **4** Under a treaty signed in 1832, U.S. government orders the Seminole Indians to leave Florida. **[1818:HIST/2]** **5** U.S. and Spain settle territorial claims.	Kaffirs (Bantu people) and white settlers of Cape Colony in South Africa. **8** Parliament defeats O'Connell's motion to repeal union of Great Britain and Ireland. **[1829:HIST/5]** **9** Sir Robert Peel becomes Prime Minister of Great Britain. He sets forth the principles of the British Conservative Party in his Tamworth Manifesto.		**4** Berlioz's symphony, *Harold en Italie,* is based on Byron's poem. **[1812:ARTS/4]** **5** Pushkin publishes "The Queen of Spades," a popular short story. **6** Balzac publishes *Le Père Goriot.* **7** Delacroix paints "Les Femmes d'Alger."
1835			
1 Mexico rejects Texans' petition for statehood. Texas Revolution breaks out when Mexicans try to disarm Americans in Gonzales. Samuel Houston is made commander of Texan army. **2** Unsuccessful attempt to assassinate Jackson is first attack on the life of a U.S. President. **3** Seminole Indian War begins when Seminoles refuse to move to territory beyond the Mississippi. Seminoles attack and massacre U.S. troops. **[1842:HIST/2]** **4** Gold is found on Cherokee land in Georgia. Cherokee Indians are forced to cede lands to U.S. **[1838:HIST/3]**	**5** Municipal Corporations Act ensures a uniform plan of government in most cities and boroughs in England. **6** Juan Manuel de Rosas establishes a dictatorship in Argentina. **7** Mexico establishes highly centralized government. **8** Turks put an end to Tripoli's independence. Turkish governor replaces Karamanli ruler. **9** Conspiracy forces Milosh Obrenovich, autocratic ruler in Serbia, to summon a popular assembly and grant a constitution.	**1** A chair of Sacred Music is established at Oberlin College.	**2** Charles Dickens, Eng. writer, publishes his first book, *Sketches by Boz,* a collection of short stories. **3** Dan. author Hans Christian Andersen publishes the first volume of his fairy tales. **4** Pol. poet Zygmunt Kasiński's *Undivine Comedy* is the first literary work to deal with class war between rich and poor. **5** Elias Lönnrot compiles, writes, and edits *Kalevala,* the national epic of Finland.
1836			
1 Texas declares its independence. Mexican army under Santa Anna massacres Texan forces at the Alamo and at Goliad. Houston's army defeats the Mexicans and captures Santa Anna at the Battle of San Jacinto. Texas becomes an independent republic with Houston as president. **2** Arkansas becomes 25th state. **3** Wisconsin Territory is formed from western part of the Michigan Territory. **4** Martin Van Buren (Demo-	**5** Andrés Santa Cruz, President of Bolivia, invades Peru and establishes a Peru-Bolivia confederation. **[1839:HIST/5]** **6** Boer farmers and cattlemen leave Cape Colony, South Africa, to escape British rule and found Transvaal, Natal, and the Orange Free State. **[1838:HIST/6]** **7** Unsuccessful plot to kill King Louis Philippe in 1835 results in more repressive laws by the French government. The King gains personal power by splitting the liberal movement and ap-	**1** Ralph Waldo Emerson publishes *Nature,* in which he explains the basic tenets of the Transcendentalist movement. **2** Architect Robert Mills designs the U.S. Treasury Building and the Washington Monument. **3** Thomas Cole paints "The Course of Empire," a series of five huge paintings.	**4** Ger. Romantic composer Robert Schumann composes *Fantasy in C Major.* **5** Russ. novelist Nikolai Vasilyevich Gogol stages his satirical play, *The Inspector General.* **6** Dickens publishes *Pickwick Papers,* which describe the humorous adventures of the imaginary Pickwick Club. **7** Mikhail Ivanovich Glinka composes *A Life for the Tsar,* often

Science & Technology		Miscellaneous		
America	**Elsewhere**	**America**	**Elsewhere**	
widely used in air conditioners and refrigerators. **4** Amalgam (a mercury alloy) is introduced as a filling material for decayed teeth.	the halogens can replace hydrogens in organic compounds.	settlement. **3** Americans begin to eat tomatoes, which had been considered poisonous and had been used ornamentally as "love apples."		
1 Burden invents a horseshoe machine that is later used to make most of the horseshoes needed by the Union Army during the Civil War. **2** America's first cast iron bridge is built over Dunlap's Creek in Brownsville, Pa. Sculpture of Hans Christian Andersen reading to children	**3** Coriolis describes the Coriolis effect (the deflection of a moving body with respect to the Earth's surface, caused by the Earth's rotation), a concept important in the study of weather systems.	**1** Nearly 30,000 people see the 10-mile foot race at Union Course on Long Island, N.Y. For a purse of $1000, 9 contestants run the course in less than an hour. Henry Stannard wins the race in 59 min. 44 sec. **2** Fire destroys 530 buildings in New York City, resulting in a loss of more than $20 million. **3** *New York Herald* is established by James Gordon Bennett. It is the first newspaper to specialize in reporting on crime and society news. **4** Samuel Colt designs a pistol with a revolving cartridge cylinder. Cheaply mass-produced with interchangeable parts, the rapid fire and handsized revolver is especially useful for men on horseback.	**5** The polka is first danced in Prague, Czechoslovakia.	**1835**
1 John Ericsson, Swed.-Amer. inventor, patents a screw propeller with blades. **2** Asa Gray, N.Y. botanist, publishes *Elements of Botany*. **3** Thomas H. Sumner, Mass. navigator, devises an accurate and fairly simple way for sailors to determine their position at sea.	**4** Daniell invents the Daniell cell—an improved electric cell which provides an even, continuous current. **5** Louis Agassiz, Swiss naturalist, while studying glaciers in the Alps, concludes that polar ice caps once covered most of Europe. **6** Francis Baily, Eng. astronomer, gives detailed descriptions of the bright spots (Baily's beads) along the Moon's edge during a total eclipse.	**1** A First and Second Reader compiled by William Holmes McGuffey is published for use in public schools. Except in New England, *McGuffey's Readers* become standard elementary school textbooks for nearly 100 years. **2** Mary Lyon founds Mount Holyoke Female Seminary (later Mount Holyoke College) at South Hadley, Mass. **3** Massachusetts child labor law requires chil-	**4** University of London is founded. It is the first institution of higher learning not connected with any particular religious group. **5** Schopenhauer publishes *On the Will in Nature*.	**1836**

191

	History and Politics		The Arts	
	America	**Elsewhere**	**America**	**Elsewhere**
	crat) is elected President. Since none of the four Vice-Presidential candidates receives an electoral majority, the Senate, for the first and only time, chooses Richard M. Johnson (Democrat) for the office.	pointing weak men to office.		considered Russia's first opera. 8 Thomas Carlyle, Scot. historian, publishes *Sartor Resartus*.
1837	1 Michigan becomes 26th state. 2 U.S. troops under Zachary Taylor defeat the Seminoles at the Battle of Okeechobee. [1835:HIST/3] 3 Canadian militia cross the Niagara River and seize on the U.S. side the *Caroline*, a steamer in the service of Canadian rebels. Pres. Van Buren declares that neutrality laws should be observed. 4 Act of Congress increases Supreme Court membership from seven to nine.	5 Victoria becomes Queen of Great Britain and Ireland. 6 Provincial revolts and separatist movements occur in Brazil until direct monarchial government is reestablished in 1840. 7 Constitutional conflict leads to unsuccessful rebellions against Britain's colonial government in Upper and Lower Canada. [1840:HIST/5] 8 Crowns of Hanover and Great Britain are separated after a union of 123 years. 9 Benjamin Disraeli is elected to the British Parliament.	1 Hawthorne's *Twice-Told Tales,* his first signed work, brings the author public recognition. 2 Painter George Catlin exhibits his "Gallery of Indians," a series of more than 500 paintings and sketches of various American Indians. 3 Alexander Davis publishes *Rural Residences,* which popularizes Gothic revival architecture for country homes. 4 Emerson publishes *The American Scholar,* in which he asserts America's literary independence from England.	5 Dickens publishes *Oliver Twist,* an immediate bestseller. 6 Berlioz's *Requiem—Grand Messe des Morts* calls for 600 singers, a full orchestra, 4 brass bands, and 16 kettledrums. 7 Scot. author John Gibson Lockhart publishes a biography of his father-in-law, *Memoirs of the Life of Sir Walter Scott.* 8 Carlo Blasis becomes Director of the Imperial Ballet, Milan, and revolutionizes technique of Ital. dancers.
1838	1 Iowa Territory is formed from part of Wisconsin Territory. 2 Congress adopts "gag resolutions" against anti-slavery petitions and motions. 3 U.S. troops forcibly move the Cherokee Indians from Georgia to Indian Territory (eastern Oklahoma). 4 Some northern states pass Personal Liberty Laws which obstruct the Fugitive Slave Act. Southern slaves develop a system of escape routes to the North, known as the Underground Railroad. [1793:HIST/2]	5 Political reform movement known as Chartism begins in Great Britain, seeking more power for laborers and parliamentary reform. [1839:HIST/6] 6 Boers defeat the Zulus at the Battle of Blood River, Natal. 7 British help the Afghans repulse an attack by the Persians against Herat, Afghanistan. 8 Ottoman Sultan, supported by Russia, forces the repeal of Serbia's constitution and establishes a ruling senate with complete power. [1835:HIST/9]	1 Frances Anne Kemble writes *Journal of a Residence on a Georgia Plantation in 1838–1839,* which contains an account of contemporary black music. 2 T. Cole paints "Shroon Mountain Adirondacks," a Hudson River School classic. 3 Sully goes to London to paint a life-sized portrait of Queen Victoria. 4 Music is taught in Boston schools.	5 Dickens's novel, *Nicholas Nickleby,* appears in serial form. 6 Thorvaldsen completes "Christ and the Twelve Apostles," his most famous sculpture. 7 Soprano Jenny Lind, known as the "Swedish Nightingale," is a smash hit in her debut as Agathe in Weber's *Der Freischütz* (1820) at the Stockholm Royal Theater. 8 Brentano publishes one of his most popular works, a fairy tale entitled *Gockel, Hinkel und Gackeleia.*
1839	1 Maine tries to prevent Canadian lumbering in Aroostock territory claimed by	4 Political conflict and civil war ends the Central American Federation, which dis-	1 Henry Wadsworth Longfellow publishes the Romantic novel	4 Stendhal publishes *The Charterhouse of Parma,* a popular

Science & Technology		Miscellaneous		
America	Elsewhere	America	Elsewhere	
	7 Theodor Schwann, Ger. physiologist, discovers the digestive enzyme pepsin.	dren to attend school for at least 3 months a year until they are 15. Manufacturers are not allowed to hire children in their mills for more than 9 months a year.		
1 James Dana, N.Y. geologist, publishes *System of Mineralogy*. **2** Thomas Davenport, Vt. inventor, patents a crude electric motor. **3** Charles Page, Mass. physicist, designs an early induction coil.	**4** Baer describes embryonic structures in his work *On the Development of Animals*. **5** Von Struve publishes *Micrometric Measurement of Double Stars*. **6** Encke discovers a small gap in Saturn's outer ring. This gap is now known as Encke's Division.	**1** Novelist Nathaniel Hawthorne reports that young officers at the Charlestown Navy Yard in Massachusetts had started wearing moustaches, a fashion from England. **2** Blacksmith John Deere invents the first plow with a steel moldboard, necessary for plowing heavy, sticky prairie soil. This improvement eventually revolutionizes prairie farming. **3** P.T. Barnum convinces the public that Joyce Heth, a woman weighing 46 lbs., was the nurse who brought George Washington into the world and is, therefore, 161 years old. She is Barnum's first successful hoax.	**4** Ger. educational reformer Friedrich Fröbel opens his first kindergarten in Germany.	**1837**
1 Morse introduces the Morse code. **2** Charles A. Spencer, N.Y. scientist, makes America's first microscope. **3** John Torrey and Asa Gray publish *Flora of North America* (-1843). **4** Chauncey Jerome, Conn. clockmaker, invents a one-day, brass movement clock that is so inexpensive and accurate that it soon floods the British and American markets and gives rise to the expression, "Yankee ingenuity."	**5** Lyell publishes *Elements of Geology*.	**1** Steamer *Moselle* explodes on the Ohio River near Cincinnati, killing 100 people. **2** Charles Wilkins (for the U.S. Navy) sails on a 6-vessel expedition to the Pacific Ocean and the South Seas. During the 4-year voyage, he discovers that the land in the Antarctic Ocean is actually a continent.	**3** Fr. philosopher Auguste Comte gives the basic social science of sociology its name. **4** First traveling post office operates between Birmingham and Liverpool, England.	**1838**
1 Charles Goodyear, Conn. inventor, produces vulcanized rubber when	**6** Darwin summarizes his trip in *Journal of Researches into the Geology*	**1** John Lowell, Jr. founds the Lowell Institute in Boston to provide	**5** Amer. traveler John Lloyd Stephens discovers and examines (along with	**1839**

History and Politics		The Arts	
America	**Elsewhere**	**America**	**Elsewhere**

both Maine and New Brunswick. So-called Aroostock War is averted by an agreement to refer the dispute to a boundary commission. **2** Liberty Party, the first anti-slavery party, holds national convention in Warsaw, N.Y. **3** France recognizes Texas independence. **[1836:HIST/1]**	solves into the states of Guatemala, Honduras, Nicaragua, El Salvador, and Costa Rica. **5** Chilean forces defeat Santa Cruz's forces at the Battle of Yungay, ending the Peru-Bolivia confederation. **6** Parliament rejects Chartist petition. Riots in Birmingham and elsewhere in Great Britain lead to the arrest of Chartist leaders. **[1838:HIST/5]** **7** Dutch recognize the independence of Belgium. Luxembourg and Limburg are divided between the Dutch and Belgian crowns. **8** Ibrahim Pasha defeats Turkish forces; Turkish fleet surrenders to Muhammad Ali of Egypt. **[1832:HIST/7]** **9** China prohibits the importation of opium. First Opium War between Great Britain and China begins. **[1842:HIST/9]**	*Hyperion* and the book of poems *Voices of the Night.* **2** Richard Upjohn designs the Gothic Revival Trinity Church in New York City. **3** R. Mills designs the U.S. Patent Office building.	Romantic novel. **5** Berlioz completes the choral symphony, *Roméo et Juliette.* Trinity Church in New York City

1840	**1** U.S., Britain, Holland, and Belgium recognize Texas independence. **2** Congress enacts Independent Treasury Act, establishing subtreasuries for the deposit of federal funds in major U.S. cities. All government payments are to be in specie (coined money) by 1843. **3** William Henry Harrison (Whig) is elected President, using the slogan "Tippecanoe and Tyler too." John Tyler (Whig) becomes Vice President. **[1811:HIST/1]**	**4** Muhammad Ali rejects terms of the Treaty of London. United European opposition forces him to return the Turkish fleet and to give up claims to Syria, in return for hereditary rule in Egypt. **5** British Parliament unites Upper and Lower Canada under one government by Act of Union. **6** Pedro II is declared Emperor of Brazil. His reign is a period of order and material progess. **7** Rafael Carrera becomes dictator of Guatemala. **8** British capture Chusan and Canton River forts in China. **9** Dost Muhammad of Afghanistan wages war against the British, who restore Shah Shuja to the throne. **[1826:HIST/6]**	**1** Sculptor Horatio Greenough executes a statue of Washington in the Neoclassical style. Public outrage at the sandaled and semi-clad depiction of the first President prevents the statue from being placed in the Capitol building. **2** Cooper publishes *The Pathfinder,* the fourth "Leatherstocking Tale." **3** Poe publishes *Tales of the Grotesque and Arabesque,* which includes his famous work "The Fall of the House of Usher."	**4** Prosper Mérimée, Fr. writer known for his classical treatment of Romantic themes, publishes *Colomba,* a popular novella. **5** Concerned about the possibility of a French invasion, Ger. poet Max Schneckenburger writes "Die Wacht am Rhein" ("Watch on the Rhine"). When music is added (1854) by Karl Wilhelm, it becomes a popular patriotic song. **6** Mikhail Yuryevich Lermontov, Russia's greatest Romantic poet, publishes *A Hero of Our Times,* a realistic novel influential in the development of Russian prose. **7** Donizetti composes *The Daughter of the Regiment,* a comic opera.
1841	**1** Harrison dies one month after inauguration. Tyler be-	**4** New Zealand is made a separate British colony.	**1** Andrew Jackson Downing, horticulturist	**6** R. Browning publishes "Pippa Passes,"

Science & Technology		Miscellaneous		
America	**Elsewhere**	**America**	**Elsewhere**	

Science & Technology		Miscellaneous		
he accidentally spills India rubber and sulfur on a hot stove. (Patented in 1844.) **2** Audubon publishes *Birds of North America.* **3** Harvard Astronomical Observatory is established with William Bond as director. A 15-in. refracting telescope is added in 1847. **4** Isaac Babbitt, Mass. inventor, produces Babbitt metal, an alloy used for lining bearings. **5** Baltimore College of Dental Surgery opens.	*and Natural History of the Various Countries Visited by HMS Beagle, 1832–36.* **7** Carl Gustav Mosander, Swed. chemist, discovers the element lanthanum. **8** Schwann describes the cell as the basic unit of life. **9** Louis Daguerre, Fr. physicist, invents the daguerreotype process, the first form of photography.	free public lectures by eminent scholars. **2** First baseball diamond is laid out at Cooperstown, N.Y., by Abner Doubleday. **3** First "normal" school is started in Lexington, Mass., offering a two-year course to high school graduates preparing to be teachers. **4** Josephine Amelia Perkins is the first lady horse thief on record. Born in England, she stole her first horse from her father. In America her career developed. She was eventually jailed.	Frederick Catherwood) the antiquities of the ancient Mayan culture in Central America. **6** Henley Royal regatta, a rowing race, is established at Henley-on-Thames, England. **7** First Grand National (steeple-chase) race is run at Aintree, England. **8** Scot. inventor Kirkpatrick Macmillan builds an early model of the bicycle. **9** Prussia restricts child labor to a maximum of 10 hours a day.	
1 American Society of Dental Surgeons is organized in New York City. **2** John W. Draper, Eng.-Amer. chemist, takes the first photographs of the Moon. **3** Graphite is produced commercially in Ticonderoga, N.Y.	**4** James Joule, Eng. physicist, publishes *On the Production of Heat By Voltaic Electricity,* in which the Joule effect is introduced.	**1** An order by the President establishes the 10-hour day for federal employees. This has long been a goal of U.S. labor. **2** First use of the expression *O.K.* It referred to "Old Kinderhook," birthplace of President Martin Van Buren, and was the name of a Democratic Club in New York City. **3** Steamboat *Lexington* catches fire near Eaton's Neck, N.Y.; 140 people die. **4** First steamship line with scheduled transatlantic sailings is established by Samuel Cunard, a Canadian. **5** Sixth national census shows a population of more than 17 million. About 600,000 immigrants have arrived since 1830.	**6** Emigration from Great Britain to the U.S. for the past 10 years is 75,810; from Ireland, 207,381. **7** Rowland Hill establishes the penny post for letters under 1/2 ounce to any point in the United Kingdom. This replaces the earlier system of charging by size, shape, and weight of letters.	**1840**
1 Hitchcock completes a second, more detailed geo-	**3** James Braid, Eng. surgeon, investigates the	**1** Earliest commercial use of oil begins about	**5** Ross leads an expedition to Antarctica and	**1841**

comes first Vice President to succeed to Presidency.

2 Tyler twice vetoes a bill creating a national bank with state branches. Whigs denounce Tyler, whose entire Cabinet except for Daniel Webster resigns.

3 Congress passes Preemption Act. Settlers on surveyed government land have the right, after about 14 months of residence, to buy it before anyone else can.

5 Britain, France, Austria, Russia, and Prussia agree to close the Straits (Bosporus and Dardanelles) to all but Turkish warships in time of peace.

6 British seize Hong Kong and Chinkiang on the Grand Canal.

7 Peru makes unsuccessful attempt to annex Bolivian territory.

8 Gen. Baldomero Espartero is made regent by the Cortes (Parliament) and becomes virtual dictator of Spain.

and architect, publishes *Treatise on Landscape Gardening,* which emphasizes the relationship between a dwelling and its surroundings.

2 Cooper publishes *The Deerslayer,* the fifth "Leatherstocking Tale."

3 James Russell Lowell, writer and poet, publishes *A Year's Life,* a work inspired by his wife, poetess Maria White.

4 Catlin publishes *Letters and Notes on the Manners, Customs, and Condition of the North American Indians,* compiled while doing his many Indian paintings. **[1837:ARTS/2]**

5 Longfellow publishes *Ballads and Other Poems,* which includes "The Wreck of the Hesperus."

a dramatic idyll.

7 Schumann composes *Symphony No. 1 in B Flat Major* (revised in 1851) and *Symphony No. 4 in D Minor* (*Spring Symphony*).

8 Dickens publishes *The Old Curiosity Shop* and *Barnaby Rudge.*

9 Italy's prima ballerina, Carlotta Grisi, dances the title role in *Giselle,* an outstanding ballet written by Adolphe Adam and Théophile Gautier, choreographed by Jean Corelli and Jules Perrot.

1842

1 Dorr's Rebellion in Rhode Island leads to new state constitution with liberalization of voting requirements.

2 U.S. troops, after destroying the Seminoles' crops and villages, force the Indians to sign peace treaty. Seminoles are moved to Indian Territory in the West (eastern Oklahoma).

3 Webster-Ashburton Treaty between the U.S. and Britain ends Northeast boundary dispute and establishes U.S.-Canadian border from Maine to Lake of the Woods (northern Minnesota). **[1839:HIST/1]**

4 Congress passes Whig tariff law with high protective levels.

5 Parliament rejects second Chartist petition. **[1838:HIST/5]**

6 French make treaties with native chiefs of the Ivory Coast.

7 British repulse the Boers in Natal, South Africa, and reestablish control.

8 Afghans massacre British and Indian troops and murder Shah Shuja. Dost Muhammad again ascends the throne at Kabul after the British evacuation of Afghanistan. **[1840:HIST/9]**

9 Treaty of Nanking ends Opium War. China cedes Hong Kong to Britain and opens its ports to foreign trade.

1 Emerson becomes editor of *The Dial,* the influential publication of the Transcendentalist movement. **[1836:ARTS/1]**

2 Showman Edwin P. Christy founds the Christy Minstrels.

3 The New York Philharmonic, is founded. It is the oldest symphony orchestra in America.

4 Ger. Romantic composer Richard Wagner successfully stages his opera, *Rienzi,* in Dresden.

5 Some of Tennyson's best works are included in *Poems*: "Locksley Hall," "Morte d'Arthur," "Ulysses," etc.

6 Fr. artist Théodore Rousseau establishes the Barbizon school of landscape painting with "Under the Birches, Evening."

7 Fr. novelist Eugène Sue publishes *Les Mystères de Paris,* a sensational bestseller that describes the Paris underworld.

Science & Technology

America

logical survey of Mass.
2 Coke, a coal product, is manufactured in Connellsville, Pa.

P. T. Barnum and Tom Thumb

Elsewhere

therapeutic value of hypnosis.
4 Sir Joseph Whitworth, Eng. engineer, devises the standard screw thread.

Miscellaneous

America

this time. "Rock oil" skimmed from the surface of streams in northwestern Pennsylvania is renamed "Seneca Oil," and sold as patent—or "Indian"—medicine.
2 Steamboat *Erie* burns on Lake Erie; 175 persons are killed.
3 *New York Tribune* is published by Horace Greeley. It becomes the most influential newspaper in the North and West, until the Civil War.
4 Brook Farm, a cooperative program based on an economy of farming and handcrafts, is founded in West Roxbury, Mass., by George Ripley, a Unitarian Minister and a Transcendentalist.

Elsewhere

takes possession for Great Britain of all of the continental land and islands he discovers.
6 First law is passed protecting workers in France.
7 Earthquake in Shinano, Japan, kills about 12,000 people.
8 *Punch,* an illustrated periodical, is published in London. It becomes famous for its satiric humor, caricatures, and cartoons.
9 Travel agent Thomas Cook leads his first tour from England to Europe.

---

1 Crawford Long, Ga. physician, performs the first successful surgery on a patient anesthetized with ether, but does not publicize his results until 1849.
2 Samuel Dana, N.H. chemist, describes the usefulness of phosphates (in manure) as a fertilizer.
3 Henry discovers the oscillatory (back and forth movement) nature of an electrical discharge. He also experiments with wireless communication.
4 James Bogardus, N.Y. inventor, designs a dry gas meter.
5 Matthew F. Maury, Va. oceanographer, charts ocean currents.

6 Christian Doppler, Aust. physicist, states the Doppler effect, which relates the frequency of a sound or light wave to motion.
7 Darwin publishes *Structure and Distribution of Coral Reefs.*
8 Anders Adolf Retzius, Swed. anatomist and anthropologist, proposes the cranial index, a method of determining race by skull size.
9 Lord William Thomson Kelvin, Brit. scientist, publishes *On the Uniform Motion of Heat in Homogeneous Solid Bodies.*
10 Hermann von Helmholtz, Ger. physicist, writes on the relation between nerve fibers and nerve cells.
11 Werner von Siemens, Ger. scientist, invents an electroplating process.

1 Horse race at the Union Course on Long Island attracts thousands of spectators. "Fashion" (the North's entry) beats "Boston" (the South's entry) for a purse of $20,000.
2 Massachusetts law regulates the work day for children under 12 years. They are limited to a 10-hour day.
3 Barnum's American Museum opens in New York City. P.T. Barnum exhibits General Tom Thumb and other freaks as well as many hoaxes, attracting the public with extravagant advertising.
4 Explorer John Frémont leads an expedition to explore the route to Oregon beyond the Mississippi River, as far as South Pass in Wyoming.

5 Fire destroys much of Hamburg, Germany; damage reaches $35 million.
6 *Illustrated World* is published weekly in London. It is the first periodical to make extensive use of woodcuts and engravings.
7 Mine Act in England forbids women and children to work in the mines.

1842

History and Politics		The Arts	
America	**Elsewhere**	**America**	**Elsewhere**

1843

America

1 U.S. sends diplomatic representative to Hawaii.
2 Settlers begin great migration westward over the Oregon Trail to the Oregon Territory.
3 Mexican Pres. Santa Anna declares that U.S. annexation of Texas will mean war with Mexico. British and French intrigues to make Texas an independent buffer state against U.S. expansion arouse U.S. concern. Southerners push for the annexation of Texas. [1845:HIST/2]

Elsewhere

4 Uprising in Spain drives Gen. Espartero from power. Isabella II is declared of age as Queen of Spain.
5 Gambia is separated from Sierra Leone and made a separate British colony. Britain annexes Natal to Cape Colony.
6 British take control of the province of Sind in the lower Indus Valley.
7 British settlers in New Zealand wage war against the Maoris concerning land.
8 Serbia's popular assembly elects Alexander Karageorgevich to the throne.

The Arts — America

1 Poe publishes the short stories "The Murders in the Rue Morgue," "The Pit and the Pendulum," and "The Tell-Tale Heart."

Edgar Allan Poe, U.S. poet, short-story writer, and critic

The Arts — Elsewhere

2 Dickens publishes *Martin Chuzzlewit* and *A Christmas Carol.*
3 Wordsworth is appointed poet laureate of England.
4 Eng. critic and artist John Ruskin publishes the first volume of *Modern Painters* (–1860, 5 vols.).
5 Wagner's Romantic style is shown in the premiere of *The Flying Dutchman,* an opera.
6 Mendelssohn completes the music to *A Midsummer Night's Dream,* including the famous "Wedding March." [1826:ARTS/3]

1844

America

1 Secretary of State John C. Calhoun negotiates treaty of annexation with Texas government.
2 Britain and U.S. argue about Oregon boundary, which was unofficially set at latitude 54°40′N by U.S. settlers. [1827:HIST/2]
3 James K. Polk (Democrat) is elected President; George M. Dallas (Democrat) is elected Vice President.
4 U.S. and China sign treaty of peace, friendship, and commerce.

Elsewhere

5 Dominicans successfully revolt against Haitian rule; Santo Domingo (eastern two-thirds of Hispaniola) proclaims its independence as the Dominican Republic.
6 French defeat the Moroccans at the Battle of Isly. Treaty of Tangiers forces the Sultan of Morocco to renounce his ally, the leader of Algeria.
7 Britain's House of Lords releases O'Connell, who was arrested (1843) and convicted for conspiracy in advocating a free Ireland. [1829:HIST/5]

The Arts — America

1 Stephen Collins Foster, song composer, writes "Open Thy Lattice, Love."
2 John Henry Belter, Ger. born furniture maker, introduces the Victorian Rococo furniture style to the U.S. [1858:ARTS/2]
3 Poe publishes the short story "The Premature Burial."
4 Chopin attends the European debut of Amer. pianist Louis Gottschalk and predicts his success.

The Arts — Elsewhere

5 Alexandre Dumas *père,* Fr. novelist, publishes *The Three Musketeers,* a swashbuckling adventure tale.
6 Fr. painter Jean-François Millet exhibits "The Milkmaid."
7 Inspired by Elizabeth Barrett's *Poems,* Robert Browning begins a correspondence that results in their famous courtship and marriage (1846).
8 William Makepeace Thackeray, Eng. novelist, publishes *Barry Lyndon,* a satirical romance.

1845

America

1 Florida becomes 27th state.
2 Texas accepts annexation

Elsewhere

4 Spain institutes a new constitution.
5 Seven Catholic cantons of

The Arts — America

1 The transition from the 4-stringed "bonjo" to the modern 5-

The Arts — Elsewhere

5 Dumas *père* publishes *The Count of Monte Cristo,* a popu-

Science & Technology		Miscellaneous		
America	Elsewhere	America	Elsewhere	
1 Oliver Wendell Holmes, Mass. physician, suggests that since puerperal fever (a disease associated with childbirth) is so contagious, doctors should be careful not to spread the disease from one patient to the next. He stresses that doctors should put on clean clothes and wash their hands before delivering a baby. **[1848:SCI/7]** **2** Alexander Bache, Pa. physicist, heads the reorganized U.S. Coast Survey. **3** Congress grants $30,000 for Morse to erect a 40-mile telegraph line between Baltimore and Washington, D.C. **4** A comet appears over North America sparking new interest in astronomy.	**5** Hamilton devises the system of complex numbers based on *i*, the square root of -1. **6** Samuel H. Schwabe, Ger. astronomer, discovers that sunspot activity follows an eleven-year cycle. **7** Joule determines the mechanical equivalent of heat (the amount of work necessary to generate a unit of heat). **8** Wheatstone successfully measures electrical resistance with a device later known as the Wheatstone bridge.	**1** Rowing is introduced at Harvard when William Weeks, a student, buys and outfits a shell. **2** Soap powder, "Babbitt's Best Soap," is introduced by Benjamin T. Babbitt. **3** Frémont's second expedition surveys the route to Oregon and he maps and names the Great Basin, the independent system of lakes and rivers divided from the ocean by the mountains. **4** New word *millionaire* is used by newspapers for the first time in reporting the death of Pierre Lorillard, banker and tobacco grower.	**5** First workers' cooperative societies, called Pioneers of Rochedale, are organized in England. **6** British Archaeological Association and the Royal Archaeological Institute of Great Britain are founded. **7** Scot. church leader Thomas Chalmers leads the Scottish Disruption when 474 clergy withdraw from the general assembly to form the United Free Church of Scotland. **8** Danish philosopher Søren Kierkegaard preaches a religion of acceptance and suffering on the part of the individual; his teaching is a forerunner of the philosophy of existentialism.	**1843**
1 Morse sends the first telegraph message, "What hath God wrought!" from Washington, D.C., to Baltimore. **2** Charles Wilkes, N.Y. scientist, publishes the results of the U.S. Exploring Expedition (1838–42) to Antarctica and the Pacific Northwest. **3** Iron is used for railroad tracks.	**4** Darwin publishes *Geological Observations on Volcanic Islands*. **5** Coriolis publishes *Treatise on the Mechanics of Solid Bodies*. **6** William Siemens, Ger. scientist, develops a mechanical copying method. **7** Robert Chambers, Scot. publisher, anonymously describes his theory of evolution in *Vestiges of the Natural History of Creation*. This work influenced Darwin's theories. **[1859:SCI/5]**	**1** Celebrated news hoax led by poet and writer Edgar Allan Poe and printed in the *New York Sun* reports a balloon crossing of the Atlantic bringing passengers from Europe to America. **2** First private bath in an American hotel is installed in the New York Hotel, and the first bridal suite is available at the Irving House in New York City.	**3** Danish educator, Bishop Nikolai Grundtvig founds the first institute for adult education in Denmark. Young people of every class attend the voluntary residential folk high schools in which they are encouraged to educate themselves and others. **4** Young Men's Christian Association (YMCA) is founded in England by George Williams. **5** Political philosopher Friedrich Engels publishes *The Condition of the Working Class in England* in Leipzig, Germany. **6** First public baths and wash-houses open in Liverpool, England. **7** Factory Act in England forbids children under 13 to work more than 6½ hours a day.	**1844**
1 Horace Wells, Conn. dentist, fails in a public attempt to remove a	**4** Adolf Kolbe, Ger. chemist, synthesizes acetic acid from carbon	**1** One of the earliest labor organizations, the Industrial Congress of the	**6** Failure of the potato crop causes the Great Famine in Ireland; before	**1845**

History and Politics
The Arts

America
Elsewhere
America
Elsewhere

History and Politics — America	History and Politics — Elsewhere	The Arts — America	The Arts — Elsewhere
to the U.S. and becomes 28th state. **3** U.S. envoy is sent to Mexico to settle Texas boundary and to negotiate the purchase of New Mexico and California. Mexico refuses to see him and begins military operations to stop U.S. annexation of Texas.	Switzerland form the *Sonderbund,* a league to protect their interests and prevent the establishment of a more centralized Swiss government. **6** Sikh army from the Punjab crosses the Sutlej River to invade British India. **7** France and Britain oppose Rosas's plan to make Paraguay and Uruguay dependent Argentine states. French and British naval forces blockade the Rio de la Plata for five years. **[1835:HIST/6]**	stringed banjo occurs. **2** Margaret Fuller publishes the feminist work *Woman in the Nineteenth Century.* **3** Poe publishes *The Raven and Other Poems* and *Tales.* **4** The Southern Musical Convention is organized to bring rural singers together for several days of singing.	lar adventure novel. **6** The Portland Vase, the finest existing Roman cameo glass, is restored after being smashed earlier in the year. **7** Wagner composes the opera, *Tannhäuser.* **8** Ingres completes a portrait of the Countess Haussonville. **9** Scot. artists David Octavius Hill and Robert Adamson begin a series of calotype (photographic) portraits.
1846 **1** Mexican War begins. U.S. forces under Gen. Taylor defeat the Mexicans at Palo Alto and Resaca de la Palma and capture Monterrey (Mexico). U.S. naval force occupies Monterey (Calif.) and San Francisco. **2** Michigan becomes first state to enact law abolishing capital punishment. **3** Oregon boundary is established at latitude 49°N. **[1844:HIST/2]** **4** Congress fails to enact the Wilmot Proviso, which bans slavery from any territory acquired from Mexico. **5** U.S. and New Granada sign commercial treaty, giving U.S. right of way across the Isthmus of Panama. **6** Iowa becomes 29th state.	**7** British government repeals the Corn Laws, which restricted the export and import of grain. **8** British forces defeat the Sikhs at Aliwal and Sobraon. By the Treaty of Lahore, the Sikhs are forced to cede Kashmir and to pay an indemnity of 55 million rupees. **9** British Possessions Act gives Canada the right to establish tariffs. **10** British and French are repulsed at Tamatave while protesting the government's order that foreigners are subject to Madagascar's native law.	**1** Architect James Renwick designs the Smithsonian Institution building in Gothic Revival style. **2** Herman Melville, writer, publishes his first novel, *Typee,* dealing with his life among a primitive Polynesian tribe. **3** Playwright Cornelius Mathews writes *Witchcraft, or the Martyrs of Salem.* **4** Poe publishes the short story "The Cask of Amontillado." **5** Emerson's *Poems* include "Woodnotes" and "Give All to Love."	**6** Fyodor Mikhailovich Dostoevsky, one of Russia's greatest novelists, publishes *Poor Folk,* the first Russian social novel. **7** Eng. painter and writer Edward Lear publishes *Book of Nonsense,* a classic in children's literature that popularizes the limerick. **8** Mérimée publishes *Carmen,* a novella. **[1875:ARTS/7]** **9** Berlioz composes the popular symphony, *La Damnation de Faust.* **10** Eng. painter John C. Horseley designs the first painted Christmas card. **11** Belg. instrument maker Antoine Joseph Sax patents the saxophone.
1847 **1** U.S. forces under Gen. Taylor defeat the Mexicans under Gen. Santa Anna at Buena Vista. U.S. forces under Gen. Winfield Scott capture Veracruz, defeat the Mexicans at Cerro Gordo, Churubusco, Molino del Rey, and Chapultepec, and enter Mexico City. Peace negotiations with Mexico begin. **2** All of California comes under U.S. control.	**3** Radical Irish group tries to secure repeal of the union of Great Britain and Ireland. British Parliament suspends Habeas Corpus Act for Ireland. **4** Swiss federal forces defeat the forces of the *Sonderbund,* which is then dissolved, and the central government is strengthened. **[1845:HIST/5]** **5** Liberia becomes a free and independent republic.	**1** Longfellow writes "Evangeline", one of his most famous poetic works. **2** Melville's novel *Omoo* depicts life in Tahiti. **3** The Christy Minstrels begin a ten year engagement at Mechanic's Hall on Broadway.	**4** Each of the Brontë sisters publishes a successful and controversial semiautobiographical novel: Charlotte, *Jane Eyre;* Emily, *Wuthering Heights;* Anne, *Agnes Grey.* **5** Thackeray publishes *Vanity Fair* (-1848). **6** Liszt gives his final piano concert and de-

| Science & Technology | | Miscellaneous | | |
America	Elsewhere	America	Elsewhere	
tooth painlessly from a patient anesthetized with nitrous oxide (laughing gas). Although earlier private attempts were successful, this public demonstration failed because Wells began the operation before the patient was completely anesthetized. **2** Alfred Beach, inventor, establishes *Scientific American* magazine. **3** Erastus Bigelow, Mass. inventor, builds power looms for weaving carpets and tapestries.	disulfide. **5** Rudolf Virchow, Ger. pathologist, publishes an early description of leukemia.	United States, is organized in New York City. **2** First formal rules for baseball are written by Alexander Joy Cartwright. **3** First written examinations begin in elementary schools in Boston. **4** Congress puts presidential election day in the first week in November, after harvest but while roads are still passable. **5** U.S. Naval Academy ("Naval School") opens at Annapolis, Md.	its end, the population is reduced from 8 million to 6.5 million. **7** Fire in a theater in Canton, China, kills 1670 people. **8** Eng. explorer John Franklin leads an expedition to discover the Northwest Passage.	
1 William T. G. Morton, Boston dentist, publicly demonstrates the effectiveness of ether as an anesthetic. John C. Warren, New England's leading surgeon, performs the operation. Morton's claim that he discovered ether leads to years of controversy. [1842:SCI/1] **2** Elias Howe, Mass. inventor, patents a lockstitch sewing machine. [1832:SCI/2]	**3** The planet Neptune is discovered by Ger. astronomers Johann Galle and Heinrich d'Arrest. **4** Ascanio Sobrero, Ital. chemist, synthesizes nitroglycerin. **5** Hugo von Mohl, Ger. botanist, identifies the principal cellular substance and names it *protoplasm*. **6** Louis Agassiz moves to America.	**1** First recorded baseball game is played at Elysian Field in Hoboken, N.J., between the New York Nine and the Knickerbockers. The New York Nine win: 23-1. **2** Smithsonian Institution for scientific research is established by Congress with £1,000,000 left by the will of James Smithson, an Eng. chemist.	**3** Henry Rawlinson opens up ancient Babylonian and Assyrian history by deciphering the Persian cuneiform inscriptions (written with wedge-shaped letters) at Behistun, Iran. **4** *Daily News,* first cheap English newspaper is founded, with author Charles Dickens as editor.	1846

Smithsonian Institution designed by architect James Renwick

America	Elsewhere	America	Elsewhere	
1 Joseph Leidy, Pa. paleontologist, suggests that the environment affects changes (evolution) within a species. **2** Edward Jarvis, Mass. physician, publishes a widely read book that popularizes public health. **3** American Medical Association is established in Philadelphia with Jonathan Knight, Conn. phy-	**7** J. Herschel publishes his extensive observations of the Southern sky. [1833:SCI/3] **8** Babbage makes his little-known invention of the ophthalmoscope. **9** Sir James Simpson, Eng. physician, publishes *Account of a New Anaesthetic Agent,* in which the use of chloroform in childbirth is established.	**1** Adhesive postage stamps are first used. **2** Irish immigration reaches 105,000 (3 times that of the preceding year) because of the potato famine in Ireland.	**3** United Presbyterian Church of Scotland is established. **4** British Factory Act restricts the working day to 10 hours for women and children between 13 and 18 years of age. **5** Influenza epidemic kills about 15,000 in London.	1847

	History and Politics		The Arts	
	America	**Elsewhere**	**America**	**Elsewhere**
		6 British defeat the Kaffirs in South Africa and set up British Kaffraria (now part of Transkei) as a native preserve. **7** French suppress the Berbers in Algeria.		votes himself to composing and conducting. **7** Charles Baudelaire, Fr. poet and critic who inspires the Symbolist movement, publishes his only novel, the autobiographical *La Fanfarlo*. **8** Eng. painter George Frederic Watts exhibits "Alfred Inciting the Saxons," one of the best of his early works.
1848	**1** Treaty of Guadalupe Hidalgo ends Mexican War. Mexico gives up claims to Texas, recognizes Rio Grande as the border, and cedes to the U.S. present-day California, Arizona, Nevada, Utah, and parts of New Mexico, Colorado, and Wyoming in exchange for $15 million and U.S. payment of its citizens' claims against Mexico. **2** Free-Soil Party is formed, opposing slavery in new U.S. territory. **3** Wisconsin becomes 30th state. **4** Zachary Taylor (Whig) is elected President; Millard Fillmore (Whig) is elected Vice President. **5** Gold is discovered at Sutter's Mill on the South Fork of the American River in California's Sacramento Valley. Pres. Polk confirms rumors of the discovery in a farewell message to the public.	**6** February Revolution by workers causes the abdication of Louis Philippe in France. National Assembly convenes; workers demonstrate. Prince Louis Napoleon Bonaparte (later Napoleon III) is elected President of the French Republic. **7** Switzerland becomes one federal union under a new constitution. **8** Revolutions occur in Vienna. Austrian Emperor abdicates in favor of his nephew who becomes Emperor Franz Josef. **9** Liberal revolutions sweep the German states. Frankfurt Parliament meets to draft a constitution for a united Germany. **10** Political and social rebellions occur in Italy, Bohemia, Hungary, Denmark, and Schleswig-Holstein. **11** British defeat the Boers at Boomplaats and establish the Orange River Sovereignty. **12** Nasir ad-Din becomes Shah of Persia. **13** Austrian troops defeat the Sardinian forces of Charles Albert at the Battle of Custozza.	**1** Foster's "Oh! Susanna" becomes a popular song among the '49ers and establishes the songwriter's reputation. **2** J.R. Lowell publishes the poems "Vision of Sir Launfal" and "Fable for Critics." **3** The Musical Fund Society begins its seasonal orchestral concerts in Boston's Tremont Temple.	**4** Eng. artists John Everett Millais, William Holman Hunt, and Dante Gabriel Rossetti establish the Pre-Raphaelite Brotherhood to oppose contemporary trends in painting. **5** Daumier's new style in lithographs establishes him as one of the first Impressionists. **6** Millet completes the first of his famous peasant portraits, "The Winnower." **7** Eng. novelist Mrs. Elizabeth Cleghorn Gaskell wins acclaim for her description of class struggles in *Mary Barton*.
1849	**1** U.S. Department of the Interior is created to meet the needs of Western settlers. **2** Congress establishes the Minnesota Territory. **3** California convention adopts a constitution that forbids slavery and requests ad-	**6** British defeat the Sikhs at Gujarat, India, and annex the Punjab region. **[1845:HIST/6]** **7** Charles Albert of Sardinia is defeated by the Austrians at the Battle of Novara. He goes into exile. **8** Giuseppe Garibaldi, Ital.	**1** Whittier publishes *Leaves from Margaret Smith's Journal*, his only novel. **2** Melville shows his love for the sea in the novels *Mardi* and *Redburn*.	**6** Gustave Courbet establishes the Realism movement in France with his paintings, "The Stone-Breakers," showing laborers in a quarry, and "Burial at Ornans," depicting a

Science & Technology		Miscellaneous		
America	**Elsewhere**	**America**	**Elsewhere**	

sician, as president.
4 Maria Mitchell, Mass. astronomer, discovers a comet and determines its orbit.
5 Richard M. Hoe, industrialist, develops rotary and web printing presses.
6 Samuel M. Kier, Pa. businessman, sells bottled petroleum as a medicine.

10 Henry Sorby, Eng. geologist, publishes work on the role of sulfur and phosphorus in crops.

---

1 American Association for the Advancement of Science (AAAS) is established in Philadelphia with William Redfield, Conn. meteorologist, as president.
2 Gray publishes *Manual of Botany,* listing all known plants in the northern U.S.
3 Maria Mitchell is the first woman elected to the American Academy of Sciences.
4 George P. Bond, astronomer, discovers Hyperion, the eighth moon of Saturn.
5 Bogardus constructs a 5-story factory building using cast iron throughout.

6 Louis Pasteur, Fr. chemist and microbiologist, establishes the study of stereochemistry.
7 Ignaz Philipp Semmelweis, Hung. physician, discovers the cause of puerperal fever: medical students are carrying the infection from cadavers (of women who died from the disease) to healthy women. He orders all medical students to wash their hands before examining patients; within months, the mortality rate drops to near zero. **[1843:SCI/1]**
8 Virchow coins the terms *thrombosis* for a condition which produces masses in the blood vessels, and *embolus* for a portion of such a mass which may detach and impair blood circulation.
9 Kelvin originates the absolute temperature scale, later measured in degrees Kelvin.

1 John B. Curtis of Bangor, Me., manufactures the first chewing gum commercially sold.
2 John Humphrey Noyes establishes the Perfectionist Community at Oneida, N.Y.
3 "Air conditioning" is installed in the Broadway Theater in New York City. The management promises "3000 Feet of Cool Air per Minute."
4 *Ocean Monarch* catches fire off Carnarvonshire, Wales; 200 Americans die.
5 Women's Rights Convention is held at Seneca Falls, N.Y. This is the beginning of the modern feminist movement, led by Lucretia Mott and Elizabeth Cady Stanton.
6 Medical school for women opens with 12 students. Known as the Boston Female Medical School, it becomes part of the Boston University School of Medicine in 1874.

7 Ger. economist and philosopher Karl Marx and Friedrich Engels issue the *Communist Manifesto,* an appeal to the workers of all countries to unite in the struggle against capitalist exploitation.

Karl Marx, German economist and philosopher

1848

---

1 George Corliss, N.Y. inventor, patents an efficient steam engine with four valves (instead of one).
2 Jeffries Wyman, Mass. anatomist, describes the similarities in the skel-

5 Armand Fizeau, Fr. physicist, measures the speed of light as 195,344 miles per second, an error of 5%.
6 Johann von Lamont, Anglo-Ger. astronomer, publishes *Handbook of*

1 Tom Hyer, the unofficial heavyweight boxing champion, fights Yankee Sullivan, an Englishman, and knocks him out.
2 More than 400 buildings (within 15 city blocks) and 27 steamships

7 Eng. archaeologist Sir Henry Layard excavates the site at Nineveh, ancient capital of Assyria (northern Iraq). About 25,000 tablets are found, including state documents and literary, religious, and

1849

History and Politics		The Arts	
America	**Elsewhere**	**America**	**Elsewhere**

<table>
<tr>
<td>

mission to the Union.
4 Sectional conflict deepens between pro- and anti-slavery factions.
5 The possibility of instant riches in the California gold fields creates a gold rush as thousands of prospectors head west by both land and sea routes. Known as "forty-niners," the prospectors sometimes find riches but often fail. The influx of Americans to the new territory overwhelms the Spanish presence.

</td>
<td>

patriot, fights for Mazzini's short-lived Roman Republic against the French. He makes famous retreat.
9 Venice surrenders to Austria.
10 Frankfurt Parliament adopts constitution. Frederick William IV, King of Prussia, is chosen "Emperor of the Germans" but refuses the crown. German unification flounders.
11 Hungary declares its independence with Louis Kossuth as president. Austrians, aided by Russians, defeat the Hungarian army at Vilagos, and Hungary again comes under Hapsburg rule.

</td>
<td>

3 Henry David Thoreau publishes *A Week on the Concord and Merrimack Rivers,* which sells only 200 copies.
4 Poe publishes the poems "Annabel Lee" and "The Bells."
5 The Mendelssohn Quintette Club, the first chamber music organization in the U.S., gives its first concert.

</td>
<td>

peasant funeral with more than 40 life-size figures.
7 Berlioz composes religious music to *Te Deum.*
8 Liszt composes *Tasso,* a symphonic poem.
9 Scribe produces *Adrienne Lecouvreur,* a melodrama.
10 Ruskin praises Gothic style in *The Seven Lamps of Architecture.*

</td>
</tr>
<tr>
<td>

1850

1 Pres. Taylor dies and Fillmore becomes President.
2 Congress bitterly debates the rights of states and territories to permit or prohibit slavery. Compromise of 1850 passes: California is admitted as a free state; New Mexico and Utah territories are formed and allowed to make their own decision about slavery; more effective Fugitive Slave Act is set up; and slave trade is abolished in the District of Columbia.
3 Clayton-Bulwer Treaty is signed. U.S. and Britain agree to neutrality of canal project across the Isthmus of Panama; neither country is to occupy any part of Central America.

</td>
<td>

4 Taiping Rebellion against the Manchu (Ch'ing) dynasty begins in Kwangsi province, China. Hung Hsiu-ch'uan proclaims himself Emperor and leads rebels against Chinese government.
[1864:HIST/14]
5 Great Kaffir War breaks out on the eastern frontier of Cape Colony, South Africa. British defeat the Kaffirs in 1853 and annex more territory.
6 Frederick William IV presents Prussian Union plan for a confederation of Prussia and the smaller German States. Austria opposes it and forces its abandonment in the Treaty of Olmütz, which restores the German Confederation. **[1816:HIST/6]**
7 Prussia and Denmark sign the Peace of Berlin, in which both reserve their rights to Schleswig-Holstein.

</td>
<td>

1 Hawthorne publishes the classic novel *The Scarlet Letter,* which attacks Puritan hypocrisy.
2 James Renwick designs St. Patrick's Cathedral in New York City.
3 Foster writes "Camptown Races."
4 Melville's novel *White-Jacket* causes an uproar about the abuses in the U.S. Navy.
5 The Spanish introduce silversmithing to the Navajo Indians. It soon becomes one of their major art forms.
6 Emerson publishes *Representative Men.*

</td>
<td>

7 E.B. Browning publishes *Sonnets from the Portuguese,* a collection of 44 sonnets that includes "How do I love thee?/Let me count the ways" (No. 43).
8 Wagner, in political exile for more than a year, is unable to attend the first performance of his opera, *Lohengrin,* conducted by Liszt.
9 Rossetti publishes the poem, "The Blessed Damazel," and exhibits the painting, "Ecce Ancilla Domini."
10 Millet is criticized for the socialist themes in his paintings, "The Sower" and "The Binders."
11 Dickens and others accuse Millais of blasphemy for his painting, "Christ in the House of His Parents."

</td>
</tr>
</table>

Science & Technology		Miscellaneous	
America	**Elsewhere**	**America**	**Elsewhere**
etons of apes and human beings. **3** Benjamin Gould, Mass. astronomer, establishes the *Astronomical Journal.* **4** Henry analyzes the first weather data sent by telegraph.	*Terrestrial Magnetism.* **7** Carl August von Steinheil, Ger. physicist, is instrumental in establishing the Austrian telegraph system.  Herman Melville, U.S. novelist	are destroyed in a St. Louis, Mo., fire. Damage is estimated at $6 million. **3** Pacific Railroad Company is chartered. It becomes the first railroad west of the Mississippi River. **4** Elizabeth Blackwell receives her medical degree from a medical school in Geneva, N.Y. She is the first woman in the world to receive an M.D. **5** To satisfy a $15 debt owed to J.R. Chapin, Walter Hunt of New York spends 3 hrs. bending wire into various forms and designs the first modern safety pin. **6** California's giant redwood trees are named Sequoias in honor of Sequoya. [1821:ARTS/1]	scientific works. **8** Scot. explorer and missionary David Livingstone crosses the Kalahari Desert in Africa and discovers Lake Ngami.

America	**Elsewhere**	**America**	**Elsewhere**	
1 William and George Bond discover the innermost or "crepe" ring of Saturn. It is officially called the "c" ring. [1969:SCI/4] **2** William Bond makes the first clear daguerreotype (a type of photograph) of the Moon.	**3** Sir William Armstrong, Eng. engineer, invents the hydraulic accumulator, thus ending hydraulic machinery's dependence on a convenient water source. **4** Rudolf Clausius, Ger. physicist, states the second law of thermodynamics: "Heat cannot of itself pass from a colder body to a hotter body." **5** Helmholtz's measurements of the velocity of a nerve impulse leads to his theory of the conservation of energy. **6** Lamont discovers that the Earth's magnetic field undergoes periodic fluctuations.	**1** U.S. population is 23.1 million, including about 3.2 million slaves and about 1.7 immigrants. **2** First overland mail delivery west of the Missouri River is organized on a monthly basis from Independence, Mo., to Salt Lake City, Utah. **3** Fugitive Slave Act requires citizens of the free states to turn in runaway slaves. **4** Cholera epidemic sweeps through the Middle West after passing through the South the year before. **5** Woman's Medical College of Pennsylvania is the first regularly organized school for the medical education of women. [1848:MISC/6] **6** First national convention of women advocating woman suffrage is held in Worcester, Mass. In July the first woman's rights convention meets in Seneca Falls, N.Y.	**7** Eng. scientist and explorer Francis Galton explores Damaraland in Southwest Africa. **8** Eng. philosopher Herbert Spencer publishes *Social Statistics,* which marks the beginning of sociology. **9** Ship *Royal Adelaide* is wrecked off Margate, England; about 400 people are lost. **10** Arctic expedition under Erasmus Ommanney sets out to search for explorer John Franklin, missing on an expedition to find the Northwest Passage in 1845; later expeditions map the north coast of Canada.	**1850**

History and Politics | The Arts

	America	Elsewhere	America	Elsewhere
1851	1 Gen. Narciso Lopéz leads an expedition of Spanish refugees and Southerners from New Orleans to Cuba in an unsuccessful attempt to free the Cubans from Spanish rule. Lopéz is captured and executed. 2 Congress authorizes the coinage of three-cent pieces and reduces postage rates. A half ounce letter can now be sent 3000 miles for three cents. 3 Sioux Indians give all their land in Iowa and most of their land in Minnesota to the U.S. 4 Maine enacts prohibition law, which forbids the manufacture and sale of alcoholic liquors in the state. 5 Charles Sumner becomes U.S. Senator from Massachusetts. He leads the fight against slavery.	6 Victoria, Australia, is made a separate British colony and is granted self-government in 1855. 7 Supported by Brazil and Uruguayan liberals, Justo Jośe de Urquiza, Argentine general, forces Manuel Oribe to end his eight-year siege of Montevideo. 8 Louis Napoleon carries out his coup d'etat in France; plebiscite authorizes a new constitution. [1848:HIST/5]	1 Melville publishes the classic *Moby Dick.* 2 Hawthorne publishes *The House of the Seven Gables,* based on a curse supposedly placed upon his family during the Salem witch trials. 3 Foster publishes "Oh! Boys, Carry Me 'Long" and "Old Folks at Home." 4 Emmanuel Leutze paints "Washington Crossing the Delaware." Artist Worthington Whittredge posed as Washington. 5 Calvert Vaux and Andrew Downing collaborate on the landscape design of the U.S. Capitol grounds. 6 T.U. Walter designs the dome atop the U.S. Capitol building.	7 Giuseppe Verdi, one of Italy's greatest composers, produces *Rigoletto,* an opera that includes the aria, "La Donna è mobile." 8 Ruskin's 3-volume *The Stones of Venice* (–1853) calls for a return to the Gothic style. 9 Millais receives international acclaim for his painting, "The Return of the Dove to the Ark."
1852	1 Democrats and Whigs adopt party platforms accepting Compromise of 1850. Democrats also endorse Virginia and Kentucky Resolutions of 1798. Free Soil Party opposes the Compromise and slavery itself. 2 Franklin Pierce and William R. King are elected President and Vice President, respectively, on the Democratic ticket.	3 British recognize the independence of the Transvaal (South African Republic). 4 Plebiscite in France approves new constitution and the establishment of the Second Empire. Pres. Louis Napoleon proclaims himself Emperor Napoleon III. 5 New constitution is established to rule the six provinces of New Zealand. 6 Count Camillo Benso di Cavour becomes Premier of Sardinia. He introduces progressive reform and supports the Risorgimento, the movement that led to the unification (kingdom) of Italy in 1870. 7 In alliance with Brazil and Uruguay, Urquiza defeats Rosas at the Battle of Monte Caseros. Argentine designs on Uruguay disappear when Rosas flees to England.	1 Hawthorne writes *Life of Benjamin Pierce,* a campaign biography for the future president. 2 Harriet Beecher Stowe, writer and philanthropist, publishes *Uncle Tom's Cabin,* a novel that had a profound influence on the abolition of slavery. 3 Foster publishes "My Old Kentucky Home." The same year he makes his only trip to the South, an area with which he is often associated.	4 Dickens publishes *Bleak House,* a satire on the delays and corruption in the Court of Chancery. 5 Eng. poet Matthew Arnold publishes *Empedocles on Etna, and Other Poems.* 6 Fr. writer and critic Théophile Gautier publishes *Enamels and Cameos,* a collection of his poems. 7 Ivan Turgenev, Russ. novelist, publishes *Sportsman's Sketches,* the first in a series of character studies. 8 Alexandre Dumas *fils* produces *Camille,* a play based on a novel he had written four years earlier. 9 Thackeray pub-

Science & Technology		Miscellaneous		
America	**Elsewhere**	**America**	**Elsewhere**	
1 Isaac Singer, N.Y. inventor, patents a continuous-stitch sewing machine. **2** Page designs an electric locomotive. **3** William Channing and Moses Farmer invent an electric fire alarm system and install it in Boston. (Patented in 1857.)	**4** Helmholtz invents the ophthalmoscope. **5** William Siemens invents a water meter. **6** G. Dollond is honored for his invention of an atmospheric recorder that is able to measure various weather conditions simultaneously. **7** Von Mohl suggests that a plant's secondary cell walls have a fibrous structure.	**1** Mass. passes the first law that allows towns to tax inhabitants for the support of free libraries. **2** Fire destroys 2500 buildings in San Francisco; property damage is estimated at $12 million. **3** First American chapter of the Young Men's Christian Association (YMCA) is organized in Boston. 24 chapters already exist in Great Britain. **4** First baseball uniforms are worn by the New York Knickerbockers. Outfits consisted of straw hats, white shirts, and blue full-length trousers. **5** Schooner-yacht *America* beats 14 British vessels in a 60-mi. yacht race around the Isle of Wight. The trophy won becomes known as "The America's Cup." **6** When glass eyes are introduced, many people believe that they will restore sight to the blind.	**7** Cholera epidemic in Jamaica, West Indies. **8** China's population is 430 million, Germany's 34 million, France's 33 million, and Great Britain's 20.8 million. **9** First horse-drawn double-decker omnibus is introduced in England. **10** Jewish schools are accepted in England.	**1851**

Washington Crossing the Delaware, painting by Emmanuel Leutze

1 James Dana describes his theory of cephalization: the more advanced (i.e., more highly evolved) animals have greater development in the head region. **2** Horse-drawn steam pumpers (fire engines) are invented by Alexander Latta, Ohio engineer. **3** Elisha Otis, Vt. inventor, designs a passenger elevator. **4** Samuel Wetherill, Pa. chemist, develops a commercially successful way of removing zinc oxide from ore. **5** Sparrows are imported from Germany to help control caterpillars in the U.S. in an example of biological control. **6** Mount Sinai Hospital opens in New York City.	**8** Henri Giffard, Fr. engineer, makes a successful flight in a steam-powered airship. **9** Abraham Gesner, Can. physician, discovers and names kerosene. **10** Sir Edward Frankland, Eng. chemist, establishes the theory of valency. **11** Joule and Lord Kelvin (William Thomson) discover that a gas which is allowed to expand will automatically cool (Joule-Thomson effect). **12** Rudolf Albert von Kölliker, Ger. embryologist, determines the cellular origin of spermatozoa.	**1** Mass. passes the first effective school attendance law, requiring all children between ages 8 and 14 to attend school at least 12 weeks a year, 6 of them consecutive. **2** Yale and Harvard hold the first intercollegiate rowing race on a 2-mi. course at Lake Winnepesaukee, N.H. Harvard wins by 4 lengths. **3** Caroline Fry Marriage Association advertises "wives for poor and deserving young men." Matrimonial agencies are becoming popular. **4** Educator George Ticknor and Edward Everett with a combination of private donations, civic funds, and gifts of books, help found the Boston Public Library.	**5** Safety matches are invented in Sweden. **6** British troopship *Birkenhead* is wrecked on the way to Cape of Good Hope; 454 are lost. **7** Livingstone begins exploring the Zambezi River in South Africa. **8** Ger. explorer Heinrich Barth explores Lake Chad in central Africa.	**1852**

History and Politics		The Arts	
America	**Elsewhere**	**America**	**Elsewhere**
	[1835:HIST/6] **6** Anglo-Burmese War be-War begins; British occupy the Irrawaddy River delta. [1826:HIST/5]		lishes *History of Henry Esmond,* a detailed historical novel.

1853

1 Congress authorizes the coinage of three-dollar gold pieces and reduces the amount of silver in all coins except the silver dollar. **2** Washington Territory is formed from part of the Oregon Territory. **3** U.S. fleet under Commodore Matthew C. Perry arrives in Edo Bay (now Tokyo Bay), Japan. Perry seeks protection for shipwrecked U.S. seamen and the opening of Japanese ports to trade. [1854:HIST/1] **4** U.S. purchases from Mexico for $10 million a 30,000-square-mile area (the Gadsden Purchase) in what is now southern New Mexico and Arizona. The territory was the last addition to the U.S. continental boundaries (the contiguous states). **5** Congress authorizes survey for a transcontinental railroad route to the Pacific.	**6** Britain and Burma make peace. British annex the province of Pegu in southern Burma. **7** British annex the Mahratta state of Nagpur in central India. **8** Turkey rejects Russian protection of Orthodox subjects of the Ottoman Sultan. Russia and France argue over the privileges of Orthodox and Roman Catholic monks in the Holy Places in Palestine. Russia occupies the Turkish states of Moldavia and Wallachia (the Danubian Principalities). Turkey declares war on Russia. Russian fleet destroys Turkish squadron and transports off Sinope; Crimean War begins.	**1** Charles Lewis Tiffany, jeweler, establishes Tiffany and Company, a firm which remains world famous for its exquisite jewelry designs. **2** Stowe defends the authenticity of her earlier work in *The Key to Uncle Tom's Cabin.* [1852:ARTS/2] **3** Gottschalk makes his American debut in New York City.	**4** Verdi composes the operas *Il Trovatore* and *La Traviata.* **5** Thackeray publishes *The Newcomes.* **6** Liszt popularizes a new musical form with the composition of 15 *Hungarian Rhapsodies* (–1854). **7** Kingsley publishes *Hypatia,* a historical novel set in 5th-century Alexandria. **8** Mrs. Gaskell publishes her most popular novel, *Cranford.* **9** Fr. urban planner Georges Eugène Haussmann begins reconstructing the *grands boulevards* of Paris.

1854

1 U.S. and Japan sign the Treaty of Kanagawa, declaring peace, friendship, and commerce. **2** Kansas-Nebraska Act, introduced by Sen. Stephen A. Douglas, repeals the Missouri Compromise of 1820. Congress establishes the territories of Kansas and Nebraska. All territories can decide whether to permit or prohibit slavery. Act is condemned by abolitionists. **3** Republican Party is formed as a reaction against the Kansas-Nebraska Act. It calls for the abolition of slavery, high protective tariffs, and a transcontinental railroad. **4** Massachusetts Emigrant Aid Society is organized to encourage anti-slavery emigration to Kansas.	**7** France and Britain conclude an alliance with Turkey and declare war on Russia. Allied troops land in Crimea and begin siege of Sevastopol. Allies defeat Russian forces at Alma River, Balaklava, and Inkerman. Russia evacuates the Danubian Principalities, which are then occupied by neutral Austrian forces. **8** By the Bloemfontein Convention, British withdraw from the territory north of the Orange River. Boers establish the Orange Free State in South Africa. [1848:HIST/10]	**1** Thoreau publishes *Walden; or, Life in the Woods,* about his idyllic two years in the wilderness. **2** Foster writes "Jeanie with the Light Brown Hair." **3** Seba Smith publishes *Way Down East,* a humorous portrayal of the New England Yankee. **4** Benjamin Shillaber, humorist, publishes *Life and Sayings of Mrs. Partington.* **5** Whittier publishes the poem "Maud Muller."	**6** Tennyson publishes "The Charge of the Light Brigade." **7** Ger. composer Johannes Brahms composes *Piano Concerto No. 1 in D Minor.* **8** Dickens publishes *Hard Times,* a novel. **9** Gérard de Nerval publishes *Des Filles du feu (Girls of Fire),* one of the first Fr. Surrealistic novels. **10** Millet paints "The Reaper." **11** Hunt's religious painting, "The Light of the World," is a public success.

Science & Technology		Miscellaneous		
America	**Elsewhere**	**America**	**Elsewhere**	
7 American Society of Civil Engineers is founded in New York City.				
1 James Coffin, Mass. meteorologist, describes three distinct wind zones in the northern hemisphere. **2** Otis improves the elevator by adding safety devices to keep the car from falling if the ropes break. **3** Charles Davis, Mass. naval officer, publishes the *American Nautical Almanac*.	Florence Nightingale, English nurse known as the "Lady with the Lamp"	**1** Antioch College, which welcomes male and female students, opens in Ohio. **2** New York Central Railroad is formed by consolidating 10 small railroads connecting New York City and Buffalo, N.Y. **3** Yellow fever epidemic hits New Orleans, La. During the next two years more than 5000 people are killed by the disease. **4** Baltimore & Ohio Railroad is completed to the Ohio River, and its first trains begin operating from Baltimore, Md., to Wheeling, W.Va. For the first time Chicago, Ill., is connected by rail to the East.	**5** Immigrant ship *Annie Jane* is wrecked off Scotland; 348 people die. **6** Vaccination against smallpox is made compulsory in England. **7** Queen Victoria allows chloroform to be administered to her during the birth of her seventh child. It becomes accepted as anesthetic in Britain. **8** First railroad through the Alps from Vienna, Austria, to Trieste, Italy, begins operation. **9** Earliest man-carrying glider is designed by Sir George Cayley and is flown by his coachman about 500 yds. across a valley in Yorkshire, England. **[1884:MISC/5]**	**1853**
1 James Dana publishes the results of the Wilkes Expedition (1838–42). **2** Horace Smith and Daniel Wesson invent the Smith and Wesson revolver and a device that is later used in Winchester repeating rifles. **3** David Alter, Pa. physician, discovers that the elements in a gas can be identified by using a spectroscope. **4** A railroad suspension bridge is built at Niagara Falls. The first train crosses a year later. **5** New York Children's Hospital opens.	**6** Florence Nightingale, Eng. nurse, departs for Turkey to treat the British soldiers fighting in the Crimean War. **7** Brewster publishes the memoirs of Sir Isaac Newton. **8** The use of the Bunsen burner is introduced by Bunsen, although he did not invent it. **9** Nathanael Pringsheim, Ger. botanist, discovers the existence of separate sexes in algae. **10** Alfred Russel Wallace, Eng. naturalist, publishes *On the Law Which Has Regulated the Introduction of New Species*.	**1** Arrival of 13,000 Chinese marks the beginning of large-scale immigration from China. The highest number in any previous year has been 42. Chinese workers are employed largely in building the transcontinental railroad. **2** Astor Library opens in New York City. John Jacob Astor left $40,000 in his will to be used for its establishment. **3** First "fire-proof" building, Harper & Bros. publishing headquarters in New York City, is built using wrought-iron beams set in masonry walls. **4** Paper collars are invented by Walter Hunt.	**5** Ship *City of Glasgow* is lost in the Atlantic between London and Philadelphia with 450 people on board. **6** Pope Pius IX declares the dogma (or doctrine) of the Immaculate Conception of the Blessed Virgin Mary to be an article of faith. **7** Eng. explorers Richard Burton and John Speke travel to the interior of Somaliland in northeast Africa.	**1854**

	History and Politics		The Arts	
	America	**Elsewhere**	**America**	**Elsewhere**
	5 U.S. ministers to Britain, France, and Spain draw up the Ostend Manifesto saying that the U.S. should seize Cuba by force if Spain refuses to sell it. **6** Native American, or Know-Nothing Party, wins many local offices in New York, Massachusetts, and Delaware.			
1855	**1** Settlement of Kansas under Douglas doctrine of "popular sovereignty" leads to bloody war between pro- and anti-slavery factions for control of the territorial government ("Bleeding Kansas"). **[1854:HIST/2]** **2** William Walker with a small force lands in Nicaragua, overthrows the government, and makes himself president in 1856. He is forced out of power by a coalition of Central American states in 1857. **3** Pres. Pierce signs act establishing the first U.S. Court of Claims. Citizens can press claims against the federal government without petitioning Congress.	**4** Sardinia enters the Crimean War on the side of Turkey, Britain, and France. French troops capture the fortress of Malakhov, and the Russians are forced to abandon Sevastopol. On the Asiatic front the Russians capture Kars. Austria threatens war if Russia refuses to accept allied peace terms. **5** Alexander II becomes Czar of Russia and begins negotiating a peace to end the Crimean War. **6** Dost Muhammad signs Treaty of Peshawar with the British. **[1842:HIST/8]** **7** British colony of Victoria enacts law restricting Chinese immigration.	**1** George Inness, painter, executes "The Lackawanna Valley" in typical Hudson River School style. **[1865:ARTS/2]** **2** Longfellow writes "The Song of Hiawatha." **3** Walt Whitman, poet, anonymously publishes *Leaves of Grass,* a collection of 12 poems including "Song of Myself." **4** Evert A. Duyckinck and his brother George publish the exhaustive two volume *Cyclopaedia of American Literature.* **5** Carl Zerrahn, conductor, organizes the Boston Philharmonic Orchestra.	**6** Dickens publishes *Little Dorrit,* a popular novel that criticizes debtor's prison and other social injustices. **7** Eng. novelist Anthony Trollope publishes *The Warden,* the first of six books set in the imaginary county of Barsetshire. **8** Tennyson's "Maud" contains his greatest love lyrics. **9** Turgenev's *A Month in the Country* is a masterpiece of psychological character study. **10** Kingsley publishes *Westward Ho!,* an anti-Catholic historical novel set in 16th-century England. **[1864:ARTS/5]**
1856	**1** Pres. Pierce recognizes pro-slavery legislature in Kansas Territory. **2** Border Ruffians (pro-slavery) sack Lawrence, Kans. In return, abolitionist John Brown, with four of his sons and three other men, murders five pro-slavery colonists at Pottawatomie Creek. Civil war continues between Free State and pro-slavery factions until federal troops restore peace. **[1855:HIST/1]** **3** Sen. Sumner makes anti-slavery speech bitterly criticizing Sen. Andrew P. Butler and Stephen A. Douglas. Rep. Preston S. Brooks, Butler's	**5** Crimean War ends with the Congress of Paris. Russia agrees to the neutralization of the Black Sea. Danubian Principalities (now Rumania) are placed under joint guarantee of the European powers. Turkey is admitted to the European concert and the integrity of its empire is recognized. Ottoman Sultan guarantees the rights of his Christian subjects. **6** British and French forces besiege Canton, China. **7** Persians seize Herat, part of Afghan territory. British declare war on Persia. **8** Britain annexes Oudh, In-	**1** Emerson credits his Anglo-Saxon ancestors with his literary individuality in the work *English Traits.* **2** Stowe publishes *Dred: A Tale of the Great Dismal Swamp,* in which she suggests that slavery is causing the deterioration of society.	**3** Hugo's best lyric poem, *Les Contemplations,* expresses grief at the death by drowning of his daughter (1843). **4** Ingres paints "La Source." **5** Millais' sentimental masterpiece, "The Blind Girl," is his greatest success. **6** Russ. composer Aleksandr Sergeyevich Dargomyzhsky produces the opera, *Rusalka.*

Science & Technology		Miscellaneous		
America	**Elsewhere**	**America**	**Elsewhere**	
1 Maury publishes *The Physical Geography of the Sea,* the text that establishes the science of oceanography. **2** James Francis, "Father of Modern Hydraulic Engineering," publishes *Lowell Hydraulic Experiments.* **3** Kier builds America's first oil refinery in Pittsburgh. **4** James Sims, surgeon, organizes the Women's Hospital of New York City. **5** John C. Dalton, Mass. physician, operates on living animals to demonstrate internal anatomy and physiology to his students. **6** Benjamin Peirce, astronomer, publishes *Physical and Celestial Mechanics,* the first text in this field.	**7** Brewster publishes the memoirs of Sir Isaac Newton. **8** The use of the Bunsen burner is introduced by Bunsen, although he did not invent it. **9** Nathanael Pringsheim, Ger. botanist, discovers the existence of separate sexes in algae. **10** Alfred Russel Wallace, Eng. naturalist, publishes *On the Law Which Has Regulated the Introduction of New Species.*	**1** U.S. citizenship laws provide that all children born abroad of U.S. citizens are assured of citizenship. **2** First oil business in the U.S., the Pennsylvania Rock Oil Co., is formed by George H. Bissell and Johathan J. Eveleth. **3** *Frank Leslie's Illustrated Newspaper* (later *Leslie's Weekly*), most successful of the early illustrated papers, begins publication in New York City. **4** Coal mine explodes in Coalfield, Va., killing 55 people. **5** Horseback riding by women becomes popular. In Boston and New York many riding academies are set up to help women adjust to sidesaddle.	**6** Fr. engineer and diplomat Ferdinand de Lesseps is granted the concession by France to build the Suez Canal. **7** George Audemars receives the first patent for the production of "artificial silk" (rayon). **8** Livingstone discovers the Victoria Falls on the Zambezi River.	**1855**
1 David E. Hughes, Brit.-Amer. inventor, patents a printing telegraph. **2** Borax is discovered in Calif. **3** Farmer discovers an inexpensive and commercially successful way of coating metal objects with aluminum by using electrolysis.	**4** Friedrich Siemens, Anglo-Ger. scientist, patents a metallurgic heat regeneration process. **5** Sir William Crookes, Eng. chemist and physicist, studies cathode rays. **6** Sir William Perkin, Eng. chemist, patents the method for making mauve, the dye.	**1** First recorded observance of Children's Day is held in the Universalist Church of the Redeemer in Chelsea, Mass. **2** Gail Borden, Tex. inventor, receives a patent for condensing milk. **3** First street trains in New England begin running between Boston and Cambridge, Mass. They are pulled by steam engines. **4** Hurricane destroys the island of Ile Dernière, killing more than 400 people. **5** Western Union Com-	**7** "Big Ben," 13½-ton bell at the Houses of Parliament, is cast at the Whitechapel Bell Foundry in England. It is named after Sir Benjamin Hall, Director of Public Works. **8** Remains of prehistoric man, including a skull, are found in the Neanderthal Valley near Düsseldorf, Germany. **9** Longest bare-knuckle boxing match takes place in Melbourne, Australia, between James Kelly and Jack Smith. The 186-round fight lasts for 6	**1856**

History and Politics		The Arts	
America	**Elsewhere**	**America**	**Elsewhere**
nephew, severely beats Sumner with a cane in the Senate chamber. Sumner's slander and Brooks's brutality show the deep rift between North and South. **4** James Buchanan and John C. Breckinridge are elected President and Vice President, respectively, on the Democratic ticket.	dia, and makes Natal, South Africa, a separate crown colony. **9** Britain grants self-government to Tasmania.		

1857

America	Elsewhere	America	Elsewhere
1 Dred Scott decision by the U.S. Supreme Court holds that a Negro slave's residence in free territory does not make him free. It declares the Missouri Compromise unconstitutional and says that Congress has no right to prohibit slavery in the territories. [1820:HIST/1] **2** Indians and whites under John D. Lee, Mormon fanatic, massacre about 140 non-Mormon emigrants at Mountain Meadows, Utah. **3** Kansas elects Free State legislature. Pro-slavery delegates meet at Lecompton, Kans., and draw up constitution rigged so that slavery could not be eliminated from the territory. **4** Pres. Buchanan consents to Lecompton Constitution in Kansas, thus splitting the Democratic Party. **5** U.S. and Japan sign treaty opening port of Nagasaki to U.S. trade. (Shimoda and Hakodate were opened in 1854.)	**6** Indian Mutiny (Sepoy Rebellion) begins. Sepoy soldiers in the Bengal army rebel against British officers at Merrut, India. Sepoys capture Delhi, Kanpur, and Lucknow. Atrocities on both sides embitter relations between Indians and British. **7** British and Persians sign peace treaty. Persia gives up its claim to Herat and recognizes the independence of Afghanistan. **8** British and French occupy Canton, China, after Royal Navy destroys Chinese fleet. **9** Italian National Society, supported by Garibaldi and Cavour, works for the unification of Italy. **10** Mexico adopts liberal constitution, secularizing church property and reducing the privileges of the army. The reforms lead to civil war between liberals and conservatives.	**1** Frederick Law Olmsted and Calvert Vaux design Central Park in New York City. **2** Frederick E. Church, painter of the Hudson River School, paints "Niagara," keeping with his theme of natural wonders. **3** Melville publishes *The Confidence Man.* **4** *Atlantic Monthly,* a periodical which evolved into a proving ground for many U.S. writers, is founded. Oliver Wendell Holmes coins the magazine's name. **5** Upjohn helps found the American Institute of Architects and serves as its president until 1876.	**6** Gustave Flaubert, one of France's greatest Realists, publishes *Madame Bovary.* **7** After publishing a collection of his poetry in *Les Fleurs du mal,* Baudelaire is fined for offending public morality and six of his poems are banned. **8** Eng. author Thomas Hughes publishes *Tom Brown's Schooldays,* a book that greatly influences the public school system in England. **9** In London, the National Portrait Gallery and the Museum of Ornamental Art open. **10** Björnstjerne Martinius Björnson, Norw. novelist, publishes *Sunny Hill.*

1858

America	Elsewhere	America	Elsewhere
1 Minnesota becomes 32nd state. **2** Abraham Lincoln debates Sen. Douglas on the slavery issue during senatorial contest in Illinois. Douglas wins re-election, but Lincoln gains national reputation. **3** People of Kansas reject the Lecompton Constitution, and the territory becomes non-slaveholding. [1857:HIST/3] **4** U.S. and China sign treaty of peace, friendship, and commerce.	**6** British Parliament transfers the powers (governmental and commercial) of the East India Company to the crown. British East India Company is dissolved in 1873. [1784:HIST/4] **7** Treaty of Tientsin ends war between Britain and China. China opens more ports to foreign trade. **8** British recapture Delhi and Lucknow and put down the Indian Mutiny. [1857:HIST/6] **9** Felice Orsini, Ital. patriot,	**1** Longfellow publishes "The Courtship of Miles Standish." **2** Belter opens a factory in New York City where he makes exquisitely carved furniture. [1844:ARTS/2] **3** Holmes's "The Autocrat of the Breakfast Table," the first of his "Breakfast-Table" works, appears in *Atlantic Monthly.*	**4** William Morris, Eng. poet and artist, publishes *The Defense of Guinevere, and Other Poems* based on the Arthurian legends. **5** Charles François Gounod, Fr. composer, produces *Le Médecin malgré lui (The Mock Doctor),* an opera based on a comedy (1666) by Molière. **6** Trollope publishes *Doctor Thorne,* the most humorous of his

212

Science & Technology		Miscellaneous		
America	**Elsewhere**	**America**	**Elsewhere**	
		pany is established. **6** H.L. Lipman receives a patent for a pencil with an eraser attached.	hrs., 15 mins. **10** Black Forest railroad with 40 tunnels begins operation in Germany.	
1 Charles Darwin writes to Asa Gray outlining for the first time his theories of evolution and natural selection. [1859:SCI/5] **2** William Kelly, Pa. inventor, patents a steel-making process that is similar to that of Bessemer. The Kelly and Bessemer ideas are later combined and called the Bessemer Process. **3** Louis Agassiz publishes *Contributions to the Natural History of the United States* (–1862). In his "Essay on Classification," Agassiz proposes an early version of the biogenetic law stating that changes during the embryonic development of a single animal are similar to changes that occurred in that species over thousands of years. [1866:SCI/9]	**4** Charles de la Tour, Fr. scientist, discovers that yeasts are living plants that reproduce by budding. **5** Henry Bessemer, Eng. inventor, develops a steel-making process that uses blasts of air to remove impurities. **6** Bunsen publishes work in which he examines methods of measuring the volume of gases. **7** Pasteur determines that fermentation is caused by microbes and that yeast is able to reproduce without oxygen. (Pasteur effect.) **8** Clausius makes important advances in the theory of electrolysis.	**1** First pageant of decorated floats in the New Orleans Mardi Gras is instituted by the Mystic Kiewe of Lomus, a secret organization established in that year. [1827:MISC/5] **2** First baseball association is formed when 25 amateur baseball clubs become the National Association of Baseball Players. **3** American Chess Association is formed at the First American Chess Congress held in New York City. Paul Morphy, a 20-year-old from New Orleans, La., wins the chess championship, becoming the first American international chess master.	**4** Charles T. Newton discovers the remains of the Mausoleum (a monument to King Mausolus of Caria, Asia Minor) at Halicarnassus, one of the Seven Wonders of the Ancient World. Louis Pasteur, French chemist and microbiologist	**1857**
1 Cyrus W. Field, Mass. financier, lays the first successful transatlantic telegraph cable. Messages are exchanged between Queen Victoria and President Buchanan, but a few weeks later, the cable stops working. **2** Hamilton E. Smith invents a mechanical washing machine. **3** Harvard University establishes a chemistry department and research lab.	**5** Virchow publishes *Cellular Pathology as Based upon Physiological and Pathological Histology,* a milestone of cell biology. **6** Kelvin patents the mirror galvanometer for use as a telegraph receiver on the transatlantic cable. **7** Lyell determines that Mount Etna was formed by a series of volcanic eruptions. **8** Friedrich August von Kekule, Ger. chemist, shows that carbon is able	**1** Religious revival, starting in New York and Pennsylvania, sweeps across the country. It is accompanied by daily prayer meetings in every major city, and conversions to the various churches reach great numbers. **2** Stagecoach service and mail delivery begins between San Francisco, Calif., and St. Louis, Mo., over a 2812-mi. route. **3** Macy's department	**4** Burton and Speke discover Lake Tanganyika and Lake Victoria Nyanza in Africa. **5** Ship *Austria* burns in the Atlantic between Hamburg, Germany, and New York City; 471 people die. **6** S.S. *Great Eastern* is launched, the largest ship up to this time.	**1858**

America	Elsewhere	America	Elsewhere

5 U.S. troops suppress the Mormon militia and restore order in the Utah Territory. Opposed to non-Mormon settlers, the Mormons had rebelled in 1857 against the appointed non-Mormon territorial governor.

tries unsuccessfully to assassinate Napoleon III. Orsini is executed.
10 By the Treaty of Aigun, China cedes the north side of the Amur River to Russia.
11 British Columbia is founded.
12 Serbian Diet deposes Alexander Karageorgevich and recalls Milosh Obrenovich as king.
13 Emperor Napoleon III meets Sardinian Premier Cavour at Plombières, France, and promises military aid against Austria.

Barsetshire novels.
7 Hiroshige exhibits "One Hundred Views of Edo," a series of color prints.
8 Björnson's novel, *Arne,* includes a good description of the *halling,* a lively solo dance popular in Norway.

1859

1 Oregon becomes 33rd state.
2 Abolitionist John Brown with 21 men seizes the U.S. arsenal at Harpers Ferry, W. Va., hoping to start slave insurrection. U.S. Marines capture the raiders. Brown is hanged for murder, treason, and conspiracy. He becomes a martyr to the North, a traitor to the South.
3 Southern convention at Vicksburg, Miss., urges repeal of all laws, state and federal, prohibiting the importation of slaves. Pres. Buchanan's message to Congress asserts U.S. enforcement of slave importation laws.
4 Kansas ratifies anti-slavery constitution at Wyandotte.

5 Sardinia rejects Austria's ultimatum to demobilize. Austrian forces invade Piedmont. France declares war on Austria. Sardinians and French defeat the Austrians at Magenta and Sofferino. Napoleon III and Emperor Franz Josef sign armistice at Villafranca di Verona. By the Treaty of Zürich, Austria keeps Venetia and Sardinia gains Lombardy.
6 Britain undertakes administrative reforms to strengthen its government in India.
7 China refuses admission of foreign diplomats to Peking.
8 Queensland is separated from New South Wales and made a British colony in Australia.
9 Insurrection overthrows the last Emperor of Haiti.

1 Washington Irving completes the five-volume biography, *George Washington.*
2 Adelina Patti, Span. soprano considered the most popular singer of the time, makes her operatic debut in New York City.
3 Stowe publishes *The Minister's Wooing,* a romance loosely based on her sister's life.
4 Daniel Emmett composes "Dixie" and "Turkey in the Straw."

5 Dickens publishes *A Tale of Two Cities,* an extremely popular historical novel.
6 Edward FitzGerald, Eng. writer, anonymously publishes a poetic version of *the Rubáiyát of Omar Khayyám.*
7 Verdi's *A Masked Ball* is heavily censored because of references to the assassination of Sweden's King Gustav III.
8 Jacques Offenbach, creator of the opérette, a type of Fr. comic opera, stages *Orpheus in the Underworld.*
9 George Eliot (Mary Ann Evans), Eng. novelist and poet, publishes *Adam Bede,* a novel.
10 Tennyson publishes the first four *Idylls of the King* (–1885), a series of 12 poems based on the legends of King Arthur.
11 Gounod's opera, *Faust,* is performed.
12 Wagner's *Tristan*

Science & Technology		Miscellaneous		
America	**Elsewhere**	**America**	**Elsewhere**	
4 The first West Coast medical college is established at the University of the Pacific by Elias S. Cooper.	to form four bonds. **9** Perkin synthesizes glycine, the first amino acid to be produced in the laboratory. **10** Pringsheim founds the *Annals of Scientific Botany.* **11** Nightingale bases *Notes on Matters Affecting the Health, Efficiency and Hospital Administration* on her Crimean War nursing experience. **[1854:SCI/6]** **12** Sorby publishes work urging microscopic studies in geology. **13** Wallace develops his evolutionary theory of survival of the fittest, and mails a copy to Darwin. **[1859:SCI/5]**	store is established in New York City. Its successful use on a large scale of a fixed-price policy, developed in smaller New York City stores since 1840, establishes an American retail sales custom.		
1 Louis Agassiz establishes the Museum of Comparative Zoology at Harvard. **2** Edwin L. Drake, N.Y. industrialist, drills America's first successful oil well at Titusville, Pa. **3** Samuel Gross, Pa. physician, publishes *System of Surgery.* **4** Farmer experiments with incandescent lighting and develops a platinum filament that burns briefly in what may be the world's first incandescent lamp. **[1879:SCI/4]**	**5** Darwin publishes his famous *Origin of Species,* in which his theories of evolution and natural selection are presented. **6** Humboldt dies while working on the fifth volume of *Kosmos,* a thorough account of the current knowledge of the Universe. **7** Bunsen determines that each element gives off a certain wavelength of light, a concept important for studying the Sun and other stars. **8** James Clerk Maxwell, Eng. physicist, proposes that Saturn's rings are made up of tiny particles.	**1** Industrialist and inventor Peter Cooper establishes the Cooper Union, an institute mainly for adult education in the arts and sciences, in New York City. **2** Fifth Avenue Hotel in New York City installs the first passenger elevator in an American hotel. Many guests still prefer stairs. **3** Michael Phelan of New York City becomes the first national billiards champion by defeating John Seercriter of Detroit, Mich., in a 2000-point match for a $15,000 prize. **4** Amherst defeats Williams, 66 to 32, in the first intercollegiate baseball game. **5** Harvard wins the first intercollegiate regatta over Yale and Brown at Worcester, Mass.	**6** Marx publishes *Critique of Political Economy.* **7** Work begins on the Suez Canal under de Lesseps' direction. **8** Ship *Royal Charter* sinks in the Irish Sea; approximately 450 people die.	**1859**

History and Politics		The Arts	
America	**Elsewhere**	**America**	**Elsewhere**
			und Isolde, a musical drama, is completed. (First performance, 1865.)

	History and Politics — America	History and Politics — Elsewhere	The Arts — America	The Arts — Elsewhere
1860	**1** Abraham Lincoln (Republican) is elected President, defeating Stephen A. Douglas (Democrat), John C. Breckinridge (National Democrat), and John Bell (Constitutional Union). Hannibal Hamlin (Republican) is elected Vice President. Lincoln receives no support from slave states; vote is purely sectional. **2** Sen. John J. Crittenden proposes resolution for amending the Constitution in order to conciliate the North and South. The Crittenden Compromise, calling for 36°30′ parallel as the boundary between free and slave states, is rejected by Lincoln and by Congress in 1861. **3** South Carolina secedes from the Union, affirming the doctrine of states' rights and condemning the North's and Lincoln's attack on slavery. **4** South Carolina troops capture the U.S. arsenal at Charleston.	**5** Garibaldi with 1000 volunteers, called the Redshirts, conquers Sicily and Naples (the two Sicilies). **6** Victor Emmanuel II, King of Sardinia, joins forces with Garibaldi and defeats the Papal army at Castelfidardo. **7** Plebiscites in Parma, Modena, Romagna, Tuscany, Sicily, Naples, and the Papal States result in vote for union with Sardinia. **8** By the Treaty of Turin, Sardinia cedes Nice and Savoy to France. **9** Russians found Vladivostok. **10** Muslim Druses massacre many Christian Maronites in Lebanon. France intervenes to restore order. **11** British and French troops occupy Peking after defeating the Chinese at the Battle of Pa-li-ch'iao. Chinese concede a legation quarter for foreign embassies. [1859:HIST/7] **12** Maoris of New Zealand refuse to sell their lands; war breaks out.	**1** Foster publishes the song "Old Black Joe." **2** Congress commissions Leutze to paint "Westward the Course of Empire Takes Its Way" to decorate a staircase in the U.S. Capitol building. **3** Emerson publishes *The Conduct of Life,* a series of essays which present the author's moral and ethical codes.	**4** Edgar Degas, Fr. artist, completes his first classical painting, "Young Spartans Exercising." **5** Wilkie Collins, one of England's first mystery novelists, publishes *The Woman in White.* **6** Thackeray establishes *The Cornhill Magazine,* a monthly literary journal. **7** Eliot publishes *The Mill on the Floss,* a novel. **8** Swiss art historian Jakob Burckhardt publishes his most famous work, *The Civilization of the Renaissance in Italy.*
1861	**1** Mississippi, Florida, Alabama, Georgia, Louisiana, Texas, Virginia, Arkansas, North Carolina, and Tennessee secede from the Union. [1860:HIST/3] **2** Confederate States of America, a new Southern union, is formed in Montgomery, Ala. Jefferson Davis and Alexander H. Stephens are elected President and Vice President, respectively. **3** Confederates fire on Fort	**9** Albert, Prince Consort of Queen Victoria, whom he married in 1840, dies. Victoria withdraws from public for three years. **10** Czar Alexander II emancipates the Russian serfs. **11** France, Britain, and Spain intervene in Mexico to force the liberal government of Benito Juárez to pay its debts. **12** King of Naples surrenders to Garibaldi at Gaeta.	**1** Mathew B. Brady, photographer, starts a photographic record of the Civil War. **2** Actress Adah Menken shocks Bostonian audiences when she appears nearly naked on stage. **3** Henry Timrod, "laureate of the Confederacy," publishes the poem "Ethnogenesis," which praises the	**5** Eng. author Charles Reade's finest novel, *The Cloister and the Hearth,* is a historical romance based on the life of the father of Erasmus. **6** Édouard Manet, Fr. artist who marks the transition from Realism to Impressionism, exhibits "Spanish Singer." **7** Dickens publishes

Science & Technology		Miscellaneous		
America	**Elsewhere**	**America**	**Elsewhere**	
1 Gray reviews Darwin's *Origin of the Species,* gives his approval, and becomes a major American supporter of the theories of evolution. **2** Louis Agassiz, though his earlier work (1857) seemed to support evolution, bitterly attacks Darwin's theories. He rejects the idea that all animals have a common ancestor, and lists breaks or "missing links" in the evolutionary chain. **3** Alvan Clark, Mass. astronomer, discovers that Sirius is a binary (double) star. **4** Cotton production in the U.S. is more than 2 billion pounds per year.	**5** Jean J. Lenoir, Fr. engineer, builds the first practical gas engine. **6** Maxwell publishes work on the kinetic theory of gases. **7** Nightingale founds the world's first nursing school.	**1** Pony Express begins fast overland mail service from St. Joseph, Mo., to Sacramento, Calif., a distance of more than 1900 mi. When the transcontinental telegraph is completed a year later, the Pony Express is discontinued. **2** A $5 chemistry set, the "Youth's Chemical Cabinet," is advertised as being perfectly safe. The set includes experiments, none of which calls for strong acids or other dangerous materials. **3** Olympia Brown, admitted to St. Lawrence University, becomes the first woman to study theology along with men. **4** Croquet is introduced from England and becomes very popular. **5** Excursion steamer *Lady Elgin* and the schooner *Augusta* collide on Lake Michigan; about 400 people die. **6** U.S. Secret Service is established. **7** First kindergarten in English is established in Boston by Elizabeth P. Peabody. A German kindergarten had been started in Wisconsin in 1856.	**8** English Church Union is founded. **9** John C. Heenan, an American, and Tom Sayers, an Englishman, fight a championship boxing match in England. The fight ends when the crowd breaks into the ring. It is the last fight with bare fists in England. **10** First British Open Golf Championship is held, won by W. Park.	**1860**
1 Otis patents a steam-powered elevator. **2** Holmes invents the stereoscope. **3** Telegraph wires are strung between New York and San Francisco, making instant coast-to-coast communication possible. **4** Eberhard Faber, Ger.-Amer. manufacturer, opens a factory in New York for the mass production of pencils.	**5** W. Siemens patents an open-hearth furnace heated by gas. **6** Crookes discovers the element thallium.	**1** There are now more than 30,000 miles of railroad tracks in the U.S. **2** Vassar College is established in Poughkeepsie, N.Y., by Matthew Vassar. Vassar is the first women's college with facilities equal to those found in men's colleges. **3** American balloonist Thaddeus Lowe makes a record balloon voyage from Cincinnati, Ohio, to	**7** Russia's population is 76 million, Great Britain's 23 million, Ireland's 5.7 million, and Italy's 25 million. **8** First horse-drawn trams (streetcars) appear in London.	**1861**

History and Politics		The Arts	
America	**Elsewhere**	**America**	**Elsewhere**
Sumter, Charleston, S.C., forcing Union troops to evacuate. U.S. Civil War begins. **4** Pres. Lincoln proclaims blockade of Confederate ports. **5** Confederates defeat Union troops at the First Battle of Bull Run, Manassas, Va. **6** Kansas becomes 34th state. **7** Congress creates Dakota, Colorado, and Nevada Territories. **8** West Virginia breaks away from Virginia; it becomes the 35th state in 1863.	Kingdom of Italy is proclaimed by first Italian Parliament, with Victor Emmanuel II as king. **13** Spain governs the Dominican Republic to protect it from Haitian attack. Spain withdraws in 1865. **14** Poles demonstrate in Warsaw against Russian rule. **15** William I becomes King of Prussia. **16** Danubian Principalities of Moldavia and Wallachia unite to form Rumania. **17** British annex Lagos, Nigeria. **18** Russia makes unsuccessful attempt to take control of the Japanese islands of Tsushima.	creation of the Confederate states. **4** Longfellow translates *Divine Comedy of Dante Alighieri* into English.	*Great Expectations.* **8** Eliot publishes *Silas Marner,* a novel about a miser whose life is changed by the love of a young girl. **9** Fr. artist Gustave Doré illustrates Dante's *Inferno* in a romantic, though somewhat bizarre style. **10** Concerned with what he considers widespread ugliness, Morris establishes a company to renew interest in the finer things such as exquisite textiles and stained glass. **11** Royal Academy of Music, London, is founded.
1862			
1 Union forces capture Forts Henry and Donelson and defeat the Confederates at Pea Ridge, Ark. **2** Union vessel *Monitor* and Confederate *Merrimack* engage in first sea battle between ironclad warships. Battle is inconclusive. **3** Union fleet under Admiral David G. Farragut defeats Confederate fleet near the mouth of the Mississippi and captures New Orleans. **4** Union army of Tennessee under Gen. Ulysses S. Grant forces Confederates to withdraw at the Battle of Shiloh, Tenn. **5** Union forces under Gen. George B. McClellan and Confederate forces under Gen. Robert E. Lee engage in inconclusive Seven Days' Battles in Virginia. **6** Confederates under Gen. Stonewall Jackson and Gen. Lee defeat Union forces at the Second Battle of Bull Run, Va. **7** Gen. Lee's invasion of the North is halted by Gen. McClellan at the Battle of Antietam, Md. Gen. Lee wins the Battle of Fredericksburg, Va.	**8** Otto von Bismarck becomes Prime Minister of Prussia. He advocates the unification of Germany under Prussian leadership. **9** Otto I attempts to discard the Greek constitution and is deposed by a military revolt. **[1833:HIST/8]** **10** British and Spanish troops withdraw from Mexico, where Napoleon III plans to establish a Catholic empire under French leadership. **11** Risorgimento embarks upon Italy's annexation of Venetia (in Austria's possession), Rome (occupied by French troops), and parts of the Papal States (under French protection). **12** Nicaragua, Honduras, and San Salvador make unsuccessful attempt to form a Central American union. **13** Taiping rebels are suppressed near Shanghai and Ningpo.	**1** Julia Ward Howe writes "Battle Hymn of the Republic." **2** Theodore Thomas develops the first highly professional orchestra in the country. **3** J.R. Lowell publishes the poem "Washers of the Shroud." **4** Charles F. Browne publishes *Artemus Ward: His Book,* the title character being the author's penname.	**5** Hugo publishes *Les Misérables,* a complex novel describing the adventures of a poor French peasant. **6** Sarah Bernhardt, Fr. actress, makes her debut at Comédie Française. **7** Hebble's drama, *Die Niebelungen Trilogie,* includes "The Horned Siegfried," "Siegfried's Death," and "Kriemhild's Revenge." **8** Ingres paints "Turkish Bath." **9** Turgenev publishes *Fathers and Sons,* his greatest novel. **10** Verdi composes the grand opera, *La Forza del Destino.*

Science & Technology		Miscellaneous		
America	**Elsewhere**	**America**	**Elsewhere**	

Sarah Bernhardt, French actress

the South Carolina coast in 9 hrs.

4 U.S. mails begin to carry merchandise as well as letters.

5 First federal income tax of 3% on incomes over $800 is enacted. Increased in the following years, it supplies about one fifth of the federal government revenues by 1865.

6 Congress abolishes flogging in the Army.

---

1 The *Monitor,* an ironclad, steam-powered warship designed by John Ericsson, is launched. It features a screw propeller and a revolving gun turret.

2 Abraham Jacobi, "Father of American Pediatrics," opens America's first children's clinic in New York City.

3 Richard J. Gatling, N.C. inventor, patents the 10-barrel "Gatling gun," a machine gun that fires 250 shots per minute.

4 James Dana publishes *Manual of Geology.*

5 Colt's Connecticut factory is producing 1000 guns a day.

6 Kelvin suggests that the Sun and Earth were much hotter one million years ago.

7 Lenoir constructs the first automobile with an internal combustion engine.

8 Jean Foucault, Fr. physicist, measures the speed of light as 185,150 miles per second, an error of 0.6%.

1 Morrill Land-Grant College Act provides for the endowment of colleges of agriculture and industry.

2 Congress authorizes the first U.S. legal tender bank notes; by 1865 more than $400 million in "greenbacks" have been issued.

3 Pacific Railway Act authorizes the Union Pacific Railroad to build a line from Nebraska to Utah to meet the Central Pacific, which is building eastward from California.

4 Borden patents a process for concentrating fruit juice.

5 Swiss banker and philanthropist Jean Henri Dunant proposes the foundation of an international relief organization—the Red Cross. **[1881:MISC/2]**

1862

History and Politics		The Arts	
America	**Elsewhere**	**America**	**Elsewhere**

1863

History and Politics — America

1 Lincoln issues Emancipation Proclamation, freeing slaves in seceding states.
2 Congress creates the Arizona and Idaho Territories.
3 Confederate army under Gen. Lee defeats Union army at the Battle of Chancellorsville, Va. Gen. Lee begins invasion of the North.
4 Union forces under Gen. George G. Meade defeat Confederate forces under Gen. Lee at the Battle of Gettysburg, Pa. Gen. Lee retreats into Virginia.
5 Union forces under Gen. Grant capture Vicksburg, Miss.
6 Union forces are beaten at the Battle of Chickamauga, Ga., but win the Battle of Chattanooga, Tenn.
7 At dedication of national cemetery at the Gettysburg battlefield, Pres. Lincoln gives his *Gettysburg Address.*
8 Pres. Lincoln offers amnesty to all Southerners taking loyalty oath.

History and Politics — Elsewhere

9 Poles in Russian Poland rise in the so-called January Revolution, which spreads to Lithuania and White Russia. [1864:HIST/11]
10 German Confederation demands that the duchies of Schleswig and Holstein be forcibly taken from Denmark. Saxon and Hanoverian troops enter Holstein.
11 George I, a Danish prince, is chosen King of Greece.
12 Internal disorder leads to civil war in Uruguay.
13 New Granada is renamed the United States of Colombia. [1830:HIST/6]
14 French troops capture Mexico City. Austrian archduke Maximilian is proclaimed Emperor of Mexico.
15 Ismail Pasha becomes ruler of Egypt. He begins modernization of the country.
16 French establish a protectorate over Cambodia.
17 Civil war breaks out in Afghanistan after the death of Dost Muhammad.

The Arts — America

1 Foster composes the song "Beautiful Dreamer."
2 Samuel Langhorne Clemens, author and humorist, adopts the Mississippi riverboat term "Mark Twain" as a penname.
3 "Harvest of Death," a photograph by Timothy O'Sullivan, shows the Confederate dead in Gettysburg on July 4, 1863.
4 Longfellow publishes *Tales of a Wayside Inn,* the first poem of which is the classic "Paul Revere's Ride."
5 Emerson writes "Boston Hymn" in praise of the Emancipation Proclamation.
6 Thomas Bishop writes the words to the Civil War ballad "When Johnny Comes Marching Home."

The Arts — Elsewhere

7 Rejected by the Académie, Manet's "Le Déjeuner sur l'Herbe" ("Luncheon on the Grass") is an instant success when exhibited at Salon de Refusés (Salon for Rejects), marking the start of modern art.
8 Fr. science fiction pioneer Jules Verne publishes his first novel, *Five Weeks in a Balloon.*
9 Georges Bizet, Fr. composer, produces *The Pearl Fishers,* an opera.
10 Ernest Renan, Fr. historian, publishes the controversial *Life of Jesus.*
11 Kingsley publishes *The Water-Babies,* a popular children's book.
12 Eng. artist and novelist Samuel Butler begins *Hudibras* (–1878), a mock heroic satire of Puritanism.

1864

History and Politics — America

1 Gen. Grant is made Commander-in-Chief of the Union armies.
2 Armies of Grant and Lee fight the inconclusive, but destructive, Battles of the Wilderness, Spotsylvania, and Cold Harbor in Virginia. Union army suffers far greater casualties than Confederate.
3 Union army under Gen. William Tecumseh Sherman captures and burns Atlanta. Sherman's army marches through Georgia to the sea, destroying everything in its path, and captures Savannah.
4 Union army defeats Confederate army at Nashville, Tenn.
5 Nevada becomes 36th state.
6 Montana Territory formed from part of Idaho Territory.
7 Union navy under Admiral Farragut defeats Confeder-

History and Politics — Elsewhere

10 Britain turns over the Ionian Islands to Greece.
11 Russians crush revolts and begin "Russification" programs in Poland.
12 Austria and Prussia declare war on Denmark, which is easily defeated. Denmark cedes Schleswig, Holstein, and Lauenburg to Austria and Prussia. [1863:HIST/10]
13 Russia establishes the zemstvo system. Local assemblies (zemstvos), on which landowners, townspeople, and peasants are represented, levy taxes for education, public health, roads, and so forth. Russia reforms its judiciary, too.
14 Chinese provincial armies suppress the Taiping Rebellion and recapture Nanking.
15 Allied expedition of British, Dutch, French, and U.S. warships bombard and silence Choshu forts at Shimonoseki,

The Arts — America

1 John Quincy Adams Ward, sculptor, completes "Indian Hunter," which now stands in New York City's Central Park.

The Arts — Elsewhere

2 Anton Bruckner, Aust. composer, completes *Symphony in D Minor* and *Mass No. 1 in D Minor.*
3 Verne publishes *A Journey to the Center of the Earth.*
4 Dickens publishes *Our Mutual Friend,* his last full-length novel.
5 In response to anti-Catholic attacks by Kingsley, Cardinal John Henry Newman publishes *Apologia pro vita sua,* a widely acclaimed history of the development of his religious ideas.
6 Dostoevsky publishes *Notes from the Underground.*

Science & Technology		Miscellaneous		
America	**Elsewhere**	**America**	**Elsewhere**	
1 National Academy of Sciences (NAS) is founded in Washington, D.C., with Alexander Bache as president. **2** Alexander Holley, N.Y. engineer, purchases the American rights to the Bessemer steelmaking process and produces America's first Bessemer steel two years later.	**3** Lyell's *The Geological Evidence of the Antiquity of Man* lends support to Darwin's theory of evolution. **4** William Huggins, Eng. astronomer, uses his newly invented stellar spectroscope to show that stars are similar to the Sun. **5** Ivan Sechenov, Russ. psychologist, describes a theory of behavior on which Pavlov later bases his work.	**1** First Union conscription act makes all men 20 to 35, and unmarried men to 45 years old, subject to military service. It is easy to avoid actual service, though, by paying $300 for a substitute to enlist for 3 years. **2** Ebenezer Butterick of Sterling, Mass., invents the first paper dress patterns sold in U.S. **3** Traveler's Insurance Company is founded in Hartford, Conn., as the first traveler's accident insurance company. **4** Roller skating is introduced into America by James L. Plimpton, who invents the 4-wheel skate. **5** Joe Coburn wins the American boxing championship from Mike McCoole in a 63-round match in Charleston, Md.	**6** Scarlet fever epidemic kills more than 30,000 people in England. **7** Grand Prix de Paris is first run at the Longchamp race course. **8** Football (soccer in America) Association is founded in London. **9** Eng. explorers John Speke and James Grant travel down the Nile River to Gondokoro, Central Africa.	**1863**
1 William F. Durfee, Mass. engineer, produces Bessemerlike steel by using the Kelly process. **2** Salmon hatchery opens in New York City. **3** Pennsylvania Railroad begins using steel for its rails. **4** Thomas Doughty invents the periscope.	**5** Maxwell suggests that electromagnetic waves travel at the speed of light in his work *A Dynamical Theory of the Electromagnetic Field.* This work refutes the theory of luminiferous ether. [1638:SCI/1] **6** Pasteur develops a pasteurization method for wine. This method is eventually applied to milk. **7** Julius von Sachs, Ger. botanist, determines that starch is the first visible product of photosynthesis.	**1** First Baptist social union composed entirely of laymen is established in Tremont Temple, Boston. It reflects the growing influence of businessmen in church affairs, especially in administrative posts. **2** The "Pullman Car," the first comfortable railroad sleeping car is built by George Pullman. **3** "In God We Trust," appears on a U.S. coin, the 2¢ piece, for the first time. **4** First croquet club is founded in Brooklyn, N.Y. **5** Travers Stakes is established at the first race track in Saratoga, N.Y. **6** Knights of Pythias, a fraternal order, is founded in Washington, D.C. **7** Two-train collision	**8** Metropolitan Railway opens in London. **9** Geneva Convention establishes the neutrality of battlefield medical facilities. [1881:MISC/2] **10** Eng. theologian and author Cardinal Newman publishes *Apologia pro Vita Sua.* **11** Eng. explorer Samuel White Baker discovers Lake Albert, a source of the Nile, in Central Africa. **12** Cyclone destroys most of Calcutta, India; about 70,000 people die.	**1864**

	America	Elsewhere	America	Elsewhere
	ate navy at the Battle of Mobile Bay, Ala. Confederate blockade-running is stifled in the Gulf. **8** Lincoln (Republican) wins reelection as President, defeating Gen. McClellan (Democrat). Andrew Johnson is elected Vice President on the Republican ticket. **9** Cheyenne and Arapaho warriors, women, and children are massacred at Sand Creek, Colo.	thereby halting the anti-foreign movement in Japan.		
1865	**1** Gen. Sherman's army marches northward through South and North Carolina, ravaging the country. Confederates evacuate Columbia and Charleston, S.C. [1864:HIST/3] **2** Lee is made General-in-Chief of all Confederate armies. **3** Deprived of food and supplies and caught between Sherman in the south and Grant in the north, Confederates under Lee abandon Petersburg and Richmond and retreat westward. **4** Union forces under Grant pursue and surround Lee, who surrenders to Grant at Appomattox Court House, Va. Other Confederate armies follow suit. Civil War ends. **5** Pres. Lincoln is shot and killed by John Wilkes Booth in Ford's Theater, Washington, D.C. Johnson is inaugurated as President. **6** Thirteenth Amendment to the Constitution, abolishing slavery, is ratified by 27 states, including eight formerly Confederate states. **7** Colorado militia suppress the Cheyenne and Arapaho Indians who have been on the warpath. [1864:HIST/9]	**8** Florence replaces Turin as the capital of the kingdom of Italy. [1870:HIST/9] **9** Peru declares war on Spain, which had not recognized Peru's independence. Peru concludes alliances with Chile, Bolivia, and Ecuador. **10** By the Treaty of Gastein, Austria is to administer Holstein and Prussia is to administer Schleswig. Lauenburg goes to Prussia in return for a money payment to Austria. [1864:HIST/12] **11** War breaks out between the Boers of the Orange Free State and the Basutos. **12** Madagascar reverses its anti-European policy and welcomes missionaries and traders. **13** Paraguay wages war against Brazil, Argentina, and Uruguay. [1870:HIST/10] **14** Wellington replaces Auckland as the capital of New Zealand.	**1** Mary Mapes Dodge publishes *Hans Brinker; or The Silver Skates.* **2** Inness breaks from the Hudson River School with the paintings "Delaware Valley" and "Peace and Plenty." **3** In the last issue of *The Liberator,* Garrison declares "my vocation as an abolitionist is ended." [1831:ARTS/5] **4** Tony Pastor, "father of American vaudeville," opens a variety theater in New York City featuring entertainment for men only. **5** Whitman publishes *Drum Taps,* a collection of Civil War poems. **6** J.Q.A. Ward sculpts "Freedman" in honor of the freed slaves.	**7** Lewis Carroll (Charles Lutwidge Dodgson), Eng. novelist, publishes the classic children's story, *Alice's Adventures in Wonderland,* with illustrations by Tenniel. **8** Leo Tolstoy, Russ. novelist, publishes *War and Peace* (–1869). **9** Manet's painting, "Olympia," creates a stir when many critics claim it is obscene. **10** Algernon Charles Swinburne, Eng. poet and critic, wins acclaim for *Atalanta in Calydon,* a drama written in classical Greek style. **11** Doré prepares illustrations for the Bible.
1866	**1** Congress passes Civil Rights Act over Pres. Johnson's veto. **2** Congress passes Fourteenth Amendment, which	**6** Bismarck concludes alliance with Italy and accuses Austria of violating the Treaty of Gastein. Prussia invades Holstein and declares the German Confederation at an end. Austro-Prussian War,	**1** Franz Schwartzer, Missouri eccentric, opens a zither factory. **2** The Metropolitan Museum is founded in New York City. **3** Joseph Jefferson be-	**9** Offenbach composes the operetta, *La Vie Parisienne.* **10** Claude Monet, Fr. artist and leading Impressionist, paints "Camille, The Green

Science & Technology		Miscellaneous		
America	**Elsewhere**	**America**	**Elsewhere**	

The Mad Tea-Party from Lewis Carroll's *Alice in Wonderland*

near Shohola, Pa., kills 65 people.

Science & Technology		Miscellaneous		
America	**Elsewhere**	**America**	**Elsewhere**	
1 Linus Yale, Jr., Conn. locksmith, invents the cylinder lock. **2** In *From the Earth to the Moon,* Jules Verne, Fr. author, predicts that America will lead the conquest of space. **3** Massachusetts Institute of Technology (MIT) opens with 15 students. **4** Alexander Agassiz, Swed.-Amer. zoologist, publishes *Embryology of the Starfish.* **5** Maria Mitchell is appointed by Vassar College as America's first woman professor of astronomy. **6** Samuel Van Syckel installs an oil pipeline near Titusville, Pa. The pipe is 5 miles long and made of wrought iron.	**7** Kekule discovers the ringed structure of benzene. **8** Joseph Lister, Brit. surgeon, applies a carbolic acid dressing to a wound in a successful effort to prevent infection. **9** Sachs determines that chlorophyll is not spread throughout a plant but is instead located in certain cell structures known as chloroplasts. **10** Semmelweis, his ideas rejected by the European medical community, dies of puerperal fever, the disease that he fought to eradicate his entire life. **[1848:SCI/7]** **11** Sorby invents a microscope for studying inorganic pigments.	**1** Union Stockyards open in Chicago, Ill. They become the largest in the U.S., serving the cattle industry over a wide area. Chicago becomes the world's greatest meat-producing and meat-packing center. **2** First fire department with paid firefighters is established in New York City. **3** Interest in baseball takes tremendous upsurge after the war. There are 91 clubs included in the national association. **4** First railroad train holdup takes place at dawn in North Bend, Ohio, when an Ohio and Mississippi train is derailed. Male passengers are robbed and the express car is looted. **5** River steamer *Sultana* explodes and sinks at Memphis, Tenn., killing about 1400 people.	**6** Edward Whymper climbs the 14,780-ft. Matterhorn in the Alps. **7** Marquis of Queensberry rules governing boxing are outlined in England. They include the use of gloves instead of bare knuckles, the 10-second count for a knockout, and the 3-minute round. **8** Eng. lawyer John Macgregor advocates canoeing as a sport. **9** Eng. religious leader William Booth founds a religious organization which later is named the Salvation Army (1878).	**1865**
1 Henry A. House, Conn. manufacturer, develops a 12-horsepower steam automobile. **2** Congress legalizes the metric system but does not require its use.	**7** Robert Whitehead, Eng. engineer, invents the torpedo. **8** Ernst Haeckel, Ger. biologist, proposes the biogenetic law: ontogeny recapitulates phylogeny,	**1** Congress passes a Civil Rights Act, which grants the same rights to all natural-born Americans (except Indians), including Negroes, who had been denied such rights.	**7** Eng. physician Elizabeth Garrett Anderson opens a dispensary (a medical clinic) for women and children in London. **8** Eng. archaeologist Charles Wilson begins to	**1866**

223

History and Politics

America | Elsewhere

The Arts

America | Elsewhere

History and Politics — America	History and Politics — Elsewhere	The Arts — America	The Arts — Elsewhere
contains the "due process" and "equal protection" clauses securing the civil rights of Negroes. [1868:HIST/3] 3 Congress passes Freedman's Bureau Bill over Pres. Johnson's veto. Military can try persons accused of depriving newly freed Negroes of their civil rights. 4 Eight hundred Irish-Americans, part of the Fenian movement to free Ireland from Britain, cross the Niagara River and defeat Canadian militia. They are arrested by U.S. officials but released. Raids continue to 1871, drawing attention to the Fenian cause. 5 U.S. government tries to build road from Ft. Laramie to the mines of Montana, across the Sioux Indians' hunting grounds. Sioux massacre U.S. troops at Ft. Philip Kearny, Wyo.	or Seven Weeks' War, begins. Italy declares war on Austria. Italians are defeated on the land, at Custozza, and on the sea, near Lissa. Prussians defeat the Hanoverians at Langensalza and the Austrians at Königgrätz (Sadowa). Preliminary peace at Nikolsburg is followed by the Treaty of Prague. Austria cedes Venetia to Italy. Prussia annexes Hanover, Hesse, Nassau, Frankfurt, and Schleswig-Holstein. Treaty of Vienna ends Austro-Italian War. 7 Cretans revolt against Turkish rule. 8 Serbia and Montenegro conclude secret alliance. 9 Carol I becomes first King of Rumania. 10 Boers defeat the Basutos, who cede territory. [1865:HIST/11] 11 Japan signs tariff agreement with the U.S., Britain, France, and the Netherlands.	comes the most popular actor in the U.S. with his depiction of Rip Van Winkle. 4 Artist Winslow Homer reflects the American mood of reconciliation in his painting "Prisoners from the Front." 5 J.Q.A. Ward sculpts "The Good Samaritan" in honor of the discovery of anesthesia. The sculpture stands in the Boston Public Gardens. 6 Alexander Wheelock Thayer publishes the first volume of *The Life of Beethoven.* 7 Alexander Gardner publishes *Photographic Sketch Book of the Civil War.* 8 Whittier's best known poem, "Snowbound," earns him $10,000.	Dress," a portrait of his future wife. 11 Bedřich Smetana, founder of the Czech. school of music, composes *The Bartered Bride,* an opera. 12 Dostoevsky publishes *Crime and Punishment.* 13 Swinburne publishes *Poems and Ballads.* 14 Léo Delibes, Fr. composer, introduces high quality symphonic music for ballet in *La Source.* 15 Paul Verlaine, Fr. lyric poet, publishes a collection of his poetry in *Poèmes Saturniens.* 16 Charles de Coster, Belg. novelist, publishes *The Glorious Adventures of Tyl Eulenspiegel.*
1867 1 Nebraska becomes 37th state. 2 Congress passes three Reconstruction Acts over Pres. Johnson's vetoes. Acts divide the South (except Tennessee) into five military districts in which army commanders control voter eligibility and registration. 3 Congress passes Tenure of Office Act over Pres. Johnson's veto. It forbids the President to remove any officials without the consent of the Senate. 4 U.S. buys Alaska from Russia for $7.2 million (less than two cents an acre) through the efforts of Secretary of State William H. Seward. 5 Congress sets up reservations in Indian Territory (now Oklahoma) for the Five Civilized Tribes (Cherokees, Chickasaws, Choctaws, Creeks, and Seminoles).	6 Garibaldi is defeated by French and Papal forces at the Battle of Mentana while attempting to capture Rome. 7 Austro-Hungarian Dual Monarchy is established by the *Ausgleich,* a compromise between Hungarian pressure for independence and Emperor Franz Josef's desire for a strong Hapsburg Empire. 8 North German Confederation under Prussian leadership replaces the German Confederation. 9 Serbia signs secret treaties with Rumania and Greece. Last Turkish troops leave Serbia. 10 British North America Act establishes the Dominion of Canada, consisting of the provinces of Ontario, Quebec, New Brunswick, and Nova Scotia. 11 Napoleon III withdraws support from Maximilian, who is captured and executed. Juárez restores order in Mex-	1 The New England Conservatory of Music in Boston is founded. 2 Horatio Alger publishes *Ragged Dick; or, Street Life in New York,* the first of many "rags to riches" stories for boys. 3 George W. Harris publishes *Yarns,* a collection of tall tales about the Southwest. 4 Sidney Lanier publishes *Tiger-Lilies,* a romance interwoven with the author's Civil War experience. 5 *Slave Songs of the United States,* the first collection of Negro spirituals published, includes the still popular "Michael Row the Boat Ashore."	6 Johann Strauss (the younger), Aust. composer known as the "Waltz King," writes *The Blue Danube,* one of the most popular tunes of the 19th century. 7 Europeans get their first taste of Japanese art at the Paris World's Fair. 8 Wagner composes *Die Meistersinger von Nürnberg.* 9 Russ. composer Modest Mussorgsky composes *Night on Bald Mountain.* 10 Fr. novelist Émile Zola, founder of the Naturalist movement, defends Manet's unconventional style in *Revue du XIXᵉ Siècle (Review of the 19th Century).* 11 Henrik Ibsen Norw. playwright,

Science & Technology		Miscellaneous		
America	Elsewhere	America	Elsewhere	
3 Thaddeus S. Lowe, balloonist and inventor, opens a factory in New Orleans to produce artificial ice for commercial use. **4** America's first refrigerated railroad car is built in Detroit, Mich. **5** Sims performs the first successful artificial insemination of a human being at the New York Women's Hospital. **6** American Society for the Prevention of Cruelty to Animals (ASPCA) is established in New York City by Henry Bergh.	that is, as an embryo develops, it goes through all the stages in the evolution of that species. [1857:SCI/3] **9** Gregor Johann Mendel, Aust. monk, publishes his laws of heredity, based on extensive genetic crossings of pea plants. **10** Werner von Siemens invents a generator that is set in motion by an electromagnet. **11** Sir Joseph Lockyer, Eng. astronomer, begins stereoscopic studies of the Sun. **12** Hamilton's *The Elements of Quaternions,* a complex mathematical work, is published one year after his death.	[1875:HIST/2] **2** First Young Women's Christian Association (YWCA) opens in Boston. The organization had its beginnings in England. **3** Steamship *Great Eastern* reaches U.S. completing the laying of the second Atlantic cable between England and America. First cable laid in 1858 was not effective. **4** Congress authorizes the issuance of a 5¢ coin, known as a "nickel." Piece is minted of copper and nickel with not more than 25% nickel. **5** Cholera epidemic strikes many cities. About 200 people die each day in St. Louis, Mo., during the worst of the epidemic. **6** National Labor Union is organized in Baltimore, Md. Ira Steward and George McNeill lead the movement for an 8-hour workday.	excavate the site of ancient Jerusalem. **9** Eng. athlete and journalist J.G. Chambers founds the Amateur Athletic Club. **10** Fire in Quebec, Canada, destroys about 2500 buildings.	
1 Alpheus Hyatt, Mass. naturalist, founds the *American Naturalist* magazine. **2** Beach exhibits a pneumatic subway that is propelled through a tube by a fan. Although this concept is largely ignored at the time, it is revived and modified 90 years later.	**3** Sir James Dewar, Eng. chemist, determines the structural formula of benzene. **4** Alfred Nobel, Swed. chemist, patents dynamite. **5** Huggins discovers that some nebulae are composed of luminous gases. **6** Zénobe Gramme, Belg. engineer, patents an alternating current device. **7** Helmholtz publishes the *Handbook of Physiological Optics.* **8** Virchow publishes work on the pathology of tumors.	**1** Ku Klux Klan, formed in 1865 by Confederate officers as a social club, is formally organized at Nashville, Tenn. The name comes from the Greek word for circle, *kyklos.* **2** First elevated railroad begins operating in New York City. Built by the West Side Elevated Railroad Co., its single track runs from Battery Place to 30th St. **3** Howard University is chartered in Washington, D.C. Named after Gen. Oliver O. Howard, its first president, it is the first predominantly Negro college to offer comprehensive university facilities. **4** "Ruthless" wins the first annual Belmont Stakes for winnings valued at $1850. **5** Record for long-distance walking is set by	**6** Pierre Michaux begins to manufacture bicycles in France. He and his son had earlier developed the velocipede "boneshaker," so called because its wooden wheels with iron rims give a rough ride over cobblestones. **7** Marx publishes volume 1 of *Das Kapital,* a work on the economic, social and political relations in society and containing the ideas on which modern communism is based. Volumes 2 and 3 are published after Marx's death. **8** Ships *Rhone* and *Wye* and many small vessels are wrecked in a storm in St. Thomas, West Indies; about 1000 people die. **9** Livingstone begins exploring the Congo River in East Africa to discover its source.	**1867**

History and Politics		The Arts	
America	**Elsewhere**	**America**	**Elsewhere**
	ico and is elected president. **[1863:HIST/14]** **12** Shogunate (military rule) is abolished in Japan; power is returned to the emperor.		publishes *Peer Gynt,* a tragedy.

1868

America (History and Politics)

1 Pres. Johnson is impeached by the House of Representatives for violating the Tenure of Office Act and for abusing his veto power. He is tried and acquitted by the Senate. **[1867:HIST/3]**
2 Congress readmits Arkansas, North Carolina, South Carolina, Georgia, Florida, Alabama, and Louisiana to the Union. **[1870:HIST/1]**
3 Fourteenth Amendment is ratified by 29 states.
4 Burlingame Treaty between the U.S. and China encourages Chinese immigration to the West.
5 Wyoming Territory is formed out of parts of the Dakota, Utah, and Idaho Territories.
6 Gen. Ulysses S. Grant and Rep. Schuyler Colfax are elected President and Vice President, respectively, on the Republican ticket.
7 Congress passes bill providing eight-hour working day for federal employees.

Elsewhere (History and Politics)

8 Benjamin Disraeli, an imperialist and Tory leader, becomes British Prime Minister but loses the office to William Evart Gladstone, an anti-imperialist and Liberal Party leader, during the year.
9 Russian troops capture the city of Samarkand in central Asia.
10 Revolution deposes Queen Isabella II of Spain. Provisional government annuls reactionary laws and establishes universal suffrage and a free press.
11 Prince Michael of Serbia is assassinated. He is succeeded by his cousin Milan.
12 Basutoland (now Lesotho) is proclaimed British territory.
13 Meiji dynasty is restored in Japan, and the imperial capital is moved from Kyoto to Edo, renamed Tokyo. Emperor places government in the hands of Westernizers, who begin to modernize Japan.
14 British military force defeats Ethiopians near Magdala and rescues imprisoned British subjects.

America (The Arts)

1 Episcopal clergyman Phillips Brooks writes the hymn "O Little Town of Bethlehem."
2 Adah Menken publishes *Infelicia,* a collection of poems dedicated to Charles Dickens.

Robert Browning, English poet and dramatist

Elsewhere (The Arts)

3 Brahms composes *A German Requiem,* one of the most important choral works of the 19th century, and "Lullaby," perhaps his most popular and best-known tune.
4 *The Ring and the Book,* a collection of 12 monologues, brings R. Browning long-overdue recognition.
5 Collins publishes *The Moonstone,* a mystery novel that features one of literature's first detectives.
6 J. Strauss composes *Tales From the Vienna Woods.*
7 Dostoevsky publishes *The Idiot,* a novel.
8 Lawrence Alma-Tadema, Dutch painter, exhibits "The Visit."

1869

America (History and Politics)

1 Congress adopts Fifteenth Amendment, stating that the right to vote shall not be denied or abridged because of "race, color, or previous condition of servitude." **[1870:HIST/2]**
2 Congress enacts Public Credit Act, which provides for payment of U.S. debts in gold. Greenbacks (paper money) worth $356 million are left in circulation.
3 Prohibition Party is founded in Chicago. It supports the temperance cause—legislative prohibition of the manufacture, transportation, and sale of alcoholic

Elsewhere (History and Politics)

5 Napoleon III reintroduces parliamentary government in France.
6 Cortes (legislative body) sets up a constitutional monarchy in Spain.
7 Hudson's Bay Company transfers its territory to the Dominion of Canada.
8 Red River Rebellion begins. Alarmed by Canadian surveys of their lands, métis (halfbreeds) led by Louis Riel capture Ft. Garry (now Winnipeg) and set up provisional government.
9 Britain, France, and Italy take financial control of Tunisia. The beys (Turkish gover-

America (The Arts)

1 Mark Twain publishes *The Innocents Abroad,* a collection of letters written during the author's tour of Europe and the Holy Land.
2 Louisa May Alcott publishes *Little Women,* one of the most popular girls' books ever written.
3 Josh Billings, humorist, begins publication of *Josh Billings' Farmer's Allminax,* a parody of *The Old Farmer's Almanac.*

Elsewhere (The Arts)

4 Richard Dodderidge Blackmore, Eng. novelist, publishes *Lorna Doone.*
5 William Schwenck Gilbert, Eng. writer, publishes *Bab Ballads,* a collection of poems.
6 Peter Ilyich Tchaikovsky, Russ. composer, produces *Romeo and Juliet,* a lyrical fantasy overture.
7 Aleksandr Borodin, Russ. composer, begins work on his opera, *Prince Igor.* (Completed in 1890 by Rimsky-Korsakov.)

226

Science & Technology		Miscellaneous		
America	**Elsewhere**	**America**	**Elsewhere**	
		Edward P. Weston who covers the distance from Portland, Me., to Chicago, Ill., in 26 days, winning $10,000.		
1 Thomas Alva Edison, creator of more than 1000 inventions, patents an electric voting machine. **2** Mahlon Loomis, N.Y. inventor, demonstrates wireless communication with a telegraph and an aerial he had invented. **3** George Westinghouse, N.Y. manufacturer, invents air brakes. (Improved in 1872.) **4** Christopher L. Sholes, Pa. printer, patents and names the first practical typewriter.	**5** Bunsen invents the filter pump. **6** The plastid, a specialized cell structure, is described by Pringsheim and von Sachs. **7** Pasteur finds the microbe responsible for silkworm disease and devises a way to combat it. **8** Lockyer discovers the previously unknown element helium in the Sun's atmosphere. **9** Darwin publishes *The Variation of Animals and Plants Under Domestication.* **10** Frankland does expollution.	**1** New England Woman's Club is founded. Its objective is to concentrate and promote the efforts of women to win recognition of their rights. **2** Congress passes a bill limiting the work hours of federally employed laborers and mechanics to an 8-hour day. The concept was still something new, although ineffectual 8-hour laws had been passed in Illinois, New York, and Missouri. **3** Popularity of ice skating leads to the meeting of an American skating congress in Pittsburgh, Pa., to establish regulations for the sport. **4** New sport of "velocipeding" (cycling) becomes popular. Schools for all ages and both sexes are set up throughout the large cities. **5** First annual track and field meet (indoors) is held by the New York Athletic Club.	**6** Skeleton of Cro-Magnon man (a forerunner of modern man in Europe and the first successor to the Neanderthal man) is found in France. **7** Badminton, developed from the ancient Asian game of battledore and shuttlecock, becomes popular in England. **8** Earliest recorded bicycle race takes place at the Parc de St. Cloud in Paris. **9** Earthquake in Peru and Ecuador kills nearly 25,000 people and causes $300 million worth of damage.	**1868**
1 The world's first transcontinental railroad line is completed as the last spike is hammered in at Promontory, Utah, by officials of the Union Pacific and Central Pacific Railroads. Union Pacific crews had laid track eastward from California while Central Pacific had worked westward from Nebraska.	**2** Dmitry Mendeleyev, Russ. chemist, publishes the classic *Principles of Chemistry,* in which he proposes the periodic law and devises the periodic table of elements. **3** Virchow founds the German Anthropological Society. **4** Due to his antiseptic techniques, Lister reduces the death rate by two thirds at the Male Accident Ward in Glasgow. **5** Gramme invents the Gramme dynamo, an important step in the developing electrical industry.	**1** Noble Order of Knights of Labor is formed secretly in Philadelphia by a group of garment cutters. Later a national organization, its membership includes skilled and unskilled workers. **2** Arabella Mansfield is admitted to the Iowa bar as the first woman lawyer since Margaret Brent. **3** Explorer John Wesley Powell navigates the Colorado River for more than 1000 mi. and explores the Grand Canyon.	**6** Suez Canal opens, connecting the Mediterranean and the Red Sea. The north-south waterway provides a sea-level passage about 105 mi. long for sea-going vessels. **7** First postcards are introduced in Austria. **8** Debtors' prisons are abolished in Britain. **9** Ger. explorer Gustav Nachtigal travels through the Sudan and the Sahara in northern Africa. **10** First Vatican Council meets in Rome. **[1870:MISC/9]** **11** Fr. chemist H. Mège-	**1869**

227

	History and Politics		The Arts	
	America	Elsewhere	America	Elsewhere
	beverages. **4** Wyoming Territory grants women the right to vote (suffrage) and to hold public office. National Woman Suffrage Association, led by Susan B. Anthony and Elizabeth Cady Stanton, and the American Woman Suffrage Association, led by Lucy Stone, are separately organized to work for women's voting rights.	nors) had contracted heavy debts and failed to meet them. **10** Turks suppress Cretan revolt, preventing annexation of Crete by Greece.		
1870	**1** Virginia, Mississippi, Texas, and Georgia (for the second time) are readmitted to the Union. **2** Fifteenth Amendment is ratified by 29 states. It gives the right to vote to black men, but not to women. **[1920:HIST/5]** **3** Congress passes act creating the Department of Justice. **4** Northerners, called "carpetbaggers," and white Southerners, called "scalawags," join the Republican Party to carry out the congressional Reconstruction program in the South, sometimes meddling in the region's political affairs to their own benefit. **[1874:HIST/1]**	**5** Red River Rebellion collapses before the advance of Canadian troops. Manitoba becomes a province of Canada. **6** British Parliament passes Gladstone's Irish Land Act protecting the tenant from arbitrary eviction. **7** Throne of Spain is offered to Hohenzollern prince, a relative of King William I of Prussia. Prince rejects offer after French protest. Bismarck's "Ems dispatch" provokes France to declare war on Prussia. German armies win victories at Wörth, Wissembourg, Vionville, and Gravelotte. Napoleon III and his army surrender at Sedan. **8** Bloodless revolution in Paris deposes Napoleon III; Third Republic of France is formed. Germans begin siege of Paris. Cities of Metz and Strasbourg surrender to the Germans. **9** Italian troops enter Rome, which becomes the capital of Italy in 1871. Italy annexes Papal States. **10** War of the Triple Alliance ends with Paraguay devastated and much of its male population killed.	**1** J.Q.A. Ward sculpts "Shakespeare," now in Central Park. **2** John F. Kensett, Hudson River School painter, paints "Storm Over Lake George," famous for its minute color gradations. **3** Homer Martin paints "Lake Sanford" in the typical Hudson River School manner. **[1895:ARTS/3]** **4** *The Luck of Roaring Camp, and Other Sketches* by Bret Harte brings the author international fame. **5** Playwright Bronson Howard writes *Saratoga,* an American comedy of manners. **6** Thomas Bailey Aldrich publishes *The Story of a Bad Boy,* which influences Mark Twain.	**7** Verne publishes *Twenty Thousand Leagues Under the Sea.* **8** Paul Cézanne, revolutionary Fr. artist called "Father of Modern Painting," completes "Snow at Estaque," a landscape that shows the influence of Impressionism. **9** In France, the Société Nationale de Musique is established to challenge German influences and to encourage the development of French orchestral music.
1871	**1** William Marcy ("Boss") Tweed, Tammany leader, is indicted for fraud in New York City. The Tweed Ring	**6** William I of Prussia is proclaimed Emperor of Germany at Versailles. Paris surrenders. French National As-	**1** Henry James, influential writer of the period, publishes "A Passionate Pilgrim,"	**6** In celebration of the opening of the Suez Canal, Verdi composes the opera, *Aida.*

228

Science & Technology		Miscellaneous		
America	**Elsewhere**	**America**	**Elsewhere**	
	6 Lord Rayleigh (b. John William Strutt), Eng. physicist, explains the electromagnetic theory in layman's terms. **7** Lockyer founds the science magazine *Nature*. **8** Pringsheim discovers conjugation, a primitive form of sexual reproduction. **9** Sir Francis Galton, Eng. scientist, publishes *Hereditary Genius,* in which he states that a person's mental and physical capacities are genetically determined.	**4** First all-professional baseball team, the Cincinnati Red Stockings, is founded. Baseball has been played only by amateurs since 1839. **5** First intercollegiate football game is played at New Brunswick, N.J., between Rutgers and Princeton. Rutgers wins 6 to 4.	Mouries invents margarine.	
1 Federal Meteorological Service is established as part of the U.S. Army Signal Corps. **2** Edison invents the stock ticker. **3** John W. Hyatt, N.Y. printer, patents a process for making Celluloid. **4** Peirce publishes *Linear Associative Algebras,* thus establishing a new branch of mathematics. **5** Tolbert Lanston, Ohio inventor, patents a padlock. **6** Edward DeSmedt, N.Y. scientist, paves a road in Newark, N.J., with asphalt pavement.	**7** Pasteur discovers a way to produce unspoilable beer. **8** Bunsen invents the ice calorimeter, a heat measuring device. **9** Charles W. Thomson, Scot. naturalist, discovers ocean invertebrates that were previously thought to be extinct. **10** Wallace publishes *Contributions to the Theory of Natural Selection.*	**1** Census shows a population of 39.8 million, of whom 4.9 million are freed Negroes and 2.3 million immigrants who have arrived since 1860. **2** Boardwalk in Atlantic City, N.J., is completed, the first in America. **3** Great Atlantic and Pacific Tea Company (The "A&P") is organized. It becomes the largest single chain of grocery stores in volume of business. **4** Roller skating spreads throughout the country. By 1863, 4 rollers have been added to "parlor skates" and a young skater, William H. Fuller, develops the art of figure skating, which he displays on a world tour. **5** John D. Rockefeller, after combining several Cleveland refineries in 1867, forms Standard Oil Company of Ohio. **6** Cartoon using the donkey as a symbol of the Democratic Party is printed for the first time in *Harper's Weekly*.	**7** Elementary education is made compulsory in England. **8** Ger. archaeologist Heinrich Schliemann begins excavating the site of ancient Troy in Asia Minor. **9** First Vatican Council pronounces the dogma (or doctrine) of papal infallibility (pope cannot make a mistake in matters of faith and morals). **10** Swed. Arctic explorer N.A. Nordenskjold explores the interior of Greenland. **11** English warship *Captain* sinks off Finisterre, France; 472 people are lost.	**1870**
1 Simon Ingersoll, Conn. farmer, invents a pneumatic drill that uses the power of compressed air	**3** Mendeleyev revises the periodic table and correctly predicts that the empty spaces will be filled	**1** First professional baseball association is formed, National Association of Professional Baseball	**6** Henry Morton Stanley, a British-born naturalized American citizen, working as a reporter for	**1871**

History and Politics		The Arts	
America	**Elsewhere**	**America**	**Elsewhere**

defrauded the city of at least $30 million, profited from tax favors, and bought votes. Tweed is convicted in 1873; his henchmen flee to Europe to escape jail.
2 Pres. Grant appoints the first Civil Service Commission, which begins reform of the civil service and the spoils system.
3 Congress enacts Indian Appropriation Act, nullifying all Indian treaties and making all Indians wards of the nation.
4 U.S. Army suppresses the Apache Indians and forces them onto reservations in New Mexico and Arizona. Many resist confinement and begin raids on white settlers.
5 U.S. and Britain sign the Treaty of Washington, providing for arbitration of the *Alabama* claims and the San Juan boundary dispute.
[1872:HIST/2]

sembly accepts the Treaty of Frankfurt, which ends the Franco-Prussian War. France agrees to pay an indemnity of five billion francs and cedes Alsace-Lorraine to Germany. [1870:HIST/7]
7 Radical Parisians, opposed to the French National Assembly, establish municipal council, the Commune of Paris. French army defeats the *communards,* who erect barricades, shoot hostages, and burn the Tuileries Palace.
8 Italian Parliament passes the Law of Guarantees, granting the Pope special rights, an annual income, and the Vatican and other palaces.
9 Cape Colony annexes Basutoland in South Africa.
10 British Columbia becomes a province of Canada.
11 Act of Parliament legalizes labor unions in Britain.
12 Bismarck initiates the *Kulturkampf,* the struggle by the German government to control the Roman Catholic Church.
13 Feudalism is abolished in Japan.

telling of an American's first exposure to England.
2 Whitman's essay "Democratic Vistas" deals with his theory of democracy and urges literary freedom.
3 Alcott publishes *Little Men.*
4 A photographic survey of the Yellowstone area by William H. Jackson is instrumental in that region becoming a national park.
5 *Atlantic Monthly* pays Harte $10,000, the most yet paid to an Amer. writer, for 12 contributions.

Its premiere at the Cairo Opera House features the great Ital. soprano, Teresa Stolz.
7 Sullivan composes the hymn, "Onward! Christian Soldiers."
8 Arthur Rimbaud, Fr. poet, writes "The Drunken Boat," a masterpiece of imagery and metaphor.
9 Lear's most famous poem, "The Owl and the Pussycat," is published.
10 Camille Saint-Saëns composes France's first symphonic poem, *Omphale's Spinning Wheel.*
11 Eliot's novel, *Middlemarch: A Study of Provincial Life,* is acclaimed for its excellent character development.
12 Dostoevsky writes *The Possessed,* a novel.
13 Albert Hall, an amphitheater that seats 8000 persons, opens in London.

1872

1 Congress passes Amnesty Act, which restores civil rights to almost all citizens in the South.
2 International tribunal awards $15.5 million to the U.S. for damage done by the *Alabama* and other Confederate cruisers built in England during the Civil War. San Juan Islands in the strait between Vancouver Island and Washington are awarded to the U.S. by the German Emperor, arbitrator in the dispute between Britain and the U.S.
3 Grant (Republican) is re-elected President; Henry Wilson (Republican) is elected Vice President. Horace Greeley, New York newspaper editor, loses as the presidential candidate of the Democratic and Liberal Republican Parties.

230

5 Ballot Act in Britain makes voting secret for the first time.
6 Balkan nationalities and Russia thwart Turkish plan for the reorganization of the Ottoman Empire.
7 Carlist insurrection in Spain fails.
8 Ismail Pasha extends Egyptian rule in the Sudan.
9 Compulsory military service is introduced in Japan.
10 Three Emperors' League, an alliance among Germany, Austria-Hungary, and Russia, is formed in Berlin. It aims to preserve peace between Austria-Hungary and Russia and to isolate Germany's enemy France.

1 Henry Hobson Richardson, leading Romanesque revival architect, in the U.S., designs Trinity Church in Boston.
2 Paul Hamilton Hayne publishes *Legends and Lyrics,* which contains the best poetry of the postwar South.

3 Mussorgsky completes a revised version of *Boris Godunov,* an opera based on Pushkin's tragedy. [1825:ARTS/7]
4 Carroll publishes *Through the Looking-Glass,* a fantasy.
5 Thomas Hardy, Eng. novelist, publishes *Under the Greenwood Tree,* the first of his "Wessex" novels.
6 Butler publishes *Erewhon,* a satire.
7 Max Liebermann, leader of Ger. Impressionist movement, exhibits his painting, "Women Plucking Geese."
8 Bernhardt is acclaimed for performance as Cordelia in Shakespeare's *King Lear.*

Science & Technology

America

to cut through rock.
2 Luther Burbank, horticulturist, begins his experiments with plant breeding and hybrids. The hybrid "Burbank potato" is an instant commercial success.

Studio photograph of American horticulturist Luther Burbank and his young wife, circa 1910

Elsewhere

by unknown elements yet to be discovered.
4 Darwin's *The Descent of Man and Selection in Relation to Sex* applies evolution to humans.

Miscellaneous

America

Players, which replaces the amateur National Association.
2 Barnum produces the circus, "The Greatest Show on Earth," in Brooklyn, N.Y.
3 Civil War leads to a revival of interest in rifle shooting and to the formation of the National Rifle Association.
4 Large portions of the center of Chicago burn to the ground. About 300 people are killed, 90,000 left homeless, and property damage is $196 million.
5 Fire in Michigan and Wisconsin burns more than 2 million acres. About 1000 people die, and 350 homes are destroyed, mostly in Peshtigo, Wisc.

Elsewhere

the *New York Herald,* finds Livingstone at Ujiji in Central Africa. Livingstone, unheard from for years, had set out to discover the source of the Nile River.
7 Yellow fever epidemic in Buenos Aires kills 13,614 people in 5 months.
8 Germany's population is 41 million; France's, 36 million; Japan's, 33 million; Great Britain's, 26 million; Ireland's, 5.4 million; and Italy's, 26.8 million.
9 *Oceanic,* of the White Star Line, is launched, the first of the large modern luxury liners.
10 Brit. educator Anne Clough provides a residence for the first woman students at Cambridge; it becomes Newnham College in 1880.

America

1 Eadweard Muybridge, Eng.-Amer. motion picture pioneer, designs the "zoopraxiscope," a crude forerunner of the movie projector.
2 Henry Draper, Va. astronomer, begins using photography in his studies of nebulae.
3 *Popular Science Monthly* begins publication.
4 Frank Hamilton, Vt. physician, publishes *Principles and Practice of Surgery.*
5 Edward Weston, Eng.-Amer. scientist, builds a dynamo that is commercially successful for use in electroplating.

Elsewhere

6 Georg Cantor, Ger. mathematician, defines irrational numbers in terms of rational numbers.
7 Ferdinand Cohn, Ger. botanist and microscopist, publishes *Researches on Bacteria,* which establishes bacteriology as a science.

America

1 Jehovah's Witnesses are organized by Charles Taze Russell, a layman member of the Presbyterian Church. Among other names the group is first known as the International Bible Students. **[1931:MISC/1]**
2 Yellowstone National Park is established.
3 Montgomery Ward & Company, the first mail-order house, opens for business in Chicago.
4 Fire in Boston rages for 3 days and destroys more than 800 buildings. Property damage is $75 million.
5 Four weeks after sailing from New York City to Genoa, the *Mary Celeste* is found abandoned in the Atlantic Ocean. All aboard are missing.

Elsewhere

7 First International Association soccer game takes place between Scotland and England.
8 Construction begins on the St. Gotthard tunnel in the Alps. When finished in 1882, the 9¼-mi.-long tunnel will connect Switzerland and Italy.
9 Jesuits are expelled from Germany.

1872

	History and Politics		The Arts	
	America	Elsewhere	America	Elsewhere
	4 *New York Sun* accuses several prominent Republicans of accepting bribes in the form of stock from Crédit Mobilier, the construction company that built the Union Pacific Railroad. **[1873:HIST/2]**			
1873	**1** Coinage Act of Congress makes gold the U.S. monetary standard and eliminates all silver currency. Advocates of silver call it "the Crime of '73." **2** Investigation by Congress of the Crédit Mobilier scandal results in the censure of two U.S. Representatives, but no prosecutions. The scandal is one of many instances of corruption in Grant's administration. **3** American schooner *Virginius* is seized by Spanish officials in Cuba on suspicion of carrying men and arms to the Cuban revolutionaries. Fifty-three members of the crew, including some Americans, are executed.	**4** Judicature Act in Britain consolidates all superior courts into one supreme court of judicature. **5** Monarchist majority of French National Assembly elects Marie Edmé Patrice de MacMahon president of the Third Republic for a seven-year term. **6** Radical majority in the Cortes (legislative body) proclaims the first Spanish republic, which lasts until 1874. **7** Prince Edward Island becomes a province of Canada. **8** Peru and Bolivia conclude secret treaty of alliance. **9** German troops evacuate France.	**1** Mark Twain and Charles Dudley Warner collaborate on *The Gilded Age*. The title of this work has become an epithet for the 1870–98 period of economic expansion in the U.S. **2** Organist Clarence Eddy gives a recital at the Vienna Exposition.	**3** Pierre-Auguste Renoir, Fr. Impressionist painter, completes "Monet Painting in His Garden." **4** Hardy publishes *Far From the Madding Crowd* (-1874), his first successful novel. **5** Bruckner composes *Symphony No. 3 in D Minor* (*Wagner Symphony*). **6** Rimbaud publishes *A Season in Hell,* combining prose and poetry. **7** Verne publishes *Around the World in Eighty Days*. **8** Antonín Dvořák, Bohemian composer, receives acclaim for his cantata, *Hymnus*.

Republican Party symbol by cartoonist Thomas Nast

	History and Politics		The Arts	
1874	**1** Carpetbaggers seize control of Arkansas's government until federal troops restore order. **2** Territorial government in the District of Columbia is abolished and replaced by a commission of three regents. **3** Greenback Party is formed in Indianapolis, Ind. Its members are chiefly farmers of the West and South who want an inflated currency to wipe out farm debts.	**5** Disraeli becomes British Prime Minister for the second time. **[1868:HIST/8]** **6** Spanish generals proclaim Queen Isabella's son King of Spain as Alfonso XII. **7** Revision of Switzerland's constitution increases the government's powers, especially in military and court matters. **[1848:HIST/6]** **8** Europe considers Ottoman Empire bankrupt; Turkish government can pay only half	**1** Cartoonist Thomas Nast establishes the elephant as a symbol for the Republican Party in a cartoon appearing in *Harper's Weekly*. **[1870:MISC/6]** **2** Louis Comfort Tiffany opens a factory in which he makes elegant glass objects. **3** Aldrich publishes *Cloth of Gold,* a collection of poems.	**4** The first exhibition of Impressionist paintings is held in Paris. The movement takes its name from "Impression: Sunrise" (1872), a painting by Monet. **5** Mussorgsky composes *Pictures from an Exhibition*. **6** Saint-Saëns composes *Danse Macabre,* a symphonic poem. **7** Pedro Antonio de

232

Science & Technology		Miscellaneous		
America	**Elsewhere**	**America**	**Elsewhere**	
		6 First ski club is founded at Berlin, N.H.		
1 William Osler, Canadian physician, discovers blood platelets. **2** Louis Agassiz establishes the Anderson School of Natural History on Penikese Island, Mass. This is the first American school to concentrate its studies on oceanography. **3** Andrew Hallidie, Calif. engineer, invents cable cars for use on the hills of San Francisco.	**4** Cantor establishes set theory with his demonstration that the "set" of rational numbers is countable, while the "set" of real (rational and irrational) numbers is infinite and uncountable. **5** Johannes Diederik van der Waals, Dutch chemist, publishes *On the Community of the Liquid and Gaseous State.* **6** Camillo Golgi, Ital. physician, introduces a staining method for studying nerve tissue. **7** Thomson describes the environment deep beneath the ocean in his work *The Depths of the Sea.* **8** Maxwell publishes his *Treatise on Electricity and Magnetism,* the cornerstone of the modern electromagnetic theory.	**1** Epidemics of yellow fever, cholera, and smallpox sweep through many southern cities. **2** Free delivery of mail is provided in all cities with a population of at least 20,000. The first penny postcards are also issued at this time. **3** Bellevue Hospital in New York City opens the first school of nursing, with instruction based on the teachings of Florence Nightingale. **[1860:SCI/7]** **4** Bethlehem Steel Company begins manufacturing in Pittsburgh, Pa. Iron ore shipments from mines near Marquette, Mich., amount to more than one million tons a year. **5** Rabbi Isaac Meyer Wise, advocate of Reform Judaism, organizes the Union of Hebrew Congregations in 1873 and the Hebrew Union College in 1875, both in Cincinnati. **6** Yale, Princeton, Columbia and Rutgers Universities meet to draw up the first rules for football.	**7** British steamer *Atlantic* is wrecked off Nova Scotia; 481 people die. **8** Modern game of lawn tennis is devised and introduced in England by Maj. Walter C. Wingfield. The game is first called Sphairistiké and has a court shaped like an hourglass, wider at the base lines than at the net. **9** Aust. explorers Payer and Weyprecht discover Franz Josef Land, a group of islands in the Arctic Ocean.	**1873**
1 Edison invents a quadriplex telegraph system which allows four messages to be sent over one wire at the same time. **2** Andrew T. Still, Kans. physician, establishes osteopathy, a branch of medicine that stresses the importance of healthy bones and muscles to one's overall health. **3** Philadelphia Zoologi-	**6** Virchow introduces a standard procedure for doing autopsies. **7** Jacobus van't Hoff, Dutch physical chemist, discovers the tertrahedral shape of the carbon atom.	**1** First Chautauqua Assembly meets at Chautauqua Lake, N.Y. Originally formed to train church workers and Sunday school teachers during summer months, the program eventually includes entertainment and general education. **2** National Woman's Christian Temperance Union (W.C.T.U.) is formed in Cleveland to	**4** British Factory Act institutes a 56½-hr. work week. **5** Archaeological excavations begin in Greece at the site of the ancient Olympic games.	**1874**

History and Politics		The Arts	
America	Elsewhere	America	Elsewhere

	America	Elsewhere	America	Elsewhere
	4 Seventy-five Negroes are killed when they assault the court house at Vicksburg, Miss. Whites had ousted a carpetbag sheriff.	interest on its debt. **9** Canada introduces ballot voting. **10** Boundary between Bolivia and Chile is fixed at parallel 24°. Chileans obtain right to work the nitrate fields in Atacama, which belongs to Bolivia. **11** Britain annexes the Fiji Islands. **12** British suppress the Ashantis in Ghana.		Alarcón, Span. author, publishes *The Three-Cornered Hat*, a short novel. **8** J. Strauss composes *Die Fledermaus*, an operetta. **9** Björnson receives international recognition for his drama, *The Bankrupt*. **10** Verdi composes *Requiem Mass* in memory of Alessandro Manzoni.
1875	**1** Congress passes Specie Resumption Act, providing for the resumption of specie payments (coins) on January 1, 1879. Greenbacks in circulation are reduced from $382 million to $300 million. **2** Congress passes Civil Rights Act, guaranteeing Negroes equal rights in public places and the right to serve on juries. [1883:HIST/3] **3** U.S.-Hawaii treaty recognizes reciprocal commercial rights. Hawaii agrees to cede no territory to any third power. **4** Secretary of the Treasury Benjamin H. Bristow investigates the conspiracy of distillers and public officials, known as the Whiskey Ring, to defraud the federal government of liquor taxes. More than $3 million in taxes are recovered; 238 persons are indicted and 110 convicted.	**5** Charles Stewart Parnell is elected to the British Parliament and begins movement for Irish independence. **6** British Parliament passes Public Health Act. **7** France adopts a republican constitution. **8** Socialist Workingmen's Party is formed at Gotha, East Germany. **9** Uprisings occur in Bosnia and Herzegovina against Turkish rule. **10** Khedive of Egypt sells his 176,000 shares in the Suez Canal Company to the British government. **11** War breaks out between Ethiopia and Egypt. **12** Kuang Hsü becomes Emperor of China.	**1** Inness's painting "Autumn Oaks" reflects the intensity of his Swedenborgian conversion. **2** Richardson designs the ornate N.Y. state capitol building in Albany. **3** Thomas Eakins, important portraitist of the period, paints "The Gross Clinic," which realistically portrays a medical school class. **4** Lanier publishes "Corn," a poem about farming in the Old South, and "The Symphony," a poem about the industrial North.	**5** Gilbert and Sullivan collaborate on their first major success, *Trial by Jury,* an operetta. **6** Tolstoy publishes *Anna Karenina,* a pessimistic novel. **7** Bizet composes *Carmen,* his most famous opera. [1846:ARTS/8] **8** Paris Opéra is built. Its designer is Charles Garnier. **9** Hung. composer Karl Goldmark produces the opera, *The Queen of Spades.*
1876	**1** House of Representatives votes to impeach Secretary of War William W. Belknap after investigation indicates he accepted annual bribes from the trader at an Indian post. Belknap resigns and is acquitted by the Senate. **2** Sioux and Cheyenne Indians, led by Chiefs Sitting Bull, Crazy Horse, and Gall, kill 264 cavalrymen and their leader, Gen. George A. Custer, at the Battle of Little Bighorn, Mont. **3** Colorado becomes 38th	**6** Disraeli secures for Queen Victoria of England the title Empress of India. **7** Serbia and Montenegro declare war on Ottoman Empire. Turks put down rebellion in Bulgaria. **8** Ethiopians defeat Egyptians at Gura. **9** Cape Colony concludes treaties with native chiefs as far as the frontier of Angola. **10** British occupy the city of Quetta, Pakistan, as a safeguard against Russian southward advance.	**1** Mark Twain publishes the classic novel *The Adventures of Tom Sawyer.* **2** Henry James publishes *Roderick Hudson,* the story of the failure of an Amer. sculptor in Rome.	**3** Wagner's musical-dramatic masterpiece, *The Ring of the Nibelung,* is first performed at the specially built Festspielhaus (theater) in Bayreuth (Ger.). The *Ring* consists of four parts: *Das Rheingold* (1869), *Die Walküre* (1870), *Siegfried* (1876), and *Götterdämmerung* (1876). **4** Renoir paints "Le Moulin de la galette." **5** Tchaikovsky com-

Science & Technology		Miscellaneous		
America	Elsewhere	America	Elsewhere	
cal Garden, America's first zoo, opens to the public. **4** Joseph Glidden, N.H. farmer, invents barbed wire. **5** Robert Thurston, R.I. engineer, establishes a mechanical engineering research laboratory at the Stevens Institute of Technology in New Jersey.		promote prohibition (stopping the manufacture and sale of alcoholic drinks) by educational, social, and political means. **3** First streetcar to operate by electricity begins running in New York City.		
1 Elihu Thomson, Eng.-Amer. engineer, operates the world's first radio. **2** Weston establishes a New Jersey factory that produces dynamoelectric machinery. **3** Edwin T. Klebs, Ger.-Amer. bacteriologist, discovers *pneumococcus,* the bacterium that causes lobar pneumonia. **4** James Sargent and Halbert Greenleaf patent a time lock for use in bank vaults. **5** George F. Green, Mich. inventor, patents an electric dental drill. **6** Samuel F. O'Reilly invents an electric tattooing machine. (Patented in 1891.)	**7** Charles Laveran, Fr. physician, publishes his work on military hygiene. **8** Cohn discovers the bacterial endospore. **9** Darwin publishes two works: *Climbing Plants,* which suggests that plant climbing is an adaptation, and *Insectivorous Plants,* which studies the digestive systems of such plants. **10** The Siemens brothers form the company responsible for the first telegraph cable between the U.S. and Britain.	**1** By this year, refrigerator cars are used regularly to ship meat from Midwest stockyards to the East. **2** Mary Baker Eddy publishes *Science and Health* (later adding *With Key to the Scriptures*), the basic text of Christian Science. **3** Steel manufacturer Andrew Carnegie builds the first factory to use the Bessemer steel-making process. **4** First Kentucky Derby is held at Churchill Downs. The winner is "Aristides" for a purse of $2850.	**5** Religious orders are abolished in Prussia: two years earlier the clergy was put under state control; universities are separated from religious connections in Austria. **6** Earthquake in Venezuela and Colombia kills about 16,000 people. **7** London Medical School for Women is founded. **8** First roller-skating rink opens in London. **9** Matthew Webb is the first to swim the English Channel, in 21 hrs. 45 min. **10** Stanley traces the Congo River to the Atlantic Ocean.	**1875**
1 Alexander Graham Bell, Scot.-Amer. inventor, patents the telephone. The first words transmitted by telephone were addressed to his assistant, Thomas A. Watson, "Mr. Watson, come here. I want you!" **2** Josiah Willard Gibbs, Conn. physicist later considered one of America's greatest scientists, publishes *On the Equilibrium of Heterogeneous Substances* in which he pro-	**7** Darwin publishes *The Effects of Cross and Self Fertilization in the Vegetable Kingdom,* in which the functions of separate sexes in plants are examined. **8** Haeckel's *The Generation of Waves in the Small Vital Particles* views heredity from a molecular standpoint. **9** Eduard Strasburger, Ger. cytologist, publishes the basic fundamentals of mitosis in *On Cell Forma-*	**1** Centennial Exposition is held in Philadelphia to celebrate the 100th anniversary of the Declaration of Independence. Fifty nations send exhibits that are housed in 180 buildings on 236 acres of land. **2** First major baseball league, the National League, is founded. There are teams in Boston, Chicago, Cincinnati, Ohio, Hartford, New York City, Philadelphia, and St. Louis.	**6** Famine in India lasts 2 years; about 5 million people die. **7** Schliemann excavates the site of ancient Mycenae in southern Greece. **8** Presbyterian churches in England join with the English congregation of the United Presbyterian Church of Scotland to form the Presbyterian Church of England. **9** Cyclone followed by a tidal wave kills about 200,000 people in Bakar-	**1876**

History and Politics		The Arts	
America	**Elsewhere**	**America**	**Elsewhere**

state.
4 In presidential election, Democrat Samuel J. Tilden receives about 250,000 more popular votes than Republican Rutherford B. Hayes. Electoral vote is Tilden 184 to Hayes 163, with returns from Florida, Louisiana, South Carolina, and Oregon in dispute. Fight for delegates and charges of corruption result in Congress deciding the vote. [1877:HIST/1]
5 Prohibition amendment to the Constitution is proposed in the House.

11 Japan recognizes Korea as independent of China. Korean ports are opened to the Japanese.
12 Abd al-Hamid II becomes Ottoman Sultan after his uncle and brother are deposed by the Young Turks, a liberal reformist group.

Peter Ilyich Tchaikovsky, Russian composer

poses *Swan Lake,* a ballet.
6 Stéphane Mallarmé, Fr. poet, publishes *L'Après-midi d'un faune.*
7 Ital. composer Amilcare Ponchielli produces *La Gioconda,* an opera famous for its ballet, "Dance of the Hours."

1877

1 Congress sets up Electoral Commission (8 Republicans, 7 Democrats) to break presidential deadlock. It awards all disputed returns to Hayes, thereby giving him a majority of one in the electoral vote. Hayes is declared President. William A. Wheeler (Republican) is declared Vice President.
2 In *Munn* v. *Illinois,* the Supreme Court upholds the Granger laws, establishing the principle of public regulation of businesses that serve the public interest.
3 Nez Percé Indians, led by Chief Joseph, fight U.S. forces and retreat across 1600 miles of Washington, Oregon, Idaho, and Montana. Forced to surrender, Joseph's band is sent to a reservation in Indian Territory.
4 Reconstruction era ends when last federal troops leave the South. Carpetbag rule ends; southern states regain control of their governments.

5 Russia declares war on Ottoman Empire. Last Russo-Turkish War begins. Russians invade Rumania and capture Plevna, Bulgaria. [1878:HIST/5]
6 British annex the Transvaal (the South African Republic) and Walvis Bay on the coast of Southwest Africa. War breaks out between the British and Kaffirs.
7 Japanese army suppresses Satsuma Rebellion.
8 Porfirio Díaz becomes President of Mexico and remains in power until 1911.

1 Twain and Harte collaborate on the play *Ah Sin.*
2 The Philadelphia Conservatory of Music is founded.
3 Albert Bierstadt, Ger. born painter of the Hudson River School, paints "Mount Corcoran."
4 Theodore Thomas takes over as conductor of the New York Philharmonic.

5 Auguste Rodin, one of France's greatest sculptors, exhibits "Age of Bronze," a life-sized work.
6 Tchaikovsky composes *Symphony No. 4,* often considered his masterpiece, and *Eugene Onégin,* an opera based on Pushkin's poem. [1822:ARTS/7]
7 Zola publishes *The Drunkard,* a bestseller about alcoholism.
8 Flaubert publishes *Trois Contes,* three short stories.
9 Brahms composes the pastoral *Symphony No. 2 in D Major.*

1878

1 Congress passes Bland-Allison Act over Pres. Hayes's veto. It requires Treasury to buy from two to four million dollars' worth of silver bullion for coinage.

5 Russo-Bulgarian force defeats the Turks at Shipka Pass. Turks appeal to Russians for armistice. Russians seize Adrianople. British fleet arrives at Constantinople, at

1 After their temporary disappearance during the Civil War, showboats are revived and feature vaudeville.
2 Henry James pub-

3 Gilbert and Sullivan produce the operetta, *H.M.S. Pinafore,* at the London Opéra Comique Theater.
4 Hardy publishes

Science & Technology		Miscellaneous		
America	Elsewhere	America	Elsewhere	

poses the "phase rule" and applies the laws of thermodynamics to physical chemistry.
3 Ericsson publishes *Solar Investigations* and describes a solar-powered electric motor.
4 American Chemical Society is founded in New York City.
5 Edison establishes an industrial research laboratory (America's first) in Menlo Park, N.J. He invents the carbon microphone and patents a mimeograph machine.
6 Centennial Exhibition in Philadelphia celebrates electrical progress. [1876:MISC/1]

tion and Cell Division.
10 Emil Theodor Kocher, Swiss surgeon, treats goiter by excising the thyroid gland.
11 Nobel patents a powerful plastic dynamite called blasting gelatin.
12 Robert Koch, Ger. bacteriologist, discovers the life cycle of the anthrax bacillus.
13 In his work *The Geographical Distribution of Animals,* Wallace divides the world into 6 regions according to their type of animal life and establishes the boundary (Wallace's Line) between the sharply different Oriental and Australian regions.

3 Train is derailed on a bridge over the Ashtabula River in Ohio; 91 people die.
4 James Gordon Bennett, publisher of the *New York Herald*, introduces polo in New York City from England.
5 Fire in a Brooklyn, N.Y., theater kills 289 of the 1200 people in the audience.

ganj, India.
10 Joe Goss of England defeats Tom Allen, an American, in 27 rounds at Covington, Ky., to become the world's heavyweight boxing champion.

1877

1 Charles Brush, Ohio scientist, invents the Brush electric arc lamp, a storage battery, and a dynamoelectric machine.
2 Emile Berliner, Ger.-Amer. inventor, develops a microphone for use in the telephone.
3 Copper wire is invented.
4 Asaph Hall, Conn. astronomer, discovers two moons of Mars. He names them Deimos and Phobos.
5 Charles J. Glidden, Mass. engineer, designs the world's first telephone exchange.
6 Weston installs an electric streetlight in Newark, N.J.

7 Lister wires a kneecap—an operation that, without antiseptic technique, would have proven fatal.
8 Maxwell publishes *Theory of Heat.*
9 Lord Rayleigh publishes *The Theory of Sound.*
10 Koch publishes work detailing bacterial preservation techniques and experimental methodology.

1 Baltimore and Ohio Railroad workers strike in protest against wage reductions. The move spreads quickly to other Eastern, later Western railroads, and riots occur in several cities. This is the first general railroad strike in the country.
2 Charles Elmer Hires begins making and distributing a drink called root beer.
3 First intercity telephone communication takes place between Salem, Mass., and Boston, and Chicago, and Milwaukee.
4 Pres. Rutherford B. Hayes initiates the Easter egg hunt on the capitol grounds in Washington, D.C.

5 Education for children 6 to 9 years of age is made compulsory in Italy.
6 All-England Lawn Tennis Championship is first played at Wimbledon, England. First champion is Spencer Gore.
7 Swiss theologian Louis Lucien Rochet founds the "Blue Cross" to fight alcoholism.

1878

1 Albert A. Michelson, Ger.-Amer. physicist, measures the speed of light with great accuracy. His measurement is 186,508 miles per second,

6 Joseph Swan, Eng. chemist, develops bromide paper for use in photography.

1 Yellow fever epidemic kills about 14,000 people in the southern U.S.
2 First regular telephone exchange opens in New Haven.

8 Ger. engineer Karl Benz builds a motorized tricycle with a top speed of 7 mph.
9 British ship *Princess Alice* sinks after a colli-

History and Politics		The Arts	
America	Elsewhere	America	Elsewhere

America	Elsewhere	America	Elsewhere
2 Labor organizations join with advocates of cheap money to form the Greenback-Labor Party. [1874:HIST/3] **3** U.S.-Samoa treaty reserves Pago Pago Harbor as a coaling station for U.S. Navy ships. **4** Democrats win control of both houses of Congress for first time since 1858.	the Sultan's request. Treaty of San Stefano ends Russo-Turkish War. Britain and Austria-Hungary force Russia to revise treaty at the Congress of Berlin. Serbia, Montenegro, and Rumania become independent states. Austria occupies Bosnia and Herzegovina. Britain occupies Cyprus. Russia acquires Ardahan, Batum, and Kars. Bulgaria becomes three territories. **6** War breaks out between Britain and Afghanistan. **7** Two unsuccessful assassination attempts on Emperor William I enables Bismarck to enact anti-socialist law in Germany.	lishes *Watch and Ward* and *The Europeans*.	*The Return of the Native,* a novel. **5** Eleanora Duse, Ital. actress, wins acclaim for her performance in Zola's *Thérèse Racquin* (1867). **6** Ger. artist Max Klinger exhibits two series of pen-and-ink drawings, "Scenes from the Life of Christ" and "The Glove." **7** Eng. actress Ellen Alicia Terry joins Henry Irving's Company (–1902) at the Lyceum Theater, London. **8** Dvořák composes the first of his *Slavonic Dances*.
1879 **1** U.S. resumes specie payment. Greenbacks are worth their face value in gold. **2** Pres. Hayes vetoes bill restricting Chinese immigration; he calls it a violation of the Burlingame Treaty of 1868. California adopts new constitution with a provision prohibiting the employment of Chinese workers. **3** By act of Congress, women lawyers are permitted to argue cases before the Supreme Court. **4** Uprising of Ute Indians is suppressed. By a treaty in 1880, the Utes are moved from Colorado to Utah. **5** Pres. Hayes vetoes five attempts by Democratic Congress to pass rider forbidding the President to use troops in congressional elections.	**6** Germany concludes defensive alliance with Austria. **7** Ismail Pasha is deposed; his son Tewfik Pasha succeeds him as Khedive of Egypt. [1863:HIST/15] **8** Zulus defeat the British at Isandhlwana but are defeated at Ulundi, South Africa. Peace is made with the Zulu chiefs. **9** British overrun Afghanistan. By the Treaty of Gandamak, the Afghans cede Khyber Pass and other areas to the British. British occupy Kabul after British envoy is murdered. **10** Gladstone attacks Disraeli's pro-Turkish, imperialist, and domestic policies. [1880:HIST/5] **11** Bolivia rescinds Chile's right to work nitrate fields. War of the Pacific begins when Chile declares war on Bolivia and Peru. [1874:HIST/10]	**1** James publishes *Daisy Miller*. **2** Frank Stockton publishes *Rudder Grange,* an adventure story of a family who live on a boat. **3** Construction of the state capitol in Hartford, Ct., is completed. The building, a mixture of Gothic and Romanesque architecture, was designed by Richard Upjohn. **4** George Washington Cable publishes *Old Creole Days,* a collection of seven short stories. **5** Clarence Eddy plays 100 organ recitals in Chicago without repeating a work.	**6** Ibsen's *A Doll's House* is the first play to portray a woman who leaves an unhappy marriage to make a life on her own. **7** Dostoevsky writes *The Brothers Karamazov,* a novel. **8** Rodin exhibits the sculpture, "St. John the Baptist Preaching." **9** George Grove, Eng. musicologist, publishes the first edition of *Dictionary of Music and Musicians* (–1889). **10** George Meredith, Eng. writer known for psychological insight in character development, publishes *Egoist*. **11** Brahms composes *Rhapsodies* for piano.

an error of less than 0.001%. 2 Edison patents the phonograph. He records "Mary had a little lamb" on a cylinder wrapped in tin foil. 3 Hughes invents an improved carbon microphone and gives it its name. 4 Clarence King, geologist, publishes *Systematic Geology,* the results of a ten-year survey along the 40th parallel from Colorado to California. 5 Durfee establishes America's first copper refinery in Ansonia, Conn.		3 Edison Electric Light Company is formed in New York City. 4 Forerunner of the Wild West Show is the exhibition of Dr. W.F. Carver, who returns to New York from California to show his skill in firing a gun while riding a horse. 5 National Archery Association is formed. 6 A.A. Pope manufactures the first bicycles, called "wheels." 7 Celebrated $3 million robbery of the Manhattan Savings Institution in New York City is credited to "Western" George L. Leslie.	sion in the Thames River in London; about 700 people die. 10 One of a pair of red granite Egyptian obelisks known as "Cleopatra's Needles" is moved from Alexandria (where they were brought from Heliopolis in 14 B.C.) to London. The other is later brought to New York City. 11 Bicycle Touring Club is founded in England.	
1 Saccharin, an artificial sweetener 500 times stronger than sugar, is discovered by Constantine Fahlberg, Russ.-Amer. scientist. 2 Alpheus Hyatt establishes an oceanographical laboratory at Annisquam, Mass. [1930:SCI/2] 3 George Eastman, N.Y. industrialist, patents a process for making dry photographic plates. 4 Edison invents the first practical electric incandescent lamp. He uses a carbon filament that glows for 40 hours in a vacuum. Edison also experiments with a platinum filament burning in a vacuum. 5 George B. Selden, engineer, develops a three-cylinder internal combustion engine and uses it to power a "horseless carriage." 6 Brush installs electric arc lamps on the streets of Cleveland, Ohio. 7 Archeological Institute of America is founded in Boston by Charles E. Norton, Mass. educator.	8 Pringsheim publishes work on the effect of light on chlorophyll. 9 Swan, working independently of Edison, invents the carbon-filament incandescent lamp. 10 Jean-Martin Charcot, Fr. neurologist, publishes *Lectures on the Diseases of the Nervous System,* which presents much new research on the brain and nerves.	1 Richard Henry Pratt founds the Carlisle Indian School in Pennsylvania, one of the most successful schools for Indians in the U.S. 2 Mary Baker Eddy founds the Church of Christ, Scientist in Boston. 3 Radcliffe College is established in Cambridge, Mass. 4 Frank W. Woolworth opens his first successful 5-and-10-cent store in Lancaster, Pa.	5 De Lesseps founds the Panama Canal Company to build a canal through the Isthmus of Panama. It becomes bankrupt 10 years later. 6 London's first telephone exchange is established. 7 First large-scale skiing contest is held at Huseby Hill in Oslo, Norway.	**1879**

19th U.S. President Rutherford B. Hayes speaking in Louisville, Kentucky (*Harper's Weekly* engraving)

History and Politics

The Arts

America

Elsewhere

America

Elsewhere

1880

1 James A. Garfield and Chester A. Arthur are elected President and Vice President, respectively, on the Republican ticket. [1881:HIST/1]
2 U.S. and China sign immigration treaty which gives the U.S. the right to "regulate, limit, or suspend" (but not exclude) laborers from China.
3 Supreme Court rules that exclusion of Negroes from jury duty is unconstitutional.
4 National Farmers' Alliance, forerunner of the Populist Party, is formed in Chicago to unite farmers against discriminatory legislation.

5 Disraeli resigns as British Prime Minister after Tory party loses general election. Gladstone becomes Prime Minister.
6 France makes Tahiti a colony.
7 Major European nations and the U.S. decide at the Madrid Conference to recognize the independence of Morocco and to maintain equal trade opportunities for all.
8 Tewfik Pasha accepts French-British control over Egypt's finances.
9 Boers revolt against the British in the Transvaal and proclaim a new republic. [1881:HIST/11]
10 Chile seizes Atacama region from Bolivia and Tacna-Arica region from Peru.
11 Conference in Sydney considers formation of federation of colonies in Australia.

1 Inness's painting "The Coming Storm" gains fame for its depiction of ominous clouds.
2 Joel Chandler Harris uses the Amer. Negro dialect in his work *Uncle Remus: His Songs and His Sayings*.
3 Cable publishes the novel *The Grandissimes*.

The Thinker, statue by Auguste Rodin

4 Rodin exhibits his sculpture, "The Thinker."
5 Guy de Maupassant, Fr. master of the short story, publishes "Ball of Fat."
6 Camille Pissarro, Fr. Impressionist, paints "The Outer Boulevards."
7 Tchaikovsky composes the *1812 Overture,* the orchestral *Italian Capriccio,* and *Serenade for Strings in C Major.* [1812:HIST/7]
8 Gilbert and Sullivan's comic opera, *The Pirates of Penzance,* opens in London after a New York premiere.
9 Zola causes a scandal with the publication of *Nana,* a novel describing prostitution and vice.

1881

1 Pres. Garfield is shot in a railroad station in Washington, D.C. He dies 11 weeks later, and Arthur succeeds to the presidency.
2 Supreme Court declares that federal income tax instituted in 1862 is constitutional (*Springer* v. *United States*). Court says Congress never intended it as the direct tax prohibited in the Constitution.
3 Sen. Roscoe Conkling resigns from office in a dispute with Republican administration over patronage issue. Conkling's Republican faction, called "Stalwarts," which had supported a third term for Grant in 1880, loses influence in New York politics when the state legislature refuses to reelect Conkling.

4 Gladstone passes the Land Act to meet the Irish demand for the "three F's"—fair rent, fixity of tenure, and freedom of sale. Parnell is imprisoned for inciting Irishmen to intimidate tenants. [1875:HIST/5]
5 French seize Bizerte and Tunis. Bey of Tunis accepts a French protectorate. French subdue uprisings in Tunisia and later in Algeria (1883).
6 Three Emperors' League is secretly renewed. [1872:HIST/10]
7 Greece receives Thessaly and part of Epirus, promised her at the Congress of Berlin. [1878:HIST/5]
8 Serbia signs secret treaty with Austria.
9 Alexander II of Russia is assassinated by a member of the People's Will, a terrorist group of the populist movement.
10 Boers defeat the British at Laing's Neck and Majuba Hill. By the Treaty of Pretoria, Britain grants the Transvaal internal self-government.

1 Mark Twain publishes *The Prince and the Pauper*.
2 James publishes *The Portrait of a Lady,* a bestselling novel.
3 Tony Pastor opens the Fourteenth Street Theater in New York City, the first vaudeville theater to feature family entertainment.
4 Helen Hunt Jackson publishes *A Century of Injustice* about the mistreatment of the Indians.
5 The Boston Symphony Orchestra is founded.

6 Richard D'Oyly Carte, a sponsor of Gilbert and Sullivan since 1875, builds the Savoy Theater, London, for their operettas which, as a result, are sometimes called the "Savoy Operas."
7 Anatole France, Fr. writer, publishes *The Crime of Sylvester Bonnard,* a novel.
8 Offenbach's grand opera, *Tales of Hoffmann,* is first performed a year after his death. [1821:ARTS/5]

Science & Technology

America

1 Bell invents the photophone, a device that transmits sound on a beam of light, and uses it to send the first wireless telephone message.
2 Thomson patents a three-phase alternating current generator.
3 Othneil C. Marsh, N.Y. paleontologist, publishes *A Monograph on the Extinct Toothed Birds of North America* which claims that birds evolved from reptiles. This concept helps fill a gap in Darwin's chain of evolution.
4 Edison patents a magnetic ore separator.
5 American Society of Mechanical Engineers is established in New York City.

Elsewhere

6 Strasburger states that new nuclei are only produced by the division of old nuclei.
7 Josef Breuer, Aust. psychologist, states his theories on psychosomatic illnesses.
8 Adolf von Baeyer, Ger. chemist, produces the dye indigo in the laboratory.
9 Laveran identifies the parasite responsible for human malaria.

Miscellaneous

America

1 Andrew Carnegie begins the establishment of Carnegie libraries. Eventually, he donates 2500 library buildings at a cost of $60 million in many English-speaking countries. The donations are given on condition that the libraries will be supplied and supported by the communities in which they are built.
2 American branch of the Salvation Army is established in Philadelphia. At first, the organization's unusual missionary methods are resented. [1865:MISC/9]
3 Census shows a population of 50.1 million, including about 2.8 million immigrants.

Elsewhere

4 Game of bingo is developed from the Italian lotto game of tumbula.
5 Parcel post is introduced in England.
6 First girl's high schools open in England.
7 Employer's Liability Act gives workers compensation for accidents caused by employer's negligence.

1880

Science & Technology

America

1 Michelson invents the "interferometer," a device that uses light waves to measure distance. He publishes *Relative Motion of the Earth and the Luminiferous Ether* and suggests that luminiferous ether may not exist.
2 Frederick E. Ives, Conn. inventor, produces the first color photographs.
3 Hiram Maxim, Maine engineer, invents a self-regulating electrical generator.
4 Bell invents an electric probe for locating bullets in the human body. The probe is widely used until x-rays are introduced.
5 William J. Morton, N.Y. physician, uses electric current as a form of medical therapy.
6 Thomson and Edwin Houston patent a system of arc lighting.
7 First lighted buoy is placed in New York harbor.

Elsewhere

8 Carlos Finlay, Cuban physician, suggests that mosquitoes are the carriers of yellow fever.
9 Cohn's *Bacteria, the Smallest of Living Organisms* is published.
10 Pierre Curie, Fr. physicist, discovers the piezoelectric effect.
11 Pasteur vaccinates a herd of sheep against anthrax.
12 Van der Waals clarifies the ideal-gas law, arriving at the formula later known as the van der Waals equation.

Miscellaneous

America

1 Educator and reformer Booker T. Washington, a former slave, organizes and becomes president of the Normal and Industrial Institute for Negroes (later Tuskegee Institute).
2 Philanthropist Clara Barton establishes the National Society of the Red Cross. She is its president until 1904, and in 1884 is responsible for the Geneva International Convention allowing the Red Cross to be of service in peacetime emergencies, as well as in war. [1862:MISC/5; 1864:MISC/9]
3 Barnum and J.A. Bailey create their circus, known as "The Barnum and Bailey Greatest Show on Earth."
4 United States Lawn Tennis Association is established. The National championship is held in Newport, R.I., and Richard D. Sears wins the first men's singles title.

Elsewhere

5 Flogging as a form of punishment is abolished in the British Army and Navy. For a long time it had been one of the most common methods of keeping discipline in the armed forces.
6 Fire in Vienna, Austria, burns the Ring Theater, leaving more than 600 people dead.
7 Canadian Pacific Railway is founded.
8 London's population is 3.3 million; Paris', 2.2 million; Berlin's, 1.1 million; Vienna's, 1 million; Tokyo's, 800,000; and St. Petersburg's, 600,000. India's population is 253 million.
9 Violent storm and a tidal wave in China and Indochina kill about 300,000 people.

1881

241

History and Politics		The Arts	
America	**Elsewhere**	**America**	**Elsewhere**

1882

America

1 Congress passes Chinese Exclusion Act, which bars Chinese laborers from entering the U.S. for ten years. Influx of cheap Chinese labor, especially in California, had led to race riots. **[1879:HIST/2]**
2 U.S. recognizes the independence of Korea and signs trade agreement.
3 Congress passes act barring the entry into the U.S. of "undesirables" such as convicts, paupers, and the insane. A head tax of 50 cents, set on every immigrant, is later increased.
4 Rivers and Harbors Bill passes over Pres. Arthur's veto and authorizes more than $18 million for public works.
5 Grover Cleveland is elected Mayor of Buffalo and then Governor of New York, as a Democrat. He wins reputation for uncovering political corruption.

Elsewhere

6 Fenians seeking Irish independence from England murder British secretary and undersecretary to Ireland in Phoenix Park, Dublin. Irish extremists blow up public buildings in England.
7 Italy, Germany, and Austria-Hungary form the Triple Alliance.
8 Prince Milan, with Austrian support, proclaims himself King of Serbia.
9 Nationalist and military revolt in Egypt results in British naval bombardment of Alexandria. British troops defeat Egyptians at the Battle of Tel al Kabir and capture Cairo.
10 Italian government takes over port of Assab on the Red Sea.
11 Boers begin expansion westward to the Kalahari Desert.

America

1 John W. Root, architect of the influential Chicago school, designs the 10-story, fireproof Montauk Building in Chicago.
2 Ignatius Donnelly publishes *Atlantis,* in which he claims that the legendary continent was the cradle of civilization.
3 Ibsen's *A Doll's House* is performed in English for the first time, in Milwaukee. **[1879:ARTS/6]**
4 Francis J. Child, scholar, publishes the exhaustive work, *The English and Scottish Popular Ballads.*

Elsewhere

5 Fr. physiologist Étienne-Jules Marey makes the first motion picture by using a "rifle-camera" that exposes 12 images in one second.
6 Wagner completes his final work, the opera, *Parsifal.*
7 Verlaine's *Art Poétique* is popular among young Symbolists.
8 Manet completes his last major painting, "A Bar at the Folies-Bergère."
9 In *An Enemy of the People,* Ibsen explores the evils of political corruption.
10 Nikolay Rimsky-Korsakov, Russ. composer, completes the opera, *The Snow Maiden.*
11 Berlin Philharmonic Orchestra is founded.

1883

America

1 Pendleton Act establishes Civil Service Commission to administer competitive examinations for the selection of persons for federal jobs. It is intended to reform the spoils system by introducing a merit system.
2 Tariff bill reduces internal excise taxes an average of five percent but retains protective tariffs on most imports.
3 Supreme Court declares Civil Rights Act of 1875 unconstitutional (except for jury duty), stating the federal government can protect political, not social, rights.
4 Congress authorizes the Secretary of Navy to build three steel cruisers and a dispatch boat—the beginning of the modern U.S. Navy.
5 Congress reduces letter postage to two cents per half ounce.

Elsewhere

6 Paul Kruger is elected President of the South African Republic (the Transvaal region).
7 Bismarck begins a program of social reform to weaken the socialists' power in Germany and then a policy of economic nationalism.
8 Radical nationalist group revolts unsuccessfully against the Serbian government.
9 Rumania forms secret alliance with Austria, the result of Rumanian fear of Russia.
10 Mahdi Muhammad Ahmad with his army defeats Anglo-Egyptian force in the Sudan. **[1884:HIST/6]**
11 French seize the city of Hue, in Annam, South Vietnam.
12 German trading firm gains a cession of land at Angra Pequena (now Lüderitz, South West Africa or Namibia).

America

1 Albert P. Ryder paints "Toilers of the Sea," typical of his vivid yellow seascapes.
2 Eakins paints "The Swimming Hole."
3 Twain publishes the realistic *Life on the Mississippi.*
4 Theodore Thomas begins the Young People's Symphony Concerts in New York City.
5 Howard Pyle writes and illustrates *The Merry Adventures of Robin Hood.*
6 Cyrus Curtis, editor, founds *Ladies' Home Journal.*
7 *Life* magazine is established.

Elsewhere

8 Scot. writer Robert Louis Stevenson publishes *Treasure Island,* a popular adventure novel that features Long John Silver, a pirate modeled after his friend, poet William Ernest Henley.
9 In *Also Sprach Zarathustra,* Ger. philosopher Friedrich Wilhelm Nietzsche proclaims, "God is dead."
10 Delibes composes *Lakmé,* an opera.
11 Emmanuel Chabrier, Fr. composer, completes *España,* an orchestral rhapsody notable for its bold brass and percussion passages.
12 Royal College of Music, London, is founded.

Science & Technology		Miscellaneous		
America	**Elsewhere**	**America**	**Elsewhere**	
1 Edison patents a 3-wire electrical system which is still in use. 2 World's first hydroelectric plant, designed by Edison, opens in Appleton, Wis. 3 Nikola Tesla, electrical engineer, discovers the rotating magnetic field, the basis of nearly all devices that use alternating current. 4 Schuyler S. Wheeler, N.Y. industrialist, invents the electric fan. 5 Silk sutures replace catgut thread in surgical operations.  Thomas Alva Edison, U.S. inventor	6 Balfour Stewart, Scot. physician, suggests the existence of the ionosphere. 7 Koch isolates the bacterium responsible for tuberculosis. 8 Strasburger coins the terms *cytoplasm* and *nucleoplasm*.	1 First Labor Day celebration is held in New York City. Peter J. McGuire, founder of the United Brotherhood of Carpenters, suggests a holiday honoring working people. 2 William Horlick of Racine, Wis., produces the first malted milk, a mixture of the extract of wheat and malted barley to which milk is added. 3 Irishman Phil Casey brings handball to the U.S. 4 National Croquet Association is founded. 5 Boxing becomes popular nationwide through the efforts of world bareknuckle champion John L. Sullivan, who tours the U.S. and gives exhibitions using gloves under the Marquis of Queensberry rules. **[1865:MISC/7]** 6 Knights of Columbus, a fraternal organization of Catholic men, is founded in New Haven.	7 Married Women's Property Act in Britain gives married women the right of separate ownership of property of all kinds. 8 Education is made compulsory, free, and nonsectarian in France. 9 Cyclone followed by tidal wave in Bombay, India, kills nearly 100,000 people.	**1882**
1 Edison discovers that an electrical current can be sent through space. Called the "Edison effect," this discovery is the basis of electronics. 2 Maxim invents the Maxim machine gun. 3 Klebs discovers the bacillus (a rod-shaped type of bacterium) that causes diphtheria. 4 Edison demonstrates an electric trolley that receives its power from an electrified "third rail."	5 Kocher discovers that the adverse effects of thyroid gland removal are reduced if a small portion of the gland is left intact. 6 Julius Hann, Aust. meteorologist, publishes *Handbook of Climatology.* 7 Galton publishes *Inquiries into Human Faculty.* 8 Sir Victor Horsley, Eng. physiologist, studies the role of the thyroid gland in growth. 9 Golgi discovers the Golgi apparatus—a cell structure thought to take part in cellular secretion. 10 Paul Ehrlich, Ger. scientist, publishes *The Requirement of the Organism for Oxygen,* which states that different tissues have different oxygen needs.	1 U.S. and Canadian railroads adopt four standard time zones proposed by Charles F. Dowd of the U.S. and Sandford Fleming of Canada. 2 Army scout and showman William "Buffalo Bill" Cody organizes his first Wild West Show. 3 Journalist and publisher Joseph Pulitzer buys the *New York World.* Under his direction sensational journalism, including crime stories, large headlines, comic strips, strong editorials (as well as a 2¢ price) increase circulation in the next 4 years from 20,000 to 250,000. 4 First annual New York Horse Show opens at Gilmore's Gardens in New York City.	6 Orient Express—Paris to Istanbul—makes its first run. 7 Ger. statesman Otto Bismarck introduces sickness insurance in Germany. Other social welfare programs, including accident and old age insurance, are put into effect to improve the situation of German workers. 8 Volcanic explosion of Krakatoa, an island in Indonesia between Java and Sumatra, kills 36,419 people. The immensity of the cataclysm creates tidal waves around the world, and dust and debris thrown into the atmosphere tint sunsets red for decades. 9 Two earthquakes in Ischia, an island in the Tyrrhenian Sea, kill about 2000 people.	**1883**

History and Politics		The Arts	
America	**Elsewhere**	**America**	**Elsewhere**
	13 Treaty of Ancón restores peace between Peru and Chile. [1879:HIST/11]		**13** Brahms composes *Symphony No. 3 in F Major.*

1884

America (History and Politics)

1 Act of Congress establishes a Bureau of Labor in the Department of the Interior.
2 Anti-Monopoly Party joins with Greenback-Labor Party to form the People's Party, which supports many liberal measures, including a graduated income tax.
3 Independent Republicans, called "Mugwumps" (Indian word for "chiefs"), walk out of Republican National Convention. They refuse to support Republican presidential nominee James G. Blaine, who they feel is corrupt, and back the Democratic choice.
4 Grover Cleveland and Thomas A. Hendricks are elected President and Vice President, respectively, on the Democratic ticket.
5 Southern Negroes, prevented from voting by the Ku Klux Klan, appeal to the Supreme Court, which rules that interference with a citizen's right to vote is a federal offense.

Elsewhere (History and Politics)

6 Gen. Charles G. Gordon is sent to Khartoum to evacuate the Egyptian garrison. He attempts to defeat the Mahdi.
7 Trade-Union Act legalizes unions in France.
8 Russia conquers city of Merv in central Asia and advances to the frontier of Afghanistan.
9 Britain and France establish separate protectorates in Somalia.
10 Berlin Conference of 14 nations discusses free trade and navigation on the Congo and Niger and the neutrality of African territory.
11 London Convention defines the relations of South African Republic to Great Britain. British fear Boer and German expansion and conclude protective treaties with native chiefs of Bechuanaland (now Botswana).
12 France establishes protectorates over Tonkin (northern Vietnam) and Annam (central Vietnam). It had made a colony of Cochin China (southern Vietnam) in 1867.
13 Bismarck proclaims a protectorate of South West Africa.
14 Bolivia and Chile sign truce at Valparaiso. Chile acquires Atacama, rich in nitrate deposits. [1879:HIST/11]

America (The Arts)

1 Helen Jackson publishes *Ramona,* inspired by her work on Indian missions. [1881:ARTS/4]
2 Winslow Homer's rescue theme in the painting "The Life Line" brings the artist fame.
3 Twain publishes the classic *The Adventures of Huckleberry Finn.*
4 Sarah Jewett, writer, publishes *A Country Doctor,* a novel about a New England girl's desire to become a doctor.

Elsewhere (The Arts)

5 Massenet composes *Manon,* his greatest opera.
6 Georges Seurat, founder of Fr. Neo-Impressionism, completes "Une Baignade, Asières." When it is rejected by the Salon, he helps establish Société des Artistes Indépendents, a group influential in the development of modern art.
7 The first volume of *Oxford English Dictionary* (–1935) is published.
8 César Franck, founder of modern Fr. instrumental school, composes *Prélude, choral et fugue,* for piano.
9 Renoir completes the first in a series of "Bathers" portraits (–1887).
10 Frédéric-Auguste Bartholdi, Fr. sculptor, designs the Statue of Liberty.
11 Rodin sculpts "The Burghers of Calais."
12 Edward Coley Burne-Jones, Eng. Pre-Raphaelite painter, exhibits "King Cophetua and the Beggar Maid."

1885

America (History and Politics)

1 Contract Labor Act forbids the immigration of laborers under contract to work for cost of transit. Skilled, domestic, and professional workers are exempted.
2 Congress forbids unauthorized fencing of public lands

Elsewhere (History and Politics)

6 Russian and Afghan troops clash over disputed border, causing serious Anglo-Russian crisis. British occupy Port Hamilton, Korea, because of military attack against Vladivostok. Matter is settled by negotiations in 1886.
7 Bulgaria annexes Eastern Rumelia. Serbia, which also claims the area, declares war

America (The Arts)

1 William Dean Howells, novelist, publishes *The Rise of Silas Lapham,* the story of a self-made man's attempts to fit into Boston society.
2 Ralph A. Blakelock, Hudson River School painter, paints "Moonlight."
3 Maud Powell, vio-

Elsewhere (The Arts)

7 Richard Francis Burton, Eng. explorer and Orientalist, translates *The Thousand and One Nights,* or *Arabian Nights' Entertainments* (–1888), a collection of folk tales that includes "Sindbad the Sailor," "Aladdin and the Magic Lamp," and "Ali Baba and the

Science & Technology		Miscellaneous		
America	Elsewhere	America	Elsewhere	

		5 Brooklyn Bridge, largest suspension bridge in the world up to this time, is completed from lower Manhattan to Brooklyn, N.Y. It is 1595 ft. long and cost $15 million.		
1 Frank J. Sprague, Conn. electrical engineer, builds a direct-current motor for use in locomotives. 2 Ottmar Mergenthaler, Ger.-Amer. inventor, patents a typesetting machine which he calls Linotype because it casts one line of characters at a time. 3 Dorr E. Felt, Wis. manufacturer, invents the first adding machine that is consistently accurate. 4 Lewis E. Waterman, N.Y. inventor, patents a practical fountain pen. 5 Telephone wires are strung between New York and Boston. 6 Electrical Exhibition and National Conference of Electricians draws more than 280,000 spectators in Philadelphia. 7 Smokeless gunpowder is developed.	8 Svante Arrhenius, Swed. chemist, publishes his dissociation theory, an important step in the study of electrolysis. 9 Wladimir Köppen, Ger. meteorologist, devises a world map of temperature zones. 10 Bessel determines that the star Sirius follows an elliptical orbit. 11 Van't Hoff publishes *Studies in Chemical Dynamics,* in which many chemical concepts are clarified.	1 Mississippi State College for Women, first state-supported women's college, is chartered at Columbus, Miss. 2 Series of tornadoes in the midwest destroys approximately 10,000 buildings and kill about 800 people. 3 Lewis E. Waterman manufactures the first practical fountain pens. 4 First U.S. baseball championship is won by Providence of the National League at the Polo Grounds, N.Y. Providence beats the American Association title winners, the New York Metropolitans, 3 to 0. 5 Glider flight is made by John J. Montgomery, who launches his glider from a 300-ft. hill near Otay, Calif., and covers a distance of 600 ft. [1853:MISC/9] 6 Last part, the capstone, is placed on the Washington Monument. It is dedicated in February 1885 and opens in October 1888.	7 First underground railroad (deep tube) begins operating in London.	**1884**
1 Charles S. Tainter, Mass. inventor, designs the Dictaphone, a device that records dictation. 2 William Stanley, N.Y. engineer, invents the electric transformer. 3 Charles Van Depoele, Belgian-Amer. scientist, invents an electric drill. 4 Statue of Liberty is lighted with electric arc	6 Dewar invents the Dewar flask, often called the vacuum or Thermos bottle. 7 Pasteur administers the first successful rabies vaccination.	1 Large immigration from eastern and southern Europe, known as the "New Immigration," starts. Many immigrants in the following years are Jews from Russia, escaping persecution. 2 First self-service restaurant opens in New York City. 3 Washington Monu-	5 Ger. inventor Gottlieb Daimler develops an internal combustion engine and Karl Benz builds a single-cylinder engine for a motor-car. 6 Francis Galton proves the permanence and individuality of fingerprints.	**1885**

	History and Politics		The Arts	
	America	Elsewhere	America	Elsewhere
	in the West. Cattle and railroad companies had fenced in great areas for themselves. **3** Land-hungry frontier farmers seek to obtain the unassigned lands in western Oklahoma—lands not assigned to any Indian tribe. **4** Apache Indians under Geronimo leave their Arizona reservation and resume their war against the whites. **[1886:HIST/2]** **5** Pres. Cleveland recommends the suspension of the minting of silver dollars. He fears silver is undermining the U.S. Treasury's gold reserves.	on Bulgaria. Serbs are decisively defeated at the Battle of Slivnitza. Bulgarian invasion is halted only by Austria's intervention to save Serbia. **[1881:HIST/8]** **8** Mahdi captures Khartoum, massacring Gen. Gordon and the garrison. The dervishes (followers of the Mahdi) take control of all Sudan except for the Red Sea fortresses. **9** Italians capture Massawa, a port on the Red Sea. **10** Spain proclaims a protectorate over Río de Oro and Spanish Guinea (now Equatorial Guinea). **11** Congo Free State is established under the personal rule of King Leopold II of Belgium. **12** Germany proclaims a protectorate over East Africa after signing treaties with black Africans. **13** Britain proclaims protectorates over Bechuanaland (now Botswana) and southeastern New Guinea.	linist, makes her German and American debuts. **4** Howard Pyle writes and illustrates *Pepper and Salt.* **5** William LeBaron Jenney, Chicago School architect, designs the Home Insurance Company building, an early skyscraper. **6** Winslow Homer paints the seascape "Fog Warning."	Forty Thieves." **8** Gilbert and Sullivan produce *The Mikado,* a two-act comic opera. **9** Stevenson publishes *A Child's Garden of Verse.* **10** Gustave Mahler, Aust. composer, completes the orchestral *Songs of a Wayfarer.* **11** Fr. poet Jean Moréas publishes the first definition of Symbolism. **12** The Rijksmuseum (Royal Art Museum) opens in Amsterdam.
1886	**1** New Presidential Succession Act is passed providing that, in the event of the death, resignation, or inability to serve of the President and Vice President, the Cabinet officers in order of the creation of their offices will succeed to the presidency. **2** Apache Chief Geronimo surrenders to Gen. Nelson A. Miles. Apache Indian wars end in the Southwest. **3** House of Representatives defeats bill permitting unlimited and free coinage of silver. **[1878:HIST/1]** **4** Illinois police attempt to break up meeting of labor leaders protesting unfair treatment of strikers; a bomb explodes; Haymarket Square riot in Chicago occurs with seven policemen and four workmen killed. **5** Supreme Court rules that legal "persons" in the Fourteenth Amendment refer not	**6** Gladstone's Home Rule Bill, establishing a separate Irish legislature, is defeated in the British Parliament. **7** Georges Ernest Boulanger becomes Minister of War in France. He appeals to French desire for revenge against Germany. **8** Serbia is forced to make peace; Eastern Rumelia remains part of Bulgaria. **[1885:HIST/7]** **9** Lagos is separated from the Gold Coast and set up as a British colony. **10** Anglo-German agreement defines the coastal frontier between the Gold Coast (British) and Togoland (German). **11** British annex upper Burma. **12** Portugal claims all territory between Angola in West Africa and Mozambique in East Africa.	**1** Henry James publishes two novels: *The Bostonians* and *Princess Casamassima.* **2** The Statue of Liberty, a gift of the French people, is dedicated in N.Y. harbor. The sonnet "The New Colossus" by Emma Lazarus is inscribed on a plaque at the statue's base. **3** Louis Sullivan and Dankmar Adler, Chicago School architects, design Chicago's Auditorium Building, a major departure from the usual theater layouts. **4** The art of stained glass windows is revived by John LaFarge with his work "Red and White Peonies." **5** Frances E.H. Burnett, Anglo-Amer. author, publishes *Little*	**7** Henri Rousseau, Fr. primitive painter, makes his debut with "Carnival Evening." **8** Seurat's masterpiece, "Sunday Afternoon on the Island of La Grande Jatte," exemplifies the technique of *pointillism,* the use of tiny brushstrokes to create an illusion of shimmering color. **9** Verlaine publishes Rimbaud's *Illuminations,* a collection of prose poems (pre-1873). **10** Rodin exhibits the sculpture, "The Kiss." **11** Stevenson publishes *The Strange Case of Dr. Jekyll and Mr. Hyde* and *Kidnapped,* two popular novels. **12** Saint-Saëns composes *Carnival of Animals,* a popular orches-

Science & Technology		Miscellaneous		
America	**Elsewhere**	**America**	**Elsewhere**	

lamps.

5 Weston invents a magnetic speedometer, the forerunner of the modern automobile speedometers.

The Statue of Liberty crated for shipment from France to the United States

ment is dedicated. It is 585 ft. high and costs $1.3 million. The top may be reached by both an elevator and a stairway of 898 steps.

4 William B. Curtis, weightlifting strongman, is reported to have hoisted 3239 lbs., with a harness.

---

1 Bell develops wax disks for use with a modified version of Edison's phonograph.

2 Westinghouse establishes the Westinghouse Electric Company and builds America's first commercially successful alternating current power plant in Buffalo, N.Y.

3 James E. Keeler, Ill. astronomer, discovers that Saturn's rings are made up of tiny pieces of meteors. His telescope was built by Alvan Clark, Mass. astronomer.

4 Ives develops a halftone photoengraving process.

5 Thomson patents an electrical resistance welding process.

6 The U.S. Forest Service is established as the Division of Forestry, U.S. Department of Agricul-

8 Ernst von Bergmann, Latv. surgeon, introduces steam sterilization of surgical instruments and dressings.

9 Nobel discovers ballistite, a smokeless nitroglycerin powder.

10 François-Marie Raoult, Fr. chemist, proposes his theory of solutions, now known as Raoult's law.

11 Élie Metchnikoff, Russ. microbiologist, describes phagocytosis, an important part of the body's defense system.

12 Henri Moisson, Fr. chemist, isolates the element fluorine.

1 Bomb explodes in Haymarket Square, Chicago, after police break up an anarchist meeting protesting the treatment of strikers at the McCormick Harvesting Machine Company the day before. Seven police and 4 workers die; 70 police are wounded.

2 American Federation of Labor is founded at Columbus, Ohio. Twenty-five trade unions participate, but unskilled workers are not represented. Labor leader, Samuel Gompers, is elected president.

3 First settlement house, the Neighborhood Guild, is established in New York City by Dr. Stanton Coit. Settlement houses provide many social services for poorer residents of the cities.

5 English Lawn Tennis Association is founded.

6 Amateur Golf Championship is started in England; Horace Hutchinson is the first champion.

1886

247

History and Politics		The Arts	
America	**Elsewhere**	**America**	**Elsewhere**

	America	Elsewhere	America	Elsewhere
	only to individuals but to corporations, as well.		*Lord Fauntleroy.* **6** Harrison Grey Fiske, playwright, writes and produces *Hester Crewe,* the production of which stars his wife, Minnie Maddern Fiske.	tral piece for children. **13** Hardy publishes *The Mayor of Casterbridge,* a novel.
1887	**1** Congress passes Interstate Commerce Act. President establishes Interstate Commerce Commission, government's first regulatory agency, to regulate all transportation and business extending beyond state borders. **2** Tenure of Office Act of 1867 is repealed. **3** Congress passes Dawes Act, providing for the granting of Indian reservation land to individual tribesmen. **4** U.S.-Hawaii treaty of 1875 is renewed and ratified with an amendment giving the U.S. exclusive right to build a naval base at Pearl Harbor. **5** Electoral Count Act makes each state responsible for its own electoral votes, thus avoiding disputed national elections. [1876:HIST/4] **6** Hatch Act grants federal aid for the study of agriculture in a state with a land-grant college. **7** U.S. discusses control of Samoa with Britain and Germany. (Germans claim right to islands.) No decision is reached.	**8** Queen Victoria of England celebrates her Golden Jubilee (50 years of English reign). **9** Boulanger leaves office with the fall of the French cabinet. [1886:HIST/7] **10** Ferdinand of Saxe-Coburg is elected ruling Prince of Bulgaria. **11** Russo-German reinsurance treaty replaces the dying Three Emperors' League, which Russia refuses to renew. **12** Britain and Germany compete for control of East Africa, especially the island of Zanzibar. **13** British annex Zululand in order to put down Zulu uprisings. **14** French form Cochin China, Annam, Tonkin, and Cambodia into the union of Indochina. **15** China recognizes Portugal's rights to Macao on the South China Sea.	**1** "The Goophered Grapevine," a short story by Charles W. Chesnutt, is the first work by a black author to be published in *Atlantic Monthly.* **2** Charles F. McKim, architect, popularizes the "Shingle Style" of residential architecture with the design of the Low House in Bristol, R.I. **3** LaFarge completes "Ascension," a large mural for the Church of the Ascension, New York City. **4** Joseph Kirkland, novelist, publishes *Zury: The Meanest Man in Spring County.*	**5** Arthur Conan Doyle, Eng. author, introduces the world's most popular detective, Sherlock Holmes, in the mystery novel, *A Study in Scarlet.* **6** Verdi composes his best tragic opera, *Otello.* **7** Pierre Loti, Fr. novelist, publishes *Madame Chrysanthème.* **8** André Antoine, Fr. actor, founds the influential Théâtre-Libre, Paris. **9** Klinger paints "The Judgment of Paris."
1888	**1** Congress establishes the U.S. Department of Labor. **2** Kentucky and Massachusetts adopt the Australian ballot system. Voters mark a printed ballot in secret in a curtained booth for the first time. **3** Benjamin Harrison and Levi P. Morton are elected President and Vice President, respectively, on the Republican ticket. Although Cleveland (Democrat) has more popular votes, he receives only 168 electoral votes to	**6** German Emperor William I dies and is succeeded by his son Frederick III, who dies in June and is succeeded by his son William II, the "Kaiser." **7** Convention of Constantinople, attended by all major European powers, declares the Suez Canal neutral and open to all merchant and war vessels in time of peace and war. **8** Arabs on the coast of East Africa rebel against the German and British colonists. **9** British treaty with the	**1** John Philip Sousa, composer and bandmaster, writes the military march "Semper Fidelis" for the Marines. **2** "Casey at the Bat," a popular ballad by Ernest Lawrence Thayer, is publicly recited for the first time by actor DeWolf Hopper. **3** Bronson Howard writes the Civil War drama *Shenandoah,* his most successful play.	**6** Claude Debussy, Fr. composer who revolutionizes 20th century music, completes *La Damoiselle élue,* a cantata based on a poem by Rossetti. [1850:ARTS/9] **7** Van Gogh paints "Portrait of Père Tanguy" and "Self-Portrait in Front of an Easel." **8** Belg. artist James Sydney Ensor completes "Entry of Christ into Brussels," a paint-

Science & Technology		Miscellaneous		
America	Elsewhere	America	Elsewhere	
ture. Bernhard E. Fernow serves as its first chief. **7** Electric motors are installed on sewing machines.		**4** First Tournament of Roses is held in Pasadena, Calif.		
1 Michelson-Morley experiment discredits the luminiferous ether theory and shows that the speed of light is constant. This experiment paves the way for Einstein's theory of relativity. [1905:SCI/13] **2** Tolbert Lanston, inventor, patents a typesetting machine that casts one piece of type at a time; he calls it the Monotype. **3** Berliner designs an improved phonograph and develops a process for duplicating disk records. **4** Hannibal W. Goodwin, N.Y. clergyman, invents Celluloid photographic film. **5** Bauxite, source of aluminum, is discovered in Ga. **6** Pennsylvania Railroad operates an electrically lighted train between Chicago and New York.	**7** Horsley becomes the first to remove a spinal tumor. **8** Bunsen invents the vapor calorimeter, a heat-measuring device.	**1** Melvile Dewey founds the State Library School in Albany, N.Y. Earlier he had devised a decimal system of library cataloguing; his teachings and methods contribute to library efficiency throughout the U.S. **2** Mail is delivered free to all communities with a population of at least 10,000. **3** First successful electric trolley line is built by Frank J. Sprague in Richmond, Va. Its 40 cars operate on 12 miles of track. **4** Foxburg Golf Club is founded in Foxburg, Pa. John Mickle Fox brought the game back with him after seeing it played in Scotland. There had been clubs called "golf clubs" earlier but there is no record of their members' playing golf. [1786:MISC/3]	**5** Stanley discovers Lake Albert Nyanza in Central Africa. **6** Yellow River overflows in Honan, China, leaving more than 900,000 people dead. George Eastman, U.S. philanthropist and inventor in the field of photography	**1887**
1 William S. Burroughs, N.Y. inventor, patents a commercially successful adding machine. **2** Clinton H. Merriam, N.Y. physician, establishes the National Geographic Society and publishes the first *National Geographic Magazine*. **3** Tesla invents an alternating current induction motor. **4** Angus Macdonald, Mass. engineer, heads a crew that keeps telephone	**10** Helmholtz describes weather fronts and speculates about their relationship to storms. **11** Bergmann publishes *The Surgical Treatment of Brain Disorders,* the cornerstone of brain surgery. **12** Johannes Warming, Dan. botanist, publishes *On the Vegetation of Greenland.* **13** Emile Hansen, Dan. botanist, describes new methods of obtaining	**1** Yellow fever epidemic in Jacksonville, Fla., lasts for almost 6 months. More than 4500 cases are reported; more than 400 persons die. **2** George Eastman perfects the Kodak hand camera, making possible the first amateur photography. The camera is preloaded with enough roll film for 100 round photographs 2 in. in diameter. When the film has been exposed it is returned	**5** Norw. arctic explorer Fridtjof Nansen leads an exploring party across Greenland.	**1888**

History and Politics		The Arts	
America	**Elsewhere**	**America**	**Elsewhere**
Harrison's 233. 4 Union Labor Party, United Labor Party, Industrial Reform Party, Equal Rights Party, and Prohibition Party nominate candidates for the presidential election this year. 5 New York State establishes electrocution for murderers condemned to die.	king of the Matabele tribe gives Cecil John Rhodes exclusive mining rights in Matabeleland and Mashonaland in South Africa. 10 Privy council is made an advisory body to the Japanese Emperor. 11 British privy council upholds the exclusion of the Chinese from Australia. 12 British establish a protectorate over Brunei, northwest Borneo. 13 Austrian and pro-Russian political factions fight for power in Serbia.	4 Edward Bellamy, writer, publishes *Looking Backward, 2000-1887.* 5 Donnelly's *The Great Cryptogram* attempts to show that Francis Bacon was the author of Shakespeare's plays.	ing that stirs such controversy that he is expelled from Les Vingt ("The Twenty"), a group of progressive artists. 9 Rimsky-Korsakov composes *Scheherazade*, one of the most popular symphonic suites ever written. 10 Cézanne's mature style is shown by the landscape, "L'Estaque."
1889 1 Kansas, North Carolina, Tennessee, and Michigan pass the first antitrust laws. New Jersey law authorizes the incorporation of holding companies within the state, which becomes the home of many large corporations. [1890:HIST/1] 2 Oklahoma (Indian Territory) is opened to white settlement. 3 Dakota Territory is divided into North and South Dakota. They are admitted to the Union as the 39th and 40th states, respectively. 4 Montana becomes 41st state. 5 Washington becomes 42nd state. 6 First Pan-American Conference meets in Washington, D.C., with the U.S. and 17 Latin American nations (all except the Dominican Republic) taking part. Inter-American organization, later called the Pan-American Union, is established (1890) to offer technical and informational service to all the nations. 7 U.S., Britain, and Germany conclude treaty providing for the neutrality of Samoa and setting up a tripartite protectorate.	8 Naval Defense Act provides that the British fleet should be as strong as the French and Russian fleets combined. 9 Boulanger wins election in Paris but fails to seize control of the government at crucial moment. He flees to Belgium to escape arrest for treason. 10 Italy and Ethiopia conclude treaty of friendship and cooperation. 11 Turks put down uprising in Crete, encouraged by Greece. 12 Military leaders depose Emperor Pedro II and proclaim Brazil a republic. [1840:HIST/6] 13 British South Africa Company, headed by Rhodes, is granted a charter with rights and powers of government in territory north of the Transvaal and west of Mozambique. 14 Emperor grants a new Japanese Constitution. 15 Crown Prince Rudolf is found dead in his hunting lodge at Mayerling, near Vienna.	1 The first Celluloid film in the U.S., *Fred Ott's Sneeze,* is made by William Kennedy Laurie Dickson. 2 Twain publishes *A Connecticut Yankee in King Arthur's Court.* 3 John Brisben Walker founds *Cosmopolitan Magazine.* 4 Angus Macdonald poses for "The Spirit of Service," a painting commemorating the Telephone Company's efforts to keep the lines up during the Blizzard of 1888. [1888:SCI/4] 5 Sousa composes "Washington Post March." 6 Loie Fuller, dancer, originates the "serpentine dance" using colored lights and lengths of silk for effect. 7 *The Wall Street Journal* is established. 8 William Holabird, Chicago School architect, designs the Tacoma Building, the first skyscraper with an all steel skeleton.	9 Gerhart Hauptmann, Pol. Naturalist writer, is an overnight success with the performance of his tragedy, *Before Dawn.* 10 "The Yellow Christ" and "Bonjour Monsieur Gauguin!" show Gauguin's *synthétisme,* a primitive style of painting with bright colors and dark, bold outlines. 11 Richard Strauss, leading Ger. composer, completes *Don Juan,* a symphonic poem. 12 Van Gogh paints "Starry Night." 13 Tchaikovsky composes *Sleeping Beauty,* a ballet. 14 Tennyson publishes a collection of poems that includes "Crossing the Bar."

Science & Technology		Miscellaneous		
America	**Elsewhere**	**America**	**Elsewhere**	

lines in service between Boston and New York. This preserves the lines of communication between these cities during the great blizzard.
5 Van Depoele patents carbon brushes for use in railway motors.
6 America's first seismograph is installed at the Lick Observatory in California.
7 Oliver Shallenberger invents a successful electric meter that measures alternating current.
8 Pullman Car Co. builds an electric locomotive for hauling freight.
9 Incubators are used for premature infants.

yeast which revolutionize the brewing industry.
14 Heinrich R. Hertz, Ger. physicist, proves that heat and light are forms of electromagnetic radiation.

with the camera to the factory. Prints and re-loaded camera are then returned to the owner.
3 Artificial straws for drinking are patented by M.C. Stone.
4 Blizzard on the east coast lasting 36 hours paralyzes New York City; 400 people die; property damage is extensive; transportation is stopped; and the city is cut off from the rest of the world. **[1888:SCI/4]**

1889

1 As the first director of the Johns Hopkins Hospital and Clinic, Osler establishes clinical training as part of the medical school curriculum. Osler further stresses the importance of a humane and personal approach to medical practice.
2 Charles M. Hall, Ohio scientist, patents an inexpensive process of producing aluminum by electrolysis.
3 Electric sewing machines are marketed by Singer.
4 Otis Brothers install an electric elevator in New York City.
5 Hoagland Laboratory opens in Brooklyn, N.Y., to study bacteria.

6 Shibasabura Kitasato, Jap. physician, becomes the first to isolate the tetanus bacillus.
7 Oskar Minkowsky, Lith. physiologist, determines that insulin is secreted by the pancreas.

Nellie Bly, U.S. newspaper reporter and world traveler.

1 First classes begin at Barnard College for Women, founded as part of Columbia University, New York City.
2 A dam above Johnstown, Pa., breaks when the Conemaugh River is swelled by heavy rains. Four towns are destroyed; the river covers Johnstown with 30 ft. of water; about 2300 people die.
3 First safety bicycles are produced in quantity. Bicycling becomes very popular.
4 Football coach Walter Camp selects the first all-American football team.
5 Last bare-knuckle boxing championship fight takes place in Richburg, Miss., between John L. Sullivan and Jake Kilrain. Sullivan wins in 75 rounds.
6 Nellie Bly, a reporter for the *New York World,* starts on round-the-world trip. She beats the time of Jules Verne's fictional journey *Around the World in Eighty Days* when she reaches home in 72 days, 6 hours, 11 minutes, and 14 seconds.

History and Politics		The Arts	
America	**Elsewhere**	**America**	**Elsewhere**

1890

America (History and Politics)

1 South Dakota, Kentucky, and Mississippi pass antitrust laws, followed by North Dakota, Oklahoma, Montana, Louisiana, Illinois, Minnesota, Missouri, and New Mexico in 1891.
2 Congress passes Sherman Antitrust Act, which declares illegal every contract, combination (in the form of trust or otherwise), or conspiracy in restraint of interstate or foreign trade.
3 Congress establishes Oklahoma Territory from lands not assigned to the Indians.
4 Idaho becomes 43rd state.
5 Wyoming becomes 44th state.
6 Sherman Silver Purchase Act requires the U.S. Treasury to purchase monthly 4,500,000 ounces of silver for coinage and to issue treasury certificates redeemable in either silver or gold. [1893:HIST/5]
7 Congress passes McKinley Tariff Act, raising duties to new highs. It is meant to protect industry, not to raise revenue.
8 U.S. troops massacre 200 Sioux Indians at the Battle of Wounded Knee, S. Dak.

Elsewhere (History and Politics)

9 Swiss government introduces social insurance.
10 Emperor William II dismisses Bismarck as Chancellor of Germany. They differ on Russo-German policy and on who should rule the empire.
11 French defeat the King of Dahomey (now Benin) in West Africa.
12 Anglo-Portuguese agreement defines the frontier between Angola and South Africa.
13 Britain gives the island of Heligoland to Germany in exchange for East African claims, including Uganda.
14 Rhodes becomes Prime Minister of Cape Colony, South Africa.
15 Britain and Germany recognize the French protectorate over Madagascar, established in 1885.
16 Japan holds its first general election.
17 Luxembourg is separated from the Netherlands and is no longer ruled by the Dutch king.

America (The Arts)

1 *Poems by Emily Dickinson* is published posthumously by the poet's sister Lavinia.
2 Clyde Fitch, playwright, writes *Beau Brummel.*
3 Jacob A. Riis, writer, publishes *How the Other Half Lives,* a shocking portrayal of slum life.
4 Howells publishes the pro-labor novel *A Hazard of New Fortunes.*
5 *Robin Hood,* a light opera composed by Reginald DeKoven, begins a run of more than 3,000 performances.
6 James A. Hearne, playwright, publishes *Margaret Fleming,* a play about marital infidelity.
7 Sullivan designs the 10-story steel frame Wainwright Building in St. Louis, Mo.

Elsewhere (The Arts)

8 Ibsen publishes *Hedda Gabler,* a play.
9 Marius Petipa, influential in modern classical Russ. ballet, choreographs *Sleeping Beauty.*
10 Eng. caricaturist John Tenniel's most famous cartoon, "Dropping the Pilot," lampoons Bismarck's forced resignation.
11 Knut Hamsun (K. Pederson), Nor. writer, publishes *Hunger.*
12 Pierre Mascagni composes the popular Italian opera, *Cavalleria Rusticana.*
13 Tchaikovsky composes *Queen of Spades,* an opera based on a Pushkin short story.
14 Debussy's *Suite bergamasque* (–1905) includes his most famous work, "Clair de lune."

1891

America (History and Politics)

1 Congress creates the Circuit Courts of Appeals to relieve the Supreme Court's case load.
2 Mob lynches 11 Italian immigrants indicted for the murder of the New Orleans police chief after the acquittal of three of them. Italy protests and recalls its minister to the U.S., and the U.S. recalls its minister to Italy. [1892:HIST/3]
3 Forest Reserve Act permits the President to close public lands to settlement for the establishment of national parks.
4 Indian Territory land ceded to the U.S. by the Sauk, Fox, and Potawatomi Indians is opened to settlement by presidential procla-

Elsewhere (History and Politics)

6 German Social Democratic Party adopts Marxist theories at the Congress of Erfurt, Germany.
7 Germany, Austria-Hungary, and Italy renew the Triple Alliance. France and Russia begin negotiations for alliance to counter-balance the Triple Alliance.
8 Menelik II, Emperor of Ethiopia, denounces Italian protectorate over Ethiopia.
9 Italians defeat and push back the Mahdists in Eritrea.
10 Belgians defeat the native king in the Congo. The Katanga Company is formed to mine Congolese copper. [1885:HIST/11]
11 By treaty, the British and Dutch set the boundaries of their territories in Borneo.

America (The Arts)

1 Stanford White, architect, designs Madison Square Garden in New York City.
2 Melville completes the novelette *Billy Budd* (pub. 1924) 5 months before his death.
3 Emily Dickinson's *Poems: Second Series* is published.
4 Ambrose Bierce publishes *In the Midst of Life,* which includes the short story "An Occurrence at Owl Creek Bridge."
5 Charles Ives composes *Variations on America,* his best-known work.
6 Donnelly's *Caesar's*

Elsewhere (The Arts)

8 Oscar Wilde, flamboyant Ir. writer, publishes *The Picture of Dorian Gray,* his only novel.
9 Henri de Toulouse-Lautrec, Fr. artist, produces his first poster, the famous "La Goulue at the Moulin Rouge."
10 Doyle publishes *The Adventures of Sherlock Holmes.*
11 James M. Barrie, Eng. writer, publishes *The Little Minister,* a popular novel.
12 Monet exhibits "Haystacks," a series of 15 paintings that show the different effects of light and weather on the same

Science & Technology		Miscellaneous		
America	**Elsewhere**	**America**	**Elsewhere**	
1 When California's citrus trees face total destruction by the cottony cushion scale insects, ladybird beetles (ladybugs) are imported from Australia for biological control.	**2** J. Alfred Ewing, Eng. physicist, discovers hysteresis, a property of magnetic materials. **3** Sach's *History of Botany from the 16th Century to 1860,* an authoritative account, is published. **4** Ehrlich establishes the field of immunology by standardizing the diphtheria antitoxin made by Ger. scientist Emil von Behring.	**1** Child labor grows in the South: almost 23,000 children work in the factories of 13 southern states. **2** Sequoia and Yosemite National Parks are established in California by the federal government, largely through the efforts of John Muir and Robert U. Johnson. **[1849:MISC/6]** **3** Psychologist and philosopher William James publishes *Principles of Psychology,* which revolutionizes the study of psychology in the U.S. **4** Smoking for men at social functions gains acceptance, but smoking by women in the company of men is still condemned.	**5** Free elementary education is established in England.	**1890**
1 Osler publishes *Principles and Practice of Medicine,* which remains a standard text in America. **2** George E. Hale, Ill. astronomer, invents the spectroheliograph and uses it to photograph sunspots. **3** Westinghouse standardizes alternating current at 60 cycles per second. **4** James Keeler, astronomer, confirms that Saturn's rings are not solid but are made of tiny meteor particles. **5** Tesla invents the Tesla coil for producing high-voltage, high-frequency electric current. It is later widely used in	**8** Alfred Werner, Fr. chemist, publishes his coordination theory, which allows for a simpler classification of inorganic chemical compounds. **9** Dewar liquefies large amounts of oxygen.	**1** University of Chicago is founded with an endowment from John D. Rockefeller. **2** First correspondence school opens in Scranton, Pa., to teach miners working methods that will make coal mines safer. **3** Whitcomb L. Judson takes out a patent on a slide fastener (zipper). **4** Physical-education professor James A. Naismith of Springfield, Mass., invents basketball as an indoor substitute for baseball and football. **5** Edison patents his kinetoscopic camera, which takes moving pictures on a strip of film. The film, called a peep show, is	**7** In Java, Dutch anthropologist Eugene Dubois discovers *Pithecanthropus erectus* (Java Man). **8** Earthquake in Japan kills about 10,000 people. **9** Widespread famine in Russia. **10** British steamer *Utopia* sinks off Gibraltar; 574 people die.	**1891**

History and Politics		The Arts	
America	**Elsewhere**	**America**	**Elsewhere**

	History and Politics — America	History and Politics — Elsewhere	The Arts — America	The Arts — Elsewhere
	mation. **5** U.S. Navy captures Chilean ship carrying arms from California to rebels in Chile. Mob at Valparaiso, Chile, attacks U.S. sailors on shore leave and kills two. War seems imminent until Chile apologizes and pays indemnity to the injured and to relatives of the dead in 1892.	**12** Boulanger commits suicide while in exile. [1889:HIST/9]	*Column* predicts the development of TV, radio, and poison gas. **7** Hamlin Garland, writer, publishes *Main-Travelled Roads,* a collection of stories about Midwestern farm life.	subject. **13** Hardy publishes *Tess of the D'Urbervilles,* a novel that shocks Victorian morals.
1892	**1** Leaders of farm and labor organizations form the Populist, or People's, Party, which calls for free coinage of silver, a graduated income tax, government ownership of railroads, postal banks, and other measures designed to strengthen political democracy. **2** Chinese Exclusion Act is extended for ten years. [1882:HIST/1] **3** U.S. pays $25,000 indemnity to the families of the Italians lynched at New Orleans in 1891. **4** Strikers at Carnegie steel plant in Homestead, Pa., protesting pay cuts and demanding recognition of their union, kill ten Pinkerton detectives and wound many others hired by management to break the strike and the union. Pennsylvania militia restores order; strike is broken. **5** Federal troops restore order in Idaho silver mines when strikers clash with non-union workers. **6** Grover Cleveland and Adlai E. Stevenson are elected President and Vice President, respectively, on the Democratic ticket. Democrats advocate tariff for revenue only and repeal of the Silver Purchase Act of 1890.	**7** Gladstone again becomes British Prime Minister and struggles to obtain Home Rule for Ireland. **8** Development of a Franco-Russian alliance is delayed by the Panama Canal scandal in France and great famine in Russia. **9** Abbas II, son of Tewfik Pasha, becomes the last Khedive of Egypt. He opposes complete British rule of Egypt. **10** French and Liberians sign treaty defining border between the Ivory Coast and Liberia. **11** Belgians defeat Arab slaveholders and traders in the upper Congo. **12** British suppress Angoni and Arab uprisings in Nyasaland (now Malawi). **13** Nationalist movement grows in India. **14** Denmark enacts new social legislation: Health Insurance Law and Old-Age Pension Law (1891). **15** Giovanni Giolitti becomes Premier of Italy. **16** Hirobumi Ito becomes Prime Minister of Japan. **17** Britain proclaims a protectorate over the Gilbert and Ellice Islands in the Pacific.	**1** Joel Chandler Harris publishes *Nights with Uncle Remus.* **2** Dvořák is appointed director of the National Conservatory of Music in New York City. **3** Edward MacDowell, piano composer, creates the orchestral *Indian Suite,* based on actual Indian tunes.	**4** Rudyard Kipling, Eng. author, publishes *Barrack-Room Ballads,* a collection that includes "Gunga Din" and "The Road to Mandalay." **5** Tchaikovsky composes the lively ballet, *Nutcracker Suite.* **6** Wilde publishes *Lady Windermere's Fan,* a light comedy. **7** Belg. author Maurice Maeterlinck writes *Pelléas et Mélisande,* generally considered the best Symbolist drama ever written. **8** Hauptmann writes *The Weavers,* a tragedy about the Silesian weavers' revolt (1844). **9** Jean Sibelius establishes himself as a major Finn. composer with *Kullervo Symphony.* **10** Ibsen writes the play, *The Master Builder.* **11** Ruggero Leoncavallo, Ital. composer, completes the opera, *I Pagliacci.*
1893	**1** Congress creates the rank of ambassador under the Diplomatic Appropriations Act. **2** Gold reserves in the U.S.	**9** France makes Laos a protectorate and rules it as part of Indochina. [1887:HIST/14] **10** Independent Labour	**1** Katherine Lee Bates, author, writes the words to the patriotic hymn "America	**7** Doyle "kills" Sherlock Holmes in *The Memoirs of Sherlock Holmes.* The public is

Science & Technology		Miscellaneous		
America	**Elsewhere**	**America**	**Elsewhere**	
radios and televisions. **6** Granville Hall, Mass. psychologist, establishes the American Psychological Assoc. **7** Edward Acheson, Pa. inventor, discovers carborundum, an abrasive hard enough to polish diamonds.		seen by one person at a time, looking into a lighted box while turning a crank. **6** First marathon race is run from Hopkinton, Mass., to Boston, a distance of 26 mi., 385 yds., the same distance run by Pheidippides in 490 B.C. to carry the news from Marathon to Athens that 10,000 Athenians had repulsed an invasion by 30,000 Persians.		
1 Boll weevils enter Texas from Mexico and soon infest most of the cotton fields in the South. **2** George Nuttall, Calif. biologist, discovers a gas-producing bacterium, *Bacillus aerogenes.* **3** Acetylene gas is produced by Thomas L. Willson, N.C. chemist. Ferris Wheel at World's Columbian Exposition in Chicago	**4** Moisson invents the electric furnace. **5** Kocher's *Chirurische Operationslehre* is published. It soon becomes a standard surgical text. **6** Warming publishes an overview of tropical, temperate, and polar plants. **7** Metchnikoff publishes *The Comparative Pathology of Inflammation.*	**1** George W.G. Ferris designs his Ferris Wheel for the World's Columbian Exposition held in Chicago in 1893. It carries 40 passengers 250 ft. high in its 36 cars. **2** First electric automobile, made by William Morrison of Des Moines, is driven in Chicago. **3** Cyclone rips through Kansas; 31 persons die and 2 towns are completely destroyed. **4** Tool and bicycle makers Frank and Charles Duryea of Mass. construct the first gasoline automobile. **5** Fire in Milwaukee destroys $5 million worth of property over 26 acres. **6** Coal mine explosion in Krebs, Okla., leaves 100 dead. **7** James J. ("Gentleman Jim") Corbett knocks out John L. Sullivan at New Orleans, La., to become the first heavyweight boxing champion under the Marquis of Queensberry rules. **[1865:MISC/7]**		**1892**
1 Attempts to have America switch to the metric system are defeated in Congress.	**6** Sigmund Freud, Aust. physician and psychologist, and Josef Breuer, publish *The Psychic*	**1** World's Columbian Exposition opens in Chicago to celebrate the 400th anniversary of the	**8** Benz constructs a 4-wheel car. **9** Nansen leads an expedition to the North Pole.	**1893**

History and Politics		The Arts	
America	**Elsewhere**	**America**	**Elsewhere**
Treasury fall below $90 million, touching off financial panic. **3** Supreme Court declares Chinese Exclusion Act constitutional. **4** U.S. Minister to Hawaii proclaims the islands a U.S. protectorate. Pres. Cleveland refuses annexation of the islands, requested by Hawaiian provisional government. **[1894:HIST/4]** **5** Cleveland calls a special session of Congress and secures repeal of the Sherman Silver Purchase Act of 1890. **6** Cherokee land between Kansas and Oklahoma, purchased by the government in 1891, is opened to settlement. **7** U.S.-Canadian agreement provides for surveillance of illegal immigrants into the U.S. through Canadian ports on West coast. **8** Colorado adopts women's suffrage.	Party is founded in Bradford, England. **11** France and Russia accept military convention (a dual alliance) to remain in force as long as the Triple Alliance. **[1891:HIST/7]** **12** British give Natal, a province in South Africa, internal self-government. **13** Riff tribes of Morocco attack Spanish possessions on the coast. **14** British crush uprisings against the British South Africa Company in Matabele. **15** Kruger is reelected President of the South African Republic. **16** Siam's boundaries are established; Siamese claims to Laos are renounced. **17** New Zealand adopts women's suffrage. **18** British House of Lords defeats Gladstone's second Irish Home Rule Bill.	the Beautiful." **2** Sousa composes "The Liberty Bell." **3** Stephen Crane, novelist, writes *Maggie: A Girl of the Streets*. **4** L.C. Tiffany develops favrile glass, an elegant type of stained glass with which he makes screens, lampshades, and other items. **[1874:ARTS/2]** **5** Henry Blake Fuller, novelist, publishes *The Cliff-Dwellers*, often considered the first American "city novel." **6** Paul Laurence Dunbar, black author, publishes *Oak and Ivy*, a poetry volume.	outraged and demands that the detective be resurrected. **[1905:ARTS/7]** **8** Verdi's comic opera, *Falstaff*, combines elements from Shakespeare's *Merry Wives of Windsor* and *Henry IV*. **9** Aubrey Beardsley, Eng. artist, illustrates a new edition of Sir Thomas Malory's *Le Morte d'Arthur* (1485). **10** Engelbert Humperdinck, Ger. composer, completes *Hansel und Gretel*, a fairytale opera. **11** Giacomo Puccini, Ital. composer, completes *Manon Lescaut*, an opera. **[1731: ARTS/4]** **12** Intrigued by Negro spirituals, Dvořák composes *Symphony No. 9 (From the New World)*. **[1892:ARTS/2]** **13** *Mrs. Warren's Profession*, a play by Ir. playwright George Bernard Shaw, is banned in England (–1924). **[1905:ARTS/19]**
1894 **1** Government sells bonds to replenish gold reserve. **2** Coxey's Army, a band of jobless men led by Jacob S. Coxey, marches to Washington, D.C., to petition Congress for public works programs to help the unemployed. Coxey is arrested for trespassing, and the army disbands. **3** American Railway Union, led by Eugene V. Debs, boycotts all Pullman railway cars as sympathy gesture for Pullman strikers protesting wage cuts. Railroad traffic out of Chicago comes to a halt. Court injunction is issued against strikers, and federal troops break the strike on grounds of interference with	**7** Alfred Dreyfus, Fr. general staff officer, is convicted on false treason charge and deported to Devils Island off French Guiana. His case splits France between right and left factions. Dreyfus is exonerated in 1906. **8** Nicholas II becomes last Czar of Russia. **9** Japanese troops occupy Seoul. Korea and Japan declare war on China and win victories at Ping-yang, Yalu River, and Port Arthur. **10** Serbia's constitution is restored. **11** Franco-German agreement establishes the northern frontier of Cameroon in Africa. **12** Italians capture Kassala	**1** Twain publishes *Tom Sawyer Abroad* and *The Tragedy of Pudd'nhead Wilson*. **2** Actor Richard Mansfield produces *Arms and the Man*, the first production of G.B. Shaw in the U.S. **3** Holabird's design of the Marquette Building includes an all glass façade. **4** Walter Damrosch, organizes the Damrosch Opera Company, which tours the U.S. presenting Wagner operas. **5** Margaret M. Saunders, author, publishes the classic children's	**6** Eng. writer Anthony Hope (Anthony Hope Hawkins) publishes *The Prisoner of Zenda*, a novel. **7** Shaw satirizes war in his play, *Arms and the Man*. **8** George du Maurier, Eng. writer, publishes *Trilby*, a novel that introduces the mysterious hypnotist, Svengali. **9** Beardsley illustrates an English version of Wilde's drama, *Salome* (1893). **10** Toulouse-Lautrec paints "Au Salon de la Rue de Moulins," one of his best works, and

256

Science & Technology		Miscellaneous		
America	**Elsewhere**	**America**	**Elsewhere**	

2 Michelson standardizes the meter, basing his measurement on the wavelength of red cadmium light. This measurement is universally accepted in 1925.

3 Leo H. Baekeland, chemist, develops *Velox,* the first photographic paper sensitive enough to be printed by artificial light.

4 Thomas C. Chamberlin, geologist, establishes the *Journal of Geology.*

5 Chlorine is used to treat sewage in Brewster, N.Y.

Mechanism of Hysterical Phenomena, the foundation of psychoanalysis.

7 George Fitzgerald, Ir. physicist, and Hendrik Lorentz, Dutch physicist, propose the Lorentz-Fitzgerald contraction, which states that objects become smaller as they approach the speed of light. This is a forerunner to the theory of relativity.

8 Hertz publishes *Electric Waves.*

9 Wilhelm Wien, Ger. physician, publishes work on radiation emission.

10 Rudolf Diesel, Ger. engineer, artificially produces 80 atmospheres of pressure.

discovery of America.

2 Automobile manufacturer Henry Ford builds his first successful gasoline engine.

3 Fire in Minneapolis leaves 1500 persons homeless and destroys $2 million worth of property.

4 Hurricane in southern U.S. devastates Charleston, S.C., and Savannah, Ga.; about 1000 people die.

5 A relay race is first run at the University of Pennsylvania.

6 Early film studio is built in West Orange, N.J., by the Edison Laboratories. It is a small building pivoted so that it can turn with the sun.

7 Ice hockey is introduced from Canada at Yale and Johns Hopkins Universities.

---

1 Simon Lake, inventor, launches *Argonaut I,* a small, hand-powered submarine.

2 Lowell Observatory is built at Flagstaff, Arizona.

3 Boston Board of Health begins medical examinations of school-children.

4 Thomson patents an electrical resistance furnace.

5 Still establishes the *Journal of Osteopathy.*

6 William H. Park, N.Y. physician, opens the world's first antitoxin laboratory and clinic in New York City.

7 Sir William Ramsay, Eng. chemist, and Lord Rayleigh, discover the chemically inert element argon.

8 Diesel invents the diesel engine.

9 Kitasato and Alexandre Yersin, Swiss bacteriologist, separately discover the bubonic plague bacterium.

1 In a year of unemployment and labor discontent, a riot among striking miners in Pennsylvania leaves 11 dead; 136,000 coal miners strike for higher wages in Ohio; 12,000 New York clothing workers strike against the piecework and sweatshop systems; and railroad strikes paralyze 50,000 mi, of railroads in the midwest.

2 Fire at Chicago's Columbian Exposition destroys nearly all the buildings; property damage is estimated at $2 million.

3 United States Golf Association is established;

1894

| History and Politics | | The Arts | |
America	Elsewhere	America	Elsewhere
interstate commerce. Debs is jailed for violating the injunction. **4** U.S. recognizes Hawaiian Republic established by provisional government. (U.S. forces withdrew in 1893, ending U.S. protectorate.) **5** Democratic Silver Convention, led by William Jennings Bryan, adopts free-coinage plank on silver-gold ratio of 16 to 1. **6** Congress passes first graduated income tax law. It is part of Wilson-Gorman Tariff Act, which lowers duties to about 40 percent. **[1895:HIST/2]**	from the dervishes in Sudan. **13** Turks begin campaign to wipe out Armenians. **14** French establish a protectorate over Dahomey (now Benin). **15** British establish a protectorate over Uganda. **16** Sadi Carnot, President of France's Third Republic, is assassinated by an Italian anarchist.	tale *Beautiful Joe*, the story of a dog.	produces a series of 16 lithographs of Fr. singer Yvette Guilbert. **11** Kipling publishes *The Jungle Book*, the story of Mowgli. **12** Alphonse Mucha, Czech. artist, prepares an Art Nouveau poster of Sarah Bernhardt.
1895 **1** Minority of House Democrats issue an appeal for the immediate return to the free coinage of silver at silver-gold ratio of 16 to 1. **2** Supreme Court declares income tax unconstitutional in *Pollack* v. *Farmers Loan and Trust Company*. **3** Supreme Court upholds the use of the injunction as a strike-breaking device. **4** Pres. Cleveland calls on U.S. citizens not to give aid to Cuban rebels fighting against Spanish rule. **5** U.S. interference in the British-Venezuelan boundary dispute is based on the application of the Monroe Doctrine. **[1823:HIST/1]**	**6** Treaty of Shimonoseki ends Sino-Japanese War. China recognizes the independence of Korea and cedes to Japan Formosa and the Pescadores Islands. Intervention by Russia, France, and Germany forces Japan to return Port Arthur and the Liaotung Peninsula to China. **[1894:HIST/9]** **7** Sir Leander Starr Jameson leads unsuccessful raid into the Transvaal to overthrow the Boer government. **8** Cuba fights Spain for its independence. **9** Italians advance into Ethiopia but are defeated at Amba Alagi. **10** Macedonian revolutionaries murder Bulgarian Premier Stefan Stambulov. **11** Turks massacre Armenians. **12** France unites its west African possessions under a governor-general.	**1** Stephen Crane publishes his best-known work, *The Red Badge of Courage*. **2** *Field and Stream* magazine begins publication. **3** Breaking with the Hudson River School, Homer Martin introduces Impressionism to the U.S. with the painting "The Harp of the Winds."	**4** Wilde writes *The Importance of Being Earnest*, a comedy. **5** Auguste and Louis Lumière, Fr. film pioneers, give the first public showing of a movie, *Lunch Break at the Lumière Factory*. Later, they produce the first newsreels, documentaries, and comedy films. **6** Edvard Munch, Norw. painter, produces "The Cry," a lithograph. **7** Leo Ivanov and Petipa choreograph *Swan Lake* for its first complete performance, in St. Petersburg. **[1876:ARTS/5]** **8** H.G. Wells, Eng. writer, publishes *The Time Machine*, a popular science fiction novel. **9** Joseph Conrad, Pol.-born writer in England, publishes *Almayer's Folly*, his first novel.
1896 **1** Utah becomes 45th state. **2** Supreme Court rules in *Plessy* v. *Ferguson* that "separate but equal" facilities for whites and blacks are constitutional. Ruling marks	**6** Ethiopians defeat the Italians at the Battle of Adua. Italians sign the Treaty of Addis Ababa, recognizing the independence of Ethiopia and retaining their colony of	**1** Sousa composes "The Stars and Stripes Forever." **2** Dickinson's *Poems: Third Series* is published.	**7** Chekhov writes *The Seagull*, a play considered a failure until performed by Stanislavsky's Moscow Art Theater (1898).

Science & Technology		Miscellaneous		
America	Elsewhere	America	Elsewhere	

Guglielmo Marconi, Italian physicist and inventor

| | | its first amateur championship and first open championship are held in 1895.
4 Sunday comics first appear.
5 Fire in Hinckley, Minn., burns more than 160,000 acres of forest and kills about 500 people there and in 18 neighboring towns. | | |

| **1** Hale organizes the Yerkes Observatory at Lake Geneva, Wis.
2 Percival Lowell, astronomer, publishes *Mars*.
3 Morley determines the atomic weight of oxygen.
4 Pneumatic (air-filled) rubber tires are produced by the Hartford Rubber Works in Connecticut.
5 Baltimore & Ohio Railroad begins using electric locomotives.
6 National Medical Association is formed by a group of black doctors who claim that their interests are not adequately represented by the American Medical Association.
7 Lewis B. Halsey begins commercial production of pasteurized milk. | **8** Guglielmo Marconi, Ital. physicist, invents a wireless telegraph system.
9 Ramsay isolates helium from the mineral cleveite.
10 Wilhelm Röntgen, Ger. chemist, discovers x-rays.
11 Fr. photographic engineers Auguste and Louis Lumière invent the Cinématographe, loosely based on Edison's Kinetoscope.
12 Yersin develops a serum to fight bubonic plague.
13 Warming classifies plants by their ecological environment.
14 One of the greatest scientific teams in history is formed when Pierre Curie marries the Pol. physicist Marie Sklodowska.. | **1** Negro Baptist groups merge to form the National Baptist Convention of the U.S.A.
2 Sears, Roebuck Company opens a mail-order business. Along with Montgomery Ward, which had been established in 1872, it soon revolutionizes the sale of goods to people living in rural areas.
3 Woodville Latham demonstrates his moving-picture projector, the Panoptikon, which combines Edison's kinetoscope with the magic lantern. [1891:MISC/5]
4 First professional football game is played at Latrobe, Pa., when the Latrobe team hires a substitute quarterback for $10 in expenses. Up to this time the Latrobe team had shared the profits from its games.
5 First U.S. Open Golf Championship is won by Horace Rawlins. | **6** Spanish cruiser *Reina Regenta* sinks near Gibraltar; 400 die. | **1895** |

| **1** Maxim and House build the unsuccessful Maxim steam-powered flying machine.
2 Edmund B. Wilson, biologist, describes cellu- | **9** Moritz Cantor, Ger. mathematician, publishes a complete history of mathematics from ancient times through 1800.
10 Marconi receives | **1** *New York World* publishes "The Yellow Kid," forerunner of modern comic strips. The words are printed on the boy's bright yellow shirt instead | **8** Nobel Prizes are established for achievements in physics, physiology and medicine, chemistry, literature, and peace. | **1896** |

259

History and Politics

The Arts

America	Elsewhere	America	Elsewhere

start of "Jim Crow" era, legalizing segregation.

3 Bryan delivers his "Cross of Gold" speech at the Democratic National Convention in Chicago. Free-silver Democrats nominate him for President. Populist Party also nominates Bryan. **[1894:HIST/5]**

4 Congress passes resolution granting belligerent rights to Cuban rebels. Spain rejects offer that President be peace arbitrator.

5 William McKinley and Garret A. Hobart are elected President and Vice President, respectively, on the Republican ticket. Republican platform endorses the gold standard. Republicans retain control of Congress.

Eritrea.

7 Kaiser William II sends "Krugar telegram," congratulating Krugar for the successful repulsion of the British in the Transvaal. Implication of German interference causes anger in England. **[1895:HIST/7]**

8 Cretans, supported by the Greeks, rebel against Turkish rule.

9 Sir Wilfrid Laurier becomes Prime Minister of Canada as liberal leader.

10 Horatio Herbert Kitchener begins the reconquest of the Sudan as commander of the Anglo-Egyptian army.

11 British defeat the Ashantis in central Ghana.

12 Transvaal and the Orange Free State conclude a military alliance.

13 British put down revolts by the Matabele and Mashona tribes in Rhodesia.

3 Cass Gilbert, architect, gains public recognition with his design of the Minnesota State Capitol Building.

4 The first, close-up, prolonged embrace on the screen, *The John Rice-May Irwin Kiss,* scandalizes audiences across the country.

5 P.L. Dunbar gains recognition with *Lyrics of Lowly Life.*

6 Motion pictures are introduced into vaudeville shows.

8 Hilaire Belloc, Brit. writer, publishes *The Bad Child's Book of Beasts,* a collection of poems for children.

9 Puccini composes the opera, *La Bohème.*

10 Edward Elgar, Eng. composer, completes *Enigma Variations,* allegedly based on a familiar melody that has never been identified.

11 Toulouse-Lautrec produces his most significant work, "Elles," a series of 11 lithographs.

12 Henryk Sienkiewicz, Pol. writer, publishes *Quo Vadis,* an historical adventure novel about Rome at the time of Nero (A.D. 54–68).

13 Gabriele D'Annunzio, Ital. poet, publishes *The Triumph of Death.*

1897

1 National Monetary Conference meets at Indianapolis and endorses existing gold standard. Appointed commission submits plan for monetary system to Congress. With free-silver issue settled, the U.S. begins decade of prosperity.

2 President vetoes bill requiring literacy test for immigrants.

3 Congress passes the Dingley Tariff, which increases duties on imported goods to new highs.

4 Supreme Court declares that an association of 18 railroads established to set transportation rates is a violation of the Sherman Antitrust Act.

5 Congress votes for relief of Americans destitute in Cuba. Imprisoned Americans are released. U.S. anti-Spanish sentiment increases; many peo-

6 Crete proclaims union with Greece. Turkey declares war on Greece. European powers intervene and force Turkey to evacuate Crete. Peace settlement creates autonomous Cretan state.

7 Germany occupies Kiaochow Bay, North China, following the murder of two missionaries in Shantung.

8 Anglo-Egyptian forces capture Sudanese territory.

9 Treaty between Ethiopia and France defines the Somali frontier.

10 British give up claims to much territory in Somaliland.

11 Italians cede Kassala to the Egyptians. **[1894:HIST/12]**

12 Zululand becomes part of Natal in South Africa.

13 Gold deposits begin to draw prospectors to the Klondike region of Canada's Yukon Territory.

1 Rudolph Dirks, cartoonist, creates "Katzenjammer Kids," the first newspaper comic strip to enclose words in balloons and to have a continuous cast of characters.

2 DeKoven composes *The Highwayman.*

3 Dankmar Alder designs the Chicago Stock Exchange Building.

4 Ellen Glasgow, novelist, publishes her first novel, *The Descendant.*

5 Amy Marcy Beach, leading woman composer of the period, publishes *Symphony in E-Minor.*

6 *First Symphony,* by Russ. composer Sergei Rachmaninoff, is poorly received, though later recognized as one of his greatest works.

7 Henri Matisse, one of France's most important 20th century artists, paints the Impressionistic "The Dinner Table."

8 Rousseau paints "The Sleeping Gypsy."

9 Edmond Rostand, Fr. dramatist, produces *Cyrano de Bergerac,* an exceptionally successful play that features Benoît Constant Coquelin in the title role.

10 Wells publishes *The Invisible Man,* a popular science fiction novel.

11 Bram Stoker, Ir.

Science & Technology		Miscellaneous		
America	**Elsewhere**	**America**	**Elsewhere**	
lar differentiation in *The Cell in Development and Inheritance.* **3** James F. Kemp, geologist, publishes *Handbook of Rocks.* **4** Samuel P. Langley, astronomer, builds the first successful motorized model airplane. It flies 3000 and 4200 feet in separate tests. **5** Wallace Sabine, Ohio physicist, devises a reverberation equation that becomes the basis of acoustics. **6** Marsh publishes *Dinosaurs of North America.* **7** Successful offshore oil wells are drilled near Santa Barbara, Calif. **8** Edison invents the fluoroscope, an instrument that is later used for viewing x-ray images. He also invents the fluorescent lamp.	English patent 7777 for his wireless telegraph system. **11** Ramsay publishes *The Gases of the Atmosphere.* **12** Magnus G. Retzius, Swed. anatomist and anthropologist, publishes *The Human Brain,* the most complete work on this topic to his time. **13** Henri Becquerel, Fr. physicist, discovers radioactivity. **14** Lord Ernest Rutherford, Eng. chemist and physicist, discovers alpha and beta waves. **15** Konstantin Tsiolkovsky, Russ. scientist, discusses some possible problems of space travel in *Exploration of Cosmic Space by Means of Reaction Devices.*	of outside of the frame as in earlier cartoons. **2** Rural free mail delivery is established. **3** "Book" matches become popular. Invented in 1892 by Joshua Pusey, the Diamond Match Company bought his patent in 1895. **4** First U.S. hockey league, the Amateur Hockey League, is organized in New York City. **5** Athlete James B. Connolly becomes the first Olympic champion in 1500 years at the revival of the Olympic games in Athens, Greece. **6** First moving picture on a public screen is shown at Koster and Bial's Music Hall in New York City. **7** Former baseball player William Ashley ("Billy") Sunday begins a career of evangelism. He conducts 300 revivals in major cities and is heard by 100 million people before his death in 1935.	**9** Earthquake and tidal wave kill about 27,000 in Japan. **10** First Alpine ski school is founded at Lilienfeld, Austria. **11** Alfred Harmsworth, Eng. journalist, founds the London *Daily Mail.*	
1 Yerkes Observatory installs a refracting telescope with a 40-in. lens—the world's largest. It was designed by Alvan Clark and built by George Hale. **2** Lake launches *Argonaut II,* a 36-ft.-long gasoline-powered submarine with wheels for rolling along the ocean floor. **3** William Morton produces the first full-length x-ray of a living human body. **4** William Hillebrand, geologist, determines the chemical make-up of the Earth's crust. **5** Steinmetz publishes *Theory and Calculation of Alternating Current Phenomena,* a work so advanced that it is years before scientists are able to understand it.	**7** Vilhelm Bjerknes, Norw. meteorologist, proposes the theory of air masses, a cornerstone of modern weather forecasting. **8** Joseph J. Thomson, Scot. physicist, discovers the electron. **9** Christiaan Eijkman, Dutch physician, determines that the disease beriberi is caused by a dietary deficiency. **10** Karl F. Braun, Ger. physicist, invents the oscilloscope. **11** Freud defines the "Oedipus complex" and suggests that dreams play an important psychological role. **12** Ivan Petrovich Pavlov, Russ. physiologist, publishes *Lectures on the Work of the Principal*	**1** Congregational minister Charles M. Sheldon publishes *In His Steps,* a collection of sermons in which he tells young people what they would do in a year if they copied Jesus Christ. **2** First practical subway is completed in Boston. **3** Corbett is defeated by Bob Fitzsimmons, an Englishman, in a 14-round boxing match. It is the first match photographed by a moving picture camera.	**4** Severe famine in India. **5** Marconi establishes the Wireless Telegraph Company.	**1897**

	History and Politics		The Arts	
	America	**Elsewhere**	**America**	**Elsewhere**
	ple advocate intervention in Cuban rebellion.			writer, publishes *Dracula,* a classic Gothic horror tale about the mysterious vampire, Count Dracula.
1898	**1** U.S. battleship *Maine* arrives at Havana, Cuba, to protect American residents and property and is blown up in the harbor. **2** McKinley signs congressional resolution declaring Cuba independent and authorizing use of army and navy to force Spain to leave Cuba. U.S. blockades Cuban ports. Spain and U.S. declare war on each other, and Spanish-American War begins. **3** U.S. fleet under Admiral George Dewey destroys Spanish fleet at the battle of Manila Bay in the Philippines. **4** U.S. forces defeat Spanish forces at Guantánamo Bay, El Caney, and San Juan Hill in Cuba. **5** U.S. fleet destroys Spanish fleet off Santiago, Cuba. Santiago surrenders to U.S. **6** U.S. forces capture Puerto Rico and Guam. **7** U.S. and Filipino forces capture the city of Manila. **8** Treaty of Paris ends Spanish-American War. Spain gives up claim to Cuba and cedes to the U.S. Puerto Rico, Guam, and the Philippines (the latter for a payment of $20 million). U.S. is recognized as world power. **9** Eugene V. Debs helps form the Social Democratic Party, later called the Socialist Party. **[1894:HIST/3]** **10** U.S. annexes Hawaii.	**11** First German Navy law marks the start of Germany's naval expansion. **12** Social Democratic Party is formed among the industrial workers in Russia. **13** Greek government defaults on its obligations; international commission is set up to control Greece's finances. **14** Kitchener's Anglo-Egyptian army defeats the Mahdists in the Sudan. His army captures Khartoum. **15** Kitchener's Anglo-Egyptian army arrives at Fashoda (now Kodok) on the Nile in the south Sudan. French forces occupying Fashoda evacuate, averting war between Britain and France. **16** A confederation, the Greater Republic of Central America, is proposed but fails after El Salvador opposes it. **17** Kruger is reelected President of the South African Republic. **18** "The Boxers," an antiforeign organization, is established in China. **19** News of the rich gold strikes in Canada's Yukon Territory creates a stampede of 100,000 prospectors, despite the remoteness of the Klondike region where the strike is centered.	**1** Ethelbert Woodbridge Nevin, composer, composes the popular piano piece "The Rosary." **2** S. Lanier publishes *Music and Poetry,* which argues for music education and chairs of music at universities. **3** James publishes *The Two Magics,* which contains the supernatural tale "The Turn of the Screw." **4** Dunbar publishes the novel *The Uncalled.* **5** The National Institute of Arts and Letters is founded.	**6** Konstantin Stanislavsky, Russ. director who wins international acclaim for his technique of "method acting," founds the Moscow Art Theater. **7** Arturo Toscanini, Ital. conductor, is appointed musical director of La Scala Theater, Milan. **8** Wells publishes *The War of the Worlds,* a science fiction novel. **9** Chekhov writes *Uncle Vanya,* a play. **10** Rimsky-Korsakov composes *Sadko,* an opera that includes the popular "Song of India." **11** In *What Is Art?* Tolstoy claims that his earlier works, as well as those of Shakespeare, Wagner, and others, are invalid as art forms because they do nothing to better man's moral, spiritual, or social condition. **12** In *The Ballad of Reading Gaol,* Wilde describes his imprisonment (1895–97).
1899	**1** Congress ratifies the Treaty of Paris. Filipinos, disappointed by terms of the treaty, begin three-year rebellion against American rule. **[1898:HIST/8]** **2** U.S. participates in first peace conference at The Hague with 25 other nations. U.S. upholds the Monroe Doctrine in the Western	**6** South African (Boer) War begins between British and Boers over territorial and political rights. Boers defeat British at Nicholson's Nek, Stormberg, Magersfontein, and Colenso, and besiege Ladysmith in Natal. Britain sends reinforcements. **7** First peace conference at The Hague establishes a Per-	**1** Frank Norris, Naturalist novelist, publishes *McTeague.* **[1924:ARTS/10]** **2** "Maple Leaf Rag" by composer Scott Joplin helps popularize the ragtime style. **3** Booth Tarkington, novelist, publishes his first work *The Gentle-*	**8** Ensor's isolation and cynicism are reflected in his bizarre painting, "Portrait of the Artist Surrounded by Masks." **9** Méliès directs the films, *Cleopatra* and *Christ Walking on the Waters.* **10** Russ. ballet pro-

Science & Technology		Miscellaneous		
America	**Elsewhere**	**America**	**Elsewhere**	
6 America's first hospital for crippled children opens in St. Paul, Minn.	*Digestive Glands.* **13** Shiga Kiyoshi, Jap. bacteriologist, discovers the bacterium responsible for dysentery.			
1 New York State Pathological Laboratory for the Study of Cancer opens. **2** John J. Abel, Ohio pharmacologist, extracts epinephrine (adrenalin) from the adrenal glands of a sheep. This is the first hormone to be isolated in a laboratory. **3** *Argonaut II* is the first submarine to travel in the open seas—300 miles from Virginia to New York City. **4** John Holland, "Father of the Modern Submarine," launches the *Holland,* a 53-ft.-long, cigar-shaped vessel. It is powered by electricity when underwater and by a gasoline engine when on the surface. **5** Fernow establishes the first college of forestry at Cornell University, Ithaca, N.Y. **6** Keeler's photographs prove that the most common type of galaxy has a spiral shape. **7** Tesla demonstrates a remote-controlled boat.	**8** Marie Curie discovers the elements polonium and radium, and coins the term *radioactivity.* **9** Philipp Lenard, Ger. physicist, determines that a given substance absorbs electrons according to its density. **10** Dewar liquefies hydrogen. **11** Sir Ronald Ross, Eng. bacteriologist, determines that malaria is transmitted by mosquitoes. **12** Ramsay and Eng. chemist Morris Travers discover the elements neon, krypton, and xenon. **13** Fritz Haber, Ger. chemist, publishes *The Theoretical Basis of Technical Electrochemistry.* **14** Valdemar Poulsen, Dan. engineer, invents the telegraphone, an early form of the tape recorder. **15** Jules Bordet, Belg. bacteriologist, discovers hemolysis, a disease-fighting process of the blood.	**1** First Food and Drug Act is passed because of public outcry against the meat supplied for U.S. troops fighting in the Spanish-American War.	**2** Ger. inventor Ferdinand von Zeppelin designs and builds a dirigible (a lighter-than-air craft). Two years later, he flies the first Zeppelin airship, 420 ft. long and 38 ft. in diameter. **[1900:MISC/8]** **3** Richard Kandt begins to explore Rwanda and Burundi in Central Africa. **4** French steamer *La Bourgogne* and British sailing ship *Cromartyshire* collide off Nova Scotia; 560 people are lost.	**1898**
1 Frederick W. Taylor, Pa. engineer, develops a process of heat-treating steel that increases its strength and cutting ability by 300%. **2** America's first tuberculosis hospital opens in Denver, Colo. **3** George W. Crile, surgeon, develops new, more	**5** Freud publishes *The Interpretation of Dreams,* in which many of his most important theories are first presented. **6** Dewar obtains hydrogen in solid form. **7** Leo Frobenius, Ger. ethnologist, begins publication of *Problems of Culture,* which studies	**1** Educator John Dewey begins a revolution in education with the publication of *The School and Society.* Among other concepts, Dewey believes that education begins with actual experience rather than with learning traditional subjects. **2** James J. Jeffries be-	**5** Although it has been used for centuries, aspirin is introduced as a "modern" medicine.	**1899**

History and Politics

The Arts

America

Elsewhere

America

Elsewhere

History and Politics		The Arts	

America (History and Politics)

Hemisphere.
3 Treaty between the U.S., Germany, and Britain recognizes U.S. interests in Samoa east of longitude 171°W. American Samoa is placed under control of the U.S. Navy.
4 U.S. annexes Wake Island in the central Pacific for use as a cable station.
5 Secretary of State John Hay sets forth his Open Door Policy with regard to China, stressing freedom of trade for U.S. merchants. Hay asks six major powers to preserve China's integrity as a nation and not to interfere with the free use of Chinese ports for trade.

Elsewhere (History and Politics)

manent Court of International Justice and Arbitration.
8 Cipriano Castro becomes dictator of Venezuela after leading a revolt.
9 Anglo-Egyptian convention forms the condominium government of the Anglo-Egyptian Sudan.
10 Somalis raid British and Italian possessions in Ethiopia and the Red Sea area.
11 Anglo-German agreement establishes the Togoland-Gold Coast boundary.

America (The Arts)

man from Indiana.
4 Charles Dana Gibson, illustrator, features his famed "Gibson Girl" in his book of sketches *The Education of Mr. Pipp.*
5 Eakins paints "Between Rounds."
6 The sousaphone, a bass tuba designed for parade use, is developed and named for John Philip Sousa.
7 Homer's painting "The Gulf Stream" shows the insignificance of man in relation to nature.

Elsewhere (The Arts)

ducer Sergei Pavlovich Diaghilev establishes *World of Art,* an important periodical.
11 Monet begins his famous series of paintings, "Water-Lily Pool" (–1906).
12 Maurice Ravel, Fr. composer, completes the orchestral *Pavane for a Dead Princess.*
13 D'Annunzio publishes *In Praise of Sky, Sea, Earth, and Heroes,* a collection of some of his best poetry.

1900

America (History and Politics)

1 U.S. forces help relieve Peking during Boxer Rebellion in China. Hay reaffirms the Open Door Policy. **[1899:HIST/5]**
2 Congress enacts Gold Standard Act, making other forms of money redeemable in gold.
3 Foraker Act declares Puerto Rico an unorganized territory and establishes a civil government for the island.
4 Hawaii is made a territory of the U.S.
5 Social Democratic Party nominates Debs for President. **[1898:HIST/9]**
6 Populist and Democratic Parties both nominate Bryan for President. Bryan runs on a platform of free silver and anti-imperialism.
7 First direct primary election is held in Minneapolis, Minn.
8 Carry Nation, temperance advocate, denounces saloons and liquor and supports prohibition laws.
9 People's (Anti-Fusion) Party, Socialist Laborites, and Prohibitionists nominate candidates for President, but together receive less than 3% of the popular vote.
10 McKinley (Republican) is reelected President; Theodore

Elsewhere (History and Politics)

12 Umberto I, King of Italy, is assassinated by an anarchist at Monza. He is succeeded by his son, Victor Emmanuel III.
13 Bernhard von Bülow becomes Chancellor of Germany.
14 Macedonian revolutionaries murder several Rumanians, creating tension between the two regions and Bulgaria.
15 Russians fail to secure a naval base in southern Korea.
16 Boxers seize Peking and besiege foreigners there. International expeditionary force fights its way through from Tientsin, lifts the siege, and ends the Boxer Uprising.
17 Anglo-German Yangtze accord maintains the Open Door Policy in Chinese territory in which Britain and Germany have influence.
18 Italy and Ethiopia sign treaty defining the borders of their respective territories in Ethiopia.
19 Italy gives France unrestricted authority in Morocco in exchange for authority in Tripoli.
20 British forces begin the conquest of northern Nigeria.
21 Spain and France sign treaty defining the borders of Spanish Guinea (now Equato-

America (The Arts)

1 Jack London publishes *The Son of the Wolf,* a short story collection.
2 L. Frank Baum, writer and dramatist, publishes *The Wonderful Wizard of Oz,* which is adapted for the stage in 1901. **[1939:ARTS/4]**
3 Theodore Dreiser writes the novel *Sister Carrie.*
4 Playwrights David Belasco, "bishop of Broadway," and John L. Long collaborate on the play *Madame Butterfly.*
5 Tarkington publishes the immensely popular *Monsieur Beaucaire.*
6 Josephine Peabody, writer, publishes the play *Fortune and Men's Eyes.*
7 J.L. Allen publishes *The Reign of Law.*
8 E. Glasgow publishes *The Voice of the People,* the first of several books tracing Virginia's history from 1850.
9 The Philadelphia Orchestra is founded.

Elsewhere (The Arts)

10 Pablo Picasso, one of the most famous Span. painters in the 20th century, exhibits "Le Moulin de la Galette."
11 Beatrix Potter, Eng. author, creates one of the most popular characters in children's literature with *The Tale of Peter Rabbit.*
12 Colette, prominent Fr. author, publishes the first of four autobiographical *Claudine* novels.
13 Fr. composer Gustave Charpentier completes *Louise,* his only opera.
14 Académie des Goncourts is established to award an annual prize, *Prix Goncourt,* for meritorious writing.
15 Conrad publishes *Lord Jim,* a popular sea novel.
16 Rimsky-Korsakov composes *The Tale of Tsar Saltan,* an opera best remembered for "The Flight of the Bumblebee."
17 Arthur Thomas Quiller-Couch compiles *The Oxford Book of*

Science & Technology		Miscellaneous		
America	**Elsewhere**	**America**	**Elsewhere**	
successful methods for treating shock, particularly that resulting from surgery. **4** Jacques Loeb, Ger.-Amer. physiologist, uses chemicals to cause unfertilized sea urchin eggs to develop into larvae. This process, known as parthenogenesis, proves that cell division is controlled chemically.	culture from a purely scientific standpoint. **8** Eng. physiologists William Bayliss and Ernest Starling demonstrate peristalsis (waves of muscle contractions, like those involved in swallowing).	comes world heavyweight boxing champion after knocking out Bob Fitzsimmons. **3** President William McKinley is the first president to ride in an automobile when he takes a spin in a Stanley Steamer. **4** The Gideons, Christian Commercial Men's Association of America, is organized by 3 traveling salesmen in Jamesville, Wisc. First Gideon Bible is placed in the Superior Hotel, Iron Mountain, Mont., in 1908.		
1 Work begins on the New York subway. **2** General Electric establishes a research laboratory in Schenectady, N.Y. **3** Reginald A. Fessenden, physicist, transmits spoken words by radio waves. **4** Elmer A. Sperry, N.Y. electrical engineer, establishes a laboratory in Washington, D.C., for electro-chemical research. **5** Jesse Lazear dies from yellow fever as he is studying the cause of the disease with Walter Reed and others. [1901:SCI/2] **6** There are more than a million miles of telephone lines in the U.S. **7** The U.S. Navy accepts Holland's submarine and rejects Lake's.	**8** Max Planck, Ger. physicist, proposes the quantum theory—that energy occurs in tiny packets called quanta. **9** Niels Bohr, Dan. physicist, proposes a theory of atomic structure in which electrons orbit around a nucleus. **10** Hugo de Vries, Dutch botanist, discovers and reveals the importance of Mendel's work, and studies evolution by studying mutations. **11** Léon Teisserenc de Bort, Fr. meteorologist, suggests that the atmosphere is divided into two layers: the troposphere (lower) and the stratosphere (higher). **12** Karl Landsteiner, Aust. pathologist, discovers that differences in blood types may cause the body's rejection of certain blood transfusions. **13** William Bateson, Eng. geneticist, proposes the now-accepted theory of vertebrate evolution. **14** Köppen devises a mathematical system of climate classification. **15** Kiyoshi develops an antiserum to combat dysentery.	**1** International Ladies' Garment Worker's Union is founded in New York City. Its goal is to shorten the 70-hour workweek and to change a system in which women sewing at home can earn only up to 30¢ a day. **2** U.S. population is 75.9 million, including 3.6 million immigrants that arrived since 1890. New York is the largest city, with a population of 3.4 million; Chicago is second, with 1.6; followed by Philadelphia, with 1.2. Life expectancy is 48 years for males and 51 years for females. **3** Olds Company of Detroit begins the first mass production of automobiles, turning out 400 cars in the first year. **4** Survey of Protestant religious groups shows reformed and evangelical denominations with large followings: Methodists 6 million; Baptists 5; Lutherans 1.5; Presbyterians 1.5; and Christian Scientists, 80,000. **5** Cyclone kills 6000 at Galveston. Winds up to 120 mph drive Gulf waters over land. Looters	**8** First trial flight of the dirigible *Zeppelin* (LZ-1) made in Germany. [1898:MISC/2] **9** Brazil produces most of the world's rubber. **10** First Browning revolvers are manufactured. **11** Eng. archaeologist Sir Arthur Evans begins excavations in Crete. His discoveries bring to light ancient Minoan culture. **12** D.F. Davis presents the international tennis cup bearing his name. **13** World Exhibition is held in Paris.	**1900**

History and Politics		The Arts	
America	**Elsewhere**	**America**	**Elsewhere**
Roosevelt (Republican) is elected Vice President. Republicans retain control of the House and Senate. **11** State Department completes negotiations for the purchase of the Danish West Indies.	rial Guinea). **22** British and the chiefs of Uganda sign treaty, making the kingdom of Buganda a province of the Uganda protectorate and transforming it into a constitutional monarchy. **23** British win victories against the Boers, seizing Ladysmith and Bloemfontein. British annex the Orange Free State and the Transvaal. Boers continue guerrilla warfare. **24** Border between Burma and China is established.		*English Verse 1250–1900.* **18** *Finlandia,* a popular patriotic work by Sibelius, is performed in Helsinki.

1901

America	**Elsewhere**	**America**	**Elsewhere**
1 Pres. McKinley signs the Army Reorganization Bill. U.S. Army Dental Corps and Army Nurse Corps are established. **2** Congress passes the Platt Amendment, making Cuba a U.S. protectorate. Cuba had to append it (1902) to its constitution before U.S. withdrawal from the island. Amendment is repealed in 1934. **3** U.S. military rule in the Philippine Islands ends and a civil government is formed. **[1902:HIST/3]** **4** Insular Cases are decided by the Supreme Court, which states that territory acquired by the U.S. might be subject to the jurisdiction of the U.S. without being part of it. **5** Pres. McKinley is shot by an anarchist at the Pan-American Exposition in Buffalo, N.Y. He dies, and Theodore Roosevelt becomes President. **6** U.S. citizenship is granted to the Indians of the Five Civilized Tribes (Cherokees, Creeks, Choctaws, Chickasaws, and Seminoles). **7** U.S. and Britain sign the second Hay-Pauncefote Treaty, which gives the U.S. the right to build, operate, and fortify any canal across the Isthmus of Panama. **8** Secretary of War Elihu Root estblishes the Army War College.	**9** Commonwealth of Australia is created, with Sir Edmund Barton as Prime Minister. **10** Queen Victoria of Great Britain and Ireland dies and is succeeded by her son Edward VII. **11** Social Revolutionary Party is founded in Russia. It calls for the overthrow of the autocracy, a classless society, and socialization of the land. **12** Russian troops occupy Manchuria under the pretext of restoring order after the Boxer Uprising in China. **[1900:HIST/16]** **13** Kingdom of Ashanti is annexed to the British Gold Coast colony. **14** Anglo-German treaty defines the border between German East Africa and Nyasaland (now Malawi). **15** Boxer protocol forces China to pay an indemnity of $333 million to the foreign powers and to permit the stationing of foreign troops in Peking. **16** New Zealand annexes the Cook Islands. **17** Hirobumi Ito, Prime Minister of Japan, tries unsuccessfully to negotiate a peace settlement with Russia.	**1** Albert Paine, playwright, publishes *The Great White Way,* the title of which becomes a popular nickname for Broadway. **2** Scott Joplin composes "The Easy Winners." **3** Norris publishes *The Octopus,* a realistic novel about California wheat growers. **4** Riis publishes the autobiographical work *The Making of an American.* **5** Lafcadio Hearn writes *A Japanese Miscellany,* his fourth book on Jap. culture. **6** Clyde Fitch writes the plays *The Climbers* and *Captain Jinks of the Horse Marines.* **7** Harrison Grey Fiske opens the Manhattan Theater in New York City.	**8** Ger. novelist Thomas Mann explores middle class values in his first novel, *Buddenbrooks.* **9** Kipling publishes *Kim,* a social novel about an Indian orphan. **10** Shaw publishes the play, *Caesar and Cleopatra.* **11** Munch paints "White Night." **12** Arthur Schnitzler, Aust. writer and psychiatrist, publishes *None But the Brave,* a novel. **13** Elgar composes the first of his famous *Pomp and Circumstance* marches (–1930). **14** Chekhov writes *The Three Sisters,* a play. **15** Maeterlinck publishes *The Life of the Bee,* a philosophical essay. **16** Selma Lagerlöf, Swed. novelist, publishes *Jerusalem.*

Science & Technology		Miscellaneous		
America	**Elsewhere**	**America**	**Elsewhere**	

Theodore Roosevelt, 26th U.S. President

found with finger rings cut from hands of the dead. Property damage amounts to $20 million.

6 New baseball league, the American League, is formed in Chicago.

7 Most Americans travel with help of horse and mules or by bicycles. According to one report, the automobile is "an expensive luxury item for the man who does not need one. It is well named the 'devil wagon.' "

---

1 National Bureau of Standards is established.

2 Walter Reed, surgeon, discovers that yellow fever is caused by a virus and is spread by mosquitoes.

3 Clarence McClung, Pa. zoologist, proposes that an extra (or "X") chromosome determines sex.

4 Eugene L. Opie, pathologist, discovers that the islets of Langerhans (part of the pancreas) are related to diabetes mellitus.

5 Oil is discovered in Texas.

6 Peter C. Hewitt, N.J. electrician, invents a mercury vapor arc lamp.

7 Otis Brothers install an escalator in Gimbels Department Store in Philadelphia, Pa.

8 Meades Ranch, Kansas, is selected as the geodetic center of the U.S.

9 Willis Carrier invents a forerunner of the air conditioner.

10 Lake launches the 60-ft.-long submarine, the *Protector*.

11 Victor Grignard, Fr. chemist, describes the preparation of various organic compounds using organic forms of magnesium (Grignard reagents).

12 Landsteiner demonstrates the existence of three blood groups: A, B, and O.

13 Carl von Linde, Ger. engineer, develops a method for extracting pure liquid oxygen from liquid air.

14 Sir Frederick Hopkins, Eng. biochemist, discovers the amino acid tryptophan.

15 Metchnikoff publishes *Immunity in Infectious Diseases*.

16 Adolf Windaus, Ger. chemist, begins research on cholesterols, which eventually leads him to an understanding of Vitamin D.

17 Nobel Prize, Chemistry: Van't Hoff, for his laws of chemical dynamics and osmotic pressure.

18 Nobel Prize, Physics: Röntgen, for his discovery of x-rays.

19 Nobel Prize, Physiology or Medicine: Von Behring, for his discovery of the diphtheria antitoxin.

1 U.S. Steel Corporation is organized by financiers headed by Elbert H. Gary and J.P. Morgan.

2 First significant oil strike in Texas at Spindletop, near Beaumont. Control of state changing, with oilmen taking over from cattlemen and railroadmen.

3 First American Bowling Club tournament is held in Chicago.

4 President Theodore Roosevelt urges "Speak softly and carry a big stick" to emphasize the need for strong official policy. The saying becomes very popular, particularly among cartoonists.

5 King C. Gillette begins manufacturing modern safety razor with disposable blades.

6 Fire in Jacksonville, Fla., destroys 1700 buildings, causes $11 million damage, and leaves 10,000 persons homeless.

7 "Iron Man" Joe McGinnity is expelled from the National League for stepping on an umpire's toes, spitting in his face, and punching him. After being fined and officially reprimanded, he is later reinstated because of the fans' pleas.

9 China's population is 350 million; India's, 294; Russia's, 146; Germany's, 56.3; Japan's, 45.4; Great Britain and Ireland's, 41.4; France's, 38.9; Italy's, 32.4; Austria's, 26.1.

10 First British submarine is launched.

11 Boxing is recognized as a legal sport in England.

12 Wilhelm Maybach, technical director at the Daimler works, builds the first Mercedes car.

13 Marconi sends messages by wireless telegraphy from Cornwall to Newfoundland.

14 Eng. colonial administrator Cecil Rhodes' Transcontinental Telegraph Company line reaches Ujiji from Abercorn in eastern Africa.

1901

History and Politics		The Arts	
America	**Elsewhere**	**America**	**Elsewhere**

1902

America (History and Politics)

1 U.S. signs treaty with Denmark for the purchase of the Danish West Indies, but Danish Parliament rejects it. [1917:HIST/2]
2 Maryland passes the first state workmen's compensation law.
3 Chinese Exclusion Act is extended to prohibit the immigration of Chinese from the Philippine Islands. [1892:HIST/2]
4 Congress establishes the permanent Census Bureau.
5 Congress declares the Philippine Islands an unorganized territory.
6 Pres. Roosevelt appoints commission to settle the strike by anthracite coal miners demanding union recognition, an eight-hour day, and a wage increase—first federal government action on behalf of labor.
7 Oregon becomes the first state to adopt the use of the initiative and referendum. People can initiate popular vote on laws and override rulings by the legislature.
8 Congress passes the Spooner Act, authorizing the financing and building of the Panama Canal. [1901:HIST/7]
9 Reclamation Act provides funds from the sale of public lands to finance the irrigation of arid Western areas. President is given authority to retain public lands for public use as parks.

Elsewhere (History and Politics)

10 Sultan introduces program of reforms to pacify revolutionaries in Macedonia. Bulgarian, Serbian, and Greek bands continue to instigate revolution in Macedonia.
11 Anglo-Japanese alliance recognizes the independence of China and Korea and Japan's special interests in Korea.
12 Treaty of Vereeniging ends the South African (Boer) War. Boers accept British sovereignty.
13 Triple Alliance between Germany, Austria, and Italy is renewed for another six years.
14 British, German, and Italian naval forces blockade Venezuela in order to press their claims for payment of foreign properties damaged during civil disturbances in Venezuela.
15 Colombia refuses to recognize Panama's declaration of independence.
16 Britain and Ethiopia sign treaty defining the border of Sudan. Ethiopia gives up claims to territory on the Nile River.
17 Portuguese troops suppress native rebellion in Angola.
18 Arthur James Balfour becomes British Prime Minister.
19 International Arbitration Court opens at The Hague, Holland.

America (The Arts)

1 Edith Wharton, writer, publishes *The Valley of Decision.*
2 Owen Wister, novelist, publishes *The Virginian,* the novel which created many of the themes of U.S. cowboy folklore.
3 Frank Lloyd Wright, architect, completes the Ward Willitts House in Illinois, the first of his "prairie style" homes.
4 Alfred Stieglitz, "father of modern photography," founds the Photo-Secession, an organization designed to promote photography as an art form.
5 Ives completes his second symphony, which is not performed until 1951.
6 H. James publishes *The Wings of the Dove.*
7 Clyde Fitch writes his best known work, *The Girl With the Green Eyes.*

Elsewhere (The Arts)

8 Doyle publishes *The Hound of the Baskervilles,* a Sherlock Holmes mystery set shortly before the detective's death (1893).
9 John Masefield, Eng. poet, publishes *Salt-Water Ballads,* a collection that includes "Sea Fever."
10 Méliès directs the film, *A Trip to the Moon.*
11 Kipling publishes *Just So Stories,* a collection of animal fables for children.
12 Barrie publishes *The Admirable Crichton,* a humorous play about a butler who becomes the ruler of a desert island.
13 Conrad publishes *Heart of Darkness,* a story based on his voyages on the Congo River in Africa.
14 Debussy's only complete opera, *Pelléas et Mélisande,* is based on a libretto by Maeterlinck. [1892:ARTS/7]
15 Maxim Gorki, Russ. author, writes the tragedy, *The Lower Depths.*
16 Eng. composer Frederick Delius, inspired by America's mountains, composes the orchestral *Appalachia.*

1903

America (History and Politics)

1 Wisconsin enacts the first direct primary law.
2 U.S. signs treaty with Colombia to dig the Panama Canal, but Colombian Senate rejects it.
3 U.S. Department of Com-

Elsewhere (History and Politics)

10 Dutch government uses troops to break up railroad and dock strikes, inciting the forces of trade-unionism and socialism.
11 Giovanni Giolitti becomes Italian Premier. He in-

America (The Arts)

1 Jack London publishes *Call of the Wild.*
2 Victor Herbert, composer, completes the operetta *Babes in Toyland.*
3 Willa Cather, poet

Elsewhere (The Arts)

10 Paul Klee, Swiss artist prominent in the development of modern art, produces the etching, "Two Men Meet, Each Supposing the Other to Be of Higher

Science & Technology		Miscellaneous		
America	**Elsewhere**	**America**	**Elsewhere**	
		8 *New York in a Blizzard,* one of the first panoramic films, is shown. A new device on motion-picture cameras makes it possible to rotate ("pan") the camera.		
1 Fessenden invents a very sensitive electrolytic detector that greatly increases the range of wireless communication. **2** Gibbs publishes *Elementary Principles in Statistical Mechanics,* a work later applied to research in quantum mechanics. **3** Florence M. Bailey, N.Y. ornithologist, publishes *Handbook of Birds of the Western United States.* **4** Walter Sutton, geneticist, claims that chromosomes occur in pairs and carry the units of heredity. **5** Charles W. Stiles, physician, discovers the hookworm, a widespread parasite in the South. **6** William C. Gorgas, Ala. army surgeon, controls an epidemic of yellow fever in Havana, Cuba, by killing mosquitoes and destroying their breeding areas. **7** Telegraph cable is laid from California to Hawaii.	**8** Robert Bosch, Ger. engineer, invents the spark plug. **9** Landsteiner discovers the AB blood group. **10** Marie and Pierre Curie determine the properties of radium. **11** Lord Rutherford discovers the positively-charged proton and determines that radioactivity is the process by which one element decomposes into another element. **12** Nobel Prize, Chemistry: Emil Fischer, Ger. chemist, for his research into sugars and purines. **13** Nobel Prize, Physics: Dutch physicists Pieter Zeeman and Hendrik Lorenz for their discovery of the Zeeman effect (the effect of magnetism on radiation). **14** Nobel Prize, Physiology or Medicine: Ross, for discovering the life cycle of the malaria parasite.	**1** About 150,000 United Mine Workers in Pennsylvania strike when mine operators refuse their request for a 20% wage increase and an 8-hour day. Strike is settled in March 1903 when the miners are given a 10% increase in wages. The operators continue to reject the union. **2** Pres. Theodore Roosevelt publishes *Outdoor Pastimes of an American Hunter,* marking the beginning of an interest in open-air living. He is joined by Stewart Edward, John Muir, and John Burroughs, who publish many books and articles on outdoor living. **3** Blue uniforms of U.S. Army are changed for olive drab. Experience during Spanish-American war showed that blue is too easily seen. **4** First postseason football game is held at the Tournament of Roses. Michigan beats Stanford, 49-0. **5** National Education Association adopts simplified spellings for 12 words: *program, tho, altho, thoro, thorofare, thru, thruout, catalog, prolog, decalog, demagog, pedagog.*	**6** King Edward VII establishes the Order of Merit, limited to 24 British subjects at any one time. **7** Martinique volcanic fire destroys the town of St. Pierre in the West Indies. **8** J.M. Bacon is the first to cross the Irish Channel in a balloon. **9** Education Act in England brings denominational schools (those affiliated with particular religions) under the state system.	**1902**
1 Orville Wright and Wilbur Wright, Ohio bicycle makers, launch the world's first successful manned flight in a motorized airplane. The flight, at Kitty Hawk, N.C., cov-	**7** William Einthoven, Dutch physiologist, invents the electrocardiograph, an instrument used to record heart contractions by detecting electrical changes.	**1** First trip by automobile across the U.S. is completed. A Packard car arrives in New York City 52 days after leaving San Francisco. **2** Boston, of the Ameri-	**9** Ger. explorer Hans Meyer climbs and explores Chimborazo, a 20,702-foot volcano in the Andes in Ecuador. **10** First Tour de France bicycle race.	**1903**

| History and Politics | | The Arts | |
America	Elsewhere	America	Elsewhere
merce and Labor is established. **4** Treaty between the U.S. and Britain creates joint commission to settle the Alaskan boundary dispute. Commission gives the U.S. ocean outlets of the Alaskan panhandle. **5** Expedition Act gives antitrust cases precedence in Circuit Courts. **6** Supreme Court declares Congress has the right to prohibit the transfer of lottery tickets from one state to another—first time federal police power exceeds that of the states. **7** Elkins Act strengthens the Interstate Commerce Act of 1887, forbidding railroads to deviate from published rates and holding railroad companies liable in cases of rebating. **8** Pres. Roosevelt orders warships to Panama to protect "free and uninterrupted transit" across the isthmus. Panama Canal Company helps separatist movement in Panama against Colombia. U.S. recognizes the independent Republic of Panama. **9** U.S. and Panama sign Hay-Bunau-Varilla Treaty, which gives the U.S. a 10-mile strip of land across Panama for $10 million and an annual payment of $250,000.	troduces social, agrarian, and labor reform. **12** Russian Social Democratic Party at its London congress splits into Mensheviks and Bolsheviks. Vladimir Ilyich Lenin leads radical wing of the Bolsheviks and advocates revolution. He hopes to destroy capitalism and establish an international socialist state. **13** Peter I becomes King of Serbia, restoring the Karageorgevich dynasty to the throne. **14** Bolivia cedes the Arce territory to Brazil. **15** Panama proclaims itself an independent republic. **16** French Congo is divided into four colonies: Gabon, Chad, Ubangi-Shari, and Middle Congo.	and novelist, publishes her first book of poems, *April Twilights.* **4** Stieglitz founds the quarterly magazine *Camera Work.* **5** Kate Douglas Wiggin, novelist, publishes *Rebecca of Sunnybrook Farm.* **6** Howard Pyle writes and illustrates *The Story of King Arthur and His Knights.* **7** Edwin S. Porter, first film director to use dramatic editing, directs *The Life of an American Fireman,* the first U.S. documentary, and *The Great Train Robbery,* which sets many patterns for future Westerns. **8** Arnold Daly, actor, produces a very successful version of Shaw's *Candida.* **9** *The Pit,* a novel by Frank Norris set in Chicago, is published posthumously.	Rank." **11** In *Man and Superman,* a play that includes the popular dream scene, "Don Juan in Hell," Shaw introduces his theory of "life force." **12** Hugo von Hofmannsthal, Aust. writer, publishes *Elektra.* **13** Butler's greatest work, the autobiographical *The Way of All Flesh,* criticizes domineering parents and excessively rigid religions. **14** Picasso paints "La Vie," a work representative of his celebrated "blue period." **15** Käthe Kollwitz, Ger. artist, begins "The Peasant War" (–1908), a series of revolutionary etchings.
1904 **1** Supreme Court rules that Puerto Ricans are not aliens, though they are not classified as U.S. citizens. **[1917:HIST/3]** **2** William Howard Taft becomes Secretary of War. **3** Socialist Party nominates Debs for President. **4** Supreme Court rules the holding company of Northern Securities violates the Sherman Antitrust Act of 1890. **5** U.S. protests the seizure of asphalt holdings in Venezuela. **6** People's Party, Socialist	**9** France and Britain sign Entente Cordiale, ending antagonisms between them. **10** Japan breaks diplomatic relations with Russia and attacks Port Arthur, bringing on the Russo-Japanese War. Japanese defeat Russians at Liaoyang and Sha-ho, China. **11** Serbia becomes nationalistic and anti-Austrian. **12** France concludes a secret treaty with Spain to partition Morocco. **13** Treaty between Bolivia and Chile formally ends the War of the Pacific. Chile ac-	**1** George M. Cohan, composer, playwright, and producer, writes the Broadway show *Little Johnny Jones,* which includes the songs "Give My Regards to Broadway" and "The Yankee Doodle Boy." **2** Jack London publishes *The Sea Wolf.* **3** Joel Chandler Harris publishes *The Tar Baby.* **4** H. James publishes *The Golden Bowl.*	**8** Barrie publishes *Peter Pan.* **9** Puccini composes the opera, *Madama Butterfly.* **10** G.K. Chesterton, Eng. writer, publishes *The Napoleon of Notting Hill,* a political novel. **11** Max Beerbohm, Eng. writer and caricaturist, publishes *Poets Corner,* a collection of drawings. **12** Yeats writes the play, *On Baile's*

Science & Technology

America | Elsewhere

Miscellaneous

America | Elsewhere

ered 852 ft. and lasted 59 seconds.

2 An experimental electrical trolley is installed in Scranton, Pa. It runs in the streets and is powered by overhead wires.

3 Sutton publishes *The Chromosomes in Heredity* and concludes that chromosomes carry genes.

4 A marine biology station, later known as Scripps Institution of Oceanography, is established in La Jolla, Calif.

5 Theobald Smith, pathologist, demonstrates anaphylaxis, an intense reaction to an injected substance.

6 Michael Owens invents a bottlemaking machine.

8 Ramsay shows that helium is produced during the radioactive decay of radium, an important concept in nuclear reactions.

9 Rutherford determines the properties of alpha rays.

10 Richard Zsigmondy, Ger. chemist, develops the ultramicroscope for studying tiny particles.

11 J.J. Thomson publishes *Conduction of Electricity Through Gases*.

12 Poulsen invents a device which generates continuous radio waves, an important step in the growth of radio communication.

13 Nobel Prize, Chemistry: Arrhenius, for his theory of ionization.

14 Nobel Prize, Physics: Becquerel, for his discovery of radioactivity, and Marie and Pierre Curie, for their discovery of radioactive phenomena.

15 Nobel Prize, Physiology or Medicine: Finsen, for his founding of phototherapy (the treatment of disease by light).

can League, wins the first annual World Series, beating Pittsburgh, 5 to 3.

3 *The Passion Play,* one of the longest motion pictures shown up to this time, runs for 30 min. Average films run between 3 and 4 min.

4 Richard Stieff designs the first teddy bears, named after Pres. Theodore Roosevelt.

5 Henry Ford organizes and becomes president of the Ford Motor Company.

6 First male motion-picture star appears in *The Great Train Robbery*. He is known as Max Aronson, "Broncho Billy," Max Anderson, and G.M. Anderson.

7 Fire in Iroquois Theater, Chicago, during a performance by comedian Eddie Foy, kills 588 people. Disaster leads to new theater codes: more fire walls, better and more exits, unobstructed alleyways, and fireproof scenery.

8 First Pacific cable opens. President Roosevelt sends a message around the world; it comes back to him in 12 min.

11 Eng. suffragist leader Emmeline Pankhurst founds the National Women's Social and Political Union.

12 First motor taxis appear in London.

13 Number of battleships in service: Great Britain, 67; France, 39; Germany, 27; Italy, 18; Russia, 18; Japan, 5.

14 Regulations in Britain set a 20 mph speed limit for automobiles.

---

1 Osler establishes the National Tuberculosis Association, later known as the American Lung Association. He publishes *Aequanimitas,* a collection of his lectures.

2 Hall publishes *Adolescence,* a 2-volume psychology text.

3 Rockefeller Institute for Medical Research opens in New York City.

4 Gorgas begins controlling yellow fever in Panama.

5 Hale organizes the

8 Sir James Jeans, Eng. physicist, publishes *The Dynamical Theory of Gases*.

9 Arthur Korn, Ger. physicist, becomes the first to transmit a photograph by telegraphic circuit.

10 John A. Fleming, Eng. engineer, builds the first electron tube and uses it to change alternating current to direct current.

11 Johan Vogt, Norw. geologist, publishes *The*

1 Fire in Baltimore destroys 2600 buildings in an 80-block area of the business district. Fire burns for 30 hrs.; it is the biggest fire since the great Chicago fire in 1871. Loss is estimated at $80 million.

2 "Hero Fund" of $5 million is established by Carnegie for those who risk their lives to rescue others and for survivors of those who lose their lives attempting a rescue.

3 First section of the

9 Rolls-Royce Company is founded in England.

10 10-hour work day is established in France.

11 Serious famine in northern Nigeria.

12 Steamer *Norge* is wrecked on Rockall Reef, east of Scotland; 590 persons are lost.

1904

History and Politics		The Arts	
America	**Elsewhere**	**America**	**Elsewhere**

Laborites, and Prohibitionists again nominate separate candidates for President. [1900:HIST/9]

7 Theodore Roosevelt and Charles W. Fairbanks are elected President and Vice President, respectively, on the Republican ticket. Republicans remain in control of the House and Senate.

8 Pres. Roosevelt asserts right of the U.S. to intervene in Latin American affairs in order to maintain order and to prevent European intervention. It becomes known as the Roosevelt Corollary to the Monroe Doctrine of 1823.

quires Atacama. [1883:HIST/13]

14 Rafael Reyes becomes President of Colombia.

15 Hereros and Hottentots rebel against German rule in German South West Africa (now Namibia). They are suppressed by 1907.

16 Dutch subdue the Achinese in northern Sumatra, thus completing pacification of the island.

5 Scott Joplin composes "The Cascades."

6 O. Henry, the penname for short story writer William Sidney Porter, publishes *Cabbages and Kings,* a collection of stories about Latin America.

7 Hearn publishes *Japan, an Attempt at an Interpretation,* a collection of essays which foresee a war between the U.S. and Japan.

Strand, for the opening of the Abbey Theater (Dublin).

13 Romain Rolland introduces the novel cycle into Fr. literature with the publication of *Jean Christophe* (-1912).

14 Chekhov writes *The Cherry Orchard,* a play.

15 "Christ of the Andes," a huge bronze statue designed by Arg. sculptor Mateo Alonzo, is dedicated as a symbol of peace between Chile and Argentina.

16 London Symphony Orchestra gives its first performance.

1905

1 Pres. Roosevelt initiates peace conference at Portsmouth, N.H., that ends the Russo-Japanese War. He is awarded the Nobel Peace Prize (1906) for his role as mediator.

2 Industrial Workers of the World, radical labor organization, is founded in Chicago by Debs.

3 U.S. signs agreement with Santo Domingo assuming charge of finances with the purpose of satisfying European creditors of Santo Domingo.

4 U.S. signs an extradition treaty with Sweden and Norway.

5 Elihu Root succeeds John Hay as Secretary of State.

6 New York legislature holds last of 57 hearings investigating scandals in the life insurance business in New York state. Hearings lead to

8 German Emperor William II visits Tangier and declares support for Morocco's independence and integrity. France had offered to make Morocco a protectorate.

9 Japanese seize Port Arthur from the Russians, who are then defeated at Mukden, China. Russian fleet is destroyed at Tsushima. Treaty of Portsmouth ends Russo-Japanese War. Japan receives the Liaotung Peninsula and the railroads in southern Manchuria.

10 Workers petitioning Czar Nicholas II are fired upon by Russian troops ("Bloody Sunday"). General strike forces Nicholas to sign October Manifesto promising representative government and civil liberties.

11 Greeks in Crete, demanding union with Greece, rebel against Turks.

1 Stieglitz opens Little Galleries of the Photo-Secession, also called "291" from its N.Y.C. street number. The gallery is important in introducing modern art to the U.S. and promoting photography as an art form. [1902:ARTS/4]

2 Thomas Dixon, novelist, publishes *The Clansman,* a sympathetic look at the Ku Klux Klan. [1915:ARTS/3]

3 Zane Grey, writer of "dime" novels, publishes *The Spirit of the Border.*

4 Wharton's *The House of Mirth* brings the writer public recognition.

5 The first nickelodeon in the U.S.

11 Matisse exhibits "Woman With the Hat," a sensational painting that prompts one critic to refer to Matisse and other painters at the Salon d'Automne as "les fauves" ("the wild beasts"). Fauvism, the first major art movement in the 20th century, is marked by the use of bold colors.

12 In *Biography for Beginners,* Edmund Clerihew Bentley, Eng. writer, introduces the "clerihew," a 4-line biography consisting of two rhyming couplets.

13 A famous trio is formed by Span. cellist Pablo Casals, Fr. pianist Alfred-Denis Cortot, and Fr. violinist Jacques Thibaud.

Science & Technology		Miscellaneous		
America	**Elsewhere**	**America**	**Elsewhere**	

Mount Wilson Observatory in California.
6 Diesel engines are brought to America.
7 Charles D. Perrine, astronomer, discovers the sixth moon of Jupiter.

Albert Einstein, German physicist, 1921 Nobel Prize Winner

Molten Silicate Solution, an important work on igneous rocks.
12 Freud publishes *Psychopathology of Everyday Life.*
13 Ludwig Prandtl, Ger. physicist, discovers the boundary level of fluids.
14 V. Bjerknes publishes *Weather Forecasting as a Problem in Mechanics and Physics.*
15 Starling coins the term *hormone.*
16 Nobel Prize, Chemistry: Ramsay, for discovering the elements helium, neon, argon, krypton, and xenon.
17 Nobel Prize, Physics: Rayleigh, for isolating the element argon.
18 Nobel Prize, Physiology or Medicine: Pavlov, for his research in digestive gland physiology.

New York City subway begins service. The line later becomes the first subway to run underground and in underwater tunnels.
4 First "perfect" major league game pitched by Cy Young of Boston Americans who does not allow a single Philadelphia player to reach first base.
5 Frank J. Marshall of Brooklyn wins the international masters' chess tournament without losing a game.
6 Popularity of jiu-jitsu started by Pres. Roosevelt, who has a Japanese instructor come regularly to the White House.
7 Woman arrested in New York City for smoking a cigarette while riding in an open automobile.
8 First Olympic Games held in U.S. as part of Exposition in St. Louis, Mo. U.S. wins 21 events.

1 Lowell predicts the existence of "Planet X" beyond Neptune.
[1930:SCI/1]
2 McClung determines that females have "XX" sex chromosomes while males have "XY."
3 Albert Einhorn, physician, produces "procaine," a local anesthetic commonly known by its trade name, Novocain.
4 Crile performs the first direct blood transfusion.
5 Frederick G. Cottrell, Calif. chemist, invents an electrical precipitator that removes dust and particles from the air. It is later used as a pollution control device.
6 U.S. Supreme Court rules that states may legally require vaccinations.
7 *Mrs. Winslow's Soothing Syrup,* popular for

10 Richard Willstätter, Ger. chemist, determines the structure of the pigment chlorophyll.
11 John Scott Haldane, Scot. physiologist, determines that breathing is regulated by the effect of carbon dioxide on the brain.
12 Freud publishes *Jokes and Their Relation with the Unconscious* and *Three Essays on the Theory of Sexuality.*
13 Albert Einstein, Ger. physicist, proposes the special theory of relativity and the equation $E = MC^2$. In other papers, he explains Brownian movement and proposes the quantum theory of light to explain the photoelectric effect.
14 Marconi patents the horizontal directional

1 First Rotary Club is founded in Chicago. Clubs consist of at least one member of each business or profession and meetings are held at each member's office in rotation.
2 In this and the following year, George Santayana, teacher of philosophy at Harvard University, publishes his 5-volume *The Life of Reason.*
3 New York Central's "Twentieth Century Limited" and the Pennsylvania Railroad's long-distance train travel between New York City and Chicago in 18 hours. Chicago and North-western Railway runs the first train equipped with electric lights, from Chicago to California.

8 Cullinan diamond, at more than 3000 carats, is the largest diamond.
9 Motor buses first used in London.

1905

History and Politics		The Arts	
America	**Elsewhere**	**America**	**Elsewhere**
wide reform. **7** Supreme Court rules unconstitutional a New York state law regulating the hours of bakery workers.	**12** Alberta and Saskatchewan become provinces in Canada. **13** Norwegian Storting (Parliament) declares the dissolution of the union with Sweden; Sweden acquiesces after the decision is ratified by plebiscite. Norway becomes a monarchy and Haakon VII is elected King of Norway. **14** Native uprising breaks out in the French Congo. **15** Reform movement begins in Persia, protesting the incompetent shah, the corrupt government, and the spread of foreign interests. **16** Sinn Fein (Irish nationalist movement) is organized in Dublin. **17** British New Guinea becomes an Australian possession as the Territory of Papua. **18** Sun Yat-sen organizes a revolutionary league, the T'ung Meng Hui, to expel the Manchus from China.	opens in Pittsburgh. **6** Vachel Lindsay, poet, publishes *The Trees of Laughing Bells,* a collection of poems. **7** Jack London publishes *The Game,* about the tragic life of a prizefighter. **8** Cather publishes *The Troll Garden,* a collection of short stories. **9** Tarkington publishes *The Conquest of Canaan.* **10** Daly is arrested and later acquitted for producing Shaw's *Mrs. Warren's Profession.*	**14** Franz Lehár, Hung. composer, completes his best-known opera, *The Merry Widow.* **15** Wilde's *De Profundis,* a bitter letter written (while imprisoned) to Douglas, is published. [1898:ARTS/12] **16** Doyle succumbs to public pressure and publishes *The Return of Sherlock Holmes.* [1893:ARTS/7] **17** Rainer Maria Rilke, Ger. poet considered a founder of modern literature, publishes *Das Stunden-Buch,* a poem cycle. **18** Shaw writes *Major Barbara.* **19** Michel Fokine, influential Russ. choreographer, composes *The Dying Swan* for ballerina Anna Pavlova.
1906			
1 Congress passes Employers' Liability Act, but the Supreme Court declares it unconstitutional in 1908. **2** Pure Food and Drug Act prohibits the sale of adulterated (impure) foods and drugs and requires statement of contents on labels. **3** Meat Inspection Act is passed by Congress as a result of public disclosure of unclean conditions in Chicago meat-packing plants. **4** Pres. Roosevelt sends U.S. troops to quell revolt and restore order in Cuba. **5** Railroad Rate Bill gives federal government the right to set rates for interstate commerce. **6** Supreme Court rules that witnesses in antitrust cases may be compelled to testify against their corporations and hand over relevant documents. **7** Troops put down anti-Negro riot in Atlanta, Ga., which is placed under martial law.	**8** Algeciras Conference reaffirms French and Spanish control in Morocco. **9** First Duma (representative assembly) meets to reform laws in Russia. Czar Nicholas II dissolves it after ten weeks. Piotr Arkadevich Stolypin becomes Russian Premier; he suppresses revolutionary movement. **10** Britain, France, and Italy sign pact defining their spheres of influence in Ethiopia and agree not to interfere with one another. **11** Lagos is annexed to the British protectorate of southern Nigeria. **12** British ultimatum forces Turkey to renounce claims to the Sinai Peninsula, which becomes Egyptian territory. **13** French Supreme Court of Appeals exonerates Dreyfus, who is reinstated as a major and awarded the Legion of Honor. [1894:HIST/7] **14** Sir Henry Campbell-Bannerman becomes British	**1** Upton Sinclair, writer, publishes *The Jungle.* The book's lurid description of the meat packing industry causes the passage of food inspection laws. **2** Cohan writes two shows: *Forty-five Minutes from Broadway,* which features the song "Mary's a Grand Old Name," and *George Washington, Jr.,* which includes the song "You're a Grand Old Flag." **3** Herbert composes *The Red Mill.* **4** Jack London publishes *White Fang.* **5** O. Henry's *The Four Million* includes his most famous work "The Gift of the Magi." **6** Edward Stratemeyer, writer, founds the Stratemeyer Literary Syndicate which, under	**7** John Galsworthy, Eng. writer, publishes *The Man of Property,* the first novel in the series, *The Forsyte Saga.* **8** Ralph Vaughan Williams, prominent Eng. composer, completes the first of his *Norfolk Rhapsodies* and publishes *The English Hymnal.* **9** Monet begins his "Les Nymphéas" series of paintings (–1926). **10** Paul Claudel, prominent Fr. writer, writes the autobiographical play, *Partage de midi.* **11** Hermann Hesse, Ger. writer, publishes *Beneath the Wheel,* a novel. **12** Georges Rouault, Fr. artist, paints "Before a Mirror," a watercolor in which a prostitute symbolizes the

Science & Technology		Miscellaneous		
America	Elsewhere	America	Elsewhere	

easing a baby's teething pain, is shown to contain morphine.

8 Perrine discovers the seventh moon of Jupiter.

9 Wilson describes the importance of the chromosomes in determining sex and other characteristics.

aerial.

15 The International Conference on Electrical Units is held in Berlin, Germany.

16 Nobel Prize, Chemistry: Baeyer, for his research on organic dyes.

17 Nobel Prize, Physics: Lenard, for his cathode ray research.

18 Nobel Prize, Physiology or Medicine: Koch, for his tuberculosis research and development of the field of bacteriology.

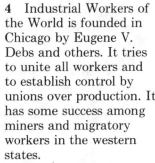
Marie Curie, Polish chemist and physicist in France, in her laboratory

4 Industrial Workers of the World is founded in Chicago by Eugene V. Debs and others. It tries to unite all workers and to establish control by unions over production. It has some success among miners and migratory workers in the western states.

5 Severe yellow fever epidemic in New Orleans lasts from July to Oct. Finally brought under control by U.S. government's antimosquito campaign. There are 3000 cases, about 400 deaths.

6 Number of registered automobiles rises to 77,988, as compared to only 300 ten years earlier. Automobile is still considered a toy by most people.

7 A 5¢ cinema in Pittsburgh shows *The Great Train Robbery.*

---

1 Lee DeForest, "Father of the Radio," invents the "triode," a 3-element vacuum tube.

2 Fessenden broadcasts the first radio program of voice and music.

3 Edison invents the "cameraphone," a device that synchronizes a phonograph and a projector for sound motion pictures.

4 Ernest F. Alexanderson, electrical engineer, invents a high-frequency generator that produces powerful, continuous-wave radio signals.

5 Albert I, prince of Monaco, founds the Oceanographic Institute.

6 Jeans publishes *Theoretical Mechanics.*

7 Bordet discovers the bacterium that causes whooping cough.

8 Enrico Forlanini, Ital. inventor, builds the first hydrofoil boat.

9 Following Pierre Curie's sudden death in a traffic accident, Marie Curie is appointed to her late husband's position, thus becoming the first woman professor at the Sorbonne.

10 Sir Charles Sherrington, Eng. physiologist, publishes *The Integrative Action of the Nervous System,* in which he divides the sense organs into three general groups.

11 Max Wolf, Ger. astronomer, discovers Achilles, an asteroid that follows Jupiter's orbit.

1 The word *muckraker,* taken from Bunyan's *Pilgrim's Progress,* first used by Pres. Roosevelt. It refers to authors who bring about reform by exposing unpleasant or corrupt aspects of American life.

2 "Typhoid Mary," a carrier of typhoid fever who has worked as a cook in institutions and private homes, is finally found after 8 years. Although healthy, she is confined by health authorities for 23 years, until her death.

3 Most severe earthquake in U.S. history, followed by fire, destroys most of San Francisco's central area. Damage is estimated at about $400 million, and nearly 700 persons are killed.

4 Pres. Roosevelt dedicates Devil's Tower, Wyoming, the first national monument. A natural tower of rock, it tapers

5 Russia's army numbers 13 million; Germany's, 7.9; France's, 4.8; Italy's, 3.1; Great Britain's (including colonial forces), 1.1.

6 Norw. explorer Roald Amundsen navigates the Northwest Passage and determines the position of the magnetic North Pole.

7 Italian steamer *Sirio* is wrecked off Cape Palos, Spain; 350 persons die.

8 British Patent Act provides greater protection for inventors.

9 Earthquake in Valparaiso, Chile; 20,000 are killed.

10 Clemens von Pirquet introduces the term *allergy* to medicine.

11 London's population is 4.5 million; Paris' 2.7; Berlin's 2; Tokyo's 1.9; and Vienna's 1.3.

12 Coal mine explosion and fire kills 1060 people in Courrières, France.

1906

History and Politics		The Arts	
America	**Elsewhere**	**America**	**Elsewhere**
	Prime Minister. He introduces many liberal reforms. **15** Giolitti is reelected Italian Premier. **16** Aga Khan III establishes the All-India Muslim League and works for Muslim support of British rule in India.	various pennames, pumps out series of children's books like *Tom Swift, The Bobbsey Twins, The Hardy Boys,* and *Nancy Drew.*	decay of society. **13** Dmitri Merezhkovsky, Russ. writer, publishes *Gogol and the Devil,* an important critical work.
1907 **1** Japan in "Gentlemen's Agreement" recognizes the right of the U.S. to refuse Japanese laborers entry into the U.S. **2** U.S. Marines land in Honduras to protect U.S. lives and property threatened by revolutionaries. **3** Second Hague Peace Conference upholds the Monroe Doctrine by stating that armed force must not be used to collect any debts owed by a North or South American nation. **4** Oklahoma, formerly Oklahoma and Indian Territories, becomes 46th state. Congress refuses to allow state to be named after Sequoyah, Indian creator of the Cherokee alphabet. **5** Alabama and Georgia adopt state prohibition laws. **6** Secretary of War Taft directs the Panama Canal Commission to appoint George W. Goethals chief engineer of the canal project. **7** U.S. Navy ("Great White Fleet") sails to Pacific and around the world to exhibit U.S. naval power. **8** Central American Peace Conference meets in Washington, D.C., and establishes a Central American court of justice.	**9** Universal direct suffrage, demanded by the socialists, is instituted in Austria. **10** Anglo-Russian Entente settles issues over Persia, Afghanistan, and Tibet. **11** Second Duma is dissolved; third Duma, elected by an electoral change, is controlled by the Russian government. **[1906:HIST/9]** **12** Military forces put down peasant uprising in Moldavia. **13** Triple Alliance between Germany, Austria, and Italy is renewed for another six years. **14** French bombard and occupy Casablanca, Morocco, after anti-foreign outbreaks. **15** Transvaal and the Orange Free State are granted self-government by the British. **16** British and French agree on the independence of Siam (now Thailand), but also claim spheres of influence. **17** France and Japan sign treaty guaranteeing Open Door Policy in China. **18** Russia and Japan agree to special spheres of influence in Manchuria. **19** New Zealand becomes a dominion within the British Empire. **20** Gustavus V becomes King of Sweden. **21** Honduras is defeated in short war with Nicaragua.	**1** Florenz Ziegfeld, theatrical producer, produces *The Follies of 1907,* an elaborate show featuring comedy, dancing girls, and a musical score by Victor Herbert. **2** John French Sloane, painter, paints the melancholy "Wake of the Ferry." **3** Thomas Joseph Shahan, Roman Catholic priest, founds *The Catholic Encyclopedia.* **4** O. Henry publishes two collections of short stories: *Heart of the West* and *The Trimmed Lamp.* **5** Joel Chandler Harris founds *Uncle Remus's Magazine.*	**6** John Millington Synge, Ir. writer, produces *The Playboy of the Western World,* a play that causes a riot at its premiere at the Abbey Theater, Dublin. **7** Picasso paints "Les Demoiselles d'Avignon." A landmark in modern art, its distorted geometric figures and unconventional style mark the beginning of Cubism. **8** Rilke's lyric poems, *Neue Gedichte* (–1908), represent a major break with traditional styles. **9** Vaslav Nijinsky, outstanding Russ. ballet dancer and choreographer, makes his debut in *La Source* at the Mariinsky Theater. **10** Rimsky-Korsakov wins international acclaim for his opera, *The Golden Cockerel.* **11** Strindberg publishes *The Ghost Sonata,* a mystical drama. **12** Gorki publishes *Mother,* a novel. **13** Conrad publishes *The Secret Agent,* a novel. **14** Aristide Maillol, Fr. sculptor, exhibits "Portrait Head of Renoir."
1908 **1** Supreme Court rules that a labor union's boycott of industry restricts trade and is	**9** King Carlos I is assassinated in a public square in Lisbon.	**1** Ezra Pound, influential writer of the period, publishes his first	**9** Chesterton publishes *The Man Who Was Thursday,* a popu-

Science & Technology		Miscellaneous		
America	**Elsewhere**	**America**	**Elsewhere**	
	12 Nobel Prize, Physics: J.J. Thomson, for his research into the conduction of electricity by gases. **13** Nobel Prize, Physiology or Medicine: Golgi and Span. scientist Santiago Ramon y Cajal, for their research on the nervous system and cell distribution.	from 1000 ft. at the base to 275 ft. at the top.	**13** 12½-mile long Simplon Tunnel connects Italy and Switzerland in the Alps. **14** H.M.S. *Dreadnought* is launched, a battleship armed with heavy-caliber guns in turrets; speed 20 knots. **15** Typhoon at Hong Kong kills about 10,000 people.	
1 Osler and Thomas McCrae publish the seven-volume *Modern Medicine, Its Theory and Practice.* **2** Thomas Hunt Morgan, geneticist, discovers that chromosomes have a definite function in heredity. **3** General Electric introduces the tungsten filament lamp. **4** Nettie Stevens, geneticist, determines that the fruit fly *(Drosophila melanogaster)* has 4 chromosomes. **5** DeForest develops a high-frequency electric scalpel for use in surgery. **6** Nobel Prize, Physics: Albert Michelson, for his experiments to determine the speed of light and for invention of precision optical instruments.	**7** Hopkins determines that vitamins are essential for good health, and that certain amino acids, also essential to health, are only supplied through one's diet. **8** Ejnar Hertzsprung, Dan. astronomer, establishes the relationship between a star's size and its color. **9** Karl Schwarzschild, Ger. astronomer, suggests the existence of black holes in space. **10** Alfred Adler, Aust. psychiatrist, publishes *Study of Organic Inferiority and Its Physical Compensation,* in which he suggests that a person with a physical disability often tries to make up for it subconsciously. **11** J.S. Haldane devises a method which enables a deep sea diver to rise to the surface safely. **12** Nobel Prize, Chemistry: Eduard Buchner, Ger. biochemist, for showing that alcoholic fermentation is the result of enzymes in the yeast. **13** Nobel Prize, Physiology or Medicine: Laveran, for his research on diseases caused by protozoa.	**1** George W. Goethals, of the Army Corps of Engineers, is appointed to direct construction of the Panama Canal. **2** First fleet of taximeter cabs, imported from Paris, arrives in New York City. **3** Mother's Day is observed for the first time in Philadelphia through the efforts of Anna M. Jarvis, who arranges a special church service. **4** Financial Panic of 1907 begins with the fall of the stock market; many banks fail throughout the country. A study by Congress of the currency and banking systems ultimately leads to the Federal Reserve Act of 1913. **5** First public showing of early talking and color motion pictures in Cleveland. Audience sees and hears some grand opera, a bullfight, and a political speaker. **6** 361 miners killed when a coal mine explodes in Monongah, W.Va. **7** Florence Lawrence is probably the first motion picture actress to be treated as a star, and her career (as the "Biograph Girl" and "the IMP") is considered the beginning of the star system.	**8** *Lusitania,* one of the world's largest steamships, sails to New York City on its first voyage. Sets speed record of 5 days, 54 minutes, from Queenstown, Ireland. **9** Medical examinations of school children are started in Britain. **10** Robert Baden-Powell founds the Boy Scouts in England. **11** Auguste and Louis Lumière develop a process for color photography. The brothers are chemists, manufacturers of photographic materials, and inventors of a motion-picture camera.	**1907**
1 Loeb raises unfertilized frog eggs to maturity in a startling example	**11** Jeans publishes *The Mathematical Theory of Electricity and Magne-*	**1** Ford introduces his Model T, which costs $850. By 1909 his com-	**7** Olympic Games are held in London. **8** Earthquake in south-	**1908**

History and Politics — America

illegal—first time Sherman Antitrust Act is applied to labor unions. **[1890:HIST/2]**

2 Congress passes bill regulating child labor in Washington, D.C., hoping the separate states will do the same.

3 Root-Takahira Agreement between the U.S. and Japan upholds the Open Door Policy in China. **[1899:HIST/5]**

4 Supreme Court upholds Oregon's law limiting women's working hours in industry.

5 Socialist Party nominates Debs for President for the third time.

6 Republican Party nominates Pres. Roosevelt's choice, Taft of Ohio, for President. Roosevelt refused (1907) to run for a third term in office.

7 Democratic Party nominates Bryan for President. **[1896:HIST/3]**

8 William Howard Taft and James S. Sherman are elected President and Vice President, respectively, on the Republican ticket.

History and Politics — Elsewhere

10 Austria annexes Bosnia and Herzegovina. Turkish-Serbian-Montenegrin-Greek alliance is sought to oppose Austria. Austria fails to allow Russian warships passage through the Dardanelles. International conference is called to consider Austria's actions.

11 Crete proclaims union with Greece.

12 Revolution by the Young Turks in the Ottoman Empire forces restoration of the constitution of 1876.

13 Ferdinand I proclaims Bulgaria independent and himself czar.

14 Juan Vicente Gomez becomes dictator of Venezuela.

15 King Leopold II turns over the Congo to the Belgian government. Investigations had revealed mistreatment of Congolese rubber workers and illegal leasing concessions.

16 Shah dissolves Persia's assembly and has many liberal leaders killed. Revolutionaries seize Tabriz following the establishment of martial law at Tehran.

17 Dutch put down native uprising to gain control of the island of Bali.

18 Canberra is chosen as the capital of Australia.

19 China's Emperor and dowager Empress die. Power passes to reactionary prince.

The Arts — America

book of poems, *A Lume Spento,* at his own expense in Venice.

2 Van Wyck Brooks, writer, attacks the old Puritan traditions in *The Wine of the Puritans.*

3 D.W. Griffith, film director, directs his first movie, *The Adventures of Dolly,* a melodrama about an infant kidnapped by Gypsies.

4 Cohan's Broadway show *Fifty Miles from Boston* includes the song "Harrigan."

5 Edward B. Sheldon, playwright, publishes *Salvation Nell,* the dramatization of which is directed by Harrison Fiske, and stars his wife Minnie Maddern Fiske.

6 Zona Gale, writer, publishes *Friendship Village,* a collection of short stories.

7 O. Henry publishes *The Gentle Grafter.*

8 Toscanini becomes director of the Metropolitan Opera, N.Y.C.

The Arts — Elsewhere

lar allegorical novel.

10 Israel Zangwill, Eng. writer, portrays America as the land of opportunity in his play, *The Melting Pot.*

11 Scot. author Kenneth Grahame publishes *The Wind in the Willows,* a classic in children's literature.

12 Oscar Straus, Aust. composer, completes his most famous work, *The Chocolate Soldier,* an operetta.

13 Georges Braque, Fr. artist and cofounder of Cubism, paints "Houses at L'Estaque."

14 Vasily Kandinsky, Russ. artist, paints "Blue Mountain."

15 Constantin Brancusi, Rom. pioneer in abstract sculpture, exhibits "The Kiss."

16 Bennett publishes *Old Wives' Tale,* a novel.

17 Jules Romains, Fr. writer, publishes *La Vie unanime,* a collection of poems, and establishes the literary movement, *Unanimisme.*

18 Schönberg's *Second String Quartet* marks the start of his experimentation with atonal composition.

19 Can. novelist Lucy Maud Montgomery publishes *Anne of Green Gables.*

1909

History and Politics — America

1 Negro and white leaders meet in New York and form the National Association for the Advancement of Colored People (NAACP) to fight for Negro rights.

2 Sixteenth Amendment to the Constitution is sent to the states for ratification. It

History and Politics — Elsewhere

9 German Chancellor Bülow resigns. He lost the confidence of Emperor William II after allowing the Emperor's foreign policy toward Britain to be printed in the London *Daily Telegraph.* German public opinion was seen as anti-British.

The Arts — America

1 Gertrude Stein, writer, publishes *Three Lives,* the story of three working class women.

2 Wright designs the Robie House, Chicago, his "prairie style" masterpiece.

The Arts — Elsewhere

7 Schönberg completes *Three Piano Pieces,* his first atonal composition.

8 Wells publishes *Tono-Bungay,* a social satire, and *Ann Veronica,* a novel based on his conflicts with Shaw

Science & Technology		Miscellaneous		
America	**Elsewhere**	**America**	**Elsewhere**	

of parthenogenesis.
2 Leo Baekeland, chemist, invents Bakelite, a plastic.
3 Growing public concern about the use of natural resources prompts Roosevelt to call the First National Conservation Congress. A Commission is appointed to inventory America's natural resources.
4 Weston invents a cadmium battery that standardizes electromotive force (EMF).
5 Berliner invents a light-weight engine for airplanes.
6 GE patents the electric iron and toaster.
7 Percy Bridgman, physicist, begins experiments in high-pressure physics (6000–400,000 atmospheres).
8 Edison produces an improved nickel-iron-alkaline storage battery.
9 Hiram Maxim invents the silencer for use on firearms.
10 The 47-story Singer Building in New York City is America's first skyscraper.

The Singer Building in New York City

tism.
12 Bayliss publishes *The Nature of Enzyme Action.*
13 Pierre Boule, Fr. paleontologist, reconstructs the first complete skeleton of a Neanderthal man.
14 Nobel Prize, Chemistry: Lord Rutherford, for his research into the breakdown of elements by x-rays and the study of radioactive elements.
15 Nobel Prize, Physics: Gabriel Lippmann, Lux. physicist, for producing the first color photographic plate.
16 Nobel Prize, Physiology or Medicine: Ehrlich and Metchnikoff, for their work on immunology.

pany is turning out 19,000 automobiles a year. Ford makes his operation so efficient that by 1926 the price drops to $310.
2 Sky advertising introduced when a plane flies over New York City towing a box kite rigged with a dummy on a trapeze and a banner advertising a theatrical attraction.
3 Moviehouses called nickelodeons, first established in 1905 by John P. Harris and Harry Davis, now number about 8000 throughout the country. Usually set up in empty stores, they show continuous movies with piano accompaniment; tickets cost 5¢. **[1905:ARTS/5]**
4 Lt. Thomas W. Selfridge, of the U.S. Signal Corps, is the first person to die in an airplane accident. He is a passenger with Orville Wright, who is seriously injured in the crash.
5 Jack Johnson, Negro stevedore from Galveston, defeats the world heavyweight champion, Tommy Burns of Canada in Sydney, Australia.
6 "Directoire" or "sheath" gown imported from Paris. Police had to rescue first woman to wear one in Chicago. Very narrow skirts without petticoats became the style, along with enormous "Merry Widow" hats, huge dotted veils, boned collars, and "fishnet" stockings.

ern Calabria and Sicily kills 150,000 people.
9 All adults are permitted to vote in Australian elections.
10 Japanese steamer *Matsu Maru* sinks after a collision near Hakadate, Japan, killing 300 people.

				1909

1 Charles R. Stockard, biologist, tests the effects of certain chemicals on animal embryos. He experimentally produces several monstrosities.
2 T. H. Morgan begins genetic experiments with *Drosophila melanogaster*

4 Haber devises a method for making ammonia, using nitrogen from the air.
5 Charles Nicolle, Fr. bacteriologist, discovers that typhus is spread by the body louse.
6 Andrija Mohorovičić,

1 3 million acres of public lands in the West are set aside by Pres. William Howard Taft for conservation purposes.
2 Lincoln Penny, issued by the Philadelphia Mint, replaces the Indian-head penny which had been in

9 Trade Boards Act ends "sweating" (employing workers at low wages, for long hours, and under unfavorable conditions) in British industry.
10 British steamer *Waratah*, sailing from Sydney, Australia, to

History and Politics		The Arts	
America	**Elsewhere**	**America**	**Elsewhere**

<table>
<tr>
<td>

grants Congress power to levy and collect an income tax. [1913:HIST/1]

3 Congress enacts Payne-Aldrich Tariff setting high protective rates. Pres. Taft is severely criticized for his defense of the tariff.

4 To protect U.S. investment and maintain balance of foreign control in China, Pres. Taft requests participation of U.S. banks in the international development of China.

5 Tennessee passes a prohibition law.

6 Government land (700,000 acres) in Washington, Montana, and Idaho is opened for settlement.

7 U.S. cruisers and troops help rebel forces overthrow Nicaragua's dictator.

8 Gifford Pinchot, head of the National Conservation Commission, makes first systematic listing of resources on public lands.

</td>
<td>

10 British, French, Russian, and Italian occupation troops withdraw from Crete.

11 British Parliament enacts the Old-Age Pension Law.

12 Turks massacre Armenians at Adana in southern Turkey.

13 Turkey recognizes Austria's annexation of Bosnia and Herzegovina and is paid compensation. [1908:HIST/10]

14 Albert I becomes King of the Belgians.

15 Young Turks depose Sultan Abd al-Hamid II and put Muhammad V on the throne.

16 Civil war breaks out in Honduras and lasts until 1911.

17 Riff tribesmen attack the Spanish at Melilla on the coast of Morocco.

18 Russian force invades northern Persia and seizes Tabriz.

19 Siam (now Thailand) surrenders to Britain its suzerainty over Kedah, Perlis, Kelantan, and Terengganu on the Malay Peninsula.

</td>
<td>

3 Pound publishes two volumes of verse, *Personae* and *Exultations*.

4 Jack London publishes the semiautobiographical novel *Martin Eden*.

5 Griffith's film *The Lonely Villa*, starring "America's Sweetheart" Mary Pickford, introduces the climactic chase scene to motion pictures.

6 Lewis Wickes Hine, photographer, publishes "Child Labor in the Carolinas" and "Day Laborers Before Their Time," two photo journals which reveal the injustice of child labor.

</td>
<td>

and other members of the Fabian Society.

9 Diaghilev founds the Ballets Russes, a Paris-based ballet company that tours the U.S. and Europe. Fokine is its first choreographer; Nijinsky is the lead dancer.

10 Vaughan Williams composes *Fantasia on a Theme by Tallis*.

11 Galsworthy publishes *Strife*, a novel about an industrial strike.

12 Ignacy Jan Paderewski, Pol. pianist and composer, is named director of the Warsaw Conservatory.

13 In preparation for his first U.S. tour, Rachmaninoff composes *Piano Concerto No. 3 in D Minor* and *Island of the Dead*.

14 Maurice Chevalier, Fr. entertainer, makes his debut at Folies Bergère, a music hall in Paris.

</td>
</tr>
<tr>
<td>

1910

1 Democratic and Republican progressives oppose dictatorial power of House Speaker and pass ruling that Rules Committee be elected by the House rather than appointed by the Speaker.

2 Interstate Commerce Commission orders a reduction in Pullman car rates and in railroad freight rates.

3 Congress establishes postal savings bank system.

4 Pres. Taft dismisses Pinchot for publicly criticizing the administration's handling of coal lands in Alaska. [1909:HIST/8]

5 Roosevelt makes speeches advocating a "New Nationalism." He is angered by scandals in the conservation program and by liberal Republican policies.

6 Mann-Elkins Act strengthens powers of the In-

280

</td>
<td>

10 George V becomes King of Great Britain and Ireland, succeeding his father Edward VII.

11 Revolution in Portugal forces the abdication of the king. A republic is established with Teófilo Braga as president.

12 Nicholas I proclaims himself king of the independent state of Montenegro.

13 Turkish army puts down revolt in Albania, which seeks its independence.

14 Russia and Austria agree to maintain the status quo in the Balkans.

15 French Equatorial Africa (formerly called French Congo) is established.

16 British establish the Union of South Africa; it consists of the Cape of Good Hope, Natal, the Orange Free State, and the Transvaal. It

</td>
<td>

1 Charles W. Eliot, Harvard University president, edits *The Harvard Classics*, a 50-volume sampling of world literature.

2 Lee DeForest produces a radio program from the Metropolitan Opera House, N.Y., starring singer Enrico Caruso.

3 Anna Pavlova, ballerina, makes her first appearance in New York City.

4 John A. Lomax, ballad and folk song collector, publishes *Cowboy Songs and Other Frontier Ballads*.

5 O. Henry publishes *Whirligigs*, which includes one of his most amusing stories, "Ransom of Red Chief."

</td>
<td>

8 Kandinsky founds the Abstract Expressionist movement with his painting, "First Abstract Watercolor," and his book, *Concerning the Spiritual in Art*.

9 Theater director Max Reinhardt's production of Sophocles' *Oedipus Rex* marks a revival of classical Greek drama in Germany.

10 Rousseau exhibits "Yadivigha's Dream," an exotic painting portraying a nude resting on a sofa in the middle of a jungle.

11 Eng. writer E.M. Forster publishes *Howard's End*, a humorous social novel.

12 Russ. composer Igor Stravinsky com-

</td>
</tr>
</table>

Science & Technology

America

(fruit flies).
3 Incandescent lamps are used in automobile headlights. They replace carbide flame jets.

William Howard Taft, 27th U.S. President

Elsewhere

Yugoslav geophysicist, discovers the boundary layer between the Earth's crust and the mantle. This layer is later known as the Mohorovičić Discontinuity, or Moho.
7 Wilhelm Johannsen, Dan. geneticist, introduces the word *gene* to describe the units of heredity. He also coins the genetic terms *genotype* and *phenotype*.
8 Ettore Bugatti, Ital. car designer, founds the company which makes the world's first race cars.
9 Nobel Prize, Physics: Braun and Marconi, for their separate development of the wireless telegraph.
10 Nobel Prize, Physiology or Medicine: Kocher, for research on the thyroid gland.

Miscellaneous

America

use for 50 years.
4 When women take up automobile driving, a new field opens for fashion designers. Special clothes for motoring include a long veil to keep a lady's hat in place. "Automobile wrinkles" are soothed away by the application of raw, freshly cut cucumbers.
6 First substantial animated cartoon is shown. *Gertie the Dinosaur* is made up of 10,000 drawings by newspaper cartoonist Winsor McCay.
7 Arctic explorer Robert E. Peary, his Negro aide, Matthew Henson, and four Eskimos are the first to reach the North Pole.
8 Freud lectures in the U.S. on psychoanalysis.

Elsewhere

London vanishes; 300 persons on board are lost.
11 Girl Guides is founded in Britain by Baden-Powell and his sister, Lady Agnes.
12 Eng. aviator Henri Farman completes the first 100-mi. flight.
13 Women are admitted to German universities.
14 First permanent waves are given by London hairdressers.
15 Fr. aviator Louis Blériot makes the first plane flight across the English Channel from Calais, France, to Dover, England.

America

1 In response to the Conservation Congress of 1908, 38 of the 46 states have formed local conservation agencies.
2 Steinmetz publishes *Engineering Mathematics* to help scientists understand the calculations involved in his electrical theories. [1897:SCI/5]
3 Francis P. Rous, pathologist, discovers that some cancers can be caused by a virus.
4 T. H. Morgan discovers that some inherited characteristics are sex-linked.
5 George A. Hughes begins production of a practical electric cooking range.
6 In *Future of Electricity,* Steinmetz warns about air pollution from

Elsewhere

8 Marie Curie publishes *Traité de Radioactivé.*
9 Georges Claude, Fr. chemist, invents the neon light.
10 After testing hundreds of compounds, Ehrlich discovers arsphenamine, the 606th, a cure for syphilis.
11 Ramsay discovers the inert element radon.
12 Karl von Frisch, Aust. zoologist, proves that fish can distinguish between colors.
13 Nobel Prize, Physics: Van der Waals, for his mathematical description of the liquid and gaseous states of matter.

America

1 U.S. population is 91.9 million; 8.7 million immigrants have arrived since 1900. Of people over 25 years old, fewer than half have completed grade school, and about 4% have graduated from college.
2 Halley's Comet passes the sun without catastrophe. Many believed that the earth would pass through the comet's tail and be destroyed.
3 Father's Day, started by Mrs. John B. Dodd, is celebrated for the first time in Spokane, Wash.
4 First President to pitch a ball to open the baseball season is William Howard Taft. He starts the game between Washington and Philadelphia in the American League.

Elsewhere

8 There are 122,000 telephones in use in Great Britain.
9 H.H. Crippen, an American who is called the English wife poisoner, is hanged for murder.
10 Evans finishes the excavation of Cnossus, Crete.
11 Brazil produces nine-tenths of the world's rubber and three-fourths of the world's coffee.

1910

terstate Commerce Commission over railroads. It also places telephone, telegraph, and cable companies under the jurisdiction of the ICC.

7 Mann Act prohibits the transportation of women from one state to another for immoral purposes.

8 Congress requires U.S. Representatives to file reports of campaign contributions.

9 Long-time dispute between the U.S. and Britain over Newfoundland fishing rights is settled by the International Court of Arbitration at The Hague. U.S. is awarded privileges in Newfoundland waters; a commission is formed to settle fishing disputes.

becomes a dominion within the British Empire. Louis Botha is chosen its first Prime Minister.

17 Japan annexes Korea.

18 Russia and Japan agree on spheres of influence in Manchuria.

19 Northern Territory comes under direct rule of the Commonwealth of Australia.

20 Eleutherios Venizelos becomes Premier of Greece.

6 Victor Herbert composes *Naughty Marietta.*

7 James Gibbons Huneker, musician and writer, publishes *Promenades of an Impressionist.*

pletes *The Firebird,* a ballet.

13 Rabindranath Tagore, Bengali poet, publishes his most famous works, *Gītāñjalī,* a collection of poetry, and *Gorā,* a novel.

14 Puccini composes the opera, *The Girl of the Golden West.*

15 Maurice de Vlaminck, Fr. Fauvist, paints "The Flood, Ivry" and "Self-Portrait."

1911

1 Robert M. La Follette, Senator from Wisconsin, helps found the National Progressive Republican League, which seeks adoption of direct primaries, direct elections of senators, and state constitutional reform.

2 U.S. troops are sent to Mexican border to protect U.S. citizens and property; fighting during Mexican Revolution occurs so close to border that U.S. citizens gather to watch.

3 Supreme Court, under the Sherman Antitrust Act, orders the dissolution of the Standard Oil Company ("unreasonable" restraint of trade) and the American Tobacco Company (monopoly).

4 Senate passes bill for direct election of senators under federal supervision.

5 U.S., Britain, Japan, and Russia sign treaty abolishing the hunting of seals for 15 years in the North Pacific.

6 U.S. abrogates (cancels) the treaty of 1832 with Russia. Treaty allowed Russia to exclude Jewish-American citizens.

7 Illinois passes first state law to assist mothers with dependent children.

8 French advance into Morocco. German gunboat *Panther* arrives to protect German interests. Germany agrees to a French protectorate in Morocco; in return France cedes to Germany territory in French Equatorial Africa.

9 War breaks out between Turkey and Italy. Italian fleet bombards Tripoli, which is annexed by Italy after the Turks are defeated.

10 Alsace-Lorraine is granted a new constitution by the Germans.

11 Russians invade and occupy northern Persia.

12 British and Belgians define the boundary between the Belgian Congo and Uganda.

13 India's capital is moved from Calcutta to Delhi.

14 Revolutionary army overthrows the Manchu government in southern China. The Republic of China is established, with Sun Yat-sen as president.

15 Ramsay MacDonald becomes leader of the Labor Party in the British House of Commons.

16 Piotr Arkadevich Stolypin, Russ. Premier and Minis-

1 Henry Bacon, architect, designs the Lincoln Memorial in the classical revival style.

2 The will of journalist Joseph Pulitzer calls for the establishment of the now coveted Pulitzer Prizes.

3 Irving Berlin, songwriter, writes his first hit song, "Alexander's Ragtime Band."

4 Charles Sumner Greene and his brother Henry Mather, architects, design the Culberton House, Pasadena, which popularizes the mission revival style in California.

5 Wharton publishes her best known work, *Ethan Frome.*

6 Dreiser gains public recognition with his novel *Jennie Gerhardt.*

7 W(illiam) C(hristopher) Handy, blues composer, writes "Memphis Blues."

8 Joyce Kilmer, poet, publishes *Summer of Love,* his first volume of poetry.

9 Scott Joplin com-

11 Chesterton publishes *The Innocence of Father Brown,* the first in a popular series of detective novels.

12 Béla Bartók, Hung. composer, completes *Duke Bluebeard's Castle,* an opera.

13 Marc Chagall, Russ. painter, begins "Homage to Apollinaire" (-1912).

14 R. Strauss and Hoffmannsthal collaborate on the opera, *Der Rosenkavalier.*

15 The stenciled letters in Braque's painting, "The Portuguese," symbolize his theory that art is more than simple representation of an object.

16 Stravinsky composes *Petrushka* for the Ballets Russes.

17 Matisse exhibits "The Red Studio," a Fauve masterpiece.

18 Katherine Mansfield, New Zealand writer, publishes *In a German Pension,* a collection of short stories.

Science & Technology		Miscellaneous		
America	**Elsewhere**	**America**	**Elsewhere**	
burning coal and water pollution from releasing untreated sewage into the rivers. **7** Electric washing machines are introduced.		**5** Barney Oldfield records the fastest speed ever traveled by man when he covers a mile at 133 mph in a Benz car at Daytona Beach, Fla. **6** Boy Scouts of America and the Camp Fire Girls are established. **7** First air meet is held at Los Angeles. Audiences of about 35,000 people a day watch all air speed records broken by Louis Paulham of France and Glenn Curtiss of the U.S. Although many want to fly, only 5 airplanes have been sold to individuals in the 3 years since the first commercially made plane was produced.		
1 Robert A. Millikan, physicist, measures the electrical charge of an electron in his famous "oil drop" experiment. **2** Walter B. Cannon, first physician to use x-rays to study physiology, publishes *The Mechanical Factors of Digestion*. **3** Carrier invents the air conditioner. **4** Harry F. Reid, Md. seismologist, suggests that earthquakes are caused by movements of faults in the Earth's crust. **5** John M. Browning, Utah gunsmith, invents the Browning automatic pistol. **6** Taylor publishes *Principles of Scientific Management*. **7** Glenn H. Curtiss, N.Y. aviator, invents the hydroplane. **8** Franz Boas, Ger.-Amer. anthropologist, publishes *The Mind of Primitive Man*. **9** Elmer Sperry invents the gyrocompass. **10** Isaac N. Lewis, Pa. inventor, develops the Lewis machine gun that is widely used on World War I warplanes.	**11** Charles T.R. Wilson, Scot. physicist, invents the cloud chamber and uses it to photograph the trails (paths) left by electrons. **12** Sir Owen Richardson, Eng. physicist, proves that hot metals emit electrons. **13** Victor F. Hess, Aust. physicist, concludes that electrical conductivity increases with altitude. This concept leads to his discovery of cosmic rays. **14** Heinrich Wieland, Ger. chemist, distinguishes between different forms of nitrogen in organic compounds. **15** Rutherford publishes his nuclear theory of atoms. **16** Claudius Dornier, Ger. aircraft builder, constructs the first all-metal aircraft. **17** Nobel Prize, Chemistry: Marie Curie, for her discovery of radium and polonium. **18** Nobel Prize, Physics: Wien, for discovering the laws governing heat radiation. **19** Nobel Prize, Physiology or Medicine: Allvar	**1** Carnegie establishes the Carnegie Corporation of New York with an endowment of $125 million to support educational projects. **2** Electric self-starter for automobiles is demonstrated by General Motors. Invented by Clyde J. Coleman in 1899, it has been improved by Charles F. Kettering. With the new starter it is no longer necessary to crank the engine to get it running. **3** Possible extermination of fur seals in the North Pacific prompts the U.S., Great Britain (for Canada), Russia, and Japan to agree not to catch seals for 15 years. **4** Robert "Bobby" Jones, the golfer, wins his first title at age 9: the Junior Championship of Atlanta. **5** As a result, in part, of the fire at the Triangle Shirtwaist factory, New York City, which kills 146 workers, Int'l Ladies' Garment Worker's Union succeeds in improving working conditions and safety for its members.	**7** Shops Act requires that workers in shops in England receive a half day off each week. **8** China's population is 325 million; India's, 315; Russia's, 167; Germany's, 65; Japan's, 52; Great Britain's, 40.8; Ireland's, 4.3; France's, 39.6; Italy's, 34.6. **9** Amundsen reaches the South Pole. **10** World Missionary Conference of Protestant Churches is held in Edinburgh, Scotland. This is the beginning of the modern ecumenical (universal Christian unity and church union) movement. **11** Yangtze River, China, overflows; 100,000 die. **12** Copyright Act requires copies of all new British publications to be given to the British Museum and to five other copyright libraries. **13** On Aug. 9, temperature in London reaches an unheard-of 100°F.	**1911**

	History and Politics		The Arts	
	America	Elsewhere	America	Elsewhere
		ter of the Interior, is assassinated by a revolutionary terrorist. **17** Karl von Sturgkh is named Premier of Austria.	poses the folk opera *Treemonisha.* **10** Kate Douglas Wiggin publishes *Mother Carey's Chicken.*	
1912	**1** New Mexico becomes 47th state. **2** Arizona becomes 48th state. **3** U.S. troops occupy Tientsin, China, to protect U.S. interests. **4** Socialist Party nominates Debs for President for the fourth time. **5** U.S. Marines land in Cuba to protect U.S. lives and property. **6** Conservative Republicans win control of the Republican National Convention; Taft is renominated; Roosevelt delegates withdraw and nominate Roosevelt as the candidate of the Progressive Party (Bull Moose Party). **7** U.S. Marines land in Nicaragua to protect U.S. interests after rebels massacre Nicaraguan soldiers. Marines open railroad and telegraph system in Nicaragua and capture Leon, stronghold of the rebels. **8** Alaska becomes an organized U.S. territory. **9** Woodrow Wilson and Thomas R. Marshall are elected President and Vice President, respectively, on the Democratic ticket. **10** Massachusetts passes first minimum wage law for women and children (invalidated by the Supreme Court in 1923). **11** New York passes 54-hour week labor law; Congress passes eight-hour day labor law for federal employees.	**12** By the Treaty of Fez, the sultan of Morocco agrees to French protectorate. French and Spanish divide Morocco into four zones (French Morocco is nine tenths of the country). **13** Treaty of Lausanne ends the war between Italy and Turkey. Turks abandon Tripoli. **14** First Balkan War begins between the Balkan countries (Montenegro, Serbia, Bulgaria, and Greece) and Turkey. Bulgarians defeat Turks at Lulé Burgas; Serbians overrun northern Albania. Armistice is declared between Turkey, Bulgaria, Serbia, and Montenegro. **15** Albanians declare their independence. **16** Chinese Emperor abdicates. Sun Yat-sen, China's first President, resigns in favor of Yüan Shih-kai. **17** Japan and Russia sign secret treaty defining their spheres in northeastern Asia. **18** British government introduces a bill for home rule in Ireland. It is attacked for its injustice to Protestant Ulster. **19** Christian X becomes King of Denmark.	**1** James Weldon Johnson, writer and poet of the "Harlem Renaissance," publishes the novel *Autobiography of an Ex-Colored Man.* **2** Zane Grey publishes his popular work *Riders of the Purple Sage.* **3** Dirks renames his comic strip "The Captain and the Kids." [1897:ARTS/1] **4** Carl Laemmle founds Universal Pictures Company. **5** Leopold Stokowski, conductor, becomes the musical director of the Philadelphia Orchestra. **6** Mack Sennett forms the Keystone Company. **7** Edna St. Vincent Millay publishes *Renascence and Other Poems.* **8** Pound, now the dominant figure in English verse, becomes the London correspondent for the U.S. quarterly *Poetry.* **9** John Sloane depicts New York City life in the paintings "Sunday, Woman Drying Their Hair" and "McSorley's Bar." **10** Amy Lowell, poet, publishes *A Dome of Many-Colored Glass,* her first volume of poetry.	**11** Shaw writes *Pygmalion,* a popular play about a Cockney girl who is changed into a lady by Professor Henry Higgins. **12** Picasso and Braque begin using colored paper and other unusual substances in their paintings, marking the start of Synthetic Cubism. **13** Guillaume Apollinaire, Fr. writer, coins the term "Orpheism" to describe the introduction (esp. by Braque) of vibrant color in Cubism. **14** Amedeo Modigliani, Ital. artist, exhibits "The Head," an elongated sculpture. **15** Nijinsky choreographs and dances the title role in *L'Après-midi d'un faune.* **16** Marcel Duchamp, Fr. artist, introduces action into Cubism with his controversial painting, "Nude Descending a Staircase No. 2." **17** Edwin Landseer Lutyens, Eng. architect, designs the Capitol at New Delhi, India. **18** Bruno Walter (Ger.) conducts the first performance of Mahler's *Ninth Symphony.*
1913	**1** Sixteenth Amendment (income tax) to the Constitution becomes law. **2** Webb-Kenyon Interstate Liquor Act states that liquor	**12** Raymond Poincare is elected President of France. **13** Count Stephen Tisza becomes Premier of Hungary. He seeks to block secessionist	**1** The International Exhibition of Modern Art (the "Armory Show") in New York City has an enormous	**8** Marcel Proust, Fr. novelist, publishes *Swann's Way,* the first of 8 volumes in his epic masterpiece, *Remem-*

Science & Technology		Miscellaneous		
America	Elsewhere	America	Elsewhere	
	Gullstrand, Swed. ophthalmologist, for his research into the light-refracting structures of the eye.	**6** Calbraith P. Rodgers makes the first cross-country airplane flight in 82 hr., 4 min.		
1 Alfred Sturtevant, Ala. biologist, determines that genes are lined up in a row on the chromosomes. **2** Henrietta S. Leavitt, astronomer, discovers Cepheid variables, a type of pulsating star. **3** U.S. Public Health Service is established. **4** Western Union and Western Electric develop a multiplex telegraph that allows eight messages to be sent over one wire at the same time. **5** *U.S.S. Jupiter,* America's first electric ship, is launched. **6** Harvey Cushing, Ohio brain surgeon, publishes *The Pituitary Body and Its Disorders.* **7** Loeb publishes *The Mechanistic Conception of Life* in which he uses chemistry and physics to explain the origin of life. **8** William Burton, chemist, introduces the thermal cracking process of refining petroleum. **9** Curtiss invents a "flying boat," or seaplane. **10** Nobel Prize, Physiology or Medicine: Alexis Carrel for developing a method of suturing blood vessels.	**11** Max von Laue, Ger. physicist, proves that x-rays are a form of electromagnetic radiation. **12** Henry G. Moseley, Eng. physicist, proposes the law which states that atomic number is based on the number of protons in the nucleus. He sets 92 as the total number of elements. **13** Sir William Bragg, Eng. scientist, makes the first accurate measurement of x-ray wavelengths. He also uses x-rays to study crystal structure. **14** Casimir Funk, Pol. biochemist, identifies the first vitamin. He names it *vitamin* for Latin *vita* "life" + *amine,* because he thought they were amines. **15** Alfred Wegener, Ger. geologist, proposes that the modern continents were once part of a huge land mass which eventually split up. This theory is called continental drift. **16** Frederick Soddy, Eng. chemist, publishes *Matter and Energy.* **17** Starling publishes *Principles of Human Physiology.* **18** Nobel Prize, Chemistry: Grignard, for his organic reactions, and Paul Sabatier, Fr. chemist, for his use of nickel to add hydrogens to organic compounds.	**1** Jim Thorpe, an American Indian, wins both the decathlon and the pentathlon at the Olympics in Sweden. He is called the world's greatest athlete. Later, his medals and honors are taken away when it is discovered that he had played semiprofessional baseball as a summer job while in college. **2** Spreading fad for ragtime introduces a series of "animal dances." Among them are: fox trot, crab step, kangaroo dip, camel walk, fish walk, chicken scratch, lame duck, snake, grizzly bear, turkey trot, and the bunny hug. **3** Attendance at motion-picture theaters reaches 5 million daily. **4** Capt. Albert Louis makes the first parachute jump in the U.S. from an airplane. **5** Congress authorizes an 8-hour day for all workers under federal contract. **6** First automobile driver jailed for speeding. **7** Textile workers in Lawrence, Mass., strike for more than 2 months when their wages are lowered following new hours law. law. **8** *Life* magazine lists the slang expressions of the year: *flossy; beat it!; peeved; sure!; classy; It's a cinch; What do you know about that?; fussed;*	*speedy; peachy; nutty; getting your goat.* **9** Swiss inventor Edwin Brandenberger develops a process for making Cellophane. **10** Brit. polar explorer Robert F. Scott reaches the South Pole one month after Amundsen. He and 4 others die on their way back. **11** On its maiden voyage, the steamship *Titanic* collides with an iceberg in the Atlantic Ocean and sinks with a loss of more than 1500 lives. **12** C. Dawson announces discovery of remains of Piltdown man, believed to be 50,000 years old near Lewes, England. **[1953:MISC/14]** **13** First regular air service between Berlin and Friedrichshaven, Ger., in a dirigible. **14** Olympic Games are held in Stockholm, Sweden. **15** Explorers Vilhjalmur Stefansson and R. Anderson explore the Canadian Arctic. **16** London has 400 motion picture theaters, as compared to 90 in 1909. **17** Fr. photographer Charles Pathé produces the first news film. **18** Royal Flying Corps established in Britain (later named R.A.F.). **19** Germany claims to have 30,000 millionaires.	**1912**
1 Elmer McCollum, biochemist, isolates vitamins A and B. **2** Frederick A. Kolster invents a practical radio-	**13** Kasimir Fajans, Pol. chemist, discovers the element protactinium. **14** Friedrich Bergius, Ger. chemist, develops a	**1** Dayton Flood in the Miami Valley, Ohio, kills more than 400 people; property damage is $100 million. More than 200	**8** There are 802 divorces in the United Kingdom; 14,000 in the U.S. **9** Alsatian doctor and missionary Albert	**1913**

History and Politics

America

can not be shipped into states where its sale is illegal.
3 Congress makes the U.S. Department of Commerce and Labor two separate departments, both with Cabinet status.
4 Seventeenth Amendment to the Constitution becomes law, providing for direct election of U.S. Senators by the people, instead of by state legislatures.
5 Pres. Wilson officially recognizes the new Chinese Republic.
6 Congress passes Underwood Tariff Act which reduces average duties to 30 percent.
7 Webb Alien Land Bill is enacted in California. It excludes Japanese from land ownership.
8 Pres. Wilson signs Federal Reserve Act which divides the country into 12 districts, each with a federal reserve bank.
9 Pres. Wilson announces policy of "watchful waiting" in Mexican affairs. He asks for the resignation of Mexican dictator Victoriano Huerta, and announces U.S. support of Mexican revolutionists.
10 Supreme Court upholds Minnesota law regulating railroad rates within the state.
11 Supreme Court upholds the constitutionality of the Mann Act, popularly called the White Slave Traffic Act. [1910:HIST/7]

Elsewhere

tendencies of Serbian and Rumanian minorities in Hungary.
14 King George I of Greece is assassinated.
15 Turks refuse to give up control of the Aegean Islands and Crete.
16 Major powers at London conference create an independent Albania.
17 Serbia, cut off from the sea, demands from Bulgaria more of Macedonia. Bulgaria attacks Serbia and, in turn, is attacked by Rumania, Greece, and Turkey. In second Balkan War, Bulgaria loses territory by the Treaty of Bucharest.
18 Mario García Menocal becomes President of Cuba. He initiates "businessman government" that is criticized as corrupt.
19 South Africa passes immigration law restricting the entry of Asiatics.
20 China recognizes the autonomy of Outer Mongolia, which had been secured by treaty between Russia and Outer Mongolia in 1912.
21 French nationalists clamor for the return of Alsace-Lorraine. [1871:HIST/6]

The Arts

America

impact on American art. When the show arrives in Chicago, an effigy of Matisse's painting "Blue Nude" is burned.
2 Robert Frost, New England poet, publishes his first book of poems, *A Boy's Will.*
3 The 60-story Woolworth Building in New York City, designed by Cass Gilbert, is completed.
4 Cather publishes *O Pioneers!* about the Nebraska settlers.
5 Ellen Glasgow writes about the grooming of a Southern belle in her novel *Virginia.*
6 Sennett begins directing the Keystone comedies, which introduce classic slapstick humor to the U.S. cinema.
7 New York's Palace Theater begins a 20-year reign as the outstanding vaudeville house in the U.S.

Elsewhere

brance of Things Past (–1927).
9 Apollinaire publishes "Alcools," his best poem, and *The Cubist Painters,* a work that defines Cubism in both art and literature.
10 Scandal follows the Paris premiere of Stravinsky's ballet, *The Rite of Spring.*
11 Duchamp produces the first mobile—a bicycle wheel on a kitchen stool. Called a "ready-made," it is an early Dadaist work. [1916:ARTS/14]
12 Eng. poet Robert Bridges is named Poet Laureate.
13 D.H. Lawrence, Eng. novelist, publishes the semiautobiographical *Sons and Lovers.*
14 Sax Rohmer, Eng. writer, publishes the first in a series of Fu Manchu novels.
15 Giorgio De Chirico, Ital. painter, exhibits the ominous "The Soothsayer's Recompense."

1914

America (History and Politics)

1 Pres. Wilson signs order establishing permanent civil government in the Panama Canal Zone. Goethals becomes first governor of the Canal Zone.
2 U.S. Marines are detained by Mexican authorities at Tampico, Mexico. Mexico apologizes but U.S. commander demands special 21-gun salute to the U.S. flag by Mexicans. Pres. Wilson orders U.S. fleet to Tampico. Congress authorizes use of force to protect U.S. rights. U.S.

Elsewhere (History and Politics)

7 Austrian Archduke Francis Ferdinand and his wife are assassinated at Sarajevo by a Serbian nationalist. Austria-Hungary demands that Serbia suppress anti-Austrian agitation.
8 Austria-Hungary rejects British peace initiative and declares war on Serbia. Germany, alarmed at Russian mobilization, declares war on Russia. Great Britain declares war on Germany, which refused to guarantee the neutrality of Belgium. World War

America (The Arts)

1 Tarkington publishes *Penrod,* a Twain-like portrayal of boyhood.
2 Edgar Rice Burroughs, novelist, publishes *Tarzan of the Apes,* the first of many books about an infant abandoned in the jungle and reared by apes.
3 Charlie Chaplin, actor, director, and producer, introduces his famous tramp outfit in the film *Kid Auto*

Elsewhere (The Arts)

13 James Joyce, Ir. novelist, publishes *The Dubliners,* a collection of short stories.
14 Raymond Duchamp-Villon, Fr. sculptor, completes his Cubist masterpiece, "The Horse."
15 Beniamino Gigli, Italy's greatest tenor, makes his debut as Enzo in the opera, *La Gioconda.* [1876:ARTS/7]
16 Alfano composes

Science & Technology		Miscellaneous		
America	**Elsewhere**	**America**	**Elsewhere**	
compass and installs radio beacons in lighthouses on the New Jersey coast. **3** DeForest's 3-element vacuum tube is used as a *repeater* to amplify weak signals. **4** Bela Schick, pediatrician, develops the Schick test for determining immunity to diphtheria. **5** Henry Russell, astronomer, describes a theory of the origin of stars. **6** Francis X. Decrum, Pa. neurologist, publishes *The Clinical Manual of Mental Diseases.* **7** Igor Sikorski, Russ.-Amer. engineer, builds and flies the first multi-engine airplane. **8** William D. Coolidge, Mass. physicist, invents a hot-filament cathode tube that produces x-rays. **9** Frank Mallory, pathologist, isolates the bacterium that causes whooping cough. **10** Sturtevant develops a method of mapping chromosomes. **11** Meades Ranch, Kansas, is selected as the geodetic center of North America. **[1901:SCI/8]** **12** George D. Birkhoff, mathematician, proposes the ergodic theorem, an important concept in modern dynamics.	process for transforming coal dust into gasoline. **15** Johannes Fibiger, Dan. pathologist, causes the growth of cancer cells in rats, a major breakthrough in cancer research. **16** Friedrich A. Paneth, Aust. chemist, and George Charles de Hevesy, Ger. chemist, introduce radioactive tracing. **17** Johannes Stark, Ger. physicist, discovers the Stark effect (the splitting of spectral lines when the light source is subjected to an electric field). **18** Hertzsprung establishes a luminosity scale helpful for determining intergalactic distances. **19** Soddy and Lord Rutherford put forth the theory of atomic disintegration of radioactive elements, and coin the term *isotope.* **20** Nobel Prize, Chemistry: Alfred Weiner, Swiss chemist, for his research on the linkage of atoms in molecules.	people also die in floods along the Indiana River and elsewhere in the West and South as a result of heavy rain for 5 days. **2** Walter Johnson pitches 56 consecutive innings, allowing no runs, and sets a record for the baseball season. **3** Domestic parcel post system begins. **4** Ford Motor Company sets up the first moving assembly line and is soon producing 1000 Model T's per day. Ford pays workers an unheard-of minimum wage of $5 a day and establishes a 40-hr. workweek. **5** Hollywood becomes the center of the motion-picture industry, replacing New York City. **6** 150,000 garment workers strike in New York City. Strike ends 3 months later and workers win wage concessions, reduced hours, and recognition of their union. **7** In first Army-Notre Dame football game, little-known Notre Dame defeats Army by using the forward pass. This victory helps popularize the game by showing that a small, clever team can beat a large, powerful one.	Schweitzer opens a hospital in Lambaréné, French Congo. **10** Zippers (in use since 1891) become popular. **11** *Imperator,* German gas turbine liner, begins service. It weighs 52,100 tons. **12** First woman magistrate is appointed in England. **13** Coal mine fire in Mid Glamorgan, Wales, kills 439 people.	
1 Edwin C. Kendall, Conn. biochemist, isolates "thyroxin," a hormone produced by the thyroid gland. **2** John Watson publishes *Behavior; An Introduction to Comparative Psychology* and calls for the use of animals in psychological experiments. **3** Edwin H. Armstrong, N.Y. electrical engineer, patents the regenerative (feedback) circuit. **4** Walter S. Adams, as-	**12** Owen Richardson publishes *The Electron Theory of Matter.* **13** Haber, working for the World War I German government, plays an important role in the development of chemical warfare. **14** Sir Arthur Stanley Eddington, Eng. astrophysicist, publishes *Stellar Movements and the Structure of the Universe,* suggesting that spiral nebulae are galaxies.	**1** Panama Canal is completed. It is 40 mi. long from Atlantic to Pacific and cost about $365 million. **2** Mack Sennett begins production of the first 6-reel motion picture. A comedy called *Tillie's Punctured Romance,* it stars Marie Dressler and Charlie Chaplin. **3** The Yale Bowl, seating almost 80,000, opens in New Haven, Conn. It is the first large football	**8** Brit. explorer Ernest Shackleton leads an expedition to the Antarctic. **9** Canadian steamer *Empress of Ireland* sinks after a collision in the St. Lawrence River; 1042 persons are killed.	**1914**

History and Politics		The Arts	
America	Elsewhere	America	Elsewhere

History and Politics		The Arts	
America	**Elsewhere**	**America**	**Elsewhere**
naval forces bombard and occupy Veracruz, Mexico. **3** Pres. Wilson and Huerta accept offer by Argentina, Brazil, and Chile ("ABC countries") to arbitrate U.S.-Mexico dispute. Huerta is forced to resign as Mexico's President, and crisis dissolves. **4** Pres. Wilson issues proclamation of U.S. neutrality in war between major European powers (World War I). He offers to negotiate peace between the warring nations. **5** Federal Trade Commission is established and seeks to regulate interstate commerce. **6** Clayton Antitrust Act strengthens Sherman Antitrust Act of 1890. It seeks to restrict use of court injunctions in labor disputes and exempts labor and farm organizations from antitrust laws.	I breaks out between the Allies (Britain, France, Russia, Belgium, and Serbia) and the Central Powers (Austria-Hungary and Germany). Japan and Montenegro join the Allies, and Turkey joins the Central Powers. Italy, Portugal, Rumania, and the U.S. later side with the Allies. **9** German troops occupy Liège and Brussels and force the British to retreat at the Battle of the Mons. Russians are defeated at Tannenberg, East Prussia. British halt German advance toward the Channel ports of Dunkirk and Calais at the first Battle of Ypres. Trench warfare begins along the entire Western Front. Russians force the Austrians back to Galicia. Austrians capture but lose Belgrade. Germans capture Lódź in Poland. British bombard the Dardanelles forts, declare war on Turkey, and annex Cyprus. **10** British unite the protectorates of southern and northern Nigeria to form the colony and protectorate of Nigeria. [1906:HIST/11] **11** Japan declares war on Germany, violates China's neutrality, and seizes Tsingtao. **12** Expeditionary force from New Zealand captures German Samoa.	*Races at Venice.* **4** Stanton Macdonald-Wright, painter of the synchromist movement, paints "Synchromy in Orange: To Form." **5** Morgan Russell, painter of the synchromist movement, paints "Abstraction on Spectrum (Organization 5)." **6** Handy composes "St. Louis Blues." **7** Eugene O'Neill, leading playwright of the period, writes his first play, *The Web.* **8** Sennett parodies Griffith's last minute rescues in the film *Barney Oldfield's Run for Life.* **9** Elmer Rice, playwright, publishes *On Trial,* the first play to use the "flashback" technique. **10** Gertrude Stein publishes the abstract *Tender Buttons.* **11** Kilmer's poem "Trees" begins with the famous lines "I think that I shall never see/ A poem as lovely as a tree." **12** Frost publishes *North of Boston,* which includes the poem "Mending Wall."	*The Legend of Sakuntala,* an opera based on Indian folk tales. **17** Aleksandr Yakolevich Taïrov establishes the Kamerny Theater, Moscow. **18** Kokoschka paints "The Bride of the Wind." **19** In a letter to *The Times* (London), Fokine outlines his theories of choreography. **20** Klee paints "Hammamet with the Mosque." **21** Vaughan Williams composes *London Symphony.* **22** Marc's "Fighting Forms" is a pure abstract painting. **23** Chagall paints "The Praying Jew."
1915 **1** U.S. states that loss of U.S. ships and lives is a violation of neutrality for which Germany will be held responsible. **2** Pres. Wilson vetoes U.S. Senate bill requiring literacy tests for all immigrants. **3** Congress combines Revenue Cutter Service and Lifesaving Service to establish U.S. Coast Guard. **4** *Lusitania* and *Arabic* sinkings with loss of American lives bring strong protest notes from Pres. Wilson. Changes occur in German	**11** World War I continues. British sink German cruiser *Blücher.* Germany begins submarine blockade of Britain. British and French battleships are sunk at the Dardanelles. Russians seize Przemyśl, Poland. German Zeppelins (airships) raid England. Italian forces fail to break through the Austrian lines at the Battles of the Isonzo. British and French forces land at Saloniki, Greece. German troops occupy Warsaw. British defeat the Turks in Mesopotamia.	**1** Ruth St. Denis and Ted Shawn found the Denishawn School of Dance and Related Arts. **2** Max Weber, painter, paints "Chinese Restaurant" in the Cubist style. **3** Griffith directs the 3-hour spectacle *The Birth of a Nation,* starring actress Lillian Gish. The film, known for its music and authentic set and costume design, is based	**12** W. Somerset Maugham, Eng. writer, publishes *Of Human Bondage,* a semiautobiographical novel about a medical student. **13** Franz Kafka, Aust. writer, completes "Metamorphosis," a short story. **14** Conrad publishes *Victory,* a novel. **15** Ivor Novello, Welsh composer, writes "Keep the Home Fires Burning," a popular,

Science & Technology

America

tronomer, uses a spectroscope to determine that the companion of Sirius is extremely dense—about one ton per cubic inch.

5 Burbank publishes the 14-volume *Luther Burbank, His Methods and Discoveries and Their Practical Applications.*

6 The last known passenger pigeon dies in the Cincinnati Zoo.

7 Ives develops a process for making color movies.

8 Charles Lawrence, aeronautical engineer, develops the first successful air-cooled airplane engine. This makes long-distance flights possible.

9 Cadillac develops a practical V-8 engine.

10 Houston (Tex.) becomes the country's only inland port when the Houston Ship Canal opens.

11 Nobel Prize, Chemistry: Theodore Richards for determining the atomic weights of more than 60 elements.

Elsewhere

15 Edward Kleinschmidt, Ger. inventor, invents the teletypewriter.

16 Sir Henry Dale, Eng. physiologist, isolates acetylcholine, a chemical which plays an important role in the transmission of nerve impulses.

17 Nobel Prize, Physics: Von Laue, for studying the diffraction of x-rays by crystals.

18 Nobel Prize, Physiology or Medicine: Robert Bárány, Aust. physiologist, for his research on the physiology and pathology of the ear.

Miscellaneous

America

stadium and shows the increasing popularity of the sport.

4 Cotillion, once the most fashionable dance of society, takes second place to the waltz and the two-step.

5 Lassen Peak, California, long supposed extinct, emits steam and ash. On June 8 and 14, steam rises to 10,000 ft. It is the only active volcano in the U.S.

6 Federal Trade Commission is established to prevent monopolies in business and to maintain competition in commerce.

7 Walter Hagen wins the U.S. Golf Association Open.

Elsewhere

Scene from *The Birth of a Nation*, motion picture directed by D.W. Griffith

---

America

1 Irving Langmuir, chemist, builds a mercury-vapor condensation pump that is able to create a nearly perfect vacuum.

2 Hermann Muller, geneticist, publishes *The Mechanism of Mendelian Heredity,* a classic in genetics.

3 Hiram Maxim establishes the American Radio Relay League to encourage communication among amateur radio operators.

Elsewhere

11 Anton Flettner, Ger. engineer, invents a military tank operated by remote control.

12 Bayliss publishes *Principles of General Physiology,* the most complete text on this topic of its time.

13 Nobel Prize, Physics: William Bragg and Lawrence Bragg, for their use of x-rays to determine crystalline structure.

America

1 Taxi industry begins when automobile owners discover that people will pay for a short automobile ride. Fare is a "jitney" (a nickel), and cars are soon called jitneys. Drivers are known as *hackers* or *hackies* in the East, *cabbies* in the Midwest.

2 First transatlantic radiotelephone communication is sent between Arlington, Va., and the Eiffel Tower, in Paris.

3 Eighty-acre tract in

Elsewhere

8 Ger. aviator Hugo Junkers develops the first fighter airplane.

9 Leipzig (Germany) railroad station is completed; it is the largest in Europe.

10 Two passenger trains and a troop train collide in Gretna, Switzerland; 227 are killed.

11 Brit. archaeologist Aurel Stein on an expedition to South Mongolia, discovers Marco Polo's "city of Etzina."

12 Earthquake in Avez-

1915

	America	Elsewhere	America	Elsewhere

America (History and Politics)

submarine warfare.

5 U.S. Marines are sent to Haiti to protect U.S. property and lives. U.S.-Haitian treaty provides for U.S. supervision of Haitian finances and constabulary (military district).

6 U.S. merchant ships are sunk by German submarines.

7 Interstate Commerce Commission decides that railroads can not own steamship lines on the Great Lakes.

8 Bryan resigns as Secretary of State. He opposed Wilson's strong notes of protest to Germany, fearing U.S. involvement in World War I.

9 Pres. Wilson reluctantly agrees to U.S. loans to warring nations.

10 U.S. declares embargo on the exportation of arms to Mexico, except to territories controlled by Mexican President Venustiano Carranza.

Elsewhere (History and Politics)

Austro-German forces drive the Russians out of Poland and hold Eastern Front extending from Riga to Chernovtsy. Bulgarians join Central Powers and overrun Serbia and Montenegro. French advance at Artois on the Western Front, but sustain heavy losses. Germans occupy Russian Baltic ports. Sir Douglas Haig is made Commander-in-Chief of all British forces in France.

12 Russians invade northern Persia to break German control at Tehran.

13 Czar Nicholas II assumes command of the Russian army. Czarina Alexandra Feodorovna takes control in St. Petersburg, Russia, and comes under the influence of the notorious adventurer Grigori Yefimovich Rasputin.

14 Japan presents China with Twenty-one Demands. They are designed to make China a Japanese protectorate.

15 South Africans under Louis Botha conquer the German colony of South West Africa (now Namibia).

America (The Arts)

on Dixon's *The Clansman.* [1905:ARTS/2]

4 William Fox founds the Fox Film Company, which eventually evolves into Twentieth-Century Fox.

5 Elie Nadelman, sculptor, creates "Man in the Open Air," a mannequin-like figurine.

6 The first motion picture serials (e.g., *The Perils of Pauline*) appear.

7 Chaplin stars in *The Tramp.*

8 Edgar Lee Masters, poet and novelist, publishes the popular *Spoon River Anthology.*

9 George Cram Cook, writer, organizes The Provincetown Players.

10 Douglas Fairbanks, actor and producer, has his first starring role in the film *The Lamb.*

11 Charles T. Griffes composes the piano piece "The White Peacock."

Elsewhere (The Arts)

patriotic war song.

16 John Buchan, Eng. novelist, publishes *Thirty-nine Steps,* a thriller that introduces the detective, Richard Hannay.

17 Duchamp begins the Dadaist "The Large Glass, or The Bride Stripped Bare by Her Bachelors, Even." When the glass is broken (1923), he proclaims, "Now it is complete."

18 Raoul Dufy, popular Fr. Fauvist, paints "Homage to Mozart."

19 Eng. poet Rupert Brooke publishes *1915,* a collection of wartime sonnets that includes "The Soldier."

20 Juan Gris, Span. Cubist, paints "La Place Ravignan, Still Life in Front of an Open Window."

21 Rolland publishes the humanitarian pamphlet, "Above the Battle"; he is awarded the Nobel Prize in Literature.

1916

America (History and Politics)

1 Resolutions restricting travel by U.S. citizens on Allied ships in war zone are tabled by Congress.

2 Senate ratifies treaty with Nicaragua, giving U.S. sole rights to build canal across Nicaragua; U.S. secures two naval bases there.

3 Mexican revolutionary Francisco ("Pancho") Villa leads guerrilla band on raids into New Mexico and Texas, killing 17 Americans. U.S. troops under Gen. John J. Pershing pursue Villa into Mexico without success. U.S.-Mexican Commission is set up to settle differences.

4 Pres. Wilson sends ultimatum stating that unless Germany stops submarine attacks on unarmed ships, the U.S. will sever relations.

Elsewhere (History and Politics)

12 World War I continues. Germans attack the French at the indecisive Battle of Verdun. British launch offensive at the Battle of the Somme and use tanks for the first time on the Western Front. Germany declares war on Portugal. French capture Corfu as a refuge for Serbian troops. Austrians seize Scutari and Berat in Albania. Russians capture Lutsk, Poland, and Chernovtsy, Rumania. Italians fight Austrians at indecisive Battles of the Isonzo. Paul von Hindenburg becomes commander of all German armies. Allies blockade Greek ports and begin massive offensive in Macedonia. Rumania declares war on Austria-Hungary and invades Transylvania. Bulgarian-Ger-

America (The Arts)

1 Norman Rockwell, illustrator begins to create the cover illustrations for *The Saturday Evening Post,* continuing until 1963.

2 Carl Sandburg, poet, causes an uproar in poetry circles with his publication of *Chicago Poems.*

3 Man Ray, avant-garde painter, executes "The Rope Dancer Accompanies Herself with Her Shadows."

4 Morton Schamberg, Precisionist painter, paints "Machine."

5 Griffith directs *Intolerance,* a spectacular film that interweaves four stories, known for its magnificent sets.

Elsewhere (The Arts)

14 The term "Dada" is coined to describe a new, outrageous, and somewhat nihilistic movement in art.

15 Jean Arp, Fr. Dadaist, prepares "Squares Arranged According to the Laws of Chance" (-1917), an early paper collage.

16 Joyce publishes the semiautobiographical novel, *Portrait of the Artist as a Young Man.*

17 Lawrence publishes *Women in Love,* a novel.

18 Sergei Prokofiev, Russ. composer, causes a scandal with his *Scythian Suite.*

19 Tristan Tzara,

Science & Technology		Miscellaneous		
America	**Elsewhere**	**America**	**Elsewhere**	
4 Joseph Goldberger, physician, discovers that pellagra is caused by a vitamin deficiency. **5** Stockard publishes *The Origin of Blood*. **6** George Shull, botanist, develops a highly successful variety of hybrid corn. **7** In *Climate and Evolution*, William Matthew suggests that animals once moved from continent to continent via natural land bridges. **8** Western Electric develops a jamming device to interfere with wartime enemy radio communication. **9** A. Bell in New York calls T. Watson in San Francisco in the first transcontinental telephone call. **10** Margaret Sanger publishes *Family Limitation* and is jailed for supporting birth control.		northwestern Colorado and northeastern Utah, an area rich in fossils, is set aside to establish Dinosaur National Monument. It is enlarged to 200,000 acres in 1938. **4** Ford plant in Detroit produces its one millionth automobile. **5** In Cambridge, Mass., Norman Taber runs the mile in 4:12.6, nearly 2 seconds under the old record. **6** Excursion steamer *Eastland* capsizes at its pier in Chicago: 852 people die. **7** Jess Willard takes the heavyweight boxing championship from Jack Johnson in a 23-round fight at Havana, Cuba.	zano, Italy; 30,000 people die.	
1 Millikan confirms Planck's constant photoelectrically by using a wavelength of light and the charge of an electron. **2** National Park Service is established as part of the U.S. Department of the Interior. **3** Electric clocks are introduced. **4** Gilbert N. Lewis, chemist, proposes a shell theory of electron orbits to explain valence and bonding. **5** Alexanderson invents a selective tuner for radio receivers. **6** John Watson proposes that learning is actually a series of conditioned responses. **7** Rous develops a pro-	**13** Owen Richardson publishes *The Emission of Electricity from Hot Bodies*. **14** Peter Debye, Dutch physical chemist, uses powdered forms of solids to study their crystalline structure. **15** Karl M.G. Siegbahn, Swed. physicist, discovers the M series of spectral lines. **16** August Krogh, Dan. physiologist, publishes *The Respiratory Exchange of Animals and Man*. **17** Sherrington publishes *Mammalian Physiology*. **18** Einstein proposes a general theory of relativity to explain all laws of physics in terms of mathematical equations.	**1** Child labor laws in South Carolina raise the minimum age of children for work in mills, factories, and mines, from 12 to 14. **2** Michigan, Montana, Nebraska, South Dakota, and Utah prohibit the sale of alcoholic drinks. By this date, through political means and the influence of the clergy, the Anti-Saloon League has been largely responsible for dry laws in 24 states with a combined population of about 32.5 million people. **3** Margaret Sanger, Fania Mandell, and Ethel Burne open America's first birth control clinic in Brooklyn.	**9** Severe rationing of food in Germany; people line up in Paris to receive milk. **10** Summer Time (daylight saving) begins in Britain. **11** Treatment of war casualties leads to the development of plastic surgery. **12** French cruiser *Provence* sinks in the Mediterranean Sea; 3100 persons die. **13** Military tanks are used for the first time in Europe.	**1916**

291

History and Politics

America

5 National Defense Act authorizes expansion of the Army and National Guard.
6 U.S. Marines land in Santo Domingo to settle internal conflict; occupation lasts until 1924.
7 Congress passes Warehouse Act authorizing crop-financing loans.
8 Jones Act restates U.S. intention to grant independence to the Philippine Islands when a stable government is formed.
9 Federal Farm Loan Bank Act helps farmers get credit.
10 Charles Evans Hughes leaves the Supreme Court to run for President on the Republican ticket.
11 Wilson and Marshall are reelected President and Vice President, respectively, on the Democratic ticket. For three days the outcome is uncertain until the final count in California shows the state has gone Democratic by less than 4000 votes.

Elsewhere

man forces capture Bucharest.
13 Turks defeat British in Mesopotamia, invade Persia, but are stopped by the Russians.
14 German fleet inflicts heavy damage on British fleet at the Battle of Jutland (Skagerrak).
15 German warships raid English coast and ravage Allied commerce in the Atlantic. German long-range bombers begin strategic bombing of enemy cities.
16 Russian right-wing patriots, including the Czar's cousin, assassinate Rasputin. [1915:HIST/13]
17 Husayn ibn Ali leads a successful revolt against the Turks in Arabia and proclaims himself King of the Arabs.
18 China recognizes Japan's claims in southern Manchuria and Inner Mongolia.
19 Belgian forces capture Ruanda and Urundi and German forts on Lake Tanganyika in Africa.

The Arts

America

6 Ring Lardner, writer, publishes *You Know Me, Al,* a collection of humorous short stories about a baseball player.
7 O'Neill's play, *Bound East for Cardiff,* is produced.
8 Adolph Zukor, film producer, becomes president of what is now Paramount Pictures.
9 Edwin Arlington Robinson, poet, publishes *The Man Against the Sky,* a volume of poetry.
10 Kilmer publishes *The Circus and Other Essays.*
11 E.L. Masters publishes *The Great Valley.*
12 Amy Lowell publishes *Men, Women, and Giants.*
13 Ellen Glasgow publishes the novel, *Life and Gabriella.*

Elsewhere

Rom. poet and cofounder of Dadaism, publishes the first Dadaist poems.
20 Vicente Blasco Ibáñez, Span. writer, publishes *The Four Horsemen of the Apocalypse,* a popular novel.
21 Enrique Granados, Span. composer, completes *Goyescas,* an opera inspired by the works of Goya.
22 Fr. writer Henri Barbusse is awarded the Prix Goncourt for his war novel, *Under Fire.*
23 Max Brod, Czech. writer, publishes *The Redemption of Tycho Brahe,* a historical novel.

1917

America (History and Politics)

1 Supreme Court upholds the constitutionality of the Webb-Kenyon law. [1913:HIST/2]
2 U.S. and Denmark ratify American purchase of the Danish West Indies (Virgin Islands) for $25 million.
3 Puerto Rico becomes U.S. territory whose inhabitants are U.S. citizens.
4 Immigration Act with literacy test for immigrants is passed over Pres. Wilson's veto. [1915:HIST/2]
5 Pres. Wilson outlines to the Senate in "Peace without Victory" speech his Ten Points for establishing an international organization to prevent future war.
6 Pres. Wilson severs diplomatic relations with Germany on the same day U.S. liner *Housatonic* is sunk after it ignores warning by German submarine.
7 Publication of secret Ger-

Elsewhere (History and Politics)

13 World War I continues. Germany begins unrestricted submarine warfare and repeatedly attacks British convoys in the North Sea. German and Austrian troops drive the Russians back and recapture Halicz, Tarnopol, Stanislav, and Chernovtsy on the Eastern Front. Germans overrun Latvia and conquer the Baltic Islands. French offensive at Aisne and Champagne fails. French suffer heavy losses; mutinies erupt in the French army. British offensive at Ypres fails to break German Western Front. Austro-German forces defeat the Italians at the Battle of Caporetto. China declares war on Germany and Austria.
14 Revolution breaks out in Russia, forcing Czar Nicholas II to abdicate. Revolutionaries, headed by Aleksandr Kerensky, set up moderate government. Bolsheviks, led

America (The Arts)

1 Ferdinand "Jelly Roll" Morton publishes the jazz composition "Jelly Roll Blues."
2 Henry Kimball Hadley, composer, writes the opera *Azora, the Daughter of Montezuma.*
3 Cohan writes the World War I song "Over There" for which Congress honors him in 1940.
4 Gallery "291" closes. [1905:ARTS/1]
5 E.A. Robinson publishes *Merlin,* the first part of his King Arthur trilogy.
6 V. Lindsay publishes *The Chinese Nightingale and Other Poems,* which includes "In Praise of Johnny Appleseed."
7 H. Garland publishes the autobio-

Elsewhere (The Arts)

14 Fr. composer Erik Satie and Fr. writer Jean Cocteau collaborate on *Parade,* a ballet choreographed by Leonide Massine and designed by Picasso. In his review of *Parade,* Apollinaire coins the word "Surrealism."
15 Apollinaire publishes *Les Mamelles de Tirèsias,* one of the first Surrealist plays.
16 T.S. Eliot, Amer.-born Eng. poet, publishes "The Love Song of J. Alfred Prufrock," his first major work.
17 Reinhardt establishes the Salzburg Festival, Austria.
18 Piet Mondrian and Theo van Doesburg, Dutch artists, establish *De Stijl* (-1931), an avant-garde review of art.

Science & Technology		Miscellaneous		
America	**Elsewhere**	**America**	**Elsewhere**	
cess for storing blood, giving rise to the idea of blood banks. **8** Edwin P. Hubble, astronomer, publishes *A Photographic Investigation of Faint Nebulae.* **9** Shull establishes *Genetics,* a scientific journal. **10** Gustav Elmen develops "permalloy," an easily magnetized metal that is widely used in electronic and communication equipment. **11** "Heparin," a natural anticoagulant produced by the liver, is discovered. **12** National Research Council is established by the National Academy of Sciences.		**4** First permanent annual Rose Bowl game is held between Washington State College and Brown University; Washington State wins, 14 to 0. In 1923, this game is officially called the "Rose Bowl Game." **5** Lawyer and writer Louis D. Brandeis appointed to the Supreme Court, the first Jew to become a Justice. **6** Grover Cleveland of the Philadelphia Phillies sets a record for most shutouts pitched in one season: 16 games. **7** Brig. Gen. John Thompson invents the submachine gun, popularly called the "Tommy gun." **8** First professional golf tournament is held at Bronxville, N.Y., by the Professional Golfers' Association, formed earlier in the year.		
1 Mount Wilson Observatory installs a 100-in. reflecting telescope. **2** Millikan publishes *The Electron.* **3** Harlow Shapley, astronomer, develops a general law based on Cepheid variables for determining stellar distances. **4** Radios are used for ground-to-air and air-to-air communication. **5** Eight-cylinder *Liberty* engines are developed. Incorporating the best parts of other patented engines, the *Liberty* engines are soon in great demand. **6** Max Mason, mathematician, invents a submarine detector. **7** Ralph Parker, physician, develops a vaccine for Rocky Mountain Spotted Fever.	**8** Julius Wagner von Jauregg, Aust. neurologist, successfully treats paralysis by introducing malaria into the patient's system. **9** Henry D. Dakin, Eng. chemist, publishes *Handbook of Chemical Antiseptics.* **10** Einstein proposes his theory of a static (unchanging) universe. He also describes stimulated emission of radiation, the basis of lasers and masers. **11** Nobel Prize, Physics: Charles G. Barkla, Eng. chemist, for discovering the x-ray radiation of elements.	**1** Federal Fuel Administrator orders all electric advertising signs shut off every Sunday and Thursday. **2** First baseball game played in New York's Polo Grounds results in the arrest of managers John McGraw of the Giants and Christy Mathewson of the Cincinnati Reds for violating New York's Blue Law against Sunday ball playing. **3** There are 4.8 million motor vehicles registered in the U.S.; 435,000 of them are trucks. In this year, 1.7 million passenger cars and 181,348 commercial vehicles are produced, and there are 25,500 garages and 13,500 repair shops to service them. Average price of a new car is $750. **4** Congress adopts the	**7** Agnes Maude Royden becomes the assistant preacher at the City Temple, London, the first Englishwoman to have a permanent pulpit. **8** French ammunition ship *Mont Blanc* and Belgian steamer *Imo* collide in Halifax Harbor, Canada; 1600 die. **9** Quebec (Canada) railroad bridge 1800 ft. long is completed. **10** Swiss psychologist Carl G. Jung publishes *The Psychology of the Unconscious.* **11** Trans-Siberian Railroad, begun in 1891, is completed; it is 5787 mi. long, linking Moscow with Vladivostok. **12** Women in factories cut their hair as a safety precaution, and "bobbed hair" sweeps Britain and the U.S.	**1917**

History and Politics

America

man note proposing German-Mexican alliance helps Pres. Wilson gain House approval to arm merchant ships.
8 Pres. Wilson calls for special session of Congress. He signs resolution declaring war on Germany.
9 Senate adopts cloture rule, permitting majority to end debate.
10 Congress passes Selective Service Act authorizing registration of all men, Espionage Act, War Revenue Act, and Trading with the Enemy Act.
11 Gen. Pershing is appointed head of the American Expeditionary Force in France.
12 Congress adopts the Eighteenth Amendment to the Constitution and sends it to the states for ratification. [1919:HIST/2]

Elsewhere

by Leon Trotsky and Lenin, overthrow Kerensky's government, seize power in Russia, and conclude an armistice with the Germans on the Eastern Front.
15 Thomas Edward Lawrence ("Lawrence of Arabia"), Brit. adventurer, leads Arab forces in their revolt against Turkish domination.
16 Turks are defeated by the British at Baghdad and retreat from Persia.
17 Balfour Declaration pledges British support to the Zionists for the creation of a Jewish national homeland in Palestine.
18 Finland proclaims its independence.
19 Mexico adopts a new, more socialistic, constitution.

The Arts

America

graphical *A Son of the Middle Border*.
8 Tarkington reveals the joys of male adolescence in *Seventeen*.
9 Patrick Henry Bruce, painter of the synchromist movement, paints "Composition III."
10 Charles Demuth, Precisionist painter, paints the abstract "Bermuda No. 2—The Schooner."
11 Buster Keaton, actor and director, establishes his comedy trademark of deadpan expressions in the film *The Butcher Boy*.
12 Kilmer publishes *Main Street and Other Poems*.
13 Joseph Hergesheimer, author, publishes the novel *The Three Black Pennies*.

Elsewhere

19 Siegfried Sassoon, Eng. poet, is acclaimed for his antiwar *The Old Huntsman*.
20 Chirico's "Grand Metaphysical Interior" and Carrà's "Drunken Gentlemen" mark the start of the school of metaphysical painting.
21 Paul Valéry, Fr. writer, publishes "La Jeune Parque," his most famous poem.
22 "The Wild Swans at Coole" establishes Yeats as a major poet.

1918

America — History and Politics

1 Pres. Wilson outlines to Congress the Fourteen Points, which he feels are indispensable as a basis for peace.
2 U.S. enacts more war mobilization measures. War Finance Corporation is created to support war industries. Sedition Act broadens Espionage Act of 1917, providing heavy penalties for those who obstruct war effort.
3 U.S. troops attack German lines and capture Belleau Wood. Half million U.S. troops under Gen. Pershing defeat Germans at Saint Mihiel. U.S. forces help Allies stop German advance at Château-Thierry, Aisne-Marne, and Meuse-Argonne. Wilson's Fourteen Points are accepted by Germany and the Allies as the basis of peace negotiations, and an armistice is signed.
4 Pres. Wilson announces that he will attend the Paris peace conference. He is criticized by many for his "egotism" and for not including

Elsewhere — History and Politics

8 Marshal Ferdinand Foch assumes unified command of the British, French, and American armies in World War I. Russia signs separate peace Treaty of Brest-Litovsk with Central Powers. Germany concentrates its forces on Western Front. Allies stop German counter-offensive at the second Battle of the Marne and break the Hindenburg Line. German fleet mutinies; Germans revolt in Kiel and Hamburg. Austria and Turkey collapse under Allied offensives. Italians win decisive victory over the Austrians at Vittorio Veneto, which leads to Austro-Hungarian surrender on Nov. 3.
9 Kaiser William II abdicates and flees from Germany. New German government accepts U.S. Pres. Wilson's Fourteen Points as the basis of peace negotiations. Armistice is signed at Compiègne, France, ending the fighting in World War I. German fleet surrenders to

America — The Arts

1 Robert Lee Ripley, cartoonist, begins his syndicated "Believe It or Not" series of strange and unusual facts.
2 *Stars and Stripes,* the official newspaper of the U.S. Armed Forces, is established.
3 Thomas "Fats" Waller, entertainer, composes "Squeeze Me," his first successful song.
4 While a soldier, Irving Berlin writes the show *Yip, Yip, Yaphank* about army life. The show includes the song "Oh, How I Hate to Get Up in the Morning."
5 George Gershwin, composer, writes the song "Swanee" for the Broadway show *Sinbad.*
6 Rosa Ponselle, singer, becomes the leading soprano with

Elsewhere — The Arts

11 With the publication of the manifesto, *After Cubism,* Fr. painters LeCorbusier (Charles-Edouard Jeanneret) and Amédée Ozenfant establish Purism.
12 Max Beckmann, Ger. Expressionist painter, completes the nightmarish "The Night."
13 Gustav Holst, Ger. composer, completes *The Planets,* an orchestral suite.
14 Almost 30 years after his death, poems by Eng. writer Paul Manley Hopkins are published.
15 Paul Nash, Eng. artist, paints "The Menin Road," an abstract work inspired by war-ravaged countrysides.
16 Satie composes his greatest work, *Socrate,* chamber music inspired

Science & Technology		Miscellaneous		
America	**Elsewhere**	**America**	**Elsewhere**	

Buster Keaton, master silent film comedian

Fourteenth Amendment, which outlaws the manufacture or sale of alcoholic drinks. By this time 29 states have Prohibition laws. The Amendment is to take effect in January 1920.

5 Four women arrested for picketing for woman's suffrage (the right to vote) in front of the White House are sentenced to 6 months in prison.

6 Rep. Jeannette Rankin, Republican from California, is the first woman member in the House of Representatives.

13 Guatemala City, Guatemala, is ruined by an earthquake.

14 Almost 550 people are killed when a troop train is derailed near the mouth of the Mt. Cenis Tunnel in Modane, France.

1918

1 Armstrong designs the super-heterodyne circuit.

2 Browning invents an automatic rifle.

3 Shapley determines that the Milky Way is about 100,000 light years in length. He also calculates that the Sun is about 30,000 light years from the center of the galaxy.

4 Herbert M. Evans, biochemist, determines that human beings have 48 chromosomes.

5 Robert G. Aitken, astronomer, publishes *The Binary Stars.*

6 Jesse M. Coulter, botanist, publishes *Plant Genetics.*

7 Bell invents a hydrofoil boat that goes 60 mph during a test run.

8 Arthur Dempster, physicist, develops a mass spectrometer for studying atomic nuclei.

9 The United States is divided into four time

11 Radio communication between England and Australia is achieved for the first time.

12 Eddington publishes *Report on the Relativity Theory of Gravitation.*

13 Starling concludes that the force of muscular contraction is directly related to the extent to which the muscle is stretched.

14 Nobel Prize, Chemistry: Haber, for his method of synthesizing ammonia (Haber-Bosch process).

15 Nobel Prize, Physics: Planck, for his formulation of the quantum theory.

1 Influenza epidemic, traveling west from Europe, begins in eastern U.S. and spreads to 46 states. Before it ends in 1919, about 500,000 people die. Throughout the world at least 20 million people die, and one billion are ill.

2 First scheduled airmail service begins between New York City and Washington, D.C. Stamps cost 24¢ (reduced to 6¢ several months later).

3 Lt. Douglas Campbell shoots down his 5th German airplane, becoming the first American-trained "ace."

4 Daylight saving time goes into effect. [1918:SCI/9]

5 An anti-submarine device, a huge steel net stretched underwater across the Narrows in New York harbor since the beginning of the war, is removed.

7 Stefansson returns from his 5-year voyage to north of the Arctic Circle.

8 Ger. philosopher Oswald Spengler begins publishing of *The Decline of the West.*

9 Women over 30 years old gain the vote in Britain.

10 Food shortage in Britain leads to the establishment of national food kitchens and rationing. Prime Minister appeals to women to help with the harvest.

11 Brit. archaeologists H.R.H. Hall and Leonard Woolley begin excavations in ancient sites in Babylonia (present-day Iraq).

12 Hong Kong race track grandstand collapses; 600 die.

13 World-wide influenza epidemic strikes; by 1920 nearly 20 million people die.

America	Elsewhere	America	Elsewhere

an active Republican or a Senator on the peace commission.
5 Supreme Court rules that conscription (compulsory enrollment of men for military service) is authorized by the Constitution in Article I.
6 Socialist leader Debs is sentenced to ten years in prison for publicly denouncing the government's prosecution of persons charged with sedition under the Espionage Act.
7 U.S. forces are rushed to Koblenz after the outbreak of a left-wing revolution in Germany.

British.
10 Austria, Hungary, Poland, and Czechoslovakia are proclaimed independent republics.
11 Montenegro unites with Serbia. The united "Kingdom of Serbs, Croats, and Slovenes" is proclaimed.
12 Great Civil War begins in Russia between the Reds (Bolsheviks) and the Whites (Mensheviks) for control of the government. Czar Nicholas II and his family are executed.
13 Iceland becomes a sovereign state in union with Denmark.

the Metropolitan Opera.
7 Joseph Stella, painter of the synchromist movement, paints "Brooklyn Bridge," the first of a series on that structure.
8 Maxwell Bodenheim, bohemian poet and novelist, publishes *Minna and Myself,* his first volume of poetry.
9 H.K. Hadley composes the opera *Bianca*.
10 Cather publishes *My Antonia.*

by Plato's *Dialogues* (c.384–360 B.C.).
17 Fernand Léger, Fr. Cubist, completes "Engine Rooms," one of his celebrated "machine paintings."
18 Darius Milhaud, Fr. pioneer in polytonal composition, collaborates with Claudel to produce *Man and his Desire,* a ballet.

1919

1 Pres. Wilson urges the establishment of the League of Nations at the Paris peace conference. Commission under Wilson drafts League's Covenant consisting of 26 articles.
2 Eighteenth Amendment to the Constitution is ratified, prohibiting the manufacture, sale, import, or export of liquor in the U.S.
3 Pres. Wilson submits the Treaty of Versailles with Covenant of the League of Nations to the Senate for ratification.
4 Communist Labor Party (now American Communist Party) is formed in Chicago after split with Socialist Party.
5 Pres. Wilson makes nationwide tour on behalf of the League of Nations and peace treaty, hoping public favor will force its ratification. He becomes ill on tour and returns to Washington, D.C., where he suffers a stroke.
6 Congress passes Volstead Act over Pres. Wilson's veto. It provides enforcement of the Eighteenth Amendment. Bootleggers (illegal distillers and liquor sellers) immediately begin operations.
7 Calvin Coolidge, Governor of Massachusetts, calls out National Guard to end Bos-

10 Allies and Germany sign the Treaty of Versailles, ending World War I. Outstanding figures in the negotiations leading to the treaty are Woodrow Wilson for the U.S., Georges Clemenceau for France, David Lloyd George for England, and Vittorio Emanuele Orlando for Italy— the so-called "Big Four." Austria signs the Treaty of Saint Germain, Hungary signs the Treaty of Trianon, Bulgaria signs the Treaty of Neuilly, and Turkey signs the Treaty of Sèvres.
11 Nationalist Congress at Sivas affirms the unity of Turkey and opposes Allied occupation.
12 Geneva, Switzerland, is chosen as the seat of the League of Nations.
13 Perpetual neutrality of Switzerland is recognized by the Treaty of Versailles.
14 By treaty, Italy supports Greek claims in Thrace and Epirus.
15 Germany's provisional government crushes the Spartacist (socialists and Communists) revolt in Berlin.
16 Germany adopts a democratic federal constitution at Weimar and becomes known as the Weimar Republic.
17 Rumanians invade Hungary and occupy Budapest,

1 Charlie Chaplin, D.W. Griffith, Douglas Fairbanks, and Mary Pickford combine their assets to form United Artists Corporation.
2 During a European tour by the Southern Syncopated Orchestra, jazz attains greater respectability when Swiss conductor Ernest Ansermet praises the jazz soprano saxophonist Sidney Bechet.
3 The Eastman School of Music is founded.
4 John Reed, writer, publishes *Ten Days That Shook the World,* a first-hand account of the Russian Revolution.
5 Francis Picabia paints "Universal Prostitution."
6 George Gershwin writes the score to the musical *La, La Lucille.*
7 Paul Whiteman, musician and bandleader, forms a band that features "symphonic jazz."
8 The will of Augustus D. Juilliard, banker and industrialist, authorizes the founding of the Juilliard School

12 Robert Wiene, Ger. film maker, directs *The Cabinet of Dr. Caligari,* a classic silent horror film.
13 Arthur Bliss, prominent Eng. composer, experiments with using the voice as a musical instrument in *Rhapsody*.
14 At the request of Diaghilev, DeFalla revises an earlier work and produces *The Three-Cornered Hat,* a ballet choreographed by Massine and designed by Picasso.
15 Joan Miró, leading Span. Surrealist, paints "Montroig (The Olive Grove)."
16 Proust's *Within a Budding Grove,* the second volume in *Remembrance of Things Past,* is awarded the Prix Goncourt.
17 Duchamp completes "L.H.O.O.Q.," a reproduction of "Mona Lisa" (1502) to which he has added a moustache and goatee. It is considered an example of artistic nihilism.
18 Shaw writes the antiwar drama, *Heartbreak House.*

Science & Technology		Miscellaneous		
America	**Elsewhere**	**America**	**Elsewhere**	
zones (Eastern, Central, Mountain, and Pacific) by the Interstate Commerce Commission. **10** Walter Dandy, surgeon, injects air into the spaces in the brain to provide contrast in x-rays.		**6** Estimated casualties of World War I: Total Allies: of 42.1 million who served, 5.1 million dead; 12.8 million wounded; 4.1 million prisoners or missing. Central Powers: of 6.5 million who served, 8.5 million dead; 21.1 million wounded; 7.7 million prisoners or missing. U.S.: of 4.3 million who served, 126,000 dead (50,000 in battle and the rest of disease, especially influenza); 234,000 wounded, 4500 prisoners or missing.	 Babe Ruth, American baseball great	

1 Radio Corporation of America (RCA) is established. **2** T. H. Morgan publishes *The Physical Bases of Heredity*. **3** Robert H. Goddard, "Father of American Rocketry," suggests using rockets to reach the Moon in *A Method of Reaching Extreme Altitudes*. **4** John Watson publishes *Psychology from the Standpoint of a Behaviorist* and calls for behavioral conditioning as a research technique. **5** Cottrell develops a process for removing helium from natural gas. **6** Edwin Slosson publishes *Creative Chemistry*, a book that popularizes the subject by explaining it in everyday language. **7** Langmuir proposes the concentric shell theory of electrons and describes chemical bonds which he calls "covalent." **8** After 30 years of work, Ernest W. Brown completes accurate lunar tables based on his theory of the motion of the Moon. **9** Glenn L. Martin invents the Martin Bomber, a warplane.	**10** Knud Rasmussen, Danish-Eskimo explorer, presents much new scientific knowledge in his work *Greenland by the Polar Sea*. **11** Rutherford produces the first artificial decomposition of an element. **12** K. von Frisch determines that bees have a well-developed sense of smell and that they communicate with each other through body movements. **13** Sergi Voronoff, Russ. physician, claims to be able to rejuvenate people by grafting glands of monkeys to them. **14** Francis W. Aston, Eng. chemist, invents the mass spectrograph, an instrument used to study isotopes and determine atomic weights. **15** Nobel Prize, Physics: Stark, for discovering the Stark effect. **[1913:SCI/17]** **16** Nobel Prize, Physiology or Medicine: Bordet, for his discovery of the immunity processes in blood.	**1** Goodyear Tire and Rubber Company balloon, the "Wing Foot," crashes into the Illinois Trust and Savings Bank at LaSalle and Jackson Sts., Chicago; 12 killed, 28 hurt. **2** Babe Ruth hits a 587-foot home run in a game between the Boston Red Sox and the New York Giants in Tampa. **3** Father Divine's Peace Mission movement gains national attention through its activities at Sayville, Long Island, N.Y. Viewed as God in the flesh by his followers, Father Divine combines evangelism with social philosophy, stressing racial equality and economic cooperation. **4** Jack Dempsey becomes the world heavyweight boxing champion when he defeats Jess Willard in Toledo, Ohio. **5** First municipal airport opens, at Tucson, Ariz. **6** "Sir Barton" is the first horse to win the Triple Crown—the Kentucky Derby, the Preakness, and the Belmont Stakes. **7** Daily air-mail service begins between New York City and Chicago. **8** Development of me-	**10** Austria abolishes the death penalty. **11** J.W. Alcock and A.W. Brown make the first nonstop flight across the Atlantic in 16 hrs. 27 min. Ross and Keith Smith fly from London to Australia in 135 hrs. **12** Women over 20 years of age are given the vote in Germany. **13** Span. matador Juan Belmonte kills 200 bulls in 109 bullfights.	**1919**

ton police strike. **8** Pres. Wilson refuses to accept amendments to the Treaty of Versailles, and the Senate fails to ratify it. U.S. never joins the League of Nations. **9** House of Representatives refuses to seat Berger of Wisconsin because of his pacifist opposition to World War I. He is tried and sentenced to a 20-year prison term for sedition.	forcing Hungarian Communist dictator Béla Kun to flee. **18** Benito Mussolini founds the *Fasci di combattimento,* whose followers stand for aggressive nationalism in Italy. **19** Russia gives Vilnius to Lithuania. Germans withdraw from Latvia. **20** Finland establishes a democratic republic after driving the Russians out. **21** Allied powers make German South West Africa a mandate to the South African Republic. **[1915:HIST/15]**	of Music in New York, now one of the most prominent music schools in the world. **9** James Branch Cabell, novelist, publishes *Jurgen,* a novel that brings the author fame. **10** Hergesheimer publishes *Java Head.* **11** Amy Lowell publishes *Pictures of the Floating World.*	**19** Brit. artist Augustus John paints the large mural, "Canadians Opposite Lens." **20** Maugham publishes *The Moon and Sixpence,* a novel. **21** Walter Gropius, Ger. architect, establishes Bauhaus, a school of architectural design.
1920 **1** "Red scare" results in nationwide raids by federal agents, with mass arrests of "anarchists," Communists, and labor agitators. **2** For the second time, the Senate rejects the Treaty of Versailles and the Covenant of the League of Nations. **[1919:HIST/8]** **3** Socialist Party nominates Debs, who is serving a ten-year prison sentence, for President for the fifth time. **[1918:HIST/6]** **4** Water Power Act establishes the Federal Power Commission to regulate generation of electricity from waterways on public lands and from navigable streams. **5** Nineteenth Amendment to the Constitution is ratified, granting suffrage (right to vote) to women. **6** National Labor Party, formed in 1919, changes its name to Farmer-Labor Party. **[1924:HIST/7]** **7** Warren G. Harding and Calvin Coolidge are elected President and Vice President, respectively, on the Republican ticket. Harding campaigns from his front porch and promises a return to "normalcy." **8** Pres. Wilson receives the Nobel Peace Prize. **9** Supreme Court rules Congress may assume powers by means of treaty, despite restrictions of the Tenth	**11** British Parliament enacts new Home Rule Bill, establishing separate parliaments for northern (Ulster) and southern Ireland. **12** Wolfgang Kapp leads right-wing uprising (the Kapp Putsch) and seizes government buildings in Berlin, Germany. **13** Czechoslovakia, Yugoslavia, and Rumania form the Little Entente to prevent the restoration of the Hapsburgs and to force Hungary's observance of the World War I peace treaty. **14** German East Africa becomes a British mandate and is renamed Tanganyika. British East Africa is renamed Kenya and is made into a Crown Colony. **15** By the Treaty of Sèvres, Turkey renounces sovereignty over Mesopotamia (now Iraq) and Palestine (including Trans-Jordan), both of which become British mandates. The Levant States (now Syria and Lebanon) become French mandates. **[1923:HIST/13]** **16** Venustiano Carranza, President of Mexico, is assassinated during a revolt. Álvaro Obregón becomes President of Mexico. **17** German Workers' Party is renamed the National Socialist German Workers', or Nazi, Party. **18** China's national government loses power during civil	**1** F. Scott Fitzgerald, important novelist of the period, publishes his first novel, *This Side of Paradise.* **2** Sinclair Lewis, novelist, publishes *Main Street,* about the cultural vacuum of a small Midwestern town. **3** E.A. Robinson publishes *Lancelot,* the second book of his King Arthur trilogy. **4** O'Neill publishes two plays: *Emperor Jones* and the Pulitzer Prize-winning *Beyond the Horizon.* **5** Hugh Lofting, children's writer, publishes *The Story of Dr. Doolittle,* the first of a series of books about a doctor who talks to and treats animals. **6** Sandburg's *Smoke and Steel,* a collection of poems for the "ordinary person," is published. **7** Joseph "King" Oliver, cornetist, organizes a jazz band in Chicago and invites Louis Armstrong to join as second cornetist. **8** Pound publishes *Hugh Selwyn Mauberley,* one of his more important poetic works.	**9** Tzara introduces Dadaism to the public by reading from a newspaper while an electric bell is ringing so loudly that no one can hear what he is saying. This demonstration is not well received. **10** Czech. writer Karel Čapek writes *R.U.R. (Rossum's Universal Robots),* a science fiction drama, coining the word *robot.* **11** Agatha Christie, Eng. detective novelist, introduces Hercule Poirot in *The Mysterious Affair at Styles.* **12** Max Ernst, Ger. Surrealist, exhibits the collage, "Here Everything is Still Floating." **13** Sigrid Undset, Norw. novelist, publishes the historical trilogy, *Kristin Lavransdatter* (–1922). **14** Leon Theremin, Sov. engineer, invents one of the first electronic musical instruments, the theremin. **15** E. Phillips Oppenheim, Eng. novelist, publishes *The Great Impersonation.*

Science & Technology		Miscellaneous		
America	**Elsewhere**	**America**	**Elsewhere**	

Man O'War, prizewinning race horse, with his jockey

chanical rabbit by Oliver Smith of California marks the beginning of modern greyhound racing.
9 War Department officially adopts the shoulder insignia, called a "patch," to distinguish different Army units in battle.

1920

America (Science & Technology)

1 Using his interferometer, Michelson makes the first accurate measurement of the size of a star. He calculates that Betelgeuse has a diameter of 240 million miles—about 300 times that of the Sun.
2 KDKA, America's first commercial radio station, begins operation in Pittsburgh, Pa., by broadcasting the results of the presidential election.
3 Cushing pioneers new techniques in brain surgery.
4 George Whipple, physician, experimentally cures anemia in dogs by feeding them large amounts of raw liver.
5 William D. Harkins, Pa. chemist, proposes the existence of an uncharged, subatomic particle which he calls the "neutron."
6 Lead tetraethyl is introduced as an antiknock agent in gasoline for internal combustion engines.
7 In *Easy Lessons in Einstein,* Slosson explains the theory of relativity in a simple, unconfusing manner.

Elsewhere (Science & Technology)

8 Soddy publishes *Science and Life,* in which he anticipates the usefulness of isotopes for determining geological age.
9 Eddington publishes *Space, Time, and Gravitation.*
10 Nikolay Vavilov, Soviet botanist, suggests that a plant species shows the greatest variation in its place of origin.
11 Otto Nordenskjöld, Swed. geographer, publishes a wealth of scientific data about Antarctica in his work *Scientific Results of the Swedish South Polar Expedition.*
12 Émile Coué, Fr. pharmacist, introduces a form of psychotherapy in which the patient repeats "Everyday, and in every way, I am becoming better and better."
13 Nobel Prize, Chemistry: Walther Nernst, Ger. physical chemist, for his formulation of the third law of thermodynamics (all molecular motion stops at absolute zero: $-273°C$).
14 Nobel Prize, Physics: Charles Guillaume, Swiss physicist, for his invention of Invar, an alloy of iron containing nickel.
15 Nobel Prize, Physiology or Medicine: Krogh, for his work on the pro-

America (Miscellaneous)

1 Women get the vote when the Nineteenth Amendment to the Constitution is ratified. By this time, 15 states have women's suffrage laws.
2 The U.S. now has more than 265,000 miles of railroad tracks.
3 Chicago Grand Jury indicts 8 members of the Chicago White Sox for fixing the World Series between the White Sox and the Cincinnati Reds. In 1920 the players are found not guilty of the charge, but they are not allowed to play baseball again.
4 Arkansas River overflows, causing $25 million property damage, $15 million in Pueblo, Colo., alone, which is largely destroyed by the flood. More than 1500 persons are either killed or missing.
5 William T. Tilden wins Wimbledon Lawn Tennis Championships; dominates world tennis until 1925.
6 "Man O' War," thoroughbred racing horse, retires after winning 20 of his 21 races, including the Belmont and the Preakness.

Elsewhere (Miscellaneous)

7 World population is 1.8 billion.
8 Water skiing as a sport is developed on Lake Annecy, France.
9 Olympic Games are held in Antwerp, Belgium. There are 24 sports, 154 events, 2606 participants, 29 nations.
10 Marconi opens the public broadcasting station in Britain.
11 Skeletal remains of the Peking Man, discovered in a cave near Peking, China, are considered to be about 350,000 years old.
12 There are 663,000 motor vehicles licensed in Great Britain, as compared to 8.8 million in the U.S.
13 3747 divorces are granted in the British courts; 95,763 convictions for drunkenness.
14 Mexican Alfredo Codona, the great aerialist, is the first to perfect a triple somersault.
15 Use of religion in Turkey for political ends is made punishable by death.
16 Earthquake in Kansu, China, kills 100,000 people.
17 First airplane flight from London to South Africa across the Sahara Desert.

History and Politics		The Arts	
America	**Elsewhere**	**America**	**Elsewhere**
Amendment. **10** U.S. Naval Court of Inquiry·clears U.S. Marines of the charge of killing natives in Haiti.	war which lasts until 1926. **19** Chaim Weizmann becomes head of the World Zionist Organization.		

1921

America (History and Politics)

1 Congress passes Quota Act, limiting immigration.
2 Congress passes Budget and Accounting Act. It provides for annual submission to Congress of a budget for the next year and an accounting of the last year's expenses.
3 Joint resolution of Congress declares World War I ended. Separate U.S. treaties with Germany, Austria, and Hungary are signed and ratified.
4 Department of Agriculture enforces regulations of the Packers and Stockyards Act to stop manipulation of prices in meat-packing industries.
5 End of wartime boom causes business depression and high unemployment. National conference proposes job program.
6 Ku Klux Klan promotes "white supremacy" and seeks to control politics in many southern communities.
7 Congress overrides President's veto of resolution which limits the size of the army to 175,000 men.
8 Ex-Pres. Taft is sworn in as Chief Justice of the U.S. Supreme Court.
9 California's Supreme Court declares the state's Alien Poll Tax Law unconstitutional and a violation of the treaty between the U.S. and Japan.
10 Senate ratifies Colombian treaty, agreeing to pay Colombia $25 million for the loss of Panama and granting free access to the Panama Canal.
11 Pres. Harding grants pardons to Debs and 23 others convicted under the Espionage Act. [1918:HIST/6]

Elsewhere (History and Politics)

12 British government grants southern Ireland Dominion status as the Irish Free State. [1920:HIST/11]
13 Rif tribes led by Abd el-Krim defeat a Spanish army at Anual, Morocco.
14 Giolitti fails to be re-elected Italian Premier. Mussolini gains power when the Fascists win seats in the government. [1919:HIST/18]
15 Greek advance against the Turks is stopped at the Battle of Sakarya in northwest Turkey.
16 Paris conference of Allies establishes German reparation payments for damages during World War I. Germany's liability is set at about $33 billion.
17 Ibn Saud conquers territory in Arabia and puts an end to the Rashid and Shalan dynasties.
18 Faisal I is proclaimed King of Iraq.
19 Plebiscite determines that Upper Silesia remain part of Germany. [1922:HIST/13]
20 Charles I tries twice to regain the Hungarian throne, but fails.
21 Takashi Hara, Jap. Prime Minister, is assassinated by a fanatic.
22 William Lyon Mackenzie King becomes Prime Minister of Canada.
23 France and Poland sign treaty providing for mutual help in case of attack.
24 Turkey and Afghanistan conclude treaty of alliance.
25 By the Treaty of Kars, Turkey recognizes Armenia as a Soviet republic.
26 Eduard Beneš is elected Premier of Czechoslovakia.

America (The Arts)

1 John Dos Passos, novelist and playwright, publishes the antiwar novel *Three Soldiers.*
2 Rudolph Valentino, actor known as the "great lover," stars in his first successful film, *The Four Horsemen of the Apocalypse.*
3 Ben Hecht, novelist and playwright, publishes *Erik Dorn,* a novel about post World War I Berlin.
4 DeWitt Wallace, publisher, founds *Reader's Digest.*
5 William Carlos Williams, poet and writer, publishes the poem "Sour Grapes."
6 Tarkington studies the feminine character in *Alice Adams.*
7 O'Neill publishes *Anna Christie.*
8 Marc Connelly, playwright, publishes *Dulcy,* his first successful play.
9 J.B. Cabell publishes *The Figures of Earth.*
10 H. Garland publishes *A Daughter of the Middle Border.*
11 Owen Davis, playwright, publishes *The Detour.*
12 Stuart Davis, important "between the wars" painter, paints "Lucky Strike."

Elsewhere (The Arts)

13 George Grosz, Ger. artist, paints "Nachkriegsidyll," a satire on German post-war society.
14 Luigi Pirandello, Ital. writer, produces *Six Characters in Search of an Author,* a drama that introduces the "theater within a theater" concept.
15 Aldous Huxley, Eng. writer, publishes *Crome Yellow,* a novel.
16 Sov. artist Chaim Soutine paints the powerful and violent "Gnarled Trees."
17 Aust. film maker Fritz Lang directs *Destiny,* a fictional history.
18 Walter de la Mare, Eng. writer, publishes *Memoirs of a Midget.*
19 Yeats publishes *Michael Robartes and the Dancer,* a collection that includes his famous poem, "Easter 1916."
20 Karel and Josef Čapek collaborate on *The Insect Play,* a comic fantasy.
21 Ernst paints the Surrealist "The Elephant of the Célèbes."
22 Picasso paints "Three Musicians."
23 Lytton Strachey, Eng. biographer, publishes *Queen Victoria.*
24 Arthur Waley, Eng. orientalist, translates *The Nō Plays of Japan.*

1922

America (History and Politics)

1 Arms Conference at Washington, D.C., guarantees the

Elsewhere (History and Politics)

11 By the Treaty of Rapallo, Germany and Russia

America (The Arts)

1 The Motion Picture Producers and Dis-

Elsewhere (The Arts)

12 Joyce publishes *Ulysses,* a literary

Science & Technology		Miscellaneous		
America	**Elsewhere**	**America**	**Elsewhere**	
	cesses of blood regulation in capillaries.			
1 Langmuir and Lewis independently propose atomic theories. **2** Albert W. Hull, physicist, invents the magnetron, a vacuum tube that produces microwaves. **3** Adams uses a spectroscope to study and determine the distances of 2000 stars. **4** Harkins produces an isotope of oxygen. **5** John Larson, psychiatrist, invents the "polygraph" (lie detector). **6** Alvan L. Barach, physician, designs a vented oxygen tent. **7** James B. Collip isolates pure insulin.	**8** Otto Stern, Ger. physical chemist, uses a molecular beam to determine certain properties of molecules. **9** Frederick Banting, Can. physician, and Charles Best, Amer. physiologist, discover insulin and use it to treat diabetes in dogs. **10** V. Bjerknes publishes the classic meteorological work *On the Dynamics of the Circular Vortex with Applications to the Atmosphere and to the Atmospheric Vortex and Wave Motion.* **11** Ernst Kretschmer, Ger. psychiatrist, publishes *Physique and Character,* in which he suggests that body build is closely related to mental state. **12** Hermann Rorschach, Swiss psychiatrist, publishes *Psychodiagnostics,* in which he introduces his famous inkblot test for study of personality. **13** Nobel Prize, Chemistry: Soddy, for his research in radioactivity and isotopes. **14** Nobel Prize, Physics: Einstein, for his discovery of the photoelectric effect, and for his many contributions to theoretical physics.	**1** Nicola Sacco and Bartolomeo Vanzetti are convicted of murder during a Mass. shoe factory robbery. Worldwide protest results, because many people believe the immigrant laborers are convicted for their anarchist beliefs rather than for murder. They are executed in 1927. **2** President Warren G. Harding proclaims November 11, Armistice Day, a national holiday. First burial ceremony is held at the Tomb of the Unknown Soldier (Tomb of the Unknowns) at Arlington National Cemetery, Va. **3** National Birth Control League and Voluntary Parenthood League are combined to form the American Birth Control League in New York City; League is headed by Margaret Sanger. **4** Knee-length skirts for women become the fashion, causing much comment in the press. **5** First prize fight with million-dollar receipts from paid admissions is held between Jack Dempsey and George Carpentier in Jersey City. Dempsey wins by a knockout in the 4th round. **6** Unemployment throughout the U.S. is 5.7 million. Widespread wage cuts in many industries include those of New York Central railroad employees (by 22½%) and clothing workers (by 15%).	**7** Russia's population is 136 million; Japan's, 78; Germany's, 60; Great Britain's, 42.7; France's, 39.2; Italy's, 38.7. **8** ZR-2, a British dirigible, breaks in two on a trial trip near Hull, Eng.; 62 die. **9** Swiss physician M.O. Bircher-Benner recommends the intake of more uncooked foods in his book, *The Fundamentals of Our Nutrition.* **10** Cuban chess player José Raoul Capablanca wins world championship from German player Emanuel Lasker, who has been champion since 1894. **11** Steamer *Hong Kong* is wrecked in the South China Sea; 1000 are lost.	**1921**
1 Philo T. Farnsworth, 15-year-old Idaho school-	**8** Banting and Best publish *Internal Secretions of*	**1** Station WEAF, New York City, broadcasts first	**9** Gliding flights lasting up to 3 hours are accom-	**1922**

America | ## Elsewhere | ## America | ## Elsewhere

History and Politics — America

U.S. Open Door Policy in China. Nine major powers also sign treaties limiting warships, restricting the use of submarines, and outlawing poison gas.

2 Fordney-McCumber Tariff raises duties on manufactured goods and puts high, protective tariffs on farm products.

3 Oklahoma is placed under martial law to control violence and curb Ku Klux Klan activity. [1921:HIST/6]

4 Supreme Court unanimously upholds Nineteenth Amendment to the Constitution.

5 U.S. government suit under the Sherman Antitrust Act against the American Sugar Refining Co. ends when the New York Circuit Court files a dissolution and injunction order.

6 Supreme Court declares the Federal Child Labor Law unconstitutional.

7 Senate committee recommends the U.S. military occupation in Haiti continue, but with a reduced Marine Corps force.

8 U.S. and Japan sign Yap Treaty, permitting U.S. cable and radio stations in the Yap islands.

9 Pres. Harding denounces the lawlessness of laborers and employers during the coal and railroad strikes.

10 Albert B. Fall, U.S. Secretary of the Interior, leases, without competitive bidding, the Teapot Dome oil reserves in Wyoming and the Elk Hills oil reserves in California to private interests. Senate begins investigation of what becomes the Teapot Dome scandal. [1924:HIST/2]

History and Politics — Elsewhere

mutually cancel all pre-war debts and renounce all war claims.

12 Britain ends its protectorate over Egypt, which is declared independent under King Fuad I.

13 Uprising by Poles in Upper Silesia forces the League of Nations to partition the territory. Poland receives the larger, more industrial part; Germany the remainder.

14 Mussolini orders the "March on Rome" by the Fascists. Italian King asks Mussolini to form government and grants him dictatorial powers. [1921:HIST/14]

15 Kemal Atatürk proclaims Turkey a republic. He is elected its first president.

16 Union of Soviet Socialist Republics is formed, consisting of the Russian Socialist Federal Soviet Republic (RSFSR), the Ukraine, Belorussia, and Transcaucasia.

17 Reactionary nationalists in Germany assassinate Walter Rathenau, Ger. Foreign Minister.

18 German mark (money) begins to collapse because of heavy reparation payments. [1921:HIST/16]

19 King Constantine I of Greece is deposed and exiled. His eldest son, George II, succeeds him.

20 Mohandas Karamchand Gandhi is arrested and sentenced to six years' imprisonment for civil disobedience. He seeks a free, united India.

21 Sino-Japanese agreement on Shantung is ratified. Shantung is returned to China, and Kiaochow is returned to Japan.

The Arts — America

tributors of America is created to serve as Hollywood's public relations organization. It is headed by Will H. Hays.

2 Robert Flaherty, "father of the documentary," produces *Nanook of the North,* a classic documentary about the Eskimo.

3 O'Neill writes *The First Man* and *The Hairy Ape.*

4 Fitzgerald publishes *The Beautiful and the Damned.*

5 Expressionist painter John Marin paints "Lower Manhattan" and "Off York Island, Maine."

6 Emily Post, social behavior expert, publishes the bestseller *Etiquette: The Blue Book of Social Usage.*

7 Lewis publishes *Babbitt,* a novel that explores U.S. middle class ideals.

8 Charles Sheeler, Precisionist painter, completes the starkly realistic "Church Street 'El.' "

9 George S. Kaufman, playwright, and Marc Connelly collaborate on the Hollywood satire *Merton of the Movies.*

10 e.e. cummings, poet, publishes *The Enormous Room,* about his brutal treatment in a French detention camp.

11 Elliot Paul, novelist, publishes *Indelible.*

The Arts — Elsewhere

masterpiece that develops the plot through the technique of "inner monologue" or "stream of consciousness."

13 F.W. Murneau, Ger. film maker, introduces the use of negative images (white trees, black sky) in *Nosferatu,* a horror classic based on *Dracula.*

14 T.S. Eliot founds *Criterion* (–1939), a literary review in which he publishes one of his most famous poems. "The Waste Land."

15 Hesse publishes *Siddhartha,* a lyric novel about Buddha.

16 Paul Hindemith, prominent Ger. composer, completes *The Young Maid,* a cycle of songs based on the poetry of George Trakl (Aust.).

17 Virginia Woolf, Eng. author, publishes the novel, *Jacob's Room.*

18 The tomb of Tutankhamen ("King Tut") is discovered in Egypt. It yields some of the world's greatest art treasures.

19 Arthur Wing Pinero, Eng. playwright, publishes *The Enchanted Cottage,* one of the most popular of his later works.

1923

America (History and Politics)

1 U.S. troops on the Rhine in Germany are ordered to return by Pres. Harding.

2 Gov. Alfred E. Smith repeals New York state's Prohibition enforcement act. Federal authorities take over enforcement.

Elsewhere (History and Politics)

11 French and Belgian troops occupy the Ruhr area to enforce war reparations from Germany.

12 Adolf Hitler, leader of the Nazi Party, leads unsuccessful coup d'etat ("Beer Hall Putsch") in Munich,

America (The Arts)

1 Thomas Wolfe, writer, publishes the play *Welcome to Our City.*

2 Cohan writes the play *The Song and Dance Man.*

3 Cecil B. DeMille,

Elsewhere (The Arts)

12 Sean O'Casey, Ir. playwright, completes *The Shadow of a Gunman,* a tragicomedy about the conflicts between the Irish Republican Army (IRA) and the British.

Science & Technology		Miscellaneous		
America	**Elsewhere**	**America**	**Elsewhere**	

boy, designs an image dissector system that is later developed into television.
2 Evans discovers vitamin E and claims that it is vital to sexual fertility. He produces giant rats by giving them injections of a pituitary hormone.
3 McCollum discovers vitamin D in cod liver oil. He uses the oil in the successful treatment of rickets.
4 Sabine publishes *Collected Papers on Acoustics.*
5 Ship-to-shore radio-telephone communication begins.
6 Alfred C. Lane, geologist, begins experiments to determine the age of the Earth.
7 Joseph Erlanger and Herbert Gasser amplify the electrical impulses in a single nerve fiber and study these impulses with an oscilloscope.

Tutankhamen ("King Tut") mask of gold

the Pancreas.
9 The British Broadcasting Corporation is founded.
10 Lewis Fry Richardson, Eng. meteorologist and mathematician, publishes *Weather Prediction by Numerical Process,* in which he describes a method which becomes more practical with the invention of the computer.
11 Aleksandr I. Oparin, Soviet scientist, suggests that the first forms of life arose from the spontaneous combining of molecules in the prehistoric atmosphere.
12 Hermann Julius Oberth, Ger. scientist, writes *The Rocket into Interplanetary Space,* in which the concept of escape velocity is introduced.
13 Hopkins discovers glutathione, a sequence of three amino acids essential for the utilization of oxygen by the cell.
14 Nobel Prize, Chemistry: Aston, for his discovery of isotopes using a mass spectrograph. [1919:SCI/14]
15 Nobel Prize, Physics: Bohr, for his research into atomic structure.
16 Nobel Prize, Physiology or Medicine: Archibald Hill, Eng. physiologist, and Otto Meyerhof, Ger. biochemist, for their research into the chemistry of muscle movements.

commercially sponsored radio program.
2 Herbert T. Kalmus makes the first successful use of the Technicolor process; it is not widely used in motion pictures until 20 years later.
3 Semi-dirigible, the *Roma,* explodes after hitting high tension wires at Hampton Roads Army Airbase, Va., killing 34 of its 45-member crew. Despite continued disasters, supporters of lighter-than-air craft do not give up their programs.
4 First mechanical switchboard is installed in the New York City telephone system; exchange is called "Pennsylvania."
5 Marriages in U.S., 1,126,000; divorces, 148,000.
6 20-ton meteor falls near Blackston, Va., causing a 500-sq.-ft. opening in the earth. A loud explosion and gigantic flames seen for miles accompany the crash.
7 Oldest American international team golf match, the Walker Cup match between U.S. and Great Britain, is established at the National Golf Links of America, Southhampton, L.I., N.Y.
8 Lt. Harold Harris becomes the first member of the Caterpillar Club by parachuting from a defective plane during a flight test in Dayton, Ohio. Club is made up of those who have escaped death using a parachute.

plished in Germany; first experimental congress for gliding held in France.
10 Brit. watchmaker John Howard invents the self-winding watch.
11 Dr. Marie Stopes holds a series of meetings in Queen's Hall, London, advocating birth control.
12 Lady Margart Rhondda is allowed to take a seat in the House of Lords, but this decision is changed.

---

1 Arthur H. Compton, physicist, discovers the "Compton effect": the wavelength of an x-ray is changed when the x-ray strikes electrons and is diffracted as it passes through a crystal.

9 Working separately, Johannes Brønsted, Dan. chemist, and Thomas Lowry, Eng. chemist, define an acid as a compound that gives up a proton and a base as a compound that accepts a

1 About 13.3 million automobiles are registered, almost triple the number in 1917.
2 Radio broadcast of Pres. Coolidge's speech to the Congress is the first of an official presidential

6 Enrigue Triboschi of Argentina swims the English Channel from France to England in 16 hr. 33 min.
7 Aeroflot, national airline of Soviet Union, is founded.

1923

America	Elsewhere	America	Elsewhere

America (History and Politics)

3 Payment of British war debt to the U.S. begins.

4 Pres. Harding dies suddenly in San Francisco on his return trip from Alaska. Coolidge is sworn in as President by his father in Vermont.

5 U.S. and Turkey sign treaty of friendship and commerce, and an extradition treaty.

6 Intermediate Credits Act expands credit to farmers and encourages farm cooperatives in an effort to ease agricultural depression. [1921:HIST/5]

7 Pres. Coolidge's first annual message to Congress announces support for a World Court, enforcement of Prohibition, and lower taxes. This is the first official presidential message ever broadcast.

8 Senate ratifies arbitration treaties with France, Britain, Norway, Portugal, and Japan.

9 Senate subcommittee, headed by Sen. Thomas J. Walsh, investigates leasing of naval oil reserves at Teapot Dome and Elk Hills. [1922:HIST/10]

10 Pres. Coolidge pardons 31 persons convicted under the Espionage Act of speaking against the government during World War I. [1921:HIST/11]

Elsewhere (History and Politics)

Germany. He is imprisoned at Landsberg, where he writes *Mein Kampf* ("My Struggle"), in which he condemns democracy and expresses hatred for the Jews and Slavs.

13 By the Treaty of Lausanne, Turkey gives up all claims to non-Turkish territories lost as a result of World War I.

14 Greek army deposes King George II. [1922:HIST/19]

15 Lithuanian forces occupy the Memel Territory, forcing the French to withdraw.

16 Allies evacuate Constantinople (Istanbul) and the Turks take control.

17 Rhodesia (now Zimbabwe) becomes a self-governing British Crown Colony.

18 Miguel Primo de Rivera leads successful coup d'etat in Spain. He dissolves the Cortes (legislative body) and establishes a military dictatorship.

19 Redistribution Bill increases the seats in Canada's House of Commons from 235 to 245.

20 Gustav Stresemann becomes German Chancellor. He tries to remove the harsh penalties on Germany set by the Treaty of Versailles.

21 Stanley Baldwin becomes British Prime Minister. His ministry ends when voters reject his protective tariff policy, but he is returned to office in 1924.

America (The Arts)

film director and producer, releases the Biblical spectacle *The Ten Commandments.*

4 Martha Graham, important figure in modern dance, makes her solo debut in the *Greenwich Village Follies.*

5 Ben Hecht and Charles MacArthur, playwright, collaborate on the play *Twentieth Century.*

6 Buddy Rich, drummer, tours the U.S. and Australia as a child prodigy on the drums.

7 Elmer Rice publishes the satirical play *The Adding Machine.*

8 *Time* magazine begins publication.

9 e.e. cummings publishes *Tulips and Chimneys,* a book of poems.

10 *Safety Last,* the first film to use physical danger as a source of humor, stars comedian Harold Lloyd.

11 Wallace Stevens, poet, publishes *Harmonium,* which includes the poems "Sunday Morning" and "The Emperor of Ice-Cream."

Elsewhere (The Arts)

13 Felix Salten, Aust. novelist, publishes *Bambi,* a popular children's story written as an allegory for adults.

14 Schönberg composes the atonal *Piano Suite,* the first work based entirely on his revolutionary 12-tone system.

15 P.G. Wodehouse, Eng. author, publishes *Leave It to Psmith,* a humorous novel.

16 Dorothy L. Sayers, Eng. novelist, introduces detective Lord Peter Wimsey in *Whose Body?*

17 Maurice Utrillo, Fr. artist, paints "Ivry Town Hall."

18 Beckmann produces the woodcuts, "Before the Mirror" and "Charnel House."

19 A. Huxley publishes *Antic Hay,* a satirical novel.

20 Ottorino Respighi, Ital. composer, completes the comic opera, *Belfagor.*

21 Molnár publishes *The Red Mill,* a play.

22 William Archer, Scot. critic, publishes *The Old Drama and the New: An Essay in Re-Valuation.*

1924

America (History and Politics)

1 Congress passes Soldiers' Bonus Bill over Pres. Coolidge's veto. Most veterans are paid 20-year annuities.

2 Fall is indicted for conspiracy and for accepting bribes, the result of Senate hearings on the Teapot Dome scandal. After a series of trials and mistrials, he is found guilty and sent to prison in 1931.

3 U.S. prohibits the exportation of firearms to Honduras and to Cuban rebels.

4 Second Quota Law cuts immigration to half of 1921 quota. It provides for a na-

Elsewhere (History and Politics)

11 Fascists under Mussolini gain tighter control of Italian government in elections.

12 Lenin dies and power struggle begins within the Soviet Party for control of the government. Joseph Stalin, Lev Kamenev, and Grigori Zinoviev form a triumvirate of successors against Leon Trotsky. Britain, France, and Italy recognize the new Soviet regime. [1926:HIST/13]

13 Tangier in Morocco becomes an international zone administered by Britain, France, and Spain.

America (The Arts)

1 George Gershwin and his lyricist brother Ira collaborate on the score for the show *Lady Be Good,* which includes the songs "Fascinating Rhythm" and "The Man I Love."

2 Paul Whiteman commissions G. Gershwin to write the symphonic jazz-style "Rhapsody in Blue."

3 Oscar Hammerstein II, author and lyricist, produces the show

Elsewhere (The Arts)

13 Wodehouse publishes *The Inimitable Jeeves,* one in a series of comic novels featuring Jeeves, the ultimate butler, and Bertie Wooster, the suave bachelor.

14 Murneau's film, *Last Laugh,* stars Emil Jannings in his most famous role, that of an aging hotel doorman.

15 Bulg. novelist Michael Arlen becomes an overnight sensation after the publication of

Science & Technology		Miscellaneous		
America	**Elsewhere**	**America**	**Elsewhere**	

America (Science & Technology)

2 George Dick and Gladys Dick isolate the scarlet fever toxin and develop an effective antitoxin.

3 DeForest demonstrates *phonofilm,* sound-on-film motion pictures, at the Rivoli Theater, N.Y.

4 Norbert Wiener, mathematician, describes Brownian movement by means of mathematical formulas.

5 Louis A. Bauer, astronomer, analyzes the Earth's magnetic field.

6 G. Lewis Randall and Merle Randall publish *Thermodynamics and the Free Energy of Chemical Substances,* a widely used text.

7 The bulldozer is invented.

8 Nobel Prize, Physics: Robert Millikan for measuring the charge of an electron and for working on the photoelectric effect.

Elsewhere (Science & Technology)

proton.

10 Theodor Svedberg, Swed. chemist, invents the ultracentrifuge.

11 Korn transmits a photograph from Rome, Italy, to Bar Harbor, Maine.

12 Fr. bacteriologists Albert Calmette and Camille Guérin discover the tuberculosis vaccine BCG (Bacillus Calmette-Guérin).

13 Freud publishes his theories on the human mind in *The Ego and the Id.*

14 Louis Victor, Prince de Broglie, Fr. physicist, proposes the wavelike properties of electrons.

15 Edward Neville da Costa Andrade, Eng. physicist, publishes *The Structure of the Atom.*

16 Nobel Prize, Chemistry: Fritz Pregl, Aust. chemist, for his methods of microanalysis of organic compounds.

17 Nobel Prize, Physiology or Medicine: Banting and John J.R. Macleod, Eng. scientist, for their production of insulin for use in diabetic therapy.

America (Miscellaneous)

message. Transmission is so clear that a rustling noise can be heard as the President turns the pages of his address.

3 Col. Jacob Schick receives a patent for the first electric shaver.

4 *The Covered Wagon,* voted one of the 10 best movies of the year by *Film Daily,* sets the style for and popularity of Westerns.

5 DuPont Company acquires the rights to manufacture Cellophane; first U.S.-made Cellophane is produced in 1924.

Elsewhere (Miscellaneous)

8 Finnish runner Paavo Nurmi runs the mile in 4 min. 10.4 sec.

9 Earthquake in Japan destroys Yokohama and half of Tokyo; about 100,000 people die.

1924

America (Science & Technology)

1 Vladimir Zworykin, Russ.-Amer. engineer, patents the iconoscope, a forerunner of television.

2 Hubble determines that Cepheid variables (stars) in the Andromeda nebula are hundreds of thousands of light-years beyond the Milky Way. This is conclusive proof that there are other galaxies besides our own.

3 KDKA, Pittsburgh radio station, experiments with short wave, transatlantic broadcasts.

Elsewhere (Science & Technology)

8 Broglie draws parallels between electrons and light waves.

9 Erwin Schrödinger, Aust. physicist, introduces a theory of atomic structure based on wave mechanics.

10 Meyerhof publishes *The Chemical Dynamics of Life Phenomena.*

11 Nobel Prize, Physics: Siegbahn, for his discovery of x-ray spectroscopy.

12 Nobel Prize, Physiology or Medicine: Einthoven, for his invention of

America (Miscellaneous)

1 Test flight for transcontinental air mail made in 27 hr. from New York City to San Francisco. Best time in 1848 was 3 mo. (by ship to Panama, overland across the Isthmus, by ship to San Francisco); in 1869, 7½ days by railroad.

2 Congress passes act making all native-born Indians full U.S. citizens.

3 RCA demonstrates wireless telegraph transmission of photographs from New York City to

Elsewhere (Miscellaneous)

9 Olympic Games are held in Paris. There are 3092 participants from 44 nations, 24 sports, and 137 events. First Winter Olympics held at Chamonix, France, include 8 sports, 16 events and 293 participants from 16 nations.

10 Ger. mass murderer Fritz Hartmann (26 victims) is sentenced to death by beheading.

11 Dan. polar explorer Knud Rasmussen completes the longest dog-sled

305

America	Elsewhere	America	Elsewhere

America (History and Politics)

tional origins plan to begin in 1929. The law also excludes all Asians and is bitterly resented by the Japanese.

5 Dawes Plan on German reparations goes into effect. It provides that reparation payments begin at one billion marks and rise over a period of four years to 2.5 billion marks a year.

6 Rogers Bill consolidates the diplomatic and consular services.

7 Progressive Party, backed by the American Federation of Labor, Farm-Labor Party, and Socialist Party, nominates Sen. La Follette of Wisconsin for President.

8 Calvin Coolidge and Charles G. Dawes are elected President and Vice President, respectively, on the Republican ticket.

9 U.S. Marines land at Shanghai, China, to help suppress civil war.

10 J. Edgar Hoover becomes director of the Bureau of Investigation (renamed the Federal Bureau of Investigation in 1935).

Elsewhere (History and Politics)

14 The caliphate (government by the caliph) is abolished in Turkey.

15 Separatist movement in the Rhineland collapses after the assassination of the president of the Palatinate government.

16 British institute a policy of separate administration for the Sudan.

17 Arab forces under Ibn Saud capture Mecca. [1921:HIST/17]

18 James Barry Munnik Hertzog becomes Prime Minister of the Union of South Africa until 1939.

19 Gandhi is released from prison. Hindu-Muslim relations remain unsettled in India. [1922:HIST/20]

20 Communist uprising is suppressed in Estonia.

21 Anglo-French agreement establishes the border between Anglo-Egyptian Sudan and French Equatorial Africa.

22 Gaston Doumergue becomes President of France.

23 London conference adopts the Dawes Plan for the reorganization of the German Reichbank under Allied supervision.

24 Greece is proclaimed a republic.

America (The Arts)

Rose Marie.

4 O'Neill publishes *All God's Chillun Got Wings* and *Desire Under the Elms.*

5 William Faulkner, poet and novelist, publishes *The Marble Faun.*

6 Maxwell Anderson and Laurence Stallings, playwrights, publish the war play *What Price Glory?*

7 Kaufman and Connelly collaborate on the play *Beggar on Horseback.*

8 Robinson Jeffers, poet, publishes *Tamar and Other Poems.*

9 Sidney Howard, playwright, publishes *They Knew What They Wanted.*

10 Erich von Stroheim, director and actor, directs *Greed,* based on Norris's *McTeague.*

11 Samuel Goldwyn and Louis B. Mayer form the film company Metro-Goldwyn-Mayer.

12 Harry Cohn founds Columbia Pictures.

Elsewhere (The Arts)

The Green Hat.

16 Arthur Honegger, Fr. composer, completes *Pacific 231,* an orchestral interpretation of a moving locomotive.

17 A.A. Milne, Eng. humorist, publishes *When We Were Very Young,* a collection of stories for his son, Christopher.

18 Noel Coward, Eng. playwright, produces and stars in *The Vortex.*

19 E.M. Forster publishes *A Passage to India,* a novel about the clash between Eastern and Western cultures.

20 Richard Hughes, Eng. novelist, writes *Danger,* the world's first radio drama, broadcast by the BBC.

21 René Clair, Fr. film maker, directs the Surrealistic *Entr'acte.*

22 Tzara publishes the *Dadaist Manifesto.*

23 The opening of Tsukiji Little Theater, Tokyo, marks the start of Japan's modern theater movement.

1925

America (History and Politics)

1 Nellie Tayloe Ross becomes Governor of Wyoming; she is the first woman governor in the U.S.

2 Congress passes resolution declaring Swains Island in the Pacific under the sovereignty of the U.S.

3 Senate ratifies 20-year-old treaty which recognizes the right of Cuba to the Isle of Pines.

4 Pres. Coolidge calls for a plebiscite to settle the Tacna-Arica boundary dispute between Chile and Peru.

5 U.S. and Canada agree to improve the St. Lawrence River between Montreal and Lake Ontario.

6 U.S. charges Mexican government with failure to pro-

Elsewhere (History and Politics)

12 Albania becomes a republic under President Zog.

13 Norway's capital, Christiania, is renamed Oslo.

14 Cyprus is made a British Crown Colony.

15 Boundary between Northern Ireland and the Irish Free State (now the Republic of Ireland) is established. [1921:HIST/12]

16 By the Treaty of Locarno, Germany agrees to demilitarize the Rhineland and to establish fixed borders with France and Belgium.

17 Reza Khan is proclaimed Shah of Iran; he changes his name to Reza Shah Pahlavi, thus founding the Pahlavi dynasty.

18 Paul von Hindenburg is

America (The Arts)

1 Fitzgerald publishes *The Great Gatsby.*

2 Dreiser publishes *An American Tragedy,* based on a real murder case.

3 Ernest Hemingway, novelist, publishes *In Our Time.*

4 G. Stein's *The Making of Americans* includes the line "Rose is a rose is a rose is a rose."

5 *The New Yorker* magazine is founded.

6 Richard Rodgers, composer, and Lorenz Hart, lyricist, write the score to *The Garrick Gaieties.*

7 Valentino stars in

Elsewhere (The Arts)

13 Sergei Eisenstein, Sov. director, presents *Potemkin,* a powerful film.

14 *The Trial,* a pessimistic novel by Kafka, is published.

15 Ernst Barlach, Ger. Expressionist sculptor, exhibits "Death."

16 Dimitri Shostakovich, Sov. composer, completes his first symphony.

17 Cocteau writes *L'Ange Heurtebise,* a poem about his conflict with an angel.

18 Inspired by Georg Büchner's tragedy, *Woyzeck* (1836), Aust.

Science & Technology		Miscellaneous		
America	**Elsewhere**	**America**	**Elsewhere**	
4 Harvard Observatory publishes the *Standard Draper Catalog,* which lists and describes 225,000 stars. **5** The portable electrocardiograph is introduced. It uses vacuum tubes to amplify the weak electrical signals produced by the heart. **6** Harry Steenbock, Wis. scientist, discovers that sunlight increases the amount of vitamin D in certain foods. After tests prove that it is the ultraviolet part of sunlight which has this effect, Steenbock patents a process of using artificial ultraviolet light to increase the vitamin D content in food. **7** Rudolf Matas, surgeon, introduces the use of intravenous saline solution to prevent dehydration.	the electrocardiograph. [1903:SCI/7]	London; process takes about 25 min. per photograph. **4** After a sensational trial, Nathan Leopold and Richard Loeb are sentenced to life imprisonment for the kidnapping of Bobby Franks. Leopold and Loeb, intelligent and well educated, apparently decided to kill someone just to see how it would feel and picked a young boy at random. **5** There are 2.5 million radios in the U.S.; in 1920 there were only 5000 sets, used mostly by professionals. **6** Temperature drops 79 degrees in one day in Helena, Mont. **7** Football's "The Four Horsemen"—Layden, Stuhldreher, Miller, and Crowley—star as Notre Dame upsets Army. **8** Tornado destroys 35 towns in Illinois, Indiana, Tennessee, Kentucky, and Missouri; 800 people die, 3000 are injured, and 15,000 are homeless.	journey ever made across the Arctic. **12** Ger. airship pioneer Hugo Eckener flies his Z-R-3 across the Atlantic to Lakehurst, N.J. **13** R.C. Andrews discovers skulls and skeletons of Mesozoic (70–220 million years ago) dinosaurs in the Gobi Desert, Mongolia.	
1 Millikan discovers that cosmic rays are absorbed (not produced) by the atmosphere. **2** Cushing publishes *The Life of Sir William Osler.* It is awarded the Pulitzer Prize in 1926. **3** Whipple demonstrates that iron is a major factor in the formation of red blood cells. **4** The meter is standardized. [1893:SCI/2] **5** Berliner invents acoustic tiles for soundproofing. **6** Zworykin patents an electronic color television. **7** Collip isolates parathormone, a hormone produced by the parathyroid gland, and uses it to treat	**13** Werner Heisenberg, Ger. physicist, develops the theory of "new quantum" or "matrix mechanics". **14** Dutch physicists Samuel Goudsmit and George Uhlenbeck discover that electrons spin on their axes. **15** Eddington publishes *Internal Constitution of Stars,* a work on astrophysics. **16** Bertil Lindblad, Swed. astronomer, suggests that the apparent motion of stars in space is owing to the rotation of the Milky Way galaxy. **17** Sir Edward V. Appleton, Eng. physicist, dis-	**1** Charleston becomes popular dance step with professional entertainers and the public. Children dance it for pennies on side streets and in front of theaters at intermission. **2** Trinity College in North Carolina agrees to change its name to Duke University to meet terms of a $40 million trust fund established by James B. Duke, tobacco millionaire. **3** U.S. Army dirigible *Shenandoah* is wrecked in a storm near Ava, Ohio; 14 are killed. **4** Crossword puzzles become very popular. **5** Tennessee school-	**9** Copy of the Bible cost equivalent of about $2,000 in 14th century; in 1455, $500; in 17th century, $100; by 1925, $3. **10** London Bible Society distributes 10.5 million bibles in 566 languages. **11** Women become legal voters in India. **12** United Church of Canada is founded. **13** First traffic lights installed in London. **14** 1.6 million radio sets in use in Great Britain. **15** Alexander Alekhine, blindfolded, plays 28 simultaneous games of chess.	**1925**

History and Politics

The Arts

America

Elsewhere

America

Elsewhere

History and Politics — America	Elsewhere	The Arts — America	Elsewhere
tect U.S. lives and property. **7** U.S. agrees to drastic reduction of war debts owed by European countries. **8** U.S. troops enter Panama territory to subdue laborers demanding lower rents. **9** Supreme Court again upholds the constitutionality of the Volstead Act. **10** Court martial finds Col. William ("Billy") Mitchell guilty of insubordination, sentencing him to a five-year suspension from duty. He had sharply criticized military leaders for neglect of U.S. air power. Mitchell resigns from the army in 1926. **11** James J. ("Jimmy") Walker is elected Mayor of New York City.	elected German President. **19** U.S.S.R. adds the new republics of Uzbekistan, Turkmenistan, and Kazakhstan to its federation. [1922:HIST/16] **20** French and Spanish begin offensive to subdue the Riffs under Abd el-Krim. [1921:HIST/13] **21** League of Nations halts Greek invasion of Bulgaria. **22** Turkey puts down revolts by the Kurds. Turkey makes an alliance with the U.S.S.R. **23** Japan grants universal male suffrage. **24** Norway takes official possession of the islands of Spitsbergen. **25** City of Dakar becomes an autonomous area in French West Africa. **26** Druses (religious sect) seize Damascus in Syria from the French.	*The Eagle.* **8** Ernst Lubitsch directs the comedy film *Lady Windermere's Fan.* **9** DuBose Heyward, writer, publishes *Porgy,* on which *Porgy and Bess* is later based. [1935:ARTS/1] **10** Crèvecoeur's unpublished work, *Sketches of Eighteenth Century America,* is discovered in an attic in France. Its description of 18th century life is of great value to historians. [1782:ARTS/1] **11** Otto Harbach, composer, produces the show *No, No, Nanette.* **12** Chaplin stars in *The Gold Rush.*	composer Alban Berg produces the atonal opera, *Wozzeck.* **19** Soutine paints the gruesomely realistic "Side of Beef." **20** Heinrich Mann, Ger. writer, completes the social trilogy, *Das Kaiserreich (The Poor,* 1917; *The Patrioteer,* 1918; *The Chief,* 1925). **21** Emil Ludwig, Ger. biographer, publishes *Napoleon.* **22** Ger. film maker G.W. Pabst directs *Joyless Street.* **23** Ivan Alekseyevich Bunin, Sov. novelist, publishes *Mitya's Love.* **24** Wells, Shaw, and others establish The Film Society of London, the world's first.
1926 **1** U.S. fails to join the Permanent Court of International Justice and Arbitration at The Hague. [1899:HIST/7] **2** Congress passes Revenue Act, reducing income and inheritance taxes and abolishing many nuisance taxes. **3** U.S. and Cuba sign an extradition treaty in Havana. **4** Congress creates the Army Air Corps. **5** Senate ratifies World War debt funding agreements with European countries. **6** U.S. Circuit Court of Appeals at New York City rules that foreign ships carrying liquor may be searched and seized within the 12-mile limit. U.S. ships with liquor may be seized anywhere. **7** U.S. marines land in Nicaragua to put down insurrection. **8** Supreme Court upholds President's exclusive power to dismiss executive officials, thus voiding the Tenure of Office Act of 1867. **9** Congress passes Air Commerce Act, providing for the Bureau of Air Commerce to	**11** Eamon De Valera resigns as President of the Sinn Fein (Irish nationalist movement). He forms the Fianna Fail (Soldiers of Destiny) Party, which takes control of the Irish government in 1932. **12** Military dictatorship is established in Portugal. **13** Kamenev and Zinoviev join forces with Trotsky in order to check Stalin's growing power in the U.S.S.R. [1927:HIST/12] **14** King resigns as Canadian Prime Minister because of customs scandal, but he is returned to office the same year in national elections. **15** Paul Joseph Goebbels is made Nazi Party leader in Berlin, Germany. **16** Ibn Saud proclaims himself King of Hijaz and Najd. **17** Chiang Kai-shek leads Chinese Nationalist army on Northern Expedition—a military campaign that overthrows the Manchu dynasty in China. **18** French and Spanish forces defeat the Riffs; Abd el-Krim surrenders. [1925:HIST/20]	**1** Hemingway publishes the novel *The Sun Also Rises.* **2** O'Neill publishes *The Great God Brown.* **3** Georgia O'Keeffe paints "Black Iris," an abstract work in which the flowers assume human anatomical shapes. **4** Faulkner publishes his first novel, *Soldier's Pay.* **5** Moss Hart, playwright, writes the Hollywood satire *Once in a Lifetime.* **6** Edna Ferber, writer, publishes *Show Boat.* **7** George and Ira Gershwin write the shows *Tiptoes,* which stars Gertrude Lawrence, and *Oh, Kay,* which features the song "Someone to Watch Over Me." **8** Whiteman's trio "The Rhythm Boys," made up of Harry Barris, Al Rinker, and Bing Crosby, becomes	**13** Milne publishes *Winnie-the-Pooh,* one of the most popular children's books ever written. **14** Christie's detective novel, *The Murder of Roger Ackroyd,* creates controversy by use of a trick device. **15** O'Casey's treatment of Irish heroes in *The Plough and the Stars,* a realistic play about the Easter Rising (1916), sparks riots in Dublin. **16** Alfred Hitchcock, Eng. film maker known for his gripping thrillers, directs *The Lodger.* **17** Scot. poet Hugh MacDiarmid publishes his masterpiece, *A Drunk Man Looks in the Thistle.* **18** Gide publishes *The Counterfeiters,* a work he calls his "only novel." **19** Van Doesburg publishes the *De Stijl* manifesto. **20** Puccini's *Turan-*

Science & Technology		Miscellaneous		
America	**Elsewhere**	**America**	**Elsewhere**	

tetany. **8** Arrowheads discovered in New Mexico prove that America was inhabited long before the time of Columbus. **9** American Telephone and Telegraph (AT&T) and General Electric (GE) jointly establish Bell Laboratories for research in physics. **10** First international radio broadcast is made between London and Maine. **11** John Watson publishes *Behaviorism,* a book that sparks popular interest in psychology. **12** The Rivoli and the Rialto, in New York, are the world's first air-conditioned theaters.	covers the layer of the ionosphere which reflects radio waves (Appleton layer). **18** Wolfgang Pauli, Aust. physicist, proposes the exclusion principle, which deals with the number of electrons able to occupy the same energy level of a given atomic nucleus. **19** Nobel Prize, Chemistry: Zsigmondy, for his study of colloids (suspended microscopic particles).	teacher John T. Scopes arrested for teaching theory of evolution, forbidden by state law. "Monkey trial" attracts enormous attention; Scopes is convicted and fined $100. **6** Electric percolators are introduced. **7** First dry ice made commercially is manufactured by Prest-Air Devices Company, Long Island City, N.Y. **8** National Spelling Bee started by the *Louisville (Ky.) Courier Journal.*		
1 Michelson measures the speed of light as 186,284 miles per second, an error of less than 0.00001%. **2** George Minot, William Murphy, and George Whipple use a diet rich in raw liver to cure patients suffering from pernicious anemia, a usually fatal disease. Later, Minot and Edwin Cohn prepare a liver extract that remains the basic treatment for this disease until 1948. **3** T. H. Morgan publishes *Theory of the Gene.* **4** Goddard launches the first liquid-fuel rocket. **5** James Sumner, Mass. biochemist, is the first to crystallize an enzyme (urease). **6** Paul de Kruif, Mich. bacteriologist, publishes *The Microbe Hunters,* a popular book about bacteriology. **7** Thorndike publishes *Measurement of Intelligence.* **8** Museum of Science and Industry opens in	**11** Enrico Fermi, Ital. physicist, publishes landmark work on ideal gases. **12** Paul A.M. Dirac, Eng. physicist, applies the theory of relativity to quantum mechanics. He also proposes the existence of the positron. **13** John L. Baird, Scot. inventor, televises images of moving objects. **14** Otto Loewi, Ger. physician, determines that a chemical (later shown to be acetylcholine) is involved in the transmission of nerve impulses. **15** Max Born, Ger. physicist, formulates the mathematical basis of the quantum theory. **16** Nobel Prize, Physics: Jean-Baptiste Perrin, Fr. physicist, for proving the atomic nature of matter. **17** Nobel Prize, Physiology or Medicine: Fibiger, for discovering a parasite that causes cancer.	**1** Radio Corporation of America, American Telephone and Telegraph Company, and British General Post Office hold first successful transatlantic radiotelephone conversation between New York City and London. **2** Ellsworth and Ital. explorer Umberto Nobile fly over North Pole in airship *Norge,* a 3393-mile journey from Spitsbergen, Norway to Alaska. **3** Book-of-the-Month Club begins enrolling members, with 40,000 the first year. **4** Congress establishes the Army Air Corps. **5** RCA organizes the National Broadcasting Company (NBC) as the first nationwide entertainment radio broadcasting network; Columbia Broadcasting System is set up in 1927. **6** Distinguished Flying Cross is established for anyone who, "while serving in the armed services, distinguishes himself by	**10** Brit. aviator Alan Cabham flies from England to Cape Town, South Africa, and back to investigate the feasibility of long-distance air routes. **11** Child adoption is made legal in Britain. **12** U.S.S.R.'s population is 148 million; Japan's 85 million; Germany's 64 million; and Britain's 45 million. **13** H. Bierkottes swims the English Channel in 12 hr. 4 min.	**1926**

America | ## Elsewhere | ## America | ## Elsewhere

oversee the civil aviation industry. Act includes the licensing of aircraft and pilots.
10 Progressive Party wins seats in Congress in fall elections.

19 Campaign begins against the Mafia, a secret criminal organization that has dominated Sicilian politics for 50 years.
20 Antanas Smetona leads successful coup against the socialist government in Lithuania and becomes president.
21 Russia and Germany sign treaty of neutrality and friendship, extending the Rapallo Treaty of 1922.

the band's top attraction.
9 Harbach and Hammerstein write the show *The Desert Song*.
10 Philip Barry, dramatist, writes the play *White Wings*.
11 Hart Crane, poet, publishes *White Buildings*.
12 Sandburg publishes *Abraham Lincoln: The Prairie Years*.

dot, Italy's only Impressionistic opera, is completed by Franco Alfano.
21 Kurt Weill, Ger. composer, completes *The Protagonist,* a one-act opera.

1927

1 U.S. sends warships to Chinese ports to bring U.S. citizens out of China.
2 Conference to limit naval armament, called by Pres. Coolidge, ends in stalemate at Geneva, Switzerland.
3 Supreme Court rules unconstitutional a Texas law forbidding Negroes to vote in Democratic primary elections.
4 Dwight W. Morrow becomes Ambassador to Mexico. He improves relations between the U.S. and Mexico, securing Mexican concessions on oil lands used before 1917.
5 Supreme Court declares that lease of the Teapot Dome oil reserves to a private company by former Secretary of the Interior Fall was illegal and fraudulent. Oil fields are restored to the U.S. government. **[1924:HIST/2]**
6 U.S. Marines land in Nicaragua to protect U.S. lives and property during civil war.
7 Pres. Coolidge announces he will not run for President in 1928.
8 Senate refuses to seat Senator-elect William S. Vare on grounds of excessive campaign expenditures.

9 Italy signs treaties with Albania and Hungary, trying to undermine the Little Entente and its supporter, France. Yugoslavia signs friendship treaty with France.
10 Pres. Hindenburg rejects German responsibility for World War I.
11 Trotsky and his followers are expelled from the Communist Party and exiled to the provinces. Stalin gains control.
12 Carlos Ibáñez del Campo becomes President of Chile. He rules as a dictator and initiates many public works projects until forced into exile in 1931.
13 Atatürk is reelected President of Turkey and reelected again in 1931 and 1935.
14 Nanking falls to the Chinese Communists. Chiang's Chinese Nationalists recapture the city and make it their capital (1928). Japanese intervention in Shantung stops northward advance of Chinese Nationalists toward Peking. **[1926:HIST/17]**
15 Australian Parliament officially meets at Canberra, the capital, for the first time.
16 Allied military control of Germany ends. League of Nations now supervises the problems of German armament.
17 Socialist uprising and general strike occurs in Vienna, Austria, after acquittal of Nazis for political murder.

1 Duke Ellington, bandleader and composer, organizes a band which begins a five-year stand at Harlem's Cotton Club.
2 Thornton Wilder, author, publishes *The Bridge of San Luis Rey*.
3 Lewis publishes *Elmer Gantry*.
4 DeMille produces his second Biblical epic *The King of Kings*.
5 The Academy of Motion Picture Arts and Sciences is founded.
6 E.A. Robinson publishes *Tristram,* thus completing his King Arthur trilogy.
7 Cather publishes *Death Comes to the Archbishop*.
8 Paul Green, writer, publishes *In Abraham's Bosom*.
9 Frankie Trumbauer, saxophonist, and Bix Beiderbecke, cornetist, record a popular version of "Singin' the Blues."
10 Gaston Lachaise, abstract sculptor, executes "Standing Woman (Elevation)," a rather buxom female nude.
11 Isadora Duncan publishes *The Art of Dance*.

12 Mazo de la Roche, Can. author, publishes *Jalna,* the first of 15 popular novels about the Whiteoak family of Jalna.
13 Woolf publishes *To the Lighthouse*.
14 Kafka's novel, *Amerika,* is published.
15 Clair directs the silent film classic, *The Italian Straw Hat*.
16 Hesse publishes the novel, *Steppenwolf*.
17 Pabst incorporates both acted and documentary scenes in his film, *The Love of Jeanne Ney*.
18 Soutine paints "Page Boy at Maxim's," one of his well-known "page-boy" series.
19 In *New Harmonic Theory,* Alois Hába (Czech.), describes the use of microtones in musical composition.
20 François Mauriac, Fr. novelist, publishes *Thérèse Desqueyroux*.
21 Chagall prepares 100 etchings for LaFontaine's *Fables*.
22 Henry Williamson, Eng. novelist, publishes *Tarka the Otter,* a nature tale.
23 Stravinsky composes the oratorio, *Oedipus Rex*.

Science & Technology		Miscellaneous		
America	**Elsewhere**	**America**	**Elsewhere**	

Chicago.
9 Hubble develops a method for classifying external galaxies (those beyond the Milky Way).
10 Roy C. Andrews, Wis. naturalist, publishes *On the Trail of Ancient Man.*

heroism or extraordinary achievement in aerial flight."
7 Polar explorer Richard E. Byrd with Floyd Bennett makes first successful airplane flight over the North Pole.
8 Gertrude Ederle at 19 is the first woman to swim the English Channel, in 14 hr. 31 min.
9 Air-mail service starts between New York City and Boston.

Science & Technology		Miscellaneous		
America	Elsewhere	America	Elsewhere	**1927**

America (Science & Technology)

1 Hermann J. Muller, geneticist, uses x-rays to cause genetic mutations.
2 Frank A. Hartman isolates "cortin" from the adrenal glands and suggests that absence of this hormone may cause Addison's disease.
3 Clinton Davisson and Lester Germer discover that electrons are diffracted when they pass through a crystal. This discovery supports the wave theory of electron behavior.
4 The pentode (a 5-element vacuum tube) is developed. It permits distortion-free amplification of sound.
5 An 8000-ft. well, the deepest in the world, is drilled in Orange County, Calif.
6 The Holland Tunnel, designed by Clifford M. Holland, opens to vehicular traffic. More than 1½ miles long, the tunnel travels under the Hudson River and connects New York with New Jersey.
7 Synchronized sound and action motion pictures are developed for commercial use in theaters.
8 Nobel Prize, Physics: Arthur Compton for discovering the Compton effect. [1923:SCI/1]

Elsewhere (Science & Technology)

9 Georges Lemaître, Belg. cosmologist, proposes the big bang theory to explain the origin of the Universe.
10 Pavlov publishes *Conditioned Reflexes,* based on his experiments in which dogs, fed at the sound of a bell, salivated at the sound of the bell alone.
11 Rudolf Geiger, Ger. meteorologist, publishes *The Climate Near the Ground,* founding the study of microclimatology.
12 John B.S. Haldane, Eng. geneticist, publishes *Animal Biology.*
13 Jan Hendrik Oort, Dutch astronomer, further clarifies Lindblad's theory about the rotation of the Milky Way galaxy. [1925:SCI/16]
14 Baron Edgar Adrian, Eng. electrophysiologist, publishes *The Basis of Sensation,* in which he makes numerous revelations about nerve cells.
15 George P. Thomson, Eng. physicist, proves the wave nature of electrons, an important property used to determine atomic structure.
16 Nobel Prize, Physics: C.T.R. Wilson, for inventing the cloud chamber. [1911:SCI/12]

America (Miscellaneous)

1 Aviator Charles A. ("Lucky Lindy") Lindbergh flies across the Atlantic from New York to France, a 3600-mile, 33½-hr. solo flight in the *Spirit of St. Louis.*
2 Tremendous floods in the Mississippi Valley cover 4 million acres, causing property loss of $300 million. 600,000 are homeless for many weeks; several hundred drown.
3 15 millionth Model T car is produced by the Ford Motor Company, and its production is discontinued.
4 First Golden Gloves amateur boxing matches held, sponsored by the New York *Daily News.*
5 Ruth Snyder and her lover, Judd Gray, murder her husband, Albert. Killers executed at Sing Sing prison in 1928.
6 Babe Ruth sets home run record when he hits 60 for the season.
7 First successful airplane flight from San Francisco to Honolulu made by 2 Army Air Corps pilots, Lts. Lester J. Maitland and Albert F. Hegenberger.

Elsewhere (Miscellaneous)

8 Brit. explorer Henry Watkins leads an expedition to Edge Island, Spitsbergen, Norway.
9 Alekhine becomes world chess champion.

Charles A. Lindbergh, U.S. aviator nick named "Lucky Lindy"

	History and Politics		The Arts	
	America	**Elsewhere**	**America**	**Elsewhere**
1928	**1** Socialist Party nominates Norman M. Thomas for President. **2** McNary-Haugen Bill for relief of farmers is vetoed by Pres. Coolidge on grounds it would fix prices and stimulate overproduction. **3** Flood Control Bill provides $325 million to curb flooding in the Mississippi River valley. **4** Jones-White Merchant Marine Bill provides $250 million loan for ship construction by private companies. **5** Democrats nominate Gov. Smith of New York for President. He calls for repeal of the Eighteenth Amendment. **6** U.S. signs Briand-Kellogg Pact, outlawing war. Eventually, 63 nations sign it. **7** Herbert Hoover and Charles Curtis are elected President and Vice President, respectively, on the Republican ticket. Hoover wins 40 of the 48 states. **8** Congress appropriates $32 million to enforce Prohibition during the next year.	**9** Stalin issues Five Year Plan for rapid industrialization and collectivization of farms in the U.S.S.R. **10** Britain recognizes the Chinese Nationalist government at Nanking. **11** Bolivia and Paraguay argue over ownership of the Chaco territory. **12** Obregón is reelected President of Mexico but is assassinated within a few weeks. **13** Stefan Radich, leader of the Croatian Peasant Party, is assassinated in the Yugoslavian Parliament. Croatians establish separatist parliament at Zagreb. **14** Pres. Zog of Albania is proclaimed king as Zog I. **15** Tangier statute is revised, and Spain is given more control in the zone. **[1924:HIST/13]** **16** Iuliu Maniu becomes Rumanian Premier and enacts liberal reforms. **17** Italian government abolishes universal suffrage and signs friendship treaties with Greece and Ethiopia. **18** Britain recognizes Trans-Jordan as an independent state but retains control of the country's defenses, finances, and foreign affairs. **19** Antonio Carmona is elected President of Portugal. **20** King Fuad I of Egypt suspends the constitution and dissolves parliament, following parliament's introduction of a measure forbidding the king to rule without parliament.	**1** Eddie Cantor, entertainer, stars in the Broadway show *Whoopee*, which features the song "Makin' Whoopee." **2** Demuth's painting "I Saw the Figure 5 in Gold" is based on a poem by William Carlos Williams. **3** Alexander Calder, developer of mobiles and stabiles, creates "Romulus and Remus," a wire sculpture. **4** Stephen Vincent Benét writes *John Brown's Body*, a highly acclaimed narrative on the Civil War. **5** Jerome Kern and Hammerstein write the score for *Show Boat*, which includes the song "Ol' Man River." **6** Robert E. Sherwood publishes the comedy *The Queen's Husband*. **7** Kaufman and playwright Morris Ryskind collaborate on *Animal Crackers*. **8** Hecht and MacArthur collaborate on *The Front Page*, a play which influences the public's image of the newspaper world. **9** Claude McKay, writer of the "Harlem Renaissance," publishes *Home to Harlem*. **10** Sinclair publishes *Boston*. **11** O'Neill publishes *Strange Interlude*.	**12** Span. painter Salvador Dali collaborates with Span. director Luis Buñuel on the Surrealist film, *An Andalusian Dog*. **13** Dan. film maker Carl Dreyer directs *The Passion of Joan of Arc*, a silent film classic. **14** Ger. playwright Bertolt Brecht and composer Kurt Weill join forces on *Threepenny Opera*, adapted from Gay's *Beggar's Opera*. **[1728:ARTS/2]** **15** Ravel composes the ballet, *Bolero*. **16** Banned as obscene, Lawrence's *Lady Chatterley's Lover* is published in abridged form. Uncensored versions are not published until 1929 (Paris), 1959 (U.S.), and 1960 (England). **17** Picasso's "Le Surréalisme et La Peinture" is hailed as one of the first Surrealist paintings. **18** A. Huxley publishes the novel, *Point Counter Point*. **19** Federico García Lorca, prominent Span. writer, publishes *The Gypsy Ballads*, a collection of 18 poems. **20** Evelyn Waugh, Eng. novelist, publishes the satirical *Decline and Fall*.
1929	**1** U.S. envoys meet in Paris with German Committee on Reparations to revise Dawes Plan. **[1924:HIST/5]** **2** Pres. Hoover's proposal concerning the Tacna-Arica boundary dispute is accepted by both Peru and Chile. **3** Agricultural Marketing Act establishes Federal Farm Board to stabilize farm prices. **4** U.S. District Court at Chi-	**12** Tacna-Arica controversy is settled; Chile receives the province of Arica and Peru receives the province of Tacna. **13** National Revolutionary Party is organized in Mexico; it becomes the chief political party. **14** Alexander I, King of Yugoslavia, dissolves the parliament, abolishes the constitution, and becomes dictator	**1** The Academy Awards, or Oscars, are presented for the first time to honor outstanding achievement in filmmaking. Emil Jannings wins the Oscar for best actor and Janet Gaynor wins for best actress. **2** Hemingway publishes the novel *A*	**11** Erich Maria Remarque, Ger. writer, publishes *All Quiet on the Western Front*. **12** Robert Graves, Eng. writer, publishes *Good-Bye to All That*, an outstanding autobiographical war novel. **13** R.C. Sherriff, Eng. playwright, publishes the popular war drama,

Science & Technology		Miscellaneous		
America	Elsewhere	America	Elsewhere	

1928

Science & Technology — America

1 T. Chamberlin and Forest R. Moulton publish their hypothesis that the solar system originally consisted of the Sun orbited by innumerable minute bodies (planetesimals) which united to form the planets and satellites.
2 Alexanderson demonstrates a television set.
3 Philip Drinker and Louis Shaw invent the "iron lung."
4 Margaret Mead, anthropologist, publishes *Coming of Age in Samoa.*
5 Sikorski develops a commercially successful amphibian airplane.
6 Mount Palomar Observatory installs a 200-in. reflecting telescope designed by George Hale.
7 In *Anthropology and Modern Life,* Boas attacks theories of racial superiority.
8 Vesto Slipher, astronomer, discovers that spiral nebulae are spinning with great velocity as they speed away from Earth.
9 John Von Neumann, mathematician, develops as part of his theory of games, the minimax theorem, a strategy for minimizing a player's maximum loss.
10 Oscar Riddle, N.Y. zoologist, determines that prolactin, a hormone from the pituitary gland, causes the production of milk in the breasts.

Science & Technology — Elsewhere

11 Sir Chandrasekhara Raman, Ind. scientist, determines that light changes wavelength when it passes through a transparent substance.
12 Juan de la Cierva, Span. engineer, demonstrates his invention, a type of aircraft called the "autogiro."
13 The "rabbit test," the first reliable pregnancy test, is developed.
14 Baird demonstrates color television.
15 Sir Alexander Fleming, Eng. bacteriologist, discovers penicillin, founding the field of antibiotic therapy.
16 Karl Ziegler, Ger. chemist, explains the chemical procedure for making artificial rubber.
17 Han Fischer, Ger. biochemist, produces the blood pigment hemin in the laboratory.
18 Ger. chemists Otto Diels and Kurt Alder develop the Diels-Alder reaction for making synthetic rubber and plastics.
19 Jeans proposes that matter is constantly being formed throughout the Universe.
20 J.B.S. Haldane publishes *Science and Ethics.*

Miscellaneous — America

1 Walt Disney releases first Mickey Mouse cartoon, *Plane Crazy*; he also produces *Steamboat Willie,* first animated film to use sound.
2 Station WGY, Schenectady begins scheduled television broadcasts.
3 Pickwick Stages, Inc., bus manufacturers of Los Angeles, completes first "nite coaches"—buses equipped with sleeping facilities for transcontinental travel.
4 *New York Times* mounts first animated electric sign in U.S. around Times Building, Times Square, N.Y. Used to report election returns, it is called the "zipper" because of the way it encircles the building.
5 U.S. wins top honors in 9th Olympic Games, at Amsterdam, scoring a total of 131 points.
6 First sound film, *The Lights of New York,* is released by Warner Bros.
7 First coast-to-coast bus line is Yelloway Bus Line with service from Los Angeles to New York City; 3433-mi. trip takes 5 days, 14 hr.

Miscellaneous — Elsewhere

8 Olympic Games in Amsterdam: 22 sports, 120 events, 3015 participants. Women participate for the first time.
9 Kohl, Fitzmaurice, and Huenefeld are the first to fly the Atlantic from east to west in 35½ hrs.
10 High tide causes Thames River to overflow its banks.
11 Amundsen dies while trying to rescue Ital. explorer Nobile, whose airship has crashed in the Arctic.
12 Joe Davis wins the British Professional Billiards championship.
13 British steamer *Vestris* sinks in a gale off the Virginia coast; 110 persons die.

1929

Science & Technology — America

1 Hubble measures the red shift and discovers that the galaxies are moving away from each other. This *universal recession of galaxies* indicates that the universe is expanding.
2 Edward A. Doisy, biochemist, isolates "theelin," a female sex hormone, from the urine of pregnant women.

Science & Technology — Elsewhere

12 Oberth publishes *Way to Space Travel,* a work far ahead of its time.
13 Kathleen Lonsdale, Eng. crystallographer, uses x-rays in discovering the arrangement of molecules in benzene compounds.
14 George Gamow, Soviet physicist, proposes

Miscellaneous — America

1 On his first expedition to the Antarctic, Byrd flies over the South Pole.
2 First American experiment in creation of a garden community in Radburn, N.J. The community is designed to eliminate many of the dangers and hazards of city.
3 Milam Building, San

Miscellaneous — Elsewhere

9 Presbyterian churches in Scotland unite to form the Church of Scotland.
10 Brit. politician Margaret Bondfield becomes the first British woman Privy Councillor (advisor to the king).
11 Airship *Graf Zeppelin* flies around world, (21,255 miles) in 20 days, 4 hr., 14 min.

History and Politics

America

cago rules that the Standard Oil Company of Indiana and fifty-one related companies are guilty of violating the Sherman Antitrust Act.
5 National origins plan goes into effect. U.S. consuls are told to reject any immigrant who might become a "public charge." [1924:HIST/4]
6 Pres. Hoover meets with important businessmen at the White House in order to stabilize the nation's business. Stock market crash brings depression, with unemployment and business failures.
7 U.S. warships arrive in Shanghai, China, to protect U.S. lives and property.
8 Pres. Hoover signs bill authorizing a $160 million cut in the income tax.
9 Interstate Commerce Commission announces plan to merge all railroads into 19 operating units.
10 U.S. Treasury Department announces plans for better Prohibition enforcement.
11 Huey P. Long, Governor of Louisiana, is impeached on charges of bribery and misconduct, but he is not convicted.

1930
1 Senate ratifies London Naval Treaty, in which the U.S., Britain, and Japan agree to limit cruiser construction.
2 War Department amends Army regulations to make any violation of the federal prohibition law a military offense.
3 Pres. Hoover signs Smoot-Hawley Tariff, raising duties to an all-time high. U.S. undergoes a sharp decline in international trade, and The Depression deepens.
4 Hughes becomes Chief Justice of the U.S. Supreme Court. [1916:HIST/10]
5 Supreme Court rules that buying bootleg liquor is not a violation of the Eighteenth Amendment.

Elsewhere

of the country. He changes name of the Kingdom of Serbs, Croats, and Slovenes to Yugoslavia.
15 Trotsky is exiled from the U.S.S.R.
16 French troops withdraw from the Rhineland after an international settlement is reached at The Hague.
17 Arabs attack Jews in Palestine following a dispute about Jewish use of the Wailing Wall in Jerusalem.
18 Aristide Briand presides over his last cabinet (11th) as Premier of France.
19 Hitler appoints Heinrich Himmler head of the SS, or *Schutzstaffel*, the Nazi Party's black-shirted elite corps.
20 British and Indian leaders hold Round Table Conference about the dominion status of India.
21 Thirty-one Communist leaders are arrested in India for sedition.
22 Russia, Poland, Rumania, Estonia, and Latvia sign pact renouncing war.

9 Hitler's Nazi Party emerges as the majority party in the German national elections, winning 107 seats in the Reichstag. Ger. Chancellor, Heinrich Brüning, forms right-wing coalition government.
10 Worldwide economic depression occurs and fosters the rise of political extremists in many countries. [1931:HIST/7]
11 By the Treaty of Ankara, Turkey and Greece agree on naval parity (equality) in the eastern Mediterranean.
12 Constantinople is officially renamed Istanbul.
13 Ras Tafari becomes Emperor Haile Selassie of Ethiopia.
14 In protest against India's

The Arts

America

Farewell to Arms.
3 Hoagy Carmichael, composer, writes the song "Star Dust."
4 Humorists James Thurber and E.B. White write *Is Sex Necessary?*, a spoof of scientific sex manuals.
5 Gypsy Rose Lee makes her burlesque debut in Kansas City.
6 The score for the movie *Gold Diggers of Broadway,* by composer Joe Burke and lyricist Al Dubin, includes the song "Tiptoe Through the Tulips."
7 Rodgers and Lorenz Hart write the score to *Spring is Here.*
8 Thomas Wolfe publishes the autobiographical *Look Homeward, Angel.*
9 Elmer Rice publishes the Pulitzer Prize winning play *Street Scene.*
10 "Amos 'n' Andy," a popular radio show heard each weekday through the 1930s, makes its national premiere.

1 Sinclair Lewis becomes the first American to win the Nobel Prize in Literature.
2 Grant Wood, painter, exhibits his most famous work, "American Gothic."
3 Dashiell Hammett, writer of detective fiction, publishes *The Maltese Falcon,* which introduces the character Sam Spade. This work has a profound impact on mystery writers in the U.S. and Europe.
4 The Gershwin brothers score the shows *Girl Crazy,* which includes the songs "I Got Rhythm"

Elsewhere

Journey's End.
14 Brecht, Weill, and Hindemith collaborate on the radio cantata, *The Lindbergh Flight.* [1927:MISC/1]
15 Dali paints the Surrealist "Illumined Pleasures" and "Accommodations of Desire."
16 Woolf publishes "A Room of One's Own," a long essay.
17 Giraudoux publishes *Amphitryon 38,* a novel.
18 Vicki Baum, Aust. novelist, publishes *Grand Hotel.*
19 R. Hughes publishes *A High Wind in Jamaica.*
20 Coward completes *Bitter Sweet,* one of his most popular musicals.
21 Hitchcock directs *Blackmail,* the first successful British sound film.

11 W.H. Auden, Eng. poet, wins acclaim for *Poems,* a collection that includes "Paid on Both Sides."
12 Salvatore Quasimodo, Ital. writer, publishes *Waters and Land,* a collection of poetry that establishes him as the leader of the introverted and symbolic Hermetic poets.
13 In Germany, von Sternberg (Amer.) directs *The Blue Angel,* a sound film starring Marlene Dietrich and Emil Jannings.
14 Clair collaborates with Marcel Carné on *Under the Roofs of*

Science & Technology		Miscellaneous		
America	**Elsewhere**	**America**	**Elsewhere**	

3 Bell Laboratories experiments with transmitting color TV signals.
4 Clarence Birdseye introduces fresh-tasting, quick-frozen foods.
5 Adenosine triphosphate (ATP) is isolated from muscle.
6 Robert M. Yerkes, psychologist, publishes *The Great Apes* and establishes the Yale Laboratories of Primate Biology (Florida) to study animal behavior and intelligence.
7 Manfred J. Sakel, psychiatrist, introduces insulin shock as a treatment for schizophrenia.
8 Alexanderson measures the altitude of an airplane by using reflected radio waves. This is an early use of radar.
9 Karl Lashley, psychologist, links brain size with intelligence in *Brain Mechanism and Intelligence.*
10 University of Pennsylvania establishes a department of Medical Physics (biophysics).
11 Kodak introduces 16mm color movie film.

the "liquid drop" model of atomic nuclei—the basis of the modern theories of fission and fusion.
15 Adolf Butenandt, Ger. biochemist, determines the chemical structure of estrone, a female sex hormone.
16 Walther Bothe, Ger. physicist, determines that cosmic rays are not solely composed of gamma rays, as previously thought.
17 A. Fleming discovers lysozyme, an antibacterial substance found in tears and saliva.
18 Eddington publishes the philosophical work *Science and the Unseen World.*
19 Nobel Prize, Physics: Broglie, for his electron wave theory.
20 Nobel Prize, Physiology or Medicine: Eijkman, for discovering vitamin B, and Hopkins, for discovering vitamin A.

Antonio, completed. It is the most modern office building of its time; an attempt is made to air-condition the whole building.
4 Stock market begins its decline.
5 Patent issued to Sabastiano Lando for coin-operated vending machine that cannot be defrauded.
6 Before the stock market crash, 60% of U.S. citizens had annual incomes of less than $2000, estimated as the bare minimum for the "basic necessities of life."
7 The "St. Valentine's Day Massacre" takes place in Chicago when 6 members of the notorious Moran gang are lined up against a garage wall and shot by a rival gang.
8 In first instrument flight, Lt. James Doolittle flies entirely by radio signals received in his airplane.

12 14th edition of *Encyclopaedia Britannica* is published.

American Gothic, painter Grant Wood's most famous work

1 Clyde W. Tombaugh, Ill. astronomer, discovers Pluto. [1905:SCI/1]
2 Woods Hole Oceanographical Institute is established. [1879:SCI/2]
3 Bell Laboratories develops a two-way television communication system.
4 Compton suggests that cosmic rays are made of particles.
5 Vannevar Bush, electrical engineer, develops a differential analyzer, the first analog computer.
6 America's first planetarium, Adler Planetarium, opens in Chicago.
7 Hans Zinsser, bacteriologist, develops an effective immunization against

12 Dirac publishes *Principles of Quantum Mechanics.*
13 Paul Karrer, Swiss chemist, determines the function and structure of vitamin A.
14 Pyotr Kapitsa, Soviet physicist, tries to smash an atom by overcoming the magnetic forces that hold it together.
15 Auguste Piccard, Swiss physicist, builds a balloon with an airtight cabin.
16 Bernard Lyot, Fr. astronomer, invents the coronagraph, a telescope that produces an artificial solar eclipse, allowing astronomers to study the Sun's corona.

1 Population is 122.7 million; life expectancy is 61 years. One of every five Americans owns an automobile.
2 Publisher William Randolph Hearst owns 33 newspapers with total circulation of 11 million.
3 318 prisoners at the Ohio State Penitentiary at Columbus burn to death when a fire breaks out. The prison, built to accommodate 1500, has about 4300 inmates.
4 New York City's Bank of the United States closes because of stock market crash. Bank has 60 branches and almost half a million depositors. During this year more

9 Earthquake destroys much of the city of Pegu, in central Burma.
10 Viktor Barna of Hungary wins world table tennis championship.
11 Brit. aviator Amy Johnson (later Mollison) flies solo from London to Australia in 19½ days.
12 Picture telegraphy service begins between Britain and Germany.
13 Hurricane in Santo Domingo, Dominican Republic, kills 2000 persons, injures 6000.
14 Amer. railroad tycoon E.S. Harkness gives £2 million to the British Prime Minister "for the benefit of Britain."
15 Youth Hostels Asso-

1930

History and Politics

The Arts

America

Elsewhere

America

Elsewhere

6 Congress establishes the Veterans Administration to aid former servicemen and their dependents.

7 Pres. Hoover asks Congress for $100 to $150 million for public works programs, announcing there are 4.5 million people unemployed. Congress appropriates $116 million for construction work and $45 million for drought relief.

8 State Department makes public Undersecretary of State J. Reuben Clark's memorandum on the Monroe Doctrine. It repudiates the Roosevelt Corollary of 1904 and emphasizes U.S. doctrine to protect Latin American countries from the aggression of European powers.

---

salt tax, Gandhi leads Indians on 200-mile march to obtain salt from the sea. He is arrested and imprisoned without trial, but is released in 1931.

15 Iraq suppresses Kurdish revolt in the north.

16 Greece calls first Balkan conference at Athens to try to establish better relations among the Balkan states.

17 Carol II proclaims himself King of Rumania.

18 British Parliament debates Passfield White Paper, which suggests restricting Jewish immigration to Palestine.

19 Last Allied troops leave the Rhineland.

20 Canada gives preferential tariff treatment to Britain.

21 Maxim Maximovich Litvinov becomes Foreign Minister of the U.S.S.R. He pursues a policy of collective security and cooperation with the great powers.

---

and "Embraceable You," and Ryskind and Kaufman's political satire *Strike Up the Band,* featuring the song "I've Got a Crush on You."

5 Chic Young, cartoonist, develops the popular newspaper comic strip "Blondie."

6 Katherine Anne Porter, novelist and short story writer, publishes *Flowering Judas,* a collection of stories.

7 Faulkner publishes *As I Lay Dying.*

8 The Marx Brothers star in the comedy film *Animal Crackers.* [1928:ARTS/7]

9 Edward Hopper paints "Early Sunday Morning."

10 Maxwell Anderson publishes the historical drama *Elizabeth the Queen.*

Paris, a popular comedy film known for its innovative sound effects.

15 Brecht and Weill complete *The Rise and Fall of the City of Mahagonny,* a satirical opera.

16 Ital. novelist Ignazio Silone publishes *Fontamara,* a novel.

17 Shostakovich composes *The Golden Age,* a ballet that features the popular "Polka."

18 Zoltán Kodály, Hung. composer, completes *Marosszek Dances,* folk dances for orchestra.

19 In *Murder at Vicarage,* Christie introduces the popular detective, Miss Jane Marple.

20 Masefield succeeds Bridges as Poet Laureate of England.

1931

1 Wickersham Commission reports that enforcement of the Eighteenth Amendment is breaking down. It recommends revision, but not repeal of the law.

2 Congress passes Veterans Compensation Act over President Hoover's veto. It permits cash loans equal to half the 1924 bonus allowances to soldiers.

2 Supreme Court rules that Minnesota's "Press Gag" law is unconstitutional.

4 Pres. Hoover proposes a one-year moratorium on all World War debts and reparations in order to break the worldwide depression. Congress and U.S. financial leaders support it.

5 New York state legislature investigates charges of malfeasance and political corruption against Mayor Walker of New York City. Walker denies charges. [1932:HIST/3]

---

6 British Parliament enacts the Statute of Westminster, recognizing the autonomy of the dominions of the British Empire and establishing the British Commonwealth of Nations.

7 Austrian Credit-Anstalt (institution) collapses, thus beginning financial failures throughout central Europe. Economic hardship increases social and political tension.

8 King Alfonso XIII of Spain is deposed and a second republic is established.

9 Atatürk launches a program of internal reform and "Westernization" in Turkey.

10 Haile Selassie introduces a constitution in Ethiopia.

11 Mukden Incident occurs. Japanese army seizes Chinese arsenal at Mukden (now Shen-Yang), China, and overruns southern Manchuria.

12 Egypt and Iraq sign friendship treaty, the first step binding Egypt to the other Arab countries.

---

1 Two architectural landmarks in New York City, the 77-story, stainless steel capped Chrysler Building and the 102-story Empire State Building, are completed.

2 Duke Ellington composes the popular song "Mood Indigo."

3 Pearl Buck, novelist, publishes *The Good Earth,* the Pulitzer Prize winning story of a Chinese peasant and his wife.

4 Hoagy Carmichael composes "Georgia on My Mind," a song later recorded by jazz vocalist Mildred Bailey.

5 Hammett publishes the mystery novel *The Glass Key.*

6 The Marx Brothers star in the film *Monkey Business.*

7 Faulkner publishes *Sanctuary,* his first suc-

---

11 Ninette de Valois, Eng. dancer and choreographer, founds the Vic-Wells Ballet Company, later (1956) the Royal Ballet.

12 Clair directs *Le Million,* a musical comedy film.

13 Carl Zuckmayer, Ger. playwright, completes one of his best satires, *The Captain of Köpenick.*

14 Cocteau completes the surrealist fantasy film, *The Blood of a Poet.*

15 Frans Eemil Sillanpää, Finn. writer, publishes *The Maid Silja,* his best-known novel.

16 James Bridie, Scot. playwright, completes *The Anatomist,* a mystery based on an actual criminal case.

17 Lang directs the film, *M,* starring Peter

Science & Technology — America

typhus.

8 Edison Pettit and Seth Nicholson, astronomers, use a thermocouple to measure accurately the surface temperature of the Moon.

9 John H. Northrup, N.Y. scientist, crystallizes two digestive enzymes, pepsin and trypsin.

10 Quartz-crystal clocks are introduced.

11 Nobel Prize, Physiology or Medicine: Karl Landsteiner for discovering the major human blood types.

Science & Technology — Elsewhere

17 Arne Tiselius, Swed. biochemist, develops electro-phoresis for separating proteins in suspension.

18 Sir Frank Whittle, Eng. aviator, patents his design of a jet engine.

19 Nobel Prize, Chemistry: Hans Fischer, for his research into the chemistry of chlorophyll and the blood pigment hemin.

20 Nobel Prize, Physics: Raman, for his work on light diffusion.

Miscellaneous — America

than 1300 banks are forced to close.

5 American Lutheran Church formed at Toledo, Ohio, by union of 3 Lutheran groups from N.Y., Iowa, and Ohio.

6 Capt. Frank M. Hawks makes first transcontinental glider flight from San Diego, Calif., to New York City. He is towed by a biplane on a 500-ft. line; flight takes 7 days.

7 Irish Sweepstakes, a lottery for several Irish hospitals, begins and soon becomes popular in U.S. In 5 years, it is the most successful lottery in the world.

8 Robert "Bobby" Jones is first golfer to win the 4 most important golf matches: U.S. Amateur Tournament; British Open; British Amateur; and U.S. Open.

Miscellaneous — Elsewhere

ciation is founded in Britain.

1931

Science & Technology — America

1 Karl Jansky, engineer, determines that the source of mysterious radio interference is the stars.

2 Ernest O. Lawrence, physicist, invents the cyclotron, a particle accelerator that is popularly known as an "atom smasher."

3 Harold C. Urey, Ind. chemist, discovers deuterium, a hydrogen isotope often called "heavy hydrogen."

4 Linus Pauling, chemist, proposes the theory of *resonance* to explain the structure of benzene.

5 Julius A. Nieuland, chemist, produces neoprene, a synthetic rubber.

6 Charles Thornthwaite, climatologist, develops a system of classifying climates based on moisture, temperature, and seasonal variation.

7 Percy Bridgman, Mass. physicist, conducts

Science & Technology — Elsewhere

11 A. Piccard ascends to a height of almost 10 miles in the airtight cabin of his balloon. [1930:SCI/15]

12 Butenandt determines the chemical structure of androsterone, a male sex hormone.

13 Pauli suggests the existence of the neutrino, a subatomic particle.

14 Fajans publishes *Radio-elements and Isotopes*.

15 Physicians in Denmark report that vitamin E may keep pregnant women from having miscarriages.

16 Nobel Prize, Chemistry: Bergius and Carl Bosch, Ger. chemist, for their invention of high-pressure methods for making ammonia and liquefying coal.

17 Nobel Prize, Physiology or Medicine: Otto Warburg, Ger. biochemist, for his work on the oxy-

Miscellaneous — America

1 International Bible Students Association becomes Jehovah's Witnesses; in 1939 organization is incorporated under the name Watch Tower Bible and Tract Society. [1872:MISC/1]

2 Unemployment is estimated at between 4 and 5 million. Bank panic spreads. In September, 305 banks close; in October, 522.

3 "Star-Spangled Banner" is officially made U.S. anthem.

4 Clyde Pangborn and Hugh Herndon make first nonstop transpacific flight; 4860-mi. trip from Japan to Washington State takes about 41 hrs.

5 Alphonse ("Scarface Al") Capone, Chicago gangster, who has a yearly income of at least $20 million, is imprisoned for income tax evasion.

6 New School for Social

Miscellaneous — Elsewhere

9 China's population is 410 million; India's 338 million; U.S.S.R.'s 168 million; Japan's 75 million; Germany's 64 million; and Great Britain's 46 million.

10 Australian explorer G.H. Wilkins captains *Nautilus* submarine, navigating it under the Arctic Ocean.

11 First trans-African railroad, Benguela to Katanga, is completed.

12 King George V accepts the 2 millionth British telephone for use at Buckingham Palace.

13 Northern face of Matterhorn in the Alps climbed for first time by Franz and Toni Schmid.

History and Politics		The Arts	
America	Elsewhere	America	Elsewhere

	America	Elsewhere	America	Elsewhere
		13 Joseph Aloysius Lyons helps form the United Australia Party and is elected Prime Minister of Australia. **14** Norway annexes the east coast of Greenland, disputing Denmark's claim to all of Greenland. **15** Gabriel Terra becomes President of Uruguay and rules as a dictator. **16** James Ramsay Macdonald, Brit. Prime Minister, forms a coalition government, with Conservative and Liberal support. **17** Smetona is reelected President of Lithuania.	cessful novel. **8** Elmer Rice publishes the play *Counsellor-at-Law*. **9** The appearance of "Dick Tracy" by Chester Gould introduces new elements (humor, gadgetry, science fiction) into comic strips. **10** Ogden Nash, writer of humorous poetry, publishes his first collection, *Hard Lines*.	Lorre. **18** Tzara's poetry, *L'Homme approximatif,* marks his break with Dadaism. **19** Eng. composer William Turner Walton completes the oratorio, *Belshazzar's Feast*. **20** Coward glorifies contemporary British history in *Cavalcade*.
1932	**1** Reconstruction Finance Corporation (RFC) is established, headed by Charles Gates Dawes. **2** Anger over the kidnapping and death of the son of Charles A. Lindbergh forces passage of the death penalty in federal kidnapping cases. **3** Fifteen charges of corruption are leveled at Mayor Walker of New York City, who resigns from office. **4** Congress submits the Twentieth ("Lame Duck") Amendment to the states for ratification. It provides for the convening of Congress on Jan. 3 and for inauguration day on Jan. 20. Vice President-elect shall succeed to the presidency if the President-elect should die before inauguration. **5** Veterans of World War I camp out in Washington, D.C., to force Congress to pass bill for payment of their bonus certificates. Federal troops led by Douglas MacArthur disperse the "Bonus Army." **6** First unemployment insurance law is passed in Wisconsin. **7** Norris-LaGuardia Anti-Injunction Act prohibits the use of the injunction in most labor disputes. **8** Franklin Delano Roosevelt and John Nance Garner are	**10** De Valera becomes head of the Irish government after his party wins control of the *Dáil* (lower house of parliament in the Republic of Ireland). [1926:HIST/11] **11** Antonio de Oliveira Salazar becomes Premier of Portugal and rules as a dictator for the next 36 years. **12** The Kingdom of Hijaz and Najd is renamed Saudi Arabia. **13** Chaco War breaks out between Bolivia and Paraguay. **14** Germany lifts ban on Nazi storm troops. Disorders among rival political groups occur frequently. Nazi and Communist Parties gain strength in the Reichstag. Ger. Chancellor Brüning and his successors Franz von Papen and Kurt von Schleicher fail to mold parliamentary majorities without Hitler's help. **15** Croatian Peasant Party denounces the Belgrade government of Yugoslavia and demands autonomy. [1928:HIST/13] **16** Peru threatens war with Columbia over disputed territory of Leticia. **17** Japanese troops invade China following the murder of a Japanese Buddhist priest in Shanghai. Japanese seize Manchuria and make it an in-	**1** The score for the show *Americana,* by composer Jay Gorney and lyricist E.Y. "Yip" Harburg features the Depression era song "Brother, Can You Spare a Dime?" **2** James Farrell, novelist, publishes *Young Lonigan.* **3** Hemingway's *Death in the Afternoon* deals with bullfighting. **4** Faulkner publishes *Light in August.* **5** Hammett publishes *The Thin Man.* **6** Kaufman and Ferber collaborate on *Dinner at Eight.* **7** Ben Shahn paints the social commentary "The Passion of Sacco and Vanzetti." **8** Stan Laurel and Oliver Hardy, early film comedy team, star in *The Music Box.* **9** Damon Runyon, journalist, publishes *Guys and Dolls,* a collection of short stories. **10** Cole Porter's score for the show *The Gay Divorcé* includes the song "Night and Day." **11** Erskine Caldwell, author, publishes *Tobacco Road.* **12** Greta Garbo and	**14** A. Huxley publishes *Brave New World,* a novel that satirizes scientific progress by describing a bleak and dehumanized future culture. **15** Jean Renoir, Fr. film maker, directs *Bondu Saved from Drowning,* a complex film notable for its symbolic use of music. **16** Graham Greene, Eng. writer, publishes *Stamboul Train,* a popular thriller. **17** Jean Anouilh, Fr. playwright, completes *Thieves' Carnival,* a comedy. **18** Thomas Beecham, Eng. conductor, establishes the London Philharmonic Orchestra. **19** Mauriac publishes *Vipers' Tangle,* a dramatic novel. **20** Louis-Ferdinand Céline, Fr. writer, publishes *Journey to the End of Night,* a novel whose revolutionary style influences later French literature. **21** Ger. film maker Leni Riefenstahl writes, directs, and stars in *The Blue Light.* **22** Romains begins

318

Science & Technology		Miscellaneous		
America	**Elsewhere**	**America**	**Elsewhere**	
experiments on materials under high pressure—up to 100,000 atmospheres. 8 Fiberglass is introduced. 9 Ernest Goodpasture, pathologist, develops a method for growing viruses in chicken eggs. This process opens the door for the production of vaccines. 10 Guy Gilpatric, N.Y. diver, popularizes the use of rubber goggles with glass lenses.	gen consumption in cells.	Research, designed specifically for adult education, opens in New York City. 7 George Washington Bridge completed, connecting New York and New Jersey across the Hudson River. Main span is 3500 ft. long. 8 Wiley Post and Harold Gatty take off from Roosevelt Field, N.Y., in their plane "Winnie Mae" on a trip around the world. They land back at Roosevelt Field 8 days, 15 hr., and 51 min. later.		
1 Carl D. Anderson, N.Y. physicist, discovers the positron, a positively charged electron and the first known antimatter. 2 Charles G. King, Pa. biochemist, isolates vitamin C from lemon juice. 3 Armand Quick, hematologist, develops the "Quick test" to measure the clotting ability of blood. 4 Cannon publishes *The Wisdom of the Body*. 5 Carl-Gustav Rossby, Swed.-Amer. meteorologist, develops the Rossby diagram for mapping air masses. 6 Sonic locator is developed. It uses sound waves to measure the depth of water. 7 Edwin Land, Conn. physicist, invents polarizing glass. 8 Von Neumann mathematically proves the ergodic theorem and publishes a book on quantum mechanics. 9 T. H. Morgan publishes *The Scientific Basis of Evolution*. 10 RCA demonstrates electronic TV using a cathode-ray picture tube receiver. 11 Sperry Gyroscope Co. develops an automatic	13 James Chadwick, Eng. physicist, discovers the neutron. [1920:SCI/5] 14 Sir Hans Krebs, Ger. biochemist, discovers the urea cycle, a process in mammals whereby ammonia is changed to urea. 15 Sir John D. Cockcroft, Eng. physicist, and Ernest T.S. Walton, Ir. physicist, design a particle accelerator and establish its application in nuclear research. 16 Gerhard Domagk, Ger. bacteriologist, discovers that Prontosil, a sulfonamide drug, can be used to fight bacterial infections. 17 Bernhard Schmidt, Ger. astronomer, invents a telescope that can observe wide portions of the sky without distortion. 18 Sir John Eccles, Austral. physiologist, publishes *Reflex Activity of the Spinal Cord*. 19 Warburg isolates the first flavoprotein. 20 Adrian publishes *The Mechanism of Nervous Action*. 21 Nobel Prize, Physics: Heisenberg, for his work in quantum mechanics. 22 Nobel Prize, Physiology or Medicine: Adrian and Sherrington, for their	1 Aviator Amelia Earhart is first woman to fly alone across the Atlantic. Her flight from Newfoundland to Ireland takes 13½ hrs. and covers 2026 mi. 2 Depression reaches low point: monthly wages are about 60% of 1929; industry operates at half of 1929 volume, more than 5000 banks have closed since 1920; average monthly unemployment is 12 million. 3 Wisconsin passes first unemployment insurance law in U.S. 4 Experiment of progressive education on college level begins at Bennington College, Vt. A school for women, it does not use usual method of grading through credits. A similar project is under way at Teachers College, Columbia University, New York City, where graduation is based on over-all knowledge rather than on completion of certain required courses. 5 Charles Urban Yeager introduces "Bank Night" in Colorado motion-picture theaters: to attract an audience, a lottery is held for money (and, later, prizes). Later he copy-	9 Germany has 5.6 million unemployed workers; Great Britain, 2.8 million. 10 Amer. aviator Paul Codos flies from Paris to Hanoi, Indochina, in 3 days, 5 hr., 40 min. Amelia Earhart, American aviatrix	**1932**

319

History and Politics		The Arts	
America	**Elsewhere**	**America**	**Elsewhere**
elected President and Vice President, respectively, on the Democratic ticket. Roosevelt's "New Deal" program stresses federal support for the economy and for social reconstruction. **9** U.S. states that the Japanese occupation of Manchuria violates the Open Door Policy in China.	dependent protectorate called Manchukuo. [1931:HIST/11] **18** Catalonia in Spain is given its own president, parliament, and government; Catalan becomes the official language. Success by the Catalans leads to similar demands by the Basques and other groups.	John Barrymore star in the film *Grand Hotel.* **13** Josef von Sternberg directs *Shanghai Express,* a film known for its exotic sets, starring Marlene Dietrich.	the novel cycle, *Men of Good Will* (–1946, 27 vols.).
1933			
1 Twentieth Amendment to the Constitution is ratified. [1932:HIST/4] **2** Pres. Roosevelt declares a national bank holiday, suspending the activity of the Federal Reserve System and all banks. He gives first radio "fireside chat." Public confidence in the currency and the banks is restored. **3** Pres. Roosevelt appoints Frances Perkins Secretary of Labor, the first woman Cabinet member in the U.S. **4** Congress enacts a wide program of anti-depression measures, including the Emergency Banking Relief Act, Economy Act, Civilian Conservation Corps (CCC), Federal Emergency Relief Administration (FERA), and Agricultural Adjustment Administration (AAA). **5** Tennessee Valley Authority (TVA) becomes an independent government agency to develop the natural resources of the Tennessee River basin. **6** Federal Securities Act requires sworn statements about all securities for sale to be filed with the Federal Trade Commission (FTC). **7** Twenty-first Amendment to the Constitution, repealing Prohibition, is ratified. [1919:HIST/2] **8** National Recovery Administration (NRA) stimulates business and helps reduce unemployment. National Labor Board establishes the right of labor to bargain collectively. Public Works Administration	**13** Pres. Hindenburg appoints Hitler Chancellor of Germany. Nazis burn the Reichstag building and accuse the Communists of setting the fire. The democratic Weimar Republic falls; Hitler's Nazi Party wins a majority of seats in the Reichstag. German government outlaws freedom of the press, all labor unions, and political parties except the Nazis. Hitler's police, the *Gestapo,* hunts down, shoots, and jails opponents of the government. Germany withdraws from the European Disarmament Conference and from the League of Nations. Hitler begins to rearm Germany. **14** Engelbert Dollfus, Chancellor of Austria, opposes *Anschluss,* or union, between Austria and Germany. Nazi terrorism continues in Austria. [1934:HIST/16] **15** Spanish government suppresses insurrections by anarchists in Barcelona and other cities. **16** Nazi agitation spreads into the Sudetenland (northern and northwestern Czechoslovakia) and into Hungary. **17** Stalin begins great purge of the Communist Party in the U.S.S.R. He arrests, imprisons, and executes many old Bolsheviks. **18** Vidkun Quisling resigns as Norway's Minister of Defense and forms the fascist Nasjonal Samling Party, which stands for the suppression of Communism. **19** Hitler appoints Hermann	**1** Jimmy Dorsey, clarinetist and saxophonist, and his brother Tommy, trombonist, form a greatly successful jazz orchestra. **2** Composer Henry Warren and Al Dubin score the movies *42nd Street, Gold Diggers of 1933* ("We're in the Money"), and *Footlight Parade.* Busby Berkeley, choreographer, introduces the extravagant "production numbers" in these movies, using dozens of precision dancers **3** Lincoln Edward Kirstein and George Balanchine, dance innovators, found School of American Ballet, **4** Irving Berlin's score for the show *As Thousands Cheer* includes the songs "Easter Parade" and "Heat Wave." **5** Erskine Caldwell publishes *God's Little Acre.* **6** Composer Harold Arlen writes the song "Stormy Weather." **7** In the film *She Done Him Wrong,* Mae West introduces her classic line "Come up and see me sometime." **8** Gertrude Stein tells the story of her own life in *The Autobiography of Alice B. Toklas.*	**12** James Hilton, Eng. writer, publishes *Lost Horizon,* a novel set in a remote paradise, Shangri-La. **13** Fr. novelist André Malraux publishes *La Condition humaine (Man's Fate).* **14** Tómas Gudmundsson, is hailed as Iceland's outstanding poet after the publication of *The Fair Earth.* **15** Woolf publishes *Flush,* a whimsical biography of the Brownings. **16** Franz Werfel, Ger. writer, receives international praise for his epic novel, *The Forty Days of Musa Dagh.* **17** After having been arrested for supposedly revealing state secrets in an earlier novel (1932), Mackenzie publishes *Water on the Brain,* a satire of the British Secret Service. **18** Nash founds Unit One, a group dedicated to preserving formalism in art. **19** Alicia Markova, prima ballerina of England's Vic-Wells Ballet, dances the lead in *Giselle,* her favorite role. **20** Lang flees Germany after satirizing Nazism in his film, *The Last Will of Dr. Mabuse.* **21** In Germany, all books by Jewish or

Science & Technology		Miscellaneous		
America	Elsewhere	America	Elsewhere	

pilot.

12 Nobel Prize, Chemistry: Irving Langmuir for experiments and discoveries in surface chemistry.

work on the function of neurons.

rights the idea, and it spreads rapidly throughout the country.
6 Radio City Music Hall opens in New York City.
7 Mrs. Hattie T. Caraway (Democrat, Arkansas) is first woman elected to U.S. Senate.
8 First Winter Olympic Games held in U.S. open at Lake Placid, N.Y.

---

1 Armstrong develops frequency modulation (FM) radio broadcasting.
2 Farnsworth develops an electronic TV receiver.
3 Lewis produces deuterium oxide ("heavy water").
4 Tennessee Valley Authority (TVA) is created to conserve area resources.
5 Robert Van de Graaf, physicist, builds *Big Bertha,* a static electricity generator that can produce 7 million volts.
6 Otto Stern, Pol.-Amer. physicist, measures the magnetic moment of a proton.
7 Theophilus S. Painter, Tex. geneticist, develops a new method for mapping chromosomes.
8 Aldo Leopold, Iowa naturalist, publishes *Game Management* in which he applies the principles of ecology to wildlife management.
9 Donald Menzel, astrophysicist, discovers that the Sun's corona contains oxygen.
10 John Lundy, anesthesiologist, uses an intravenous barbiturate, sodium pentothal, to anesthetize a patient before surgery.
11 High-intensity mercury vapor lamps are developed.
12 Nobel Prize, Physiology or Medicine: Thomas Hunt Morgan for discov-

13 Grantly Dick-Read, Eng. obstetrician, publishes *Natural Childbirth,* which suggests that expectant mothers learn certain exercises and procedures to enable them to give birth without drugs.
14 Tadeus Reichstein, Swiss chemist, produces ascorbic acid (vitamin C) in the laboratory.
15 Geoffrey Bourne, Austral. anatomist, demonstrates the technique for detecting vitamin C in animal tissue.
16 Eddington publishes *The Expanding Universe,* a cosmological work for the layman.
17 Otto R. Frisch, Aust. scientist, determines the magnetic moment of the proton.
18 O. Richardson publishes *Molecular Hydrogen and Its Spectrum.*
19 J.B.S. Haldane publishes *The Causes of Evolution.*
20 Nobel Prize, Physics: Schrödinger and Dirac, for developing useful applications of the atomic theory.

1 Affected seriously by the depression, 2000 rural schools do not open for the fall semester; 200,000 teachers are out of work; and about 2.3 million children are not in school; in addition, a number of colleges and universities are forced to close.
2 President Franklin D. Roosevelt begins practice of speaking directly to the American people by means of radio in "fireside chats."
3 National Guard is made part of the U.S. Army in wartime and in national emergencies.
4 Great Lakes are linked with the Gulf of Mexico when Illinois Waterway opens.
5 Frances Perkins, Secretary of Labor, becomes first woman cabinet member.
6 Civilian Conservation Corps (CCC) employs 500,000 people to improve the environment (-1942).
7 American League beats the National League, 4-2, in the first All-Star Baseball Game at Comiskey Field, Chicago, Ill., before 49,200 fans.
8 Chicago Bears beat the New York Giants, 23 to 21, for the first National Professional Football League Championship in Chicago.

9 Theory that Neanderthal man is in line of descent of *Homo Sapiens* (modern man) is rejected following discovery of Steinheim skull in western Germany.
10 Brit. racing champion Malcolm Campbell achieves automobile speed record of 272.46 mph.
11 Widespread famine in U.S.S.R.
12 British airplanes fly over Mt. Everest.

1933

History and Politics		The Arts	
America	**Elsewhere**	**America**	**Elsewhere**
(PWA) provides funds for the construction of public projects. **9** Farm Credit Act helps farmers refinance mortgages. **10** Federal Deposit Insurance Corporation (FDIC) is established. **11** National Guard is made part of the U.S. Army. **12** Fiorello LaGuardia is elected Mayor of New York City.	Göring Reich Air Minister and Prussian Prime Minister. **20** Assyrian Christians are massacred in Iraq. **21** Switzerland outlaws the wearing of political party uniforms.	**9** Sidney Kingsley, playwright, writes the medical drama *Men in White.* **10** John P. Marquand publishes *Haven's End,* a detective novel featuring the character Mr. Moto. **11** Jerome Kern and Otto Harbach compose the song "Smoke Gets in Your Eyes."	non-Nazi authors are ordered burned. Modern Art is supressed in favor of artificial Realism.

1934

History and Politics		The Arts	
America	**Elsewhere**	**America**	**Elsewhere**
1 Gold Reserve Act grants the President authority to regulate the value of the dollar. **2** Tydings-McDuffie Act grants independence to the Philippines in 1946. **3** Securities and Exchange Commission (SEC) is set up to control the trading of securities and to correct violations in the market. **4** Federal Communications Commission begins to regulate all national and international communications by telephone, radio, and cable. **5** Federal Farm Mortgage Corporation provides easier credit to farmers in debt. **6** Pres. Roosevelt initiates his "Good Neighbor Policy" with the Latin American nations; it opposes armed intervention by any foreign power. **7** Wheeler-Howard Indian Organization Act returns to various Indian tribes reservation lands which had been for sale. [1887:HIST/3] **8** U.S. troops and administrators leave Haiti. [1915:HIST/5] **9** Reciprocal Trade Agreements Act authorizes the President to raise or lower tariffs 50% for countries giving the U.S. favorable trade agreements. **10** Federal Housing Administration insures loans to homeowners by private institutions. **11** U.S. and Cuba (headed by Fulgencio Batista) sign new treaty. It cancels the	**13** Stavisky Affair, a financial scandal in France, causes right-wing riots, forcing the resignation of two successive French Premiers of the ruling left-wing coalition. Gaston Doumergue becomes French Premier and restores public confidence. **14** Red (Communist) Army under Mao Tse-tung withstands attacks by the Chinese Nationalist Army under Chiang Kai-shek. Mao leads his army on famous "Long March" (6000 miles) from south to north China. More than half the marchers die during the trek. **15** Hitler combines the offices of Ger. Chancellor and President and gives himself the title *Führer* (leader). **16** Dollfus ruthlessly suppresses a Socialist uprising in Austria. Nazis assassinate Dollfus and make an unsuccessful attempt to seize power in Vienna. Kurt von Schuschnigg becomes Chancellor of Austria. **17** Croatian terrorist kills King Alexander I of Yugoslavia. **18** Lázaro Cárdenas becomes President of Mexico. **19** Italians and Ethiopians fight over disputed area on the border of Italian Somaliland in eastern Africa. **20** Terra is reelected President of Uruguay. **21** Spanish government puts down great strike led by the socialists in Barcelona. **22** Many Nazi leaders are	**1** "King of Swing" Benny Goodman, clarinetist, organizes one of the first swing bands, which, during its ten year existence, brings great popularity to jazz dance music. **2** Lillian Hellman, playwright, completes *The Children's Hour.* **3** Paul Manship, sculptor, completes the bronze Prometheus Fountain in Rockefeller Center. **4** The summertime Berkshire Festival at Tanglewood in Lenox, Mass., is begun. **5** Farrell publishes *The Young Manhood of Studs Lonigan.* **6** Louis de Rochemont begins the documentary film series "March of Time." **7** Rex Stout, detective fiction author, publishes *Fer-de-Lance,* in which he introduces the characters Nero Wolfe and Archie Goodwin. **8** William Saroyan, author, publishes the collection of short stories, *The Daring Young Man on the Flying Trapeze.* **9** Shirley Temple, actress, stars in the film *Bright Eyes,* in which she sings "On the Good Ship Lollipop." **10** James Cain, writer, publishes the	**12** Hindemith's greatest opera, *Mathis der Maler,* causes a furor and is banned by the Nazis after being performed by the Berlin Philharmonic. **13** René Magritte, Fr. Surrealist, paints "The Rape." **14** André Breton, Fr. Surrealist writer, brings international attention to the movement with *What is Surrealism?* **15** Fr. jazz violinist Stephane Grappelli and Belg. guitarist Django Reinhardt form the popular group, Quintette of the Hot Club, France. **16** Hilton publishes *Goodbye, Mr. Chips,* a novel about a kindly schoolteacher. **17** Welsh poet Dylan Thomas publishes *Eighteen Poems.* **18** Graves publishes *I, Claudius,* a popular historical novel about ancient Rome. **19** Laurence Housman, Eng. writer, produces *Victoria Regina,* a play about Victorian England. **20** Cocteau publishes the novel, *The Infernal Machine.* **21** John Christie, Eng. musician, organizes the Glyndebourne Operatic Festival at his Sussex estate.

Science & Technology		Miscellaneous		
America	**Elsewhere**	**America**	**Elsewhere**	
ering the role of chromosomes in heredity.				
1 Federal Communications Commission (FCC) is created to regulate radio and wire communication. **2** Wallace Carothers, chemist, produces "polymer 66," later known as nylon. **3** Hubble discovers a nebula at a distance of 220 million light-years, moving away at 24,000 miles per second. **4** Fritz Zwicky and Walter Baade determine that supernovae are relatively rare and are different from novae. **5** Felix Bloch, Swed.-Amer. physicist, develops a method of polarizing neutrons. **6** Jesse W. Beams, physicist, develops an air-driven, vacuum-enclosed ultracentrifuge. **7** Ruth Benedict, N.Y. anthropologist, publishes *Patterns of Culture*. **8** Charles W. Beebe, N.Y. naturalist, descends 3028 feet into the ocean near Bermuda in a bathysphere. **9** Boston police begin using mobile 2-way radios. **10** Nobel Prize, Chemistry: Harold Urey for discovering deuterium. **[1931:SCI/3]** **11** Nobel Prize, Physiology or Medicine: George Minot, William Murphy, and George Whipple for	**12** Wernher von Braun, Ger. rocket engineer, launches two rockets which reach heights of 1.5 miles. **13** Fr. chemists Frédérick Joliet-Curie and Irène Joliet-Curie produce radioactive nitrogen, the first artificially radioactive element. **14** Pavel Cherenkov, Russ. physicist, discovers that the velocity of light in matter is less than it is in a vacuum (Cherenkov effect). **15** Andrade develops a formula which relates the viscosity of liquids to temperature. **16** Fermi announces the discovery of the 93rd element, transuranium, produced by bombarding uranium with neutrons. **17** Dorothy Hodgkin, Eng. biochemist, takes the first x-ray diffraction photograph. **18** Butenandt determines the structure of progesterone, a female sex hormone. **19** Nikolay Semenov, Soviet chemist, publishes *Chemical Kinetics and Chain Reactions*. **20** Sir Walter Haworth, Eng. chemist, synthesizes vitamin C. **21** Hevesy tracks the course of various body functions using radioactive isotopes.	**1** Congress establishes the death penalty for kidnapping across state lines, a result of the kidnap-murder of the 20-month old son of Charles A. Lindbergh in 1932. **2** Censorship of motion pictures is begun by the Catholic Legion of Decency. **3** About 130 persons die when fire breaks out on the ship *Morro Castle*, near Asbury Park, N.J. **4** Bank robber and murderer John Dillinger, public enemy no. 1, shot and killed by F.B.I. **5** First general strike takes place in San Francisco in support of the 12,000 striking dock-workers. **6** Max Baer scores a technical knockout over Primo Carnera, world's heavyweight boxing champion. Carnera, at 6 ft. 6½ in. and 260 lbs., is one of the biggest men ever to be champion. **7** U.S. golfers defeat golfers of Great Britain in the International Walker Cup Match at St. Andrews, Scotland.	**8** Dionne quintuplets, five girls, born in Callender, Ontario, Canada. They are the first known quintuplets to survive. **9** Brit. golfer Henry Cotton wins the Open Golf Championship, ending American golfers' dominance. **10** U.S.S.R. balloon *Osoaviakhim* ascends 13 mi. into stratosphere. **11** Hurricane in Honshu Island, Japan, kills more than 4000 persons. **12** S.S. *Queen Mary* is launched in Britain. It is the first British ship to exceed 1000 ft. in length; weighs 81,235 tons. **13** Regular air-mail service begins between London and Australia. **14** Women gain vote in Turkey.	**1934**

America	Elsewhere	America	Elsewhere

Platt Amendment, except for the Guantánamo base lease. [1901:HIST/2]
12 Nebraska establishes the first unicameral state legislature.

executed in Germany because of an alleged plot against Hitler and his government.

violent novel *The Postman Always Rings Twice.*
11 Al Capp, cartoonist, creates the comic strip "Li'l Abner."

22 Honegger composes *Sémiramis,* a ballet.

1935

America

1 Works Progress Administration (WPA) ends direct relief funds from the federal government but continues to make jobs for workers on public projects.
2 Soil Conservation Service is set up to stop soil erosion caused by the severe drought in the Great Plains (the "Dust Bowl").
3 Rural Electrification Administration is set up to construct power lines and to provide electricity for areas not served by private companies.
4 New National Labor Relations Board is established to oversee collective bargaining by employees and to prevent unfair labor practices by employers and unions. [1933:HIST/8]
5 Social Security Act provides a federal-state program of unemployment compensation and a federal program of old-age retirement insurance.
6 Wealth Tax Act increases income tax rates for wealthy individuals and corporations and raises gift and estate taxes.
7 Huey Long, now Senator from Louisiana and critic of Pres. Roosevelt, is assassinated in the state capital at Baton Rouge, La. [1929:HIST/11]
8 Federal Conservation Reserve Program returns 28 million acres of cropland to grassland and forests.
9 Government restricts public utility monopolies.
10 U.S. citizens are told to travel on ships of nations at war at their own risk.

Elsewhere

11 Italian forces invade Ethiopia and seize Adua. League of Nations votes sanctions against Italy.
12 Switzerland begins an extensive modernization of its army and air force.
13 Plebiscite in the Saarland favors its reunification with Germany, marking the start of Germany's expansion under Hitler. Hitler renounces the Versailles Treaty and reintroduces the military draft.
14 Chaco War between Bolivia and Paraguay ends with more than 100,000 lives lost.
15 Austria repeals anti-Hapsburg laws and restores part of the imperial property. France and the Little Entente oppose this.
16 Persia is renamed Iran.
17 King again becomes Prime Minister of Canada.
18 Nazi Party Congress issues the Nuremberg Laws, which deprive German Jews of their civic rights.
19 France concludes an alliance with the U.S.S.R. to protect against an unprovoked attack.
20 Finland tries to form a bloc of Scandinavian and Baltic countries to keep the balance between Germany and the U.S.S.R.
21 British Parliament passes the Government of India Act, which provides for a federal legislature in Delhi. Burma and Aden are separated from India.
22 Pierre Laval becomes Premier and Foreign Minister of France.

America

1 George and Ira Gershwin collaborate on their masterpiece, the opera *Porgy and Bess.*
2 Ayn Rand, author, writes *The Night of January 16,* a mystery play which features a jury picked from the audience.
3 Maxwell Anderson publishes *Winterset,* a poetic drama based on the Sacco and Vanzetti case.
4 Farrell publishes *Judgement,* the conclusion of the Studs Lonigan trilogy.
5 Mark Tobey, abstract expressionist, paints "Broadway."
6 John O'Hara, writer, publishes *Butterfield 8,* based on an actual New York murder.
7 Clarence Day, essayist, publishes the autobiographical *Life With Father.* [1939:ARTS/5]
8 John Steinbeck, novelist, publishes *Tortilla Flat,* a sympathetic study of Mexican-Americans.
9 Thomas Wolfe publishes *Of Time and the River,* a sequel to his 1929 work.
17 Clifford Odets, playwright, publishes three plays: *Waiting for Lefty, Awake and Sing,* and *Paradise Lost.*
18 Sherwood produces the play *The Petrified Forest.*

Elsewhere

12 Eng. writer Enid Bagnold publishes *National Velvet,* a popular novel about a 14-year-old girl who wins England's most prestigious race, the Grand National.
13 Hitchcock directs two classic thrillers, *The Thirty-nine Steps* and *The Man Who Knew Too Much.*
14 T.S. Eliot writes *Murder in the Cathedral,* a play about Thomas à Becket.
15 Christopher Isherwood, Eng. novelist, collaborates with Auden on the verse drama, *The Dog Beneath the Skin.*
16 García Lorca publishes *Lament for Ignacio Sanchez Mejías.*
17 Giraudoux writes the drama, *Tiger at the Gates.*
18 Bonnard paints "Still Life (Corner of a Table)," a work known for its powerful colors.
19 Prokofiev composes *Romeo and Juliet,* a ballet.
20 A.J. Cronin, Eng. physician and novelist, wins worldwide acclaim for *The Stars Look Down,* set in a Welsh coal-mining town.
21 Emlyn Williams, Welsh dramatist who designs leading roles for himself, produces *Night Must Fall,* a mystery.

Science & Technology		Miscellaneous		
America	**Elsewhere**	**America**	**Elsewhere**	
using liver extract to treat anemia. [1926:SCI/2]				

Science & Technology		Miscellaneous		
America	**Elsewhere**	**America**	**Elsewhere**	
1 Dempster discovers U-235, an isotope of uranium later used in nuclear weapons and in nuclear power plants. 2 Edward Kendall, chemist, isolates a hormone (later called *cortisone*) from the adrenal cortex. 3 Wendell M. Stanley, biochemist, crystallizes a tobacco mosaic virus. This proves that a virus contains protein and shows that matter may have both living and nonliving forms. 4 Rudolf Schoenheimer and David Rittenberg use radioactive tracers to follow the paths of certain foods during metabolism. 5 Aitken has discovered more than 3000 binary (double) stars since 1930. 6 Beams separates isotopes with his ultra-centrifuge. 7 William F. Giauque, chemist, produces temperatures within one degree of absolute zero ($-273.16°C$), theoretically the coldest possible temperature. 8 Riboflavin (vitamin B_2) is synthesized. 11 W. Maurice Ewing, Tex. geophysicist, is the first to take seismic measurements in open seas. 9 The first round-the-world telephone conversation covers more than 23,000 miles. It is routed from New York to San Francisco, Indonesia, Holland, England, and back to New York—to an office less than 50 feet from the phone where the call started.	10 Emilio Segré, Ital. physicist, and Fermi discover slow neutrons. 11 Leopold Ružička, Swiss chemist, determines the structure of testosterone, a male sex hormone. 12 Konrad Lorenz, Aust. zoologist, describes the animal learning process called imprinting. 13 Robert Watt, Scot. physicist, begins the research which leads to the development of the English and American radar systems. 14 Construction of the first commercially built electron microscope begins in England. 15 Eddington publishes *New Pathways of Science*. 16 Carrel publishes *Man, the Unknown*. 17 Nobel Prize, Chemistry: the Joliet-Curies, for their creation of artificially radioactive elements. 18 Nobel Prize, Physics: Chadwick, for discovering the neutron. 19 Nobel Prize, Physiology or Medicine: Hans Speeman, Ger. embryologist, for discovering the organizer effect in embryonic growth.	1 Pan American Airways begins transpacific air service from San Francisco to Manila. 2 Committee for Industrial Organizations is founded by heads of eight unions in the American Federation of Labor (AFL). Its goal is to develop industry-wide unions that include clerical and unskilled workers, as well as skilled workers who are eligible for the AFL. 3 Soil Conservation Service is established to try to stop soil erosion in the Great Plains, where the most destructive drought ever known in the Midwest has turned the land into a dust bowl. 4 Social Security Act establishes federal payroll tax to finance cooperative federal-state system of unemployment insurance. 5 Alcoholics Anonymous is organized in New York City. 6 Cincinnati Reds and Philadelphia Phillies play the first major league night baseball game at Crosley Field, Cincinnati.	7 Earthquake at Quetta, India, kills about 50,000 people. 8 Longest railroad bridge in world opens over the lower Zambesi River in South Africa. 9 Subway opens in Moscow. 10 Max Euwe of Holland defeats Alekhine for world chess title. 11 France's S.S. *Normandie* crosses the Atlantic in 107 hrs. 33 min. 12 Germany has regular television service. 13 First broadcast of quiz program, in Canada.	**1935**

History and Politics

America

Elsewhere

The Arts

America

Elsewhere

1936

America (History and Politics)

1 Congress passes Adjusted Compensation Act over Pres. Roosevelt's veto. It provides for immediate payment of requested veterans' benefits. [1932:HIST/5]
2 Soil Conservation and Domestic Allotment Act gives funds to farmers who practice soil conservation.
3 Socialist Party again nominates Thomas for President.
4 Republican Party nominates Gov. Alfred M. Landon for President. Republicans criticize the unconstitutionality of Pres. Roosevelt's New Deal programs.
5 Robinson-Patman Act forbids low pricing that reduces competition and encourages monopolies.
6 Walsh-Healey Public Contracts Act sets minimum employee wages for companies having government contracts. Eight-hour day, 40-hour week, and no child labor is enforced.
7 Roosevelt and Garner are reelected President and Vice President, respectively, on the Democratic ticket. Roosevelt carries every state but Vermont and Maine, winning 523 electoral votes to 8 for Landon. Congress is 80% Democratic.
8 Pres. Roosevelt opens Inter-American Conference at Buenos Aires. Latin American nations will consult with the U.S. for "mutual safety."
9 Gross national debt increases to about $34 billion; government expenditures rise because of relief programs.
10 Many Americans go to Spain to fight with the Spanish Loyalists against the Fascists.

Elsewhere (History and Politics)

11 Edward VIII becomes King of England but abdicates after the British government opposes his marriage to Mrs. Wallis Warfield Simpson. George VI, brother of Edward, becomes King.
12 Italy annexes Ethiopia. Victor Emmanuel III, King of Italy, takes the title Emperor of Ethiopia. Haile Selassie flees.
13 Rightist uprisings against Spain's government begin in Morocco and spread to Spain. Francisco Franco leads the Falangists (Spanish fascists) that oppose the Loyalists during the Spanish Civil War.
14 Germany denounces the Treaty of Locarno and reoccupies the Rhineland. [1925:HIST/16]
15 Goebbels accuses Czechoslovakia of concealing Soviet warplanes. Nazis begin campaign denouncing Czechoslovakia.
16 Stalin continues his purge trials, which last until 1939.
17 Anastasio Somoza seizes power in Nicaragua after a successful coup against the liberal regime. [1937:HIST/16]
18 Farouk becomes King of Egypt.
19 Aust. Chancellor Schuschnigg disbands the Heimwehr, a national paramilitary defense group led by his Vice Chancellor. Schuschnigg becomes leader of the Fatherland Front in Austria.
20 John Metaxas leads successful coup in Greece, dissolves parliament, and makes himself dictator.
21 Saudi Arabia and Iraq sign treaty of non-aggression. Arab High Commission is formed and opposes Jewish claims in Palestine.
22 Hitler and Mussolini sign an accord known as the "Rome-Berlin axis."

America (The Arts)

1 Margaret Mitchell, author, publishes her only book, *Gone With the Wind,* about the Civil War.
2 Kaufman and Moss Hart write the Pulitzer Prize-winning play *You Can't Take It With You.*
3 Benny Goodman becomes the first bandleader to integrate racially his band when he hires pianist Teddy Wilson and vibraphonist Lionel Hampton.
4 Count Basie, pianist and composer, organizes a band featuring Lester Young on the tenor saxophone.
5 Eugene O'Neill becomes the first American playwright to win the Nobel Prize in Literature.
6 Dos Passos completes his "U.S.A." trilogy with the publication of *The Big Money.* The earlier works include *The 42nd Parallel* (1930) and *1919* (1932).
7 Pare Lorentz produces *The Plow that Broke the Plains,* a film about the agricultural misuse of the Great Plains.
8 Orson Welles, actor, director, and producer, directs an all-black cast in *Macbeth* for the Negro People's Theater, part of the Federal Theater Project.
9 Cole Porter's score for the show *Born to Dance* includes the songs "I've Got You Under My Skin" and "You're the Top."
10 Frost's *A Further Range* wins him the Pulitzer Prize.
11 Sherwood publishes *Idiot's Delight.*

Elsewhere (The Arts)

12 Prokofiev composes the symphonic tale, *Peter and the Wolf.*
13 *Things to Come,* a futuristic British film based on the works of H.G. Wells, is directed by William Cameron Menzies (Amer.), features music by Bliss, and stars Raymond Massey (Can.) and Ralph Richardson (Brit.).
14 T.S. Eliot begins *Four Quartets* (–1942), his most religious poetry.
15 Bernanos publishes his greatest novel, *The Diary of a Country Priest.*
16 Riefenstahl directs *Triumph of the Will,* an important Nazi documentary, and *Olympia* (–1938), a two-part film about the 1936 Olympics.
17 R. Strauss composes *Olympische Hymne,* opening music for the Olympics.
18 Eng. playwright Terence Rattigan completes the farce, *French Without Tears.*
19 Mondrian paints "Composition in White, Black, and Red."
20 Rilke publishes *Sonnets to Orpheus,* 55 of his greatest works.
21 Soviet authorities condemn Shostakovich's opera, *Lady Macbeth of Mtsensk.*
22 C.S. Lewis, Eng. author, publishes *Allegory of Love: A Study in Medieval Tradition.*

Science & Technology

America

1 Robert R. Williams, chemist, synthesizes thiamine (vitamin B$_1$).

2 Carrel and Lindbergh invent the perfusion pump, a type of artificial heart for use during cardiac surgery.

3 Electroluminescence, later used in fluorescent lighting, is discovered.

4 Fiberglass fabric is used to insulate electrical wires.

5 Eugene P. Wigner, physicist, develops the theory of neutron absorption.

6 Catalytic cracking is introduced for refining petroleum.

7 George H. Brown, electrical engineer, invents the turnstile antenna. It is soon in standard use for TV and FM broadcasting.

8 U.S. Weather Bureau begins showing fronts and isolines on their weather maps.

9 Nobel Prize, Physics: Carl Anderson for discovering the positron. **[1932:SCI/1]**

Elsewhere

10 Reichstein isolates cortisone and determines its structure.

11 Albert Szent-Györgyi, Hung. biochemist, suggests the existence of a vitamin that helps maintain capillary structure.

12 Eddington examines the quantum theory in his work *Relativity Theory of Protons and Electrons.*

13 Nobel Prize, Chemistry: Debye, for his work on electrical charges within molecules.

14 Nobel Prize, Physics: Victor Hess, for discovering cosmic radiation.

15 Nobel Prize, Physiology or Medicine: Dale and Loewi, for their discovery of the chemical transmission of nerve impulses.

Franklin Delano Roosevelt, 32nd U.S. President

Miscellaneous

America

1 Boulder (Hoover) Dam on the Colorado River in Nevada and Arizona is completed, creating Lake Mead, America's largest reservoir with a capacity of more than 10 trillion gal. Dam is the highest in the world.

2 Luce publishes *Life,* weekly photographic news and feature magazine.

3 Bruno Richard Hauptmann is convicted of kidnapping and killing the Lindbergh baby (in 1932).

4 It is estimated that there are 160,000 automobile trailers on the road. Some predict that soon half the country would be living in trailers.

5 Educator Robert M. Hutchins publishes *The Higher Learning in America,* a statement of the movement against progressive education and the elective system in colleges.

6 Airship *Hindenburg* lands at Lakehurst, N.J., after the first scheduled transatlantic dirigible flight. Built by the Zeppelin Transport Company, the ship is 830 ft. long, 135 ft. in diameter, with a range of 8000 mi.

7 Baseball Hall of Fame is established at Cooperstown, N.Y.

8 S.S. *Queen Mary* arrives in New York City from England on its first voyage; it is the largest liner afloat.

Elsewhere

9 China's population is 422 million; India's 360 million; U.S.S.R.'s 173 million; Japan's 89 million; Germany's 70 million; Great Britain's 47 million; and France's 44 million.

10 S.S. *Queen Mary* crosses Atlantic in 3 days, 23 hr., 57 min.

11 Olympic Games are held in Berlin. Amer. athlete Jesse Owens wins 4 gold medals.

12 Brit. aviator Mrs. Amy (Johnson) Mollison flies from England to Cape Town in 3 days, 6 hrs., 25 min. J.A. Milinson flies from Newfoundland to London in 13 hrs., 17 min. Jean Batteu flies solo from England to New Zealand in 11 days.

1936

History and Politics

America

Elsewhere

The Arts

America

Elsewhere

1937

America — History and Politics

1 Pres. Roosevelt restricts U.S. munitions trade with Japan.
2 Congress resists Pres. Roosevelt's plan to increase the number of Supreme Court justices from 9 to 15. He is charged with "packing the court."
3 Supreme Court upholds the Social Security Act and other New Deal legislation.
4 Neutrality Act prohibits the exporting of munitions to nations at war and the use of U.S. ships for carrying munitions into war zones.
5 Farm Security Administration is empowered to make 40-year loans at 3% interest to help farmers, tenants, and laborers.
6 Judicial Procedure Reform Act permits federal judges to retire at 70 with full pensions after serving 10 or more years.
7 Supreme Court rules the federal government can regulate local dealings of labor unions.
8 Housing Act gives loans to local communities for low-cost construction and for rent subsidies.
9 U.S. signs agreement with Brazil, guaranteeing funds to Brazil to improve its economy.
10 Japanese planes bomb and sink U.S. gunboat *Panay* in Chinese waters. Japan apologizes.

Elsewhere — History and Politics

11 Neville Chamberlain becomes British Prime Minister. He tries to secure peace in Europe through a policy of "appeasement," making concessions to Germany and Italy.
12 Franco's Falangists merge with the Nationalists and conquer northwestern Spain. Loyalist Spanish government moves from Valencia to Barcelona. British, French, Italian, and German warships help Franco blockade the entire Spanish coast.
13 Hitler encourages Nazi demonstrations in Austria.
14 Fascist groups unite to form the Hungarian National Socialist Party.
15 Kyosti Kallio is elected President of Finland.
16 Somoza becomes President of Nicaragua and begins program against Communists and other radicals.
17 France suppresses nationalist revolt in French Morocco.
18 Japanese troops seize Peking, Tientsin, and other Chinese cities. Japanese bomb Chinese cities; Japanese navy blockades South China. League of Nations condemns Japan. Chinese forces abandon Shanghai to the Japanese. Japanese attack on U.S. and British ships near Nanking produces tense international situation. Japan apologizes and pays indemnity. [1938:HIST/19]
19 New constitution in Brazil gives the president dictatorial powers.
20 Mussolini visits Libya and is proclaimed protector of Islam. Italy withdraws from the League of Nations.

America — The Arts

1 Steinbeck publishes *Of Mice and Men.*
2 Artie Shaw, clarinetist, forms an early swing band which, the next year, features singer Billie Holiday as vocalist.
3 Bil Baird and his wife Cora lead a revival of puppet theater in the U.S.
4 Benét publishes his best known short story "The Devil and Daniel Webster."
5 Marquand publishes *The Late George Apley.*
6 Count Basie composes the swing tune "One O'Clock Jump."
7 The Marx Brothers star in *A Day at the Races.*
8 Laurel and Hardy star in the film *Way Out West.*
9 The Gershwin Brothers score the film *Shall We Dance?,* which includes the song "Let's Call the Whole Thing Off."
10 Rodgers and Lorenz Hart compose the score for the show *Babes in Arms,* which includes the songs "The Lady is a Tramp" and "Johnny One Note."
11 Odets publishes the play *Golden Boy.*
12 Walt Disney produces the first feature-length cartoon, *Snow White and the Seven Dwarfs,* with music by Frank Churchill.

Elsewhere — The Arts

13 Picasso's mural, "Guernica," is painted to protest the destruction of that city during the Spanish Civil War.
14 The first two acts of Berg's opera, *Lulu,* are performed. This atonal opera uses Schönberg's 12-tone system. [1979:ARTS/16]
15 J.R.R. Tolkien, Eng. writer, publishes the fantasy novel, *The Hobbit.*
16 Eng. composer Benjamin Britten wins an international reputation with *Variations on a Theme of Frank Bridge,* for string orchestra.
17 J. Renoir directs *Grand Illusion* and *The Lower Depths,* two popular films.
18 Giraudoux bases his play, *Électra,* on classical Greek mythology.
19 Pol. violinist Bronislaw Hubermann establishes the Israel Philharmonic Orchestra, Tel Aviv.
20 Shostakovich returns to official favor with his *Fifth Symphony.*
21 C.S. Forester publishes *The Happy Return,* the first in a series of novels featuring Captain Horatio Hornblower.
22 Braque paints "Woman with a Mandolin" and "The Yellow Tablecloth."
23 Malraux publishes *L'Espoir (Man's Hope).*

1938

America — History and Politics

1 Pres. Roosevelt proposes appropriations for military expansion to keep the country defensively strong.
2 House of Representatives shelves the Ludlow Resolution, which calls for a na-

Elsewhere — History and Politics

13 Disorders break out in Austria, forcing Chancellor Schuschnigg to resign. German army invades Austria. Arthur Seyss-Inquart becomes Chancellor and proclaims the *Anschluss* (union)

America — The Arts

1 Thornton Wilder publishes the Pulitzer Prize-winning play *Our Town.*
2 Hemingway publishes *The Fifth Column and the First*

Elsewhere — The Arts

12 Daphne du Maurier, Eng. novelist, publishes *Rebecca.*
13 Jean-Paul Sartre, leading Fr. Existentialist, publishes *Nausea,* his first novel.

Science & Technology		Miscellaneous		
America	Elsewhere	America	Elsewhere	

Science & Technology — America

1 Grote Reber, astronomer, builds world's first radio telescope to receive cosmic radio waves.

2 Anderson discovers the muon (mu meson), a subatomic particle that is heavier than an electron but lighter than a proton.

3 Best and Taylor publish *The Physiological Basis of Medical Practice.*

4 George Beadle and Edward Tatum develop the *one gene-one enzyme theory* which states that all chemical reactions in the cell are controlled by enzymes and that each enzyme is controlled by a single gene.

5 Theodosius Dobzhansky publishes *Genetics and the Origin of the Species,* a book that establishes evolutionary genetics as a science.

6 Max Theiler, physician, develops a vaccine for yellow fever.

7 Land establishes the Polaroid Corporation.

8 Polykarp Kusch and Isidor I. Rabi develop the magnetic resonance method of studying atomic nuclei.

9 Dow Chemical begins manufacturing polystyrene plastic products.

10 National Cancer Institute is established.

11 Franz Weidenreich, anthropologist, discovers the skull of the Peking Man.

12 Nobel Prize, Physics: Clinton Davisson (Amer.) and George Thomson (Eng.) for discovering diffraction of electrons by crystals.

Science & Technology — Elsewhere

13 Segré produces technetium, the first manmade element not found in nature.

14 Krebs discovers the tricarboxylic acid (or Krebs) cycle, a process whereby higher mammals produce energy from digested food.

15 Lev D. Landau, Soviet physicist, shows that liquid helium exhibits the least resistance against surfaces of any of the elements.

16 Walter R. Dornberger, Ger. engineer, directs the building of the Ger. V-2 rocket, widely used in World War II.

17 Erwin W. Müller, Ger. physicist, invents the field-emission microscope.

18 The Nobel Institute of Physics is founded in Stockholm, Sweden.

19 Nobel Prize, Chemistry: Haworth, for his research on carbohydrates and vitamin C, and Karrer, for the chemical analysis of vitamins A and B_2.

20 Nobel Prize, Physiology or Medicine: Szent-Györgyi, for his research into the role of vitamin C and other nutrients in the cell.

Miscellaneous — America

1 During winter of 1936–37, more than 500,000 workers quit their jobs; many engage in new, illegal sit-down strikes.

2 Explosion destroys a school building in New London, Tex.; 294 persons are killed.

3 Harlem River Houses built, one of the first public housing projects in New York City. They were 4- and 5-story walk-ups strung together.

4 Golden Gate Bridge is completed; main section is 4200 ft. long. It is longest span bridge up to this time.

5 Minimum wage law for women is upheld by the U.S. Supreme Court.

6 Dirigible *Hindenburg* explodes near mooring at Lakehurst, N.J., killing most passengers and crew.

7 World's largest flower blooms in New York City Botanical Gardens. It is the giant calla lily, 8½ ft. high, 4 ft. in diameter, and 12 ft. in circumference.

8 Joe Louis wins the heavyweight boxing championship when he knocks out James J. Braddock. Louis is the 2nd Negro to hold the title. [1908:MISC/6]

9 Amelia Earhart disappears while on a flight across the Pacific Ocean.

Miscellaneous — Elsewhere

10 U.S. has 2 million domestic refrigerators; Great Britain 3000.

11 Skeletal remains of an infant found on the island of Java; belongs to group known as Pithecanthropus, or Java man.

12 Alekhine regains world chess title from Euwe.

Science & Technology — America

1 Chester Carlson produces the first xerographic copy using a modified form of inkless electrostatic printing. [1958:SCI/1]

2 Hans A. Bethe, physi-

Science & Technology — Elsewhere

13 Swiss chemists Arthur Stoll and Albert Hofman make the drug LSD.

14 Sir Neville Mott, Eng. physicist, explains the theory behind the effect of light on photo-

Miscellaneous — America

1 Floods and landslides cause 144 deaths in Southern California. Thousands of homes are destroyed; nearly $60 million in property lost.

2 Committee for Indus-

Miscellaneous — Elsewhere

8 Great Britain has 1.7 million private automobiles; Germany 1.3 million; Italy 1.1 million; and France 800,000.

9 Lajos Biro of Hungary invents the ballpoint pen.

History and Politics		The Arts	
America	**Elsewhere**	**America**	**Elsewhere**

tional referendum to decide a declaration of war.

3 Agricultural Adjustment Administration extends government financing of farmers and sets up crop insurance corporations.

4 Congress establishes the House Committee on Un-American Activities to investigate Communist, Fascist, Nazi, and other "un-American" organizations.

5 Revenue Act reduces taxes on large corporations, while raising those on small companies.

6 Temporary National Economic Committee investigates monopolies, price-fixing, and restraint of trade.

7 Civil Aeronautics Authority becomes independent agency to oversee non-military transport in the U.S.

8 Federal Food and Drug Administration tightens regulations on food, drug, and cosmetics. **[1906:HIST/2]**

9 Fair Labor Standards Act raises scale of minimum wages and lowers scale of maximum hours. It also forbids child labor in industries engaged in interstate trade.

10 U.S. protests Japanese violations of the Open Door Policy in China.

11 Most Americans accept Munich Pact as a means to maintain peace in Europe. **[1938:HIST/15]**

12 For the first time since 1928, Republicans gain seats in Congress during elections.

---

of Austria and Germany. Opponents of the Nazis are put in concentration camps and Schuschnigg is imprisoned until 1945.

14 Hitler demands self-determination for the Sudetenland. Riots break out in Czechoslovakia.

15 France and Britain, led by Chamberlain, give in to Hitler's demands; the Munich Pact is signed, permitting occupation by Germany of the Sudetenland.

16 Poland and Hungary seize, respectively, the Teschen district and parts of Slovakia.

17 Rumania suspends its constitution and suppresses all political parties in order to check the fascist groups. Many Iron Guardists (terrorists) are imprisoned following the discovery of a plot against the king.

18 Spanish Nationalists make bombing raids against Barcelona. Nationalists capture Lerida, cutting Spain in half. **[1937:HIST/12]**

19 Japanese capture Tsingtao, Canton, and Hankow. Chinese government and army retreat up the Yangtze River to Chungking, the new Chinese capital.

20 United Party wins South African elections, and Hertzog remains Premier.

21 Italy enacts anti-Semitic legislation.

22 New constitution establishes the sovereign nation of Ireland (Eire) within the British Commonwealth of Nations.

23 Ismet Inönü succeeds Atatürk as President of Turkey.

Forty-nine Short Stories, which include "The Snows of Kilimanjaro" and "The Short Happy Life of Francis Macomber."

3 Nobel Prize, Literature: Pearl Buck.

4 Lyonel Feininger, Cubist painter, completes his most famous work, "Dawn."

5 Aaron Copland, composer, writes *Billy the Kid,* a ballet based on U.S. folklore.

6 Walter Piston composes the ballet *The Incredible Flutist.*

7 Richard Whiting, composer, and Johnny Mercer, lyricist, score two movies: *Hollywood Hotel,* with the song "Hooray for Hollywood," and *Jezebel,* with "You Must Have Been a Beautiful Baby."

8 Ella Fitzgerald, singer, and the band led by Chick Webb, drummer, achieve fame with the song "A-Tisket A-Tasket."

9 Glenn Miller forms a jazz band which soon is world famous.

10 Ralph Rainger, composer, and Leo Robin, lyricist, write "Thanks for the Memory," adopted by actor and comedian Bob Hope as his theme.

11 Eugene Ormandy, as conductor and musical director of the Philadelphia Orchestra, raises the orchestra to international status.

---

14 Pierre Teilhard de Chardin, Fr. philosopher, completes *The Phenomenon of Man,* a religious work on evolution.

15 Shaw wins an Oscar for his screenplay of *Pygmalion.*

16 Howard Spring, Welsh novelist, publishes the best-selling *O Absalom!*

17 Eisenstein and Prokofiev collaborate on the film, *Alexander Nevsky.*

18 Grosz paints "A Piece of My World II," a work critical of Nazism.

19 Greene publishes *Brighton Rock,* a thriller.

20 Miró paints "Nursery Decoration."

21 Elizabeth Bowen, Ir. writer, publishes *The Death of the Heart,* a popular novel.

1939

1 Supreme Court rules that sit-down strikes are illegal.

2 Pres. Roosevelt asks Congress for $535 million defense appropriation over two years. **[1938:HIST/1]**

3 Roosevelt administration consolidates many existing

---

12 Nazi troops occupy Bohemia and Moravia; Czechoslovakia disappears as a state. Slovakia and Carpatho-Ukraine declare their independence.

13 Italian forces invade and conquer Albania. Italy signs

---

1 Victor Fleming directs the film *Gone With the Wind,* starring Vivien Leigh, Clark Gable, Leslie Howard, Olivia de Havilland, and Hattie McDaniel (who be-

---

14 The English translation of Hitler's *Mein Kampf* is published. Begun during a 1923 imprisonment, it expresses his hatred of the Jews and his plan for world domination.

Science & Technology

Miscellaneous

America

Elsewhere

America

Elsewhere

Science & Technology — America

cist, theorizes that stars get their energy by nuclear fusion.

3 After more than 70 people die from a popular antibiotic, Congress enacts the Federal Food, Drug and Cosmetic Act, which bans potentially dangerous drugs.

4 DuPont markets the first nylon product—a toothbrush.

5 Tom D. Spies, physician, proves that pellagra is a deficiency disease; he treats it with niacin.

6 Albert Einstein and Leopold Infeld publish *The Evolution of Physics.*

7 Robert E. Gross, physician, surgically repairs a congenital heart defect.

8 Congress enacts the Venereal Disease Control Act which provides federal funds for the prevention, treatment, and control of VD.

9 In *Physiological Genetics,* Richard Goldschmidt describes his theories of intersexuality.

10 N.Y. requires premarital blood tests.

11 The radio altimeter is developed. It uses reflected radio waves to measure an airplane's altitude.

12 Calvin Bridges, geneticist, maps 1024 genes on the X-chromosome of *Drosophila,* the common fruit fly.

Science & Technology — Elsewhere

graphic film.

15 A living coelacanth, a fish thought to have been extinct for 60 million years, is caught off the African coast.

16 Fritz Zernike, Dutch physicist, invents the phase-contrast microscope, which enables scientists to study living cells and cell structures.

17 Nobel Prize, Physics: Fermi, for his creation of radioactive elements by neutron bombardment.

Miscellaneous — America

trial Organization, expelled from A.F.L., creates independent group called Congress of Industrial Organizations (C.I.O.); leading unions are steel, auto, and mine workers. John L. Lewis elected its president. [1935:MISC/2]

3 "Invasion from Mars," a radio play produced by actor Orson Welles, causes panic when listeners think account of an attack from Mars is an actual news broadcast.

4 Pres. Roosevelt signs Wage and Hours Act; raises minimum wage for workers engaged in interstate commerce from 25¢ to 40¢ an hour. Hours limited to 44 a week the 1st year, to 40 after the 3rd.

5 Tropical hurricane strikes without warning in New England, taking an estimated 460 lives; property damage, $150 million.

6 National Safety Council records more than 32,000 deaths in automobile accidents for the year. About ⅓ involved pedestrians; almost 9000 deaths result from collisions between vehicles.

7 Tennis player Don Budge accomplishes the Grand Slam, winning all 4 major singles tennis championships in Australia, France, Great Britain, and the U.S.

Miscellaneous — Elsewhere

10 Gas masks issued to British civilians during the Munich crisis with Germany.

11 S.S. *Queen Elizabeth* is launched in England. A 1000-ft. liner, it carries 2288 passengers.

Science & Technology — America

1 Doisy discovers and isolates vitamin K.

2 Sikorski develops a practical helicopter.

3 The Rossby number is devised to help explain the Coriolis effect. [1835:SCI/3]

Science & Technology — Elsewhere

14 Ernst Boris Chain, Ger. pathologist, and Howard Walter Florey, Austral. pathologist, isolate pure penicillin.

15 Paul Müller, Swiss chemist, discovers the insect-killing properties of

Miscellaneous — America

1 Three branches of the Methodist Church, with about 7.5 million members, reunite after splits of main body in 1830 and 1844.

2 U.S. submarine *Squalus* sinks off Hampton

Miscellaneous — Elsewhere

9 Balloons with suspended cables are used as barriers against aircraft attacks in Britain. Radar stations are used to give early warning of approaching enemy aircraft.

10 Earthquake in Ana-

1939

History and Politics

America

government agencies, many of them formed by the New Deal.

4 Congress passes amendments to Social Security Act that broaden it to provide benefits to the dependents and survivors of workers. [1935:HIST/5]

5 WPA workers are reduced. [1935:HIST/1]

6 Pres. Roosevelt urges arbitration with Germany, Poland, and Italy to avoid war. In radio "fireside chat," he declares U.S. neutrality.

7 Hatch Act prohibits political-campaign activities by most federal employees.

8 Amendments to U.S.-Panama treaty end U.S. guarantee of the neutrality and sovereignty of Panama.

9 After 30 Americans drown when a Ger. submarine sinks the Brit. passenger ship *Athenia*, Secretary of State Cordell Hull asks Americans to travel to Europe only when absolutely necessary.

10 Congress repeals prohibition of arms exports and authorizes sale of arms to nations at war on a "cash and carry" basis. [1937:HIST/4]

11 Pres. Roosevelt orders all U.S. ports and waters closed to submarines of nations at war.

Elsewhere

military alliance with Germany.

14 Hitler demands that Gdańsk (Danzig) be united with Germany, but Poland refuses to give up the city. Germany annexes the Memel Territory and without warning invades Poland, bringing about the start of World War II between the Allies and the Axis powers. German *Blitzkrieg* (lightning war), using surprise air and tank attacks, crushes Polish defenses. Britain and France (the Allies) declare war on Germany and set up a blockade.

15 U.S.S.R. invades Poland, which is partitioned between Germany and the U.S.S.R. Soviet forces seize Lithuania, Latvia, and Estonia, and invade Finland.

16 Japan continues its undeclared war in China. Manchukuan (Japanese) forces fight Soviets on the Mongolian border. Japan demands that Britain give up her support of the Chinese Nationalists and help Japan establish a "new order" in the Far East. Japanese blockade the British and French at the port of Tientsin.

17 France transfers the sanjak (district) of Alexandretta to Turkey.

18 Sir Robert Gordon Menzies, leader of the United Australian Party, becomes Prime Minister of Australia.

19 Chamberlain appoints Sir Winston Churchill First Lord of the Admiralty.

20 Ger. battleship *Graf Spee* sinks Brit. cargo ships in the South Atlantic before it is put out of action by three Brit. cruisers off the coast of Uruguay.

The Arts

America

comes the first black to win a major Academy Award). [1936:ARTS/1]

2 Irving Berlin releases the popular patriotic song "God Bless America," sung by Kate Smith.

3 Steinbeck publishes *The Grapes of Wrath.*

4 The score of the movie *The Wizard of Oz*, by Yip Harburg and Harold Arlen, features the song "Over the Rainbow," sung by Judy Garland.

5 Russel Crouse and Howard Lindsay dramatize *Life With Father*. [1935:ARTS/7]

6 Trumpeter Harry James hires singer Frank Sinatra as lead vocalist for his newly formed band.

7 Marjorie Kinnan Rawlings, novelist, publishes *The Yearling.*

8 Saroyan publishes *The Time of Your Life,* for which he refuses the Pulitzer Prize.

9 Sandburg's 4 volume *Abraham Lincoln: The War Years* wins 1940 Pulitzer Prize.

10 Kaufman and Moss Hart collaborate on *The Man Who Came to Dinner.*

11 Katherine Anne Porter publishes the short story collection, *Pale Horse, Pale Rider.*

12 Coleman Hawkins, saxophonist, records the jazz masterpiece "Body and Soul."

13 Nathanael West publishes *The Day of the Locust.*

Elsewhere

15 Isherwood publishes *Good-bye to Berlin,* a novel.

16 Eng. pianist Myra Hess organizes daily concerts at London's National Gallery (–1946).

17 Joyce publishes *Finnegans Wake,* a unique novel.

18 Brecht writes *Mother Courage and Her Children,* a drama.

19 Popular war songs in England: "Roll Out the Barrel," "Hang Out the Washing on the Siegfried Line," "The Last Time I Saw Paris"; in Germany: "Wir fahren gegen England," "Bomben auf England," "Lili Marlene."

20 Richard Llewellyn, Welsh novelist, publishes *How Green Was My Valley,* a bestseller about a Welsh mining family.

21 Carol Reed, Brit. film maker, directs the mystery, *Night Train.*

22 Braque completes one of his best figure paintings, "Painter and Model."

23 Picasso paints "Night Fishing Antibes."

24 Giraudoux writes *Ondine,* a play adapted from a fantasy by La-Motte-Fouqué. [1811:ARTS/4]

25 Henry Moore, England's leading avant-garde sculptor, exhibits "Reclining Figure."

1940

America — History and Politics

1 U.S. does not renew its commercial treaty with Japan.

2 U.S. sends surplus war supplies in reply to Brit. Prime Minister Churchill's appeal for aid.

Elsewhere — History and Politics

13 German armies invade Denmark, Norway, Holland, Belgium, and Luxembourg. Dutch and Belgian armies surrender. British expeditionary forces of 250,000 evacuates the beaches of Dunkirk.

America — The Arts

1 Popular radio shows of the period include *The Shadow, Gangbusters, Fibber McGee and Molly,* and *The Jack Benny Show.*

2 Alfred Hitchcock's

Elsewhere — The Arts

16 Greene publishes *The Power and the Glory,* a novel about the conflicts faced by an alcoholic priest.

17 Thomas publishes *Portrait of the Artist as*

Science & Technology

America

4 Leo Szilard, physicist, proves that a chain reaction occurs during nuclear fission.
5 Pauling publishes *The Nature of the Chemical Bond, and Structure of Molecules and Crystals.*
6 F. Bloch and Luis Alvarez measure the magnetic moment of a neutron.
7 Max Delbrück, biologist, develops a simple process for growing bacteriophages, viruses that attack bacteria.
8 Philip Levine and Rufus Stetson discover the Rh factor in human blood. **[1940:SCI/1]**
9 Color television is demonstrated.
10 U.S. Weather Bureau adopts "bar" and "millibar" as units of atmospheric pressure.
11 Bethe calculates the amount of energy produced by the Sun.
12 At the urging of Wigner, Szilard, and Teller, Einstein urges Pres. Roosevelt to develop an atomic bomb.
13 Nobel Prize, Physics: Ernest Lawrence for inventing the cyclotron. **[1931:SCI/2]**

Elsewhere

DDT.
16 Henrik Dam, Dan. biochemist, discovers vitamin K and establishes its role in blood clotting.
17 Sir Bernard Lovell, Eng. astronomer, publishes *Science and Civilization,* his first of many works.
18 Marguerite Perey, Fr. chemist, discovers the element francium.
19 Hannes Alfvén, Swed. astrophysicist, presents a theory relating magnetic storms and the aurorae (northern lights).
20 Frisch coins the term *fission.*
21 Nobel Prize, Chemistry: Butenandt, for his work on the sex hormones.
22 Nobel Prize, Physiology or Medicine: Domagk, for his discovery of the antibacterial effects of prontosil, the first sulfa drug.

Miscellaneous

America

Beach, N.H., with 59 men aboard; 33 saved.
3 Pan American World Airways begins regular transatlantic passenger flights with *Dixie Clipper,* a "flying boat" carrying 22 passengers from New York to Lisbon, Portugal; flight takes about 24 hrs.
4 King George VI and Queen Elizabeth of Great Britain arrive in Washington, D.C. They are first British sovereigns to visit U.S.
5 Nylon stockings are sold for the first time.
6 World Fairs in New York City and San Francisco attract millions of visitors. They see wonders of the future, and line up to take "death-defying" rides on the roller coaster and the parachute jump.
7 Lincoln Ellsworth surveys a large part of eastern Antarctica.
8 Baseball game is first televised.

Elsewhere

tolia, Turkey, claims 45,000 victims.
11 Eng. racing driver John Cobb drives at 368.85 mph, at Bonneville Salt Flats, Utah.
12 Floods in northern China leave 10 million homeless, starving, or drowned.
13 Streamlined diesel train travels at 133.6 mph between Hamburg and Berlin.
14 Earthquake in Chile strikes an area of 50 sq. mi.; 30,000 persons killed.
15 Trans-Iranian Railroad opens, from Caspian Sea to the Persian Gulf.
16 More than 125 persons die when two trains collide near Magdeburg, Germany.
17 Of 1,484,811 criminal offenses in the U.S., 24,402 are crimes against persons; in England and Wales there are 303,771 crimes, 2,899 against persons.
18 Malcolm Campbell sets water speed record of 141.7 mph.
19 Severe earthquake in northern Turkey destroys the city of Erzingnan; about 100,000 casualties.
20 British submarine *Thetis* sinks in Liverpool Bay, England; 99 persons die.

Night scene at 1939 New York World's Fair

---

1 K. Landsteiner and Alexander Wiener discover the Rh factor in human blood. **[1939:SCI/8]**
2 Peter Goldmark, engineer, develops a commercially practical system for

12 Many of Europe's greatest scientists flee to the United States.
13 Jeans publishes *Introduction to the Kinetic Theory of Gases.*
14 Hellmuth Walter,

1 Population is 131.6 million. More than 56% of people live in places of 2500 or more population. Life expectancy is 63 years.
2 Alien Registration

8 The George Cross is instituted by King George VI; given for acts of great heroism or courage shown in extreme danger.
9 There are 264,000 divorces in the U.S.; 8396 in

1940

3 Pres. Roosevelt asks Congress for defense appropriation·of $4.26 billion and for production of 50,000 airplanes a year.
4 Pittman Resolution allows the sale of arms to Latin American nations.
5 Smith Act (Alien Registration Act) requires the registration of all aliens and makes it illegal to advocate the overthrow of the U.S. government by force.
6 U.S. gives 50 outdated destroyers to Britain in exchange for 99-year leases on naval and air bases in Newfoundland and the West Indies.
7 Congress creates the Selective Service System, the first U.S. peacetime program of compulsory military service. It requires all men between ages 21 and 36 to register. [1941:HIST/8]
8 Pres. Roosevelt orders an embargo on shipments of scrap iron and steel to all nations except Britain and those in the Western Hemisphere.
9 John L. Lewis asks all members of the Congress of Industrial Organizations to support Wendell Willkie, Republican candidate for President. Lewis says he will resign CIO presidency if Roosevelt is reelected.
10 Roosevelt is reelected President. Henry A. Wallace is elected Vice President. Democrats also retain control of Congress. Lewis resigns as President of the CIO.
11 U.S. Office of Production Management for Defense is set up to coordinate work in defense plants. It is authorized to send aid to countries fighting the Axis Powers.
12 National Defense Advisory Commission coordinates U.S. civilian defense protection.

Germans invade France and enter Paris. Occupied France (Vichy) under Henri Pétain signs an armistice with Germany. Vichy government breaks off relations with British government. British sink or capture French fleet at the Battle of Oran to prevent it from falling into German hands.
14 Italy declares war on Britain and France. Italy and France conclude an armistice.
15 Germans bomb London. German and British planes fight air battles over Britain. British begin night bombing of Germany.
16 Germany blockades Britain, and German submarines attack Allied shipping in the North Atlantic.
17 Churchill becomes Brit. Prime Minister after Chamberlain resigns; he gives his famous "blood, toil, tears, and sweat" speech to rally the British.
18 Italian forces attack the British in North Africa.
19 Hungary, Rumania, and Bulgaria join the Axis Powers (Germany, Italy, and Japan).
20 Japanese forces occupy French Indochina.
21 U.S.S.R. annexes Estonia, Latvia, and Lithuania. Finland surrenders to the Soviets.
22 Free French forces under Charles de Gaulle capture Duala in West Africa.
23 British push back Italians in Egypt and invade Libya.
24 Trotsky is assassinated in Mexico City by alleged Stalinist agent.
25 Hitler appoints Goering *Reichs-Marschall* (marshal of the empire).
26 British forces reopen the Burma Road, used to carry war supplies into Burma.

first U.S. film, *Rebecca*, wins the Oscar for Best Picture.
3 Carson McCullers, novelist, publishes *The Heart is a Lonely Hunter*.
4 Mae West and W.C. Fields star in the classic comedy *My Little Chickadee*.
5 Hemingway publishes his most popular work, *For Whom the Bell Tolls*.
6 The Museum of Modern Art sets up a separate department of photography.
7 Kaufman and Moss Hart write *George Washington Slept Here*.
8 Bob Hope, Bing Crosby, and Dorothy Lamour star in the film *Road to Singapore*, the first of 7 "road movies."
9 Important abstract expressionist painters of the time include Lore MacIver, Morris Graves, and Hans Hofmann.
10 John Ford wins an Oscar for directing *The Grapes of Wrath*.
11 Thurber publishes *Fables for Our Time*.
12 Raymond Chandler, author, publishes *Farewell, My Lovely*.
13 Disney's *Fantasia*, an animated expression of classical music, features Stokowski conducting the Philadelphia Orchestra.
14 Richard Wright, black author, publishes *Native Son*.
15 Now in the U.S., Auden publishes his best work, *Another Time*.

a Young Dog, a collection of his short stories.
18 O'Casey criticizes Fascism in his play, *The Star Turns Red*.
19 C.P. Snow, Brit. novelist, publishes *Strangers and Brothers*, the first novel in a series of 11 (-1970).
20 Picasso's lithograph, "Dove," is selected as the symbol of the World Peace Congress.
21 Klee's painting, "Death and Fire," predicts his own cremation later this year.
22 Munch paints "Between Clock and Bed, Self-Portrait."
23 Ernst paints "Europe After the Rain" (-1942), a work known for its "calm violence."
24 Arthur Koestler, Brit. novelist, describes Stalin's "purge trials" in *Darkness at Noon*. [1936:HIST/16]
25 David Low, Eng. cartoonist, completes a series of anti-Hitler cartoons.
26 Prehistoric drawings that are at least 20,000 years old are found in the Lascaux Caves in France.

1941			

1 Pres. Roosevelt delivers his "Four Freedoms" speech, outlining what is needed for

15 Germany increases its air attacks on Britain. Blockade by German submarines men-

1 The Mount Rushmore National Monument in South Dakota

13 Coward completes one of his best comedies, *Blithe Spirit*.

Science & Technology		Miscellaneous		
America	**Elsewhere**	**America**	**Elsewhere**	
broadcasting color TV. **3** V. Zworykin and James Hillier invent the electron microscope. **4** Lawrence builds a giant cyclotron and produces mesons from atomic nuclei. **5** Selman A. Waksman, bacteriologist, prepares the antibiotic actinomycin from soil bacteria. **6** Pauling and Delbrück determine that antigens cause the body to produce antibodies. **7** Fritz A. Lipmann, biochemist, proposes that ATP (adenosine triphosphate) is a common form of energy in many cells. **8** Evans uses radioactive iodine to prove that iodine is used by the thyroid gland. **9** Congress establishes the Fish and Wildlife Service to develop and administer a wildlife conservation program. **10** Edwin McMillan, chemist, discovers element number 93, neptunium, the first of the transuranic elements. **11** George Washington Carver Foundation for Agricultural Research is established at Tuskegee Institute (Ala.) in honor of the former slave who is best known for discovering 300 uses for the peanut.	Ger. engineer, invents a propulsion system for submarines. **15** N.M. Gregg, Austral. ophthalmologist, discovers that German measles during pregnancy may cause birth defects in the unborn child.  Sir Winston Churchill, British statesman and author, photographed with homburg and cane	(Smith) Act requires registration and fingerprinting of aliens. Registration shows approximately 5 million aliens. **3** First large-scale urban college building of modern design, Hunter College, is built in New York City. **4** Oglethorpe University (Ga.) deposits a bottle of beer, an encyclopedia, and a movie fan magazine along with thousands of other objects in its "Crypt of Civilization," a time capsule not to be opened until the year 8113. **5** Suspension bridge over the Narrows at Tacoma, Wash., called "Galloping Gertie," collapses because of wind vibration. Bridge tumbles into Puget Sound. **6** Cornelius Warmerdam is first to pole-vault 15 ft. Two years later he sets new record, 15 ft. 7-3/4 in. **7** 40-hr. work week, part of Fair Labor Standards Act of 1938, goes into effect.	Great Britain.	
1 E. McMillan and Glenn T. Seaborg lead a team of scientists that	**14** Sir Harold Spencer, Eng. astronomer, determines that the Sun is	**1** Congresswoman Jeannette Rankin, a pacifist, casts the only vote in	**9** China's population is 450 million; India's 389 million; U.S.S.R.'s 182	**1941**

History and Politics

America

postwar peace.

2 Lend-Lease Act lends war matériel to friendly nations.

3 U.S. agrees to defend Greenland for Denmark in exchange for the right to build and maintain military bases there.

4 Office of Price Administration and Civilian Supply is set up. It immediately freezes steel prices and later announces tire rationing to conserve rubber.

5 Pres. Roosevelt orders the freezing of all German, Italian, and (later) Japanese assets in the U.S.

6 U.S. forces land in Iceland to defend it against possible attack.

7 Pres. Roosevelt and Brit. Prime Minister Churchill, at secret meeting off Newfoundland, enunciate the Atlantic Charter, pledging to destroy Nazi tyranny.

8 Selective Service System repeals the 900,000-man limitation of the Army and extends the length of service of draftees to 18 months.

9 U.S. lends the U.S.S.R. $1 billion worth of war matériel.

10 Ger. submarines sink U.S. destroyers *Kearny* and *Reuben James*. More than 100 Americans are lost.

11 Joseph C. Grew, Ambassador to Japan, informs Pres. Roosevelt that Japan might attack the U.S.

12 Japanese naval and air forces make surprise attack on U.S. naval base at Pearl Harbor, Hawaii (Dec. 7). Eighteen U.S. warships are sunk or damaged, about 170 planes are destroyed, and about 2000 Americans are killed.

13 U.S. declares war on Japan.

14 After Germany and Italy declare war on the U.S., Congress passes resolution recognizing a state of war between the U.S. and these nations.

Elsewhere

ace British supplies. Germany attacks Yugoslavia, Greece, and Crete and wins quick victories. German armies invade the U.S.S.R., occupy Riga, and seize Minsk, Tallinn, and Smolensk. Germans begin the siege of Leningrad, Moscow, and Sevastopol and seize Kiev, Orel, Odessa, and Karkov. Soviets move their government to Kuibyshev, but Premier Stalin remains in Moscow. Marshal Semyon Timoshenko begins Soviet counteroffensive and helps relieve Moscow.

16 Gen. Erwin Rommel (the "Desert Fox") leads his special German tank corps (the Afrika Corps) into Libya and captures Tobruk. British begin counteroffensive against the Germans in North Africa.

17 British navy sinks Italian warships at the Battle of Cape Matapan. German battleship *Bismarck* sinks British dreadnought *Hood* off the coast of Iceland. British air and naval forces destroy the *Bismarck* after 1½ hour-bombardment. German submarines make "wolf pack" attacks on Allied ships.

18 Finland permits Germany to move troops through to attack the U.S.S.R. **[1940:HIST/21]**

19 Japan declares war on the U.S., Britain, Australia, Canada, New Zealand, and South Africa. Japanese bomb British at Hong Kong and occupy Bangkok.

20 Many Latin American nations declare war on the Axis Powers.

21 U.S.S.R. and Japan conclude a neutrality agreement.

22 Japanese sink British battleship *Prince of Wales* and cruiser *Repulse*.

23 Fifty French hostages are executed for the murder of a German officer at Nantes, France.

The Arts

America

is completed. Begun in 1927, sculptor Gutzon Borglum designed the 60 ft. tall faces of former presidents Washington, Jefferson, T. Roosevelt, and Lincoln.

2 Orson Welles directs and stars in *Citizen Kane,* a film which introduces many new techniques.

3 Rodgers' and Lorenz Hart's score for the show *Pal Joey* includes the song "Bewitched, Bothered and Bewildered."

4 Howard Fast, novelist, publishes *The Last Frontier,* a historical novel about the mistreatment of the Indians.

5 Bruno Walter becomes the conductor of the Metropolitan Opera.

6 Gypsy Rose Lee publishes the mystery novel, *The G-String Murders.*

7 Robert Sherwood publishes *There Shall Be No Night,* a Pulitzer Prize-winning account of the Soviet invasion of Finland.

8 "Doomsday," a painting by impressionist Karl Knaths, shows Cubist influences.

9 Billy Strayhorn, arranger-composer for Duke Ellington, composes the band's theme song, "Take the 'A' Train."

10 Eudora Welty, writer, publishes *A Curtain of Glass,* a collection of short stories.

11 Cain publishes *Mildred Pierce.* **[1945:ARTS/5]**

12 Greta Garbo, at the height of her career, retires to a reclusive life in New York.

Elsewhere

14 Werfel describes the miracle of Bernadette of Lourdes in *The Song of Bernadette,* thus fulfilling a promise he had made to God for safe passage to America.

15 Graham Vivian Sutherland, Eng. painter, completes "Somerset Maugham," the first in a series of Expressionist portraits. He is appointed official war artist (–1944).

16 Turkish-born Canadian photographer Yousuf Karsh produces a world-famous portrait of Churchill.

17 Hauptmann publishes the powerful, four-part drama, *Die Atridentetralogie* (–1948).

18 Henry Moore produces drawings of refugees in London's air-raid shelters.

19 Shostakovich dedicates his Seventh Symphony to the besieged city of Leningrad. **[1941:HIST/15]**

Science & Technology

America

discovers an isotope of plutonium. In the next 10 years, Seaborg identifies elements 94 through 102.

2 Manhattan Project, under the direction of Leslie Groves, begins top-secret research to develop an atomic bomb.

3 Eleanor J. Macdonald, epidemiologist, establishes the world's first cancer registry in Connecticut.

4 LORAN (*long range aid to navigation*) uses fixed radio signals to determine position at sea.

5 Since 1946, Zwicky has discovered 18 supernovae.

6 National Nutrition Program begins; vitamins and minerals are added to milk, bread, and other common foods.

7 An electron microscope is used to obtain the first photograph of a virus. The virus, only 4 ten-millionths of an inch in diameter, is magnified 65,000 times.

8 FCC authorizes TV broadcasting. By the end of the year, 1 million sets are sold.

9 Bush heads the newly-formed Office of Scientific Research and Development.

10 Aerosol spray cans are introduced.

11 Joseph H. Keenan, engineer, publishes *Thermodynamics*.

12 Radioactive iodine is used to treat cancer of the thyroid.

13 RCA develops the "alert receiver," a radio that is turned on or off by a special radio wave signal.

Elsewhere

about 93 million miles from the Earth.

15 Jaroslav Heyrovsky, Czech chemist, publishes *Polaragraphie,* in which polarography is introduced as a method of chemical analysis.

16 Whittle designs the first turbojet engine.

17 Victor Hasselblad, Swed. inventor, develops the Hasselblad camera. It is the first $2\frac{1}{4}'' \times 2\frac{1}{4}''$ single-lens reflex camera with interchangeable lenses.

Miscellaneous

America

Congress against declaring war on Japan after Pearl Harbor attack.

2 Water from $200 million Colorado Aqueduct begins flowing to Los Angeles and other southern California cities. Aqueduct carries water more than 250 mi., generating power to lift the water 1617 ft.

3 Gasoline curfew begins in 17 eastern states. Gasoline stations are closed from 7 a.m. to 7.

4 Lou Gehrig, baseball's "Iron Man," dies in New York City. As first baseman for the New York Yankees, he played in 2130 consecutive games.

5 A 6-ton granite monument over the site of time capsule is unveiled in Flushing Meadow, Queens, N.Y. A souvenir of the New York World's Fair, capsule contains artifacts and information about 20th-century culture to be recovered in the year 6939.

6 First woman to pay the death penalty in California dies in San Quentin's gas chamber. Mrs. Ethel Leta Spinelli, 52, alias "The Duchess," was convicted of killing one of her own gang.

7 New York Yankee centerfielder Joe DiMaggio hits safely in 56 consecutive games, a major-league record.

8 Famous wartime phrase "Praise the Lord and pass the ammunition" said by Howell M. Forgy, chaplain on the U.S. cruiser *New Orleans,* which is attacked at Pearl Harbor.

Elsewhere

million; Germany's 110 million; Japan's 105 million; Great Britain's 41 million; and France's 40 million.

10 Double Summer Time is introduced in Britain.

11 A Ferry Command aircraft crosses the Atlantic from the west in 8 hr. 23 min.

12 "Utility" clothing and furniture are encouraged in Britain; clothes rationing starts.

13 Brit. engineer Donald Bailey invents the portable military bridge.

14 Air Training Corps is established in Britain.

15 British A.R.P. (Air Raid Precaution) is reorganized as Civil Defence.

History and Politics

America

Elsewhere

The Arts

America

Elsewhere

1942

America (History and Politics)

1 U.S.-Filipino troops under Gen. MacArthur retreat to the Bataan peninsula in the Philippines. Japanese force them to withdraw after strong U.S. resistance at Corregidor. U.S. prisoners are forced to make "Bataan Death March" to prison camps.
2 Government wartime agencies take control of housing, alien property, shipping and transportation, foreign relief, censorship, and scientific research.
3 Japanese defeat U.S. fleet at the Battle of Java Sea.
4 Gen. MacArthur is made commander of Allied forces in Southwest Pacific.
5 U.S. carrier-based planes bomb Gilbert and Marshall Islands. U.S. bombers led by Major Gen. James H. Doolittle make surprise raid on Tokyo and other Japanese cities. U.S. warplanes defeat the Japanese at the Battle of the Coral Sea, halting southward Japanese advance. Japanese naval forces are crippled at the Battle of Midway.
6 U.S. Marines invade Japanese-held island of Guadalcanal and win major victory in 1943. Marine and Army forces attack Japanese on New Guinea, the Solomon Islands, and Butaritari in the central Pacific.
7 Congress enacts measures forming Women's auxiliary corps of the Army, Navy, Marines, Air Force, and Coast Guard.
8 U.S. B-17s make first bombing attacks in Europe.
9 U.S. troops under Lieut. Gen. Dwight D. Eisenhower invade North Africa with support from British naval and air units.
10 Congress lowers the draft age to 18.
11 U.S. begins strict rationing of food and materials needed for the war effort.

Elsewhere (History and Politics)

12 German forces seize Sevastopol and Maikop and reach Stalingrad. Soviets counterattack at Rzhev and Kharkov.
13 German troops move into unoccupied parts of France. Crews scuttle French fleet at Toulon to prevent German possession of it.
14 British 8th Army under Field Marshal Bernard L. Montgomery halts strong Axis drive at the Battle of El Alamein in Egypt and forces the Germans to retreat across North Africa to Tunisia. [1941:HIST/16]
15 Japanese forces capture Manila, Singapore, and Rangoon. The Burma Road between Lashio and Mandalay is closed by Japanese troops. [1940:HIST/26]
16 Chinese Nationalist armies win victories over the Japanese in Kiangsi Province, China.
17 Quisling becomes Premier of Norway; he helped the Germans conquer Norway in 1940.
18 British bomb German submarine base at Saint-Nazaire, France, and the German cities of Lübeck and Cologne.
19 Germans murder the male population of Lidice, Czechoslovakia, in retaliation for the murder of Ger. Gestapo Chief Reinhard Heydrich by Czech patriots.
20 German submarines sink more than 6¼ million tons of Allied shipping. British convoys suffer heavy losses in the Mediterranean.
21 Brit. Prime Minister Churchill discusses opening a second front with Sov. Premier Stalin.
22 Canada severs relations with the French Vichy government.
23 Gen. Franco keeps Spain a neutral nation.
24 Nazis begin systematic murder of Jews in gas chambers.

America (The Arts)

1 Irving Berlin's show *This is the Army* features the songs "This is the Army, Mr. Jones" and "I Left My Heart at the Stage Door Canteen." He also writes the popular holiday song "White Christmas" for the film *Holiday Inn.*
2 Rodgers and Lorenz Hart score the show *By Jupiter.*
3 Elliot Paul publishes *The Last Time I Saw Paris.*
4 James Cagney wins an Oscar for his portrayal of Cohan in the film *Yankee Doodle Dandy.*
5 Steinbeck publishes *The Moon is Down,* about Norway under Nazi rule.
6 Copland composes the ballet *Rodeo,* staged and choreographed by Agnes deMille.
7 William L. White, journalist, publishes *They Were Expendable,* about a patrol boat squadron in the Pacific.
8 Thurber publishes *My World and Welcome to It,* which includes the tale, "The Secret Life of Walter Mitty."
9 Marsden Hartley, Expressionist painter, paints "Mt. Katahdin, Autumn, No. 1."
10 Mary McCarthy, novelist, publishes *The Company She Keeps.*
11 Now a U.S. citizen, Schönberg, composes "Ode to Napoleon."
12 Lloyd Douglas, Lutheran clergyman, publishes *The Robe,* a novel based on the New Testament.
13 Wilder publishes *The Skin of Our Teeth.*

Elsewhere (The Arts)

14 Albert Camus, Fr. writer, publishes *The Stranger,* a novel, and *The Myth of Sisyphus,* an essay that concludes that the human situation is absurd—the basis of "theater of the absurd."
15 Aram Khachaturian, Sov. composer, completes *Gayane,* a ballet that features the popular "Sabre Dance."
16 Jean Genêt, radical Fr. writer, publishes *Our Lady of the Flowers,* a novel based on his underworld experiences.
17 Luchino Visconti, Ital. film maker, directs the Realistic masterpiece, *Obsession,* based on Cain's novel.
18 Coward collaborates with Eng. director David Lean on the war film, *In Which We Serve.*
19 Jan de Hartog, Dutch writer, publishes *Captain Jan: A Story of Ocean Tugboats,* his best known novel.
20 C.S. Lewis publishes *The Screwtape Letters,* an extremely popular Christian novel.
21 Antoine de Saint-Exupéry, Fr. writer and aviator, publishes *Flight to Arras,* an adventure novel based on a 1940 reconnaissance mission.
22 Quasimodo publishes *And Suddenly It's Evening,* a collection of poetry.
23 Cronin publishes *The Keys of the Kingdom,* one of his most important novels.
24 Prokofiev composes the epic opera, *War and Peace.*

Science & Technology		Miscellaneous		
America	**Elsewhere**	**America**	**Elsewhere**	**1942**

Science & Technology

America

1 Szilard and Fermi produce the first nuclear reaction and split the atom.
2 Bell Aircraft, under the direction of founder Lawrence Bell, builds and tests the first U.S. jet, the XP-59.
3 Henry Kaiser and Howard Hughes design the *Spruce Goose,* an 8-engine airplane with room for 700 people.
4 Seaborg, now directing the top-secret "Plutonium Project," develops a process for removing plutonium from uranium.
5 Martin's *Mars,* a huge flying boat, can travel at 200 mph and has a 7000 mile range.
6 Sonobuoys are used to detect submarines.
7 Radio "signals" (interference) are received from the Sun.
8 Reber makes radio maps of the sky.
9 Gamow and Teller develop a theory to explain the structure of red giant stars.
10 Magnetic recording tape is introduced.
11 Bruno Rossi, physicist, calculates that the half-life of a meson is 3 millionths of a second.
12 Russian Academy of Sciences awards honorary memberships to Americans for the first time: W. Cannon, E. O. Lawrence, and G. Lewis.
13 U.S. and Canada establish the Nutrition Foundation, recognizing nutrition as a formal science.

Elsewhere

14 Sister Elizabeth Kenny, Austral. nurse, publishes *Kenny Concept of Infantile Paralysis and Its Treatment.*
15 Fr. chemists prepare the first usable antihistamines.
16 Erich von Drygalski, Ger. geographer, publishes *Gletscherkunde,* an important work on glaciers.

Miscellaneous

America

1 F.B.I. captures German saboteurs brought by submarines to coasts of Florida and Long Island, N.Y. 6 are executed and 2 imprisoned.
2 Rationing of foods and materials needed for the war effort begins; sugar, coffee, fuel oil, gasoline, butter, meats, cheese, canned foods, and, finally, shoes are rationed.
3 Coconut Grove, a nightclub in Boston, is destroyed by fire; 487 people die; most suffocate when trapped by exit doors that open inward.
4 First V-mail sent overseas from New York City to London.
5 Gasoline rationing in 17 eastern states. Limit is 3 gallons a week for non-essential driving. A coupon system begins in July.
6 First all-star bowling tournament is held.
7 France's greatest ocean liner, *Normandie,* burns and capsizes at a New York City pier; cause is never discovered.
8 Army-Navy football game usually seen by 100,000 in Philadelphia is played at Annapolis, Md., before fewer than 12,000 fans. By presidential order, tickets are sold only to residents within a 10-mi. radius of the stadium.

Elsewhere

9 *Queen Mary* rams a British cruiser; 388 persons aboard the cruiser die.
10 Island of Malta awarded the George Cross for heroism under constant German air attack.
11 Great Britain produces 23,671 aircraft, 8611 tanks, and 173 major vessels, totaling 299,920 tons.
12 Cyclone destroys Bengal, India; 40,000 lives lost.
13 Mildenhall Treasure, a hoard of Roman silverware, is discovered in Suffolk, Eng.
14 Mine explosion in Honkeiko, Manchuria, kills 1549 persons.

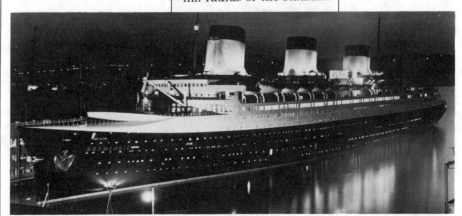

S.S. Normandie, French ocean liner at night

History and Politics		The Arts	
America	**Elsewhere**	**America**	**Elsewhere**

1943

America (History and Politics)

1 Pres. Roosevelt confers with Brit. Prime Minister Churchill at Casablanca, Morocco, concerning military strategy. They agree to demand unconditional surrender from the Axis Powers.

2 Gen. Eisenhower becomes Commander-in-Chief of all Allied forces in North Africa. U.S. forces capture Bizerte, Tunisia, and combine with the British to drive the Axis forces out of Africa.

3 U.S. bombers sink Japanese convoy of 22 ships at the Battle of Bismarck Sea.

4 U.S. forces recapture Attu, Kiska, and Agattu in the Aleutian Islands.

5 Burma declares war on the U.S.

6 U.S. naval and amphibious forces begin island-hopping operations in the Pacific, capturing key bases. Japanese are forced to retreat on New Guinea.

7 Gen. Eisenhower directs the invasions of Sicily and Italy. U.S. 7th Army under Gen. George S. Patton, Jr. conquers Sicily. U.S. forces land south of Naples and push back German and Italian defenses.

8 U.S. planes bomb Rome and Rumania's Ploesti oilfields.

9 Pres. Roosevelt attends war conferences in Quebec (with Churchill), Tehran (with Churchill and Stalin), and Cairo (with Churchill and Chiang Kai-shek).

10 U.S. Marines capture Tarawa and Butaritari in the Pacific.

11 Gen. Eisenhower is named Supreme Commander of the Allied Expeditionary Force that plans an invasion of Western Europe.

12 U.S. bombers sink Japanese ships at Rabaul on New Britain Island (now a port on Papua New Guinea).

13 Pres. Roosevelt repeals Chinese Exclusion Acts.
[1882:HIST/1]

Elsewhere (History and Politics)

14 Soviet armies relieve Leningrad of a 17-month German siege and force the German 6th army to surrender near Stalingrad (now Volgograd). Soviets recapture Kursk, Belgorod, Rostov, Kharkov, Rzhev, and Viazma. German counteroffensive brings some success, but Soviet armies cross the Dnieper River and recapture Smolensk and Kiev.

15 Allied forces make amphibious invasion in southern Italy. Ital. King Victor Emmanuel III dismisses Premier Mussolini, who is placed under arrest. Germans free Mussolini and make him head of puppet government in northern Italy. Italian government of new Premier Pietro Badoglio surrenders, and Italy joins the Allies.

16 British 8th Army occupies Tripoli as Axis forces retreat across Tunisia. Axis resistance ends in North Africa when German forces surrender at Tunis and Bizerte.

17 Allied offensives in the South Pacific capture Rendova Island and Japanese air bases at Munda, Salamaua, Lae, and Finschhafen. Japanese organize a new land-based air force of more than 700 planes.

18 Yugoslav guerrilla forces led by Marshal Josip Tito (Broz) fight German occupation troops near Trieste.

19 Allies begin "round-the-clock" bombing of German cities and munitions and aircraft plants in the Ruhr Valley.

20 Chiang Kai-shek is made President of the Chinese Nationalist Republic.

21 Inönü is reelected President of Turkey.

22 Iran declares war on Germany and joins the United Nations.

23 Soviets announce that henceforth Communist Parties in other countries are autonomous.

America (The Arts)

1 Betty Smith, novelist and playwright, publishes *A Tree Grows in Brooklyn*.

2 Isamu Noguchi, sculptor, creates the rather bizarre "Monument of Heroes."

3 Ernie Pyle, journalist, publishes *Here is Your War*, a compilation of syndicated articles written while he was a war correspondent.

4 Richard Rodgers and lyricist Oscar Hammerstein II begin their successful partnership when they produce *Oklahoma!*, which features the song "Oh, What a Beautiful Morning," and choreography by Agnes DeMille.

5 Leonard Bernstein, conductor and composer, becomes the assistant conductor of the N.Y. Philharmonic.

6 Saroyan publishes *The Human Comedy*.

7 Robert Motherwell, painter, brings abstract expressionism in a new direction with his most famous work, "Pancho Villa, Dead and Alive."

8 "Pharmacy," a work by assemblage sculptor Joseph Cornell, incorporates mirrors to give unusual effects.

9 Thomas Hart Benton, painter, paints "July Hay," a work typical of his pastoral American scenes.

10 U.S. Army engineers complete the Pentagon building. This 5-sided building, headquarters of the Department of Defense, remains the largest office building in the world.

Elsewhere (The Arts)

11 The bombing of a Milan church knocks out a wall, revealing da Vinci's "Last Supper."
[1495:ARTS/2]

12 Simone de Beauvoir, Fr. Existentialist writer, publishes the novel, *She Came to Stay*.

13 Saint-Exupéry publishes *The Little Prince*, a children's story for adults.

14 Sartre completes the Existentialist philosophical statement, *Being and Nothingness*, and the play, *The Flies*.

15 Chagall paints "Between Darkness and Light."

16 Brancusi exhibits "Flying Turtle," an abstract sculpture.

17 Maillol sculpts "The River."

18 Now in his "American phase," Mondrian paints "New York City" and "Broadway Boogie Woogie."

19 Hesse publishes *Magister Ludi*, a novel.

20 Eng. author H.E. Bates writes *How Sleep the Brave*, a popular war novel published under the pseudonym, "Flying Officer X."

Science & Technology

America

1 The tiny town of Oak Ridge, Tenn., is suddenly populated by 50,000 scientists and aides, all conducting secret atomic research.

2 ACTH (adrenocorticotropic hormone) is isolated from the pituitary gland by Choh Hao Li.

3 Waksman discovers the antibiotic streptomycin and uses it to cure tuberculosis.

4 Large-scale production of penicillin begins to meet the demand as the drug is being used to treat a variety of infectious diseases.

5 Kaiser develops techniques of prefabrication that allow him to build a 100,000-ton *Liberty* ship in 4 days.

6 Charles Huggins, surgeon, uses synthetic female sex hormones in the successful treatment of prostate cancer, proving that chemicals may be effective against cancer.

7 Oppenheimer organizes the Manhattan Project's top-secret Weapons Laboratory in Los Alamos, N.Mex.

8 Alvarez develops a radar-controlled bombsight.

9 Polyethylene plastic is introduced.

10 C.K. Seyfert, astronomer, describes Seyfert galaxies, unusual spiral galaxies beyond the Milky Way.

11 Shapley announces that there are at least 75,000 external galaxies, each with more than a billion stars.

12 Nobel Prize, Physics: Otto Stern for discovering the magnetic moment of a proton and for developing a molecular beam.

13 Nobel Prize, Physiology or Medicine: Doisy for determining the chemical structure of vitamin K.

Elsewhere

14 Jacques-Yves Cousteau, Fr. oceanographer, invents the aqualung, an underwater breathing device.

15 A. Hofman mistakenly swallows LSD and discovers the drug's intense hallucinogenic effects. [1938:SCI/13]

16 Willem Kolff, Dutch inventor, makes an artificial kidney machine.

17 Nobel Prize, Chemistry: Hevesy, for his development of radioactive tracing.

18 Nobel Prize, Physiology or Medicine: Dam, for his discovery of vitamin K.

Miscellaneous

America

1 U.S. Supreme Court reverses 1940 decision and holds that children cannot be required to salute the flag in school if their religion prohibits it; case brought by Jehovah's Witnesses.

2 "Big Inch," world's longest oil pipeline, is dedicated. It is 1300 mi. long, from Texas to Pennsylvania.

3 Infantile paralysis (polio) epidemic kills 1151 persons and cripples thousands.

4 Postal-zone numbering system starts in 178 cities. Use of numbers expected to speed up mail deliveries.

5 In salvage drives, 255,513 tons of tin cans, 6 million tons of newspaper, and more than 26 million tons of iron and steel scrap are collected for use in essential industries.

6 Standard male outfit of "hepcats" and young Negroes is the zoot suit. It includes a long, one-button jacket with broad, padded shoulders, high-waisted trousers that grip the ankles, a knee-length key chain, and a broad-brimmed hat.

7 Detroit Red Wings win last 4 games in the Stanley Cup finals, defeating the Boston Bruins 2-0 to become National League hockey champions.

8 Jitterbug is the most popular dance. As part of the dance the man swings his partner over his back and between his legs.

9 Two trains collide near Rennert, N.C.; 72 persons are killed.

Elsewhere

10 Accident in underground war shelter in London kills 178 people, mostly women and children. Most suffocate when one trips on stairs, causing others to pile up behind.

11 Explosion in a field is followed by the formation of new volcano in Mexico; grows to 900 ft. in a month.

12 Earthquake in Turkey kills 493 people, injures 767, and destroys 3000 buildings.

13 Women in England no longer required to wear hats in law courts.

1943

History and Politics		The Arts	
America	**Elsewhere**	**America**	**Elsewhere**

1944

America (History and Politics)

1 U.S. planes bomb Berlin for the first time.
2 U.S. Marines establish footholds in the Marshalls and Marianas, island groups in the Pacific.
3 Gen. Joseph ("Vinegar Joe") Warren Stilwell, commander in Southeast Asia, leads U.S.-Chinese forces in successful campaign against Japanese-Burmese forces.
4 U.S. 5th Army helps drive the Germans out of Rome.
5 U.S. troops establish beachheads at Utah Beach and Omaha Beach during Allied invasion of Western Europe (D-day). Gen. Omar N. Bradley leads U.S. 1st Army into Normandy, France, and captures Cherbourg. U.S. 3rd Army under Gen. Patton sweeps through northern France, relieves Bastogne during the Battle of the Bulge, and crosses the Rhine into southern Germany. U.S. 7th Army invades southern France and fights up the Rhône River.
6 U.S. long-range superfortresses bomb southern Japan. U.S. forces heavily damage Japanese at the Battle of the Philippine Sea.
7 U.S. forces under Gen. MacArthur return to the Philippines at Leyte. Japanese fleet is heavily damaged at 6-day Battle of Leyte Gulf.
8 Roosevelt is reelected President for a fourth term. Harry S. Truman is elected Vice President on the same Democratic ticket.
9 Pres. Roosevelt signs Serviceman's Readjustment Act ("G.I. Bill of Rights"), establishing benefits for veterans after the war.

Elsewhere (History and Politics)

10 Soviets seize Odessa and advance into Rumania. Sevastopol is liberated, and the Germans are driven out of the Crimea. Rumania surrenders to the Soviets. Bulgaria signs armistice with the Soviets.
11 Allied navies destroy many German submarines and warships.
12 Allies land at Anzio and Nettuno, Italy. U.S.-British troops enter Rome.
13 Allied invasion of Normandy, France, begins on June 6 (D-Day). About 156,000 British, Canadian, and U.S. troops under Gen. Eisenhower and Gen. Montgomery land on Normandy beaches. British and Canadian troops capture Caen. Allied tanks drive through German defenses. French underground forces rise against the Germans. Brussels is liberated. German V-1 and V-2 rockets prove ineffective against Allies. Strong German counteroffensive in the Belgian Ardennes creates "bulge" in the Allied lines. At the Battle of the Bulge, Allied counterattacks halt the Germans and push them back.
14 Dumbarton Oaks Conference among delegates from the U.S., the U.S.S.R., and the British Commonwealth proposes a permanent international peace organization called the United Nations.
15 German officers make unsuccessful attempt to assassinate Hitler.
16 Soviet and Yugoslav forces occupy Belgrade.
17 Allies occupy Athens and try to settle Greek civil war.
18 Polish underground forces in Warsaw attack German occupation troops.

America (The Arts)

1 Tennessee Williams, dramatist, publishes *The Glass Menagerie*, his first successful work.
2 Lillian Hellman publishes *The Searching Wind*.
3 Charles Jackson, novelist, publishes *The Lost Weekend*.
4 Bing Crosby stars in the film *Going My Way*.
5 Vincente Minnelli directs the film *Meet Me in St. Louis*, starring his future wife, Judy Garland.
6 Copland composes the ballet *Appalachian Spring*, with choreography by Martha Graham.
7 Howard Fast publishes *Freedom Road*.
8 Mary (Coyle) Chase, playwright, publishes *Harvey*, about a drunkard and his imaginary companion, a rabbit.
9 The popular radio show, *The Adventures of Ozzie and Harriet*, starring Ozzie and Harriet Nelson, debuts.
10 Jerome Robbins, dancer and choreographer, creates the ballet *Fancy Free*, with music by Leonard Bernstein.
11 Arshile Gorky, abstract expressionist, paints "The Liver is the Cock's Comb."
12 Robert Lowell, poet, publishes *Land of Unlikeness*, his first book of poems.
13 Saul Bellow, novelist, publishes *Dangling Man*, the diary of an army inductee.

Elsewhere (The Arts)

14 Anouilh completes *Antigone*, a play.
15 Jimmy "Trump" Davidson's Big Band introduces Dixieland Jazz to Canada.
16 Brecht writes the drama, *The Caucasian Chalk Circle*.
17 Colette publishes the novel, *Gigi*.
18 John Van Druten, Eng. playwright, produces *I Remember Mama*.
19 Diego Rivera, Mex. muralist, completes "The Rug Weaver."
20 Eng. writer Osbert Sitwell publishes *Left Hand! Right Hand!*, the first volume of his autobiography (–1950, 5 vols.).
21 Lehmann publishes *The Ballad and the Source*, a novel written from the perspective of a teenage girl.
22 Eisenstein directs the film, *Ivan the Terrible (Part II*, 1958).
23 Alberto Moravia, Ital. writer, publishes *Agostino (Two Adolescents)*, a novel.
24 Helpmann choreographs and dances the lead in Bliss' ballet, *Miracle in the Gorbals*.
25 Maugham's *The Razor's Edge* is a novel about an American war veteran.
26 Werfel writes *Jakobowsky and the Colonel*, a play.

1945

America (History and Politics)

1 Pres. Roosevelt, Brit. Prime Minister Churchill, and Soviet Premier Stalin meet at Yalta in the Crimea.
2 U.S. troops cross the

Elsewhere (History and Politics)

12 British-Chinese-U.S. forces defeat Japanese army in Burma.
13 U.S.S.R. declares war on Japan and begins invasion of

America (The Arts)

1 Dizzy Gillespie, trumpeter and composer, organizes an orchestra featuring the "bop" style of jazz.

Elsewhere (The Arts)

14 George Orwell, Eng. novelist, publishes *Animal Farm*, a satirical condemnation of Communism.

Science & Technology

America

1 Howard Aiken, mathematician, invents the *Mark I,* an automatic calculator that is the forerunner of the digital computers.
2 Uranium pile is built at Oak Ridge, Tenn.
3 Robert B. Woodward, "Father of Modern Organic Synthesis," synthesizes quinine.
4 Alfred Blalock and Marie Taussig introduce a surgical technique for saving "blue babies."
5 Baade examines and describes stars in distant galaxies.
6 Oswald Avery, bacteriologist, proves that DNA is the genetic material responsible for heredity.
7 Theodore Von Kármán, "Father of the Supersonic Age," helps establish the Jet Propulsion Laboratory in Calif.
8 Clarence C. Little, biologist, proposes that cancer is caused by a combination of genetic and environmental factors.
9 Silicone resins are introduced as insulation capable of withstanding very high temperatures.
10 Von Neumann publishes *Theory of Games and Economic Behavior.*
11 Nobel Prize, Physics: I.I. Rabi for discovering the resonance method of studying atomic nuclei.
12 Nobel Prize, Physiology or Medicine: Joseph Erlanger and Herbert Gasses for describing the different functions of single nerve fibers in the same nerve cord.

Elsewhere

13 Schrödinger publishes *What is Life?,* using physical and chemical laws to explain biological phenomena.
14 DDT is used to control a typhus outbreak in Naples, Italy.
15 Daniel Bovet, Ital. pharmacologist, discovers the antihistamine, pyrilamine.
16 H.C. van de Hulst, Dutch astronomer, predicts the existence of radio waves emitted by hydrogen in interstellar space. [1951:SCI/13]
17 Nobel Prize, Chemistry: Hahn, for discovering nuclear fission.

Dwight David Eisenhower, Five-Star General, 34th U.S. President

Miscellaneous

America

1 Congress creates new rank, General of the Army ("five-star general"), for Generals Eisenhower, Henry ("Hap") Arnold, MacArthur, and George C. Marshall.
2 Declaration of Independence and other historic documents, sent from Washington, D.C., for safekeeping in December 1941, are displayed again at the Library of Congress.
3 Ammunition ships explode in Port Chicago, Calif.; 300 persons die.
4 Meat rationing ends, except for steak and choice cuts of beef.
5 New York Hospital, New York City, establishes the first eye bank, which stores human corneas to be used to restore sight in certain kinds of blindness.
6 Major hurricane with winds up to 134 mph strikes the Atlantic coast from Cape Hatteras, N.C., to Canada, killing 390 at sea and about 50 on land. Damage estimated at $50 million.
7 Fire destroys the main tent of Ringling Brothers Barnum & Bailey Circus at an afternoon performance in Hartford, Conn., attended by 7000 spectators. Blazing canvas falls on the audience; 167 are killed, more than 175 injured.

Elsewhere

8 First nonstop flight from London to Canada.
9 "Blackout" restrictions relaxed in Britain.
10 British Commonwealth armed forces total 8.7 million; Britain supplies 4.5 million.

Douglas MacArthur, U.S. Army Five-Star General

1944

---

1 The first atomic bomb, code-named *Trinity,* is exploded near Alamogordo, N. Mex. Three weeks later, a U-235 atomic bomb

12 Von Braun and his staff surrender to American forces and are quickly moved to the U.S., where they use V-2 rockets for

1 U.S. armed forces total 7.2 million. War casualties: 292,000 killed or missing; 613,611 wounded.

8 Women win the vote in France.
9 "Black Markets" for food, clothing, and cigarettes develop throughout

1945

History and Politics		The Arts	
America	**Elsewhere**	**America**	**Elsewhere**

History and Politics

America

Rhine at Remagen, enter the Ruhr Valley in Germany, and capture Mannheim, Frankfurt am Main, and Nuremberg. They reach the Elbe River; at Torgau, they meet Soviet troops marching from the east.

3 U.S. B-29s bomb Tokyo. U.S. Marines seize Iwo Jima in the western Pacific. U.S. 6th Army lands on Luzon, and Gen. MacArthur enters Manila, liberating the Philippines. Heavy Japanese air attacks fail to thwart successful U.S. invasion of Okinawa.

4 Pres. Roosevelt dies of a cerebral hemorrhage; Vice President Truman becomes President.

5 After Germany's surrender, the U.S. takes control of southwestern Germany and one sector of Berlin.

6 United Nations opens in San Francisco. Senate ratifies UN Charter by a vote of 89 to 2.

7 U.S. drops atomic bomb on Hiroshima, Japan, killing or injuring about 135,000 people. After U.S. drops second atomic bomb on Nagasaki, Japan announces its unconditional surrender on Aug. 14 (V-J Day) and signs document aboard U.S. battleship *Missouri* in Tokyo Bay. U.S. forces under Gen. MacArthur take over supervision of Japan.

8 U.S. troops enter Korea south of the 38th parallel to replace Japanese.

9 War Production Board lifts ban on the manufacture of consumer goods. Military plane production is cut in half. National Wage Stabilization Board replaces National War Labor Board.

10 Pres. Truman asks Congress for special admission of displaced persons to the U.S.

11 Lend-Lease program ends; U.S. aid to the Allies amounts to about $49 billion. [1941:HIST/2]

Elsewhere

Manchuria.

14 Potsdam Conference attended by Pres. Truman, Prime Minister Churchill, and Premier Stalin, sends unconditional surrender demand to Japan; it is rejected. [1945:HIST/7]

15 Soviet armies smash through the German Vistula defense line, conquering eastern Germany to the Oder River and Czechoslovakia. Allied forces in the west smash through Siegfried Line, overrunning western Germany. [1945:HIST/2]

16 U.S. and British forces break German resistance in northern Italy. German divisions surrender. Mussolini is captured and shot by Italian anti-Fascists.

17 Hitler commits suicide in underground Reichs Chancellery. German emissaries sign unconditional surrender at Rheims, France, on May 7. The end of World War II is proclaimed the next day (V-E Day).

18 Allied Control Commission divides both Germany and Berlin into four occupation zones under U.S., British, French, and Soviet military administration.

19 Clement R. Attlee becomes British Prime Minister.

20 Gen. de Gaulle is elected provisional President of France.

21 Marshal Tito becomes head of the new federal government of Yugoslavia.

22 International tribunal is set up at Nuremberg, Germany, to try Nazi military and civilian leaders for war crimes. [1946:HIST/16]

23 Ho Chi Minh, Vietnamese Communist leader, proclaims Vietnam an independent republic. French oppose it.

24 Premier Quisling of Norway is convicted of high treason and shot. [1942:HIST/17]

25 Allied military occupation of Japan begins under Gen. MacArthur.

The Arts

America

2 Richard Wright publishes his autobiography, *Black Boy.*

3 Bernstein and lyricists Betty Comden and Adolph Green score the show *On the Town,* which includes the song "New York, New York."

4 Stravinsky completes his composition of *Symphony in Three Movements.*

5 Joan Crawford wins an Oscar in the title role of *Mildred Pierce.*

6 E.B. White publishes the children's classic *Stuart Little.*

7 Thurber publishes *The Thurber Carnival,* a collection of writings and drawings.

8 Steinbeck publishes *Cannery Row.*

9 Rodgers and Hammerstein produce *Carousel,* based on Molnar's *Liliom* (1909).

10 Crouse publishes *State of the Union,* a satirical play based on the presidential hopeful Wendell Willkie.

11 "Baptismal Scene" by painter Mark Rothko is an example of abstract surrealism.

12 Milton Avery, artist, paints the abstract landscape "Swimmers and Sunbathers."

13 Popular radio shows include *The Red Skelton Show, The Green Hornet, Superman, Inner Sanctum, The Fred Allen show, One Man's Family,* and *Queen for a Day.*

Elsewhere

15 Gabriela Mistral, Chilean poet, is the first Latin-American woman to win the Nobel Prize in Literature.

16 Translations of Icel. novelist Halldór Laxness' *Salka Valka* (1930–32) and *Independent People* (1935) bring him international acclaim.

17 Dutch painter Hans van Meegeren is convicted of forging paintings of 17th-century artist Jan Vermeer.

18 Britten composes *Peter Grimes,* an outstanding opera inspired by George Crabbe's poem, *The Borough* (1810).

19 Sartre writes *No Exit,* a play.

20 Roberto Rossellini, Ital. film maker, directs *Rome, Open City,* a movie that creates Neorealism.

21 Rattigan's best-known social drama, *Separate Tables,* is produced.

22 Cocteau and René Clément direct the fantasy film, *The Beauty and the Beast.*

23 Roland Pettit, Fr. dancer and choreographer, founds the Ballets des Champs-Elysées.

24 Ivo Andrić, Yugo. writer, publishes *The Bridge on the Drina,* a historical novel.

25 John Betjeman, Eng. poet, publishes *New Bats in Old Belfries.*

26 Ital. writer Carlo Levi causes a sensation with his novel, *Christ Stopped at Eboli.*

Science & Technology		Miscellaneous	
America	**Elsewhere**	**America**	**Elsewhere**

America (Science & Technology)

(equal to 20,000 tons of TNT) is dropped on Hiroshima, Japan. Three days after this, a plutonium-based A-bomb is dropped on Nagasaki, Japan. Both cities are destroyed and more than 130,000 people are dead or missing as a result of the most powerful weapons ever used in a war.

2 Langmuir experiments with *cloud-seeding,* using chemicals such as silver iodide or solid carbon dioxide (dry ice) to cause rain or snow artificially.

3 Vitamin A is synthesized.

4 F. Bloch, William Hansen, and Martin Packard devise the principle of nuclear magnetic resonance (nuclear induction).

5 Woodward determines the chemical structure of penicillin by using a spectroscope.

6 Rossby identifies and studies jet streams, winds in the upper atmosphere.

7 Spies proves that folic acid (a B-vitamin) is necessary for proper development of red blood cells.

8 Weather radar is developed.

9 FCC sets aside 13 channels for commercial TV broadcasting.

10 Ralph Linton, Pa. anthropologist, publishes *The Cultural Background of Personality.*

11 Nobel Prize, Physics: Wolfgang Pauli for discovering the Pauli exclusion principle.

Elsewhere (Science & Technology)

high altitude research.

13 K. Lonsdale becomes the first woman elected to the Royal Society of London.

14 Nobel Prize, Physiology or Medicine: Fleming, Chain, and Howard W. Florey, Austral. pathologist, for their discovery and purification of penicillin.

America (Miscellaneous)

2 Rationing of shoes, butter, and tires ends.

3 On a foggy Saturday morning a B-25 bomber flies into the Empire State Building in New York City at the 78–79th floors; 13 persons die.

4 Medal of Freedom is established. Awarded to civilians for meritorious act or service; first recipient is Anna Rosenberg.

5 First large-scale department store sales demonstration televised at Gimbel Bros. department store in Philadelphia.

6 U.S. ship loaded with aerial bombs explodes at Bari, Italy; at least 360 persons killed.

7 First railroad car with observation dome is used by Chicago, Burlington & Quincy Railroad. Dome is 19½ ft. long and extends the full width of railroad car.

Elsewhere (Miscellaneous)

Europe.

10 Family allowances are introduced in Britain.

11 War casualties (1939–45) Great Britain, 244,723 killed; 277,090 wounded. Rest of British Commonwealth, 109,929 killed; 197,908 wounded. Germany, 3 million military and civilian dead or missing; about 1 million wounded. U.S.S.R. estimates 20 million military and civilian dead.

Charles de Gaulle, French General, later President, reviewing troops

History and Politics		The Arts	
America	**Elsewhere**	**America**	**Elsewhere**

1946

America (History and Politics)

1 Government lifts most price and wage controls.
2 Strike by United Mine Workers begins. Pres. Truman seizes mines after employers reject government negotiated contract.
3 Chinese Communists tell the U.S. to stop supplying arms to the Nationalist Chinese. U.S. gives up trying to mediate the civil war in China.
4 Bernard Baruch, U.S. Representative to the UN Atomic Energy Commission, formulates plans for international control of atomic energy.
5 U.S. grants independence to the Philippines, which leases military bases to the U.S.
6 Army and Navy are permitted to manufacture atomic weapons.
7 Henry Wallace, Secretary of Commerce since 1945, is forced to resign because of his public opposition to Pres. Truman's foreign policy. Wallace favors cooperation with the Soviets, despite increasing "hard line" from Truman administration.
8 U.S. holds trials of German war criminals at Nuremberg, Germany.
9 U.S. announces it will keep troops in South Korea until Soviet troops leave North Korea and a free government is established for a unified country.
10 UN accepts donation of $8.5 million from John D. Rockefeller, Jr. to purchase the site for the UN headquarters in New York City.
11 Churchill makes speech at Fulton, Mo., warning of Soviet expansionism and coining the phrase the "Iron Curtain." This marks the start of the "cold war."

Elsewhere (History and Politics)

12 Chinese civil war continues between Nationalists and Communists.
13 Trygve Halvdan Lie of Norway is elected the first UN Secretary General.
14 De Gaulle resigns as French President and is succeeded by Georges Bidault.
15 King Victor Emmanuel III of Italy abdicates and is succeeded by his son, Umberto II, who is forced to abdicate after a referendum approving a republican government. Premier Alcide de Gasperi forms a coalition government.
16 International tribunal at Nuremberg convicts 22 Nazi leaders of war crimes. Goering commits suicide by poison before his scheduled execution.
17 Beneš is reelected President and Klement Gottwald is named Premier of Czechoslovakia.
18 Communists proclaim Albania a republic with Enver Hoxha as Premier and Bulgaria a republic with Georgi Dimitrov as Premier.
19 Poland establishes a unicameral parliament, as advocated by the Communists, and nationalizes all large industries.
20 Juan Domingo Péron is elected President of Argentina.
21 Communist-dominated Socialist Unity Party takes control of the Soviet zone in Germany (now East Germany).
22 Britain offers independence to British India.
[1947:HIST/16]
23 International tribunal in Tokyo begins trying major Japanese war criminals.

America (The Arts)

1 Taylor Caldwell, novelist, publishes *This Side of Innocence.*
2 Robert Penn Warren, writer, publishes *All the King's Men,* a novel based on Louisiana politician Huey Long.
3 Gertrude Stein writes of the U.S. soldiers who visited her in wartime Paris in *Brewsie and Willie.*
4 Irving Berlin's score for the show *Annie Get Your Gun* includes the songs "There's No Business Like Show Business," "Doin' What Comes Natur'lly," and "Anything You Can Do."
5 O'Neill publishes *The Iceman Cometh,* considered his best work by some.
6 Robert Lowell's *Lord Weary's Castle* includes the poem "In the Cage."
7 Stokowski becomes the director of the New York Philharmonic.
8 Howard Hawks directs Humphrey Bogart and Lauren Bacall in the film *The Big Sleep.*
9 Alfred Hitchcock directs the film *Notorious,* starring Ingrid Bergman and Cary Grant.
10 McCullers publishes the novel *A Member of the Wedding.*
11 Charles Burchfield, artist, paints "The Sphinx and the Milky Way."

Elsewhere (The Arts)

12 Sutherland's religious masterpiece, "The Crucifixion," marks the start of his "thorn period" of painting.
13 Beauvoir publishes *All Men Are Mortal,* an Existentialist view of death.
14 Coward and Lean collaborate on *Brief Encounter,* selected at the first annual Cannes (France) Film Festival as the best British picture of the year.
15 Giraudoux's play, *The Madwoman of Chaillot,* is produced.
16 Fadeyev publishes *The Young Guard,* a novel about Red guerrilla fighters in the Ukraine. After complaints from Communist authorities, he revises the book (1951), playing up the role of the party leaders.
17 Vittorio De Sica, Ital. film maker, directs *Shoeshine,* winner of an Academy Award for best foreign film.
18 Nikos Kazantzakis, Greek novelist, writes *Zorba the Greek.*
19 Pierre Boulez, influential Fr. composer, completes *Sonatine,* a 12-tone work for piano and flute.
20 Rattigan's play, *The Winslow Boy,* wins a New York Critics Award.

1947

America (History and Politics)

1 Pres. Truman states the principle of Soviet containment (Truman Doctrine). Soviets attack the U.S. as "war-

Elsewhere (History and Politics)

12 Britain nationalizes coal mines, cable and radio communications, and electrical supply industry.

America (The Arts)

1 Wallace Harrison, architect, designs the United Nations building in New York City.

Elsewhere (The Arts)

12 *The Diary of a Young Girl,* written by Anne Frank during the Nazi persecution of the

Science & Technology		Miscellaneous		
America	**Elsewhere**	**America**	**Elsewhere**	
1 John P. Eckert and John Mauchly develop ENIAC (Electronic Numerical Integrator And Calculator), the first electronic digital computer. **2** Edward M. Purcell develops an accurate method of measuring nuclear magnetic resonance (NMR). **3** M. Delbrück and Alfred Hersey independently discover that genetic material (DNA) from different viruses can combine to produce a third virus. **4** Atomic Energy Commission is established. **5** Printed circuits are developed. **6** Willard F. Libby, Colo. chemist, proves that tritium, a hydrogen isotope, can be produced by cosmic radiation. **7** Joshua Lederberg, a pioneer in bacterial genetics, publishes *Gene Recombination in Escherichia coli.* **8** Carbon-13, an isotope, is discovered. **9** Fairey Aviation Co. builds a pilotless rocket missile. **10** Nobel Prize, Physics: Percy Bridgman for experiments in high pressure physics. **11** Nobel Prize, Chemistry: James Sumner, John Northrup, and Wendell Stanley for work with enzymes. **12** Nobel Prize, Physiology or Medicine: Hermann Muller for producing genetic mutations by using x-rays.	**13** Baird devises a method for producing three-dimensional television images. **14** Sir Cyril Hinshelwood, Eng. chemist, publishes *The Chemical Kinetics of the Bacterial Cell.* **15** Lemaître publishes *Hypothesis of the Primeval Atom.*	**1** Mother Frances X. Cabrini is canonized; she is first U.S. citizen to become a saint in the Catholic Church. **2** U.S. Army plane crashes into the Manhattan Company Building in New York City; 5 persons die. **3** After 10-month trial of 24 major Nazis for crimes against peace, humanity, and the laws of war at Nuremberg, Ger., 12 are sentenced to death. **4** Trial of high-ranking Japanese leaders results in sentences of hanging for 7 and life imprisonment for 16 others. **5** Hotel fire in Atlanta kills 127 and injures about 100. Winecoff Hotel had no outside fire escapes or sprinkler system. **6** The "ranch-type" home becomes popular; many find the low-slung, single-story homes appealing. **7** Byrd leads an expedition to the South Pole. **8** Train accident near Ogden, Utah, kills 48 persons; another near Naperville, Ill., kills 47.	**9** China's population is 455 million; India's 311 million; U.S.S.R.'s 194 million; Japan's 73 million; West Germany's 48 million; Italy's 47 million; Britain's 46 million; Brazil's 45 million; and France's 40 million. **10** Williamson diamond mine in Tanganyika, Africa, is the world's largest. **11** Women win the vote in Italy. **12** Mikhail Botvinnik of the U.S.S.R. considered world's finest chess player.	**1946**
1 Von Neumann develops EDVAC (Electronic Discrete Variable Automatic Computer) which is	**11** Dennis Gabor, Hung. engineer, develops the technique of holography—a photographic pro-	**1** U.S. Supreme Court upholds state law permitting pupils at parochial schools to ride on public	**8** Scrolls dating from approximately 22 B.C. to A.D. 100 are discovered in Wadi Qumran, near the	**1947**

mongers" in the UN General Assembly.

2 Congress approves economic and military assistance for Greece and Turkey.

3 Secretary of State Marshall proposes the European Recovery Program (the Marshall Plan) to give economic aid to certain war-torn European nations.

4 Wartime draft ends.

5 U.S. ratifies peace treaties with Italy, Hungary, Bulgaria, and Rumania.

6 Congress enacts the Labor Management Relations Act (Taft-Hartley Labor Act) over Pres. Truman's veto. It limits power of labor unions and puts restrictions on use of the strike, closed shop, and political activities.

7 Hoover Commission is formed to correct government inefficiency.

8 Presidential Succession Act designates the Speaker of the House, President pro tempore of the Senate, and Cabinet members according to rank as next in succession after the Vice President.

9 National Security Act unifies all branches of the armed services into a new Department of Defense. James V. Forrestal becomes the first Secretary of Defense.

10 UN gives the U.S. trusteeship over the Carolines, the Marshalls, and the Marianas—island groups in the Pacific.

11 Pres. Truman initiates a loyalty program for civil servants; federal government is attacked for loose security.

13 Communist parties in Europe establish *Cominform* (Communist Information Bureau).

14 De Gaulle heads a new party, *Rassemblement du Peuple Français,* to unify French non-Communists. Vincent Auriol becomes President of France.

15 Communists begin political agitation to gain control of Czechoslovakia; they extend their control in Hungary.

16 British India is divided into the independent states of India (Hindu) and Pakistan (Muslim). Jawaharlal Nehru becomes Prime Minister of India.

17 U.S. and Britain send help to Greece to prevent Communist takeover.

18 Allied peace treaty with Italy awards Venezia Giulia to Yugoslavia and establishes the free territory of Trieste.

19 U.S.S.R. and her satellites refuse aid from the Marshall Plan. [1947:HIST/3]

20 Nikolai Aleksandrovich Bulganin becomes Soviet Deputy Premier and succeeds Stalin as Minister of the Armed Forces.

21 Communists gain control of Manchuria in Chinese civil war with the Nationalists.

2 Tennessee Williams publishes the Pulitzer Prize winning work, *A Streetcar Named Desire.*

3 James Michener, author, publishes *Tales of the South Pacific,* the basis for the Broadway show *South Pacific.* [1949:ARTS/2]

4 Now a U.S. citizen, Thomas Mann publishes *Doctor Faustus,* an allegorical novel about the rise of Nazism.

5 A copy of the first edition of the *Bay Psalm Book* is sold in New York for $151,000—at the time, the highest price ever paid for any book.

6 Arthur Miller publishes *All My Sons.*

7 Arshile Gorky paints the abstract work "The Betrothal II."

8 Auden publishes *the Age of Anxiety,* which wins him a Pulitzer Prize.

9 Bruno Walter becomes the conductor of the New York Philharmonic Symphony Orchestra.

10 Laura Hobson, writer, publishes *Gentleman's Agreement.*

11 Virgil Thomson, composer, composes the opera *The Mother of Us All,* with a libretto by Gertrude Stein.

Jews in the Netherlands, is published.

13 Gottfried von Einem, Swiss composer, completes *Danton's Death,* an opera based on Büchner's drama, *Danton's Tod* (1835).

14 Genêt's complex drama, *The Maids,* establishes him as a leading figure in the "theater of the absurd."

15 Lean directs the film, *Oliver Twist,* and collaborates with Coward on *This Happy Breed.*

16 Hartog writes *The Fourposter,* his most popular comedy.

17 Beecham establishes the Royal Philharmonic Orchestra, London.

18 Marcel Marceau, Fr. mime, creates Bip, a white-face clown based on Pip from *Great Expectations.*

19 Quasimodo publishes *Day After Day,* a collection of social poems that includes the grim, anti-Fascist "On the Willow Branches."

1948

1 Congress approves four-year recovery expenses for the Marshall Plan. [1947:HIST/3]

2 U.S. recognizes the new state of Israel. Ralph Bunche succeeds in working out an Arab-Israeli armistice.

3 Whittaker Chambers accuses Alger Hiss, Pres. of the Carnegie Endowment for International Peace and a for-

12 Gandhi is fatally shot by a Hindu fanatic in New Delhi.

13 British mandate over Palestine ends. Jewish state of Israel is proclaimed, with David Ben-Gurion as Prime Minister and Chaim Weizmann as President. Arab armies from Lebanon, Syria, Jordan, and Egypt attack

1 Miles Davis, trumpeter, leads a nine-piece combo that pioneers "cool" jazz.

2 Agnes DeMille stages *Fall River Legend,* starring ballet dancer Nora Kaye and featuring a score by Morton Gould.

3 Irwin Shaw, dram-

13 Waugh satirizes California's morticians in *The Loved One.*

14 Rouault produces "Miserere," a series of etchings.

15 Alan Stewart Paton, S. African novelist, publishes *Cry, the Beloved Country,* describing a South Africa torn

Science & Technology

America

able to store programs in its memory.

2 Aiken produces an improved, all-electronic calculator, the Mark II.

3 Lipmann isolates coenzyme A, important in cellular metabolism.

4 Heparin is synthesized.

5 Land introduces the Polaroid camera for instant photographs.

6 Reports of "flying saucers" receive widespread publicity.

7 Libby develops radiocarbon (carbon-14) dating and uses this method to determine the age of several ancient artifacts.

8 The X-1, a rocket-powered airplane designed by L. Bell, makes the first supersonic flight.

9 Pi-mesons (pions) and K-mesons (kaons) are discovered.

10 Henry Kessler, physician, publishes *Cineplasty,* which describes his development of muscle-controlled artificial limbs.

Elsewhere

cess with many scientific uses.

12 Bovet discovers synthetic drugs which produce a nonpoisonous, curarelike effect.

13 Adrian publishes *The Physical Background of Perception.*

14 Nobel Prize, Physics: Appleton, for discovering the Appleton layer of the atmosphere.

Jackie Robinson, Brooklyn Dodgers baseball player

Miscellaneous

America

school buses. This is the first of many cases in this period on separation of church and state in relation to schools.

2 Tornado kills 167 persons and injures more than 1300 others in Texas and Oklahoma.

3 Almost 500 persons die when a ship explodes in Texas City, Tex. The city itself is nearly destroyed by the blast.

4 Labor Management (Taft-Hartley Act) opposed by unions and others because it is designed to swing power in management-union relationships away from "excess" privileges unions have gained during recent years.

5 Severe hurricane sweeps in from Gulf of Mexico, causing widespread damage in Florida, Mississippi, and Louisiana, killing at least 100 people.

6 Jack R. ("Jackie") Robinson becomes first Negro major-league baseball player in this century when he signs with Brooklyn Dodgers.

7 Heavy snowfall in North Atlantic states causes 80 deaths; New York City has 25.8 in.

Elsewhere

Dead Sea.

9 Floods in wake of typhoon kill 2000 persons on Honshu Island, Japan.

10 Norw. ethologist Thor Heyerdahl sails on raft, *Kon Tiki,* from Peru to Polynesia in attempt to prove that the Polynesians may have come from South America.

11 Cobb establishes a world ground speed record of 394.196 mph.

12 Most severe winter in Britain since 1894.

13 Francis Steele reconstructs the laws of Hammurabi, King of Babylonia, 18th century B.C., from the archaeological excavations at Nippur, in present-day Iraq.

---

1 John Bardeen, Walter Brattain, and William Shockley invent the transistor.

2 Goldmark develops the long-playing (LP) phonograph record.

3 Vitamin B$_{12}$ is isolated from liver extract and is used as the primary treatment for pernicious

13 Lovell determines that meteors are natural phenomena of the solar system.

14 Eric Jacobsen, Dan. pharmacologist, introduces the drug disulfiram for treatment of alcoholism. A patient having taken the drug becomes violently ill if he con-

1 General Motors Corporation signs first sliding wage scale union contract with United Automobile Workers; it includes clause that adjusts wages to cost-of-living index.

2 Idlewild International Airport in New York City, largest in the world up to this time, dedicated

7 World Council of Churches organized in Amsterdam at a meeting of representatives of 147 churches from 44 countries.

8 Bread rationing ends in Britain.

9 Chinese refugee ship *Kiangya* explodes; about 1000 believed dead.

1948

History and Politics		The Arts	
America	**Elsewhere**	**America**	**Elsewhere**

History and Politics — America

mer State Dept. official, of being a Communist Party member.
4 Selective Service Act authorizes the registration of all men between 18 and 25 and the drafting of men to create an army of 837,000.
5 Vanderberg Resolution favors U.S. participation in security pacts under UN auspices.
6 Republican Party again nominates Gov. Thomas E. Dewey of New York for President; he was first nominated in 1944.
7 Progressive Party, opposing Pres. Truman's foreign policy, nominates Vice Pres. Wallace for President. Communist Party supports Wallace.
8 Southern Democrats bolt the Democratic Party to support civil rights platform. They nominate Gov. J. Strom Thurmond for President on the States' Rights ticket.
9 Truman is reelected President. Sen. Alben W. Barkley of Kentucky is elected Vice President. Democrats also take control of Congress.
10 Communist Party leaders in the U.S. are indicted and charged with instigating the overthrow of the U.S. government.
11 U.S. helps airlift food and other supplies to West Berlin, blockaded by the Soviets in hope of forcing the Western powers to give up control of the area. [1949:HIST/4]

History and Politics — Elsewhere

Israel.
14 Burma becomes an independent republic.
15 Luigi Einaudi is elected President of Italy.
16 *Cominform* accuses Tito of deviating from the correct Communist line and expels Yugoslavia. [1947:HIST/13]
17 Soviet blockade of all rail and road traffic between Berlin and the West leads to large-scale airlift of supplies by Western powers to West Berlin. [1948:HIST/11]
18 Organization of American States (OAS) is established to work with the UN to promote peace, economic growth, and national sovereignty.
19 Daniel François Malan, advocate of apartheid (racial segregation), becomes Prime Minister of South Africa.
20 Hungary's Communist government arrests and convicts (1949) Roman Catholic Cardinal Jozsef Mindszenty on charges of treason. He is given life imprisonment.
21 Chinese Communists conquer most of northern China.
22 British Nationality Act gives British citizenship to all citizens of the Commonwealth.
23 International tribunal at Tokyo sentences former Japanese Prime Minister Hideki Tojo to death.
24 Communist parties gain full control of Czechoslovakia and Hungary. [1947:HIST/15]

The Arts — America

atist, publishes the novel, *The Young Lions.*
4 Gore Vidal, writer, publishes *The City and the Pillar.*
5 Norman Mailer, novelist, publishes *The Naked and the Dead.*
6 Faulkner publishes *Intruder in the Dust.*
7 Eero Saarinen, architect, designs the 630 ft. tall stainless steel Gateway Arch in St. Louis, the tallest monument in the U.S.
8 James Gould Cozzens, novelist, publishes *Guard of Honor,* a Pulitzer Prize winning novel about racial discrimination on an Air Force base.
9 David Smith, abstract sculptor, creates the stainless steel work, "The Royal Bird."
10 Bradley W. Tomlin, abstract expressionist, paints the black and white "Tension by Moonlight."
11 Maxwell Anderson publishes the historical drama *Anne of the Thousand Days.*
12 The School of American Ballet becomes the New York City Ballet with Lincoln Kirstein as its first director.

The Arts — Elsewhere

by racial strife.
16 Christopher Fry, Brit. dramatist, writes *The Lady's Not For Burning.*
17 Graves publishes *The White Goddess,* a novel.
18 De Sica directs *Bicycle Thief,* winner of the Academy Award for best foreign film.
19 Moira Shearer, Eng. ballerina, stars with Helpmann and Massine in the ballet film, *The Red Shoes.*
20 When Genêt is sentenced to life imprisonment as a habitual criminal, a group of influential writers intercedes in his behalf and he is released.
21 Visconti's *The Earth Trembles* wins the Grand Prize at the Venice Film Festival.
22 Greene publishes the novel, *The Heart of the Matter.*

1949

History and Politics — America

1 Pres. Truman outlines his "Point Four" proposal for U.S. technical aid to underdeveloped countries. He also proposes a program of domestic legislation called the "Fair Deal," which favors repeal of the Taft-Hartley Labor Act, farm price supports, expansion of social security, low rent public housing, and more civil rights laws.
2 Hoover Commission recommends streamlining the ex-

History and Politics — Elsewhere

10 North Atlantic Treaty Organization (NATO) is established to safeguard the West against Soviet aggression.
11 Socialist Unity Party adopts a constitution creating the German Democratic Republic (East Germany). The Federal Republic of Germany (West Germany) is established, with Konrad Adenauer as Chancellor.
12 Hungary nationalizes all

The Arts — America

1 Maxwell Anderson publishes *Lost in the Stars,* a dramatization of *Cry, the Beloved Country.* [1948:ARTS/15]
2 Rodgers and Hammerstein produce the show *South Pacific,* starring Mary Martin, and featuring the songs "Some Enchanted Evening," "Younger than Springtime," and

The Arts — Elsewhere

9 Orwell foresees a grim future in his satirical masterpiece, *1984,* a novel that introduces the "Big Brother" concept of totalitarian government.
10 Rossellini's film, *Stromboli,* stars Swed. actress Ingrid Bergman.
11 Genêt's prison experiences are the basis of his play, *Death-*

Science & Technology

America

anemia.

4 Aureomycin and chloromycetin, two antibiotics, are developed.

5 Oak Ridge National Laboratory begins to develop peaceful uses for atomic energy.

6 E. Kendall and Philip Hench use an adrenal hormone (later shown to be cortisone) to treat rheumatoid arthritis.

7 N. Wiener publishes *Cybernetics: or, Control and Communication in the Animal and the Machine.* This establishes cybernetics as a science and provides much of the technology required for developing computers.

8 Gerard Kuiper, astronomer, discovers Miranda, the fifth moon of Uranus. In another study, he detects carbon dioxide in the atmosphere of Mars.

9 U.S. Public Health Service devises a simple test for diabetes mellitus.

10 Richard P. Feynman, physicist, develops a corrected and improved theory of quantum electrodynamics.

11 U.S. Air Force begins Project Blue Book to investigate "flying saucer" reports.

12 Yale University scientists develop a nylon respirator to replace the iron lung.

Elsewhere

sumes an alcoholic beverage.

15 D. Hodgkin takes x-ray photographs of vitamin B_{12} and uses the photos to analyze its structure.

16 Sir Fred Hoyle, Eng. astronomer, with Thomas Gold and Hermann Bondi, propose the steady-state theory, which states that the Universe is constantly expanding.

17 A. Piccard designs the bathyscaphe, a chamber in which scientists can descend to great depths beneath the sea.

18 The Soviet Union officially sanctions the genetic theories of biologist Trofim D. Lysenko. His theories, which directly oppose those of Darwin and Mendel, cause Soviets to ignore many of the great achievements of genetics, such as the production of hybrid grains.

19 Nobel Prize, Chemistry: Tiselius, for separating the proteins found in blood serum.
[1930:SCI/17]

20 Nobel Prize, Physics: Patrick M.S. Blackett, Eng. physicist, for his work on cosmic radiation and his explanation of nuclear disintegration.

21 Nobel Prize, Physiology or Medicine: Müller, for discovering DDT.

Miscellaneous

America

by Pres. Truman. (Renamed Kennedy Airport in 1963.)

3 Eddie Arcaro is the first jockey to win the Kentucky Derby four times.

4 First motion-picture newsreel in color is taken in Pasadena, Calif., at the Tournament of Roses Parade and the Rose Bowl.

5 First woman army officer sworn in.

6 Stan Musial of the St. Louis Cardinals wins the Most Valuable Player Award for the third time.

Elsewhere

10 World Health Organization (WHO) organized; first meets in Geneva, Switzerland.

11 Women win the vote in Belgium.

12 Brit. explorer Wilfred Thesiger crosses the Arabian desert and reaches the Oman steppes.

Harry S. Truman, 33rd U.S. President

---

1 Eckert and Mauchly build BINAC (Binary Automatic Computer), the first computer with self-checking devices.

2 American Cancer Society and National Cancer Institute warn that cigarette smoking may cause cancer.

3 Commercial production of ACTH begins. It is used to treat arthritis, rheumatic fever, and

12 K. von Frisch discovers that bees use the Sun as a compass.

13 Alexander Todd, Eng. biochemist, synthesizes ATP.

14 Igor V. Kurchatov, Soviet nuclear physicist, develops the first Soviet atomic bomb.

15 Nobel Prize, Physics: Hideki Yukawa, Jap. physicist, for demonstrating the existence of the

1 Brief bathing suits for women, called "bikinis," are introduced to the American fashion scene.

2 Under the Smith Act of 1940, 11 leaders of U.S. Communist Party are sentenced to fines and prison terms for conspiracy to overthrow the U.S. government by force.

3 U.S. Air Force jet flies across the country in 3 hr. 46 min.

6 Earthquake in Ecuador kills 6000 people, destroys 50 towns.

7 Clothes rationing ends in Britain.

8 The Danzig-Warsaw Express is derailed near Nowy Dwor, Poland; more than 200 persons reported killed.

9 Waterfront fire in Chungking, China, kills 1700 people.

1949

America	Elsewhere	America	Elsewhere

ecutive branch. Pres. Truman signs Reorganization Act. **[1947:HIST/7]**
3 U.S. occupation forces in W. Germany are replaced by U.S. civilian commission.
4 U.S. airlift ends after Soviets withdraw Berlin blockade.
5 Senate ratifies agreement establishing the North Atlantic Treaty Organization (NATO).
6 U.S. military advisers remain after U.S. occupation troops leave Korea.
7 Eleven U.S. Communist Party leaders are found guilty of conspiracy to overthrow the government and sentenced to prison terms. **[1948:HIST/10]**
8 Permanent headquarters of the UN is dedicated in New York City.
9 Hiss is tried on two counts of perjury concerning his dealings with Chambers. Jury is unable to reach a decision, but at a second trial (1950) Hiss is found guilty and given a five-year prison term. **[1948:HIST/3]**

major industries.
13 Communists take full control in Rumania.
14 Soviet bloc countries break all economic relations with Yugoslavia. Marshal Tito concludes economic agreements with the West. **[1948:HIST/16]**
15 Greece's civil war ends with the defeat of Communist rebel forces.
16 South African law makes marriage between whites and nonwhites illegal.
17 United States of Indonesia is established, headed by Sukarno
18 Communist Chinese drive the Nationalists off the Chinese mainland. Communists proclaim the People's Republic of China, with Mao Tse-tung as Chairman and Chou En-lai as Premier and Foreign Minister. Chiang Kai-shek establishes Nationalist government on the island of Formosa (now Taiwan).
19 Ireland (Eire) declares itself a republic.
20 Soviet and U.S. troops withdraw from Korea. Two governments (north and south) compete to unify and control the country. UN warns Korean civil war likely.

"There is Nothing Like a Dame." **[1947:ARTS/3]**
3 Arthur Miller publishes the Pulitzer Prize winning *Death of a Salesman.*
4 Nobel Prize, Literature: William Faulkner.
5 Composer Jule Styne and Leo Robin compose the score to *Gentlemen Prefer Blondes,* which includes the song "Diamonds are a Girl's Best Friend."
6 Franz Kline, abstract expressionist, produces the black and white painting "Nijinsky (Petrushka)."
7 Johnny Marks, songwriter, writes the popular holiday song, "Rudolph, the Red-Nosed Reindeer."
8 Philip C. Johnson, architect, designs the famous "Glass House" in New Canaan, Ct. The house is completely transparent except for a solid column containing the bathroom.

watch, and his autobiography, *The Thief's Journal.*
12 Britten composes the audience-participation opera, *The Little Sweep,* or, *Let's Make an Opera.*
13 Reed and Greene collaborate on the wartime spy movie, *The Third Man.*
14 Beauvoir publishes the feminist treatise, *The Second Sex.*
15 Léger completes the painting, "Homage to Louis David."
16 Arp exhibits "Human Concretion," a cast stone sculpture.
17 Edith Sitwell, Eng. poet, publishes *The Canticle of the Rose,* a collection.
18 Ugo Betti, prominent Ital. playwright, produces *Corruption in the Palace of Justice,* winner of the Italian Drama Institute Prize.
19 Cesare Pavese, Ital. critic and novelist, describes his wartime imprisonment for anti-Fascist activities in *The Political Prisoner.*

1950

1 U.S. recognizes new state of Vietnam. U.S. advisers are sent to teach the use of weapons to the Vietnamese.
2 Sen. Joseph R. McCarthy of Wisconsin charges the State Department has been infiltrated by Communists. **[1954:HIST/1]**
3 Pres. Truman authorizes the use of U.S. forces in Korea, following the invasion of South Korea by North Korean troops. A naval blockade of Korea is ordered.
4 Guam becomes a territory administered by the U.S., and Guamanians are made U.S. citizens.
5 Congress passes the McCarran Act (Internal Security Act) over Pres. Truman's

13 French Foreign Minister Robert Schuman proposes the integration of western European coal and steel industries (Schuman Plan).
14 Gen. Eisenhower becomes Supreme Allied Commander in Europe.
15 Korean War begins after an attack by the North Korean army against South Korea. UN asks members to send aid to South Korea. North Korean forces seize most of Korean peninsula, except for area around Pusan. Allied troops launch counteroffensive, landing behind enemy lines at Inchon. UN forces under Gen. MacArthur cross the 38th parallel and push north to the Yalu River on

1 Popular radio shows include *The Lone Ranger, Guiding Light, Dragnet, You Bet Your Life, Jack Armstrong, the All American Boy, Stella Dallas,* and *Ma Perkins.*
2 Jackson Pollock, abstract expressionist, paints "Lavender Mist," the first "drip" or "action" painting.
3 Charles Shulz, cartoonist, creates the popular "Peanuts" comic strip featuring Charlie Brown.
4 Lee Simonson publishes *The Art of Scenic Design.*
5 Tennessee Williams

14 C.S. Lewis publishes *The Lion, the Witch and the Wardrobe,* the first of seven novels in his popular children's series, *The Chronicles of Narnia.*
15 Johnny Dankworth, Brit. jazz band leader, forms his influential bebop Septet.
16 Pierre Schaeffer, Fr. composer, completes *Symphony for One Man Only,* the first major "concrete music."
17 Pavese publishes his novel, *The Moon and The Bonfires.*
18 T.S. Eliot writes the play, *The Cocktail*

Science & Technology

America

gout.

4 Atomic Energy Commission designs a breeder-reactor that produces power by nuclear fusion, creating more fuel than it uses.

5 Waksman prepares neomycin, an antibiotic.

6 Maria Goeppert-Mayer, physicist, develops a nuclear shell theory.

7 Kuiper discovers Nereid, the second moon of Neptune; he later proposes his condensation theory of the universe.

8 Von Braun publishes *Space Flight—A Program for International Scientific Research.*

9 National Bureau of Standards builds an atomic clock that is accurate to within one second in 3 million years.

10 Thomas Park, a leader in the study of population dynamics, publishes *Principles of Animal Ecology.*

11 Nobel Prize, Chemistry: William Giauque for experiments in low-temperature physics.

Elsewhere

meson.

16 Nobel Prize, Physiology or Medicine: Walter Rudolf Hess, Swiss physiologist, for his work in determining the functions of various parts of the brain, and Antonio de Egas Moniz, Port. neurosurgeon, for his development of the prefrontal lobotomy—a radical brain operation performed on certain psychotic patients.

Miscellaneous

America

4 U.S. wins unofficial championship of the 14th Olympic games in London with a team score of 547 points.

5 Fighter plane rams an airliner, killing 55 persons.

Roman Catholic pontiff Pope Pius XII (Eugenio Pacelli)

Elsewhere

---

1 University of Illinois demonstrates a 300-million-volt betatron.

2 Atomic Energy Commission develops an inexpensive radiation-exposure meter.

3 FCC licenses CBS for color TV broadcasts. RCA objects, claiming that its system is more sophisticated and effective than that of CBS.

4 Truman approves the development of a hydrogen bomb. Scientists are divided on this issue and several, notably Bethe and Szilard, warn that use of such powerful nuclear weapons could destroy all life on Earth

11 Oort suggests that comets originate from huge clouds of matter that orbit the Sun.

12 Alfvén publishes many of his early articles in *Cosmical Electrodynamics.*

13 Nobel Prize, Physics: Cecil Powell, Eng. physicist, for his photographic method of tracking nuclear particles and his subsequent discovery of pions (pi mesons).

1 National Council of the Churches of Christ is formed; unites 25 Protestant and 4 Eastern Orthodox groups. Membership is 32 million.

2 Population is 150.6 million. People living in cities make up 64% of population. Since 1940 many Southern Negroes have moved to the north.

3 The bikini bathing suit no longer popular; dresses become more wearable and natural. Young people wear their hair short, dress in dungarees and ballet shoes.

4 "Man O' War" named greatest horse of the first half of the 20th century.

10 London's population is 8.3 million; Tokyo's, 5.3; Moscow's, 4.1; Shanghai's, 3.6; Calcutta's, 3.5; and Berlin's, 3.3. World population is about 2.3 billion.

11 UN reports that of 800 million children in the world, more than half are undernourished.

12 Severe earthquake damages Assam, India; 20,000-30,000 people killed.

13 Record crowd of 199,854 attends World Soccer game (Brazil vs Uruguay) in Rio de Janeiro.

14 Pope Pius XII proclaims first Roman Catho-

1950

History and Politics

The Arts

America

Elsewhere

America

Elsewhere

veto. It provides for the registration of Communists and Communist-front organizations.

6 Two Puerto Rican nationalists make unsuccessful attempt to kill Pres. Truman.

7 Federal Communications Commission authorizes color television broadcasting.

8 Pres. Truman authorizes the Atomic Energy Commission to produce the hydrogen bomb (H-bomb).

9 Pres. Truman orders Army to seize railroads to prevent a general strike, following rail union's rejection of wages. Railroads are returned to the owners after new contract is accepted in 1952.

10 U.S. signs military aid pact with France, Cambodia, Laos, and Vietnam.

11 Defense Production Act grants the President emergency powers over wages and prices.

12 U.S. bars trade shipments to Communist China.

the Manchurian border. North Korea, now aided by China, drives back UN forces to 38th parallel. [1951:HIST/9]

16 René Plevan becomes Premier of France and works for European political unity.

17 Somaliland becomes a UN trust territory under Italian control.

18 King Gustavus V of Sweden dies and is succeeded by his son Gustavus VI.

19 East Germany and Poland recognize the Oder-Neisse line as their permanent border. West Germany protests but recognizes it in 1971.

20 Czechoslovakia holds trials against government officials accused of anti-Soviet, pro-Western tendencies. Western journalists are barred from the country.

21 Adnan Menderes becomes Premier of Turkey, and Celâl Bayar becomes President.

22 Riots break out in Johannesburg against South African government's apartheid (racial segregation) policies.

23 Rajendra Prasad is elected India's first President.

publishes the comedy *The Rose Tattoo*.

6 Isaac Asimov, science fiction author, publishes *Pebble in the Sky* and *I, Robot*.

7 Jack Kerouac, leading author of the "Beat movement," publishes *The Town and the City*.

8 Leroy Anderson writes the holiday song "Sleigh Ride."

9 Conrad Richter, novelist, publishes *The Town*.

10 Gian Carlo Menotti, opera composer, writes the Pulitzer Prize winning opera *The Consul*.

11 Leonard Bernstein writes the score to *Peter Pan*, which stars Mary Martin in the title role. [1904:ARTS/8]

12 Isaac Singer publishes the novel *The Family Moskat*.

13 In Stuart Davis's "Little Giant Still Life," the words become the entire painting.

Party.

19 Max Ophüls, Ger. film maker, directs *Ronde,* a movie based on *Reigen*.

20 On the day of his death, Beckmann completes the triptych, "Argonauts."

21 Jap. film director Kurosawa Akira receives international acclaim for *Rashomon*.

22 Giacometti sculpts "Composition with Seven Figures and One Head."

23 Wolfgang Fortner, Ger. composer, completes *Phantasie über B-A-C-H,* a 12-tone work for two pianos, 9 solo instruments, and orchestra.

24 Fry writes the verse drama, *Venus Observed*.

25 Eng. novelist Nevil Shute publishes *A Town Like Alice* and *The Legacy*.

26 Cocteau directs the film, *Orphée*.

1951

1 Twenty-second Amendment to the Constitution is ratified; it states no person may be elected President more than twice.

2 Pres. Truman relieves Gen. MacArthur of his Far Eastern commands. Gen. Matthew B. Ridgway replaces him as commander of UN forces in Korea. At joint session of Congress, Gen. MacArthur urges military action against Communist China. Gen. Ridgway sends North Korea a proposal to negotiate a cease-fire agreement. UN adopts U.S. resolution calling for no more arms shipments to Communist China and North Korea.

3 Selective Service Bill lowers draft age to 18½ and

9 North Korean-Chinese forces break through UN lines at 38th parallel, capture Seoul, the capital of South Korea, and reject UN peace proposal. UN troops recapture Seoul and halt new North Korean offensive. Armistice talks fail at Kaesong and are later renewed at Panmunjom, where they stall.

10 France, West Germany, Italy, Belgium, Holland, and Luxembourg set up a single market for coal and steel as proposed by the Schuman Plan. [1950:HIST/13]

11 Churchill again becomes British Prime Minister. He ends nationalization of the auto and steel industries, but retains other socialist measures set up by the Labour

1 James Jones, novelist, publishes *From Here to Eternity,* a portrayal of pre-Pearl Harbor army life in Hawaii.

2 Dave Brubeck, pianist and composer, forms the Dave Brubeck Quartet, which includes saxophonist Paul Desmond. The quartet soon becomes the most popular jazz combo in the world.

3 Now living in New York, Dali paints "The Crucifixion of St. John of the Cross."

4 Rodgers and Hammerstein's *The King and I* features the songs "Getting to

13 Samuel Beckett, Ir. writer, publishes *Molloy,* the first volume in his novel trilogy (*Malone Dies,* 1951; *The Unnamable,* 1953).

14 Peter Ustinov, Eng. actor and playwright, produces *The Love of Four Colonels*.

15 Malraux publishes *The Voices of Silence,* a history and philosophy of art.

16 Vaughan Williams composes *The Pilgrim's Progress,* an opera.

17 Greene publishes *The End Of the Affair,* a novel.

18 Britten and Forster collaborate on the

Science & Technology		Miscellaneous	
America	**Elsewhere**	**America**	**Elsewhere**

Science & Technology — America

by blanketing the planet with a cloud of deadly radiation.

5 Archaeological discoveries in La Jolla, Calif., indicate that North America has been inhabited for at least 40,000 years.

6 Congress establishes the National Science Foundation.

7 Although Americans are spending more than $100 million a year on antihistamines, research shows that the drugs neither prevent nor cure the common cold, but merely relieve some symptoms.

8 Brookhaven National Laboratory (N.Y.) begins research on peaceful uses of atomic energy.

9 AN-FO, a low cost, powerful explosive, replaces dynamite in industrial blasting.

10 Nobel Prize, Physiology or Medicine: P. Hench (Amer.), E. Kendall (Amer.), and T. Reichstein (Swiss) for discovery of cortisone and its medical uses.

Miscellaneous — America

5 Paul Mantz flies from Burbank, Calif., to New York City in 4 hrs., 52 min., 58 sec.; a new transcontinental record for gasoline-powered planes.

6 Richard (Dick) Button, 19, world figure skating champion, selected as top U.S. amateur athlete.

7 Nine men wearing Halloween masks hold up Brink's, Inc., a Boston armored car service, and escape with $1 million in cash and $500,000 in checks.

8 Longest vehicular tunnel, the Brooklyn-Battery tunnel in New York City, opens to traffic.

9 Payment of $3.9 million in court-approved claims resulting from Ringling Bros. Barnum & Bailey Circus fire in Hartford, Conn. **[1944:MISC/8]**

Miscellaneous — Elsewhere

lic dogma since 1870—that the Virgin Mary, after her death, was assumed into heaven bodily as well as spiritually.

15 Floods in eastern and southern China leave one million people homeless; 500 die.

1951

Science & Technology — America

1 Walter Zinn, nuclear physicist, designs an experimental breeder-reactor that is built near Idaho Falls, Ida.

2 Woodward synthesizes two steroids: cortisone and cholesterol.

3 Rachel Carson publishes *The Sea Around Us,* which in effect launches the ecological movement.

4 Levine discovers a new blood factor, the "J" factor, in the blood of some cancer victims.

5 National Geographic Society estimates that there are 300 million stars in the Milky Way.

6 Fluoridated water is shown to reduce tooth

Science & Technology — Elsewhere

16 Eight years after his death, Vavilov's *The Origin, Variation, Immunity, and Breeding of Cultivated Plants* is published in English. **[1920:SCI/11]**

17 Oort devises a new method for mapping the galaxy.

18 E.W. Müller invents the field-ion microscope.

19 Bernardo Houssay, Arg. biochemist, publishes *Human Physiology.*

20 Nikolaas Tinbergen, Dutch zoologist, publishes *The Study of Instinct,* an important work on animal behavior.

21 Nobel Prize, Physics: Cockcroft and Walton, for their work on the transmutation of elements

Miscellaneous — America

1 First transcontinental television broadcast is Pres. Truman's address at Japanese Peace Conference in San Francisco.

2 Missouri River and its tributaries flood more than 1 million acres of farm land in Kansas, Oklahoma, Missouri, and Illinois. Property damage estimated at more than $1 million.

3 Employment of women reaches highest point—even more than during World War II.

4 First commercial color telecast presented by the Columbia Broadcasting System (CBS), New York City. **[1950:SCI/3]**

5 First horse to win $1

Miscellaneous — Elsewhere

7 British submarine *Affray* sinks in the English Channel; 75 persons die.

8 Gordion, the capital of Phrygia (present-day Turkey) 4000 to 3000 B.C., is excavated.

9 Provisions of Witchcraft Act of 1735 repealed in Britain.

10 China's population is 490 million; India's, 375; the U.S.S.R.'s, 190; Pakistan's, 76; Great Britain's, 50; West Germany's, 48; Italy's, 48; France's, 42; and South Africa's, 11.7.

America	Elsewhere	America	Elsewhere

America (History and Politics)

lengthens military service to two years.

4 Supreme Court upholds the Smith Act, under which eleven Communists in the U.S. were convicted. [1940:HIST/5; 1949:HIST/7]

5 Mutual Security Agency, headed by W. Averell Harriman, is set up to offer U.S. economic, military, and technical aid to other countries.

6 U.S.-Japanese treaty allows the U.S. to maintain military bases in Japan.

7 Julius Rosenberg and Ethel Rosenberg are found guilty and sentenced to death for conspiring to transmit classified military documents to the Soviets. They are executed in 1953.

8 Pres. Truman declares the state of war with Germany is officially ended. [1941:HIST/14]

Elsewhere (History and Politics)

government.

12 Czech Communist Party undergoes a purge of the "Titoist" elements in it. [1950:HIST/20]

13 Muhammad Mussadegh, Premier of Iran, nationalizes Iran's oil industry. Britain objects and asks the International Court of Justice at The Hague to rule against it. [1953:HIST/16]

14 Australia, New Zealand, and the U.S. sign defense treaty (ANZUS).

15 King Abdullah of Jordan is assassinated in Jerusalem.

16 De Valera again becomes Prime Minister of Ireland.

17 Allies sign peace treaty with Japan at San Francisco. U.S.S.R., Czechoslovakia, and Poland refuse to sign.

America (The Arts)

Know You" and "Shall We Dance?"

5 Lyricist Alan Jay Lerner and Frederick Loewe, composer, write the score to the show *Paint Your Wagon.*

6 Willem de Kooning, abstract expresssionist, paints the black and white "Night Square."

7 Jerome D. Salinger, novelist, publishes his best known work, *Catcher in the Rye.*

8 James Brooks, abstract expressionist, paints "Tondo," a circular painting 82 in. in diameter.

9 William Styron, novelist, publishes *Lie Down in Darkness,* about the decline of a Southern family.

10 Menotti composes *Amahl and the Night Visitors,* the first opera written specifically for TV.

11 Capote publishes *The Grass Harp.*

12 Stravinsky composes the Neoclassical opera *The Rake's Progress,* inspired by Hogarth's engravings.

Elsewhere (The Arts)

opera, *Billy Budd.*

19 Brit. architect Basil Spence's design for the new Coventry Cathedral (–1962) incorporates the ruins of the original 14th-century structure.

20 Kodály's collection of folk music is used to establish the *Corpus Musicae Popularis Hungariae.*

21 Nellie Sachs, Ger. writer, completes *Eli: A Mystery Play of the Suffering of Israel.*

1952

America (History and Politics)

1 Pres. Truman seizes steel mills to prevent strike by 600,000 CIO steelworkers. Supreme Court rules seizure is unconstitutional because Pres. Truman does not have approval from Congress. Steelworkers go on strike, which is settled by negotiations.

2 Congress passes the McCarran-Walter Act (Immigration and Nationality Act) over Pres. Truman's veto. It abolishes race as a barrier to immigration but retains the national origins quota system.

3 Pres. Truman announces he will not run for a second term.

4 Democratic Party drafts

Elsewhere (History and Politics)

10 European Coal and Steel Community is officially created. [1950:HIST/13]

11 European Defense Community (EDC) is formed by Italy, Holland, Belgium, Luxembourg, France, and West Germany.

12 King George VI of England dies and is succeeded by his daughter Queen Elizabeth II. Prime Minister Churchill announces that Britain has made an atomic bomb.

13 East Germany plans to rearm to defend itself against aggression.

14 Vincent Massey is first native-born Canadian to become Governor-General of

America (The Arts)

1 Kurt Vonnegut, Jr., author, publishes his first novel, *Player Piano.*

2 The architectural firm of Skidmore, Owings, and Merrill designs the Lever House (New York), which sets the style of office building design for the next 10 years.

3 Cecil B. DeMille's film spectacle *The Greatest Show on Earth* wins the Oscar for Best Picture.

4 Steinbeck publishes *East of Eden.*

5 Ralph Ellison, au-

Elsewhere (The Arts)

13 Christie writes *The Mousetrap,* a phenomenally successful play that has a record 8862 performances at London's Ambassador Theatre (–1973).

14 Beckett's *Waiting for Godot* is the most famous play in the "theater of the absurd."

15 Angus Wilson, Eng. writer, publishes his first novel, *Hemlock and After.*

16 Eng. abstract sculptor Barbara Hepworth completes "Evocation," one of several

Science & Technology		Miscellaneous		
America	**Elsewhere**	**America**	**Elsewhere**	

decay by two thirds.

7 UNIVAC I is the first mass-produced computer.

8 Robert Leighton, physicist, announces the discovery of a negatively-charged proton, or *anti-proton*.

9 An additional 70 broadcast frequencies are made available for TV in the ultra-high frequency (UHF) range.

10 Antabuse, a drug that prevents alcoholics from drinking, is introduced.

11 A video camera is developed that records both pictures and sound on magnetic tape.

12 Reuben Kahn, physician, develops a "universal reaction" blood test for early detection of several diseases.

13 Purcell detects radio "signals" coming from hydrogen in space.

14 Nobel Prize, Chemistry: E. McMillan and G. Seaborg for discovering and studying transuranic elements.

15 Nobel Prize, Physiology or Medicine: M. Theiler for developing a vaccine for yellow fever. [1937:SCI/6]

using artificially accelerated particles.

million is "Citation"; total earnings: $1,085,760.

6 World heavyweight championship won by Jersey Joe Walcott when he knocks out Ezzard Charles. At 37, Walcott is oldest man to win the title.

Queen Elizabeth II and the Duke of Edinburgh

---

1 Teller successfully tests a hydrogen bomb, the world's first thermonuclear weapon.

2 Cobalt-60 is used for radiation treatments of cancer.

3 James D. Watson discovers the protein structure of the coat of tobacco mosaic virus.

4 In *Creation of the Universe,* Gamow describes his version of the big bang theory.

5 Research shows that the genetic material of viruses is DNA.

6 John Enders, Thomas Weller, and Frederick

12 Rosalind Franklin, Eng. biophysicist, produces a photograph of DNA that proves it has a double helix structure. Her work is the basis for the 1953 Watson-Crick research.

13 Lovell publishes *Radio Astronomy.*

14 Soviet physicists Nikolay Basov and Alexandr Prokhorov propose the maser principle, a concept which leads to the development of the maser and the laser.

15 Nobel Prize, Chemistry: Eng. chemists Archer J.P. Martin and Richard

1 More than 2000 new television broadcasting stations open. About 65 million people watch presidential nominating conventions.

2 Panty raids are carried on at college campuses throughout the country.

3 Pres. Truman signs "G.I. Bill of Rights" for Korean veterans; provides benefits similar to those given to World War II veterans.

4 U.S.S. *United States* sets a transatlantic eastward crossing record, 3 days, 10 hrs., 40 min.

5 Eddie Arcaro is first

10 Olympic Games held in Helsinki, Finland. U.S. wins 43 gold medals; U.S.S.R. and Hungary 22 each.

11 Two express trains crash into a commuter train in England, killing 112 people.

12 Concern in Britain over horror comic books.

13 Brit. archaeologist Kathleen Kenyon excavates the ancient site of Jericho.

14 Last London tram (streetcar) runs.

15 Racing driver John Cobb killed while establishing water-speed record

1952

History and Politics · The Arts

America	Elsewhere	America	Elsewhere
Gov. Adlai E. Stevenson of Illinois for President. Sen. John J. Sparkman of Alabama is chosen Democratic nominee for Vice President. **5** Progressive and American Labor, Socialist Workers, Socialist, Prohibition, and America First parties nominate presidential candidates. **6** Pres. Truman signs "G.I. Bill of Rights" for veterans of the Korean War. Korean veterans receive benefits similar to those given to World War II veterans. **7** Gen. Eisenhower and Sen. Richard M. Nixon of California are elected President and Vice President, respectively, on the Republican ticket. Eisenhower is the first Republican president since Hoover's election in 1928. Republicans gain control of Congress. **8** Pres.-elect Eisenhower, fulfilling his campaign promise, makes three-day inspection of UN forces in Korea. **9** Puerto Rico adopts its own constitution and becomes a commonwealth.	Canada. **15** Armistice ends Korean War, and the battle line (near 38th parallel) becomes the boundary between North and South Korea. Syngman Rhee is reelected President of the Republic of Korea (South Korea); he was first elected in 1948. **16** Mau Mau (terrorist Kikuyu tribesmen) uprising begins in Kenya. The Mau Mau hope to drive out white European settlers and to take control from the British. **[1956:HIST/10]** **17** King Farouk of Egypt abdicates following a successful coup led by Gen. Muhammad Naguib, who becomes President of a newly formed Egyptian republic. **18** Ibáñez again becomes President of Chile. **19** Hussein I, grandson of King Abdullah, becomes King of Jordan. **20** Eritrea is made an autonomous part of Ethiopia. **21** Adolfo Ruiz Cortines is elected President of Mexico.	thor, publishes *The Invisible Man,* the story of a young black searching for his place in society. **6** Herman Wouk, novelist, publishes *The Caine Mutiny.* **7** Flannery O'Connor, writer, publishes *Wise Blood,* a novel about a religious fanatic. **8** Thomas Costain, novelist, publishes *The Silver Chalice,* a novel about the Holy Grail. **9** Louis Auchincloss, author, publishes *Sybil.* **10** Hemingway publishes *The Old Man and the Sea.* **11** Howard Fast publishes *Spartacus,* about a Roman slave revolt. **12** Bernard Berenson, art historian, publishes the monumental work, *Italian Painters of the Renaissance.*	groups of small, white marble figurines. **17** *The African Queen,* a Brit. film based on C.S. Forester's novel (1935), stars Humphrey Bogart and Katharine Hepburn (Amer.). **18** Fernandel, Fr. comedian, stars in the film, *The Little World of Don Camillo.* **19** George Auric, Fr. composer, completes the music to *Moulin Rouge,* a film biography of Toulouse-Lautrec. **20** Dylan Thomas publishes the immensely popular *Collected Poems.* **21** Anouilh completes *The Waltz of the Toreadors,* a play about an aging couple. **22** Waugh publishes *Men at Arms,* the first novel in his war trilogy (*Officers and Gentlemen,* 1955; *Unconditional Surrender,* 1961).
1953 **1** U.S. blockade of Formosa is lifted, permitting attacks by Nationalists on China's mainland. **2** New Cabinet-level Department of Health, Education, and Welfare is created, with Mrs. Oveta Culp Hobby of Texas as Secretary. **3** U.S. Communist Party is ordered to register with the Department of Justice as an organization controlled and directed by the U.S.S.R. **4** Pres. Eisenhower announces the U.S. will not interfere physically in the affairs of countries behind the Iron Curtain. Sec. of State John Foster Dulles states U.S. moral opposition to Soviet subjugation of eastern European nations. **5** Refugee Relief Act allows more than 200,000 victims of Communist persecution to be	**11** Georgi Maksimilanovich Malenkov succeeds Stalin as Soviet Premier. Lavrenti Pavlovich Beria, former chief of Soviet secret police and Deputy Premier, is expelled from the Communist Party, arrested for conspiracy, tried secretly, and shot. Soviets suppress riots by East German workers. **12** Dag Hammarskjöld of Sweden succeeds Trygve Lie as UN Secretary General. **13** Chancellor Adenauer of West Germany negotiates peace treaty with Western allies, obtaining recognition of West Germany's full sovereignty. **14** René Coty is elected President of France. **15** Yugoslav Parliament appoints Tito President. **16** Muhammad Reza Shah Pahlavi flees from Iran after	**1** William Burroughs, writer of the "Beat movement," publishes *Junkie: Confessions of an Unredeemed Drug Addict,* based on his own experiences. **2** James A. Baldwin, black author, publishes the autobiographical work, *Go Tell It On the Mountain.* **3** Arthur Miller publishes *The Crucible* about the Salem witch trials. **4** The Broadway musical *Kismet* features the songs "Stranger in Paradise" and "Baubles, Bangles, and Beads." **5** Hugh Hefner, publisher, founds the men's magazine, *Playboy.*	**14** Poulenc and Bernanos collaborate on *The Fearless Heart,* one of the 20th century's best operas. **15** Ian Fleming, Eng. writer, publishes *Casino Royale,* the first of 13 novels featuring secret agent 007, James Bond. **16** Mizoguchi Kenji directs *Ugetsu monogatari,* one of Japan's finest films. **17** Khachaturian composes *Spartacus,* a ballet. **18** H. Moore exhibits "King and Queen," one of his best-known sculptures. **19** Max Frisch, Swiss writer, completes the play, *Don Juan, or the Love of Geometry.*

Science & Technology		Miscellaneous		
America	**Elsewhere**	**America**	**Elsewhere**	

Robbins prepare a culture of poliomyelitis virus. This makes research on a vaccine possible.
7 Donald Glaser, physicist, designs a bubble chamber for observing nuclear reactions.
8 Jacob Bjerknes, meteorologist, uses high-altitude photographs in preparing weather forecasts.
9 Floyd Lewis, surgeon, uses hypothermia (lowering a patient's body temperature) in open-heart surgery.
10 Nobel Prize, Physics: F. Bloch and E. Purcell for independently developing the nuclear resonance method of measuring the magnetic fields of atomic nuclei.
11 Nobel Prize, Physiology or Medicine: S. Waksman for discovering streptomycin and its use against tuberculosis.

L.M. Synge, for developing the analyzation method of paper partition chromatography.
16 Eng. scientists claim that when a woman eats the weed gromwell, it will render her sterile for several days.

Ernest Hemingway, U.S. writer, in 1934 photograph

American-born jockey to win 3000 races.
6 Mine sweeper *Hobson* collides with aircraft carrier *Wasp* and sinks during night maneuvers in mid-Atlantic; 176 persons lost.
7 The *Revised Standard Version* of the Bible for Protestants is published; it has been edited by 32 scholars, who have worked since 1937. Also Confraternity of Christian Doctrine publishes first 8 books of Old Testament for Roman Catholics.
8 Hollywood develops three-dimensional movies. Natural Vision (3-D) films must be viewed through special eye glasses; after brief success the novelty wears off.
9 Unidentified flying objects (UFOs) reported flashing across night skies all over the country. They are detected visually and on radar near Washington, D.C.

of 206.89 mph at Loch Ness, Scotland.
16 Brit. scholar Michael Ventris deciphers "Linear B," the Greek language used in Crete from 1400 to 1150 B.C.
17 Two trains crash near Sakvice, Czechoslovakia; more than 100 people die.

1953

1 Murray Gell-Mann, physicist, proposes "strangeness," a characteristic of some subatomic particles.
2 Lipmann determines the structure of coenzyme A.
3 Charles Townes, physicist, develops the MASER (Microwave Amplification by Stimulated Emission of Radiation).
4 J. Watson discovers that the bases in DNA are arranged in a definite order.
5 Gamow proposes that the genetic code is based on groups of three nucleotides.
6 Transistorized hearing aids are introduced.
7 H. Urey and Stanley Miller produce an amino acid in the laboratory,

12 Francis Crick, Eng. biophysicist, and James Watson propose the double-helix structure of DNA.
13 Kurchatov and his staff detonate Russia's first thermonuclear bomb.
14 Jacques Piccard, Swiss engineer, and his father Auguste, design the *Trieste,* a bathyscaphe capable of descending to a depth of seven miles underwater.
15 Sir Peter Medawar, Eng. zoologist, discovers that if a young animal is injected with foreign cells, it has a better chance of accepting future skin grafts and transplants.
16 Cousteau publishes *The Silent World.*
17 Guilo Natta, Ital. chemist, develops meth-

1 Maj. Charles E. Yeager reaches air speed record of more than 1600 mph in a Bell Aircraft X-1A rocket-powered plane.
2 Fashion designers become interested in men's clothes. Bermuda shorts for the businessman are promoted and worn during summer months.
3 First atomic artillery shell is fired at the proving grounds in Nevada.
4 Senator Wayne Morse speaks for a record 22 hr., 26 min. in the U.S. Senate.
5 New York Yankees defeat the Brooklyn Dodgers in the 50th annual World Series. Yankees are the first team to win 5 consecutive World Series.
6 First broadcast by an

11 Storm followed by floods devastates North Sea coastal areas in northwest Europe. The Netherlands hardest hit with 1794 deaths.
12 Edmund Hillary of New Zealand and Tenzing Norgay of Nepal are the first to climb 29,028-ft. Mt. Everest.
13 British ferry *Princess Victoria* sinks in the Irish Sea; 133 lives lost.
14 Brit. scientist William le Gros Clark proves Piltdown Man a hoax. [1912:MISC/13]
15 South Korean ferry *Chang Tyong-Ho* founders off Pusan; 249 persons reported killed.

359

History and Politics

America

Elsewhere

The Arts

America

Elsewhere

admitted to the U.S. in the next three years.

6 U.S. gives Spain $226 million in aid in return for military bases in that country.

7 Congress proposes giving individual Indians the same civil status as U.S. citizens, thus ending all limitations on Indian tribes.

8 Federal jury in New York City convicts 13 Communists of conspiring to teach the overthrow of the U.S. government.

9 U.S. gives France financial aid to help her fight the Viet Minh rebels in Vietnam.

10 Senate enacts bill returning offshore oil fields to the states.

clash with the supporters of Premier Mussadegh; he returns after loyalists oust the Premier. Shah dissolves parliament and orders new elections. Iran signs agreement allowing international oil companies to sell Iranian oil (1954). **[1925:HIST/17]**

17 Demilitarized zone (DMZ) is established between North and South Korea. UN-Communist military commission is set up to enforce the armistice. **[1952:HIST/15]**

18 Monarchy is abolished in Egypt.

19 Jomo Kenyatta is imprisoned by the British as an instigator of the Mau Mau uprising.

20 Moshe Sharett is elected Prime Minister of Israel.

21 Federation of Rhodesia and Nyasaland is created, composed of the British colony of Southern Rhodesia and the British protectorates of Northern Rhodesia and Nyasaland.

6 Tennessee Williams publishes *Camino Real.*

7 de Kooning paints the abstract "Woman VI."

8 Leon Uris, novelist, publishes *Battle Cry,* a bestseller about the Marines during World War II.

9 Styron publishes *The Long March* about a brutal Marine Corps training camp.

10 Martinů's opera, *The Marriage,* opens in New York.

11 Henry Dixon Cowell composes *Seven Rituals of Music,* often considered his greatest work.

12 Asimov completes his "Foundation Trilogy" with the publication of *Second Foundation.*

13 Richard Wright publishes *The Outsider.*

20 Dylan Thomas writes *Under Milk Wood,* a radio play.

21 Magritte paints "Golconda."

1954

1 Senate censures Sen. McCarthy for contempt of a Senate subcommittee, misconduct and abuse of certain Senators, and insults to the Senate during his investigations of alleged Communism in the government and the U.S. Army. "McCarthyism" comes to mean political accusations using sensational tactics and unsupported evidence.

2 Senate approves U.S.-South Korea Mutual Defense Treaty.

3 Four Puerto Rican nationalists, shouting for Puerto Rican independence, fire shots in the House of Representatives, wounding five Congressmen.

4 Sec. of State Dulles shifts U.S. foreign policy from one of Soviet containment (Truman Doctrine) to one of massive retaliation by the U.S. if it is attacked by the Soviets.

5 U.S.-Japanese Mutual Defense Treaty permits the

10 Big Four (Britain, France, U.S.S.R., and U.S.) Foreign Ministers confer in Berlin. Soviets reject any plan for German reunification.

11 British offer Cyprus limited self-government.

12 Crimea is made a part of the Soviet Ukraine.

13 Viet Minh (Communist) forces of Ho Chi Minh defeat the French at the Battle of Dienbienphu in North Vietnam, marking the end of French power in Indochina. Geneva settlement divides Vietnam into two parts—North Vietnam under Ho Chi Minh and South Vietnam under Bao Dai.

14 Gamal Abdal Nasser seizes power in Egypt. Naguib is arrested.

15 Southeast Asia Treaty Organization (SEATO) is formed as a defense pact against further Communist gains in Southeast Asia.

16 Józef Cyrankiewicz be-

1 Jacques D'Amboise, dancer, stars in Balanchine's ballet *Western Symphony.*

2 Nora Kaye becomes the prima ballerina with the American Ballet Theater.

3 Robert H. W. Welch, Jr. publishes *The Life of John Birch,* based on the 1945 execution of the title character by Chinese Communists. **[1958:ARTS/3]**

4 Evan Hunter, writer, publishes *The Blackboard Jungle,* based on his teaching experience at a New York vocational school.

5 The increasing popularity of television entertainment causes radio programmers to adopt a largely musical format.

6 Odets publishes *The*

14 Tolkien publishes the epic fantasy trilogy, *The Lord of the Rings* (–1955).

15 William Golding, Eng. novelist, publishes *Lord of the Flies,* the story of a group of boys stranded on a desert island.

16 Iris Murdoch, Brit. writer, publishes *Under the Net,* a novel.

17 Brendan Behan, Ir. author, writes *The Quare Fellow,* a popular play based on his imprisonment (1942–46).

18 Kingsley Amis, Eng. writer, publishes *Lucky Jim,* an extremely popular social comedy that features the antihero, Jim Dixon.

19 Federico Fellini, Ital. film maker, directs *La Strada.*

Science & Technology		Miscellaneous		
America	**Elsewhere**	**America**	**Elsewhere**	
supporting their theory that all life evolved from chemicals. **8** Charles S. Draper, aeronautical engineer, develops a highly accurate inertial guidance system for airplanes. Modified versions are later used in ships and spacecraft. **9** Alfred Charles Kinsey publishes the controversial *Sexual Behavior in the Human Female.* **10** The heart-lung machine, developed in 1951 by J. Andre-Thomas, is used during open-heart surgery so that the heart can be emptied of blood for a short time. **11** A means is developed of transmitting color TV signals that can be received by both color and black-and-white sets.	ods for the preparation of a variety of plastics now used for films, fibers, and artificial rubber. **18** Sir Frank Burnet, Austral. virologist, publishes *Viruses and Man.* **19** Whittle publishes *Jet: The Story of a Pioneer.* **20** Martin helps develop gas chromatography, a technique for studying chemical vapors. **21** Nobel Prize, Physics: Zernike, for his invention of the phase-contrast microscope.	educational television station, KUHI, operated by the University of Houston, Tex. **7** U.S. Air Force Globemaster crashes near Tokyo, killing 129 men. **8** Tornadoes in Waco and San Angelo, Tex., kill 124 people; others in Ohio and Flint, Mich., kill 139; and another in Worcester, Mass., kills 86. **9** Golfer Ben Hogan wins the Masters Tournament, and the U.S. and the British Open championships. **10** Maureen Connolly, age 19, is first woman to win a "grand slam" in tennis: the British, U.S., Australian, and French singles championships in one year.		
1 The *Nautilus,* the world's first nuclear-powered submarine, is launched. **2** Jonas Salk, physician, develops injectible Salk vaccine for infantile paralysis (poliomyelitis). After schoolchildren in Pittsburgh are vaccinated, a nationwide program begins. [1954:MISC/4] **3** American Cancer Society reports higher death rates among cigarette smokers. Tobacco industry cites 36 specialists who deny that lung cancer is caused by cigarette smoking. **4** RCA develops a flashlight-sized atomic battery. **5** Almost 9 million people are examined for TB by portable x-rays developed by the Atomic Energy Commission. **6** Plant fossils are discovered in the Great	**15** J.B.S. Haldane publishes *The Biochemistry of Genetics.* **16** Lovell publishes *Meteor Astronomy.* **17** Kurchatov designs an icebreaker powered by nuclear energy. **18** Nobel Prize, Physics: Bothe, for his invention of new methods for detecting subatomic particles, and Born, for his extensive research into quantum mechanics and nuclear physics.	**1** Atomic Energy Act allows development of peaceful atomic energy projects by private companies, which are also allowed to own nuclear materials. **2** Twenty-six comic-book publishers adopt voluntary code to eliminate obscene, vulgar, and horror comics. **3** U.S. Supreme Court, in *Brown* v. *Board of Education of Topeka,* rules that segregation in public schools violates Fourteenth Amendment. Lower courts ordered to use "all deliberate speed" in admitting Negro children to public schools. **4** Hurricane Carol strikes Long Island, N.Y., and New England killing 68 people; property losses estimated at $500 million. Hurricane Edna veers inland at Cape Hatteras,	**7** Flash flood in Iran kills 2000 religious pilgrims. **8** Brit. athlete D. Leather is first woman to run a mile in under 5 minutes. **9** Temple of Mithras (Roman god, 3rd century B.C.) uncovered during rebuilding in London. **10** Gordon Richards of England is the first professional jockey to be knighted. **11** Typhoon off Hakodate, Japan, kills 1600 people. **12** Eng. athlete Roger Bannister is first to run a mile in under 4 minutes—3 min. 59.4 sec. **13** Locust plague in Morocco. Within 6 weeks citrus crop valued at $14 million is destroyed. **14** Italian mountaineering expedition climbs 28,250-ft. Mt. Godwin	**1954**

History and Politics		The Arts	
America	**Elsewhere**	**America**	**Elsewhere**

<table>
<tr><td></td><td>

gradual rearming of Japan.
6 U.S. signs pact with Nationalist China (now Taiwan).
7 Communist Control Act deprives U.S. Communists of rights enjoyed by ordinary citizens.
8 U.S. and Canada announce construction of Distant Early Warning (DEW) Line of radar stations across northern North America. It begins operation in 1957.
9 U.S. authorizes construction of the St. Lawrence Seaway in cooperation with Canada.

</td><td>

comes Premier of Czechoslovakia, serving until 1970.
17 Johannes G. Strijdom becomes Prime Minister of South Africa and pursues a policy of apartheid.
18 National Liberation Army attacks French offices in Batna calling for an independent Algeria under Muslim control.
19 Pierre Mendes-France becomes Premier of France.
20 Mao Tse-tung is reelected Chairman of the central government of the People's Republic of China.

</td><td>

Flowering Peach.
7 Nobel Prize, Literature: Ernest Hemingway.
8 Wilder publishes *The Matchmaker,* on which *Hello Dolly!* is based. [1964:ARTS/4]
9 Menotti composes the Pulitzer Prize-winning opera, *The Saint of Bleecker Street.*
10 Jasper Johns, pop artist, paints the photo-realistic "Flag."
11 The first Newport Jazz Festival takes place.
12 Now a U.S. citizen, Isherwood publishes *The World in the Evening.*
13 Elia Kazan directs the film *On the Waterfront,* featuring Oscar-winning performances by Marlon Brando and Eva Marie Saint.

</td><td>

20 Satyajit Ray, Ind. film maker, directs *On the Road,* the first movie in his "Apu" trilogy (*The Unvanquished,* 1956; *The World of Apu,* 1959).
21 Henry de Montherlant, Fr. writer completes *Port-Royal,* a drama set in a 17th-century Fr. convent.
22 Churchill is so offended by his portrait by Sutherland that he orders it never be shown or copied. It is later destroyed by his widow.
23 Jean Dubuffet, Fr. painter who develops *art brut* ("raw art"), completes "The Gypsy" and "La Vache," one of his "cow" paintings.
24 Picasso begins a series of 15 variations on a painting by Delacroix. [1834:ARTS/7]

</td></tr>
<tr><td>

1955

</td><td>

1 U.S. begins economic aid to South Vietnam, Laos, and Cambodia.
2 Congress authorizes the President to use force, if necessary, to protect Nationalist China against Communist attack.
3 Federal employees who are "security risks" continue to be dismissed, an ongoing policy since 1953.
4 American Federation of Labor (AFL) and the Congress of Industrial Organizations (CIO) merge. George Meany is elected President of the AFL-CIO and is reelected until he retires in 1979.
5 House extends Selective Service to 1959. U.S. military reserves are to be raised from 800,000 to 2,900,000 by 1960.
6 Blacks boycott segregated city bus lines in Montgomery, Ala. Dr. Martin Luther King, Jr., boycott leader, gains national prominence for advocating passive resistance to

</td><td>

12 Warsaw Pact is formed by Albania, Bulgaria, Czechoslovakia, East Germany, Hungary, Poland, Rumania, and the U.S.S.R. It is the Soviet bloc's equivalent to NATO. [1949:HIST/10]
13 Malenkov resigns and is succeeded by Bulganin as Soviet Premier.
14 Bandung Conference in Indonesia expresses new nationalism among 29 African and Asian nations.
15 Pres. Perón is ousted during a bloodless coup in Argentina.
16 Churchill resigns and is succeeded as British Prime Minister by Sir Anthony Eden.
17 Muslim rebels continue to revolt against the French in Algeria. France refuses UN intervention.
18 Anti-Greek riots occur in Istanbul and Izmir, increasing the tension between Turkey and Greece over control of

</td><td>

1 Tennessee Williams publishes *Cat on a Hot Tin Roof.*
2 Lawrence Welk, bandleader, begins a weekly TV show with a completely musical format.
3 Marian Anderson, contralto, becomes the first black to sing at the Metropolitan Opera.
4 Arthur Mitchell, dancer and choreographer, becomes the first black to dance with a major company (N.Y.C. Ballet).
5 The American Shakespeare Festival Theater in Stratford, Conn., modeled on the old Globe Theater in London, opens.
6 Jim Henson creates Kermit the Frog, the first of the Muppets.
7 MacKinlay Kantor,

</td><td>

14 Greene speculates about the U.S. role in Vietnam in his novel, *The Quiet American.*
15 Swed. film maker Ingmar Bergman directs *Smiles of a Summer Night.*
16 W. Lewis publishes *The Human Age,* an allegory begun in 1928.
17 Rebecca West, Eng. writer, publishes *A Train of Powder,* an account of the Nuremberg trials.
18 Dylan Thomas' early stories are published in *Adventures in the Skin Trade.*
19 Bernard Buffet, Fr. Realist, paints "The Circus."
20 O'Casey completes the play, *The Bishop's Bonfire.*

</td></tr>
</table>

Science & Technology		Miscellaneous		
America	**Elsewhere**	**America**	**Elsewhere**	

Lakes. Analysis shows that the fossils are about 2 billion years old.

7 Brookhaven announces plans for the world's largest atom-smasher—almost 10 times larger than any other.

8 In the U.S. and Europe, there is increasing concern about the dangers of fallout, especially when radioactive *strontium-90* is detected in food.

9 Woodward synthesizes strychnine and lysergic acid.

10 Lawrence develops bevatron.

11 Basic Oxygen Process of steelmaking is introduced in the U.S.

12 Plastic contact lenses are developed.

13 Atomic-powered locomotives are designed.

14 Nobel Prize, Chemistry: L. Pauling for describing chemical bonds.

N.C., roars northward, kills 22, causes property damage of $50 million. Most violent hurricane of year is Hazel which causes 99 deaths.

5 Largest warship built to this time, 59,650-ton aircraft carrier, U.S.S. *Forrestal,* launched at Newport News, Va.

6 Average American's favorite meal is fruit cup, vegetable soup, steak and potatoes, peas, rolls and butter, pie à la mode.

Austen (K2) in the Himalayas, world's second highest mountain.

---

1 After two hurricanes devastate the East coast, the National Hurricane Center is established in Miami, Fla.

2 Severo Ochoa, biochemist, discovers an enzyme that produces RNA in the laboratory. He also proves that cellular energy is stored in phosphate compounds (such as ATP).

3 Gregory Pincus, biologist, develops an effective oral contraceptive (birth control pill).

4 Albert Sabin, virologist, develops an effective oral polio vaccine.

5 GE Research Laboratory produces industrial-quality synthetic diamonds.

6 Bernard Burke and Kenneth Franklin detect radio waves coming from Jupiter.

7 Thorazine and reser-

12 Frederick Sanger, Eng. biochemist, determines the structure of the protein insulin.

13 Burnet publishes *Principles of Animal Virology.*

14 The First International Conference on the Peaceful Uses of Atomic Energy meets in Geneva, Switzerland. 1,200 scientists from 72 countries attend. The U.S. offers 440 lbs. of nuclear "fuel" for use in experimental reactors.

1 Polio cases, which have been rising for almost a generation, drop sharply as a result of vaccination of children.

2 Automobile deaths over Christmas weekend set a record of 609.

3 Ordination of women ministers approved by Presbyterian Church.

4 Rock 'n' roll music is attacked as "immoral" and contributing to juvenile delinquency.

5 More than 1 billion comic books are sold a year, at an estimated cost of $100 million.

6 Rains in northern California and Oregon cause $150 million damage; 74 people killed.

7 U.S. Air Force Academy opens.

8 Estimate is that U.S. has 4000 atomic bombs stockpiled, Soviet Union 1000, enough to kill

10 Prince Philip, Duke of Edinburgh, establishes an award for young people, for outstanding performance in fields such as rescue work, study, crafts, adventure, and physical fitness.

11 Diamonds artificially manufactured under heat of 2700° centigrade.

12 Execution of Ruth Ellis for murdering her lover and new evidence in the Evans-Christie murders (1950) strengthen movement in Britain for abolition of capital punishment.

13 82 people die in a disaster at the Le Mans auto race in France.

14 Brit. aviator Walter Gibb, in Canberra, Australia, flies at an altitude of 65,876 ft.

15 Commercial television broadcasting begins in Britain.

1955

History and Politics

The Arts

America

Elsewhere

America

Elsewhere

segregation in public places. National Association for the Advancement of Colored People (NAACP) encourages and supports segregation movement throughout the country.
7 Congress passes $3.25 billion foreign aid bill.
8 Interstate Commerce Commission (ICC) forbids racial segregation on interstate buses and trains.
9 All federal defense programs are to be run by the Civil Defense Coordinating Board.
10 Supreme Court orders public school desegregation to begin at once.
11 House bill increases salaries of congressmen and federal judges by 50 percent.

Cyprus.
19 Pres. Ho Chi Minh of North Vietnam concludes economic agreement with Chinese Communist leaders.
20 Ngo Dinh Diem wins controlled referendum against Bao Dai and becomes ruler of South Vietnam. Monarchy is abolished.
21 Communist and nationalist forces fight over offshore islands in the Formosa (Taiwan) Straits. Nationalists leave Tachen Islands, which are taken over by the Communists.
22 Egyptian forces raid Israel from the Gaza Strip; Syrian and Jordanian forces raid Israel in the east. Israeli forces retaliate. UN condemns border fighting.

author, publishes the Civil War novel *Andersonville,* about a Confederate prison camp.
8 Marianne Moore, poet, publishes *Predilections.*
9 Patrick Dennis publishes *Auntie Mame.* [1966:ARTS/15]
10 Thomas Merton, Trappist monk, publishes *No Man Is an Island.*
11 Nabokov publishes the bestseller, *Lolita.*
12 Eudora Welty publishes *The Bride of Innisfallen.*
13 Popular Broadway musicals this year include *Silk Stockings* and *Damn Yankees.*

Elvis Presley, popular American singer

1956

1 Southern Congressmen call on states to resist "by all lawful means" the Supreme Court ruling against segregation in the public schools. Virginia challenges the ruling, amending its laws to permit public funds for private schools. Federal court in Louisiana nullifies state's laws opposing ruling.
2 Agricultural (Soil Bank) Act pays farmers to take cropland out of production in order to reduce crop surpluses.
3 Federal Aid Highway Act authorizes a 13-year intra- and interstate highway building program to be funded by tolls paid by motorists.
4 Democratic Party nominates Stevenson for President. Sen. Estes Kefauver, former chairman of the Senate crime investigating committee of 1950–51, wins Democratic vice presidential nomination over Sen. John F. Kennedy of Massachusetts.
5 States' Rights, Prohibition, Socialist Labor, and Socialist parties nominate presidential candidates.
6 Eisenhower and Nixon are reelected President and Vice

9 Nikita Sergeyevich Khrushchev, Communist Party leader, denounces Stalin at the 20th Communist Party Congress in Moscow, beginning a period of "de-Stalinization" in the U.S.S.R. and Eastern Europe.
10 Fighting between the Mau Mau and British ends in Kenya, with about 11,500 Kikuyu tribesmen killed.
11 Soviet troops brutally suppress anti-Communist revolution in Hungary. Some 190,000 refugees flee from the country. János Kádár becomes head of the new Communist regime in Hungary.
12 Nasser becomes President of Egypt. He nationalizes the Suez Canal after the U.S. and Britain withdraw financing of the Aswan High Dam. Britain and France send troops to retake the canal. UN orders ceasefire and helps clear canal of sunken ships, which is reopened in 1957.
13 Spain ends its Moroccan protectorate; France grants independence to Morocco.
14 Franco-German accord transfers the Saar region to West Germany.

1 Elvis Presley, singer, achieves national fame with the song "Heartbreak Hotel." For the next 16 months, Elvis has at least one song on the Top Ten, including such hits as "Hound Dog," "Don't Be Cruel," and "Love Me Tender."
2 Movies and movie stars are allowed to appear on TV for the first time.
3 Broadway musicals include Lerner and Loewe's *My Fair Lady,* starring Julie Andrews and Rex Harrison, and featuring the songs "I've Grown Accustomed to Her Face" and "I Could Have Danced All Night," and *The Most Happy Fella,* the score by Frank Loesser featuring the song "Standing on the Corner."
4 Wallace Harrison designs the fish-shaped First Presbyterian Church in Stamford, Conn., an outstanding

12 John Osborne, Eng. playwright, is established as the first of the "angry young men" with the English Stage Company's production of his influential drama, *Look Back in Anger.*
13 Casals organizes an annual music festival in Puerto Rico.
14 Oscar Niemeyer, Braz. architect, designs the President's Palace and other buildings in the capital, Brasilia.
15 Jøern Utzon, innovative Dan. architect, designs the Sydney (Australia) Opera House (–1973).
16 Bagnold writes *The Chalk Garden,* her best play.
17 Ingmar Bergman directs the film, *The Seventh Seal.*
18 Camus publishes *The Fall,* a novel.
19 Genêt writes *The Balcony,* a drama.
20 Kawabata Yasunari, Jap. novelist, publishes *Snow Country,* his best-known work.

Science & Technology		Miscellaneous		
America	**Elsewhere**	**America**	**Elsewhere**	
pine prove to be effective drugs for controlling some mental disorders. **8** National Geographic Society suggests that blue-green areas on Mars are living plants. **9** Electricity for public use is produced on a limited, experimental basis at a nuclear reactor. **[1951:SCI/1]** **10** Nobel Prize, Physics: Willis Lamb for work on the hydrogen spectrum; P. Kusch for measuring the magnetic moment of an electron. **11** Nobel Prize, Chemistry: Vincent du Vigneaud for synthesizing a hormone.		everyone on earth several times over. **9** General Motors becomes the first corporation to earn more than $1 billion in one year.		
1 Stanley "creates" a virus in his laboratory. **2** The neutrino, a subatomic particle with no charge, is observed. **3** A team of scientists, working under E.O. Lawrence, discovers the antineutron. **4** Earl Sutherland, physiologist, discovers cyclic-AMP (adenosine monophosphate), a chemical important in carbohydrate metabolism. **5** Robert Hofstadter, physicist, measures the diameter of a proton: 3×10^{-14} inches. **6** The 5th edition of Einstein's *The Meaning of Relativity* includes his last paper, *The Non-Symmetric Field*. **7** Michael DeBakey, heart surgeon, introduces plastic tubing as replacements for diseased blood vessels. **8** National Cancer Institute suggests that increased rates of lung cancer may be due to air pollution. **9** National Academy of Sciences reports that any	**15** A. Piccard publishes *In Balloon and Bathyscaphe.* **16** G. Bourne publishes *Biochemistry and Physiology of Bone.* **17** England opens the world's first major atomic power plant for the production of electricity. **18** Charles T.R. Wilson proposes a theory of thunderstorm electricity.	**1** First transatlantic telephone cable begins operation; two cables, each 2250 mi. long, stretch from Newfoundland to Scotland. **2** Tornadoes in midwest kill at least 45 persons and damage $15 billion worth of property. **3** In worst commercial air disaster up to this time, 128 people die when 2 airliners crash into the Grand Canyon after a mid-air collision. **4** First transcontinental helicopter flight nonstop from San Diego to Washington, D.C., in 37 hrs. A crew of 5 flies 2610 mi. **5** Approximately 6 million cars and 1 million trucks come off assembly lines. About 1 out of 8 cars is a station wagon. **6** First gorilla born in captivity, a female weighing 4½ lbs., at the zoo in Columbus, Ohio. **7** Ringling Brothers Barnum & Bailey Circus performs its last show under canvas. Rising costs force the circus to close. **8** Don Larsen, New	**10** Olympic Games held in Melbourne, Australia. **11** At least 126 persons die near Mahbubnagar, India, when bridge collapses under a train. **12** German Evangelistic Churches begin revision of Lutheran text of New Testament. **13** Ital. ocean liner *Andrea Doria* sinks after colliding with the *Stockholm,* off Nantucket Island, Mass.; 52 persons, mostly passengers on the Italian ship, dead or unaccounted for; more than 1600 rescued. **14** About 1100 people die when 7 army ammunition trucks explode at Cali, Colombia, South America. **15** Palace of Emperor Diocletian (Roman emperor A.D. 285–305) is excavated at Split, Yugoslavia. **16** Brit. test pilot Peter Twiss flies 1132 mph in a plane called Fairy Delta. **17** Coal mine fire kills 262 people in Marcinelle, Belgium.	**1956**

History and Politics

America

President on the Republican ticket, winning by a landslide. Eisenhower is the first Republican to win reelection since McKinley in 1900. Democrats win control of Congress.
7 Defense Department sets up emergency operation to transport 15,000 Hungarian refugees to the U.S. [1956:HIST/11]
8 *Daily Worker,* U.S. Communist newspaper, is shut down by the IRS for nonpayment of taxes. It resumes publishing after partial payment.

Elsewhere

15 Sudan and Pakistan become independent republics.
16 British exile Archbishop Makarios becomes leader of the Greek Cypriots seeking the union of Cyprus with Greece. [1959:HIST/16]
17 Guerrilla forces under Fidel Castro land in Cuba and begin campaign against the dictatorship of Fulgencio Batista.
18 Rhee is reelected President of South Korea.

The Arts

America

example of modern church design.
5 Billie Holiday publishes *Lady Sings the Blues.*
6 Vidal publishes *Visit to a Small Planet.*
7 Allen Ginsberg publishes *Howl,* a poetic work which discusses the basic tenets of the "Beat movement."
8 John Barth, novelist, publishes *The Floating Opera.*
10 O'Neill's autobiographical tragedy, *Long Day's Journey Into Night,* is published posthumously.
11 Dizzy Gillespie and his band are sent by the U.S. State Department on a goodwill tour—the first jazz musicians to be subsidized by the government.

Elsewhere

21 Ravi Shankar, Indian sitarist and composer, begins tours which stimulate Western interest in Indian classical music.
22 Roger Vadim, Fr. film maker, directs *And God Created Woman.*
23 Friedrich Dürrenmatt, Swiss playwright, completes *The Visit,* a tragicomedy.

1957

America (History and Politics)

1 Pres. Eisenhower proposes plan (Eisenhower Doctrine) to supply Middle Eastern countries with economic and military aid in order to help them fight Communist aggression.
2 Gov. Orval Faubus of Arkansas calls out state National Guard to prevent integration at Central High School, Little Rock. Pres. Eisenhower sends federal troops to enforce court-ordered desegregation. Nine black students enter school guarded by troops.
3 U.S. occupation forces leave Japan.
4 Senate committee investigates labor racketeering. AFL-CIO finds Dave Beck guilty of misuse of union funds and expels both him and the Teamsters union. James R. Hoffa succeeds Beck as President of the Teamsters. Beck is found guilty of federal income tax evasion in 1959.
5 F.B.I. Chief J. Edgar Hoover accuses U.S. Communist Party of adopting a new,

Elsewhere (History and Politics)

10 Israel withdraws its troops from the Gaza Strip and the Sinai Peninsula. UN emergency forces patrol Gaza border to keep peace.
11 Hammarskjöld is reelected UN Secretary General.
12 Eden resigns and is succeeded by Harold Macmillan as British Prime Minister.
13 Belgium, France, Italy, Luxembourg, the Netherlands, and West Germany establish the European Economic Community (EEC), also called the Common Market.
14 Berlin Declaration by the U.S., Britain, France, and West Germany calls for a free and reunited Germany.
15 Vyacheslav Mikhailovich Molotov, Soviet Foreign Minister, and Malenkov are expelled from the Central Committee of the Communist Party after an unsuccessful attempt to oust Khrushchev.
16 Franco announces that the monarchy will be restored in Spain after his death.

America (The Arts)

1 Jack Kerouac publishes his best-known work, *On the Road.*
2 Jerome Robbins directs *West Side Story,* a show which blends music, dancing, and acting into a unified art form. The music, composed by Bernstein with lyrics by Stephen Sondheim, features the songs "Tonight," "Maria," and "I Feel Pretty."
3 John Cheever, writer, publishes *The Wapshot Chronicle,* a novel about suburban life.
4 Dr. Seuss, penname of children's writer Theodor Seuss Geisel, publishes *The Cat in the Hat* and *The Grinch that Stole Christmas.*
5 *A Death in the Family* by novelist James Agee is published posthumously.
6 James Jones pub-

Elsewhere (The Arts)

12 John Braine, Eng. novelist, publishes *Room at the Top,* the popular story of a working-class hero.
13 Sartre coins the term "anti-novel" to describe a new, radical type of avant-garde novel.
14 Brit. saxophone players Tubby Hayes and Ronnie Scott establish the Jazz Couriers (-1959).
15 Sutherland completes a tapestry for the new Coventry Cathedral.
16 LeCorbusier designs the Tokyo Museum of Art (-1960).
17 Durrell publishes *Justine,* the first novel in the *Alexandria Quartet* (*Balthazar,* 1958; *Mountolive,* 1958; *Clea,* 1960).
18 Henri-Georges Adam, Fr. sculptor, completes "Beacon of the Dead," at Ausch-

Science & Technology		Miscellaneous		
America	**Elsewhere**	**America**	**Elsewhere**	

radiation, even tiny amounts, can cause genetic damage.
10 Atomic Energy Commission develops atomic-powered rockets.
11 U.S. Army Map Service determines that, at the equator, the Earth's circumference is 24,902 miles.
12 Dobzhansky publishes *The Biological Basis of Human Freedom.*
13 Nobel Prize, Physics: J. Bardeen, W. Brattain, and W. Shockley for inventing the transistor.
14 Nobel Prize, Physiology or Medicine: Dickinson Richards (Amer.), André Cournand (Amer.), and Werner Forssmann (Ger.) for developing a technique of cardiac catheterization to examine the heart's interior.

York Yankees right-hander, pitches first no-hit, no-run game in World Series history.
9 Floyd Patterson at 21 becomes the youngest man to win the heavyweight boxing championship.

Lawrence Durrell, English novelist and poet, author of the *Alexandria Quartet*

1 America's first large nuclear power plant opens in Shippingport, Pa.
2 Arthur Kornberg, physician, synthesizes DNA.
3 Based on studies of Sputnik's orbits, Robert Jastrow determines that the Earth's atmosphere is 40 times denser than originally thought.
4 Rose Ichelson isolates and cultivates a microorganism that causes multiple sclerosis.
5 Borazon, a boron-nitrogen compound harder than diamond, is developed.
6 Federation of American Scientists urges a worldwide ban on nuclear weapon tests.
7 Gibberellins, a group of plant growth hormones, are isolated.
8 Perceptron, a bionic computer that prints, writes, and responds to spoken commands, is developed.
9 John Bardeen, Leon

13 The Russians launch *Sputnik 1,* the first artificial satellite. One month later, *Sputnik 2* is launched with a passenger, a dog named Laika, aboard.
14 Lovell completes the design and construction of the world's largest radio telescope at Jodrell Bank, England. The telescope is used to track Sputnik 1. Lovell also publishes *The Exploration of Space by Radio.*
15 The International Geophysical Year (IGY) begins, a program of geophysical research involving more than 70 countries and thousands of scientists.
16 Prince Buu Hoi, Vietnamese physicist, discovers dibenzpyrene, a substance in cigarette smoke thought to cause cancer.
17 Eccles publishes *The Physiology of Nerve Cells.*
18 Eng. virologists discover interferon, a sub-

1 Transcontinental speed record (Long Beach, Calif., to Brooklyn, N.Y.) is set by Maj. John H. Glenn, Jr., in a F8U-1P jet, in 3 hr., 23 min., 8.4 sec.
2 Office of Education publishes two-year survey of education in Soviet Union showing that emphasis on scientific and technical education in U.S.S.R. is far ahead of that in U.S.
3 Hurricane Audrey and a tidal wave strike the Louisiana and Texas coasts, leaving 531 dead and missing.
4 Don Bowden is first American to run mile in less than 4 min.—3 min., 58.7 sec., at Stockton, Calif.
5 World's longest suspension bridge to date, the Mackinac Straits Bridge between Michigan's upper and lower peninsula, opens. Bridge cost $100 million.

10 *Mayflower II,* replica of 1620 Pilgrim vessel, leaves England under command of Alan Villiers, for voyage to Plymouth, Mass. Voyage takes 53 days, 14 less than original trip.
11 Japan wins world table tennis championship in Stockholm, Sweden.
12 175 people killed near Kendal, Jamaica, when train plunges into a ravine.
13 Donatier Gutierrez of Mexico wins long distance swim championship from Naples to Capri, Italy.
14 Death toll in 10-week smallpox epidemic in Calcutta is 946.
15 Tokyo-London jet speed record set by British Canberra twin jet Aries V; flies a 5942.5-mi. route across North Pole in 17 hr. 42 min.
16 Floods along Yi, Shu, and Yellow rivers in China kill 557 persons.
17 World Jewish popula-

1957

America	Elsewhere	America	Elsewhere

America (History and Politics):

more liberal constitution in order to gain acceptance in the U.S. **[1954:HIST/8]**

6 U.S. proposes a 10-month halt to nuclear testing as first step toward disarmament.

7 *Mayflower II* lands at Plymouth, Mass., after 54-day voyage across the North Atlantic from Plymouth, England. It duplicates the first crossing by the Pilgrims in 1620.

8 Senate subcommittee holds hearings on U.S. preparedness to withstand Soviet military attack.

9 Congress enacts Civil Rights Act, the first civil rights legislation since Reconstruction (1866–77). It prohibits discrimination in public places based on race, color, religion, or national origin.

Elsewhere (History and Politics):

17 Adenauer is reelected Chancellor of West Germany.

18 Antonin Novotný becomes President of Czechoslovakia. His government is repressive.

19 Military junta overthrows Pres. Gustavo Rojas Pinilla dictator of Colombia since 1953.

20 Ghana becomes an independent nation within the British Commonwealth of Nations.

21 Turkish troops move toward Syrian border. Soviets warn Turkey not to attack Syria.

America (The Arts):

lishes *Some Came Running*.

7 Gypsy Rose Lee publishes her autobiography, *Gypsy*.

8 Meredith Willson's score for the show *The Music Man*, starring Robert Preston, includes the songs "76 Trombones" and "Till There Was You."

9 Ayn Rand publishes *Atlas Shrugged,* a novel about a "mind strike," in which all creative people withhold their ideas.

10 Edward Villella, dancer, joins the N.Y.C. Ballet and stars in *Prodigal Son*.

11 Jan Muller, figurative painter, paints the haunting "The Temptation of Saint Anthony."

Elsewhere (The Arts):

witz.

19 Ingmar Bergman directs the film, *Wild Strawberries*.

20 The Brit. film *The Bridge Over the River Kwai* wins Academy Awards for best picture, best director (Lean), and best actor (Guinness).

21 Shute describes a nuclear holocaust in his novel, *On the Beach*.

22 H. Moore prepares a sculpture (–1958) for the UNESCO headquarters, Paris.

1958

America (History and Politics):

1 Supreme Court orders states not to delay public school desegregation, citing the situation in Little Rock in 1957. Gov. Faubus of Arkansas defies Supreme Court ruling by closing four high schools and reopening them as private schools.

2 U.S. adopts neutrality in Indonesian civil war.

3 During goodwill tour in South America, Vice Pres. Nixon is greeted angrily by demonstrators in Venezuela and Peru. U.S. troops are sent to Caribbean.

4 Under Eisenhower Doctrine, U.S. Marines are sent to Lebanon to restore order after uprising by Arab nationalists. **[1957:HIST/1]**

5 Defense Reorganization Act centralizes defense structure so U.S. can respond more quickly to a nuclear attack by the U.S.S.R.

6 Sherman Adams resigns as Assistant to Pres. Eisenhower

Elsewhere (History and Politics):

10 Revolt in Algeria creates political crisis in France. De Gaulle becomes French Premier. Constitution for a Fifth French Republic is approved by French Assembly, which names De Gaulle President.

11 Amintore Fanfani becomes Italian Premier.

12 Foreign Ministers of Britain, France, and the U.S. reject Soviet Premier Khrushchev's demand for the end of four-power occupation of Berlin.

13 John George Diefenbaker becomes Prime Minister of Canada.

14 Support from Perón helps Arturo Frondizi become President of Argentina.

15 Chile legalizes the Communist Party.

16 Hendrik Frensch Verwoerd is elected Prime Minister of South Africa; he strengthens the country's apartheid policies.

17 France agrees to with-

America (The Arts):

1 J. Edgar Hoover publishes *Masters of Deceit*.

2 MacLeish publishes the verse drama, *J.B.*.

3 Welch publishes *The Blue Book of the John Birch Society,* in which he puts forth the basic tenets of his newly founded ultraconservative organization. **[1954:ARTS/3]**

4 Barbara Tuchman, writer and historian, publishes *The Zimmerman Telegram,* about the German suggestion that Mexico invade the U.S. during World War I.

5 Tennessee Williams publishes *Suddenly Last Summer*.

6 Truman Capote publishes *Breakfast at Tiffany's*. **[1961:ARTS/9]**

7 Duke Ellington

Elsewhere (The Arts):

18 Because of intense political pressure from Soviet leaders after the publication of his novel, *Dr. Zhivago,* Boris Pasternak refuses the Nobel Prize in Literature.

19 T.H. White, Eng. novelist, publishes *The Once and Future King,* a four-part version of Sir Thomas Malory's *Le Morte d'Arthur* (1485).

20 Behan writes *The Hostage,* his best play and an important work in the "theater of the absurd."

21 Fr. dramatist Eugène Ionesco completes *The Bald Prima Donna,* an "anti-play" in the "theater of the absurd."

22 Shelagh Delaney, Eng. playwright, completes the highly ac-

Science & Technology		Miscellaneous		
America	**Elsewhere**	**America**	**Elsewhere**	

Cooper, and John Schrieffer develop the BCS theory of superconductivity.
10 Penicillin is synthesized.
11 *Nautilus* is refueled. It had used 8.3 lb. of uranium fuel to travel 60,000 miles.
12 Nobel Prize, Physics: Tsung-Dao Lee and Chen Ning Yang for disproving the law of the conservation of parity.

stance produced by the body to prevent multiple viral infections.
19 Carlos Chagas, Braz. biophysicist, isolates Fraction X, a protein involved in the transmission of impulses from the brain to the muscles.
20 Rudolf Mössbauer, Ger. physicist, describes the Mössbauer effect that occurs when some atomic nuclei give off or take in gamma radiation.
21 Nobel Prize, Physiology or Medicine: Bovet, for his discovery of antihistamines and muscle-relaxing drugs.

6 Sack dress, unfitted material that drapes the body, is the fashion this year.
7 George Metesky is arrested in Waterbury, Conn., as the "mad bomber"; he had planted 32 bombs in the New York City area in the past 16 years.
8 Robert Strom, 10, of New York City, science enthusiast, wins $192,000 after completing 3 rounds on TV quiz program, "The $64,000 Question."
9 Bob Butowski, an Occidental College senior, sets new pole-vault record of 15 ft. 8½ in. at Palo Alto, Calif.

tion is 11.8 million: U.S., 5.2 million; U.S.S.R., 2 million; Israel, 1.5 million; Britain, 450,000; and Argentina, 400,000.
18 385 persons die in Alpine mountain-climbing accidents this year.
19 Juan Manuel Fangio, Arg. race-car driver, wins the Grand Prix of France, the Monte Carlo Grand Prix, the Grand Prix of Portugal, and the German Grand Prix.
20 22 persons die when a bus plunges down a mountain near San Salvador, El Salvador, after its brakes fail.
21 Tineke Lageberg, 16, of Holland, swims the 220-yd. butterfly in world record time of 2 min. 38.1 sec., in West Germany.
22 Regular air service established between London and Moscow.
23 Smallpox epidemic in Iraq; 300 persons die.

Nautilus, the world's first nuclear-powered submarine

1 Xerox produces its first commercial copying machine. [1938:SCI/1]
2 Pauling presents the UN with a petition signed by 11,021 scientists demanding an end to nuclear weapons testing. He claims that present radiation will cause 5 million birth defects or cases of cancer in the next 300 generations.
3 National Aeronautics and Space Administration (NASA) is established with T. Keith Glennan as administrator.
4 *Bionics* is coined to describe artificial machines or systems that work and/or look like living systems.
5 Stereo LPs are introduced.
6 Federal Aviation Agency (FAA) is established to ensure air safety.
7 *Nautilus* makes the

13 The Soviets launch Sputnik 3. Much scientific data is obtained from this unmanned satellite.
14 The Mohole Project, a part of the IGY research, proposes to drill a hole through the Earth's crust to the mantle.
15 Viktor A. Ambartsumian, Armenian astronomer, publishes *Theoretical Astrophysics,* a textbook which addresses many of the modern astronomical problems.
16 Nobel Prize, Chemistry: Sanger, for determining the chemical structure of insulin.
17 Nobel Prize, Physics: Cherenkov, for discovering the Cherenkov effect, and Ilya Frank and Igor Tamm, Soviet physicists, for providing the theoretical justification of the Cherenkov effect.
[1934:SCI/14]

1 National Defense Education Act is signed; authorizes low-interest, long-term tuition loans to college and graduate students.
2 Pan-American World Airways begins transatlantic jet service. Regular commercial jet flights begin in U.S. This year, for first time, airlines carry more transatlantic passengers than ships do.
3 U.S. churches report large increases in membership since 1950; those with greatest percentages of gain are Roman Catholic Church, Southern Baptist Convention, Churches of Christ, and Methodists: a total of 13 million new members.
4 Fire in Our Lady of the Angels Roman Catholic school in Chicago kills 87 children and 3 nurses.
5 An Air Force KC-135

7 Supreme Religious Center for World Jewry is dedicated in Jerusalem, Israel.
8 Under First Offenders Act no adult is to be imprisoned in Britain if there is a more appropriate way of dealing with him or her.
9 Brit. explorer Vivian Fuchs reaches South Pole traveling overland.
10 There are 160 electronic computers in use in Europe (1000 in U.S.).
11 First parking meters used in London.
12 World Exhibition in Brussels.
13 Severe famine in Eritrea and Tigre, Ethiopia, following drought and locusts.

1958

History and Politics — America

after Democrats and Republicans criticize him for accepting gifts from a Boston industrialist. "Conflict of interest" is cited.
7 Pres. Eisenhower signs antirecession bill to stimulate housing construction.
8 Nelson A. Rockefeller is elected Governor of New York. He is reelected in 1962, 1966, and 1970.
9 Presidential pension law provides income for the first time to former Presidents.

History and Politics — Elsewhere

draw troops from Tunisia except for Bizerte.
18 Egypt and Syria merge to form the United Arab Republic, with Nasser as President. U.S.S.R. agrees to loan Egypt $100 million toward the building of the Aswan High Dam.
19 Iraq and Jordan form Arab Union. Gen. Abdul Karim Kassem leads coup that overthrows the Iraqi monarchy. King Faisal II is assassinated and Iraq is proclaimed a republic, with Kassem as Premier. Arab Union is dissolved.
20 Chinese Communists shell off-shore islands of Quemoy and Little Quemoy, outposts of the Chinese Nationalists. Negotiations for a cease-fire fail.
21 West Indies Federation is formed by 10 British territories.
22 Castro increases his "war" against the Batista regime in Cuba.
23 Muhammad Ayub Khan becomes President of Pakistan after a military coup.

The Arts — America

composes the song "Satin Doll."
8 Uris writes about the struggle to establish Israel in his book, *Exodus*.
9 Auchincloss publishes *Venus in Sparta*.
10 Hannah Arendt, writer, publishes *The Human Condition*.
11 John D. MacDonald, writer, publishes *The Executioners*.
12 John Barth publishes *The End of the Road*.
13 Abraham Rattner, painter, paints "Song of Esther" in the abstract expressionist style.
14 George Garrett publishes *King of the Mountain*.
15 D'Amboise stars in Balanchine's ballet *Stars and Stripes*.
16 Stravinsky completes *Threni*, his first fully serial composition.
17 Alvin Ailey, dance director, choreographs *Blue's Suite*.

The Arts — Elsewhere

claimed *A Taste of Honey*.
23 Harold Pinter, Eng. playwright, baffles audiences with his drama, *The Birthday Party*.
24 Arnold Wesker, Eng. dramatist, completes *Chicken Soup With Barley*, the first of three Socialist plays about Jews in London (*I'm Talking About Jerusalem*, 1960; *Chips With Everything*, 1962).
25 Genêt writes the violent drama, *The Blacks*.
26 Jorge Amado, Braz. novelist, publishes *Gabriela, Clove and Cinnamon*.

1959

History and Politics — America

1 Alaska becomes 49th state.
2 Hawaii becomes 50th state.
3 Virginia Supreme Court rules that state's laws against school integration are unconstitutional. Desegregation of schools in Norfolk and Arlington begins.
4 Supreme Court upholds injunction under the Taft-Hartley Act, ending 116-day steel strike in Pittsburgh.
5 Vice Pres. Nixon engages in famous "kitchen debate" with Soviet Premier Khrushchev in Moscow.
6 Supreme Court rules that a person can be tried for the same offense in both state and federal courts (double jeopardy).
7 New York City studies the possibility of becoming the

History and Politics — Elsewhere

15 Castro's forces topple Batista's government in Cuba. Castro executes Batista's supporters and sets up a totalitarian regime. Batista flees to the Dominican Republic.
16 Settlement among Britain, Greece, and Turkey provides for the independence of Cyprus. Makarios returns from exile and is elected President of Cyprus.
17 Soviets demand peace treaty between East and West Germany. Western powers seek the reunification of Germany on the basis of free elections. Foreign ministers confer in Geneva and fail to reach a resolution.
18 Rómulo Betancourt is elected President of Venezuela. He initiates economic and educational reforms.

The Arts — America

1 Styne and Sondheim collaborate on the score of *Gypsy*, starring Ethel Merman, and featuring the songs "Let Me Entertain You" and "Everything's Coming Up Roses."
2 Rodgers and Hammerstein's *The Sound of Music*, starring Mary Martin, features the songs "Do-Re-Mi," "My Favorite Things," and "Climb Ev'ry Mountain."
3 Lorraine Hansberry, playwright, publishes *Raisin in the Sun*, which becomes the first drama by a black woman to be produced on Broadway.
4 Edward Albee,

The Arts — Elsewhere

11 Günter Grass, Pol.-Ger. writer, publishes *The Tin Drum*.
12 Anouilh completes *Becket, or The Honor of God*, a play about Thomas à Becket's conflicts with Henry II.
13 Eng. writer Alan Sillitoe publishes *The Loneliness of the Long Distance Runner*.
14 François Truffaut, Fr. film maker, is named best director by the Cannes Film Festival for his New Wave movie, *The 400 Blows*.
15 Theodor Adorno, Ger. music critic, publishes *Theory of Modern Music*.
16 Magritte paints "The Castle of the Pyrenees."

Science & Technology

America

first underwater crossing of the North Pole.

8 Explorer I is America's first satellite. Results sent back from this unmanned vehicle lead to the discovery of the Van Allen belts—high energy radiation surrounding the Earth—by Explorer's designer, James Van Allen.

9 Vanguard I, an unmanned satellite, proves that the Earth is pear-shaped with a bulge in the Southern Hemisphere.

10 Project Mercury is organized to put a man in orbit.

11 Project Score, an unmanned probe, transmits a prerecorded message from Pres. Eisenhower—the first voice received from outer space.

12 Nobel Prize, Physiology or Medicine: G. Beadle and E. Tatum for proving that genes are the units of heredity; and J. Lederberg for work in bacterial genetics.

Lorraine Hansberry, American playwright

Elsewhere

Miscellaneous

America

piloted by Col. Harry Burrell, sets a New York-to-London speed record of 5 hr., 27 min., 42.8 sec., for an average speed of 630.2 mph.

6 School bus collides with a car and plunges into The Big Sandy River near Prestonburg, Ky. The driver and 27 children are drowned.

Elsewhere

America

1 *Trieste,* a deep-sea bathyscaphe, dives to a record depth of 18,000 ft.

2 *Savannah,* the world's first nuclear-powered commercial cargo ship, is launched.

3 GE demonstrates a radio-optical telescope tracking station for following and monitoring space vehicles.

4 International Atomic Energy Agency is formed to explore peaceful uses of atomic energy.

5 Heat produced in a nuclear reaction is converted directly into electricity via a plasma thermocouple.

6 Lick Observatory (Calif.) installs a reflecting telescope with a 120-in. mirror.

Elsewhere

16 The Soviets launch three important unmanned spacecrafts: Luna 1, the first spacecraft to reach escape velocity; Luna 2, which lands on the Moon; and Luna 3, which photographs the dark side of the Moon.

17 Louis S.B. Leakey, Eng. anthropologist, and his wife Mary, discover the fossil remains of a manlike creature that lived about 1.75 million years ago.

18 Lovell publishes *The Individual and the Universe,* based on a series of lectures given by the author over British radio.

19 Burnet publishes *The Clonal Selection Theory of Acquired Immunity.*

20 Iosif S. Shklovsky,

America

1 Nationwide steel strike lasts 116 days; longest steel strike in U.S. history.

2 Alaska, with Juneau as capital, becomes 49th state. Its area is 86,400 sq. mi., making it the largest state; its population is 191,000, smallest of any state.

3 Hawaii becomes 50th state. Population is about 656,000; land area is 6424 sq. mi., consisting of 8 major and 7 minor islands. Population is Japanese, Caucasian, Hawaiian, Filipino, and Chinese.

4 U.S.S. *George Washington* is commissioned; first nuclear submarine able to carry and launch missiles.

5 American Football

Elsewhere

10 Pope John XXIII calls for Vatican Council II, first ecumenical council since 1870.

11 DeBeers Corporation in Johannesburg, South Africa, manufactures a synthetic diamond.

12 Alfred Dean lands a 2664-lb. shark at Ceduna, Australia.

13 First British drive-in bank opens in Liverpool.

14 Flood caused by collapse of Malpasset Dam in Fréjus, France, leaves 412 persons dead.

15 British hovercraft crosses English Channel in 2 hrs.

16 Great Britain has 10.4 million television sets; West Germany, 2 million; France, 1.5 million.

1959

America	Elsewhere	America	Elsewhere

51st state.

8 Christian A. Herter succeeds Dulles as Secretary of State.

9 Federal court rules unconstitutional the Arkansas law under which Gov. Faubus shut the Little Rock public schools. [1958:HIST/1]

10 Soviet Premier Khrushchev visits the U.S. and holds talks with Pres. Eisenhower.

11 Pres. Eisenhower makes 3-week trip to 11 countries in Europe, Asia, and Africa.

12 Supreme Court refuses to reconsider lower court ruling against travel to Red China by U.S. citizens.

13 St. Lawrence Seaway is opened.

14 Gus Hall becomes Secretary General of U.S. Communist Party.

---

19 Violent anti-European riots occur in Kinshasa. Belgium announces a program for eventual independence for the Belgian Congo (now Zaire).

20 Pres. de Gaulle offers Algerians the right to choose independence during elections held within four years after peace is restored in Algeria.

21 Pres. Nasser criticizes Soviet interference in Arab affairs. Arab League states pro-Communist government in Iraq threatens Arab unity.

22 Chinese Communist forces occupy Lhasa, Tibet. Chinese Premier Chou En-lai dissolves the Tibetan government. Dalai Lama seeks asylum in India, and the Chinese install the Panchen Lama in his place as ruler in Tibet.

23 De Valera becomes President of Ireland.

24 Black Africans revolt against British rule in Nyasaland (now Malawi).

---

dramatist, publishes *The Zoo Story.*

5 Construction of the Solomon Guggenheim Museum is completed. It is the only building designed by Frank Lloyd Wright in New York City.

6 Robert Rauschenberg, pop artist, creates "Monogram," the most spectacular of the "combine paintings" in which real objects are attached to the canvas.

7 Philip Roth, writer, publishes *Goodbye Columbus.*

8 D.H. Lawrence's *Lady Chatterley's Lover* is published after a 30-year ban because of obscenity. **[1928:ARTS/16]**

9 Berry Gordy, Jr., entrepreneur, founds Motown Records, the company responsible for most of the great "Soul" groups of the 1960s.

10 Burroughs further explores the world of the drug addict in *Naked Lunch.* **[1953:ARTS/1]**

---

17 Tony Richardson, Brit. Neorealist film maker, directs *Look Back in Anger.*

18 John Arden, Brit. playwright, writes *Serjeant Musgrave's Dance.*

19 Henze's ballet, *Undine,* combines classical and jazz elements.

20 Alain Resnais, Fr. New Wave film maker, directs *Hiroshima mon amour.*

21 Clément directs the film thriller, *Purple Noon.*

22 Ionesco writes the play, *Rhinoceros.*

23 Miró prepares a mural for the UNESCO building, Paris.

24 Stockhausen composes *Kontakte,* electronic music.

1960

1 Blacks stage sit-ins in South to force desegregation of lunch counters and other public places.

2 U-2 photographic reconnaissance plane piloted by Francis Gary Powers is shot down over Soviet territory. Premier Khrushchev denounces U.S. spying missions. Powers is imprisoned by the Soviets and released in 1962 in exchange for convicted Soviet spy Rudolf Abel. Pres. Eisenhower suspends U-2 flights.

3 Premier Castro confiscates U.S. property in Cuba. U.S. places an embargo on exports to Cuba.

---

11 Israeli agents capture Adolf Eichmann, Ger. Nazi official, in Argentina. He is tried and hanged (1962) for crimes against Jews and against humanity during World War II.

12 Belgian Congo gains independence. Katanga province secedes, and civil disorder breaks out.

13 UN troops go to the Congo to restore order. Joseph Kasavubu becomes the Congo's first President, defeating his rival Patrice Lumumba with the help of Col. Mobutu Sese Seko.

14 Walter Ulbricht becomes East German Communist

---

1 Harper Lee, writer, publishes the Pulitzer Prize-winning novel, *To Kill a Mockingbird.*

2 Chubby Checker, singer, causes an international dance craze with his recording of "The Twist."

3 William Shirer, journalist, publishes *The Rise and Fall of the Third Reich,* a history of Nazi Germany.

4 Hitchcock releases the suspense thriller *Psycho,* starring Anthony Perkins and Janet Leigh.

5 John Updike,

---

15 Fr. director Jean-Luc Godard's *Breathless,* an experimental film produced without a script, marks the official start of the New Wave movement in film making.

16 Bolt writes *A Man For All Seasons,* a play based on the life of Sir Thomas More.

17 Fellini directs the film, *La Dolce Vita.*

18 The *Complete Works* of Mex. writer Mariano Azuela includes *Los de abajo* (1916), an important novel about the Mexi-

Science & Technology		Miscellaneous		
America	**Elsewhere**	**America**	**Elsewhere**	
7 Christian Anfinsen, biochemist, publishes *Molecular Basis of Evolution*. **8** National Radio Astronomy Observatory (W.Va.) announces plans to listen for radio signals from intelligent beings on other planets. **[1958:SCI/11]** **9** NASA selects seven astronauts. **10** Vanguard II, the first weather station in space, transmits photographs of the cloud cover. **11** Pioneer IV, a lunar probe, misses the Moon and enters orbit around the Sun. **12** Two monkeys, Abel and Baker, return safely from a space flight that reaches an altitude of 300 miles. **13** Explorer VI returns the first TV pictures of Earth. **14** Nobel Prize, Physics: E. Segré and O. Chamberlain for proving the existence of antiprotons. **15** Nobel Prize, Physiology or Medicine: S. Ochoa and A. Kornberg for synthesizing RNA and DNA.	Soviet astronomer, suggests that the moons of Mars may actually be satellites launched by Martians. Scientists throughout the world scoff. **21** Nobel Prize, Chemistry: Heyrovsky, for his development of polarography. **[1941:SCI/15]**	League is formed. **6** St. Lawrence Seaway opens. It is world's largest inland waterway; ships travel 135 mi. from Montreal to Lake Ontario and through other Great Lakes, 2,300 mi. inland from Atlantic Ocean. **7** Truck loaded with 6½ tons of dynamite and ammonium nitrate explodes, 11 persons killed, 100 injured. 8 blocks in Rosebury, Ore., leveled by blast. **8** National Council of Churches announces that church membership is 109.5 million. **9** American Soap Box Derby is won by Barry Townsend, an Indiana 13-year-old.		
1 Theodore Maiman, physicist, develops the first LASER (*Light Amplification by Stimulated Emission of Radiation*). **2** Neuristors, tiny bionic devices that act like nerve cells, are developed. **3** Quasars, or QSOs (quasi-stellar objects), are detected by Alan Sandage and other radio-astronomers at Palomar Observatory. **4** Meter is standardized based on the wavelength of red-orange light from krypton-86. **5** Birth control pills are made available to the	**17** Sputnik 5 is launched by the Soviets. Two dogs and six mice survive the journey. **18** Derek Barton, Eng. chemist, discovers a chemical reaction that simplifies the synthesis of aldosterone, an adrenal gland enzyme. **19** Jane van Lawick-Goodall, Eng. zoologist, begins her study of the behavior of African chimpanzees. **20** The International System of Units (SI), based on the metric system, is adopted as the worldwide standard at the	**1** First successful underwater launching of Polaris missiles; they are fired from submerged atomic submarine at targets more than 1100 mi. away. **2** Population is 179.3 million. Shifts in population cause a change in number of seats in House of Representatives for 25 states; trend is mainly westward, with California gaining 8 seats. **3** Automobile industry begins shift to compact cars to meet falling sales and imports of foreign economy and sports models.	**9** Brasilia, a planned modern city, is new capital of Brazil, replacing Rio de Janeiro. **10** Coal mine explosion kills 437 persons in Coalbrook, South Africa. **11** Archaeologists begin saving treasures in the Aswan High Dam region of Nubia (Egypt) before flooding begins. **12** More biblical texts are discovered in the Dead Sea region. **[1947:MISC/8]** **13** Air France Boeing 707 jet crashes at Orly Airport, Paris; 130 persons die.	**1960**

America	Elsewhere	America	Elsewhere

History and Politics — America

4 Pres. Eisenhower makes goodwill tours in Far East and Latin America.
5 Social Security coverage is extended to the needy aged.
6 Pres. Eisenhower's foreign policies are denounced by Soviet Premier Khrushchev at UN General Assembly.
7 Republican presidential nominee Nixon and Democratic nominee Kennedy engage in four televised debates.
8 Soviets shoot down U.S. RB-47 reconnaissance bomber, charging continual U.S. spying missions.
9 Sen. Kennedy and Sen. Lyndon Baines Johnson are elected President and Vice President, respectively, on the Democratic ticket. Kennedy receives 303 electoral votes, Nixon 219, and Sen. Harry F. Byrd of Virginia 15 from "Dixiecrats." Kennedy becomes, at 43, the youngest man ever elected President and the first Roman Catholic President.
10 U.S. warns North Vietnam and Communist China not to intervene militarily in Laos.

History and Politics — Elsewhere

leader.
15 Cyprus gains independence. Conflicts begin between the Greek Cypriot majority, who want unification with Greece, and the Turkish Cypriot minority.
16 France explodes its first atomic bomb in southwestern Algeria.
17 Organization of American States (OAS) imposes sanctions on the Dominican Republic. Pres. Rafael Trujillo Molina is accused of instigating an attempt on the life of Pres. Betancourt of Venezuela. Trujillo resigns and Joaquin Balaguer becomes President.
18 Viet Cong, backed by North Vietnam, establish the National Front for the Liberation of South Vietnam.
19 Austria, Denmark, Great Britain, Norway, Portugal, Sweden, and Switzerland form the European Free Trade Association (EFTA) as a counterpart to the Common Market. [1957:HIST/13]
20 The Central African Republic, Gabon, Ivory Coast, Mauritania, Mali, Upper Volta, Niger, Nigeria, Chad, Dahomey (now Benin), Cameroon, Malagasy, Senegal, Somalia, Togo, and the Congo Rupublic (Brazzaville) become independent nations.

The Arts — America

writer, publishes *Rabbit, Run,* a novel about a former high school athlete's problems coping with life.
6 Broadway musicals this year include *The Fantasticks* ("Try to Remember"), *Oliver!* ("As Long As He Needs Me"), *Bye Bye Birdie* ("Put on a Happy Face"), and Lerner and Loewe's *Camelot.*
7 E.L. Doctorow publishes *Welcome to Hard Times.*
8 Lillian Hellman publishes *Toys in the Attic.*
9 Arthur Kopit, playwright, writes *Oh Dad, Poor Dad, Mama's Hung You in the Closet and I'm Feelin' So Bad.*
10 John Barth publishes the novel *The Sot-Weed Factor.*
11 Albee publishes *The Death of Bessie Smith* and *The Sandbox.*
12 Vidal publishes *The Best Man.*
13 Jack Tworkov, abstract expressionist, paints "Boon," using his characteristic colored stripes.
14 Scott O'Dell, novelist, publishes *Island of the Blue Dolphin.*

The Arts — Elsewhere

can Revolution.
19 Marie Rambert, Brit. dancer and choreographer, publishes *Dancers of Mercury: The Story of Ballet Rambert,* the history of England's oldest ballet company, founded 1926.
20 Michelangelo Antonioni directs *L'Avventura,* a classic in modern film making.
21 Pinter writes the popular drama, *The Caretaker.*
22 Arden writes *The Happy Haven,* a farce about an old folks' home.
23 Dan. novelist Isak Dinesen (Karen Blixen) publishes *Shadows on the Grass.*
24 Britten composes the opera, *A Midsummer Night's Dream.* [1595:ARTS/2]
25 Hepworth completes "Meridian," a huge sculpture.

1961

History and Politics — America

1 U.S. breaks diplomatic relations with Cuba, calling it a "Soviet satellite." About 1500 Cuban exiles trained by the U.S. make unsuccessful attempt to invade Cuba and overthrow Premier Castro ("Bay of Pigs"). Failure is blamed on the CIA and lack of air support.
2 Pres. Kennedy establishes the Peace Corps to give trained manpower and technical assistance to underdeveloped countries.
3 Pres. Kennedy proposes the Alliance for Progress to

History and Politics — Elsewhere

12 East German Communists build wall dividing East and West Berlin.
13 UN Secretary General Hammarskjöld is killed in a plane crash in Northern Rhodesia (now Zambia) while on a mission to the Congo.
14 UN forces disarm Katangese rebels. Col. Mobutu begins attack on Katanga and its leader Moise Kapenda Tshombe.
15 Africans rebel against Portuguese rule in Angola.
16 Union of South Africa leaves the British Common-

The Arts — America

1 Pete Seeger composes "Where Have All the Flowers Gone."
2 *Tropic of Cancer* and *Tropic of Capricorn,* two novels by Henry Miller, are published in the U.S. after a 30-year ban because of obscenity.
3 Harold Robbins, author, publishes *The Carpetbaggers.*
4 Robert Heinlein, science fiction author, publishes *Stranger in a Strange Land.*

The Arts — Elsewhere

14 Cinéma Vérité, a film movement characterized by realistic, often unrehearsed, action and dialogue, is exemplified by Jean Rouch's *Chronicle of a Summer* (Fr.). Other major films (directors) include: *Knife in the Water* (Polanski); *The Job* (Olmi); *Last Year at Marienbad* (Resnais); *Boccaccio '70* (Fellini); *Through A Glass Darkly* (Bergman); *Jules and Jim* (Truf-

Science & Technology		Miscellaneous	
America	**Elsewhere**	**America**	**Elsewhere**

America (Science & Technology)

public.

6 Atomic hydrogen maser is developed.

7 X-15, an experimental rocket-powered airplane, is flown at 2196 mph.

8 *Triton,* a nuclear submarine, travels around the world under water.

9 Woodward synthesizes chlorophyll.

10 Robert Pound, physicist, detects a red shift caused by the Earth's gravitational field.

11 Pioneer 5 is launched to study radiation and magnetic fields between Earth and Venus.

12 Tiros 1 is the first weather satellite launched.

13 Midas 2 satellite will provide early warning in case of missile attacks.

14 Echo 1, a huge, metal-covered plastic balloon, is launched. A passive communications satellite, it reflects radio signals from one place on Earth to another.

15 Nobel Prize, Physics: D. Glaser for inventing the bubble chamber.

16 Nobel Prize, Chemistry: W. Libby for developing radiocarbon dating.

Elsewhere (Science & Technology)

11th General Conference on Weights and Measures.

21 Nobel Prize, Physiology or Medicine: Burnet and Medawar, for discovering that the body acquires immunological tolerance to tissue transplants.

John Fitzgerald Kennedy, 35th U.S. President

America (Miscellaneous)

4 Thirty persons killed and heavy damage done as Hurricane Donna ravages the Atlantic Coast from Florida to New England.

5 16-year-old chesswonder, Bobby Fischer, successfully defends his U.S. chess championship in a tournament in New York City.

6 Alan Freed, originator of the term "rock 'n' roll" and the person who popularized the new music, is arrested on charges of commercial bribery. 7 other persons involved in "payola" scandals also arrested.

7 United Airlines and Trans World Airlines planes collide in fog over New York City, killing 134 in air and on ground.

8 Women's transcontinental air race is won by Mrs. Aileen Saunders. She flies 2709 mi. in 18 hr. 27 min.

Elsewhere (Miscellaneous)

14 Three women ordained as priests in the Swedish Lutheran Church.

15 Earthquake sets off tidal wave and fire, destroys most of Agadir, Morocco; 10,000-12,000 people die.

16 Tokyo's population is 9.6 million; London's, 8.1; Shanghai's, 6.2; Moscow's, 5; Mexico City's, 4.8; Buenos Aires's, 4.5; and Bombay's, 4.1.

17 152 children die in Syria in a movie-house fire.

18 Olympic games in Rome, Italy.

19 Earthquakes, volcanic eruptions, and tidal waves strike Chile; 5700 people die.

1961

America (Science & Technology)

1 Alan Shepard is America's first man in space. He reaches an altitude of 115 miles in a 15 minute flight aboard Freedom 7, a Mercury Mission capsule.

2 Carl Sagan, astrophysicist, publishes *The Atmosphere of Mars and Venus.*

3 Institute for Space Studies (N.Y.) holds a two-month seminar on the origin of the solar system.

4 Gell-Mann develops

Elsewhere (Science & Technology)

12 Yuri Gagarin, Soviet cosmonaut, becomes the first man in space aboard Vostok 1. Four months later, Vostok 2 is launched with cosmonaut Gherman Titov aboard. Vostok 2 stays in space for 24 hours.

13 The Soviet Sputnik 8-Venera 1 project includes the first launching from a satellite in orbit around the Earth.

14 J. Piccard publishes *Seven Miles Down.*

15 Watson and Crick

America (Miscellaneous)

1 Twenty-third Amendment to the Constitution allows residents of the District of Columbia to vote in presidential elections.

2 First intercontinental ballistic missile (ICBM) fired; travels 4200 mi.

3 78 persons die when a TWA constellation crashes in Hinsdale, Ill., 4 minutes after take-off from Chicago's Midway Airport.

4 A.J. Foyt, Jr., wins the Indianapolis Speed-

Elsewhere (Miscellaneous)

10 Modern English prose translation of the New Testament, the *New English Bible,* is published in London.

11 China's population is 660 million; India's, 435; the U.S.S.R.'s, 209; Japan's, 95; Pakistan's, 94; Brazil's, 66; West Germany's, 54; Great Britain's, 53; Italy's, 50; and France's, 47.

12 The *rand,* decimal currency is introduced into South Africa; equal to about 100 cents and

give U.S. aid toward relief of Latin American economic and social problems.
4 Newton N. Minow, Chairman of the Federal Communications Commission, calls TV a "vast wasteland" and asks for more educational programs.
5 Congress of Racial Equality (CORE) sponsors the "Freedom Riders," interracial groups that seek to end segregation on interstate bus routes in the South. Demonstrations are made against *de facto* segregation in the North.
6 Black Muslims (black nationalist and religious group) under Malcolm X advocate black power and separation of the races.
7 Senate voices concern about growing influence of the John Birch Society, a right-wing, secret society dedicated to fighting Communism.
8 Pres. Kennedy and Soviet Premier Khrushchev hold talks on Berlin, Laos, and disarmament. He asks Congress for defense funds to counter growing Soviet threat in Europe.
9 Pres. Kennedy accepts full responsibility for unsuccessful Cuban invasion.
10 Pres. Kennedy proposes $1.8 billion, 10-year, space exploration program.
11 David Dean Rusk becomes Secretary of State, and Robert Strange McNamara becomes Secretary of Defense.

wealth of Nations and becomes a republic.
17 Trujillo is assassinated. [1960:HIST/17]
18 U.S.S.R. resumes nuclear testing, exploding a 50-plus megaton bomb in the Arctic region.
19 Organization for Economic Cooperation and Development (OECD) is formed by Western nations to expand world trade and to aid underdeveloped countries.
20 Kenyatta is released from prison in Kenya. [1953:HIST/19]
21 Algerian Muslim rebels fight French troops for self-rule.
22 Tunisians besiege French naval installations at Bizerte; Tunisia breaks relations with France.
23 Army officers take control of Syria; the country withdraws from the United Arab Republic. [1958:HIST/18]
24 India annexes the Portuguese colonies of Goa, Damao, and Diu.
25 Military junta overthrows the civilian government in South Korea.

5 Neil Simon, playwright, publishes the comedy play, *Come Blow Your Horn*.
6 J.D. Salinger publishes *Franny and Zooey*.
7 Steinbeck publishes *The Winter of Our Discontent,* a novel about the moral collapse of a New England aristocrat.
8 Arthur Miller writes the screenplay *The Misfits* as a vehicle for his wife, actress Marilyn Monroe.
9 The film *Breakfast at Tiffany's* features the song "Moon River" by composers Henry Mancini and Johnny Mercer. [1958:ARTS/6]
10 Vonnegut publishes the novel *Mother Night*.
11 Reuben Nakian, abstract sculptor, completes the terra cotta "Leda and the Swan."
12 Popular Broadway shows this year include *How to Succeed in Business Without Really Trying,* with Robert Morse and Rudy Vallee and a score by Frank Loesser, and *Carnival,* starring Anna Maria Alberghetti, and featuring a score by Bob Merrill.
13 Uris publishes *Mila 18,* about the Warsaw uprising.

faut); *Accatone!* (Pasolini).
15 Jorge Luis Borges, Arg. writer, comes to international attention when he and Beckett share the prestigious Formentor Prize.
16 Scot. writer Muriel Spark publishes her best-known novel, *The Prime of Miss Jean Brodie*.
17 Osborne produces *Luther,* a play based on the life of Martin Luther.
18 Museum of the Chinese Revolution opens in Peking.
19 Pop Art becomes popular in England.
20 Murdoch publishes *A Severed Head,* a novel.
21 Uwe Johnson, Ger. "anti-novelist," publishes *The Third Book About Achim*.

1962

1 U.S. troops on training mission in Vietnam are ordered to fire if fired upon by enemy troops. New U.S. military command, known as Military Assistance Command (MAC) is set up in South Vietnam. U.S. Army officers are killed by Communist guerrillas near Saigon.
2 U.S. reconnaissance planes discover the existence of Soviet missile and bomber bases

10 France and Algeria sign truce, ending seven years of civil war between Muslims and French in Algeria. Pres. de Gaulle of France recognizes Algeria's sovereignty following a unanimous vote for independence by the Algerians.
11 Burmese diplomat U Thant becomes UN Secretary General.
12 Georges Pompidou be-

1 Andy Warhol, leading painter of the pop art movement, paints "Green Coca-Cola Bottles" and "Marilyn Monroe."
2 Richard Stankiewicz, junk sculptor, unveils "Untitled," an abstract conglomeration of rusty machinery.
3 Jim Dine, pop artist, creates "Five

14 Aleksandr Solzhenitsyn, Sov. novelist, publishes *One Day in the Life of Ivan Denisovich,* the story of life in a forced-labor camp.
15 Anthony Burgess, Eng. novelist, publishes *A Clockwork Orange,* a popular work that incorporates both Surrealism and science fiction.

Science & Technology

America

the *Eight-Fold Way,* a method of grouping subatomic particles into families.
5 Chicago Heart Association begins recording children's heart sounds as a means of detecting defects.
6 Kennedy states the U.S. goal in its space program: "landing an American on the Moon in this decade."
7 Virgil "Gus" Grissom is America's second man in space as he makes a 16-minute flight aboard the Mercury Mission's Liberty Bell 7.
8 Transit 4A, a communications satellite, is the first spacecraft to use nuclear power.
9 Nobel Prize, Physics: R. Hofstadter for describing the structure of protons and nucleons.
10 Nobel Prize, Chemistry: Melvin Calvin for describing the chemical reactions of photosynthesis.
11 Nobel Prize, Physiology or Medicine: Georg von Békésy for discoveries about the inner ear and hearing.

Elsewhere

propose that each amino acid has a specific, 3-base DNA code.
16 François Jacob and Jacques-Lucien Monod, Fr. biologists, suggest the existence of messenger RNA (mRNA), a substance that carries genetic information to the ribosome (the cell structure where proteins are made).
17 Nobel Prize, Physics: Rudolf L. Mössbauer, for discovering the Mössbauer effect, used to measure the magnetic fields of atomic nuclei.

Actress Marilyn Monroe

Miscellaneous

America

way Memorial Day 500-mile auto race and a prize of $111,400.
5 447 homes, including some owned by well-known Hollywood figures, are destroyed by fire in the Bel Air-Brentwood suburbs of Los Angeles.
6 Roger Maris of the New York Yankees hits his 60th home run, sets record for a 162-game schedule. (Babe Ruth's record of 60 homers in a 154-game schedule remains.)
7 American Unitarian Association and the Universalist Church of America merge to form the Unitarian Universalist Association, with combined membership of 190,000.
8 74 Army recruits are killed when a chartered Imperial Airlines Constellation crashes and burns near Richmond, Va.
9 Wilma Rudolph runs the 220-yd. dash in 25 sec., a women's world indoor record.

Elsewhere

1.40 U.S. dollars.
13 Antonio Abertando is first to swim English Channel non-stop both ways. He is in the water 43 hr., longer than any other channel swimmer.
14 Tanganyika conference moves to protect African wildlife.
15 Farthing, bronze coin equal to 1/4 of a penny, is discontinued in Britain.

---

1 Woodward synthesizes tetracycline, a widely used antibiotic.
2 Carson publishes *Silent Spring,* a book about the effects of chemical pesticides that sparks interest in controlling environmental pollution.
3 Marshall Nirenberg, biochemist, discovers the genetic code (DNA structure) for an amino acid.

14 Great Britain and the U.S. launch the Ariel satellite, the first international space project.
15 A thorough description of the research taking place at Jodrell Bank is given in Lovell's *The Exploration of Outer Space.*
16 The Soviets launch two manned spacecrafts: Vostok 3, with cosmonaut

1 Rt. Rev. John Melville Burgess is consecrated as suffragan bishop of Massachusetts, the first U.S. Negro bishop of the Protestant Episcopal Church to serve a predominantly white diocese.
2 More than $1 million is taken during the robbery of a mail truck at Plymouth, Mass.
3 Wilt Chamberlain of

10 World population is about 3.1 billion. Of the world's adult population of 1.6 billion, about 66% are literate.
11 20 years after beginning of nuclear age, Great Britain and the U.S.S.R. each have 39 atomic reactors in operation.
12 French jet crashes and burns in Paris; 130 die.

1962

History and Politics		The Arts	
America	**Elsewhere**	**America**	**Elsewhere**

History and Politics — America	History and Politics — Elsewhere	The Arts — America	The Arts — Elsewhere
in Cuba. Pres. Kennedy demands removal of installations and orders a blockade of Cuba. Soviet Premier Khrushchev agrees to dismantle bases and remove missiles. U.S. lifts blockade. **3** Congress passes constitutional amendment (24th) forbidding the use of a poll tax or other tax as a requirement for voting in federal elections. [1964:HIST/1] **4** U.S. removes its military tanks from the Berlin Wall; Soviets remove theirs. **5** Billie Sol Estes, Texas agricultural financier involved in business deals with the Department of Agriculture, is found guilty of and sentenced to 8 years in prison for swindling a Pecos farmer. Other state and federal indictments against him are for theft, mail fraud, false statements, and criminal antitrust violations. **6** Felix Frankfurter and Charles E. Whittaker retire from the Supreme Court. Pres. Kennedy appoints Arthur J. Goldberg and Byron R. White to the Court. **7** Trade Expansion Act gives President right to reduce tariffs and to assist companies hurt by lower duties. **8** Pres. Kennedy forbids racial discrimination in federally built housing. **9** Supreme Court rules that public schools can not require the recitation of prayers since it violates the First Amendment.	comes Premier of France. **13** Fighting continues between central government forces of the Congo and Katangese. [1961:HIST/14] **14** Burundi becomes an independent kingdom ruled by the mwami (Tutsi king). **15** Uganda and Trinidad-Tobago become independent nations. **16** Tanganyika (now the main part of Tanzania) becomes a republic within the British Commonwealth of Nations. Julius K. Nyerere is elected President. **17** Eritrea becomes a province of Ethiopia. Eritreans opposing the union begin guerrilla war against Emperor Haile Selassie's forces. **18** Chinese Communist forces invade India, seize territory, and announce ceasefire. **19** Pakistan adopts new constitution, establishing an Islamic republic with two federal provinces (East and West Pakistan) and two official languages (Bengali and Urdu).	Toothbrushes on Black Ground," a "combine painting." **4** Barbara Tuchman publishes *The Guns of August,* about the early battles of World War I. **5** Kubrick directs *Lolita,* a film based on Nabokov's novel. **6** Joseph Heller, novelist, publishes *Catch-22,* about the misadventures of an officer during World War II. **7** Bob Dylan, folk rock singer, achieves recognition with his song "Blowin' in the Wind." **8** Ken Kesey, writer, publishes *One Flew Over the Cuckoo's Nest.* **9** Nobel Prize, Literature: John Steinbeck. **10** Tennessee Williams publishes *The Night of the Iguana.* **11** Albee publishes *Who's Afraid of Virginia Woolf?* **12** Katherine Anne Porter publishes her only novel, *Ship of Fools.* **13** Johnny Carson, entertainer, begins as host of *The Tonight Show,* a talk show which introduces much new talent.	**16** Britten's most famous choral work, *War Requiem,* is based on the Catholic funeral Mass and the poems of Wilfred Owen. **17** Shostakovich revises an earlier work to produce his greatest opera, *Katerina Ismailova.* **18** Doris Lessing, Eng. writer, publishes *The Golden Notebook,* a popular novel. **19** BBC starts the satirical review of the news, *That Was The Week That Was,* with David Frost as host. **20** Major films (directors) include: *Winter Light* (Bergman); *Divorce—Italian Style* (Germi); *The Loneliness of the Long Distance Runner* (Richardson); *Lawrence of Arabia* (Lean); *Trial of Joan of Arc* (Bresson).
1963 **1** Pres. Kennedy proposes major medical-hospital plan for the aged to be funded through Social Security. [1965:HIST/3] **2** Supreme Court rules states must provide free legal counsel for all defendants in criminal cases. **3** Civil rights demonstrations occur throughout the country. Medgar W. Evers, Field Secretary for the NAACP, is shot and killed in	**11** U.S.S.R., Britain, and the U.S. sign treaty that prohibits nuclear testing in the atmosphere, in space, and underwater, but permits it underground. **12** Malaya, Singapore, Sarawak, and Sabah unite to form the Federation of Malaysia. Singapore becomes independent in 1965. **13** Military coup overthrows the government of Ngo Dinh Diem of South Vietnam.	**1** Sylvia Plath, poet, describes her various suicide attempts in her morbid autobiography, *The Bell Jar.* **2** Vonnegut publishes *Cat's Cradle.* **3** Roy Lichtenstein, pop artist, paints the comic-strip-like "Whaam." **4** Larry Rivers, pop artist, paints the "Dutch Masters and	**14** John LeCarré, Eng. novelist, publishes *The Spy Who Came in from the Cold.* **15** Rolf Hochhuth, Ger. dramatist, stirs international controversy with *The Deputy,* a political play. · **16** For the first time in history, a British group—the Beatles—dominates England's pop music charts. Their

Science & Technology		Miscellaneous		
America	**Elsewhere**	**America**	**Elsewhere**	
4 Semiconductor lasers are developed. **5** Cardioversion, the use of electric shock to restore normal heartbeat, is introduced. **6** University of Illinois installs a radio telescope with a 600 × 400 ft. antenna. **7** Pres. Kennedy signs the Communications Satellite Act which establishes COMSAT, a private corporation to coordinate America's role in the development of a worldwide system of communication satellites. **8** John Glenn becomes the first American to orbit the Earth. His 3 orbits aboard Friendship 7 cover 81,000 miles in less than 5 hours. **9** OSO-1, an orbiting solar observatory, is launched. **10** Ranger 4 lunar probe strikes the Moon. **11** M. Scott Carpenter completes 3 orbits aboard Aurora 7. **12** Telstar 1, the first privately financed satellite, relays TV programs from the U.S. to Europe. **13** Walter Schirra lands within 5 miles of his target after completing 6 orbits—160,000 miles—aboard Sigma 7.	Andrian Nikolayev; and Vostok 4, with cosmonaut Pavel Popovich. At one point, the two crafts come within 3.1 miles of each other. **17** Thalidomide, a sedative, is proven responsible for thousands of birth defects, disproving the belief that a fetus is protected from drugs taken by the mother. **18** Cousteau publishes *The Living Sea,* a work about underwater life. **19** Hevesy publishes *Adventures in Radioisotope Research.* **20** Nobel Prize, Chemistry: Max Perutz and John Kendrew, Eng. biochemists, for their determination of the structures of hemoglobin and myoglobin. **21** Nobel Prize, Physics: Landau, for his research into the superfluidity of liquid helium. **[1937:SCI/15]** **22** Nobel Prize, Physiology or Medicine: Crick, Watson (Amer.), and Maurice Wilkins, Eng. geneticist, for their roles in determining the structure and function of DNA.	the Philadelphia Warriors becomes first basketball player to score 100 points in a game. **4** World's fair, Century 21 Exposition, opens in Seattle. The 600-ft. Space Needle with a revolving restaurant on top is a popular attraction. **5** Arnold Palmer is voted Player of the Year by the Professional Golf Association. **6** Jim Beatty runs the indoor mile in less than 4 minutes—3:58.9—in Los Angeles. **7** Supreme Court rules that reading of prayers in New York City schools is unconstitutional. **8** U.S. successfully defends the America's Cup. *Weatherly* defeats the Australian sloop *Gretel* in 4 out of 5 races off Newport, R.I. **9** John Uelses is the first to pole-vault 16 ft.	**13** Avalanche down Huascarán, an extinct volcano in South America, kills more than 3000 people. **14** Gary Player is first nonresident of U.S. to win the Professional Golf Association championship. **15** Coal mine gas explosion kills 298 persons in Saarland, West Germany. **16** Vatican Council II opens in Rome, called by Pope John XXIII (in 1959) to promote Christian unity. **17** 163 persons killed and 400 injured in Japan when train crashes into wreckage of collision between freight train and commuter train. **18** Of the 230 million people in Africa, 29 million are Roman Catholics, 19 million Protestants, and 5 million from Coptic and Orthodox churches. There are a total of 2000 sects among Africa's religions. **19** Rod Laver (Australia) wins grand slam of tennis—all four major championships, Australian, French, British, and American. **20** Earthquake in northwestern Iran kills 10,000 people. **21** British weather reports give temperatures in Celsius as well as Fahrenheit.	
1 Maarten Schmidt, astronomer, studies the red shift of quasars and determines that these galaxies are the farthest objects from Earth and are moving away with incredible speed. **2** Lasers are used in delicate eye surgery. **3** Computers are used to determine a new, "highest" prime number: $2^{11,213} - 1$.	**15** The United Nations establishes the World Weather Watch, a program whereby standardized meteorological observations and forecasts are achieved through international cooperation. **16** The Russians launch two manned spacecraft: Vostok 5, with cosmonaut Valery Bykovsky; and Vostok 6, which carried the first woman in space,	**1** Controversial book, *The American Way of Death,* by Jessica Mitford, attacks American funeral and burial customs. It creates a great deal of interest in low-cost, dignified burials. **2** U.S. nuclear-powered submarine *Thresher* is lost in the Atlantic Ocean with 129 men on board. **3** Catholic Church approves the use of vernacu-	**8** Explosion in coal mine in Omuta, Japan, kills 447 people. **9** Teaching machines first used in British schools. **10** Hurricane and resulting tsunamis (large sea waves) leave 22,000 dead in East Pakistan. 4000 people die in Cuba and Haiti in a hurricane. **11** Britain has coldest winter since 1740.	**1963**

History and Politics

America

Jackson, Miss. Riots break out in protest. Dr. King leads massive March on Washington in support of equal rights for blacks and delivers his famous speech, "I have a dream . . . ."
4   U.S. and the U.S.S.R. agree to set up a "hot line," a direct telephone link between Washington and Moscow, to prevent the start of nuclear war by accident.
5   Sir Winston Churchill is made an honorary U.S. citizen.
6   U.S. sends task force to the Caribbean during Haitian-Dominican crisis.
7   U.S. protests the flights of two Soviet reconnaissance planes over Alaska.
8   U.S. aid to South Vietnam continues. U.S. recognizes the South Vietnamese provisional government following the overthrow of Ngo Dinh Diem's government.
9   Pres. Kennedy is assassinated (Nov. 22) in Dallas while riding in a motorcade with Gov. John B. Connally of Texas, who is severely wounded. Vice Pres. Johnson is sworn in as President. Lee Harvey Oswald, presumed assassin of Pres. Kennedy and held in police custody, is murdered by nightclub owner Jack Ruby.
10   Special commission, headed by Chief Justice Earl Warren, is named by Pres. Johnson to investigate Pres. Kennedy's assassination.

Elsewhere

Diem is murdered.
14   Organization of African Unity (OAU) is formed by 32 African countries to promote unity and economic cooperation.
15   France vetoes Britain's entry into the Common Market.
16   Ludwig Erhard becomes Chancellor of West Germany.
17   John Profumo resigns as British Secretary of War because of involvement in spy scandal. British Prime Minister Macmillan resigns and is succeeded by Sir Alex Douglas-Home.
18   Haitian exiles fail to overthrow Pres. Francois ("Papa Doc") Duvalier, dictator in Haiti since 1957.
19   Tshombe flees following successful UN operations in Katanga province. [1961:HIST/14]
20   Civil war breaks out between Greek and Turkish Cypriots over Turkish rights on Cyprus.
21   Federation of Rhodesia and Nyasaland ends. Nyasaland becomes independent (1964) as country of Malawi.
22   Sukarno proclaims himself President-for-life of Indonesia.
23   Harold Adrian Russell Philby, Soviet spy with the British intelligence service, defects to the U.S.S.R.
24   Levi Eshkol becomes Prime Minister of Israel.

The Arts

America

Cigars" series.
5   Rauschenberg's painting "Estate" takes a new direction called pop expressionism.
6   John Chamberlain, junk sculptor, creates "Silverheels," a bizarre assemblage of discarded auto parts.
7   Marisol, sculptor, creates "The Family," a combination of wood, sculpture, painting, and articles of clothing.
8   Red Grooms, realist artist, paints "Coney Island."
9   Mary McCarthy's novel *The Group* follows the lives of eight Vassar graduates.
10   Susan Sontag publishes *The Benefactor,* a novel about people who are unable to distinguish reality from fantasy.
11   Auchincloss publishes *Powers of Attorney,* a collection of short stories.
12   Edward Gorey, writer and illustrator, publishes *The West Wing* and *The Insect God.*
13   Popular TV series of the time include *The Twilight Zone, Mr. Ed, Perry Mason, Dr. Kildare, Gunsmoke, Leave It to Beaver, Bonanza, The Beverly Hillbillies,* and *The Dick Van Dyke Show.*

Elsewhere

biggest hits: "Please, Please Me" and "Love Me Do." In future years, the Beatles (Paul McCartney, John Lennon, George Harrison, and Ringo Starr) are extremely influential in the development of popular music.
17   Frederick Ashton, Eng. choreographer, produces *Marguerite and Armand,* a ballet featuring Rudolf Nureyev (defected from U.S.S.R. in 1961) and Eng. ballerina Margot Fonteyn.
18   Chagall designs murals for the ceiling of Paris Opéra.
19   Tanizaki Junichirō, Jap. novelist, publishes *Seven Japanese Tales.*
20   Britten composes *Symphony in D Major* for Sov. cellist Mstislav Rostropovich.
21   Natalia Ginzburg, Ital. writer, receives Italy's most prestigious literary award, the Strega Prize, for *Family Sayings.*
22   Soviet authorities begin a campaign to suppress "artistic rebels."
23   Major films (directors) include: *Tom Jones* (Richardson); *The Leopard* (Visconti); *8½* (Fellini); *The Silence* (Bergman).

1964

History and Politics — America

1   Twenty-fourth Amendment to the Constitution is ratified. [1962:HIST/3]
2   Pres. Hoffa of Teamsters is convicted of fraud in the misuse of union funds and of jury tampering. He begins 13-year prison term in 1967 and retains Teamsters presidency until 1971 when he resigns.
3   Supreme Court rules that both houses of a bicameral

History and Politics — Elsewhere

11   Aleksei Nikolayevich Kosygin succeeds Khrushchev as Soviet Premier and shares power with Leonid Ilyich Brezhnev, General Secretary of the Communist Party.
12   Northern Rhodesia becomes independent as the republic of Zambia, with Kenneth Kaunda as President.
13   Kenya becomes independent, with Kenyatta as Pres-

The Arts — America

1   The Supremes, a Motown trio headed by singer Diana Ross, record a string of hit songs including "Baby Love," "Stop in the Name of Love," and "Come See About Me."
2   "Beatlemania" sweeps the U.S. as the album *Meet the Beatles* sells two million copies

The Arts — Elsewhere

12   Beatlemania spreads throughout the world as the Beatles break all existing sales and popularity records with such hits as "She Loves You" and "I Want to Hold Your Hand."
13   Swiss composer Rolf Lieberman completes *Symphonie des*

Science & Technology		Miscellaneous		
America	**Elsewhere**	**America**	**Elsewhere**	

4 DeBakey develops a mechanical heart that is implanted in the chest to help the patient's own heart.
5 Arecibo Observatory, Puerto Rico, installs a radio telescope with the world's largest antenna—1000 ft. in diameter.
6 Woodward synthesizes colchicine, a pain reliever for patients with gout.
7 America's first commercial hydrofoil boat, the *Albatross,* is launched.
8 Polaroid introduces color film.
9 Enders, Weller, and Robbins develop an effective measles vaccine.
10 FDA claims that there is no direct cause-and-effect relationship between birth control pills and blood clots.
11 Chrysler tests 50 experimental gas turbine cars.
12 Color TV is relayed via satellite for the first time.
13 Gordon Cooper completes 22 orbits in 34 hours and 20 minutes aboard Faith 7. He is the first astronaut to control his flight manually, and he lands almost directly on his splashdown target.
14 Nobel Prize, Physics: E. Wigner (Amer.), M. Goeppert-Mayer (Amer.), and J. H. Jensen (Ger.) for work with atomic nuclei.

cosmonaut Valentina Tereshkova.
17 Martin Schwarzbach, Ger. geologist, publishes *Climates of the Past.*
18 Nobel Prize, Physiology or Medicine: Alan Hodgkin and Andrew Huxley, Eng. biophysicists, and Eccles, for their research into the chemistry of nerve impulses.

lar languages—English in the U.S.—in place of Latin for parts of the Mass and for the sacraments.
4 Most expensive motion picture to date, *Cleopatra,* opens in New York City and in theaters nationwide; film cost $37 million.
5 John Pennel is the first to pole-vault 17 ft.; using a fiberglass pole, he clears 17 ft. ¾ in.
6 Elizabeth Ann Bayley Seton is first U.S.-born person to be beatified (the step before sainthood) by the Roman Catholic Church. **[1975:MISC/2]**
7 Jack Nicklaus, is the youngest man to win the Masters golf tournament in Augusta, Ga.

12 Ferry capsizes and sinks in upper Nile, Egypt; more than 200 people die.
13 Religious denominations in India: Hindu, 366 million; Moslem, 47 million; Christian, 10 million; and Buddhist, 3 million.
14 Greek liner *Lakonia* sinks in the North Atlantic; 150 lives lost.
15 Tigran Petrosian (U.S.S.R.) wins world chess championship; keeps title until 1969.
16 Earthquake in Skopje, Yugoslavia, kills 1100 people.
17 Education report in Britain recommends that children not be allowed to leave school before age 16.

The Beatles, world-famous British singing group

				1964

1 Gell-Mann proposes the existence of quarks, three basic particles that make up the subatomic particles called hadrons. He also discovers the omega-minus particle whose existence had been predicted by an open position in one family of the *Eight-Fold Way.* **[1961:SCI/4]**

15 J. Piccard designs the mesoscaphe, a sightseeing bathyscaphe.
16 John Hutchinson, Eng. botanist, publishes *The Genera of Flowering Plants.*
17 A. Hodgkin publishes *Conduction of the Nervous Impulse.*
18 The Soviets launch Voshkod 1, the first 3-

1 Report by surgeon general's special committee, *Smoking and Health,* strongly links cigarette smoking with cancer (as well as other diseases) and calls for federal regulation.
2 California becomes the state with the largest population.
3 There are 162 million

11 Pope Paul VI makes pilgrimage to the Holy Land.
12 At 18th Olympic Games in Japan, strong swimming and track and field teams win 36 gold medals for the U.S. Soviet Union takes 30 gold medals, Japan 16.
13 British scientists leave England in large

History and Politics

America

Elsewhere

The Arts

America

Elsewhere

state legislature must be apportioned by population.

4 Senate invokes cloture to end 75-day filibuster by southern Senators of Civil Rights Act. Congress passes Act which prohibits discrimination in public places for reason of color, race, religion, or national origin.

5 Warren Commission Report states there was no conspiracy in the assassination of Pres. Kennedy. It finds Oswald a lone assassin. [1963:HIST/9 & 10]

6 Republican Party nominates Sen. Barry M. Goldwater of Arizona for President.

7 Three North Vietnamese PT boats attack U.S. destroyer *Maddox* in international waters in the Gulf of Tonkin. U.S. jets bomb PT boat bases and oil depot in North Vietnam. Congress passes resolution (Tonkin Gulf Resolution) which gives Pres. Johnson power to use any action necessary to repel armed attack on U.S. forces.

8 Economic Opportunity Act provides funds for youth programs, Job Corps, and community action programs in poverty-stricken areas.

9 Johnson and Sen. Hubert H. Humphrey of Minnesota are elected President and Vice President, respectively, on the Democratic ticket. Johnson wins 486 electoral votes to Goldwater's 52. Only Roosevelt, in 1936, won more electoral votes.

10 District of Columbia votes for the first time in a presidential election.

ident.

14 Island of Malta becomes independent within the British Commonwealth of Nations.

15 Tshombe returns to the Congo, and Pres. Kasavubu names him Premier of a government of national reconciliation.

16 Zanzibar and Tanganyika unite to form the republic of Tanzania.

17 UN intervention brings a ceasefire between Greek and Turkish Cypriots. [1963:HIST/20]

18 Nehru dies and Shri Lal Bahadur Shastri becomes Prime Minister of India.

19 Political fighting among socialists, leftists, and conservatives in Italy brings four-year period of social unrest and instability.

20 Ian Smith is elected Prime Minister of Rhodesia (now Zimbabwe).

21 Harold Wilson becomes British Prime Minister after Douglas-Home resigns.

22 Eisaku Sato becomes Prime Minister of Japan.

23 China supports Pakistan's proposal to permit Kashmir to choose its own allegiance in a referendum.

24 Faisal becomes King of Saudi Arabia.

25 Gustavo Díaz Ordaz is elected President of Mexico.

in one month.

3 Edward Durell Stone, architect, designs the John F. Kennedy Center for the Performing Arts in Washington, D.C.

4 Broadway musicals this year include *Hello Dolly,* starring Carol Channing, *Fiddler on the Roof,* starring Zero Mostel, and *Funny Girl,* starring Barbara Streisand and featuring a score by Styne and Merrill that includes the song "People."

5 Cheever continues his study of suburbia in the novel *The Wapshot Scandal.*

6 Larry Poons, exponent of op art, paints "Nixes Mate."

7 Kubrick directs *Dr. Strangelove,* a satirical film about the nuclear threat, starring Peter Sellers.

8 Michelangelo's "Pietà" is brought to New York for the Vatican exhibit at the World's Fair. [1498:ARTS/1]

9 *Mary Poppins,* a film starring Dick Van Dyke and Julie Andrews, becomes the most successful Disney film to date.

10 Paddy Chayefsky writes *The Americanization of Emily.*

11 Isherwood publishes *A Single Man,* a highly regarded novel about the loneliness of a homosexual intellectual.

Echanges, an unusual work calling for 156 machines conducted by a computer.

14 Lessing publishes *Children of Violence,* a novel.

15 Britten composes *Curlew River,* a work that combines elements from Japanese Nō and English medieval dramas.

16 As discothèques become more popular, jobs for live musicians begin to disappear.

17 Sartre refuses the Nobel Prize in Literature.

18 Peter Weiss, Ger. writer, completes the play, *Marat/Sade.*

19 De Sica's Oscar winning film, *Yesterday, Today and Tomorrow,* stars Marcello Mastroianni and Sophia Loren. Other major films (directors) include: *The Umbrellas of Cherbourg* (Demy); *A Hard Day's Night* (Beatles); *Red Desert* (Antonioni); *The Gospel According to Saint Matthew* (Pasolini).

1965				
1 Viet Cong attack U.S. military compound in South Vietnam. Pres. Johnson orders air raids on North Vietnam and sends U.S. troops to	**11** Rhodesia unilaterally declares its independence from Britain, which calls it an act of rebellion and imposes oil embargo.	**1** Frank Herbert, science-fiction author, publishes the highly acclaimed novel *Dune.* **2** Arthur Schlesinger,	**15** Weiss writes *The Investigation,* a play based on the Frankfurt trials of Auschwitz war criminals.

Science & Technology		Miscellaneous		
America	**Elsewhere**	**America**	**Elsewhere**	
2 U.S. Navy begins its *Sealab* experimental program to determine if people can live and work for extended periods at the bottom of the ocean. **3** Nuclear-powered lighthouse is built in Chesapeake Bay. **4** A fluid computer that uses liquids and gases instead of electricity is developed. **5** U.S. Public Health Service charges that insecticides have killed thousands of fish in the Mississippi River since 1960. **6** Muriel Roger, geneticist, transplants individual genes from one cell to another. **7** Methadone therapy is introduced as treatment for heroin addiction. **8** Polio vaccinations have cut new cases from 35,592 in 1953 to fewer than 100 in 1964. **9** Echo 2 is launched. It is the first communications satellite that will be used jointly by the U.S. and the Soviet Union. **10** Ranger 7 crashes into the Moon after taking 4316 photographs. **11** Nimbus 1, an experimental weather satellite, is launched. **12** OGO-1, an orbiting geophysical observatory, is launched. **13** Mariner 4 is launched on a 325-million-mile journey to photograph Mars. **14** Nobel Prize, Physiology or Medicine: Konrad Bloch (Amer.) and Feodor Lynen (Ger.) for discoveries about fatty acid and cholesterol metabolism.	man space mission. The cosmonauts aboard include Vladimir Komarov, Konstantin Feoktistov, and Boris Yegorov. **19** Cousteau publishes *World Without Sun.* **20** W. Hess publishes *The Biology of the Mind.* **21** The Mohole project is suspended due to its great expense and technological difficulties. **22** Following a change of power in the Soviet Union, Lysenko loses his influence over the scientific community. Soon, the more conventional genetic theories are allowed to be taught in Russia. **23** Nobel Prize, Chemistry: D. Hodgkin, for her determination of the chemical structures of penicillin and vitamin B_{12}. **24** Nobel Prize, Physics: Basov, Prokhorov, and Charle Townes (Amer.), for their work in quantum electronics that led to the development of the laser and maser. **[1952:SCI/14; 1953:SCI/3]** **25** Nobel Prize, Physiology or Medicine: Feodor Lynen, Ger. biochemist, and Konrad Bloch, Amer. biochemist, for their research on cholesterol and fatty acid metabolism.	television sets in use; more than 500 million radios. **4** Earthquake strikes Alaska at Anchorage, the state's largest city; 117 persons die. **5** Six persons win $100,000 each in the first legalized sweepstakes in U.S. horseracing history at Rockingham Park, N.H. **6** Verrazano-Narrows Bridge between Brooklyn and Staten Island, N.Y., opens. It is 6690 ft. long. **7** Popular rock 'n' roll dances have animal names: the Dog, the Monkey, the Chicken; favorites are the Watusi and the Frug. **8** New York World's Fair opens. General Motors' Futurama (as in 1939) is the most popular attraction. **9** Thieves steal jewels from collection of rare stones in Museum of Natural History, New York City. Value of jewels, $410,000; they include world's largest sapphire, the 565-carat Star of India. **10** Cassius Clay (later known as Muhammad Ali) wins the heavyweight boxing title from Sonny Liston, but World Boxing Association withdraws recognition of Clay's title when he plans a rematch with Liston.	numbers for the U.S.— the "Brain Drain." **14** Prison sentences totaling 307 years given to 12 mail-train robbers in England; for 1963 holdup that netted bandits £2.5 million. **15** 300 spectators killed in riots at soccer match in Lima, Peru.	
1 Arno Penzias and Robert Wilson discover radio waves going in all directions through the universe. This finding	**13** Loris S. Russell, Can. scientist, claims that dinosaurs were warm-blooded animals. **14** In a fine example of	**1** Series of 37 tornadoes sweep through midwest killing 271 persons, injuring 5000. **2** 105 cadets resign from	**8** Elizabeth Lane becomes first woman to be appointed High Court Judge in England. **9** Mont Blanc Tunnel	**1965**

History and Politics

America

fight. U.S. halts bombing and makes peace effort to end Vietnam War. North Vietnam rejects U.S. terms, and U.S. resumes bombing and builds up troops in Vietnam. Large antiwar demonstrations break out in the U.S. U.S. B-52s begin mass bombing of Viet Cong.

2 Dr. King leads march from Selma to Montgomery, Ala., to protest discrimination against blacks in voting registration.

3 Medicare is established; it provides hospital and medical care for persons 65 or older, financed through Social Security.

4 Blacks riot for six days in the Watts section of Los Angeles. National Guard restores order.

5 Cabinet-level Department of Housing and Urban Development is created, with Dr. Robert C. Weaver as Secretary (he is the first black Cabinet member).

6 John V. Lindsay is elected Mayor of New York City on the Republican-Liberal ticket.

7 Malcolm X, preaching brotherhood between blacks and whites, is shot and killed in New York City. **[1961:HIST/6]**

8 McCarran-Walter Act is amended, abolishing the national origins quota system. **[1952:HIST/2]**

9 Goldberg resigns from the Supreme Court to become U.S. Ambassador to the UN. Abe Fortas is appointed to the Court.

10 Voting Rights Act expands registration of black voters, especially in the South. Federal offices are set up to prevent abuses by registrars.

Elsewhere

12 India and Pakistan fight for control of Kashmir.

13 Gen. Suharto opposes pro-Chinese policies of Pres. Sukarno, crushes Communist coup, and replaces Sukarno as ruler of Indonesia.

14 Houari Boumedienne leads successful coup against the regime of Ahmed Ben Bella and becomes President of Algeria.

15 Premier Mobutu overthrows Pres. Kasavubu and assumes control of the Congo (now Zaire). **[1964:HIST/15]**

16 Civil war breaks out between rightists and leftists in the Dominican Republic. OAS forms peace-keeping force and works out a compromise agreement.

17 De Gaulle is reelected President of France.

18 King Constantine II of Greece dismisses Premier George Papandreou, who allegedly heads the Aspida (Greek army officers wishing to depose the king and set up a leftist regime).

19 Nicolae Ceaușescu is made chief of the Communist Party in Rumania. He becomes head of state in 1967.

20 Fighting occurs between Iraqi troops and the Kurds, who want a unified and autonomous Kurdistan.

21 Gambia gains independence.

22 Nikolai Viktorovich Podgorny becomes President of the Presidium (now the Politburo) of the Supreme Soviet.

The Arts

America

Jr., biographer, publishes *A Thousand Days* about Kennedy's administration.

3 Jerzy Kosinski, writer, publishes *The Painted Bird,* based on his nightmarish childhood in Nazi-occupied Europe.

4 Petula Clark, singer, makes the popular recording of the song "Downtown."

5 Paul Zindel, author, writes the Pulitzer Prize-winning play, *The Effect of Gamma Rays on Man-in-the-Moon Marigolds.*

6 *Ariel,* a collection of poems by Sylvia Plath, is published posthumously by her husband, Eng. poet Ted Hughes.

7 Sonny Bono and his wife Cher, singers, achieve fame with their song "I Got You, Babe."

8 The Astrodome, the first completely covered stadium in the world, opens in Houston, Texas.

9 The Broadway musical *Man of La Mancha* stars Richard Kiley and features the song "The Impossible Dream."

10 Neil Simon writes the play *The Odd Couple.*

11 Claude Brown, writer, tells of his Harlem upbringing in *Manchild in the Promised Land.*

12 Robert Indiana, pop artist, paints "The Demuth Five."

13 Dali creates his first major sculpture, a bronze bust of Dante.

14 Alex Haley ghostwrites *The Autobiography of Malcolm X.*

Elsewhere

16 Pinter completes the popular play, *The Homecoming.*

17 Henze and Auden collaborate on the opera, *Bassarids,* based on *Bacchae,* a play by Euripedes (c. 480–406 B.C.).

18 The Rolling Stones establish themselves as a major Eng. rock group with the hit record, "Satisfaction."

19 Onuora Nzekwu, Nigerian novelist, publishes *High Life for Lizards.*

20 Behan's memoirs are published in *Confessions of an Irish Rebel.*

21 David Mercer, Eng. playwright, completes *The Generations,* a trilogy of social dramas.

22 To celebrate the 750th anniversary of the Magna Charta, Auden writes the play, *Left-Handed Liberty.*

23 Boulez composes *Éclat,* for 15-piece chamber orchestra.

24 The Beatles continue their popularity with such hits as "Nowhere Man" and "Michelle."

25 Fontana completes the sculpture, "Spatial Concept (White and White)."

America

Elsewhere

America

Elsewhere

lends support to the big bang theory.

2 Schmidt discovers quasar 3C-9, the fastest and most distant galaxy yet detected. It is speeding away from the Milky Way at 80% of the speed of light, or about 150,000 miles per second.

3 Sandage discovers blue galaxies. They are similar to quasars, but do not give off radio waves.

4 As UFO sightings increase, Joseph Hynek and other scientists claim that UFOs may be signs of intelligent life on other planets.

5 NASA's high-altitude research laboratory (a modified jet) carries 30 scientists from 5 countries in a race with a total eclipse over the South Pacific.

6 V. Grissom and John Young manually maneuver Gemini 3 during its three orbits of the Earth.

7 Early Bird is the first commercial communications satellite launched by INTELSAT (International Telecommunications Satellite Organization).

8 Edward White is the first American to walk in space when he spends 23 minutes outside the Gemini 4 spacecraft.

9 G. Cooper and Charles Conrad complete 120 orbits in an 8-day flight aboard Gemini 5.

10 Gemini 7, piloted by Frank Borman and James Lovell is launched on a 14-day mission.

11 Pioneer 6 is launched to study interplanetary space.

12 Nobel Prize, Chemistry: R. Woodward for developing methods of synthesizing organic substances.

international cooperation, a British Skylark space probe equipped with German and Belgian instruments is launched from an Italian site.

15 France becomes the third country with space exploration capabilities with its launching of the satellite A-1.

16 The Soviet space probe Venera 3 becomes the first probe to land on another planet's surface when it strikes Venus.

17 The Soviets launch Voshkod 2. Cosmonauts Pavel Belyayev and Aleksey Leonov, make the first walk in space during this mission.

18 Tetrahydracannabinol (THC), the active ingredient in marijuana, is synthesized in Israel.

19 G.P. Thomson writes of his father in *J.J. Thomson and the Cavendish Laboratory in His Day.*

20 Nobel Prize, Physics: Shin'ichirō Tomonago, Jap. physicist, for making the theory of quantum electrodynamics consistent with the theory of relativity.

21 Nobel Prize, Physiology or Medicine: Jacob, Monod, and Andre Lwoff, Fr. biologist, for their discovery of the genetic control over the production of proteins and enzymes.

U.S. Air Force Academy in cheating scandal.

3 Robert Manry of Cleveland, Ohio, reaches Falmouth, England, after an 11-week singlehanded crossing of the Atlantic Ocean, in his 13½-ft. boat, *Tinkerbelle.*

4 U.S. spends more than $26.2 billion for public school education—$654 per student.

5 At about 5:15 P.M. on Nov. 9, massive power failure in northeastern U.S. blacks out New York State, most of New England, and parts of New Jersey and Pennsylvania, affecting nearly 30 million people.

6 There are more than 5 million color television sets in U.S.; networks predict that by end of 1966, all evening programs will be broadcast in color.

7 Membership in religious bodies is 120.9 million: Protestants, 66.8 million; Roman Catholics, 44.8 million; Jews, 5.5 million; Eastern Orthodox, 3 million; Eastern rite Catholics, 497,527; and Buddhists, 60,000.

opens, linking France and Italy. Burrowing 7.2 mi. through Europe's highest mountain (15,781 ft.), took 6-1/2 yrs. to build and cost $60 million.

10 Cyclone strikes East Pakistan; 12,000-20,000 people die.

11 Britain agrees to adopt the metric system over ten years.

12 First flight around the world over both the North and South Poles.

13 Roof of newly built church in Rijo, Mexico, collapses during early morning mass, killing 58 persons.

14 Soviet Union displays giant airplane, said to be largest and heaviest in world. It is 187 ft. long, with a wingspan of 211 ft., and can carry 720 passengers or 80 tons of cargo.

15 People's Republic of China wins 5 out of 7 world championship titles in table tennis series.

16 Snowslide sweeps a bus carrying ski tourists more than 150 ft. down a mountain road near Obertauren, Austria; 140 persons die.

17 Death penalty abolished in Britain.

18 Cigarette advertising on commercial television banned in Britain.

History and Politics

America

1 Cabinet-level Department of Transportation is established.
2 Interstate Commerce Commission approves the merger of the New York Central and Pennsylvania railroads.
3 U.S. increases its military strength in Vietnam and its bombing of the North; Hanoi and Haiphong are heavily bombed. U.S. supports the regime of Premier Nguyen Cao Ky of South Vietnam and helps plan national elections. North Vietnam rejects major U.S. peace offensive. U.S. forces attack enemy targets in Cambodia for the first time.
4 Race riots occur in slum areas of Chicago, Cleveland, and other cities. Congress authorizes funds to assist rebuilding programs.
5 Ku Klux Klan makes attacks against blacks and civil rights workers in the South.
6 Supreme Court upholds Voting Rights Act of 1965.
7 Pres. Johnson signs law extending U.S. fishing territorial limit to 12 miles off the coast.
8 Congress enacts truth in packaging law, requiring clear and correct statement of ingredients in about 8000 drug, cosmetic, and food products.
9 Supreme Court rules that a person accused of a crime must be informed of his constitutional rights, including the right to remain silent, before being questioned.
10 Edward W. Brooke is elected Senator from Massachusetts. He is the first black U.S. Senator since Reconstruction (1866–77).
11 Pres. Johnson makes 17-day tour of the Far East.

Elsewhere

12 Power struggle in Communist China brings the start of the Cultural Revolution (1966-69). Mao Tse-tung directs purge of bourgeois bureaucrats ("Peking Black Gang") and Communist leaders with Western, capitalistic tendencies. Red Guards are formed to attack Chinese dissidents and to check factional fighting and disorder.
13 Government of Pres. Kwame Nkrumah of Ghana is overthrown. Nkrumah takes refuge in Guinea.
14 Pres. de Gaulle withdraws French forces from NATO and asks U.S. and NATO forces to leave France.
15 UN ends South Africa's mandate over South West Africa.
16 U Thant is reelected UN Secretary General.
17 Indira Gandhi, daughter of Nehru, succeeds Shastri as Prime Minister of India.
18 British Guiana becomes the independent country of Guyana.
19 Conflicts (cultural and linguistic) between Flemings and Walloons disrupt Belgium's government.
20 Prime Minister Verwoerd of South Africa is assassinated and is succeeded by Balthazar Johannes Vorster. [1958:HIST/16]
21 Kurt Georg Kiesinger replaces Erhard as Chancellor of West Germany.

The Arts

America

1 Harry M. Petrakis, novelist, publishes *A Dream of Kings,* one of several stories about Greek immigrants in Chicago.
2 Woody Allen, actor and filmmaker, releases the movie *What's Up, Tiger Lily,* a Japanese spy film to which Allen dubs a ludicrous dialogue.
3 Jacqueline Susann, writer, publishes *Valley of the Dolls.*
4 Auchincloss publishes *The Embezzler.*
5 Robert Crichton publishes *The Secret of Santa Vittoria.*
6 Elia Kazan publishes *The Arrangement.*
7 John Barth publishes the novel *Giles Goat-Boy.*
8 Duke Ellington composes "In the Beginning God," religious jazz that is played in churches throughout the U.S. and Europe.
9 William Manchester, writer, publishes *The Death of a President,* a controversial biography of John F. Kennedy.
10 Tolkien's *The Lord of the Rings* trilogy enjoys a cultish popularity in the U.S. [1978:ARTS/9]
11 Albee publishes *A Delicate Balance.*
12 Capote publishes *In Cold Blood,* the lurid story of a Kansas mass murder.
13 Claes Oldenburg, pop sculptor, creates the appropriately named "Soft Toilet."
14 Malamud publishes *The Fixer.*
15 Broadway musicals this year include *Cabaret,* starring Joel Grey and Lotte Lenya, *I Do!*

Elsewhere

20 Eng. playwright Tom Stoppard's comedy, *Rosencrantz and Guildenstern Are Dead,* is based on characters from *Hamlet.*
21 Amado publishes the novel, *Doña Flor and Her Two Husbands.*
22 Cyprian Ekwenski, Nigerian social novelist, publishes *Lokotown and Other Stories.*
23 Mikhail Baryshnikov, Sov. dancer, makes his professional debut as a soloist with the Kirov company.
24 Jean Rhys, Br. novelist, publishes *Wide Sargasso Sea,* a novel that wins several awards.
25 Bolt writes the play, *Vivat! Vivat Regina!*
26 Major films (directors) include: *Blow-Up* (Antonioni); *Fahrenheit 451* (Truffaut); *Persona* (Bergman); *Is Paris Burning?* (Clément); *Alfie* (Gilbert); *The Birds, the Bees and the Italians* (Germi); *La Guerre Est Finie* (Resnais).
27 Hepworth completes "Four-Square," a huge, walk-through sculpture.

Science & Technology

America

1 America's SST (supersonic transport) will be built by Boeing and GE. Lockheed and Pratt & Whitney had competed for the contract.

2 Honeywell Corp. invents a laser gyroscope.

3 Research indicates that glaucoma may be hereditary.

4 Sagan uses radar to study the surface of Mars. He also publishes *Intelligent Life in the Universe.*

5 RCA introduces integrated circuits in its new TVs.

6 Cygnus A, a galaxy located about 500 million light-years from Earth, is identified as probably the most powerful source of radio waves in the universe.

7 Johns Hopkins University Hospital (Md.) performs two sex-change operations.

8 The Sierra Club leads opposition to a dam planned for the Colorado River in the Grand Canyon.

9 Pres. Johnson's Science Advisory Committee publishes *Effective Use of the Sea.*

10 Neil Armstrong and David Scott, astronauts aboard Gemini 8, rendezvous and dock with an unmanned target vehicle.

11 Surveyor 1 achieves a soft landing on the Moon and sends back 11,237 photographs.

12 Gemini 9, piloted by T. Stafford and Eugene Cernan, achieves a rendezvous but is unable to dock with a target vehicle. Cernan completes more than 2 hours of EVA (extravehicular activity, i.e., a space walk).

13 Gemini 10, piloted by J. Young and Michael Collins achieves rendezvous with two separate

Elsewhere

18 Audouin-Charles Dollfus, Fr. astronomer, discovers Janus, a moon of Saturn.

19 Crick publishes *Of Molecules and Men.*

20 Takeshi Hirayama, Jap. physician, reports that drinking milk may help prevent stomach cancer.

21 Lorenz publishes *On Aggression,* in which he suggests that animals, like human beings, have certain warlike tendencies.

22 The Soviets launch three unmanned space probes: Luna 9, which lands on the Moon and sends back photos; Luna 10, the first spacecraft to circumnavigate the Moon; and Luna 13, which also achieves a lunar landing.

23 Nobel Prize, Physics: Alfred Kastler, Fr. physicist, for the discovery of optical methods for studying atomic resonance.

Miscellaneous

America

1 Truth-in-packaging Law requires clear and accurate statement of ingredients and amounts; bans use of confusing phrases like "giant half quart"; law covers about 8000 drug, cosmetic, and food products.

2 New York Central and Pennsylvania railroads combine, creating biggest merger in U.S. history.

3 Violence erupts in slum areas of 16 cities throughout the country. Whites battle Negroes in a month of shootings, robberies, burnings, and looting.

4 Motor Vehicle Safety Act sets standards for all American automobiles built after 1968.

5 Uniform Time Act establishes that daylight-saving time is to be observed throughout the country from the last Sunday in April until the last Sunday in October.

6 There are 78 million passenger cars and 16 million trucks and buses registered; they travel a total of 910 billion miles per year. The number of deaths due to automobiles so far in the century is three times that of military deaths in all U.S. wars.

7 In air crash near coast of Spain, a U.S. B-52 bomber drops 4 unarmed hydrogen bombs, 3 on land and 1 into the sea; last is recovered after 3 months.

8 Jim Ryun sets world record of 3 min. 51.3 sec. for mile run.

Elsewhere

9 Indian airliner crashes into Mont Blanc, France, in fog; 117 people die. British airliner catches fire and crashes into Mt. Fuji, Japan; 124 killed.

10 Salazar suspension bridge, 3322 ft. long, opens in Lisbon.

11 Floods ravage northern Italy; thousands of art treasures ruined in Florence and Venice.

12 West Germany's autobahn system totals more than 2000 mi. of roads.

13 Miniskirts come into fashion.

14 Supermarkets open in Europe and the Far East.

15 England defeats West Germany to win soccer's World Cup.

16 Jack Brabham (Australia) is first to win world driving championship in a car that he has built.

17 German mountain-climbing team makes first ascent of the direct route on the north face of Switzerland's 13,036-ft. Eiger mountain.

18 Salvation Army celebrates its 100th anniversary.

19 Brit. yachtsman Francis Chichester arrives in Sydney, Australia, 107 days after sailing 14,100 mi. alone from London.

20 Earthquake in eastern Turkey kills 2477 people.

1966

History and Politics		The Arts	
America	**Elsewhere**	**America**	**Elsewhere**
		I Do!, with Mary Martin and Robert Preston, and *Mame*, with Angela Lansbury and Beatrice Arthur. **16** George Segal, pop sculptor, completes "The Diner," the patrons of which are plaster figures. **17** Chagall designs the mural "The Triumph of Music" for the Metropolitan Opera House. **18** William Gass, novelist, publishes *Omensetter's Luck*. **19** Sartog's *Against Interpretation* argues that art should be an emotional rather than intellectual experience.	
1967 **1** U.S. forces attack Viet Cong in Mekong River delta. U.S. suffers heavy losses near Con Thien, just south of the DMZ. U.S.-South Vietnamese troops stop 5-day attack by Viet Cong-North Vietnamese on Loc Ninh near Cambodia. Pres. Johnson restricts bombing in North. U.S. peace talks with Hanoi begin in Paris. U.S. troops capture hill near Dak To after bloody 19-day battle. Antiwar protesters march in Washington, D.C. **2** Twenty-fifth Amendment to the Constitution is ratified. It gives the President authority (with congressional approval) to appoint a Vice President when that office becomes vacant. **3** Riots occur in black areas of Cleveland, Detroit, Newark, Boston, New Haven, and other cities. **4** House denies Congressman Adam Clayton Powell, Jr. of New York his seat for misuse of House funds. Powell is overwhelmingly re-elected in a special election. **5** Thurgood Marshall becomes first black to sit on the Supreme Court. **6** Puerto Rico votes to re-	**10** Nguyen Van Thieu is elected President of South Vietnam; Nguyen Cao Ky becomes Premier. **11** Ibos of Nigeria proclaim the republic of Biafra. Nigeria wages war against Biafra and regains control in 1970 after inflicting sever hardship on the Biafrans. **12** Ernesto ("Che") Guevara, Cuban revolutionary and Castro's close friend, leads unsuccessful guerrilla movement against the government of Bolivia. **13** Gibraltar votes for continued British control. [1968:HIST/12] **14** Egypt blockades the Israeli port of Elat. Israel attacks Egypt, Syria, and Jordan, occupying the Gaza Strip, the Sinai Peninsula, and the Golan Heights in the so-called Six-Day Israeli-Arab War. UN obtains cease-fire on all three fronts. **15** Greek and Turkish Cypriots fight on Cyprus, causing Turkey to threaten an invasion of the island and war with Greece. UN arranges a settlement. **16** Military junta, headed by George Papadopoulos	**1** Ira Levin, novelist, publishes *Rosemary's Baby*. **2** Composer Burt Bachrach and Hal David, lyricist, collaborate on a number of songs, including "Walk on By" and "What the World Needs Now," that are popularized by singer Dionne Warwicke. **3** *Hello Dolly!* is revived with an all black cast that includes Pearl Bailey and Cab Calloway. **4** Richard Anuszkiewicz, op artist, paints "Inflexion." **5** Uris publishes *Topaz*, a spy novel. [1969:ARTS/8] **6** Mailer publishes *Why Are We in Vietnam?*, on which the film *The Deer Hunter* is loosely based. [1978:ARTS/3] **7** Svetlana Alliluyeva, Joseph Stalin's daughter, publishes *Twenty Letters to a Friend*. **8** Jann Wenner, en-	**16** Herbert von Karajan, Aust. conductor, establishes the annual Easter Music Festival in Salzburg. **17** The Beatles release *Sgt. Pepper's Lonely Hearts Club Band*, a pivotal album that features such hits as "A Day in the Life" and "A Little Help From My Friends." **18** Ustinov completes the drama, *Halfway Up the Tree*. **19** BBC produces Galsworthy's *The Forsyte Saga* for TV. **20** Tibor Dery, Hung. author, publishes *The Portuguese Princess*, a collection of short stories. **21** Major films (directors) include: *Belle de Jour* (Buñuel); *Weekend* (Godard); *La Chinoise* (Godard); *King of Hearts* (Boulanger); *Magical Mystery Tour* (Beatles). **22** Erik Bruhn, Dan. dancer and choreographer, is appointed director of the Royal

Science & Technology		Miscellaneous		
America	**Elsewhere**	**America**	**Elsewhere**	

targets.
14 Lunar Orbiter 1 studies potential landing sites for upcoming manned missions to the Moon.
15 Gemini 12, last of the Gemini series, is piloted by J. Lovell and Edwin "Buzz" Aldrin. Aldrin completes two EVAs for a total of 5½ hours in space.
16 Nobel Prize, Chemistry: Robert Mulliken for developing the molecular-orbital theory of bonding.
17 Nobel Prize, Physiology or Medicine: C. Huggins, for discovering a hormonal treatment of prostate cancer, and F. Rous, for discovering a cancer-causing virus.

Twiggy, fashion model from Great Britain

1 Kornberg synthesizes biologically active DNA.
2 Jastrow publishes *Red Giants and White Dwarfs,* a best-seller that traces the origin of life.
3 Tennessee's "Monkey Law" is repealed. [1925:MISC/5]
4 3-D holographic movies are developed.
5 The hormones found in birth control pills are used to treat acne.
6 Electroencephalographs (EEG) are teamed with computers to test the hearing of infants.
7 Flu vaccinations are tested on 500,000 soldiers.
8 Computers are used to generate electronic music.
9 Aspirin is found to be a possible cause of ulcers.
10 High blood cholesterol is determined a factor in heart disease.
11 10 million children are vaccinated against measles.
12 Antilymphocytic serum (ALS) is used to prevent rejection of tissue grafts.
13 FDA approves a high-protein flour that

20 Christiaan Barnard, South African surgeon, performs the first human heart transplant.
21 Gordon Murray, Can. surgeon, claims that he successfully repaired a severed spinal cord.
22 Anthony Hewish and S.J. Bell, Eng. astronomers, discover the first pulsar—a star which emits recordable radiation in short pulses.
23 The Soviets launch Soyuz 1. Cosmonaut Vladimir Komarov dies when the craft becomes tangled with its parachute during reentry.
24 The Soviet probe Venera 4 transmits important data about Venus and its atmosphere before its impact with the planet.
25 Nobel Prize, Chemistry: Eng. chemists Ronald Norrish and George Porter, and Ger. chemist Manfred Eigen, for their development of methods for studying rapid chemical reactions.

1 Albert de Salvo, the "Boston Strangler," who admits to 13 murders, is sentenced to life imprisonment.
2 12 billion cans of beer and 5.3 billion cans of soft drinks are consumed during year.
3 Trapped in the capsule of Saturn 1-B rocket on the ground, astronauts Grissom, White and Chaffee are killed when fire sweeps through it.
4 U.S. population reaches 200 million. Projected date for a population of 500 million is—barring catastrophes—the year 2015.
5 Mickey Mantle of the New York Yankees hits his 500th career home run.
6 Drought in southern Florida endangers wildlife in the Everglades.
7 Peggy Fleming wins world championship for women's figure skating in Vienna.

11 Fire in department store in Brussels kills 322 people.
12 People's Republic of China explodes its first hydrogen bomb.
13 "Expo 67" opens in Montreal, Canada.
14 Soviet team wins Women's International Chess Tournament in West Germany.
15 Chichester finishes his solo voyage around the world in 226 days; trip in *Gypsy Moth IV* covers almost 30,000 mi. [1966:MISC/19]
16 Twiggy, a British model, takes world fashion by storm.

1967

History and Politics		The Arts	
America	**Elsewhere**	**America**	**Elsewhere**
main a commonwealth rather than be a U.S. state or independent country. **7** U.S. Attorney General prohibits unauthorized wiretapping and electronic eavesdropping by federal agencies, except in cases of national security. **8** Gen. Lewis B. Hershey, Director of the Selective Service System, cancels draft deferments for college students who interfere with military recruiting. **9** Black mayors are elected in Gary, Ind., and Cleveland.	seizes power in Greece, suspends the constitution, and enforces strict censorship. King Constantine II fails to oust the junta and flees to Rome. **17** Anastasio Somoza Debayle is elected President of Nicaragua. **18** Tshombe's airplane is hijacked and flown to Algeria where Tshombe is held captive. Congolese troops fight pro-Tshombe rebels at Kisangani on the Congo River. **19** Malaysia, Singapore, Thailand, and the Philippines form the Association of Southeast Asian Nations for economic and cultural cooperation.	trepreneur, begins publication of *Rolling Stone* magazine. **9** Robert Massie, biographer, publishes *Nicholas and Alexandra,* about the end of the Russian monarchy. **10** James Jones publishes *Go to the Widow-Maker.* **11** Broadway musicals this year include *You're a Good Man, Charlie Brown* and *Hair,* the first show to emphasize rock music, featuring the song "Aquarius." **12** Chaim Potok publishes *The Chosen.* **13** Styron publishes *The Confessions of Nat Turner.* **14** Stephen Birmingham, writer, publishes *Our Crowd: The Great Jewish Families of New York.* **15** Herbert Ferber creates "Environmental Sculpture," a sculptural room into which the viewer enters.	Swedish Ballet. **23** *Margarita,* a novel begun by Sov. writer Mikhail Bulgakov in 1928, is published. **24** Frisch publishes the novel, *A Wilderness of Mirrors.* **25** Hochhuth writes *Soldiers,* a political play that criticizes Churchill. **26** The Royal Shakespeare Company sets a box-office record of more than $1 million in sales.
1968 **1** Viet Cong and North Vietnamese attack (the Tet Offensive) more than 100 cities, towns, and military bases in South Vietnam, including Saigon, Hue, and Khe Sanh. U.S. and North Vietnam hold peace talks in Paris. Pres. Johnson ends all bombing of North Vietnam. **2** U.S.S. *Pueblo,* naval intelligence ship, is seized (Jan.) by North Korean patrol boats and taken to Wonsan, Korea. It is accused of violating Korean waters. U.S. appeals to UN. Negotiations bring release of *Pueblo* (Dec.). **3** Dr. King is assassinated in Memphis. Racial riots occur in about 125 cities. Escaped convict James Earl Ray pleads guilty to the murder and is sentenced (1969) to 99 years.	**10** Alexander Dubček succeeds Novotný as First Secretary of the Communist Party in Czechoslovakia. Dubček initiates a democratization of Czech life. Soviet and other Warsaw Pact countries invade Czechoslovakia and arrest Dubček and other Czech leaders. Soviets force the repeal of major reforms. **11** UN General Assembly approves nuclear non-proliferation treaty; it condemns Portugal's colonial policies in Africa and South Africa's apartheid. **12** Spain closes its border with Gibraltar. **13** Rev. Ian Paisley leads Protestant extremists on anti-Catholic marches in Northern Ireland. Violence erupts between Catholics and Protestants.	**1** Kubrick's science fiction extravaganza *2001: A Space Odyssey* wins an Oscar for special effects. **2** Tom Wolfe, writer, publishes the psychedelic novel *The Electric Kool-Aid Acid Test.* **3** Bachrach and Hal David score the show *Promises, Promises,* featuring the song "I'll Never Fall in Love Again." **4** Classification of movies by "G," "PG," "R," and "X" is begun. **5** Vidal publishes *Myra Breckenridge.* **6** *The Producers,* a film written, directed, and starring Mel Brooks, wins him an Oscar for Best Original	**15** Solzhenitsyn publishes the novel, *Cancer Ward.* **16** Stockhausen composes *Spiral,* electronic music for soloist with short wave receiver. **17** Shoji Hamada, Jap. artist, is awarded the prestigious Order of Culture Medal for reviving the art of ceramics in Japan. **18** Desmond Morris, Brit. writer, publishes *The Naked Ape,* a study of evolution. **19** Swed. novelist Pär Fabian Lagerkvist, winner of the 1951 Nobel Prize, publishes *Marianne.* **20** The Beatles release a full-length musical cartoon, *Yellow*

Science & Technology		Miscellaneous		
America	**Elsewhere**	**America**	**Elsewhere**	

is made from fish.

14 Mariner 5 studies Venus and finds that its atmosphere contains no oxygen.

15 Bios 2, a biological research satellite, carries living plants and animals for experiments in space. On its reentry, it is caught in midair by a recovery aircraft.

16 Surveyor 5 lands in the Moon's Sea of Tranquility, gathers data and transmits photographs.

17 Surveyor 6 lifts off from the Moon's surface after gathering information. It moves several feet to a new location, lands, and gathers more data.

18 Nobel Prize, Physics: H. Bethe for describing the nuclear reactions involved in the energy production of stars.

19 Nobel Prize, Physiology or Medicine: Haldan Hartline (Amer.), George Wald (Amer.), and Ragnar Granit (Swed.) for discoveries about the eye and perception of color.

8 Fire on aircraft carrier U.S.S. *Forrestal* off North Vietnam kills 134 persons.

9 U.S. has 74 nuclear-powered submarines in commission.

10 Mrs. Billie Jean King wins almost every American and international tennis match open to women.

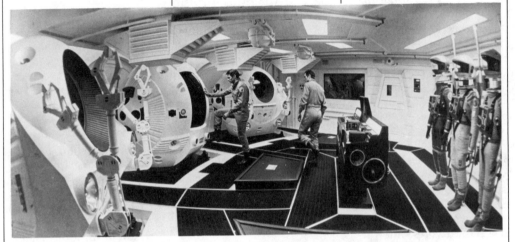

Scene from Stanley Kubrick's popular science-fiction film, *2001: A Space Odyssey*

1968

1 Norman Shumway, surgeon, performs America's first successful heart transplant.

2 James Watson publishes *The Double Helix,* describing the DNA molecule.

3 Geneticists reveal that some male criminals have an extra Y chromosome. Thus they are XYY instead of the normal XY.

4 Surgeons experiment with animal hearts for transplants to human beings.

5 Denton Cooley, surgeon, performs 17 heart transplants.

6 Mumps vaccine, developed in 1966, is approved for human use.

7 When the National Institutes of Health confirm

14 Paulo Maffei, Ital. astronomer, discovers two nearby galaxies, later named Maffei I and Maffei II.

15 Lovell describes the various aspects of constructing the great radio telescope in his work *The Story of Jodrell Bank.*

16 The Soviet Soyuz 3, manned by cosmonaut Georgi T. Beregovoi, links up in space with the unmanned Soyuz 2.

17 The Soviet supersonic transport Tu-144, the largest and heaviest aircraft of its time, makes its first flight. The craft was designed by the Soviet engineer Andrei Tupolev.

18 Boris V. Timofeyev, Soviet scientist, claims to

1 U.S. B-52 bomber carrying four unarmed hydrogen bombs crashes near Thule, Greenland, scattering bomb fragments, some radioactive, over ice.

2 Arthur Ashe wins U.S. tennis title at Forest Hills, N.Y. Tournament is open for first time to both amateurs and professionals, and Ashe is first Negro to win men's title.

3 Methodist and Evangelical United Brethren Churches merge to form United Methodist Church, second largest Protestant body in U.S., with more than 11 million members.

4 Atomic Energy Commission explodes experimental hydrogen bomb,

9 Student unrest causes wide confusion and changes in university life.

10 Foundations of the Temple of Herod (King of Judea 37–4 B.C.) found in Israel.

11 Skull of 28-million-year-old ape is discovered in Egypt.

12 Hugh Porter of Britain wins world cycling championship in Rome.

13 Europe's population is 455 million, excluding the Soviet Union, with a population of 239 million.

14 Olympic Games in Mexico City have more than 6000 competitors from 112 countries.

15 There are 25 million TV sets in U.S.S.R.; 20.5 million in Japan; 19 million in Great Britain; 13.5

History and Politics

America

4   Sen. Robert F. Kennedy of New York is assassinated in Los Angeles. Sirhan Bishara Sirhan, Jordanian Arab, is convicted of the murder (1969) and sentenced to life imprisonment (1972).
5   Kerner Commission Report cites white racism as the major cause of civil disorder by the blacks. [1967:HIST/3]
6   Poor People's March, planned by the late Dr. King, takes place in Washington, D.C.
7   Democratic Party nominates Vice Pres. Humphrey for President and Sen. Edmund S. Muskie of Maine for Vice President, despite violent protests by antiwar supporters of Sen. Eugene J. McCarthy of Minnesota.
8   Richard M. Nixon and Spiro T. Agnew are elected President and Vice President, respectively, on the Republican ticket. Nixon wins 301 electoral votes; Humphrey 191 electoral votes; and former Gov. George C. Wallace of Alabama, candidate of the American Independent Party, 46 electoral votes.
9   Congress enacts gun control law banning interstate sale of rifles, shotguns, and ammunition.

Elsewhere

14   Student demonstrations and labor strikes against France's educational and political systems nearly topple Pres. de Gaulle's government.
15   Pierre Elliott Trudeau, Liberal Party leader, becomes Prime Minister of Canada.
16   Lebanese and Israelis make terrorist attacks along each other's border.
17   Nauru, UN trust territory administered by Australia, and Mauritius, British colony, gain their independence.
18   Marcello Caetano becomes Premier of Portugal after Salazar suffers a stroke.
19   Spanish Guinea becomes independent as Equatorial Guinea.
20   Greek and Turkish Cypriots hold talks at Nicosia, Cyprus.
21   Britain restricts immigration of Asians, Africans, and West Indians who hold British citizenship.

The Arts

America

Screenplay.
7   Barth publishes *Lost in the Funhouse.*
8   Isaac Abrams becomes the major exponent of psychedelic art with his "Untitled" works.
9   Vonnegut publishes *Welcome to the Monkey House.*
10   e.e. cummings' *Complete Poems* are published posthumously.
11   Neil Simon writes *Plaza Suite,* a series of one-act plays.
12   Auchincloss publishes *A World of Profit* about a wealthy east coast family.
13   Mike Nichols directs the film *The Graduate,* starring Dustin Hoffman and Anne Bancroft.
14   *Guess Who's Coming to Dinner,* a film about an interracial marriage, stars Katharine Hepburn, Spencer Tracy, and Sidney Poitier.

Elsewhere

Submarine. Their biggest hit this year is "Hey Jude."
21   Orff composes *Prometheus,* an opera.
22   Stoppard writes *The Real Inspector Hound,* a one-act comedy.
23   Major films (directors) include: *Oliver!* (Reed); *Stolen Kisses* (Truffaut); *Charlie Bubbles* (Finney); *Playtime* (Tati); *Closely Watched Trains* (Menzel); *One Plus One* (Godard); *War and Peace* (Bondartchuk); *Barbarella* (Vadim).
24   C. Day-Lewis is appointed Poet Laureate of England.
25   Yasunari Kawabata, Jap. writer, is the first Japanese author to win the Nobel Prize in literature.

1969

America (History and Politics)

1   U.S.-North Vietnamese peace talks in Paris are expanded to include Viet Cong and South Vietnamese government.
2   House votes to reseat Congressman Powell but fines him for misuse of federal funds. [1967:HIST/4]
3   Federal grand jury indicts eight antiwar protesters for conspiring to incite a riot at the 1968 Democratic National Convention in Chicago. Trial of the "Chicago 8" begins. They are acquitted (1970) on conspiracy to riot charge.
4   Pres. Nixon announces withdrawal of U.S. troops from Vietnam. U.S. B-52s intensify their bombing of

Elsewhere (History and Politics)

13   Pres. de Gaulle resigns; Georges Pompidou is elected President of France.
14   Soviet and Chinese forces clash along the Ussuri River in Manchuria.
15   Omar Herrera Torrijos becomes ruler of Panama.
16   British troops restore order in Northern Ireland following clashes between Protestants and Catholics in Belfast and Londonderry. Irish Republican Army (IRA) splits into two groups: the majority devoted to a united Ireland and the "provisionals" advocating terrorist activities, if necessary, to bring about unification.
17   Yasir Arafat, leader of Al

America (The Arts)

1   Mario Puzo, novelist, publishes *The Godfather,* about the rise of a New York underworld chieftain.
2   Philip Roth publishes the controversial novel, *Portnoy's Complaint.*
3   Penelope Ashe, writer, publishes *Naked Came the Stranger.*
4   Lillian Hellman publishes the autobiographical work, *An Unfinished Woman.*
5   Robert Guccione, publisher, founds *Penthouse* magazine.
6   *Oh! Calcutta!,* a

Elsewhere (The Arts)

17   Olivier Messiaen, Fr. composer, completes the oratorio, *The Transfiguration of Our Savior Jesus Christ.*
18   The Rolling Stones release an album and a movie, both entitled *Gimme Shelter.* Other popular musical groups include the hard-rock Led Zeppelin and the soft-rock Crosby, Stills, and Nash.
19   Rembrandt's "Self-Portrait" sells for $1,256,000 at Christie's, London.
20   Williamson publishes *The Gale of the*

Science & Technology		Miscellaneous		
America	**Elsewhere**	**America**	**Elsewhere**	

that birth control pills can cause blood clots and other health hazards, the FDA orders that warnings be included with the pill packages. **8** Congress recommends that the U.S. switch to the metric system within 10 years. **9** Surveyor 8, last in its series, soft-lands on the Moon and sends back TV pictures. **10** OAO-2, the most sophisticated orbiting astronomical observatory developed, is launched. **11** Apollo 8 achieves the first manned lunar orbit (10 revolutions). Astronauts aboard are F. Borman, William Anders, and J. Lovell. **12** Nobel Prize, Chemistry: Lars Onsager for discovering the basis of irreversible chemical processes, such as those that occur in the cell. **13** Nobel Prize, Physiology or Medicine: Robert Holley H. Gobind Khorana, and Nirenberg for determining how enzymes affect the development and function of a cell.	have detected algaelike life forms in meteorites. **19** Soviet Union refuses to allow doctors to perform heart transplants.	largest yet tested in U.S., 3800 ft. below Nevada desert. Man-made "earth-quake" is felt in California coastal cities. **5** Nuclear submarine U.S.S. *Scorpion* sinks in Atlantic Ocean; 99 persons die. **6** Direct airline service begins between U.S.S.R. and the U.S. by Aeroflot, the Soviet airline, and Pan American World Airways. **7** Crimes of violence have increased 57% since 1960. **8** Disney's Mickey Mouse celebrates his 40th birthday. **[1928:MISC/1]**  Astronaut Edwin Aldrin walking on the moon	million in West Germany; and 10 million in France. **16** Earthquake strikes Iran, killing 12,000 people.	
1 Neil Armstrong is the first man on the Moon. While M. Collins pilots Apollo 11 in orbit around the Moon, Armstrong and E. Aldrin fly the Lunar Module to the surface where they remain for more than 21 hours. In Armstrong's first words from the Moon, "It's one small step for a man, one giant leap for mankind." **2** Edward Condon, physicist, publishes the government-sponsored *Scientific Study of UFOs.* Popularly known as "The Condon Report," it rejects the idea that UFOs are vehicles from other	**12** Charles McCusker, Austral. physicist, identifies a quark. **[1964:SCI/1]** **13** D. Hodgkin determines the three-dimensional structure of insulin. **14** Sir Bernard Katz, Eng. scientist, publishes *The Release of Neural Transmitter Substances.* **15** Hutchinson publishes *Evolution and Phylogeny of Flowering Plants.* **16** J. Piccard designs the submarine *Ben Franklin,* which is used to study the Gulf Stream. **17** Sweden and Denmark ban the use of DDT because of the insecticide's bad environmental	**1** Massive leakage from offshore oil-drilling installations near Santa Barbara, Calif., causes widespread property damage, water pollution, and wildlife destruction. **2** Woodstock Music and Art Fair, a 3-day rock concert, is held near Bethel, N.Y.; an estimated 400,000 people attend. **3** Rains in California cause mud slides that destroy or damage 10,000 homes and kill 100 persons. **4** In a game marking the centennial of collegiate football Rutgers de-	**10** The *Concorde,* Anglo-French supersonic aircraft, makes first test flight. **11** Rain and hurricane winds cause Greek airliner to crash into 2000-ft. mountain near Athens; 90 persons die. **12** Approximately 225 million telephones in use in the world. **13** Boris Spassky (U.S.S.R.) defeats Tigran Petrosian to win world chess championship.	**1969**

History and Politics		The Arts	
America	**Elsewhere**	**America**	**Elsewhere**

<table>
<tr>
<td>

Communist sanctuaries in Cambodia.

5 Warren Earl Burger becomes Chief Justice of the Supreme Court, succeeding Earl Warren, who retires.

6 Lindsay is reelected Mayor of New York City as the candidate of the Liberal and Independent parties.

7 Car driven by Sen. Edward M. Kennedy of Massachusetts plunges off bridge on Chappaquiddick Island, Martha's Vineyard. His passenger, Mary Jo Kopechne, drowns. Kennedy survives but his political future is marred.

8 House of Representatives and the U.S. Army investigate the massacre (1968) of South Vietnamese civilians at My Lai, South Vietnam. Many U.S. soldiers are indicted, but only Lt. William L. Calley is convicted and found guilty (1971) of premeditated murder. Federal court later overturns the conviction and the army releases Calley (1974).

9 Large antiwar demonstrations take place, including Vietnam Moratorium Days in Washington, D.C.

10 U.S. and the U.S.S.R. begin preliminary Strategic Arms Limitation Talks (SALT) in Helsinki.

11 Department of Agriculture halts the use of DDT in residential areas—first step toward its total ban in 1971.

12 Vice Pres. Agnew accuses network television and the press of biased news coverage.

</td>
<td>

Fatah, becomes head of the Palestine Liberation Organization (PLO).

18 Expulsion by Honduras of thousands of illegal immigrants from El Salvador causes war between the two countries. OAS settles dispute.

19 Portuguese fight nationalist rebels in Angola, Mozambique, and Portuguese Guinea (now Guinea-Bissau).

20 Willy Brandt, Mayor of West Berlin from 1957-66, succeeds Kiesinger as Chancellor of West Germany.

21 South Africa ignores UN call to give up its mandate over South West Africa (now Namibia). [1966:HIST/15]

22 Gen. Muhammad Gaafur al-Nimeiry leads successful coup against the civilian government of Sudan and establishes himself as President in 1971.

23 Col. Muammar al-Quaddafi takes control of Libya.

24 Golda Meir succeeds Eshkol as Prime Minister of Israel.

</td>
<td>

Broadway show by Kenneth Tynan, shocks audiences with its frontal nudity. Other shows include *Coco,* starring Katharine Hepburn and featuring a score by Lerner and André Previn.

7 Neil Simon writes the play *The Last of the Red Hot Lovers.*

8 Hitchcock releases the film *Topaz.*

9 Vonnegut publishes *Slaughter House Five.*

10 Woody Allen produces the film *Take the Money and Run.*

11 Menotti composes *Help! Help! The Globolinks!,* an opera about an alien invasion.

12 Bachrach composes "Raindrops Keep Falling on My Head" for *Butch Cassidy and the Sundance Kid,* a film starring Paul Newman and Robert Redford.

13 Arthur Mitchell establishes the Dance Theater of Harlem.

14 Gwen Davis writes *The Pretenders.*

15 Malamud publishes *Pictures of Fidelman,* a collection of short stories.

16 Michael Crichton, author, publishes *The Andromeda Strain.*

</td>
<td>

World, the 15th and final novel in the series, *Chronicle of the Ancient Sunlight.*

21 Humphrey Searle, Brit. composer, completes the opera, *Hamlet.*

22 Nathalie Sarraute, Fr. novelist, publishes *Entre la vie et la mort.*

23 Félicien Marceau, Fr. writer, completes the play, *La Babour.*

24 Major films (directors) include: *Satyricon* (Fellini); *Women in Love* (Russell); *Z* (Costa-Gavras); *A Gentle Woman* (Bresson); *The Damned* (Visconti).

25 Philippe Jullian, Fr. writer and artist, publishes *Dreamers of Decadence,* a study of Surrealist painters.

26 Solzhenitsyn is expelled from the Soviet Writers' Union.

</td>
</tr>
<tr>
<td>

1970

1 Postal Service, an independent agency, replaces Post Office Department.

2 Paris peace talks continue, and public pressure builds to end Vietnam War. National Guard troops fire on 1000 antiwar protesters at Kent State University in Ohio; four students are killed. U.S. withdraws more troops from Vietnam.

3 U.S. casts its first veto in

</td>
<td>

12 Anwar al-Sadat becomes President of Egypt.

13 Norodom Sihanouk, Cambodian head of state, is overthrown by Gen. Lon Nol, who tries unsuccessfully to suppress Communist guerrillas in Cambodia.

14 Prime Minister Trudeau of Canada institutes martial law for six months following terrorist attacks by the Front de Libération du Québec

</td>
<td>

1 Robert Altman directs the popular film *M*A*S*H,* starring Donald Sutherland and Elliott Gould.

2 Erich Segal, a teacher at Yale, publishes *Love Story.*

3 Hemingway's *Islands in the Stream* is published posthumously.

4 "Doonesbury," a sa-

</td>
<td>

15 The Beatles, the most influential and best-selling popular music group in history, disband.

16 In Christie's novel, *Curtain,* Hercule Poirot dies.

17 Borges publishes *Doctor Brodie's Report,* a chilling tale.

18 Mishima Yukio, Jap. novelist, publishes

</td>
</tr>
</table>

Science & Technology		Miscellaneous		
America	Elsewhere	America	Elsewhere	

planets. As a result of this report, the U.S. Air Force discontinues Project Blue Book. **[1948:SCI/13]**
3 Ribonuclease is the first enzyme to be synthesized.
4 The fourth or "D" ring of Saturn is discovered.
5 Gerald Edelman, biochemist, determines the structure of an antibody, gamma globulin.
6 National Audubon Society begins a national campaign to ban DDT because the chemical is killing the bald eagles.
7 Fossil skull found in Antarctica proves "without question" the theory of continental drift.
8 Arthur Jensen, psychologist, stirs widespread debate by his published claims that blacks are genetically less intelligent than whites.
9 J. McDivitt, D. Scott, and Russel Schweickart test the Lunar Module in docking with their craft, Apollo 9.
10 Apollo 12's Lunar Module brings C. Conrad and Alan Bean to the Moon's surface while R. Gordon remains aboard the Apollo craft.
11 Nobel Prize, Physics: M. Gell-Mann for classifying subatomic particles. **[1961:SCI/4]**

effects.
18 The Soviet Soyuz 4, with cosmonaut Vladimir Shatalov, and Soyuz 5, with cosmonauts Aleksey Yeliseyev, Yevgeny Khrunov, and Boris Volynov, are launched within a day of each other. The two spacecraft rendezvous in space and transfer passengers. The Soviets launch three more manned spacecraft which conduct numerous tests, including the welding of metals in space. The spacecraft and cosmonauts are: Soyuz 6, with Georgi Shonin and Valery Kubasov; Soyuz 7, with Anatoly Filipchenko, Vladislav Volkov, and Viktor Gorbatko; and Soyuz 8, with V. Shatalov and A. Yeliseyev.
19 Nobel Prize, Chemistry: Barton and Odd Hassel, Norw. chemist, for their research into three-dimensional organic structures.

feats Princeton, 27-0. Rutgers also won the 1869 game, 6 goals to 4.
5 New York Mets baseball team tops an almost incredible late season pennant rush by winning the World Series in 5 games.
6 Several traditionally all-male colleges, including Yale, Bowdoin, and Colgate, admit women students.
7 U.S. government removes cyclamates (artificial sweeteners) from market; laboratory experiments link food additives to cancer.
8 Hurricane Camille, the strongest to strike the U.S. since 1937, devastates Mississippi Gulf Coast.
9 Pants suits become acceptable for everyday wear by women.

Golda Meir, Prime Minister of Israel

1 Khorana synthesizes a complete gene.
2 Environmental Protection Agency (EPA) is established to enforce the Clean Air Act of 1970.
3 National Weather Service (NWS) replaces the Weather Bureau. NWS is part of the newly created National Oceanic and Atmospheric Administration (NOAA).

15 Japan becomes the fourth country with space exploration capabilities with its launching of the satellite Osumi I.
16 China becomes the fifth country with space exploration capabilities with its launching of the satellite China 1.
17 The Soviet Soyuz 9, with cosmonauts Vitaly Sevasyanov and A. Niko-

1 448 universities and colleges are either closed or on strike.
2 Chartered plane carrying 43 players and coaches of Marshall University football team crashes in West Virginia; 75 persons die.
3 World's most valuable stamp, the 1856 British Guiana one cent, sold at a New York City auction

13 In Guatemala, archaeologists unearth a 5-ft. statue, estimated to date from 700–300 B.C.
14 Japan World Exhibition, "Expo 70," in Osaka.
15 Dance-hall fire in Saint-Laurent-du-Pont, France, kills 146 young people.
16 Tony Jacklin is first British golfer to win U.S. Open championship in 50

1970

America	Elsewhere	America	Elsewhere

America (History and Politics)

the UN Security Council. It rejects a resolution for all UN members to sever ties with Rhodesia.

4 U.S. troops are sent into Cambodia to destroy North Vietnamese "sanctuaries."

5 Congress creates the National Railroad Passenger Corporation (Amtrak), a federal corporation authorized to operate passenger trains between U.S. cities.

6 Senate rejects Pres. Nixon's second nominee for the Supreme Court (his first was rejected in 1969). His third choice, Harry A. Blackmun, is approved.

7 Congress establishes U.S. Office of Management and Budget.

8 Former Gov. Wallace of Alabama urges Southern governors to defy integration order of the federal government.

9 Pres. Nixon names the first two women generals in U.S. history.

10 Congress establishes the Environmental Protection Agency (EPA), bringing under single management the 15 federal agencies dealing with pollution problems.

11 Commission on Civil Rights says presidential policy on school integration is inadequate.

Elsewhere (History and Politics)

(FLQ), Canadian group advocating independence for Quebec.

15 Salvador Allende Gossens becomes the first freely elected Marxist president in the Western Hemisphere as President of Chile.

16 Poles riot over poor economic conditions. Edward Gierek replaces Władysław Gomułka as First Secretary of the Communist Party.

17 Jordanian government forces fight 10-day civil war with Palestinian commandos. Other Arab countries arrange cease-fire.

18 Israel makes reprisals against Arab guerrilla attacks from Egypt, Jordan, Syria, and Lebanon.

19 Prime Minister Smith declares Rhodesia a republic. **[1965:HIST/11]**

20 Edward Richard George Heath, Conservative Party leader, becomes British Prime Minister.

21 Conference of non-aligned nations at Lusaka, Zambia, supports liberation movements everywhere, and the admission of Communist China to the UN; and denounces U.S. policy in Vietnam.

22 PLO members hijack four international jetliners en route to New York. Passengers are held hostage until Britain, West Germany, and Switzerland release seven commandos held captive for earlier hijackings.

America (The Arts)

tirical comic strip created by Garry Trudeau, has its debut in 30 newspapers.

5 Saul Bellow publishes *Mr. Sammler's Planet.*

6 Ursula LeGuin, science-fiction author, publishes *The Lathe of Heaven.*

7 Mae West returns to the screen for the film *Myra Breckenridge.* **[1968:ARTS/5]**

8 Irwin Shaw writes *Rich Man, Poor Man.*

9 Zelazny publishes the science-fiction novel *Nine Princes in Amber.*

10 Uris publishes *QB VII,* a novel based on Nazi war crimes and the subsequent trials.

11 David Reuben, physician, publishes *Everything You Always Wanted to Know About Sex But Were Afraid to Ask.*

12 Popular Broadway shows this year include Sondheim's *Company,* starring Dean Jones, *Two by Two,* with music composed by Richard Rodgers, and *Applause,* starring Lauren Bacall.

13 Todd Rundgren, musician, writes and records the song "Hello, It's Me."

14 Vonnegut writes the play *Happy Birthday, Wanda June.*

Elsewhere (The Arts)

Sun and Steel and *Sea of Fertility.*

19 London Contemporary Dance Theater is the first modern dance company in England.

20 Ir. actor Michael MacLiammoir writes and stars in the one-man show, *Talking About Yeats.*

21 Hochhuth criticizes the U.S. in his play, *Guerrillas.*

22 C.P. Snow writes *Public Affairs,* a collection of essays on science and culture.

23 Anouilh completes the play, *Les Poissons rouges.*

24 Major films (directors) include: *Zabriskie Point* (Antonioni); *Medea* (Pasolini); *The Clowns* (Fellini); *Bed and Board* (Truffaut); *The Wild Child* (Truffaut); *Sympathy for the Devil* (Godard); *Rider on the Rain* (Clément); *The Passion of Anna* (Bergman).

25 Shiko Munakata, Jap. wood-block artist, receives his country's highest award, the Order of Culture.

26 Eng. actor Laurence Olivier is made a baron, the first actor awarded this honor.

1971

America (History and Politics)

1 *New York Times* publishes classified Pentagon papers about U.S. involvement in Vietnam. Supreme Court upholds the right of the *Times* and the *Washington Post* to publish the papers. Daniel Ellsberg, who disclosed the papers, is indicted on charges of unauthorized possession of secret documents.

Elsewhere (History and Politics)

11 East Pakistan declares its independence as Bangladesh. India supports Bangladesh and sends troops to help East Pakistanis fight invading West Pakistani army. West Pakistani troops surrender in Bangladesh, and a cease-fire is declared.

12 Women in Switzerland are given the right to vote for

America (The Arts)

1 Two religiously inspired Broadway shows are hits this year: *Godspell,* featuring the song "Day by Day," and *Jesus Christ Superstar,* with the song "I Don't Know How to Love Him."

2 Carole King, singer, releases *Tapestry,* one

Elsewhere (The Arts)

15 V.S. Naipaul, Trinidadian novelist, publishes *In A Free State.*

16 Solzhenitsyn's novel, *August 1914,* is an underground sensation in the U.S.S.R.

17 David Williamson, Australian playwright, completes *The Remov-*

Science & Technology		Miscellaneous		
America	**Elsewhere**	**America**	**Elsewhere**	

4 Bethe discovers neutron stars.
5 Pauling suggests that large doses of vitamin C may help prevent common colds and the flu.
6 After great success as an experimental treatment for Parkinson's disease, L-dopa is approved as a prescription drug.
7 National Air Quality Control Act calls for a 90% reduction in automobile pollution.
8 Lysosomes, structures in the human cell, are synthesized.
9 GE synthesizes a gem-quality diamond.
[1955:SCI/5]
10 Bell Telephone introduces the Picturephone.
11 Scientists experimenting with the Lassa fever virus stop their research when they discover that the virus is one of the most deadly known.
12 20 million Americans take part in activities and demonstrations against pollution to celebrate Earth Day.
13 Nimbus 4, a research weather satellite, is launched.
14 When an oxygen line breaks causing two fuel cells to fail, Apollo 13 cancels its planned lunar landing. The astronauts, J. Lovell, Fred Haise, and John Swigert safely return to Earth using the life support system aboard the Lunar Module.

layev, tests the abilities of humans to endure long periods of time in space.
18 The Soviet Union's Venera 7 is the first probe to transmit data from the surface of Venus.
19 The Soviet Union's Luna 16 and Luna 17 gather a wealth of scientific data from the Moon.
20 Nobel Prize, Chemistry: Luis Leloir, Arg. biochemist, for his work on how sugars are broken down into carbohydrates.
21 Nobel Prize, Physics: Alfvén and Fr. physicist Louis Néel, for their work on magnetism and plasma physics.
22 Nobel Prize, Physiology or Medicine: Katz, Swed. scientist Ulf von Euler, and Amer. scientist Julius Axelrod, for their discoveries concerning the substances at the end of nerve fibers.

for $280,000.
4 Population is 205 million.
5 Hospital care costs reach average of $81 per day.
6 A copy of the second draft of the U.S. Constitution, printed in 1787, is sold for $160,000.
7 Curt Flood, St. Louis Cardinals' outfielder, files suit charging baseball with violation of antitrust laws, challenging the "reserve clause."
8 Police officials in Philadelphia recruit 19-year-old youths for city's police force.
9 Oleomargarine heir Michael James Brody, Jr., 21, is besieged by requests after he announces that he will give away part of his $6.8 million inheritance to any worthy person.
10 Report shows that "Sesame Street," nationwide TV program, helps to improve skills of preschool children.
11 A drifting Navy cargo ship, *Yancey,* tears a 375-ft. gap in the Chesapeake Bay bridge-tunnel during a storm.
12 University of California charges tuition for the first time in the school's 102-yr. history.

years.
17 Aswan High Dam, Egypt, completed at cost of more than $800 million.
18 Cyclones and floods kill 500,000 people in East Pakistan; 30,000 die in earthquakes, floods, and landslides in Peru; earthquake at Gediz, Turkey, kills 1087.
19 Margaret Smith Court (Australia) wins grand slam of women's tennis—British, French, Australian, and U.S. titles.
20 Heart pacemaker powered by nuclear energy used for first time in France; device should work without refueling for at least 10 years.
21 Israeli archaeologists uncover first evidence of the destruction of Jerusalem by Roman troops in A.D. 70.
22 Two British pilots win $28,000 prize for 12,000-mi. London to Sydney air race.
23 236 persons killed near Buenos Aires when express train crashes into standing commuter train.
24 People's Republic of China's population is 760 million; India's, 550 million; U.S.S.R.'s, 243 million.

---

1 Edward O. Wilson, biologist, publishes *The Insect Societies.* It is soon acclaimed the definitive work on social insects.
2 Woodward synthesizes vitamin B$_{12}$.
3 Plans for an American supersonic transport (SST) are abandoned.

13 A primitive tribe called the Tasaday is discovered in a remote mountain region of the Philippines. The tribe uses Stone Age tools, and has no words in its language for "hate" or "war."
14 Britain launches the satellite Prospero.

1 U.S. Supreme Court rules that hiring policies must be the same for men and women.
2 Laura Baugh, 16, wins U.S. Women's Amateur Golf championship in Atlanta; she is youngest women's amateur title holder.
3 Longest trial in Cali-

12 Church of England and Roman Catholic Church end 400-year dispute when they agree on the meaning of the sacrament of Holy Communion.
13 Japanese Boeing 727 and F-86 fighter collide in mid-air; death toll is 162.
14 Chichester crosses

1971

	History and Politics		The Arts	
	America	**Elsewhere**	**America**	**Elsewhere**

History and Politics — America

[1973:HIST/6]
2 Twenty-sixth Amendment to the Constitution is ratified. It lowers the minimum voting age in all elections from 21 to 18.
3 Pres. Nixon imposes 90-day freeze on wages, prices, and rents. He devalues the dollar (8.57%) by cutting its tie with gold. Pay Board and Price Commission are set up to curb inflation.
4 Supreme Court upholds the busing of children to integrate public schools where state laws have allowed segregation.
5 U.S. blockades North Vietnam to cut off its war matériel from China and the U.S.S.R. North Vietnam's ports are mined and its rail and highway links to China are bombed.
6 Gov. Rockefeller of New York orders state troopers and police to storm Attica State Correctional Facility, ending 4-day prisoner-rebellion in which 1200 convicts held 38 guards hostage.
7 Lewis F. Powell, Jr. and William H. Rehnquist become Supreme Court Justices.
8 Ten black activists are convicted of firebombing a Wilmington, Del., store and draw prison terms of from 29 to 34 years.
9 Supreme Court rules that conscientious objectors who seek draft exemption must show they oppose all wars, not just the Vietnam War.
10 Congress ends the funding of the supersonic transport project.

History and Politics — Elsewhere

the first time.
13 Brian Faulkner, Unionist Party leader, becomes Prime Minister of Northern Ireland. IRA and the Ulster Defense Association increase their terrorist attacks after Faulkner imprisons IRA and other militants.
14 UN votes to admit Communist China and expel Nationalist China (Taiwan).
15 Gen. Idi Amin seizes power in Uganda.
16 Austrian diplomat Kurt Waldheim is elected UN Secretary General.
17 Erich Honecker replaces Ulbricht as First Secretary of the East German Communist Party.
18 Lin Piao leads unsuccessful coup against Mao Tsetung. He dies mysteriously in an airplane crash in Mongolia.
19 Pres. Mobutu changes his country's name from Congo to Zaire. [1965:HIST/15]
20 Sixty-three nations sign treaty prohibiting the installation of nuclear weapons on the seabed beyond any nation's 12-mile coastal zone.
21 Jean-Claude Duvalier becomes President-for-life of Haiti upon the death of his father. [1963:HIST/18]
22 Pres. Boumedienne nationalizes (with compensation) the French oil and natural gas companies in Algeria.

The Arts — America

of the bestselling record albums of the 1970s.
3 Norman Lear, TV producer, brings controversial topics to the situation comedy with his hit series *All in the Family,* starring Carroll O'Connor and Jean Stapleton, adapted from a British TV series.
4 Joseph Wambaugh, author of police stories, publishes *The New Centurions.*
5 Jerzy Kosinski publishes *Being There,* about the influence of TV on American life.
6 Kubrick directs *A Clockwork Orange,* starring Malcolm McDowell.
[1962:ARTS/15]
7 James Jones publishes *The Merry Month of May.*
8 Updike publishes *Rabbit Redux,* a sequel to his earlier work.
[1960:ARTS/5]
9 Neil Simon writes the play *The Prisoner of Second Avenue.*
10 Philip Roth publishes the political satire *Our Gang.*
11 Shapiro publishes *Edsel,* his first novel.
12 Harold Robbins publishes *The Betsy.*
13 James Whitehead publishes *Joiner,* a novel about professional football.
14 The film *Love Story,* stars Ryan O'Neal and Ali McGraw.
[1970:ARTS/2]

The Arts — Elsewhere

alist, acclaimed in London as the best play of the year.
18 Fr. clothing designer Yves Saint Laurent abandons the exclusive world of *haute couture* for ready-to-wear fashions.
19 Brit. rock musician Elton John achieves superstar status with his albums, *Tumbleweed Connection* and *Madman Across the Water.*
20 Major films (directors) include: *The Decameron* (Pasolini); *The Garden of the Finzi-Continis* (De Sica); *Death in Venice* (Visconti); *The Conformist* (Bertolucci); *Investigation of a Citizen Above Suspicion* (Petri); *The Go-Between* (Losey); *Traffic* (Tati); *Claire's Knee* (Rohmer).
21 Colin Davis is appointed director of the Royal Opera, Covent Garden, England.
22 Karsh publishes *Faces of Our Time,* a collection of photographs of famous people.
23 *I Breathe a New Song,* an anthology of Eskimo poetry, is published.

1972

America (History and Politics)
1 U.S. B-52s bomb Haiphong and Hanoi. U.S. destroyers shell coastal areas of North Vietnam. Quang Tri falls to the North Vietnamese. Henry A. Kissinger, Pres. Nixon's Assistant for Na-

Elsewhere (History and Politics)
9 Mujibur Rahman becomes Prime Minister of Bangladesh; tries to rebuild his country and to normalize relations with Pakistan. Zulfikar Ali Bhutto takes control in Pakistan. [1971:HIST/11]

America (The Arts)
1 Wambaugh publishes *The Blue Knight,* on which the TV series starring George Kennedy is based.
2 Ira Levin publishes *The Stepford Wives.*

Elsewhere (The Arts)
15 Richard George Adams, Brit. novelist, publishes *Watership Down,* an allegorical rabbit tale based on bedtime stories he created for his daughters.

Science & Technology

America

4   NSF reports that animals and plants taken from the Atlantic Ocean have high levels of the cancer-causing industrial pollutant PCB (polychlorinated biphenyl).

5   DES (diethylstilbesterol) is linked to cancer in women whose mothers took the drug during pregnancy. A synthetic estrogen (hormone), DES had been prescribed to prevent miscarriages.

6   Detergents containing phosphates are shown to cause water pollution.

7   C.H. Li synthesizes human growth hormone.

8   A powerful underground nuclear test explosion causes 22 earthquakes and hundreds of aftershocks at Amchitka, Alaska.

9   A. Shepard and Edgar Mitchell descend to the Moon's surface and collect 98 lb. of Moon rocks before returning to Apollo 14, piloted by astronaut Stuart Roosa.

10   Mariner 9 orbits Mars and returns 6876 photographs of the planet's surface.

11   Apollo 15 carries a 4-wheel Lunar Rover to the Moon. Driven by D. Scott and James Irwin, the vehicle travels more than 17 miles on the Moon's surface. Alfred Worden, meanwhile, performs a 38-minute EVA in deep space.

12   Nobel Prize, Physiology or Medicine: E. Sutherland for work with cyclic-AMP.

Elsewhere

15   Japan launches its second and third satellites, Tansei and Shinsei.

16   Two Soviet space probes, *Mars 2* and *Mars 3*, eject landers to the Martian surface. Both landers stop functioning after a brief period.

17   The Soviet *Soyuz 10*, with cosmonauts V. Shatalov, A. Yeliseyev, and Nikolai Rukavishnikov, link up with the *Salyut 1* space station.

18   The Soviet *Soyuz 11* docks with *Salyut 1*. Cosmonauts V. Volkov, Georgi Dobrovolsky, and Viktor Patsayev are found dead in their craft after reentry.

19   J. Piccard publishes *The Sun Beneath the Sea*.

20   Nobel Prize, Chemistry: Gerhard Herzberg, Can. physicist, for his research on the structure of molecules and free radicals.

21   Nobel Prize, Physics: Gabor, for his development of holography. **[1947:SCI/11]**

Miscellaneous

America

fornia history closes in Los Angeles when Charles M. Manson and 3 of his female followers are convicted of first-degree murder in the slaying of actress Sharon Tate and 6 other persons.

4   Joe Frazier defeats Muhammad Ali (Cassius Clay) to win the world heavyweight boxing championship in New York City. It is Ali's first loss after 31 professional wins.

5   U.S. Supreme Court rules federal and state aid to parochial schools is unconstitutional.

6   Cigarette advertisements banned from television.

7   Henry Aaron hits 600th career home run, the 3rd baseball player ever to reach that mark.

8   The "Jesus movement" is a much-publicized part of religion in America.

9   Earthquake in southern California kills 62 people, injures hundreds, and causes more than $1 billion damage in Los Angeles and surrounding areas.

10   Tennis star Mrs. Billie Jean King is first woman athlete to win $100,000 in one year.

11   Justice Department reports that nearly half of nation's major crimes are committed by juveniles.

Elsewhere

the Atlantic Ocean alone in *Gypsy Moth IV*, covering 4000 mi. in 22 days.

15   *Nisseki Maru*, 372,400-ton tanker, launched in Japan, largest ship built to date.

16   Cyclone and tidal wave in Bay of Bengal, India, kills 10,000 people.

17   Egyptian scientists discover drawings dating back to 6000 B.C. in caves in Egypt's western desert.

Muhammad Ali (Cassius Clay), heavyweight boxing champion

---

1   Hexachlorophene, a widely used germ killer, is banned when research shows it may damage the nervous system.

2   DDT is banned.

3   Work begins on a re-

14   The Soviet Luna 20 lands on the Moon, obtains a sample of lunar soil, and successfully returns to Earth.

15   12 European nations agree not to dump gar-

1   4 Episcopal bishops defy church law and ordain 11 women as priests.

2   Coal mine waste waters burst through a 200-ft. high makeshift dam in Logan County, W.Va.;

11   Spanish charter jet carrying West German tourists crashes on takeoff at Tenerife, Canary Islands, killing all 155 persons aboard.

12   Tutankhamun (14th

1972

America

tional Security Affairs, states "peace is at hand." U.S. continues to pull more troops out of Vietnam.

2 Police arrest five men for breaking into the Democratic Party National Headquarters in the Watergate office complex, Washington, D.C. Republicans deny Democratic charges that "Watergate burglars" were sanctioned by Pres. Nixon's campaign officials. John N. Mitchell, U.S. Attorney General, resigns as head of the Committee to Re-elect the President. [1973:HIST/1]

3 Pres. Nixon visits Communist China and the U.S.S.R.

4 Supreme Court rules that the death penalty as administered in the U.S. is "cruel and unusual punishment" and unconstitutional.

5 Constitutional Amendment prohibiting sex discrimination against women is sent to the states for ratification. [1978:HIST/7]

6 Wallace campaigns for the Democratic presidential nomination, is shot in Maryland, and is paralyzed from the waist down.

7 Sen. George S. McGovern of South Dakota wins the Democratic nomination for President. His running mate Sen. Thomas F. Eagleton of Missouri is replaced by former Peace Corps Director Sargent Shriver after Eagleton reveals he has been treated for manic depression.

8 Nixon and Agnew are re-elected President and Vice President, respectively. Nixon receives 521 electoral votes, McGovern 17, as the Democrats suffer their worst defeat in the most one-sided election since 1936.

Elsewhere

10 British troops fire on illegal Catholic protesters in Londonderry and kill 13 ("Derry Massacre"). Britain imposes direct rule over Northern Ireland and suspends its government; Faulkner resigns. [1971:HIST/13]

11 Ceylon declares itself a republic and changes its name to Sri Lanka.

12 Opposition to Pres. Allende's socialist programs in Chile increases.

13 Pres. Ferdinand Edralin Marcos imposes martial law in the Philippines and arrests many Filipinos as Communist subversives.

14 Gough Whitlam, Labour Party leader, becomes Prime Minister of Australia, ending 23 years of rule by the Liberal-Country Party.

15 Eight Arab terrorists kill two Israeli athletes and take nine others hostage at Olympic Games in Munich. During shootout with West German police, five terrorists and all the hostages are killed.

16 Kakuei Tanaka succeeds Sato as Prime Minister of Japan.

17 Prime Minister Trudeau of Canada remains in office after his Liberal Party gains parliamentary majority with help from the new Democratic Party.

18 Norman Eric Kirk, Labour Party leader, becomes Prime Minister of New Zealand, ending 12 years of rule by the National Party.

19 Chinese, Soviet, North Vietnamese, and Mongolian representatives convene at Peking to arrange economic and military aid for North Vietnam.

20 Margaret II becomes Denmark's first ruling queen since the reign of Margaret I in the early 15th century.

America

3 Popular Broadway musicals this year include *Pippin* and *Grease*.

4 The film *Cabaret* wins actress Liza Minnelli and director Bob Fosse Academy Awards.

5 Elia Kazan publishes *Assassins*.

6 Eudora Welty publishes *The Optimist's Daughter*.

7 Wadsworth Atheneum in Hartford, Ct., opens the Tactile Gallery, an art exhibition for the blind.

8 The film *Lady Sings the Blues,* starring Diana Ross, is loosely based on Billie Holiday's autobiography. [1956:ARTS/5]

9 Gloria Steinem, feminist, founds *Ms.* magazine.

10 Ralph Bakshi, cartoonist, makes the film *Fritz the Cat,* the first X-rated cartoon.

11 Bette Midler, singer, releases *The Divine Miss M,* a record album that revives songs from the previous 40 years.

12 Helen Reddy, singer, causes a feminist sensation with her recording of "I Am Woman."

13 Irwin Allen, film writer and producer, produces *The Poseidon Adventure,* the first of a series of "disaster movies," a popular film genre of the 1970s.

14 Robert Moog, engineer, patents the Moog synthesizer, an electronic musical instrument which can duplicate the sounds of various instruments with remarkable accuracy.

Elsewhere

16 England's National Theater Touring Company makes its debut at the Globe Theater with a production of John Ford's *'Tis Pity She's a Whore* (1630).

17 Williamson's *Jugglers Three* wins the Melbourne Critic's "Erik Award" as the best Australian play of the year.

18 Beckett writes *The Lost Ones,* a parable.

19 Stoppard satirizes the academic world in his play, *Jumpers.*

20 Michelangelo's "Pietà" at St. Peter's is defaced by a lunatic. It is later restored and placed in a glass case for protection.

21 Karen Kain, Can. ballerina, and Rudolf Nureyev dance the leads in a Canadian production of the ballet, *Swan Lake.*

22 Major films (directors) include: *The Discreet Charm of the Bourgeoisie* (Buñuel); *Roma* (Fellini); *Canterbury Tales* (Pasolini); *Cries and Whispers* (Bergman); *Chloe in the Afternoon* (Rohmer); *The Working Class Goes to Paradise* (Petri); *The Mattei Affair* (Rosi); *And Now For Something Completely Different* (Monty Python).

23 Betjeman is named Poet Laureate of England.

24 Asturias, winner of the 1967 Nobel Prize, publishes *Viernes de dolores.*

Science & Technology

Miscellaneous

America

Elsewhere

America

Elsewhere

usable, manned rocket-powered craft launched from a high-flying airplane. The space shuttle would be able to navigate in space and return to Earth under its own power.

4 The U.S. and 90 other countries agree to stop dumping pollutants into the oceans.

5 Westinghouse is selected to build a $700 million breeder-reactor near Oak Ridge, Tenn.

6 Acupuncture, an ancient Chinese medical practice, is used for the first time to anesthetize an American patient before surgery.

7 The controversy continues about whether cigarette smoking by a pregnant woman results in her having a smaller baby.

8 FDA proposes a ban on the use of antibiotics used to fatten cattle and other animals.

9 Pioneer 10 is launched to explore the asteroid belt and Jupiter. This probe will be the first man-made object to leave the solar system.

10 J. Young, Charles Duke, and Thomas Mattingly pilot Apollo 16 to America's fifth manned lunar landing.

11 Apollo 17 is the last manned Moon landing. Astronauts E. Cernan and Harrison Schmitt spend almost 75 hours on the Moon while Ronald Evans orbits overhead.

12 Nobel Prize, Physics: J. Bardeen, L. Cooper, and J. Schrieffer for their theory of super-conductivity.

13 Nobel Prize, Chemistry: C. Anfinsen, Stanford Moore, and William Stein for their molecular studies of proteins and enzymes.

bage in the Atlantic Ocean.

16 Heinrich K. Erben, Ger. paleontologist, suggests that dinosaurs died out when their egg shells became thin and brittle.

17 The establishment of a European Molecular Biology Laboratory is agreed upon by 12 western European countries. The laboratory would develop new methods for studying the molecular basis of life.

18 Nobel Prize, Physiology or Medicine: Rodney Porter, Eng. immunologist, for his research into the chemical structure of antibiotics.

107 people die, 57 are missing.

3 Don Johnson bowls 6 straight strikes to win the $100,000 Bowling Proprietors Association U.S. Open in New York City.

4 Six largest cigarette manufacturers agree to include a health warning in their cigarette advertisements.

5 New York City Court of Appeals upholds right of New York City woman to be an umpire in professional baseball.

6 Hurricane Agnes causes $1.7 billion damage to eastern U.S.

7 Military draft ends; armed forces become all-volunteer.

8 Roberto Clemente is 11th baseball player to reach 3000 base hits; later dies in plane crash.

9 U.S. tennis team wins Davis Cup for 5th straight year.

10 First woman rabbi in U.S., Sally J. Priesand, ordained in Cincinnati.

century B.C. Egyptian king) exhibition in London is visited by 1.6 million people.

13 Richard Leakey, Brit. anthropologist, discovers a 2.5 million-year-old human skull in northern Kenya, Africa.

14 5,000 people killed in earthquake in Iran.

15 Winter Olympics held at Sapporo, Japan; U.S.S.R. wins 8 gold medals. Summer olympics in Munich, Ger.; U.S.S.R. wins 50 gold medals; Amer. swimmer Mark Spitz captures a record 7 gold medals.

16 Train carrying religious pilgrims is derailed and catches fire near Saltillo, Mexico, killing 204 people and injuring more than 1000.

17 "Sierra Leone," largest diamond (969.8 carats) discovered to date, is unearthed in Sierra Leone, Africa.

18 Earthquake in Managua, Nicaragua, destroys the city, leaving up to 12,000 dead.

19 118 die in fire in nightclub on top floor of department store in Osaka, Japan.

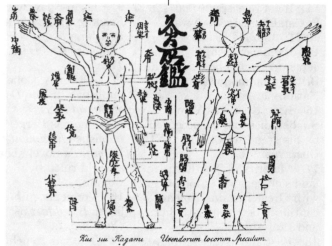

Kiu su Kagami   Urendorum locorum Speculum.

Chinese anatomical chart indicating points for application of acupuncture

History and Politics		The Arts	
America	**Elsewhere**	**America**	**Elsewhere**

1973

America (History and Politics)

1 Senate committee, headed by Sen. Samuel J. Ervin, holds televised hearings on the Watergate affair. Former White House counsel John W. Dean III admits to playing a major role in the cover-up of the burglary and says Nixon and his aides knew about it. Chief White House advisers John D. Ehrlichman and H. R. (Bob) Haldeman resign. Grand jury indicts Mitchell and Maurice H. Stans, finance chairman of Nixon's re-election campaign, for perjury and obstruction of justice. (Stans is acquitted in 1974.) Archibald Cox, special prosecutor to investigate the Watergate affair, sues Pres. Nixon to obtain taped presidential conversations. Nixon fires Cox; U.S. Attorney General Elliot L. Richardson resigns in protest. Judge John J. Sirica sentences seven Watergate break-in defendants to prison terms. House Judiciary Committee investigates possible impeachment of Pres. Nixon. Leon Jaworski becomes new special prosecutor. Taped Watergate conversations are released to Judge Sirica; there are "gaps" in some conversations. [1974:HIST/2]

2 U.S. ends military draft.

3 Vice Pres. Agnew resigns pleading no contest to charges of income tax evasion. Gerald R. Ford, Republican leader in the House, becomes Vice President.

4 U.S. and South Vietnam sign cease-fire with North Vietnam and Viet Cong, ending Vietnam War.

5 Kissinger becomes Secretary of State.

6 Government charges against Ellsberg are dismissed.

7 Members of the American Indian Movement make Indian grievances known during 70-day seizure of trading post and church at Wounded Knee, S. Dak. [1890:HIST/8]

Elsewhere (History and Politics)

8 Greece abolishes the monarchy. Pres. Papadopoulos is ousted by a coup led by Gen. Phaedon Gizikis. [1974:HIST/18]

9 Perón returns to Argentina and is reelected President, with his third wife, María Estela (Isabel) Martínez de Perón as Vice President. [1955:HIST/15]

10 Great Britain, Ireland, and Denmark become members of the Common Market.

11 Chilean armed forces overthrow Pres. Allende, who apparently commits suicide. Four-man junta, headed by Gen. Augusto Pinochet Ugarte takes control. Mass arrests remove socialists and Marxists from power in Chile.

12 Egyptian and Syrian forces attack Israeli positions in the Sinai and on the Golan Heights. Israeli counterattacks push Egyptians and Syrians back. UN arranges cease-fire. Arab-Israeli peace conference opens in Geneva, Switzerland.

13 Arab oil-producing countries ban oil exports to the U.S., Europe, and Japan in retaliation for their support of Israel. Organization of Petroleum Exporting Countries (OPEC) is formed. Arab oil embargo (and later the doubling of oil prices) precipitates energy crisis in the West.

14 India releases 90,000 Pakistani prisoners-of-war. [1971:HIST/11]

15 Bahamas becomes an independent republic within the British Commonwealth of Nations.

16 King Gustavus VI of Sweden dies and is succeeded by his grandson Charles XVI Gustavus.

17 Majority of Northern Ireland's citizens votes for union with Great Britain. Violence continues between Catholics and Protestants.

18 East and West Germany formally establish diplomatic relations.

America (The Arts)

1 The 110-story World Trade Center, designed by architect Ieoh Ming Pei, is completed in N.Y.C., briefly becoming the tallest building in the world.

2 Malamud publishes the short story collection, *Rembrandt's Hat*.

3 George Lucas directs *American Graffiti*, a film that causes a wave of 1950s nostalgia.

4 *The Exorcist*, a horror film starring Linda Blair, is the biggest money-maker of a series of movies dealing with demons and the occult.

5 Billy Joel, musician and songwriter, releases the *Piano Man* album.

6 Bruce Springsteen, rock musician, releases the album *Greetings from Asbury Park*.

7 Stevie Wonder, singer and songwriter, releases the popular songs "You Are the Sunshine of My Life" and "All in Love is Fair."

8 Erica Jong, writer, publishes *Fear of Flying*.

9 Irwin Shaw writes *Evening in Byzantium*.

10 Jerzy Kosinski publishes *The Devil Tree*.

11 Arthur A. Cohen publishes *In The Days of Simon Stern*.

12 Thomas Berger publishes *Regiment of Woman*, a novel about a world ruled by woman.

13 Vonnegut publishes *Breakfast of Champions*.

14 Thomas Pynchon, writer, publishes *Gravity's Rainbow*.

Elsewhere (The Arts)

15 Peter Shaffer. Eng. playwright, completes *Equus*, an internationally acclaimed drama.

16 Swed. writers Harry Martinson and Eyvind Johnson share the Nobel Prize in Literature.

17 Elton John releases the album, *Yellow Brick Road*.

18 André Laplante, Can. piano virtuoso, wins an international competition in Paris.

19 *The Rocky Horror Show*, a film that later takes on cultish popularity in the U.S., wins the London *Evening Standard* award as best musical. Other major films (directors) include: *Last Tango in Paris* (Bertolucci); *Brother Sun Sister Moon* (Zeffirelli); *The Hireling* (Bridges); *Day for Night* (Truffaut); *The Bitter Tears of Petra von Kant* (Fassbinder).

20 Britten composes the opera, *Death in Venice*.

21 Kain and her partner, Frank Augustyn represent Canada at the 2nd International Ballet Competition, Moscow.

22 Hung. poet Laszlo Nagy publishes *Hiding in Poems*, a collection.

23 To celebrate the opening of the New London Theater, Ustinov stars in *The Unknown Soldier and his Wife*.

24 Gregor Piatigorsky, Russ. cellist, marks his 70th birthday with a concert in New York City.

Science & Technology

America

1 A "cold star" is discovered that has 30,000 times more energy than the Sun. Scientists think that this star is in its early stages of development.
2 Center for UFO Studies is established in Evanston, Ill.
3 Scientists at Massachusetts Institute of Technology determine the structure of transfer-RNA (tRNA).
4 Marijuana is used as a treatment for glaucoma.
5 SSTs are thought to harm the ozone layer in the stratosphere.
6 Rabies vaccine is developed.
7 Congress approves the Alaska pipeline.
8 Monocytes, a type of white blood cell, are proposed as a key to conquering cancer.
9 Endangered Species Act prohibits the federal government from supporting any activities or projects that may be harmful to any endangered species.
10 Pioneer 11 is launched to fly by Jupiter and Saturn.
11 Skylab 1, an unmanned craft, is launched. Its heat shield is ripped away and the solar panels fail to extend properly.
12 Skylab 2, with astronauts C. Conrad, Joseph Kerwin, and Paul Weitz aboard, docks with Skylab 1. In 3 EVAs, the astronauts install a parasol to replace the shield. The mission lasts 28 days.
13 Skylab 3, manned by A. Bean, Owen Garriot, and Jack Lousma, completes a 59-day mission that involves 3 EVAs for a total of 13¾ hours.
14 Mariner 10 is launched to fly by both Venus and Mercury.

Elsewhere

15 A team of Belgian geneticists determines the sequence of molecules in a gene.
16 The Soviet Union launches *Soyuz 12,* with cosmonauts Vasily Lazarev and Oleg Makarov. This is Russia's first manned flight since the ill-fated *Soyuz 11.*
17 The Soviet Union launches *Soyuz 13,* a manned craft equipped with a telescope for studying the stars.
18 Nobel Prize, Chemistry: Geoffrey Wilkinson, Eng. chemist, and Ernst Otto Fischer, Ger. chemist, for their research on methods of bonding metals to organic compounds.
19 Nobel Prize, Physics: Brian Josephson, Eng. physicist, Leo Esaki, Jap. physicist, and Ivar Giaever, Amer. physicist, for their work on conductors and semiconductors.
20 Nobel Prize, Physiology or Medicine: Tinbergen, K. von Frisch, and Lorenz, for their research into animal behavior.
21 Lubos Kohoutek, Czech. astronomer, discovers a comet, now called Kohoutek. Skylab 3 astronauts gathered much data on the comet.

Miscellaneous

America

1 Conservative Jews allow women in the minyan—10 or more adult Jews required for communal worship.
2 14 states restore the death penalty.
3 "Secretariat" is horse racing's first triple crown winner since "Citation" in 1948.
4 Presbyterians form a new church, the National Presbyterian Church, with 75,000 worshipers from 275 churches in 14 southern and border states.
5 Mississippi River floods 11 million acres in 7 states; damage estimated at $322 million. At least 11 flood-related deaths reported and 35,000 people are homeless.
6 Boston Bruins center Phil Esposito wins National Hockey League's scoring title for third straight year, combining 55 goals with 75 assists for a total of 130 points.
7 Chris Evert, 18, wins last five tournaments of the U.S. Lawn Tennis Association (USLTA).
8 Juan V. Corona, convicted of killing 25 farm workers in California, is sentenced to 25 consecutive life terms in prison.
9 American Hospital Association publishes a 12-point patient bill of rights.
10 Ford Motor Company fined $7 million for violating Clean Air Act by improperly servicing 1973 model cars during tests for emission controls.
11 Population is 210.1 million, an increase of 1.6 million during 1972.
12 American League allows 10th player, the designated hitter, to bat in place of the pitcher.

Elsewhere

13 One of longest total eclipses of the sun in modern times is visible for up to 7 min., over a path stretching from Brazil across the Atlantic Ocean through Africa.
14 Soviet Union defeats Sweden to win World Ice Hockey Tournament, their 10th title in 11 years.
15 Smallpox epidemic in Bangladesh kills 1000 people.
16 A Soviet TU-144 supersonic jet liner (SST) explodes at Le Bourget airport near Paris; explosion seen by 300,000 spectators at air show.
17 Cambridge University varsity crew defeats Oxford University in their 148th race on the Thames.
18 Death penalty, abolished in Northern Ireland, replaced by life imprisonment.
19 A Boeing 707 jet crashes and explodes in thick fog in Kano, Nigeria; 176 persons die, all are Nigerian Muslims returning from a pilgrimage to Mecca.
20 Helgafell volcano erupts on island of Heimaey, Iceland. More than 100 homes burn and island's 5000 inhabitants flee to mainland.
21 Kenya bans hunting of elephants and sale of ivory.

1973

History and Politics		The Arts	
America	**Elsewhere**	**America**	**Elsewhere**

1974

America (History and Politics)

1 Supreme Court rules that presidential executive privilege is not unlimited.
2 House Judiciary Committee holds televised impeachment hearings against Pres. Nixon. He is charged with taking part in a conspiracy to obstruct justice in the Watergate cover-up, with failure to fulfill his constitutional oath through apparent abuses of power, and with unconstitutional defiance of Committee subpoenas. House recommends the three articles of impeachment. Pres. Nixon resigns and is succeeded by Vice Pres. Ford.
3 U.S. ends all price and wage controls.
4 Rockefeller becomes Vice President.
5 Federal judge dismisses charges against Indian leaders who participated in the takeover at Wounded Knee. [1973:HIST/7]
6 Pres. Ford issues an unconditional pardon to Nixon for all federal crimes he may have committed as President.
7 Former United Mine Workers President W. A. (Tony) Boyle is convicted of murder in the 1969 murders of union rival Joseph A. Yablonski, his wife, and a daughter.
8 Central Intelligence Agency (CIA) is charged with foreign and domestic abuse of its power.
9 Pres. Ford proposes conditional amnesty to draft evaders and deserters of the Vietnam War.
10 Boston school committee rejects court-ordered busing plan for desegregation.
11 U.S. is hit by a recession.

Elsewhere (History and Politics)

12 Egyptian forces withdraw to east side of Suez Canal; Israelis withdraw to west side and evacuate Syrian territory captured in the 1973 war. UN-patrolled buffer zone is set up along the Canal.
13 OPEC ends its oil embargo against the U.S. but continues it against Denmark and the Netherlands.
14 General strike sponsored by militant Protestants forces the collapse of Catholic-Protestant coalition government in Northern Ireland. British again take over rule. [1972:HIST/10]
15 Perón dies and is succeeded by his wife Isabel as President of Argentina.
16 Cypriot National Guard overthrows the Makarios government in Cyprus. Turkey invades northern Cyprus to protect Turkish Cypriots. UN arranges cease-fire. Negotiations among Turkey, Greece, and Cyprus break down, and Turkey renews attacks against Greek Cypriots. Makarios returns to Cyprus.
17 Helmut Schmidt becomes Chancellor of West Germany following Brandt's resignation as a result of a spy scandal.
18 Gizikis government in Greece turns over power to civilian government headed by Constantine Karamanlis. Political parties are allowed to operate freely.
19 Military junta, headed by Gen. António de Spínola, seizes power in Portugal. Spínola recognizes the independence of Portugal's colonies in Africa (Guinea-Bissau, in particular). Rightists and leftists fight for control; Spínola resigns and is succeeded by Gen. Francisco da Costa Gomes, who heads a leftist government in Portugal.
20 Army officers depose Emperor Haile Selassie and seize control of Ethiopia.
21 Yitzhak Rabin succeeds Meir as Prime Minister of Israel.

America (The Arts)

1 Peter Benchley, writer, publishes *Jaws,* a novel about a huge shark that terrorizes a Long Island beach resort.
2 Irwin Allen directs *The Towering Inferno,* a three-hour disaster spectacle with an all-star cast that includes Steve McQueen and Paul Newman. A second disaster movie, *Earthquake,* introduces "Sensurround," a technique intended to produce more realism.
3 *Godfather 2* wins Oscars for Best Picture, Best Director (Francis Ford Coppola), and Best Supporting Actor (Robert DeNiro).
4 The 110-story Sears Tower in Chicago is completed, becoming the tallest building in the world.
5 Stephen King novelist, publishes *Carrie,* a suspense story later made into a movie starring Sissy Spacek and Piper Laurie.
6 Among the popular rock groups of the time are Chicago, Steeley Dan, Yes, Jefferson Starship, Santana, The Eagles, and Utopia.
7 Journalists Carl Bernstein and Bob Woodward publish *All the President's Men,* about their investigation of the Watergate case.
8 *Upstairs, Downstairs,* a popular TV series produced by the BBC, is a huge success in the U.S.
9 Richard Condon, writer, publishes *Winter Kills.*
10 Mel Brooks produces *Blazing Saddles,* a parody of Westerns, starring Gene Wilder.

Elsewhere (The Arts)

11 Solzhenitsyn is tried for treason and exiled from the U.S.S.R. after the publication (1973) of *The Gulag Archipelago 1918–1956.*
12 LeCarré publishes *Tinker, Tailor, Soldier, Spy,* an adventure novel that introduces George Smiley, a British secret agent.
13 Margaret Lawrence's *The Diviners* is acclaimed as Canada's best English-language novel of the year.
14 Seven volumes of poetry by Nobel Prize (1971) winning Chilean poet Pablo Neruda are published.
15 Sov. authorities allow the publication of a heavily censored version of Vasily Shukshin's satirical novel, *The Red Snowball Tree.*
16 Valery and Galina Panov, Sov. ballet dancers, appear together outside the U.S.S.R. for the first time in 15 years.
17 The Royal Academy celebrates the 100th anniversary of the first Impressionism exhibit with "Impressionism—Its Masters, Precursors, and Its Influence in Britain." [1874:ARTS/4]
18 Can. pianist Oscar Peterson tours the U.S.S.R.
19 Alan Ayckbourn, Eng. playwright, completes *Absurd Person Singular.*
20 Major films (directors) include: *The Cars That Ate Paris* (Weir); *Scenes From A Marriage* (Bergman); *Fear Eats the Soul* (Fassbinder); *A Thousand and One Nights* (Pasolini).

Science & Technology

America

1 Freon, a fluorocarbon used as a propellant in many aerosol sprays, is said to endanger the ozone layer.

2 Safe Drinking Water Act sets water pollution standards. When drinking water supplies throughout the U.S. are tested, cancer-causing chemicals are found in all samples.

3 National Research Act is passed to set standards and limits on research involving human beings.

4 High-energy neutrons, produced in cyclotrons, are used to treat cancer.

5 *New England Journal of Medicine* reports that males who smoke large amounts of marijuana have lower levels of testosterone (male sex hormone).

6 A government report indicates that moderate drinkers live longer than nondrinkers. It also states that heavy drinkers have higher rates of mouth, throat, and liver cancer.

7 National Academy of Sciences urges a ban on genetic experiments with bacteria, especially those involving *E. coli,* a helpful type of bacteria that lives in the intestines.

8 Vinyl chloride, commonly used in making plastics, is shown to cause cancer.

9 SMS-1, a weather satellite, is placed in synchronous orbit, that is, it always stays over the same spot on Earth.

10 Nobel Prize, Chemistry: Paul Florey for experiments with macromolecules.

11 Nobel Prize, Physiology or Medicine: Albert Claude (Amer.), Christian de Duve (Belg.), and George Palade (Amer.) for work on cell biology.

Elsewhere

12 West Germany launches Helios 1, a space probe designed to study the Sun.

13 Douglas Bevis, Eng. obstetrician, claims to have knowledge of three European "test-tube" babies. The mother's ovum was fertilized in a laboratory test-tube and then implanted in the mother.

14 Barnard performs the first "extra heart" implant. The operation involves the implantation of a second heart to help relieve the burden on the patient's own heart. **[1967:SCI/20]**

15 Russia launches *Soyuz 14,* which links up with the *Salyut 3* space station. Cosmonauts P. Popovich and Yuri Artyukhin perform physiological experiments.

16 The flight of Russia's *Soyuz 15,* with cosmonauts Gennadi Sarafanov and Lev Demin, ends early because of unexpected storms on the Sun's surface.

17 Russia launches *Soyuz 16.* Cosmonauts A. Filipchenko and N. Rukavishnikov rehearse the planned Russian-American flight.

18 Nobel Prize, Physics: Hewish and Martin Ryle, Eng. astronomer, for their pioneer work in radio astronomy.

Miscellaneous

America

1 "Streaking," in which a participant unexpectedly appears nude before a mass of people, spreads from college campuses to public parks, concerts, and nationally televised awards presentations.

2 Little League Baseball, Inc., bars foreign teams from future Little League world series; accepts girl players.

3 Federal Trade Commission requires advertisers to support claims about nutritional value with information including a food's vitamin, protein, and caloric content.

4 U.S. Olympic Committee adopts a bill of rights for athletes.

5 U.S. Lawn Tennis Association names Jimmy Connors as No. 1 men's singles player and Chris Evert as No. 1 women's player.

6 Air Force SR-71 jet plane flies from New York City to London in 1 hr., 55 min., 42 sec., reaching speeds of 2000 mph.

7 Gasoline shortage inconveniences Americans through winter months; year-round Daylight-Saving Time adopted to save fuel. (Law later repealed.)

8 Aaron passes Babe Ruth's record of 714 career home runs.

9 Golfer Johnny Miller establishes 1-yr. money-winning record of $346,933.

10 Frank Robinson, of the Cleveland Indians, is the first black manager in major league baseball.

11 More than $1.9 billion spent by moviegoers; *The Sting* and *The Exorcist* earn the most money.

Elsewhere

12 World's population is 3.7 billion.

13 Brit. train robber Ronald Briggs stays in Rio de Janeiro when his Brazilian wife has a child. As father of a Brazilian child, Briggs, who faces a 30-yr. sentence, cannot now be expelled from Brazil. **[1964:MISC/14]**

14 Earthquake in Pattan, Pakistan, affecting more than 1000 sq. mi., kills 5000 people.

15 Soviet Union's national hockey team defeats Team Canada in their best-of-eight series.

16 Pope Paul VI opens Holy Year of the Roman Catholic Church, the 25th since 1450. (The first Holy Year was proclaimed in 1300.)

17 Cyclone Tracy with winds up to 160 mph strikes Darwin, Australia, killing 50 persons and destroying 90% of the city.

18 A 2200-year-old merchant ship which sank outside Kyrema, Cyprus, goes on display; oldest vessel ever recovered from underwater.

19 170 people die as fire sweeps through São Paolo, Brazil, high-rise building.

20 Large quantity of historical manuscripts, philosophical works, and medical texts more than 2000 years old discovered in ancient tombs in China.

21 Smallpox epidemic kills 10,000–20,000 people in India.

22 Turkish jetliner crashes in a forest near Paris; all 346 passengers and crew are killed in worst aviation disaster to date.

1974

History and Politics

America

Elsewhere

The Arts

America

Elsewhere

1975

History and Politics — America

1 Mitchell, Ehrlichman, and Haldeman are found guilty of perjury, conspiracy, and obstruction of justice in the Watergate cover-up. They are given prison terms. Judge Sirica releases from prison several convicted Watergate figures.

2 U.S. evacuates troops, civilians, and refugees from South Vietnam. Congress approves $405 million to aid Vietnamese refugees.

3 U.S. cuts off economic and military aid to Turkey. [1974:HIST/16]

4 Cambodian Communist forces fire on and seize U.S. merchant ship *Mayaguez* in the Gulf of Siam. U.S. Marines recapture ship and crew; 38 Americans die.

5 John Paul Stevens becomes Supreme Court Justice following the retirement of William O. Douglas, who served on the Court longer than any other Justice (since 1939).

6 Richard J. Daley wins his sixth term as Mayor of Chicago.

7 IRS and SEC investigate U.S. corporations for illegal political contributions, foreign and domestic.

8 Two assassination attempts are made against Pres. Ford in California.

9 FBI agents capture Patricia C. (Patty) Hearst, who was kidnaped in 1974 by members of the Symbionese Liberation Army, a radical terrorist group.

10 Hoffa mysteriously disappears; FBI begins search. [1957:HIST/4]

11 Municipal Assistance Corporation (Big MAC) lends New York City money to pay its bills, thus avoiding default by the city.

12 Daniel Patrick Moynihan becomes U.S. Ambassador to the UN.

History and Politics — Elsewhere

13 Turkish Cypriots proclaim a separate state in northern Cyprus.

14 King Faisal of Saudi Arabia is assassinated in Riyadh. Khalid ibn Abdul Aziz, brother of Faisal, becomes king.

15 Civil war breaks out in Eritrea between Ethiopian forces and secessionist guerrillas. [1962:HIST/17]

16 Communist Khmer Rouge seize control of Cambodia; Pres. Lon Nol flees.

17 Portugal grants independence to Angola, Mozambique, Cape Verde, and São Tomé and Príncipe.

18 Leftist Muslims and rightist Christians battle in Lebanon.

19 Suez Canal is reopened to shipping after having been closed by Egypt during the 1967 Arab-Israeli War.

20 Soviet bloc and Western nations sign agreement at Helsinki, pledging to work for economic cooperation and to promote peace and human rights (Helsinki Accord).

21 South Vietnamese government surrenders to Communist Viet Cong and North Vietnamese.

22 Communist Pathet Lao takes control of Laos, abolishing its 600-year-old monarchy.

23 Juan Carlos I becomes the first King of Spain in 44 years.

24 Papua New Guinea, Surinam, and the Comoro Islands become independent nations.

25 Sikkim abolishes its monarchy.

26 Israeli-Egyptian agreement provides for Israel's withdrawal from the oil fields in the Sinai. Egypt permits non-military shipments to and from Israel through the Suez Canal.

The Arts — America

1 Beverly Sills, soprano, has her debut at the Metropolitan Opera in Rossini's *The Siege of Corinth.*

2 Vincent Bugliosi publishes *Helter Skelter,* based on the Charles Manson murders.

3 The film *Jaws,* starring Robert Shaw, Roy Scheider, and Richard Dreyfuss, breaks box office records across the U.S. and causes a nationwide "Jawsmania." [1974:ARTS/1]

4 The film *One Flew Over the Cuckoo's Nest* is the first movie since 1934 to win the top four Oscars: Best Picture, Best Actor (Jack Nicholson), Best Actress (Louise Fletcher), and Best Director (Milos Forman). [1962:ARTS/8]

5 Bellow publishes *Humboldt's Gift.*

6 Edward Albee publishes the Pulitzer Prize-winning *Seascape.*

7 Norman Lear satirizes soap operas in his controversial serial *Mary Hartman, Mary Hartman,* starring Louise Lasser.

8 Wambaugh publishes *The Choirboys.*

9 Judith Rossner, novelist, publishes *Looking for Mr. Goodbar,* the story of a schoolteacher who, by night, frequents N.Y.C.'s singles bars.

10 *A Chorus Line,* a musical featuring music by Marvin Hamlisch and lyrics by Edward Kleban, opens on Broadway.

11 Bruce Springsteen releases the hit album *Born to Run.*

The Arts — Elsewhere

12 Naipaul publishes *Guerrillas,* one of his best novels.

13 Osborne writes the play, *The Picture of Dorian Gray.*

14 Nureyev's interpretation of *Sleeping Beauty* brings great success to the London Festival Ballet.

15 In popular music, Scot. rock groups The Bay City Rollers and The Average White Band are performing before sell-out crowds. The Bee Gees, an Australian trio, abandon their earlier "soft rock" sound and record "Jive Talkin'," a hit that helps popularize disco music.

16 Eng. novelist Anthony Powell publishes *Hearing Sweet Harmonies,* the 12th and final volume in his satirical series, *The Music of Time.*

17 *El Paso de los Ganos,* a novel by Peruvian writer Ciro Alegría, is published.

18 Ital. film producer Carlo Ponti is found guilty of defaming Pope Pius XII in *Massacre in Rome.* Other major films (directors) include: *Seven Beauties* (Wertmuller); *Dersu uzala* (Kurosawa); *Picnic at Hanging Rock* (Weir); *The Magic Flute* (Bergman); *Monty Python and the Holy Grail.*

Science & Technology

America

1 Thalidomide, a drug linked to birth defects, proves to be an effective treatment for leprosy.
2 Paleontologists discover the oldest American fossil—a 620-million-year-old marine worm.
3 National Cancer Institute links cancer to pollution.
4 Heart valves from pigs are used to replace defective valves in human hearts.
5 University of California astronomers discover a new galaxy that is at least 10 times larger than the Milky Way and about 8 billion light-years away from Earth.
6 E. O. Wilson publishes *Sociobiology: The New Synthesis,* which argues that social behavior patterns are controlled by genes.
7 Virus DNA is recombined in a test tube.
8 Use of synthetic estrogens is linked to cancer.
9 Scientists claim to have discovered a monopole (a single magnetic pole) in cosmic rays.
10 In the *Apollo Soyuz Test Project,* Apollo 18 docks with Soyuz 19. Astronauts T. Stafford, Donald Slayton, and Vance Brand join the Russian cosmonauts for a joint news conference from space.
11 Viking 1 and Viking 2 are launched and are scheduled to land on Mars about a year later.
12 Nobel Prize, Physiology or Medizine: David Baltimore, Renato Delbecco, and Howard Temin for discovering how certain cancer-causing viruses affect genes.

Elsewhere

13 Godfrey Hounsfield, Eng. engineer, designs an x-ray scanner capable of giving clear cross sections of a patient's body, and thus providing the means for a faster, more accurate diagnosis.
14 The European Space Agency (ESA) is formed to promote international cooperation for space projects. The member nations are: Belgium, Britain, Denmark, France, Holland, Italy, Spain, Switzerland, Sweden, and West Germany.
15 The Russian space probes *Venera 9* and *Venera 10* study the surface and atmosphere of Venus, and eventually land on the planet's surface.
16 The Soviet Soyuz 17, with cosmonauts Alexei Gubarev and Georgi Grechko, links up with the Salyut 4 space station. The cosmonauts do x-ray studies of the Sun.
17 The Soviet Soyuz 18, with cosmonauts P. Klimuk and V. Sevastynov, links up with the Salyut 4 space station. The cosmonauts spend just under 63 days in space.
18 Nobel Prize, Chemistry: Eng. chemist John Cornforth and Swiss chemist Vladimir Perlog, for their research in stereochemistry.
19 Nobel Prize, Physics: Dan. physicists Aage Bohr and Ben Mottleson, and Amer. physicist James Rainwater, for their extensive work on atomic nuclei.

Miscellaneous

America

1 Eastern Airlines Boeing 747 crashes at Kennedy Airport, New York City, killing 113 people; highest single-aircraft toll in U.S. to date.
2 Elizabeth Seton is first U.S.-born saint in Roman Catholic Church.
3 Jackie Tonawanda, a woman, is denied a boxing license by the New York State Athletic Commission.
4 The Tombstone *Epitaph,* a newspaper first published in 1880, closes. Paper covered many shootouts, brawls, and Indian uprisings, including the gunfight at the O.K. Corral.
5 Insurance companies dropping malpractice insurance coverage for doctors because losses in suits are so high.
6 Vaughn Booker, sentenced to life for murdering his wife, is ordained an Episcopal deacon at Graterford State Prison, Penn.
7 New Roman Catholic missal, *The New American Sunday Missal,* published; provides use of single volume for Sunday mass.
8 Metric Conversion Act suggests voluntary change to metric system.
9 Chris Evert wins $40,000, the highest prize in the history of women's tennis, on the Virginia Slims tour.
10 National Association of Broadcasters agrees to assign a two-hour period of prime television time to programs suitable for family viewing.
11 55 nuclear power plants in operation, providing 7.5% of country's electricity. Within 25 years 830 reactors planned, producing 50% of nation's electricity.

Elsewhere

12 Earthquake in Turkey kills 2312, injures 3372; quake levels town of Lice.
13 Well-preserved body of a man more than 2000 years old discovered buried in China; body is 5 ft. 4 in. tall, weighs 115 lb., and has complete set of teeth.
14 An engineer and his assistant fall asleep at controls of express train in Zagreb, Yugoslavia; crash kills 153 people.
15 European basketball league finishes first season; Israeli Sabres in first place from among 5 teams.
16 Chartered Boeing 707, returning Moroccan workers home after vacation in France, plunges into mountainside in Morocco; all 188 aboard killed.
17 British scientists and explorers complete expedition down 2700-mi. Congo River (later Zaire River), held to commemorate anniversary of Stanley's navigation of the river 100 years ago.
18 In Dhanbad, India, coal mine explosion and flooding from nearby reservoir leave 372 persons dead.
19 World population passes 4 billion.
20 U.S. Air Force plane crashes after take-off near Saigon, Vietnam, killing 172 persons; most are Vietnamese children.
21 Heavy rains flood southern Thailand, killing 131 people and leaving more than 10,000 homeless; many rubber plantations and mines destroyed.

1975

History and Politics

America

Elsewhere

The Arts

America

Elsewhere

1976

1 Consolidated Rail Corporation (Conrail), a private, government-financed corporation, takes control of the freight service of six bankrupt Northeast railroads.
2 U.S. vetoes UN Security Council resolution condemning Israeli policies in occupied territories. U.S. also vetoes resolution for the establishment of a Palestinian state.
3 U.S. celebrates the 200th anniversary (bicentennial) of its independence. Six million persons view parade of tall ships from 31 countries on the Hudson River.
4 U.S. intelligence agencies are charged with unlawful investigation and surveillance of U.S. citizens.
5 Senators Walter F. Mondale (Democrat) and Robert J. Dole (Republican) engage in the first televised debate between U.S. vice presidential candidates.
6 U.S. vetoes admission of Vietnam to the UN, saying Hanoi government has failed to account for 800 U.S. servicemen still listed as missing in action.
7 Presidential candidates Ford (Republican) and James Earl (Jimmy) Carter, Jr. debate political issues on public television. Before becoming the Democratic presidential nominee, Carter was Governor of Georgia (1971–75).
8 Carter and Mondale are elected President and Vice President, respectively. Carter wins 297 electoral votes, Ford 240, and former Gov. Ronald W. Reagan of California (1967–75) one electoral vote.
9 U.S. and the U.S.S.R. sign treaty limiting the size of underground nuclear explosions. Some on-site inspection of compliance is approved for the first time.

10 Military junta, headed by Gen. Jorge Rafael Videla, overthrows Pres. Isabel Perón of Argentina.
11 Chinese Premier Chou En-lai and Communist Party Chairman Mao Tse-tung die. Mao's widow and three other revolutionaries ("Gang of Four") make unsuccessful attempt to seize power. Hua Kuo-feng becomes Premier and Chairman.
12 North and South Vietnam are reunited as one nation after 22 years, with Hanoi as capital. Saigon is renamed Ho Chi Minh City.
13 Cease-fire halts civil war between Christians and Muslims in Lebanon.
14 Sihanouk resigns and Khieu Samphan becomes head of state of Cambodia, which is renamed Kampuchea.
15 Pro-Palestinian terrorists hijack Air France plane to Entebbe Airport, Uganda. Israeli commando raid frees 103 hostages.
16 Blacks in Soweto, Johannesburg, and Cape Town riot against South Africa's apartheid policy.
17 Transkei becomes the first black African homeland to gain independence in South Africa.
18 Parti Québécois wins majority of seats in Quebec's parliament. René Lévesque becomes Premier of Quebec.
19 Supporters of black majority rule wage guerrilla war against the white government of Rhodesia. **[1977:HIST/17]**
20 Portugal holds its first free presidential election in half a century.
21 James Callaghan succeeds Wilson as British Prime Minister.
22 José López Portillo is elected President of Mexico, replacing Luis Echeverria Álvarez.

1 Nobel Prize, Literature: Saul Bellow.
2 Stevie Wonder releases the immensely popular album, *Songs in the Key of Life.*
3 Woodward and Bernstein publish *The Final Days,* about Nixon's last days in the White House.
4 *Network,* a film that presents a rather unusual view of the TV world, features Oscar-winning performances by Peter Finch, Faye Dunaway, and Beatrice Straight.
5 *Rocky,* a film starring Sylvester Stallone, wins the Oscar for Best Picture.
6 Uris publishes *Trinity,* a novel based on the conflict in Ireland.
7 Peter Benchley publishes *The Deep,* a suspense novel about deep-sea diving.
8 Erma Bombeck, humorist, publishes *The Grass Is Always Greener Over the Septic Tank,* an amusing look at suburban life.
9 Alex Haley publishes *Roots: The Saga of an American Family,* in which he traces his ancestry back to the African slave trade.
10 Ira Levin publishes *The Boys from Brazil.*
11 Vonnegut publishes *Slapstick.*
12 Christo, artist, designs "Running Fence," a curtain of fabric stretching 24 miles along the Pacific coast.
13 Neil Simon writes *California Suite,* a series of one-act plays.
14 Doctorow publishes *Ragtime.*
15 Potok publishes *In the Beginning.*

16 Hochhuth writes *Death of a Hunter,* a play based on Hemingway's life.
17 Puzo's *Back Room Boys* (1969) is produced by the BBC.
18 Paul Mark Scott, Eng. writer, publishes *The Raj Quartet,* four historical novels about British rule in India.
19 Marian Engel, Can. novelist, publishes *Bear,* called by one critic "the strangest and most impossible love story ever."
20 Peter Frampton, Brit. rock star, is an international sensation. He is elected "artist of the year" in a rock music poll conducted by *Rolling Stone Magazine* (Amer.). Bob Marley and the Wailers, a Jamaican group, popularize reggae music.
21 Ayckbourn completes the comedy, *The Norman Conquests.*
22 Fr. writer Patrick Grainville wins the Prix Goncourt for his novel, *Les Flamboyants.*
23 Claiming harassment by tax officials, Ingmar Bergman announces plans to move from Sweden. His film, *Face to Face,* stars actress Liv Ullman.

Science & Technology

America

1 A mysterious illness kills 29 people and affects 182 others, most of whom are attending an American Legion convention in Philadelphia. Known as "Legionnaire's Disease," it has scientists baffled.

2 After 51 people are paralyzed, a national vaccination program against swine flu is discontinued. 35 million people were vaccinated.

3 Stanford University (Calif.) scientists produce a subatomic particle that possesses the property known as *charm*.

4 The chronon (T_{ch}) is selected as the smallest unit of time. It is 4.4×10^{-24} second.

5 Lyme arthritis, a new, infectious form of arthritis, is discovered near Lyme, Conn. The disease is thought to be spread by virus-carrying insects.

6 A malaria-causing organism is cultured in the lab—the first step in the development of a vaccine.

7 Kitts Peak astronomers determine that Pluto is covered with methane ice and may once have been a moon of Neptune.

8 Pioneer 10 travels through Saturn's rings and heads toward a 1987 examination of Pluto.

9 Viking 1 and Viking 2 land on Mars and begin sending back information about the planet's surface.

10 Nobel Prize, Physics: Burton Richter and Samuel Ting for their 1974 discovery of the subatomic psi particle.

11 Nobel Prize, Physiology or Medicine: Baruch Blumberg and Daniel Gajdusek for discoveries about the origin and spread of infectious diseases.

Elsewhere

12 Indonesia launches the communication satellite Palapa from Cape Canaveral in Florida.

13 The 143 member nations of the World Meteorological Organization (WMO) develop methods to standardize weather data.

14 The Soviet Soyuz 21 links up with the Salyut 5 space station. Cosmonauts B. Volynov and Vitaly Zholobov study the effects of weightlessness on plants and animals.

15 The Soviet Soyuz 22, with cosmonauts V. Bykovsky and Vladimir Aksenov, photographs the Earth's surface.

16 The Soviet Soyuz 23, with cosmonauts Vyacheslav Zudov and Valery Rozhdestvensky, fails to make its planned link up with the Salyut 5 space station and is forced to make the first Soviet water landing.

Miscellaneous

America

1 Women win 13 of 32 Rhodes Scholarships awarded to Americans; first time scholarships—established in 1902—are open to women.

2 *Argo Merchant,* a Liberian tanker, runs aground off Nantucket Island, Mass.; spills 5 million gallons of oil into the sea.

3 .Survey of 17,000 high school seniors in 130 schools finds that 53% have tried marijuana. Of those who have experimented with it, 32% considered themselves current users.

4 Pan-American airliner completes world's longest nonstop commercial flight, covering 8,088 mi. in 13 hr., 31 min.

5 Departmental of Health, Education, and Welfare (HEW) finds Americans generally healthy. Life expectancy for white women, 79.2 yr.; nonwhite women, 72 yr.; white men 67.4 yr.; nonwhite, 62 yr. Among younger persons, accidents and homicides are major causes of death.

6 Patricia Hearst's trial begins. (In 1974 she had been kidnapped by the Symbionese Liberation Army, a terrorist group, which she later joined.) Charged with robbing a San Francisco bank, she is found guilty and sentenced to 25 years in prison. (Her sentence is later reduced.)

7 Worst West Coast drought in 70 years ends; since 1975 only 0.59 in. of rain has fallen in southern California .

Elsewhere

8 Shower of more than 100 meteorites in China, including largest stone ever seen falling onto the earth; fragments collectively weigh 3894 lbs.

9 Col. Valérie André is first woman general in French armed forces.

10 Thieves steal estimated $10–15 million in cash and valuables from bank in Nice, France; underground looting operation is biggest bank robbery in history.

11 British archaeologists excavate 8 tombs of 10th century B.C. on Crete.

12 Winter Olympics held at Innsbruck, Austria, where 1054 athletes from 37 countries compete.

13 Remains of 5 ships belonging to Spanish Armada (1588) found underwater along Irish and Scottish coasts.

14 France gives U.S. gifts worth $4 million for country's bicentennial.

15 Norwegian freighter *Berge Istra* is lost en route from Brazil to Japan. Loss of 224,000-ton vessel, with insurance claims of $27 million, is one of costliest disasters in maritime history.

16 3250-year-old mummy of Ramses II (1292–1225 B.C., king of ancient Egypt) flown to Paris for preservation treatment.

17 6 women in British Columbia and Ontario, Canada, ordained as priests in Anglican Church.

18 A 10-mi. long, 120-yd. wide tunnel, world's longest, is completed; runs under St. Gotthard range from Switzerland to Italy.

19 Earthquake in China kills 655,000 people.

1976

History and Politics

America

Elsewhere

The Arts

America

Elsewhere

1977

America (History and Politics)

1 Pres. Carter pardons most draft evaders of the Vietnam War period.
2 Congress creates new Cabinet-level Department of Energy. James R. Schlesinger is named its first secretary.
3 Justice Department investigates alleged illegal bribery by South Korean officials to influence members of Congress ("Koreagate").
4 Congress grants Pres. Carter authority to eliminate or consolidate federal agencies that duplicate services.
5 Travel bans on U.S. citizens to Cuba, Vietnam, Cambodia, and North Korea are lifted.
6 Andrew J. Young, Jr., U.S. Representative from Georgia, is appointed U.S. Ambassador to the UN.
7 Pres. Carter makes "human rights" a part of U.S. foreign policy.
8 U.S. extends its territorial fishing zone to 200 miles.
9 Pres. Carter and Gen. Torrijos sign new Panama Canal treaties. [1978:HIST/2]
10 Thomas Bradley, Mayor of Los Angeles since 1973, is reelected. A black, he defeats 11 white opponents.
11 Edward I. Koch is elected Mayor of New York City.
12 U.S. imports exceed exports by $26.72 billion—the largest trade deficit in its history. High oil consumption in U.S. makes energy conservation necessary (energy crisis).
13 Pres. Carter stops the manufacture of the B-1 bomber and urges development of the cruise missile.

Elsewhere (History and Politics)

14 Soviets harass and arrest political and human rights activists in the U.S.S.R., Czechoslovakia, and other Soviet bloc countries.
15 Britain, Canada, and other nations set 200-mile fishing limits.
16 Pol Pot becomes leader of the Cambodian Communist Party.
17 Prime Minister Smith of Rhodesia agrees to work out a settlement for black majority rule.
18 Morarji R. Desai, head of the Janata Party, succeeds Gandhi as Prime Minister of India.
19 Menachem Begin becomes Prime Minister of Israel following Rabin's resignation as a result of U.S. bank fund scandal. Begin and Pres. Sadat of Egypt meet in Israel and then in Egypt to discuss ways to end the Arab-Israeli conflict and to establish peace.
20 Military leaders depose Bhutto and take control of Pakistan.
21 Ethiopia and Somalia wage war over Ogaden region.
22 French territory of Afars and Issas becomes the independent republic of Djibouti.
23 Brezhnev replaces Podgorny as President of the U.S.S.R., becoming the first Soviet leader to be both Communist Party chief and President.
24 Military leaders seize power in Thailand. Thai and Cambodian troops fight along the border.
25 Bophuthatswana becomes the second black African homeland to be granted independence by South Africa. [1976:HIST/17]
26 Angolans, including Katangan exiles, invade Shaba (formerly Katanga) province in Zaire.
27 French leftists gain control in elections of most of France's large cities.

America (The Arts)

1 The TV dramatization of *Roots* breaks records for audience size.
2 Bakshi produces the feature length cartoon fantasy *Wizards*.
3 David Mamet, playwright, produces *American Buffalo*.
4 Erich Segal publishes *Oliver's Story*, a sequel to *Love Story*.
5 Colleen McCollough, writer, publishes *The Thorn Birds*.
6 Paul Erdman publishes *The Crash of '79*.
7 *Annie*, a musical based on the comic strip "Little Orphan Annie," opens on Broadway.
8 Howard Fast publishes *The Immigrants*.
9 Zeffirelli produces the highly acclaimed TV drama *Jesus of Nazareth*, starring Robert Powell.
10 Cheever publishes the best-selling novel, *Falconer*.
11 The film *Saturday Night Fever*, starring John Travolta, helps to popularize disco dance music.
12 Billy Joel's album *The Stranger* includes the Grammy winning song "Just the Way You Are."
13 George Lucas directs *Star Wars*, a film which signals the beginning of a new, more polished science-fiction genre in films.
14 Neil Simon writes the semi-autobiographical play, *Chapter Two*.
15 The film *Annie Hall* wins Oscars for Best Picture, Best Director (Woody Allen), and Best Actress (Diane Keaton).

Elsewhere (The Arts)

16 Tolkien's novel, *The Silmarillion*, originally written as a preface to *Lord of the Rings*, is published.
17 Didier Decoin, Fr. novelist, wins the Prix Goncourt for *John l'Enfer*.
18 Georg Solti, Hung. conductor and music director of the Chicago Symphony, is appointed principal conductor of the London Philharmonic.
19 Yoshimi Usui, Jap. author, creates a stir with *The Circumstances of the Incident*, a novelized account of the suicide (1972) of Yasunari Kawabata.
20 Amado publishes the novel, *Tieto do Agreste*.
21 The Sex Pistols and other "punk rock" or "new wave" music groups gain popularity.
22 In Paris, the Georges Pompidou National Centre of Art and Culture opens.
23 In London, the art exhibit, "Pompeii A.D. 79," gives a glimpse of life at that time.
24 Norman Morrice, Eng. dancer and choreographer, becomes artistic director of the Royal Ballet, London.
25 *Padre Padrone*, a movie directed by Paolo and Vittorio Taviani (Ital.), is the first film to win both the Grand Prize and the International Critics' Prize at Cannes.
26 Jacques Brel, Bel.-born songwriter and performer, records his last album, *Brel*, the year's biggest hit in France.

Science & Technology

America

1 Methanogens are identified as a totally separate and previously unknown form of life that existed about 3.5 billion years ago.
2 Astronomers aboard NASA's Airborne Observatory discover rings around Uranus.
3 Charles Kowal, astronomer, discovers Chiron, a "miniplanet" orbiting the Sun.
4 Fluorocarbons are banned as aerosol propellants because of evidence that they harm the ozone in the atmosphere. [1974:SCI/1]
5 After extensive hearings, FDA declares that laetrile is not a vitamin and is of no value in treating cancer.
6 *Enterprise*, the space shuttle, successfully completes several test flights and landings.
7 A previously unknown type of bacterium is identified as the cause of Legionnaire's disease.
8 FDA claims saccharin may cause cancer.
9 Upsilon, a subatomic particle, is detected.
10 HEAO-1, a High Energy Astronomy Observatory, is launched into Earth orbit to study x-rays and gamma rays.
11 Voyager 1 and Voyager 2 are launched on a journey that will bring them near Jupiter and Saturn in 1979 and 1980.
12 Nobel Prize, Physics: John Van Vleck (Amer.), Philip Anderson (Amer.), and Nevill Mott (Eng.) for developments in solid state electronics.
13 Nobel Prize, Physiology or Medicine: Rosalyn Yalow, Roger Guillemin, and Andrew Schally for research on the action of hormones.

Elsewhere

14 After analyzing the genetic structure of certain viruses, Eng. scientists conclude that more information is stored in DNA than was previously thought.
15 An outbreak of venereal disease affects horses in England, Ireland, and France.
16 The Soviet Soyuz 24, with cosmonauts V. Gorbatko and Yuri Glazkov, links up with the Salyut 5 space station.
17 The Soviet Soyuz 26 docks with the Salyut 6 space station. Cosmonauts G. Grechko and Yuri Romanenko spend 96 days in space, during which they conduct many astrophysical experiments.
18 Nobel Prize, Chemistry: Ilya Prigogine, Belg. chemist, for his work on nonequilibrium thermodynamics.

Star Wars character See-Threepio

Miscellaneous

America

1 Blizzard with 60-mph winds sweeps through Midwest into the East; Buffalo, N.Y., is completely isolated.
2 Steve Cauthen, 17, is first jockey in horse racing to reach $6 million in purse earnings in one year.
3 Mysterious legionnaires' disease, which killed 29 persons in Philadelphia in 1976, spreads, afflicting 48 persons in 19 states.
4 St. Louis Cardinal outfielder Lou Brock sets new base-stealing record of 893, passing record held since 1928 by Ty Cobb.
5 Convicted murderer Gary Gilmore shot to death by firing squad at Utah State Prison; first person to suffer the death penalty in U.S. since 1967.
6 John Neumann made a saint in the Roman Catholic Church; first American male to be selected.
7 U.S. Supreme Court rules that spanking of students by school officials is not a violation of pupils' constitutional rights.
8 Americans explore forms of spiritualism: 6 million active in transcendental meditation; 5 million practice yoga; 3 million follow the charismatic movement; 3 million involved in mysticism; and 2 million in Eastern religions.
9 George Willig, amateur mountain climber, scales the 1350-ft. South Tower of New York City's World Trade Center.
10 Trans-Alaska pipeline system begins operation; 789-mi. pipeline costs $7.7 billion. [1973:SCI/7]

Elsewhere

11 At least 300 people, mostly young children, starve to death because of serious drought in Haiti.
12 Roman Catholic Church prohibits ordination of women as priests.
13 Earthquake in Rumania destroys Bucharest, the capital; death toll is 1541; 11,275 injured and 80,000 homeless.
14 Sahaharu Oh of the Tokyo (Japan) Yomiuri Giants baseball team hits 756th career home run, bypassing Henry Aaron's record of 755.
15 Armed robbers in Paris, France, hijack a truck carrying $3.5 million shipment of new coins; described as "heaviest holdup in world."
16 Cyclone strikes India; estimated 20,000 people killed, 2 million homeless. Storm brings tidal waves 18 ft. high and 100 mph winds.
17 Tomb of Philip II, King of Macedon and father of Alexander the Great, discovered in Greece.
18 Earthquake in Iran kills 589 people, injures 700; 3 villages destroyed.
19 The Temple Scroll, one of longest of the Dead Sea Scrolls first found in 1947, is published in Israel.
20 Pan American and KLM 747s collide on runway at Tenerife, Canary Islands. All 249 on KLM plane and 333 of 394 aboard Pan Am jet killed; total is highest for any kind of aviation disaster.

1977

History and Politics | The Arts

America | Elsewhere | America | Elsewhere

1978

America (History and Politics)

1 U.S. and Communist China establish full diplomatic relations.

2 Senate ratifies new Panama Canal treaties; one treaty gives Panama full control of the Canal at the end of 1999; the other gives the U.S. the right to defend the Canal's neutrality.

3 Mideast peace talks, arranged by Pres. Carter, are held by Egyptian Pres. Sadat, Israeli Prime Minister Begin, and Pres. Carter at Camp David, Md. Major agreement is reached, including the drafting of a peace treaty between Israel and Egypt. [1979:HIST/23]

4 Pres. Carter invokes the Taft-Hartley Act to end coal strike. Mine workers and coal operators sign new contract, ending 110-day strike, the longest continuous walkout by miners.

5 New 15-cent stamp goes into use, approved by the Postal Rate Commission.

6 Pres. Carter calls for voluntary anti-inflation program.

7 Congress extends ratification of the Equal Rights Amendment (ERA) to 1982. [1972:HIST/5]

8 California voters approve Proposition 13, which drastically cuts property taxes; it reduces state revenues from $12 billion to $5 billion.

9 U.S. dollar falls in value against Western European and Japanese currencies.

10 Pres. Carter signs law making 70 the mandatory retirement age for most Americans.

11 Supreme Court allows the drilling for oil and natural gas off the Mid-Atlantic coast.

12 Supreme Court requires the Univ. of California Medical School (at Davis) to admit Allan P. Bakke. He claimed the school's minority-admissions program made him a victim of "reverse discrimination."

Elsewhere (History and Politics)

13 Bulent Ecevit is named Premier of Turkey.

14 Belgian and French paratroopers repulse rebels in Shaba, Zaire.

15 Leftist Sandinista guerrillas fight Nicaraguan National Guard in effort to overthrow the regime of Pres. Somoza. [1979:HIST/18]

16 Red Brigades, Ital. revolutionary group, kidnap and murder former Premier Aldo Moro. Communists are given a direct rule in Italy's government.

17 Military officers seize power in Afghanistan.

18 Filipinos protest against the dictatorial rule of Pres. Marcos. [1972:HIST/13]

19 Antonio Guzman is elected President of the Dominican Republic, narrowly defeating Pres. Balaguer.

20 Dominica, Tuvalu (formerly the Ellice Islands), and the Solomon Islands become independent nations.

21 Fighting breaks out between Yemen and Southern Yemen.

22 Leading human rights activists are convicted of "anti-Soviet agitation" and sentenced to prison in the U.S.S.R.

23 Coalition government of Portugal collapses because of discord between political parties.

24 Pieter Willem Botha succeeds Vorster as Prime Minister of South Africa. Guerrillas of South West African People's Organization (SWAPO) fight for Namibia's independence.

25 Violent riots break out in Iran against the rule of the Shah. Self-exiled Muslim leader Ayatollah Ruhollah Khomeini in Paris warns of civil war if an Islamic republic is not installed in Iran. [1953:HIST/16; 1979:HIST/16]

America (The Arts)

1 Dolly Parton, singer, wins the Country Music Association's Entertainer of the Year Award for the song "Here You Come Again."

2 The Vietnam War is the subject of two important movies: *The Deer Hunter* starring Robert DeNiro, winner of the Best Picture Oscar, and *Coming Home*, featuring Oscar-winning performances by Jane Fonda and Jon Voight.

3 Nobel Prize, Literature: Isaac Bashevis Singer.

4 David Mamet publishes *The Water Engine*.

5 Robert Ludlum, writer, publishes *The Holcroft Covenant*.

6 Marilyn French, writer, publishes *The Women's Room*.

7 John Irving, novelist, publishes *The World According to Garp*.

8 James Michener publishes *Chesapeake*.

9 Bakshi's animated version of Tolkien's *Lord of the Rings* introduces a technique in which live actors are filmed, after which the footage is painted over to give the impression of a "realistic painting in motion."

10 Broadway musicals this year include *On the Twentieth Century*, with a score by Betty Comden and Adolph Green, and *The Act*, which wins actress Liza Minnelli a Tony award.

11 Seiji Ozawa becomes the first foreigner to conduct China's Central Philharmonic Orchestra.

Elsewhere (The Arts)

12 Greene publishes the spy novel, *The Human Factor*.

13 Sov. conductor Gennady Rozhdestvensky is appointed chief conductor of the BBC Symphony Orchestra.

14 M.M. Kaye, Eng. author, publishes *The Far Pavilions*, a historical novel.

15 Bulg. defector Georgi Markov, author of the play, *The Assassins*, dies after being stabbed by a poison-tipped umbrella.

16 Grass publishes *The Flounder*, a novel based on the effects of the women's movement.

17 Ir. flutist James Galway has a best-selling hit record in England, "Annie's Song."

18 The third volume of Solzhenitsyn's *The Gulag Archipelago* is published.

19 ABBA, the most popular rock group since the Beatles, begins an international tour.

20 Patrick Modiano, Fr. novelist, is awarded the Prix Goncourt for *Rue des boutiques obscures*.

21 André Laplante, pianist, is the first Canadian to receive a medal at the *International Tchaikovsky Competition* in Moscow.

Science & Technology

America

1 Widespread controversy surrounds claims that a human being has been cloned.

2 Chromosomes are discovered in parts of the cell other than the nucleus. Until this discovery, scientists thought all chromosomes were in the nucleus.

3 Interferon is used experimentally to treat 150 patients with "hopeless" cases of cancer.

4 Texas Instruments introduces magnetic bubble memories for computers.

5 Vitamin C is proposed as a cancer-preventing drug.

6 AMA concludes a 14-year study that shows that cigarette smoking causes heart disease and may cause cancer.

7 Plasma Physics Laboratory at Princeton University conducts controlled fusion experiments.

8 Construction of the Tellico Dam in Tennessee is halted because it threatens the last known habitat of the snail darter, an endangered species of fish. Construction resumes in 1979.

9 James Cristy, astronomer, discovers Charon, a moon of Pluto.

10 Pioneer-Venus Probes 1 and 2 are launched to study the atmosphere of Venus.

11 Nobel Prize, Physics: A. Penzias and R. Wilson for discovering background cosmic radiation which supports the big bang theory.

12 Nobel Prize, Physiology or Medicine: Daniel Nathans (Amer.), Hamilton Smith (Amer.), and Werner Arber (Swiss) for discovery of restriction enzymes and their effect on genes.

Elsewhere

13 Scot. scientists immunize tomatoes against the tobacco mosaic virus.

14 Eng. scientists determine that women who bear children before the age of 20 have lower incidence of breast cancer than older women.

15 The nuclear-equipped Soviet satellite *Cosmos 954* falls from space and crashes in a remote area of Canada. Radioactive debris is detected.

16 The Soviet Soyuz 27 docks with Salyut 6. Cosmonauts Vladimir Dzhanibekov and O. Makarov spend several days with the Soyuz 26 cosmonauts already aboard Salyut 6. [1977:SCI/17]

17 The Soviet Soyuz 28 docks with Salyut 6. Cosmonaut A. Gubarev and the first non-Russian cosmonaut, Vladimir Remek, a Czech, visit with the Soyuz 26 cosmonauts already aboard Salyut 6.

18 The Soviet Soyuz 29, with cosmonauts Vladimir Kovalenkov and Alexander Ivanchenkov, docks with Salyut 6. The cosmonauts spend 96 days 10 hours aboard the space station.

19 The Soviets launch Soyuz 30, with cosmonauts P. Klimuk and Miroslaw Hermaszewski, a Pole, and Soyuz 31, with cosmonauts V. Bykovsky and Sigmund Jaehn, an East German. Both missions successfully dock with the Salyut 6 space station, where the Soyuz 29 cosmonauts are still conducting tests.

20 Nobel Prize, Chemistry: Peter Mitchell, Eng. biochemist, for his research on how cells use energy.

21 Nobel Prize, Physics: Kapitsa, for his work on low-temperature physics.

Miscellaneous

America

1 Three balloonists complete first transatlantic crossing from Presque Isle, Me., to Miserey, France, traveling 3233 mi. in 137 hr. 18 min.

2 Federal Communications Commission studies' children's television to see if TV industry is showing reasonable amount of children's shows, including educational programs.

3 Nancy Lopez wins 5 consecutive golf tournaments and sets earnings record of $153,336 for a first-year professional golfer.

4 *Star Wars* is all-time leader in worldwide film rentals; takes in $202 million, passing record set by *Jaws*.

5 Boxing match between Muhammad Ali and Leon Spinks seen in more U.S. homes than any other event in television's history—34.7 million.

6 Brig. Gen. Mary Clarke is first woman named by Army to two-star rank of major general.

7 Tracy Caulkins, 15, from Nashville, Tenn., sets U.S. records in 14 individual events during year and wins 5 gold medals at World Swimming Championships in Germany.

8 Irene Miller and Vera Komarkova are first Americans and first women to climb Annapurna One, a 26,545-ft. mountain in Nepal.

9 Mass murder-suicides at Peoples Temple, Jonestown, Guyana, total 911.

10 Federal judge in Ohio rules that high school girls should not be prevented from participating with boys on same sports teams.

Elsewhere

11 Mary Simpson, Amer. Episcopal priest, is first woman to preach at Westminster Abbey, London.

12 Month-long heat wave in India kills more than 200 people; temperatures range between 105° and 115° Fahrenheit, remaining in high nineties at night.

13 Japanese explorer Naomi Uemura completes 500-mi. trip over frozen Arctic Ocean to North Pole; first to make trip alone.

14 Virus that attacks the brain strikes parts of northern India, killing 480 people in one month.

15 Soviet Union finishes first in World Gymnastics Championships in France.

16 Shroud of Turin, believed by many to be burial garment of Jesus Christ, studied by scientists.

17 World chess champion Anatoly Karpov of Soviet Union defeats Viktor Korchnoi, who resigns in 32nd game of the match.

18 Earthquake in northeast Iran kills 25,000 people; lasts 90 sec., measures 7.7 on Richter scale.

19 Bernard Hinault of France wins 2500-mi. Tour de France, world's most important bicycle endurance race. Race is run in 22 stages of more than 100 mi. each over 23 days.

20 Naomi Jones of England is first woman to sail around world alone: over 30,000 mi. in 272 days.

21 Fire sweeps through packed movie theater in Abadan, Iran, killing 430 persons.

22 Argentina wins World Cup soccer championship, defeating the Netherlands, 3–1.

1978

413

History and Politics

America

Elsewhere

The Arts

America

Elsewhere

1979

America (History and Politics)

1 Department of Energy sues nine large U.S. oil companies for allegedly overcharging customers nearly $1 billion since 1973.
2 New Cabinet-level Department of Education is established, with Shirley M. Hufstedler as its first secretary.
3 Large anti-nuclear rallies are held in Washington, D.C., and New York City.
4 Gasoline sales on odd-even days are instituted in many states.
5 Jane M. Byrne becomes first woman to be elected Mayor of Chicago.
6 Cuban Pres. Castro visits the U.S. for the first time in 19 years and addresses UN General Assembly.
7 Supreme Court upholds voluntary "affirmative action" programs.
8 Shah of Iran is admitted to the U.S. to undergo surgery. He leaves for Panama following uproar over his stay in the U.S.
9 U.S. suspends Iranian oil imports and Iranian assets in the U.S. in retaliation for the holding of 50 U.S. hostages in Teheran. [1979:HIST/16]
10 U.S. embassy in Islamabad, Pakistan, is stormed. Anti-American protests occur also in India, Bangladesh, Turkey, and Libya.
11 Congress approves a $1.5 billion federal loan guarantee plan for Chrysler Corporation—largest government bailout ever of a U.S. company.
12 U.S. annual inflation rate is 13.3%, the highest in 33 years.
13 Senate delays ratification of the new Strategic Arms Limitation Treaty between the U.S. and the U.S.S.R. (SALT II).

Elsewhere (History and Politics)

14 Vietnamese forces seize Phnom Penh, Cambodia. Pol Pot's government falls, and thousands of Cambodians flee to Thailand.
15 Morocco takes possession of all of Western Sahara after Mauritania gives up its claim to the southern part.
16 Iranian revolution forces the Shah to leave Iran. Ayatollah Khomeini returns to proclaim an Islamic republic. Trials and executions of former officials of the Shah take place. Iranians storm U.S. embassy in Teheran and hold employees, vowing not to return the U.S. hostages until the Shah is returned to stand trial.
17 Vietnamese refugees on cargo ships ("boat people") seek asylum in Indonesia, Malaysia, and other countries.
18 Sandinista guerrillas capture Managua, Nicaragua. Pres. Somoza flees.
19 Panama takes possession of the Canal Zone.
20 Ugandans aided by Tanzanian forces liberate Uganda from the dictatorial rule of Gen. Amin.
21 Margaret Hilda Thatcher, Conservative Party leader, becomes Britain's first woman Prime Minister.
22 Joseph Clark, Conservative Party leader, becomes Canada's youngest Prime Minister.
23 Egypt and Israel sign peace treaty.
24 Blacks vote for the first time in Rhodesian national elections. Bishop Abel Muzorewa is elected the first black Prime Minister and renames the country Zimbabwe. British governor takes control of Zimbabwe-Rhodesia during a transition period to a new government.
25 Soviet military forces invade Afghanistan and overthrow the Kabul government.

America (The Arts)

1 Norman Mailer publishes *The Executioner's Song*, the Pulitzer Prize-winning story of convicted killer Gary Gilmore.
2 Tom Wolfe publishes *The Right Stuff*, a detailed account of the training and private lives of the original seven astronauts.
3 *The Rose*, a film starring Bette Midler, is loosely based on the life of singer Janis Joplin.
4 Bob Woodward and Scott Armstrong publish *The Brethren*, an inside look at the Supreme Court.
5 Ken Follet, writer, publishes *Triple*.
6 Jerzy Kosinski publishes *Passion Play*.
7 Isaac Bashevis Singer publishes *Old Love*, a collection of short stories.
8 Christopher Lasch publishes *The Culture of Narcissism*, about the "me generation."
9 "The Icebergs," a painting created by Frederic E. Church in 1861, is auctioned for $2.5 million, the most ever paid for a painting by an American.
10 Coppola directs *Apocalypse Now*, a Vietnam War film spectacle starring Martin Sheen and Marlon Brando, based on Conrad's *Heart of Darkness*.
11 Dustin Hoffman and Meryl Streep win Oscars for their roles in *Kramer vs. Kramer*.
12 Sally Field wins the Oscar for Best Actress in *Norma Rae*, a film about a woman labor organizer.

Elsewhere (The Arts)

13 LeCarré publishes *Smiley's People*, the last case for his famous secret agent, George Smiley.
14 Fr. photographer Henri Cartier-Bresson publishes a book of his candid photographs to coincide with the start of a two-year tour.
15 Elton John is the first rock star from the West to tour the U.S.S.R.
16 The Paris Opéra gives the first performance of the complete *Lulu*, an opera unfinished at the time of its composer's (Berg) death.
17 Tate Gallery (Eng.) is criticized for its "over-emphasis" on abstract art.
18 BBC produces the historical-scientific series, *The Voyages of Charles Darwin*.
19 *Ten Thousand Leaves of the Shōwa Period* is an anthology of Japanese poets, 1926–71.
20 The Paris-Moscow Exhibition, Paris, features avant-garde works by Soviet artists.
21 Communist Party leader Leonid I. Brezhnev is awarded the prestigious Lenin Prize, the U.S.S.R.'s highest literary award, for his trilogy published in 1978.
22 Junji Kinoshita writes *The Mandarin Festival*, acclaimed as the Japanese play of the year.
23 Shaffer completes *Amadeus*, a drama based on the Mozart-Salieri intrigue.

Science & Technology

America

1 Researchers at Mass. General Hospital discover that cancer cells form a protective cocoon around the tumor, preventing the body's own defenses from fighting the disease.

2 A black hole is discovered at the center of the Milky Way.

3 Doctors in Maryland use a metal cylinder to replace an 8-inch section of a woman's spine removed earlier because of cancer.

4 Gasohol—a mixture of gasoline and alcohol—gains more widespread use as a substitute for gasoline.

5 Antimatter particles are detected in the upper atmosphere. This is the first time they have been found anywhere but in a laboratory.

6 Trace amounts of nitrosamines, chemicals that may cause cancer, are found in most brands of beer.

7 MIT researchers discover that the DNA molecule spirals to the left, not to the right as was previously believed.

8 Using a 6-beam laser fusion instrument, scientists produce a temperature of 67 million °F (19 million °C).

9 A hybrid ape is born at the Atlanta Zoo. The parents: a gibbon (44 chromosomes) and a siamang (50 chromosomes).

10 Pioneer 11 discovers two new moons and two new rings around Saturn.

11 Viking 1 discovers that Jupiter has a ring and a 14th moon.

12 Nobel Prize, Physiology or Medicine: Allan M. Cormack and Godfrey N. Hounsfield (Eng.) for development of x-ray procedure known as CAT-scan (Computed Axial Tomography).

Elsewhere

13 The Soviet Soyuz 32 docks with the Salyut 6 space station. Cosmonauts Vladimir Lyakhov and V. Ryumin spend a record 175 days in space. During that time, Soyuz 33, with cosmonauts N. Rukavishnikov and Georgi Ivanov, a Bulgarian, makes an unsuccessful attempt to dock with Salyut 6.

14 Mary Leakey discovers humanlike footprints in Tanzania that are estimated to be 3.6 million years old.

15 Chin. dentists claim a 90% success rate for replanting teeth.

16 Scott Tremain, Eng. astronomer, and Peter Goldreich, Amer. astronomer, suggest the existence of undetected moons which somehow keep the particles that compose Uranus's rings in their correct paths.

17 Scientists discover a giant worm off the Galápagos Islands which appears to absorb nutrients directly from the ocean. The worm may require a new zoological classification.

18 Chin. physicians claim to have constructed a workable hand for a 25-year-old man. The hand, composed of a stainless-steel palm covered with grafted muscle and skin, uses two toes, transplanted from the recipient's foot, as fingers.

19 Nobel Prize, Chemistry: Herbert Brown, Amer. chemist, and Georg Witteg, W. Ger. chemist, for their work on the chemistry and various pharmaceutical applications of boron and phosphorus.

Miscellaneous

America

1 Wreck of 17-century Spanish galleon *Concepción* discovered off coast of Dominican Republic.

2 Blizzards strike Midwest; Chicago reports winter's accumulation of almost 80 in. of snow.

3 Pope John Paul II makes tour with stops in Boston; New York City; Philadelphia; Des Moines; Chicago; and Washington, D.C.

4 Lou Brock, St. Louis Cardinal, gets his 3000th hit; Carl Yastrzemski, Boston Red Sox, hits his 400th major league home run; Pete Rose, Philadelphia Phillies, is all-time leader in National League singles with 2427.

5 Dime-sized, silver and copper disk found near Bar Harbor, Me., in 1961, is identified as Norse penny minted between 1065 and 1080. It is the first datable Viking artifact found in North America.

6 Three Mile Island nuclear plant near Middletown, Pa., damaged in accident; major catastrophe looms; evacuation plans prepared for people living 10 to 20 mi. downwind of plant.

7 272 persons on American Airlines DC-10 jet and 3 on ground are killed when plane loses engine and crashes at O'Hare Field, Chicago; worst accident in U.S. aviation history.

8 Bryan Allen of California makes first man-powered flight across English Channel; pedals a craft 22 mi. from English to French coast.

9 Tracy Austin, 16, wins women's singles tennis title in Queens, N.Y., becoming youngest women's champion in U.S. Open history.

Elsewhere

10 Volcano, Mount Sinila, erupts in Java; 175 persons killed, many die from inhaling poisonous gases.

11 Soviet Union's national hockey team defeats Amer. National Hockey League All-Stars to win Challenge Cup series.

12 Mother Teresa, of India, is awarded the Nobel Peace Prize for her work among the sick and the poor.

13 Octuplets—5 girls and 3 boys—born in Naples; 5 die within a short time.

14 Hurricane David kills 1100 persons in the Caribbean, causing billions of dollars in damage.

15 Eighteen sailors drown and scores are injured when storm strikes more than 300 boats competing in yacht race in the English Channel and the Irish Sea.

16 Pope John Paul II visits Poland; first time a pope has visited a communist country.

17 Air New Zealand jet crashes into mountain in Antarctica; all 257 aboard killed.

History and Politics

America

Elsewhere

The Arts

America

Elsewhere

1980

History and Politics — America

1 U.S. negotiates through other countries for release of Americans held hostage by Iranians in Teheran. U.S. rescue mission fails with plane-helicopter collision in Iranian desert.

2 FBI exposes bribery of public officials in Abscam undercover operation.

3 Pres. Carter signs Crude Oil Windfall Profits Tax, possibly the largest single tax ever imposed on an industry.

4 125,000 Cuban refugees are held at U.S. army bases prior to resettlement in U.S. [1980/MISC:18]

5 Thousands of Haitians flee to U.S.

6 Chrysler Corporation receives government-guaranteed $400 million loan.

7 U.S. acquires military bases in Oman and Somalia.

8 Ronald W. Reagan and George Bush are elected President and Vice President respectively on the Republican ticket, defeating Jimmy Carter and Walter Mondale (Democrats) and John B. Anderson and Patrick J. Lucey (Independents).

9 U.S. defense network's computer system mistakenly triggers alarm against nuclear attack.

10 Following acquittal of four Miami police officers charged with beating to death a black insurance executive, race riot in Miami leaves 18 persons dead and property damage of $100 million.

11 Congress overrides Pres. Carter's veto and rejects his proposal to levy $4.62 on each barrel of imported oil. First overriding of veto by a Congress controlled by the President's own party since 1952.

12 House of Representatives expels Congressman Michael J. Myers, convicted in Abscam scandal. First expulsion from House since the Civil War.

History and Politics — Elsewhere

13 Former Shah of Iran leaves home-in-exile on Cantadora Island, Panama, for Cairo, Egypt, where he dies of lymphatic cancer.

14 Afghan rebels wage guerrilla war against Soviet troops in Afghanistan.

15 Cambodia wracked by civil war between Pol Pot's forces and Vietnamese invaders.

16 Chao Chi-yang (Zhao Ziyang) replaces Hua Kuo-feng (Hua Guofeng) as Premier of China.

17 Polisario Front with Algerian aid fights Moroccan-occupation forces in Western Sahara.

18 Pres. William R. Tolbert killed during military coup in Liberia.

19 Helmut Schmidt is re-elected Chancellor of West Germany.

20 Soviet Prime Minister Aleksei N. Kosygin resigns after 16 years in post. He dies shortly thereafter.

21 Nationwide strikes in Poland force government to allow workers to set up independent trade union known as Solidarity, led by Lech Walesa.

22 Rhodesia becomes independent nation of Zimbabwe, officially ending 90 years of white rule. Robert G. Mugabe is elected Prime Minister.

23 Government of Uganda is overthrown by the military.

24 Iraqi forces invade Iran's oil-rich Khuzistan province.

25 Zenko Suzuki is elected Prime Minister of Japan, succeeding the late Masayoshi Ohira.

26 Voters in Quebec reject separatism.

27 Large-scale political violence erupts in El Salvador.

28 Anglo-French condominium of New Hebrides becomes independent nation of Vanuatu.

29 Proposed merger of Libya with Syria fails.

The Arts — America

1 Museum of Modern Art in New York shows "Pablo Picasso: A Retrospective." It is the first time the almost 1,000 items, representative of the artist's work in various media, have been exhibited together. "Guernica," Picasso's antiwar mural long housed at the Museum, will be sent to Spain in accordance with his wishes.

2 Eugene Ormandy ends his 44-year tenure as musical director of the Philadelphia Orchestra.

3 Mikhail Baryshnikov becomes director of the American Ballet Theater.

4 Metropolitan Museum of Art in New York opens its new American Wing, featuring an enclosed sculpture garden and a series of period rooms.

5 The 20-volume, sixth edition of Grove's Dictionary of Music and Musicians is published. The 4-volume first edition (1889) set codes and standards musical encyclopedists have followed ever since.

6 Academy Award-winning composer and conductor John Williams is appointed musical director of the Boston Pops Orchestra, succeeding the late Arthur Fiedler.

The Arts — Elsewhere

7 Mex. architect Louis Barragán, designer of the residential garden complex "El Pedregal," is awarded the Pritzker Architectural Prize.

8 Jap. film director Akira Kurosawa, makes a comeback with the tragedy *Kagemusha,* which takes top honors at the Cannes Film Festival.

9 A long crack is found in Leonardo da Vinci's "Last Supper" (finished 1497). [1495:ARTS/2]

10 The Comédie Française in Paris celebrates its 300th anniversary.

11 The Paris Opéra and La Scala (Milan) enter into a formal partnership, agreeing to share production costs and selected activities.

12 Nobel Prize for Literature is awarded to Polish-born American Czeslaw Milosz.

13 French-born American author Marguerite Yourcenar becomes the first woman elected to the prestigious French Academy.

14 Da Vinci's 36-page notebook of drawings and writings, known as the *Codex Leicester,* is sold at Christie's in London for $5.28 million, the highest auction price ever paid for a manuscript. Purchaser Armand Hammer says he will bequeath the *Codex* to the Los Angeles County Museum of Art.

Science & Technology		Miscellaneous		
America	**Elsewhere**	**America**	**Elsewhere**	**1980**

Science & Technology

America

Elsewhere

Miscellaneous

America

Elsewhere

1980

Science & Technology — America

1 Government-supported United States Synthetic Fuels Corporation is created to develop synthetic energy sources.

2 New York Blood Center scientists report finding a successful, experimental vaccine against hepatitis B.

3 Technicians finish cleaning damaged nuclear reactor at Three Mile Island. Radiation level is acceptable and residents are permitted to return to the area.

4 Voyager 1 photographs previously undetected 13th and 14th moons in orbits around Saturn, as well as 15th and 16th moons around Jupiter.

5 U.S. declares a state of emergency at the Love Canal in Niagara Falls, N.Y., an area contaminated by toxic chemical wastes.

6 Experiments by U.S. physicists indicate the subatomic particle known as the "neutrino" appears to have mass, helping to explain how the galaxies are held together by gravity.

7 Volunteers at Duke University emerge from pressure tank after 28 days, setting a world record simulating a dive 2132 feet below sea level.

8 World's largest oil rig—Shell's "Cognac" offshore drilling platform—begins operations off the coast of Louisiana. Rig's daily peak oil production is 50,000 barrels of oil and 150 million cu. ft. of gas.

Science & Technology — Elsewhere

9 Soviets launch several Soyuz spacecraft that dock with Salyut space station before returning to Earth. Soviet cosmonauts set new 185-day record for stay in space.

10 Fifteen nations sign agreement to protect marine life in the Antarctic, clearing way for development of mineral resources in Antarctica.

11 Anthrax epidemic in south-central Russia is result of biological mishap.

12 Engineers successfully cap oil well off east coast of Mexico, stopping world's worst oil spill of more than 3.1 billion barrels of crude oil.

13 Aegyptopithecus is thought to be oldest known ancestor of man and apes after examination of primate fossils found at the edge of the Sahara Desert in Egypt.

14 Nobel Prize for physics is awarded to Americans James W. Cronin and Val L. Fitch for discoveries concerning the symmetry of subatomic particles.

15 Nobel Prize for medicine is awarded to Americans Baruj Benacerraf and George D. Snell and to Frenchman Jean Dausset for research in cell immunology and the discovery of HLA antigens.

16 Nobel Prize for chemistry is awarded to Americans Paul Berg and Walter Gilbert and to Englishman Frederick Sanger for the development of methods used to diagram the structure and function of DNA.

Miscellaneous — America

1 Winter Olympics held in Lake Placid, N.Y., are won by E. Germany, with U.S.S.R. second, and U.S.A. third. Summer Olympics are held in Moscow, but several countries (including the U.S.) boycott the games to protest Soviet invasion of Afghanistan.

2 Mt. St. Helens, a volcano in Washington state, erupts and continues to erupt intermittently throughout the year.

3 U.S. population approximates 226,550,000.

4 Price of silver plummets after Hunt brothers of Dallas fail to cover their $100 million loan.

5 U.S. balloonists Max Anderson and his son, Kris, make first nonstop balloon flight across North America, traveling more than 3100 miles in 4 days.

6 Wildlife refuges, totaling 40 million acres, are set up in Alaska under U.S. federal protection. Development of oil, gas, and mineral resources is barred for at least 20 years.

7 Genuine Risk becomes second female horse in history to win the Kentucky Derby.

8 Pittsburgh Steelers win the Super Bowl. Philadelphia Phillies win the World Series.

9 Newly opened National Herb Garden in Washington, D.C. features 7000 selected plants in a series of gardens.

10 CBS-TV names Dan Rather to succeed Walter Cronkite as chief anchorman, following Cronkite's retirement in 1981.

Miscellaneous — Elsewhere

11 Major diamond field is discovered in Western Australia.

12 Pope John Paul II reaffirms his opposition to divorce at synod of Roman Catholic bishops in Rome. The Vatican also condemns euthanasia.

13 UNESCO reports that almost one-third of the world's population is illiterate.

14 Gold bullion prices soar to record heights on international markets, reaching $835 an ounce on the London market.

15 Islamic militants who raided Grand Mosque in Mecca in 1979 are publicly executed.

16 *O Canada* becomes the national anthem of Canada.

17 Floating oilfield platform in North Sea collapses in severe storm. Metal fatigue is blamed for the accident.

18 About 10,000 Cubans jam the Peruvian embassy in Havana, seeking visas to leave their country. Pres. Castro grants them safe passage out of Cuba when other countries agree to take them. Boatlift brings thousands of Cubans to Key West, Fla. [1980:HIST/4]

19 Nobel Peace Prize is awarded to Adolfo Perez Esquivel, Argentine leader of human rights organization based in Buenos Aires.

History and Politics

America

Elsewhere

The Arts

America

Elsewhere

1981

History and Politics — America

1 Upon the inauguration of recently elected Ronald Reagan, the 52 Amer. hostages held for 444 days are freed by Iran, eventually returning to a heroes' welcome. In return, the U.S. agrees to release $8 billion in Iranian assets frozen after the U.S. embassy in Teheran was seized by militant Iranian students.

2 Pres. Reagan, shot and seriously wounded in Washington, recuperates slowly after surgery. His would-be assassin, John W. Hinckley, Jr., is found not guilty by reason of insanity.

3 Reagan fires striking air traffic control workers after the 15,000 union members reject an 11% pay raise and walk out. Reagan says, "The law is the law, and the law says they cannot strike." Replacements are hired and trained.

4 Sandra Day O'Connor begins her term as the first woman justice on the U.S. Supreme Court. She favors the death penalty and the right of women to have abortions.

5 Reagan expands the powers of the Central Intelligence Agency, permitting pursuit of "pertinent" domestic intelligence.

6 The President resumes sales of wheat to Russia that had been embargoed by Pres. Jimmy Carter after the Russian invasion of Afghanistan in 1979.

7 U.S. Navy jets shoot down 2 Libyan warplanes over the Mediterranean Sea. The U.S. says the Libyans fired first.

8 In the biggest naturalization ceremony ever held, 9700 immigrants are sworn in as U.S. citizens at Los Angeles Memorial Coliseum.

History and Politics — Elsewhere

9 Pope John Paul II is shot and seriously wounded as he greets worshipers in St. Peter's Square, Vatican City. The gunman, a Turkish radical convicted of murder who escaped from prison, receives a life sentence.

10 Egypt's Pres. Anwar Sadat is assassinated by extremists opposed to his peace treaty with Israel. Vice Pres. Hosni Mubarak assumes presidency.

11 Queen Elizabeth's 55th birthday ceremony is marred when an unemployed teenager fires pistol blanks.

12 François Mitterrand is elected France's first Socialist President.

13 In Poland, Gen. Wojciech Jaruzelski overthrows Premier Jozef Pinkowski to become Poland's leader.

14 Bishop Jean Marie Lustiger is named Archbishop of Paris, the first convert from Judaism to Roman Catholicism to hold that post.

15 Spain's Civil Guards attempt a coup by storming parliament, but fail. King Juan Carlos rallies most military commanders around the cause of democracy.

16 The U.S. embassy in El Salvador is heavily damaged by rocket fire. Both leftists and rightists claim responsibility.

17 In London, hundreds of youths riot in a demonstration that police link to racial tensions and high unemployment.

18 Ten Irish Republican Army hunger strikers die in protest against conditions in Belfast's Maze Prison.

19 An Israeli air raid destroys Iraqi nuclear reactor.

The Arts — America

1 John Updike wins the National Book Critics Circle Award, American Book Award, and Pulitzer Prize for *Rabbit Is Rich.* Other U.S. bestsellers include Dee Brown's *Bury My Heart at Wounded Knee,* Erica Jong's *Fanny,* James Michener's *The Covenant,* and Martin Cruz Smith's *Gorky Park.*

2 Cable TV, magazines, and computers join forces. *Reader's Digest* offers the database "The Source," while *Playboy* and *Penthouse* produce cable versions of their men's magazines.

3 Film actress Natalie Wood drowns in a mysterious yachting accident off the California coast.

4 Hoagy Carmichael, composer of "Stardust" and other timeless hits, dies at 82. In his heyday Carmichael worked with jazz greats Benny Goodman and Louis Armstrong.

5 Film star Meryl Streep receives widespread critical acclaim for her portrayal of the mysterious Sarah in *The French Lieutenant's Woman.*

6 Barbara Mandrell is named Entertainer of the Year by the Country Music Association amid a popular resurgence of country music.

The Arts — Elsewhere

7 A symphony written by Wolfgang Amadeus Mozart when he was 9 is uncovered in a private collection in Germany.

8 Italy begins a $3 million restoration of Michelangelo's frescoes in the Sistine Chapel.

9 A new translation of the prophecies of the 16th-century astrologer Nostradamus, forecasting a gloomy end to the 20th century, is a French bestseller.

10 The Rolling Stones play for 2 million fans in a smash U.S. tour. Scalpers command as much as $500 for a pair of $15 seats.

11 A British film about the Summer Olympics, *Chariots of Fire,* is a critical and commercial success. Meanwhile, Australian films go global with *Gallipoli,* a worldwide hit about Australia's participation in the ill-fated World War I campaign.

12 Pablo Picasso's self-portrait brings $5.3 million at a Sotheby's auction in New York City, the highest price paid to date for a 20th-century painting.

13 Photographs of rural France by Eugene Atget draw large crowds to an exhibition at New York's Museum of Modern Art.

14 Nobel Prize, Literature: Elias Canetti—born in Bulgaria, resident of England, and writer in German. His best-known work is *Die Blendung (Tower of Babel).*

15 The novel *Two Women of China* by China's Hualing Nieh is published in Beijing and New York to critical acclaim.

Science & Technology

America

1 IBM introduces its model of the personal computer (PC), destined to revolutionize office automation and move corporations away from mainframe computers, a market dominated by IBM. Small companies begin to "clone" the IBM PC.

2 The first test-tube baby in the U.S. is born. The mother's egg was fertilized in a laboratory, then implanted in her womb.

3 Scientists identify the virus that causes the fatal condition called AIDS (Acquired Immune Deficiency Syndrome). Initially confined to homosexual men and Haitian immigrants, AIDS begins to emerge as an epidemic among other groups.

4 The space shuttle *Columbia* becomes the first spaceship to be used a second time. After an April flight circling the Earth 36 times, it is refitted and completes another space mission in November. A fleet of space shuttles is under construction.

5 Voyager 2 passes by Saturn, transmitting photographs of the planet's rings and moons.

6 One-month-old inflatable dome of the Hubert H. Humphrey Metrodome in Minneapolis, Minn., collapses under the weight of a foot of snow.

7 North Dakota moves ahead of Kansas as the nation's leading wheat producer because of a Kansas frost. But bumper crops lead to hard times as the glut lowers grain prices.

Elsewhere

8 France inaugurates high-speed rail service as the bullet-nosed TGV (Train à grande vitesse) train begins carrying passengers from Paris to Lyons at 162 mph.

9 Deep-sea divers salvage a safe from the sunken Italian liner *Andrea Doria,* which sank in 1956 after a collision with the Swedish liner *Stockholm.* Jewelry and other valuables are recovered.

10 The first sun-powered aircraft flies across the English Channel. Earlier attempts failed because of cloudy skies.

11 Amid growing debate over genetic engineering, the German drug firm Hoechst invests $50 million in DNA research at Massachusetts General Hospital in Boston.

12 Researchers conclude that Kenyan monkeys use a rudimentary form of language.

13 The U.S.S.R. drills the world's deepest hole, about 35,500 ft. deep, near Murmansk, for scientific research.

14 African elephants are decimated by poachers of ivory, now selling at $34 per pound. The World Wildlife Fund says 1 African elephant in 10 is slaughtered each year.

15 Severe earthquakes shake Iran, Pakistan, and Peru.

Miscellaneous

America

1 U.S. auto production reaches a 20-year low; only 6.2 million new cars are built, and the Big 3 auto makers suffer huge losses. Analysts blame Japanese competition, recession, and high interest rates.

2 The Supreme Court rules that exempting women from the military draft does not violate the Constitution.

3 During a dance at the new Hyatt Regency Hotel in Kansas City, Kan., suspension rods supporting bridge-like walkways that span the 4-story lobby snap, and 2 walkways collapse on the crowd in the lobby. Dancers and spectators are among the 113 killed.

4 *Washington Post* reporter Janet Cooke is forced to return a Pulitzer Prize upon the finding that her story about an 8-year-old heroin addict was untrue.

5 Aspartame, a new artificial sweetener, is introduced after FDA approval.

6 Honolulu has the highest cost of living of any American city. Rising prices are driven by wealthy tourists and development financed by Japanese investors.

7 The Oakland Raiders beat the Philadelphia Eagles, 27-10, in Super Bowl XV.

8 The Los Angeles Dodgers defeat the N.Y. Yankees 4 games to 2 to win the World Series.

9 George Washington's dentures are stolen from the National Museum of American History. They are made of gold and ivory, not wood, as popularly believed.

Elsewhere

10 Prince Charles (32) and Lady Diana Spencer (20) are married in an elegant royal wedding at St. Paul's Cathedral in London. After an hour-long ceremony, the royal couple returns by gilded carriage to Buckingham Palace where they appear on a balcony and kiss.

11 Sweden releases a Russian submarine that ran aground in Swedish waters. Radiation monitors indicate that the sub was carrying nuclear weapons.

12 European Monetary System nations agree to realign their currencies.

13 China emerges as a force in world bridge competition. Leader Deng Xiaoping hosts foreign bridge players as China is inaugurated into the World Bridge Federation.

14 World Chess Champion Anatoly Karpov of the U.S.S.R. retains his crown by defeating challenger Viktor Korchnoi, a Soviet émigré living in Switzerland.

15 China and India begin talks in Moscow to resolve their long-standing dispute over their border in the Himalayas.

16 The Caribbean islands of Antigua and Barbuda unite to form a single independent nation, ending 350 years of British rule.

17 After 25 years in office, Finland's Pres. Urho Kekkonen resigns because of ill health.

18 Jack Sutcliffe, the Brit. serial killer known as the Yorkshire Ripper, gets life in prison for murdering 13 prostitutes.

19 Canada goes without mail for 43 days as postal employees go on strike. Business communications are crippled.

1981

History and Politics

America

1982

1 Pres. Reagan proposes that the U.S. and the Soviet Union reduce their nuclear arsenals by one-third. Strategic Arms Reduction Talks (START) begin in Geneva, Switzerland.

2 Pres. Reagan orders an embargo on Libyan oil, reflecting Washington's growing impatience with Libya's support for international terrorism.

3 The Equal Rights Amendment to the U.S. Constitution is defeated as only 35 of the required 38 states approve it within the 10-year limit for ratification.

4 A federal judge in Arkansas rules it is unconstitutional to require schools to teach "creationism" if they teach the theory of evolution.

5 Violent disorders erupt in Miami, Fla., after the shooting of a young black man by a policeman.

6 Federal agents round up more than 5000 illegal immigrants in 9 major cities. Washington says it wants to make jobs available for legal residents.

7 The UN adopts the Law of the Sea Treaty, but the U.S. rejects it. A key provision imposes limits on seabed mining.

8 In midterm congressional elections, Republicans retain a majority in the Senate but lose seats in the Democrat-controlled House.

9 Pres. Reagan orders reinstatement of the U.S. military draft registration for 18-year-olds.

Elsewhere

10 The U.S. and NATO denounce Poland for instituting martial law and the Soviet Union for supporting it. Economic and diplomatic sanctions are decreed against Poland.

11 After a 9-month cease-fire, heavy fighting breaks out in the Middle East. Israel, which annexed Syria's Golan Heights late in 1981, invades Lebanon in an effort to destroy forces of the Palestinian Liberation Organization based there. Israel subsequently rejects peace plans put forth separately by Pres. Reagan and the Arab League.

12 Some 600 Palestinians are massacred by Christian militia at the Sabra and Shatila refugee camps in Lebanon.

13 Israel cedes the last of the Sinai it promised to return to Egypt under the terms of their peace treaty.

14 Great Britain and Argentina go to war over the Falkland Islands in the South Atlantic. Long held by Britain, the Falklands are occupied by the Argentine military in an attempt to annex them. Britain dispatches a large military force and defeats the Argentines in 10 days. Argentine crowds riot, and the military government falls.

15 In an address to the Organization of American States, Pres. Reagan proposes a Caribbean Basin Initiative to improve the region's economy.

16 Polish labor leader Lech Walesa is freed after 11 months of internment for leading the outlawed Solidarity union.

17 An era ends in the Soviet Union when Pres. Leonid Brezhnev dies after 18 years as the U.S.S.R.'s leader. He is succeeded by Yuri Andropov, former KGB chief.

The Arts

America

1 EPCOT Center—the Experimental Prototype Community of Tomorrow—opens at Disney World in Florida. Under a geodesic dome called Spaceship Earth, EPCOT offers educational exhibits of the future.

2 Hollywood's Steven Spielberg releases another blockbuster with *E.T. the Extra-Terrestrial*. *E.T.* sets box-office records and popularizes the catchphrase, "E.T., phone home."

3 It was a banner year for the movie industry—box-office receipts rose 9% over 1981 to almost $3 billion.

4 Critics and audiences alike purr over *Cats,* the Brit. musical that makes its Broadway debut. Andrew Lloyd Webber based the show on poet T.S. Eliot's *Old Possum's Book of Practical Cats.*

5 Washington agrees to deregulate television commercials. The old rules limited TV ads to a maximum of 8 minutes per hour.

6 Actor Vic Morrow and 2 Vietnamese children are killed when a helicopter crashes during the on-location shooting of a movie scene.

7 The Getty Museum of Malibu, Calif., erects 3 new exhibition halls. While other museums struggle to raise money, the Getty Museum remains well funded.

8 Primitive art from the Pacific, the Americas, and Africa gains an elegant showcase with the opening of the Michael Rockefeller wing of New York's Metropolitan Museum. Michael, son of former N.Y. Governor Nelson Rockefeller, died

Elsewhere

9 British producer-director Richard Attenborough brings *Gandhi* to the screen after 20 years of seeking support for the project. The 3½-hour epic is widely hailed as one of the year's most beautiful and graceful films.

10 Sophia Loren spends 17 days in jail for tax fraud. The Italian actress, who was living in France, says she returned to Italy to pay her debt lest she be forbidden to return forever.

11 The Ger. film *Das Boot (The Boat),* directed by Wolfgang Petersen, a powerful drama depicting the futility and fear of World War II submarine warfare, is acclaimed worldwide.

12 Classical music finds a stylish new home in London's Barbican Centre, a $300 million hall with remarkable acoustics.

13 Nobel Prize, Literature: Gabriel Garcia Márquez, the Colombian novelist best known for *One Hundred Years of Solitude.*

14 Graham Greene's latest novel, *Monsignor Quixote,* pays tribute to Cervantes in its account of a Spanish priest and his "Sancho Panza," the Communist mayor of his village.

15 Piano maestro Artur Rubinstein, who began performing as a child, dies in Geneva, Switzerland, at 95.

Science & Technology

America

1 Medical history is made at the University of Utah Medical Center in Salt Lake City when doctors successfully implant a permanent artificial heart designed by Dr. Robert K. Jarvik in 61-year-old Barney Clark.
2 The space shuttle *Columbia* lands safely after orbiting the Earth for 7 days.
3 Apple Computer becomes the first personal computer firm to reach $1 billion in annual sales.
4 The Solar One power plant, the world's most powerful solar-based system, opens in California's Mojave Desert.
5 NASA orbits Landsat 4, an advanced observation satellite important for scientific research purposes.

Elsewhere

6 Soviet cosmonauts aboard the Salyut space station break the all-time endurance record, spending 186 days circling the Earth.
7 The U.S. Department of Justice charges 18 Japanese businessmen with conspiring to steal computer secrets from IBM.
8 The *Mary Rose,* flagship of England's King Henry VIII, is brought to the surface off Portsmouth, Eng., 437 years after it sank in battle against the French. Most of its oak frame is intact, and historians begin sifting through its artifacts from Tudor England.
9 A 300,000-year-old skull is found in Ethiopia by University of California scientists. It shows evidence of the practice of scalping.
10 The longest lunar eclipse since 1736 is seen in the Western Hemisphere. The Moon appears reddish orange from volcanic dust surrounding the Earth.
11 The Super Proton Synchrotron in Geneva, Switzerland, is converted into a proton-antiproton collider to aid in meson research.
12 Subway tunneling in Mexico City reveals early Aztec pyramids.
13 Paleontologists in Antarctica make the first discovery of mammal fossils on the continent.

Miscellaneous

America

1 The government settles a major antitrust suit that ends American Telephone and Telegraph's virtual monopoly on telephone service. AT&T is broken up into 7 "Baby Bell" companies offering regional phone service, while the parent company faces the prospect of competition for its long-distance service.
2 In another antitrust action, the government decides to let IBM remain in one piece despite competitors' claims that it is dominating the market.
3 Seven Chicagoans die after taking Tylenol capsules laced with cyanide. The maker of Tylenol recalls 264,000 bottles.
4 The Dow Jones Industrial average tops the 1000 level for the first time as Wall Street is bullish over sliding interest rates.
5 Braniff Airlines, the nation's 8th largest air carrier, surprises the business world by declaring bankruptcy.
6 Toxic waste dumps are identified as a major hazard by the Environmental Protection Agency, which lists more than 400 sites as clean-up priorities.
7 National Football League players go on strike against the league's 28 teams, demanding a share of the gate and TV revenues. They settle 2 months later, receiving relatively little of what they asked for.
8 The St. Louis Cardinals beat the Milwaukee Brewers 4 games to 3 in the World Series.
9 The San Francisco 49ers win the NFL championship by beating the Cincinnati Bengals, 26-21, in Super Bowl XVI.
10 The New York Islanders capture their 3rd consecutive National Hockey League crown.

Elsewhere

15 The International Whaling Commission votes to ban all commercial whaling, beginning in 1986.
16 Princess Grace of Monaco, the former actress Grace Kelly, dies after an auto crash.
17 China's population tops 1 billion, nearly one-fourth of the world's population.
18 Ending some 450 years of absolute separation between the Roman Catholic and Anglican churches, Pope John Paul II and the Archbishop of Canterbury join in an emotional religious service. Britain and the Vatican resume diplomatic relations.
19 Princess Diana gives birth to a boy, William, 2nd in line to the Brit. throne after his father, Prince Charles.
20 Queen Elizabeth awakens to find a stranger in her Buckingham Palace bedroom. He is removed by servants after talking to the Queen for several minutes.
21 Italy takes soccer's World Cup, defeating West Germany, 3-1, in the final game.
22 Britain's Laker Airlines, pioneer of discount transatlantic flights, declares bankruptcy.
23 An earthquake in Yemen leaves more than 2800 dead.
24 The DeLorean auto company, headquartered in Northern Ireland, goes bankrupt. The innovative, stainless-steel–bodied car sold poorly because of its high price.
25 Nobel Prize, Peace: Disarmament advocates Alva Myrdal and Alfonso Garcia Robles.

History and Politics		The Arts	
America	**Elsewhere**	**America**	**Elsewhere**
		while on an expedition in Polynesia.	

	America	Elsewhere	America	Elsewhere
1983	**1** Pres. Reagan describes the Soviet Union as an "evil empire" in a speech in which he also opposes a nuclear arms freeze and favors outlawing abortion. **2** Reagan proposes an anti-ballistic missile system, later dubbed "Star Wars." At a cost of billions of dollars, it would use powerful laser beams and other advanced technology to stop incoming nuclear missiles. **3** A congressional committee condemns the U.S. World War II policy of interning Japanese Americans. Financial compensation for the victims is recommended. **4** Harold Washington becomes the first black man elected as Mayor of Chicago, Ill. **5** A blue-ribbon panel finds the nation's educational standards "are being eroded by a rising tide of mediocrity," threatening the nation's future. **6** U.S. Marines and Army Rangers invade and subdue the tiny island nation of Grenada after the U.S. decides that Caribbean political and economic stability is threatened by Grenada's leftist government. **7** Pres. Reagan defends military and economic aid to Contra rebels fighting against the Sand-	**9** More than 200 U.S. Marines die when a suicide bomber drives an explosives-filled truck into the Marine compound in Beirut, Lebanon. Two minutes later, a second truck blows up a French paratroop barracks, killing 58. Months earlier, the U.S. Embassy in Lebanon had been destroyed by a suicide trucker. **10** A South Korean civilian jetliner en route from New York to Seoul strays off course over Soviet territory and is shot down by a Sov. fighter plane. All 269 crew and passengers die, and the incident strains U.S.–Sov. relations. Pres. Reagan calls it a "horrifying act of violence." **11** About 1 million illegal aliens, mostly Hispanic, cross the southern U.S. border during the year. Most are fleeing the poverty of Mexico or the political turmoil of Central America. **12** Right-wing death squads in El Salvador are condemned by the U.S. State Department. **13** A landslide Tory victory in Brit. elections assures Margaret Thatcher a 2nd term as Prime Minister. **14** Philippine opposition leader Benigno Aquino is gunned down at Manila's airport when he re-	**1** New York's Metropolitan Opera celebrates its 100th birthday with an 8-hour musical extravaganza televised live. Nearly 100 opera stars of the past 40 years sing excerpts from 46 operas. **2** Cable television increasingly threatens the former monopoly of broadcast TV. Cable is watched in 25 million homes, a 16% share of the TV marketplace. **3** Videocassette recorders (VCRs) are catching on throughout the U.S. By midyear 7 million homes have a VCR, and they are selling at a rate of 250,000 a month. VHS (video home system) format dominates over Sony's Beta format. Movie-rental stores begin to attract an increasing volume of business. **4** TV's long-running situation comedy *M*A*S*H* airs its final episode; it is seen by 125 million viewers, the largest TV audience ever for a non-sports program.	**7** Conflict erupts between Britain and Greece over possession of the Elgin Marbles. Greece, original home of the famous sculptures from Athens' Parthenon, wants them returned, but Great Britain, whose Lord Elgin brought them to the British Museum in the early 19th century, says they will stay in England. **8** Iraq seeks the return from France's Louvre Museum of the stele bearing the 3700-year-old Code of Hammurabi. **9** Nobel Prize, Literature: Britain's William Golding, author of *The Lord of the Flies*. **10** The year's major foreign film is Ingmar Bergman's *Fanny and Alexander,* a period saga of a middle-class family in a small Swedish town. **11** Among the year's notable English-language novels in Canada is Morley Callaghan's *A Time for Judas,* an unusual retelling of the Christ story.

Science & Technology		Miscellaneous		
America	**Elsewhere**	**America**	**Elsewhere**	
		11 The Rev. Sun Myung Moon, Korean-born founder and leader of the Unification Church, is convicted of income tax evasion, signaling the decline of the "Moonie" movement. **12** The 1982 World's Fair opens in Knoxville, Tenn. Millions come to see the exhibits featuring the theme "Energy Turns the World." **13** A government survey of income tax returns shows the IRS is twice as likely as taxpayers to make mathematical errors. **14** Nobel Prize, Economics: University of Chicago's George J. Stigler for his studies of industrial structures, markets, and public regulation.		
1 Sally Ride becomes the first American woman in space, as a crew member on the 2nd mission of the space shuttle *Challenger*. **2** Health officials assure a nervous public that there is little risk of catching AIDS via blood transfusions. **3** The American Medical Association calls for a ban on boxing, saying it leads to chronic brain damage. A study of 38 boxers found more than half had brain tissue loss. **4** The U.S. offers to buy all homes and businesses in Times Beach, Mo., site of a toxic waste dump. **5** The Jet Propulsion Laboratory in Pasadena, Calif., reports the detection of solid objects orbiting the star Vega, the first such solar system known outside ours. **6** Mercur, a new gold mine near Salt Lake City, Utah, produces its first gold. Getty Oil has invested $80 million in the mine, which is expected to yield 80,000 oz. a year for 14 years. **7** Margaret Mead's pioneering anthropology studies in Samoa are challenged	**8** The Pacific Ocean warming current known as "El Niño" upsets weather patterns worldwide, causing heavy rains in coastal Peru, drought in northern Australia, and other weather anomalies in North America and Europe. **9** The Milky Way emits gamma rays, according to German astronomer H. Mayer-Hasselwinder, who studied satellite findings for 4 years. **10** A global oil glut forces the Organization of Petroleum Exporting Countries to lower its benchmark price from $34 to $29 a barrel. **11** Apple Computer unveils a new computer device called a "mouse"; it allows users to point an arrow in order to access computer functions rather than entering complicated instructions on a keyboard. **12** Spread over 176 acres, the International Horticultural Exhibition, held near Munich, Germany, every 10 years, draws 8 million visitors. **13** French researchers find that the effectiveness of cor-	**1** The National Council of the Churches of Christ issues a new Bible that no longer refers to God in masculine terms only. God is called either "Father" or "Mother" or "the One." References to "mankind" are replaced by "humankind" or "humanity." **2** Hurricane Alicia whips through southern Texas, leaving 17 dead and damage of $1.3 billion. **3** For the first time in its 132-year history, the America's Cup, yachting's most prestigious prize, leaves the U.S. It is won by an Australian vessel that comes from behind in 4 races to beat the defending *Liberty*. **4** Chanting the theme of "Jobs, Peace, and Freedom," some 250,000 Americans converge on Washington to mark the 20th anniversary of the 1963 civil rights march. **5** Washington Public Power Supply System says it cannot repay $2.25 billion in bonds, making it the largest default in municipal-bond history.	**11** Nobel Prize, Peace: Lech Walesa, for leading a nonviolent drive toward democracy in Poland. But like many other Soviet-bloc winners, he cannot travel to Oslo for the ceremony; his wife accepts it for him. **12** Chiang Ching, Chairman Mao's 69-year-old widow, has her death sentence in China commuted to life in prison. **13** Klaus Barbie, the Nazi nicknamed "The Butcher of Lyons," is discovered hiding in La Paz, Bolivia. He is extradited to France where it is revealed that he was helped by U.S. officials to escape to Bolivia after World War II. **14** Former Japanese Prime Minister Kakuei Tanaka is convicted of taking million-dollar bribes from Lockheed Aircraft to arrange the sale of its planes to a Japanese airline. **15** France intervenes in the civil war of its former African colony Chad, whose government is under attack by rebels supported by Libya.	**1983**

History and Politics		The Arts	
America	**Elsewhere**	**America**	**Elsewhere**
inista government of Nicaragua. Some lawmakers call Contra support an illegal violation of laws banning covert aid to rebels. **8** The birthday of Martin Luther King, Jr., is declared a national holiday, to be observed on the 3rd Monday of January.	turns to rally opponents of Pres. Ferdinand Marcos; Aquino's assassination sets off a political crisis. **15** Chile's government lifts the "state of emergency" that has been in effect since 1978.	**5** Stylish skyscrapers spring up in the big cities. New York City boasts 3 new giants: the pediment-capped AT&T Building, the granite-and-glass IBM Center, and the futuristic Trump Tower. Chicago, Ill., long home to innovative commercial architecture, adds a central atrium with glass elevators to the Chicago Board of Trade. **6** TV anchorwoman Christine Craft wins $500,000 in a sex discrimination case against a Kansas City, Mo., station. Craft says she was demoted for being "too old, too unattractive, and not deferential enough to men." The judgment is later reversed on appeal.	**12** One of Europe's most innovative productions is Christophe Willibald Gluck's opera *Orpheus and Eurydice,* produced as a ballet at Basel, Switzerland, with choreography by Heinz Spoerli. He also designs the set, which depicts Hell as an endless treadmill through an industrial maze. **13** Brit. musicmakers going strong in the U.S. include David Bowie, Duran Duran, Def Leppard, Sting, Eurythmics, and Boy George, prompting U.S. popular music lovers to call it the 2nd British invasion—akin to that led by the Beatles in the 1960s.
1984			
1 Pres. Ronald Reagan and Vice Pres. George Bush are easily reelected over Democratic candidate Walter Mondale; they carry 49 of 50 states. N.Y. Rep. Geraldine Ferraro is Mondale's running mate, the first woman chosen by a major party to run for Vice President. **2** Pres. Reagan goes to China to promote trade, signing accords easing U.S.-China commercial relations. **3** The U.S. Supreme Court tightens rules for political asylum, holding that those seeking refuge in the U.S. must show "clear probability" of persecution in their native country. **4** Pres. Reagan undergoes successful surgery for a small nonmalignant polyp on his colon. **5** Seven chemical firms agree to pay $180 million to Vietnam veterans if they drop claims related to Agent Orange, the herbicide used in Vietnam and linked to cancer and nerve damage. **6** The Civil Rights Commission votes to end use of numerical quotas in employment promotions of African Americans.	**10** Konstantin Chernenko succeeds Yuri Andropov, who dies in office, as the Soviet Union's Secretary General of the Communist Party. **11** U.S. sends $3 billion in aid to counter instability in Central America. Targets are Sandinistas in Nicaragua, rebels in El Salvador, and area-wide poverty. **12** The U.S. Central Intelligence Agency directs the mining of harbors in Nicaragua. Congress and the UN pass measures criticizing the action, and the World Court rules that the U.S. should stop its support of the mining. **13** Five El Salvador ex–National Guards are convicted of murdering 4 U.S. church women who run a refugee center. **14** Cuba agrees to take back more than 2500 criminals and mentally ill refugees who entered the U.S. in the "Mariel boatlift." **15** Great Britain agrees to return Hong Kong to China in 1997 when Britain's 99-year lease on the crown colony runs out.	**1** Donald Duck, comic icon of children worldwide, marks his 50th birthday at Florida's Disney World. **2** Pop singer Michael Jackson begins the year with 8 Grammy awards; sales of his *Thriller* album will eventually break all records, topping 37 million copies. **3** Michael Jackson's hit stirs greater demand for videos, a new genre of movie shorts that feature popular songs. The new all-videos cable channel MTV draws a large young audience. **4** Bruce Springsteen stirs millions with *Born in the U.S.A.,* an album, featuring a song of the same name, reflecting his bittersweet view of U.S. society. **5** *Amadeus,* a comic but moving tale of Mozart's life through the eyes of his jealous competitor Salieri, is one of the top films of the year.	**12** Nobel Prize, Literature: Jaroslav Seifert, an 83-year-old poet from Czechoslovakia. **13** George Orwell's classic novel *1984* becomes a best-seller once again; his grim forecasts about totalitarianism have not come to pass. **14** France's Prix Goncourt is awarded to playwright Marguerite Duras, who was distinguished earlier by her film *Hiroshima Mon Amour.* **15** Hugh Hudson's movie *Greystoke: The Legend of Tarzan, Lord of the Apes* offers an offbeat, aristocratic tilt to the Edgar Rice Burroughs story. **16** Another well-received Brit. film is Roland Jaffe's *The Killing Fields,* a chilling examination of wartime genocide in Cambodia. **17** Germany's contribution to world cinema is *Heimat,* Edgar Reitz's

424

Science & Technology		Miscellaneous		
America	Elsewhere	America	Elsewhere	

for ignoring biological hereditary factors. Prof. Derek Freeman, an Australian, titles his book *Margaret Mead and Samoa: The Making and Unmaking of an Anthropological Myth,* but his work is denounced by many as a personal attack.

ticosteroids in treating asthma is improved if the drugs are taken upon waking.
14 Southwest of Tahiti, an unmanned computer-controlled earthquake monitoring station is thrust deep into a borehole 500 ft. below the sea bed, itself 18,000 ft. below the ocean surface. The object is to improve forecasting of earthquakes in the Pacific Basin.

6 Jesse Jackson announces that he is running for the Democratic Presidential nomination.
7 General Motors and Toyota form a partnership to produce compact cars in California. Just 4 years after declaring bankruptcy Chrysler repays its federally guaranteed loan, 7 years ahead of the due date.
8 Lefty Steve Carlton of the Philadelphia Phillies becomes baseball's all-time leading strikeout pitcher.
9 The Washington Redskins defeat the Miami Dolphins, 27-17, in Super Bowl XVII.
10 The N. Y. Islanders sweep to their 4th straight Stanley Cup, beating the Edmonton Oilers.

16 More than 600 Muslims in the Indian state of Assam are killed by students protesting Muslim immigration from Bangladesh.
17 A UN Food and Health Agency warns that some 22 African nations face catastrophic food shortages that could lead to mass famine.
18 Raúl Ricardo Alfonsin is sworn in as President of Argentina, ending 8 years of military rule.
19 During a historic visit to his native Poland, Pope John Paul II salutes Polish nationalism.

---

1 U.S. orders "passive-restraint" airbags or automatic seatbelts on all new U.S. cars by 1989.
2 Nonsmokers can get cancer by inhaling smoke from other people's cigarettes, declares Surgeon Gen. C. Everett Koop.
3 Nobel Prize, Chemistry: Bruce Merrifield of Rockefeller University in recognition of his research into peptides.
4 Bell Labs announces a computer chip with a megabyte of memory, capable of storing 4 times as much data as its predecessor.
5 NASA space-shuttle mission repairs and reorbits the Solar Max satellite that gathers information about the Sun.
6 James Fixx, running-for-fitness guru and author of a book on the sport, dies of a heart attack while running in Vermont.
7 A prototype of the controversial B-1 bomber crashes in the Mohave Desert; the Pentagon

11 The compact disc (CD), developed by the Dutch company Phillips and Japan's Sony, is hailed as the music recording medium of the future.
12 Cosmonaut Svetlana Savitskaya becomes the first woman to walk in space and the first woman to make 2 trips into space.
13 In the most infamous industrial accident ever, toxic methyl isocyanate leaks from an insecticide plant in Bhopal, India, and poisons the city. Thousands are blinded, and more than 3500 eventually die. A $15 billion lawsuit is filed against plant owner Union Carbide.
14 Fr. scientists report a breakthrough in AIDS research, focusing on a virus called LAV, which they suspect is a cause of the disease.
15 West Germany bans leaded gasoline and orders catalytic converters on all autos beginning in 1988. Supporters of the environ-

1 The Los Angeles Summer Olympic Games open with Hollywood glitz—an enormous symphony, a huge marching band, gospel singers, breakdancers, and 84 pianists. The U.S. dominates the games, which are boycotted by the Soviet Union and some other Communist nations in retaliation for the U.S. boycott of Moscow's 1980 games.
2 The Supreme Court holds that exhibiting a publicly financed nativity scene does not violate the First Amendment.
3 An unidentified Vietnam combat casualty is buried at Arlington National Cemetery's Tomb of the Unknown Soldier.
4 The National Conference of Catholic Bishops says that capitalism fails to provide a just economic system. Bishops cite homelessness and hunger in a wealthy nation and ask the government to play a bigger role in correcting the problems.

14 Nobel Prize, Peace: Bishop Desmond Tutu for using nonviolence against apartheid in South Africa.
15 China marks its 35th year as a Communist state by turning toward capitalism. State companies are free to compete; prices are left to supply and demand.
16 Brit. Prime Minister Margaret Thatcher escapes death when a bomb explodes in her hotel, but 5 others die in the blast at a Conservative Party conference. The IRA claims responsibility.
17 Italian police crack down on the Mafia. More than 50 suspects are arrested in the biggest raid on organized crime since World War II.
18 Foreign aid pours into Ethiopia to help feed starving millions.
19 Bolivia's president is briefly kidnapped during an abortive military coup.
20 Chile's rightist government led by Augusto Pinochet Ugarte rounds up

1984

425

	America	Elsewhere	America	Elsewhere

America (History and Politics)

7 Nearly 80 banks fail, the highest number since 1938.

8 The Federal Deposit Insurance Corporation must cover $4.5 billion in bad-loan losses at Continental Illinois Bank, one of its largest payouts ever.

9 Dr. Kathryn Sullivan, in a mission on the space shuttle *Challenger,* becomes the first U.S. woman to walk in space.

Elsewhere (History and Politics)

16 Brian Mulroney, a Progressive Conservative, is elected Canada's Prime Minister, replacing Liberal John N. Turner.

17 Israeli political rivals Shimon Peres and Yitzhak Shamir form unity government and agree to alternate as Prime Minister.

18 Libyan diplomats are expelled from the U.K. after a London policewoman is killed during an anti-Libyan protest at Libya's embassy.

19 U.S. and South American banks lend Argentina $500 million to help pay its debts.

20 The oil-rich Pacific sultanate of Brunei achieves full independence from the U.K.

21 Indian Army troops put down a Sikh uprising by storming a Sikh temple in the sacred city of Amritsar. Possibly in retaliation, Indira Gandhi, India's Prime Minister, is later assassinated by 2 Sikh members of her personal guard. Her son Rajiv succeeds her.

America (The Arts)

6 Other movie megahits include *Indiana Jones and the Temple of Doom* and *Ghostbusters.*

7 *Ironweed* by William Kennedy wins the Pulitzer Prize for fiction.

8 A 48-page collection of unpublished William Faulkner poems is given to the Univ. of Mississippi.

9 The New Orleans World's Fair closes, widely considered a national flop and a financial fiasco.

10 Singer Marvin Gaye is fatally shot by his father, the Rev. Marvin Gaye, Sr., after a dispute at home.

11 Vanessa Williams becomes the first Miss America to resign, after nude photos of her are published in *Penthouse* magazine.

Elsewhere (The Arts)

singular 16-hour epic of 60 years of family life.

18 The State Gallery in Stuttgart, West Germany, a new art showcase, is the architectural handiwork of Britain's James Stirling. Witty and novel, it draws almost as much attention as the art it houses.

19 An untouched Mayan tomb is discovered in Petan, Guatemala.

20 West Germany pays more than $10 million for a 12th-century illuminated manuscript of the Duke of Saxony.

1985

America (History and Politics)

1 In his State of the Union message, Pres. Ronald Reagan begins his second term by calling for reform in federal income tax policy as part of his "Second American Revolution."

2 The U.S. becomes the world's leading debtor nation, owing foreigners $130 billion. It marks the first time since 1914 that the U.S. has owed more than it is owed.

3 Pres. Reagan undergoes surgery to remove a cancerous growth from his colon. During the 8-hour operation, Vice Pres. George Bush acts as President.

4 U.S. curbs trade with South Africa, adding pressure on the apartheid government to change its racist policies.

Elsewhere (History and Politics)

10 Uruguay inaugurates a civilian President after 12 years of military rule.

11 Mikhail Gorbachev succeeds Konstantin Chernenko as Chairman of the Soviet Union's Communist Party.

12 South Africa declares a state of emergency to try to deal with escalating protests by blacks against the apartheid system.

13 Palestinian terrorists attack El Al passengers at airports in Rome and Vienna, hurling hand grenades and firing submachine guns. The attacks kill 19 people and wound 110.

14 Pres. Reagan's visit to a military cemetery in Bitburg,

America (The Arts)

1 Pulitzer Prizes are awarded to Alison Lurie for *Foreign Affairs* and to Studs Turkel for *The Good War: An Oral History of World War II.*

2 Neil Simon wins his 3rd Tony for the Broadway play *Biloxi Blues,* recounting his experiences in World War II.

3 Pop star Madonna captures a vast audience and makes her first movie, *Desperately Seeking Susan.*

4 Big Hollywood hits of the year include *Out of Africa, Prizzi's Honor,* and *Kiss of the Spider Woman.*

Elsewhere (The Arts)

12 Johann Sebastian Bach's 300th birthday is marked by performances in his hometown of Leipzig, Germany, and dozens of other cities in Europe and the U.S.

13 In one of the boldest art thefts of the century, 5 gunmen hold guards and visitors at gunpoint at the Marmottan Museum in Paris and escape with major Impressionist works, including Claude Monet's *Impression, Sunrise* and Renoir's *Bathers.*

14 A new record price ($10.4 million) for a single painting is set in Lon-

Science & Technology		Miscellaneous		
America	**Elsewhere**	**America**	**Elsewhere**	

says the program will continue.

8 New York's Gov. Mario Cuomo signs the nation's first bill to curb acid rain.

9 A baboon's heart is implanted in "Baby Fae," a California infant born with a defective heart. She dies 20 days later.

10 In Louisville, Ky., surgeons perform the world's second permanent artificial heart transplant. William Schroeder's heart is replaced by an 11-oz. plastic and metal device.

mentally conscious Green Party demand the new standards, citing the dying Black Forest and the poisoned Rhine River.

16 Brazilian scientists uncover a freshwater snail that can function either as male or female.

17 A Fr. cargo ship carrying 450 tons of uranium sinks off the Belgian coast after colliding with a ferry. The French Environmental Ministry tests the waters and finds them free of radioactivity.

18 Thousands of migrating caribou drown attempting to cross flooded rivers in Canada.

19 A Brit. tanker runs aground and leaks 5000 tons of oil that foul Texas beaches.

5 American Indian leader Dennis Banks gives up after 9 years on the run and is sentenced to 3 years in prison for his part in a 1973 riot.

6 New York becomes the first state to require the wearing of seatbelts in automobiles.

7 The movie industry creates a new rating, PG-13, meaning some scenes may be unsuitable for children under 13.

8 The Boston Celtics beat the Los Angeles Lakers for the NBA title.

9 The U.S. Supreme Court rules that the civic group the Jaycees cannot exclude women.

10 Los Angeles Olympics organizer Peter Ueberroth is named commissioner of Major League Baseball.

11 Standard Oil of California buys Gulf Oil for $13 billion in the biggest corporate merger to date.

12 The Detroit Tigers dominate the San Diego Padres in the World Series, winning 4 games to 1.

13 The Los Angeles Raiders beat the Washington Redskins, 38-9, in Super Bowl XVIII.

thousands of political opponents as Pinochet reimposes a state of siege.

21 The U.S. quits UNESCO, claiming mismanagement and hostility toward democratic principles.

22 In a postscript to the Vietnam War, William Westmoreland, the former U.S. commander, files a libel suit after a TV program suggests that he falsified enemy troop casualty estimates.

23 David Lange becomes Prime Minister of New Zealand after his Labour Party wins elections with an anti–nuclear-weapons platform.

1985

1 Obesity is called a major killer, particularly among those who are more than 20% overweight, a category that includes 34 million Americans.

2 Teenage computer hackers break into confidential files at American Telephone & Telegraph and the Pentagon.

3 The world's largest particle accelerator goes into operation in Batavia, Ill. The enormous device produces subatomic energy levels 3 times greater than anything in the past.

4 The cold snap of the century hits the U.S. citrus crop. Two days of sub-

8 The International Civil Aviation Organization says 1985 is the worst year in the history of commercial flight, with more than 1400 killed.

9 The Soviet Union sends a cosmonaut crew to its vacant Salyut 7 space station to repair it and perform experiments.

10 French scientists uncover a drug that combats AIDS, but researchers at the Pasteur Institute acknowledge the test sample was very small.

11 Slow-moving, 500-pound ancient turtles are threatened by fires on one of the Galapagos islands.

1 Retailer Montgomery Ward quits the catalog and mail-order business after 113 years, ending an American tradition.

2 Coca-Cola markets a controversial new formulation of its soft drink, but after sales plummet it brings back the original, now dubbed "Coke Classic."

3 Philadelphia police try to subdue the radical group Move by dropping a bomb on its headquarters, causing extensive fires and 11 deaths.

4 Texaco is ordered to pay Pennzoil a record $11 billion in damages for undermining

12 New Zealand declares itself a nuclear-free zone and excludes U.S. Navy warships unless they prove they have no nuclear weapons aboard.

13 Palestinian terrorists seize control of the Italian cruise ship *Achille Lauro* near Port Said, Egypt, demanding the release of Palestinians held by Israel. American Leon Klinghoffer is killed during the hijack.

14 Israeli Gen. Ariel Sharon loses a libel suit against *Time* magazine in which he claimed *Time* linked him to revenge massacres of Palestinians by Lebanese Christians.

History and Politics   The Arts

	America	Elsewhere	America	Elsewhere

5 U.S. Supreme Court bars a moment of silence in public schools, declaring it fosters religious activity in schools, which was declared unconstitutional in 1962.

6 Pres. Reagan meets Soviet leader Mikhail Gorbachev in a Geneva summit, the first U.S.–Soviet summit in 6 years. Gorbachev insists that the U.S. halt the "Star Wars" antimissile system, but Reagan refuses.

7 Three members of a Navy family are convicted of spying for the Soviet Union.

8 Growing numbers of homeless Americans face winter. Only 91,000 shelter beds exist in the nation, while estimates of homeless range from 350,000 to 1 million.

9 The Gramm-Rudman bill, requiring a balanced budget for the federal government by 1991, becomes law.

West Germany, stirs anger because some Nazi SS troops are buried there. American and European Jewish groups protest the visit.

15 Violence at soccer matches outrages Europe and Asia. A clash between Brit. and Ital. fans in Brussels, Belgium, results in 38 deaths. In Peking, after China loses to Hong Kong, thousands wreck cars and property, mostly owned by foreigners.

16 After one year, Brit. coal miners end their strike and return to work under pressure from the Thatcher government.

17 The body of missing Nazi Josef Mengele is exhumed from a grave near São Paulo, Brazil. Investigators are "99%" sure it is the "Angel of Death" from the Auschwitz death camp.

---

5 Tourists flock to Tupelo, Miss., Elvis Presley's birthplace, to mark the 8th anniversary of the death of "The King."

6 Capital Cities Communications buys the American Broadcasting Company for $3.5 billion, the largest deal ever in the entertainment industry.

7 Tipper Gore, wife of Tenn. Sen. Albert Gore, tries to clean up rock lyrics, urging warning labels on "offensive" albums. Rocker Frank Zappa speaks out in opposition, calling it censorship.

8 Divers off the Florida coast recover millions of dollars in treasure from the wreck of the Spanish galleon *Nuestra Señora de Atocha,* which sank in a hurricane 363 years earlier.

9 Random House agrees to pay Edmund Morris $3 million to write Pres. Reagan's authorized biography.

10 The Boston Pops orchestra celebrates its centennial with a 15-city national tour.

11 European masters—France's Henri Rousseau and Russia's Marc Chagall—are honored by shows at New York's Museum of Modern Art; the Guggenheim Museum showcases Wassily Kandinsky.

---

don with the auction of Andrea Mantegna's *Adoration of the Magi.*

15 The "Live Aid" rock concert is broadcast from Philadelphia and London to help starving millions in East Africa. About $50 million is raised for famine relief.

16 *Shoah,* a monumental documentary film by France's Claude Lanzmann, is released after a decade's work. Almost 10 hours long, it documents Hitler's extermination program for Jews.

17 Nobel Prize, Literature: 72-year-old French novelist Claude Simon, author of 15 novels.

18 Christo's latest extravaganza of outdoor sculpture is Paris's Pont Neuf, wrapped in 44,000 sq. yds. of cloth.

19 Rainer Fassbinder's play *Garbage, the City and Death,* is canceled before it opens at a Frankfurt theater due to its anti-Semitic content.

20 A previously unknown 9-stanza love poem said to be by William Shakespeare is discovered by U.S. scholar Gary Taylor while working in Oxford, England. Controversy rages over the attribution.

1986

1 In the worst catastrophe in U.S. space history, the space shuttle *Challenger* explodes 74 seconds after liftoff, killing all 7 astronauts aboard. One victim is Christa McAuliffe, a schoolteacher who had volunteered under the "teacher-in-space" program.

2 Pres. Ronald Reagan authorizes an air attack on Libya for its terrorism, specifically the

---

10 Defeated in a popular election and heavily denounced by widespread protests against him, Pres. Ferdinand Marcos flees the Philippines. He is succeeded by Corazon Aquino, widow of a slain anti-Marcos politician.

11 While walking home from a movie in Stockholm, Sweden's Premier Olaf Palme is fatally shot by an unknown assailant.

---

1 The Rock and Roll Hall of Fame inducts its first 10 members: Chuck Berry, James Brown, Ray Charles, Buddy Holly, Sam Cooke, the Everly Brothers, Fats Domino, Jerry Lee Lewis, Little Richard, and Elvis Presley.

2 Among pop music's biggest albums are Paul

---

11 Nobel Prize, Literature: Nigerian author Wole Soyinka, who becomes the first black African to receive the prize.

12 Fire destroys part of Hampton Court, King Henry VIII's elegant palace near London.

13 Author Kingsley Amis wins Britain's Booker Prize for *The Old*

Science & Technology		Miscellaneous		
America	Elsewhere	America	Elsewhere	

Science & Technology — America

freezing weather in central Florida ruin 90% of the orange and grapefruit crop.
5 Manville Corp. offers $2.5 billion to settle thousands of asbestos-related health claims in the largest health settlement proposal made by a U.S. company.
6 Nobel Prize, Physiology or Medicine: two Univ. of Texas scientists, Michael S. Brown and Joseph L. Goldstein, for their research into cholesterol, a growing concern of health-conscious Americans.
7 Divers find the hull of the luxury liner *Titanic,* which hit an iceberg and sank in the North Atlantic in 1912. The vessel was in 12,000 ft. of water.

Science & Technology — Elsewhere

12 Tampons are sold in China for the first time.
13 Nobel Prize, Physics: West Germany's Klaus von Klitzing for research into the properties of electrical resistance.

Miscellaneous — America

Pennzoil's bid to acquire Getty in 1984.
5 Gen. William Westmoreland, U.S. commander during the Vietnam War, drops his libel suit against CBS, which had implied he exaggerated the size of the Viet Cong forces.
6 An airline crash in Maine kills Samantha Smith, 13, who visited the Soviet Union at the Kremlin's invitation after she wrote a letter advocating peace.
7 Power blackouts across Louisiana leave 70,000 people without electricity.
8 Pete Rose surpasses Ty Cobb's all-time record for career base hits, singling for the 4129th hit of his career.
9 San Francisco 49ers beat the Miami Dolphins, 38-16, in Super Bowl XIX.
10 The Kansas City Royals defeat the St. Louis Cardinals 4 games to 3 in the World Series.
11 Libby Riddles becomes the first woman to win the grueling Iditarod Trail Dog Sled Race in Alaska.

Miscellaneous — Elsewhere

15 Peru says it will not pay its debts to foreign banks. "Peruvians come first and the banks come second," said Pres. Alan Garcia Perez.
16 *Rainbow Warrior,* the protest boat of environmental organization Greenpeace, is blown up and sinks in Auckland, New Zealand. The French government admits that its agents sank the ship.
17 More than 500 passengers and crew die when a Japanese Airlines jumbo jet crashes into a mountain in Japan, the worst single plane disaster ever.
18 An Air India jet explodes in flight over the Atlantic killing all 329 aboard. India blames radical Sikhs, claiming they hid bombs aboard the jet.
19 Mexico City is devastated by a powerful earthquake measuring 7.8 on the Richter scale. About 5000 die, and damages run into the billions of dollars.
20 In Africa's worst railroad disaster, 392 people die and 370 are injured as an Ethiopian train derails and plunges down a ravine.
21 The Tesero Dam in Italy collapses, killing 264.

1986

Science & Technology — America

1 William Schroeder dies after 620 days of life with an artificial heart.
2 On its journey to outer space, the Voyager 2 space probe comes within 50,000 mi. of Uranus.
3 U.S. oil prices tumble to $10 a barrel, benefiting drivers but damaging the economy of Texas, where

Science & Technology — Elsewhere

9 The Soviet Union's Chernobyl nuclear plant, near the city of Kiev, has a major accident, believed the worst in nuclear power history. An explosion starts a fire that releases radioactivity into the air and causes at least 31 deaths.
10 Nobel Prize, Physics: West German scientist Ernst Ruska, for his 1930s

Miscellaneous — America

1 The 100th birthday of the Statue of Liberty is marked in New York Harbor with a sensational display of fireworks, warships, dozens of tall sailing ships, and speeches by Pres. Reagan and Pres. François Mitterrand of France, the country that presented the statue to the U.S.

Miscellaneous — Elsewhere

16 Nobel Prize, Peace: author and human rights campaigner Elie Wiesel, a survivor of the Holocaust.
17 Elaborate ceremonies mark the royal wedding of Prince Andrew, 4th in line to the Brit. throne, and his redheaded bride Sarah Ferguson, as 300 million worldwide watch on TV.

429

History and Politics

America

bombing of a West Berlin disco popular with American GIs. Libyan assets are frozen, and U.S. trade with Libya is banned.

3 The Iran-Contra scandal erupts in Washington. The Reagan administration confirms it sold arms to Iran, then apparently diverted the money illegally to aid rebels in Nicaragua.

4 Wall Street is struck by insider trading scandals. Ivan Boesky, one of Wall Street's biggest players, pays a $100 million fine for dealings based on illegally obtained information.

5 The Supreme Court upholds affirmative action, which gives hiring preference to minorities.

6 The AIDS epidemic is growing, says Surgeon Gen. C. Everett Koop, who urges safe-sex practices, including teenage abstinence and adult use of condoms, to help prevent the spread of the disease.

7 The national debt passes the $2 trillion mark, having doubled in 5 years.

8 Manufacturing in the U.S. declines as a percentage of the gross national product as industrial firms transfer production to lower-wage countries; service industries increase in the national economy, creating 10 million jobs in 7 years.

9 Immigration reform legislation signed by Pres. Reagan gives legal status to immigrants who settled in the U.S. before 1982 and toughens penalties for employers who hire illegal aliens.

Elsewhere

12 The U.S. and the Soviet Union hold meetings in Switzerland aimed at reducing the number of nuclear weapons.

13 The Reykjavík, Iceland, peace summit between Pres. Reagan and Sov. leader Mikhail Gorbachev collapses over the U.S. commitment to the Star Wars missile system.

14 Kurt Waldheim, President of Austria and former UN Secretary General, acknowledges a Nazi past. As a young German army officer, he says he was a translator but had no part in war crimes.

15 France elects Jacques Chirac, a Conservative, as Prime Minister to serve with Socialist Pres. François Mitterrand.

16 India hangs 3 Sikhs for assassinating Prime Minister Indira Gandhi.

17 Arab gunmen kill 21 Jewish worshipers at a synagogue in Istanbul, Turkey.

18 Nonaligned African nations meet in Zimbabwe, spending much of the conference criticizing South Africa's apartheid policy and the West's failure to adopt sanctions against South Africa.

The Arts

America

Simon's *Graceland,* Whitney Houston's self-titled first album, and Steve Winwood's *Back in the High Life.*

3 Painter Andrew Wyeth sells 240 watercolors, temperas, and drawings whose existence until now was known only to him and his subject, Helga.

4 Pulitzer Prizes go to J. Anthony Lukas for *Common Ground* and to Larry McMurtry for *Lonesome Dove.*

5 Robert Penn Warren is officially named poet laureate of the U.S., the first so designated.

6 Director Spike Lee brings *She's Gotta Have It* to movie screens, while Paul Newman stars in *The Color of Money,* a sequel to his famous pool-playing film of 1961, *The Hustler.*

7 In a nostalgic throwback to the 1940s and 1950s, diners that sport elegant decor and elaborate menus become fashionable as eateries.

8 The men's fashion industry marks the centennial of the tuxedo, created when tobacco magnate Griswold Lorillard shortened his dress coat for a dance in Tuxedo, N.Y.

9 Three big advertising firms—BBDO International, Doyle Dane Bernbach Group, and Needham Harper Worldwide—merge to form the Omnicon Group, the world's largest agency.

10 Fashion designer Aldo Gucci pleads guilty to a $7 million tax fraud.

Elsewhere

Devils, the tale of an elderly Welsh couple.

14 The colorful *Rossano Gospels* is returned to southern Italy after a brief stay at New York City's Pierpont Morgan Library.

15 Germany's Gottfried Boehm is awarded the prestigious Pritzker Architecture Prize.

16 Edouard Manet's *Rue Mosnier with Street Pavers* fetches $11 million at an auction in London, a record for an Impressionist work.

17 Pope John Paul II pays a historic visit to Rome's main synagogue, a gesture seen as a step toward the Vatican's recognition of Israel.

18 Beauty parlors, once considered "decadent" and "bourgeois" in China, emerge in Beijing and other big cities.

19 Italy's La Scala opera company draws record crowds in Vancouver, British Columbia.

Science & Technology

America

unemployment and bank failures rise sharply.

4 The federal government makes the environmental danger from toxic wastes a priority by enacting a $9 billion cleanup law.

5 *Voyager,* a lightweight experimental airplane, circles the Earth nonstop without refueling. Its 25,000-mi. trip takes 9 days, using 1500 gal. of fuel.

6 The U.S. Census Bureau predicts that 6.2 billion people will inhabit the Earth by the year 2000. The forecast also estimates that 170 cities in the world will have a population of more than 2 million.

7 Tylenol pain reliever capsules injected with cyanide cause 4 deaths on the East and West coasts. Manufacturer Johnson & Johnson, which had brought its brand back after a similar drug-tampering problem in 1982, develops improved packaging and a new form of pill called a "caplet."

8 A mild but rare earthquake centered in Ohio shakes up an area from New York to Wisconsin.

Elsewhere

invention of the electron microscope.

11 Halley's Comet, which can be seen from Earth every 76 years, is observed closely by several space probes, including the Soviet Union's Vega and the European Space Agency's Giotto.

12 Europe faces a major ecological disaster as a warehouse fire in Basel, Switzerland, spills 1000 tons of chemicals into the Rhine River. Switzerland, Germany, France, and the Netherlands all close Rhine water-processing plants.

13 The Soviets say they will resume nuclear testing in response to the U.S. refusal to halt testing.

14 England and France finally agree to build a tunnel (the "Chunnel") under the English Channel. The idea has been discussed since the early 1800s, but Britain previously vetoed it for financial or security reasons.

15 The world's largest indoor shopping mall achieves success in Alberta, Canada. The West Edmonton Mall boasts 836 stores and 20 movie theaters, plus restaurants and rides.

16 Record high prices for ivory provoke greater poaching among African wildlife. Elephant herds dwindle while the black rhinoceros population almost vanishes.

Miscellaneous

America

2 William Rehnquist takes the oath as Chief Justice of the Supreme Court, succeeding retiring Chief Justice Warren Burger. Antonin Scalia takes Rehnquist's seat as Associate Justice.

3 General Motors becomes the biggest U.S. company in annual sales, replacing Exxon.

4 Studies claim that 13% of American adults are illiterate.

5 Asians now account for half of all legally admitted foreigners.

6 A 4000-mi. "Hands Across America" human chain places a dramatic focus on U.S. problems of poverty and homelessness, raising funds for their relief.

7 Martin Luther King Day is observed for the first time as a federal holiday.

8 A group of Dartmouth College students opposed to the college's divestiture of South African investments fight with students supporting divestiture.

9 The most comprehensive tax reform bill since World War II becomes law, simplifying individual rates and raising corporate taxes.

10 Hormel meat workers settle after a bitter yearlong strike.

11 Dodge Morgan sails solo around the world in a record 150 days.

12 New federal legislation weakens existing gun-control law.

13 Jack Nicklaus wins his 6th Masters golf title, an all-time record.

14 The Chicago Bears defeat the New England Patriots, 46-10, in Super Bowl XX.

15 The N.Y. Mets beat the Boston Red Sox 4 games to 3 in the World Series.

Elsewhere

18 The Iran-Iraq war continues, causing heavy casualties on both sides.

19 After a 2-year stay in the Soviet Union, Soviet dictator Joseph Stalin's daughter, Svetlana Alliluyeva, returns to the U.S., where she had lived for 17 years.

20 Pakistan arrests and then frees opposition leader Benazir Bhutto, daughter of the country's former President.

21 Nicholas Daniloff, an American journalist held as a spy by the Soviet Union, is freed as the U.S. releases Gennadi Zakharov, a Soviet physicist held as a spy by the U.S.

22 Japan's Prime Minister Yasuhiro Nakasone stirs flap by commenting on U.S. ethnic divisions, implying that blacks are less intelligent than whites.

23 After Paris experiences its worst riots in 18 years, Conservative Premier Jacques Chirac yields to angry student protests and plans to reform universities.

24 Japanese saboteurs cut rail communication lines near Tokyo, disrupting 1 million commuters.

25 An earthquake in El Salvador's capital of San Salvador devastates the city, killing more than 1500 and leaving hundreds of thousands homeless.

History and Politics

America

Elsewhere

The Arts

America

Elsewhere

1987

1 Pres. Ronald Reagan and Soviet leader Mikhail Gorbachev sign a treaty in Washington to eliminate short- and medium-range nuclear weapons.
2 Congressional committees investigating the Iran-Contra Affair blame White House "secrecy, deception, and disdain for the law." Investigators claim that the U.S. sold weapons to Iran and used the profits illegally to buy arms for Contra guerrillas fighting the Nicaraguan government.
3 An Iraqi warplane fires on the U.S. Navy frigate *Stark,* killing 37 American sailors. Iraq calls it an accident and apologizes.
4 The Reagan administration proposes the government's first trillion-dollar budget.
5 William Casey resigns as chief of the CIA after undergoing brain tumor surgery; Pres. Reagan appoints FBI Director William Webster to replace him.
6 U.S. Marine Sgt. Clayton Lonetree, a former guard at the U.S. embassy in Moscow, is sentenced to 30 years in prison for spying for the Soviet Union.
7 The newly constructed U.S. embassy in Moscow is found to contain Soviet bugging devices.
8 After contentious hearings, conservative federal judge Robert Bork is denied confirmation to the U.S. Supreme Court by the Senate.
9 The Dow Jones industrial average plunges 508 points—22.6%—on "Black Monday," by far the largest one-day loss in history.

10 Bloody riots escalate in the Gaza Strip and West Bank as Palestinians resist Israeli occupation. Israeli forces respond with gunfire.
11 U.S. bars entry to Austria's Pres. Kurt Waldheim on the grounds that he took part in Nazi war crimes during World War II.
12 Former Nazi Klaus Barbie is convicted by a French court of crimes against humanity and sentenced to life in prison.
13 A young German, Mathias Rust, flies unchallenged over Soviet airspace and lands his plane in Red Square, Moscow. He is sentenced to 4 years in a Soviet labor camp.
14 Organization of Petroleum Exporting Countries limits its oil production to 16 million barrels a day at $18 a barrel.
15 Philippine voters approve a constitution confirming the government of Pres. Corazon Aquino.
16 Brazil announces it will no longer make interest payments on debts to foreign commercial banks.
17 Anglican Church envoy Terry Waite disappears in Lebanon while seeking the release of Western hostages.
18 Libya and Chad agree to a cease-fire in their border war.
19 Nobel Prize, Peace: Costa Rica's Pres. Oscar Arias Sánchez for his efforts in Central America.
20 Portugal agrees to turn over its former colony of Macao to China in 1999.

1 Van Gogh's *Irises* is auctioned for a record $53.9 million at Sotheby's in New York City. He painted it only days after entering a mental asylum in France.
2 CBS-TV anchorman Dan Rather storms off the set to protest his newscast being cut short for a tennis match. CBS network goes blank for 6 minutes.
3 Nearly half the homes in the U.S. are now hooked up to cable TV.
4 Cultural critic Tom Wolfe's first novel, *The Bonfire of the Vanities,* is hailed as a sharp dramatization of class conflicts and social behavior in New York City.
5 Profits from actor Paul Newman's "Newman's Own" salad dressing funds numerous charities, including a Connecticut camp for children with serious illnesses.
6 *Snow White and the Seven Dwarfs* is re-released by Disney on its 50th anniversary.
7 Oliver Stone's Vietnam War movie, *Platoon,* wins 4 Oscars, including best picture.
8 George Gershwin is honored on the 50th anniversary of his death with a month of concerts at the Brooklyn Academy of Music.
9 A new operatic work, *Nixon in China,* premieres at the Houston Grand Opera.
10 Beijing's Central Philharmonic makes its U.S. debut in a 24-city tour.
11 The 10th anniversary of Elvis Presley's death spurs TV specials, books, and releases of new collections of his music.

12 The Pushkin Museum in Moscow hosts a major exhibition of the works of Russian-born Marc Chagall to mark the 100th anniversary of his birth. It is the first showing of modern art in the Soviet Union in 50 years.
13 French director Maurice Pialat wins the Cannes Film Festival best-film award for *Under Satan's Sun.*
14 Nobel Prize, Literature: Joseph Brodsky, exiled Soviet-born poet and essayist.
15 The Irish rock group U2 reaches superstardom, selling out at almost every stop on its world tour.
16 Herbjorg Wassmo wins the Nordic Literature Prize for her novel *Sensitive Sky,* the first Norwegian woman so honored.
17 Berlin marks its 750th year with visits from Pres. Reagan, Queen Elizabeth, French Pres. François Mitterrand, and Soviet leader Mikhail Gorbachev.
18 Brit. productions continue to dominate the world of musicals, with *Les Miserables* winning Broadway's Tony Award as best musical.
19 Penelope Lively wins the Booker Prize, Britain's top literary award, for her novel *Moon Tiger.*
20 Restoration of Michelangelo's Sistine Chapel at the Vatican stirs criticism that it is endangering or even altering the fresco.

Science & Technology

America

1 Los Angeles is rocked by a severe earthquake that causes 6 deaths and widespread damage.

2 Utah's Great Salt Lake rises to its highest recorded level in history, causing $250 million in damage to shoreline property.

3 Expanded possible uses of superconductors make the news, promising scientific and technological revolution.

4 Some 34 nations sign a treaty in Montreal to reduce or eliminate production of ozone-destroying chemicals.

5 Garbage scow *Mobro* leaves New York City waters with a cargo no one wants—3186 tons of refuse for landfill. Turned away by 6 states and 3 nations, *Mobro* returns to port after 5 months, and the garbage is finally burned in a Brooklyn incinerator.

6 Radon is named the leading U.S. air and water pollution problem by the Environmental Protection Agency.

7 Congress overrides Pres. Reagan's veto of the $20 billion Clean Water Bill, making it law.

8 A human growth hormone is transplanted into pig embryos to increase the size and value of hogs for slaughter, a procedure that stirs ethical and scientific debate.

9 First Lady Nancy Reagan undergoes a mastectomy after a biopsy reveals cancerous cells.

Elsewhere

10 A mysterious 2500-year-old dog cemetery is uncovered near Israel's coast. The carefully buried dogs were a breed similar to today's greyhounds.

11 The World Health Organization estimates that 5 to 10 million people now carry the AIDS virus.

12 Meteorologists observe a large ozone "hole" in the stratosphere over Antarctica; they link it to special south polar weather and high atmospheric concentrations of industrial chlorofluorocarbons.

13 Archaeologists in Peru locate the ancient site of an immense cache of gold objects. Most of the 1900-year-old treasures have recently been stolen by grave robbers.

14 NEC (Nippon Electric Corp.) unveils one of the world's fastest supercomputers. It has peak speeds of 1.3 billion calculations per second.

15 Because of movement in the Earth's geologic plates, Hawaii is approaching Japan at the rate of 3.2 in. a year. At that rate, Hawaii will bump into Tokyo in 76,051,800 years.

16 Sov. cosmonaut Yuri Romanenko returns safely to Earth after a record 326 days in orbit.

17 Konica markets color film with an ASA speed of 3200.

Miscellaneous

America

1 Television evangelist Jim Bakker resigns his *Praise the Lord* TV ministry after admitting to an extramarital sexual encounter.

2 At least 36 states pass laws against the often vicious breed of dogs known as "pit bulls," many linked to bite-related deaths. The new bills require owners to secure and leash the dogs; some violations may be treated as felonies.

3 The U.S. Supreme Court upholds a voluntary affirmative action plan for public employees to correct sex discrimination.

4 Alan Greenspan is named Federal Reserve Board chairman, replacing Paul Volcker.

5 Del. Democratic Sen. Joseph Biden quits the race for President amid publicity he apparently plagiarized speeches and misstated his educational qualifications.

6 Former White House aide Michael Deaver is convicted of perjury for lying about the extent of his lobbying efforts.

7 Chrysler Corp. buys American Motors Corp. and its Jeep trademark for $1.5 billion.

8 Japan's Honda Motors sells 100,000 Acuras in the U.S., spurring Toyota and Nissan to bring out their luxury Lexus and Infiniti models.

9 An Amtrak train collides with 3 diesel engines north of Baltimore, leaving 16 people dead and dozens injured.

10 *Stars & Stripes,* the U.S. racing yacht skippered by Dennis Conner, regains the America's Cup by taking 4 straight races from Australia's *Kookaburra III* off Fremantle, Australia.

11 Al Unser wins his 4th Indianapolis 500 auto race.

12 The New York Giants beat the Denver Broncos, 39-20, in Super Bowl XXI.

Elsewhere

13 Russians mark the 70th anniversary of the Bolshevik Revolution.

14 A British ferry capsizes in the English Channel off the Belgian coast; of 543 aboard, more than 185 are lost.

15 A rush-hour fire in London's busiest subway and train station, King's Cross, leaves 30 dead.

16 A bomb explosion kills 11 people and injures more than 60 others in Enniskillen, Northern Ireland. The Irish Republican Army claims responsibility.

17 Jean Bokassa, former Emperor of the Central African Republic, is sentenced to death for the murder of political opponents.

18 After weeks of political violence, South Korea's Pres. Chun Doo Hwan promises direct popular election of the next President.

19 Gary Kasparov retains his world chess championship in a match with Anatoly Karpov in Madrid.

20 Pope John Paul II visits 9 U.S. cities in a 10-day tour.

21 Chinese police crush an independence rally in Lhasa, Tibet; 19 die.

22 A passenger ferry and an oil tanker collide and sink off the Philippines' Mindoro Island, killing about 1500.

23 U.S. and Mongolia establish diplomatic relations.

24 Zimbabwe's House of Assembly abolishes 20 seats reserved for whites.

1987

433

History and Politics

America

1 Vice Pres. George Bush is elected 41st President of the U.S., soundly defeating the Democratic candidate, Massachusetts Gov. Michael Dukakis.

2 U.S. indicts Panamanian leader Manuel Noriega on drug-smuggling charges.

3 A U.S. Navy cruiser in the Persian Gulf shoots down an Iranian commercial jetliner after mistaking it for an attack plane. All 290 people aboard are killed.

4 A Pan Am 747 bound from Frankfurt via London to New York City explodes in midair and crashes into the Scottish village of Lockerbie, killing all 259 people aboard and 11 on the ground. Terrorists are suspected, and new airline security measures are put in place worldwide.

5 The U.S. Senate confirms Anthony M. Kennedy as an associate justice of the Supreme Court.

6 Lt. Col. Oliver North is indicted in the Iran-Contra Affair, along with former National Security Adviser John Poindexter and other participants. The charge is conspiracy to defraud the U.S. by planning to illegally supply arms to the Nicaraguan Contras, guerrillas working to overthrow the leftist government.

7 Lyn Nofziger, former top political aide to the Reagan White House, is convicted of illegal lobbying and sentenced to 90 days in jail.

8 The Arizona Senate convicts Gov. Evan Mecham of misconduct in office and removes him from office.

9 Congress passes and Pres. Reagan signs a bill establishing the cabinet-level Department of Veterans Affairs.

Elsewhere

10 Nicaragua's protracted civil war ends. The Sandinista government signs a truce with Contra rebels, pledges ongoing talks, and releases 3300 prisoners.

11 Australia celebrates the bicentennial of the continent's settlement by Europeans.

12 The Palestine Liberation Organization votes to recognize the existence of Israel and proclaims an independent state of Palestine. U.S. then begins dialogue with the PLO.

13 Israel's 2 major parties form a coalition government under Yitzhak Shamir. During a Washington visit, Shamir rejects Reagan's Middle East peace plan.

14 Nobel Prize, Peace: the UN Peacekeeping Forces.

15 Pakistan's Pres. Mohammed Zia is killed in a midair plane explosion. Later, Benazir Bhutto becomes Prime Minister, the first woman to rule a modern Muslim nation.

16 The Soviet Union, the U.S., Afghanistan, and Pakistan sign a treaty for the withdrawal of 100,000 Soviet troops from Afghanistan.

17 An Israeli court convicts John Demjanjuk, the alleged "Ivan the Terrible," of taking part in Nazi death-camp murders during World War II and sentences him to death.

18 An international panel of historians concludes that Austrian Pres. Kurt Waldheim was aware of war crimes committed by his German Army unit in World War II but had not committed any himself.

19 The 8-year Iran-Iraq War ends with a cease-fire on Aug. 20.

The Arts

America

1 Superman marks the 50th anniversary of his first appearing in *Action Comics.* A birthday exhibit at the Smithsonian Institution is one of many tributes to the enduring U.S. supermyth.

2 A record price for contemporary art is reached when Jackson Pollock's *The Search* sells for $4.8 million at a Sotheby's auction in New York City.

3 Toni Morrison wins the Pulitzer Prize for fiction for *Beloved,* a novel about a runaway slave who kills her daughter rather than let her be captured and raised as a slave.

4 Two centuries of American fashion are exhibited at Cincinnati's Art Museum.

5 Climbing attendance at Broadway theaters is led by the success of *Phantom of the Opera* and the Tony-winning *M. Butterfly.*

6 Rodeos become big business as U.S. corporations begin to underwrite large cash prizes for competitors.

7 Massachusetts's Worcester Art Museum holds an exhibit of 100 historic works from its photography archives, 150 years after Louis Daguerre helped invent photography.

8 A 22-week strike of movie and television writers ends with ratification of a 4-year contract.

9 Director Martin Scorsese's controversial movie *The Last Temptation of Christ* is attacked by many religious organizations for portraying Jesus as a man with doubts about his mission on Earth.

Elsewhere

10 Egypt's Sphinx is starting to show its age after 4600 years. Despite restoration begun in 1981, a 700-lb. chunk falls off.

11 *The Last Emperor,* the epic film by Italian director Bernardo Bertolucci, wins a near-record 9 Oscars.

12 Tokyo Disneyland becomes Japan's favorite playland. It resembles its American counterpart but with a Japanese style—visitors are greeted by a smiling "Mickey-San."

13 Nobel Prize, Literature: Egypt's Naguib Mahfouz, a novelist and playwright.

14 Pop star Michael Jackson goes prime time on Russian TV in a show sponsored by Pepsi Cola that airs the first U.S. commercials on Soviet television.

15 In Britain, 5 new books and a TV miniseries mark the centennial of Jack the Ripper, the unidentified 19th-century psychopath who slashed prostitutes to death.

Science & Technology

America

1 Aspirin is found to reduce heart attacks, according to a National Heart, Lung, and Blood Institute study. Using aspirin regularly, it says, reduces the risk of heart attack by as much as 47%.

2 Dermatologists say women patients are clamoring for the new drug Retin-A, which can actually smooth out minor skin wrinkles.

3 A *New York Times* study reports that despite new awareness of nutrition, most Americans still love junk food. And while 46% of women say they pay close attention to their health needs, only 31% of men do so.

4 Half the nation's agricultural counties are declared disaster areas because of severe drought. Farmers say it is the driest year since the mid-1930s.

5 An Ashland Oil fuel tank collapses near Pittsburgh, Pa., fouling the Monongahela River with 1 million gal. of oil.

6 DuPont announces it will stop production of chlorofluorocarbons (CFCs), thought to threaten the Earth's ozone layer.

Elsewhere

7 Discovery of charcoal among prehistoric stone tools in Chile indicates that humans may have inhabited the Americas 33,000 years ago, challenging the theory that the first "Americans" came from Asia into Alaska 11,000 years ago.

8 Hurricane Gilbert, the most severe storm on record in the Western Hemisphere, wreaks destruction on Jamaica and throughout the Caribbean and Mexico.

9 A new Airbus A320, considered one of the most advanced commercial airliners on the market, crashes during a demonstration flight in France.

10 Mexico City is called the world's most smog-polluted city, with heavy concentrations of sulfur, lead, mercury, and carbon monoxide.

11 An Occidental Petroleum oil platform explodes in the North Sea; more than 160 workers are killed.

12 Greek bicyclist Kanellos Kanellopoulos pedals a human-powered superlight plane 74 mi. across the Aegean Sea.

13 The first fiber-optic cable across the Atlantic takes its first call. It can handle 40,000 calls at once.

14 Two Soviet cosmonauts safely return to Earth after being stranded in orbit for 25 hours with a dwindling supply of air.

15 Fax machines emerge as an integral business tool around the world. The advent of cheap machines that can transmit documents over telephone lines begins to change the way the business world communicates.

16 Security concerns for computer records and data grow as unauthorized entry into computer systems becomes an international problem.

Miscellaneous

America

1 The ever-expanding membership of the American Association of Retired Persons and demonstrations by the Gray Panthers underline the increasing influence of older people in the U.S.

2 In his book *For the Record,* former White House Chief of Staff Donald Regan says that Pres. Reagan's public moves were dictated by the stars. First Lady Nancy Reagan called her astrologer for White House advice, Regan alleges.

3 Kohlberg Kravis Roberts, a New York investment firm, buys RJR Nabisco, the food and tobacco conglomerate, for $25 billion, and Philip Morris buys Kraft Foods for $13.1 billion, the two largest corporate mergers in U.S. history.

4 Once high-flying Wall Street brokerage house Drexel Burnham Lambert pleads guilty to violations of federal securities laws and is fined $650 million.

5 The White House begins random drug testing for presidential employees after reports of off-duty cocaine use by 3 White House guards.

6 The U.S. Supreme Court rules that public-school officials have broad powers to censor school newspapers.

7 The Washington Redskins beat the Denver Broncos, 42-10, in Super Bowl XXII.

8 Winning Colors, a filly, wins the Kentucky Derby.

9 A year after Jim Bakker quit TV evangelism in a sex scandal, Jimmy Swaggart, a TV evangelist who had attacked Bakker, resigns his position after reports that he consorted with a prostitute.

10 "No Smoking" signs go up on Northwest Airlines

Elsewhere

13 Antarctica becomes a tourist mecca. Some 35 travelers pay $35,000 each for a tour of a South Pole research unit, where the average summer reading is −47°F.

14 Professional tennis player Steffi Graf of West Germany wins the Grand Slam by taking titles at Wimbledon and the Australian, French, and U.S. opens.

15 The Soviet Union's liberal policy of *glasnost* exposes Russians to more than political dissent; amid efforts to enliven its economy, Moscow gets its first American pizzeria.

16 Dissident Roman Catholic Archbishop Marcel LeFebvre defies papal orders by consecrating 4 bishops in Switzerland. The Vatican excommunicates him.

17 Three Italian Air Force jets collide during an air show in Ramstein, West Germany, killing 50 people and injuring 350.

18 Thousands of Kurds flee Iraq for Turkey amid reports the Iraqis used poison gas to drive them out.

19 Khalil al-Wazir, the military leader of the Palestine Liberation Organization, is killed in his Tunisian home, perhaps by Israeli special forces.

20 Fans jam Calgary, Alberta, Canada, for the Olympic Winter Games, in which nearly 1800 athletes from 57 nations compete.

21 The Edmonton Oilers win their 4th Stanley Cup in 5 years.

22 In the Olympic Summer Games in Seoul, South Korea, U.S. diver Greg Louganis repeats his 1984 triumphs by taking 2 gold medals.

1988

435

	History and Politics		The Arts	
	America	**Elsewhere**	**America**	**Elsewhere**
1989	**1** Republican George Bush succeeds Ronald Reagan as President. **2** The oil tanker *Exxon Valdez* runs aground in the Gulf of Alaska, causing the largest oil spill in U.S. history, killing thousands of fish, birds, and other wildlife. Exxon, Alaska, and the U.S. government spend billions of dollars on the cleanup, but the coastal ecological system is devastated, and the Alaskan fishing industry suffers heavy losses. **3** U.S. military forces enter Panama and capture Pres. Manuel Noriega, who is taken to the U.S. to answer a drug indictment. **4** A gun turret explosion on the battleship *Iowa* kills 47 American sailors. The Navy begins an investigation to determine the cause. **5** The U.S. Supreme Court declares that the Constitution protects the rights of protesters to burn the U.S. flag. **6** Pres. Bush signs a law authorizing a bailout of troubled U.S. savings and loan institutions, a measure that will initially cost taxpayers more than $165 billion. **7** Former U.S. National Security Council staff member Oliver North is fined $150,000 and given 2 years probation for his role in the Iran-Contra scandal. **8** Richard M. Daley, son of legendary Chicago mayor Richard J. Daley, is elected the city's mayor.	**10** Crown Prince Akihito becomes Emperor of Japan upon the death of his father Emperor Hirohito. **11** The notorious Berlin Wall separating East and West Germany is breached; hundreds of thousands of East Germans migrate west. **12** Thousands of Chinese troops move into downtown Beijing to rout pro-democracy demonstrators. An estimated 300 to 400 students and workers are killed in what becomes known as the Tiananmen Square Massacre. In response, Pres. Bush suspends U.S. military sales to China. **13** F.W. de Klerk succeeds the ailing P.W. Botha as President of South Africa. **14** For the first time since the Russian Revolution of 1917, Russian voters have a choice of parties and candidates in parliamentary elections. **15** Soviet troops clash with nationalist demonstrators in Tbilisi, the capital of the Soviet Republic of Georgia. **16** Leaders of the Angolan government and rebel forces agree to a cease-fire, trying to end their 14-year-old war. **17** Two U.S. Navy jets shoot down 2 Libyan warplanes off the Libyan Coast. **18** Martial law is ordered in the Tibetan capital of Lhasa after violent confrontations between Tibetan demonstrators and Chinese troops. **19** Romanian dictator Nicolae Ceausescu is overthrown and	**1** Filmmaker Woody Allen wins critical acclaim for *Crimes and Misdemeanors,* a drama/comedy on the meaning of life. Director Spike Lee offers *Do the Right Thing,* a powerful film about racism. Writer/director Steven Soderbergh debuts with the much-discussed *sex, lies, and videotape.* **2** The comic book hero Batman becomes a national phenomenon with the release of the movie *Batman,* starring Michael Keaton and Jack Nicholson. **3** E.L. Doctorow's *Billy Bathgate,* a tale of organized crime in the 1930s, is hailed as his best novel. **4** Chinese art draws thousands to U.S. museums when the exhibit "Masterworks of the Ming and Qing: Painting from the Forbidden City" tours 5 U.S. cities. **5** European masters Goya, Hals, Veláquez, and Canaletto are featured in well-attended U.S. shows. **6** Interest in American artists continues strong, with record sales for works by sculptor Frederic Remington and painter Frederick Edwin Church. **7** The "Fakes Phenome-	**9** The year's highest priced painting is Pablo Picasso's *Pierrette's Wedding,* which brings $51.3 million at a Paris auction house; another Picasso sells for almost $48 million in New York City. **10** Claudio Abbado, conductor of the Vienna Philharmonic, succeeds Herbert von Karajan as music director of the Berlin Philharmonic. **11** Nobel Prize, Literature: Camilo José Cela, who is immensely popular in his native Spain. **12** The bicentennial of the French Revolution turns Paris's Champs-Elysées boulevard into a festival, with costumed paraders from the U.S., Europe, Asia, and Africa. **13** Legendary rock groups the Rolling Stones and the Who each reunite to stage glitzy world concert tours. **14** The centennial of silent film star Charlie Chaplin is marked by film festivals worldwide in his honor. **15** Canada's most talked about book is Erik Nielsen's *The House Is Not a Home,* the candid memoirs of a former legislator and cabinet minister.

436

Science & Technology		Miscellaneous		
America	Elsewhere	America	Elsewhere	

Miscellaneous — America (continued)

flights, the first such ban by a U.S. carrier.

11 "Hypermarkets" become the rage—the mega-size retail stores as big as 5 football fields that sell everything from bananas to bedroom sets. Kmart and Walmart set up dozens of these "malls without walls."

12 A new law stipulates that U.S. companies must provide 60 days' notice of major layoffs or closings.

Science & Technology — America

1 A major earthquake rocks northern California, causing at least 67 deaths and $6 billion in damage. As an internationally telecast World Series game is about to begin in San Francisco, buildings topple, a lane falls on the Bay Bridge, and elevated freeways collapse.

2 Alar, a chemical that delays the ripening of apples, is reported to be carcinogenic. Shoppers avoid the fruit until Alar's maker stops selling it for food treatment.

3 Hurricane Hugo devastates the Caribbean, then slams into South Carolina before heading north.

4 Univ. of Cincinnati scientists report that even minor exposure to lead can stunt growth in children and make them lose their balance.

5 Photographs taken by the Voyager 2 satellite show that Neptune has at least 6 moons besides the 2 already known.

6 The space shuttle *Atlantis* returns to Earth after launching the Galileo spacecraft on a 6-year exploration voyage to Jupiter.

7 Cigarette smoking increases the risk of eye cataracts, says a Johns Hopkins University study.

8 The U.S. space shuttle *Atlantis* and its 5-member crew deploy the Magellan

Science & Technology — Elsewhere

10 A weather satellite spots a huge circular scar on the earth near Prague, Czechoslovakia. It is believed to be a 200-mi. wide crater from a meteorite that smashed into Earth 100 million years ago.

11 India's Supreme Court rules that Union Carbide must pay $470 million to victims of the 1984 poisonous-gas leak from its chemical plant in Bhopal, India.

12 Fears of nuclear contamination rise after a Soviet nuclear submarine sinks off the Norwegian coast following a fire on board.

13 The world's oldest known beer brewery, 5400 years old, is found in the ruins of an ancient Egyptian city on the Nile.

14 A ring of computer spy-hackers from West Germany breaks into computer systems in Europe, Japan, and the U.S. Those arrested are charged with stealing secrets and passing them to the Russians.

15 A strong, 6.8-magnitude earthquake strikes Mexico City and Acapulco, cracking buildings and frightening Mexicans who experienced a devastating earthquake in 1985.

16 The World War II German battleship *Bismarck* is located in 15,000 ft. of water off the French coast by Rob-

Miscellaneous — America

1 A gunman armed with a submachine gun opens fire on a Stockton, Calif., schoolyard, killing 5 children before committing suicide. Another gunman, armed with an assault rifle, kills 7 coworkers at a Louisville, Ky., printing plant before killing himself. Congress reacts with bills against the ownership of assault weapons, but the National Rifle Association lobbies against the measures, which leads to a deadlock.

2 A United Airlines DC-10 crashes into an Iowa field after a complete hydraulic control failure. Of the 296 people on board, 112 die.

3 African Americans win 2 high-profile elections: David Dinkins is the first black elected Mayor of New York City; Virginia's Douglas Wilder becomes the country's first elected black governor.

4 Pete Rose, Cincinnati Reds manager, is banned from baseball for life for betting on games.

5 Pete Rozelle retires as National Football League Commissioner after 29 years.

6 In pro football's Super Bowl XXIII, the San Francisco 49ers beat the Cincinnati Bengals, 20-16.

Miscellaneous — Elsewhere

7 Iranian leader Ayatollah Khomeini issues a *fatwa* calling on Muslims to kill author Salman Rushdie for writing *The Satanic Verses,* a novel some Muslims consider blasphemous. Rushdie goes into hiding.

8 Fighting intensifies between Christian and Muslim factions in Beirut, Lebanon; shelling takes hundreds of lives.

9 Nobel Prize, Peace: the Dalai Lama, Tibet's exiled religious and secular leader.

10 A French DC-10 flying from the Congo to Paris explodes, killing 171 passengers and crew. Authorities suspect a bomb was the cause.

11 In Colombia, leading presidential candidate Luis Carlos Galan is assassinated by the Medellín drug cartel, spurring a government drive to crack down on the powerful drug lords.

13 A mail train and an express train carrying religious pilgrims crash head-on in Bangladesh, killing 179 people and injuring 1000.

14 West Germany's Boris Becker and Steffi Graf win the men's and women's singles tennis titles at Wimbledon. Each also wins the U.S. Open.

1989

History and Politics		The Arts	
America	Elsewhere	America	Elsewhere

History and Politics — America

9 Pres. Bush announces a new program to curb illegal drug trafficking and use.

History and Politics — Elsewhere

executed in bloody revolution.
20 East European nations start turning away from Communism, with non-Communist opposition parties taking office in several countries.
21 Arab countries of the Middle East try to strengthen their ties through establishment of the Arab Maghreb Union and the Arab Cooperative Council.

The Arts — America

non" dominates the fashion world in part because of pressure from animal-rights groups. Fake furs, fake ivory, and fake reptile hides are hot sellers.
8 In performance art, Montana celebrates its state centennial with a 60-mi. cattle drive. Some 3000 riders and 200 covered wagons drive a herd of more than 2800 cattle across mountains and prairies.

1990

History and Politics — America

1 The U.S. faces a major military crisis when Iraq invades Kuwait. Pres. George Bush attempts diplomatic resolution but also dispatches approximately 400,000 U.S. military personnel to the Persian Gulf.
2 In midterm elections, Democrats increase their majority in the House and Senate and hold their own in the gubernatorial races.
3 The U.S. Court of Appeals overturns most of Oliver North's Iran-Contra felony convictions.
4 David Souter of New Hampshire becomes an associate justice of the U.S. Supreme Court, replacing retiring Justice William J. Brennan, Jr.
5 Discrimination against the disabled is banned under the Americans with Disabilities Act.
6 Pres. Bush approves $1 billion for food and medicine for the Soviet Union to enable it to meet its severe economic crisis and food shortage.
7 The House of Representatives defeats a proposed constitutional amendment making desecration of the U.S. flag a crime, following a Supreme Court decision overturning federal legislation protecting the flag.
8 Pres. Bush, whose campaign slogan in 1988 was "Read my lips—no new taxes," upsets supporters by acknowledging that reducing the federal budget deficit would require "tax-revenue increases." The legislation he signs includes higher taxes on

History and Politics — Elsewhere

10 Iraq invades its oil-rich neighbor Kuwait and proclaims it part of Iraq. The UN and leading world nations denounce the move as aggression, but Iraqi Pres. Saddam Hussein refuses to withdraw. International military forces led by the U.S. assembles in Saudi Arabia to oppose Iraq.
11 Germany, divided since the end of World War II in 1945, is reunited as the barriers between East and West Germany disappear. West German Chancellor Helmut Kohl becomes Chancellor of the reunited Germany.
12 Margaret Thatcher resigns as Great Britain's Prime Minister and is succeeded by fellow Conservative John Major.
13 Nelson Mandela, South African black nationalist leader, is freed after almost 3 decades in prison. South African Pres. F.W. de Klerk lifts the 30-year ban on Mandela's African National Congress, the main group seeking black majority rule, and begins talks with Mandela.
14 Lech Walesa, shipworker turned political leader, is elected President of Poland.
15 Mikhail Gorbachev is elected to a 5-year term as Soviet President.
16 Lithuania leads restive Soviet republics in moving toward independence.
17 The Soviet Union pulls its troops out of Czechoslovakia.
18 Romania bans the Communist Party, the first East European country to do so.

The Arts — America

1 The top price for fine art at Christie's in New York reaches $82.5 million for Vincent Van Gogh's *Portrait du Dr. Gachet,* while Pierre Auguste Renoir's *Au Moulin de la Galette* sells for $78.1 million at Sotheby's. Both paintings are bought by a Japanese collector.
2 The Contemporary Arts Center in Cincinnati and its director are tried on obscenity charges stemming from exhibits of Robert Mapplethorpe's photography; a jury acquits them.
3 Two burglars disguised as police officers break into the Isabella Stewart Gardner Museum in Boston and steal a dozen masterworks by Vermeer, Rembrandt, Degas, and Manet, valued at $200 million.
4 *A Chorus Line* closes after 15 years, the longest run in the history of the Broadway theater. New hits on Broadway include *Buddy,* a salute to early rock 'n' roller Buddy Holly, and John Guare's *Six Degrees of Separation.*
5 Rap music engenders controversy as an album by 2 Live Crew is ruled obscene by a Florida court.

The Arts — Elsewhere

10 The world's 3 leading tenors join for a benefit concert in Rome: Plácido Domingo, Luciano Pavarotti, and José Carreras.
11 "Monet in the 90s," a landmark exhibition of paintings by the French Impressionist, makes the rounds of major museums in Europe and the U.S.
12 Archaeologists digging at the site of the ancient Canaanite city of Ashkelon in Israel uncover a 3500-year-old calf figurine, the oldest such object known. They speculate it might have been a prototype of the biblical "golden calf."
13 A rare bark-paper book, known as a codex, is discovered at a Mayan site in El Salvador that was buried in volcanic ash about A.D. 600.
14 Nobel Prize, Literature: Mexican poet Octavio Paz, who concentrated on writing after a career as a diplomat.
15 Parisians welcome the Bastille Opera, a glass-and-tile structure deemed an architectural and acoustical triumph.
16 The young Soviet pianist Yevgeny Kissin makes his U.S. debut in New York City. Critics say he lives up to his reputation as a technical vir-

Science & Technology — America

spacecraft on a 15-month trip to Venus.

9 The drug AZT (azidothymidine) is reported effective in delaying the onset of AIDS for those infected with the virus who have not yet shown symptoms.

Science & Technology — Elsewhere

ert Ballard, the same man who in 1985 located the *Titanic*. He says the *Bismarck* is in one piece, suggesting it was scuttled.

Science & Technology — America

1 NASA reports a major manufacturing flaw in the main mirror of the Hubble Space Telescope that renders its pictures fuzzy and disappointing.

2 The Environmental Protection Agency reports a 90% drop in lead and 28% decline in carbon monoxide in the air since 1980.

3 An oil tanker dumps nearly 400,000 gal. of oil into the Pacific Ocean near Huntington Beach, Calif., endangering beaches and wildlife.

4 Joseph Hazelwood, skipper of the oil tanker *Exxon Valdez,* is acquitted in an Alaska court on most charges related to the biggest oil spill in U.S. history.

5 General Motors unveils the Saturn, a compact car aimed at a young market.

6 In an important court decision, Eastman Kodak is ordered to pay Polaroid more than $900 million for patent infringements.

7 Ruling in an important case in the debate over euthanasia, the U.S. Supreme Court upholds the decision of a Missouri court to permit parents of 33-year-old Nancy Beth Cruzan, who has been in a coma for 7 years, to discontinue life-support.

8 The Food and Drug Administration approves Simp-

Science & Technology — Elsewhere

10 China completes history's biggest census. Its population of 1,133,682,501 is growing at 1.4% a year.

11 Ninety-three nations pledge to stop, by the year 2000, the manufacture of chemicals that may be destroying the Earth's atmosphere's protective ozone level.

12 The space probe Galileo glides past Venus and takes 80 pictures showing details as small as 25 mi. across. The close encounter gives Galileo a gravity-aided boost toward its primary target, Jupiter, which it should reach in 1995.

13 The 20th anniversary of Earth Day, created to heighten awareness of threats to the environment, is celebrated around the world.

14 Onboard explosions damage a Norwegian tanker, sending flaming oil into the Gulf of Mexico.

15 Two Soviet cosmonauts spend 6 months aloft on the Soviet space station Mir.

16 A powerful earthquake in Iran takes an estimated 40,000 lives.

Miscellaneous — America

1 Top Wall Street brokerage firm Drexel Burnham Lambert is fined for insider trading and files for bankruptcy. Drexel's chief junk-bond dealer, Michael Milken, is sentenced to 10 years in prison.

2 The U.S. unemployment rate reaches 5.9%, its highest level in 3 years.

3 Atlanta, Ga., is chosen as the site for the 1996 Summer Olympics.

4 In a New York City trial, Imelda Marcos, wife of former Philippine Pres. Fernando Marcos, is acquitted of charges of racketeering, fraud, and obstruction of justice.

5 Rabbi Meir Kahane, the driving force behind the militant Jewish Defense League and leader of a small anti-Arab political party in Israel, is assassinated in New York City.

6 In Jacksonville, Fla., construction worker James Pough shoots 8 people fatally with an assault weapon and then kills himself.

7 After intervention by the Dept. of Labor, striking coal miners in Virginia agree to a new contract, ending a bitter strike.

8 Two well-known European carmakers, Jaguar and Saab, are bought by U.S. automakers. Ford buys Jaguar for $2.5 billion; General

Miscellaneous — Elsewhere

13 Great Britain joins Europe's monetary system.

14 Mary Robinson takes office as the first woman President of Ireland.

15 Some 1500 Muslim pilgrims are killed in a stampede as they approach the holy sites in the city of Mecca, Saudi Arabia.

16 Japan's Emperor Akihito expresses his "deepest regret" for Japan's occupation of Korea from 1910 to 1945.

17 Bolivia, Colombia, Peru, and the U.S. agree to cooperate in a campaign against illegal drugs.

18 After 75 years of South African rule, South-West Africa becomes the independent state Namibia.

19 After years of negotiation, pro-Western North Yemen and pro-Soviet South Yemen unite into the Republic of Yemen.

20 Alberto Fujimori, an engineer of Japanese descent, is elected President of Peru.

21 Nobel Prize, Peace: Soviet leader Mikhail Gorbachev for his leadership in international peace efforts.

22 Great Britain and Argentina restore full diplomatic relations, which had been severed in 1982 during the Falklands War.

23 In Canada, foreign ministers of NATO and Warsaw

1990

	History and Politics		The Arts	
	America	Elsewhere	America	Elsewhere
	the wealthy and higher excise taxes on airline tickets, gasoline, and alcohol. **9** Estimated costs for the federal rescue of the U.S. savings and loan industry rise to $500 billion.	**19** Nicaraguan Sandinista Pres. Daniel Ortega is defeated by Violetta Barrios Chamorro in national elections. **20** Pres. Samuel K. Doe of Liberia is killed during the civil war provoked by his corrupt regime. **21** Singapore's Lee Kuan Yew leaves office after 3 decades as Prime Minister.	**6** Ellis Island, the historic U.S. entrance point for immigrants in New York Harbor, is the home of the new Ellis Island Immigration Museum. **7** Author John Updike brings his series of novels centered on Harry "Rabbit" Angstrom to a close with *Rabbit at Rest*. **8** The movies bring the comics to life with *Dick Tracy*. Other popular films include *Pretty Woman* and *Postcards from the Edge*. **9** U.S. architects receive big contracts overseas, exporting U.S. designs to Europe and Asia, where many favor the American look.	tuoso with a romantic streak. **17** *Cinema Paradiso*, from Italy, wins an Oscar in the U.S. as best foreign-language film.
1991	**1** The U.S. leads an allied military force in the 6-week Persian Gulf War, which frees Kuwait from the Iraqi occupation begun in 1990. After diplomacy fails to persuade the Iraqis to pull back, the U.S. obtains UN approval for a multination attack force. **2** In a campaign code-named Desert Storm, U.S. troops and forces from 34 other nations attack Iraq and occupied Kuwait. Iraq fires SCUD missiles into Israel and Saudi Arabia. In battle, large numbers of Iraqi troops are killed or surrender, while Allied losses are light. Pres. Bush tells Congress that "Kuwait is liberated." **3** Clarence Thomas wins confirmation to the U.S. Supreme Court after televised hearings into charges of sexual harassment brought by Anita Hill, a law professor and former colleague. **4** Five U.S. Senators are criticized in an ethics probe centering on favors allegedly done for Charles Keating, owner of the failed Lincoln Savings and Loan Association. Keating is later convicted of fraud. **5** Four white policemen are indicted by a Los Angeles, Calif., grand jury in the beating of a	**8** Economic and political crises trigger the breakup of the Soviet Union, which separates into republics. Most of the 15 new nations ally in a loose confederation called the Commonwealth of Independent States. Soviet Pres. Mikhail Gorbachev survives a coup d'etat, but his power is weakened and he is later forced to resign. **9** The former Soviet republics of Estonia, Latvia, and Lithuania have their independence recognized by the Soviet government. **10** The Warsaw Pact powers of Eastern Europe dissolve their defense alliance, originally formed to counter NATO. **11** Poland, Hungary, and Czechoslovakia sign a pact to work together to convert their economies from Communist to free-market systems. **12** Jean-Bertrand Aristide is overthrown by military leaders after becoming Haiti's first democratically elected president. **13** Nelson Mandela is elected president of the African National Congress in its first national conference permitted by South Africa in 32 years. Pres. Bush lifts U.S. economic sanctions against South Africa.	**1** Philanthropist Walter Annenberg makes a gift worth $1 billion to New York City's Metropolitan Museum: his unmatched collection of more than 50 Impressionist and Post-Impressionist works. **2** Rap music, reflecting inner-city social conditions, extends its influence to mainstream America through artists such as M.C. Hammer, 2 Live Crew, and Run-DMC. Country star Garth Brooks is the dominant solo performer on the concert and recording scene. **3** Feminist writer Susan Faludi's *Backlash: The Undeclared War Against American Women*, argues that politics and mass culture pressure women to return to traditional roles of subservience. **4** The 200th anniversary of Mozart's death spurs musical tributes around the world; the largest is at New York's Lincoln Center. **5** New York City's Carnegie Hall celebrates its centennial.	**10** Art auction prices plunge because of the global recession, but Degas's *Racehorses* fetches just under $10 million at Christie's auction in London. **11** A highlight of British theater is the joint appearance in Chekhov's *Three Sisters* of sisters Vanessa and Lynn Redgrave and their niece Jemma Redgrave. **12** Nobel Prize, Literature: Nadine Gordimer, outspoken critic of apartheid in her native South Africa. **13** American architect Robert Venturi completes a new wing of London's National Gallery. **14** A Tate Gallery exhibit in London adds recognition to the 20th-century sculptor Sir Anthony Caro, showing his favorite medium, steel. **15** Brit. publishing magnate Robert Maxwell dies in an apparent suicide; his body is found floating near his yacht off the Canary Islands. Re-

Science & Technology		Miscellaneous		
America	Elsewhere	America	Elsewhere	
lesse, a low-calorie fat substitute. **9** The U.S. space shuttle *Atlantis,* with a 5-member crew, completes a secret military mission.		Motors buys 50% of Saab for $600 million. **9** Jose Canseco of the Oakland Athletics signs a 5-year, $23.5-million contract that makes him baseball's highest-paid player. **10** The New England Patriots football team and 3 of its players are fined for demeaning a female sports reporter. **11** The San Francisco 49ers trounce the Denver Broncos, 55-10, in Super Bowl XXIV. **12** The Cincinnati Reds take 4 straight games from the Oakland Athletics to win the World Series.	Pact countries meet together in a historic summit. **24** Russians get their first taste of American-style fast food when a McDonald's opens in Moscow. Lines were long until prices were doubled. **25** West Germany wins the World Cup soccer tourney.	
1 Four men and 2 women seal themselves in Biosphere 2, a large metal and glass greenhouse in Arizona, in a scheduled 2-year study of the ecology of closed systems. **2** During a 6-day flight, the space shuttle *Atlantis* puts the Gamma Ray Observatory into orbit. **3** Both Pan Am and Eastern Airlines go out of business. **4** Pres. Bush is hospitalized for 2 days for an irregular heartbeat. **5** A radar image of the planet Venus taken by the Magellan spacecraft shows huge volcanoes and large craters. **6** Alzheimer's disease emerges as a major U.S. public health issue. Some 4 million Americans suffer from the incurable disease that claims 100,000 lives yearly. Symptoms are a gradual loss of memory, speech, and orientation. **7** A fire in a chicken-processing plant in Hamlet, N.C., claims the lives of 25 workers. **8** Computers continue to	**10** Scientists find the site of an asteroid crash 65 million years ago that they suspect caused the extinction of the dinosaurs. The evidence points to an asteroid that blasted a crater more than 100 mil. in diameter on Mexico's Yucatan peninsula, raising so much dust that sunlight was blocked, plant life withered, and the plant-eating dinosaurs died. **11** Japan again assumes the title of the world's largest automaker, turning out almost 10 million cars compared to 6 million in the U.S. **12** European scientists produce a significant amount of energy from controlled nuclear fusion for the first time, at a pan-European lab in Oxfordshire, England. **13** In Japan, Mt. Unzen, a volcano dormant for 2 centuries, suddenly erupts, killing 38 persons. **14** Mt. Pinatubo volcano near Manila erupts, showering the Philippines with ash and killling about 435. **15** Tropical storm Thelma causes flooding in the Phil-	**1** After his arrest in Milwaukee, mass murderer Jeffrey Dahmer confesses to killing at least 11 people. Human heads and various other body parts are found in his apartment. **2** George Hennard goes on a shooting spree that kills 27 (including himself) in a Killeen, Tex., restaurant. **3** William Kennedy Smith, nephew of Sen. Edward Kennedy, is acquitted of rape charges in Palm Beach, Fla. **4** The U.S. Supreme Court rules that use of a forced confession in a criminal case does not automatically void the conviction. **5** Conservative writer and TV personality Pat Buchanan starts his campaign for the 1992 Republican presidential nomination. **6** Los Angeles Lakers basketball star Magic Johnson discloses that he has the HIV virus that causes AIDS and retires as a player. **7** Led by superstar Michael Jordan, the Chicago Bulls capture their first National Basketball Association championship, de-	**10** Pope John Paul II names 22 new cardinals, including 2 Americans—Archbishops Anthony Bevilacqua of Philadelphia and Roger Mahoney of Los Angeles. **11** Winnie Mandela, wife of South African black leader Nelson Mandela, is sentenced to 6 years in prison for her role in kidnapping and assault incidents. She appeals the verdict. **12** Travel and emigration by Soviet citizens is eased by the government in the midst of an economic crisis. **13** Taiwan's Pres. Lee Teng-hui declares an end to 43 years of emergency rule. **14** Rajiv Gandhi, son of Indira Gandhi, campaigning to regain the prime ministership of India, is assassinated. **15** China and Vietnam renew diplomatic relations, severed in 1979 when Vietnam invaded Cambodia. **16** Middle East peace talks begin in Madrid, Spain, attended by representatives from Israel and its Arab neighbors—Egypt, Jordan,	**1991**

History and Politics

America

black motorist, Rodney King. The brutal beating, captured on videotape by an amateur, is widely seen on television.

6 U.S. indicts 2 Libyan intelligence operatives in the 1988 bombing of a Pan Am flight over Lockerbie, Scotland, in which 270 people died.

7 An appeals court reverses the Iran-Contra convictions of John Poindexter; all charges against Oliver North are dropped.

Elsewhere

14 In the aftermath of the Persian Gulf war, more than 1 million Kurds are driven out of Iraq and flee to Iran and Turkey.

15 The republics of Croatia and Slovenia declare their independence as Yugoslavia disintegrates.

The Arts

America

6 The Huntington Library in San Marino, Calif., agrees to makes its photographs of the Dead Sea Scrolls available to the public.

7 New York City Opera presents Bernd Alois Zimmermann's *Die Soldaten,* considered extremely difficult to perform.

8 Broadway's big hit is the British import *Miss Saigon,* with Neil Simon's *Lost in Yonkers* also acclaimed.

9 Archaeologists locate underground burial chambers of Arizona's Mongollan Indians, who disappeared before Europeans reached North America.

Elsewhere

ports circulate in England about his financial problems.

16 Critics hail *Turbulence,* a novel by China's Jia Pingwa about 2 peasant lovers in the years after Chairman Mao's death.

17 *Liverpool Oratorio* by former Beatle Paul McCartney and film-score composer Carl Davis is well received in its Liverpool, England, debut.

1992

America (History and Politics)

1 Gov. Bill Clinton of Arkansas, a Democrat, defeats incumbent Republican Pres. George Bush in a presidential race influenced by the third-party candidacy of Texas billionaire Ross Perot, who nets 19% of the popular vote.

2 U.S. Marines are ordered to Somalia in East Africa with the mission of feeding the starving and restoring order among battling warlords.

3 In June, the U.S. and Russia agree to further nuclear arms reductions, with each nation to reduce significantly the number of its land-based, multi-warhead nuclear missiles.

4 Four white policemen are acquitted of all serious charges in the videotaped beating of Los Angeles black motorist Rodney King. The jury verdict triggers widespread looting and violence in which 52 people die and property damages reach $21 billion. Later, a U.S. grand jury indicts the 4 officers on federal charges.

5 Manuel Noriega, ousted president of Panama, is convicted in Miami of drug trafficking, money laundering, and racketeering, and is sentenced to 40 years in prison.

Elsewhere (History and Politics)

10 Leaders of Canada, Mexico, and the U.S. sign the North American Free Trade Agreement (NAFTA), which will eliminate most trade restrictions.

11 Nations of the Western Hemisphere mark the 500th anniversary of Columbus's landing in the New World.

12 Thousands flee Haiti by boat bound for the U.S. as a military junta that overthrew elected Pres. Jean-Bertrand Aristide cracks down on opponents. The U.S., in a policy shift, sends the Haitians back home.

13 El Salvador's government and rebel forces sign a pact ending more than a decade of civil war.

14 White voters in South Africa approve by a 3-to-1 margin a referendum approving the development of a constitution embracing racial equality.

15 The disintegration of Yugoslavia continues with factions warring in Bosnia and Herzegovina.

16 Pres. George Bush and Israeli Pres. Yitzhak Rabin agree on a $10 billion U.S. loan guarantee for Israel.

America (The Arts)

1 Johnny Carson retires as host of NBC's *The Tonight Show* after nearly 30 years.

2 A young Elvis Presley is portrayed on a postage stamp; some $20 million worth are kept by collectors.

3 Pulitzer Prize–winning poet Mona Van Duyn is the first woman chosen as U.S. poet laureate.

4 The hit TV show *Murphy Brown* becomes controversial when the campaigning Vice Pres. Dan Quayle says it undermines U.S. moral values by presenting its star as a single mother.

5 Serious historical novels, most notably Susan Sontag's *The Volcano Lover,* attract a wide audience. David McCullogh's *Truman* elevates the reputation of the former President.

6 Moviemaker Spike Lee offers the controversial *Malcolm X,* Woody Allen releases *Husbands and Wives,* and Clint

Elsewhere (The Arts)

9 Euro Disney opens near Paris, a $4 billion park that resembles its U.S. cousins. But losses mount as European tourists find it disappointing.

10 Nobel Prize, Literature: Derek Walcott, a Caribbean native who divides his time between teaching in Boston and writing in Trinidad.

11 Bible Lands Museum opens in Jerusalem, Israel, with the purpose of dramatizing the people and events of the Bible in its original environment.

12 Italian television stages a live production for a world audience of *Tosca* at the various sites in Rome named in the opera.

13 UNESCO begins a 5-year project to photograph the world's cultural and natural wonders before they are further harmed by war or environmental problems.

14 Windsor Castle near London sustains $100 million damages in fire. As the result of a contro-

Science & Technology		Miscellaneous		
America	**Elsewhere**	**America**	**Elsewhere**	
be miniaturized: Hewlett-Packard introduces a hand-held model that weighs less than a pound. **9** The Bush administration initiates a study to find ways to cut the rapid rise in U.S. health costs.	ippines, killing more than 3000 people. **16** Oceanographers discover a new species of whale in the Pacific Ocean near South America. **17** The Soviet space station Mir continues to receive astronauts and serve as a space laboratory while the U.S.S.R. undergoes political turmoil. **18** A major earthquake kills 400 persons in Afghanistan and 300 in Pakistan.	feating the Los Angeles Lakers. **8** The Minnesota Twins win baseball's World Series 4 games to 3 over the Atlanta Braves. **9** The New York Giants beat the Buffalo Bills, 20-19, in pro football's Super Bowl XXV.	Lebanon, Syria, and Palestinians from the Israeli-occupied territories. **17** Edith Cresson is named the first woman Prime Minister of France. **18** The trial of Manuel Noriega, deposed leader of Panama, on drug-trafficking and money-laundering charges, begins in Miami, Fla. **19** Nobel Prize, Peace: Aung San Suu Kyi, for her nonviolent campaign for democracy in her homeland of Myanmar (formerly Burma).	
1 Pioneer 10 continues to send back deep-space data 20 years after its launch. Five billion miles out, the probe still has 7 functioning instruments. **2** Dell Computer brings out a trend-setting 3.5-lb. laptop, accelerating the use of these small computers. **3** Hurricane Andrew devastates a 25-mi.-wide strip of southeast Florida. The storm kills 18, leaves 250,000 homeless, and causes damage estimated above $10 billion. **4** U.S. launches the Mars Observer, an unmanned spacecraft designed to orbit and study Mars.	**5** Archaeologists uncover Ubar, a 5000-year-old trading city famous for its frankincense, under the desert sands in Oman. **6** The Earth Summit conference on the world's environment draws 118 world leaders and 35,000 visitors to Rio de Janeiro, Brazil. **7** Researching ancient climate data, oceanographers drill the Earth's deepest hole 1.2 mi. into the seabed off the Galápagos Islands. **8** The Middle East sees a rare sight—snow, up to 2 ft. deep in Jordan and Israel. **9** A sculptured head of a giant bird that was one of the main Mayan gods is discovered in what was the ancient Mayan city of Nakbe. **10** The Greek tanker *Aegean Sea* runs aground off Spain's Atlantic port of La Coruña, causing a gigantic oil spill that fouls more than 50 mi. of the coast. **11** A strong earthquake centered in Cairo, Egypt, kills about 550 people. **12** Zimbabwe announces a national emergency as a	**1** Vietnam agrees to give U.S. all documents and belongings relating to U.S. military personnel missing during the Vietnam War. **2** John Gotti, leader of an organized crime family, is convicted in Brooklyn, N.Y., of racketeering, murder, and other crimes. **3** Former Secretary of State Clark M. Clifford is charged with crimes in connection with the Bank of Credit and Commerce International scandal. **4** A constitutional amendment is approved by the states prohibiting Congress from instituting midterm pay raises. Congress originally passed the measure in 1789. **5** Pres. Bush vetoes the proposed "motor-voter" law that would simplify voter registration. **6** U.S. deports IRA member Joseph Doherty to Northern Ireland to face sentencing in the murder of a Brit. soldier. **7** U.S. unemployment soars to 7.8%, its highest rate since 1983.	**16** The Church of England allows the ordination of women priests. **17** French truckers protest new licensing regulations by blockading more than 150 of France's most traveled highways. **18** Bloody religious conflicts erupt in India after Hindus desecrate a historic Muslim mosque. **19** Brazil's Pres. Fernando Collor de Mello resigns to avoid impeachment trial on corruption charges. **20** Expo 92, called the largest world's fair in history, attracts millions of tourists to Seville, Spain. **21** Peru's Pres. Alberto Fujimoro dissolves Congress and censors the press as he attacks Shining Path rebels and drug traffickers. **22** Europe hosts both Olympics, with the XVI Winter Games in Albertville, France, and the XXV Summer Games in Barcelona, Spain. **23** Presidents Yeltsin and Mitterrand sign a treaty welcoming political, economic, and military coopera-	**1992**

443

History and Politics		The Arts	
America	**Elsewhere**	**America**	**Elsewhere**
6 Navy Secretary H. Lawrence Garrett III resigns over the 1991 Las Vegas Tailhook scandal in which women were assaulted by Navy personnel. **7** By a 5-4 margin the Supreme Court reaffirms the core of a woman's constitutional right to abortion but upholds parts of a Pennsylvania law restricting access to abortion. **8** Ten women claim sexual harassment by Republican Sen. Bob Packwood of Oregon. **9** U.S. begins military airlift of emergency food and medical supplies to the Commonwealth of Independent States, the former Soviet Union.	**17** China explodes its largest underground nuclear weapon. **18** France and Germany agree to form a joint army corps. **19** A car bomb explosion at the Israeli embassy in Buenos Aires, Argentina, kills almost 30 people. The Islamic Jihad, a radical Arab organization based in Lebanon, claims responsibility. **20** The UN Security Council votes for sanctions against Libya until it turns over agents linked to 2 airline bombings.	Eastwood is director and star of the western *Unforgiven*. **7** Musicals dominate the Broadway theater scene, with *Crazy for You, Jelly's Last Jam,* and a revival of *Guys and Dolls* all drawing large, enthusiastic audiences. **8** The most talked about museum show is "Henri Matisse: A Retrospective," at the Museum of Modern Art in New York City. Matisse's *Harmony in Yellow* is auctioned for $14.5 million at Christie's, a record for Matisse.	versy in Britain over who will pay for repairs, Queen Elizabeth agrees to start paying income taxes. **15** A retrospective show of the Belgian artist René Magritte begins an international tour in London. **16** Show-business entrepreneur Andrew Lloyd Webber pays almost $18 million for a Canaletto painting, *Old Horse Guards,* at a London auction.
1993			
1 A terrorist bomb explodes in New York City's 110-story World Trade Center, killing 6 and injuring hundreds. The FBI arrests Muslim fundamentalists in a terrorist plot to bomb New York sites. **2** Dr. David Gunn is shot dead by "right-to-life" advocate Michael Griffin outside an abortion clinic in Pensacola, Fla. **3** The Family and Medical Leave Act passes, Pres. Bill Clinton's first legislative victory. **4** The President and First Lady Hillary Clinton push for national health care reform, but the controversial bill succumbs to political pressure. **5** White House aide Vincent Foster is found shot to death. Police call it a suicide. **6** Janet Reno is confirmed as	**13** Czechoslovakia divides into 2 separate nations, the Czech Republic and Slovakia. **14** Israel and the Palestine Liberation Organization sign accord toward Palestinian self-rule. Terrorists on both sides try to derail plan. **15** UN forces establish peace in the Somalian civil war, but some fighting continues. Most U.S. troops are withdrawn. **16** Russian President Boris Yeltsin routs foes in a bloody Moscow showdown. Parliament is shelled and 125 die. Yeltsin remains in power but loses face in December parliamentary elections to the top vote-getting Liberal Democrats, led by Russian ultra-nationalist Vladimir Zhirinovsky. **17** Civil war in Bosnia and	**1** Steven Spielberg's dinosaur spectacular, *Jurassic Park,* grosses a world record $725 million in 16 weeks. Spielberg scores again with the acclaimed drama *Schindler's List,* the story of the heroism of a German Catholic businessman who saved more than 1000 Jews from the Auschwitz death camp. **2** The 1993 Oscar for the best picture goes to *Schindler's List;* Tom Hanks takes best actor for his portrayal of an AIDS victim in *Philadelphia;* Holly Hunter wins best actress for her performance in *The Piano.* **3** The National Book	**11** European Impressionists bring top prices at spring sales in London and New York City. Cézanne's *Still Life with Apples* sells for $28.6 million at Sotheby's in New York. **12** London heralds the opening of Andrew Lloyd Webber's new musical, *Sunset Boulevard,* based on Billy Wilder's 1950 film. **13** At the Cannes Film Festival, first prize is shared by Jane Campion of New Zealand for *The Piano* and Chen Kaige of China for *Farewell My Concubine.* **14** Russian conductor Mstislav Rostropovich returns from 20 years'

Science & Technology		Miscellaneous		
America	Elsewhere	America	Elsewhere	

Elsewhere (Science & Technology):

devastating drought affects most of southern Africa.

13 An earthquake in Turkey kills nearly 500 persons and demolishes hundreds of buildings.

America (Miscellaneous):

8 IBM says it will "downsize" by eliminating 25,000 jobs in 1993.

9 A 9-day strike at a General Motors plant in Lordstown, Ohio, causes temporary layoffs of 42,900 GM workers.

10 Nobel Prize, Economics: University of Chicago's Gary S. Becker for his studies about how economics impacts individual and family decisions.

11 Big-name companies Trans World Airlines and the R.H. Macy chain of retail stores file for bankruptcy protection.

12 Former heavyweight boxing champion Mike Tyson is convicted of rape in Indianapolis and sentenced to prison.

13 Major League Baseball Commissioner Fay Vincent resigns at the request of club owners.

14 The Washington Redskins take Super Bowl XXVI by defeating the Buffalo Bills 37-24.

15 The Pittsburgh Penguins take ice hockey's Stanley Cup for the second year in a row.

Elsewhere (Miscellaneous):

tion between Russia and France.

24 Egypt's Boutros Boutros-Ghali begins a 5-year term as UN Secretary-General.

25 Nobel Prize, Peace: Rigoberta Menchú of Guatemala for her campaign for social justice.

1993

America (Science & Technology):

1 Computer users in record numbers join the Internet, the information superhighway that links people and computers worldwide. Meanwhile, price wars bring down the cost of home personal computers and software.

2 The blurry Hubble Space Telescope is brought into focus by astronauts from the U.S. space shuttle *Endeavour,* whose astronauts fit new optics and devices that correct the $3 billion observatory.

3 A remarkable chain of 20 comets strung like a chain of pearls is discovered by astronomers at Mount Palomar, Calif. Named Comet Shoemaker-Levy, they

Elsewhere (Science & Technology):

8 The ozone layer, which shields the Earth from harmful solar ultraviolet light, deteriorates to record low levels. Ozone thinning over Antarctica now covers an area about the size of North America—15% larger than ever before.

9 Amtrak begins testing a German-built high-speed express train between New York and Washington. In tests it clocks more than 250 mph.

10 Vitamin supplements lower the risk of dying from cancer and other diseases, according to a major study by Chinese and American scientists. Daily vitamin A pills, for example, greatly

America (Miscellaneous):

1 The "Great Flood of 1993" washes out thousands of homes, farms, and businesses in nine states in the Midwest. The toll is at least 50 dead, 70,000 homeless, and $12 billion in property damage.

2 David Koresh, leader of the Branch Davidians, and more than 70 of his followers die when 100 federal agents attack his cult's compound in Waco, Tex. Four agents died in an earlier attack.

3 An Atlanta jury finds General Motors negligent in designing the fuel tank for its pickup truck and orders GM to pay $105 million to the victims' families.

4 Rodney Peairs is acquit-

Elsewhere (Miscellaneous):

9 Queen Elizabeth opens Buckingham Palace to tourists to help pay for repairs to Windsor Castle, which was damaged by fire in 1992. But there are other royal troubles. The marriage of Prince Charles to Princess Diana moves nearer to separation. London tabloids publish stories linking Charles romantically with an old girlfriend.

10 Japan's Crown Prince Naruhito marries Masako Owada, the first career woman in the Japanese royal family.

11 Western Europe's economic slump is the worst in 20 years.

12 RU-486, the French-made abortion pill that is

445

History and Politics | The Arts

America	Elsewhere	America	Elsewhere

History and Politics — America

the first woman U.S. Attorney General.

7 Senate committee reports "no compelling evidence" that U.S. prisoners of war are held in Vietnam.

8 The Pentagon says 83 women were sexually assaulted by Navy personnel at the rowdy Tailhook Convention in Las Vegas.

9 The "motor-voter" law, vetoed by Pres. Bush in 1992, is enacted; citizens can register to vote while getting a driver's license.

10 Homosexuals are permitted in U.S. armed forces under "don't ask, don't tell" procedure.

11 Congress passes the North American Free Trade Agreement, which links Canada, the U.S., and Mexico in a "free-trade zone."

12 U.S. corporations scale down: Sears lays off 50,000; Boeing, 20,000; McDonnell Douglas, 8700.

History and Politics — Elsewhere

Herzegovina persists despite constant cease-fire efforts.

18 Israel and the Vatican agree to establish diplomatic relations.

19 The U.S., Russia, and more than 100 other nations sign a treaty outlawing chemical weapons.

20 South Africa says elections open to all races will be held in 1994, clearing the way for black majority rule.

21 British and Irish Prime Ministers announce a peace pact to end years of bloodshed in Northern Ireland.

22 UN Commission blames the Salvadoran Army for human rights abuses, including hundreds of deaths, during El Salvador's civil war.

23 Kim Campbell becomes the first woman Prime Minister of Canada.

The Arts — America

Award for fiction goes to E. Annie Proulx for *The Shipping News.*

4 Whitney Houston wins a Grammy for best album of the year, *The Bodyguard.*

5 TV's Emmy awards include the comedy series *Seinfeld,* the drama series *Picket Fences,* and the comedy review *Saturday Night Live.*

6 Tony awards for the best in theater are given to the musical *Kiss of the Spider Woman* and *Angels in America.*

7 CBS's *60 Minutes* remains the nation's most popular TV show.

8 Nobel Prize, Literature: Toni Morrison for her novels portraying the experiences of black women.

9 The Norman Rockwell Museum opens in Stockwell, Mass., honoring the popular illustrator.

10 TV's David Letterman quits NBC after 11 years to sign with CBS for $16 million.

The Arts — Elsewhere

exile to lead the Washington National Symphony before 100,000 music lovers in Moscow's Red Square.

15 Russian chess grand master Gary Kasparov trounces England's Nigel Short in a disputed world championship in London.

16 Neo-Nazi music is outlawed in Germany. Police seize tapes and CDs by right-wing rock groups that glorify Nazism and racism.

17 Carol Shields's *The Stone Diaries* is acclaimed Canada's best English-language novel of the year.

18 Paris's Louvre Museum opens its Richelieu Wing, adding 70% to its exhibition space. Culture Minister Jacques Toubon calls it "the world's largest cultural space."

19 Harold Pinter directs the British premiere of David Mamet's controversial drama, *Oleanna.*

20 Shakespeare's Globe Theater in London, the birthplace of Elizabethan theater, is being recreated at a cost of $30 million.

1994

History and Politics — America

1 In midterm elections, Republicans gain control of the House and Senate for the first time in 40 years, weakening the power of Democratic Pres. Bill Clinton.

2 Powerful Illinois Democrat Dan Rostenkowski, House Ways and Means chairman, loses in the election after being indicted for felonies that include fraud and embezzlement. House Speaker Tom Foley of Washington also loses.

3 Clinton ends 19-year-old trade embargo against Vietnam.

4 Former CIA agent Aldrich Ames is sentenced to life in prison for spying for the former U.S.S.R.

5 Former football hero and actor O.J. Simpson pleads not

History and Politics — Elsewhere

11 Deposed Pres. Jean-Bertrand Aristide is restored to office in Haiti after its military junta resigns under threat of U.S. invasion.

12 Russian troops battle the breakaway republic of Chechnya in southern Russia.

13 After winning South Africa's first election open to all races, Nelson Mandela is inaugurated as the nation's first black President.

14 The Irish Republican Army declares a cease-fire in its military campaign to end British rule in Northern Ireland.

15 In the face of an enormous wave of Cuban refugees who are temporarily detained at Guantanamo Bay, the U.S. agrees to

The Arts — America

1 Singer Barbra Streisand's first live concerts in nearly 30 years are pop music's hottest ticket. Shows in New York, Los Angeles, and London are sellouts, despite a new high in ticket prices: $350.

2 In an operatic concert in Los Angeles, Luciano Pavarotti, Plácido Domingo, and José Carreras win raves for "Encore! The Three Tenors."

3 The entertainment industry's wedding of the year unites megastar singer Michael Jackson and Lisa Marie Presley, Elvis's daughter.

The Arts — Elsewhere

11 *Chant,* a collection of Gregorian chants recorded by Spanish Benedictine monks, becomes a surprise best-selling recording worldwide.

12 Albert Camus's final novel, *Le premier homme (The First Man),* is released 34 years after the Nobel Prize–winning author's death.

13 British theater productions receive an enthusiastic welcome in the U.S. There is a surreal revival of *An Inspector Calls,* a successful London production of the U.S. favorite *Carousel,* and Andrew Lloyd Web-

Science & Technology		Miscellaneous		
America	Elsewhere	America	Elsewhere	

would last only until 1994, when the chain would crash into Jupiter.

4 The Food and Drug Administration says second-hand smoke causes 6,000 U.S. deaths yearly.

5 The measles epidemic in the U.S. is finally over, thanks to a campaign of widespread inoculation.

6 Having a vasectomy greatly increases a man's chances of developing prostate cancer, according to two important studies.

7 Nobel Prize, Chemistry: Dr. Kary B. Mullis, along with Canadian Dr. Michael Smith, for discovering a chemical technique that makes possible the use of DNA for individual identification; in Medicine: Drs. Richard J. Roberts and Phillip A. Sharp for discovering so-called split genes, vital in the diagnosis of cancer; and in Physics: Drs. Russell A. Hulse and Joseph H. Taylor for discovering the first known binary pulsar.

reduce a woman's risk of breast cancer.

11 The U.S. adopts the UN Convention of Biological Diversity, requiring every nation to protect the Earth's species, their habitats, and the environmental systems that support them.

12 Russia's space station Mir remains the longest-running space show. Though several Russian cosmonauts finally return to Earth, others stay aboard Mir for more than one year.

13 Archaeologists in Israel uncover a stone monument with text in Aramaic mentioning King David and his descendants—the only known reference to him outside the Bible.

ted of manslaughter after he shoots to death a Japanese exchange student who knocked on his door in Baton Rouge, La., seeking directions.

5 The Dow Industrials rose 452 points, or 13%. Mutual funds hit all-time highs, with 1300 new listings in the year, more than 4300 total, and assets of $1.8 trillion. Yet about 15% of Americans live below the poverty line, the highest rate in 30 years.

6 Tennis's top-ranked Monica Seles is stabbed in the back by an obsessed German fan of Steffi Graf and has to leave the tennis tour.

7 Cincinnati Reds owner Marge Schott is suspended from baseball for one year for making racist and anti-Semitic remarks.

8 The Chicago Bulls beat the Phoenix Suns for their 3rd straight NBA championship, the first team to "three-peat" since the Boston Celtics of 1964–66. Their star guard, Michael Jordan, later announces his retirement in the wake of the tragedy of his father's murder.

used in Europe, will be reviewed by the FDA for possible sale and use in the U.S.

13 Nobel Prize, Peace: South Africa's Nelson Mandela and Pres. F.W. de Klerk.

14 The Organization of American States imposes an embargo on Haiti, trying to force its military rulers to reinstate ousted Pres. Jean-Bertrand Aristide.

15 Colombian drug king Pablo Escobar is killed by police in Medellín.

16 Fidel Castro's daughter wins political asylum in the U.S.

17 The Colombian volcano Galeras erupts while scientists are exploring the crater. Nine people die.

18 At least 44 persons are trampled to death by a wild elephant rampaging through Indian villages.

19 Central India is struck by a devastating earthquake, killing nearly 10,000.

1994

1 The Los Angeles region is rocked by a strong earthquake that kills 60 people, injures more than 9000, and leaves 20,000 homeless. Damage comes to more than $13 billion.

2 The disclosure that Ronald Reagan has Alzheimer's disease heightens concern about the degenerative illness that afflicts 4 million elderly Americans.

3 After leaving 800 dead in Haiti, tropical storm Gordon sweeps across Florida and North Carolina, wrecking shoreline property.

4 Anti-smoking campaigns become widespread as some cities pass laws banning

8 A remarkable civil-engineering feat contemplated for almost 200 years is finally completed—the $15 billion Channel Tunnel (or "Chunnel"), linking England and France.

9 Cosmonaut Valery Polyakov spends all of 1994 aboard the Russian space station Mir. He plans to remain in space 430 days to record the longest human space flight in history.

10 Richard Leakey, noted paleontologist, resigns as director of Kenya's Wildlife Service under political pressure from the Kenya government.

11 In northern Chile, the

1 The U.S. hosts the world's most popular sporting event, soccer's World Cup, a 31-day tourney in 9 cities that ends with Brazil beating Italy for the championship.

2 Four Arab defendants are convicted for the 1993 bombing of New York City's World Trade Center.

3 Jacqueline Kennedy Onassis, widow of Pres. Kennedy, noted for her glamour and style, dies in New York City.

4 Stephen G. Breyer joins the U.S. Supreme Court as an associate justice, succeeding Harry Blackmun.

5 Figure skater Tonya

9 Nobel Prize, Peace: shared by Israeli's Yitzhak Rabin and Palestine Liberation Organization Chairman Yasir Arafat.

10 French commandos storm a hijacked airliner at Marseilles airport, freeing 170 hostages and killing 4 Islamic militants.

11 Presidents and Prime Ministers gather in Normandy, France, to mark the 50th anniversary of D-Day, the Allied invasion of Europe that led to the defeat of Germany, ending World War II in Europe.

12 Pres. Clinton signs pact with Russia and Ukraine in

History and Politics		The Arts	
America	**Elsewhere**	**America**	**Elsewhere**

History and Politics — America

guilty to charges of murdering his former wife and a male friend. Simpson's trial becomes an unprecedented media circus.

6 Major league baseball players go on strike, ending play in midseason and causing cancellation of the World Series.

7 U.S. Surgeon Gen. Joycelyn Elders resigns after making controversial statements related to sex education.

8 The U.S. Supreme Court rules that pro-life protesters can be barred from getting too close to abortion clinics and can be sued for blocking access.

9 A gunman opposed to abortion kills 2 people and wounds 5 at 2 Massachusetts abortion clinics.

10 Former Pres. Richard M. Nixon dies, and his funeral is attended by the 5 living U.S. presidents—Bill Clinton, George Bush, Ronald Reagan, Jimmy Carter, and Gerald Ford.

History and Politics — Elsewhere

admit some Cuban immigrants, while Cuba agrees to deter their boat departures.

16 Israel grants partial Palestinian self-rule in Jericho and Gaza.

17 Israel and Jordan sign an agreement ending a state of war that lasted nearly 50 years.

18 After the mysterious plane crash that kills President Juvénal Habyarimana, the African nation of Rwanda collapses in bloody tribal slaughter and starvation. Estimates of the dead reach 500,000 by June. UN forces try to restore order as the U.S. and other nations airlift food.

19 Kim Jong Il assumes the presidency of North Korea upon the death of his father, longtime ruler Kim Il Sung.

20 U.S. ends dispute with North Korea over its refusal to permit international inspections of its nuclear development sites.

21 In Angola, government and rebel forces sign a peace pact ending almost 2 decades of civil war.

22 Leaders of 34 Western Hemisphere nations agree to set up a free-trade zone by 2005.

23 A guerrilla group called the Zapatista National Liberation Army takes over most of Mexico's southern state of Chiapas, declaring war on the government.

24 Ernesto Zedillo is elected President of Mexico.

The Arts — America

4 *Forrest Gump* is Hollywood's biggest moneymaker, attracting moviegoers with its positive vision of life. Second is *The Lion King,* Disney's animated jungle saga.

5 The veteran rock groups the Rolling Stones and Pink Floyd undertake concert tours that gross more than $100 million each.

6 The 25th anniversary of the Woodstock "peace and love" gathering prompts a rain-soaked rerun, Woodstock '94, a 3-day rock festival drawing more than 300,000 to music and mud.

7 A new entertainment company is formed by a show business dream-team: moviemaker Steven Spielberg, former Walt Disney studio chief Jeffrey Katzenberg, and recording industry mogul David Geffen.

8 Best-selling novelist John Updike abandons Americana in *Brazil,* a tale of romantic adventure along the Amazon River.

9 Anna Quindlen, popular Pulitzer Prize-winning columnist for the *New York Times,* resigns to write fiction and raise her family.

10 Kurt Cobain, lead singer for the group Nirvana and an alleged drug user, commits suicide.

The Arts — Elsewhere

ber's London stage version of a classic film, *Sunset Boulevard.*

14 Zlata Filopovic, 13, whom some call "Bosnia's Anne Frank," publishes *Zlata's Diary,* her best-selling account of her family's experience during the siege of Sarajevo.

15 Britain's Royal Ballet unveils a radical new staging of *The Sleeping Beauty* for audiences in New York and Washington. Reaction is mixed.

16 At a London auction, a manuscript illustrated by Leonardo da Vinci commands more than $30 million, a record price for manuscripts.

17 The Canadian play *Nothing Sacred* by George Walker, winner of the 1994 Performing Arts Award, wins outstanding reviews at Toronto's Winter Garden Theatre.

18 Nobel Prize, Literature: Japanese novelist Kenzaburo Oe, who becomes the 2nd Japanese to win this prize.

1995

History and Politics — America

1 Republicans take control of both the House of Representatives and the Senate for the first time in 40 years. New House Speaker Newt Gingrich pushes a legislative agenda that he calls the Contract with America. Success is mixed for the Republicans' program, with defeats of a term-limit bill, a constitutional amendment requiring a balanced

448

History and Politics — Elsewhere

11 The United Nations celebrates its 50th anniversary while facing peacekeeping problems in the republics of the former Yugoslavia, Angola, and other trouble spots. In Africa, UN peacekeepers leave Somalia, but another force is sent to Angola.

12 Presidents of Serbia, Croatia, and Bosnia-Herzegovina, under pressure from their American hosts, agree in Dayton Accords to end their warfare.

The Arts — America

1 The art world embraces computerization, with many museum collections becoming viewable on CD-ROM disks and via Internet sites.

2 Controversy over public funding for the arts continues, with the Republican Congress initiating large cuts in support for the National Endowment for the Arts.

The Arts — Elsewhere

12 Bulgarian-American artist Christo and his wife, Jeanne-Claude, create an eye-catching new work, *Wrapped Reichstag,* in Berlin, Germany, by swathing the historic German parliament building in silver-colored fabric. Drawing nearly 1 million visitors to Berlin, the exhibit remains in place for a month.

Science & Technology		Miscellaneous		
America	**Elsewhere**	**America**	**Elsewhere**	

smoking in office buildings, stores, and restaurants. Still, 48 million continue puffing, and 400,000 U.S. deaths yearly are linked to smoking.

5 Food and Drug Administration extends approval of Prozac, the best-selling antidepressant drug, to treat bulimia and obsessive-compulsive disorder.

6 Congress, under budget pressure, votes to halt spending in 1994 on the Superconducting Super Collider, a $10 billion Texas project that was to be the world's largest scientific instrument.

7 Archaeologists in Colorado find an 8000-year-old skeleton in a cave, the first confirmation that humans lived at high elevations in prehistoric America.

European Southern Observatory moves ahead in its efforts to build the world's most powerful astronomical telescope.

12 Comet Shoemaker-Levy 9 collides with Jupiter and causes spectacular explosions as its several parts strike the planet.

Harding pleads guilty to conspiracy charges arising from an assault on her rival Nancy Kerrigan at the U.S. national championships.

6 In hockey, The New York Rangers beat the Vancouver Canucks 4 games to 3 to win the Stanley Cup, the team's first since 1940.

7 The National Hockey League postpones the start of the 1994–95 season while players and owners negotiate a new contract.

8 The Dallas Cowboys beat the Buffalo Bills, 30-13, for the second time in a row to win Super Bowl XXVII.

Moscow to dismantle Ukraine's nuclear weapons.

13 Two U.S. Army helicopters flying UN aid to Iraq's Kurds are accidentally shot down over Iraq by U.S. Air Force jet fighters.

14 Asian and African nations find a new source for weaponry in U.S. arms makers, who, with the Cold War over, seek clients overseas.

15 About 900 lives are lost when an Estonian ferry sinks in the Baltic Sea after the bow door fails, letting seawater enter the vessel.

16 German automakers follow Japan in setting up "transplants" in the U.S. BMW opens a new plant in South Carolina, while Mercedes-Benz has one in Alabama.

17 New Zealand sailors win the Whitbread Round-the-World Race, sailing 32,000 mi. from Southampton, England, and back.

18 Sweden and Finland vote to seek membership in the European Union (formerly the Common Market), while Norwegian voters turn down membership.

1 A vaccine against chicken pox is approved by the Food and Drug Administration, and vaccination of all young children, as well as of children currently under 14 who have not contracted the disease, is recommended.

2 More than 7 million Americans subscribe to online computer services that help users access the Internet.

12 Concern about the ozone layer of the Earth's atmosphere accelerates after an enormous hole reappears in the layer over Antarctica. A World Meteorological Organization report claims that ozone levels in the stratosphere are declining about 5% per decade.

13 The importance of the ozone layer is underscored by the award of the Nobel

1 A terrorist car bomb explodes in Oklahoma City, Oklahoma, killing 169 and injuring hundreds. Former army buddies Timothy McVeigh and Terry Nichols are later arrested and charged with the attack.

2 Sheikh Omar Abd al-Rahman and nine other Islamic extremists are convicted of the 1993 bombing of the World Trade

13 Delegates from 185 countries attend the UN's World Conference on Women, held in Beijing, China. Speakers include U.S. First Lady Hillary Clinton, who calls for action to end abuses against women around the world.

14 Denmark hosts the UN's World Summit for Social Development, which examines poverty and social inequalities.

History and Politics		The Arts	
America	**Elsewhere**	**America**	**Elsewhere**

History and Politics

America

budget, and a welfare-reform bill but success with other measures.

2 Pres. Clinton vetoes Republican legislation for the first time, rejecting a spending bill that would reduce funds for education and job training.

3 Wrangling between Pres. Clinton and Congress over the nation's budget leads to a monthlong partial shutdown of the federal government.

4 A Senate committee begins extensive investigation of the so-called Whitewater Affair, concerning real estate dealings of Pres. and Mrs. Clinton, and launches reviews of questionable activities by various cabinet members.

5 Republican Senator Bob Packwood resigns amid accusations of sexual misconduct. Democratic Representative Mel Reynolds soon follows under similar circumstances.

6 Several prominent senators, including Democrats Sam Nunn of Georgia and Bill Bradley of New Jersey, as well as Republican Alan Simpson of Wyoming, announce that they will not seek reelection in 1996.

7 The United States establishes formal diplomatic relations with Vietnam.

8 In Washington, Pres. Clinton hosts a ceremony at which Israel and the Palestine Liberation Organization sign an agreement to begin a second phase of Palestinian autonomy.

9 Louis Farrakhan, Nation of Islam leader, organizes and promotes the "Million Man March" to Washington, D.C.; its aim is to encourage black men to take more social responsibility and to thereby strengthen black families.

10 The nation's affirmative-action programs are heatedly debated by both liberals and conservatives. The courts, in restricting the reach of affirmative action, seem to mirror the sentiments of the public, which generally feels that affirmative action is reverse discrimination.

Elsewhere

13 Attempt by the rebel republic of Chechnya to break away from Russia results in destructive fighting with many casualties.

14 Israeli prime minister Yitzhak Rabin is assassinated by a right-wing Jewish extremist opposed to Rabin's peace overtures to the Palestinians.

15 The World Trade Organization, created to oversee international trade, is formed, with 125 members.

16 Mexico receives emergency $20 billion loan from United States in effort to stabilize its economy and avoid defaulting on its debt.

17 Voters in Bermuda retain island's colonial status by turning down independence from the United Kingdom.

18 Vietnam celebrates the 20th anniversary of the fall of Saigon to North Vietnamese forces and the end of the Vietnam War. Robert McNamara, U.S. secretary of defense during the war, publishes memoir in which he concludes that the United States erred in joining the fighting.

19 Japan notes 50th anniversary of the atomic bombing of Hiroshima and other engagements in the last year of World War II with large ceremonies. Japan acknowledges its aggression in Asia during this era.

20 An especially active hurricane season causes crippling damage in several Caribbean nations.

21 Tensions and genocidal warfare between majority Hutu and minority Tutsi in Rwanda and Burundi lead to huge death tolls and massive refugee problems in eastern Africa.

22 Voters in Quebec narrowly turn down complete independence for the Canadian province, avoiding a constitutional crisis and keeping Quebec in Canada's federal union.

23 After serving as president of France since 1981, François Mitterand is succeeded by Jacques Chirac. A Socialist, Mitterand strengthened France's commitment to European unity.

The Arts

America

3 Among major museums, New York City's Metropolitan Museum of Art marks its 125th anniversary with a retrospective exhibition of its architecture, while the Smithsonian Institution starts a $100 million fund-raising drive.

4 Despite funding problems, American museums present numerous popular exhibitions, which help swell attendance to record levels. The most important exhibitions include the Metropolitan's Goya show, a traveling exhibit of American painter John Singleton Copley, Washington's National Gallery of Art's display of the paintings of Vermeer, and the Museum of Modern Art's Piet Mondrian and Jacob Lawrence exhibits in New York City.

5 The New York City Ballet premiers Jerome Robbins' *West Side Story Suite*, based on the popular 1950s Broadway musical by Leonard Bernstein.

6 Funding for dance companies remains a problem, as exemplified by the move of the Joffrey Ballet, long associated with New York City, to Chicago in exchange for more substantial financial support.

7 Robert Hass becomes the U.S. poet laureate and spearheads an initiative that establishes National Poetry Month, to be observed for the first time in April 1996.

8 Superstars Clint Eastwood and Meryl Streep team up to bring the popular novel *Bridges of Madison County* to the silver screen.

Elsewhere

13 During the year, three paintings—two by Pablo Picasso and one by Vincent van Gogh—are sold for more than $20 million each.

14 Swiss architect Mario Botta is acclaimed for his design for the San Francisco Museum of Modern Art, which is the largest such museum in the western U.S.

15 The Canadian city of Vancouver wins praise for its new public library and theater for the performing arts, both designed by architect Moshe Safdie.

16 Irish poet Seamus Heaney receives the Nobel Prize for literature for his works of "lyrical beauty and ethical depth" that often depict violence in Northern Ireland.

17 Germany's Günter Grass publishes a sweeping historical novel, *A Wide Field*, that attempts to incorporate the themes of German history from the late 19th century to the fall of the Berlin Wall.

18 Dance companies from 13 countries mark the 50th anniversary of the United Nations with the United We Dance Festival, held in San Francisco.

19 Mel Gibson's *Braveheart*, an action-adventure film about a Scottish chieftain, proves particularly popular in Scotland, with audiences cheering the main character's battles against the English.

20 Several theater productions that enjoy great success in London, including *Indiscretions* and *Hamlet*—the latter staring Ralph Fiennes—are also well received in New York. Andrew Lloyd Webber's *Sunset Boulevard* wins a Tony

Science & Technology		Miscellaneous	
America	**Elsewhere**	**America**	**Elsewhere**
3 Microsoft, which already provides the operating system for more than 75% of personal computers, introduces its new Windows 95 operating system with a worldwide marketing campaign. The Justice Department begins investigating whether Microsoft has an unfair competitive advantage over its business rivals. **4** The use of cellular phones booms, with about 10% of Americans using them and with thousands of new customers signing up each day. **5** The AIDS death toll in the United States since the disease was first identified in 1981 passes 300,000. Researchers continue to develop new drugs to fight the condition. **6** Pres. Clinton vetoes legislation from Congress that calls for cuts in federal health-care funding, including Medicare, the health-insurance program primarily for people 65 and older, and Medicaid, the program for low-income Americans. **7** After a six-year journey, the spacecraft Galileo reaches Jupiter. Its orbiter is scheduled to gather scientific information about the planet for two years. **8** The National Aeronautics and Space Administration launches seven space-shuttle flights during the year but is under pressure to reduce costs. **9** U.S. scientists study the Arctic floor for indications of global warming, and for the first time the navy permits civilians to use its nuclear submarines for such research. **10** Peregrine falcons, which had been endangered since the 1970s due to the effects of pesticide use, are removed from the endangered species list by the Fish and Wildlife Service.	Prize for chemistry to three scientists, one from Germany and two from the U.S., who predicted the existence of an ozone hole caused by chlorofluorocarbons. **14** An international report on global climate establishes that human activity, such as the burning of fossil fuels, is warming the world's atmosphere, which could seriously affect life on Earth. **15** Concern about overfishing leads to a meeting of fishing nations and the adoption of a UN convention that limits the catches of certain species if populations reach a level that threatens future harvesting. **16** An American space shuttle docks successfully with the Russian space station *Mir* for the first time, initiating a new phase of space exploration. A second space-shuttle docking during the year delivers supplies and equipment to *Mir*. **17** The UN renews the Nuclear Non-Proliferation Treaty; China and France conduct underground nuclear tests. **18** A disease outbreak in Zaire is recognized as the deadly Ebola virus, first identified almost 20 years previously. The epidemic dies out after two months. **19** In Kenya, fossils of the earliest known hominid to walk upright, *Australopithecus anamensis*, are unearthed and are dated to 3.9 to 4.2 million years ago. **20** Archaeologists in the Valley of the Kings in Egypt find a huge royal burial ground dating from the time of Ramses II in the 13th century B.C. **21** Use of the Internet continues to climb rapidly, with users worldwide estimated at 35 million by the end of the year; sales of personal computers for home use remain strong.	Center in New York City that killed six. **[1993:HIST/1]** **4** After a sensational trial that became a media event, football star and actor O.J. Simpson is found not guilty of stabbing to death his ex-wife and her companion Ronald Goldman. The announcement of the verdict attracts a gigantic television audience. **5** The Supreme Court issues rulings that endanger the legality of federal affirmative-action programs. Ruth Bader Ginsburg and Stephen Breyer join the Supreme Court and often vote with the liberal minority. They are the first justices appointed by a Democratic president in more than two decades. **6** The Federal Trade Commission sets new disclosure regulations for telemarketers in an effort to end telemarketing fraud. **7** The Federal Bureau of Investigation releases statistics showing that serious crime declined for the third consecutive year in 1994. **8** Major League Baseball players' strike, begun in 1994, ends. Cal Ripken Jr. breaks Lou Gehrig's record of 2,130 consecutive games played. **9** The University of Connecticut's women's basketball team sparks fan and media interest in the sport when it becomes the first undefeated team to win the women's NCAA championship. **10** The ninth Special Olympics Games are staged in New Haven, Connecticut, and are opened by President and Mrs. Clinton. **11** Pres. Clinton, with South Korea's president, Kim Young Sam, dedicates the Korean War Veterans Memorial in Washington, D.C.	**15** Members of Aum Shinrikyo, a Japanese religious cult, release nerve gas in Tokyo subways, killing 12 people and injuring more than 5,000. **16** The Kobe-Osaka region in Japan is hit by a strong earthquake that kills more than 5,000 people and leaves hundreds of thousands homeless. **17** Great Britain's Queen Elizabeth II urges Prince Charles and Princess Diana to divorce and end their publicly troubled marriage. **18** Voters in Ireland endorse changing the nation's constitution to end the prohibition of divorce. **19** A subway fire in Baku, the capital of Azerbaijan, results in the death of about 300. **20** National Hockey League lockout ends, bringing U.S. and Canadian teams back to the ice for a shortened season. **21** Miguel Indurain of Spain becomes the first rider to win the Tour de France, the world's most famous cycling event, five consecutive times. **22** Britain's courts hold that the country's military forces can discharge homosexuals. **23** While on a visit to the Philippines, Pope John Paul II celebrates World Youth Day with a mass for 4 million people. He also visits Africa, several European countries, and the United States during the year.

History and Politics		The Arts	
America	**Elsewhere**	**America**	**Elsewhere**
		9 Disney makes a major impact with two high-grossing animated films. *Pocahontas* is popular particularly with young girls; *Toy Story* is the first feature to rely completely on computer animation. **10** Controversy over the lyrics in rap music lead Time Warner, a power in the music business, to sell its share in a rap-music label. **11** The Rock and Roll Hall of Fame and Museum opens in Cleveland. Among those performing at the dedication of the I. M. Pei–designed building are Chuck Berry and Bruce Springsteen.	award as best musical for its Broadway version. **21** Japanese architect Tadao Ando, noted for his use of geometric forms, receives the prestigious Pritzker Prize.

1996

America	Elsewhere	America	Elsewhere
1 Pres. Bill Clinton approves legislation ending the shut-down of the federal govern-ment. The White House and Congress eventually reach final agreement on a fiscal-year 1996 budget. **2** Pres. Clinton signs comprehensive welfare-reform act that transforms the Amer-ican welfare system. States now can require those who receive welfare benefits to work and can put time limits on benefits. **3** Another scandal rocks the Clinton administration after it is revealed that the White House improperly accessed confidential FBI files on more than 300 people, including many Republicans. **4** Sen. Bob Dole clinches the Republican presidential nomination by winning early state primaries. Jack Kemp, a former NFL quarterback, U.S. representative, and cabinet member, is picked as his running mate at the Republican convention. **5** Dole resigns from the Senate to concentrate on campaigning and is succeeded as Senate majority leader by Trent Lott of Mississippi.	**13** Palestinians choose Yasir Arafat of the Palestine Lib-eration Organization (PLO) as president of the new Palestinian National Authority government that will control the West Bank and Gaza Strip regions. **14** The Organization of American States and individual nations condemn U.S. legislation against Cuba passed in the wake of Cuba's shooting down two planes flown by anti-Castro Cuban exiles. **15** A Liberal Party–National Party coalition wins elections in Australia; John Howard becomes the nation's new prime minister. **16** Russia signs an economic-integration agreement with Belarus, Kazakhstan, and Kyrgyzstan. **17** Taiwan holds its first democratic presidential election in spite of threatening military exercises by Communist China. **18** The United Nations makes an agreement with Iraq that allows Iraq to export oil for the first time since the Gulf War of 1990–91. **19** At year's end, Kofi Annan of Ghana is selected as the UN's new secretary-general. **20** Israel's political leadership shifts from center-left to center-	**1** Architecture's Pritzker Prize for 1996 goes to Spanish architect Jose Rafael Moneo, known in the United States for the Davis Museum at Wellesley College in Massachusetts. **2** The market for American paintings is strong, with John Singer Sargent's *Cashmere* selling at auction for more than $11 million, by far the most ever paid for a work by an American artist. **3** Productions from New York City's Lincoln Center dominate the ballet world, highlighted by presentations of Peter Martins's *Reliquary*, a tribute to George Balan-chine and Igor Stravin-sky, and Merce Cunningham's *Ocean*, performed in a park. **4** U.S. poet laureate Robert Hass is appointed for a second term. Poetry enjoys a boom with publishers. **5** Novelist William Kennedy, a chronicler of Irish-American life in	**11** Wislawa Szym-borska becomes the fifth Pole to win the Nobel Prize for literature. A poet who supported and then rejected Stalinism after World War II, she is cited as a "Mozart of poetry." **12** Previous literature Nobelists publish new works during the year. Poet Derek Walcott presents *The Bounty*, and Japan's Kenzaburo Oe completes a trilogy with his new novel, *On the Day of Grandeur.* **13** Canadian Margaret Atwood's historical novel, *Alias Grace,* is nominated for Britain's prestigious Booker Prize, which ultimately goes to Graham Swift for his novel *Last Orders.* **14** Italy's Umberto Eco enjoys success with his new novel, *Island of the Day Before*; the popular Mexican novelist Carlos Fuentes explores Mexican-American relations and other issues in *The Glass Curtain.*

Science & Technology		Miscellaneous		
America	Elsewhere	America	Elsewhere	
11 The reintroduction of wolves into Yellowstone National Park causes controversy in the West, where wolves have historically been considered a threat to livestock.		**12** John F. Kennedy Jr., a founder of *George*, a new political-affairs magazine, becomes the magazine's editor-in-chief.		
1 Archaeologists in Jamestown, Virginia, uncover and excavate the site of the colony's original settlement. **2** Scientists find evidence that Native Americans in the Southwest used hallucinogenic plants in their ceremonies as long as 4,000 years ago. **3** Personal computers become faster and contain more memory, while competition results in lower prices. **4** The space shuttle *Columbia* makes the two longest flights in the history of the space-shuttle program. The first conducts experiments focusing on the effects of microgravity, while the second releases two scientific platforms but is unable to perform scheduled space walks. **5** Highlights of other shuttle missions include taking a Japanese astronaut to help retrieve a Japanese satellite platform; successfully testing space tethers; two dockings with Russia's *Mir* space station;	**9** Artifacts discovered in Australia backdate the earliest time that humans lived there to between 115,000 and 175,000 years ago. Fragments of the world's earliest rock art are also found. **10** The passage of the comet Hyakutake (named after the Japanese amateur astronomer who first spotted it) close to Earth (9.3 million miles) gives astronomers the opportunity to use the most modern instruments to study a comet. **11** Russia's *Mir* space station is more like a hotel, receiving visitors from the United States, France, and the European Space Agency (ESA) during the year. The scientific community fears that Russia's financial problems may limit the *Mir's* activities and Russian participation in international space research and exploration. **12** The ESA's Infrared Space Observatory (ISO) reports new findings on the rapid formation of stars in distant galaxies, while its Solar and Heliospheric	**1** The Dallas Cowboys win Super Bowl XXX by defeating the Pittsburgh Steelers. **2** Atlanta, Georgia, hosts the 26th Summer Olympic Games. In the first act of violence since the 1972 Munich games, a pipe bomb explodes, killing 1 and injuring more than 100 spectators. **3** Alan Greenspan, the powerful and influential chairman of the Federal Reserve Board, is nominated for a third four-year term. **4** Brothers Lyle and Eric Menendez are convicted of killing their parents; a California jury rejects their defense that they acted out of fear that their parents would kill them. **5** Ted Kaczynski, a former math professor known as the Unabomber for his mail-bomb attacks over nearly 20 years that resulted in three deaths and many injuries to university personnel and industrial figures, is apprehended in Montana. **6** The Freemen, an anti-government, antitax militia group, resists law enforcement officials for 81 days	**16** Britain's royal family suffers two divorces: Prince Andrew and Sarah Ferguson, Duchess of York, receive a divorce; then Prince Charles and Princess Diana obtain theirs a few months later. Diana receives a substantial settlement and loses the title of royal highness but can still be known as princess. **17** Britain agrees to return the Stone of Scone, the symbol of the Scottish monarchy, to Scotland after holding it for 700 years under the coronation chair in England. **18** Cuban Air Force jets shoot down two unarmed planes flown by Cuban exiles belonging to the Brothers to the Rescue group, killing four, further straining U.S.-Cuban relations and sparking protests among anti-Castro groups in the United States. **19** A deranged gunman in Scotland kills 16 kindergartners and their teacher before committing suicide. **20** Islamic militants in Egypt are blamed for a	**1996**

453

History and Politics

America

6 For the first time in five years, Congress raises the U.S. minimum wage. The two-stage increase will total 90 cents, bringing the minimun wage to $5.15 in 1997.

7 Congress removes restrictions on telephone and cable-television service in an effort to increase competition.

8 Incumbent Democrats Bill Clinton and Al Gore are reelected president and vice president as the nation enjoys sustained prosperity; Republicans retain control of the House and Senate. The Reform Party's Ross Perot–Pat Choate ticket runs a distant third.

9 Madeleine Albright is designated as secretary of state, becoming the first woman to hold the office.

10 House Speaker Newt Gingrich is found by a House ethics subcommittee to have violated House rules by diverting tax-exempt donations to political uses.

11 Senate ratifies strategic arms reduction treaty, START II, with Russia, but Moscow seeks modifications.

12 Pres. Clinton appoints retired four-star general Barry McCaffrey to head the Office of National Drug Control Policy and increases spending for drug-control efforts.

Elsewhere

right as Benjamin Netanyahu and his Likud Party defeat incumbent Shimon Peres and the Labor Party. As prime minister, Netanyahu takes a harder line in peace negotiations with the PLO and expands Jewish settlements in the West Bank and Gaza.

21 Netanyahu and Palestinian National Authority leader Arafat hold a two-day summit and agree to continue negotiating.

22 Russian president Boris Yeltsin needs a runoff election to retain office; he later undergoes heart surgery.

23 The leaders of Bosnia and Herzegovina, Serbia, and Croatia agree to resolve their differences over putting the 1995 Balkan treaty into effect.

24 Bulgarian opposition leader Peter Stoyanov of the Union of Democratic Forces party wins the country's presidential election. The opposition leader in neighboring Romania, Emil Constantinescu, also wins his country's presidency.

25 Following elections in which there was no clear winner, New Zealand's National and New Zealand First parties form a coalition government with Jim Bolger continuing as prime minister.

26 South Korea goes on high alert after a North Korean submarine is discovered off its east coast; South Korean military forces hunt down the sub's crew and commando passengers.

The Arts

America

Albany, New York, publishes his sixth novel about life there.

6 Country-western singer Garth Brooks becomes the recording industry's all-time top-selling soloist, far surpassing Elvis Presley.

7 Hostess Rosie O'Donnell introduces a popular new talk show; veteran talk-show host Phil Donohue retires.

8 Cable television, with a wealth of channels directed at special audiences, continues to draw viewers away from the network channels.

9 The Broadway season features two innovative musicals. *Bring in da Noise, Bring in da Funk* uses dance and music to explore African-American history, while *Rent*, with its roots in *La Bohème*, wins both a Tony and a Pulitzer Prize.

10 Among regional theaters, Houston's Alley Theater marks its 50th anniversary and receives a special Tony award.

Elsewhere

15 The novels of Jane Austen are still popular in movies, with Gwyneth Paltrow playing the title role in *Emma*. Other notable films are the dark comedy *Fargo* and *The English Patient*.

16 Actors Daniel Auteuil and Catherine Deneuve star together in two well-received films, *Ma Saison Preferée* ("My Favorite Season") and *Les Voleurs* ("The Thieves").

17 The macarena, a new dance craze based on Latin rhythms, achieves worldwide popularity.

18 Canadian Alanis Morissette achieves enormous success in the United States and wins a Grammy for her first album, *Jagged Little Pill*.

and testing a large inflatable antenna.

6 The Galileo spacecraft transmits historic and informative images of Jupiter's moons. NASA sends the Mars Global Surveyor off to map Earth's nearest planetary neighbor and later dispatches the Mars Pathfinder, which is to land on the planet and conduct experiments.

7 Researchers at Cornell and Stanford universities share the Nobel Prize for physics for their discovery of superfluidity in helium-3, a breakthrough in low-temperature physics.

8 Immune-system research, focused on how T-cells recognize cells infected by a virus, brings a Nobel Prize for medicine to an American and a Swiss scientist.

Observatory (SOHO) delivers new data on the composition of the Sun.

13 India and Japan launch satellites to conduct scientific observations.

14 A meteorite discovered in Antarctica in 1984 may contain proof that primitive life existed on Mars more than 3.5 billion years ago. Deposits in the rock, although much smaller than the smallest found on Earth, are similar to Earth fossils of bacteria.

15 A report from the UN Intergovernmental Panel on Climate suggests that the Earth's climate is warming because of human activity and may become considerably warmer during the next century.

16 A drought in Mongolia leads to forest and grasslands fires that consume more than 20 million acres. The United States sends a satellite station to help the nation track its fires.

17 Eruptions of Montserrat's Soufrière Hills volcano force the evacuation and relocation of many of the Caribbean island's residents.

18 Bovine spongiform encephalopathy (BSE), commonly known as mad-cow disease, is a disease that when transmitted to humans manifests itself as Creutzfeldt-Jakob disease (CJD). BSE, believed to be transmitted by eating contaminated beef, becomes a major concern in Europe, where 11 people in Britain and 1 in France die of the disease. Cattle detected with the disease are destroyed.

before surrendering at their stronghold in Montana.

7 Dan Rostenkowski, former chairman of the U.S. House Ways and Means Committee, is sentenced to prison after pleading guilty to mail fraud.

8 Abortion continues to be a contentious issue, and anti-abortion protesters condemn Pres. Clinton's veto of a bill outlawing late-term abortions.

9 The New York Stock Exchange Dow Jones industrial average breaks the 6,000 ceiling for the first time.

10 The U.S. Supreme Court rules that states may not stop local governments from passing legislation protecting homosexuals from discrimination.

11 The Oakland, California, school board votes to recognize a variety of black English, known as "Ebonics," as a distinct language.

12 An auction of the memorabilia from the estate of Jacqueline Kennedy Onassis, including many belongings of the late Pres. Kennedy, brings in more than $34 million.

13 TWA Flight 800 from New York's Kennedy Airport explodes in midair minutes after takeoff, killing 230 passengers and crew.

14 A major reform of U.S. telecommunications law, the first since the 1930s, aims to increase competition in the industry by removing distinctions among different kinds of communications companies.

15 Another part of the telecommunications legislation requires that television sets manufactured in or imported into the United States have a "V chip," a device that would allow viewers to block programming they consider offensive, such as violence- or sex-oriented programs.

terrorist attack on Greek tourists that leaves 18 dead.

21 Thailand's King Bhumibol Adulyadej celebrates his 50th anniversary as monarch. The world's longest-reigning ruler, he is regarded as a symbol of the nation.

22 The Nobel Peace Prize goes to José Ramos Horta and Roman Catholic Bishop Carlos Ximenes Belo for their efforts to end the violence between Indonesia and rebel groups in East Timor. The area was annexed by Indonesia in 1976 after Portuguese colonial rule ended.

History and Politics		The Arts	
America	**Elsewhere**	**America**	**Elsewhere**

1997

America (History and Politics)

1 Pres. Bill Clinton and Vice Pres. Al Gore take the oath of office for a second term. The Republicans control both the Senate and the House in the new Congress.

2 Speaker Newt Gingrich, a Republican, is reprimanded by the House of Representatives and fined $300,000 for using tax-exempt donations for political purposes.

3 Controversy over Democratic fund-raising activities during the 1996 elections grows amid reports that Vice Pres. Gore played a key role of questionable legality. The Senate holds hearings on campaign-finance abuses. Attorney General Reno resists Republican pressure to appoint a special counsel to look into money-raising tactics by the president and vice president during the campaign.

4 James McDougal, a partner with Pres. and Mrs. Clinton in the Whitewater real estate affair, is sent to prison after being convicted for fraudulently obtaining loans and other charges.

5 A conference in Philadelphia called the Presidents' Summit for America's Future draws Pres. Clinton and former presidents Ford and Carter to help encourage American volunteerism.

6 Showing a spirit of compromise, Pres. Clinton and the Republican Congress agree on a plan to balance the nation's budget and also reduce taxes for families within five years. The country's robust economy makes it easier for the two sides to reconcile their differences.

7 Congress, however, thwarts Clinton by refusing to grant him "fast-track" authority to negotiate U.S. trade agreements with foreign countries, a power that Congress had ceded to previous administrations. Congress also refuses to confirm several high-level appointments by the president.

8 Arizona governor Fife Symington resigns after his conviction in federal court on fraud charges.

456

Elsewhere (History and Politics)

12 Under the leadership of Tony Blair, Britain's Labour Party triumphs in the country's general election, deposing Prime Minister John Major and the Conservative Party. Blair broadened Labour's appeal by attracting Britain's new middle class, moving Labour away from its traditional identification with labor unions, and calling his party "New Labour."

13 Scotland and Wales, accepting the opportunity presented in a Labour campaign promise, vote to establish their own regional legislatures.

14 British colonial rule over Hong Kong ends after 156 years, and China takes control. The city known for its capitalist tradition will now be a "Special Administrative Region" of China.

15 Khmer Rouge leader Pol Pot, thought by many to be responsible for more than 1 million deaths in Cambodia, is captured by government forces.

16 The severity of Asia's economic crisis is evident when the International Monetary Fund arranges a $57 billion bailout for South Korea.

17 Reflecting the changing face of Europe, NATO invites the former Soviet-bloc nations of the Czech Republic, Hungary, and Poland to join the alliance.

18 Russian soldiers finish withdrawing from the breakaway republic of Chechnya.

19 Israel's prime minister Benjamin Netanyahu and Palestinian leader Yasir Arafat agree on the conditions for Israeli withdrawal from the city of Hebron.

20 Mexico's dominant political party, the PRI, loses its majority in the lower house of the national legislature for the first time since the end of the 1920s.

21 A long standoff in Peru between Peruvian military and Tupac Amaru guerrillas holding more than 70 prominent hostages at the Japanese embassy ends as soldiers take the embassy. Only one hostage dies during the attack.

22 Cheddi Jagan, longtime leader of Guyana, dies and is succeeded as prime minister by

America (The Arts)

1 *Cats*, a musical by Andrew Lloyd Webber based on the poems of T. S. Eliot, becomes the longest-running show in Broadway history.

2 Paintings by popular American artists Winslow Homer, John Singer Sargent, and Andrew Wyeth all sell at record prices. Traveling exhibitions of the works of Sargent, the Peale family, and Thomas Moran draw large crowds.

3 Robert Pinsky succeeds Robert Hass as U.S. poet laureate and says that he would like to see poetry accorded greater prominence in high school and college literature programs.

4 Poet Adrienne Rich stirs controversy when she refuses to accept the National Medal of Arts because of her belief that government puts power into the hands of too few people.

5 The National Book Award for fiction goes to Charles Frazier for *Cold Mountain*, a novel set in the Confederate South during the Civil War and featuring a tired and determined veteran who leaves the front lines to return home.

6 The movie *Titanic* opens, portraying one of the great maritime disasters of the 20th century, one that had been the subject of several earlier films. Starring Leonardo DiCaprio and Kate Winslet, it conveys the rampant confusion after the luxury passenger ship hits an iceberg.

7 A Broadway presentation *Titanic* attempts to capture the story on stage and wins a Tony award for best musical.

8 Disney's influence spreads to Broadway with

Elsewhere (The Arts)

12 Impressionist and modern art sell at near-record prices, with works by Renoir, Picasso, and Cezanne fetching nearly $50 million each.

13 Italy's Dario Fo receives the Nobel Prize for literature. Noted primarily for his plays, many of them one-man shows in which he also starred, Fo was long barred from entering the United States because of his support of the Communist Party.

14 Arundhati Roy of India wins Britain's highest literary award, the Booker Prize, for his novel *The God of Small Things*, which examines conflict in the turbulent Indian state of Kerala.

15 Colombia's Gabriel García Márquez, a Nobel winner for literature, explores the impact of the drug culture in his country in *News of a Kidnapping*.

16 Singer Elton John rewrites "Candle in the Wind," a song originally written about Marilyn Monroe, to salute Princess Diana of Britain. John performs the song at her funeral and the recording made there becomes the best-selling single of all time. Profits from its sales are directed to some of Diana's favorite charities.

17 Britain's Spice Girls, a quintet of five young women, becomes internationally popular with young teens.

18 Canadian singer and songwriter Sarah MacLachlan spearheads Lilith Fair, a show featuring female performers that tours Canada and the U.S. with great success.

19 A world tour by Australian pianist David Helfgott, whose struggle with mental illness was

Science & Technology

America

1 NASA's Mars Pathfinder spacecraft lands on Mars and sends out its Sojourner rover to gather chemical and geological data about the planet's surface. Thousands of photographs are sent back from Pathfinder and Sojourner.

2 Later in the year, the Mars Global Surveyor arrives and goes into orbit above Mars in preparation for a photographic mapping mission that will last a Martian year (nearly two Earth years).

3 The Hubble Space Telescope sends spectacular images back to Earth, including one of a bright star in the Milky Way galaxy that is 10 million times as bright as our Sun.

4 Astronauts from the space shuttle *Discovery* visit Hubble and during five extravehicular activities make repairs and install updated equipment, including an imaging spectograph, a near-infrared camera, and a multiobject spectrometer. The Hubble is then sent into a higher orbit.

5 The Cassini mission to Saturn is launched, despite antinuclear protests of its use of plutonium for power. It will take seven years to reach Saturn, a voyage that will include flybys of Venus and Jupiter. The craft will study Saturn's atmosphere, rings, and moons, as well as send a Huygens probe down to the surface of Titan, Saturn's largest moon.

6 Microsoft invests $150 million in Apple Computer, its former strong rival that had lost much of its market share to Microsoft, and also agrees to pay for licensing agreements.

7 Use of the Internet by people with personal computers continues to explode, with U.S. usage rising more than 100% during the year.

8 Deaths from AIDS decline sharply in the U.S.,

Elsewhere

12 The Hale-Bopp Comet, named after the two astronomers who first saw it in 1995, makes its closest approach to Earth. Far brighter than the better-known Halley's Comet and larger than most, Hale-Bopp attracts professional and amateur astronomers around the world. It also inspires unusual behavior such as in the mass suicide in California. **[1997:MISC/4]**

13 The Russian space station *Mir* faces numerous problems that threaten its usefulness in space. A fire in an oxygen-generating unit sends clouds of smoke through the station before burning out. Twice more during the year, malfunctions interrupt the station's air supply. *Mir* is disabled again when a supply ship crashes into it, damaging a solar panel and a science module. The near-catastrophes cause U.S. congressmen to complain that American astronauts might not be safe conducting experiments on *Mir*.

14 Biotechnologists in Scotland announce the successful cloning of a sheep, which they name Dolly. The experiment is hailed for its scientific achievement and criticized for raising the possibility of human cloning, which many opponents consider unnatural.

15 The rapidly expanding use of the Internet leads to concern both by the public and governments about issues of on-line privacy and intellectual copyright. Legal issues remain murky not only because of the nature of the medium but also because Internet use so often crosses the frontiers of nations that have conflicting laws.

16 Delegates from more than 150 countries attend a UN conference on climate change in Kyoto, Japan, and agree on a treaty to restrict

Miscellaneous

America

1 In separate trials, Timothy McVeigh and Terry Nichols are found guilty of the 1995 Oklahoma City bombing. McVeigh receives a death sentence. **[1995:MISC/1]**

2 O.J. Simpson is judged guilty in a civil trial for the death of his ex-wife Nicole Brown and her friend Ronald Goldman. Earlier, he had been found innocent in a criminal trial. **[1995:MISC/4]**

3 Fashion mogul Gianni Versace is murdered in Florida; murder suspect Andrew Cunanan, also wanted for four other murders, commits suicide as police close in.

4 In California, 39 members of a group known as Heaven's Gate commit suicide, believing that they will be received by an alien spacecraft behind the Hale-Bopp Comet. **[1997:SCI/12]**

5 Communications giant Ted Turner pledges $1 billion to further the causes of the United Nations.

6 Following 1995's Million Man March **[1995:HIST/9]** African-American women stage in Philadelphia a Million Woman March stressing unity.

7 Golfer Tiger Woods bursts upon the sports scene by winning his first major title, the Masters Tournament, by a record score and heightening spectator interest in the sport.

8 Major League Baseball celebrates the 50th anniversary of Jackie Robinson breaking the modern color barrier by playing for the Brooklyn Dodgers.

9 The fifth-year Florida Marlins best the Cleveland Indians in the World Series, 4 games to 3, winning the world title sooner than any other expansion baseball team.

10 Latrell Sprewell, a star player for the National Basketball Association's Golden State Warriors, stuns

Elsewhere

17 Diana, Princess of Wales and ex-wife of Britain's Prince Charles, dies with her companion in an automobile accident in Paris. Her funeral draws worldwide media coverage.

18 Queen Elizabeth II of Great Britain and Prince Phillip mark their 50th wedding anniversary.

19 Switzerland's government, banks, and businesses agree to create a fund to reimburse Holocaust victims whose deposits in Swiss institutions had disappeared or whose assets had been taken by the Nazis and sent to Switzerland.

20 Meeting in Denver, Colorado, the Summit of Eight, composed of the world's leading industrial nations, discusses the expansion of NATO, Middle East tensions, and the state of the environment.

21 Under the banner of the World Trade Organization, 65 countries agree to allow foreign competition in their domestic telephone operations.

22 The Nobel Prize for peace goes to the International Campaign to Ban Landmines and its leader, Jody Williams. More than 120 nations sign a treaty banning the use and manufacture of land mines. The U.S. does not sign the treaty because it believes the mines are still needed on the South Korea–North Korea border area.

23 Continued violent eruptions of a volcano on the British Carribean colony of Montserrat make the island almost inhabitable and destroy most of the island's infrastructure. Many residents relocate to the nearby island of Antigua.

24 Islamic militants in Egypt are blamed for an armed attack on tourists at a temple near Luxor that results in 70 deaths. The

9 The U.S. signs a new cooperative regional-security agreement with Japan.

10 The U.S. extends indefinitely the deadline by which it will remove its peacekeeping troops from Bosnia; Pres. Clinton visits the area to show his support.

11 The Supreme Court affirms the legality of the line-item veto law, which Pres. Clinton uses for the first time to kill some provisions of the balanced-budget act.

his wife, Janet Jagan, who is subsequently elected president.

23 In Zaire, rebel leader Laurent Kabila topples the government of President Mobutu Sese Seko, ruler since 1965. Kabila changes the country's name to Democratic Republic of the Congo, its original designation, and assumes the presidency. The ailing Mobutu soon dies in exile.

24 Liberia's long civil war ends, and rebel leader Charles Taylor becomes the country's president.

the opening of the spectacular *The Lion King* in a historic theater renovated by the entertainment company.

9 The television series *Ellen* creates controversy when its main character reveals that she is a lesbian. The show's star, Ellen DeGeneres, also states that she is gay off screen.

10 Trumpet virtuoso Wynton Marsalis wins the Pulitzer Prize for music for *Blood on the Fields*, a jazz oratorio exploring the issue of slavery. It is the first jazz work to receive a Pulitzer.

11 Rap music dominates the popular-music scene, with rivalries between East and West Coast rap entrepreneurs creating headlines.

portrayed in the film *Shine*, is a popular triumph but receives poor reviews from the critics.

20 Architecture's Pritzker Prize goes to Norway's Sverre Fehn, noted for his Modernist structures that also reflect Scandinavian tradition.

21 *Riverdance* and *Lord of the Dance*, two shows featuring Irish step dancing, tour the world to great acclaim. Their success sparks renewed interest in Irish culture.

22 The Cannes Film Festival, the world's most prestigious film festival, holds its 50th gathering in the south of France. The top prize, the *Palme d'Or* (Golden Palm), is shared by the movies *Taste of Cherry* from Iran and *The Eel* from Japan.

1998

1 Pres. Clinton is embroiled in several cases with sexual overtones. He agrees to pay $850,000 to settle a sexual-harassment charge leveled against him by Paula Corbin Jones, and an administration employee, Kathleen Willey, claims on television that the president made sexual advances on her.

2 Former White House intern Monica Lewinsky testifies before a grand jury about her relationship with Pres. Clinton, who also testifies and then admits publicly that his earlier denials had misled the American public.

12 The Protestant and Roman Catholic factions in war-torn Northern Ireland agree on a framework for peace after more than 25 years of conflict. Voters in Ireland and Northern Ireland overwhelmingly approve the agreement. Former U.S. senator George Mitchell plays a key mediating role; Prime Minister Blair of Britain and U.S. president Clinton also contribute substantially.

13 The agreement's historic importance is underlined when John Hume and David Trimble, Northern Ireland's Protestant and Catholic leaders, receive the Nobel Peace Prize.

1 An Andy Warhol portrait of actress Marilyn Monroe sells for more than $17 million, one of the highest prices for post–World War II art. A Winslow Homer seascape is bought by Microsoft founder Bill Gates for about $30 million.

2 An exhibition of Van Gogh's works from the Van Gogh Museum in Amsterdam draws large crowds to Washington's National Gallery before the show travels to Los Angeles.

3 The New York City Ballet marks its 50th

14 Italy's Renzo Piano takes architecture's Pritzker Prize, which salutes both his early Modernist structures, such as the Georges Pompidou Center in Paris, and more recent works, such as the conversion of a factory in Turin, Italy, into a convention center.

15 The works of European painters, ranging from Old Masters to contemporary artists, bring near-record prices. A Van Gogh self-portrait goes for more than $79 million, while a Monet

primarily because of new drug regimes that fight HIV, the virus that causes AIDS.

9 The average life expectancy for Americans rises above 76 years for the first time.

10 Congress and Pres. Clinton agree on legislation to manage American wildlife refuges that balances the concerns of strict environmentalists with those of hunters and recreation enthusiasts.

11 The U.S. approves legislation that protects dolphins, often caught in the past by the nets of foreign tuna boats, and certifies foreign tuna fishermen as "dolphin safe," which allows them access to the U.S. tuna market.

emissions of carbon dioxide and other greenhouse gases. U.S. business interests claim that the treaty's conditions will cause an economic downturn in America.

17 Scientists remain concerned about climate conditions in the Antarctic, where the ozone hole continues to widen and ice breakup suggests that warming is continuing.

18 Studies in the Arctic find that pollution is threatening the environment and the area's human populations.

19 DNA tests on a Neanderthal fossil from Germany seem to indicate that the Neanderthals were unrelated to modern humans and did not breed with them.

20 Fossils found in Spain may be from a species that predates both Neanderthals and modern humans. Anthropologists are divided about the significance of the new find.

the sports world by fighting with his coach, P.J. Carlesimo, and is suspended without pay.

11 The Green Bay Packers win the National Football League's Super Bowl XXXI, trouncing the New England Patriots.

12 In a title bout, former heavyweight boxing champion Mike Tyson is disqualified for biting opponent Evander Holyfield, the reigning champ.

13 Spring flooding of the Red River devastates North Dakota. The federal government later passes a more than $8 billion flood-relief bill.

14 Congress and Pres. Clinton agree on legislation that gives financial stability to the Medicare program, which provides health care for the elderly and disabled.

15 Sexual-misconduct scandals rock the U.S. military establishment from the highest officer levels down to senior enlisted personnel. Frequent allegations of mistreatment of new recruits are made.

16 Mormons mark the 150th anniversary of their trek west to Utah with a recreation of the historic migration.

violence against tourists casts a shadow over one of Egypt's most important industries.

25 India stages a state funeral for Nobel Peace Prize and Templeton Prize winner Mother Teresa, who worked with the poor in India for decades.

26 The Templeton Prize goes to Pandurang Athavale, a Hindu who leads a self-help program among India's rural poor.

27 World chess champion Garry Kasparov of Russia loses a heralded match with Deep Blue, IBM's chess-programmed computer that he had defeated in 1996.

---

1 NASA marks its 40th anniversary and begins the construction in space of the International Space Station (ISS). U.S. astronauts join an American section to a previously launched Russian section.

2 Astronauts conduct several space-shuttle flights, including two to the Russian space station *Mir*, where astronaut Andrew Thomas spends more than four months.

3 John Glenn, the first American astronaut to orbit the Earth **[1962:SCI/8]**, who went on to long service as a U.S. senator, becomes the

12 To initiate construction of the International Space Station (ISS), Russia launches its *Zarya* module, to which the American module *Unity* is later joined. Additional modules will be added before the station's scheduled completion in 2004.

13 The Russian space station *Mir* avoids the dangerous malfunctions that plagued it in 1997 and hosts several new American and Russian astronauts.

14 Computer technicians race the calendar to make necessary programming changes so computers

1 Weather events triggered by the Pacific Ocean's El Niño current cause record precipitation in California and especially severe tornadoes in the southeast U.S.

2 In a year of giant mergers and acquisitions, Chrysler Corporation, one of Detroit's Big Three auto makers, agrees to merge with Germany's Daimler-Benz. Exxon, the nation's largest energy company, acquires Mobil, the second biggest. Corporate combinations are also frequent in the telecommunications and financial industries.

13 A huge ice storm descends on eastern Canada and the northeastern U.S., causing billions of dollars of damage and leaving some areas without power for weeks.

14 The weather event known as El Niño, originating in a change in climatic conditions in the Pacific Ocean, reaches a peak. Its Western Hemisphere effects include both unusually heavy precipitation in some areas and severe drought in others.

15 An undersea earthquake in the Pacific

1998

History and Politics		The Arts	
America	**Elsewhere**	**America**	**Elsewhere**

3 Pres. Clinton's efforts to establish executive and lawyer-client privileges to shield associates from an independent-counsel investigation are denied by a federal judge.

4 The House of Representatives votes to impeach Pres. Clinton for lying under oath and obstructing justice in matters regarding his relationship with White House intern Monica Lewinsky.

5 The Supreme Court declares unconstitutional the line-item veto authority of the president.

6 After much wrangling, Congress and Pres. Clinton agree on a budget that will produce a surplus. Other legislation signed into law included new funds for teacher training and a six-year mass-transit and road-building program.

7 Terrorist bombings of the U.S. embassies in Tanzania and Kenya on the same day result in hundreds of deaths and the indictment in the U.S. of Osama bin Laden, a wealthy Saudi and suspected terrorist leader purportedly living in Afganistan.

8 In November elections, Republicans maintain control of both houses of Congress, but Democratic gains in the House lead Speaker Newt Gingrich, who had predicted Republican gains, to resign as speaker and from the House as well.

9 Republican governor George W. Bush of Texas easily wins reelection and immediately becomes the favorite for the Republican presidential nomination in 2000.

10 Independent candidate Jesse Ventura, once a professional wrestler known as "the Body," shocks traditional politicians by winning the gubernatorial race in Minnesota.

11 Although economic crisis in Asia weakens markets for U.S. exports, driving the trade deficit higher, most economic indicators show that the American economy is continuing its period of high prosperity.

14 Israel marks its 50th anniversary of independence as its population nears 6 million. Further progress toward domestic peace is made with the signing of the Wye River Memorandum during an Israeli-Palestinian meeting in the U.S.

15 While being threatened with renewed bombing by the U.S., Iraq reaches an agreement with the United Nations that permits UN arms inspectors unlimited access to potential Iraqi weapons locations, an agreement Iraq later rescinds. The U.S. and Britain soon launch air strikes against Iraqi installations.

16 In Indonesia, severe economic problems and recession spur student protests and charges of corruption against Pres. Suharto, who had been reelected to a 7th five-year term early in the year. Suharto soon resigns and is succeeded by Vice Pres. Habibie.

17 India and Pakistan detonate underground nuclear devices, heightening tensions in the Indian subcontinent.

18 An era ends in Germany as Chancellor Helmut Kohl loses national elections after 16 years in office. He is succeeded by Gerhard Schroeder.

19 Yugoslavia's restive province of Kosovo, inhabited mainly by ethnic Albanians, becomes a battleground when Kosovar rebels clash with Serbian troops sent in to "pacify" the region. Although a fragile cease-fire is in place by year's end, large sections are held by the rebels of the Kosovo Liberation Army (KLA).

20 Tensions among various ethnic groups and political factions in Georgia, a former Soviet republic, are heightened by an unsuccessful assassination attempt on Pres. Eduard Shevardnadze and a sharp downturn in the economy.

21 Russia endures a year of crisis, in which Pres. Boris Yeltsin's health declines as he changes prime ministers three times, the economy worsens dramatically, and the nation pleads for foreign aid and

anniversary by introducing new works, and the American Ballet Theatre enjoys success with a revival of *Le Corsaire*, a 19th century work.

4 Conductor and composer Andre Previn debuts in opera with *A Streetcar Named Desire*, drawn from the play by Tennessee Williams. Presented by the San Francisco Opera, Previn's work is hailed by critics.

5 The centennial of composer George Gershwin's birth sparks acclaimed performances of *Porgy and Bess*. A salute to Gershwin is televised.

6 The movie *Titanic* captures 11 Academy Awards, including best picture and best director (James Cameron). The movie's soundtrack recording sells more than 10 million copies.

7 Several top rock groups, including the Beastie Boys and the Dave Matthews Band, gather for a concert to support freedom for Tibet.

8 On the 30th anniversary of Martin Luther King Jr.'s assassination, several books, including Taylor Branch's *Pillar of Fire*, examine the legacy of the civil rights leader.

9 Norman Mailer celebrates the 50th anniversary of his classic World War II novel, *The Naked and the Dead*, and publishes selections from various works in *The Time of Our Time*. Tom Wolfe brings out a critically well-received second novel, *A Man in Full*.

10 The Broadway theater season is dominated by two musicals adapted from other media. *Ragtime*,

reaches a new height at more than $30 million and a Mondrian canvas brings $40 million.

16 Students from Russia's Vaganova Ballet Academy, affiliated with the Kirov Ballet, tour the U.S. with Kirov Ballet members, while the Kirov Opera appears at New York City's Metropolitan Opera.

17 Italy's Andrea Bocelli, a blind operatic tenor, continues his huge success as a recording artist and makes a triumphal concert tour of the U.S.

18 Precarious finances lead London's Royal Opera Company to announce a yearlong closing.

19 International opera stars Luciano Pavarotti and Placido Domingo mark their 30th anniversaries at the Metropolitan Opera and also perform at a Three Tenors concert in France that is broadcast to a worldwide TV audience.

20 Portuguese author Jose Saramago receives the Nobel Prize for literature, the first awarded to a Portuguese-language writer, and publishes a new novel, *All the Names*. Best known as a novelist, he also writes nonfiction, plays, and poetry.

21 Great Britain's Booker Prize goes to Ian McEwan for his short satirical novel *Amsterdam*. Shortly before his death, Ted Hughes, the nation's poet laureate, publishes a collection called *Birthday Letters*, examining his life with his wife, U.S. poet Sylvia Plath, and how her suicide affected him.

22 Germany celebrates the centennial of the birth of Marxist playwright Bertolt Brecht, who wrote

Science & Technology		Miscellaneous	
America	**Elsewhere**	**America**	**Elsewhere**

Science & Technology — America

oldest person (77) to make a voyage into outer space. His presence on the shuttle *Discovery* brings NASA much favorable publicity and the opportunity to study the effects of space travel on older people.

4 The FDA approves the use of Viagra, or sildenafil citrate, the first pill for male impotence. The drug enjoys huge sales and publicity.

5 The drug tamoxifen is certified by the FDA to help prevent breast cancer, despite potentially severe side effects that include uterine cancer and blood clots.

6 Studies of health care in the U.S. continue to find severe public dissatisfaction with the services of health-maintenance organizations (HMOs). Efforts by Pres. Clinton and Democrats in Congress to pass a patients' bill of rights are successfully blocked by health insurers and most congressional Republicans.

7 Two scientists at the University of Hawaii successfully clone mice from cells around a developing egg. They then clone additional generations of mice from the first clones.

8 Three physicists at U.S. universities share the Nobel Prize for physics for their research into the properties of subatomic particles.

9 Scientists at the University of California at Santa Barbara and at Northwestern University share the Nobel Prize for chemistry for developing methods for theoretical studies of molecules.

10 U.S. archaeologists establish that England's early American colonies on Roanoke Island and at Jamestown, Virginia, faced some of the driest conditions in a millennium, which may help account for their survival problems.

Science & Technology — Elsewhere

worldwide will recognize that a different century is being entered in 2000. The effort to address the so-called Y2K problem costs governments and businesses billions of dollars to update computer systems.

15 Numerous scientific institutions in Japan and the U.S. announce jointly that an atomic particle known as a neutrino has mass.

16 An international agreement known as the Protocol for the Protection of the Antarctic Environment becomes effective, aiming at high-level protection of the Antarctic, the scene of important scientific research, such as the study of the ozone layer.

17 For his pioneering studies of welfare economics, Amartya Sen of Britain's Cambridge University receives the Nobel Prize for economics.

18 An Italian anthropologist working in Eritrea unearths a 1-million-year-old skull that may provide a link between early *Homo sapiens* and other species such as *Homo erectus*.

19 Archaeologists in the Czech Republic discover evidence in a 25,000-year-old settlement that, contrary to long-held beliefs, women and children helped men with prehistoric hunting, especially of small game.

20 In Cambodia, aerial radar scans of the area around Angkor locate more ancient temples, built earlier than those already found, and a web of water-control projects, including reservoirs and canals.

Miscellaneous — America

3 Unemployment in the U.S. falls to its lowest rate since 1970 as the nation's economy continues to grow rapidly.

4 Reacting to complaints from the public and a government report, Congress passes and Pres. Clinton signs a broad-based reform of the Internal Revenue Service. The legislation reduces the power of the IRS and gives taxpayers more rights in tax disputes.

5 In the largest settlement in U.S. history, the tobacco companies reach agreement with 46 states (earlier, four states made separate settlements) to pay the states more than $205 billion over 25 years, while the states agree to withdraw lawsuits seeking damages for medical treatment of smokers. The tobacco companies also agree to numerous other marketing restrictions.

6 The body of the Vietnam War's Unknown Soldier is identified, removed from Arlington National Cemetery, and returned to his family.

7 The Denver Broncos claim their first National Football League championship, winning 31–24 over the Green Bay Packers in Super Bowl XXXII.

8 Mark McGwire of the National League's St. Louis Cardinals breaks Roger Maris's Major League single-season record **[1961:MISC/6]** by hitting 70 home runs.

9 The American League's New York Yankees win baseball's World Series, trouncing the National League's San Diego Padres in four straight games.

10 Led by Michael Jordan, the Chicago Bulls of the National Basketball Association capture their third consecutive championship by defeating the Utah Jazz.

11 The National Hockey League's Stanley Cup is won

Miscellaneous — Elsewhere

Ocean near Papua New Guinea creates three tsunamis, or tidal waves, that kill more than 2,000 people and cause extensive damage.

16 British Petroleum acquires Amoco in the most expensive purchase of a U.S. company by a foreign corporation.

17 Russia reburies Czar Nicholas II and the imperial family, 80 years after their execution by communist Bolshevik rebels.

18 President Nelson Mandela of South Africa marries Graca Machel, the widow of the president of nearby Mozambique.

19 The two biggest banks in Switzerland announce they will settle claims brought on behalf of Holocaust survivors and their heirs who had held accounts with them.

20 Britain's Sir Sigmund Sternberg, a leader of the International Council of Christians and Jews, is chosen for the Templeton Prize for championing understanding among adherents of different religions.

21 Pope John Paul II receives a tumultuous welcome on a visit to Cuba and conducts an outdoor mass in Havana for a huge throng.

22 A U.S. Air Force jet severs a ski-lift cable in Italy, killing 20 riders in a cable car that plunges to the ground.

23 France, the host country, wins soccer's World Cup for the first time, upsetting defending champion Brazil in the finals, which are watched by a worldwide TV audience of more than 1.5 billion.

24 The city of Nagano, Japan, hosts the XVIII Winter Olympic Games. Snowboarding is an official sport for the first time.

461

History and Politics		The Arts	
America	Elsewhere	America	Elsewhere
	investment from Western nations. **22** Sierra Leone, ruled by military junta since 1997, restores its democratic government with the help of troops from the Economic Community of West African States Monitoring Group (ECOMOG).	spun out of an E. L. Doctorow novel, competes with *The Lion King*, based on Disney's movie, which had opened in 1997 and which wins the Tony Award for best musical. **11** *Seinfeld*, a TV show about the day-to-day lives of four friends in New York City, and the most popular program of the 1990s, airs its final episode, which is seen by more than 75 million people. **12** The law remains a hit with TV audiences, with the drama-comedy *Ally McBeal* and *The Practice* both achieving high ratings. **13** The animated show *South Park* draws many young viewers but is criticized for its violence and vulgarity.	*Threepenny Opera* **[1928:ARTS/14]** with formal ceremonies and revivals. **23** Polish literature Nobelist Czeslaw Milosz publishes *A Road-Side Dog*, a collection of stories, essays, and poems about his memories of Europe during the World War II era. **24** South Africa's Nadine Gordimer, also a Nobel Literature Prize recipient, examines her country's current politics in a new novel, *The House Gun*.
1999			
1 In only the second impeachment trial for a U.S. president, Bill Clinton is acquitted after being tried by the Senate on charges of lying under oath and obstruction of justice concerning his efforts to disguise the nature of his relationship with White House intern Monica Lewinsky. The first impeachment trial was that of Pres. Andrew Johnson. **[1868:HIST/1]** **2** The House of Representatives chooses Dennis Hastert, a Republican from Illinois, as Speaker of the House. **3** The surging U.S. economy results in a budget surplus, which leads to disputes in Congress about using the money. Republicans pass a tax cut, which President Clinton vetoes, citing other needs for the money, such as supporting the Social Security system. **4** Protestors in Seattle disrupt the meeting of the World Trade Organization with violent street demonstrations against globalization and the WTO. The demonstrators allege substandard labor practices and working	**10** Canada creates a huge new territory, called Nunavut, from the eastern parts of the Northwest Territories. Most of the population is Inuit, and the territory's name means "Our Land" in the dominant language. **11** Australian voters affirm in a national referendum that the British sovereign should continue to be Australia's nominal head of state. **12** The North Atlantic Treaty Organization (NATO) accepts the former communist countries of Czech Republic, Hungary, and Poland as members. Later in the year, the alliance's 19 members celebrate its 50th anniversary in ceremonies in Washington, D.C. **13** During a year of turmoil in Russia that includes renewed fighting in Chechnya, President Boris Yeltsin overcomes an impeachment attempt but later resigns unexpectedly, turning over the presidency to his prime minister, Vladimir Putin. **14** Responding to "ethnic cleansing" by Yugoslavia in the province of Kosovo, NATO forces launch a successful bombing campaign that helps force	**1** The debate continues over true ownership of artworks taken from Jewish owners during the Nazi era and subsequently acquired by museums and private collectors. U.S. customs agents prevent the return of some paintings to Austria and the Seattle Art Museum returns a Matisse canvas to the family of a Jewish collector who had lost it to the Nazis in 1941. **2** Internet technology begins to play an important role in the art world, with on-line auctions being held by such sites as eBay and Amazon.com. **3** A new record is set for an American artist's work when George Bellows's *Polo Crowd* sells for more than $27 million. **4** The centennial of Ernest Hemingway's birth is marked with various celebrations and the publication of an unfinished work, *True at*	**14** The Pritzker Prize goes to British architect Sir Norman Foster, who is noted for his futuristic buildings with innovative treatment of light. **15** The works of European artists of the Impressionist and Modern schools command the year's top prices at auction. Two Picasso portraits sell for more than $45 million each, and a Cezanne still life soars over $60 million. **16** Europe also confronts the issue of ownership of Holocaust-era art collections. The Austrian branch of the Rothschild banking family finally recovers artworks confiscated by the Nazis and holds a spectacular auction of them that brings nearly $90 million. **17** German novelist Günter Grass takes the Nobel Prize for literature, with the award citation saluting his ability to

462

Science & Technology		Miscellaneous		
America	Elsewhere	America	Elsewhere	

11 In Montana, the site of a camp made by the Lewis and Clark expedition in 1805 while exploring the Louisiana Purchase is identified by archaeologists.

for the second year in a row by the Detroit Red Wings, who take four straight games from the Washington Capitals in the championship series.

12 Michigan authorities arrest Dr. Jack Kevorkian for murder after he performs an act of euthanasia that is later broadcast on TV. Previously, Kevorkian had publicly acknowledged helping people to commit suicide.

25 A Swissair flight goes down in the Atlantic Ocean off Nova Scotia, Canada, resulting in the deaths of all 229 people on the plane.

1999

1 NASA's Mars exploration program suffers setbacks as two space vehicles, one collecting information on the planet's atmosphere and the other designed to explore its surface, lose contact with Earth as they enter Mars' atmosphere.
2 The U.S. space program enjoys success in deploying the Chandra X-ray Observatory and in repairing the Hubble Space Telescope.
3 NASA's *Lunar Prospector,* which is deliberately crashed onto the lunar surface, determines that the Moon has a small core.
4 Microsoft suffers a setback in the antitrust suit filed against it by the federal government when the presiding judge rules that Microsoft is a monopoly that deploys its marketing muscle to intimidate competitors.
5 Internet use continues to explode, with the number linked to the World Wide Web perhaps as high as 90

13 Nations around the world prepare for the anticipated effects of the Y2K (Year 2000) computer problem—the need to reprogram computers and computer-dependent activities to recognize the change to a new century. The key role of computers in society lead to some predictions of widespread communications, banking, and transportation breakdowns.
14 The UN establishes an Internet Worldwide Y2K Watch to coordinate reports from more than 170 countries about Y2K events.
15 Russia's financial problems take a toll on its space program, with the *Mir* space station in danger of being permanently abandoned.
16 After studying data gathered by the Hubble Space Telescope, an international team of astronomers declares that the universe is 12 billion to 15 billion years old.

1 Two boys at Columbine High School in Littleton, Colorado, bring weapons to the school and shoot to death 12 students and a teacher before killing themselves. The event brings new demands for gun control and for an investigation of a wave of shootings in U.S. schools.
2 John F. Kennedy Jr., founder of the magazine *George* and son of the assassinated president, dies with his wife, Carolyn, and her sister when a plane he is piloting crashes in waters near Martha's Vineyard.
3 Michael Jordan, widely considered basketball's greatest player, retires from the National Basketball Association's Chicago Bulls.
4 Interest in women's soccer soars as the American team wins the Women's World Cup, held in the United States for the first time.
5 For the first time, the Dow Jones Industrial Average closes above 10,000

12 Doctors Without Borders, an organization that sends medical personnel to trouble spots around the world, receives the Nobel Peace Prize in recognition of its "pioneering humanitarian work."
13 Two Libyan suspects in the 1988 bombing of Pan Am Flight 103 over Scotland are brought to the Netherlands to stand trial. Libya resisted turning over the suspects until an acceptable neutral nation was chosen as a trial site and until their delivery resulted in a suspension of UN sanctions against Libya.
14 A Swiss psychiatrist and an English adventurer complete the first nonstop around-the-world balloon trip in 19 days in the *Breitling Orbiter 3*.
15 Spanish golfer José María Olazabal captures the prestigious Masters tournament in Georgia.
16 Winnipeg, Canada, hosts the Pan-American Games, with 41 countries represented; Canadian

History and Politics		The Arts	
America	**Elsewhere**	**America**	**Elsewhere**

conditions in many of the WTO member countries.

5 The Senate refuses to ratify the Comprehensive Test Ban Treaty. Senate Republicans oppose the nuclear-testing treaty, claiming that it has insufficient protections for the United States.

6 Competition for the 2000 presidential nominations begins in earnest, with Democrats Vice Pres. Gore and former senator. Bill Bradley and several Republicans, including Texas governor George Bush, son of the former president George H. W. Bush, and Senator. John McCain, announcing their candidacies.

7 First Lady Hillary Clinton causes a stir when she decides to "explore" seeking the U.S. Senate nomination for the Democrats in New York state.

8 U.S. relations with China are severely strained after U.S. jets mistakenly bomb the Chinese embassy in Belgrade and kill several staff members during the air campaign over Yugoslavia.

9 Former President Jimmy Carter represents the United States as ownership of the Panama Canal is formally transferred to Panama in ceremonies in the Panama Canal Zone.

Yugoslavia into a peace treaty and then send ground troops into Kosovo to maintain peace.

15 Eleven members of the European Union begin using the euro, the EU's new currency that according to plan will replace national monies in the early 2000s.

16 The African National Congress dominates South Africa's parliamentary and provincial elections and chooses Thabo Mbeki to follow Nelson Mandela as the country's president.

17 After the country reinstates civilian rule, Nigeria elects its first president since 1983.

18 Celebrations and parades mark the 50th anniversary of communist rule in China, but the nation fails to gain admission to the World Trade Organization.

19 China assumes control of Macao from Portugal, which had held the island since the 16th century. Terms of the transfer make Macao a Special Administrative Region with autonomy.

20 Following a pro-independence vote in East Timor, a region annexed by Indonesia in 1976, pro-Indonesia forces rampage against the population. The national government does little to stem the violence, and the UN sends in a peacekeeping force.

21 In Pakistan, former prime minister Benazir Bhutto and her businessman husband are convicted of corruption. Pakistan's military leaders later overthrow her successor as prime minister and install a military government.

First Light, edited by his son Patrick.

5 The Harry Potter books, by British author J. K. Rowling, captivate young American readers, and the stories about a boy training to be a wizard dominate the best-seller lists.

6 The New York City Ballet marks its 50th anniversary with new works by Peter Martins and Christopher Wheeldon and revivals of George Balanchine and Igor Stravinsky ballets.

7 The centennial of the birth of jazz great Duke Ellington is celebrated by both the New York City Ballet and the Lincoln Center Jazz Orchestra. Ellington music festivals are held around the country.

8 New York City's Metropolitan Opera premiers an American opera, *The Great Gatsby*, by John Harbison, based on the F. Scott Fitzgerald novel.

9 George Lucas augments his hugely successful *Star Wars* series of movies with a new title, *Star Wars: Episode I—The Phantom Menace,* which is popular with viewers but not critics.

10 Other popular movies include *American Beauty*, which examines modern family life, and the low-budget *The Blair Witch Project*.

11 The movie *Titanic*, which opened in 1997 **[1997:ARTS/6]**, becomes the highest-grossing film in history.

12 Television's largest audience tunes in when former White House intern Monica Lewinsky appears on the show *20/20* and talks about her relationship with Pres. Clinton.

show "the intertwined roots of good and evil." His best-known novel in English translation is *The Tin Drum* (1959).

18 For his novel *Disgrace*, centered on contemporary urban South Africa, author J. M. Coetzee receives Britain's Booker Prize for the second time.

19 The Australian Ballet stages an adaptation of Igor Stravinsky's *Rite of Spring* reflecting the heritage of the aborigines.

20 The playwright William Shakespeare remains a movie favorite following the success of 1998's *Shakespeare in Love*, with the release of *A Midsummer's Night Dream* as well as *Titus*, a contemporary-dress version of the play *Titus Andronicus*.

21 The atmosphere of World War II in Italy is evoked in Franco Zeffirelli's *Tea with Mussolini*.

22 Hits on the London stage, notably Judi Dench in *Amy's View*, also appear in New York City theaters.

Science & Technology		Miscellaneous	
America	**Elsewhere**	**America**	**Elsewhere**

America — Science & Technology

million in the U.S. Shopping on-line also expands exponentially, both for individual consumers and between businesses.

6 Rockefeller University's Guenter Blobel receives the Nobel Prize for physiology or medicine for proteins research that will help the production of drugs. A researcher at California Institute of Technology wins the Nobel Prize for chemistry for devising a method for observing atoms in a molecule moving through a chemical reaction.

7 The first vaccine for the prevention of Lyme disease becomes available in the U.S.

8 The first White House Conference on Mental Health convenes in Washington, D.C., as part of an effort to have psychological problems receive treatment equal to that given to physical illnesses.

9 Builders on a construction site in Miami, Florida, unearth a circle cut into limestone. Archaeologists date pottery and other materials to A.D. 1200–1500 and speculate that the circle may have been part of a chief's home.

10 The bald eagle, the national bird of the United States, is removed from the endangered species list.

11 Pres. Clinton bans logging and road building from large sections of the national forest system, an act opposed by timber companies and many states in the West.

12 Geologists discover a fault system under Los Angeles and believe that it caused significant earthquakes in the last 10 years.

Elsewhere — Science & Technology

17 Astronomers also confirm the finding of a multiplanetary system beyond our solar system.

18 The European Union (EU) leads the way in voicing concerns about the use of genetically modified plant and animal products in food for humans.

19 An expedition co-led by Americans finds the bodies of three children sacrificed about A.D. 1500 in Inca rituals atop a volcanic mountain in Argentina.

20 At the ancient Mayan city of Palenque in the jungles of Mexico, archaeologists discover a tomb with painted murals and numerous sculptures dating to the 8th century A.D.

21 Excavations in Kenya uncover stone tools about 2.3 million years old, about 700,000 years older than similar finds of stone tools.

22 South of Cairo, Egypt, scientists find a cemetery of such richly ornamented mummies that the area becomes known as the Valley of the Golden Mummies.

America — Miscellaneous

and then above 11,000 as the nation's economy continues to boom.

6 Dr. Jack Kevorkian, noted for assisting terminally patients to commit suicide, is convicted of murder for administering a lethal injection to one of his patients.

7 A series of strong storms, punctuated by Hurricane Floyd, batter North Carolina, causing more than 50 deaths and billions of dollars in damage.

8 Statistics published in 1999 indicate that the United States has the highest incarceration rate in the world, with more than 460 people imprisoned per 100,000 of population. The decrease in the number of patients in mental hospitals is responsible for part of the increase in the prison population.

9 Kansas removes the topic of evolution from statewide tests, leaving decisions about teaching evolution and creationism to local school authorities.

10 Minnesota governor Jesse Ventura, a former professional wrestler elected on the Reform Party ticket, makes headlines throughout the year with outspoken statements on such topics as religion—holding that it was for the weak-minded—and obesity, claiming that overweight people lacked willpower.

11 Several members of the Freemen, a fringe group that does not recognize state or federal laws, are sentenced in Montana to prison for fraud.

Elsewhere — Miscellaneous

athletes make their best showing in Games history.

17 A severe earthquake in western Turkey results in more than 15,000 deaths and causes massive destruction. Within a month, an aftershock in Turkey kills hundreds more, and an earthquake in Athens, Greece, kills more than 100.

18 An Egyptian passenger plane crashes into the Atlantic Ocean off Nantucket Island, Massachusetts, killing all 217 aboard. There is speculation that one of the pilots may have been committing suicide.

19 Chinese authorities continue to harass and arrest members of the Falun Gong sect, which believes that exercise and meditation can help release spiritual forces.

20 Germany celebrates the 10th anniversary of the dismantling of the Berlin Wall. [1989:HIST/11]

21 In Britain, Prince Edward marries a commoner at Windsor Castle and takes the title of Earl of Wessex.

22 In the worst storm in more than 20 years, India's east coast is hit by an enormous cyclone that kills more than 10,000 and causes widespread damage.

23 New Zealand's former prime minister, Mike Moore, becomes head of the World Trade Organization.

24 Two Arab nations greet new rulers. Abdullah, the oldest son of King Hussein of Jordan, succeeds his father as monarch, and Hassan II of Morocco is succeeded by his son, Mohamed VI.

History and Politics		The Arts	
America	**Elsewhere**	**America**	**Elsewhere**
		13 Other top-rated television programs are *The Sopranos*, a series about organized-crime figures with personal problems, and the quiz show *Who Wants to Be a Millionaire*.	

	America	Elsewhere	America	Elsewhere
2000	**1** In the presidential primaries, Vice Pres. Al Gore bests challenger and former U.S. senator Bill Bradley to secure the Democratic nomination, while Texas governor George W. Bush, the son of former president George Bush, outlasts Sen. John McCain of Arizona for the Republican nomination. **2** Gore's running mate, Sen. Joe Lieberman, is the first Jew nominated for vice president. Bush picks businessman Dick Cheney, a former congressman and Reagan and elder Bush administration official, as his running mate. **3** In the most disputed presidential election in U.S. history, Republican Bush wins the electoral vote after the vote count in Florida is resolved, while Al Gore wins the overall popular vote. **4** The election's outcome remains in doubt for more than a month as the result in Florida is disputed well into December. Lawsuits and countersuits pose the threat that Congress will have to decide the victor, but a 5–4 U.S. Supreme Court decision limits the actions that Gore can take, and he finally concedes to Bush. **5** President-elect Bush moves rapidly to nominate cabinet members who have broad experience and Republican ties; several members served in Congress and/or previous administrations, while others, such as secretary of state–designate Colin Powell, are nationally respected. **6** In a preelection decision, Pres. Clinton leaves the issue of a nuclear missile–defense shield for the next administration. Among the objections to such a	**11** Russian president Boris Yeltsin announces his retirement as the new year begins and is followed, after elections, by his chosen successor, Vladimir Putin, who faces formidable economic problems as well as the continuing rebellion in Chechnya. **12** Yugoslav president Slobodan Milosevic loses an election he calls to validate his rule, then tries to manipulate voting returns before conceding to Vojislav Kostunica. Initially not well known, Kostunica is the candidate of a coalition of opposition parties and becomes popular by appealing to Serbian nationalism. **13** Pres. Hugo Chavez of Venezuela continues his program of changing the nation, wins approval of a new constitution, and is reelected president for a six-year term. He hosts a meeting of the OPEC heads of state and presses to maintain high oil prices. **14** The Middle East remains unsettled as the longtime leader of Syria, Hafez al-Assad, dies and is succeeded by his son Bashar; Israel withdraws from South Lebanon; and prospects of an Israeli-Palestinian peace fade when violence between the two factions escalates. **15** Pope John Paul II, celebrating a Holy Year to begin the new millennium, visits Jerusalem and prays at the Wailing Wall as part of an effort to resolve historic Roman Catholic differences with the Jews and to bring peace to the Middle East. **16** Mexico's Institutional Revolutionary Party (PRI) loses its first presidential election since the party was established in 1929. Opposition winner Vincente Fox Quesada promises changes in the way Mexico is governed.	**1** The American art world is stunned by the revelation that the two leading auction houses, Sotheby's and Christie's, conspired for years to fix fees. **2** Seattle opens its Experience Music Project, an unusual building by Frank Gehry housing interactive music exhibits. **3** The publication of the fourth volume in J. K. Rowling's Harry Potter series, *Harry Potter and the Goblet of Fire*, results in a marketing firestorm and debates about whether, at 700-odd pages, it should be considered an adult or children's book. **4** The antics of the cartoon characters Snoopy, the imaginative beagle, and Charlie Brown, the ever-hopeful loser, end with the death of *Peanuts* creator Charles Schulz, who stipulates that no one else may draw his characters. **5** White rap singer Eminem enjoys huge success with teenagers while drawing severe criticism from adults for the violence and sexual imagery in his songs and performances. **6** Popular entertainment spreads to the Internet through the explosive growth of a site called Napster, which offers users the opportunity to freely exchange music files at no cost. Music-industry companies sue Napster, charging copyright violation.	**11** The Tate Modern Gallery opens and immediately becomes a London destination immensely popular with the public. **12** Spanish architect Santiago Calatrava opens his Science Museum in Valencia, the centerpiece in a multibuilding cultural complex. **13** Dutch architect Rem Koolhaas, noted for his unconventional ideas about buildings and urban planning, wins the Pritzker Prize. Koolhaas was cited for the influence of his books on the role of contemporary architecture. **14** Gao Xingjian, a Chinese playwright and novelist living in exile in France, receives the Nobel Prize for literature. Although hailed as a key 20th-century Chinese dramatist, much of his work has been barred from the stage there since the 1980s. **15** Britain's Booker Prize goes to popular Canadian author Margaret Atwood for her novel *The Blind Assassin*, which concerns two sisters. Atwood, previously nominated three times, is the second Canadian to win the award. **16** Already immensely popular, British author J. K. Rowling reaches a worldwide audience with the publication of *Harry Potter and the Goblet of Fire*, the fourth in a series about a boy training to be a wizard.

Science & Technology		Miscellaneous		
America	Elsewhere	America	Elsewhere	
1 The Y2K problem, a fear that society will be disrupted by the failure of computer systems that did not recognize the changeover to a new century, does not materialize. Problems are minor and generally scattered. **2** Two rival teams, one private and one backed by the federal government, almost complete decoding the human genome, mapping the billions of chemical combinations that make up each human's chromosomes. Scientists around the world, but concentrated in the U.S., had been working on the project for more than 10 years. Interpreting the data will continue for years, with vast benefits expected, especially in understanding and curing disease. **3** NASA's Mars Global Surveyor finds evidence that there may be current sources of liquid water at or near the surface of Mars and that the planet once had numerous lakes and shallow seas. **4** The space-shuttle program's Radar Topography Mission achieves a breakthrough in the science of remote sensing and produces topographic maps of Earth that are 30 times as precise as the best currently available. **5** NASA's TRACE (Transition Region and Coronal Explorer) mission finds evidence of why the Sun's corona is so much hotter than its surface and sends back images of immense coils of hot, electrified gas, called coronal loops. **6** Scientists at the Fermi National Accelerator Laboratory confirm the	**10** Worldwide, the Y2K problem has much less impact than anticipated, after governments, organizations, and businesses spend billions of dollars to reprogram their computer systems. **11** The European Space Agency (ESA) sends aloft the third module for the International Space Station. Called the *Zvezda,* it is launched from Kazakhstan and provides much of the computing systems for the ISS. The ESA will also contribute a space laboratory and the Automated Transfer Vehicle for the project. **12** An international crew composed of an American commander and two Russian cosmonauts are the first to take up residence in the ISS. **13** A NASA spectrometer detects an Antarctic ozone hole that is three times bigger than the U.S. land mass and is the largest ever observed. Scientists believe that ozone-destroying gases are reaching a peak in the Earth's stratosphere. **14** The Near Earth Asteroid Rendezvous mission, launched by NASA, makes a close orbit of the asteroid Eros and sends images and data back to Earth. **15** The ESA and the European Union (EU) reach agreement on space policies that will benefit science and commerce in the EU. **16** The world focus on the AIDS epidemic is increasingly directed at Africa, where HIV/AIDS infection runs as high as 35% in some areas. In Africa, HIV infection is generally passed	**1** Stock-market indexes dip sharply, while the national economy slows after several years of rapid growth. **2** Alan Greenspan, widely credited for his powerful role in shaping the U.S. economy, is nominated for a fourth four-year term as chairman of the Federal Reserve Board. **3** James Heckman of the University of Chicago and Daniel McFadden of the University of California share the Nobel Prize for economics. They are recognized for developing methods of statistical analysis. **4** The Federal Trade Commission approves the $110 billion merger of America Online and Time Warner, which establishes the world's largest entertainment and media company. **5** Elian Gonzalez, a six-year-old Cuban refugee rescued at sea, becomes an international figure as anti-Castro family members in the U.S. attempt to gain custody rather than return him to his father in Cuba. Federal agents take him into custody in a raid on a Florida relative's home, and he eventually returns to Cuba with his father. **6** The tires on Ford's Explorer sport utility vehicle are blamed for numerous accidents and deaths, leading to the recall by tiremaker Firestone of millions of tires and to the filing of many damage lawsuits. **7** The detention of scientist Wen Ho Lee ends with the collapse of the federal	**16** Extravagant millennial celebrations around the world salute the new century. **17** South Korea's President Kim Dae Jung receives the Nobel Peace Prize for his efforts to promote human rights and democracy in South Korea and to reconcile with North Korea. His efforts include an historic visit to the North. **18** Britain's royal family basks in favorable media attention as Queen Mother Elizabeth turns 100 and Prince William, older son of Prince Charles, turns 18. **19** Demonstrators protesting against increasing globalization disrupt international monetary conferences in Washington, D.C., and Melbourne, Australia. **20** Environmentalists and conservationists mark the 30th anniversary of Earth Day with gatherings around the world. **21** Many blame global warming for both droughts, such as those in Africa, the Indian subcontinent, and North America, and floods, as in southern Africa and the southeastern U.S. **22** German and U.S. negotiators agree to establish a $5 billion fund, equally contributed by the German government and industry, to compensate victims of the Holocaust. **23** Pope John Paul II issues a papal apology for the errors made by the Roman Catholic Church during the past 200 years. **24** The Templeton Prize for Religious Progress, named for donor Sir John	**2000**

America

defense shield is that it might violate arms-control treaties.

7 As Pres. Clinton's power diminishes during the last months of his administration, that of his wife, Hillary Rodham Clinton, increases as she secures the Democratic nomination for the U.S. Senate from New York and then trounces her Republican opponent, Rick Lazio, in the election.

8 The Census Bureau launches the 2000 Census with one goal being a more complete and accurate count than was achieved in 1990. For the first time, Americans can indicate more than one race in their heritage.

9 In an important decision, the U.S. Supreme Court reaffirms the validity of *Miranda v. Arizona*, protecting people against self-incrimination.

10 In another decision, the Court holds unconstitutional a Nebraska state law banning late-term abortions, thereby invalidating such laws in 30 states.

Elsewhere

17 Peru's president, Alberto Fujimori, wins a third term in a fraud-tainted election, but scandals in his administration and widespread protests result in his resignation while on a trip to Japan.

18 In a historic breakthrough, the leaders of North and South Korea meet for the first time since the Korean War, even though a formal peace treaty has never been signed. Later, small groups of families separated by Korea's division are able to reunite for visits.

19 Congo (formerly Zaire) remains in turmoil as Laurent Kabila's government battles several different groups of rebels in a civil war that threatens to involve most the nations in southern and central Africa.

20 Tensions in Northern Ireland increase over the issue of disarmament by Catholic partisans, but Protestants and Catholics finally agree to govern together.

America

7 With the closing of the long-running *Cats*, Broadway theater looks for new musicals. The Disney adaptation of the opera *Aida,* with music by Elton John and Tim Rice, proves popular; *Seussical: The Musical,* based on characters from the Dr. Seuss books, receives extensive media attention.

8 Two serious films make a strong showing with audiences: *Traffic* explores the drug problem in the U.S. through a variety of characters and *Pollock,* directed by and starring Ed Harris, examines the difficult life of abstract expressionist painter Jackson Pollock. Both films are nominated for the best-picture Academy Award.

9 Julia Roberts's performance in *Erin Brockovich,* a movie based on a real-life crusading reformer, earns her a nomination for the Academy Award for best actress, while the film garners a best-picture nomination. Its director, Steven Soderbergh, also directs *Traffic.* Tom Hanks draws critical acclaim for his portrayal of a marooned crash survivor in *Cast Away.*

10 A new type of TV show, "reality-based" programming that seeks to capture real-life tension-filled situations, begins with *Survivor,* which generates outstanding ratings and several similar programs.

Elsewhere

17 Alan Ayckbourn's *Comic Potential,* a success in London, is also well-received off-Broadway in New York City.

18 Sales of fine art remain below the high prices of the late 1980s and early 1990s, but works of some artists still bring notable prices. Cezanne's *Still Life with Fruit and Pot of Ginger* auctions for $18 million in a London sale, while a Francis Bacon, *Portrait of George Dyer Talking,* establishes a new record for the artist, $6.6 million.

Science & Technology — America

existence of the subatomic tau neutrino, which physicists had anticipated for years. Additional experiments are needed to determine the mass of the neutrinos.

7 The National Academy of Sciences issues a cautionary report on the potential dangers of genetically engineered food, both crops and animals. Although the Academy found no health risks in existing products, it warned that problems might develop if laboratory strains bred with wild strains.

8 Studies indicate that American children are taking increased amounts of mood-altering psychiatric drugs, including antidepressants and stimulants. Critics condemn the overmedication of children, while supporters claims that many children suffer from severe problems that are helped by the drugs.

9 Computer giant Microsoft loses an important round in its defense against federal charges of monopolistic business practices when a federal judge holds that the company should be split into two parts. The company immediately appeals the decision.

Science & Technology — Elsewhere

through heterosexual contact.

17 Canadian researchers announce that transplants of insulin-producing cells hold out the possibility that diabetes can be cured.

18 Arvid Carlsson (Sweden), Paul Greengard (U.S.), and Eric Kandel (U.S.) share the Nobel Prize for physiology or medicine for advancing the understanding of "signal transduction in the nervous system."

19 Scientists in the U.S.— Alan Heeger and Alan MacDiarmid—and Japan— Hideki Shirakawa—share the Nobel Prize for chemistry for developing a conductive polymer, or type of plastic, that conducts electricity like a metal would.

20 The Nobel Prize for physics is shared three ways by Jack Kilby of the U.S. for inventing the computer chip, or integrated circuit, and Zhores Alferov of Russia and Herbert Kroemer of the U.S. for inventing components used in electronic devices.

Miscellaneous — America

government's charge that he may have passed nuclear-weapons secrets to China. His arrest had led to claims that he was targeted because of his Asian heritage.

8 Vermont becomes the first state to recognize the legality of same-sex "civil unions," commonly known as "gay marriages."

9 The western U.S. is ravaged by numerous forest fires, with well over 5 million acres burned during the year.

10 Tiger Woods rules in men's professional golf, winning three major championships—the U.S. and British opens and the PGA championship.

11 Venus Williams, only 20, dominates women's tennis, taking the Wimbledon and U.S. Open titles, as well as two gold medals in the Olympics. Men's star Pete Sampras sets a new record of 13 major titles by winning at Wimbledon.

12 The St. Louis Rams win professional football's Super Bowl, defeating the Tennessee Titans.

13 For the first time since the 1950s, major league baseball has a "subway" World Series with two New York teams. The American League Yankees take their crosstown rivals, the National League Mets, 4 games to 1.

14 The Los Angeles Lakers, led by Shaquille O'Neill and Kobe Bryant, capture the National Basketball Association championship over the Indiana Pacers, their first title since 1988.

15 The National Hockey League's New Jersey Devils triumph over the Dallas Stars in the Stanley Cup finals.

Miscellaneous — Elsewhere

Templeton, goes to physicist Freeman Dyson, who believes that "technology must be guided and driven by ethics."

25 The *Kursk*, a Russian nuclear submarine, sinks suddenly in the Barents Sea after an apparent onboard explosion, killing all 118 aboard. Russian President Putin is criticized for delays in accepting international offers of help.

26 An Air France Concorde passenger jet catches fire during takeoff and crashes, killing a total of 113. It is the first accident experienced by the Concorde fleet.

27 At the Summer Olympic Games in Sydney, Australia, Australian Cathy Freeman lights the Olympic torch and then becomes the first Aborigine to capture a gold medal when she wins the 400-meter race.

Index

470

Albany 1664:H1.
Albatross 1963:S7.
Albce, Edward (b.1928) 1959:A4, 1960:A11, 1962:A11, 1966:A11, 1975:A6.
Alberghetti, Anna Maria (b.1936) 1961:A12.
Albert, Lake 1864:M11, 1887:M5.
Albert, Prince (1819–61) (Brit.) 1861:H9.
Alberta 1905:H12.
Albert Hall 1871:A13.
Albert I (1848–1922) 1906:S5.
Albert I (1875–1934) (Belgium) 1909:H14.
Albright, Madeleine 1996:H9.
Alcazarquivir, Battle of 1578:H3.
Alchemist, The 1610:A4.
Alchemy 1606:S2.
Alcium 1798:A1.
Alcock, J. W. 1919:M11.
alcohol 1974:S6.
alcoholic beverages 1789:M4.
alcoholics 1951:S10.
Alcoholics Anonymous 1935:M5.
alcoholism 1948:S14.
Alcools 1913:A9.
Alcotl, Louisa May (1832–88) 1869:A2, 1871:A3.
Alder, Dankmar 1897:A3.
Alder, Kurt (1902–58) 1928:S18.
Aldine Press 1494:A4, 1495:A4, 1597:A3.
aldostorone 1960:S18.
Aldrich, Thomas Bailey (1836–1907) 1870:A6, 1874:A3.
Aldrin, Edwin "Buzz" (b.1930) 1966:S15, 1969:S1.
Aldrovandi, Ulisse (1522–1605) 1574:S1.
Alegría, Ciro (1909–67) 1975:A17.
Alekhine, Alexander (1892–1946) 1925:M15, 1927:M9, 1935:M10, 1937:M12.
"alert receiver" 1941:S13.
Aleutian Islands 1785:H7, 1943:H4.
Alexander, William (1726–83) 1773:S1.
Alexander I (1777–1825) (Russ.) 1801:H7, 1808:H6.
Alexander II (1818–81) (Russ.) 1855:H5, 1861:H10, 1881:H9.
Alexander I (1888–1934) (Yugoslavia) 1929:H14, 1934:H17.
Alexander Nevsky 1938:A17.
Alexanderson, Ernest F. (1878–1975) 1906:S4, 1916:S5, 1928:S2, 1929:S8.
"Alexander's Ragtime Band" 1911:A3.
Alexander VI (1481?–1503) (pope) 1493:H3, 1495:H1, 1502:H3.
Alexandretta 1939:H17.
Alexandria Quartet 1957:A17.
Alfano, Franco (1876–1954) 1914:A16, 1926:A20.
Alfie 1966:A26.
Alfonsin, Raúl Ricardo 1983:M18.
Alfonso XII (1857–85) (Span.) 1874:H6.
Alfonso XIII (1886–1941) (Span.) 1931:H8.
"Alfred Inciting the Saxons" 1847:A8.
Alfvén, Hannes (b.1908) 1939:S19, 1950:S12, 1970:S21.
algae 1855:S9.
algebra 1545:S4, 1591:S1, 1824:S4.
Algeciras Conference 1906:H8.
Alger, Horatio (1832–99) 1867:A2.
Algeria 1830:H4, 1881:H5, 1954:H18, 1955:H17, 1958:H10, 1959:H20, 1961:H21, 1962:H10.
Algerine War 1815:H2.
Ali Muhammad 1964:M10, 1971:M4, 1978:M5.

"Ali Baba and the Forty Thieves." 1885:A7.
Alice Adams 1921:A6.
Alice's Adventures in Wonderland 1865:A7.
Alien and Sedition Acts 1798:H2, 1798:H3, 1802:H2.
Alien Poll Tax Law 1921:H9.
Alien Registration Act 1940:H5, 1940:M2.
Allegory of Love: A Study in Medieval Tradition 1936:A22.
"Allegory of Painting" 1665:A3.
Allen, Bryan 1979:M8.
Allen, Ethan (1738–89) 1762:S1, 1775:H3.
Allen, Irwin (b.1916) 1972:A13, 1974:A2.
Allen, J. L. (1849–1925) 1900:A7.
Allen, Tom 1876:M10.
Allen, Woody (b.1935) 1966:A2, 1969:A10, 1977:A15, 1989:A1, 1992:A6.
Allen, Zachariah (1795–1822) 1821:S1, 1829:S3, 1834:S1.
Allende 1972:H12, 1973:H11.
Allende Gossens, Salvador (1908–73) 1970:H15.
allergy 1906:M10.
All For Love 1677:A1.
All God's Chillun Got Wings 1924:A4.
Alliance for Progress 1961:H3.
Allied Expeditionary Force 1943:H11.
Alliluyeva, Svetlana (b.1926) 1967:A7, 1986:M18.
All-India Muslim League 1906:H16.
"All in Love is Fair" 1973:A7.
All in the Family 1971:A3.
All Men Are Mortal 1946:A13.
All My Sons 1947:A6.
All Quiet on the Western Front 1929:A11.
All-Star Baseball Game 1933:M7.
Allston, Washington (1779–1843) 1804:A1, 1811:A1, 1819:A3.
All's Well That Ends Well 1602:A2.
All the King's Men 1946:A2.
All the President's Men 1974:A7.
All Women Are Like That 1790:A5.
Almanza, Battle of 1707:H4.
Alma River, Battle of 1854:H7.
Alma-Tadema, Lawrence (1836–1912) 1868:A8.
Almayer's Folly 1895:A9.
Almeida, Francisco de (1450?–1510) 1507:H3.
Almenara, Battle of 1709:H3.
Alonzo, Mateo (1878–) 1904:A15.
alpha rays 1903:S9.
alpha waves 1896:S14.
Alsace-Lorraine 1871:H6, 1911:H10, 1913:H21.
Alsop, George 1666:A1.
Also Sprach Zarathustra 1853:A9.
Altdorfer, Albrecht (1480?–1538) 1532:A3.
Alter, David (1807–81) 1854:S3.
alternating current 1867:S6, 1882:S3, 1886:S2, 1888:S3, 1888:S7, 1891:S3, 1904:S10.
Altman, Robert (b.1925) 1970:A1.
aluminum 1887:S5, 1889:S2.
Alvarez, Luis (b.1911) 1939:S6, 1943:S8.
Alvarez de Piñeda, Alonso 1519:H2.
Alzheimer's disease 1991:S6, 1994:S2.
Amadeus 1979:A23.
Amado, Jorge (b.1912) 1958:A26, 1966:A21, 1977:A20.
Amahl and the Night Visitors 1951:A10.
amalgam 1834:S4.

Amateur Athletic Club 1866:M9.
Amati, Andrea (1596–1684) 1564:A4.
Amba Alagi, Battle of 1895:H9.
Ambartsumian, Viktor A. (b.1908) 1958:S15.
Amberg, Battle of 1796:H6.
ambergris 1725:S1.
Ambroise, Peaco of 1563:H1.
Ambrosio, or the Monk 1796:A8.
Amelia 1752:A5.
America 1499:H1, 1507:H1.
America 1851:M5.
America Online 2000:M4.
Americana 1932:A1.
American Academy of Arts and Sciences 1780:A1, 1785:S5.
American Academy of Fine Arts 1795:A1.
American Academy of Sciences 1848:S3.
American Antiquarian Society 1812:A1.
American Anti-Slavery Society 1833:H3.
American Association for the Advancement of Science (AAAS) 1848:S1.
American Association of Retired Persons 1988:M1.
American Ballet Theater 1980:A8.
American Bible Society 1816:M1.
American Birth Control League 1921:M3.
American Board of Commissioners for Foreign Missions 1810:M2.
American Bowling Congress 1895:M7.
American Buffalo 1977:A3.
American Chemical Society 1876:S4.
American Chess Association 1857:M3.
"American Childers" 1757:M1.
American Communist Party 1919:H4.
"American Company" 1752:A4.
American Company of Booksellers 1801:M2.
American Dictionary of the English Language 1828:A2.
"American Eclipse" 1823:M2.
American Entomology; or Descriptions of the Insects of North America 1824:S1.
American Expeditionary Force 1917:H11.
American Federation of Labor 1886:M2, 1924:H7, 1935:M2, 1955:H4.
American First Party 1952:H5.
American Football League 1959:M5.
American Geological Society 1819:S2.
"American Gothic" 1930:A2.
American Graffiti 1973:A3.
American Grove, The 1785:S6.
American Hospital Association 1973:M9.
American Independent Party 1968:H8.
American Indian 1500:A1, 1587:M1, 1632:A1, 1643:A1, 1665:M1, 1799:A3, 1821:A1, 1837:A2, 1841:A4, 1850:A5, 1881:A4.
American Indian church 1660:M2, 1670:M1.
American Indian Movement 1973:H7.
American Institute of Architects 1857:A5.
Americanization of Emily, The 1964:A10.
American Journal of Sciences and Arts 1818:S1.
American Law Journal 1808:M1.

American League 1900:M6, 1903:M2, 1973:M12.
American Lung Association 1904:S1.
American Lutheran Church 1930:M5.
American Magazine and Historical Chronicle 1743:A1.
American Magazine and Monthly Chronicle, The 1757:A2.
American Medical Association 1847:S3, 1895:S6.
American Medical Botany 1817:S2.
American Mercury 1784:A2.
American Minerva, The 1793:A5.
American Museum 1842:M3.
American Naturalist 1867:S1.
American Nautical Almanac 1853:S3.
American Philosophical Society 1727:M1, 1743:S1, 1771:S1.
American Poems, Selected and Original 1793:A1.
American Psychological Assoc. 1891:S6.
American Radio Relay League 1915:S1.
American Railway Union 1894:H3.
American Review and Literary Journal 1799:A2.
American Revolution 1775:H2, 1781:H2, 1783:H1.
American Scholar, The 1837:A4.
Americans with Disabilities Act 1990:H5.
American Shakespeare Festival Theater 1955:A5.
American Shooter's Manual 1827:M2.
American Soap Box Derby 1959:M9.
American Society for the Prevention of Cruelty to Animals 1866:S6.
American Society for the Return of Negroes to Africa 1817:M3.
American Society of Civil Engineers 1852:S7.
American Society of Dental Surgeons 1840:S1.
American Society of Mechanical Engineers 1880:S5.
American Spelling Book, The 1783:M1.
American Sugar Refining Co. 1922:H5.
American Sunday School Union 1824:M5.
American Telephone and Telegraph 1925:S9, 1982:M1, 1985:S2.
American Tobacco Company 1911:H3.
American Tract Society 1817:M2.
American Tragedy, An 1925:A2.
American Turf Register and Sporting Magazine 1829:M2.
"American Turtle" 1775:S1.
American Unitarian Association 1961:M7.
American Way of Death, The 1963:M1.
American Weekly Mercury 1719:A1.
American Woman Suffrage Association 1869:H4.
America's Cup 1962:M8, 1983:M3.
"The America's Cup" 1851:M5.
"America's Sweetheart" 1909:A5.
"America the Beautiful" 1893:A1.
Amerika 1927:A14.
Ames, Aldrich 1994:H4.
Amiens, Treaty of 1802:H4.
Amin, Idi (b.1925?) 1971:H15, 1979:H20.
amino acid 1858:S9, 1901:S14, 1907:S7, 1922:S13, 1953:S7, 1961:S15.
Amis, Kingsley (b.1922) 1954:A18, 1986:A16.

ammonia 1786:S8, 1909:S4, 1918:S14, 1931:S16, 1932:S14.
Amnesty Act 1872:H1.
Amontons, Guillaume (1663–1705) 1687:S3, 1695:S2, 1699:S2, 1702:S1.
"Amos 'n' Andy" 1929:A10.
Ampère, André (1775–1836) 1825:S8.
amphibian airplane 1928:S5.
Amphitryon 1690:A3.
Amphitryon 38 1929:A17.
amplifier 1927:S4.
Amritsar, Treaty of 1809:H7.
Amsterdam 1672:H1.
Amtrak 1970:H5.
Amundsen, Roald (1872–1928) 1906:M6, 1911:M9, 1912:M10, 1928:M11.
Amur River 1858:H10.
analog computer 1930:S5.
Analysis of the Phenomena of the Human Mind 1825:M6.
analytical engine 1834:S5.
anaphylaxis 1903:S5.
Anatomie générale 1801:S5.
Anatomist, The 1931:A16.
anatomy 1543:S2, 1611:S3, 1615:S1, 1719:S2, 1805:S3, 1811:S2, 1865:S5.
Anatomy and Diseases of the Ear 1704:S2.
Anatomy of Plants, The 1682:S1.
Anatomy of the Brain 1810:S5.
"The Anatomy Lesson of Dr. Nicolaes Tulp" 1632:A3.
Ancón, Treaty of 1883:H13.
Andalusian Dog, An 1928:A12.
Anders, William (b.1933) 1968:S11.
Andersen, Hans Christian (1805–75) 1835:A3.
Anderson, Carl D. (b.1905) 1932:S1, 1936:S9, 1937:S2.
Anderson, Elizabeth Garrett 1866:M7.
Anderson, John B. (b.1922) 1980:H8.
Anderson, Leroy (1908–75) 1950:A8.
Anderson, Marian (b.1902) 1955:A3.
Anderson, Max 1903:M6, 1980:M5.
Anderson, Maxwell (1888–1959) 1924:A6, 1930:A10, 1935:A3, 1948:A11, 1949:A1.
Anderson, Philip (b.1924) 1977:S12.
Anderson, R. 1912:M15.
Andersonville 1955:A7.
And God Created Woman 1956:A21.
And Now For Something Completely Different 1972:A22.
Ando, Tadao 1995:S22.
André, Valérie 1976:M9.
Andrea Doria 1956:M13, 1981:S8.
Andre-Thomas, J. 1953:S10.
"Andrew Jackson" 1819:A2.
Andrew, Prince 1986:M16.
Andrews, Julie (b.1935) 1956:A3, 1964:A9.
Andrews, Roy C. (1884–1960) 1924:M13, 1926:S10.
Andrić, Ivo (1892–1975) 1945:A24.
Androboros 1714:A2.
"Andromache Mourning Hector" 1784:A5.
Andromaque 1667:A2.
Andromeda 1924:S2.
Andromeda nebula 1611:S1.
Andromeda Strain, The 1969:A16.
Andropov, Yuri 1982:H17, 1984:H10.
Andros, Sir Edmund (1637–1714) 1686:H1, 1689:H2.
androsterone 1931:S12.
Andrussovo, Treaty of 1667:H3.
And Suddenly It's Evening 1942:A22.

anemia 1920:S4, 1934:S11.
anesthesia 1842:S1, 1845:S1, 1846:S1, 1933:S10, 1972:S6.
anesthetic 1853:M7.
Anfinsen, Christian (1908–77) 1959:S7, 1972:S13.
AN-FO 1950:S9.
Angiolini, Gasparo (1723–96) 1761:A8.
Angkor, Cambodia 1998:S20.
Anglican Church 1705:M2, 1811:M5, 1976:M17.
Anglican parish 1706:M3.
Anglo-Egyptian Sudan 1899:H9, 1924:H21.
Angola 1574:H2, 1886:H12, 1890:H12, 1902:H17, 1961:H15, 1969:H19, 1975:H17, 1994:H21.
Angostura, Congress of 1819:H5.
"angry young men" 1956:A11.
animal behavior 1929:S6, 1951:S20, 1966:S21, 1973:S20.
Animal Biology 1927:S12.
Animal Crackers 1928:A7, 1930:A8.
Animal Farm 1945:A14.
animal hospital 1830:S5.
Animal Kingdom, Distributed According to Its Organization, The 1817:S5.
"animal magnetism" 1775:S6.
animated film 1909:M4, 1928:M1, 1937:A12, 1940:A13, 1968:A20, 1972:A10, 1977:A2, 1978:A9.
Ankara, Treaty of 1930:H11.
Ann 1806:A4.
"Annabel Lee" 1849:A4.
Anna Bolena 1830:A9.
Anna Christie 1921:A7.
Anna Karenina 1875:A6.
Annals of Scientific Botany 1858:S10.
Annam 1884:H12.
Annan, Kofi 1996:H19.
Annapolis Royal 1605:H1, 1710:H1, 1744:H1.
Annapurna 1978:M8.
Anne (1665–1714) (Brit.) 1702:H4.
Anne, Queen 1702:M6.
"Anne of Cleves" 1540:A1.
Anne of Cleves (1515–57) 1540:H3.
Anne of Green Gables 1908:A19.
Anne of the Thousand Days 1948:A11.
Annenberg, Walter 1991:A1.
Annie 1977:A7.
Annie Get Your Gun 1946:A4.
Annie Hall 1977:A15.
Annie Jane 1853:M5.
"Annie's Song" 1978:A17.
Ann McKim 1832:M2.
Ann Taylor 1806:A4.
Ann Veronica 1909:A8.
"An Occurrence at Owl Creek Bridge" 1891:A4.
anode 1833:S4.
Another Time 1940:A15.
Anouilh, Jean (b.1910) 1932:A17, 1944:A14, 1952:A21, 1959:A12, 1970:A23.
Anschluss 1933:H14, 1938:H13.
Ansermet, Ernest (1883–1969) 1919:A2.
antabuse 1951:S10.
Antarctic 1929:M1, 1998:S16.
Antarctica 1841:M5, 1844:S2, 1920:S11, 1939:M7, 1980:S10, 1988:M13, 1993:S8, 1998:S16.
Anthony, Susan B. (1820–1906) 1869:H4.
anthracite 1791:S5.
anthrax 1876:S12, 1881:S11, 1980:S11.
Anthropology and Modern Life 1928:S7.
antibiotics 1972:S8, 1972:S18.
antibiotic therapy 1928:S15.
antibodies 1940:S6.
Antic Hay 1923:A19.

anticoagulant 1916:S11.
Antietam, Battle of 1862:H7.
antigens 1940:S6.
Antigone 1944:A14.
antihistamine 1942:S15, 1944:S15, 1950:S7, 1957:S21.
antilymphocytic serum 1967:S12.
Anti-Masonic Party 1831:H2.
antimatter 1932:S1, 1951:S8, 1956:S3, 1979:S5.
Anti-Monopoly Party 1884:H2.
antineutron 1956:S3.
"anti-novel" 1957:A13, 1961:A21.
Antioch College 1853:M1.
"anti-play" 1958:A21.
Antiprognosticon 1642:S1.
antiprotons 1951:S8, 1959:S14.
Anti-Saloon League 1916:M2.
antiseptic technique 1848:S7, 1865:S8, 1865:S10, 1869:S4, 1877:S7, 1886:S8.
anti-slavery society 1823:M6.
anti-submarine device 1918:M6.
antitoxin laboratory 1894:S6.
Antoine, André (1858–1943) 1887:A8.
Antonioni, Michelangelo (b.1912) 1960:A20, 1964:A19, 1970:A24.
"Antony and Cleopatra" 1745:A5.
Anual, Battle of 1921:H13.
Anuszkiewicz, Richard (b.1930) 1967:A4.
"Anything You Can Do" 1946:A4.
Anzio 1944:H12.
Anzus Treaty 1951:H14.
aortic arches 1673:S2.
Apache Indians 1871:H4, 1885:H4, 1886:H2.
apartheid 1985:H4, 1986:H18.
ape 1968:M11.
apes 1849:S2.
Apianus, Petrus (1495–1552) 1524:S1.
Apocalypse Now 1979:A10.
Apollinaire, Guillaume (1880–1918) 1912:A13, 1913:A9, 1917:A14, 1917:A15.
Apollo Soyuz Test Project 1975:S10.
Apollo 8 1968:S11.
Apollo 9 1969:S9.
Apollo 11 1969:S1.
Apollo 12 1969:S10.
Apollo 13 1970:S14.
Apollo 14 1971:S9.
Apollo 15 1971:S11.
Apollo 16 1972:S10.
Apollo 17 1972:S11.
Apollo 18 1975:S10.
Apologia pro vita sua 1864:A5, 1864:M10.
Apothecaries Act 1815:M5.
Appalachia 1902:A16.
Appalachian Spring 1944:A6.
"*Appassionata*" 1804:A3.
Appert, Nicolas-François (1750?–1841) 1810:S4.
Applause 1970:A12.
Apple Computer 1982:S3, 1983:S11.
Appleton, Sir Edward V. (1892–1965) 1925:S17, 1947:S14.
Appleton layer 1925:S17, 1947:S14.
Appomattox Court House 1865:H4.
April Twilights 1903:A3.
"Apu" 1954:A20.
aqualung 1943:S14.
"Aquarius" 1967:A11.
Aqueduct 1941:M2.
Aquino, Benigno 1983:H14.
Aquino, Corazon 1986:H10, 1987:H15.
Arabian Nights' Entertainments 1885:A7.
Arabic 1915:H4.
Arab-Israeli War (1967) 1967:H14.

Arab-Israeli War (1973) 1973:H12, 1974:H12.
Arafat, Yasir (b.1929) 1969:H17, 1994:M9, 1996:H13, 1997:H19.
Arapaho Indians 1864:H9, 1865:H7.
Arbeau, Thoinot (1519–1595) 1588:A2.
Arber, Werner (b.1929) 1978:S12.
Arbuthnot, John (1667–1735) 1727:A3.
Arcaro, Eddie 1948:M3, 1952:M5.
Arc de Triomphe 1806:A5.
archaeology 1738:M4, 1808:M7, 1849:M7, 1857:M4, 1900:M11, 1918:M11, 1947:M13, 1974:M18, 1974:M20, 1975:M13, 1979:M1, 1982:S9, 1982:S13, 1984:A19, 1987:S10, 1987:S13, 1990:A12, 1991:A9, 1992:S5, 1993:S13, 1994:S7.
Archeological Institute of America 1879:S7.
Archer, William (1856–1924) 1923:A22.
Archers; or, the Mountaineers of Switzerland, The 1796:A4.
archery 1541:M3, 1828:M3.
architecture 1983:A5.
Arcimboldo, Giuseppe (1530?–1593) 1566:A3.
Arcis-sur-Aube, Battle of 1814:H5.
arc lighting 1881:S6.
Arcolo, Battle of 1796:H5.
Arden, John (b.1930) 1959:A18, 1960:A22.
Arecibo Observatory 1963:S5.
Arendt, Hannah (1906–75) 1958:A10.
Argo Merchant 1976:M2.
argon 1894:S7, 1904:S16, 1904:S17.
Argonaut I 1894:S1.
Argonaut II 1897:S2, 1898:S3.
"Argonauts" 1950:A20.
"Ariadne, Bacchus, and Venus" 1581:A2.
Arianna 1608:A3.
Arias Sanchez, Oscar 1987:H19.
Ariel 1962:S14.
Ariel 1965:A6.
Ariosto, Ludovico (1474–1533) 1502:A1, 1516:A2.
Aristide, Jean-Bortrand 1991:H12, 1992:H12, 1994:H11.
"Aristides" 1875:M4.
Aristotle 1661:S2.
"Aristotle Contemplating the Bust of Homer" 1653:A2.
arithmetic 1522:S1.
Arithmetica Logarithmica 1624:S2.
Arithmetick Vulgar and Decimal 1729:S1.
arithmetic textbook 1729:M1.
Arizona 1912:H2.
Arkansas 1682:H1, 1836:H2, 1861:H1, 1868:H2.
Arlen, Harold (1905–86) 1933:A6, 1939:A4.
Arlen, Michael (1895–1956) 1924:A15.
Armenia 1827:H6, 1894:H13, 1895:H11, 1909:H12, 1921:H25.
Armistice Day 1921:M2.
"Armory Show" 1913:A1.
Arms and the Man 1894:A7, 1984:A2.
Armstrong, Edwin H (1890–1954) 1914:S3, 1918:S1, 1933:S1.
Armstrong, Louis (1900–71) 1920:A7.
Armstrong, Neil (b.1930) 1966:S10, 1969:S1.
Armstrong, Scott (b.1945) 1979:A4.
Armstrong, Sir William (1810–1900) 1850:S3.
army 1906:M5.
Army, U.S. 1916:H5.
Army Air Corps 1926:M4.

Borges, Jorge Luis (b.1899)
1961:A15, 1970:A17.
Borgia, Cesare (1476–1507)
1502:H3.
Borglum, Gutzon (1867–1941)
1941:A1.
Boris Godunov 1825:A7, 1872:A3.
Bork, Robert 1987:H8.
Borman, Frank (b.1928) 1965:S10,
1968:S11.
Born, Max (1882–1970) 1926:S15,
1954:S18.
Borneo 1891:H11.
Born to Dance 1936:A9.
Born to Run 1975:A11.
Borodin, Aleksandr (1833–87)
1869:A7.
Borodino, Battle of 1812:H7.
boron 1808:S3, 1979:S19.
Borough, The 1945:A18.
Borromini, Francesco (1599–1667)
1631:A1.
Bort, Léon Teisserenc de
(1855–1913) 1900:S11.
Bosch, Carl (1874–1940)
1931:S16.
Bosch, Hieronymus (1450?–1516)
1495:A1.
Bosch, Robert (1861–1942) 1902:S8.
Bosnia 1718:H4, 1875:H9,
1908:H10, 1909:H13, 1993:H17,
1997:H10.
"Bosom Bottles" 1766:M1.
Bosperus 1841:H5.
Boston 1630:H1.
Boston 1928:A10.
"Boston" 1842:M1.
Boston Academy of Music 1832:A1.
Boston Americans 1904:M4.
Boston Athenaeum 1807:M1.
"Boston Blue" 1818:M1.
Boston Bruins 1973:M6.
Boston Female Medical School
1848:M6.
Boston Gazette 1719:A1.
"Boston Hymn" 1863:A5.
Bostonians, The 1886:A1.
Boston Massacre 1770:H1.
Boston Philharmonic Orchestra
1855:A5.
Boston Pops Orchestra 1980:A6,
1985:A10.
Boston Public Latin School
1635:M2.
Boston Public Library 1852:M4.
Boston Red Sox 1979:M4.
Boston Society for the Moral and
Religious Instruction of the Poor
1815:M3.
"Boston Strangler" 1967:M1.
Boston Symphony Orchestra
1881:A5.
Boston Tea Party 1773:H1,
1774:H1.
Boswell, James (1740–95) 1762:A2,
1763:A4, 1791:A7.
botanical gardens 1545:S2, 1610:S2,
1728:S1.
botany 1530:S3, 1672:S2, 1814:S1.
Botha, Louis (1862–1919)
1910:H16, 1915:H15.
Botha, Pieter Willem (b.1916)
1978:H24.
Bothe, Walther (1891–1957)
1929:S16, 1954:S18.
Botta, Mario 1995:A14.
Botticelli, Sandro (1444?–1510)
1494:A3.
bottlemaking 1903:S6.
Botvinnik, Mikhail 1946:M12.
Boulanger, Georgos Ernest
(1837–91) 1886:H7, 1887:H9,
1889:H9, 1891:H12.
Boulder 1936:M1.
Boule, Pierre (1861–1942)
1908:S13.
Boulez, Pierre (b.1925) 1946:A19,
1965:A23.

Boulogne, Edict of 1573:H1.
Boumedienne, Houari (1925?–78)
1965:H14, 1971:H22.
boundary level 1904:S13.
Bound East for Cardiff 1916:A7.
Bourne, Geoffrey (b.1909) 1933:S15,
1956:S16.
Boutros-Ghali, Boutros 1992:M24.
Bovet, Daniel (b.1907) 1944:S16,
1947:S12, 1957:S21.
bow 1595:M2.
Bowden, Don 1957:M4.
Bowditch, Nathaniel (1773–1838)
1799:S1, 1802:S2, 1806:S1,
1815:S1.
Bowdler, Thomas (1754–1825)
1818:A7.
Bowen, Elizabeth (1899–1973)
1938:A21.
bowling 1591:M1, 1895:M7,
1901:M3, 1942:M6, 1972:M3.
bowling green 1732:M1.
bowls 1611:M1.
Boxer Rebellion 1900:H1.
Boxers 1900:H16, 1901:H15.
Boxers, The 1898:H18.
Boxer Uprising 1900:H16,
1901:H12.
boxing 1719:M5, 1792:M10,
1810:M4, 1816:M4, 1849:M1,
1856:M9, 1860:M9, 1863:M5,
1865:M7, 1876:M10, 1882:M5,
1889:M5, 1892:M7, 1897:M3,
1899:M2, 1901:M11, 1921:M5,
1927:M4, 1975:M3, 1978:M5,
1983:S3.
Boyacá, Battle of 1819:H5.
boyars 1564:H4, 1584:H2, 1591:H2,
1606:H2, 1610:H3.
Boyer, Jean Pierre (1776–1850)
1818:H5.
Boyle, Robert (1627–91) 1660:S2,
1661:S2.
Boyle, W. A. (Tony) (b.1901)
1974:H7.
Boylston, Zabdiel (1679–1766)
1721:S4, 1722:S1.
Boyne, Battle of 1690:H3.
Boy Scouts of America 1907:M10,
1910:M6.
Boys from Brazil, The 1976:A10.
Boy's Will, A 1913:A2.
Brabham, Jack 1966:M16.
Bracebridge Hall 1822:A5.
Braddock, Edward (1695–1755)
1755:H1.
Braddock, James J. 1937:M8.
Bradford, William (1590–1657)
1621:H1, 1621:M1, 1622:A1,
1628:A1, 1630:A2, 1685:A1,
1690:S1, 1693:S1, 1725:M1.
Bradley, Bill 1999:H6, 2000:H1.
Bradley, James (1693–1762)
1728:S4.
Bradley, Omar N. (b.1893)
1944:H5.
Bradley, Thomas (b.1917)
1977:H10.
Bradstreet, Anne (1612?–1672)
1650:A1, 1678:A1.
Bradstreet, Charles 1738:M3.
Brady, Mathew B. (1823?–96)
1861:A1.
Braga, Teófilo (1843–1924)
1910:H11.
Bragg, Lawrence (1890–1971)
1915:S13.
Bragg, Sir William (1862–1942)
1912:S13, 1915:S13.
Brahe, Tycho (1546–1601) 1560:S1,
1563:S3, 1572:S1, 1573:S1,
1577:S1.
Brahms, Johannes (1833–97)
1854:A7, 1868:A3, 1877:A9,
1879:A11, 1883:A13.
Braid, James (1795–1860)
1841:S3.
Braille, Louis (1809–52) 1834:M6.

brain 1664:S3, 1802:S8, 1879:S10,
1888:S11, 1905:S11, 1949:S16,
1957:S19.
Brain Drain 1964:M13.
Braine, John (b.1922) 1957:A12.
Brain Mechanism and Intelligence
1929:S9.
brain surgery 1920:S3.
Bramah, Joseph (1748–1814)
1784:S8.
Bramante, Donato 1505:A1,
1514:A1.
Branch Davidians 1993:M2.
Brancusi, Constantin (1876–1957)
1908:A15, 1943:A16.
Brand, Vance (b.1931) 1975:S10.
Brandeis, Louis D. (1856–1941)
1916:M5.
Brandenberger, Edwin 1912:M9.
Brandenburg 1675:H1, 1679:H2,
1681:H4, 1701:H3.
Brandenburg concertos 1721:A4.
Brando, Marlon (b.1924) 1954:A13,
1979:A10.
Brandt, Willy (b.1913) 1969:H20,
1974:H17.
Brandywine, Battle of 1777:H3.
Brant, Sebastian (1458?–1521)
1494:A2.
Braque, Georges (1882–1963)
1908:A13, 1911:A15, 1912:A12,
1912:A13, 1937:A22, 1939:A22.
Brasilia 1960:M9.
brass 1802:S4.
Brattain, Walter (b.1902) 1948:S1,
1956:S13.
Brattle, Thomas (1658–1713)
1680:S1.
Braun, Karl F. (1850–1918)
1897:S10, 1909:S9.
Braun, Wernher von (1912–77)
1934:S12, 1945:S12, 1949:S8.
Braveheart 1995:A19.
Brave New World 1932:A14.
Brazil 1500:H3, 1654:H3, 1777:H5,
1807:H6, 1822:H6, 1837:H6,
1889:H12, 1903:H14, 1937:H19,
1987:H16, 1992:M19.
Breakfast at Tiffany's 1958:A6,
1961:A9.
Breakfast of Champions 1973:A13.
"Breakfast-Table" 1858:A3.
breast cancer 1998:S5.
breathing 1905:S11.
Breathless 1960:A15.
Brecht, Bertolt (1898–1956)
1928:A14, 1930:A15, 1939:A18,
1944:A16.
Brecht, Weill, and Hindemith
1929:A14.
Breckinridge, John C. (1821–75)
1856:H4, 1860:H1.
Breda 1625:H2, 1637:H3.
Breda, Peace of 1667:H1.
breeder-reactor 1949:S4, 1951:S1,
1972:S5.
Breintnall, Joseph 1738:S4,
1746:S3.
Breisach, Battle of 1638:H4.
Breitenfeld, Battle of 1631:H1,
1642:H2.
Breitkopf, Johann (1719–1794)
1750:A6.
Brel, Jacques (1929–1978)
1977:A26.
Brenner, Lucy 1812:M2.
Brenner Pass 1772:M3.
Brent, Margaret (1600?–1671?)
1648:M3, 1869:M2.
Brentano 1838:A8.
Bresson 1962:A20, 1969:A24.
Brest-Litovsk, Treaty of 1918:H8.
Brethren, The 1979:A4.
Breton, André (b.1869)
1934:A14.
Breuer, Josef (1842–1925) 1880:S7,
1893:S6.
Brewsie and Willie 1946:A3.

Brewster, Jr., John (1766–1854)
1801:A3.
Brewster, Sir David (1781–1868)
1811:S5, 1816:S4, 1831:S4,
1855:S7.
Breyer, Stephen G. 1994:M4.
Brezhnev, Leonid Ilyich (b.1906)
1964:H11, 1977:H23, 1982:H17.
Briand, Aristide (1862–1952)
1929:H18.
Briand-Kellogg Pact 1928:H6.
bricks 1612:S1.
bridal suite 1844:M2.
Bride of Innisfallen, The 1955:A12.
"The Bride of the Wind" 1914:A18.
bridge, portable 1941:M13.
Bridge of San Luis Rey, The
1927:A2.
Bridge on the Drina, The
1945:A24.
Bridge over the River Kwai, The
1957:A20.
Bridger, James 1824:M3.
Bridges, Alan (b.1927) 1973:A19.
Bridges, Calvin (1889–1938)
1938:S12.
Bridges, Robert (1844–1930)
1913:A12, 1930:A20.
Bridgman, Percy (1882–1961)
1908:S7, 1931:S7, 1946:S10.
Bridie, James (1888–1951)
1931:A16.
Brief Description of New York, A
1670:A1.
*Briefe and True Report of the New
Found Land of Virginia,*
A1588:M1.
Brief Encounter 1946:A14.
Briggs, Henry (1561–1630) 1617:S3,
1624:S2, 1633:S3.
Briggs, Ronald 1974:M13.
Bright, Richard (1789–1858)
1827:S6.
Bright Eyes 1934:A9.
Brighton Rock 1938:A19.
Bright's disease 1827:S6.
Brihuega, Battle of 1710:H3.
Brink's 1950:M7.
Bristow, Benjamin H. (1832–96)
1875:H14.
Britain 1947:H12, 1971:S14,
1975:S14.
British African Company 1723:H1.
British and Foreign Bible Society
1804:M2.
British Archaeological Association
1843:M6.
British Broadcasting Corporation
1922:S9.
British Columbia 1858:H11,
1871:H10.
British East Africa 1920:H14.
British Empire 1798:H6, 1833:H5,
1910:H16, 1931:H6.
*British Gazette and Sunday
Monitor, The* 1780:M3.
British Guiana 1966:H18.
British Kaffraria 1847:H6.
British Mariner's Guide, The
1763:S2.
British Museum 1823:A6,
1911:M12.
British Nationality Act 1948:H22.
British North America Act
1867:H10.
British Open 1953:M9.
British Open Golf Championship
1860:M10.
British South Africa Company
1889:H13, 1893:H14.
Britten, Benjamin (b.1913)
1937:A16, 1945:A18, 1949:A12,
1951:A18, 1960:A24, 1962:A16,
1963:A20, 1964:A15, 1973:A20.
Broadway 1901:A1.
"Broadway" 1935:A5.
"Broadway Boogie Woogie"
1943:A18.

477

Brock, Lou (b.1939) 1977:M4, 1979:M4.
Brod, Max (1884–1968) 1916:A23.
Brodsky, Joseph 1987:A14.
Brody, Jr., Michael James 1970:M9.
Broglie, Louis Victor de (b.1892) 1923:S14, 1924:S8, 1929:S19.
"Broken Pitcher" 1773:A5.
bromide paper 1878:S6.
Brøonsted, Johannes (1879–1947) 1923:S9.
Brontë, Anne (1820–49) 1847:A4.
Brontë, Charlotte (1816–55)1847:A4.
Brontë, Emily (1818–48) 1847:A4.
Brooke, Edward W. (b.1919) 1966:H10.
Brooke, Rupert (1887–1915) 1915:A19.
Brooker, William 1719:A1.
Brook Farm 1841:M4.
Brookhaven 1954:S7.
Brookhaven National Laboratory 1950:S8.
Brooklyn-Battery Tunnel 1950:M8.
Brooklyn Bridge 1883:M5.
"Brooklyn Bridge" 1918:A7.
Brooklyn Dodgers 1953:M5.
Brooks, Garth 1991:A2, 1996:A6.
Brooks, James (b.1906) 1951:A8.
Brooks, Mel (b.1926?) 1968:A6, 1974:A10.
Brooks, Phillips (1835–93) 1868:A1.
Brooks, Preston S. (1819–57) 1856:H3.
Brooks, Van Wyck (1886–1963) 1908:A2.
"Brother, Can You Spare a Dime?" 1932:A1.
Brothers Karamazov, The 1879:A7.
Brother Sun, Sister Moon 1973:A19.
Brougham, Henry (1778–1868) 1802:A3, 1827:M6.
Brown, A.W. 1919:M11.
Brown, C.B. 1799:A3, 1800:A4.
Brown, Charles Brockden (1771–1810) 1798:A1.
Brown, Claude (b.1937) 1965:A11.
Brown, Dee 1981:A1.
Brown, Ebenezer 1819:M1.
Brown, Ernest W. (1866–1938) 1919:S8.
Brown, George H. (b.1908) 1936:S7.
Brown, Herbert (b.1912) 1979:S19.
Brown, John (1800–59) 1856:H2, 1859:H2.
Brown, Michael S. 1985:S6.
Brown, Olympia 1860:M3.
Brown, Robert (1773–1858) 1810:S6, 1828:S4, 1831:S5.
Brown, William Hill (1765–93) 1789:A2.
Brown, William (1752–92) 1778:S2.
Browne, Charles F. (1834–67) 1862:A4.
Browne, Patrick (1720?–90) 1756:S2.
Browne, Sir Thomas (1605–82) 1646:S1.
Brownian movement 1828:S4, 1905:S13, 1923:S4.
Browning 1918:S2.
Browning, Elizabeth Barrett 1850:A7, 1933:A15.
Browning, John M. (1855–1926) 1911:S5.
Browning, Robert 1841:A6, 1844:A7, 1868:A4, 1933:A15.
Browning, automatic pistol 1911:S5.
Browning revolvers 1900:M10.
Brubeck, Dave (b.1920) 1951:A2.
Bruce, James (1730–94) 1771:H3.

Bruce, Patrick Henry (1880–1937) 1917:A9.
Bruce, Philip Alexander 1665:A1.
Bruckner, Anton (1824–96) 1864:A2, 1873:A5.
Brueghel the Elder, Pieter (1525?–1569) 1553:A1, 1563:A2, 1566:A4, 1567:A1.
Bruhn, Erik (b.1928) 1967:A22.
Brunei 1888:H12, 1984:H20.
Brunfels, Otto (1488–1534) 1530:S3.
Brüning, Heinrich (1885–1970) 1930:H9, 1932:H14.
Brunschwig, Hieronymus (1450–1512) 1497:S1.
Brush, Charles (1849–1929) 1877:S1, 1879:S6.
Bryan, William Jennings (1860–1925) 1894:H5, 1896:H3, 1900:H6, 1908:H7, 1915:H8.
bubble chamber 1952:S7, 1960:S15.
bubonic plague 1492:M1, 1563:M1, 1575:M2, 1592:M2, 1599:M1, 1603:M1, 1625:M1, 1634:M4, 1655:M1, 1672:M1, 1711:M2, 1720:M2, 1787:M3, 1792:M8, 1894:S9, 1895:S12.
Buchan, John (1875–1940) 1915:A16.
Buchanan, James (1791–1868) 1856:H4, 1857:H4, 1859:H3.
Bucharest, Treaty of 1913:H17.
Buch der Lieder 1827:A5.
Büchner 1947:A13.
Buchner, Eduard (1860–1917) 1907:S12.
Büchner, Georg (1813–37) 1925:A18.
Buck, Pearl (1892–1973) 1931:A3, 1938:A3.
Buddenbrooks 1901:A8.
Buddha 1922:A15.
Buddhists 1965:M7.
budding 1857:S4.
Budge, Don 1938:M7.
budget, balanced 1997:H6.
Budget and Accounting Act 1921:H2.
Budinot, Elias 1828:M1.
Buell, Abel (1741?–1822) 1764:M1, 1769:S1, 1783:S1.
Buena Vista, Battle of 1847:H1.
Buenos Aires 1536:H5.
Buffet, Bernard (b.1928) 1955:A19.
Buganda 1900:H22.
Bugatti, Ettore (1881–1947) 1909:S8.
Bugliosi, Vincent (b.1934) 1975:A2.
Bulfinch, Charles (1763–1844) 1792:A4, 1795:A4, 1811:A2, 1816:A1.
Bulgakov, Mikhail (1891–1940) 1967:A23.
Bulganin, Nikolai Aleksandrovich (1895–1975) 1947:H20, 1955:H13.
Bulgaria 1885:H7, 1944:H10, 1946:H18.
Bulge, Battle of the 1944:H5.
Bull, Dixy 1632:M1.
Bull, John 1727:A3.
bulldozer 1923:S7.
Bull Moose Party 1912:H6.
Bull Run, First Battle of 1861:H5.
Bull Run, Second Battle of 1862:H6.
Bülow 1900:H13, 1909:H9.
Bunche, Ralph (1904–71) 1948:H2.
bundling 1785:M1.
Bunin, Ivan Alekseyevich (1870–1953) 1925:A23.
Bunker Hill, Battle of 1775:H5.
bunny hug 1912:M2.
Bunsen, Robert (1811–99) 1834:S6, 1855:S8, 1857:S6, 1859:S7, 1868:S5, 1870:S8, 1887:S8.

Bunsen burner 1855:S8.
Buñuel, Luis (b.1900) 1928:A12, 1967:A21, 1972:A22.
Bunyan, John (1628–1688) 1678:A2, 1681:A3, 1684:A3, 1906:M1.
Buonarrotti, Michelangelo (1475–1564) 1496:A1, 1498:A1, 1501:A1, 1504:A1, 1504:A2, 1508:A2, 1512:A1, 1534:A1, 1536:A2, 1545:A1, 1555:A1, 1557:A1, 1575:A1, 1964:A8, 1972:A20.
Burbage, James (1530?–97) 1576:A1.
Burbank, Luther (1849–1926) 1871:S2, 1914:S5.
Burchfield, Charles (1893–1967) 1946:A11.
Burckhardt, Jakob (1818–97) 1812:M6, 1860:A8.
Burden, Henry (1791–1871) 1820:S2, 1835:S1.
Bureau of Air Commerce 1926:H9.
Burger, Warren Earl (b.1907) 1969:H5, 1986:M2.
Burgess, Anthony (b.1917) 1962:A15.
Burgess, Rt. Rev. John Melville (b.1909) 1962:M1.
"The Burghers of Calais" 1884:A11.
Burgoyne, John (1722–92) 1777:H2.
"Burial at Ornans" 1849:A6.
"The Burial of Count Orgaz" 1586:A2.
Burke, Bernard (b.1928) 1955:S6.
Burke, Edmund (1729–97) 1790:M3.
Burke, Joe (1884–1950) 1929:A6.
Burkersdorf, Battle of 1762:H4.
burlesque 1929:A5.
Burlingame Treaty 1868:H4, 1879:H2.
Burma 1765:H6, 1824:H6, 1826:H5, 1852:H8, 1853:H6, 1900:H24, 1943:H5, 1945:H12, 1948:H14.
Burma Road 1940:H26, 1942:H15.
Burne, Ethel 1916:M3.
Burne-Jones, Edward Coley (1833–98) 1884:A12.
Burnet, Sir Frank (b.1899) 1953:S18, 1955:S13, 1959:S19, 1960:S21.
Burnet, William (1688–1729) 1720:H1.
Burnett, Frances E.H. (1849–1924) 1886:A5.
Burney, Charles (1726–1814) 1776:A4.
Burney, Fanny (1752–1840) 1778:A2, 1782:A6, 1796:A7.
Burns, Alexander 1833:M7.
Burns, Robert (1759–96) 1786:A4, 1790:A6, 1794:A7.
Burns, Tommy 1908:M5.
Burr, Aaron (1756–1836) 1800:H2, 1801:H1, 1804:H2, 1806:H2, 1807:H2.
Burrell, Col. Harry 1958:M5.
Burroughs, Edgar Rice (1875–1950) 1914:A2.
Burroughs, John 1902:M2.
Burroughs, William (b.1914) 1953:A1, 1959:A10.
Burroughs, William S. (1857–98) 1888:S1.
Burt, William A. (1792–1858) 1829:S1.
Burton, Richard Francis (1821–90) 1854:M7, 1858:M4, 1885:A7.
Burton, William (1865–1954) 1912:S8.
Burundi 1962:H14.
Bury My Heart at Wounded Knee 1981:A1.
buses 1905:M9, 1966:M6.

Bush, George (b.1924) 1980:H8, 1984:H1, 1985:H3, 1988:H1, 1989:H1, 1990:H1, 1991:S4, 1992:H1.
Bush, George W. 1998:H9, 1999:H6, 2000:H1–3, 5.
Bush, Vannevar (1890–1974) 1930:S5, 1941:S9.
Bushnell, David (1742–1824) 1775:S1, 1776:S1.
Butaritari 1942:H6, 1943:H10.
Butch Cassidy and the Sundance Kid 1969:A12.
Butcher Boy, The 1917:A11.
Butenandt, Adolf (b.1903) 1929:S15, 1931:S12, 1934:S18, 1939:S21.
Butler, Andrew P. 1856:H3.
Butler, Samuel (1835–1902) 1863:A12, 1872:A6, 1903:A13.
Butowaki, Bob 1957:M9.
Butter, Nathaniel 1621:M3.
Butterfield 8 1935:A6.
Butterick, Ebenezor 1863:M2.
Button, Richard (Dick) 1950:M3.
Buxar, Battle of 1764:H3.
Buxtehude, Dietrich (1637–1707) 1668:A1, 1705:A4.
Bye Bye Birdie 1960:A6.
By Jupiter 1942:A2.
Bykovsky, Valory (b.1934) 1963:S16, 1976:S15, 1978:S19.
Byrd, Harry F. (1887–1966) 1960:H9.
Byrd, Richard E. (1888–1957) 1926:M7, 1929:M1, 1946:M7.
Byrd, William (1674–1744) 1728:S3, 1737:H1.
Byrne, Jane M. (b.1934) 1979:H5.
Byron (George Gordon), Lord (1788–1824) 1807:A5, 1812:A4, 1819:A6, 1834:A4.
Cabaret 1966:A15, 1972:A4.
Cabbages and Kings 1904:A6.
Cabell, James Branch (1879–1958) 1919:A9, 1921:A9.
Cabeza de Vaca, Alvar Núñez (1490?–1557?) 1528:H1, 1536:H1, 1542:A1.
Cabham, Alan 1926:M10.
Cabinet Dictionary, The 1803:A2.
Cabinet of Dr. Caligari, The 1919:A12.
Cable, George Washington (1844–1925) 1879:A4, 1880:A3.
cable cars 1873:S3
cable television 1983:A2, 1987:A3.
Cabot, John (1450?–98) 1497:H1, 1498:H1.
Cabot, Sebastian (1483?–1557) 1527:H2.
Cabral, Pedro Alvares (1467?–1520?) 1500:H3.
Cabrillo, Juan Rodriguez (d.1543) 1542:H1.
Cabrini, Mother Frances X. (1850–1917) 1946:M1.
Cadillac, Antoine de la Mothe (1658?–1730) 1701:H1.
cadmium battery 1908:S4.
Cadwalader, Thomas (1708?–99) 1745:S1.
Caesar and Cleopatra 1901:A10.
Caesarean section 1500:S1.
Caetano, Marcollo (b.1906) 1968:H18.
Cagney, James (1904–86) 1942:A4.
Cain, James (b.1892) 1934:A10, 1941:A11, 1942:A17.
Caine Mutiny, The 1952:A6.
Cajal, Santiago Ramon y (1852–1934) 1906:S13.
Calais 1558:H1, 1564:H2, 1596:H2.
calculator 1644:S3, 1944:S1, 1947:S2.
calculus 1647:S2, 1675:S2, 1690:S2, 1695:S1, 1742:S3, 1751:S4, 1780:S3.

Calcutta 1757:H2, 1911:H13.
Calder, Alexander (1898–1976) 1928:A3.
Caldwell, Erskine (b.1903) 1932:A11, 1933:A5.
Caldwell, Taylor (b.1900) 1946:A1.
calendar 1582:M2, 1751:M4.
Calepino, Ambrogio (1435–1511) 1502:A4.
Calhoun, John C. (1782–1850) 1825:H1, 1828:H1, 1844:H1.
California 1847:H2, 1849:H3, 1964:M2, 1978:H8.
California missioin 1769:A2.
California Suite 1976:A13.
calla lily 1937:M7.
Callaghan, James (b.1912) 1976:H21.
Callaghan, Morley 1983:A12.
Calley, William L. (b.1943) 1969:H8.
Call of the Wild 1903:A1.
Calloway, Cab (1907–94) 1967: A3.
Call to the Unconverted, A 1664:A1.
Calmette, Albert (1863–1933) 1923:S12.
calorimeter 1870:S8, 1887:S8.
calotype 1845:A9.
"Calumny" 1494:A3.
Calvert, 2nd Lord Baltimore, Cecilius (1605?–75) 1634:H1.
Calvin, John (1509–64) 1532:M1, 1566:A3, 1620:M1.
Calvin, Melvin (b.1911) 1961:S10.
Calvinism 1555:H3.
Calvinist Reformation 1541:M2.
Cambodia 1863:H16, 1966:H3, 1970:H4, 1975:H16, 1979:H14, 1980:H15.
Cambrai, League of 1508:H1, 1510:H1.
Cambrai, Treaty of 1529:H1.
Cambridge University 1571:M1.
Camden, Battle of 1780:H3.
Camelot 1960:A6.
camel walk 1912:M2.
cameo glass 1845:A6.
camera 1888:M2.
camera obscura 1568:S1.
"cameraphone" 1906:S3.
Camerarius, Rudolph (1665–1721) 1694:S1.
Camerata 1580:A2.
Camera Work 1903:A4.
Cameroon 1894:H11, 1960:H20.
Camilla 1796:A7, 1852:A8.
"Camille, The Green Dress" 1866:A10.
Camino Real 1953:A6.
Camões, Luis Vaz de (1524?–1580) 1572:A1.
Camp, Walter 1889:M4.
Campbell, Lt. Douglas 1918:M3.
Campbell, Kim 1993:H23.
Campbell, Malcolm (1885–1948) 1933:M10, 1939:M18.
Campbell-Bannerman, Henry (1836–1908) 1906:H14.
Camp Fire Girls 1910:M6.
Campion, Thomas (1567–1620) 1601:A1.
Campo Formio, Treaty of 1797: H2.
"Camptown Races" 1850:A3.
Camus, Albert (1913–60) 1942:A14, 1956:A17, 1994:A12.
Canada 1837:H7, 1840:H5, 1867:H10, 1999:H10.
Canada Constitutional Act 1791:H6.
Canadensium Plantarum 1635:S2.
Canadian Pacific Railway 1881:M7.
"Canadians Opposite Lens" 1919:A19.
Canaletto (1697–1768) 1720:A2.

Canal Zone 1979:H19.
Canberra 1908:H18, 1927:H15.
cancer 1782:S2, 1898:S1, 1910:S3, 1913:S15, 1926:S17, 1941:S3, 1943:S6, 1944:S8, 1949:S2, 1951:S4, 1952:S2, 1956:S8, 1957:S16, 1958:S2, 1964:M1, 1966:S20, 1969:M7, 1971:S4, 1971:S5, 1973:S8, 1974:S2, 1974:S4, 1974:S8, 1975:S3, 1975:S8, 1977:S5, 1977:S8, 1978:S3, 1978:S5, 1978:S6, 1978:S14, 1979:S1, 1979:S3, 1979:S6.
cancer-causing virus 1966:S17, 1975:S12.
cancer of the thyroid 1941:S12.
Cancer Ward 1968:A15.
Candida 1903:A8, 1759:A4.
Canetti, Elias 1981:A14.
Cannery Row 1945:A8.
Cannes (France) Film Festival 1946:A14, 1997:A22.
canning 1820:S1.
Cannon, Walter B. (1871–1945) 1911:S2, 1932:S4, 1942:S12.
cannons 1762:S1.
Cano, Juan Sebastian del (1476–1526) 1519:H4.
canoeing 1865:M8.
Canova, Antonio (1757–1822) 1779:A5, 1801:A10.
cans 1825:S4.
Canterbury, Archbishop of 1982:M18.
Canterbury, Cathedral at 1503:A1.
Canterbury Tales 1972:A22.
Canticle of the Rose, The 1949:A17.
Cantiones sacrae 1619:A1.
Canton 1856:H6, 1857:H8.
Cantor, Eddie (1892–1964) 1928:A12.
Cantor, Georg (1845–1918) 1872:S6, 1873:S4.
Cantor, Moritz (1829–1920) 1896:S9.
Capablanca, José Raoul (1888–1942) 1921:M10.
capacitor 1745:S3.
Cape Breton Island 1713:H3.
Cape Cod 1602:H1, 1620:H1.
Cape Colony 1834:H4.
Cape St. Vincent, Battle of 1797:H5.
Capetown 1652:H4.
Cape Verde 1975:H17.
capital punishment 1823:M23, 1941:M6, 1955:M12, 1965:M17, 1973:M2, 1973:M18, 1977:M5.
Capitol 1815:A1.
Capone, Alphonse ("Scarface Al") 1931:M5.
Caporetto, Battle of 1917:H13.
Capote, Truman 1951:A11, 1958:A6, 1966:A12.
Capp, Al (1909–79) 1934:A11.
capricci 1801:A8.
"The Caprices" 1799:A5.
Captain 1870:M11.
"The Captain and the Kids" 1912:A3.
Captain Jan: A Story of Ocean Tugboats 1942:A19.
Captain Jinks of the Horse Marines 1901:A6.
Captain of Köpenick, The 1931:A13.
"Captain Samuel Chandler" 1780:A2.
Capuchins 1526:M1.
car 1885:M5, 1901:M12.
Carabobo, Battle of 1821:H4.
Caravaggio (1573–1610) 1597:A1.
Caraway, Mrs. Hattie T. 1923:M7.

carbohydrate 1937:S19, 1970:S20.
carbon 1858:S8, 1874:S7.
carbon dioxide 1648:S1, 1905:S11.
carbon-filament incandescent lamp 1879:S9.
carbon-13 1946:S8.
carbon-14 1947:S7.
carborundum 1891:S7.
carbuncular fever 1569:M1.
"Carceri d'invenzione" 1745:A6.
Cardenas, Garcia Lopez de 1540:H1.
Cárdenas, Lázaro (1895–1970) 1934:H18.
cardiac catheterization 1956:S14.
Cardinal College 1525:M2.
Cardioversion 1962:S5.
Cardona, Gerolama (1501–76) 1545:S4.
card playing 1618:M2.
Caretaker, The 1960:A21.
Carey, Mathew (1760–1839) 1785:A4, 1786:A1, 1790:A4, 1801:M2.
caricature 1566:A3.
carillon 1745:A2.
Carlisle Indian School 1879:M1.
Carlists 1834:H6, 1872:H7.
Carlos I (1863–1908) (Port.) 1908:H9.
Carlson, Chester (1900–68) 1938:S1.
Carlton, Steve 1983:M8.
Carlyle, Thomas (1795–1881) 1836:A8.
Carmen 1846:A8, 1875:A7.
Carmichael, Hoagy (1899–81) 1929:A3, 1931:A4, 1981:A4.
Carmona, Antonio (1869–1951) 1928:H19.
Carné, Marcel (b.1903) 1930:A14.
Carnegie, Andrew (1835–1919) 1875:M3, 1880:M1, 1904:M2, 1911:M1.
Carnegie libraries 1880:M1.
Carnera, Primo 1934:M6.
Carnos, Peter (1762–1822) 1784:S4.
Carnival 1961:A12.
"Carnival Evening" 1886:A7.
Carnival of Animals 1886:A12.
Carnot, Sadi (1796–1832) 1824:S8.
Carnot, Sadi (1837–94) 1894:H16.
Carol I (1839–1914) (Rumania) 1866:H9.
Carol II (1893–1953) (Rumania) 1930:H17.
Carolina 1669:H1, 1713:H1, 1837:H3.
Caroline Fry Marriage Association 1852:M3.
Caroline Islands 1947:H10.
Carothers, Wallace (1896–1937) 1934:S2.
Carousel 1945:A9.
Carpenter, M. Scott (b.1925) 1962:S11.
Carpentier, George 1921:M5.
carpetbaggers 1870:H4, 1874:H1, 1874:H4, 1877:H4.
Carpetbaggers, The 1961:A3.
carpets 1845:S3.
Carr, Benjamin (1769–1831) 1796:A4, 1800:A3.
Carrà 1917:A20.
Carracci, Annibale (1560–1609) 1604:A3.
Carranza, Venustiano (1859–1920) 1915:H10, 1920:H16.
Carrel, Alexis 1912:S10, 1935:S19, 1936:S2.
Carrera, Rafael (1814–65) 1840:H7.
Carrie 1974:A5.
Carrier, Willis (1876–1950) 1901:S9, 1911:S3.
Carroll, Lewis (1832–98) 1865:A7, 1872:A4.

cars 1900:M3, 1917:M8, 1956:M5, 1966:M6.
Carson, Johnny (b.1925) 1962:A13, 1992:A1.
Carson, Rachel (1907–64) 1951:S3, 1962:S2.
Cars That Ate Paris, The 1974:A20.
Cartagena 1740:H2.
Carter, Jr., James Earl (Jimmy) (b.1924) 1976:H7, 1976:H8, 1977:H1, 1977:H4, 1977:H7, 1977:H9, 1977:H13, 1978:H3, 1978:H4, 1978:H6, 1978:H10, 1980:H8.
Cartier, Jacques (1491–1557) 1534:H1, 1536:H2.
Cartier-Brosson, Henri (b.1908) 1979:A14.
Cartwright, Alexander Joy 1845:M2.
Caruso, Enrico 1910:A2.
Carver, Dr. W.F. 1878:M4.
Carver, George Washington (1860?–1943) 1940:S11.
Carver, John (1576?–1621) 1621:H1.
Carver, Jonathan 1778:M1.
Casablanca 1907:H14, 1943:H1.
Casals, Pablo (1876–1973) 1905:A13, 1956:A12.
"The Cascades" 1904:A5.
Cases and Observations 1788:S3.
Casey, Phil 1882:M3.
Casey, William 1987:H5.
"Casey at the Bat" 1888:A2.
Casino Royale 1953:A15.
"The Cask of Amontillado" 1846:A4.
Cassano, Battle of 1799:H4.
Cassel, Battle of 1677:H2.
Casserius, Julius (1522?–1616) 1601:S1, 1609:S2.
Cassini, Giovanni Domenico (1625–1713) 1666:S3, 1668:S1, 1675:S1, 1693:S3.
Cassini space mission 1997:S5.
Cassini's Division 1675:S1.
Cassini's Laws 1693:S3.
Cassiopeia 1572:S1.
Castelfidardo, Battle of 1860:H6.
Castiglione, Baldassare (1478–1529) 1508:A1.
cast iron 1848:S5.
cast iron bridge 1835:S2.
Castle of Otranto, The 1765:A6.
"The Castle of the Pyrenees" 1959:A16.
Castro, Cipriano (1858?–1924) 1899:H8.
Castro, Fidel (b.1926) 1956:H17, 1958:H22, 1959:H15, 1960:H3, 1961:H1, 1979:H6.
casualties, war 1945:M11.
casualties of World War I 1918:M6.
catacombs 1578:M1.
Catalogue of English Plants, The 1670:S1.
Catalonia 1932:H18.
catalytic cracking 1936:S6.
Catcher in the Rye 1951:A7.
Catch-22 1962:A6.
Catechism in the Indian Language 1653:A1.
Caterpillar Club 1922:M8.
caterpillars 1852:S5.
Catesby, Mark (1679?–1749) 1731:A1, 1731:S1, 1747:S1.
Cathedral of St. Basil the Blessed 1560:A1.
Cather, Willa (1873–1947) 1903:A3, 1905:A8, 1913:A4, 1918:A10, 1927:A7.
Catherine de' Medici (1519–89) 1560:H1, 1572:H1, 1581:A1.
Catherine II (the Great) (1729–96) (Russia) 1762:H2, 1766:H5, 1768:H5, 1773:H2, 1775:H6, 1781:H4, 1785:H5.

479

Catherine of Aragon (1485–1536) 1533:H1, 1544:H1.
Catherwood, Frederick 1839:M5.
cathode 1833:S4.
cathode ray 1856:S5, 1905:S17.
cathode tube 1913:S8.
Catholic 1647:M2, 1700:M2.
Catholic bishops 1511:M1, 1528:M1.
Catholic Church 1946:M1, 1963:M3.
Catholic Encyclopedia, The 1907:A3.
Catholicism 1554:M1, 1555:H3, 1617:M3.
Catholic League 1609:H2, 1620:H3, 1622:H4, 1626:H2.
Catholic Legion of Decency 1934:M2.
Catholic parish 1565:M1.
Catholic parochial school 1782:M1.
Catholic Relief Act 1780:H6.
Cat in the Hat, The 1957:A4.
Catlin, George (1796–1872) 1837:A2, 1841:A4.
Cato 1713:A1, 1749:A2.
Cat on a Hot Tin Roof 1955:A1.
Cato Street conspiracy 1820:H4.
Cats 1982:A4, 1997:A1, 2000:A7.
CAT-scan 1979:S12.
Cat's Cradle 1963:A2.
cattle 1496:M1, 1624:S1.
Caucasian Chalk Circle, The 1944:A16.
Caulkins, Tracy 1978:M7.
Cause of Heat and Cold 1747:S2.
Cauthen, Steve 1977:M2.
Cavalcade 1931:A20.
Cavalieri, Francesco (1598–1647) 1632:S1, 1647:S2.
Cavaliers 1642:H3, 1644:H1, 1645:H1.
Cavalleria Rusticana 1890:A12.
Cavendish, Henry (1731–1810) 1766:S3, 1785:S8, 1801:S4.
Cavendish experiment 1801:S4.
caves 1685:M1.
Cavour, Camillo Benso di (1810–61) 1852:H6, 1857:H9, 1858:H13.
Cayley, George (1773–1857) 1809:S3, 1853:M9.
Ceauşescu, Nicolae (b.1918) 1965:H19, 1989:H19.
Cecilia 1782:A6.
Cela, Camilo José 1989:A11.
célérifère 1690:M6.
Céline, Louis-Ferdinand (1894–1961) 1932:A20.
cell 1665:S1.
cell 1839:S8, 1978:S20.
cell biology 1858:S5, 1974:S11.
Cell in Development and Inheritance, The 1896:S2.
Cellini, Benvenuto (1500–1571) 1550:A4, 1562:A2.
cellophane 1912:M9, 1923:M5.
cellular differentiation 1896:S2.
cellular energy 1955:S2.
Cellular Pathology as Based upon Physiological and Pathological Histology 1858:S5.
celluloid 1870:S3, 1887:S4.
celluloid film 1889:A1.
Celsius, Anders (1701–44) 1730:S2, 1733:S1, 1736:S2, 1740:S2, 1742:S2.
censorship 1662:M2.
census 1665:M3, 1986:S6, 1990:S10.
Census Bureau 1902:H4, 2000:H8.
Centennial Exhibition 1876:S6.
Centennial Exposition 1876:M1.
Center for UFO Studies 1973:S2.
centigrade temperature scale 1742:S2.
Central African Republic 1960:H20.
Central American Federation 1839:H4.

Central American Peace Conference 1907:H8.
Central Intelligence Agency 1974:H8, 1987:H5.
Central Pacific 1862:M3.
Central Pacific Railroads 1869:S1.
Central Park 1857:A1, 1864:A1.
Centuries 1555:S1.
Century of Injustice, A 1881:A4.
Century 21 Exposition 1962:M4.
cephalization 1852:S1.
Cepheid variables 1912:S2, 1917:S3, 1924:S2.
ceramics 1968:A17.
Cerezo, Sebastian 1780:A4.
cerium 1803:S5.
Cernan, Eugene (b.1934) 1966:S12, 1972:S11.
Cerro Gordo, Battle of 1847:H1.
Cervantes, Miguel de (1547–1616) 1569:A2, 1605:A3.
Cesis, Battle of 1578:H2.
Çeşme, Battle of 1770:H4.
Ceuta 1580:H2.
Ceva, Giovanni (1647?–1734) 1678:S3, 1712:S1.
Ceylon 1795:H9, 1972:H11.
Cézanne, Paul (1839–1906) 1870:A8, 1888:A10.
Chabrier, Emmanuel (1841–94) 1883:A11.
Chacabuco, Battle of 1817:H4.
Chaco 1928:H11.
Chaco War 1932:H13, 1935:H14.
Chad 1903:H16, 1960:H20, 1983:M15, 1987:H18.
Chadwick, James (1891–1974) 1932:S13, 1935:S21.
Chaffee, Roger (1935–67) 1967:M3.
Chagall, Marc (b.1889) 1911:A13, 1914:A23, 1927:A21, 1943:A15, 1963:A18, 1966:A17, 1985:A11, 1987:A12.
Chagas, Carlos (b.1911) 1957:S19.
Chain, Ernst Boris (1908–79) 1939:S14, 1945:S14.
Chakkri dynasty 1782:H6.
Chalk Garden, The 1956:A15.
Chalmers, Lionel (1715–77) 1776:S2.
Chalmers, Thomas (1780–1847) 1843:M7.
Chamberlain, John (b.1927) 1963:A6.
Chamberlain, Neville (1869–1940) 1937:H11, 1938:H15, 1940:H17.
Chamberlain, O. 1959:S14.
Chamberlain, Wilt (b.1936) 1962:M3.
Chamberlen, Peter (1560–1631) 1630:S1.
Chamberlin, Thomas C. (1843–1928) 1893:S4, 1928:S1.
chamber music 1849:A5.
Chambers, Ephraim (1680–1740) 1728:A6.
Chambers, J.G. 1866:M9.
Chambers, Robert (1802–71) 1844:S7.
Chambers, Whittaker (1901–61) 1948:H3, 1949:H9.
Chambord, chateau at 1519:A1.
Chamisso, Aldebert von (1781–1838) 1813:A6.
Chamorro, Violetta Barrios 1990:H19.
Champagne, Battle of 1917:H13.
Champlain, Lake 1814:H2.
Champlain, Samuel de (1567–1635) 1603:H1, 1604:A2, 1608:H1, 1609:A2, 1610:A2, 1613:A1, 1632:A2.
Champollion, Jean-François (1778–1867) 1821:M4.
Champs-Élysées 1637:A2.
Chancellorsville, Battle of 1863:H3.
Chandler, Raymond (1888–1959) 1940:A12.

Chandler, Winthrop (1747–90) 1780:A2.
Chang Tyong-Ho 1953:M15.
Channing, Carol (b.1921) 1964:A4.
Channing, William Ellery 1819:M3.
Channing, William (1820–1901) 1851:S3.
Chapin, J.R. 1849:M5.
Chaplin, Charlie (1889–1977) 1914:A3, 1914:M2, 1915:A7, 1919:A1, 1925:A12, 1989:A14.
Chapman, George (1559?–1634) 1611:A1, 1615:A3.
Chapman, John 1800:M4.
Chappaquiddick Island, Martha's Vineyard 1969:H7.
Chappe, Claude (1763–1805) 1794:S3.
Chapter Two 1977:A14.
Character of a Good Ruler, The 1694:A1.
Character of the Province of Maryland, A 1666:A1.
Characters of Shakespeare's Plays 1817:A3.
Charcot, Jean-Martin (1825–93) 1879:S10.
Chardin, Jean-Baptiste-Siméon (1710–79) 1728:A4.
"The Charge of the Light Brigade" 1854:A6.
Chariots of Fire 1981:A11.
Charles, Ezzard 1951:M6.
Charles Albert (1798–1849) 1848:H12, 1849:H6.
Charles I 1632:A4, 1634:A2.
Charles I (Aust.) 1921:H20.
Charles I (1600–49) (Eng.) 1625:H1, 1628:H2, 1629:H3, 1634:H2, 1639:H2, 1640:H1, 1641:H2, 1642:H3, 1645:H1, 1646:H1, 1647:H3, 1648:H1, 1649:H1.
Charles I (Span.) 1519:H3.
Charles II 1660:A1, 1660:H1, 1669:A4.
Charles II (Brit.) 1650:H3, 1651:H1, 1660:H2, 1663:H1, 1670:H4, 1673:H3, 1678:H1.
Charles III (1685–1740) (Span.) 1703:H3.
Charles III (1716–88) (Span.) 1720:H4.
Charles V 1584:A1.
Charles V, Palace of 1526:A1.
Charles V (1500–58) (Holy Roman Emperor) 1519:H3, 1525:H2, 1526:H4, 1529:H1, 1530:H1, 1530:H2, 1535:H2, 1538:H1, 1538:H2, 1541:H1, 1545:H1, 1546:H1, 1547:H4, 1552:H1, 1556:H1.
Charles VI (1685–1740) (Holy Roman Emperor) 1703:H3, 1711:H5, 1714:H2, 1716:H2, 1731:H1.
Charles VIII (1470–98) (Fr.) 1494:H2, 1495:H1, 1498:H4.
Charles IX (1550–74) (Fr.) 1560:H1, 1574:H4.
Charles X (1757–1836) (Fr.) 1830:H4.
Charles XII (1682–1718) (Swed.) 1700:H2, 1702:H2, 1706:H5, 1708:H4, 1709:H1, 1710:H2, 1714:H3, 1717:H5.
Charles XVI Gustavus (b.1946) 1973:H16.
Charles, Prince (Brit.) 1981:M10, 1993:M9, 1996:M16.
Charleston 1706:H1, 1780:H1, 1782:H2, 1925:M1.
Charlie Brown 1950:A3.
Charlie Bubbles 1968:A23.
charm 1976:S3.
"Charnel House" 1923:A18.
Charon 1978:S9.
Charpentier, Gustave (1860–1956) 1900:A13.

Charterhouse of Parma, The 1839:A4.
Chartism 1838:H5, 1839:H6, 1842:H5.
Chase, Mary (Coyle) (b.1907) 1944:A8.
Chateaubriand, François René de (1768–1848) 1801:A5.
Château-Thierry, Battle of 1918:H3.
Chattanooga, Battle of 1863:H6.
Chatterton, Thomas (1752–70) 1764:A2.
Chautauqua Assembly 1874:M1.
Chayefsky, Paddy (b.1923) 1964:A10.
Chechnya 1995:H13.
Checker, Chubby (b.1941) 1960:A2.
checks 1608:M3, 1681:M3.
Cheever, John (1912–82) 1957:A3, 1964:A5, 1977:A10.
Chekhov 1896:A7, 1898:A9, 1901:A14, 1904:A14.
chemical bonds 1916:S4, 1919:S7, 1954:S14.
chemical dynamics 1901:S17.
Chemical Dynamics of Life Phenomena, The 1924:S10.
Chemical Kinetics and Chain Reactions 1934:S19.
Chemical Kinetics of the Bacterial Cell, The 1946:S14.
chemical reactions 1967:S25.
Chemical Society of Philadelphia 1792:S2.
chemical warfare 1914:S13.
chemical wastes 1980:S5.
chemistry 1606:S2, 1789:S6, 1810:S3, 1858:S3.
chemistry set 1860:M2.
Cheney, Dick 2000:H2.
Chénier, André (1762–94) 1819:A8.
Cherbourg 1944:H5.
Cherenkov, Pavel (b.1904) 1934:S14, 1958:S17.
Cherenkov effect 1934:S14, 1958:S17.
Chernenko, Konstantin 1984:H10, 1985:H11.
Chernobyl 1986:S9.
Cherokee Indians 1760:H3, 1768:H2, 1831:H3, 1835:H4, 1838:H3, 1867:H5, 1893:H6, 1901:H6.
Cherokee Phoenix 1828:M1.
Cherry Orchard, The 1904:A14.
Cherry Valley 1778:H4.
Cherubini, Luigi (1760–1842) 1791:A9, 1800:A8, 1809:A6, 1822:A11.
Chesapeake 1807:H1, 1978:A8.
Chesapeake Bay Bridge-Tunnel 1970:M11.
Chesnutt, Charles W. (1858–1932) 1887:A1.
chess 1561:M1, 1749:M2, 1904:M5, 1921:M10, 1925:M15, 1935:M10, 1937:M12, 1946:M12, 1963:M15, 1967:M14, 1969:M13, 1978:M17, 1981:M14, 1987:M17.
Chess Made Easy 1802:M5.
Chesterton, G.K. (1874–1936) 1904:A10, 1908:A9, 1911:A11.
Chevalier, Maurice (1888–1972) 1909:A14.
chewing gum 1848:M1.
Cheyenne Indians 1864:H9, 1865:H7, 1876:H2.
Chézy, Wilhelmine de (1783–1856) 1823:A4.
Chiang Ching 1988:M12.
Chiang Kai-shek (1887–1975) 1926:H17, 1927:H14, 1934:H14, 1943:H9, 1943:H20, 1949:H18.
Chicago 1906:H3, 1974:A6, 1979:H5.
Chicago Poems 1916:A2.
Chicago school 1882:A1, 1885:A5, 1886:A3, 1889:A8.

Chicago White Sox 1920:M3.
"Chicago 8" 1969:H3.
Chichester, Francis (1901–72)
    1966:M19, 1967:M15, 1971:M14.
Chickamauga, Battle of 1869:H6.
Chickasaw Indians 1867:H5,
    1901:H6.
Chicken 1964:M7.
chicken pox vaccine 1995:S1.
chicken scratch 1912:M2.
Chicken Soup With Barley
    1958:A24.
Chief, The 1925:A20.
"Chief Justice Oliver Ellsworth and
    His Wife, Abigail Ellsworth"
    1792:A3.
Ch'ien Lung (1711–99) 1736:H6,
    1755:H2, 1757:H4.
Child, Francis J. (1825–96)
    1882:A4.
child adoption 1926:M11.
childbirth 1630:S1, 1847:S9,
    1933:S13.
Childe Harold's Pilgrimage
    1812:A4.
child labor 1833:M8, 1836:M3,
    1839:M9, 1842:M7, 1844:M7,
    1847:M4, 1890:M1.
child labor laws 1916:M1.
children 1799:M2.
Children of Violence 1964:A14.
children's clinic 1862:S2.
Children's Day 1856:M1.
children's heart sounds 1961:S5.
Children's Hour, The 1934:A2.
Children's Magazine, The 1789:A1.
Child's Garden of Verse, A 1885:A6.
Chile 1818:H4, 1891:H5, 1958:H15,
    1970:H15, 1973:H11, 1983:H15,
    1984:M20, 1988:S7, 1994:S11.
chimpanzee 1960:S19.
China 1736:H6, 1850:H4, 1858:H7,
    1894:H9, 1898:H18, 1899:H5,
    1908:H19, 1911:H14, 1913:H20,
    1915:H14, 1927:H1, 1946:H3,
    1949:H18, 1950:H12, 1970:S16,
    1971:H14, 1972:H3, 1980:H16,
    1981:M15, 1984:M15, 1986:A18,
    1990:S10, 1992:H17, 1997:H14,
    1999:H8, H18, H19, M19.
China trade 1784:M1.
China 1 1970:S16.
Chinese 1854:M1.
Chinese Exclusion Act 1882:H1,
    1892:H2, 1893:H3, 1902:H3,
    1943:H13.
*Chinese Nightingale and Other
    Poems, The* 1917:A6.
"Chinese Restaurant" 1915:A2.
Chinese Revolution, Museum of the
    1961:A18.
Ch'ing dynasty 1636:H4, 1850:H4.
Chinkiang 1841:H6.
Chippendale, Thomas (1718?–79)
    1754:A5.
Chips With Everything 1958:A24.
Chirac, Jacques 1986:H15,
    1986:M22, 1995:H22.
Chirico, Giorgio De (b.1888)
    1913:A15, 1917:A20.
Chiron 1977:S3.
Chirurische Operationslehre
    1892:S5.
Chi-yang, Chao 1980:H16.
Chloe in the Afternoon 1972:A22.
chlorine 1774:S5, 1786:S3, 1823:S2,
    1893:S5.
chloroform 1831:S2, 1847:S9,
    1853:M7.
chloromycetin 1948:S4.
chlorophyll 1865:S9, 1879:S8,
    1905:S10, 1930:S19, 1960:S9.
chloroplasts 1865:S9.
chocolate 1620:M2, 1657:M4,
    1714:M1, 1756:M8, 1765:M1.
Chocolate Soldier, The 1908:A12.
Choctaw Indians 1867:H5,
    1901:H6.

Choirboys, The 1975:A8.
cholera 1669:M2, 1830:M4,
    1832:M6, 1832:S5, 1850:M4,
    1851:M7, 1866:M5, 1873:M1.
cholesterol 1901:S16, 1951:S2,
    1964:S25, 1967:S10.
cholesterol metabolism 1964:S14.
Chopin, Frédéric François
    (1810?–49) 1830:A7, 1844:A4.
chorales 1517:A2.
choral music 1644:A2, 1660:A2.
*Choreography, or the Art of
    Describing the Dance* 1700:A4.
Chorus Line, A 1975:A10, 1990:A4.
Chosen, The 1967:A12.
Chouans, The 1829:A3.
Chou En-lai (1898–1976) 1949:H18,
    1959:H22, 1976:H11.
Chovet, Abraham (1704–90)
    1774:S3.
"Christ and the Twelve Apostles"
    1836:A6.
Christian II (1481–1559) (Den. and
    Norw.) 1520:H1.
Christianity 1496:M2, 1499:M1,
    1637:M3, 1638:H6, 1723:M2.
Christian Science 1875:M2.
Christian X (1870–1947) (Den.)
    1912:H19.
Christie, Agatha (1890–1976)
    1920:A11, 1926:A14, 1930:A19,
    1952:A13, 1970:A16.
Christie, John (1882–1962)
    1934:A21.
"Christ in the House of His Parents"
    1850:A11.
Christmas 1644:M2.
Christmas card 1846:A10.
Christmas Carol, A 1843:A2.
"Christ of the Andes" 1904:A15.
"Christ on the Cross" 1631:A2.
Christo 1985:A18, 1995:A12.
"Christ Preaching" 1652:A1.
Christ Stopped at Eboli 1945:A26.
Christ Walking on the Waters
    1899:A9.
Christy, Edwin P. (1815–62)
    1842:A2.
Christy Minstrels 1842:A2,
    1847:A3.
chromium 1797:S6.
chromosomes 1902:S4, 1905:S9,
    1907:S2, 1907:S4, 1912:S1,
    1913:S10, 1918:S4, 1933:S7,
    1933:S12, 1938:S12, 1968:S3,
    1978:S2.
Chromosomes in Heredity, The
    1903:S3.
Chronicle of a Summer 1961:A14.
Chronicle of the Ancient Sunlight
    1969:A20.
Chronicles 1577:A2.
Chronicles of Narnia, The
    1950:A14.
chronometer 1762:S4, 1804:S1.
chronon 1976:S4.
Chrysler Building 1931:A1.
Chrysler Corporation 1979:H11,
    1980:H6, 1987:M7, 1998:M2.
Chungking 1938:H19.
"Chunnel" 1986:S14, 1994:S8.
Church, Frederick E. (1826–1900)
    1857:A2, 1979:A9.
Churches of Christ 1958:M3.
Churchill, Frank (1901–42)
    1987:A12.
Churchill, Winston (1874–1965)
    1705:A2, 1939:H19, 1940:H17,
    1941:A16, 1941:H7, 1942:H21,
    1943:H1, 1943:H9, 1945:H1,
    1945:H14, 1946:H11, 1951:H11,
    1952:H12, 1954:A22, 1955:H16,
    1963:H5, 1967:A25.
Churchman, John 1789:S2.
Church Missionary Society
    1799:M4.
church music 1000:A2, 1523:A2,
    1707:A2.

Church of Christ, Scientist
    1879:M2.
Church of England 1549:M1,
    1594:M1, 1609:M1, 1620:M1,
    1661:H3, 1687:M1, 1692:M2,
    1701:M2, 1702:M2, 1971:M12.
Church of Jesus Christ of Latter-
    day Saints 1830:M5.
Church of Scotland 1560:M1,
    1929:M9.
"Church Street 'Eli'" 1922:A8.
Churubusco, Battle of 1847:H1.
Cibber, Colley (1671–1757)
    1696:A2, 1740:A5.
cigarette 1904:M7, 1954:S3,
    1957:S16, 1965:M18, 1971:M6,
    1972:M4, 1972:S7, 1978:S6.
cigarette smoking 1949:S2,
    1964:M1, 1989:S7.
Cimarosa, Domenico (1749–1801)
    1792:A7.
Cincinnati Red Stockings 1869:M4.
Cinderella 1817:A2.
Cinema Paradiso 1990:A17.
Cinématographe 1895:S11.
Cinéma Vérité 1961:A14.
Cineplasty 1947:S10.
Cinq Mars 1826:A7.
Cintra, Convention of 1808:H5.
circuit 1914:S3.
Circuit Courts of Appeals 1891:H1.
circulating library 1731:M1.
Circumstances of the Incident, The
    1977:A19.
"The Circus" 1955:A19.
Circus and Other Essays, The
    1916:A10.
Cisalpine Republic 1797:H3.
"Citation" 1951:M5, 1973:M3.
Citizen Kane 1941:A2.
citizenship laws 1855:M1.
City and the Pillar, The 1948:A4.
"city novel" 1893:A5.
City of Glasgow 1854:M5.
Civil Aeronautics Authority
    1938:H7.
*Civil and Natural History of
    Jamaica* 1756:S2.
Civil and Penal Legislation
    1802:M6.
Civil Defense 1941:M15.
Civil Defense Coordinating Board
    1955:H9.
Civilian Conservation Corps
    1933:H4, 1933:M6.
*Civilization of the Renaissance in
    Italy, The* 1860:A8.
civil rights 1983:M4, 1984:H6.
Civil Rights Act 1866:H1, 1866:M1.
Civil Rights Act (1875) 1875:H2.
Civil Rights Act (1875) 1883:H3.
Civil Rights Act (1957) 1957:H9.
Civil Rights Act (1964) 1964:H4.
Civil Service Commission 1871:H2.
Civil War 1865:H4, 1871:M3.
Civil War, Chinese 1920:H18.
Civil War, Russian 1918:H12.
Civil War, Spanish 1936:H13,
    1937:H12, 1938:H18.
Civil War, U.S. 1861:H3, 1865:H4.
Clair, René (b.1898) 1924:A21,
    1927:A15, 1930:A14, 1931:A12.
"Clair de lune." 1890:A14.
Claire's Knee 1971:A20.
Clansman, The 1905:A2, 1915:A3.
Clap, Thomas (1703–67) 1798:S3,
    1756:S1.
Clarendon Colony 1665:H4.
Clarendon Press 1672:A3.
Clari, or the Maid of Milan
    1823:A7.
*Clarissa, or The History of a Young
    Lady* 1748:A5.
Clark, Alvan (1804–87) 1860:S3,
    1886:S3, 1897:S1.
Clark, Barney 1982:S1.
Clark, George Rogers (1752–1818)
    1779:H1.

Clark, Jeremiah (1674?–1707)
    1704:A3.
Clark, Joseph (b.1939) 1979:H22.
Clark, J. Reuben 1930:H8.
Clark, Petula (b.1932) 1965:A4.
Clark, William (1770–1830)
    1803:M3.
Clark, William le Gros (b.1895)
    1953:H14.
Clarke, Brig. Gen. Mary 1978:M6.
Clarke, John 1651:M1.
classical elementary school
    1659:M2.
classification, biological 1623:S2,
    1678:S1, 1693:S2, 1713:S2,
    1735:S2, 1753:S2, 1795:S3,
    1801:S2, 1895:S13, 1979:S17.
classification, hological 1555:S2.
Claude, Albert (b.1899) 1974:S11.
Claude, Georges (1870–1960)
    1910:S9.
Claudel, Paul (1868–1955)
    1906:A10, 1918:A18.
Claudine 1900:A12.
Clausius, Rudolf (1822–88)
    1850:S4, 1857:S8.
Clay, Cassius (b.1942) 1964:M10.
Clay, Henry (1777–1852) 1824:H1,
    1834:H2.
Clayton, John (1657–1725)
    1687:S1.
Clayton, John (1685?–1773)
    1743:S2.
Clayton, Antitrust Act 1914:H6.
Clayton-Bulwer Treaty 1850:H3.
Clea 1957:A17.
Clean Air Act of 1970 1970:S2.
Clean Water Bill 1987:S7.
Cleaveland, Parker (1780–1858)
    1816:S1.
Clemenceau, Georges (1841–1929)
    1919:H10.
Clemens, Samuel Langhorne
    (1835–1910) 1863:A2.
Clément, René (b.1913) 1945:A22,
    1959:A21, 1966:A26, 1970:A
Clemente, Roberto (1934–72)
    1972:M8.
Cleopatra 1899:A9, 1963:M4.
"Cleopatra's Needles" 1878:M10.
clergy 1875:M5.
"clerihew" 1905:A12.
Clermont 1807:S1.
cleveite 1895:S9.
Cleveland, Grover (1837–1908)
    1882:H5, 1884:H4, 1885:H5,
    1888:H3, 1892:H6, 1893:H4,
    1895:H4, 1916:M6.
Cleves, Treaty of 1666:H3.
Cliff-Dwellers, The 1893:A5.
Clifford, Clark M. 1992:M3.
climate 1884:S9, 1900:S14,
    1997:S16.
Climate and Evolution 1915:S7.
Climate Near the Ground, The
    1927:S11.
Climates of the Past 1963:S17.
climatology 1931:S6.
Climbers, The 1901:A6.
"Climb Ev'ry Mountain" 1959:A2.
Climbing Plants 1875:S9.
clinic, medical 1866:M7.
*Clinical Manual of Mental Diseases,
    The* 1913:S6.
Clinton, Bill 1992:H1, 1993:H3,
    1993:H4, 1995:H2–4, 1996:H1–3,
    1997:H1, 1998:H1–4, 1999:H1,
    2000:H6–7.
Clinton, DeWitt (1769–1828)
    1817:S1, (1769–1828) 1825:M2.
Clinton, George (1739–1812)
    1804:H3, 1808:H3.
Clinton, Hillary 1993:H4, 1999:H7,
    2000:H1.
Cliosophic Society 1765:A1.
clipper ships, 1832:M2
clock 1500:S2, 1770:S2, 1814:S3,
    1838:S4.

481

clocks 1807:M2, 1916:S3,
1930:S10.
Clockwork Orange, A 1962:A15,
1971:A6.
Clodion (Claude Michel)
(1738–1814) 1806:A5.
Cloister and the Hearth, The
1861:A5.
*Clonal Selection Theory of
Acquired Immunity, The*
1959:S19.
cloned 1978:S1.
cloning 1997:S14, 1998:S7.
Closely Watched Trains 1968:A23.
clothes 1634:M3, 1676:M1.
clothing 1639:M1.
Cloth of Gold 1874:A3.
cloud chamber 1911:S11, 1927:S16.
cloud-seeding 1945:S2.
Clough, Anne (1820–92)
1871:M10.
Clowns, The 1970:A24.
Clusius, Carolus (1526–1609)
1576:S1.
coal 1492:S1, 1709:M5, 1750:S2,
1913:S14, 1931:S16.
coasting 1713:M1.
coast-to-coast bus 1928:M7.
Cobain, Kurt 1994:A10.
Cobalt-60 1952:S2.
Cobb, John 1939:M11, 1947:M11,
1952:M15.
Cobb, Ty 1977:M4, 1985:M8.
Coburn, Joe 1863:M5.
Coca-Cola 1985:M2.
Cochin China 1884:H12.
Cockcroft, Sir John D. (1897–1967)
1932:S15, 1951:S21.
Cocktail Party, The 1950:A18.
Coco 1969:A6.
Coconut Grove 1942:M3.
Cocteau, Jean (1889–1963)
1917:A14, 1925:A17, 1931:A14,
1934:A20, 1945:A22, 1950:A26.
Code Napoleon 1804:M3.
Codex Leicester 1980:A14.
Codona, Alfredo 1920:M14.
Codos, Paul 1932:M10.
Cody, William "Buffalo Bill"
(1846–1917) 1883:M2.
coelacanth 1938:S15.
coenzyme A 1947:S3, 1953:S2.
Coercion Acts 1817:H6.
Coetzee, J. M. 1999:A18.
coffee 1517:M1, 1910:M11.
Coffin, Isaac (1759–1839) 1827:S3.
Coffin, James (1806–73) 1853:S1.
Cognac, League of 1526:H4.
Cohan, George M. (1878–1942)
1904:A1, 1906:A2, 1908:A4,
1917:A3, 1923:A2, 1942:A4.
Cohen, Arthur A. (b.1928)
1973:A11.
Cohn, Edwin (1892–1953)
1926:S2.
Cohn, Ferdinand (1828–98)
1872:S7, 1875:S8, 1881:S9.
Cohn, Harry (b.1891) 1924:A12.
Coinage Act 1873:H1.
coins 1613:M2, 1652:M2.
Coit, Dr. Stanton 1886:M3.
coke 1841:S2.
Colbert, Jean-Baptiste (1619–1683)
1661:A2.
colchicine 1963:S6.
Colden (1688–1776) 1743:S2,
1745:S2, 1751:S2.
Cold Harbor, Battle of 1864:H2.
Cold Mountain 1997:A5.
"cold star" 1973:S1.
Cole, Thomas (1801–48) 1824:A2,
1827:S2, 1836:A3, 1838:A2.
Coleman, Clyde J. 1911:M2.
Colenso, Battle of 1899:H6.
Coleridge, Samuel Taylor
(1772–1832) 1795:A7, 1797:A3,
1798:A4, 1817:A1, 1817:A4.
Colet, John (1466?–1519) 1510:M1.

Colette (1873–1954) 1900:A12,
1944:A17.
Colfax, Schuyler (1823–85)
1868:H6.
Collected Papers on Acoustics
1922:S4.
college 1568:M1.
College of Charleston 1770:M2.
College of Physicians of
Philadelphia 1787:S4.
Collegium Musicum 1844:A1.
Colles, Christopher (1738–1816)
1789:S1.
Collier, Jeremy (1650–1726)
1698:A2, 1701:A4.
Collins, Michael (b.1930) 1966:S13,
1969:S1.
Collins, Wilkie (1824–69) 1860:A5,
1868:A5.
Collinson, Peter (1694–1768)
1762:S6.
Collip, James B. (1892–1965)
1921:S7, 1925:S7.
colloids 1925:S19.
Collor de Mello, Fernando
1992:M19.
Cologne, Diet of 1512:H2.
Colomba 1840:A4.
Colombia 1902:H15, 1921:H10,
1989:M11, 1990:M17, 1993:M15,
1993:M17.
Colombo 1656:H3.
Colombo, Matteo Realdo (1516–59)
1559:S1.
Colonnade Row 1811:A2.
color, perception of 1967:S19.
Colorado 1876:H3, 1893:H8.
Colored Baptists 1725:M2.
color motion pictures 1914:S7.
color movie 1929:S11.
color photographs 1881:S2.
color television 1925:S6, 1929:S3,
1951:M4, 1965:M6.
Colt, Samuel 1835:M4, 1862:S5.
Columbia Broadcasting System
1926:M5.
Columbiad, The 1807:A1.
Columbian Exposition 1892:M1,
1894:M2.
Columbian Magazine 1786:A1.
*Columbian Songster and Free
Mason's Pocket Companion, The*
1798:A3.
Columbia Pictures 1924:A12.
Columbia River 1792:M4.
Columbia University 1754:M1.
Columbus, Christopher
(1446?–1506) 1492:H1, 1492:S2,
1493:H1, 1493:S1, 1498:H2,
1502:H1.
Combo, William (1741–1823)
1812:A5.
"combine paintings" 1959:A6,
1962:A3.
Comden, Betty (b.1915) 1945:A3,
1978:A10.
Come Blow Your Horn 1961:A5.
Comédie Française 1680:A2,
1980:A10.
comedy, English 1553:A3, 1566:A2.
Comedy of Errors 1594:A1.
"Come See About Me" 1964:A1.
comets 1531:S2, 1577:S1, 1619:S1,
1642:S1, 1680:S1, 1765:S3,
1771:S3, 1797:S5, 1811:S1,
1819:S3, 1843:S4, 1847:S4,
1950:S11, 1973:S21.
comic 1896:M1.
comic books 1952:M12.
comic literature 1808:A1.
comics 1894:M4, 1954:M2,
1955:M5.
comic strips 1897:A1, 1930:A5,
1931:A9, 1950:A3, 1970:A4.
Cominform 1948:H16.
Coming Home 1978:A2.
Coming of Age in Samoa 1928:S4.
"The Coming Storm" 1880:A1.

*Commentaries on the Laws of
England* 1765:M5.
Commerce, Department of
1913:H3.
Commerce and Labor, Department
of 1903:H3.
commercial law code 1807:M3.
Commission on Civil Rights
1970:H11.
Committee for Industrial
Organization 1935:M2, 1938:M2.
Committees of Correspondence
1772:H3.
Common, Boston 1728:M1.
common cold 1950:S7, 1970:S5.
Common Market 1957:H13,
1960:H19, 1973:H10
Common Sense 1776:M2.
Commonwealth of Independent
States 1991:H8, 1992:H9.
Commonwealth of Nations
1931:H6.
communards 1871:H7.
Commune of Paris 1871:H7.
Communications Satellite Act
1962:S7.
Communist Control Act 1954:H7.
Communist Labor Party 1919:H4.
Communist Manifesto 1948:M7.
Communist Party 1927:H11,
1948:H7, 1948:H10, 1949:H7,
1949:M2, 1953:H3, 1957:H5.
Comnynes, Philippe de
(1447?–1511) 1524:A2.
Comoro Islands 1975:H24.
compact cars 1960:M3.
compact disc 1984:S11.
Company 1970:A12.
Company She Keeps, The
1942:A10.
*Comparative Pathology of
Inflammation, The* 1892:S7.
compass 1600:S2.
*Compendious Dictionary of the
English Language* 1806:A1.
Compiègne, Armistice of 1918:H9.
Compleat Angler, The 1653:A3.
Compleat Gamester 1674:M2.
Complete Housewife, The 1761:M1.
complex numbers 1843:S5.
"Composition in White, Black, and
Red" 1936:A19.
"Composition with Seven Figures
and One Head" 1950:A22.
compounds 1808:S4, 1819:S5,
1891:S8.
*Comprehensive Natural History of
Crustaceans and Insects* 1805:S4.
*Comprehensive Pronouncing and
Explanatory Dictionary of the
English Language* 1830:A3.
compressor 1834:S3.
Compromise of 1850 1850:H2.
Compton, Arthur H. (1892–1962)
1923:S1, 1927:S8, 1930:S4.
Compton effect 1923:S1, 1927:S8.
Computed Axial Tomography
1979:S12.
computers 1834:S5, 1922:S10,
1949:S1, 1951:S7, 1958:M10,
1963:S3, 1967:S6, 1978:S4,
1989:S14, 1991:S8, 1992:S2,
1996:S3.
COMSAT 1962:S7.
Comte, Auguste (1798–1858)
1838:M3.
concentric shell theory 1919:S7.
Concerning Magnetism 1600:S2.
Concerning Money Matters 1712:S1.
Concerning Straight Lines 1678:S3.
Concerning the Spiritual in Art
1910:A8.
Concorde 1969:M10.
"concrete music" 1950:A16.
condensation theory 1949:S7.
condenser 1745:S3.
Conditioned Reflexes 1927:S10.
conditioned responses 1916:S6.

*Condition of the Working Class in
England, The* 1844:M5.
Condon, Edward (1902–74)
1969:S2.
"The Condon Report" 1969:S2.
Condon, Richard (b.1915) 1974:A9.
conduction 1906:S12.
*Conduction of Electricity Through
Gases* 1903:S11.
Conduction of the Nervous Impulse
1964:A17.
conductivity 1911:S13.
Conduct of Life, The 1860:A3.
conductors 1973:S19.
Conestoga wagon 1750:M1,
1815:M2.
"Coney Island" 1963:A8.
Confederate States of America
1861:H2.
Confederation of the Rhine
1806:H3.
Confessions 1781:A4.
*Confessions of an English Opium
Eater* 1821:A7.
Confessions of an Irish Rebel
1965:A20.
Confessions of Nat Turner, The
1967:A13.
Confidence Man, The 1857:A3.
Conformist, The 1971:A20.
Confraternity of Christian Doctrine
1952:M7.
Congo 1891:H10, 1892:H11,
1908:H15, 1960:H13, 1971:H19,
1997:H23, 2000:H19.
Congo eel 1768:S2.
Congo Free State 1885:H11.
Congo Republic 1960:H20.
Congo River 1975:M17.
Congregational Church 1620:M1,
1708:M1.
Congress of Industrial
Organizations 1938:M2, 1940:H9,
1955:H4.
Congress of Racial Equality
1961:H5.
Congreve, William (1670–1729)
1700:A3.
conical refraction 1823:S6.
conic sections 1639:S3, 1640:S1.
Conjectural Arts, The 1713:S3.
conjugation 1869:S8.
Conkling, Roscoe (1829–88)
1881:H3.
Connally, John B. (b.1917)
1963:H9.
Connecticut Colony 1639:H1.
Connecticut Courant, The 1764:A1.
"Connecticut Wits" 1793:A1.
*Connecticut Yankee in King Arthur's
Court, A* 1889:A2.
Connelly, Marc (b.1890) 1921:A8,
1922:A9, 1924:A7.
Connolly, James B. 1896:M5.
Connolly, Maureen 1953:M10.
Connor, Dennis 1987:M11.
Connors, Jimmy 1974:M5.
Conquest of Canaan, The 1905:A9.
Conrad, Charles (b.1930) 1965:S9,
1969:S10, 1973:S12.
Conrad, Joseph (1857–1924)
1895:A9, 1900:A15, 1902:A13,
1907:A13, 1915:A14, 1979:A10.
Conrail 1976:H1.
conscription 1733:M7, 1863:M1.
conservation 1681:S1, 1908:S3,
1909:M1, 1910:A1, 1933:S4,
1940:S9, 1961:M14, 1968:S8,
1969:S6.
conservation laws 1626:S1.
Conservative Party 1834:H9.
Consolidated Rail Corporation
1976:H1.
Constable, John (1776–1837)
1819:A5.
Constance, Diet of 1507:H2.
Constantine I (1868–1923) (Greece)
1922:H19.

485

Dietrich, Marlene (1904–92) 1930:A13, 1932:A13.

"Die Wacht am Rhein" 1840:A5.

Die Walküre 1876:A3.

differential analyzer 1930:S5.

diffraction of electrons 1937:S12.

digestion 1752:S2, 1822:S1, 1833:S1.

digestive gland 1904:S18.

digestive juice 1773:S5.

Dighton Rock 1774:S2.

digital computers 1944:S1, 1946:S1.

Dillinger, John 1934:M4.

DiMaggio, Joe 1941:M7.

"dime" novels 1905:A3.

Dimitrov, Georgi (1882–1949) 1946:H18.

Dine, Jim (b.1936) 1962:A3.

"The Diner" 1966:A16.

Dinesen, Isak (1885–1962) 1960:A23.

Dingley Tariff 1897:H3.

Dinkins, David 1989:M3.

Dinner at Eight 1932:A6.

"The Dinner Table" 1897:A7.

Dinosaur National Monument 1915:M3.

dinosaurs 1924:M13, 1965:S13, 1972:S16, 1991:S10.

Dinosaurs of North America 1896:S6.

Diocletian, Emperor (A.D. 285–305) 1956:M15.

"Diomed" 1808:M3.

Dionne quintuplets 1934:M8.

diphtheria 1618:M3, 1686:M1, 1748:S2, 1883:S3, 1890:S4, 1901:S19, 1913:S4.

Diplomatic Appropriations Act 1893:H1.

dipping needle compass 1775:S5.

Dirac, Paul A.M. (b.1902) 1926:S12, 1930:S12, 1933:S20.

direct current 1904:S10.

direct-current motor 1884:S1.

"Directoire" 1908:M6.

Directory 1795:H8, 1799:H3.

dirigible 1898:M2, 1912:M13, 1921:M8, 1922:M3, 1925:M3, 1936:M6, 1937:M6.

Dirks 1912:A3.

"disaster movies," 1972:A13, 1974:A2.

"The Disasters of War" 1810:A6.

disco 1977:A11.

disco music 1975:A15.

discothèques 1964:A16.

Discourse 1769:A3.

Discourse on Metaphysics 1686:M2.

Discourse on Method 1637:S1.

Discourse on the Connexion Between Chemistry and Medicine 1818:S3.

Discourse on the Usefulness of Chemistry 1751:S5.

Discours sur les sciences et les arts 1750:A7.

Discreet Charm of the Bourgeoisie, The 1972:A22.

disease 1810:S7, 1907:S13.

disease, job related 1713:S1.

diseases 1546:S1.

diseases, infectious 1976:S11.

Disney 1987:A6, 1994:A4.

Disney, Walt (1901–66) 1928:M1, 1937:A12, 1940:A13, 1964:A9, 1968:M8.

Disraeli, Benjamin (1804–81) 1826:A4, 1837:H9, 1868:H8, 1874:H5, 1876:H6, 1879:H10, 1880:H5.

dissection 1565:S1, 1770:S1, 1788:S1, 1832:S4.

dissociation theory 1884:S8.

Distant Early Warning (DEW) Line 1954:H8.

Distinguished Flying Cross 1926:M6.

District of Columbia 1961:M1, 1964:H10.

disulfiram 1948:S14.

Dittersdorf, Karl Ditters von (1739–99) 1770:A5, 1786:A7.

Diurnal Occurrences 1641:M2.

Divers Voyages 1582:A1.

Divine, Father 1919:M3.

Divine Comedy of Dante Alighieri 1861:A4.

Divine Miss M, The 1972:A11.

Diviners, The 1974:A13.

diving 1907:S11.

"diving boat" 1620:S4.

divorce 1837:M7, 1940:M9, 1980:M12.

Divorce—Italian Style 1962:A20.

divorces 1913:M8, 1920:M13, 1922:M5.

"Dixie" 1859:A4.

Dixie Clipper 1939:M3.

"Dixiecrats" 1960:H9.

Dixieland Jazz 1944:A15.

Dixon, Jim 1954:A18, 1915:A3.

Dixon, Thomas (1864–1946) 1905:A2.

Djibouti 1977:H22.

Dmitri 1604:H3, 1605:H2, 1606:H2.

DNA 1944:S6, 1946:S3, 1952:S5, 1952:S12, 1953:S4, 1953:S12, 1957:S2, 1959:S15, 1961:S15, 1962:S3, 1962:S22, 1967:S1, 1968:S2, 1975:S7, 1977:S14, 1979:S7, 1980:S16, 1981:S10, 1993:S7.

Dobrovolsky, Georgi (1928–71) 1971:S18.

Dobzhansky, Theodosius (1900–75) 1937:S5, 1956:S12.

Dockwra, William 1680:M2.

Doctor, The 1834:A2.

Doctor and Apothecary 1786:A7.

Doctor Brodie's Report 1970:A17.

Doctor Faustus 1947:A4.

Doctorow, E.L. (b.1931) 1960:A7, 1976:A14, 1989:A3.

Doctors Without Borders 1999:M12.

Doctor Thorne 1858:A6.

documentary film 1922:A2, 1934:A6.

Dodd, Mrs. John B. 1910:M3.

Dodge, Mary Mapes (1831–1905) 1865:A1.

Doe, Samuel K. 1990:H20.

Dog 1964:M7.

Dog Beneath the Skin, The 1935:A15.

Doherty, Joseph 1992:M6.

"Doin' What Comes Natur'lly" 1946:A4.

Doisy, Edward A. (b.1893) 1929:S2, 1939:S1, 1943:S13.

Dole, Robert J. (b.1923) 1976:H5, 1996:H4.

Dollfus, Audouin-Charles (b.1924) 1966:S18, 1934:H16.

Dollfus, Engelbert (1892–1934) 1933:H14.

Dollond, George (1774–1852) 1821:S6, 1851:S6.

Doll's House, A 1879:A6, 1882:A3.

Dolly (cloned sheep) 1997:S14.

dolphins 1551:S2.

Domagk, Gerhard (1895–1964) 1932:S16, 1939:S22.

Dome of Many-Colored Glass, A 1912:A10.

Dominica 1978:H20.

Dominican Republic 1844:H5, 1861:H13, 1960:H17, 1965:H16.

Dominion of New England 1686:H1.

Doña Flor and Her Two Husbands 1966:A21.

Donald Duck 1984:A1.

Don Carlos (1788–1855) 1834:H6.

Don Giovanni 1787:A4.

Donizetti, Gaetano (1797–1848) 1830:A9, 1840:A7.

Don Juan 1761:A8, 1819:A6, 1889:A11.

Don Juan, or the Love of Geometry 1953:A19.

"Don Juan in Hell" 1903:A11.

donkey 1870:M6.

"Don Manuel de Zuniga" 1784:A6.

Donne, John (1572–1631) 1615:A1.

Donnelly, Ignatius (1831–1901) 1882:A2, 1888:A5, 1891:A6.

Don Quixote 1605:A3.

"Don't Be Cruel" 1956:A1.

Doolittle, James H. (b.1896) 1929:M8, 1942:H5.

"Doomsday" 1941:A8.

"Doonesbury" 1970:A4.

Doppler, Christian (1803–53) 1842:S6.

Doppler effect 1842:S6.

Doré, Gustave (1832–83) 1861:A9, 1865:A11.

"Do-Re-Mi" 1959:A2.

Dornberger, Walter R. (b.1895) 1937:S16.

Dornier, Claudius (1884–1969) 1911:S16.

Dorr's Rebellion 1842:H1.

Dorsey, Jimmy (1904–57) 1933:A1.

Dorsey, Tommy (1905–56) 1933:A1.

Dos Passos 1936:A6.

Dost Muhammad (1793–1863) 1826:H6, 1840:H9, 1842:H8, 1855:H6, 1863:H17.

Dostoevsky, Fyodor Mikhailovich (1821–81) 1846:A6, 1864:A6, 1866:A12, 1868:A7, 1871:A12, 1879:A7.

Douai-Rheims Bible 1582:M1.

Doubleday, Abner (1819–93) 1839:M7.

double-decker omnibus 1851:M9.

Double Helix, The 1968:S2.

Double Summer Time 1941:M10.

Doughty, Thomas 1864:S4.

Douglas, Lloyd (1877–1951) 1942:A12, 1856:H3, 1858:H2, 1860:H1, 1905:A15.

Douglas, Stephen A. (1813–61) 1854:H2.

Douglas, William O. (1898–1980) 1975:H5.

Douglas-Home, Alex (b.1903) 1963:H17.

Douglass, William (16917–1752) 1718:S1, 1721:S3, 1736:S1.

Doumerque, Gaston (1863–1937) 1924:H22, 1934:H13.

"Dove" 1940:A20.

Dover, Treaty of 1670:H4.

Dow Chemical 1937:S9.

Dow Jones Industrial Average 1999:M5.

Dowd, Charles F. 1883:M1.

Downing, Andrew Jackson (1815–52) 1841:A1, 1851:A5.

"Downtown" 1965:A4.

Doyle, Arthur Conan (1859–1930) 1887:A5, 1891:A10, 1893:A7, 1902:A8, 1905:A16.

D'Oyly Carte, Richard (1844–1901) 1881:A6.

Dracula 1897:A11, 1922:A13.

draft 1739:M7, 1972:M7, 1982:H9.

Dragnet 1950:A1.

Drake, Edwin L. (1819–80) 1859:S2.

Drake, Sir Francis (1540?–96) 1578:H1, 1579:M1, 1580:H3, 1586:H1, 1598:A2.

Draper, Charles S. (b.1901) 1953:S8.

Draper, Henry (1837–82) 1872:S2.

Draper, John W. (1811–82) 1840:S2.

Dreadnought 1906:M14.

dream 1899:S5.

Dreamers of Decadence 1969:A25.

Dream of Kings, A 1966:A1.

dreams 1897:S11.

Drebbel, Cornelius (1572–1633) 1592:S1, 1620:S4.

Dred: A Tale of the Great Dismal Swamp 1856:A2.

Dred Scott Case 1857:H1.

Dreiser, Theodore (1871–1945) 1900:A3, 1911:A6, 1925:A2.

Dresden 1759:H4.

Dresden, Battle of 1813:H4.

Dresden, Treaty of 1745:H5.

Dresden Opera 1731:A3.

Dressler, Marie 1914:M2.

dress patterns 1863:M2.

Dreyer, Carl (1889–1868) 1928:A13.

Dreyfus, Alfred (1859–1935) 1894:H7, 1906:H13.

Dreyfuss, Richard (b.1947) 1975:A3.

Dr. Faustus 1588:A3.

"D" ring 1969:S4.

Drinker, Philip 1928:S3.

drinking straws 1888:M3.

drip painting 1950:A2.

"Dropping the Pilot" 1890:A10.

drought 1749:M1, 1967:M6, 1976:M7, 1977:M11.

Dr. Strangelove 1964:A7.

drugs 1574:S1, 1806:S2, 1810:S7, 1812:S3, 1947:S12, 1957:S21, 1962:S17.

Drum Tops 1865:A5.

Drunkard, The 1877:A7.

"The Drunken Boat" 1871:A8.

"Drunken Gentlemen" 1917:A20.

drunkenness 1741:M1.

Drunk Man Looks in the Thistle, A 1926:A17.

Drury Lane Theater 1663:A3, 1672:A2, 1747:A4.

Druses 1860:H10, 1925:H26.

Dryden, John 1677:A1, 1670:A6, 1681:A5, 1690:A3.

Drygalski, Erich von (1865–1949) 1942:S16.

dry ice 1925:M7.

Dr. Zhivago 1958:A18.

Du Barry, Mme. 1770:A8.

Dubček, Alexander (b.1921) 1968:H10.

Dubin, Al (1891–1945) 1929:A6, 1933:A2.

Dubliners, The 1914:A13.

Dubois, Eugene (1858–1940) 1891:M7.

Dubuffet, Jean (b.1901) 1954:A23.

Due d'Orléans 1717:A2.

Duchamp, Marcel (1887–1968) 1912:A16, 1913:A11, 1915:A17, 1919:A17.

Duchamp-Villon, Raymond (1876–1918) 1914:A14.

"The Duchess of Alba" 1795:A8.

Duchess of Malfi, The 1614:A1.

Ducking stool 1691:M1.

Du Contrat Social 1762:M1.

Dudloy, Paul (1675–1751) 1720:S1, 1724:S1, 1725:S1.

duel 1626:M2.

Dufy, Raoul (1877–1953) 1915:A18.

Dukakis, Michael 1988:H1.

Duke, Charles (b.1935) 1972:S10.

Duke, James B. 1925:M2.

Duke Bluebeard's Castle 1911:A12.

Duke University 1925:M2.

Dulcy 1921:A8.

Dulles, John Foster (1888–1959) 1953:H4, 1954:H4.

Dumas *fils*, Alexandre (1824–95) 1852:A8.

Dumas *père*, Alexandre (1802–70) 1844:A5, 1845:A5.

Essays and Notes on Husbandry and Rural Affairs 1799:S3.
Essays: Moral and Political 1741:M6.
Essays of Elia 1823:A5.
Essays on the Principle of Population 1798:M2.
Essay Upon Projects, An 1697:M3.
Essay Upon the Government of the English Plantations on the Continent of America, An 1701:A1.
Essex Merrimac Bridge 1792:S1.
Estates-General 1614:H6, 1787:H3, 1788:H4, 1789:H6.
Esterházy, Paul 1766:A6.
Estes, Billie Sol (b.1925) 1962:H5.
Esther 1721:A5.
Estienne, Robert (1503–59) 1532:M2.
Estonia 1924:H20, 1939:H15, 1940:H21, 1991:H9.
estrogens 1975:S8.
estrone 1929:S15.
Ethan Frome 1911:A5.
ether 1842:S1, 1846:S1.
Ethica 1675:M6.
Ethiopia 1895:H9, 1896:H6, 1897:H9, 1809:H10, 1900:H18, 1906:H10, 1935:H11, 1936:H12, 1974:H20, 1984:M18.
"Ethnogenesis" 1861:A3.
Etiquette: The Blue Book of Social Usage 1922:A6.
E.T. the Extra-Terrestrial 1982:A2.
Eugene Onégin 1822:A7, 1877:A6.
Eugénie Grandet 1833:A5.
Eulenspiegel, Till 1500:A4.
Euler, Leonhard (1707–83) 1748:S3, 1769:S5, 1772:S5.
Euler, Ulf von (b.1905) 1970:S22.
Euphues 1579:A1.
Euripedes 1965:A17.
euro 1999:H15.
Euro Disney 1992:A9.
"Europe After the Rain" 1940:A23.
European Coal and Steel Community 1952:H10.
European Defense Community 1952:H11.
European Economic Community 1957:H13.
European Free Trade Association 1960:H19.
European Molecular Biology Laboratory 1972:S17.
European Monetary System 1981:M12, 1990:M13.
European Recovery Program 1947:H3.
Europeans, The 1878:A2.
European Space Agency 1975:S14, 1996:S11, S12, 2000:S11, S15.
European Union 1994:M18, 1999:H15, S18, 2000:S15.
euthanasia 1980:M12.
Euwe, Max 1935:M10.
Evangelical United Brethren Churches 1968:M3.
Evangeline 1847:A1.
evangelism 1896:M7, 1919:M3.
Evans, Herbert M. (1822–1971) 1918:S4, 1922:S2, 1940:S8.
Evans, Mary Ann 1859:A9.
Evans, Oliver (1755–1819) 1773:S4, 1784:S5.
Evans, Ronald (b.1933) 1972:S11.
Evans, Sir Arthur (1851–1941) 1900:M11, 1910:M10.
evaporation 1787:S3.
Eveleth, Jonathan J. 1856:M2.
Evelina 1778:A2.
Evening in Byzantium 1973:A9.
Evening Post, The 1706:M5.
Everett, Edward (1794–1865) 1852:M4.
Evers, Medgar W. (1925–83) 1963:H3.

Evert, Chris 1973:M7, 1974:M6, 1975:M9.
Everyman 1500:A3.
Every Man in His Humour 1598:A3.
"Everything's Coming Up Roses" 1959:A1.
Everything You Always Wanted to Know About Sex But Were Afraid to Ask 1970:A11.
"Evocation" 1952:A16.
evolution 1769:S3, 1794:S5, 1809:S4, 1844:S7, 1847:S1, 1849:S2, 1852:S1, 1857:S1, 1858:S13, 1859:S5, 1860:S1, 1860:S2, 1863:S3, 1866:S8, 1871:S4, 1880:S3, 1900:S10, 1900:S13, 1922:S11, 1953:S7.
Evolution and Phylogeny of Flowering Plants 1969:S15.
evolutionary genetics 1937:S5.
Evolution of Physics, The 1938:S6.
Ewing, J. Alfred (1855–1935) 1890:S2.
Ewing, W. Maurice (1906–74) 1935:S10.
excise tax on liquor 1684:M1.
exclusion principle 1925:S18.
Executioners, The 1958:A11.
Executioner's Song, The 1979:A1.
existentialism 1843:M8.
Exodus 1958:A8.
Exorcist, The 1973:A4, 1974:M11.
Expanding Universe, The 1933:S16.
Expedition Act 1903:H5.
Expedition of Humphry Clinker, The 1771:A7.
Experiments and Observations on Electricity 1751:S1.
Experiments and Observations on the Gastric Juice and the Physiology of Digestion 1833:S1.
Exploration of Cosmic Space by Means of Reaction Devices 1896:S15.
Exploration of Outer Space, The 1962:S15.
Exploration of Space by Radio, The 1957:S14.
Explorer I 1958:S8.
Explorer VI 1959:S13.
explosion 1906:M12, 1947:M3, 1959:M7.
export 1815:M1.
"Expo 67" 1967:M13.
"Expo 70" 1970:M14.
Expressionist 1918:A12.
"extra heart" implant 1974:S14.
Exultations 1909:A3.
Exxon 1998:M2.
Exxon Valdez 1989:H2, 1990:S4.
eye 1911:S19, 1967:S19.
eye bank 1944:M5.
eye surgery 1963:S2.
Eylau, Battle of 1807:H4.
Faber, Eberhard (1823–79) 1861:S4.
Fabian Society 1909:A8.
"Fable for Critics" 1848:A2.
Fables 1668:A2, 1927:A21.
Fables for Our Time 1940:A11.
"The Fables of LaFontaine" 1736:A4.
Fantasy in C Major 1836:A4.
Fabricius, Hieronymus (1537–1619) 1600:S1, 1603:S1.
Fabricius, Johannes (1587–1615) 1611:S2.
Fabritius, Carol (1622–1654) 1648:A1.
Faces of Our Time 1971:A22.
Face to Face 1976:A23.
factory 1814:S2.
Factory Act 1833:M8, 1844:M7, 1847:M4, 1874:M4.
Fadeyev 1946:A16.
Faerie Queene, The 1590:A1, 1596:A2.

Fahlberg, Constantine (1850–1910) 1879:S1.
Fahrenheit, Gabriel (1686–1736) 1709:S1.
Fahrenheit temperature scale 1714:S1.
Fahrenheit 451 1966:A26.
Fairbanks, Charles W. (1852–1918) 1904:H7.
Fairbanks, Douglas (1883–1939) 1915:A10, 1919:A1.
"Fair Deal" 1949:H1.
Fair Earth, The 1933:A14.
Fairey Aviation Co. 1946:S9.
Fair Labor Standards Act 1938:H9, 1940:M7.
Fair Penitent, The 1703:A5.
fairy tales 1835:A3.
Faisal I (1885–1933) (Iraq) 1921:H18.
Faisal II (1935–58) (Iraq) 1958:H19.
Faisal (Saudi Arabia) 1964:H24, 1975:H14.
Faith 7 1963:S13.
Fajans, Kasimir (b.1887) 1913:S13, 1931:S14.
Falangists 1936:H13, 1937:H12.
Falconer 1977:A10.
Falconet, Étienne-Maurice (1716–91) 1757:A4.
Falkland Islands 1982:A14, 1990:M22.
Fall, Albert B. (1861–1944) 1922:H10, 1924:H2, 1927:H5.
Fall, The 1956:A17.
"The Fall of the House of Usher" 1840:A3.
Fallen Timbers, Battle of 1794:H3.
Fallopius, Gabriel (1523–62) 1561:S1.
fallout 1954:S8.
Fall River Legend 1948:A2.
false teeth 1822:M3.
Falstaff 1893:A8.
Faludi, Susan 1991:A3.
Falun Gong sect 1999:M19.
"The Family" 1963:A7.
Family Limitation 1915:S10.
Family and Medical Leave Act 1993:H3.
Family Moskat, The 1950:A12.
"Family of Charles IV" 1800:A7.
"The Family of the Duke of Marlborough" 1777:A4.
Family Sayings 1963:A21.
Family Shakespeare 1818:A7.
famine 1497:M2, 1766:M4, 1776:M4, 1876:M6, 1891:M9, 1897:M4, 1904:M11, 1933:M11, 1958:M13, 1983:M17.
Fancy Free 1944:A10.
Faneuil Hall 1742:A2.
Fanfani, Amintore (b.1908) 1958:H11.
Fangio, Juan Manuel (b.1911) 1957:M19.
Fanshawe 1828:A1.
Fantasia 1940:A13.
Fantasia on a Theme by Tallis 1909:A10.
Fantasticks, The 1960:A6.
Faraday, Michael (1791–1867) 1821:S5, 1823:S2, 1825:S5, 1831:S6, 1833:S4.
Farewell, My Lovely 1940:A12.
Farewell to Arms, A 1929:A2.
Far From the Madding Crowd 1873:A4.
Farman, Henri (1874–1958) 1909:M10.
Farm Credit Act 1933:H9.
Farmer, Moses (1820–93) 1851:S3, 1856:S3, 1859:S4.
Farmer-Labor Party 1920:H6, 1924:H7.

Farmer's Almanac, The 1792:A1.
Farm Security Administration 1937:H5.
Farnsworth, Philo T. (1906–71) 1922:S1, 1933:S2.
Farouk (1920–65) 1936:H18, 1952:H17.
Far Pavilions, The 1978:A14.
Farquhar, George (1678–1707) 1707:A3, 1732:A1.
Farragut, David G. (1801–70) 1862:H3, 1864:H7.
Farrakhan, Louis 1995:H9.
Farrell, James (1904–79) 1932:A2, 1934:A5, 1935:A4.
Farthing 1961:M15.
Fasci di combattimento 1919:H18.
"Fascinating Rhythm" 1924:A1.
fashion 1675:M3, 1710:M3, 1842:M1, 1909:M3, 1953:M2, 1957:M6, 1967:M16.
Fashoda 1898:H15.
Fassbinder, Rainer Werner (b.1945) 1973:A19, 1974:A20, 1985:A19.
Fast, Howard (b.1914) 1941:A4, 1944:A7, 1952:A11, 1977:A8.
"Father of American Ornithology" 1747:S1.
"Father of American Rocketry" 1919:S3.
"Father of Mass Production" 1798:S1.
"Father of Modern Organic Synthesis" 1944:S3.
"Father of Modern Painting" 1870:A8.
"Father of the Supersonic Age" 1944:S7.
Fathers and Sons 1862:A9.
"The Father's Curse" 1765:A5.
Father's Day 1910:M3.
"Fat Ladies" 1829:M4.
fatty acid 1964:S14, 1964:S25.
Faubus, Orval (b.1910) 1957:H2, 1958:H1, 1959:H6.
Faulkner, Brian (b.1921) 1971:H13, 1972:H10.
Faulkner, William (1897–1962) 1924:A5, 1926:A4, 1930:A7, 1931:A7, 1932:A4, 1948:A6, 1949:A4, 1984:A8.
Faust 1808:A2, 1832:A7, 1859:A11.
Fauve 1911:A17.
Fauvism 1905:A11.
favrile glass 1893:A4.
Fawkes, Guy (1570–1606) 1605:H3.
fax machine 1988:S15.
FCC 1941:S8, 1945:S9, 1950:S3.
FDA 1963:S10.
Fear Eats the Soul 1974:A20.
Fearless Heart, The 1953:A14.
Fear of Flying 1973:A8.
February Revolution 1848:H5.
Federal Aid Highway Act 1956:H3.
Federal Aviation Agency 1958:S6.
Federal Bureau of Investigation 1924:H10.
federal capital 1788:M2.
Federal Child Labor Law 1922:H6.
Federal Communications Commission 1934:H4, 1934:S1, 1950:H7, 1978:M2.
Federal Conservation Reserve Program 1935:H8.
Federal Deposit Insurance Corporation 1933:H10, 1984:H8.
Federal Emergency Relief Administration 1933:H4.
Federal Farm Board 1929:H3.
Federal Farm Loan Bank Act 1916:H9.
Federal Farm Mortgage Corporation 1934:H5.
Federal Food, Drug and Cosmetic Act 1938:S3.

489

Federal Food and Drug Administration 1938:H8.
Federal Housing Administration 1934:H10.
Federalist, The 1788:A3.
Federalist Party 1789:H1, 1792:H1, 1796:H3, 1800:H2.
Federal Meteorological Service 1870:S1.
Federal Power Commission 1920:H4.
Federal Reserve Act 1907:M4, 1913:H8.
Federal Reserve System 1933:H2.
Federal Securities Act 1933:H6.
Federal Trade Commission 1914:H5, 1914:M6, 1933:H6, 1974:M3.
Federation of American Scientists 1957:S6.
Fehrbellin, Battle of 1675:H1.
Feininger, Lyonel (1871–1956) 1938:A4.
Felix, Treaty of 1580:H1.
Fellini, Federico (b.1920) 1954:A19, 1960:A17, 1961:A14, 1963:A28, 1969:A24, 1970:A24, 1972:A22.
Felt, Dorr E. (1862–1930) 1884:S3.
Fénelon, François (1651–1715) 1699:A3.
Fenian movement 1866:H4, 1882:H6.
Feodorovna, Alexandra (1872–1918) 1915:H13.
Feoktistov, Konstantin (b.1926) 1964:S18.
Ferber, Edna (1887–1968) 1926:A6, 1932:A6.
Ferber, Herbert (b.1906) 1967:A15.
Fer-de-Lance 1934:A7.
Ferdinand I (1861–1948) (Bulgaria) 1887:H10, 1908:H13.
Ferdinand I (1503–64) (Holy Roman Emperor) 1528:H3, 1556:H1.
Ferdinand II of Aragon (1452–1516) 1492:H2, 1504:H1.
Ferdinand II (1578–1637) (Holy Roman Emperor) 1619:H4, 1623:H3, 1626:H2, 1629:H4, 1629:H5, 1635:H2.
Ferdinand III (1608–57) (Holy Roman Emperor) 1637:H2.
Ferdinand VII (1784–1833) (Span.) 1814:H6, 1822:H7, 1823:H2.
Ferdinand VIII (Span.) 1820:H5.
Ferdinand of Austria and Bohemia 1528:H3.
Ferguson, Sarah 1986:M16.
fermentation 1857:S7, 1907:S12.
Fermi, Enrico (1901–54) 1926:S11, 1934:S16, 1935:S13, 1938:S17, 1942:S1.
Fernandel (1903–71) 1952:A18.
Fernández de Córdoba, Francisco (d.1518?) 1517:H1.
Fernow, Bernhard E. (1851–1923) 1886:S6, 1898:S5.
Ferraro, Geraldine 1984:H1.
Ferris, George W.G. (1859–96) 1892:M1.
Ferris Wheel 1892:M1.
fertility 1922:S2.
fertilization 1761:S2, 1779:S3.
fertilizer 1842:S2.
Fessenden, Reginald A. (1866–1932) 1900:S3, 1902:S1, 1906:S2.
Festspielhaus 1876:A3.
"Fête in a Park" 1718:A2.
fetus 1962:S17.
Feuillet, Raoul (1675?–1730?) 1700:A4.
fever 1666:S4.
Feynman, Richard P. (b.1918) 1948:S10.

Fez, Treaty of 1912:H12.
Fianna Fail 1926:H11.
Fibber McGee and Molly 1940:A1.
Fiberglass 1931:S8, 1936:S4.
fibers 1665:S1.
Fibiger, Johannes (1867–1928) 1913:S15, 1926:S17.
Fiddler on the Roof 1964:A4.
fiddling 1618:M2.
Fidelio 1805:A4.
Fiedler, Arthur (1894–1980) 1980:A6.
Field, Cyrus W. (1819–92) 1858:S1.
Field, Sally (b.1946) 1979:A12.
Field and Stream 1895:A2.
field-emission microscope 1937:S17.
Fielding, Henry (1707–1754) 1730:A3, 1742:A3, 1749:A3, 1752:A5.
field-ion microscope 1951:S18.
Fields, W.C. 1940:A4.
Fifteenth Amendment 1869:H1, 1870:H2.
Fifth Column and the First Forty-nine Short Stories, The 1938:A2.
Fifth Symphony 1808:A1.
Fifty Miles from Boston 1908:A4.
"Fifty-three Stages of the Tokaido" 1832:A8.
Figg, James 1719:M5.
"Fighting Forms" 1914:A22.
figure skating 1950:M6, 1967:M7.
Figures of Earth, The 1921:A9.
Fiji Islands 1874:H11.
Filipchenko, Anatoly (b.1928) 1969:S18, 1974:S17.
Fillmore, Millard (1800–74) 1848:H4, 1850:H1.
film 1893:M6.
Film Daily 1923:M4.
Film Society of London 1925:A24.
Filopovic, Zlata 1994:A14.
filter pump 1868:S5.
Final Days, The 1976:A3.
Finch, Peter (1916–77) 1976:A4.
fingerprints 1885:M6.
Finland 1721:H2, 1790:H4, 1809:H5, 1917:H18, 1919:H20, 1935:H20, 1939:H15, 1940:H21, 1941:H18.
Finlandia 1990:A18.
Finlay, Carlos (1883–1915) 1881:S8.
Finley, James (1781–1856) 1796:S2.
Finnegans Wake 1939:A17.
Finney, Albert (b.1936) 1968:A23.
Finsen 1903:S15.
fire 1631:M1, 1646:M2, 1675:M2, 1679:M2, 1740:M1, 1776:M1, 1777:S3, 1788:M1, 1834:M5, 1835:M2, 1849:M2, 1851:M2, 1871:M4, 1872:M4, 1892:M5, 1893:M3, 1901:M6, 1903:M7, 1904:M1, 1906:M3, 1930:M3, 1942:M3, 1944:M7, 1946:M5, 1949:M9, 1958:M4, 1961:M5, 1967:M11, 1970:M15, 1972:M19, 1974:M19, 1978:M21.
fire alarm 1851:S3.
Firebird, The 1910:A12.
fireboats 1800:S3.
fire code 1653:M1.
fire department 1865:M2.
fire engines 1659:S1, 1852:S2.
fire insurance 1752:M1.
"fire-proof" building 1854:M3.
"fireside chats" 1933:M2.
"fire water" 1772:S4.
"First Abstract Watercolor" 1910:A8.
First Book of Madrigals 1589:A1.
First Coalition 1793:H4.
First Folio 1623:A1.

First International Conference on the Peaceful Uses of Atomic Energy, The 1955:S14.
First Man, The 1922:A3.
first man on the Moon 1969:S1.
First Offenders Act 1958:M8.
First Universalist Congregation 1779:M2.
Fischer, Bobby 1960:M5.
Fischer, Emil (1852–1919) 1902:S12.
Fischer, Ernst Otto (b.1908) 1973:S18.
Fischer, Hans (1881–1945) 1928:S17, 1930:S19.
fish 1910:S12.
Fish and Wildlife Service 1940:S9.
fishes 1556:S2.
fish flour 1967:S13.
fishing 1577:M1, 1618:M2, 1650:S1, 1675:M1, 1742:M1.
"fishnet" stockings 1908:M6.
fish walk 1912:M2.
Fiske, Harrison Grey (1861–1942) 1886:A6, 1901:A7, 1908:A5.
Fiske, Minnie Maddern (1865–1932) 1886:A6, 1908:A5.
fission 1929:S14, 1939:S20, 1944:S17.
Fitch, Clyde (1865–1909) 1890:A2, 1901:A6, 1902:A7.
Fitch, John (1743–98) 1787:S1.
Fitch, Val L. (b.1923) 1980:S14.
FitzGerald, Edward (1809–83) 1859:A6.
Fitzgerald, Ella (b.1918) 1938:A8.
Fitzgerald, F. Scott (1896–1940) 1920:A1, 1922:A4, 1925:A1.
Fitzgerald, George (1851–1901) 1893:S7.
Fitzmaurice 1928:M9.
Fitzsimmons, Bob 1897:M3, 1899:M2.
Five-and-ten-cent store 1879:M4.
Five Civilized Tribes 1867:H5, 1901:H6.
"five-star general" 1944:M1.
"Five Toothbrushes on Black Ground" 1962:A3.
Five Weeks in a Balloon 1863:A8.
Fixer, The 1966:A14.
Fixx, James 1984:S6.
Fizeau, Armand (1819–96) 1849:S5.
Flagg, Josiah 1771:A1, 1783:S2.
Flaherty, Robert (1884–1951) 1922:A2.
Flamsteed, John (1646–1719) 1725:S2.
Flanders 1659:H1, 1668:H2.
"flashback" 1914:A9, 1954:A12.
"Flatford Mill on the River Stour" 1819:A5.
Flaubert, Gustave (1821–80) 1857:A6, 1877:A8.
flavoprotein 1932:S19.
Flaxman, John (1755–1826) 1793:A10.
Fleming, Ian (1908–64) 1953:A15.
Fleming, John A. (1849–1945) 1904:S10.
Fleming, Peggy (b.1948) 1967:M7.
Fleming, Sandford 1883:M1.
Fleming, Sir Alexander (1881–1955) 1928:S15, 1929:S17, 1945:S14.
Fleming, Victor (1883–1949) 1939:A1.
Fletcher, John (1579–1625) 1611:A3.
Fletcher, Louise (b.1934) 1975:A4.
Flettner, Anton (1885–1961) 1915:S11.
Fleurus, Battle of 1690:H4.
Fleury, André (1653–1743) 1726:H2.
Flies, The 1943:A14.

"The Flight into Egypt" 1563:A2, 1627:A1.
flight, nonstop 1944:M8.
"The Flight of Florimel" 1819:A3.
"The Flight of the Bumblebee" 1900:A16.
Flight to Arras 1942:A21.
Floating Opera, The 1956:A8.
Floating Theater, The 1831:A1.
Flodden Field, Battle of 1513:H4.
flogging 1861:M6, 1881:M5.
flood 1787:M1, 1913:M1, 1920:M4, 1951:M2, 1959:M14, 1975:M21.
Flood, Curt 1970:M7.
Flood Control Bill 1928:H3.
"The Flood, Ivry" 1910:A15.
floods 1927:M2, 1938:M1, 1939:M12, 1947:M9, 1950:M15, 1953:M11, 1957:M16, 1966:M11, 1970:M18, 1973:M5.
Flora Bostoniensis 1814:S1.
Flora Caroliniana 1788:S2.
Flora of North America 1838:S3.
Flora Virginica 1743:S3, 1762:S3.
Florence 1865:H8, 1966:M11.
Florentine militia 1506:M2.
Florey, Howard Walter (1898–1968) 1939:S14, 1945:S14.
Florey, Paul (b.1910) 1974:S10.
Florida 1566:M1, 1763:H1, 1795:H3, 1845:H1, 1861:H1, 1868:H2.
Flounder, The 1978:A16.
Flowering Judas 1930:A6.
Flowering Peach, The 1954:A6.
flowers 1576:S1.
flu 1967:S7, 1970:S5.
fluid computer 1964:S4.
fluorescent lamp 1896:S8.
fluoridated water 1951:S6.
fluorine 1886:S12.
fluorocarbons 1977:S4.
fluoroscope 1896:S8.
Flush 1933:A15.
flying boat 1942:S5.
Flying Dutchman, The 1843:A5.
"Flying Officer X" 1943:A20.
"flying saucers" 1947:S6, 1948:S11.
flying shuttle 1733:S2.
"Flying Turtle" 1943:A16.
FM 1933:S1, 1936:S7.
Fo, Dario 1997:A13.
Foch, Marshal Ferdinand (1851–1929) 1918:H8.
"Fog Warning" 1885:A6.
Fokine, Michel (1880–1942) 1905:A19, 1909:A9, 1914:A19.
Folger, Peter (1617–1690) 1676:A1.
folic acid 1945:S7.
Folies Bergère 1909:A14.
folk high schools 1844:M3.
folk rock 1962:A7.
folk song 1910:A4.
Follen, Charles 1826:M3.
Follet, Ken (b.1949) 1979:A5.
Follies of 1907, The 1907:A1.
Fonda, Jane (b.1937) 1978:A2.
Fontainebleau, Treaty of 1762:H1.
Fontamara 1930:A16.
Fontana 1965:A25.
Fontenoy, Battle of 1745:H4.
Fonteyn, Margot (b.1919) 1963:A17.
Food and Drug Act 1898:M1.
food preservation 1810:S4.
foods, quick-frozen 1929:S4.
football 1820:M2, 1822:M1, 1863:M8, 1869:M5, 1873:M6, 1889:M4, 1895:M4, 1902:M4, 1913:M7, 1914:M3, 1924:M7, 1933:M8, 1942:M8, 1969:M4, 1982:M7.
Footlight Parade 1933:A2.
Foraker Act 1900:H3.
forbidden books 1556:M2.
Forc'd Marriage, The 1670:A4.
Force Bill 1833:H1.
forceps 1630:S1.

492

493

494

495

497

INTELSAT 1965:S7.
Inter-American Conference 1936:H8.
"interferometer" 1881:S1, 1920:S1.
interferon 1957:S18, 1978:S3.
Interior, Department of the 1849:H1.
Intermediate Credits Act 1923:H6.
internal combustion engine 1826:S1, 1862:S7, 1879:S5, 1885:M5, 1920:S6.
Internal Constitution of Stars 1925:S15.
internal revenue 1791:M1.
Internal Revenue Service 1975:H7, 1982:M13, 1998:M4.
Internal Security Act 1950:H5.
International Arbitration Court 1902:H19.
International Atomic Energy Agency 1959:S4.
International Bible Students 1872:M1.
International Bible Students Association 1931:M1.
International Campaign to Ban Landmines 1997:M22.
International Conference on Electrical Units 1905:S15.
International Court of Arbitration 1910:H9.
International Court of Justice 1951:H13.
International Geophysical Year 1957:S15, 1958:S14.
International Ladies' Garment Worker's Union 1900:M1.
International Monetary Fund 1997:H16.
International Space Station 1998:S1, S12, 2000:S11, S12.
International System of Units, The 1960:S20.
International Tchaikovsky Competition 1978:A21.
Internet 1993:S1, 1995:S21, 1997:S7, S15, 1999:A2, S5, 2000:A6.
interplanetary space 1965:S11.
Interpretation of Dreams, The 1899:S5.
intersexuality 1938:S9.
Interstate Commerce Act 1887:H1, 1903:H7.
Interstate Commerce Commission 1910:H2, 1910:H6, 1915:H7, 1929:H9, 1955:H8, 1966:H2.
"The Intervention of the Sabine Women" 1799:A8.
In the Beginning 1976:A15.
"In the Beginning God" 1966:A8.
"In the Cage" 1946:A6.
In The Days of Simon Stern 1973:A11.
Int'l Ladies' Garment Worker's Union 1911:M5.
"Intolerable Acts" 1774:H1.
Intolerance 1916:A5.
Introduction to the Kinetic Theory of Gases 1940:S13.
Introduction to the Principles of Morals and Legislation, An 1789:M6.
Intruder in the Dust 1948:A6.
Invar 1920:S14.
"Invasion from Mars" 1938:M3.
inventors 1623:M2, 1906:M8.
inverse square law 1678:S2.
invertebrate 1801:S2.
Investigation, The 1965:A15.
Investigation of a Citizen Above Suspicion 1971:A20.
Invisible Man, The 1897:A10, 1952:A5.
In Which We Serve 1942:A18.
iodine 1818:S5.
Ionesco, Eugène (b.1912) 1958:A21, 1959:A22.

Ionian Islands 1797:H2, 1799:H6, 1864:H10.
ionization 1903:S13.
ionosphere 1882:S6, 1925:S17.
Iowa 1846:H6.
I Pagliacci 1892:A11.
Iphigenia in Aulis 1774:A5.
Iran 1935:H16, 1953:H16, 1978:H25, 1979:H9, 1979:H16, 1980:H1.
Iran, Shah of 1980:H13.
Iran-Contra Affair 1986:H3, 1987:H2, 1990:H3, 1991:H7.
Iran-Iraq War 1986:M17, 1988:H19.
Iraq 1933:H20, 1958:H19, 1990:H1, 1990:H10, 1991:H2, 1994:M13, 1998:H15.
Ireland 1649:H1, 1799:H5, 1801:H4, 1892:H7, 1912:H18, 1920:H11, 1921:H12, 1938:H22, 1949:H19.
Ireland, Northern 1925:H15.
I Remember Mama 1944:A18.
Irish Free State 1921:H12, 1925:H15.
Irish Home Rule Bill 1893:H18.
Irish Land Act 1870:H6.
Irish Republican Army 1969:H16, 1971:H13, 1981:H18, 1984:M16, 1987:M16, 1994:H14.
Irish Sweepstakes 1930:M7.
iris screen 1701:A3.
iron 1585:S1, 1621:S1, 1650:M2, 1715:S1, 1720:S2, 1750:S1, 1762:S2, 1775:S2, 1784:S9, 1844:S3, 1925:S3.
Iron Act of 1750 1750:S1.
"Iron Curtain" 1946:H11.
Iron Guardists 1938:H17.
"iron lung" 1928:S3, 1948:S12.
ironworks 1644:S1.
Iroquois 1720:H1.
Iroquois Confederation 1713:H2, 1722:H1, 1744:H2.
Iroquois Indians 1689:H1, 1768:H2.
irrational numbers 1872:S6, 1873:S4.
irreversible chemical processes 1968:S12.
irrigation 1941:M2.
Irving, Henry (1838–1905) 1878:A7.
Irving, John (b.1942) 1978:A7.
Irving, Washington (1783–1859) 1807:A3, 1808:A1, 1820:A1, 1822:A5, 1832:A3, 1859:A1.
Irwin, James (b.1930) 1971:S11.
"Isabella, Countess of Sefton" 1769:A5.
Isabella II (1830–1904) (Span.) 1834:H6, 1843:H4, 1868:H10.
Isabella I of Castile (1451–1504) 1492:H2, 1504:H1.
Isabella Stewart Gardner Museum 1990:A8.
Isagoge Phytoscopia 1678:S1.
Isandhlwana, Battle of 1879:H8.
Isfahan 1722:H2, 1724:H2, 1726:H3, 1728:H1, 1785:H6.
Isherwood, Christopher (b.1904) 1935:A15, 1939:A15, 1954:A12, 1964:A11.
Islamabad 1979:H10.
Island of the Blue Dolphin 1960:A14.
Island of the Dead 1909:A13.
Islands in the Stream 1970:A3.
Isle of Pines 1925:H3.
islets of Langerhans 1901:S4.
Isly, Battle of 1844:H6.
Ismail Pasha (1830–95) 1863:H15, 1872:H8, 1879:H7.
isomorphism 1819:S5.
Isonzo, Battles of the 1915:H11, 1916:H12.
isotope 1913:S19.
isotope 1921:S4, 1941:S1.
isotopes 1919:S14, 1920:S8, 1921:S13, 1922:S14, 1935:S6.

Is Paris Burning? 1966:A26.
Israel 1948:H2, 1948:H13, 1955:H22, 1957:H10, 1967:H14, 1970:H18, 1973:H12, 1988:H13, 1993:H18, 1994:H16.
Israel Philharmonic Orchestra 1937:A19.
Is Sex Necessary? 1929:A4.
Istanbul 1930:H12.
Istria 1797:H2.
Italian Capriccio 1880:A7.
"The Italian Comedy" 1716:A4.
Italian Girl in Algiers, The 1813:A4.
Italian National Society 1857:H9.
Italian Painters of the Renaissance 1952:A12.
Italian Republic 1802:H5.
Italian Straw Hat, The 1927:A15.
Italian Symphony 1833:A4.
Italy, 1831:H6, 1852:H6, 1861:H12, 1865:H8, 1870:H9, 1940:H19, 1941:H14, 1943:H15, 1975:S14.
Ito, Hirobumi (1841–1909) 1892:H16, 1901:H7.
Iturbide, Augustín de (1788–1824) 1822:H5, 1823:H3.
Ituzaingó, Battle of 1827:H5.
Ivanchenkov, Alexander (b.1940) 1978:S18.
Ivanhoe 1820:A2.
Ivan IV (1530–84) (Russ.) 1547:H2, 1549:H1, 1563:H2, 1564:H4, 1581:H2.
Ivanov, Georgi 1979:S13.
Ivanov, Leo (1884–1901) 1895:A7.
Ivan the Terrible 1944:A22.
"I've Got a Crush on You" 1930:A4.
"I've Got You Under My Skin" 1936:A9.
"I've Grown Accustomed to Her Face" 1956:A3.
Ives, Charles (1874–1954) 1891:A5, 1902:A5.
Ives, Frederick E. (1856–1937) 1881:S2, 1886:S4, 1914:S7.
ivory, 1973:M21, 1981:S13, 1986:S16.
Ivory Coast 1842:H6, 1892:H10, 1960:H20.
"Ivry Town Hall" 1923:A17.
"I Want to Hold Your Hand" 1964:A12.
Iwo Jima 1945:H3.
Jack Armstrong, the All American Boy 1950:A1.
Jack Benny Show, The 1940:A1.
Jacklin, Tony 1970:M16.
Jackson, Andrew (1767–1845) 1814:H1, 1815:H1, 1818:H2, 1821:H3, 1824:H1, 1828:H1, 1829:H1, 1831:H2, 1832:H2, 1833:H1, 1833:H2, 1834:H2, 1835:H2.
Jackson, Charles (1903–68) 1944:A3.
Jackson, Helen Hunt (1830–85) 1881:A4, 1884:A1.
Jackson, Jesse 1983:M6.
Jackson, Michael 1984:A2, 1988:A14, 1994:A3.
Jackson, Stonewall (1824–63) 1862:H6.
Jackson, William H. (1848–1942) 1871:A4.
Jacob, François (b.1920) 1961:S16, 1965:S21.
Jacobi, Abraham (1830–1919) 1862:S2.
Jacobites 1690:H3, 1715:H2, 1716:H1, 1745:H3, 1746:H2.
Jacobsen, Eric (b.1903) 1948:S14.
Jacob's Room 1922:A17.
Jaehn, Sigmund 1978:S19.
Jaffe, Roland 1984:A16.
Jahan, Shah (1592?–1666) 1628:A3.
Jakobowsky and the Colonel 1944:A26.

Jalna 1927:A12.
Jamaica 1655:H4.
James, Harry (1893–1966) 1939:A6.
James, Henry (1843–1916) 1871:A1, 1876:A2, 1878:A2, 1886:A1, 1879:A1, 1881:A2, 1898:A3, 1902:A6, 1904:A4.
James William (1842–1910) 1890:M3.
James I (1566–1625) (Eng.) 1603:H2, 1603:H3, 1606:H1, 1607:H2, 1611:H1, 1622:H3, 1625:H1, 1634:A2.
James II (1633–1701) (Brit.) 1685:H2, 1687:H2, 1688:H1, 1690:H3.
James IV (1473–1513) (Scot.) 1496:H1.
Jameson, Leander Starr (1853–1917) 1895:H7.
Jamestown, Virginia 1607:H1, 1608:M1, 1608:M2, 1610:H2, 1611:M1, 1619:H1, 1619:H2, 1996:S1, 1998:S10.
James V (1512–42) (Scot.) 1542:H2, 1542:H3.
James VI (Scot.) 1567:H1, 1603:H2.
jamming 1915:S8.
Janata Party 1977:H18.
Jane Eyre 1847:A4.
Jane Seymour 1536:H4.
Jane Taylor 1806:A4.
Janissaries 1804:H9, 1826:H4.
Jankau, Battle of 1645:H3.
Jannings, Emil (1886–1950) 1924:A14, 1929:A1.
Jansky, Karl (1905–50) 1931:S1.
Janssen, Zacharias (1580–1638?) 1590:S2.
January Revolution 1863:H9.
Janus 1966:S18.
Japan 1543:H1, 1638:H6, 1864:H15, 1867:H12, 1894:H9, 1915:H14, 1937:H18, 1939:H16, 1940:H19, 1941:H13, 1941:H19, 1943:H17, 1945:H7, 1945:H25, 1954:H5, 1957:H3, 1970:S15, 1980:H25.
Japan, an Attempt at an Interpretation 1904:A7.
Japanese-American internment 1983:H3.
Japanese art 1867:A7.
Japanese Miscellany, A 1901:A5.
Japanese Peace Conference 1951:M1.
Japanese War Crimes Trials 1946:M4.
Jarvik, Robert K. 1982:S1.
Jarvis, Anna M. 1907:M3.
Jarvis, Edward (1803–84) 1847:S2.
Jarvis, John W. (1780–1840) 1819:A2.
Jassy, Treaty of 1792:H4.
Jastrow, Robert (b.1925) 1957:S3, 1967:S2.
Jauregg, Julius Wagner von (1857–1940) 1917:S8.
Java 1811:H5, 1825:H9.
Java 1812:H2.
Java Head 1919:A10.
Java Man 1891:M7, 1937:M11.
Java Sea, Battle of 1942:H3.
Jaworski, Leon (b.1905) 1973:H1.
Jaws 1974:A1, 1975:A3, 1978:M4.
1978:H2.
Jay, John (1745–1829) 1782:H1, 1789:H2.
Jay's Treaty 1794:H4, 1797:H1.
jazz 1919:A2, 1920:A7, 1933:A1, 1934:A1, 1938:A9, 1945:A1, 1950:A15, 1951:A2, 1956:A10, 1966:A8.
Jazz Couriers 1957:A14.
J.B. 1958:A2.
Jean Christophe 1904:A13.
"Jeanie with the Light Brown Hair" 1854:A2.

Jeanneret, Charles-Edouard (1884–1965) 1918:A11.
Jeans, Sir James (1877–1946) 1904:S8, 1906:S6, 1908:S11, 1928:S19, 1940:S13.
Jeeves 1924:A13.
Jeffers, Robinson (1887–1962) 1924:A8.
Jefferson, Joseph (1829–1905) 1866:A3.
Jefferson, Thomas (1743–1826) 1774:A3, 1776:H2, 1779:M1, 1783:M3, 1784:A3, 1784:H1, 1785:H3, 1785:S2, 1790:S3, 1792:H1, 1796:H3, 1798:H3, 1800:A2, 1800:H2, 1800:H2, 1801:H1, 1801:H2, 1804:H3, 1806:H1, 1806:H2, 1807:H1.
Jefferson Starship 1974:A6.
Jeffrey, Francis (1773–1850) 1802:A3, 1817:A1.
Jeffries, James J. 1899:M2.
Jeffries, John 1785:M5.
Jehovah's Witnesses 1872:M1, 1931:M1, 1943:M1.
"Jelly Roll Blues" 1917:A1.
Jena, Battle of 1806:H4.
Jencks, Joseph (1602–83) 1659:S1.
Jenner, Edward (1749–1823) 1796:S4, 1797:S7, 1798:S7.
Jenney, William LeBaron (1832–1907) 1885:A5.
Jennie Gerhardt 1911:A6.
Jensen, Arthur (b.1923) 1969:S8.
Jensen, Jobannes H. (1907–73) 1963:S14.
Jericho 1952:M13.
Jerome, Chauncey (1793–1868) 1888:S4.
Jerusalem 1010:H3, 1866:M8, 1970:M21.
Jerusalem 1901:A16.
Jesuits 1543:M1, 1549:M2, 1566:M1, 1568:M1, 1590:M1, 1605:M1, 1615:M1, 1627:M4, 1656:M2, 1759:M2, 1767:M4, 1773:M4, 1774:M3, 1814:M4, 1872:M9.
Jesus Christ Superstar 1971:A1.
"Jesus movement" 1971:M8.
Jesus of Nazareth 1977:A9.
jet 1942:S2.
jet engine 1930:S18.
Jet Propulsion Laboratory 1944:S7.
jet streams 1945:S6.
Jet: The Story of a Pioneer 1953:S19.
jewelry 1853:A1.
Jewett, Sarah (1849–1909) 1884:A4.
Jewish 1654:M1, 1957:M17.
Jews 1492:M2, 1496:M2, 1509:M1, 1728:M2, 1742:M3, 1753:M3, 1790:M2, 1965:M7, 1973:M1.
Jezebel 1938:A7.
"J" factor 1951:S4.
"Jim Crow" 1828:A3, 1896:H2.
Jitterbug 1943:M8.
jiu-jitsu 1904:M6.
"Jive Talkin'" 1975:A15.
J.J. Thomson and the Cavendish Laboratory in His Day 1965:S19.
Joan of Arc 1801:A7.
Job, The 1961:A14.
Job Corps 1964:H8.
Jockey Club 1753:M2.
Jodrell Bank, England 1957:S14, 1962:S15.
Joel, Billy (b.1949) 1973:A5, 1977:A12.
Joffrey Ballet 1995:A6.
Johannsen, Wilhelm (1881–1927) 1909:S7.
John, Augustus (1878–1961) 1919:A19.
John, Elton (b.1947) 1971:A19, 1973:A17, 1979:A15.
John Birch Society 1958:A3.

John Birch Society 1961:H7.
John Brown's Body 1928:A4.
John Bull 1831:S3.
John F. Kennedy Center for the Performing Arts 1964:A3.
John Gilpin 1779:A2.
John I (1487–1540) (Hung.) 1528:H3.
John l'Enfer 1977:A17.
"John Mason" 1832:M3.
"Johnny Appleseed" 1800:M4.
"Johnny One Note" 1937:A10.
John Paul II, Pope (b.1920) 1979:M3, 1979:M16, 1980:M12, 1981:H9, 1982:M17, 1983:M19, 1986:A17, 1987:M20, 1991:M10, 2000:H15, 2000:M23.
Johns, Jasper (b.1930) 1954:A10.
Johns Hopkins Hospital 1889:S1.
Johnson, Amy 1930:M11.
Johnson, Andrew (1808–75) 1864:H8, 1865:H5, 1866:H1, 1866:H3, 1867:H2, 1867:H3, 1868:H1.
Johnson, Don 1972:M3.
Johnson, Earvin (Magic) 1991:M6.
Johnson, Eyvind (b.1900) 1973:A16.
Johnson, Henrietta 1700:A2.
Johnson, Jack 1908:M5, 1915:M7.
Johnson, James Weldon (1871–1938) 1912:A1.
Johnson, Lyndon Baines (1908–73) 1960:H9, 1963:H9, 1963:H10, 1964:H7, 1964:H9, 1965:H1, 1966:H7, 1966:H11, 1966:S9, 1968:H1.
Johnson, Philip C. (b.1906) 1949:A8.
Johnson, Richard M. (1780–1850) 1836:H4.
Johnson, Robert U. (1853–1937) 1890:M2.
Johnson, Samuel (1709–1784) 1737:A2, 1744:A3, 1746:A4, 1750:A4, 1755:A2, 1756:A4, 1759:A5, 1763:A4, 1775:A8.
Johnson, Thomas (1600?–1644) 1933:S1.
Johnson, Uwe (b.1934) 1961:A21.
Johnson, Walter 1913:M2.
Johnstown flood 1889:M2.
John XXIII, Pope (1881–1963) 1959:M10, 1962:M16.
Joiner 1971:A13.
Jokes and Their Relation with the Unconscious 1905:S12.
Joliet, Louis (1645–1700) 1673:H2.
Joliot, Whitcomb L. 1891:M3.
Joliet-Curie, Frédérick (1900–58) 1934:S13, 1935:S20.
Joliet-Curie, Irène (1897–1956) 1934:S13, 1935:S20.
Jones, Dean (b.1936) 1970:A12.
Jones, Hugh 1724:A1.
Jones, Inigo (1573–1652) 1605:A2, 1622:A2, 1630:A3.
Jones, James (1921–1977) 1951:A1, 1957:A6, 1967:A10, 1971:A7.
Jones, John Paul (1747–92) 1779:H3.
Jones, Margaret 1648:M1.
Jones, Naomi 1978:M20.
Jones, Paula Corbin 1998:H1.
Jones, Robert "Buddy" 1911:M4, 1930:M8.
Jones, William (1746–94) 1789:A7.
Jones Act 1916:H8.
Jonestown 1978:M9.
Jones-White Merchant Marine Bill 1928:H4.
Jong, Erica (b.1942) 1973:A8.
Jonson, Ben (1572–1637) 1598:A3, 1601:A2, 1606:A2, 1610:A4.
Joplin, Janis (1943–70) 1979:A3.
Joplin, Scott (1868–1917) 1899:A2, 1901:A2, 1904:A5, 1911:A9.
Jordan 1958:H19, 1999:M24.
Jordan, Michael 1991:M7, 1993:M8, 1998:M10, 1999:M3.

"Joseph and His Brothers" 1789:A6.
Joseph Andrews 1742:A3.
Joseph II (1741–90) (Holy Roman Emperor) 1763:H3, 1765:H4, 1767:M3, 1769:H6, 1773:M4, 1778:H7, 1781:H4, 1781:H5, 1781:M3, 1784:H1, 1785:H4.
Josephson, Brian (b.1904) 1973:S19.
Josh Billings' Farmer's Allminax 1869:A3.
Josselyn, John (1608–75) 1672:S1, 1674:S1.
Joule, James (1818–99) 1840:S4, 1843:S7, 1852:S11.
Joule effect 1840:S4.
Joule-Thomson effect 1852:S11.
Journal de Paris 1777:M2.
Journal for Pure and Applied Mathematics 1826:S3.
Journal of a Residence on a Georgia Plantation in 1838–1839 1838:A1.
Journal of Geology 1893:S4.
Journal of Mme. Knight, The 1824:A3.
Journal of Osteopathy 1894:S5.
Journal of Researches into the Geology and Natural History of the Various Countries Visited by HMS Beagle, 1832–36 1839:S6.
Journal of the Plague Year, A 1722:A6.
Journals 1735:M3.
Journey's End 1929:A13.
Journey to the Center of the Earth, A 1864:A3.
Journey to the End of Night 1932:A20.
Journey to the Western Islands of Scotland, A 1775:A8.
Joyce, James (1882–1941) 1914:A13, 1916:A16, 1922:A12, 1939:A17.
Joyless Street 1925:A22.
Juan Carlos I (b.1938) (Span.) 1975:H23.
Juárez, Benito (1806–72) 1861:H11, 1867:H11.
Jude the Obscure 1895:A10.
Judgement 1935:A4.
"The Judgment of Paris" 1887:A9.
Judicature Act 1873:H4.
Judicial Procedure Reform Act 1937:H6.
Judiciary Act 1789:H2, 1802:H2.
Judson, Whitcomb L. 1891:M3.
Jugglers Three 1972:A17.
Juilliard, Augustus D. (1836–1919) 1919:A8.
Juilliard School of Music 1919:A8.
Jules and Jim 1961:A14.
Jülich-Cleves 1609:H3, 1666:H3.
Julie, or La Nouvelle Heloise 1761:A6.
Julius Caesar 1599:A2.
Julius II (1443–1513) (pope) 1508:H1, 1510:H1, 1511:H1, 1545:A1.
Jullian, Philippe (1920–77) 1969:A25.
"July Hay" 1943:A9.
Jumpers 1972:A19.
Jung, Carl G. (1876–1961) 1917:M10.
Jungfrau 1811:M6.
Jungius, Joachim (1587–1657) 1678:S1.
Jungle, The 1906:A1.
Jungle Book, The 1894:A11.
Junichirō, Tanizaki (1886–1965) 1963:A19.
Junin, Battle of 1824:H5.
Junkers, Hugo (1859–1935) 1915:M8.
Junkie: Confessions of an Unredeemed Drug Addict 1953:A1.

junk sculpture 1962:A2, 1963:A6.
Juno 1804:S3.
Junto 1727:M1.
Jupiter 1563:S3, 1610:S4, 1664:S1, 1664:S2, 1666:S2, 1668:S1, 1904:S7, 1905:S8, 1906:S11, 1955:S6, 1972:S9, 1973:S10, 1977:S11, 1979:S11, 1980:S4.
Jupiter Symphony 1788:A6.
Jupiter U.S.S. 1912:S5.
Jurgen 1919:A9.
justice 1638:M2.
Justice, Department of 1870:H3, 1953:H3, 1977:H3.
Justine 1957:A17.
Just So Stories 1902:A11.
"Just the Way You Are" 1977:A12.
Jutland, Battle of 1916:H14.
juvenile delinquency 1971:M11.
Kabila, Laurent 1997:H23.
Kabuki 1586:A3, 1748:A2.
Kaczynski, Ted 1996:M5.
Kádár, János (b.1912) 1956:H11.
Kaesong 1951:H9.
Kaffirs 1834:H4, 1847:H6, 1850:H5, 1877:H6.
Kaffir War 1850:H5.
Kafka, Franz (1888–1924) 1915:A13, 1925:A14, 1927:A14.
Kahane, Meir 1990:M5.
Kahn, Reuben (b.1887) 1951:S12.
Kain, Karen (b.1951) 1972:A21, 1973:A21.
Kaiser, Henry (1882–1967) 1942:S3, 1943:S5.
Kakiemon, Sakaida (1596–1666) 1645:A1.
Kalahari Desert 1882:H11.
kaleidoscope 1816:S4.
Kalevala 1835:A5.
Kàlidàsa 1789:A7.
Kallio, Kyosti (1873–1940) 1937:H15.
Kalmar, War of 1611:H2, 1613:H3.
Kalmus, Herbert T. 1922:M2.
Kamenev, Lev (1883–1936) 1924:H12, 1926:H13.
Kamerny Theater 1914:A17.
Kampuchea 1976:H14.
Kanagawa, Treaty of 1854:H1.
Kandinsky, Vasily (1866–1944) 1908:A14, 1910:A8, 1985:A11.
Kandt, Richard 1898:M3.
kangaroo dip 1912:M2.
Kansas 1855:H1, 1857:H3, 1859:H4, 1861:H6, 1889:H1.
Kansas-Nebraska Act 1854:H2, 1854:H3.
Kant, Immanuel (1724–1804) 1781:A5.
Kantor, MacKinlay (1904–77) 1955:A7.
kaons 1947:S9.
Kapitsa, Pyotr (b.1894) 1930:S14, 1978:S21.
Kapp, Wolfgang (1858–1922) 1920:H12.
Kapp Putsch 1920:H12.
Karageorgevich, Alexander (1806–85) 1849:H8, 1858:H12, 1903:H13.
Karageorge (1768?–1817) 1804:H9, 1817:H5.
Karajan, Herbert von (b.1908) 1967:A16.
Karamanlis, Constantine (b.1907) 1974:H18.
Kardia, Peace of 1661:H2.
Karelia 1790:H4.
Karmin Khan (d.1779) 1750:H3, 1775:H7.
Karlowitz, Treaty of 1699:H2.
Karlsefni, Thorfinn 1010:H1.
Karlskirche 1715:A2.
Kasparov, Garry 1997:M27.
Karpov, Anatoly (b.1951) 1978:M17.
Karrer, Paul (1889–1971) 1930:S13, 1937:S19.

501

Malawi 1963:H21.
Malaysia, Federation of 1963:H12.
Malcolm X (1925–65) 1961:H6, 1965:H7.
Malenkov, Georgi Maksimilanovich (b.1902) 1953:H11, 1955:H13.
Mali 1960:H20.
Mallarmé, Stéphane (1842–98) 1876:A6.
Mallory, Frank (1862–1941) 1913:S9.
Malone Dies 1951:A13.
Malory, Sir Thomas (d.1471) 1893:A9, 1958:A19.
Malpasset Dam 1959:M14.
Malpighi, Marcello (1628–94) 1661:S3.
Malplaquet, Battle of 1709:H2.
malpractice insurance 1975:M5.
Malraux, André (1901–76) 1933:A13, 1937:A23, 1951:A15.
Malta 1551:H1, 1565:H2, 1800:H6, 1802:H4, 1803:H5, 1942:M10, 1964:H14.
malted milk 1882:M2.
Maltese Falcon, The 1930:A3.
Malthus, Thomas (1766–1834) 1798:M2.
Mame 1966:A15.
Mamelukes 1517:H2, 1766:H6, 1798:H6, 1811:H6.
Mamet, David (b.1947) 1977:A3, 1978:A4.
Mammalian Physiology 1916:S17.
mammals 1551:S1, 1556:S2, 1795:S3, 1827:S5.
mammoth 1799:M6.
Man, the Unknown 1935:S19.
Man Against the Sky, The 1916:A9.
Man and his Desire 1918:A18.
Man and Superman 1903:A11.
Manchester, William (b.1922) 1966:A9.
Manchester Guardian 1821:M5.
Manchild in the Promised Land 1965:A11.
Manchukuo 1932:H17.
Manchuria 1901:H12, 1907:H18, 1910:H18, 1916:H18, 1931:H11, 1932:H17, 1947:H21.
Manchus 1627:H5, 1636:H4, 1644:H3, 1683:H3, 1685:H3, 1722:H3, 1774:H5, 1850:H4, 1905:H18, 1911:H14, 1926:H17.
Mancini, Henry (b.1924) 1961:A9.
Mandarin Festival, The 1979:A22.
Mandela, Nelson 1990:H13, 1991:H13, 1993:M13, 1994:H13, 1998:M18.
Mandela, Winnie 1991:M11.
Mandell, Fania 1916:M3.
Mandrell, Barbara 1981:A6.
Manet, Édouard (1832–83) 1861:A6, 1863:A7, 1865:A9, 1867:A10, 1882:A8, 1986:A16.
Man For All Seasons, A 1960:A16.
manganese 1774:S6.
Manhattan Island 1612:M1, 1626:H1.
Manhattan Project 1941:S2, 1943:S7.
Manhattan Theater 1901:A7.
Manila 1571:H3, 1898:H7.
Manila Bay, Battle of 1898:H3.
"The Man I Love" 1924:A1.
"Man in the Open Air" 1915:A5.
Manitoba 1870:H5.
Maniu, Iuliu (1873–1955?) 1928:H16.
Mann, Heinrich (1871–1950) 1925:A20.
Mann, Thomas (1875–1955) 1901:A8, 1947:A4.
Mann Act 1910:H7, 1913:H11.
manned lunar orbit 1968:S19.
manned missions to the Moon 1966:S14.

Mann-Elkins Act 1910:H6.
Mannheim 1945:H2.
Man of La Mancha 1965:A9.
Man of Property, The 1906:A7.
Manon 1884:A5.
Manon Lescaut 1731:A5, 1893:A11.
"Man O' War" 1920:M6, 1950:M4.
man-powered flight 1979:M8.
Manry, Robert (b.1918) 1965:M3.
Mansfield, Arabella 1869:M2.
Mansfield, Katherine (1888–1923) 1911:A18.
Mansfield, Richard (1854?–1907) 1894:A2.
Mansfield Park 1814:A7.
Manship, Paul (1885–1966) 1934:A3.
Manson, Charles M. 1971:M3, 1975:A2.
Mantegna, Andrea 1985:A14.
Manteo 1587:M1.
mantle 1909:S6, 1958:S14.
Mantle, Mickey (b.1931) 1967:M5.
Mantz, Paul 1950:M5.
Manual of Botany 1848:S2.
Manual of Geology 1862:S4.
Manutius, Aldus (1450–1515) 1495:A4, 1597:A3.
Man Who Came to Dinner, The 1939:A10.
Man Who Knew Too Much, The 1935:A13.
Man Who Was Thursday, The 1908:A9.
Manzoni, Alessandro 1825:A6, 1874:A10.
Maoris 1843:H7, 1860:H12.
Mao Tse-tung (1893–1976) 1934:H14, 1949:H18, 1954:H20, 1966:H12, 1971:H18, 1976:H11.
Ma Perkins 1960:A1.
"Maple Leaf Rag" 1899:A2.
Map of Viginia, A 1612:S2.
Mapplethorpe, Robert 1990:A2.
maps 1513:S1, 1539:S2, 1554:S1, 1569:S2, 1616:S1, 1755:S3, 1783:S1, 1789:S1
Marat, Jean Paul (1744–93) 1793:A9.
marathon 1891:M6.
Marat/Sade 1964:A18.
Marble Faun, The 1924:A5.
Marbury v. Madison 1803:H3.
Marc 1914:A22.
Marceau, Félicien (b.1913) 1969:A23.
Marceau, Marcel (b.1923) 1947:A18.
"March of Time" 1934:A6.
March on Washington 1963:H3.
Marconi, Guglielmo (1874–1937) 1895:S8, 1896:S10, 1897:M5, 1901:M13, 1905:S14, 1909:S9, 1920:M10.
Marcos, Ferdinand Edralin (b.1917) 1972:H13, 1978:H18, 1986:H10.
Marcos, Imelda 1990:M4.
Mardi 1849:A2.
Mardi Gras 1827:M5, 1857:M1.
Marengo, Battle of 1800:H5.
"Mares and Foals in a Landscape" 1760:A3.
Marey, Étienne-Jules (1830–1904) 1882:A5.
Margaret Fleming 1890:A6.
Margaret I (1353–1412) (Den.) 1972:H20.
Margaret II (b.1940) (Den.) 1972:H20.
margarine 1869:M11.
Margarita 1967:A23.
Marguerite and Armand 1963:A17.
"Maria" 1957:A2.
Mariana Islands 1944:H2, 1947:H10.
Marianne 1969:A19.
Maria Theresa (1717–80) 1740:H3, 1741:H3, 1742:H2, 1744:H4, 1745:H5, 1765:H4, 1767:M3.

Marie Antoinette (1755–93) 1793:H3.
Marie de' Medici (1573–1642) 1610:H4, 1614:H6, 1616:H3, 1619:H3, 1622:A3, 1630:H3.
Mariel boatlift 1984:H14.
Marie Louise (1791–1847) 1810:H3.
Marignano, Battle of 1515:H1.
marijuana 1965:S18, 1973:S4, 1974:S5, 1976:M3.
"Marilyn Monroe" 1962:A1.
Marin, John (1870–1933) 1922:A5.
Mariner 4 1964:S13.
Mariner 5 1967:S14.
Mariner 9 1971:S10.
Mariner 10 1973:S14.
Maris, Roger (b.1934) 1961:M6.
Marius, Simon (1573–1624) 1610:S4, 1611:S1.
Markov, Georgi (1929–78) 1978:A15.
Markova, Alicia (b.1910) 1933:A19.
Marks, Johnny (b.1909) 1949:A7.
Marlborough, Duke of (1650–1722) 1702:H3, 1703:H2, 1704:H3, 1706:H3, 1708:H2, 1709:H2, 1711:H4.
Marley, Bob, and the Wailers 1976:A20.
Marlowe, Christopher (1564–1593) 1586:A1, 1588:A3.
Marmion 1808:A3.
Marne, Battle of the 1918:H8.
Maronites 1860:H10.
Marosszek Dances 1930:A18.
Marquand, John P. (1893–1960) 1933:A10, 1937:A5.
Marquette, Jacques (1637–75) 1673:H2.
Marquis of Queensberry 1865:M7.
"The Marriage at Cana" 1562:A3.
Marriage, The 1953:A10.
Marriage Act 1753:M1.
"Marriage à la Mode," 1743:A3.
Marriage of Figaro, The 1786:A5.
marriages 1664:M1, 1783:M7, 1922:M5.
Mars 1609:S3, 1666:S3, 1877:S4, 1948:S8, 1955:S8, 1959:S20, 1964:S13, 1966:S4, 1971:S10, 1971:S16, 1975:S11, 1976:S9.
Mars 1895:S2.
Mars Observer spacecraft 1992:S4.
Marsalis, Wynton 1997:A10.
Marsh, Othniel C. (1831–99) 1880:S3, 1896:S6.
Marshall, Frank J. 1904:M5.
Marshall, George C. 1944:M1, 1947:H3.
Marshall, Humphry (1722–1801) 1785:S6.
Marshall, John (1755–1835) 1801:H3, 1803:H3, 1819:H2.
Marshall, Thomas R. (1854–1925) 1912:H9, 1916:H11.
Marshall, Thurgood (b.1908) 1967:H5.
Marshall Islands 1942:H5, 1944:H2, 1947:H10.
Marshall Plan 1947:H3, 1947:H19, 1948:H1.
Marston Moor, Battle of 1644:H1.
Mars 2 1971:S16.
Mars 3 1971:S16.
Martin, Archer J.P. (b.1910) 1952:S15, 1953:S20.
Martin, Glenn L. (1886–1955) 1919:S9.
Martin, Homer (1836–97) 1870:A3, 1895:A3.
Martin, Hugh 1782:S2.
Martin, Mary (b.1913) 1949:A2, 1950:A11, 1959:A2, 1966:A15.
Martin Bomber 1919:S9.
Martin Chuzzlewit 1843:A2.
Martin Eden 1909:A4.
Martinson, Harry (b.1904) 1973:A16.

Martinu, Bohuslav (1890–1959) 1953:A10.
"Martyrdom of St. Bartholomew" 1720:A3.
"The Martyrdom of St. Maurice" 1582:A2.
Maruyama 1777:A5.
Marx, Karl (1818–83) 1848:M7, 1859:M6, 1867:M7.
Marx Brothers 1930:A8, 1931:A6, 1937:A7.
Mary Barton 1848:A7.
Mary Celeste 1872:M5.
Mary Hartman, Mary Hartman 1975:A7.
Mary I (1516–58) (Eng.) 1544:H1, 1553:H2, 1554:H1, 1558:H2.
Mary II (1662–94) (Brit.) 1688:H1, 1689:H3.
Mary Lamb (1764–1847) 1807:A4.
Maryland 1902:H2.
Marylebone Cricket Club 1787:M2.
Mary Poppins 1964:A9.
Mary Queen of Scots (1542–87) 1542:H3, 1559:H1, 1561:H1, 1567:H1, 1583:H1, 1585:H2, 1587:H3, 1603:H2.
"Mary's a Grand Old Name" 1906:A2.
Mascagni, Pierre (1863–1945) 1890:A12.
Masefield, John (1878–1967) 1902:A9, 1980:A20.
maser 1917:S10, 1952:S14, 1953:S3, 1960:S6, 1964:S24.
maser principle 1952:S14.
*M*A*S*H* 1970:A1, 1983:A4.
Masked Ball, A 1859:A7.
Maskelyne, Nevil (1732–1811) 1763:S2.
Mason, Lowell (1792–1872) 1822:A6.
Mason, Max (1877–1961) 1917:S6.
Mason-Dixon Line 1766:H3, 1784:S7.
Massachusetts 1888:H2, 1912:H10.
Massachusetts Bay Colony 1638:H3, 1641:H1, 1684:H1.
Massachusetts Bay Company 1629:H1, 1630:H1.
Massachusetts Emigrant Aid Society 1854:H4.
Massachusetts Institute of Technology 1865:S3.
Massachusetts Magazine 1791:A3.
Massachusetts Medical Society 1770:S1, 1781:S1.
Massacre in Rome 1975:A18.
Massasoit (1580?–1661) 1621:H2.
Massenet 1884:A5.
Massey, Raymond (b.1896) 1936:A13.
Massey, Vincent (1887–1967) 1952:H14.
Mass for the Dead 1791:A6.
Massie, Robert (b.1929) 1967:A9.
Mass in B minor 1738:A3.
Massine, Leonide (b.1896) 1917:A14, 1919:A14, 1948:A19.
Mass in F Major 1809:A6.
mass spectrograph 1919:S14, 1922:S14.
mass spectrometer 1918:S8.
Master Builder, The 1892:A10.
Masters, Edgar Lee (1869–1950) 1915:A8, 1916:A11.
Masters of Deceit 1958:A1.
Masters Tournament 1953:M9.
mastodon 1766:S2, 1801:M4.
Mastroianni, Marcello (b.1924) 1964:A19.
Matabele 1888:H9.
Matas, Rudolf (1860–1957) 1924:S7.
matches 1827:M7, 1852:M5, 1896:M3.
Matchmaker, The 1954:A8.
Mathematical Laws Applied to Triangles 1579:S1.

507

Merton, Thomas (1915–69) 1955:A10.

Merton of the Movies 1922:A9.

Mesmer, Franz Anton (1734–1815) 1775:S6.

mesons 1940:S4, 1942:S11, 1949:S15.

Mesopotamia 1915:H11, 1916:H13, 1920:H15.

mesoscaphe 1964:S15.

messenger RNA (mRNA) 1961:S16.

Messiaen, Olivier (b.1908) 1969:A17.

Messiah, The 1741:A5, 1742:A6, 1742:A1.

metabolism 1741:S1.

metallurgy 1550:S1, 1856:S4.

Metamorphoses 1626:A1.

"Metamorphosis" 1915:A13.

metaphysical painting 1917:A20.

Metaxas, John (1871–1941) 1936:H20.

Metchnikoff, Élie (1845–1916) 1886:S11, 1892:S7, 1901:S15, 1908:S16.

meteor 1807:S2, 1815:S1, 1922:M6.

Meteor Astronomy 1954:S16.

meteorites 1968:S18, 1976:M8.

Meteorological Essays and Observations 1823:S5.

Meteorological Observations and Essays 1793:S6.

meteorology 1963:S15.

meteors 1756:S1, 1948:S13.

meter 1893:S2, 1925:S4, 1960:S4.

Meteren, Emanuel van (1535–1612) 1610:A1.

Metesky, George 1957:M7.

methadone 1964:S7.

methane 1778:S4.

methanogens 1977:S1.

"method acting" 1898:A6.

Methodism 1735:M3.

Methodist Association 1743:M3.

Methodist Book Concern 1789:M1.

Methodist Church 1768:M2, 1939:M1.

Methodist Missionary Society 1813:M4.

Methodists 1738:M5, 1744:M2, 1773:M1, 1958:M3, 1968:M3.

Method of Reaching Extreme Altitudes, A 1919:S3.

métis 1869:H8.

Metric Conversion Act 1975:M8.

metric system 1790:S3, 1821:S4, 1866:S2, 1893:S1, 1960:S20, 1962:M21, 1965:M11, 1968:S8, 1975:M8.

Metro-Goldwyn-Mayer 1924:A11.

Metropolitan Museum of Art 1866:A2, 1980:A4, 1995:A2.

Metropolitan Opera 1908:A8, 1955:A3, 1983:A1.

Metropolitan Opera House 1966:A17.

Metropolitan Police 1829:M7.

Metropolitan Railway 1864:M8.

Metternich, Klemens von (1773–1859) 1810:H3, 1816:H6.

Meuse-Argonne, Battle of 1918:H3.

Mexican War 1846:H1, 1848:H1.

Mexico 1539:M1, 1810:H5, 1821:H5, 1824:H8, 1830:H2, 1835:H1, 1857:H10, 1862:H10, 1867:H11, 1914:H2, 1914:H3, 1995:H16, 1997:H20, 2000:H16.

Mexico City 1524:A1, 1988:S10.

Meyer, Hans (1858–1929) 1903:M9.

Meyer, Johann 1811:M6.

Meyerbeer, Giacomo (1791–1864) 1831:A8.

Meyerhof, Otto (1884–1951) 1922:S16, 1924:S10.

M'Fingal 1782:A2.

Michael, Prince (1862–68) (Serbia) 1868:H11.

Michael Robartes and the Dancer 1921:A19.

"Michael Row the Boat Ashore" 1867:A5.

Michaux, François (1770–1855) 1810:S2.

Michaux, Pierre 1867:M6.

Michelangelo 1981:A8, 1987:A20.

"Michelle" 1965:A24.

Michelson, Albert A. (1852–1931) 1878:S1, 1881:S1, 1887:S1, 1893:S2, 1907:S6, 1920:S1, 1926:S1.

Michelson-Morley experiment 1887:S1.

Michener, James (b.1907) 1947:A3, 1978:A8.

Michigan 1837:H1, 1846:H2, 1889:H1.

Mickey Mouse 1928:M1, 1968:M8.

Mickiewicz, Adam (1798–1855) 1832:A6.

Microbe Hunters, The 1926:S6.

microclimatology 1927:S11.

micrometer 1821:S6.

Micrometric Measurement of Double Stars 1837:S5.

microphone 1876:S5, 1877:S2, 1878:S3.

microscope 1590:S2, 1673:S3, 1838:S2, 1865:S11.

Microsoft Corporation 1995:S3, 1997:S6, 1999:S4, 2000:S9.

microtones in musical composition 1927:A19.

microwaves 1921:S2.

Midas 2 satellite 1960:S13.

Middle Congo 1903:H16.

Middle East 1982:H11, 1982:H12, 18, 1985:H13, 1987:H10, 1991:M16, 1994:H17.

Middlemarch: A Study of Provincial Life 1871:A11.

Middlesex, Lord 1745:A4.

Middlesex Canal 1793:S2.

Midler, Bette (b.1945?) 1972:A11, 1979:A3.

Midsummer Night's Dream, A 1595:A2, 1826:A3, 1843:A6, 1960:A24.

Midway, Battle of 1942:H5.

"A mighty fortress is our God" 1533:A1.

Mikado, The 1885:A8.

Milan, Prince (1854–1901) (Serbia) 1868:H11, 1882:H8.

Mila 18 1961:A13.

Mildenhall Treasure 1942:M13.

Mildred Pierce 1941:A11, 1945:A5.

mile run 1966:M8.

Miles, Nelson A. (1839–1925) 1886:H2.

Milhaud, Darius (1892–1974) 1918:A18.

Milinson, J.A. 1936:M13.

Military Assistance Command 1962:H1.

military tanks 1916:M13.

milk 1545:S1, 1864:S6, 1966:S20.

Milken, Michael 1990:M1.

"The Milkmaid" 1844:A6.

Milky Way 1610:S3, 1918:S3, 1925:S16, 1927:S13, 1951:S5, 1979:S2.

Mill, John Stuart (1806–73) 1825:M6.

Millais, John Everett (1829–96) 1848:A4, 1850:A11, 1851:A9, 1856:A5.

Millay, Edna St. Vincent (1892–1950) 1912:A7.

Millbury Lyceum Number 1 1826:M4.

Miller 1924:M7.

Miller, Arthur (b.1915) 1947:A6, 1949:A3, 1953:A3, 1961:A8.

Miller, Glenn (1904–44) 1938:A9.

Miller, Henry (b.1891) 1961:A2.

Miller, Irene (b.1936) 1978:M8.

Miller, Johnny 1974:M9.

Miller, Stanley (b.1930) 1953:S7.

Millet, Jean-François (1814–75) 1844:A6, 1848:A6, 1850:A10, 1854:A10.

"millibar" 1939:S10.

Millikan, Robert A. (1868–1953) 1911:S1, 1916:S1, 1917:S2, 1923:S8, 1925:S1.

milling machine 1798:S1.

millionaire 1843:M4.

Million Man March 1995:H9.

Million Woman March 1997:M6.

Mill on the Floss, The 1860:A7.

Mills, Robert (1781–1855) 1807:A2, 1836:A2, 1839:A3.

Milne, A.A. (1882–1956) 1924:A17, 1926:A13.

Milosevic, Slobodan 2000:H12.

Milosz, Czeslaw (b.1911) 1980:A12, 1998:A23.

Milton, John (1608–1674) 1629:A1, 1637:A4, 1667:A1, 1671:A3.

Milton 1808:A4.

mimeograph 1876:S5.

Minden 1759:H4.

Mind of Primitive Man, The 1911:S8.

Mindszenty, Jozsef (1892–1975) 1948:H20.

Mine Act 1842:M7.

mineralogy 1530:S2.

minerals 1825:S3.

mineral water 1773:S2.

Ming dynasty 1644:H3.

miniature golf 1652:M1.

miniature portraiture 1570:A1.

minimax theorem 1928:S9.

minimum wage 1937:M5, 1938:M4, 1996:H6.

"miniplanet" 1977:S3.

miniskirts 1966:M13.

minister 1629:M1.

Minister's Wooing, The 1859:A3.

Minkowsky, Oskar (1858–1981) 1889:S7.

Minna and Myself 1918:A8.

Minneapolis 1900:H7.

Minnelli, Liza (b.1946) 1972:A4, 1978:A10.

Minnelli, Vincente (b.1913) 1944:A5.

Minnesota 1858:H1, 1890:H1.

Minoan culture 1900:M11.

Minorca 1713:H4.

Minot, George (1885–1950) 1926:S2, 1934:S11.

Minow, Newton N. (b.1926) 1961:H4.

Minstrelsy of the Scottish Border 1802:A2.

mint 1792:M2.

Minuit, Peter (1580?–1638) 1626:H1.

Minutemen 1775:H2.

Mir space station 1990:S15, 1991:S17, 1993:S12, 1994:S9, 1995:S16, 1996:S11, 1997:S13, 1998:S2, S13, 1999:S15.

Miracle in the Gorbals 1944:A24.

"Miracles of St. Philip" 1509:A2.

Miranda 1948:S8.

Microcosmographia 1615:S1.

Miró, Joan (b.1893) 1919:A15, 1938:A20, 1959:A23.

miscarriage 1931:S15.

Miscellaneous Works of Freneau 1788:A1.

"Miserere" 1948:A14.

Misfits, The 1961:A8.

Misrepresentations Corrected and Truth Vindicated 1752:A3.

"missing links" 1860:S2.

missionaries 1549:M2, 1614:M3, 1622:M2.

mission revival 1911:A4.

missions 1542:M1, 1627:M4, 1701:M2, 1736:M2.

Mississippi 1817:H2, 1861:H1, 1870:H1, 1890:H1.

Mississippi Company 1717:H1, 1719:H1, 1720:H6.

Mississippi River 1673:H2, 1681:H1, 1795:H3.

Mississippi State College for Women 1884:M1.

Missouri 1820:H1, 1890:H1.

Missouri 1945:H7.

Missouri Compromise 1820:H1, 1854:H2, 1857:H1.

Miss Sara Sampson 1755:A3.

Miss Saigon 1991:A8.

Mistral, Gabriela (1889–1957) 1945:A15.

Mitchell, Arthur (b.1934) 1955:A4, 1969:A13.

Mitchell, Edgar (b.1930) 1971:S9.

Mitchell, George 1998:H12.

Mitchell, John N. (b.1913) 1972:H2, 1973:H1, 1975:H1.

Mitchell, John (1690?–1768) 1748:S1.

Mitchell, Margaret (1900–49) 1936:A1.

Mitchell, Maria (1818–89) 1847:S4, 1848:S3, 1865:S5.

Mitchell, Peter (b.1930) 1978:S20.

Mitchell, William ("Billy") (1879–1936) 1925:H10.

Mitcherlich, Eilhardt (1794–1863) 1819:S5.

Mitchill, Samuel Latham (1764–1831) 1787:S3, 1797:S1.

Mitford, Jessica 1963:M1.

Mithras 1954:M9.

mitosis 1876:S9.

Mitscherlich 1832:S9.

Mitterrand, François 1981:H12, 1986:H15, 1986:M1, 1992:M23, 1995:H22.

Mitya's Love 1925:A23.

Mobile Bay, Battle of 1864:H7.

Mobil Oil 1998:M2.

mobiles 1913:A11, 1928:A3.

Mobutu Sese Seko (b.1930) 1960:H13, 1961:H14, 1965:H15, 1971:H19, 1997:H23.

Moby Dick 1851:A1.

Model T 1908:M1, 1927:M3.

modern art 1863:A7, 1884:A6.

modern languages 1779:M1.

Modern Medicine, Its Theory and Practice 1907:S1.

Modern Painters 1843:A4.

"A Modest Proposal" 1729:A7.

Modiano, Patrick 1978:A20.

Modigliani, Amedeo (1884–1920) 1912:A14.

Mogul empire 1526:H2, 1707:H3, 1712:H4, 1739:H2.

Mohács, Battle of 1526:H3.

Mohl, Hugo von (1802–72) 1846:S5, 1851:S7.

Moho 1909:S6.

Mohole Project 1958:S14, 1964:S21.

Mohorovičić, Andrija (1857–1936) 1909:S6.

Mohorovičić, Discontinuity 1909:S6.

Moisson, Henri (1852–1907) 1886:S12, 1892:S4.

Molasses Act 1733:H2, 1736:H1.

Moldavia 1769:H3, 1774:H3, 1807:H7, 1829:H4, 1853:H8, 1907:H12.

Molecular Basis of Evolution 1959:S7.

molecular beam 1943:S12.

Molecular Hydrogen and Its Spectrum 1933:S18.

molecular-orbital theory of bonding 1966:S16.

molecular theory 1786:S2.

molecules 1811:S6, 1921:S8, 1971:S20.

509

Muhammad Ali (Egypt)
(1769?–1849) 1805:H7, 1811:H6,
1824:H4, 1833:H6, 1839:H8,
1840:H4.
Muhammad Reza Shah Pahlavi
1953:H16, 1979:H8, 1979:H16.
Muhammad V (1844–1918) (Turk.)
1909:H15.
Mühlberg, Battle of 1547:H4.
Muhlenberg, Gotthilf Henry
(1753–1815) 1778:S1.
Muir, John (1838–1914) 1890:M2,
1902:M2.
Mujibur Rahman (b.1920) 1972:H9.
Mukden, Battle of 1905:H9.
Mukden Incident 1931:H11.
Müller, Erwin W. (b.1911) 1937:S17,
1948:S21, 1951:S18.
Muller, Hermann J. (1890–1967)
1915:S2, 1927:S1, 1946:S12.
Muller, Jan (1922–58) 1957:A11.
Müller, Paul (1899–1965) 1939:S15.
Mulliken, Robert (b.1896) 1966:S16.
Mulroney, Brian 1984:H16.
multiple sclerosis 1957:S4.
multiplication 1631:S4.
mu meson 1937:S2.
mumps 1968:S6.
Munakata, Shiko (1903–75)
1970:A25.
Munch, Edvard (1863–1944)
1895:A6, 1901:A11, 1940:A22.
Munich 1972:H15.
Munich Pact 1938:H11, 1938:H15.
Municipal Assistance Corporation
1975:H11.
municipal college 1770:M2.
Municipal Corporation Act 1835:H5.
Munn v. Illinois 1877:H2.
Münster, Sebastian (1489–1552)
1544:S1.
muon 1937:S2.
Muppets 1955:A6.
Murasaki Shikibu (978?–1026?)
1000:A3.
murder 1630:M3.
Murder at Vicarage 1930:A19.
Murder in the Cathedral 1935:A14.
Murder of Roger Ackroyd, The
1926:A14.
"The Murders in the Rue Morgue"
1843:A1.
Murdoch, Iris (b.1919) 1954:A16,
1961:A20.
Murillo, Bartolomé (1618–1682)
1642:A2, 1656:A3.
Murneau, F.W. (1889–1931)
1922:A13, 1924:A14.
Murphy, William (b.1892) 1926:S2,
1934:S11.
Murphy Brown 1992:A4.
Murray, Gordon (b.1894) 1967:S21.
Murray, John 1779:M2.
Murray and Kean's 1750:A1.
muscle 1918:S13, 1922:S16.
museum 1773:S3.
Museum of Comparative Zoology
1859:S1.
Museum of Modern Art 1940:A6,
1980:A1.
Museum of Natural History
1635:M4.
Museum of Ornamental Art
1857:A9.
Museum of Science and Industry
1926:S8.
Musial, Stan 1948:M6.
music, academy of 1543:A1.
Musical Fund Society 1848:A3.
Musical Journal 1800:A3.
Musica Sacra 1724:A3.
Music Box, The 1932:A8.
music education 1898:A2.
Music in Miniature 1779:A1.
Music Man, The 1957:A8.
Music of Time, The 1975:A16.
Muskie, Edmund S. (b.1914)
1968:H7.

Muslims 1496:M2, 1499:M1.
Mussadegh, Muhammad
(1880–1967) 1951:H13,
1953:H16.
Mussolini, Benito (1883–1945)
1919:H18, 1921:H14, 1922:H14,
1924:H11, 1936:H22, 1937:H20,
1943:H15, 1945:H16.
Mussorgsky, Modest (1839–81)
1867:A9, 1872:A3, 1874:A5.
mutations 1590:S1, 1900:S10.
Mute Girl of Portici, The 1828:A5.
mutual-aid groups 1793:M3.
Mutual Security Agency 1951:H5.
Muybridge, Eadweard (1830–1904)
1872:S1.
Muzorewa, Abel (b.1925) 1979:H24.
myasthenia gravis 1671:S1.
Mycenae 1876:M7.
Myers, Michael J. (b.1943)
1980:H12.
My Fair Lady 1956:A3.
"My Favorite Things" 1959:A2.
My Lai, South Vietnam 1969:H8.
My Little Chickadee 1940:A4.
myoglobin 1962:S20.
"My Old Kentucky Home" 1852:A3.
Myra Breckenridge 1968:A5,
1970:A7.
Myrdal, Alva 1982:M24.
Mysore 1767:H3, 1831:H7.
Mysteries of Udolpho 1794:A4.
Mysterious Affair at Styles, The
1920:A11.
Myth of Sisyphus, The 1942:A14.
My World and Welcome to It
1942:A8.
Nabokov, Vladimir (b.1899)
1955:A11, 1962:A5.
"Nachkriegsidyll" 1921:A13.
Nachtigal, Gustav (1834–85)
1869:M9.
Nadelman, Elie (1882–1946)
1915:A5.
Nadir Shah (1688–1747) 1728:H1,
1730:H2, 1733:H4, 1735:H2,
1736:H4, 1739:H2, 1743:H4,
1747:H3.
Nagasaki, Japan 1570:H3, 1857:H5,
1945:H5, 1946:S1.
Naguib, Muhammad (b.1901)
1952:H17, 1954:H14.
Nagy, Laszlo (1925–78) 1973:A22.
Naipaul, V.S. (b.1932) 1971:A15,
1975:A12.
Naismith, James A. (1861–1939)
1891:M4.
Nakasone, Yasuhiro 1986:M21.
Naked and the Dead, The 1948:A5.
Naked Ape, The 1968:A18.
Naked Came the Stranger 1969:A3.
Naked Lunch 1959:A10.
Nakian, Reuben (b.1897) 1961:A11.
Namibia 1978:H24, 1990:M18.
naming streets 1679:M1.
Namur 1695:H1.
Nana 1880:A9.
Nancy Drew 1906:A6.
Nanking 1927:H14, 1928:H10.
Nanking, Treaty of 1842:H9.
Nanook of the North 1922:A2.
Nansen, Fridtjof (1861–1930)
1888:M5, 1893:M9.
Nantes 1941:H23.
Nantes, Edict of 1598:H2.
Napier, John (1550–1617) 1614:S1,
1617:S4.
Napier's bones 1617:S4.
Naples 1720:H4, 1734:H2, 1733:H1.
Napoleon Bonaparte (1769–1821)
1795:H5, 1796:H5, 1797:H3,
1798:H6, 1798:H7, 1799:H3,
1801:H5, 1802:H5, 1803:H2,
1803:H8, 1804:H4, 1805:H3,
1806:H3, 1806:H4, 1806:H5,
1806:H7, 1807:H5, 1807:M3,
1808:H6, 1808:H7, 1808:M5,
1809:H4, 1809:H6, 1810:H3,

1810:H4, 1811:H7, 1812:H7,
1812:H7, 1812:H8, 1813:H4,
1814:H5, 1815:H4, 1815:H5.
Napoleon 1925:A21.
Napoleonic Wars 1805:H5, 1806:H4,
1807:H4, 1809:H3, 1811:H3,
1812:H7, 1813:H4, 1814:H5.
Napoleon III (1808–73) (Fr.)
1848:H5, 1852:H4, 1858:H9,
1858:H13, 1859:H5, 1862:H10,
1867:H11, 1869:H5, 1870:H7,
1870:H8.
Napoleon of Notting Hill, The
1904:A10.
Napster 2000:A6.
Narrow Road to the Deep North,
The 1694:A2.
Narva, Battle of 1700:H2.
Narváez, Pánfilo de (1470?–1528)
1528:H1.
NASA 1959:S9, 1965:S5.
Naseby, Battle of 1645:H1.
Nash, John (1752–1835) 1811:A5.
Nash, Ogden (1902–71) 1931:A10.
Nash, Paul (1889–1946) 1918:A15,
1933:A18.
Nashoba 1825:M1.
Nashville, Battle of 1864:H4.
Nasir ad-Din (1831?–96) 1848:H11.
Nasjonal Samling Party 1933:H18.
Nasser, Gamal Abdal (1918–70)
1954:H14, 1956:H12, 1958:H18,
1959:H21.
Nast, Thomas (1840–1902)
1874:A1.
Natal 1836:H6, 1843:H5, 1856:H8,
1893:H12, 1897:H12.
Natchitoches 1714:H1.
Nathans, Daniel (b.1928) 1978:S12.
Nathan the Wise 1779:A7.
Nation, Carry (1846–1911)
1900:H8.
National Academy of Design
1826:A2.
National Academy of Sciences
1863:S1, 1916:S12.
National Aeronautics and Space
Administration 1958:S3, 1995:S8,
1997:S1, 1999:S1–3, 2000:S3, S5.
National Air Quality Control Act
1970:S7.
national anthem 1792:A6.
National Archery Association
1878:M5.
National Association for the
Advancement of Colored People
1955:H6.
National Association for the
Advancement of Colored People
(NAACP) 1909:H1.
National Association of Baseball
Players 1857:M2, 1871:M1.
National Association of
Broadcasters 1975:M10.
National Association of Professional
Baseball Players 1871:M1.
National Audubon Society 1969:S6.
National Baptist Convention of the
U.S.A. 1895:M1.
National Broadcasting Company
1926:M5.
National Bureau of Standards
1901:S1.
National Cancer Institute
1937:S10.
national conscription 1792:M1.
National Conservation Commission
1909:H8.
National Council of Churches
1959:M8.
National Council of the Churches of
Christ 1950:M1.
national debt 1986:H7.
National Defense Act 1916:H5.
National Defense Advisory
Commission 1940:H12.
National Defense Education Act
1958:M1.

National Democratic Party
1860:H1.
National Drug Control Policy, Office
of 1996:H12.
National Education Association
1902:M5.
National Farmers' Alliance
1880:H4.
National Gallery 1824:A2.
National Geographic Magazine
1888:S2.
National Geographic Society
1888:S2.
National Guard 1916:H5, 1933:H11,
1933:M3.
National Herb Garden 1980:M9.
National Hurricane Center
1955:S1.
National Institute of Arts and
Letters 1898:A5.
Nationalist China 1954:H6,
1955:H2.
National Labor Board 1933:H8.
National Labor Party 1920:H6.
National Labor Relations Board
1935:H4.
National Labor Union 1866:M6.
National League 1876:M2,
1901:M7, 1979:M4.
National Medical Association
1895:S6.
National Monetary Conference
1897:H1.
national monument 1906:M4.
National Nutrition Program
1941:S6.
National Oceanic and Atmospheric
Administration 1970:S3.
National Park Service 1916:S2.
National Portrait Gallery 1857:A9.
National Presbyterian Church
1973:M4.
National Progressive Republican
League 1911:H1.
National Radio Astronomy
Observatory 1959:S8.
National Railroad Passenger
Corporation 1970:H5.
National Recovery Administration
1933:H8.
National Research Act 1974:S3.
National Research Council
1916:S12.
National Revolutionary Party
1929:H13.
National Rifle Association 1871:M3.
National Science Foundation
1950:S6.
National Security Act 1947:H9.
National Socialist German Workers'
Party 1920:H17.
National Society of the Red Cross
1881:M2.
National Theater Touring Company
1972:A16.
National Tuberculosis Association
1904:S1.
National Velvet 1935:A12.
National Wage Stabilization Board
1945:H9.
National War Labor Board 1945:H9.
National Weather Service 1970:S3.
National Woman's Christian
Temperance Union 1874:M2.
National Woman Suffrage
Association 1869:H4.
National Women's Social and
Political Union 1903:M11.
Native Son 1940:A14.
NATO 1949:H10, 1982:H10,
1990:M23.
Natta, Guilo (b.1903) 1953:S17.
Natural Childbirth 1933:S13.
natural gas 1919:S5.
natural history 1778:M1, 1807:S3.
Natural History of Carolina,
Florida, and the Bahama Islands,
The 1731:S1.

511

517

Rabin Yitzhak (b.1922) 1974:H21, 1977:H19, 1992:H16, 1994:M9, 1995:H14.
Rabutin-Chantal, Marie de 1671:A2.
race cars 1909:S8.
race riots 1980:H10.
Rachmaninoff, Sergei 1897:A6, 1909:A13.
racial violence 1966:M3.
Racine, Jean (1639–1699) 1667:A2, 1677:A2.
racquets 1766:M2.
radar 1929:S8, 1935:S16, 1939:M9, 1966:S4.
radar-controlled bombsight 1943:S8.
Radburn, N.J. 1929:M2.
Radcliffe, Ann Ward (1764–1823) 1794:A4.
Radcliffe College 1879:M3.
radiation 1893:S9, 1902:S13, 1956:S9.
radiation-exposure meter 1950:S2.
Radich, Stefan (1871–1928) 1928:H13.
radio 1875:S1, 1891:A6, 1900:S3, 1906:S4, 1916:S5, 1920:S2, 1922:M1, 1923:M2, 1925:M14, 1925:S10, 1929:A10, 1933:M2, 1941:S13, 1954:A5.
radioactive decay 1903:S8.
radioactive decomposition 1913:S19, 1919:S11.
radioactive iodine 1940:S8, 1941:S12.
radioactive isotopes 1934:S21.
radioactive tracing 1913:S16, 1943:S17.
radioactivity 1896:S13, 1898:S8, 1902:S11, 1903:S14, 1921:S13, 1934:S13, 1935:S20, 1978:S15.
radio altimeter 1938:S11.
Radio Astronomy 1952:S13.
radio astronomy 1974:S18.
radio beacons 1913:S2.
radiocarbon 1947:S7.
radiocarbon dating 1960:S16.
Radio City Music Hall 1932:M6.
radio-compass 1913:S2.
Radio Corporation of America 1919:S1.
radio drama 1924:A20.
Radio-elements and Isotopes 1931:S14.
radio maps 1942:S8.
radio-optical telescope 1959:S3.
radio program 1906:S2.
radios 1917:S4, 1924:M5, 1964:M3.
radiotelephone 1922:S5, 1926:M1.
radio telescope 1937:S1, 1962:S6, 1963:S5.
radio waves 1903:S12, 1944:S16, 1955:S6.
radium 1898:S8, 1902:S10, 1903:S8, 1911:S17.
radon 1910:S11, 1987:S6.
Raeburn, Henry (1756–1823) 1794:A6.
R.A.F. 1912:M18.
Rafinesque, Constantine (1783–1840) 1830:S3.
Ragged Dick; or, Street Life in New York 1867:A2.
ragtime 1899:A2, 1912:M2.
Ragtime 1976:A14.
railroad bridge 1935:M8.
Railroad Rate Bill 1906:H5.
railroads 1826:M2, 1832:M7, 1844:S3, 1853:M8, 1856:M10, 1939:M15, 1945:M7.
railroad tunnel 1826:M5.
rainbows 1637:S1.
"Raindrops Keep Falling on My Head" 1969:A12.
Rainger, Ralph (1901–42) 1938:A10.
Rainwater, James (b.1918) 1975:S19.

Raisin in the Sun 1959:A3.
Rajputs 1562:H3.
Raj Quartet, The 1976:A18.
"A Rake's Progress" 1735:A2.
Rake's Progress, The 1951:A12.
Raleigh, Sir Walter (1554?–1618) 1584:H1, 1585:H1, 1587:H2, 1595:H1, 1603:H3, 1616:H2, 1618:H2.
Ralph Roister Doister 1553:A2.
Raman, Sir Chandrasekhara (1888–1970) 1928:S11, 1930:S20.
Ramazzini, Bernardino (1633–1714) 1713:S1.
Rambert, Marie (b.1888) 1960:A19.
Rambler 1750:A4.
Rambouillet, Marquise de (1588–1665) 1617:A1, 1659:A1.
Rameau, Jean Philippe (1683–1764) 1722:A4, 1733:A4.
Ramillies, Battle of 1706:H3.
Ramona 1884:A1.
Ramsay, Sir William (1852–1916) 1894:S7, 1895:S9, 1896:S11, 1898:S12, 1903:S8, 1904:S16, 1910:S11.
Ramses II (1292–1225 B.C.) 1976:M16.
"ranch-type" home 1946:M6.
rand 1961:M12.
Rand, Ayn (b.1905) 1935:A2, 1957:A9.
Randall, G. Lowis 1923:S6.
Randall, Merle 1923:S6.
Ranger 4 lunar probe 1962:S10.
Ranger 7 1964:S10.
Rangoon 1824:H6.
Rankin, Rep. Jeannette (1880–1973) 1917:M6, 1941:M1.
"Ransom of Red Chief" 1910:A5.
Raoult, François-Marie (1830–1901) 1886:S10.
Raoult's law 1886:S10.
rap music 1995:A10, 1997:A11.
Rapallo, Treaty of 1922:H11, 1926:H21.
"The Rape" 1934:A13.
Rape of the Lock, The 1712:A3.
"Rape of the Sabines" 1799:A8.
Raphael (1483–1570) 1504:A1, 1512:A2, 1514:A1, 1517:A1.
rap music 1990:A5.
Rapp, George 1805:M1.
Rappites 1805:M1.
Rashid dynasty 1921:H17.
Rashomon 1950:A21.
Rasht, Treaty of 1732:H4.
Rasmussen, Knud (1879–1933) 1919:S10, 1924:M11.
Rasputin, Grigori Yefimovich (1872–1916) 1915:H13, 1916:H16.
Rasselas 1759:A5.
Rastatt, Treaty of 1714:H2.
Rathenau, Walter (1867–1922) 1922:H17.
Rather, Dan (b.1931) 1980:M10, 1987:A2.
rational numbers 1872:S6, 1873:S4.
rationing 1916:M9, 1918:M10, 1941:M12, 1942:M2, 1945:M2, 1948:M8, 1949:M7.
Rattigan, Terence (b.1911) 1936:A18, 1945:A21, 1946:A20.
rattlesnake bites 1746:S3.
Rattner, Abraham (b.1895) 1958:A13.
Raucoux, Battle of 1746:H3.
Rauschenberg, Robert (b.1925) 1959:A6, 1963:A5.
Ravel, Maurice (1875–1937) 1899:A12, 1928:A15.
Raven and Other Poems, The 1845:A3.
Ravenna, Battle of 1512:H1.
Ravenscroft, Thomas (1590?–1633?) 1609:A4, 1621:A1.
Ravenscroft's Psalter 1621:A1.

Rawlings, Marjorie Kinnan (1896–1953) 1939:A7.
Rawlins, Horace 1895:M5.
Rawlinson, Henry (1810–95) 1846:M3.
Ray, James Earl (b.1928) 1968:H3.
Ray, John (1627–1705) 1670:S1, 1676:S2, 1682:S2, 1685:S1, 1693:S2, 1696:S1.
Ray, Man (1890–1976) 1916:A3.
Ray, Satyajit (b.1922) 1954:A20.
Rayleigh (b.John William Strutt), Lord (1842–1919) 1869:S6, 1877:S9, 1894:S7, 1904:S17.
rayon 1855:M7.
Razor's Edge, The 1944:A25.
Reade, Charles (1814–84) 1861:A5.
Reader's Digest 1921:A4.
reading and writing 1647:M1.
Reagan, Nancy 1987:S9.
Reagan, Ronald W. (b.1911) 1976:H8, 1980:H8, 1981:H1, 1981:H2, 1981:H3, 1982:H1, 1982:H2, 1983:H1, 1983:H2, 1984:H1, 1985:H1, 1986:H2, 1987:H1, 1988:H9, 1989:H1, 1994:S2.
Real Inspector Hound, The 1968:A22.
Realism 1849:A6, 1861:A6.
realist 1963:A8.
real numbers 1873:S4.
reaper 1832:M4, 1834:S2.
"The Reaper" 1854:A10.
Réaumur, René-Antoine Ferchault de (1683–1757) 1720:S2, 1734:S2, 1752:S2.
Réaumur scale 1730:S3.
Rebecca 1938:A12, 1940:A2.
Rebecca of Sunnybrook Farm 1903:A5.
Reber, Grote (b.1911) 1937:S1, 1942:S8.
Reciprocal Trade Agreements Act 1934:H9.
Reclamation Act 1902:H9.
"Reclining Figure" 1939:A25.
Reconstruction 1870:H4, 1877:H4, 1957:H9.
Reconstruction Acts 1867:H2.
Reconstruction Finance Corporation 1932:H1.
records 1887:S3.
recreation 1611:M1.
Recruiting Officer, The 1732:A1.
Red and the Black, The 1830:A8.
"Red and White Peonies" 1886:A4.
Red Badge of Courage, The 1895:A1.
red blood cells 1658:S2, 1925:S3.
Red Brigades 1978:H16.
Redburn 1849:A2.
Red Cross 1862:M5.
Red Desert 1964:A19.
Reddy, Helen (b.1941) 1972:A12.
Redeemed Captive, The 1707:A1.
Redemption of Tycho Brahe, The 1916:A23.
Redfield, William (1789–1857) 1848:S1.
Redford, Robert (b.1936) 1969:A12.
Red Giants and White Dwarfs 1967:S2.
Red Guards 1966:H12.
Redistribution Bill 1923:H19.
Red Mill, The 1906:A3, 1923:A21.
Red River 1803:M1.
Red River Rebellion 1869:H8, 1870:H5.
Red Rover, The 1827:A1.
"Red scare" 1920:H1.
red shift 1929:S1, 1960:S10, 1963:S1.
Redshirts 1860:H5.
Red Shoes, The 1948:A19.
Red Skelton Show, The 1945:A13.
Red Snowball Tree, The 1974:A15.
"The Red Studio" 1911:A17.

redwood trees 1849:M6.
Reed, Carol (1906–76) 1939:A21, 1949:A13, 1968:A23.
Reed, John (1887–1920) 1919:A4.
Reed Walter (1851–1902) 1900:S5, 1901:S2.
reflecting quadrant 1730:S1.
reflecting telescope 1959:S6.
Reflections on the Motive Power of Fire 1824:S8.
Reflections on the Revolution in France 1790:M3.
Reflex Activity of the Spinal Cord 1932:S18.
Reformation 1532:M1.
Reformation, Swiss 1531:H1.
Reform Judaism 1873:M5.
refrigerated railroad car 1866:S4.
refrigerator cars 1875:M1.
refrigerators 1937:M10.
Refugee Relief Act 1953:H5.
Regan, Donald 1988:M2.
Regency 1794:A2.
regenerative 1914:S3.
Regent's Park 1811:A5.
Regent Street 1811:A5.
reggae music 1976:A20.
Regiment of Woman 1973:A12.
Regnard, Jean François (1655–1709) 1695:A2.
Regulating Act 1773:H3.
Rehnquist William H. (b.1924) 1971:H7, 1986:H2.
Reichstein, Tadeus (b.1897) 1933:S14, 1936:S10, 1950:S10.
Reid, Harry F. (1859–1944) 1911:S4.
Reigen 1950:A19.
Reign of Law, The 1900:A7.
Reign of Terror 1793:H5.
Reinagle, Alexander (1756–1809) 1787:A1.
Reina Regenta 1895:M6.
Reinhardt, Django (1910–53) 1917:A17, 1934:A15.
Reinhardt's, Max (1873–1943) 1910:A9.
Reinken, Jan (1623–1722) 1702:A3.
Reitz, Edgar 1984:A17.
Relación 1542:A1.
Relative Motion of the Earth and the Luminiferous Ether 1881:S1.
Relativity Theory of Protons and Electrons 1936:S12.
relay race 1893:M5.
Release of Neural Transmitter Substances, The 1969:S14.
religion 1920:M15.
Religion, War of 1563:H1, 1568:H2, 1570:H1, 1572:H1, 1574:H3, 1576:H2, 1580:H1.
religious freedom 1636:M2.
religious liberty 1681:M1.
religious revival 1733:M3, 1858:M1.
religious tolerance 1781:M3.
Remagen 1945:H2.
Remarque, Erich Maria (1898–1970) 1929:A11.
Rembrandt van Rijn (1606–69) 1627:A1, 1632:A3, 1640:A3, 1652:A1, 1653:A2, 1969:A19.
Rembrandt's Hat 1973:A2.
Remek, Vladimir 1978:S17.
Remembrance of Things Past 1913:A8, 1919:A16.
remote-controlled boat 1898:S7.
Removal Bill 1830:H3.
Removalist, The 1971:A17.
Renaissance 1519:A1.
Renan, Ernest (1823–92) 1863:A10.
Renascence and Other Poems 1912:A7.
Reno, Janet 1993:H6.
Renoir, Jean (1894–1979) 1932:A15, 1937:A17.
Renoir, Pierre-Auguste (1841–1919) 1873:A3, 1876:A4, 1884:A9, 1907:A14, 1985:A13.

Rensselaer Polytechnic Institute 1824:S2.
Rent 1996:A9.
Renwick, James (1792–1863) 1846:A1, 1850:A2.
Reorganization Act 1949:H2.
Report on the Relativity Theory of Gravitation 1918:S12.
Report on the Subject of Manufactures 1799:S2.
Repository of Sacred Music 1810:A2.
Representative Men 1850:A6.
reproduction 1762:S5, 1869:S8.
Republican Party 1792:H1, 1854:H3, 1860:H1, 1864:H8, 1868:H6, 1872:H3, 1874:A1, 1876:H4, 1880:H1, 1884:H3, 1888:H3, 1896:H5, 1900:H10, 1904:H7, 1908:H8, 1920:H7, 1924:H8, 1928:H7, 1936:H4, 1948:H6, 1952:H7, 1956:H6, 1964:H6, 1968:H8, 1972:H8, 1982:H8, 1994:H1.
Repulse 1941:H22.
Requiem 1791:A6.
Requiem—Grand Messe des Morts 1837:A6.
Requiem Mass 1874:A10.
Requirement of the Organism for Oxygen, The 1883:S10.
Resaca de la Palma, Battle of 1846:H1.
Researches on Bacteria 1872:S7.
reserpine 1955:S7.
resistance 1843:S8.
Resnais, Alain (b.1922) 1959:A20, 1961:A14, 1966:A26.
resonance 1931:S4.
resonance method 1944:S11.
Respectable Girl, The 1749:A4.
Respighi, Ottorino (1879–1936) 1923:A20.
respiration 1747:S3.
respirator 1948:S12.
Respiratory Exchange of Animals and Man, The 1916:S16.
Ressel, Franz (1793–1857) 1829:S7.
restaurant 1643:M1, 1770:M4.
restaurant, self-service 1885:M2.
Restitution, Edict of 1629:H4.
"Rest on the Flight into Egypt" 1504:A3, 1621:A2.
restriction enzymes 1978:S12.
Retin-A 1988:S2.
Return of Sherlock Holmes, The 1905:A16.
"The Return of the Dove to the Ark" 1851:A9.
Return of the Native, The 1878:A4.
Retzius, Anders Adolf (1796–1860) 1842:S8.
Retzius, Magnus G. (1842–1919) 1896:S12.
Reuben, David (b.1933) 1970:A11.
Reuben James 1941:H10.
Revenue Act 1926:H2, 1938:H5.
Revenue Cutter Service 1915:H3.
Revere, Paul (1735–1818) 1775:H2, 1770:A2, 1770:A3, 1774:M1.
Revised Standard Version 1952:M7.
revolver 1835:M4, 1854:S2.
revolving gun turret 1862:S1.
Revue du XIXᶜ Siècle 1867:A10.
Reyes, Rafael (1850–1921) 1904:H14.
Reynolds, Joshua (1723–1792) 1746:A2, 1768:A6, 1769:A3, 1777:A4.
Rhapsodies 1879:A11.
Rhapsody 1919:A13.
"Rhapsody in Blue" 1924:A2.
Rhäticus (1514–76) 1541:S1, 1596:S1.
Rhee, Syngman (1875–1965) 1952:H15, 1956:H18.
Rheims 1945:H17.
Rheims-Douai Bible 1609:M3.

rheumatic fever 1949:S3.
rheumatoid arthritis 1948:S6.
Rh factor 1939:S8, 1940:S1.
Rhineland 1644:H2, 1925:H16, 1929:H16, 1930:H19, 1936:H14.
Rhinoceros 1959:A22.
Rhode Island 1647:H2.
Rhodes, Cecil John (1853–1902) 1888:H9, 1889:H13, 1890:H14, 1901:M14.
Rhodesia 1896:H13, 1923:H17, 1965:H11, 1970:H19, 1976:H19, 1980:H22.
Rhodesia and Nyasaland, Federation of 1953:H21.
Rhodes Scholarships 1976:M1.
rhodium 1804:S4.
Rhondda, Lady Margaret 1922:M12.
Rhone 1867:M8.
Rhymes for the Nursery 1806:A4.
Rhys, Jean (1894–1979) 1966:A24.
"The Rhythm Boys" 1926:A8.
Rialto 1925:S12.
Ribaut, Jean (1520?–65) 1562:H1.
riboflavin 1935:S9.
ribonuclease 1969:S3.
ribosome 1961:S16.
rice 1724:S2.
Rice, Elmer (1892–1967) 1914:A9, 1923:A7, 1929:A9, 1931:A8.
Rice, Thomas ("Jim Crow") (1808–60) 1828:A3.
Rich, Buddy (b.1917) 1923:A6.
Richard II 1595:A2.
Richard III 1592:A1, 1741:A3, 1750:A1.
Richards, Dickinson (1895–1973) 1956:S14.
Richards, Gordon (b.1904) 1954:M10.
Richards, Theodore (1868–1928) 1914:S11.
Richardson, Elliot L. (b.1920) 1973:H1.
Richardson, Henry Hobson (1838–86) 1872:A1, 1875:A2.
Richardson, Lewis Fry (1881–1953) 1922:S10.
Richardson, Ralph (b.1902) 1936:A13.
Richardson, Samuel (1689–1761) 1740:A4, 1744:A2, 1748:A5.
Richardson, Owen (1879–1959) 1911:S12, 1914:S12, 1916:S13, 1933:S18.
Richardson, Tony (b.1928) 1959:A17, 1962:A20, 1963:A23.
Richelieu, Armand Jean du Plessis, Duke of (1585–1642) 1616:H3, 1622:H1, 1624:H2, 1626:H3, 1628:H8, 1630:H3.
Richelieu, Cardinal 1629:M3.
Rich Man, Poor Man 1970:A8.
Richmond 1737:H1.
Richmond, Bill 1805:M2.
Richter, Burton (b.1931) 1976:S10.
Richter, Conrad (1890–1968) 1950:A9.
rickets 1922:S3.
Riddle, Oscar (1877–1968) 1928:S10.
Rider on the Rain 1970:A24.
Riders of the Purple Sage 1912:A2.
Ride, Sally 1983:S1.
Ridgway, Matthew B. (b.1895) 1951:H2.
Riefenstahl, Leni (b.1902) 1932:A21, 1936:A16.
Riel, Louis (1844–45) 1869:H8.
Rienzi 1842:A4.
Riffs 1893:H13, 1909:H17, 1921:H13, 1925:H20, 1926:H18.
rifle 1918:S2.
rifle shooting 1871:M3.
Riga 1941:H15.
Rights of Man, The 1791:M3.
Right Stuff, The 1979:A2.

Rigoletto 1851:A7.
Riis, Jacob A. (1849–1914) 1890:A3, 1901:A4.
Rijksmuseum 1885:A12.
Rilke, Rainer Maria (1875–1926) 1905:A17, 1907:A8, 1996:A20.
Rimbaud, Arthur (1854–91) 1871:A8, 1873:A6, 1886:A9.
"The Rime of the Ancient Mariner" 1798:A4.
Rimsky-Korsakov, Nikolay (1844–1908) 1869:A7, 1882:A10, 1888:A9, 1898:A10, 1900:A16, 1907:A10.
Rinaldo 1711:A3.
Ring and the Book, The 1868:A4.
Ringling Brothers Barnum & Bailey Circus 1944:M7, 1950:M9, 1956:M7.
Ring of the Nibelung, The 1876:A9.
Ring Theater 1881:M6.
Rinker, Al (b.1901) 1926:A8.
Rinuccini, Ottavio (1562–1621) 1594:A2, 1627:A2.
Rio de Janeiro 1555:H1, 1777:H5.
Rio de la Plata 1845:H7.
Rio de Oro 1885:H10.
Rio Grande 1582:H1, 1848:H1.
Ripken, Cal Jr. 1995:M8.
Ripley, George 1841:M4.
Ripley, Robert Lee (1893–1943) 1918:A1.
"Rip Van Winkle" 1820:A1.
Rip Van Winkle 1866:A3.
Rise, Progress, and Present State of Medicine, The 1792:S3.
Rise and Fall of the City of Mahogonny, The 1930:A15.
Rise and Fall of the Third Reich, The 1960:A3.
Rise of Silas Lapham, The 1885:A1.
Risorgimento 1852:H6, 1862:H11.
Rite of Spring, The 1913:A10.
Rittenberg, David (b.1906) 1935:S4.
Rittenhouse, Davi (1782–96) 1767:S1, 1769:S2, 1786:S2.
Rittenhouse, William (1644–1708) 1690:S1.
Rivals, The 1775:A5.
"The River" 1943:A17.
Rivera, Diego (1886–1957) 1944:A19.
Rivers, Larry (b.1923) 1963:A4.
Rivers and Harbors Bill 1882:H4.
Rivoli 1925:S12.
RNA 1955:S2, 1959:S15.
"road movies" 1940:A8.
"The Road to Mandalay" 1892:A4.
Road to Singapore 1940:A8.
Roanoke Island 1585:H1, 1586:H1, 1587:H2, 1590:H1.
Robbers, The 1781:A2.
robbery 1878:M7, 1962:M2, 1964:M9.
Robbins, Frederick (b.1916) 1952:S6, 1963:S9.
Robbins, Harold (b.1916) 1961:A3, 1971:A12.
Robbins, Jerome (b.1918) 1944:A10, 1957:A2.
Robe, The 1942:A12.
Robert II (970–1031) (Fr.) 1010:H2.
Robert Le Diable 1831:A8.
Robin, Leo (b.1900) 1938:A10, 1949:A5.
Robin Hood 1890:A5.
Robins, Benjamin (1707–51) 1742:S4.
Robinson, Edwin Arlington (1869–1935) 1916:A9, 1917:A5, 1920:A3, 1927:A6.
Robinson, Frank 1974:M10.
Robinson, Jack R. ("Jackie") (1919–72) 1947:M6.
Robinson, Mary 1990:M14.
Robinson Crusoe 1719:A3.
Robinson-Patman Act 1936:H5.
robot 1920:A10.
Rob Roy 1818:A8.

Rochemont, Louis de (1899–1979) 1934:A6.
Rochet, Louis Lucien 1877:M7.
Rock and Roll Hall of Fame and Museum 1995:A11.
Rockefeller, John D. (1839–1937) 1870:M5, 1891:M1.
Rockefeller, Jr., John D. (1874–1960) 1946:H10.
Rockefeller, Nelson A. (1908–79) 1958:H8, 1971:H6, 1974:H4.
Rockefeller, Michael 1982:A8.
Rockefeller Center 1934:A3.
Rockefeller Institute for Medical Research 1904:S3.
Rocket into Interplanetary Space, The 1922:S12.
rocket missile 1946:S9.
rocket-powered airplane 1960:S7.
rockets 1919:S3, 1926:S4, 1934:S12, 1947:S8.
rock music 1967:A11, 1974:A6, 1983:A13.
rock 'n' roll 1955:M4, 1960:M6, 1964:M7, 1986:A1.
"Rock oil" 1841:M1.
Rockwell, Norman (1894–1978) 1916:A1.
Rocky 1976:A5.
Rocky Horror Show, The 1973:A19.
Rocky Mountain Spotted Fever 1917:S7.
rococo 1730:A5.
Rodeo 1942:A6.
Roderick Hudson 1876:A2.
Rodgers, Calbraith P. 1911:M6.
Rodgers, Richard (1902–79) 1925:A6, 1929:A7, 1937:A10, 1941:A3, 1942:A2, 1943:A4, 1945:A9, 1949:A2, 1951:A4, 1959:A2, 1970:A12.
Rodin, Auguste (1840–1917) 1877:A5, 1879:A8, 1880:A4, 1884:A11, 1886:A10.
Roger, Muriel 1964:S6.
Rogers, Robert (1735–91) 1766:A2.
Rogers, Bill 1924:H6.
Rohmer, Eric (b.1920) 1971:A20, 1972:A22.
Rohmer, Sax (1883?–1959) 1913:A14.
Rojas Pinilla, Gustavo (b.1900) 1957:H19.
Rolfe, John (1585–1622) 1612:S3, 1613:S2.
Rolland, Romain (1866–1944) 1904:A13, 1915:A21.
roller bearings 1496:S1.
roller-skating 1863:M4, 1870:M4, 1875:M8.
rolling mill 1496:S1.
Rolling Stone Magazine 1967:A8, 1976:A20.
Rolling Stones 1965:A18, 1969:A18, 1981:A10, 1989:A13.
"Roll Out the Barrel" 1939:A19.
Rolls-Royce Company 1904:M9.
Roma 1972:A22.
Romains, Jules (1885–1972) 1908:A17, 1932:A22.
Roman Catholic Church 1958:M3, 1963:M6, 1971:M12, 1974:M16, 1975:M2, 1977:M6, 1977:M12.
Roman Catholicism 1678:H1.
Roman Catholics 1965:M7, 1975:M7.
Romanenko, Yuri (b.1944) 1977:S17, 1987:S16.
Romanesque revival 1872:A1, 1879:A3.
Romani 1831:A9.
Romania 1990:H18.
Romanov, Michael (1596–1645) 1613:H2.
Romanov dynasty 1613:H2.
Roman Republic 1793:H4, 1849:H7.
Romans, Bernard (1720–84) 1775:S3.

519

Romanticism 1801:A5, 1827:A8, 1830:A5.
Rome 1527:H1, 1862:H11, 1870:H9, 1944:H4.
Rome, Open City 1945:A20.
Romeo and Juliet 1594:A1, 1869:A6, 1935:A19.
Roméo et Juliette 1839:A5.
Rømer, Ole (1644–1710) 1676:S1.
Rommel (the "Desert Fox"), Erwin (1891–1944) 1941:H16.
Romney, George (1734–1802) 1771:A5, 1775:A6.
"Romulus and Remus" 1928:A3.
Ronde 1950:A19.
Ronsard, Pierre de (1524–1585) 1572:A2.
Röntgen, Wilhelm (1845–1923) 1895:S10, 1901:S18.
Room at the Top 1957:A12.
"A Room of One's Own" 1929:A16.
Roosa, Stuart (b.1933) 1971:S9.
Roosevelt, Franklin Delano (1882–1945) 1932:H8, 1933:H2, 1933:H3, 1933:M2, 1934:H6, 1936:H7, 1936:H8, 1937:H1, 1937:H2, 1938:H1, 1938:M4, 1939:H2, 1939:H6, 1939:H11, 1940:H3, 1940:H8, 1940:H10, 1941:H1, 1941:H5, 1941:H7, 1941:H11, 1943:H1, 1943:H9, 1943:H13, 1944:H8, 1944:H9, 1945:H1, 1945:H4.
Roosevelt, Theodor (1858–1919) 1900:H10, 1901:H5, 1901:M4, 1902:H6, 1903:H8, 1904:H7, 1904:H8, 1904:M6, 1905:H1, 1906:H4, 1906:M1, 1906:M4, 1908:H6, 1908:S3, 1910:H5, 1912:H6.
Roosevelt Corollary 1904:H8, 1930:H8.
Root Elihu (1845–1937) 1901:H8, 1605:H5.
Root, John W. (1850–91) 1882:A1.
root beer 1877:M2.
Roots 1977:A1.
Roots: The Saga of an American Family 1976:A9.
Root-Takahira Agreement 1908:H3.
Rorschach, Hermann (1884–1922) 1921:S12.
Rosamond 1733:A5.
Rosamunde 1823:A4.
"The Rosary" 1898:A1.
Rosas, Juan Manuel de (1793–1877) 1835:H6, 1845:H7, 1852:H7.
Rose, Pete 1979:M4, 1985:M8, 1989:M4.
Rose, The 1979:A3.
Rose Bowl 1916:M4, 1948:M4.
"Rose is a rose is a rose is a rose" 1925:A4.
Rose Marie 1924:A3.
Rosemary's Baby 1967:A1.
Rosenberg, Anna 1945:M4.
Rosenberg, Ethel (1916–53) 1951:H7.
Rosenberg, Julius (1918–53) 1951:H7.
Rosencrantz and Guildenstern Are Dead 1966:A20.
Rose Tattoo, The 1950:A5.
Rostenkowski, Dan 1996:M7.
Rosetta stone 1799:M5, 1821:M4.
Rosi, Francesco (b.1922) 1972:A22.
Ross, Diana (b.1944) 1964:A1, 1972:A8.
Ross, James (1800–62) 1831:M4, 1841:M5.
Ross, John (1777–1856) 1818:M5.
Ross, Nellie Tayloe (1876–1977) 1925:H1.
Ross, Sir Ronald (1857–1932) 1898:S11, 1902:S14.
Rossbach, Battle of 1757:H3.
Rossby, Carl-Gustav (1898–1957) 1932:S5, 1945:S6.

Rossby diagram 1932:S5.
Rossby number 1939:S3.
Rossellini, Roberto (1908–77) 1945:A20, 1949:A10.
Rossetti, Dante Gabriel (1828–82) 1848:A4, 1850:A9, 1888:A6.
Rossi, Bruno (b.1905) 1942:S11.
Rossini, Gioacchino Antonio (1792–1868) 1806:A6, 1813:A4, 1816:A3, 1817:A2, 1829:A4, 1975:A1.
Rossner, Judith (b.1935) 1975:A9.
Rostand, Edmond (1868–1918) 1897:A9.
Rostenkowski, Dan 1994:H2.
Rostropovich, Mstislav (b.1927) 1963:A20, 1993:A14.
Roswitha of Gandersheim 1501:A2.
Rotary Club 1905:M1.
Roth, Philip (b.1933) 1959:A7, 1969:A2, 1971:A10.
Rothko, Mark (1903–70) 1945:A11.
Rouault, Georges (1871–1958) 1906:A12, 1948:A14.
Rouch, Jean (b.1917) 1961:A14.
Roundheads 1642:H3, 1643:H2, 1644:H1.
Round Hill School 1823:M1.
Rous, Francis P. (1879–1970) 1910:S3, 1916:S7, 1966:S17.
Rousseau, Henri (1844–1910) 1886:A7, 1897:A8, 1910:A10, 1985:A11.
Rousseau, Jean-Jacques (1712–78) 1737:A1, 1750:A7, 1761:A6, 1762:M1, 1781:A4.
Rousseau, Théodore (1812–67) 1842:A6.
Roussillon 1659:H1.
Rowe, Nicholas (1674–1718) 1703:A5.
rowing 1843:M1, 1852:M2.
rowing race 1715:M1, 1775:M4, 1811:M4.
Rowlandson, Thomas (1756–1827) 1784:A7, 1812:A5.
Rowley, Thomas 1764:A2.
Rowling, J. K. 1999:A5, 2000:A3, A16.
Royal Academy 1768:A6.
Royal Academy of Dance 1661:A2.
Royal Academy of Music 1822:A10, 1861:A11.
Royal Adelaide 1850:M9.
Royal African Company 1663:H1.
Royal American Magazine 1774:M1.
Royal Archaeological Institute of Great Britain 1843:M6.
Royal Astronomical Society 1820:S7.
Royal Ballet 1931:A11, 1977:A24.
"The Royal Bird" 1948:A9.
Royal Charter 1859:M8.
Royal College of Music 1883:A12.
Royal College of Physicians 1518:S1, 1565:S1.
Royal Exchange 1565:M3.
Royal Flying Corps 1912:M18.
Royal Hospital 1685:A3.
Royal Library of France 1520:A2.
Royal Opera 1971:A21.
Royal Philharmonic Orchestra 1947:A17.
Royal Shakespeare Company 1967:A26.
Royal Society, The 1797:S7.
Royal Society of Arts 1760:A6.
Royal Society of London 1660:S4, 1661:S1, 1665:S2, 1753:S1, 1945:S13.
Royal Swedish Ballet 1967:A22.
Royden, Agnes Maude (1876–1956) 1917:M7.
Rozelle, Pete 1989:M5.
Rozhdestvensky, Gennady (b.1931) 1978:A13.
Rozhdestvensky, Valery (b.1939) 1976:S16.

Ruanda 1916:H19.
Rubáiyát of Omar Khayyám 1859:A6.
rubber 1839:S1, 1900:M9, 1910:M11, 1928:S16, 1928:S18, 1931:S5.
RU-486 1993:M12.
Rubens, Peter Paul (1577–1640) 1603:A1, 1622:A3, 1634:A2.
Rubinstein, Artur 1982:A15.
Ruby, Jack (1911–67) 1963:H9.
Rudder Grange 1879:A2.
Rudolf II (1552–1612) (Holy Roman Emperor) 1608:H3, 1611:H3, 1612:H1.
Rudolf (1858–89) (Aust.) 1889:H15.
"Rudolph, the Red-Nosed Reindeer" 1949:A7.
Rudolph, Wilma (b.1940) 1961:M9.
Rue des boutiques obscures 1978:A20.
Ruel, Treaty of 1649:H2.
Rugby football 1823:M5.
"The Rug Weaver" 1944:A19.
Ruhr Valley 1923:H11, 1943:H19, 1945:H2.
Ruisdael, Jacob van (1628–1682) 1647:A5.
Rukavishnikov, Nikolai (b.1932) 1971:S17, 1974:S17, 1979:S13.
rum 1714:M1, 1751:M3.
Rumania 1861:H16, 1878:H5, 1938:H17, 1944:H10, 1949:H13.
Rumelia 1885:H7, 1886:H8.
Rumford, Count 1779:S1.
Rump Parliament 1659:H2.
Rumsey, James (1743–92) 1787:S5, 1791:S2.
Rundgren, Todd (b.1948) 1970:A13.
"Running Fence" 1976:A12.
Runyon, Damon (1884–1946) 1932:A9.
R.U.R. 1920:A10.
Rural Electrification Administration 1935:H3.
Rural Residences 1837:A3.
Rusalka 1856:A6.
Rush, Benjamin (1745–1813) 1773:S2, 1774:S1, 1775:M3, 1786:S1, 1798:S2, 1812:S2.
Rush, William (1756–1833) 1812:A2.
Rush-Bagot Agreement 1817:H1.
Rushdie, Salman 1989:M7.
Rusk, David Dean (b.1909) 1961:H11.
Ruska, Ernst 1986:S10.
Ruskin, John (1819–1900) 1843:A4, 1849:A10, 1851:A8.
Russell, Charles Taze (1852–1916) 1872:M1.
Russell, Henry (1877–1957) 1913:S5.
Russell, Ken (b.1927) 1969:A24.
Russell, Loris S. 1965:S13.
Russell, Morgan (1886–1953) 1914:A5.
Russia 1598:H3, 1606:H2, 1610:H3, 1686:H2, 1721:H2, 1774:H3, 1783:H7, 1785:H5, 1864:H13, 1885:H6, 1906:H9, 1907:H11, 1918:H12, 1987:M13, 1999:H13.
Russian-American Company 1799:M3.
Russian Revolution 1917:H14, 1919:A4.
Russo-Japanese War 1904:H10, 1905:H1, 1905:H9.
Russo-Turkish Wars 1736:H2, 1737:H2, 1739:H3, 1768:H6, 1770:H4, 1774:H3, 1787:H5, 1788:H2, 1792:H4, 1807:H7, 1812:H6, 1828:H6, 1829:H4, 1853:H8, 1877:H5, 1878:H5.
Russwurm, John Brown 1827:M1.
Ruth, Babe 1919:M2, 1927:M6, 1961:M6, 1974:M8.

Rutherford, Lord Ernest (1871–1937) 1896:S14, 1902:S11, 1903:S9, 1908:S14, 1911:S15, 1913:S19, 1919:S11.
"Ruthless" 1867:M4.
Ružička, Leopold (1887–1976) 1935:S14.
Rwanda 1994:H18.
Ryder, Albert P. (1847–1917) 1883:A1.
Ryle, Martin (b.1918) 1974:S18.
Ryskind, Morris (b.1895) 1928:A7, 1930:A4.
Ryswick, Treaty of 1697:H1, 1697:H2.
Ryumin, V. 1979:S13.
Ryun, Jim (b.1947) 1966:M8.
Saarinen, Eero (1910–61) 1948:A7.
Saarland 1935:H13, 1956:H14.
Sabatier, Paul (1854–1941) 1912:S18.
Sabbath 1619:M2, 1676:M4.
Sabin, Albert (b.1906) 1955:S4.
Sabino, Wallace (1868–1919) 1896:S5, 1922:S4.
"Sabre Dance" 1942:A15.
saccharin 1879:S1, 1977:S8.
Sacco, Nicola (1891–1927) 1921:M1.
Sachs, Julius von (1832–97) 1864:S7, 1865:S9, 1868:S6, 1890:S3.
Sachs, Nellie (1891–1970) 1951:A21.
sack dress 1957:M6.
Sackville, Thomas (1536–1608) 1559:A1.
Sacred Congregation for the Propagation of the Faith 1622:M2.
"The Sacrifice of Isaac" 1716:A2.
Sadat, Anwar 1977:H19, 1978:H3, 1981:H10.
Sade, Marquis de (1740–1814) 1787:A5.
Sadko 1898:A10.
Safe Drinking Water Act 1974:S2.
safety lamp 1815:S4.
Safety Last 1923:A10.
safety pin 1849:M5.
safety razor 1901:M5.
Sagan, Carl (b.1934) 1961:S21, 1966:S4.
Sagan om hästen 1740:A3.
Saga of Eric the Red 1000:M1.
Sagard, Gabriel 1632:A1.
Sahagún, Bernardino de (1500?–1590) 1583:A1.
Saigon 1968:H1, 1976:H12.
saint 1975:M2.
Saint, Eva Marie (b.1929) 1594:A13.
Saint-Exupéry, Antoine de (1900–44) 1942:A21, 1943:A13.
Saint Francis Indians, village of the 1759:H2.
Saint-German, Treaty of 1570:H1, 1919:H10.
Saint Laurent, Yves (b.1936) 1971:A18.
Saint Mihiel, Battle of 1918:H3.
Saint-Nazaire 1942:H18.
Saint of Bleecker Street, The 1954:A9.
Saint-Saëns, Camillo (1835–1921) 1871:A10, 1874:A6, 1886:A12.
Sakarya, Battle of 1921:H15.
Sakel, Manfred J. (1900–57) 1929:S7.
Sakuntala 1789:A7.
Salamanca, Battle of 1812:H5.
Salazar, Antonio de Oliveira (b.1889) 1932:H11, 1968:H18.
Salbai, Treaty of 1782:H5.
Salem 1628:H1, 1629:H1, 1636:H1.
Sales, St. Francis de (1567–1622) 1610:M2.
Salinger, Jerome D. (b.1919) 1951:A7, 1961:A6.

saliva 1929:S17.
Salk, Jonas (b.1914) 1954:S2.
Salka Valka 1945:A16.
Salk vaccine 1954:S2.
Salmagundi 1807:A3.
salmon hatchery 1864:S2.
Salome 1894:A9.
Salon de Refusés 1863:A7.
salt 1641:M1.
salt-box style 1639:A2.
Salten, Felix (1869–1945)
    1923:A13.
Salt-Water Ballads 1902:A9.
salute the flag 1943:M1.
salvage drives 1943:M5.
Salvation Army 1865:M9, 1880:M2,
    1966:M18.
Salvation Nell 1908:A5.
Salyut 1 1971:S17, 1971:S18.
Salyut 3 1974:S15.
Salyut 4 1975:S16, 1975:S17.
Salyut 5 1976:S14, 1976:S16,
    1977:S16.
Salyut 6 1977:S17, 1978:S16,
    1978:S17, 1978:S18, 1978:S19,
    1979:S13.
Salzburg Festival 1917:A17.
Samoa 1878:H3, 1887:H7, 1889:H7,
    1899:H3.
Sampras, Pete 2000:M11.
Samson Agonistes 1671:A3.
Sam Spade 1930:A3.
San Antonio 1718:H2.
Sanctuary 1931:A7.
Sand, George 1832:A4.
Sandage, Alan (b.1926) 1960:S3,
    1965:S3.
Sandbox, The 1960:A11.
Sandburg, Carl (1878–1967)
    1916:A2, 1920:A6, 1926:A12,
    1939:A9.
Sand Creek 1864:H9.
San Diego de Alcala 1769:A2.
Sandinistas 1978:H15, 1979:H18,
    1983:H7, 1984:H11.
Sandwich Islands 1778:H6.
Sandys, George (1578–1644)
    1926:A1.
San Francisco 1906:M3, 1945:H6.
Sanger, Frederick (b.1918)
    1955:S12, 1958:S16, 1980:S16.
Sanger, Margaret (1883–1966)
    1915:S10, 1916:M3, 1921:M3.
San Jacinto, Battle of 1886:H1.
San Juan Capistrano 1777:A2.
San Juan Hill, Battle of 1898:H4.
San Juan Islands 1872:H2.
San Lorenzo, Treaty of 1795:H3.
San Martín, José de (1778–1850)
    1817:H4, 1818:H4, 1820:H6.
San Mateo 1568:H1.
San Salvador 1492:H1.
Sanskrit 1789:A7.
San Stefano, Treaty of 1878:H5.
Santa Anna, Antonio López de
    (1794–1876) 1833:H4, 1836:H1,
    1848:H3, 1847:H1.
Santa Cruz, Andrés (1792?–1865)
    1836:H5, 1839:H5.
Santa Fe 1610:H1.
Santana 1974:A6.
Santayana, George (1863–1952)
    1905:M2.
Santee Canal 1793:S3.
Santiago, Battle of 1898:H5.
Santo Domingo 1496:M1, 1844:H5,
    1905:H3, 1916:H6.
Santorio, Santorio (1561–1636)
    1602:S2, 1612:S4.
São Tomé and Príncipe 1975:H17.
Sarafanov, Gennadi (b.1942)
    1974:S16.
"Sarah Prince" 1801:A3.
Sarajevo 1914:H7.
Saramago, Jose 1998:A20.
Saratoga 1870:A6.
Saratoga, Battle of 1777:H2.
Saratoga, N.Y. 1802:M4.

Sardinia 1717:H2, 1720:H4,
    1859:H5, 1860:H7, 1860:H8.
Sargent, James (1824–1910)
    1875:S4.
Sargent, John Singer 1996:A2.
Sarnenbund 1832:H6.
Saroyan, William (b.1908) 1934:A8,
    1939:A8, 1943:A6.
Sarraute, Nathalie (b.1902)
    1969:A22.
Sarto, Andrea del (1486–1531)
    1509:A2.
Sartog 1966:A19.
Sartor Resartus 1836:A8.
Sartre, Jean-Paul (1905–80)
    1938:A13, 1943:A14, 1945:A19,
    1957:A13, 1964:A17.
Saskatchewan 1905:H12.
Sassoon, Siegfried (1886–1967)
    1917:A19.
Satanic Verses, The 1989:M7.
satellite 1957:S13, 1958:S8,
    1958:S9, 1958:S13, 1960:S14,
    1961:S8, 1961:S13, 1962:S12,
    1963:S12, 1964:S9, 1965:S7,
    1967:S15, 1982:S5, 1989:S5.
Satie, Erik (1866–1925) 1917:A1,
    1918:A16.
"Satin Doll" 1958:A7.
"Satisfaction" 1965:A18.
Sato, Eisaku (1901–1975)
    1964:H22.
Satsuma Rebellion 1877:H7.
Saturday Evening Post, The
    1916:A1.
Saturday Night Fever 1977:A11.
Saturn 1563:S3, 1610:S2, 1659:S2,
    1675:S1, 1837:S6, 1848:S4,
    1850:S1, 1859:S8, 1966:S18,
    1969:S4, 1973:S10, 1976:S8,
    1977:S11, 1979:S10, 1980:S4,
    1981:S4.
Saturn's rings 1886:S3, 1891:S4.
Saturn 1-B 1967:M3.
Satyricon 1969:A24.
Saudi Arabia 1932:H12.
Sauk Indians 1830:H3, 1832:H1,
    1891:H4.
Sault Sto. Marie 1668:H1.
Saunders, Aileen 1960:M8.
Saunders, Margaret M.
    (1861–1947) 1894:A5.
Saussure, Horace-Benedict de
    (1710–99) 1766:S4, 1783:S5,
    1796:S5.
Savage, Richard (1697–1743)
    1744:A3.
Savannah 1733:H1, 1778:H3,
    1779:H4, 1782:H2, 1818:S4,
    1864:H3, 1959:S2.
savings banks 1816:M8.
Savitskaya, Svetlana 1984:S12.
Savonarola, Girolamo (1452–98)
    1497:M1, 1497:A1, 1498:M2.
Savoy 1713:H4, 1720:H4, 1860:H8.
Savoy, Prince of 1704:H3, 1706:H4,
    1708:H2, 1709:H2, 1716:H2,
    1717:H3.
"Savoy Operas" 1881:A6.
Savoy Theater 1881:A6.
Sax, Antoine Joseph (1814–94)
    1846:A11.
Saxony 1706:H5, 1719:H2, 1743:H2,
    1758:H2, 1763:H3.
saxophone 1846:A11.
Say, Thomas (1787–1834) 1824:S1.
Saybrook Platform 1708:M1.
Sayers, Dorothy L. (1893–1957)
    1923:A16.
Sayers, Tom 1860:M9.
"scab" 1799:M1.
"scalawags" 1870:H4.
Scalia, Antonin 1986:M22.
Scandinavia 1539:S2.
Scarlatti, Alessandro (1660–1725)
    1679:A2, 1702:A4, 1720:A2.
Scarlatti, Domenico (1685–1757)
    1705:A3.

scarlet fever 1736:S1, 1863:M6.
scarlet fever toxin 1923:S2.
scarlet letter 1782:M4.
Scarlet Letter, The 1850:A1.
Scenes From A Marriage 1974:A20.
"Scenes from the Life of Christ"
    1878:A6.
Sceptical Chymist, The 1661:S2.
Schaeffer, Pierre (b.1910) 1950:A16.
Schally, Andrew (b.1927) 1977:S13.
Schamberg, Morton (1882–1918)
    1916:A4.
Scheele, Karl Wilhelm (1742–86)
    1772:S4, 1774:S5, 1777:S3,
    1778:S5.
Scheherazade 1888:A9.
Scheider, Roy (b.1934) 1975:A3.
Scheidt, Samuel (1587–1654)
    1624:A2.
Schelling, Friedrich (1775–1854)
    1801:M6.
Schick, Bela (1877–1967) 1913:S4.
Schick, Jacob 1923:M3.
Schick test 1913:S4.
Schiller, Johann Christoph
    Friedrich von (1759–1805)
    1781:A2, 1788:A4, 1799:A6,
    1801:A7, 1804:A2, 1808:A2.
Schindler's List 1993:A1.
Schirra, Walter (b.1923) 1962:S13.
schizophrenia 1929:S7.
Schlegel, August Wilhelm von
    (1767–1845) 1797:A5.
Schlegel, Friedrich von (1772–1829)
    1799:A4.
Schleicher, Kurt von (1882–1934)
    1932:H14.
Schlesinger, James R. (b.1929)
    1977:H2.
Schlesinger, Jr., Arthur (b.1917)
    1965:A2.
Schleswig-Holstein 1627:H4,
    1848:H9, 1850:H7, 1863:H10,
    1864:H12, 1865:H10, 1866:H6.
Schliemann, Heinrich (1822–90)
    1870:M8, 1876:M7.
Schmalkaldic League 1546:H1,
    1547:H4.
Schmid, Franz 1931:M13.
Schmid, Toni 1931:M13.
Schmidt, Bernhard (1879–1935)
    1932:S17.
Schmidt, Helmut (b.1918)
    1974:H17, 1980:H16.
Schmidt, Maarten (b.1929) 1963:S1,
    1965:S2.
Schmitt, Harrison (b.1935)
    1972:S11.
Schneckenburger, Max (1819–49)
    1840:A5.
Schnitzler, Arthur (1862–1931)
    1901:A12.
Schoenheimer, Rudolf (1898–1941)
    1935:S4.
Scholemaster, The 1570:M1.
Schönberg 1908:A18, 1909:A7,
    1923:A14, 1937:A14, 1942:A11.
Schonbrunn, Peace of 1809:H4.
Schönlein, Johann Lukas
    (1793–1864) 1828:S3.
school 1640:M1.
School and Society, The 1899:M1.
school attendance law 1852:M1.
School for Scandal 1777:A3.
School for Wives, The 1662:A3.
schoolmaster 1634:M2.
Schopenhauer, Arthur (1788–1860)
    1819:M6, 1836:M5.
Schott, Marge 1993:M7.
Schrieffer, John (b.1931) 1957:S9,
    1972:S12.
Schrödinger, Erwin (1887–1961)
    1924:S9, 1933:S20, 1944:S13.
Schroeder, Gerhard 1998:H18.
Schroeder, William 1986:S1.
Schubert, Franz Peter (1797–1828)
    1814:A4, 1823:A4.
Schulz, Charles 2000:A4.

Schuman Plan 1950:H13,
    1951:H10.
Schuman, Robert (1886–1963)
    1950:H13.
Schumann, Robert (1810–56)
    1836:A4, 1841:A7.
Schuschnigg, Kurt von (1897–1977)
    1934:H16, 1936:H19, 1938:H13.
Schütz, Heinrich 1627:A2.
Schwabe, Samuel H. (1789–1875)
    1843:S6.
Schwann, Theodor (1810–82)
    1836:S7, 1839:S8.
Schwartzer, Franz 1866:A1.
Schwarzbach, Martin (b.1907)
    1963:S17.
Schwarzschild, Karl (1873–1916)
    1907:S9.
Schweickart, Russel (b.1935)
    1969:S9.
Schweitzer, Albert (1875–1965)
    1913:M9.
science 1738:S3, 1743:S1.
Science and Civilization 1939:S17.
Science and Ethics 1928:S20.
Science and Health 1875:M2.
Science and Life 1920:S8.
Science and the Unseen World
    1929:S3.
science-fiction 1977:A13.
Science of Mechanics, The 1829:S3.
Scientific American 1845:S2.
Scientific Basis of Evolution, The
    1932:S9.
scientific method 1565:S2, 1623:S1.
Scientific Results of the Swedish
    South Polar Expedition 1920:S11.
Scientific Study of UFOs 1969:S2.
Scone, Stone of 1996:M17.
Scopes, John T. 1925:M5.
Scorpion, U.S.S. 1968:M5.
Scotland 1639:H2, 1715:H2.
Scott, David (b.1932) 1966:S10,
    1969:S9, 1971:S11.
Scott, Paul Mark (1920–78)
    1976:A18.
Scott, Robert F. (1868–1912)
    1912:M10.
Scott, Ronnie (b.1927) 1957:A14.
Scott, Sir Walter (1771–1832)
    1802:A2, 1805:A2, 1808:A3,
    1810:A5, 1814:A3, 1815:A3,
    1818:A8, 1820:A2, 1821:A9.
Scott, Winfield (1786–1866)
    1847:H1.
Scottish Disruption 1843:M7.
screw propeller 1836:S1.
Screwtape Letters, The 1942:A20.
Scribe, Augustin Eugène
    (1791–1861) 1828:A5, 1849:A9.
Scriblerus Club 1713:A2.
Scripps Institution of
    Oceanography 1903:S4.
Scythian Suite 1916:A18.
Sea Around Us, The 1951:S3.
Seaborg, Glenn T. (b.1912) 1941:S1,
    1942:S4, 1951:S14.
sea disaster 1854:M5, 1858:M5,
    1867:M8, 1891:M10, 1904:M12,
    1912:M11, 1914:M9, 1916:M12,
    1928:M13, 1952:M6, 1963:M2,
    1967:M8, 1979:M15.
"Sea Fever" 1902:A9.
Seagull, The 1896:A7.
Sealab 1964:S2.
Sea of Fertility 1970:A18.
seaplane 1912:S9.
Searching Wind, The 1944:A2.
Searle, Humphrey (b.1915)
    1969:A21.
Sears, Richard D. 1881:M4.
Sears, Roebuck Company 1895:M2.
Sears Tower 1974:A4.
Seascape 1975:A6.
sea serpent 1817:M1.
Season in Hell, A 1873:A6.
Seasons, The 1726:A3, 1801:A9.
Sea Wolf, The 1904:A2.

521

Sibelius, Joan (1865–1957)
1892:A9, 1900:A18.
Sibley, John 1803:M1.
Sicily 1720:H4, 1734:H2, 1738:H1,
1926:H19, 1943:H7.
sickness insurance 1883:M7.
Siddhartha 1922:A15.
Siddons, Sarah (1755–1831) 1782:A4.
"Side of Beef" 1925:A19.
Sidney, Philip (1554–1586) 1591:A1.
Siebenerhonkordat 1832:H6.
Siegbahn, Karl M.G. (b.1886)
1916:S15, 1924:S11.
"The Siege of Corinth" 1975:A1.
Siegfried 1876:A3.
Siegfried Line 1945:H15.
"Siegfried's Death" 1862:A7.
Siemens, Friedrich (1826–1904)
1956:S4.
Siemens, Karl 1875:S10.
Siemens, Werner von (1816–92)
1842:S11, 1861:S5, 1866:S10,
1875:S10.
Siemens, William (1823–83)
1844:S6, 1851:S5, 1875:S10.
Sienkiewicz, Henryk (1846–1916)
1896:A12.
Sierra Club 1966:S8.
Sierra Leone 1817:M3, 1998:H22.
"Sierra Leone" 1972:M17.
Sigismund I (1467–1548) (Pol.)
1506:H1.
Sigismund II (1520–72) (Pol.)
1569:H1.
Sigismund III 1566–1632) (Swed.)
1599:H1.
Sigma 7 1962:S13.
Signorelli, Luca (1445?–1523)
1499:A2.
Sihanouk 1976:H14.
Sikhs 1712:H4, 1809:H7, 1845:H6,
1846:H8, 1849:H5.
Sikkim 1975:H25.
Sikorski, Igor (1889–1972) 1913:S7,
1928:S5, 1939:S2.
Silas Marner 1861:A8.
Silbermann, Gottfried (1683–1753)
1714:A4.
Silence, The 1963:A23.
silencer 1908:S9.
Silent Spring 1962:S2.
Silent World, The 1953:S16.
Silesia 1740:H3, 1742:H2, 1745:H5,
1748:H2, 1758:H2, 1763:H3,
1921:H19, 1922:H13.
silicon 1823:S3.
silicone 1944:S9.
silk 1521:M2, 1748:M3, 1760:M6.
Silk Stockings 1955:A13.
silkworm disease 1868:S7.
Sillanpänä, Frans Eemil
(1888–1964) 1931:A15.
Silliman, Benjamin (1779–1864)
1818:S1, 1830:S4, 1831:A6.
Silliman's Journal 1818:S1.
Sillitoe, Alan (b.1928) 1959:A13.
Sills, Beverly (b.1929) 1975:A1.
Silmarillion, The 1977:A16.
Silone, Ignazio (b.1900) 1930:A16.
Silver, Long John 1883:A8.
Silver Chalice, The 1952:A8.
Silver Purchase Act 1892:H6.
Simon, Claude 1985:A17.
Simon, Neil (b.1927) 1961:A5,
1965:A10, 1968:A11, 1969:A7,
1971:A9, 1976:A13, 1977:A14,
1985:A2.
Simon, Paul 1986:A2.
Simonson, Leo (1888–1967)
1950:A4.
*Simple Cobler of Agawam in
America, The* 1647:A1.
Simplon Tunnel 1906:M13
Simpson, Mary 1978:M11.
Simpson, Orenthal James (O.J.)
1994:H5, 1995:M4, 1997:M2.
Simpson, Sir James (1811–70)
1847:S9.

Simpson, Wallis Warfield (b.1896)
1936:H11.
Sims, James (1813–83) 1855:S4.
Sinatra, Frank (b.1915) 1939:A6.
Sinbad 1918:A5.
Sincere Convert, The 1641:A1.
Sinclair, Upton (1878–1908)
1906:A1, 1928:A10.
"Sindbad the Sailor" 1885:A7.
Singapore 1819:H6, 1963:H12.
Singer, Isaac Bashevis (b.1904)
1950:A12, 1978:A3, 1979:A7.
Singer, Isaac (1811–75) 1851:S1.
Singer Building 1908:S10.
"Singin' the Blues" 1927:A9.
Single Man, A 1964:A11.
singspiel 1786:A7.
"Sinners in the Hands of an Angry
God" 1741:A2.
Sinn Fein 1905:H16, 1926:H11.
Sino-Japanese Wars 1894:H9,
1895:H6, 1937:H18, 1938:H19,
1939:H16.
Sinzheim, Battle of 1674:H3.
Sioux Indians 1851:H3, 1866:H5,
1876:H2.
"Sir Barton" 1919:M6.
"Sir Henry" 1823:M2.
Sirhan, Sirhan Bishara (b.1944)
1908:H4.
Sirica, John J. (b.1904) 1973:H1,
1975:H1.
Sirio 1906:M7.
Sirius 1860:S3, 1884:S10, 1914:S4.
"Sir John Sinclair" 1794:A6.
Sister Carrie 1900:A3.
Sistine Chapel 1508:A2, 1512:A1,
1536:A2, 1981:A8, 1987:A20.
"Sistine Madonna" 1512:A2.
Sistova, Treaty of 1791:H5.
Sitting Bull (1831?–90) 1876:H2.
situation comedy 1971:A3.
Sitwell, Edith (1887–1964)
1949:A17.
Sitwell, Osbert (1892–1969)
1944:A20.
Sivaji (1627–80) 1674:H4.
Sivas 1919:H11.
*Six Characters in Search of an
Author* 1921:A14.
Six-Day Israeli-Arab War
1967:H14.
Six Geometrical Exercises 1647:S2.
Sixteenth Amendment 1909:H2,
1913:H1.
"The $64,000 Question" 1957:M8.
skate 1863:M4.
skeletons 1849:S2.
Sketch Book, The 1820:A1, 1822:A5.
*Sketches and Eccentricities of Col.
David Crockett, of West Tennessee*
1833:M4.
Sketches by Boz 1835:A2.
*Sketches of Eighteenth Century
America* 1925:A10.
*Sketch of Old England, by a New
England Man, A* 1822:A2.
ski 1896:M10.
ski club 1872:M6.
skiing, 1879:M7.
skiing, water 1920:M8.
skin grafts 1953:S15.
Skinner, John 1829:M2.
Skin of Our Teeth, The 1942:A13.
skirts 1921:M4.
skittle 1591:M1.
sky advertising 1908:M2.
Skylab 1 1973:S11.
Skylab 2 1973:S12.
Skylab 3 1973:S13, 1973:S21.
Skylark 1919:S13.
skyscraper 1885:A5, 1889:A8,
1908:S10.
slang 1912:M8.
Slankamen, Battle of 1691:H2.
slapstick 1913:A6, 1976:A11.

Slater, Samuel (1768–1835)
1790:S2.
Slaughter House Five 1969:A9.
slave 1772:M1.
slavery 1823:M6, 1834:M4.
slaves 1518:M2, 1576:M1, 1664:M2.
Slave Songs of the United States
1867:A5.
Slavonic Dances 1878:A8.
Slayton, Donald (b.1924) 1975:S10.
Sleeping Beauty 1889:A13, 1890:A9,
1975:A14.
"The Sleeping Gypsy" 1897:A8.
sleighing 1713:M1.
"Sleigh Ride" 1950:A8.
slide fastener 1891:M3.
slide rule 1617:S4, 1633:S2.
Slipher, Vesto (1875–1969) 1928:S8.
Slivnitza, Battle of 1885:H7.
Sloane, John French (1871–1951)
1907:A2, 1912:A9.
Sloane, Sir Hans (1660–1753)
1696:S2.
Slosson, Edwin (1865–1929)
1919:S6, 1920:S7.
Slovakia 1993:H13.
Slovenia 1991:H15.
Small Drawings 1665:S1.
smallpox 1616:M1, 1667:M1,
1678:M1, 1697:M1, 1713:M2,
1721:S2, 1721:S3, 1721:S4,
1722:S1, 1722:S2, 1740:M2,
1755:M1, 1764:S1, 1765:S1,
1777:S1, 1796:S4, 1797:S7,
1800:S1, 1802:S3, 1853:M6,
1873:M1, 1957:M14, 1957:M23,
1973:M15, 1974:M21.
Smeaton, John (1724–92) 1759:S4.
smell 1919:S12.
smelting, 1709:M5.
Smetana, Bedřich (1824–84)
1866:A11.
Smetona, Antanas (1874–1944)
1926:H20, 1931:H17.
Smibert, John (1688–1751)
1729:A3, 1742:A2.
Smiles of a Summer Night
1955:A15.
Smiley's People 1979:A13.
Smirke, Robert (1781–1867)
1823:A6, 1826:M1.
Smith, Alfred E. (1873–1944)
1923:H2, 1928:H5.
Smith, Betty (1904–72) 1943:A1.
Smith, David (1906–61) 1948:A9.
Smith, Hamilton (b.1931) 1978:S12.
Smith, Hamilton E. 1858:S2.
Smith, Horace (1808–93) 1854:S2.
Smith, Ian (b.1919) 1964:H20,
1970:H19, 1977:H17.
Smith, Jack 1856:M9.
Smith, James 1802:S3.
Smith, Jedediah 1824:M1.
Smith, John (1580?–1631) 1607:H1,
1608:A1, 1609:M2, 1612:S2,
1614:H1, 1616:S1, 1624:A1,
1671:A1.
Smith, Joseph (1805–44) 1830:M3.
Smith, Kate (b.1909) 1939:A2.
Smith, Keith 1919:M11.
Smith, Oliver 1919:M8.
Smith, Samantha 1985:M6.
Smith, Seba (1792–1868) 1854:A3.
Smith, Sydney (1771–1845)
1802:A3.
Smith, Theobald (1859–1934)
1903:S5.
Smith, William (1727–1803)
1757:A2, 1721:M2.
Smith Act 1940:H5, 1949:M2,
1951:H4.
Smithson, James (1765–1829)
1846:M2.
Smithsonian Institution 1846:A1,
1846:M2.
Smoke and Steel 1920:A6.
"Smoke Gets in Your Eyes"
1933:A11.

smoking 1646:M2, 1890:M4.
Smoking and Health 1964:M1.
Smollett, Tobias (1721–1771)
1748:A3, 1751:A3, 1771:A7.
Smoot-Hawley Tariff 1930:H3.
SMS-1 1974:S9.
snail darter 1978:S8.
snake 1912:M2.
Snell, George D. (b.1903) 1980:S15.
Snell, Willebrond (1591–1626)
1617:S2, 1621:S2.
snow 1665:S1.
Snow, C.P. (b.1905) 1940:A19,
1970:A22.
"Snow at Estaque" 1870:A8.
"Snowbound" 1866:A8.
Snow Country 1956:A19.
Snow Maiden, The 1882:A10.
"The Snows of Kilimanjaro"
1938:A2.
"Snowstorm: Hannibal and his
Army Crossing the Alps"
1812:A7.
Snow White and the Seven Dwarfs
1937:A12.
snuff 1558:M1.
Snyder, Ruth 1927:M5.
soap 1524:M1, 1608:M1.
soap powder 1843:M2.
Sobraon, Battle of 1846:H8.
Sobrero, Ascanio (1812–88)
1846:S4.
soccer 1863:M8, 1872:M7,
1950:M13, 1964:M15, 1966:M15,
1978:M22, 1982:M20, 1985:H15.
social clubs 1733:M1.
Social Democratic Party 1898:H9,
1898:H12, 1900:H5.
social insects 1971:S1.
socialism 1800:M6.
Socialist Labor Party 1900:H9,
1904:H6, 1956:H5.
Socialist Party 1898:H9, 1904:H3,
1908:H5, 1912:H4, 1919:H4,
1920:H3, 1924:H7, 1928:H1,
1936:H3, 1952:H5, 1956:H5.
Socialist Unity Party 1946:H21,
1949:H11.
Socialist Workers Party 1952:H5.
Socialist Workingmen's Party
1875:H8.
social reform 1800:M7.
Social Revolutionary Party
1901:H11.
Social Security Act 1935:H5,
1935:M4, 1937:H3, 1939:H4,
1960:H5.
Social Statistics 1850:M8.
Société des Artistes Indépendants
1884:A6.
Société Nationale de Musique
1870:A9.
Society for Propagation of the
Gospel in Foreign Parts 1701:M2.
Society for the Diffusion of Useful
Knowledge 1827:M6.
Society for the Propagation of the
Gospel 1710:M2.
Society for the Propagation of the
Gospel in Foreign Parts 1752:M3.
Society for the Relief of Free
Negroes Unlawfully Held in
Bondage 1775:M3.
Society of Friends 1648:M4,
1656:M1.
Society of Jesus 1534:M1.
Sociobiology: The New Synthesis
1975:S6.
sociology 1838:M3, 1850:M8.
Socrate 1918:A16.
Soddy, Frederick (1877–1956)
1912:S16, 1913:S19, 1920:S8,
1921:S13.
sodium 1807:S4.
sodium pentothal 1933:S10.
Sofferino, Battle of 1859:H5.
soft drinks 1967:M2.
"Soft Toilet" 1966:A13.

531

"Washington Crossing the Delaware" 1851:A4.
Washington Monument 1836:A2, 1884:M6, 1885:M3.
Washington Post 1971:H1.
"Washington Post March" 1889:A5.
Wasp 1952:M6.
Wassmo, Herbjorg 1987:A16.
Waste Land, The 1922:A14.
watch 1502:S1, 1922:M10.
Watch and Ward 1878:A2.
"Watch on the Rhine" 1840:A5.
Watch Tower Bible and Tract Society 1931:M1.
water 1783:S3, 1785:S8, 1805:S2.
Water-Babies, The 1863:A11.
Water Engine, The 1978:A4.
Watergate 1972:H2, 1973:H1, 1974:H2, 1975:H1.
Waterhouse, Benjamin (1754–1846) 1792:S3, 1800:S1.
"Water-Lily Pool" 1899:A11.
Waterloo, Battle of 1815:H5.
Waterman, Lewis E. (1837–1901) 1884:S4, 1884:M3.
water meter 1851:S5.
Water Music 1740:A6.
Water on the Brain 1933:A17.
water pollution 1868:S10.
Water Power Act 1920:H4.
Waters and Land 1930:A12.
Watership Down 1972:A15.
water speed 1939:M18.
Watkins, Henry (1907–1930) 1927:M8.
Watson, James D. (b.1928) 1952:S3, 1952:S12, 1953:S4, 1953:S12, 1961:S15, 1962:S22, 1968:S2.
Watson, John (1878–1958) 1914:S2, 1916:S6, 1919:S4, 1925:S11.
Watson, Thomas A. (1854–1934) 1876:S1, 1916:S9.
Watt, James (1736–1819) 1765:S4, 1782:S3, 1790:S5.
Watt, Robert (b.1892) 1935:S16.
Watteau, Jean-Antoine (1684–1721) 1703:A3, 1716:A4, 1718:A2.
Watts, George Frederic (1817–1904) 1847:A8.
Watts, Isaac (1674–1748) 1707:A2, 1739:A1.
Watts, Los Angeles 1965:H4.
Watusi 1964:M7.
Waugh, Evelyn (1903–66) 1928:S20, 1948:A13, 1952:A22.
Waverly 1814:A3.
wave theory 1927:S3.
wax museum 1774:S3.
Way Down East 1854:A3.
Wayne, Anthony (1745–96) 1779:H2, 1794:H3, 1795:H2.
Way of All Flesh, The 1903:A13.
Way of the World, The 1700:A3.
Way Out West 1937:A8.
Way to Get Married, The 1796:A9.
Way to Space Travel 1929:S12.
W.C.T.U. 1874:M2.
wealth 1735:M2.
Wealth Tax Act 1935:H6.
weather 1686:S2, 1738:S1, 1742:S1, 1743:S4, 1746:S1, 1816:M2, 1835:S3, 1849:S4, 1851:S6, 1853:S1, 1870:S1, 1888:S10, 1897:S7, 1921:S10, 1932:S5, 1936:S8, 1939:S10, 1945:S2, 1959:S10, 1963:S15, 1964:S11, 1976:S13, 1983:S8.
Weather Bureau 1970:S3.
Weather Forecasting as a Problem in Mechanics and Physics 1904:S14.
weather forecasts 1952:S8.
Weatherly 1962:M8.
Weather Prediction by Numerical Process 1922:S10.
weather radar 1945:S8.
weather reports 1962:M21.

weather satellite 1960:S12, 1970:S13, 1974:S9.
Weaver, John (1673–1760) 1702:A2.
Weaver, Robert C. (b.1907) 1965:H5.
Weavers, The 1892:A8.
Web, The 1914:A7.
Webb, Chick (1909–39) 1938:A8.
Webb, Matthew (1848–83) 1875:M9.
Webb Alien Land Bill 1913:H7.
Webb-Kenyon Interstate Liquor Act 1913:H2, 1917:H1.
Weber, Carl Maria von (1786–1826) 1821:A4.
Weber, Max (1881–1961) 1915:A2.
Weber, Wilhelm (1804–91) 1833:S5, 1826:A5, 1838:A7.
Webster, Daniel (1782–1852) 1830:H1, 1841:H2.
Webster, John (1575–1625) 1614:A1.
Webster, Noah (1758–1843) 1783:M1, 1790:A2, 1793:A5, 1806:A1, 1828:A2.
Webster, William 1987:H5.
Webster-Ashburton Treaty 1842:H3.
wedding 1607:M1.
"The Wedding Dance" 1566:A4.
"Wedding March" 1843:A6.
Wedgwood, Josiah (1730–1795) 1739:A2.
Weekend 1967:A21.
Weekly Political Register 1816:M5.
Week on the Concord and Merrimack Rivers, A 1849:A3.
Weeks, William 1843:M1.
Wegener, Alfred (1880–1930) 1912:S15.
Weidenreich, Franz (1873–1948) 1937:S11.
weightlessness 1976:S14.
weightlifting 1885:M4.
Weill, Kurt (1900–50) 1926:A21, 1928:A14, 1930:A15.
Weimar Republic 1919:H16, 1933:H13.
Weiner, Alfred (1866–1919) 1913:S20.
Weir, Peter (b.1944) 1974:A20, 1975:A18.
Weiss, Peter (b.1916) 1964:A18, 1965:A15.
Weitz, Paul (b.1933) 1973:S12.
Weizmann, Chaim (1874–1952) 1920:H19, 1948:H13.
Welch, Jr., Robert H. W. (b.1899) 1954:A3, 1958:A3.
Welcome to Hard Times 1960:A7.
Welcome to Our City 1923:A1.
Welcome to the Monkey House 1968:A9.
welding 1886:S5.
welfare 1795:M3, 1883:M7, 1996:H2.
Welk, Lawrence (b.1903) 1955:A2.
well 1927:S5.
Weller, Thomas (b.1915) 1952:S6, 1963:S9.
Welles, Orson (b.1915) 1936:A8, 1938:M3, 1941:A2.
Wellington, New Zealand 1865:H14.
Wellington, Duke of (Arthur Wellesley) (1769–1852) 1809:H3, 1812:H5, 1815:H5, 1828:H5.
Well Meaning Society 1765:A1.
Wells, H.G. (1866–1946) 1895:A8, 1897:A10, 1898:A8, 1909:A8, 1925:A24, 1936:A13.
Wells, Horace (1815–48) 1845:S1.
Well-Tempered Clavier, The 1722:A5, 1744:A4.
Welty, Eudora (b.1909) 1941:A10, 1955:A12, 1972:A6.
Wenham, Jane 1712:M1.
Wenner, Jann (b.1946) 1967:A8.
"We're in the Money" 1933:A2.
Worfel, Franz (1890–1945) 1933:A16, 1941:A14, 1944:A26.

Werner, Alfred (1866–1919) 1891:S8.
Wertmuller, Lina 1975:A18.
Wesker, Arnold (b.1932) 1958:A24.
Wesley, John (1703–91) 1735:M3, 1738:M5, 1742:A4, 1784:M4.
Wesleyan Methodism 1784:M4.
Wessel, Johan Herman (1742–85) 1772:A5.
"Wessex" 1872:A5.
Wesson, Daniel (1825–1906) 1854:S2.
West, Benjamin (1738–1820) 1760:A2, 1763:A3, 1767:A1, 1768:A2, 1771:A3, 1772:A2, 1775:A3, 1802:A1, 1808:A2.
West, Mae (1893?–1981) 1933:A7, 1940:A4, 1970:A7.
West, Nathanael 1939:A13.
West, Rebecca (b.1892) 1955:A17.
West Berlin 1948:H11, 1948:H17.
Western Electric 1912:S4, 1915:S8.
Western Front 1914:H9, 1915:H11, 1916:H12, 1918:H8.
Western Sahara 1979:H15.
Western Symphony 1954:A1.
Western Union Company 1856:M5, 1912:S4.
West Germany 1949:H11, 1953:H13, 1974:S12, 1975:S14, 1980:H19.
West Indies 1627:H1, 1666:H4, 1740:H2, 1763:H1.
West Indies Federation 1958:H21.
Westinghouse, George (1846–1914) 1868:S3, 1886:S2, 1891:S3.
Westinghouse Electric Company 1886:S2.
Westminster, Statute of 1931:H6.
Westminster, Treaty of 1674:H1.
Westmoreland, William 1984:M22, 1985:M5.
Weston, Edward (1850–1936) 1867:M5, 1872:S5, 1875:S2, 1877:S6, 1885:S5, 1908:S4.
Westphalia, Peace of 1648:H2.
West Point Military Academy 1780:H2, 1802:M2, 1819:M2.
West Side Story 1957:A2.
West Virginia 1861:H8.
Westward Ho! 1832:A2, 1855:A10.
"Westward the Course of Empire Takes Its Way" 1860:A2.
West Wing, The 1968:A12.
Wetherill, Samuel (1821–70) 1852:S4.
Weyprecht 1873:M9.
"Whaam" 1963:A3.
whales 1991:S16.
whaling 1700:S1.
Wharton, Edith (1862–1937) 1902:A1, 1905:A4, 1911:A5.
What Is Art? 1898:A11.
What is Life? 1944:S13.
What is Surrealism 1934:A14.
What Price Glory? 1924:A6.
What's Up, Tiger Lily 1966:A2.
"What the World Needs Now" 1967:A2.
wheat 1519:S1, 1602:S1, 1618:S1, 1760:S1.
Wheatley, Philis (1753?–84) 1771:A4.
Wheatstone, Sir Charles (1802–75) 1832:S8, 1843:S8.
Wheatstone bridge 1843:S8.
Wheeler, Schuyler S. (1860–1923) 1882:S4.
Wheeler, William A. (1819–87) 1877:H1.
Wheeler-Howard Indian Organization Act 1934:H7.
"When Johnny Comes Marching Home" 1863:A6.
When We Were Very Young 1924:A17.
"Where Have All the Flowers Gone" 1961:A1.

Werner, Alfred (1866–1919) 1891:A1.
"While shepherds watched their flocks by night" 1692:A1.
Whims of Cupid and the Ballet Master 1786:A6.
Whipple, George (1878–1976) 1920:S4, 1925:S3, 1926:S2, 1934:S11.
Whirligigs 1910:A5.
Whiskey Rebellion 1794:H2.
Whiskey Ring 1875:H4.
Whist 1745:M1, 1760:M5.
Whitaker, Rev. Alexander 1613:A2.
White, Byron R. (b.1917) 1962:H6.
White, E.B. (b.1899) 1929:A4, 1945:A6.
White, Edward (1930–67) 1965:S8, 1967:M3.
White, John 1585:A1.
White, Maria 1831:A3.
White, Rev. William (1748–1836) 1808:M4.
White, Stanford (1853–1906) 1891:A1.
White, T.H. (1906–64) 1958:A19.
White, William L. (1900–73) 1942:A7.
White Buildings 1926:A11.
"White Christmas" 1942:A1.
White Fang 1906:A4.
Whitefield, George 1738:M5.
White Goddess, The 1948:A17.
Whitehall Palace 1697:M4.
Whitehead, James (b.1936) 1971:A13.
Whitehead, Robert (1823–1905) 1866:S7.
White House 1793:A2, 1815:A1.
White-Jacket 1850:A4.
Whiteman, Paul (1890–1967) 1919:A7, 1924:A2, 1926:A8.
White Mountain, Battle of the 1620:H3.
"White Night" 1901:A11.
White Nile 1771:H3.
"The White Peacock" 1915:A11.
White Plains, Battle of 1776:H3.
White Slave Traffic Act 1913:H11.
white stockings 1730:M2.
Whitewater affair 1995:H4, 1997:H4.
White Wings 1926:A10.
Whiting, Richard (1891–1931) 1938:A7.
Whitlam, Gough (b.1916) 1972:H14.
Whitman, Walt (1819–92) 1855:A3, 1865:A5, 1871:A2.
Whitney, Eli (1765–1825) 1793:M2, 1793:S4, 1798:S1.
Whittaker, Charles E. (1901–73) 1962:H6.
Whittier, John Greenleaf (1807–92) 1831:A2, 1849:A1, 1854:A5, 1866:A8.
Whittle, Sir Frank (b.1907) 1930:S18, 1941:S16, 1959:S19.
Whittredge, Worthington (1820–1910) 1851:A4.
Whitworth, Sir Joseph (1803–77) 1841:S4.
WHO 1948:M10.
Whole Book of Psalms, The 1621:A1.
Whoopee 1928:A1.
whooping cough 1906:S7, 1913:S9.
Who's Afraid of Virginia Woolf? 1962:A11.
Whose Body? 1923:A16.
Why Are We in Vietnam? 1967:A6.
Whymper, Edward (1840–1911) 1865:M6.
Wickersham Commission 1931:H1.
Wide Sargasso Sea 1966:A24.
Wieland 1798:A1.
Wieland, Heinrich (1877–1957) 1911:S14.
Wien, Wilhelm (1864–1928) 1893:S9, 1911:S18.